Second Edition

AN INTRODUCTION TO MODERN BUSINESS STATISTICS

DUXBURY TITLES OF RELATED INTEREST

Second Edition

AN INTRODUCTION TO MODERN BUSINESS STATISTICS

GEORGE C. CANAVOS

DON M. MILLER

Virginia Commonwealth University

Duxbury Press
An Imprint of Brooks/Cole Publishing Company
I(T)P® An International Thomson Publishing Company

Pacific Grove • Albany • Belmont • Bonn • Boston • Cincinnati • Detroit • Johannesburg • London • Madrid
Melbourne • Mexico City • New York • Paris • Singapore • Tokyo • Toronto • Washington

Sponsoring Editor: *Curt Hinrichs*
Project Development Editor: *Cynthia Mazow*
Marketing Team: *Marcy Perman, Laura Hubrich, Michele Mootz, and Jean Vevers Thompson*
Editorial Assistant: *Rita Jaramillo*
Production Editor: *Laurel Jackson*
Manuscript Editor: *Susan Reiland*

Interior Design: *John Ritland*
Cover Design: *Lisa Milski Devenish*
Cover Photo: *PhotoDisc*
Typesetting: *Graphic World Inc.*
Cover Printing: *Phoenix Color Corporation*
Printing and Binder: *R. R. Donnelley & Sons, Inc./Willard Mfg. Division*

For more information, contact:

BROOKS/COLE PUBLISHING COMPANY
511 Forest Lodge Road
Pacific Grove, CA 93950
USA

International Thomson Publishing Europe
Berkshire House 168-173
High Holborn
London WCIV 7AA
England

Thomas Nelson Australia
102 Dodds Street
South Melbourne, 3205
Victoria, Australia

Nelson Canada
1120 Birchmount Road
Scarborough, Ontario
Canada M1K 5G4

International Thomson Editors
Seneca 53
Col. Polanco
11560 México, D. F., México

International Thomson Publishing GmbH
Königswinterer Strasse 418
53227 Bonn
Germany

International Thomson Publishing Asia
60 Albert St.
#15-01 Albert Complex
Singapore 189969

International Thomson Publishing Japan
Hirakawacho Kyowa Building, 3F
2-2-1 Hirakawacho
Chiyoda-ku, Tokyo 102
Japan

Printed in the United States of America

10 9 8 7 6 5 4 3 2 1

Library of Congress Cataloging-in-Publication Data
Canavos, George C.
    An Introduction to modern business statistics / George C. Canavos,
Don M. Miller.—2nd ed.
      p.   cm.
    Includes bibliographical references and index.
    ISBN 0-534-35819-5
    1. Commercial statistics. 2. Statistics. I. Miller, Don M.
II. Title.
HF1017.C37 1999   98-7637
519.5′02465—dc21   CIP

In loving memory to my dearest mother,
    Alexandra,
    for her love, devotion, inspiration, and guidance;
    and for the extraordinary sacrifices she made and the
    pain and suffering she endured in caring for me as a
    child in the midst of a ravaging war.

                                                                        −G. C. C.

I would like to dedicate this book to my mother,
    Mrs. Eloise Miller:
    You have always loved me and supported me.
    You guided me to a good education and to a set of
    values that have served me well.
    I am proud to be your son.

                                                                        −D. M. M.

About the Authors

George C. Canavos and **Don M. Miller** are professors in the School of Business at Virginia Commonwealth University. Between them, they have over forty years of experience teaching statistics, management science, and forecasting to undergraduate and graduate students in business. Both earned the Ph.D. degree from the Department of Statistics at Virginia Tech. Each has considerable experience working in non-academic environments. Professor Canavos was a practicing statistician for twelve years at National Aeronautic and Space Administration's Langley Research Center. Professor Miller worked for ten years as an internal consultant in statistics and management science for Xerox Corporation and IBM Corporation. Since joining academia, they have continued to work with professionals through extensive noncredit teaching and consulting activities, primarily in the areas of design and analysis of experiments (Canavos), forecasting (Miller), and regression modelling and analysis (Canavos and Miller). They have published many original research articles in statistical and forecasting journals. Additionally, Dr. Canavos is the author of *Applied Probability and Statistical Methods,* a respected calculus-based book in statistics for engineering and science students. This blend of practical experience and rigorous theoretical preparation, shared by both authors, is the foundation for their belief that the fundamental role of statistics in business has to do with the transformation of data into useful information. Consequently, they believe that a modern statistical education for business students must stress fundamental concepts, use intuitive rather than mathematical explanations, integrate the computer thoroughly and emphasize interpretation of computer output, and motivate by illustrating the role that statistics can play in enhancing students' careers.

Brief Contents

Contents

CHAPTER 3   PROBABILITY, RANDOM VARIABLES, AND PROBABILITY DISTRIBUTIONS   110

CHAPTER 4   SOME IMPORTANT PROBABILITY DISTRIBUTIONS   154

CHAPTER 9   SIMPLE LINEAR REGRESSION ANALYSIS   390

CHAPTER 10   MULTIPLE LINEAR REGRESSION   452

CHAPTER 11   GOODNESS-OF-FIT PROCEDURES AND CONTINGENCY TABLES   526

CHAPTER 12   TIME SERIES ANALYSIS AND FORECASTING   556

CHAPTER 13   **METHODS FOR PROCESS IMPROVEMENT AND STATISTICAL QUALITY CONTROL   590**

APPENDIX   **STATISTICAL TABLES   621**

Preface

With the widespread use of the computer, data have become abundantly available to business organizations. More than ever before, there is a great need for people who can make sense of data. Those who can interpret data effectively, who can convert data to usable information, will make better decisions and exert more influence. Although statistical competence is increasingly vital, many business students want relevance, and a statistics text must clearly link statistical competence to specific, concrete business settings. Our aim in writing this second edition is to show the connection between the analysis of data and the business context from which the data arise. Statistical software is the gateway to effective statistical analysis, and we integrate it so that students experience statistical software (Excel, Minitab, and JMP IN) as an integral part of statistical practice. To provide students with needed experience in interpreting data and practice in using the computer for this purpose, we include many examples and exercises that deal with real situations and use real data sets. We emphasize fundamental concepts and interpretation and deemphasize computation and rote learning.

Intended Audience

The second edition of *An Introduction to Modern Business Statistics* is intended for a one- or two-semester course in business statistics for either undergraduate or master's students. We assume that students have access to a computer at home, in a lab, or in the classroom. Our goal is for students to understand the fundamental concepts of statistics, not just memorize formulas and steps. Thus, the book emphasizes conceptual learning. At the same time, we have sought to make our approach accessible to those who have not had strong preparation in mathematics, because calculus is not used directly in the presentation, and most of the development of concepts is intuitive rather than mathematical.

Significant Changes

This new edition differs from the first edition in four significant ways:

1. We have designed the second edition to inspire and motivate students by demonstrating the importance of statistics to their careers. Throughout the text, we reinforce the idea that statistics transforms data into information that enhances decision making and planning in many specific work settings. For instance, we have bolstered virtually all the numbered examples by adding introductory text that articulates the importance of the example in a functional area of business.

2. In the second edition, we place the computer at center stage to minimize rote computation and to facilitate conceptual learning. We feature the use of Excel, Minitab, and JMP IN. When statistical software is used to execute a statistical

method, neither traditional statistical tables nor special computational expressions are needed to learn the method. Indeed, learning to use statistical tables and computational formulas sometimes constitutes the greatest challenge to students in learning a method. To promote the learning of fundamentals, the second edition also takes the student through many methods step by step, using examples with very small data sets. Thus, we present computer output and interpretation first, then the method using small data sets and traditional statistical tables while voiding special computational expressions entirely. Chapter appendices provide clear, detailed instructions on the use of Excel, Minitab, and JMP IN.

3. We have made the second edition leaner so that a class can move through the chapters more rapidly. Some material has been eliminated, and the remaining material has been streamlined. In every chapter, entire portions have been rewritten. This streamlining has been accomplished without sacrificing substance because students' understanding of concepts remains essential. Still, the second edition is a decidedly smaller, more student-friendly book than its predecessor.

4. To address Excel's statistical limitations, we have licensed a special version of Data Analysis Plus™, a statistical add-in for Microsoft Excel. A copy of this software is contained on the CD-ROM in the back of this book.

5. We have added approximately 120 exercises based on published articles in academic journals, the popular media, or widely available sources of data. In these exercises, we provide the actual data if they are provided in the source. Many of these exercises contain large data sets, and many are revisited in chapters throughout the text.

We have made several more specific improvements as well, including the following:

- We have added another 40 or so practice exercises in several chapters, particularly in Chapters 5 through 7.

- We have added a discussion of errors in hypothesis testing, as well as of the application of decision rules to reject or fail to reject a null hypothesis. Because explicit decision rules do not often come into play in business applications, we continue to emphasize the interpretation of *P*-values as the usual end result of hypothesis testing.

- We have added a chapter covering goodness-of-fit procedures and contingency table analysis (Chapter 11).

- We have reinforced the distinction between quantitative and qualitative data, as well as the links between the type of data, the appropriate summary statistics, and the appropriate method of analysis.

- Without sacrificing substance, we have streamlined Chapter 1 by rewriting some portions and by transferring some of the process improvement material to Chapter 13. As a result, Chapter 13 is now a more complete process improvement chapter.

- The exercises remain grouped by section, but we have placed all section exercises at the end of the chapter. We have done so in response to feedback we have received from students stating that because many exercises build on previous exercises, searching for an exercise that appeared earlier in the chapter was an unnecessary annoyance.

Unique Features and Approach

The changes we have made are intended to build upon the distinctive features of the first edition. Thus, the essential themes and features of the book are unchanged. These include the following:

- An emphasis on developing an intuitive rather than a mathematical understanding of statistics.
- An emphasis on using graphical analysis as an integral component of statistical analysis that complements statistical inference. This approach is reinforced in the exercises throughout the book.
- Many data-driven exercises involving real data that stem from projects done by our former students; these exercises encourage students to get involved in *doing* statistics.
- Explicit directions for a student project that can be started early in a student's first statistics course.
- Comprehensive examples that originate from real problems.
- Case studies that involve a variety of interesting, real-world situations to which students can easily relate.
- The inclusion throughout the text of issues that arise when data are taken from a process rather than a finite population—particularly when the data are time-ordered.

Organization

The material covered in the text is sufficient to provide flexibility for several configurations. The topical coverage is arranged in a way that provides the instructor ample opportunity for greater emphasis of certain topics and deletion of others. For example, either Chapter 11 or Chapter 13 could be covered immediately after Chapter 6. If the text is used in a one-semester course, typical coverage will include Chapters 1 through 7, 8, or 9, depending on the objectives of the course and the pace that is suitable for the class. Many instructors will wish to include one of the late chapters dealing with more specialized topics. For a two-semester sequence, we suggest coverage of Chapters 1 through 7 during the first semester, and Chapters 8 through 10 plus at least two of Chapters 11 through 13 (chosen to match course objectives) during the second semester.

Chapters 1 and 2 set the stage for the material to follow. We introduce the concept of variation and the importance of identifying its sources. We also introduce the fundamental elements of statistics and show how they fit together in a statistical study. In addition, we introduce three common approaches to obtaining sample data. We discuss common sources of error in statistical studies, most of which are unrelated to sampling error. We also examine the concerns that commonly arise when data are taken from a process rather than a fixed population. Finally, we provide an overview of the considerations that arise in designing experiments. In Chapter 2, we introduce techniques for exploring and summarizing data. We begin with a discussion of the types of data and the implications for choosing appropriate descriptive statistics and methods. We also introduce the idea of a distribution and several graphical techniques for characterizing distributions. We present the basic descriptive statistics that are used throughout the book and discuss their important characteristics. Finally, we introduce graphical and tabular methods for examining the relationship between two variables. After mastering the material in Chapters 1 and 2, the student is ready to plan a significant statistics project. Explicit guidelines for such a project are provided in an appendix to Chapter 2.

Chapters 3 and 4 deal with probability. Chapter 3 covers only those aspects of formal probability that we believe are necessary to support inference. For example, we present the concepts of joint and conditional probabilities only to the extent necessary to define statistically independent or dependent events. We introduce (and emphasize) the use of cumulative probabilities, thus setting the stage for the consistent interpretation of statistical tables in the book, all of which are based on cumulative probabilities. In Chapter 4, we introduce the binomial and normal distributions. Throughout this chapter, we illustrate the use of a computer, as well as statistical tables, in dealing with these distributions.

Chapter 5 amplifies the concept of sampling discussed in Chapter 1 and introduces the crucial concept of sampling distributions. Simulations are used to help students to visualize this often-elusive concept. This chapter, which serves as a transition from probability to statistical inference, includes an introduction of the T distribution.

Chapters 6 and 7 introduce the essential concepts of statistical inference, confidence intervals, and hypothesis testing. In these chapters, we deemphasize the discussion of the case in which the values of the population standard deviations are assumed known. Because parameter values are rarely known in practice, we cover this case only to the extent needed to enhance the learning process.

Chapters 7 and 8 extend the discussion of experimental design concepts that begins in Chapter 1. Chapter 8 presents the analysis of variance procedure for comparing population/process means with independent samples and with samples selected in blocks. Chapters 6 through 8 are noteworthy for their emphasis on graphical interpretation as a visual prelude to the ensuing statistical analysis. For instance, Chapter 8 cultivates an intuitive, visually derived interpretation of such quantities as mean square for treatments and mean square for error.

Chapters 9 and 10 contain a comprehensive treatment of regression analysis and modeling, stressing conceptual understanding, diagrammatic illustration of regression topics, and interpretation of computer output.

Chapter 11 covers the traditional topics of goodness-of-fit procedures and contingency tables, introducing and using the chi-square distribution.

Chapters 12 and 13 cover two more specialized statistical topics that are particularly important in business. Chapter 12 presents forecasting methods that are commonly used to support business planning. Both univariate time series methods and causal (regression) models are discussed. Chapter 13 presents statistical quality control, expanding on the concepts first introduced in Chapter 1. This material is especially relevant today in light of the continuing drive to improve the quality of services and manufactured products.

Acknowledgments

We gratefully acknowledge the assistance of our colleagues in the VCU Department of Management, who helped us considerably in developing this book. We also thank the following reviewers for providing us with many suggestions and constructive criticisms at various stages of development: Renato Clavijo, Robert Morris College; Samuel B. Graves, Boston College; Tim Krehbiel, Miami University; Ruth Meyer, St. Cloud State University; Ravinder Nath, University of Memphis; Don R. Robinson, Illinois State University; George A. Schieren, Appalachian State University; Gerald Sievers, Western Michigan University; Richard Spinetto, University of Colorado, Boulder; and Marietta Tretter, Texas A & M University. Many improvements originated from the suggestions of our colleagues and reviewers.

We are indebted to the following former students who provided us, through their work and through class projects, the opportunity to use *real* data in many of the exercises, examples, and case studies in this book. Many of these data sets stem from interesting problems in actual work environments. We extend our thanks to Richard Ainsworth, Michele Biggs, Jared Bjarnason, Charles Blottner, Lewis Broome, Omega Brown, Heather Burke, Neil Callan, Alexis Campbell, Trent Crable, John Cotter, Aaron Dennis, Emily Dille, Patricia Douglas, Faye Eure, Richard Fauth, D. Fitzgerald, Rebecca France, K. L. Fuget, Timothy Geer, Melissa Gorman, Douglas Haag, Kim Hale, Bernadette Hendrix, Saher Itayem, Spurgeon James, Ann Kiernan, Holly Killius, Greg Martin, Martha Mitchell, Wayne Moyer, John Murphy, Kim Ogle, Phillip Perdue, Ashley Rawlings, Denise Rimes, Michael Roeder, Michael Setaro, Donna Shelton, Abbey Shipp, Robert Stewart, Scott Walker, Rebecca Ward, Chalmers Ward, Denise Weir, Tony Woo, Doug Zeigenfuss, and Wei Zhang. We are especially indebted to Bob Andrews, Bill Belew, Deborah Cowles, Quentin Custer, Steve Custer, Bill Harrison, Goerge Hoffer, Elliott Minor, Dennis O'Toole, Mike Spinelli, Steve Peterson, and Roxanne Spindle for their help in constructing case studies and extended exercises.

We also express our deep appreciation to Laurie Jackson for her fine job in managing the production process and to Susan Reiland for outstanding assistance in the copy-editing process. Finally, we thank our wives, Athena and Ada, for their continued patience, understanding, and encouragement.

George C. Canavos
Don M. Miller

Chapter 1

Introduction to Statistics and Statistical Thinking

CHAPTER OUTLINE

1.1 Introduction

Why is it that virtually all business students must take one or two courses in statistics? The reason is that the ability to analyze and convert raw data into useful information is being recognized as vital by more and more organizations. On the other hand, too many organizations find themselves data-rich but information-poor because of their apparent inability to extract meaning from data. A manager's ability to make good decisions and to improve the activities for which he or she is responsible is limited by the depth of knowledge of those activities. We call this *subject-matter knowledge*. The analysis of data guided by statistical thinking is perhaps the best vehicle available for increasing subject-matter knowledge. Thus, statistical data analysis increases managers'

Figure 1.1

Use of statistical data analysis in business

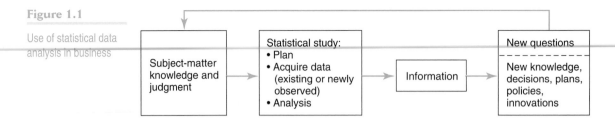

and workers' understanding of important activities, leading to better methods, decisions, plans, policies, and innovations.

Is statistics interesting? In our experience, business students often find statistics dull or tedious when it is studied as a stand-alone topic, and they fail to recognize its relevance to their future work. Think of statistics as an important tool in the effective operation of all business disciplines. For example, a financial analyst might use a statistical analysis of recent financial data to assess an investment proposal. A marketing manager might use a statistical study of recent market behavior before proposing a new marketing action. As these examples illustrate, statistics is a support discipline used to convert raw data into useful information and thus enhance one's knowledge of the subject at hand. It is essentially detective work that students find exciting when they apply it to a subject of interest to them.

Thoughtful planning of statistical studies pays great dividends. Decisions regarding the acquisition of data and their subsequent analysis are driven by current informational needs and one's subject-matter knowledge. Indeed, subject-matter knowledge and good judgment guide all phases of study, including determining the questions to be addressed, what to observe or measure, how to measure, what methods of analysis to use, and what conclusions to reach.

Fundamental to any analysis of data is an understanding of **variation.** Variation is inevitable in all phenomena. Look around you. Are all people of exactly the same height? Of course not! Some are short, some are tall, and some are in between. Are the content weights of identical-size cereal boxes *exactly* the same? They are not, provided we measure carefully enough. Can we expect variation in the annual sales totals of equally competent salespersons? Surely. No matter what phenomenon a data set represents, there will be variation among the data values. An understanding of variation and its causes is the key to increasing knowledge about the phenomenon. The knowledge gained often forms the basis for decisions we make about the phenomena that produced the data. This is what statistical analysis is all about.

We define **statistical thinking** as thought processes that recognize that variation is present in all phenomena and that the study of variation leads to new knowledge and better decisions. We discuss these principles more fully in Section 1.5. Figure 1.1 illustrates the use of statistical data analysis, guided by subject-matter knowledge and judgment, to increase knowledge as a basis for better planning, better decision making, and the development of innovations. Notice that the figure depicts a process of continual improvement. As we gain greater understanding about a phenomenon through statistical thinking and analysis, we increase subject-matter knowledge and generate new questions, thus setting the stage for further learning the next time around.

1.2 The Fundamental Elements of Statistical Analysis

In this section, we discuss the basic elements common to all statistical studies. To illustrate these elements as they are introduced, consider a simple (and real) example.

EXAMPLE 1.1

An insurance agency manager (who happened to be one of our students) wanted to better understand the buying decisions of her customers. She wished to know whether gender and income were factors in determining a customer's policy amount and type of policy ("term" or "universal").* She thought this knowledge might help her to tailor sales proposals to individual potential customers. Data for the study were obtained by selecting randomly from the agency's 1,250 customer files a sample of 51 customer records.[†] For each customer, she recorded (1) type of policy, (2) policy amount, (3) gender of customer, and (4) customer's annual income. The data are given in the accompanying table.

Take a moment to scan the data. What do you see? For one thing, you see variation. The policy amounts vary, and so do the annual incomes. On closer inspection, it appears that customers with higher annual incomes tend to have the larger policy amounts. Figure 1.2(a) depicts the policy amounts separately for female and male

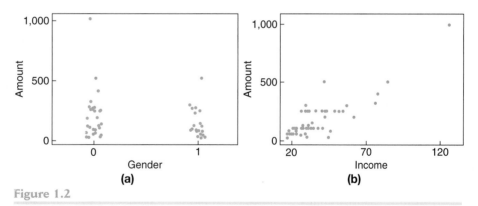

Figure 1.2

Policy amounts (a) for male and female customers, and (b) versus incomes

customers. We see that there is considerable variation among the policy amounts of the men and among those of the women, as indicated by the vertical spreads of the two sets of data values. We also see that the policy amounts for men tend to be somewhat greater than those for women, with one distinctly large policy amount. Other than that, the policy amounts for both men and women appear to overlap considerably. Figure 1.2(b) plots the policy amounts on the vertical axis against customers' annual incomes

---

* A term policy covers a specific period of time. Once the policy is purchased, the customer cannot get back the premium. A universal policy is an investment as well as an insurance policy. It may be for the lifetime of the customer and can be cashed in at any time.

† Courtesy of D. Fitzgerald.

Customer	Gender	Policy Amount ($000)	Type of Policy	Annual Income ($000)	Customer	Gender	Policy Amount ($000)	Type of Policy	Annual Income ($000)
1	1	75	1	46.0	27	0	400	1	78.5
2	0	250	1	52.0	28	1	100	0	32.7
3	0	250	1	42.5	29	1	150	0	33.5
4	1	100	1	31.0	30	0	100	1	22.0
5	1	100	0	40.5	31	1	250	1	48.8
6	1	50	0	20.0	32	0	300	1	29.0
7	0	100	1	27.5	33	0	50	1	18.0
8	0	25	0	30.0	34	1	100	0	34.4
9	1	50	1	21.0	35	1	75	0	22.8
10	1	80	0	18.0	36	0	250	0	31.4
11	0	250	1	43.5	37	1	500	1	41.7
12	1	50	1	17.0	38	0	100	1	20.8
13	0	50	1	19.0	39	1	250	0	54.7
14	1	250	1	30.0	40	0	125	0	27.3
15	0	500	1	85.0	41	0	250	1	40.2
16	0	200	0	62.0	42	1	100	1	27.0
17	0	250	1	26.0	43	0	320	0	76.5
18	1	250	1	29.0	44	1	300	0	57.0
19	0	40	0	26.0	45	0	200	1	42.1
20	1	15	0	17.0	46	0	100	1	37.5
21	0	25	1	44.5	47	0	100	1	26.0
22	0	250	1	36.0	48	1	100	1	23.0
23	0	50	1	21.0	49	0	100	1	29.5
24	0	50	1	29.0	50	0	125	1	31.0
25	1	50	1	23.0	51	0	250	1	30.5
26	0	1,000	1	126.0					

Gender: 1 = female, 0 = male; type of policy: 1 = term, 0 = universal.

on the horizontal axis. It is apparent that customers with higher annual incomes tend to have larger policy amounts. However, there is considerable overlap between the ranges for customers with lower incomes and those with moderate incomes.

Figure 1.2 seems to indicate that a customer's policy amount is related to the customer's annual income and, to a much lesser extent, gender. These data are analyzed more completely in Chapter 2. At this time, the analysis reveals the following information from these data:

1. Eighty percent of the men had term policies, but only 52% of the women had this type of policy. Thus, the type of policy seems to depend somewhat on gender.

2. The average policy amount for men is $202,000, versus $142,600 for women. This coincides with previous conclusions based on Figure 1.2(a).

3. On the average, policy amounts tend to increase by $6,870 for every additional $1,000 of annual income. This result is determined through the use of *regression analysis,* the subject of Chapters 9 and 10.

A statistical study is guided by a clear statement regarding the *aim* of the study—that is, what we wish to learn from the study. The aim guides all decisions made in its execution. In the insurance example, the aim is to learn about the relationships of customers' policy types and amounts to their income and gender.

Statistical studies support the aim by enhancing understanding of the phenomenon that is the source of the data. In general, there are two types of phenomena for which we observe data, *processes* and *populations;* the distinction between them is often important. A **process** is *a set of conditions that repeatedly come together to transform inputs into outcomes.* Examples include business processes used to serve customers, bill customers, and manufacture goods. Other familiar processes that could be studied statistically include registration at your school and going to your classes from your home or dormitory. Each of these processes involves a number of conditions that act together to create outcomes. Examples include the length of time to complete a banking transaction, the time to complete the registration process, and the time to go to your classes from your home or dormitory. In process studies, we seek to understand how a process is performing by measuring some important quantity derived from the outcomes produced by the process, usually over a period of time. In such cases, a particular set of outcomes is viewed as a sample of the possible outcomes that could be produced by the process if it continued unchanged. For example, suppose a bank manager collects a sample of times required to complete banking transactions at this bank. The observed times (outcomes) reflect the operation of the banking process over the period of observation. By noting other characteristics such as type of transaction, time of day, day of the week, and number of available employees, the manager begins to identify and understand the causes of variation in the transaction times. This knowledge provides a basis for future decisions to improve customer service at this bank.

Alternatively, we may wish to learn about some particular group of (usually) persons or objects that share a common characteristic. The term **population** denotes such a group for which we seek greater knowledge and understanding. The insurance example is a typical population study, where the agency's customers are the group about which we seek additional information based on a sample of customers. Other examples of potential populations include the current employees of a company, a large group of manufactured items scheduled for shipment, and all students at your college or university. In population studies, we wish to learn more about such a group as it exists at a particular time based on a sample from the group.

Whether the source of data is a population or a process, the essential components of a statistical study are the same. We start by identifying what we want to learn. Subject-matter knowledge guides the determination of what is to be studied. Great care must be taken to define what is to be observed in such a way that it is easily communicated to and well understood by all concerned. This is accomplished by *operationally defining* what is to be studied. An **operational definition** provides a clear and precise statement of exactly what is to be observed and how it is to be measured. It provides the same meaning over time—past, present, and future. Operational definitions prevent miscommunication and lead to consistent measurement and understanding of results. For example, an operational definition for "copier speed" that has been used at Xerox Corporation is "the number of copies of a single page that has been produced and lie in the output bin after 60 seconds, as measured by a standard stopwatch beginning when the START button is pressed." A **statistical variable** is an operationally defined characteristic of a population or process and represents the quantity to be observed or measured. Thus, "copier speed" as defined above might serve as a statistical variable in a study to compare several engineering designs for copiers. It is the variation in the observations of statistical variables that provides a basis for learning.

Suppose you wish to observe some statistical variable for a sample taken from a population. A good sample reflects the essential features of the population from which it is drawn. An important step is to construct a list of population elements from which a sample could be selected. The set of population elements that actually have an opportunity to be included in the sample is called the **sampled population.** To achieve adequate representation of the intended population, it is important to establish a set of elements that matches the intended population as closely as possible. This is important because resulting conclusions apply only to the sampled population. Their applicability to the intended population depends on how closely the sampled population matches the intended population. In the life insurance example, the sampled population is the set of customer files from which a sample was selected. Even in this illustration the sampled population might not be a perfect match for the intended population. For example, these files would not include any new policies not yet placed on file, nor would they exclude terminated policies not yet removed from the files.

Now suppose you wish to study a process rather than a population. For the time period of interest, you still must establish a set of process outcomes from which a sample of data can be selected. The **sampled process** is the set of all outcomes over the period studied from which a sample is selected. In the banking transactions example, the sampled process consists of all customer transactions at the time and date of the study from which a sample of transaction times is selected. Any conclusions about the banking process based on such data apply only to the time period of observation.

It is rarely feasible, if not impossible, to obtain data for every element of a sampled population or process (if we do, we call it a **census**) because it would be too costly or time-consuming to do so. Instead, we rely on sampling. A **sample** is a subset of a sampled population or process and usually comprises only a small portion of it. The individual elements of a sample are called **sampling units** or **experimental units.** Some people distrust conclusions based on samples. Do you? There is some wisdom to this distrust. Nevertheless, cost and time considerations often make sampling necessary; sometimes only sample information is feasible to obtain. At times there is simply no alternative to sampling if you want to obtain objective information. Another reason for sampling is to allow proper care to be given to the data-collection activity. Without adequate control and supervision, far more error may be introduced by attempting a census than could occur with a smaller, more carefully managed sampling activity.

Suppose that a census could be carried out with precisely the same methods used in sampling—the same questionnaires, the same instruments, the same training of workers, and so on. We call such a census a *100% sample*. The difference between the results derived from a sample and the (hypothetical) results of a 100% sample is called **sampling error.** Sampling error is a fact of life and an integral part of statistical analysis. This is the error usually cited in political polls by statements such as "42% of voters favor candidate A. The margin of error is plus or minus 3 percentage points." This means that the estimated proportion who favor candidate A is unlikely to be off by more than 3 percentage points from the result that would be obtained from a 100% sample. Thus, we have a high degree of confidence that the actual proportion for a 100% sample would not be lower than 39% nor higher than 45% because of sampling error. Since this source of error cannot be avoided, it is important to estimate the magnitude of sampling error associated with any statistical analysis. Many statistical methods include techniques for estimating the amount of sampling error, provided the sample has been selected in proper fashion. (Sample selection procedures are discussed in Section 1.4.)

Suppose it were feasible to observe a 100% sample. Before we could really learn from this information, we would have to summarize it or organize it graphically in a meaningful way. Our brains simply cannot efficiently handle a great deal of information: we must summarize to find meaning. For example, suppose the life insurance manager in Example 1.1 had recorded the policy amounts for all 1,250 customers of the agency. Before she could use this information effectively, she would have to summarize it in some fashion. A **parameter** is a number that summarizes some aspect of a population or process. Two parameters of considerable interest to the insurance manager were the average policy amount for male customers and the average policy amount for female customers. Two other parameters of interest were the proportions of men and women whose type of policy was term, as opposed to universal. The insurance manager obtained sample information to understand the population as it is characterized by these parameters. A parameter of a process is a number that summarizes some aspect of process behavior. For example, if a process has not undergone changes in the past, a process average is the average of all outcomes that would be produced if the process could continue unchanged. The concept of a process parameter is somewhat hypothetical because a 100% sample of *potential* outcomes is impossible. As illustrated in these examples, the purpose of many statistical methods is to shed light on key parameters of a population or process.

Just as it would be necessary to summarize if all possible data were available, it is also necessary to summarize sample data. **Statistical graphs** are plots of the sample data designed to summarize the data by revealing patterns of variation, among other aspects. They are usually accompanied by numerical summaries known as *statistics.* A **statistic** is a numerical quantity that also summarizes a sample. For example, the sample average is a statistic. Since the purpose of a statistical study is often to learn about key parameters of populations or processes, the analysis usually focuses on the statistics that correspond to these parameters. For example, because the insurance manager wishes to learn about the average policy amounts of male and female customers, she computes the averages for the men and women in the sample.

We noted in the insurance example that, for every additional $1,000 of income, customers' policy amounts tended to increase by an average of $6,870. This result was achieved by developing a statistical model. A **statistical model** is a mathematical equation that shows how one key variable is related to one or more other variables, while ignoring the lesser effects of many minor factors. The following equation was developed in the insurance example to depict the relationship between policy amounts and incomes for the sample:

$$\text{Policy amount} = -\$75{,}600 + 6.87 \times \text{Income}$$

This statistical model explains the variation among customers' policy amounts in terms of customer income, while ignoring any other factors that might influence the policy amount. It suggests that a customer's policy amount can be approximated by multiplying annual income by 6.87 and then subtracting $75,600. For example, the equation predicts that a customer with a $40,000 annual income has a $199,200 policy (since $-75{,}600 + 6.87 \times 40{,}000 = 199{,}200$). Notice that this equation predicts an additional $6,870 in policy amount for every additional $1,000 in income; this could be an important finding for the manager. The equation is only a statistical model; it does not fully account for the variation among customers' policy amounts, which may also be affected by a variety of other factors. Indeed, several customers with identical incomes differed substantially in their policy amounts, perhaps because of differences in their ages, number of dependents, and other factors. Nevertheless, this model helps to explain why some customers have greater policy amounts than others.

The use of sample information to learn about a population or process is called **statistical inference.** In this book, we examine two kinds of statistical inferences: **estimation** and **hypothesis testing.** In estimation, we use a sample statistic to estimate (guess) the value of a population or process parameter. In the insurance example, the estimated average policy for all female customers is $142,600. In hypothesis testing, we assess the validity of some claim (called an *hypothesis*) about the value of a parameter. In the insurance example, we may wish to examine a claim that "the average policy amount for all male customers is the same as the average policy amount for all female customers."

The **confidence** associated with a statistical inference is, in broad terms, the likelihood that it is correct. Closely related to confidence is statistical precision—that is, how much in error a statistical inference is likely to be. For the insurance example, consider the estimated average policy amount for women of $142,600. This estimate is based on a sample, so it is probably in error by some amount. Suppose the insurance manager determined that this error could be no more than $20,000. Then the average policy amount for all female customers could be as low as $122,600 or as high as $162,600. Now, how certain is the insurance manager that the error is no more than $20,000? This question is important. If she can be sufficiently confident that the average for all female customers lies between $122,600 and $162,600, she can plan accordingly. Otherwise, this information is not useful for planning and decision making.

The fundamental elements of statistical analyses may be summarized as follows:

THE FUNDAMENTAL ELEMENTS OF STATISTICAL ANALYSIS

A **population** is a group of elements for which understanding is desired.

A **process** is a set of conditions that repeatedly come together to transform inputs into outcomes.

A **sampled population** or **sampled process** is the set of elements or outcomes that actually had an opportunity to be included in a sample.

A **statistical variable** is a clearly and precisely defined (i.e., operationally defined), measurable version of a characteristic of interest.

A **sample** is a subset of a sampled population or process.

A **sampling unit** or **experimental unit** is an individual member of a sample for which a statistical variable is observed.

A **parameter** is a number that summarizes some aspect of a population or process.

A **statistic** is a numerical quantity that summarizes some aspect of a sample.

Sampling error is the difference between the result of a sample and the corresponding result of a 100% sample.

A **statistical model** is an equation that shows how one variable is related to one or more other variables, while ignoring the effects of other, minor factors in a system.

Statistical inference is the procedure of using sample information to learn about a population or a process.

The **confidence** associated with a statistical inference is the likelihood that it is correct or in error by no more than a stated amount.

Figure 1.3

The utilization of statistical analysis to understand populations or processes

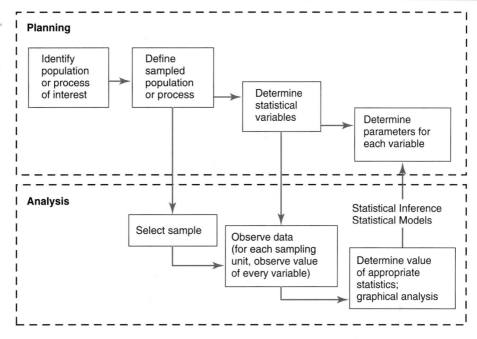

Figure 1.3 illustrates how the concepts that we have been discussing come together in our understanding of populations or processes through statistical analyses.

The following is an example of how statistical analysis is used in specific business context, in which there is a need to monitor the average of an important measurement.

EXAMPLE 1.2

A manufacturer of an electrical coil selects a sample of ten coils every half-hour and measures the resistance of each. The average resistance for these samples is monitored carefully. If a sample average strays from the historical range of variation, the process controls are checked carefully and adjustments are made if a cause can be identified. Several consecutive averages that are either unusually high or unusually low can signal that a problem (or perhaps an opportunity for improvement) might exist.

(a) Does this example deal primarily with an existing population or a process? Discuss.

(b) Describe the sampled population or process for this ongoing statistical study.

(c) Identify the sampling units.

(d) Identify the statistical variable.

(e) What parameter is of interest?

(f) Identify the relevant statistic.

(g) Can you think of any other parameters that might be of interest to this manufacturer?

(h) Can you think of some factors that might cause the sample resistance values to vary?

Solution

(a) We are concerned with the process of electrical coil production over time. We wish to learn about the process that produces the coils rather than about the coils themselves.

(b) The sampled process consists of all coils produced during each sampling period that could be selected by a sample.

(c) The sampling units are the coils selected for the samples.

(d) The statistical variable is the resistance of a manufactured coil.

(e) The parameter of interest is the average resistance of the coils being produced by this manufacturing process.

(f) The relevant statistic is the average resistance of the coils in a given sample.

(g) Another parameter that seems important is the *variation* in resistance among manufactured coils. If some have very high resistance and others very low resistance, then there may be a problem even though the average is about right.

(h) Are the coils all produced by the same machine? Is more than one gauge used to measure resistance? Are there several operators? Is there variation in raw materials?

1.3   The Evaluation of Statistical Analyses

It is important to understand how statistical analysis can be used effectively, but it is equally important to understand how a statistical analysis can be misleading. Many potential sources of error are possible with any statistical study. In addition to sampling error, a statistical report should include a discussion of other possible sources of error. A detailed discussion of possible errors in a study usually enhances credibility rather than detracting from it. Users develop confidence in the analysis and the analyst when they see that the possibility of errors is not being swept under the rug. The following sources of error can be minimized through careful planning and proper understanding of statistical methods.

A Sampled Population That Does Not Match the Intended Population

A statistical analysis is apt to be in error to the extent that the sampled population does not match the intended population. In the insurance example, the sampled population consisted of all customers on file at the time of the study. New customers not yet in the file were excluded, and customers who recently canceled but whose files had not been purged were included. Is this a serious problem? Probably not in this case, but it can be! Therefore, this judgment is required of the manager, based on subject-matter knowledge.

The problem can be serious. Consider a soft-drink taste test that may be conducted in a given city. The sampled population consists of all consumers who had the opportunity to participate in the test. Thus, the sampled population is limited to consumers in the city where the test was conducted. If it was conducted in shopping malls on a weekend, then the sampled population is further limited to consumers who patronize shopping malls on weekends. To the extent that "consumers in the tested city who frequent shopping malls on weekends" are not representative of "soft-drink consumers nationally" the conclusions of this study are in jeopardy.

Inappropriate Treatment of Data Collected over Time

One of the most common errors of statistical analyses is to ignore the fact that data may have been collected over a period of time. This is true of samples from populations as well as processes. If we fail to consider the time element as we analyze such data, we miss the opportunity to notice changes that may have occurred. Although populations tend to change more gradually than processes, both are dynamic entities that can undergo considerable change over time. Therefore, one should always check for systematic variation in data over time, even when the time span is relatively short. Usually, this is best accomplished by plotting the data in the order in which they are observed. Only if it is clear that no substantive changes have occurred over time should one act as if the data come from a source that has not changed.

Consider the insurance example, in which we averaged the policy amounts for each gender, thereby treating each group as a separate population. The current customer base includes men and women who took out their policies at various times in the past, with policy-initiation times ranging over perhaps the last 20 years. Is it possible that there have been changes in the behavior of men and women over that time? For instance, the manager might discover that the average policy amount for men who purchased a policy more than 10 years ago is less than the average policy amount of men who initiated their policies within the last 5 years. If this is the case, then how meaningful is the average of $202,000 that was computed from the sample data? By ignoring the time sequence in which policies were initiated, the manager might miss important information about trends in the customer base and reach erroneous conclusions about the future customer base.

Poor Choice of Statistical Variable

This problem lies at the base of many arguments. For example, who was the better basketball player, Magic Johnson or Larry Bird? Proponents of Bird argue that he led the NBA (National Basketball Association) or was among the leaders in many scoring categories during his career with the Boston Celtics. Johnson proponents counter that his team (the Los Angeles Lakers) won more championships under his leadership than Bird's Celtics. Who is right? There is no settling an argument like this; it all depends on what statistical variable you accept as a proxy for "good performance." This problem is pervasive in business studies. For example, how healthy is the economy? The answer depends on the statistical variable that serves as a proxy for "economic health." If you choose GDP (gross domestic product) or the value of the Standard & Poor's 500 Stock Index, you would conclude the economy is healthy. If you choose the balance of trade (which is running at a deficit), you would conclude that it is unhealthy. Indeed, astute politicians select their statistical variables very carefully to support their stands on issues!

Failure to Measure Accurately and Consistently

Data result when we measure some variable for a given sampling unit. One of the most overlooked sources of error is the failure to measure accurately and consistently. This can occur for several reasons. Measurement equipment might not be calibrated properly. People who take physical measurements might not be properly trained. Or measurement specifications might be ambiguous. Because the measurement itself can exhibit some degree of variation, it is important to minimize variation by giving adequate attention to measurement specification and the training of observers. Consider an example from one of our classes. Students were instructed to count the number of pages in a book that was circulated around the room. Very few students recorded the same number, even though all used the same book! The problem was that the term *page* had not been specified adequately. Some students counted sheets of paper, while others considered each sheet to consist of two "pages" (front and back). In surveys, inaccurate measurement often occurs because respondents do not understand a question in the way intended due to unclear wording. Similarly, the wording of a question may strongly suggest the desired answer. To combat these problems, it is a good idea to ask the same question several times, using a different wording each time.

Inappropriate Choice of Statistical Technique or Statistical Model

Much of the remainder of this book addresses this aspect of statistical analysis. In addition to learning a variety of techniques, it is essential to be able to recognize situations in which a technique, if applied, is likely to lead to erroneous or misleading conclusions. The same concern applies to the use of statistical models. Not all models characterize the relationship between variables adequately. It is important to be able to test the adequacy of any model before it is used to influence decisions.

1.4 Obtaining Data

The goal of statistical analysis is to learn as much as possible about a population or process. It is therefore desirable to obtain data that characterize the population or process as well as possible, minimizing sampling error. There are three major ways of obtaining data: (1) we may select a **random sample;** (2) we may conduct a **designed experiment;** and (3) we may use **convenience data**—data that happen to be available at the time of the desired study. In Chapter 13, we will also consider another way: that of using **rational subgroups.** These are planned samples that are selected over time and are particularly useful in assessing process performance.

1.4.1 Random Samples

The most effective way to control sampling error is to use a technique called *random sampling*. There are several variations of random sampling. In this book, we rely primarily on the idea of a simple random sample. A **simple random sample** is one in which all members of a sampled population or process have an equal and independent chance of being included in the sample. This assures that all possible samples of the same size have the same chance of being selected. A more detailed discussion of sampling procedures is given in Section 5.2. Random sampling offers several key advantages over nonrandom methods of selection:

1. *Eliminating bias.*   It ensures that the sample members are chosen without bias. Otherwise, there is the possibility that a bias is introduced, perhaps unconsciously. Although random selection does not guarantee that a sample is representative, it eliminates the risk of biased selection. It offers the additional advantage of assuring skeptics of the impartiality of the selection process.

2. *Determining confidence.* It provides a statistical basis for determining the confidence level associated with the inferences. This cannot be done if sample members are selected in any other way.
3. *Controlling sampling error.* It allows sampling error to be controlled by the choice of sample size.* Therefore, it provides a means of achieving a desired level of sampling error. With nonrandom methods of sample selection, an acceptable level of sampling error cannot be assured.

How do we choose a sample so that all sampled population or process members have equal, independent chances of selection? The basic idea is to select sample members one by one until the desired sample size is achieved and then measure or observe the characteristic of interest for each member of the sample. For example, suppose we wish to select a random sample of five employees from a department of 500 employees. To achieve randomness, we first assign the integers 1 through 500 to the 500 employees. We then let a computer randomly select five integers from 1 to 500. The sample consists of the measurements or observations made on each of the five employees whose numbers match the randomly selected integers. Specific instructions for computer selection of random numbers are provided in Section 5.2.

1.4.2   Designed Experiments

One of the key ways to learn about the causes of variation is to design an experiment. For example, a manufacturer of farm products might test the effect of a proposed fertilizer on the yield of corn. A variety of corn would be planted on a plot of ground and treated with the proposed fertilizer. The same variety of corn would also be planted on a similar plot of ground and treated with a conventional fertilizer. The eventual yields of the two plots would be compared to assess the effect of the proposed fertilizer relative to that of the conventional fertilizer. The seeds of corn to be used in the test (the experimental units) should be allocated randomly to the two plots. The randomized allocation of seeds assures that the study enjoys the benefits discussed earlier for random sampling. Now, can you identify the population to which the findings of this experiment can be properly applied? It is not simply the seeds used in the study. Instead, the population is hypothetical; it is the yield for all corn of this variety if grown under the conditions of the study (similar soil, fertilizer, water, etc.). Here, we are primarily interested in the effect of fertilizer on the process of corn growth. We use the designed experiment to increase our understanding of that process.

1.4.3   Convenience Data

We often find that the formal use of random sampling is not feasible, and we must instead rely on data that are simply available. Readily available data that have not been obtained through a genuine random sampling process are often called **convenience data.** For example, suppose we want to develop a statistical model between the selling prices of homes in a given neighborhood and their sizes (number of enclosed square feet). We could select a random sample of these homes, but we could not obtain their selling prices because their owners would not sell just to accommodate the study! So

---

* This is demonstrated in Chapter 6.

random sampling is not feasible. Instead, we observe from public records the selling prices and sizes of those homes that happen to have been sold recently. We may choose to analyze the data *as if* these homes had been selected randomly, but the analysis is vulnerable on this point. It is important to consider the possibility that the selection process that produced the available data was biased in some way. For example, if most of the homes in the sample were older homes, the statistical model might not represent the neighborhood as a whole. In general, there are two distinct disadvantages to reliance on convenience data: (1) they do not provide the advantages afforded by random sampling discussed earlier, and (2) they do not provide the opportunity to plan the selection process to gain the advantages provided by designed experiments.

1.5   Statistical Thinking for Process Management and Quality Improvement

One of the primary ways we use statistics is to gain insight into the management of business processes. In this regard, **statistical thinking** is a pattern of reasoning that allows us to understand, and thus ultimately to improve, processes through the careful analysis of the variation in data. As we have said, an understanding of variation and its causes is the key to effective process management. For example, suppose a marketing innovation has been implemented in a sales region. Would an increase in sales for three consecutive months indicate a genuine improvement? Suppose an IRS (Internal Revenue Service) analyst observes that variation in the amount of charitable contributions claimed on a sample of Forms 1040 appears to correspond to differences in adjusted annual incomes. Might there be a statistical relationship between these two quantities? There is also variation in our personal experiences. You might have noticed that on some days it takes longer to get to work or school than on other days. Does it indicate that some departure times are better than others? Statistical thinking allows us to recognize and make sound interpretations of the variation we encounter.

One of the keys to the effective interpretation of variation is an understanding of the process from which it arose. The essence of statistical thinking is to recognize that all processes produce variation, and the reduction of variation is a key to process improvement. The systematic use of statistics for the proper interpretation of variation in data in concert with subject-matter knowledge provides a means by which we increase understanding and thereby improve processes.

The following steps summarize the use of statistical thinking for increased understanding and the eventual improvement of processes:

1. State clearly the aim of the process study.
2. Understand how a process currently works. What are the inputs to the process? Who are the suppliers of inputs? What are the important factors within the process? What actions are taken? In what sequence? What decisions must be made within the process? What are the outcomes? Who are the customers of the process?
3. Assess how the process is currently performing. What level of performance can we realistically expect from the process in its current state?
4. Identify possible strategies to improve the process.
5. Test the effectiveness of the selected strategies.

Figure 1.4

The never-ending cycle of process improvement

6. If the tests indicate likely success, implement process change. If the test results are not promising, return to step 4.

7. Return to step 2 in a never-ending cycle of improvement.

The cycle of improvement is illustrated in Figure 1.4.

We have said that statistical thinking involves the careful study of the variation in data in concert with subject-matter knowledge. Let's examine the use of each in the cycle of improvement. Step 1 identifies clearly the aim of the study, and step 2 incidates the current understanding of how a process works; these two steps are based solely on current subject-matter knowledge. An understanding of the interaction of the elements within a process is essential to the effectiveness of the ensuing analysis. The primary tools for this work are the *flow diagram* and the *cause-and-effect diagram* discussed in Chapter 13.

To assess current process performance (step 3), we use subject-matter knowledge to determine what variables to study and what statistical methods to use. The primary statistical methods involved are *run charts* (introduced later in this section), *control charts* (introduced in Chapter 13), *histograms,* and *scatter diagrams* (introduced in Chapter 2). We rely on subject-matter knowledge to suggest potential strategies for improvement (step 4). Testing the effectiveness of proposed strategies (step 5) relies primarily on statistical methods, which include run charts, control charts, and, the most effective of all, *designed experiments.* An introduction to the design of experiments is presented in Section 1.6. The implementation of process change (step 6) is primarily a nonstatistical endeavor, although the results of any planned change should be tracked statistically. As we go through these steps to study, understand, and improve a process, we inevitably unearth as many questions as we answer. Each study naturally leads to another study in an ongoing cycle of process improvement (step 7). Thus, statistical thinking itself is a continuing process that never ends and that should be woven into the fabric of management practice.

To study the performance of a process (step 3), we must identify indicators of its performance. Consider a process with which you are probably familiar: driving to work (or driving to any routine destination such as school, the mall, the ballpark). For the process of driving to work, one important indicator of performance might be the length of time required. A statistical variable that is used to characterize the quality of process outcomes is called a **quality characteristic.** Much of the task of process improvement involves observing the variation of a quality characteristic, identifying the cause(s) of the variation, and acting on the process to reduce variation. Often the variation among process outcomes can be attributed to other variables within the process. For example, the time it takes to drive to work might depend on the route taken, the time of departure, the number of red lights, and the weather.

There are two types of causes of variation. **Common causes** of variation are attributed to the normal conditions under which the process operates. These conditions stem from the design of the process and cause a predictable variation in process outcomes. Common causes affect *all* outcomes. For instance, common causes of variation in the time it takes you to drive to work might include the route you take, the speed at which you drive (within your normal range), the number of red lights you encounter, and the amount of traffic. Your trip time is affected by all these variables every time you take a trip. On the other hand, **assignable causes** (also called **special causes**) are unusual occurrences that are not part of process design or the normal operating conditions. For example, you might have had a flat tire one day, or perhaps you left an hour late one day and missed the normal traffic. Assignable causes are often breakdowns in some component of the process, such as a machine that needs repair or the flat tire in our example. Assignable causes affect only one or a few outcomes. For example, most of your driving times to work or school are not affected by a flat tire, but if you have a flat tire, that trip time is likely to be much longer than normal.

A **stable process** is one in which only common cause variation is present. There are no special causes that create unusual variation. Since each common cause affects *all* outcomes, the variation among outcomes reflects the cumulative effect of all the factors of the process. If an individual outcome has a larger value than most, it cannot be explained by a single cause. Rather, the cumulative effect of *all* common causes on that outcome happened to produce a larger value. In a stable process, the *system* of causes of variation remains constant over time. Outcomes vary, but the range of variation remains essentially the same and is therefore predictable. If we observe an outcome outside the usual range of variation, then we have reason to suspect that an assignable cause has affected this individual outcome. If a process is affected by assignable causes as well as common causes such that there is a discernible pattern in the variation, it is said to be an **unstable process.** Since assignable causes are not routine process components, they cannot be foreseen. Thus, the range of variation of unstable processes is not easy to predict. If an outcome has a value outside the usual range of variation, or if there is a nonrandom pattern among the outcomes, then we have reason to suspect that a special cause is at work. A **run chart** is a very useful tool in identifying an unstable process when data are time-sequenced.

Run Charts

A **run chart** is a plot of data values in the order in which they have been observed. When we have time-sequenced data, a run chart is a simple and very useful tool in identifying instability. Consider a real example, offered by one of our students who worked in a printing company.

EXAMPLE 1.3

In plant environments, change is a way of life because of the increasing need to decrease toxic emissions. The change brings about a new set of concerns that the astute plant manager must address. For example, the level of emissions of volatile compounds in a printing plant is identified as a problem. To reduce the level, the plant manager decides to switch to the use of water-based printing inks. After changing to the new process, however, the manager became concerned about the amount of scrap being accumulated. To study this problem, the manager observed the amount of scrap (in pounds) per 1,000 yards of printed material in a sample of 23 consecutive printing runs. The sample data* are as follows (sequenced from left to right in rows):

36	31	45	14	38	15	25	46
30	21	28	24	51	15	51	12
19	10	44	22	17	36	41	

What amounts of scrap per 1,000 yards can be expected from this process if it is indeed a stable process?

Solution

It is difficult to answer this question without a run chart. (i.e., a plot of the data over time). The computer-generated run chart is given in Figure 1.5. (Computer instructions for creating run charts are given in the appendix to this chapter.) The chart indicates that the amount of scrap has varied from about 10 to just over 50 pounds per 1,000 yards printed. If the process is indeed stable and remains stable, then we can expect variation in this range in the near future.

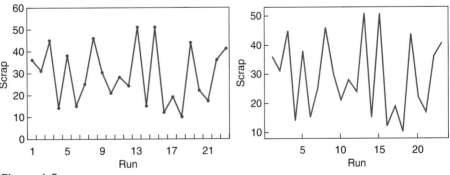

Figure 1.5

Excel and Minitab run charts for Example 1.3

---

* Courtesy of Michael Roeder.

Figure 1.6

Four run charts indicating types of unstable processes

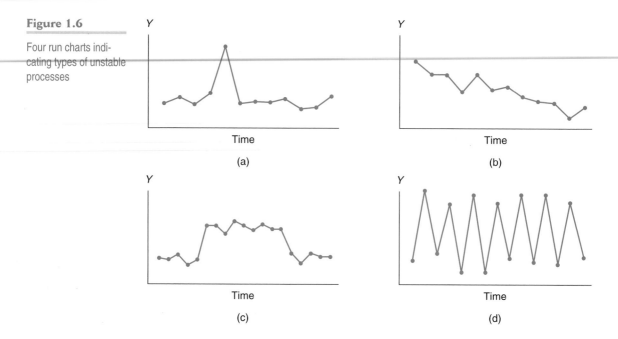

Now, based on the run chart in Figure 1.5, would you conclude that the process is stable with respect to the amount of scrap being produced? Data for a stable process should not exhibit any obvious patterns, the data values should appear to be produced in a random fashion, and there should be no data values that are radically larger or smaller than the rest. Applying these considerations to the run chart in Figure 1.5, we see that the printing process appears to be stable with respect to the amount of scrap produced.

Now, let's discuss several general types of unstable processes, illustrated in Figure 1.6.

In Figure 1.6(a), notice that one data value is much larger than the rest. This suggests that a special cause may have created unusual variation in the data. Any summary statistic, such as an average, that includes this data value would not be truly indicative of the process because a special cause is not a normal part of the process.

Figure 1.6(b) shows a consistently downward trend over the period of time observed. A decreasing or increasing trend suggests that data values do not appear to have been produced in a random fashion; thus, the presence of an assignable cause is suggested.

Figure 1.6(c) is a run chart in which an unusually long sequence of data values are all above the middle of the data. This indicates that, at some point in time, something changed within the process that caused the average to increase for a while.

In Figure 1.6(d), lower than average data values alternate with higher than average values in what is called a "sawtooth" pattern. Such a pattern sometimes indicates overcontrol, where a process is adjusted in reaction to any data value that by chance happens to lie above or below the perceived average. In addition, a sawtooth pattern can result when data from two different processes are combined (e.g., from two shifts, two machines, junior and senior salespersons, and so on).

An Introduction to the Design of Experiments

One of the principal uses of statistics is to plan for the acquisition of data and conversion of the data into useful information. This is especially true in our efforts toward process improvement. The statistical design of experiments is an extremely useful way to identify factors that contribute to the variation of outcomes in a stable process and to assess important differences among these factors. For example, if differences exist among the machines in a filling process, then an improved maintenance policy is likely to reduce the differences and thus improve the process. The fact that a process is stable does *not* imply that it is satisfactory. The most challenging aspect of process improvement is to find ways to change a stable process to reduce the variation of outcomes. In recent years managers have begun to use designed experiments more systematically toward process improvement. In this section, we introduce the principles underlying the statistical design of experiments with an example that should be familiar to you.

Suppose a college professor is interested in finding ways to improve student learning in her statistics course. She considers test grades to be an adequate measure of learning. Based on her experience in the classroom and many conversations with students, she suspects that students' grades are affected by the number of exercises they work in preparation for tests. A survey of her students indicates that the typical student completes about half of the exercises assigned. She believes that if students would work substantially more exercises, their grades would improve. To test her belief, she conducts the following experiment with her class. The 24 students in her class agree to participate as a way of learning designed experiments. The class is divided into three "study groups" consisting of eight students each. One group agrees to complete half the exercises in the chapters covered on the next test. Worked-out solutions are provided. An exercise is completed when the student has worked it correctly and believes he or she understands the solution. A second group agrees to complete 75% of the exercises, and a third group agrees to complete 100% of the exercises. The quality characteristic is the test grade assigned by the professor. Because good students tend to get higher grades on tests than poor students, students are first grouped according to their grade point averages (GPA). The 12 students with GPAs between 2.0 and 3.0 form one group; the 12 with GPAs between 3.01 and 4.0 form another group. The 12 students from each GPA group are assigned randomly to the three study groups. Therefore, each study group has balanced representation from the two GPA groups (i.e., four students from each GPA group). The random assignment is fundamental to any designed experiment because it ensures impartiality. Figure 1.7 depicts the allocation of students to groups.

Suppose the outcomes of the experiment are as given in Table 1.1. Figure 1.8 depicts the grades graphically. For each group, the actual grades are indicated by bullets and the group averages are indicated by triangles. Based on these results, what can we say about the effect of the number of exercises completed on test grades?

To analyze the results of the experiment, let's make some "apples-to-apples" comparisons. First, let's look at the test grades of students with GPAs of 2.0–3.0. As the percentage of exercises completed went from 50% to 75% to 100%, the average test grades went from 68.5 to 76.0 to 82.25. Now look at the 3.01–4.0 GPA group. For this group, average test scores went from 79.5 to 89.25 to 93.75 as the percentage of exercises completed increased. Therefore, for both GPA groups, the average test grade

Figure 1.7

Assignment of students to subgroups in a statistics class experiment

GPA = (2.0–3.0): 12 students

Random Group Assignment

Name	Assignment
A	50%
B	75%
C	100%
D	50%
E	100%
F	50%
G	75%
H	100%
I	75%
J	75%
K	50%
L	100%

GPA = (3.01–4.0): 12 students

Random Group Assignment

Name	Assignment
M	100%
N	50%
O	50%
P	75%
Q	100%
R	75%
S	50%
T	75%
U	50%
V	75%
W	100%
X	100%

Table 1.1

Results of the Statistics Test Experiment

GPA Group	Percent of Exercises	Student Test Grades				Group Average
2.0–3.0	50%	54	66	73	81	68.5
	75%	71	73	78	82	76.0
	100%	78	78	84	89	82.25
3.01–4.0	50%	74	75	84	85	79.5
	75%	83	87	93	94	89.25
	100%	88	93	96	98	93.75

Figure 1.8

Graphical depiction of the results of the statistics test experiment

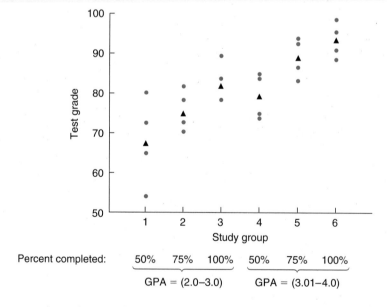

Percent completed: 50%   75%   100%   50%   75%   100%

GPA = (2.0–3.0)   GPA = (3.01–4.0)

appears to have increased substantially as the number of exercises completed increased. These results certainly suggest that test grades improve as the percentage of exercises completed increases. The fact that GPA seems to be a good predictor of the test grade is an entirely expected result. Notice that, if we compare any two groups that completed the same percentage of exercises, the 3.01–4.0 GPA group consistently had the higher average test grade. We have 68.5 versus 79.5 for the 50% groups; 76.0 versus 89.25 for the 75% groups; and 82.25 versus 93.75 for the 100% groups. In all three cases, the average test grade was about 12 points higher for the 3.01–4.0 GPA group. This result is consistent with what one would expect between two groups whose GPAs differ by about one letter grade on the average.

The discussion of the design of experiments is extended in Chapters 7 and 8.

1.7

Statistical Notation

The study of statistical methods requires the use of a certain amount of technical notation to denote parameters and statistics. We have established a consistent format for notation that (we hope) facilitates your becoming familiar with the notation. Basically, there are two rules for you to keep in mind:

1. Parameters are represented by Greek letters. For example, the mean of a population or process is always denoted by the symbol μ (the Greek letter mu). Similarly, the proportion of the items in a population that have a given characteristic (e.g., the proportion of consumers who prefer a proposed cola flavor) is always denoted by the symbol π (the Greek letter pi). In this context, π is not the ratio of the circumference to the diameter of a circle.

2. Statistics are denoted by Roman letters. For instance, the mean of a sample is denoted by the symbol $\bar{X}$ (pronounced "X bar"), and the proportion of sample members having a given characteristic is denoted by the symbol p.

Occasionally, we deviate from these rules to comply with universally accepted statistical notation. When this happens, we clearly state that we are deviating from the policy of this text. We shall mention one exception now. The universally accepted symbol for the number of members in a population is N rather than a Greek letter.

1.8

Use of Computers in Statistical Analysis

The accessibility of statistical analysis has been enhanced tremendously by the advent of computerized statistical packages. Before computers were widely available, statistical methods required extensive work on fairly crude calculators. This had the practical effect of discouraging the use of any but the most straightforward statistical methods. As such, statistical analysis was not available directly to the manager, who had no opportunity to explore and become familiar with relevant data. Now the situation has changed dramatically. Several excellent statistical packages are abundant and widely available.

However, the wide availability of computers and statistical software does not ensure good use of statistics! Computers make statistical methods readily available, but one must still be able to determine which method is appropriate (and just as important, which ones are not). One can argue plausibly that, in making statistics available, computers have also made statistics dangerous! Therefore, more than ever, it is important that a manager understand statistical thinking.

The primary purpose of this text is to teach sound statistical thinking. In doing this, we think it is also important that you be able to use statistical software and interpret the output. The needed information from most of the examples we have included for illustration is presented in the form of actual computer output from two widely available statistical software packages, Minitab and JMP IN, and the popular spread-sheet Excel, which is found in virtually all businesses and schools of business. We provide complete instruction in the chapter appendices so that you can use Minitab, JMP IN, or Excel to perform the statistical methods covered by this text.

As you learn to interpret computer output, you will find that it usually provides far more information than you want, need, or understand. The designers of statistical packages usually include virtually every bit of information that might conceivably be desired. You should simply accept this state of affairs and relax. Learn to find the information you need and ignore the rest.

1.9   Looking Ahead

Here is a brief overview of the coverage of statistical topics in this book. We have tried to make clear the linkage between topics by frequently referencing related material in other sections.

1. Chapter 2 is an introduction of techniques for exploring and summarizing data. The goal is to reveal the essential, relevant characteristics of the underlying population or process in a way that is easy to comprehend. This is an important task, often poorly executed. In addition, the concepts introduced lay the groundwork for statistical inference, presented later.

2. Chapters 3 and 4 deal with probability. *Probability* is a branch of mathematics that establishes rigorous principles for dealing with uncertainty. The basic purpose of applied statistics is to provide information to assist managers in making decisions in uncertain environments. All statistical inferences are made with some degree of uncertainty; we never know for sure the accuracy of conclusions based on sample data. Probability provides the analytical basis for determining the confidence that can be associated with statistical inferences.

3. Chapters 5–7 introduce the essential concepts of statistical inference. *Estimation* and *hypothesis testing* are the key inferential tools at the core of many statistical methods.

4. Chapters 8–10 deal with statistical modeling. The methodologies covered are *analysis of variance* and *regression analysis.*

5. Finally, Chapters 11–13 cover specialized statistical applications: *goodness-of-fit procedures* and *contingency tables, time series analysis and forecasting* and *statistical quality control for process monitoring.*

The linkage between topics is both forward and backward: forward to give some idea of where the current material leads, and backward to identify material that leads to the current topic. In addition, we introduce and emphasize a graphical approach to statistical inference beginning in Chapter 6. It is usually possible to gain considerable insight into a desired inference simply by graphing the sample data. We believe data visualization complements the statistical method quite well because, at a minimum, it provides a visual understanding of the result.

1.10 Summary

In this chapter, we explored the fundamental elements of statistical thinking and data analysis for understanding and thereby improving business activities.

Statistical analyses rely on sampling to gain information about an activity. There are three major ways by which data are obtained: simple random samples, designed experiments, and convenience data. Perhaps the greatest benefit in knowledge and understanding is realized through the careful design of an experiment.

Fundamental to any data analysis is an understanding of variation. The study of variation leads to new knowledge and thus to better decisions. In process studies, there are two kinds of variation: the normal or usual factors within a process (common causes) and the unusual factors that are not ordinarily part of the process (assignable causes). A process is stable if variation is due to only common causes. Run charts are useful devices to gauge the stability of a process.

EXERCISES FOR SECTIONS 1.2–1.3

1.1 Explain why statistical analyses are important in business.

1.2 Discuss possible flaws in statistical analyses that can lead to unsuccessful planning and decision making.

1.3 What is statistical thinking and why is it important in business?

1.4 Explain why the selection of data is important.

1.5 What characteristic is inevitable in virtually all data and why is the understanding of it important?

1.6 Explain and differentiate between a process and a population.

1.7 What is a statistical variable?

1.8 What is a sampled population or process and why should it closely match the population or process?

1.9 Explain the difference between a parameter and a statistic.

1.10 Explain the purpose of statistical inference.

1.11 Explain the difference between estimation and hypothesis testing.

1.12 What is sampling error?

1.13 Discuss potential sources of error in statistical studies and their consequences.

1.14 For the following situations, identify these statistical elements:
   (1) The population or process
   (2) The sampled population or process
   (3) The statistical variable(s)
   (4) The parameter(s) of interest
   (5) The statistic(s) of interest

(a) The American Cancer Society is interested in updating its information on the smoking habits of young adults.

(b) A bank operations analyst is interested in assessing the customer wait time before a transaction service is provided.

(c) An agency in charge of a state's lottery is interested in updating its information on the adult residents who regularly play the lottery.

(d) A manufacturer of a certain metal wishes to assess its breaking strength.

(e) A city's Chamber of Commerce wishes to update its information on the amount of money spent by those who attend conventions in the city.

1.15 A hospital administrator has observed the length of stay in days for a sample of 20 Medicare-supported patients. The 20 patients were selected from a list of all who entered the hospital in March 1998, as found in the hospital's admissions register for that month. It is of specific interest to estimate the average length of stay for all patients who entered the hospital in March 1998. The data are as follows (expressed in days). The average of these data is 7.7 days; therefore, the administrator estimates that the average length of stay for patients who entered in March was 7.7 days.

23	2	5	10	2	5	4	1	5	33
3	7	5	1	9	8	17	7	6	1

The following are specific elements of the example. Next to each specific element on the left side, place the letter of one of the following general statistical elements. (*Note:*   Not every element will necessarily be used.)

(a) population (b) process (c) sampled population or process (d) statistical variable (e) sample (f) sampling units (g) parameter (h) statistic (i) statistical inference

_____ list of Medicare patients in hospital's admissions register for March 1998	_____ length of stay
	_____ 20 patients selected from the list
_____ all Medicare patients who enter the hospital	_____ the administrator estimates that the average length of stay for all March patients was 7.7 days
_____ Medicare patients	
_____ average length of stay for sample of 20 patients	_____ average length of stay for all Medicare patients entering the hospital in March 1998

1.16 A bank operations analyst has observed the amount of money involved in a sample of 20 customer transactions. The 20 transactions were selected from a list of all transactions in August, as found in a computer file of transactions maintained by the bank. It is of specific interest to estimate the average transaction amount for all transactions in August.

The data are as follows (expressed in dollars). The average of these data is $326.80; therefore, the analyst estimates that the average transaction amount for August was $326.80.

235	202	295	104	28	25	44	58	285	338
330	750	25	1,660	950	18	47	507	625	10

Identify each of the general statistical elements listed below in the specific context of this example.

(a) population or process   (e) sampling units
(b) sampled population   (f) statistical variable
      or process   (g) statistical inference
(c) parameter   (h) sample
(d) statistic

1.17 In Exercise 1.15, the administrator estimated that the average length of stay for March 1998 was 7.7 days. Identify and describe briefly three possible sources of error in this estimate (i.e., reasons why the estimate might be in error by some amount).

1.18 In Exercise 1.16, the analyst estimated that the average transaction amount for August was $326.80. Identify and describe briefly three possible sources of error in this estimate.

1.19 For each of the following potential sampling situations, develop an operational definition for the statistical variable to be measured.

(a) The amount of time a customer waits at a fast-food restaurant

(b) The miles per gallon of gasoline for an automobile on a test trip

(c) The annual income of an applicant for a credit card

(d) A person's heartbeat rate

EXERCISES FOR SECTIONS 1.4–1.6

1.20 Identify the three basic ways of obtaining data.

1.21 Discuss the advantages of simple random samples.

1.22 Explain the need to use convenience data on certain occasions.

1.23 Identify and explain two primary tools for understanding how a process currently works and for identifying possible reasons for problems.

1.24 What is the statistical variable called that is used to characterize process outcomes and why is this variable important?

1.25 Explain the difference between common and assignable causes of variation.

1.26 Explain the difference between stable and unstable processes.

1.27 Discuss the usefulness of run charts.

1.28 Consider the process by which students study for a statistics test.

(a) Identify an appropriate quality characteristic for this process and justify your answer.

(b) Identify three common causes of variation in the quality characteristic mentioned in part (a) and justify your answer for each.

(c) Identify at least one potential assignable cause of variation and justify your answer.

1.29 Because his college basketball team is small and relatively weak on defense, a respected coach thinks his team must average at least 85 points per game on offense to be successful. After ten games, however, his offense has averaged only 75 points per game. His staff have urged him to make significant changes in either strategy, personnel, or both to increase offensive production. Do you agree that changes are needed? Justify your answer. Point totals for the first ten games are as follows:

Game	1	2	3	4	5	6	7	8	9	10
Points	61	53	61	70	71	78	81	86	96	93

1.30 One of the processes with which we are all familiar is food consumption—eating. Paula has been concerned about her weight. As a first step in controlling her weight, she recorded her daily calorie intake (number of calories per day) for the past month, as follows:

Week 1: 1,295 1,720 1,215 1,210 1,260 1,075 1,100
Week 2: 1,200 1,435 1,255 1,300 1,385 1,515 1,105
Week 3: 1,270 1,200 1,215 1,225 995 1,270 1,350
Week 4: 1,285 1,110 1,430 1,180 1,385 1,300 1,175
Week 5: 1,475 1,225

(a) Based on your knowledge of people's eating habits, identify some possible sources of variation in these data.
(b) Identify each source of variation in part (a) as either a common or a special cause of variation.
(c) Construct a run chart of Paula's daily calorie intake.
(d) Does your run chart in part (c) contain any obvious signs of process instability? Explain your answer.

1.31 Sales of hardcover books (number of books sold) in a book shop for 30 consecutive working days are as follows:

Week 1:	38	35	76	58	48	59
Week 2:	67	63	33	69	53	51
Week 3:	28	25	36	32	61	57
Week 4:	49	78	48	42	72	52
Week 5:	47	66	58	44	44	56

(a) Does the sales process appear to be stable, in your best judgment?
(b) If you were told to count the number of books sold in a day, do you think you would encounter any difficulty in deciding what constitutes a book? Explain.
(c) List as many possible causes of variation in these data as you can.
(d) Label each cause of variation listed in part (c) as either a common cause or a special cause.

1.32 Two thoroughbreds are entered in a 1-mile race. Each of the horse's times (in minutes : seconds) in the previous six 1-mile races against each other are as follows:

	Race					
	1	2	3	4	5	6
Horse A	1:39	1:37	1:36	1:33	1:31	1:30
Horse B	1:32	1:34	1:31	1:34	1:34	1:33

Based on a run chart (using the same graph), which horse would you expect to win the current race? Explain your reasoning.

1.33 A bank operations analyst has observed the number of transactions (customer deposits and withdrawals) per day over a 7-week period. The data are as follows (Monday through Friday, by week):

	Mon.	Tues.	Wed.	Thurs.	Fri.
Week 1:	64	96	75	105	169
Week 2:	67	104	74	73	202
Week 3:	70	116	89	112	230
Week 4:	68	95	121	83	168
Week 5:	55	109	99	94	157
Week 6:	52	102	72	82	123
Week 7:	68	90	105	78	179

Based on a run chart, does the transaction process appear to be stable for each day of the week? Explain your findings in the context of the causes of variation for any days that you believe are not stable.

1.34 The accompanying data represent Circuit City's annual sales for 1991–1995 (*Source:* "Circuit City 1995 Annual Report," pp. 17–18) for the following product categories: TV, VCR/Camcorders, Audio, Home office, Appliances, and Other.

Sales by Merchandise Category (as a percentage of total sales)	1991	1992	1993	1994	1995
TV	24%	23%	23%	20%	19%
VCR/ Camcorders	22%	20%	19%	17%	14%
Audio	22%	21%	20%	21%	20%
Home office	N/A	5%	7%	12%	20%
Appliances	18%	19%	19%	18%	15%
Other	14%	12%	12%	12%	12%
Total Sales (in millions of dollars)	2,366.9	2,790.2	3,269.8	4,130.4	5,582.9

(a) Describe the relative contributions of each category to 1995 sales. Based on your answer, can you say which categories are most promising for future sales? Explain.

(b) Examine the changes that have taken place in the relative contribution of each category to total sales over the 5-year period by constructing a run chart for each category's sales. What do the run charts suggest about the future contributions to sales of the six product categories?

1.35 The following data represent the percentage of product rejected during inspection of a certain type of lens for specific defects on each production day in April at an optical lens production plant:*

Production day:

1	2	3	4	5	6	7	8	9	10

Percentage rejected:

5.13	4.31	5.88	5.37	5.73	4.31	4.42	4.07	5.96	4.37

Production day:

11	12	13	14	15	16	17	18	19	20

Percentage rejected:

4.89	4.71	4.57	5.40	4.00	6.47	6.33	4.83	4.40	4.12

Using a run chart, determine whether the production process was stable during this month with regard to the percentage of product rejected.

1.36 The following data are the numbers of transactions processed per day in the months of December and January at a branch of a large bank.† The listed number represents the total number of retail and commercial transactions processed on that business day. The day of the week is also given in parentheses.

December		January	
	Number of		Number of
Date	Transactions	Date	Transactions
2 (M)	792	2 (Th)	821
3 (T)	791	3 (F)	917
4 (W)	781	6 (M)	772
5 (Th)	818	7 (T)	724
6 (F)	912	8 (W)	701
9 (M)	812	9 (Th)	776
10 (T)	782	10 (F)	891
11 (W)	911	13 (M)	804
12 (Th)	811	14 (T)	762
13 (F)	889	15 (W)	711
16 (M)	879	16 (Th)	890
17 (T)	801	17 (F)	904
18 (W)	768	21 (T)	836
19 (Th)	821	22 (W)	762
20 (F)	991	23 (Th)	803
23 (M)	798	24 (F)	961
24 (T)	891	27 (M)	792
26 (Th)	801	28 (T)	781
27 (F)	981	29 (W)	741
30 (M)	802	30 (Th)	817
31 (T)	888	31 (F)	1,011

(a) Explain why the recording of such information is important to management.

(b) Using a run chart, determine whether the business activity at this branch bank has been stable during these two months.

(c) On one graph, plot the number of transactions on the vertical axis corresponding to each day of the week on the horizontal axis. Explain your findings.

1.37 The Smithsonian Institute in Washington, DC, is open 365 days a year from 10:00 A.M. to 5:00 P.M. Visitors are admitted free of charge and have a large assortment of exhibits from which to choose. When visitors enter the Information Age Exhibit, they are counted electronically and are given a bar-coded sheet that is used to track the amount of time they spend in the exhibit. They are also given an opportunity to complete a survey, which is used to obtain demographic information, particularly the age and gender of the visitor. Typically, about 40% of the visitors complete the survey.

All of this information is processed by the Institute's computer tracking system. The system uses these data to develop a daily use report containing the number of visitors each day, the number who completed the survey, the number of male visitors, the number of female visitors, and the number of visitors in each of five age groups. The data for this exercise represent the 56-day period from September 30, 1995, to November 26, 1995, during which time 33,189 visitors passed through the exhibit. (*Source:* "Variations in Total Visitors and Average Times at the Smithsonian Institute's Information Age Exhibit," report by Phllip Perdue for Karen Lee, one of the creators of the exhibit.) They are on the book's data diskette in the file named EX0137.

The purpose of this exercise is to examine the stability of the visitation process over the period of observation.

(a) Does the visitation process appear to be stable with respect to the daily number of visitors? Develop and interpret a run chart of the number of daily visitors.

* Courtesy of Richard S. Fauth.

† Courtesy of Robert Stewart.

(b) Does the visitation process appear to be stable with respect to the daily proportion of visitors who complete the survey? Develop and interpret a run chart of the daily proportion of visitors who complete the survey.

(c) Does the daily distribution of males and females appear to be a stable process? Develop and interpret a run chart of the daily proportion of visitors who are female.

(d) Does the average time spent in the exhibit each day appear to be a stable process? Develop and interpret a run chart of the daily average visitation time.

Appendix 1

Introduction to MINITAB, EXCEL, and JMP IN

Today, the computer is an essential tool in our society; this is especially true for statistical data analysis. Virtually all of the methods in this text are facilitated by using a computer, and some of them cannot even be carried out without a computer. The benefits of using a computer far outweigh the little time that you may have to spend getting acquainted with one. The integration of the computer in a course such as statistics not only enhances your computer proficiency but also makes more time available for you to learn the concepts underlying the methods.

There are many statistical software packages available for use in either microcomputers or mainframe computers. We rely on Excel, Minitab, and JMP IN. Minitab and JMP IN are well-established statistical software packages, and Excel is a leading spreadsheet application. Minitab and JMP IN provide more extensive statistical capability and indeed are more effective as statistical software than Excel. On the other hand, Excel is probably the most familiar and widely available general business software application. Excel provides most but not all of the methods covered in this book. We have included on the book's data diskette a set of easily installed Excel macros that perform most of the methods that are absent from Excel. (Installation instructions are on the diskette.) The specific versions discussed in the chapter appendices are Minitab Release 12, JMP IN Version 3, and Excel Version 5.0 for Office 97 in Windows 95. If you are using an earlier version of Excel, JMP IN, or Minitab, you will experience some differences from the instructions in these appendices. These differences are relatively minor, and with a little trial and error you should be able to obtain the desired results. All three applications run under both Windows and Macintosh operating systems using menu interfaces with nearly identical menus, options, and outputs. All are relatively easy to learn and use.

The purpose of the chapter appendices is to show you how to use Minitab, Excel, and JMP IN for the methods presented in the text. It is *not* our purpose to teach you all there is to know about these software packages. Thus, we present only the information you need to produce the computer outputs shown in the book. In the same vein, we sometimes provide only that portion of the output that pertains directly to the method being presented. For additional information about the software, we encourage you to consult handbooks that should be available in your computer center or bookstore.

We assume that necessary information to gain access to a computer (such as identification number, account number, and password) will be provided by your instructor or other appropriate persons at your college or university. The computer instructions given here assume that you have already gained access and are ready to use Minitab, Excel, or JMP IN.

1.1 MINITAB

If you are using Minitab Release 9, 10, or 11 (the Minitab releases for Windows), you will experience some differences from the instructions in these appendices. These differences are relatively minor, and with a little trial and error, you should be able to obtain the desired results.

Minitab Windows

Minitab primarily uses two windows, the DATA window and the SESSION window.* The DATA window looks like a spreadsheet but is actually called a *worksheet*. It is used to enter and modify data but does not have spreadsheet capabilities such as formulas, filling down, etc. The SESSION window is used to view statistical outputs. When you initially start Minitab, you see a split screen, with the SESSION window in the upper half and the DATA window in the lower half. The title of the worksheet (initially "Worksheet 1") appears on the title bar of the DATA window.

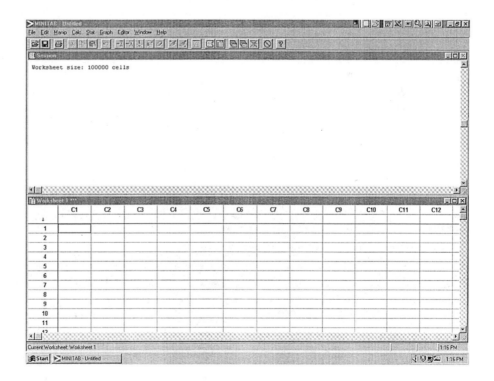

---

* The use of two other windows, the INFO window and the HISTORY window, is not described here.

Normally, both windows are viewed simultaneously. You can choose menu commands while either the DATA window or the SESSION window is active. Minitab graphs appear in separate GRAPH windows. To make any window the active window, click the WINDOW menu and choose the desired window. Your choices will include SESSION, INFO, HISTORY, WORKSHEET 1 (or whatever name you have given to the current data worksheet), and the windows for any graphs that you have created.

Providing Instructions

To choose an instruction, first click the appropriate menu item, then click the appropriate choice for that menu item. Henceforth, to describe such a choice, we direct you to "choose MENU ITEM–CHOICE." For example, to create a histogram (one of the types of graphs discussed in Chapter 2), you choose the HISTOGRAM . . . option from the GRAPH menu item. Our instructions for doing this would be: "choose GRAPH–HISTOGRAM . . ."

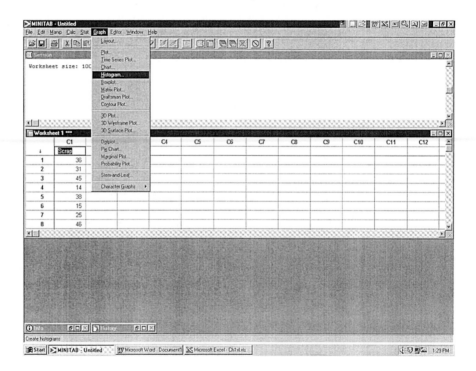

Sometimes a menu choice creates a dialogue box in which you must specify the columns of data to be used and provide more precise instructions for carrying out the method involved. In this case, simply click the appropriate choices, type in appropriate specifications, and then click the OK button when you have finished.

Entering Data

Before statistical computation can be performed by Minitab, you must enter the data. Data entry is accomplished most simply by typing directly into the DATA worksheet. Data must be entered in columns; thus, each column of data represents a variable. By default, Minitab names the columns cl, c2, c3, etc. You can create your own variable names by typing them directly into the cells above the columns of data. Names can consist of as many as 31 characters. You can always refer to a given column by its "c" designation.

Creating New Variables as Functions of Existing Variables

At times you may wish to create a new data column by performing some mathematical operation, such as addition (+), subtraction (−), multiplication (*), division (/), or exponentiation (**), on one or more existing columns. You can accomplish this by using the CALC menu. Suppose you wish to place new data in c3 that are based on the data in cl and c2. First choose CALC−CALCULATOR .... In the dialogue box, specify the column in which the results will appear; then enter the appropriate expression either by typing it or by clicking on the calculator buttons. Various math functions can be selected from the FUNCTIONS list. Here are some common expressions:

- To place the square of the data in c1 into c3, enter c1 **2.
- To place the product of the data in c1 and c2 into c3, enter c1*c2.
- To identify values of c1 that are in a given range—say, those that are positive—enter c1>0. This puts into c3 a series of 0s and 1s. For each value of c1 that is greater than 0, the corresponding value of c3 equals 1; for each value of c1 that is less than or equal to zero, the corresponding value of c3 equals 0.

Changing the Format of the Data: Stacking and Unstacking

Suppose you have entered grade point averages for samples of two male students and three female students in columns c1 and c2, respectively. For some Minitab methods, it may be necessary to reformat the data as follows: (1) place *all* the GPAs in one column—say, c3; (2) place integer values (which Minitab calls *subscripts*) in another column—say, c4—to indicate which gender is associated with each GPA value. Minitab calls this *stacking* the data. Stacking can be accomplished by choosing MANIP−STACK/ UNSTACK−STACK COLUMNS .... In the resulting dialogue box, (1) specify the columns to be stacked in the STACK THE FOLLOWING COLUMNS: area; (2) specify the column that you want to contain the stacked data in the STORE THE STACKED DATA IN area; and (3) specify the column to contain the indicators of the original sample corresponding to each data value in the stacked column (i.e., the *subscripts*) in the STORE SUBSCRIPTS IN area. An example of the original data and the stacked data that result from the preceding instructions is as follows:

Original data		Stacked data	
c1	c2	c3	c4
2.2	3.2	2.2	1
2.8	2.1	2.8	1
	3.9	3.2	2
		2.1	2
		3.9	2

To unstack data that are in the stacked format, choose MANIP−STACK/ UNSTACK−UNSTACK ONE COLUMN ... and indicate in the resulting dialogue box (1) the column containing the stacked data, (2) the columns to receive the unstacked data, and (3) the column containing the subscripts that will guide the unstacking process.

Printing Your Work and Displaying Data

To print the contents of the DATA window, make it the active window; then choose FILE–PRINT WORKSHEET . . . and specify the desired printing details in the dialogue box. To print the contents of the SESSION window, make it the active window; then choose FILE–PRINT SESSION WINDOW . . . . If you wish to print only some of the SESSION window's output (say, the statistical output of a particular analysis), select the material to be printed; then click the SELECTION button in the FILE–PRINT SESSION WINDOW dialogue box.

Saving Files

You can save a Minitab worksheet either to the hard drive of the computer you are using or to a diskette; this enables you to use it again at a later time. Select FILE–SAVE PROJECT AS . . . . In the dialogue box, select the desired drive in the SAVE IN area, and enter the desired file name in the FILE NAME: area.

Retrieving Previously Created Files

You can open previously saved Minitab files by choosing FILE–OPEN PROJECT . . . and (1) selecting the desired drive in the LOOK IN: area and (2) selecting the desired file name. If you wish to open a file saved from a different application, select ALL FILES in the FILES OF TYPE: box.

Getting Help

You can get help on the use of Minitab by choosing the HELP menu; one of the options explains how to use the other HELP options. Additionally, many dialogue boxes include a HELP button. (Sometimes they have a DESCRIBE button instead.)

Ending a Minitab Session

You can end your Minitab session by choosing FILE–EXIT.

Developing Run Charts with Minitab

To illustrate the use of Minitab to develop run charts, we use Example 1.3. The data consist of the amount of scrap per 1,000 yards of printed material for 23 consecutive runs at a printing plant. To produce a run chart as in Figure 1.5, enter the data into column c1, and name the column SCRAP. Select GRAPH–TIME SERIES PLOT . . . . In the dialogue box, specify c1 (the SCRAP values) in the GRAPH VARIABLES area (in the GRAPH 1 slot) and click OK. To print a run chart (or any graph), choose FILE–PRINT GRAPH while the graph window is active.

EXCEL

Excel contains statistical functions for most but not all of the methods discussed in this book. We have included on the book's data diskette a set of easily installed Excel macros that perform most of the methods that are absent from Excel. (Installation instructions are on the diskette.) We assume that you are familiar with the Windows 95 operating system, including opening and saving new or existing Excel files, entering data and text, creating new data through the use of formulas, and using menus and dialogue boxes. In the end-of-chapter computer appendices throughout the book, we explain how to use Excel formulas and menu choices to produce statistical results for methods presented in the book. To describe the use of Excel menus, the wording we use is "choose MENU ITEM—SELECTION." For example, to develop a histogram (a type of graph that is discussed in Chapter 2) , you choose DATA ANALYSIS . . . from the TOOLS menu. We indicate such a choice by instructing you to "choose TOOLS—DATA ANALYSIS . . . ."

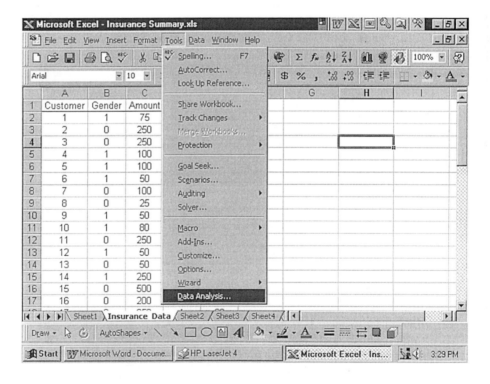

You will find that your menu choices usually produce dialogue boxes that offer many statistical and graphical options; we explain those options that you need to get the desired results. We encourage you to explore other options, too; explanations of most options can be obtained by clicking the HELP buttons in the dialogue boxes.

Most statistical methods are selected by choosing TOOLS—DATA ANALY-SIS . . . and then selecting from the list of methods that appears. You might discover that DATA ANALYSIS . . . is not available on the TOOLS menu. If this happens, you need to activate the Excel Analysis ToolPak. Select TOOLS—ADD INS . . . and, in the ADD

INS dialogue box, click the ANALYSIS TOOLPAK box and click OK. (You have to do this only once.) If DATA ANALYSIS still does not appear on the TOOLS menu, then you need to reinstall Excel using a normal installation rather than a custom installation. Similarly, all of the Excel macros are selected by choosing TOOLS–DATA ANALYSIS PLUS . . . (after they have been installed).

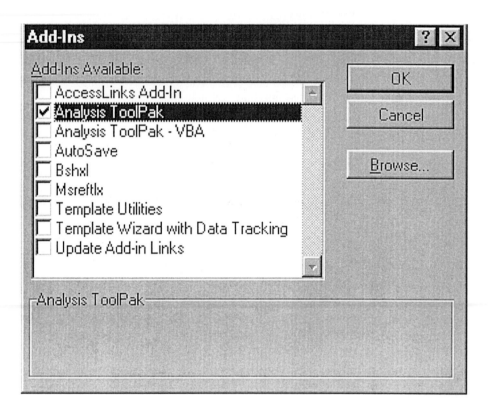

Entering Data

To enter data, type the data directly into the spreadsheet. Data for a variable are typically entered as a column, with the name of the variable (if any) appearing in the first cell. Data for a variable can also be entered as a row, with the name of the variable appearing in the first cell of the row.

Retrieving Previously Created Files

You can open previously saved Excel files by choosing FILE–OPEN . . . and selecting the appropriate directory and file name. If you wish to work with an existing data set that has been saved as a tab-delimited text file (also known as an ASCII file), open the file by choosing FILE–OPEN . . . . In the dialogue box, click the FILES OF TYPE: button (the downward arrow) and select TEXT FILES. Then select the desired file name, and click OPEN. The TEXT IMPORT WIZARD dialogue box appears next. Click the FINISH button, and the desired file opens. If a text file is not tab-delimited, you can still open it using the TEXT IMPORT WIZARD dialogue box.

Performing Arithmetic Operations

Sometimes you may wish to create a new column or row of data by performing a mathematical operation on existing columns or rows of data. Typical mathematical operations include addition (+), subtraction (−), multiplication (*), division (/), exponentiation (∧), and comparisons [equals (=), greater than (>) , less than (<), greater than or equal to (>=), less than or equal to (<=), and not equal to (< >)] on one or more existing columns or rows of data. For example:

- To place the squares of the values in cells al to a3 into cells b1 through b3: First select the cell b l; type: = a1∧2 and press the ENTER key. Then drag the fill handle for b1 (the small button on the lower right-hand corner of a selected cell) through cells b2 and b3.

- To place the product of the values in cells a1 through a3 and the corresponding values in b1 through b3 into cells c1 through c3: First select the cell c1; type: = a1*b1 and press the ENTER key. Then drag the fill handle for c1 through cells c2 and c3.

- To create a column of 0s and 1s based on the values in another column (for example, to set the values in b1 through b3 to 1 if a value in a1 through a3 is greater than or equal to 10, and to 0 otherwise): First select cell b1 and type the formula =(a1>=10) and press the ENTER key. Then drag the fill handle for b1 through cells b2 and b3.

Getting Help

Excel provides help on commands, buttons, and functions from the HELP menu. Many dialogue boxes also contain HELP buttons that explain many of the options that are available.

Developing Run Charts with Excel

To illustrate the use of Excel to develop run charts, we use Example 1.3. To produce a run chart as in Figure 1.5, enter the name SCRAP in cell a1, and enter the data into cells a2 through a24. Choose INSERT−CHART . . . . This activates the CHART WIZARD. Follow the four steps of the CHART WIZARD to produce the run chart: (1) Click the LINE chart type, then click the first option on the second row of chart subtypes (lines with markers displayed at each value); (2) in the DATA RANGE box, enter the cell range containing the data (al:a24) and click the SERIES IN COLUMNS button; (3) provide chart title and labels for the axes as desired; (4) indicate whether you wish the run chart to be placed on a new sheet or within the currently active sheet.

JMP IN

JMP IN Windows

The JMP IN DATA TABLE window is a simple spreadsheet used primarily to enter and modify data. Each column contains the data for a given variable, and each row contains all the observations for a given sampling unit. A distinct window is produced each time

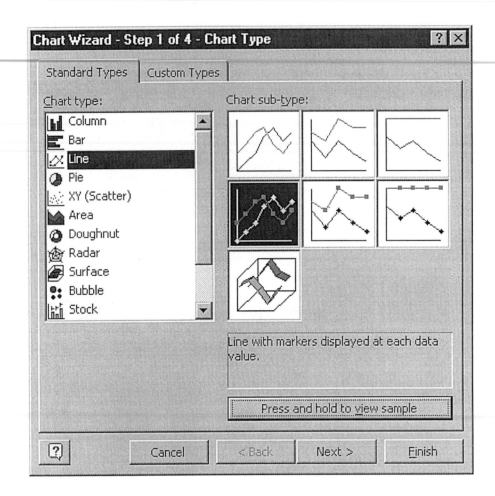

an analysis is performed or a graph is created. You can choose menu commands at any time regardless of which window is active. You can access any window from the WINDOW menu.

Providing Instructions

To choose an instruction, first click the appropriate menu item, then click the appropriate choice for that menu item. Henceforth, to describe such a choice, we direct you to "choose MENU ITEM—CHOICE." For example, to create a histogram (a type of graph presented in Chapter 2) and to determine the average and other summary measures for a variable, you choose the DISTRIBUTION OF Y option from the ANALYZE menu. Our instructions for doing this would be: "choose ANALYZE—DISTRIBUTION OF Y."

Entering Data

Consider the insurance data in Example 1.1. To enter these data into a new data table, choose FILE—NEW. Before you enter data, you must indicate the number of rows and columns you will use. (You can always add more rows and columns later.) To indicate

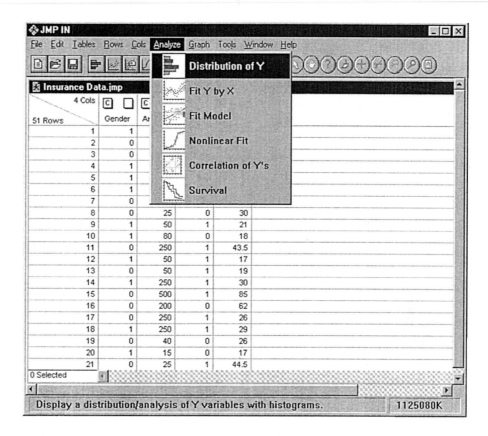

the number of rows, choose ROWS–ADD ROWS . . . . In the dialogue box, enter the number of rows to add and click the ADD button. For the insurance data, enter 51, since there are 51 sampling units. Each new data table starts with one column. To add columns for additional variables, choose COLS–ADD COLUMNS . . . . In the dialogue box, specify the number of columns to be added in the # OF COLS TO ADD box; for the insurance data enter 4 because there are 4 variables. Next, specify the placement of the new columns by clicking the appropriate button (choose from AT START, AT END, and AFTER SELECTED COL). If you want to add only one column, choose instead COLS–NEW COLUMN . . . , and simply click OK in the dialogue box.

For each variable (column of data), you must provide some essential specifications. This can be done at the time that you create a new column, or the specs can be entered or revised later directly in the data table. First select the columns by dragging the cursor over the cells containing the column names. Choose COLS–COLUMN INFO; this produces the Column Information dialogue box (one box for each selected column). Here, you specify the following information for each column:

1. COL NAME: Simply type the desired column name. For the insurance data, type Gender, Amount, Type, and Income.

2. DATA TYPE: Choose between NUMERIC (i.e., numbers only) and CHARAC-TER (i.e., labels such as M and F). For the insurance data, choose NUMERIC.

3. MODELING TYPE: Choose between CONTINUOUS, ORDINAL, and NOMI-NAL. See Section 2.2 for a discussion of these terms. Briefly, *continuous* means

the data are quantitative and are appropriate for arithmetic. *Ordinal* means that the data indicate the order of the observations (e.g., 1 indicates largest, 2 indicates second largest, etc.) but not their amounts. *Nominal* data simply indicate that observations are of the same category or different categories (e.g., male or female). For the insurance data, specify Gender and Type as NOMINAL, and specify Amount and Income as CONTINUOUS.

4. FIELD WIDTH: This indicates the maximum number of characters that can fit in the column for any observation. It is relevant only for columns with DATA TYPE: = CHARACTER.

Columns containing dates should be specified as DATA TYPE: NUMERIC. In addition, specify FORMAT: DATE AND TIME.

You can alter the information for a column at any time. If you want to change only the data type, just click the small box above and to the left of the column name (it is called a *popup box*) and select the desired type from the list that appears. To make more extensive changes, simply double-click above the column name to produce the Column Information dialogue box.

If you do not specify the data type and/or modeling type for a column, JMP IN assumes DATA TYPE: NUMERIC and MODELING TYPE: CONTINUOUS. Unless stated otherwise, it is always assumed in the chapter appendices that you have specified each variable in this manner. If another data type and/or modeling type is needed for a particular analysis or graph, this will be stated in the appendix.

Data entry is accomplished by typing directly into the DATA worksheet. Click on a cell, then type the data value. To move right to the next cell in a row, press the TAB key. To move down to the next cell in a column, press the RETURN key. You can create or change variable names by typing them directly into the cells above the columns of data.

Creating New Variables as Functions of Existing Variables

At times you may wish to create a new data column by performing mathematical operations on one or more existing columns. Consider the insurance data. Suppose you wish to place new data in COLUMN 5 that consist of the ratios of policy amounts (in COLUMN 2) to income (in COLUMN 4). First create COLUMN 5. In the Column Information dialogue box for the variable being created, choose DATA SOURCE: FORMULA and click OK. This opens the CALCULATOR window. You will see a small gray square in the Formula Display area (the large box in the lower half of the CALCULATOR window). Enter the desired expression here using standard algebraic notation. To specify a variable to be used in the calculation, select it from the Column Selector List at the upper left side of the CALCULATOR window. To insert a number, either type it from your computer's keyboard or click on the desired choice from the Keypad area at the upper center of the window; then press your keyboard's RETURN key. To insert a math operation (+, −, ÷, *, parentheses, etc.), either click on the desired choice from the Keypad area at the upper center of the window or type it from your computer's keyboard and press the RETURN key. To select a function (such as the logical operator "<"), click on the desired function from the Function Browser in the upper right portion of the window. When the desired function has been entered, click the close box in the upper left corner of the CALCULATOR window. To create the ratios of policy amount to income for the insurance data, click Amount from the Column Selector List; click the division key from the keypad; click Income; and close the calculator window.

For example:

- To create COLUMN 2 = the squares of the data in COLUMN 1: In the CALCULATOR window for COLUMN 2, (1) click COLUMN 1; (2) click the X^2 button.

- To create COLUMN 3 = the product of the data in COLUMN 1 and COLUMN 2: In the CALCULATOR window for COLUMN 3, (1) click COLUMN 1; (2) click *; and (3) click COLUMN 2.

- To create COLUMN 2 = indicators of those values of COLUMN 1 that are in a given range—say, those that are positive: (1) Click COLUMN 1; (2) click COMPARISONS—x>y. This puts into COLUMN 2 a series of 0s and 1s. For each value of COLUMN 1 that is greater than 0, the corresponding value of COLUMN 2 equals 1; for each value of COLUMN 1 that is less than or equal to zero, the corresponding value of COLUMN 2 equals 0.

Changing the Format of the Data: Stacking and Splitting

Suppose you have entered grade point averages for two male students and three female students in COLUMN 1 and COLUMN 2, respectively. At times, it may be necessary to reformat the data as follows: (1) place *all* the data in one column; (2) place indicator values in a second column (which JMP IN calls the _ID_ column) to indicate the students' gender associated with each GPA value. This can be accomplished by choosing

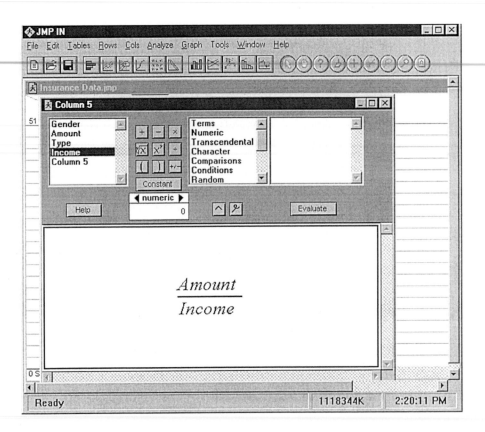

TABLES–STACK COLUMNS . . . . In the dialogue box, select the columns to be stacked; click the STACK button; and click OK. The new stacked data will be created in a new data table in a column with the default name of _STACKED_. A second column is also created; its default name is _ID_ and it contains integer values that identify the gender of the student associated with each GPA value.

The new column _STACKED_ is ordered in a surprising manner. Its first value is the first value of COLUMN 1; its second value is the first value of COLUMN 2; its third value is the second value of COLUMN 1; its fourth value is the second value of COLUMN 2; and so on. You may wish to reorder the data so that all COLUMN 1 data precede the COLUMN 2 data. To do this, select TABLES–SORT . . . . In the dialogue box, select _ID_ and click ADD; then click OK.

An example of the original data and the stacked data that result from the preceding instructions (before and after sorting) is as follows:

Original (split) data table		Stacked data table		Stacked data table (sorted)	
SAMPLE 1	SAMPLE 2	DATA	ID	DATA	ID
2.2	3.2	2.2	Column 1	2.2	Column 1
2.8	2.1	3.2	Column 2	2.8	Column 1
	3.9	2.8	Column 1	3.2	Column 2
		2.1	Column 2	2.1	Column 2
		3.9	Column 2	3.9	Column 2

To unstack data that are in a stacked format, choose TABLES—SPLIT COLUMNS . . . . In the dialogue box, select the column to be split; click the SPLIT button; select the ID column and click COL ID; and click OK. The new split data will be created in a new data table.

Printing Your Work

To print the contents of the window you are working in, choose FILE—PRINT.

Saving Files

You can save a JMP IN worksheet either to the hard drive of the computer you are using or to a diskette. Select FILE—SAVE AS . . . . In the dialogue box, type the desired file name and specify the drive, directory, and subdirectory (if any). If you wish to save in a different format, select the desired format by clicking the appropriate button at the bottom of the dialogue box.

Retrieving Previously Created Files

You can open previously saved JMP IN files by choosing FILE—OPEN . . . , selecting the desired file name in the dialogue box, and clicking OPEN. Files saved from a different application may not appear in the list of files; click the SHOW ALL FILES button.

Ending a JMP IN Session

To end your JMP IN session, choose FILE—EXIT (Macintosh users choose FILE—QUIT).

JMP IN Help

To get help, choose HELP—CONTENTS. (Macintosh users choose APPLE—ABOUT JMP . . . , where APPLE represents the apple-shaped icon on the menu bar.) This provides help regarding statistical methods in general and the JMP IN menus and calculator function in particular.

Developing Run Charts with JMP IN

Consider Example 1.3. Enter the data into COLUMN 1, and name the column SCRAP. Set the data type to NUMERIC and the modeling type to CONTINUOUS. Click the small box to the right over the column name and select "Y." (This is called the Column Role popup box. It will be explained in greater detail in Appendix 2.) Select GRAPH—OVERLAY PLOTS and click the PLOT button. This produces a run chart similar to Figure 1.5. If desired, you can adjust the scale of the horizontal axis as follows: Double-click anywhere just below the horizontal axis. In the dialogue box that appears, enter the desired MINIMUM, MAXIMUM, and INCREMENT values. For these data, the values 0, 23, and 1, respectively, are suggested.

To control the size of the run chart (and any other JMP IN graphs), click anywhere within the graph. This produces a small sizing box in the lower right corner of the graph. Click on the sizing box and drag the outline of the graph to resize it.

Chapter 2

Exploring and Summarizing Data

CHAPTER OUTLINE

Introduction

In Chapter 1, you were introduced to many of the basic elements of statistical analysis: processes, populations, parameters, samples, statistics, and so on. You were also introduced to *statistical thinking*—a pattern of analysis that leads to the acquisition and conversion of data into information that provides an opportunity to improve the effectiveness and productivity of organizations. In this chapter, we present some broadly applicable statistical techniques for exploring and summarizing data. Mastery of these methods enables you to use statistics effectively to learn about phenomena that are important to you. Indeed, at the end of this chapter, you will be prepared to carry out a statistical study using the concepts and methods of Chapters 1 and 2. Planning and executing your own statistical study are perhaps the most effective means of truly understanding statistics. There are two important limitations to the methods of this chapter, however. They do not provide a way to assess the risk associated with any conclusions you might reach, and they do not enable you to develop statistical models to facilitate decision making. Developing these capabilities is the principal objective of Chapters 3–11.

With regard to data for a variable of interest, there are several aspects that we typically wish to summarize: the distribution of the data, the location (sometimes called the center) of the data, and the variation of the data. In the following sections, we define each of these terms and discuss the most important techniques involved with each.

2.2   Types of Data

Before we discuss ways to summarize data, you need to understand the kinds of data you are likely to encounter. Data can be either *qualitative* or *quantitative;* that is, they involve either qualitative or quantitative statistical variables.

Qualitative data do not adhere to a meaningful numerical scale; rather, they consist of categories or labels that may or may not have a natural ordering. Qualitative data that have no natural order are **nominal scaled.** To illustrate, suppose a runner's competitor number in a 10-kilometer race is 319. This is simply a label that identifies the runner; it has no natural order and provides no information about the runner's order of finish or the completion time. In a market research survey on automobile purchasing behavior, the make of car owned is qualitative information because it identifies a category (such as "Ford owner" or "Toyota owner") in which the principle of order is meaningless.

Qualitative data that have a natural order but provide no information about the difference between adjacent positions are **ordinal scaled.** For example, if a runner finishes fourth in a race, the "4" identifies the order of finish for this runner in a natural sequence from first to last; but it provides no information about the difference in times between this runner and the runner that finished third and fifth. Similarly, if you rank eighth in your class, the "8" identifies your relative position in the class without providing any information about the difference between your grades and those of the persons who rank seventh and ninth.

On the other hand, **quantitative data** are numerically distinguished and ordered, and the differences among them are meaningful. That is, *quantitative data indicate an amount (how much or how many).* For example, a runner's time in a 10-kilometer race is a quantitative variable because it measures the amount of time it took the runner to finish this race. And if this runner's time is, say, 2 minutes less than that of another runner, the difference of 2 minutes is a meaningful quantity. Quantitative data may be classified as **interval scaled** or **ratio scaled.** The distinction between these scales is not pertinent to the methods presented in this book, so we do not discuss it any further.

It is important to distinguish between quantitative data and qualitative data. The choice of statistical method is often driven by the type of data involved. Many summary calculations make sense only for quantitative data, whereas others are appropriate for qualitative data. In summarizing quantitative data, we are usually interested in the average of the data and/or some measure of variation of the data. In summarizing qualitative data, we should consider first whether the data are nominal scaled or ordinal scaled. For nominal-scaled data, we are usually interested in the proportion of items in a given category. For ordinal-scaled data, a proper choice of analysis is to use a branch of statistics known as *nonparametric methods,* a topic not covered in this text.

EXAMPLE 2.1

In the life insurance study of Example 1.1, the statistical variables were policy amount, type of policy, gender, and annual income. State whether each variable is qualitative (nominal or ordinal scaled) or quantitative and justify your answer. For each variable, indicate whether it is summarized more meaningfully by an average or a proportion.

Solution

Policy amount is quantitative. It indicates *how much* money the policy will pay out upon the customer's death. Annual income is also quantitative because it indicates *how many* dollars the customer earns per year. Type of policy and gender are qualitative (both nominal scaled). Type of policy places the customer's policy into a category—either term or universal. Gender categorizes the customer as either male or female. Quantities that summarize these variables meaningfully are the *average* policy amount, the *average* annual income, the *proportion* of term policies, and the *proportion* of male customers.

2.3 Distributions of Data

To discern any meaning from a set of data, we almost always need to summarize it in some fashion. There are two basic approaches to summarizing data. One is to characterize with tables or graphs the arrangement of data between the smallest and largest values. Suppose the lowest grade in your class on a statistics test was 51 and the highest was 97. How well did the class do as a whole? That depends on how the other grades were arranged between 51 and 97. To illustrate, consider two possible situations: (1) most grades were in the 60s and low 70s, with only a few in the 80s and 90s; and (2) most grades were in the 90s and 80s, with only a few in the 60s and 50s. Although the ranges are the same, the second situation represents better overall performance. The grades are arranged in such a way that most were in the upper half of the range, unlike in the first situation. In statistics, the arrangement of data is known as the **distribution** of the data. The distribution is important because it reveals the pattern of variation and helps us to better understand the phenomenon the data represent. The second way to summarize data is to use numerical quantities called statistics (or parameters, if the data happen to constitute the entire population). For instance, you might characterize your class's performance on the statistics test by citing the average test grade. In this section, we introduce methods for characterizing distributions of data with tables and graphs. In following sections, we discuss some important statistics and considerations involved in their use.

2.3.1 Dot Diagrams for Quantitative Data

When there are only a small number of quantitative data values, their distribution can easily be demonstrated with a **dot diagram.** A dot diagram is simply a plot of the individual data values along a line segment. If two or more values coincide, they are stacked. Suppose ten persons received the following grades on a statistics test: 66, 74, 78, 78, 80, 81, 85, 88, 89, 97. To construct a dot diagram, we need a line segment that

Figure 2.1

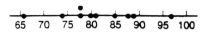

Dot diagram for ten
test grades

includes the range from 66 to 97. The ten grades are then indicated on the line segment using a dot as a plotting symbol, as in Figure 2.1. Notice that the two identical values of 78 are stacked. The dot diagram of Figure 2.1 reveals that the grades are distributed fairly symmetrically, centered roughly around a value of 80. The grades of 66 and 97 stand out somewhat from the rest.

Designed experiments often involve observing a fairly small number of data values under a common set of conditions. In this regard, dot diagrams are often an effective means of graphically displaying such data, as will be seen in Chapters 7 and 8. To illustrate, suppose a professor gave the same test to three separate classes, each of which was taught using different methods. The results already given represent Section 1. The results for Sections 2 and 3 are the following:

Section 2:	65	66	68	71	77	78	80	82	88
Section 3:	48	61	62	71	75	82	84	91	99

Figure 2.2 shows computer-generated* vertical dot diagrams for all three sections on the same graph. All three dot diagrams relate to the same line segment: the vertical axis of the graph from 40 to 100.

Figure 2.2

JMP IN and Excel dot
diagrams for the
statistics test grades
of three sections

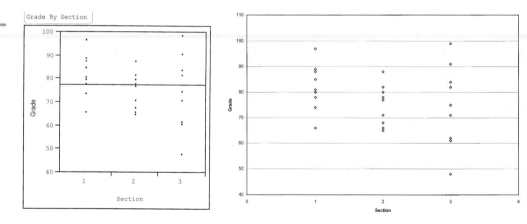

How would you compare the distribution of grades for the three sections? In Figure 2.2, it is apparent that the average grades for Sections 2 and 3 are about equal, whereas the average for Section 1 is a bit higher. At the same time, the variation among the grades of the students in Section 3 is greatest, whereas the variation in Section 2 is the smallest.

If a data set contains too many data values, dot diagrams become too crowded to be effective. If this is the case and we wish to depict a distribution, then the better approach is to group together similar data values. Instead of plotting individual values, we report the number of data values that lie in each group. This can be done using either a *frequency distribution* or a *stem-and-leaf diagram*, the subjects of the following sections.

---

* Throughout this chapter, we encourage you to use a computer to summarize data sets. Virtually all of the methods that we present can easily be done on a computer. Instructions are given in the chapter appendix.

2.3.2 Frequency Distributions

A very popular approach to demonstrate the arrangement of data is to develop a **frequency distribution.** In all likelihood, you have seen frequency distributions displayed in newspapers—*USA Today* features them virtually every day—and in other media. Frequency distributions can be developed for data involving quantitative or qualitative variables. If data involve a quantitative variable, the graphical demonstration of the frequency distrution is a **histogram.** If data involve a qualitative variable, the graphical demonstration is a **bar chart.**

Frequency Distributions for Quantitative Data: Histograms

To develop a frequency distribution when the data are quantitative, we divide the interval covered by the data into a series of nonoverlapping classes. We then count the data values contained in each class. For example, consider the following set of 20 grades, ranging from 54 to 93, on a business statistics test:

93	83	86	83	56	63	73	78	81
62	88	54	72	74	87	78	61	63
89	64							

How did the class do on the test? Notice that even for a class as small as 20 students, you must scan the data for a while, probably organizing it informally in your mind before assessing class performance.

Suppose we divide the interval covered by the data into the following five classes: 50–59, 60–69, 70–79, 80–89, 90–99. A **frequency** is the number of data values lying in a given class. By simple counting, we see that the frequencies for the five classes are 2, 5, 5, 7, and 1, respectively. Sometimes it is more helpful to know the *proportion* of data values within the classes rather than the actual count. A **relative frequency** is the proportion of the set of data values that lie within a given class. The frequencies and relative frequencies for the 20 test grades are shown in Table 2.1.

Although the frequency distribution of quantitative data may be indicated in tabular form as in Table 2.1, an often preferred method of presentation is a graph of the frequencies (or relative frequencies) against their respective class intervals. Such a graph is called a **histogram.** Computer-generated histograms for the 20 test grades are given in Figure 2.3.

A histogram allows us to visually observe the distribution of the data. For example, in Figure 2.3, you can see that the grades were distributed fairly evenly between the low 60s and the high 80s. Only three grades were outside this range: one in the 90s and two in the 50s.

In practice, most histograms are developed by a computer. The key step is to establish the classes properly. Most statistical packages use default rules to determine the classes; they should also offer the user the opportunity to specify the classes. In general, the selection of classes should be guided by the following principles:

1. The selected classes should enable the distribution of the data to be honestly portrayed.
2. The classes should be easy to understand and interpret for the first-time viewer.

It is a good idea to keep these principles in mind because a software's default process may pay inadequate attention to them. Let's consider the first principle. If a frequency distribution is to reveal the essence of the distribution of the data, it is necessary to

Table 2.1

Frequencies and relative frequencies for 20 statistics test grades

Class	Frequency	Relative Frequency
50–59	2	$\frac{2}{20} = .10$
60–69	5	$\frac{5}{20} = .25$
70–79	5	$\frac{5}{20} = .25$
80–89	7	$\frac{7}{20} = .35$
90–99	1	$\frac{1}{20} = .05$
Total	20	1.00

Figure 2.3

Minitab and Excel histograms for the 20 statistics test grades

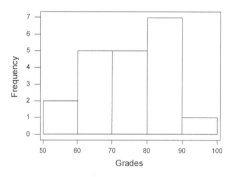
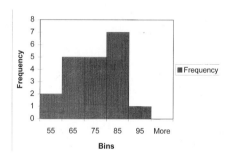

choose an appropriate number of classes. If we use too few classes, we lose sensitivity to the distribution. If we use too many classes, we get some classes that are empty or contain only one or two data values. This creates a ragged appearance (a "city skyline" effect) that obscures the overall distribution. Neither provides a satisfactory summary of the data. There is no uniquely correct number of classes. The best procedure is to start with a reasonable guess and develop an initial frequency distribution; continue to make adjustments until you are satisfied with the result. As a general rule, the number of classes should be between 5 and 15. The larger the data set, the more classes that can be used effectively.

The purpose of summarization is to make it easy for the user to quickly understand key aspects of a data set (the second principle). Therefore it is important to define class limits as naturally as possible. To accomplish this, it may be necessary to adjust the boundaries generated by a computer. In the test grades example, we are accustomed to the 10-point grading scale. Therefore, classes of 50–59, 60–69, 70–79, 80–89, and 90–99 seem more natural than those that might be determined initially by a computer. Such adjustments might change the number of classes slightly and might result in a slightly less satisfactory representation of the distribution. You must use your judgment to make tradeoffs between ease of interpretation by the user and effective portrayal of the distibution.

In contrast to dot diagrams, histograms are most effective for larger data sets consisting of, say, at least 30–35 data values.

Frequency Distributions for Qualitative Data: Bar Charts

Suppose we want to know the distribution of students among the six academic majors in a business school. Based on a sample of 30 students, we find 7 students in finance,

6 in accounting, 9 in management, 3 in MIS, 4 in marketing, and 1 in economics. Such data information is qualitative because a student's major is simply a category that does not adhere to a meaningful numerical scale. In addition to academic major, characteristics such as gender, location, opinion, party affiliation, and so on are all qualitative. To develop the frequency distribution for qualitative data, we first determine the number (frequency) or proportion (relative frequency) of individuals in each category, then graph each frequency or relative frequency using "bars" to produce a bar chart.

For the academic major example, the bar chart is given in Figure 2.4. From this figure it is clear that about 70% of these students are in finance, accounting, or management. The purpose of a bar chart, therefore, is the same as that of a histogram: to reveal the distribution of qualitative data.

Figure 2.4

Excel and JMP IN bar charts for the academic major example

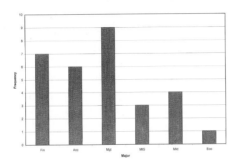
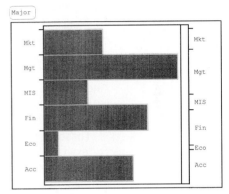

When data are qualitative, often there is no natural order to the categories, as in the example involving academic major. Hence, in determining the bar chart, we can place the categories on the horizontal axis in any order we find useful. For example, JMP IN arranges the categories alphabetically, as in Figure 2.4. If the categories are ordered according to their frequencies—the category with the highest frequency appearing first, followed by the category with the next highest frequency, and so on—the resulting bar chart is known as a **Pareto diagram.** Pareto diagrams are often used to target major problem sources (for example, those categories with the highest frequencies of problems) in process improvement actions.

2.3.3 Stem-and-Leaf Diagrams for Quantitative Data

The **stem-and-leaf diagram** (or plot) is another very simple but powerful way of organizing quantitative data to reveal their distribution. For example, Figure 2.5 is a Minitab-generated stem-and-leaf diagram for the 20 test grades given at the beginning of Section 2.3.2. For the moment, let's ignore the first column of this output and concentrate on the remaining portion. A stem-and-leaf diagram consists of two fundamental parts: the **stem** and the **leaf.** In this example, the stems are the "tens"

Figure 2.5

Minitab-generated stem-and-leaf diagram for the 20 test grades

```
  2     5  46
  7     6  12334
 (5)    7  23488
  8     8  1336789
  1     9  3
```

digits—that is, the numbers 5, 6, 7, 8, and 9 listed in a column. To the right of each stem we find the leaf values (the "units" digits). Notice that the first stem value is 5 and the leaf values are 4 and 6, thus corresponding to the grades 54 and 56. The next stem value is 6 and the leaf values are 1, 2, 3, 3, and 4, corresponding to the grades 61, 62, 63, 63, and 64, and so on. In general, all numbers with the same stem value are placed on the same row of the stem-and-leaf diagram, with the leaf values indicated in an ordered sequence to the right of the stem value. As in a histogram, the stems divide the interval covered by the quantitative data into a series of nonoverlapping classes.

Now let's return to the first column. This column provides cumulative frequencies for each stem, going from the extreme stems toward the center. The "center" stem is indicated by parentheses; the value in parentheses is its frequency. Thus, there were 2 grades for the first stem (the 50s). There were 7 grades for all stems of 6 or lower. There were 5 grades for the "center" stem. Working from the other end, there was one grade for the 9 stem (the 90s), and 8 grades for all stems of 8 or higher.

Notice that the test grades involve two-digit numbers; thus, there is a natural division between the tens digits (the stems) and the units (the leaves). For larger numbers, there are several alternatives for defining stems and leaves. For example, consider the four-digit number 1,625. One might choose a stem of 16 and a leaf of 25. Alternatively, the stem might be defined by the thousands digit; thus, the stem would be 1 and the leaf would be 625. In the end, the best choice is the arrangement that best depicts the distribution of the data.

For some data sets, one might find that there are too many leaves for a given stem. For example, if all 20 test grades had been in the 70s and 80s, using the tens digit to define the stem would produce only two rows. To achieve a better resolution of the distribution of grades, we could segment the grades that have a common stem into a "high-range group" and a "low-range group." Thus, the stems for grades in the 80s would become 8^+ for grades of 85 to 89 and 8^- for grades of 80 to 84. Similarly, the stems for grades in the 70s would be 7^+ and 7^-. This approach produces four rows of grades rather than two rows and thus provides a better resolution of the distribution of grades.

As with histograms, statistical software allows a user to intervene and adjust the initial stem-and-leaf diagram that has been determined by the software. This is necessary when the generated diagram does not appear to provide the most effective depiction of the distribution.

As an alternative to dot diagrams and histograms, a stem-and-leaf diagram is especially effective in organizing data *manually* (i.e., not on a computer) because (1) it provides the individual data values so that further, visual analysis can be performed, and (2) new data values can be added as they become available without requiring the reconstruction of the diagram.

2.3.4. The Shapes of Distributions

How would you describe the shape of the histogram of statistics test grades in Figure 2.3? It is very helpful to have a vocabulary for such a purpose. In most distributions, the data tend to concentrate around a single peak, with the peak near the center. The greatest concentration of data values creates the single peak and usually occurs near the center of the range of data. At the same time, frequencies usually decline for values far away from the single peak. Such distributions are said to be **single peaked** (or **mound shaped** because they look like the profile of a mound). For single-peaked

Figure 2.6

Three common single-peaked distribution shapes: (a) symmetric, (b) skewed to the right, (c) skewed to the left

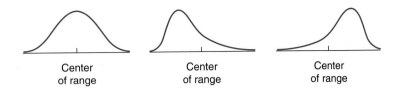

distributions, if frequencies decline symmetrically as we move away from the center in either direction, we say that the distribution is **symmetric.** An example of a single-peaked, symmetric distribution is given in Figure 2.6(a), where we adhere to the usual practice of using smooth curves to represent distributions of quantitative data. On the other hand, the greatest frequency may not lie exactly at the center of the range, and the distribution may "tail" off more slowly in one direction than in the other. In this case, we say that the single-peaked distribution is *skewed*. If the frequencies tail off more slowly to the right, we say the distribution is **skewed to the right** (or positively skewed). If the frequencies tail off more slowly to the left, we say the distribution is **skewed to the left** (or negatively skewed). Skewed, single-peaked distributions often occur when quantitative data are bounded by some limit in one direction but not in the other. For example, salaries are bounded on the low end by zero, but there is (theoretically) no upper bound. Indeed, distributions of salaries within an organization are often skewed to the right, whereas distributions of grades on a very easy test may be skewed to the left because they "pile up" near the maximum of 100. Figures 2.6(b) and (c) illustrate distributions that are skewed to the right and left, respectively.

Data sometimes are distributed in ways other than those described here. There are distributions that have no peaks and distributions that have more than one peak. In addition, there are skewed distributions that are not mound shaped. But the shapes described here are the most common and suffice to describe most of the distributions you will encounter.

2.3.5 The Value of Understanding Distributions

The following example illustrates the need for understanding distributions, especially when the data involve a quantitative variable. For many manufacturing processes, management establishes process specifications—lower and upper limits beyond which process outcomes are considered unacceptable. In this regard, frequency distributions allow us to compare the distribution of process outcomes with process specifications, as illustrated in Figure 2.7. In part (a), process outcomes vary enough that some

Figure 2.7

Distribution of process outputs versus specification limits

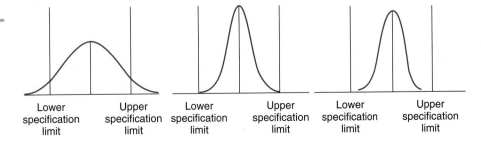

proportion of product is outside the specificaitons in one direction or the other. Part (b) shows that a reduction of variation has resulted in virtually all outcomes being acceptable. Part (c) indicates that continued reduction of variation has resulted in more outcomes that are near the target value.

Using the Computer

Data analysis is greatly aided by the use of a computer. In the following illustration, we use computer-aided analysis to study the insurance data from Example 1.1.

EXAMPLE 2.2

It was important for the insurance manager of Example 1.1 to understand how customers' insurance policy amounts were related to gender, type of policy, and income. Recall that the men seemed to prefer term policies more than the women did, the men tended to take out larger policies than the women did, and policy amount seemed to depend on income. Let's see whether these initial conclusions hold up under closer scrutiny. We now use Minitab to develop dot plots and histograms of the policy amounts and the incomes for this sample of customers. Minitab histograms for the 51 policy amounts and incomes are given in Figure 2.8. Both histograms reveal

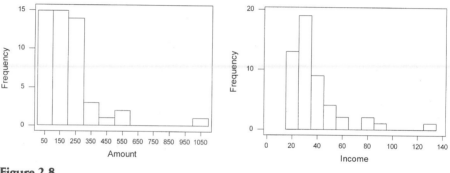

Figure 2.8

Minitab histograms for policy amounts and incomes

distributions that are distinctly skewed to the right. We may prefer to construct stem-and-leaf diagrams instead of histograms. Although not shown here, they reveal the same distribution shape as seen in the histograms.

It was also important to the manager to compare male and female customers. Let's compare the distributions of policy amounts and incomes for men versus women. Since there were only 21 women in the sample, we use dot diagrams rather than histograms. The dot diagrams are given in Figure 2.9, where "0" indicates policy amounts for men and "1" indicates policy amounts for women. The dot diagrams for policy amounts indicate that women's policies tend to be somewhat smaller than those of men, although the policies of both genders have similar ranges (except the one extremely large policy for a male). Meanwhile, the dot diagrams for income indicate that women's incomes tend to be lower than men's incomes. This raises the possibility that the only reason for the differences between the policy amounts for the genders may be the differences between their incomes.

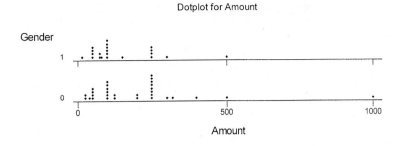

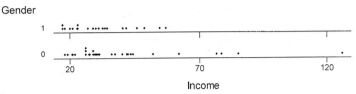

Figure 2.9

Minitab dot diagrams for policy amounts and incomes of female and male customers

We continue the computer-aided analysis of the insurance data at the end of Section 2.6.

<table>
<tr><td>**2.4**</td><td></td></tr>
</table>

Measures of Location: The Center of the Data

In the previous section, we summarized the distribution of data by using tables and graphs. In many statistical applications, it is also desirable to use numerical quantities to summarize data. As you know, these are called *parameters* and *statistics* (depending on whether the data constitute a population/process or a sample, respectively).

The two questions of most general interest concern the magnitude of the data and the variation among the data: How large are the data values? and How much do the data values vary (among themselves)? In this section, we focus on magnitude. We discuss variation in Section 2.5.

Examples of questions involving the magnitude of data are:

How well did our class do on a test?

How many sales calls do our sales representatives usually make in a month?

Are the bearings we are producing strong enough?

For each of these questions, the answer differs somewhat for each member of the data set. So the questions really deal with locating what we might call the *center* of the data—a value around which the data tend to be centered. This measure is called the **location** of the data or the **central tendency** of the data. There are three primary measures used to characterize the location of data: the mean, the median, and the mode. Each is useful under certain circumstances. We first define each of these measures; then we discuss their properties, their advantages and disadvantages, and the circumstances under which they are useful.

2.4.1   The Arithmetic Mean

The **arithmetic mean** (which we henceforth refer to simply as the **mean**) is the average value of the data. This is the average with which you are already familiar. The mean is the most commonly used measure of location and is usually the easiest to determine. It is found by summing the data values and dividing the sum by the number of data values. For example, recall the statistics test grades of the three sections illustrated in Figure 2.2:

Section 1:	66	74	78	78	80	81	85	88	89	97
Section 2:	65	66	68	71	77	78	80	82	88	
Section 3:	48	61	62	71	75	82	84	91	99	

We can easily use a computer to determine the mean grades for these sections to be, respectively:

```
MEAN = 81.600
MEAN = 75.000
MEAN = 74.778
```

To delineate clearly between samples and populations, we use the symbol $\overline{X}$ (pronounced "X bar") to represent the mean of a sample and the symbol μ (the Greek letter mu) to represent the mean of a population or process. The expressions for determining the values of $\overline{X}$ and μ are given by (2.1) and (2.2), respectively. Notice in these expressions that, as we said in Chapter 1, the number of members in a population is denoted by N, whereas the number of sampling units in a sample is denoted by n. The latter is typically called the **sample size.**

$$\text{Sample mean:} \quad \overline{X} = \frac{\sum_{i=1}^{n} X_i}{n} \tag{2.1}$$

$$\text{Population mean:} \quad \mu = \frac{\sum_{i=1}^{N} X_i}{N} \tag{2.2}$$

2.4.2   The Median

The **median** is the value that divides an ordered set of data into halves. Thus, half the data are smaller than or equal to the median, and half are equal to it or larger. To determine the median, we must first arrange the data in order (usually from low to high). For example, look at the grades of class Section 2 as given in Section 2.4.1; they are already arranged from low to high. Notice that the middle grade of 77 divides the data into two equal parts, four grades below it and four grades above it. So 77 is the median grade.

Now notice the grades of class Section 1; they are also arranged from low to high. But here there is no middle grade, because the number of grades is even. In such cases, the median is defined to be the average of the two data values nearest the center in the ordered set. For the first section, the median is 80.5, the average of the two middle grades 80 and 81.

Again, we can easily use a computer to determine medians. For example, the median grade of the third section is: MEDIAN = 75.000. There is no universal symbol for the median, and none is necessary in this book.

2.4.3   The Mode

The **mode** of a set of data is the value that occurs most frequently. Its appeal is that it is the data value that is most typical. The mode for the statistics test grades of Section 1 is 78, since this grade is most frequent. Now consider the grades of Section 2. These grades have no mode because each grade appears only once; there are no repeated values. In fact, we can encounter situations in which two or more values in a data set occur more than once but with exactly the same frequency. For example, the following data are the number of base hits in a baseball game by each of the nine starting players: 0, 0, 0, 1, 1, 2, 2, 2, 3. The most frequent values are 0 and 2, with each appearing three times. For these data, there are two modes. Though having an intuitive appeal, the mode is generally the least useful of the measures of location. Unlike the mean and the median, the mode might not be a unique value. For some data sets, the mode does not exist because each value appears once, with no duplication. Some data sets have two or more values that occur most frequently. Generally, data sets with more than one mode are said to have no unique mode because the essence of describing the typical value is really lost. This is likely to be the case for large data sets with a wide variety of values and little chance of repeated values.

In contrast, the mode is effective for summarizing data sets that contain many repeated values. For example, suppose the frequencies of selling 0, 1, 2, 3, and 4 computers per day by an office products firm over the last 30 days are 8, 14, 5, 2, and 1, respectively. For these data, it is meaningful to point out that the mode is one sale per day to indicate the most frequently occurring sales result for a day.

The concept of the mode is also useful in describing frequency distributions. Consider the distribution of the 20 test grades in Table 2.1. The most frequently occurring grades were in the 80s. The class with the greatest frequency (i.e., the most data values) is called the **modal class,** and the midpoint of the modal class is defined to be the mode.

2.4.4   A Comparison of the Properties of the Mean, Median, and Mode

We have presented three different ways to characterize the location of the data: the mean, median, and mode. A natural question is: Which one do I use? The choice depends on the needs of the specific situation. To understand this, you first must understand the characteristics of the three measures. Their characteristics differ significantly with regard to three issues: (1) sensitivity to the presence of outlier data values, (2) sensitivity to distributional shape, and (3) status of theoretical development. For the most part, these issues involve only the mean and the median.

The Effect of Outlier Data Values

Let's start by addressing the effect of data values that differ dramatically from the other values in a data set. Such data values are often known as **outliers.** For example, most families have annual incomes of less than $100,000, but a small proportion of families have annual incomes far greater than $100,000. The annual income of such an affluent family in the presence of annual incomes of typical families is an outlier value. To examine the effect of outlier values, consider the data set consisting of four annual incomes: $30,000, $40,000, $50,000, and $60,000. For these incomes, the median and the mean are both $45,000. Now observe what happens when $60,000 is replaced by $600,000 (the annual income of a very wealthy family). Notice that the median is unchanged; it is still $45,000 because the middle two numbers remain $40,000 and $50,000. This is a good characteristic if the intent is to summarize the salaries of typical families; the median serves this purpose well even in the presence of an outlier value that does not represent a typical family. But now the mean increases to $180,000 because changing $60,000 to $600,000 increased the total from $180,000 to $720,000.

The mean is affected by all data values. It can be thought of as the center of gravity—the point of balance for the data. Consequently, the mean is sensitive to outlier values in a data set. The median is not sensitive to outlier values because it depends only on the middle observations. On the other hand, since the mean utilizes *all* observations in its computation, it is affected directly by how extreme any outlier values are. In fact, the smaller the number of observations in a data set, the greater the influence of any outliers on the mean. Thus, the median is said to be **resistant** to the presence of outlier data values, but the mean is not.

The Effect of Distributional Shape

Now we turn to the effect of distributional shape. The effect of outlier values comes into play when a distribution is single peaked and skewed. Suppose Figure 2.10 represents the distribution of earnings among employees of a corporation. The distribution is single peaked and skewed to the right because, typically, top management's earnings are quite large relative to those of most employees. The few very large salaries are, in effect, outlier values. They affect the mean, but they do not affect the median. Therefore, if one desired a summary measure to represent the typical salary, the median would be preferred to the mean.

Figure 2.10

A typical distribution of employees' earnings: positively skewed, with mean greater than median and median greater than mode

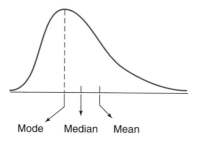

Mode   Median   Mean

In general, the mean is larger than the median and the median is larger than the mode for distributions that are single peaked and skewed to the right because the distribution contains a few outlier values in that direction. Similarly, the mean is smaller than the median and the median is smaller than the mode for distributions that are single peaked and skewed to the left. For perfectly symmetric distributions, the mean, median, and mode are the same. In general, the median is preferred to the mean as a way of measuring location for single-peaked, skewed distributions.

The effect of distributional shape on the mean, median, and mode is illustrated in Figure 2.11.

Figure 2.11

A comparison of mean, median, and mode for three distributional shapes

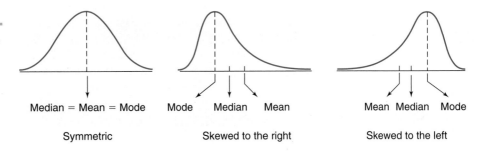

Median = Mean = Mode	Mode Median Mean	Mean Median Mode
Symmetric	Skewed to the right	Skewed to the left

Status of Theoretical Development

As you progress through this book, you will discover that statistical inference is concerned with means much more than with medians. A strong reason for this is that the theoretical development of statistics involving the mean is much beyond that for the median because the mean has been easier to work with mathematically. Because of advances in computer technology, research dealing with the median has recently become more abundant; however, such work is outside the scope of this book. Our discussion of the characteristics of the mean and the median is summarized in the following box.

A COMPARISON OF THE MEAN VERSUS THE MEDIAN

Mean	Median
Sensitive to the effect of outlier values, especially in small data sets	Not sensitive to the effect of outlier values
Less representative of "typical value" for single-peaked, skewed distributions	More representative of "typical value" for single-peaked, skewed distributions
Easier to work with theoretically	Difficult to work with theoretically

---

2.5 Measures of Variation

There is variation within almost every data set because there is variation within every population or process. Simply put, variation is the scatter or dispersion among the values in a data set. An essential task, therefore, is to measure the scatter, understand it, and identify its causes to provide a basis for action.

To understand variation and deal with it sensibly, we must first be able to measure it. In this section, we examine several important measures that are commonly used for this purpose. Specifically, we discuss the range, the mean absolute deviation, the variance, and the standard deviation. As you will see, the last three are closely related. It is important to know that in the absence of any variation in a data set, all measures of variation must equal 0. As a result, the larger the variation among the values in a data set, the larger the values of all measures of variation.

2.5.1   The Range

The **range** is defined to be *the difference between the largest and smallest values within a data set.* Its chief virtue is that it is easy to understand and to compute. Its chief drawback is its reliance on only two values in the data set; it is absolutely sensitive to the two extremes and completely insensitive to the other values. For example, the range for the data set 1, 2, 3, 7, 12 is 11. The range for the data set 1, 1, 1, 12, 12 is also 11; yet the second set has noticeably greater overall scatter than the first set. This insensitivity is a considerable drawback in using the range to measure variation in larger data sets. Before computers became widely available, the range was often used to measure variation because of its simplicity. Today it is used considerably less often in real statistical applications.

2.5.2   The Mean Absolute Deviation

Let's develop a more sensitive quantity for measuring variation—one that utilizes all the data. For this measure of variation as well as for the variance and standard deviation, we consider variation as the *degree to which values within a data set deviate from the center.* An initial strategy is to observe the deviation of each data value from the mean and then compute the average deviation. Consider the simple data set 1, 3, 7, 9, for which the mean is 5. The deviations from the mean are $(1 - 5) = -4$, $(3 - 5) = -2$, $(7 - 5) = +2$, and $(9 - 5) = +4$.

The average of these deviations is zero because, as you can see, the sum of the deviations is zero. In fact, *the sum of the deviations of the individual data values from their mean is always zero* for any data set because the positive deviations are perfectly offset by the negative deviations! This always occurs because the mean is the balance point of the data—its center of gravity. Since the average deviation from the mean is always zero, it is useless as an indicator of variation.

To overcome this problem, we focus on the *distance* of each observation from the mean, without regard to whether an observation is above or below the mean. Note that an observation's distance from the mean is always a positive number, whether it is below or above the mean. To obtain the distance from the mean, we simply ignore the sign of the deviation we computed previously; that is, we take the absolute value of each observation's deviation from the mean. By averaging these distances from the mean, we compute what is called the mean absolute deviation. Therefore, the **mean absolute deviation** (or **MAD**) is the *average of the absolute values of the deviations of observations from the mean.*

For the data set 1, 3, 7, 9, the mean absolute deviation works out to be

$$\text{MAD} = \frac{|1 - 5| + |3 - 5| + |7 - 5| + |9 - 5|}{4} = 3$$

In general, the mean absolute deviation for a sample is given by the following expression:*

---

* This expression is appropriate for sample data. The correct expression for population or process data is obtained by replacing n by N and $\overline{X}$ by μ.

$$\text{MAD} = \frac{\sum\limits_{i=1}^{n} |X_i - \bar{X}|}{n} \tag{2.3}$$

where $|X_i - \bar{X}|$ denotes the absolute value of the difference between the data value X_i and the mean of the data values $\bar{X}$.

The mean absolute deviation is a useful measure to characterize variation. It is sensitive to all data values and easy to explain. The chief drawback is that it has been difficult to develop statistical theory with the mean absolute deviation because it is a function of absolute values. As a result, the mean absolute deviation has not been utilized as a measure of variation as much as the variance and standard deviation, discussed next.

2.5.3 The Variance and Standard Deviation

In the discussion of the mean absolute deviation, we found that the average deviation from the mean is always zero for any data set. The mean absolute deviation avoids this problem by dealing with the distances from the mean, using absolute values to eliminate the negative signs. Another way to eliminate the signs of the negative deviations is to square them. Instead of computing the average distance from the mean (i.e., the mean absolute deviation), we can compute the average *squared* deviation from the mean.

The Variance

Consider the illustrative data we have been using (1, 3, 7, 9), for which the mean is 5. Assume for the moment that this data set is a population rather than a sample. (The importance of this distinction will soon be made clear.) With regard to populations, the average squared deviation from the mean is called the **variance** of the population. The variance of the data works out to be

$$\text{Variance} = \frac{(1-5)^2 + (3-5)^2 + (7-5)^2 + (9-5)^2}{4} = 10$$

The variance has one great advantage over the mean absolute deviation as a measure of variation: It lends itself easily to theoretical manipulation. As a result, it has been the chief measure of variation in the development of statistical theory.

The population or process variance is denoted by σ^2 (sigma squared) and is determined in general by Expression (2.4):

$$\sigma^2 = \frac{\sum\limits_{i=1}^{N} (X_i - \mu)^2}{N} \tag{2.4}$$

The chief importance of the population variance is that it is the primary measure of variation among the members of a population. Therefore, it is often a parameter of great interest. In almost all applications of statistics, however, we deal with *sample* data. As a result, we rarely find ourselves determining a population variance. Instead, we are interested in using sample data to *estimate* the population variance.

Suppose we are dealing with sample data. Can you anticipate what the expression for a *sample* variance looks like? Take a moment now to attempt this. [*Hint:* Examine Expression (2.4) and make adjustments in the notation to reflect sample rather than population data.] When the expression for the sample variance was derived theoretically, it turned out to be an exact counterpart of the population variance, with the sample mean $\bar{X}$ replacing μ and the sample size n replacing the population size N in Expression (2.4). However, it was shown that division by n tends to cause the resulting estimate of σ^2 to be too low; that is, over many random samples, this estimate is lower than σ^2 more often than it is higher than σ^2. This mostly undesirable condition is called *bias*. (Additional discussion of bias is provided in Chapter 5.) It has been shown that division by $(n-1)$ rather than n removes the bias. Therefore, the sample variance with division by $(n-1)$ is said to be *unbiased* and is the version that we use throughout the text. This sample variance is denoted by S^2 and is defined by the following expression:

$$S^2 = \frac{\sum\limits_{i=1}^{n} (X_i - \bar{X})^2}{n-1} \tag{2.5}$$

The numerator in Expression (2.5) is the sum of the squared deviations from the sample mean. It is called the **total sum of squares** and is denoted by SST. Thus,

$$SST = \sum\limits_{i=1}^{n} (X_i - \bar{X})^2 \tag{2.6}$$

and

$$S^2 = \frac{SST}{n-1} \tag{2.7}$$

The total sum of squares is an important quantity because it plays a crucial role in many of the statistical methods you will encounter later—notably analysis of variance and regression analysis. It measures the *total* variation among the values of a data set (whereas the variance measures, essentially, the *average* variation). Like all measures of variation, SST equals zero if there is no variation in a data set. The larger the value of SST, the greater the variation among the values in a data set.

The Standard Deviation

The numerical value of a population or sample variance is difficult to interpret because it is expressed in squared units. To reach a more interpretable measure of variation, expressed in the units of the original data, we determine the positive square root of the variance, which is known as the **standard deviation.** Notice that neither the variance nor the standard deviation is ever negative. The variance cannot be negative because it is an average of *squared* quantities. The standard deviation cannot be negative because it is the *positive* square root of the variance. As you read on in this book, you will see that the standard deviation is the primary way in which variation is assessed in most of the statistical methods you encounter.

The population or process standard deviation is denoted by σ (lowercase Greek sigma), and the sample standard deviation is denoted by S. Once a variance is known, the determination of the standard deviation is easy enough: Simply take the square root of the variance. Consequently,

$$\sigma = \sqrt{\sigma^2} \qquad \qquad \textbf{(2.8)}$$

and

$$S = \sqrt{S^2} \qquad \qquad \textbf{(2.9)}$$

Today, measures of variation such as total sum of squares, variance, and standard deviation are easily determined by a computer. Indeed, many inexpensive calculators compute the standard deviation automatically; one need only enter the data. Recall the test grades for three sections that were illustrated in Figure 2.2. The computer-determined standard deviations are as follows:

```
ST.DEV. = 8.6564
ST.DEV. = 7.9215
ST.DEV. = 16.0918
```

We can easily determine the variances by squaring the standard deviations ($S_1^2 = 74.9333$, $S_2^2 = 62.7502$, and $S_3^2 = 258.946$). Since $n = 10$ for the first section and $n = 9$ for the other two, we can also determine the total sum of squares for each section by multiplying the variance by $(n - 1)$, as suggested by Expression (2.7). Thus, $SST_1 = 674.4$, $SST_2 = 502$, and $SST_3 = 2,071.56$. The quantities developed here confirm that, as illustrated by Figure 2.2, the variation of the grades in Section 3 is the greatest, whereas the variation in Section 2 is the least.

Degrees of Freedom

There is a statistical term for the denominator of the sample variance $(n - 1)$. It is called the **degrees of freedom.** Why this name? We illustrate with an example. Suppose you ask Sue to pick any three numbers, and she chooses 2, 4, and 16. You then ask Sam to pick three numbers, adding a restriction that their average must equal 5. He chooses 0, 5, and 10. Notice that Sue was completely free to choose any three numbers, but Sam was free to choose only the first two numbers. The third had to be a number that would give a total of 15, so that the average would be 5. Because of the requirement of a fixed mean, we say that he had only 2 degrees of freedom. Now let's generalize. If he were asked to pick n numbers that must have a given average, then the number of degrees of freedom would be $n - 1$. The last number picked must be the value that causes the desired mean to be achieved. Since the sample variance is based on the deviations of data values from their mean, we say that it has $n - 1$ degrees of freedom.

The Mean Absolute Deviation Versus the Standard Deviation

How do the mean absolute deviation and the standard deviation compare as measures of variation? For any data set, the mean absolute deviation is always smaller than the standard deviation because it is less sensitive to the effect of outlier observations. (Remember, deviations from the mean are squared in the determination of variance.) Therefore, when a data set contains a few outlier observations, the mean absolute deviation might provide a more realistic measure of variation than does the standard deviation. As we have pointed out, however, the standard deviation is much more commonly used in statistical procedures because its mathematical properties have made it more amenable to theoretical development.

2.5.4   The Interpretation and Use of the Standard Deviation

The standard deviation is generally preferred to the variance as a descriptor of variation because its unit of measurement is the same as that for the data. Let's concentrate on how to interpret the standard deviation as a descriptor of variation. Suppose you found that the mean and standard deviation of sales representatives' earnings for the past year were $45,000 and $15,000, respectively. Could you explain to a manager who is unfamiliar with statistics what these results indicate about the variation among salespersons' earnings?

One way to approach this is to ask the question: What proportion of the data values can be expected to fall within a one-standard-deviation distance (or two, or three, etc.) of the mean? That is, what proportion of the salespersons can be expected to have earned between $30,000 and $60,000 (where $30,000 equals the mean minus one standard deviation, and $60,000 equals the mean plus one standard deviation)? A Russian statistician named Tchebysheff made an interesting discovery in this regard. He proved that, for *any* data set, at least 75% of the observations must lie within two standard deviations of the mean, and at least 89% of the observations must lie within three standard deviations of the mean. In general, he showed that at least $100[1 - (1/k^2)]\%$ of the observations must lie within a distance of k standard deviations of the mean. Based on his finding, therefore, we know that at least 75% of all salespersons must have earned between $15,000 and $75,000 [$15,000 = $45,000 − 2($15,000) and $75,000 = $45,000 + 2($15,000)]. We also know that at least 89% earned between $0 and $90,000.

Because Tchebysheff's finding applies to all data sets, no matter how unusual or distorted they might be, it is extremely conservative. For most data sets, we can expect much larger proportions of the data to lie within a distance of one, two, and three standard deviations of the mean—thus the reason for the important phrase "at least" in Tchebysheff's finding.

Now suppose the data have a single-peaked, symmetric distribution. An important theoretical distribution that fits this description is known as the **normal distribution;** it is examined in detail in Chapter 4. For the normal distribution, the proportions of data values that lie within a distance of one, two, and three standard deviations of the mean are as given in the following box. Experience has shown that the indicated proportions are usually roughly correct for moderately large data sets whose distributions are single peaked and symmetric or moderately skewed. Because they are based on empirical findings with many data sets, these guidelines have come to be known as the **empirical rule.** The empirical rule is illustrated for the normal distribution in Figure 2.12.

THE EMPIRICAL RULE

For moderately large data sets that conform to the normal distribution:

- 68.26% of the data values lie within one standard deviation of the mean.
- 95.44% of the data values lie within two standard deviations of the mean.
- 99.74% of the data values lie within three standard deviations of the mean.

What if a data set is severely skewed or is not single peaked? In these cases, the empirical rule can be substantially inaccurate. The real point here is to give you some

Figure 2.12

Proportions of values for normal distributions within one, two, and three standard deviations of the mean

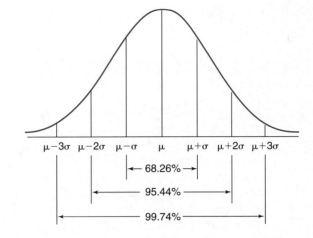

feeling for the interpretation of a standard deviation. If you find the standard deviation to be large relative to the mean, this can be an indication of considerable skewness or the presence of outliers. However, the empirical rule is at least roughly correct for a surprisingly large number of data sets.

2.6 Measures of Relative Standing

In this section, we introduce several techniques for characterizing a distribution of data. They serve as useful alternatives to frequency distributions and are also useful in indicating the standing of a particular data value relative to the entire data set. Hence, the quantities we discuss are called *measures of relative standing.*

2.6.1 Quantiles

Have you ever taken a standardized test such as the SAT, the ACT, or the GMAT? Suppose you were told that a friend scored 620 on the GMAT. Would you be impressed? Chances are good that this score does not mean much to you. What if you learned that 620 was *no less than* 92% *of the scores of those who took the test?* Doesn't this give you a fairly good idea now that your friend did rather well on this test? A **quantile** is a number that indicates the *proportion* of values in a data set that are equal to or less than this number. Quantiles may be expressed in several variations, the most common of which are **percentiles** and **quartiles.**

Percentiles

Percentiles are numbers that divide a data set into 100 ordered subgroups, each containing the same proportion of data values. Dividing a data set into 100 subgroups requires 99 percentiles. Your friend's score of 620 is the 92nd percentile for the group who took the GMAT. It means that 92% of those who took the test scored no better than 620; that is why your friend's score is very good in relative terms. As you might imagine, percentiles are useful only when a data set contains a large number of data values. Percentiles are most commonly used to indicate the relative standing of individual scores on standardized tests given to large groups of people.

Suppose the 50th percentile for the group who took the GMAT is 450. This means that 50% of the GMAT scores are less than or equal to 450 and 50% exceed 450. As such, the 50th percentile is in fact the median. We denote this as $x_5 = 450$. In general, x_q is the quantile value such that $100q\%$ of the data values are less than or equal to x_q.

Quartiles

Quartiles are numbers that divide a data set into four ordered subgroups, each containing the same proportion of data values. Since three points are required to establish four subgroups, there are three quartiles. Suppose the three quartiles of a set of SAT scores are $x_{25} = 850$, $x_5 = 1,000$, and $x_{75} = 1,160$. (We assume the computer has determined these quartile values; we focus on their interpretation.) These quartile values mean that 25% of those taking this SAT had scores less than or equal to 850, 50% had scores less than or equal to 1,000, and 75% had scores less than or equal to 1,160. In other words, the three quartiles are the same as the 25th, 50th, and 75th percentiles, respectively.

Whereas percentiles are used primarily to indicate the relative standing of an individual data value, quartiles are often used to summarize the overall distribution of a data set. We illustrate this in the following example involving the earnings of salespersons.

EXAMPLE 2.3

It is common for any organization that employs a sales force to review its compensation plan frequently to ascertain whether goals stated prior to implementation are being met. A marketing analyst has been asked to describe the earnings of the individuals on the sales force based on a firm's current compensation plan. His report includes the following points:

- Half the salespersons earned no more than $38,000; half earned more than $38,000.
- The "middle half" of all salespersons earned between $28,000 and $54,000; 25% earned no more than $28,000 and 25% earned more than $54,000.
- Five percent earned no more than $20,000; 5% earned more than $70,000.
- Minimum earnings were $13,000; maximum earnings were $88,000.

Do you find that this information provides a helpful picture of the distribution of sales earnings? Notice that the analyst has simply reported the quartiles, some percentiles, and the minimum and maximum earnings without using statistical jargon. Identify the statistical quantities he has reported.

Solution

Statistically, the marketing analyst's report says:

$$x_5 = \$38,000 \text{ (second quartile, or 50th percentile, or median)}$$

$$x_{25} = \$28,000 \text{ (first quartile or 25th percentile)}$$

$$x_{75} = \$54,000 \text{ (third quartile or 75th percentile)}$$

$$x_{05} = \$20,000 \text{ (fifth percentile)}$$

$$x_{95} = \$70,000 \text{ (95th percentile)}$$

Minimum = $13,000

Maximum = $88,000

2.6.2 Box Plots

As we have stated, quartiles are useful primarily as indicators of the distribution of a set of data. In most cases, distributions are better communicated graphically than in numerical tables. Just as histograms are effective graphical expressions of a frequency distribution, **box plots** also are effective graphical means of communicating information about a distribution using the quartiles. Thus, they allow us to provide additional information about a distribution.

Figure 2.13 is a box plot for the sales earnings example (Example 2.3). The box depicts the "middle 50%" of sales earnings; its boundaries are the first and third quartiles. The line through the center of the box depicts the median. The lines extending above and below the box indicate the distance from the first and third quartiles to the smallest and largest values, respectively. What do we learn from the box plot in Figure 2.13 about the distribution of earnings? Notice that the upper vertical line is substantially longer than the lower vertical line. This suggests that the distribution is positively skewed. Half of the salespersons earned between $28,000 and $54,000, but those in the upper 25% varied from this group by quite a bit more than did those in the bottom 25%.

Figure 2.13

Box plot for the earnings of a sales force

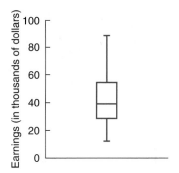

2.6.3 *Z*-values

Recall the earnings example in Section 2.5.4 for which the mean for the past year was $45,000 and the standard deviation was $15,000. Suppose one of the salespersons earned $85,000. Is this a large amount relative to the other salespersons? Apparently it is. If the empirical rule applies, more than 99% of the salespersons earned between $0 and $90,000. So this salesperson's earnings appear to be near the top 1% of earnings. This example illustrates that a data value's relative standing within the overall distribution can also be determined by knowing the mean and standard deviation of the distribution. That is, by knowing the number of standard deviations a data value lies above or below the mean, we know the data value's relative standing in the distribution. The number of standard deviations an observation lies above or below the mean is called its **Z-value.** The *Z*-value is determined by subtracting the mean ($45,000) from the salesperson's earnings ($85,000) and then dividing the difference by the standard deviation ($15,000). Thus, the Z-value corresponding to $85,000 is

$$Z = \frac{85,000 - 45,000}{15,000} = 2.67$$

This means that the salesperson's earnings were 2.67 standard deviations above the mean.

The general expression for computing a Z-value is

$$Z = \frac{X - \mu}{\sigma} \qquad\qquad \textbf{(2.10)}$$

where X is the data value of interest, μ is the mean, and σ is the standard deviation.

It is important to notice that Z-values are scale-free. The unit of measure for any Z-value is the number of standard deviations that an observation lies above or below the mean, regardless of whether the observations are measured in hours, inches, dollars, gallons, or square feet. For this reason, Z-values are very useful for comparing two scores on different scales, such as ACT and SAT scores. The transformation of a data value to its corresponding Z-value is known as a **standardizing transformation.**

The interpretation of a Z-value depends on the distribution of the data. If the distribution is such that the empirical rule applies, then interpreting a Z-value is simple. A Z-value with an absolute value of 1 or less is not at all unusual—about 68% of all data values should have Z-values that lie between +1 and −1. However, a Z-value with an absolute value of more than 3 is unusual—less than 1% of all observations would have a Z-value greater than 3 or less than −3. A negative Z-value simply indicates that an observation is below the mean; a positive Z-value indicates that an observation is above the mean. Z-values are used extensively in later chapters.

Using the Computer

Let's continue the analysis of the insurance data that was begun in Example 2.2. We now focus on the descriptive statistics for location and variation, quantiles, and box plots.

EXAMPLE 2.4

The dot plots of Example 2.2 suggested that there might be no differences between the average policy amounts of the two genders except for those caused by differences in their incomes. Table 2.2 contains Minitab and Excel output [parts (a) and (c) and (b), respectively] that include the mean, median, standard deviation, maximum value, and minimum value for customer policy amounts and incomes. Other quantities are also included, some of which are not covered in this book or have not yet been introduced. Parts (a) and (b) of the table represent the entire data set, whereas part (c) provides the same information by gender. The latter shows that, indeed, women (gender = 1) average less than men (gender = 0) for both policy amount and income. The women average $142,600 for policy amount versus $202,000 for men (we saw this result in Chapter 1, Example 1.1), and they average $31,810 in income versus $40,340 for men. Notice that the difference between their median incomes is much less ($30,000 for women versus $30,750 for men), because the medians are unaffected by the outlier income of one man ($126,000). Notice also that the men exhibit more variation among their policy amounts and incomes, as indicated by the standard deviations.

Table 2.2

Numerical Quantities for Summarizing the Insurance Data

(a)

	N	MEAN	MEDIAN	TRMEAN	STDEV	SEMEAN
amount	51	177.5	100.0	155.3	166.1	23.3
income	51	36.83	30.50	34.15	20.20	2.83

	MIN	MAX	Q1	Q3
amount	15.0	1000.0	75.0	250.0
income	17.00	126.00	23.00	42.50

(b)

Amount		Income	
Mean	177.55	Mean	36.83
Standard Error	23.26	Standard Error	2.83
Median	100	Median	30.5
Mode	250	Mode	26
Standard Deviation	166.08	Standard Deviation	20.20
Sample Variance	27583.37	Sample Variance	407.90
Kurtosis	11.27	Kurtosis	7.12
Skewness	2.75	Skewness	2.32
Range	985	Range	109
Minimum	15	Minimum	17
Maximum	1000	Maximum	126
Sum	9055	Sum	1878.4
Count	51	Count	51
Confidence Level (95.0%)	46.71	Confidence Level (95.0%)	5.68

(c)

	gender	N	MEAN	MEDIAN	TRMEAN	STDEV	SEMEAN
amount	0	30	202.0	162.5	173.5	191.4	34.9
	1	21	142.6	100.0	130.5	116.9	25.5
income	0	30	40.34	30.75	37.01	23.86	4.36
	1	21	31.81	30.00	31.27	12.23	2.67

	gender	MIN	MAX	Q1	Q3
amount	0	25.0	1000.0	87.5	250.0
	1	15.0	500.0	62.5	250.0
income	0	18.00	126.00	26.00	43.75
	1	17.00	57.00	21.90	41.10

To facilitate a comparison of the distributions based on quartiles, we provide computer-generated box plots of policy amounts by gender in Figure 2.14. Notice that the boxes, which indicate the range of policy amounts between the first and third quartiles, are about the same for the two genders. The median, indicated by a line inside each box, is somewhat lower for the women. The largest amount and one other fairly large amount for men are highlighted by asterisks to indicate that they are considered to be outlier values of varying degrees of extremity. Finally, the vertical line above each

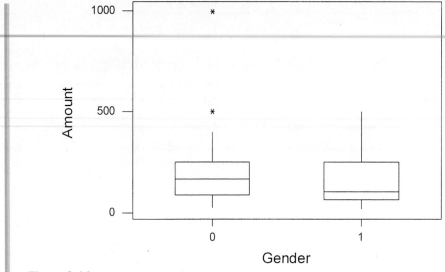

Figure 2.14

Minitab box plots for the insurance data

box is considerably longer than the line below each box. This indicates that the distributions are skewed to the right, as previously illustrated by the histograms.

2.7 Relationships Between Two Variables

We have studied techniques mostly for describing data for a single variable. For example, we discussed grades on a statistics test, the amounts of life insurance policies, and the amounts of scrap produced in printing runs. Often, however, it is of interest to study the relationship between two variables. For example, you might like to know whether students' test grades are related to the number of hours of study. An insurance manager might want to know whether the face amounts of life insurance policies tend to be higher for customers with higher incomes. A university administrator might want to know whether the proportions of out-of-state students differ for the various schools that make up the university. Insight into such relationships can contribute greatly to better understanding them.

2.7.1 Scatter Diagrams

Consider the example involving 20 statistics test grades. Does a student's test grade seem to depend on the number of hours spent studying? Suppose we define the variable X as the number of hours a student reports studying for an assigned test. We use the symbol Y to represent the test grade. The data are as follows:

Y (test grade):	54	56	63	64	62	61	63	73	78	72
X (study hours):	5	10	4	8	12	9	10	12	15	12

Y (test grade):	74	78	83	86	83	81	88	87	89	93
X (study hours):	12	20	16	14	22	18	30	21	28	24

For the process of preparing for and taking a test, the outcome is a student's test grade and the performance indicator being investigated is the number of study hours.

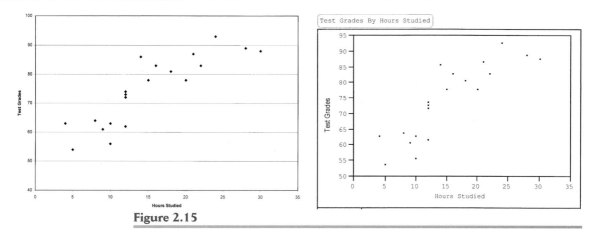

Figure 2.15

Excel and JMP IN scatter diagrams of test grades versus hours studied

Since the test grade depends (presumably) to some degree on the number of hours studied, "test grade" is called the **response variable.** Since the number of hours studied can be used to predict (to some degree) the test grade, it is called the **predictor variable.** To examine the relationship between two variables, a scatter diagram is a very useful tool. A **scatter diagram** is a two-variable plot of data values in which the horizontal axis represents the predictor variable and the vertical axis represents the response variable. The response variable must be quantitative. Computer-generated scatter diagrams for the test data are shown in Figure 2.15. What does the scatter diagram suggest to you about the relationship between test grades and the number of hours studied? Think about this before reading ahead.

Two significant points are suggested by the scatter diagrams: (1) The students who studied more tended to get higher grades. For example, compare the grades of those who studied less than 10 hours to those who studied more than 20 hours. (2) The number of hours studied is not a perfect predictor of a student's test grade. Students who studied about the same amount vary somewhat in their test grades. Why do these students' grades vary? There must be other factors that explain the variation in grades among students. Two possibilities are their aptitudes for statistical thinking and the quality of their prerequisite courses such as math courses. Simple luck may also be involved.

Statistical Association as a Basis of Action

Do the scatter diagrams in Figure 2.15 suggest that a cause-and-effect relationship exists between the number of hours of study and the test grade? If students increased their studying time, would they get better test grades? Perhaps, but cause and effect cannot be established by a scatter diagram alone. Another conceivable explanation of the relationship in the scatter diagram is that some other factor caused the students' grades to vary and at the same time caused the hours spent studying to vary. For instance, the true causative factor might be level of maturity. The argument would be that a lack of maturity causes some students to do worse on tests and also leads them to study less. It is possible that if we persuaded the less mature students to study more for the next test, their grades would not improve because they are too immature to understand the material. This explanation cannot be discounted on statistical grounds. Instead, we must rely on our subject-matter knowledge to form an opinion. For example, your experience with less mature students might lead you to believe that those who significantly increased their study time would surely improve their test grades. If you wanted solid evidence of the effect of increased studying, you could conduct a designed experiment in which some of the less mature students agreed to study, say, twice as many hours. If their grades improved in comparison to the other students who simply maintained their studying habits, then you would have convincing statistical evidence of a causal relationship.

2.7.2 Contingency Tables

Consider an example in which interest is on the distribution of female students in schools of business and schools of arts and sciences. Might the proportion of female students be related to the type of school? Suppose a random sample of 500 students enrolled in schools of business or arts and sciences was selected from comprehensive state universities throughout the United States. The breakdown of these 500 students with regard to gender and type of school is given in Table 2.3.

Table 2.3

Numbers of male and female students by two schools

	Schools of Business	Schools of Arts & Sciences	Total
Male	130	130	260
Female	70	170	240
Total	200	300	500

Notice that each row in this table is a frequency distribution of the enrollments at each type of school with respect to gender. For example, there are 70 female students in schools of business and 170 in arts and sciences. Similarly, each column is a frequency distribution for gender with respect to each type of school. For example, in the sample involving schools of arts and sciences, there were 130 male students and 170 female students. Such a two-way frequency distribution is called a **contingency table.** A detailed analysis of contingency tables is presented in Chapter 11.

What do these sample data reveal about the distribution of male and female students in these two types of schools? A contingency table can be illustrated graphically by a bar chart as in Figure 2.16. This graph reveals that the proportion of female students in schools of arts and sciences is considerably larger than that in schools of business (170 out of 300 in arts and sciences, 70 out of 200 in business). Apparently, therefore, there may be a relationship between gender and these two types of schools with regard to enrollment.

Figure 2.16

Enrollments for two types of schools by gender

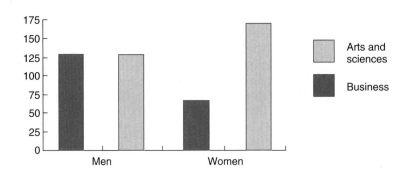

2.8 Exploring and Summarizing Data: A Comprehensive Example

The HAVCOR Corporation owned and operated 11 nursing homes. Terwilliger Plaza, the most recently opened facility, was being managed under a unique and controversial strategy. The premise was to limit the number of patients whose expenses were paid by Medicaid (a government program providing medical care for the indigent). It was believed that the nursing home would be more profitable if most patients paid either privately or with Medicare. This strategy appeared to be causing a problem, however. After 9 months, only 63% of the 120 beds in the facility were occupied, whereas about 96% of all nursing home beds statewide were occupied. The low occupancy rate was causing the owners to question the viability of the strategy. The president commissioned a statistical analysis to shed light on the problem and to predict the length of time until the facility reached its utilization goal of 97.5%.

The first step was to study the historical utilization of beds and identify any trends or patterns. The maximum possible usage in any 30-day month would occur if all 120 beds were used every day of the month. For a 30-day month, the maximum usage would be $120 \times 30 = 3,600$. The actual usage in a month is determined by adding the numbers of beds used each day over the entire month. Utilization for a month is defined as actual usage divided by the maximum usage for that month. Table 2.4 shows the monthly usage, utilization, and growth in utilization for the first 10 months that Terwilliger Plaza existed.

Table 2.4

Utilization by month at Terwilliger Plaza

Month	Usage	Utilization	Utilization Growth
Jan.	74	.02	
Feb.	291	.08	.06
Mar.	717	.19	.11
Apr.	975	.27	.08
May	1,182	.32	.05
June	1,408	.39	.07
July	1,766	.47	.08
Aug.	2,046	.55	.08
Sept.	2,083	.58	.03
Oct.	2,340	.63	.05
		Average growth in utilization:	.068

An inspection of the data reveals an obvious increasing trend: Utilization grew from .02 in January to .63 in October; this represents an average increase of .068 per month over the 10 months the facility has existed. The run chart in Figure 2.17 illustrates the trend graphically. Notice that the increasing trend is virtually a straight line. It was observed with some concern that the last two increases, .03 and .05, were somewhat less than the average. Was this an early indication that the growth rate in utilization was slowing?

The following question arose from these results: If utilization continued to grow at an average rate of .068 per month, when would full utilization be realized? At this rate of growth, 97.5% utilization would be reached in 5 months. Notice that the dotted line projection in Figure 2.17, which reflects a .068 growth rate, reaches the 97.5% level after 5 months.*

Figure 2.17

Run chart of utilization by month

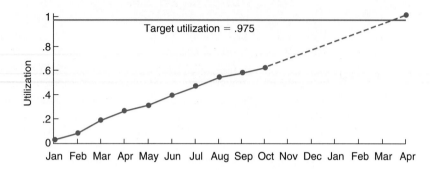

This analysis represented the first phase of the study. The second phase was to look more deeply. The utilization level is determined by the rate at which new patients are admitted to the facility (i.e., "arrive") and the lengths of time that patients stay before departing. A database was created from file records kept for each patient. The database included each patient's arrival date, source (the hospital or other agency that referred the patient to the nursing home), and length of stay. With these data, an analysis of the arrival rate and the lengths of stay was conducted.

For studying the rate of arrivals to the facility, the variable was the interarrival time—that is, the number of days between consecutive arrivals. Table 2.5 provides summary statistics for the interarrival times of the 179 patients admitted over the 10 months of operation. The average interarrival time was 1.62 days, and the standard deviation of arrival times was 1.764 days. A histogram of interarrival times is given in Figure 2.18. Notice that the distribution is quite skewed to the right; most interarrival times are 1 day or less, but go up to 8 days.

To investigate the possible change in the arrival rate from month to month, the arrivals were grouped by month so that a run chart of the numbers of arrivals per month could be examined. This run chart is given in Figure 2.19; it clearly indicates a slowing of the original rate over the last three months (which correspond to the last 50 patients).

The apparent decline in the arrival rate raised a question, so attention turned to the lengths of stay. Table 2.6 is a summary of the lengths of stay for all patients. The average length of stay for the 137 patients who have left has been 43.59 days, and the standard deviation has been 47.46 days. Although not given, the distribution of the lengths of stay is single peaked and skewed distinctly to the right (as one would expect based on a comparison of the mean and median for single-peaked distributions).

If the arrival rate has declined sharply, why has utilization continued to increase? One possibility was that the lengths of stay had increased for more recent patients. Figure 2.20 is a run chart of the lengths of stay for all patients to date, in the order in which they were admitted. The run chart indicates clearly that the lengths of stay have increased for more recent patients, thereby counterbalancing the effect of a declining arrival rate.

To look more closely at this phenomenon, the lengths of stay were divided into two groups. The first consists of the first 95 arrivals, and the second consists of the last 42

---

* This finding was supported by time series forecasting methodology, presented in Chapter 12.

Table 2.5

Minitab statistical summary of interarrival times

	N	MEAN	MEDIAN	TRMEAN	STDEV	SEMEAN
arrival interval	179	1.620	1.000	1.447	1.764	0.132

	MIN	MAX	Q1	Q3
arrival interval	0.000	8.000	0.000	3.000

Figure 2.18

Minitab histogram of interarrival times

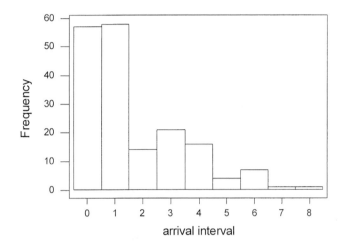

Figure 2.19

Run chart of number of arrivals by month

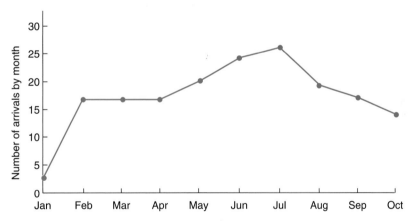

arrivals, corresponding approximately to the point at which greater lengths of stay began to occur. Table 2.7 provides a descriptive summary of lengths of stay for these two groups (where period 1 is "before" and period 2 is "after"). Notice that the mean more than doubled from 31.76 days to 70.4 days, and the median increased from 23 days to 41 days. Variation also increased, with the standard deviation of lengths of stay more than doubling from 27.73 to 68.2.

These results created serious concern. Length of stay could not continue to increase for long and thereby negate the effect of declining admissions. If the admission rate could not be restored, the prediction of full occupancy in 5 months no longer seemed likely.

Why were admissions declining? This question led to an investigation of the sources

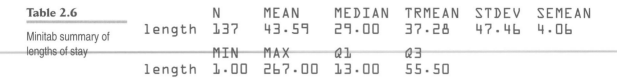

Table 2.6

Minitab summary of lengths of stay

	N	MEAN	MEDIAN	TRMEAN	STDEV	SEMEAN
length	137	43.59	29.00	37.28	47.46	4.06

	MIN	MAX	Q1	Q3
length	1.00	267.00	13.00	55.50

Figure 2.20

Run chart of lengths of stay for all patients

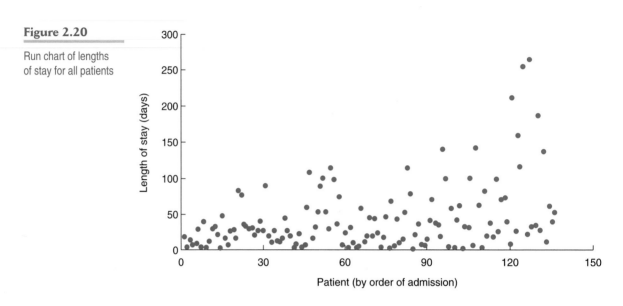

Table 2.7

Descriptive summary of lengths of stay before and after the observed upturn

	ArPeriod	N	MEAN	MEDIAN	TRMEAN	STDEV	SEMEAN
length	1	95	31.76	23.00	29.06	27.73	2.85
	2	42	70.4	41.0	63.9	68.2	10.5

	ArPeriod	MIN	MAX	Q1	Q3
length	1	1.00	115.00	12.00	44.00
	2	1.0	267.0	24.5	100.3

of patients. Table 2.8 is a frequency table indicating the distribution of sources for the patients admitted.* The table shows that the major sources were Mears Home Health, University Hospital, and Greenbrooke Hospital. This information was then broken out into a table showing frequencies by source and by time period (January–July vs. August–October), as shown in Table 2.9. The key observation was that the decline in referrals had occurred entirely among the three major sources. Referrals from the "Other" category remained high; indeed, the referral rate per month from other sources was actually higher over the last three months than in the first six. This information struck a chord with the president. HAVCOR had hired a marketing representative to

---

* The total frequency is 164 rather than 179 because the referral source was unknown for 15 patients.

Table 2.8

Frequency of patient sources

Source	Frequency	Percent
Mears Home Health	74	45.1
University Hospital	32	19.5
Greenbrooke Hospital	29	17.7
Others (21 different sources)	29	17.7
Total	164	100.0

Table 2.9

Patient frequencies by source and time period

Source	Jan.–July	Aug.–Oct.	Jan.–Oct.
Mears Home Health	52	22	74
University Hospital	24	8	32
Greenbrooke Hospital	24	5	29
Others (21 different sources)	16	13	29
Total	116	48	164

interact with hospitals and care facilities that were major sources of patients. The referrals from other sources were unsolicited by the marketing representative. A few telephone calls revealed that the marketing representative had alienated key people at each of the three major sources, who were now referring patients elsewhere. This information precipitated action; the marketing representative had to correct the situation and increase the arrival rate.

2.9 Summary

In this chapter, we examined ways to explore and summarize data. There are two basic approaches to summarizing data. One is to characterize the distribution of data between the smallest and largest values with tables or graphs, and the other is to use numerical quantities.

The distribution of data is important because it reveals the pattern with which the data are varying. The most common distribution shapes are those that concentrate around a single peak and are either symmetric or skewed (to the right or to the left). To reveal the distribution of a data set, we use dot diagrams, histograms, stem-and-leaf diagrams, and box plots.

Numerical quantities are divided into three distinct types: (1) measures of location, (2) measures of variation, and (3) measures of relative standing. Measures of location depict the value around which the data tend to be centered. There are three primary measures of location: the mean, median, and mode. Measures of variation depict the scatter or dispersion among the values in a data set. The range, mean absolute deviation, variance, and standard deviation are the primary measures of variation. Measures of relative standing depict the position of a particular data value relative to the entire data set. Quantiles and Z-values are the primary measures of relative standing.

We also discussed ways to study the relationship between two variables, Scatter diagrams and contingency tables can help us understand relationships that might exist between two variables.

EXERCISES FOR SECTION 2.2

2.1 Identify the two types of data and explain the difference between them.

2.2 If we were recording outcomes for the following variables, what type of data would we be recording?
   (a) Gender
   (b) Annual income
   (c) Order of finish in a golf tournament
   (d) Number of automobiles sold in a week by a dealer
   (e) Rank of a company's annual sales relative to the company's industry
   (f) The condition of a VCR

2.3 In Exercise 2.2, for which variables would the data be:
   (a) Qualitative, nominal scaled?
   (b) Qualitative, ordinal scaled?
   (c) Quantitative?

2.4 For the variables in parts (a), (b), (d), and (f) in Exercise 2.2, indicate whether an average or a proportion would be a more meaningful statistic and explain your choice.

EXERCISES FOR SECTION 2.3

2.5 Why is it necessary to summarize data?

2.6 Explain the approaches available to summarize data distributions.

2.7 In constructing frequency distributions for quantitative data, explain why it is not a good idea to use fewer than five classes.

2.8 Identify and describe the three common shapes of single-peaked distributions.

2.9 For the following situations, choose the most plausible of the three common shapes for single-peaked distributions and justify your choice.
   (a) Number of automobiles sold in a week by a dealer under stable economic conditions
   (b) The length of time before the first service is needed for a particular brand of VCR
   (c) Age at first marriage for men

2.10 Recall Paula's calorie intake data in Exercise 1.30 of Chapter 1.
   (a) Construct a histogram of the daily calorie intake data.
   (b) Describe the shape of your histogram in part (a).
   (c) Construct a stem-and-leaf diagram.
   (d) Use the stem-and-leaf diagram to describe the variation in her daily calorie intake.

2.11 The following data are the percent changes in profit from the first quarter to the second quarter for 15 pharmaceutical companies. Determine a dot diagram to describe the distribution of the percent changes in profits for these pharmaceutical companies over this period (all of which happened to have increased):

19	10	18	20	20	38	35	21
34	22	20	18	12	13	17	

2.12 A commercial real estate developer is considering a business expansion in Virginia. In the evaluation of potential sites, it is of interest to understand the relative wealth of the city or county in which the site is located and the relationship of that wealth to demographic conditions associated with housing. The data for this exercise are on the book's data diskette under the file name EX0212. They are 1990 data for 17 localities in Virginia under consideration by the developer. For each locality, they include the number of occupied housing units and the median income for all occupied housing units (*Source: 1990 Census of Housing, Detailed Characteristics of Housing–Virginia,* Table 67–Fuel, Occupancy, and Social Characteristics: 1990; p. 127).
   (a) Develop a frequency bar chart to highlight the relative size of the localities based on the number of occupied housing units.
   (b) Develop a frequency bar chart to highlight the relative wealth of the localities based on the median income for all occupied housing units.
   (c) Based solely on their size and relative wealth, which five localities would you recommend to the developer for additional study? Justify your recommendation.

2.13 A Richmond, Virginia, company was planning to purchase a real estate property at a price of $500,000 and wished to learn about the distribution of current lending rates for Richmond area lenders. The available data consisted of the mortgage loan rates offered at the time of purchase consideration by 32 area lenders for loan amounts over $203,150 (*Source: Richmond Times-Dispatch,* Oct. 23, 1995). They are on the book's data diskette in the file named EX0213. The data include the lender's interest rates, points, and total costs for 30-year and 15-year mortgages. The purpose of this exercise is to learn about the range of mortgage options that were available at the time and to compare the costs of 15-year and 30-year mortgages.

(a) Depict the distributions of total costs for 30-year mortgages and 15-year mortgages at the time of the decision, using appropriate graphical methods. Provide verbal descriptions of these distributions.

(b) Depict the distribution of loan rates for 30-year mortgages and 15-year mortgages, using appropriate graphical methods. Provide verbal descriptions of these distributions.

(c) To what extent do lenders' interest rates differ for 30-year and 15-year mortgages? Develop and interpret a dot diagram for the *differences* between the rates for these two types of mortgages.

2.14 Should investors use national brokers, regional brokers, or discount brokers? Key factors include the cost of a transaction, annual fees, the quality of investment advice afforded by the broker, and ease of access. The following are data (*Fortune,* Dec. 25, 1995) for a sample of 18 selected brokerage frrns thought to be representative of the three groups—6 national brokers, 4 regional brokers, and 8 discount brokers. The variables include (1) commission for 500 shares at $20 per share; (2) transaction fee; (3) number of equity analysts; (4) number of retail offices.

	Com-mission	Fee	Research Strength	Access
	500 shares @ $20	Trans-actions	Analysts	Number of Offices
NATIONAL				
A. G. Edwards	227	3.00	38	530
Dean Witter Reynolds	230	2.35	32	340
Merrill Lynch	238	4.85	260	510
Paine Webber	249	3.80	67	325
Prudential	253	0.00	60	300
Smith Barney	247	4.00	150	463
REGIONAL				
Edward Jones	230	1.95	12	3,174
Piper Jaffrey	236	4.50	32	77
Raymond James	228	3.00	29	800
Sutro & Co.	232	2.50	17	17
DISCOUNT				
Brown & Co.	29	0.00	0	10
Charles Schwab	110	0.00	0	216
Fidelity Investments	110	0.00	0	81

	Com-mission	Fee	Research Strength	Access
	500 shares @ $20	Trans-actions	Analysts	Number of Offices
Jack White	48	33.00	0	1
Muriel Siebert	60	0.00	0	4
Olde Discount	80	1.75	25	200
Pacific Brokerage	25	4.00	0	4
Waterhouse Securities	61	0.00	0	73

For each variable, compare the distributions of national brokers, regional brokers, and discount brokers by developing dot diagrams for each group. Use the same scale for each graph to facilitate comparisons. Based on your results, describe the essential differences among the three groups.

2.15 In recent years, European banks, especially those in southern tier countries, have felt increasing pressure to accommodate the procedures of the European Union and to conform to international auditing standards. As a result, government financial ministries and central banks are providing more oversight than in the past. A trend toward privatization has increased the involvement of multinational audit firms, bringing pressure for banks to conform to the performance standards set by such rating agencies as Moody's and Standard & Poor's.

In response, the Secretary General of the Bank Association of Turkey, Dr. Ekrem Keskin, and the Group Head for Research, Mr. Ahmet Acar, enlisted the support of Dr. William B. Harrison of the Middle East Technical University to study the performances of Turkish banks using internationally accepted performance standards. In particular, they compared the performances of Turkish banks to those of other southern tier countries such as Italy, Spain, Greece, and Portugal (*Source:* "A Comparison of CAMEL Performance Ratios: Turkish and Foreign and Large Bank Branching Systems with Other Banks in Turkey," report to the Bank Association of Turkey by William B. Harrison, Middle East Technical University, Ankara, Turkey).

CAMEL performance ratios were used to characterize bank performance. They derive from the Uniform Financial Institutions Rating System, adopted in the in United States in 1979, which provides a way for all depository institutions to receive a uniform basis of evaluation. They characterize five crucial aspects of a bank's performance: capital adequacy, asset quality, management ability, earnings, and liquidity (CAMEL for short). The following statistical variables were selected to measure each CAMEL component:

CAMEL Characteristic	Statistical Variable	File Name
Capital adequacy	Equity-to-assets ratio	Capratio
Asset quality	Nonperforming loans to total loans ratio	Nplratio
Management ability	Non-interest income to assets ratio	Noinasst
Earnings	Return on equity	ROE
Liquidity	Loans-to-assets ratio	Lnsassts

(*Note:* The loans-to-assets ratio is an "inverse" measure of liquidity. Larger loans-to-assets ratios signify decreased liquidity.) The data for these variables were taken from a 1992 sample of 37 Turkish banks, 5 Spanish banks, and 3 Italian banks available from the Bank Association of Turkey. The data are on the book data diskette in the file EX0215.

(a) Develop dot diagrams of the distribution of the equity-to-assets ratios of the Turkish banks and the foreign banks. Now repeat for the other four CAMEL variables.

(b) Based on the dot diagrams, do you see any substantial differences between the group of Turkish banks and the group of foreign banks?

2.16 Ethyl Corporation manufactures engine oil additives for oil manufacturers such as Valvoline. Before a customer agrees to use a proposed additive, Ethyl must establish its performance properties by conducting engine tests. These tests are conducted under controlled conditions at test sites called *stands*. Before test results can be accepted by the customer, Ethyl must demonstrate that the conditions of the stands are appropriately calibrated. To do this, Ethyl runs a standard engine test using a *reference oil*. A reference oil is one whose performance characteristics are well understood because of extensive previous testing conducted under the auspices of the American Society for Testing and Materials (ASTM) in Pittsburgh, Pennsylvania.

The prevention of rust is a key performance characteristic of engine oils. The data for this exercise provide a measurement of rust for 135 engine tests involving 3 stands and 4 reference oils. The rust measurement is an average of evaluations of the amount of rust that developed during the test on 5 different components of the engine. The

data are on the book's data diskette under the file name EX0216 (*Source:* Data maintained on the World Wide Web by the Test Monitoring Center of the American Society for Testing and Materials. The website address for these data is http://www.tmc.astm.cmri.cmu.edu/).

(a) Do the tests appear to be stable? Develop and interpret a run chart of rust for each reference oil.

(b) Does the amount of rust seem to depend on which reference oil is used? Develop and interpret dot diagrams of rust for each reference oil, using the same scale to facilitate the comparison.

(c) Does the amount of rust seem to depend on which stand was used to conduct the test? Develop and interpret dot diagrams of rust for each stand, using the same scale to facilitate the comparison.

2.17 The 1994 NCAA Women's Final Four Basketball Tournament was held on April 2–3 in Richmond, Virginia, hosted by Virginia Commonwealth University (VCU). This exercise deals with a study of the economic impact of this tournament on the Richmond–Petersburg metropolitan statistical area (MSA). (*Source:* "1994 WOMEN'S FINAL FOUR, Economic Impact of the 1994 Women's Final Four Basketball Tournament on the Richmond–Petersburg Metropolitan Statistical Area (MSA)" by D. L. Cowles, D. M. O'Toole, and M. A. Spinelli, Virginia Commonwealth University. Report and survey instruments available from the authors at Virginia Commonwealth University School of Business, Box 844000, Richmond VA, 23284-4000.) The purpose was to assist the university and the City of Richmond in future decisions to host such tournaments. The key to evaluating the tournament's economic impact lies in estimating the direct expenditures attributable to the tournament. These include expenditures by out-of-town fans staying in Richmond, the media, the competing teams, the NCAA staff, vendors, and VCU tournament-related expenditures. About 78% of all estimated direct expenditures were determined to have come from out-of-town fans. These expenditures are the focus of this exercise. The categories of fan spending that are considered for assessing economic impact included lodging, meals, entertainment, shopping, and local transportation.

It was found that a total of 11,766 tickets were sold to fans each day, of which about 75% were known to be from out of town (based on information from VCU officials). Thus, it was assumed that

8,824 out-of-town fans attended each day. A sample of 378 out-of-town fans were interviewed by trained interviewers at the Richmond Coliseum (220 on April 2 and 158 on April 3). Although true random selection was not possible, the interviewers were instructed to "choose randomly." Specific information obtained from each respondent included (variable names in capital letters):

- the number of persons in the respondent's group (GROUP)
- group stay (number of nights in Richmond) (STAY)
- total lodging expense for the group ($LODGING)
- total group expenditure for meals ($MEALS)
- total group expenditure for entertainment ($ENTER)
- total group expenditure for shopping ($SHOP)
- total group expenditure for transportation ($TRANS)
- The data are included on the book diskette in a file named EX0217. Develop histograms of the data for each variable. In each case, describe the distribution in appropriate statistical terms.

2.18 The following data are the daily closing prices of an industrial stock over a 4-week period. The market was closed for a holiday on the third Friday of the period, so there are 19 data values:

71.750	71.750	73.750	73.500	72.000
72.000	72.250	72.375	71.000	69.250
69.500	70.875	70.625	71.375	Closed
70.375	70.625	74.000	74.125	75.250

(a) Create a dot diagram for these data.
(b) Comment on the variation and stability of the stock over the data-collection period.

2.19 The daily high temperatures in Richmond, Virginia, were recorded for the month of April and are presented as follows (ordered from lowest to highest):

52 57 57 58 58 58 65 65 66 68 69 70 71 71 73
74 75 76 78 79 80 81 81 81 82 83 85 85 85 89

(a) Construct a histogram for these data.
(b) Construct a stem-and-leaf diagram for these data.
(c) Describe the distribution of April temperatures.

2.20 Consider further the temperature data in Exercise 2.19.

(a) Construct a dot diagram for these data.
(b) Describe the distribution of April temperatures using the dot diagram.
(c) These data have been ordered from lowest to highest. Do you think any meaningful information about April temperatures might have been lost as a result? Explain.

2.21 Daily high temperatures for January of the same year are recorded in degrees Fahrenheit for Richmond, Virginia. They are given in sequence from Jan. 1 to Jan. 31:

38 46 47 45 42 49 62 47 46 40 46 53 53 69 62 49
42 36 40 45 41 34 31 37 31 26 27 35 41 53 45

(a) Construct a dot diagram for these data.
(b) Construct a histogram for these data.
(c) Describe the distribution of January temperatures for the year in which these data were recorded.
(d) Would you say that these data represent a stable system with regard to temperature? Explain.
(e) Refer to Exercise 2.19. Compare the histograms of daily high temperatures for January and April. What do they tell us about the relative temperatures in the two months?

2.22 A bank operations analyst has observed the number of transactions (customer deposits and withdrawals) per day over an 11-week period.* The data are as follows (Monday through Friday, by week):

64	96	75	105	169
67	104	74	73	202
70	116	89	112	230
68	95	121	83	168
55	109	99	94	157
52	102	72	82	123
68	90	105	78	179
64	89	105	89	219
71	87	116	82	132
55	78	87	90	119
74	83	73	75	148

(a) Using one graph for all weeks, construct a dot diagram, with days of the week on the horizontal axis.

* Courtesy of Richard Ainsworth.

(b) What does the dot diagram tell you about the transaction process?

(c) Identify as many sources of variation in these data as you can, based on your knowledge of bank transactions.

(d) Identify the process or population to which inferences based on these results might apply.

(e) What does your analysis in parts (a) and (b) suggest about daily staffing needs?

2.23 As part of the same study in Exercise 2.22, the bank operations analyst has also observed the lengths of time in minutes to complete a transaction for a random sample of 50 customer transactions in the last month. The data are as follows:

2.3	.2	2.9	.4	2.8	2.4	4.4	5.8	2.8	3.3
3.3	9.7	2.5	5.6	9.5	1.8	4.7	.7	6.2	1.2
7.8	.8	.9	.4	1.3	3.1	3.7	7.2	1.6	1.9
2.4	4.6	3.8	1.5	2.7	.4	1.3	1.1	5.5	3.4
4.2	1.2	.5	6.8	5.2	6.3	7.6	1.4	.5	1.4

(a) Construct a histogram.

(b) Construct a stem-and-leaf diagram.

(c) Describe the distribution of transaction times.

(d) Identify the process or population to which inferences based on these results might apply.

2.24 The annual premiums charged by 40 companies for $25,000 of term life insurance for 35-year-old men, as reported in *Consumer Reports*, are as follows:

82	85	86	87	87	89	89	90	91	91
92	93	94	95	95	95	95	95	97	98
99	99	100	100	101	101	103	103	103	104
105	105	106	107	107	107	109	110	110	111

(a) Construct a histogram.

(b) Construct a stem-and-leaf diagram.

(c) Describe the distribution of annual premiums.

2.25 Let's return to the data of Exercise 1.31 for the daily demand for hardcover books in a book shop on 30 consecutive working days, in number of books sold.

(a) Using one graph for all weeks, construct a dot diagram by plotting the demands on the vertical axis corresponding to the weeks on the horizontal axis.

(b) Construct a histogram for the 30 working days.

(c) Describe the distribution of daily demand.

(d) Based on your answer to part (a), compare the week-to-week variations of daily demands. Explain what is apparent to you.

2.26 The average monthly sales over the past year (in thousands of dollars) of a computer company's 20 salespersons are as follows:

40.2	29.3	35.6	88.2	42.9
26.9	28.7	99.8	35.6	37.8
44.2	32.3	55.2	50.6	25.2
31.7	36.8	45.2	25.1	39.7

(a) Construct a histogram.

(b) Construct a stem-and-leaf diagram.

(c) Based on your results in parts (a) and (b), would you say that some sales representatives outperformed others? Justify your answer.

2.27 Return to Exercise 2.26.

(a) Identify as many sources of variation in the data as you can imagine (within reason), and label each as a common cause or a special cause.

(b) Which of these causes of variation are under the control of the salesperson, and which are beyond the salesperson's control?

(c) What do your answers to parts (a) and (b) suggest about using sales to judge the performance of a salesperson?

2.28 Thirty-two batteries were randomly selected from a stable manufacturing process and subjected to a life test. The following data represent the lifetimes in hours of the 32 batteries:

52.5	62.7	58.9	65.7	49.3	62.8	48.3	52.9
58.9	57.3	60.4	59.6	58.1	55.3	54.9	63.4
62.3	64.4	52.7	54.9	48.8	54.6	64.2	57.2
56.8	53.1	58.7	61.6	63.3	51.7	59.5	56.8

(a) Construct a histogram.

(b) Construct a stem-and-leaf diagram and use it to describe the distribution of the lifetimes of the batteries.

(c) Based on your work in parts (a) and (b), describe the amount of variation in the lifetimes of batteries produced by this process.

2.29 Of the last 200 beads produced by a bead manufacturer, 24 were defective. A production manager has recorded the causes of defects for these 24. The types of defect are bead diameter (BD), hole diameter (HD), bead smoothness (BS), hole smoothness (HS), color (C), and shape (S). The types of defects for the 24 defective beads are as follows:

BD	C	C	S	S	BD	C	C	HS	HD	BD	BS
BD	BS	BS	S	S	C	HS	S	S	BD	HS	C

(a) Identify the process or population to which inferences based on this information might apply.

(b) Based on this information, what would you estimate is the proportion of defective beads that would be produced if the process continued unchanged? Assume that it has been determined that the process is stable with respect to the proportion of defective beads.

(c) Construct a Pareto diagram.

(d) What does your Pareto diagram suggest about the focus of a strategy to reduce the number of defects produced?

2.30 Educational Services, Inc. is a small firm that provides tutoring to middle school and high school students. Clients are obtained through three sources: the Yellow Pages, professional referral, or referral from a previous client. The data* that follow represent sales revenues in dollars for a sample of 143 clients, broken out by source.

Client Referrals

40	300	100	120	160	140	80	110	160	180
80	710	120	220	100	250	120	20	160	120
1,340	160	280	200	560	3,940	60	600	140	840
230	160	530	200	140	480	140	120	560	120
38	180	100	220	100	220	1,040			

Yellow Pages

950	120	75	200	100	620	320	120	140	80
130	830	180	320	90	1,220	380	60	70	1,600
80	120	160	760	850	420	150	140	20	520
260	100	100	840	480	150	230	220	220	

Professional Referrals

2,200	140	480	480	150	2,840	560	530	2,470	140
160	320	80	320	180	940	580	900	1,730	100
900	360	1,560	1,050	680	4,160	200	165	300	60
1,870	390	1,920	740	140	60	140	40	540	8,320
1,020	175	1,260	710	720	1,540	4,680	1,460	400	1,120
240	360	540	1,500	3,280	880	1,120			

(a) Develop a dot diagram of the distribution of revenues for each source.

(b) Develop a stem-and-leaf diagram of the distribution of revenues for each source.

(c) Based on your diagrams from parts (a) and (b), describe and compare the distribution of revenues for each source.

2.31 Northup and Bauers is a large, highly respected law firm. The legal staff consists of partners, associates, and paralegals. The attorneys and paralegals must record their billable hours each day. This information is the basis for client billing. In a study of the work of the associates in the firm, the number of billable hours was recorded for each of the firm's 43 associates over a 9-month period. These data are:*

802	1,287	1,225	1,178	1,275	767	1,424	1,328	1,223	790
1,399	1,434	1,050	796	1,308	1,464	1,389	1,316	1,325	1,494
1,096	1,482	1,493	1,452	1,060	1,407	1,067	934	901	1,400
1,320	1,132	1,256	858	1,346	885	1,084	1,065	1,211	1,379
1,340	1,098	1,407							

(a) Develop a dot diagram of the billable hours of associates.

(b) Develop a histogram of the billable hours of associates.

(c) Based on parts (a) and (b), describe the distribution of billable hours of the associates.

(d) This is a study of the work process of the firm's associates. List several factors that might explain the observed variation in billable hours among the associates.

2.32 A study was conducted to determine the factors that influence the daily sales of an ice cream parlor. Daily sales are defined as the total cash receipts collected from the selling of ice cream, yogurt, drinks, and brownies on a given day. The data that follow† represent daily sales for the months of March, June, September, and December. These months were thought to be indicative of the entire year.

373	761	412	180	242	148	221	436	640	462
254	257	259	220	382	737	610	246	238	342
307	505	739	591	260	262	317	419	335	550
884	793	379	497	407	423	702	815	777	583
494	509	456	587	878	674	480	322	453	477
726	779	795	381	445	465	443	594	869	884
700	668	349	349	419	440	780	700	321	242
385	287	438	749	600	300	311	313	196	452
441	514	290	245	193	301	385	643	583	343
544	190	200	173	193	372	547	528	274	285
168	250	495	635	306	198	368	263	226	296
468	416	331	324	464	544	336	498	380	

(a) Develop a histogram of daily sales.

(b) Based on your histogram in part (a), describe the distribution of daily sales.

(c) List several factors that might explain some of the observed variation in daily sales.

---

* Courtesy of Douglas Haag and Timothy Geer.

* Courtesy of Alexis Campbell.

† Courtesy of Omega Brown, Abbey Shipp, and Aaron Dennis.

EXERCISES FOR SECTION 2.4

2.33 What is the purpose of measures of location?

2.34 Identify and differentiate the three primary measures of location.

2.35 Which of the measures of location is most sensitive to outlier data values? Explain.

2.36 Which measure of location corresponds to the 50th percentile?

2.37 Which measure of location would usually be preferred if the distribution is known to be single peaked and skewed? Why?

2.38 Consider the following small data sets:

(1) 3, 4, 5, 6, 7   (2) 7, 8, 9, 10, 11
(3) 1, 6, 7, 8, 9   (4) 1, 2, 3, 4, 9

(a) Compute the mean and the median.
(b) In each case, explain your finding in terms of the effect of any outlier data values.

2.39 Consider the following small data sets:

(1) 1, 2, 3, 4, 5   (2) 1, 2, 3, 4, 50   (3) 1, 200, 220, 240, 260

(a) Compute the mean and the median.
(b) In each case, explain your finding in terms of the effect of any outlier data values.

2.40 Review the distribution of data for the daily demand for hardcover books (Exercises 1.31 and 2.25).
(a) From viewing the histogram, which would you expect to be larger, the median or the mean? Explain.
(b) Compute the median and the mean to confirm or contradict your expectation in part (a).

2.41 A service manager wants to compare the average length of downtime per service call for the two copiers his company uses. They have a Suny 1000 and Saban XL100. For each copier, he has compiled the total downtime in hours for each service call in the last 6 months, obtaining the following results:

Model	Downtime (hours)
Suny 1000	7.2 3.6 5.5 4.6 3.7 3.1 2.6 7.2
Saban XL100	4.4 3.3 5.6 6.1 4.2 3.6 3.4 4.2 5.0 3.0

(a) Compute the mean and median downtimes for each model.
(b) Construct a dot diagram using the same graph for the two models. Based on this graph, is it apparent to you which model exhibits the larger variation in downtime?
(c) Based on your results in parts (a) and (b), would you expect one model to have shorter downtimes in the future than the other model? Explain.

2.42 In the production of lightbulbs, many bulbs are broken. A production manager is testing a new type of conveyor system in hopes of reducing the percentage of bulbs broken each day. For ten days he observes bulb breakage with the current conveyor. He then records bulb breakage for ten days with the new system, after allowing a few days for the operator to learn to use it. His data are as follows:

Conveyor System	Percentage of Bulbs Broken Daily
Old	8.7 11.1 4.4 3.7 9.2 6.6 7.8 4.9 6.9 8.3
New	10.8 6.2 3.2 4.6 5.3 6.5 4.6 7.1 4.9 7.2

(a) Compute the mean and median for each conveyor system.
(b) Construct a dot diagram using the same graph for the two conveyor systems. Is it apparent to you which system exhibits the larger variation in percentage of bulbs broken?
(c) Based on these results, do you think this test establishes that the new system lowers the breakage rate? Explain.

2.43 Suppose the average amount of cash (in pocket, wallet, purse, etc.) possessed by the 47 students attending a finance class meeting is $12.50. The median amount carried is $9.00.
(a) What characteristics of the distribution of cash carried by students might explain why the mean is larger than the median?
(b) Identify the process or population to which inferences based on these results might apply.

2.44 Is it true that half of the families in this country have incomes below the median family income? Why?

2.45 For the following situations, assume that the applicable distribution is single peaked and symmetric. Is it true that half the medical doctors in the country are "below average" (using any criterion of performance, such as income, medical knowledge, etc.)? Are half the college professors in your university below average (for the professors of that university)? Are half the students in your class below average (for your class—again, using any criterion of performance)? What do your answers suggest about what it means to be below average? Discuss in your own words.

2.46 Which of the measures of location can have a value that is different from all of the individual values in a data set? Construct an example to demonstrate your answer.

2.47 Which of the measures of location can have a value that is the same as the smallest value in the data set (assuming there is some variation in the data)? Construct an example to demonstrate your answer.

2.48 Refer to Exercise 2.30, concerning Educational Services, Inc. The data represent sales revenues for a sample of 143 clients, broken out by source of referral.
(a) Determine the mean and median sales

amounts for each source of referral. Do the average sales revenue amounts appear to differ for clients from the three referral sources?

(b) Compare the mean to the median sales amount for each referral source. What accounts for the large differences?

EXERCISES FOR SECTION 2.5

2.50 Identify the primary measures of variation.

2.51 Why is the value of the standard deviation easier to interpret than the value of the variance?

2.52 Which quantity, the MAD or the standard deviation, is more sensitive to outlier data values? Why?

2.53 What are the advantages and disadvantages in using the range as a measure of variation?

2.54 Which measure of variation would usually be preferred if the distribution is known to be single peaked and considerably skewed? Why?

2.55 Consider the following data sets:

(1) 0, 25, 75, 100   (2) 48, 49, 51, 52

(a) Inspect each data set. Which has the greater variation? Why?

(b) To check your thinking in part (a), determine the range, MAD, variance, and standard deviation for each data set. Explain your findings.

2.56 Consider the following data sets:

(1) 0, 2, 4, 6, 8, 10   (2) 0, 2, 5, 5, 8, 10   (3) 0, 0, 0, 10, 10, 10

(a) Inspect each data set. Which set has the greatest variation? Why?

(b) To check your thinking in part (a), determine the range, MAD, variance, and standard deviation for each data set. Explain your findings.

2.57 In Exercise 1.37, you examined the stability of the visitation process at the Information Age Exhibit of the Smithsonian Institute in Washington, D.C, based on data produced by the Institute's computer tracking system. Run charts suggested that the day of the week was a source of substantial variation in the number of visitors in a day. The data for this exercise are on the book's data diskette, in the file named EX0137. To examine this dependence further:

(a) Develop five dot diagrams of the distribution of daily total visitors, one for each day of the week and sharing the same scale. Do these diagrams suggest that the number of visitors tends to differ by the day of the week?

(b) Determine the mean, median, and standard

2.49 Refer to Exercise 2.31, concerning billable hours of the associates at the law firm Northup and Bauers.

(a) Determine the mean and median for billable hours.

(b) Explain your results in part (a) based on the distributions observed in Exercise 2.31.

deviation of the daily attendance for each day of the week.

(c) Based on your results in parts (a) and (b), describe the effect of the day of the week on the number of visitors in a day. Are you confident that the mean number of visitors varies by day of the week? If so, which day produces the most visitors on the average? Which day produces the least?

(d) Repeat the analysis of parts (b) and (c) by applying it to the daily average visitation times. Based on this analysis, describe the effect of the day of the week on the mean daily visitation time.

2.58 In Exercise 2.17, you studied the expenditures of out-of-town fans attending the 1994 Women's Final Four Basketball Tournament in Richmond, Virginia. Five categories of direct spending were included: lodging, meals, entertainment, shopping, and local transportation.

Recall that it was estimated that 8,824 out-of-town fans attended each day, and that a sample of 378 out-of-town fans were interviewed. Specific information obtained for each respondent included the variables that were listed in Exercise 2.17. The data for this exercise are on the book's data diskette, in the file named EX0217.

(a) Determine the sample means and standard deviations for the number of persons in a group, the number of nights stayed, and each of the group spending categories listed.

(b) Use the information you developed in part (a) to estimate the average dollars spent over the entire stay by out-of-town groups.

(c) Using your results for parts (a) and (b), along with the information given in this exercise, estimate the total dollar expenditures of the population of out-of-town fans.

2.59 How much money do major-league baseball players make? The salaries for all major-league baseball players in 1994 (747 players) are contained on the book data diskette in a file named EX0259 (*Source: USA Today*, Apr. 5, 1994). Salaries include prorated signing bonuses. The file also contains the player's name, his team, and his defensive position.

(a) Use an appropriate graphical method to characterize the distribution of 1994 player salaries. Based on your graph, describe the distribution.

(b) Given the shape of the distribution of 1994 player salaries, would you expect the mean to be considerably less, about the same, or considerably greater than the median? Justify your answer.

(c) Determine the mean and median of 1994 player salaries, and discuss the results in light of your answer in part (b).

2.60 It is frequently asserted that competition is the best way to control costs. This argument has been actively used as a mechanism to force more efficient management of hospitals and health-care facilities. As a result, for-profit providers have proliferated. But are they really more efficient? One commonly accepted indicator of efficiency is the financial ratio Return on Assets (ROA), defined as the financial return from investment in assets (the higher the ratio, the higher the efficiency); it is computed as

$$ROA = \frac{\text{Cash flow from operations}}{\text{Total unrestricted assets}}$$

The data consist of the 1993 RAO ratios for a sample of 76 not-for-profit hospitals and 14 for-profit hospitals in Virginia (*Source: 1994 Annual Report of the Virginia Health Services Cost Review Council*); they are as follows.

Return on Assets

Not-For-Profit					For Profit
17.2	4.1	11.38	10.41	5.19	19.2
6.12	10.85	−1.29	1.8	9.21	23.96
15.51	3.85	4.89	7.35	15.79	.52
8.82	8.21	8.12	22.12	12.26	19.32
14.87	10.67	3.83	3.93	9.16	14.15
8.66	−.26	1.01	28.17	12.26	40.44
13.05	12.18	2.87	16.92	11.39	10.41
13.67	7.98	9.41	29.78	4.98	18.19
11.96	8.18	11.88	13.39	16.77	16.85
7.25	12.92	−.77	17.45	18.26	2.01
8.75	.72	13.92	5.73	12.83	26.83
7.39	21.28	11.54	9.29	9.24	14.99
14.15	12.6	13.87	16.2	20.28	19.04
12.63	9.74	9.41	13.02	12.14	−1.04
8.76	16.26	11.75	7.91	−.18	
				14.9	

(a) Develop appropriate graphical representations of the distributions of ROA for the not-for-profit hospitals and for the for-profit hospitals. Compare the two distributions based on these graphs.

(b) Develop appropriate numerical summaries of ROA for the not-for-profit hospitals and for the for-profit hospitals (mean, median, standard deviation). Compare the two groups based on these results.

(c) Based on your results in parts (a) and (b), what do you conclude about the premise that for-profit hospitals are more efficient than not-for-profit hospitals?

2.61 In Exercise 2.14, you compared distributions of data for selected samples of national, regional, and discount brokers based on four characteristics involving cost, research strength, and access (*Source: Fortune*, Dec. 25, 1995). Now, to more sharply specify apparent differences among the three groups, determine means, medians, and standard deviations for all four characteristics. For each characteristic, compare the distributions of the three groups with regard to location and variation. The data for this exercise are on the book's data diskette, in the file named EX0214.

2.62 In Exercise 2.15, you studied data for samples of 37 Turkish banks and 8 foreign banks with respect to five performance variables (called CAMEL characteristics). The data for this exercise are on the book's data diskette, in the file named EX0215.

(a) For each group and each CAMEL variable, determine the mean, the median, and the standard deviation.

(b) For each CAMEL variable, compare the groups with respect to location and variation of their respective distributions. For which CAMEL variables do you see discernible differences between the groups? For which do the differences seem inconsequential?

2.63 Refer to Exercises 2.19 and 2.20, in which the daily high temperatures in Richmond, Virginia, in April were presented.

(a) Compute the mean, median, and mode of the daily high temperatures.

(b) Referring to the frequency table for these data (you should construct one now if you have not already done so), determine the modal class.

(c) Compute the range, MAD, and standard deviation. Comment on your findings.

(d) Determine the percentage of data values that lie within one standard deviation of the mean, within two standard deviations, and within three standard deviations. Compare these percentages to those of Tchebysheff's finding and the empirical rule.

2.64 Refer to Exercise 2.23, dealing with the transaction times for 50 customers of a bank.
   (a) Compute the mean, median, and mode. Which do you consider the best indicator of location for these data? Explain.
   (b) Compute the MAD and standard deviation.
   (c) Determine the percentage of data values that lie within one standard deviation of the mean and within two standard deviations of the mean. Compare these percentages to those of Tchebysheff's finding and the empirical rule.
   (d) Based on your answer to part (c) and the histogram of Exercise 2.23, do you think the empirical rule is appropriate here? Explain.

2.65 In Exercise 2.64, one of the transaction times was 6.3 minutes.
   (a) How many standard deviations above or below the mean is a transaction time of 6.3 minutes?
   (b) Based on Tchebysheff's finding, roughly what percentage of transaction times could be expected to exceed 6.3 minutes?
   (c) Based on the empirical rule, roughly what percentage of transaction times could be expected to exceed 6.3 minutes?

2.66 Refer to Exercise 2.24, which dealt with annual premiums for $25,000 of term life insurance charged to 35-year-old men by 40 companies.
   (a) Compute the mean, median, and mode. Which do you consider the best indicator of location for these data? Explain.
   (b) Compute the MAD and standard deviation.
   (c) Based on the mean and standard deviation, describe the amount of variation that could be expected of this data set.
   (d) Based on your answer to part (c) and the histogram of Exercise 2.24, do you think the empirical rule is appropriate here? Explain.

2.67 A manufacturing process manager thinks that differences between two machines used in producing plastic bottle caps might cause unnecessary variation in the breaking strength of the caps (measured in pounds). She measures the breaking strength for random samples of ten caps from each machine. Both samples were taken while the machine's production was stable. The data are as follows:

Machine A   .46   .50   .48   .52   .49   .50   .51   .48   .54   .50
Machine B   .44   .54   .56   .45   .47   .51   .54   .48   .58   .50

(a) Construct a dot diagram for these two machines using the same graph. Is it apparent to you that the locations and variations of breaking strengths are not the same?
(b) Compute the mean and median for each sample. What do they suggest to you about the two machines?
(c) Compute the range and standard deviation for each sample. What do they suggest to you about the two machines?
(d) Based on your answers to parts (a) and (c), would you expect the empirical rule to apply to these samples? Explain your thinking.

2.68 The following data are the sales amounts for a random sample of 30 recent invoices selected from all invoices in the last month at Kathy's Korner, a young women's apparel shop:

.99	5.00	8.23	11.00	14.99	18.88	21.50	24.50
24.99	28.88	29.98	30.00	31.00	33.73	34.53	34.88
36.00	37.76	39.99	41.64	42.00	44.72	46.26	47.00
48.00	54.44	64.87	73.24	99.98	103.52		

(a) Identify the process or population to which inferences based on these data might apply.
(b) Construct a histogram.
(c) Determine the mean, median, MAD, and standard deviation.
(d) Explain why the mean is larger or smaller than the median.

2.69 To obtain some idea about the length of introductory statistics textbooks, a statistics professor selected ten different texts from her bookshelf and recorded the number of pages in each. The following are the number of pages from the oldest book to the newest:

312   608   780   786   894   982   1,029   1,098   1,156   1,245

(a) Construct a run chart. What is your conclusion?
(b) Determine the mean, median, MAD, and standard deviation.
(c) If you had to predict the number of pages in a more recent book than these, what would be your prediction relative to this mean? Explain.

2.70 The following data are the waiting times in minutes of the last 15 patients in a doctor's office (in the order in which the patients arrived):

37   19   21   39   25   27   43   15   41   29   31   17   33   23   35

(a) Construct a run chart. Is any pattern apparent to you? Explain.

(b) Compute the mean and standard deviation of these patient waiting times.

(c) If you had to plan, what would be your best prediction of the waiting time of the next patient? Explain your prediction.

2.71 Given here are the waiting times in minutes of the last 15 patients in a dentist's office (in the order in which the patients arrived):

17 15 23 19 21 27 25 33 29 31 35 39 37 41 45

(a) Construct a run chart. Is any pattern apparent to you? Explain.

(b) Compute the mean and standard deviation of these patient waiting times.

(c) If you had to plan, what would be your best prediction of the waiting time of the next patient? Explain your prediction.

2.72 In what essential way does Exercise 2.70 differ from Exercise 2.71, and how does this affect your use of the mean and standard deviation for prediction?

EXERCISES FOR SECTION 2.6

2.73 Explain why measures of relative standing are useful.

2.74 Upon graduation, suppose you receive a starting salary of $29,500. You learn that this salary corresponds to the 60th percentile of the starting salaries for your field of study. Explain what this means.

2.75 With reference to Exercise 2.74, suppose you also learn that the average starting salary is $28,500 and the standard deviation is $2,000. Determine your Z-value and explain what it means.

2.76 Suppose the middle 50% of monthly sales of a particular brand of television at a discount retailer is between 80 and 120 sets. Determine the first and third quartiles and explain what they mean.

2.77 With reference to Exercise 2.76, suppose the middle 80% of monthly sales is between 50 and 150 sets. Determine the 10th and 90th percentiles and explain what they mean.

2.78 Suppose a retailer in Exercise 2.76 sells on average 100 TV sets a month with a standard deviation of 20 sets. In a particular month, the retailer sells 75 sets. Assuming a stable situation, explain how the retailer did that month in relative terms.

2.79 Refer to Exercise 2.23. Construct a box plot for these data. Is your finding consistent with your answer in Exercise 2.23? Explain.

2.80 Refer to Exercise 2.24. Construct a box plot for these data. Is your finding consistent with your answer in Exercise 2.24? Explain.

2.81 Refer to Exercise 2.28. Construct a box plot for these data. Is your finding consistent with your answer in Exercise 2.28? Explain.

2.82 In Exercise 2.16, you constructed dot diagrams for data involving the testing of the performance characteristics of 4 engine oils in 3 test facilities called stands. These data are used by Ethyl Corporation and other manufacturers of engine oil additives to calibrate their testing facilities. The data for this exercise are on the book's data diskette, in the file named EX0216.

(a) Develop and interpret (1) box plots of rust for the 4 reference oils and (2) box plots of rust for the 3 stands.

(b) How would you rate the effectiveness of box plots vs. that of dot diagrams for comparing these distributions?

2.83 Refer to Exercise 2.68. Construct a box plot for these data. Is your finding consistent with your answer in Exercise 2.68? Explain.

2.84 Refer to Exercises 2.30 and 2.48, concerning Educational Services, Inc. The data represent sales revenues for a sample of 143 clients, broken out by source of referral. Construct a box plot for each referral source. Are your findings consistent with those of Exercise 2.30? Explain.

2.85 Refer to Exercises 2.31 and 2.49, concerning the billable hours of associates at the law firm of Northup and Bauers. Construct a box plot of the distribution of billable hours, and compare it to your findings in Exercise 2.31.

2.86 Refer to Exercise 2.32, concerning the daily sales at an ice cream parlor. Construct a box plot of the distribution of daily sales, and compare it to your findings in Exercise 2.32.

EXERCISES FOR SECTION 2.7

2.87 The following data represent the power generated daily (in thousands of megawatts) for ten consecutive days in August by a regional utility and the atmospheric high temperature (in degrees Fahrenheit) on the same days:*

Day:	1	2	3	4	5	6	7	8	9	10
Temp.:	99	99	97	97	97	76	84	81	96	95
Power:	153	158	148	138	149	112	124	103	136	124

(a) Construct a scatter diagram for power and daily high temperature.

(b) What does the scatter diagram suggest to you about the relationship between the power generated on a given day and the high temperature that day? Explain your thinking.

(c) Does the high temperature on a given day govern the amount of power generated that day? Or is it the other way around? Is it possible that neither directly affects the other?

(d) Are your answers in parts (b) and (c) based on statistical analysis or on subject-matter knowledge? Explain.

(e) For another August day in which the high temperature was 88°, what amount of power would you predict would be generated? (*Hint:* Make your prediction subjectively, based on the scatter diagram.)

(f) Based on this analysis, what prediction would you make for an April day with a high temperature of 55°?

2.88 Express Graphics is a printing firm. Express prints a wide variety of packaging, including flip-top boxes for cigarettes, detergent boxes, and boxes for cosmetics, pharmaceuticals, and fast foods. The jobs vary in size, configuration, print quality, and type of paper used. The firm completes about 200 jobs a month. To assess the effectiveness of the current pricing process, a manager is interested in the degree of correspondence between the target selling price (X) of a job and the eventual billed amount (Y). Data for a random sample of 15 jobs completed in the last month are as follows:[†]

Billed Amount	Target Selling Price
$6,417	$5,295
85	83
2,178	2,336

---
* Courtesy of K. L. Fugett.

† Courtesy of Jared Bjarnason.

Billed Amount	Target Selling Price
127	123
4,349	4,285
115	76
381	125
122	44
328	551
543	469
2,577	1,882
404	545
15,090	13,596
292	929
1,045	633

(a) Create a scatter diagram for these data.

(b) Interpret the scatter diagram. What does it indicate about the correspondence between target selling prices and actual billed amounts?

(c) Use the scatter diagram to estimate subjectively the billed amount of a job whose target selling price is $5,000.

2.89 In Exercise 2.12, you analyzed 1990 data for 17 Virginia localities under consideration by a commercial real estate developer who is considering expansion. Now the developer wishes to understand the relationships of wealth to demographic characteristics related to real estate. The relevant data are for the same 17 localities; they are on the book's data diskette in file EX0212. Wealth is represented by the median income for all occupied housing units. The demographic characteristics are the proportion of housing units that are renter-occupied, the proportion of housing units with incomes below the poverty line, and the proportion of housing units that have a telephone. Develop and interpret scatter diagrams of the relationships between wealth and each of the three demographic variables.

2.90 In Exercise 2.13, you studied data for 30-year and 15-year mortgage rates offered by 32 Richmond, Virginia, lenders for loan amounts over $203,150. To what extent does a lender's total cost for 30-year mortgages correspond to its total cost for a 15-year mortgage? That is, if a lender's total cost is high (or low) for a 15-year mortgage, can we expect the cost to be high (or low) for that lender's 30-year mortgage? Develop and interpret a scatter diagram. The data for this exercise are on the book's data diskette, in the file named EX0213 (*Source: Richmond Times-Dispatch,* Oct. 23, 1995).

2.91 In Exercises 2.14 and 2.61, you compared distributions of data (*Source: Fortune*, Dec. 25, 1995) for selected samples of national, regional, and discount brokers based on four characteristics involving commissions cost, fees, research strength, and access. The data for this exercise are on the book's data diskette, in the file named EX0214.

To what extent do commissions, fees, and research strength correspond to size? Develop scatter diagrams between commissions cost and number of offices, between transaction fees and number of offices, and between number of analysts and number of offices. Discuss your findings.

2.92 In Exercises 2.15 and 2.62, you studied data for samples of 37 Turkish banks and 8 foreign banks. Recall that officials of the Bank Association of Turkey wished to compare Turkish banks with banks of other European southern tier countries. The officials also were interested in the relationship between bank performance and bank size for Turkish banks. They decided to use the number of branches and assets as measures of a bank's size. These additional data are on the book's data diskette, in the file named EX0215.

(a) To what degree do number of branches and assets agree as measures of size? Develop a scatter diagram for number of branches versus assets, and describe the relationship.

(b) To investigate the relationship between one of the CAMEL measures and size, develop a scatter diagram between the ratio of non-interest income to assets (Noinasst) and assets, and describe the relationship you see (if any).

2.93 It is a general perception in the hospital industry that a large proportion of Medicaid patient-days is undesirable, because the reimbursement rate is generally lower than other pay rates. Additionally, it is known that the medically indigent tend to seek care later in the disease process; so it might be expected that they require a higher utilization of resources. As a result, many providers either limit or refuse outright the treatment of Medicaid patients. But can the proportion of Medicaid patient-days truly be shown to have an impact on a hospital's resource allocation and financial performance? The data for this exercise are provided by the Virginia Health Services Cost Review Council *(1994 Annual Report: Efficiency and Productivity—Performance Profiles of Hospitals)* and are stored on the book data diskette, in a file named EX0293. The sample consists of all Virginia acute-care hospitals that provided usable data for 1993 (67 of

100). The variables reported by the Review Council are:

Medicaid Participation Variables

- M/TRatio: Proportion of Medicaid patient-days (ratio of Medicaid patient-days to total patient-days)
- McaidDys: Medicaid patient-days
- TPatDys: Total patient-days

Resource Utilization Variables

- Hrs/Adm: Paid hours per adjusted admission—the number of hours for which employees were paid divided by the number of patients admitted
- ALoS: Average length of stay—total patient-days divided by the number of admissions

Financial Performance Indicators

- Debt: Cash debt coverage—cash flow from operations plus interest paid/current debt service; this indicates the ability to repay long-term debt. (Higher is better.)
- TotMargn: Total profit margin—operating and non-operating profit
- ROA: Return on assets—financial return on investment in assets plus cash flow from operations and total unrestricted assets

(a) Develop a scatter diagram of the relationship between the proportion of Medicaid patient-days and each of the indicators of resource utilization and financial performance. In each case, describe the apparent relationship, if any.

(b) Based on the scatter diagrams in part (a), would you say that treating Medicaid patients puts hospitals at a disadvantage, either in terms of resource utilization or reduced financial performance? Explain.

2.94 The following data represent the total annual sales and before-tax profits (both in billions of dollars) for all manufacturing corporations in the United States over the period 1980–1989 (*Source: Statistical Abstract of the United States*, 1994).

Year	1980	1981	1982	1983	1984
Sales	1,897	2,145	2,039	2,114	2,335
Before-tax profits	145	159	108	133	166

Year	1985	1986	1987	1988	1989
Sales	2,331	2,221	2,378	2,596	2,745
Before-tax profits	137	129	173	216	189

(a) Develop a scatter diagram for before-tax profits (the response variable) and sales (the predictor variable). What does this diagram suggest about the relationship between sales and before-tax profits for U.S. manufacturing corporations?

(b) If it were reported that U.S. manufacturing corporations had total sales of $2,450 billion in 1990, what would you estimate to be their 1990 total before-tax profits? Base your estimate on the scatter diagram you developed in part (a).

2.95 In Exercise 2.16, you studied data involving the testing of the performance characreristics of engine oils. These data are used by manufacturers of engine oil additives to calibrate their testing facilities. They can also be used to evaluate the performance properties of a proposed additive. The data for this exercise represent 64 test runs for reference oil 1002 over the period 1993–1995; they are stored on the book's data diskette under the file name EX0295. The performance characteristics of interest here are the rate of sludge formation (SLUDGE) and the average amount of wear on the eight lobes of a camshaft (CAMWEAR). Use these data to characterize the performance of reference oil 1002 as follows.

(a) Since the test runs were conducted sequentially over a 3-year period, there is some concern over the stability of the testing process. Develop run charts of each performance characteristic and discuss the apparent stability or instability exhibited.

(b) Determine and interpret the mean and standard deviation for each characteristic.

(c) The manufacturer is interested in learning whether camshaft wear is related to sludge formation. Develop a scatter diagram for these two characteristics to shed light on this question. What would you tell the manufacturer of reference oil 1002 about the relationship between camshaft wear and sludge formation?

2.96 A personnel manager administers an aptitude test to all new sales representatives. Sales management is interested in the extent to which the test is able to predict eventual sales success. The following are the test scores and the average weekly sales for eight sales representatives who took the test a year ago:

Average sales:	8	12	28	24	18	16	15	12
Test scores:	55	60	85	75	80	85	65	55

(a) Construct a scatter diagram.

(b) Interpret the scatter diagram and describe any apparent relationship between a sales representative's test score and his or her average sales.

(c) Is the prediction of sales representatives' average sales helped by basing predictions on test scores? If so, how much? (*Note:* No method has yet been presented for answering this question.)

2.97 In a recent study involving a random sample of 300 automobile accidents, the information was classified by the size of the automobile and whether a fatality had occurred:

	Small	Medium	Large
At least one fatality	42	35	20
No fatality	78	65	60

Based on a graphical analysis, is it apparent to you that the size of an automobile is relevant to the occurrence of a fatality? Explain.

2.98 A production process uses four machines in its three-shift operation. A random sample of 135 breakdowns was classified according to machine and the shift in which the breakdown occurred. The data are as follows:

	Machine			
Shift	A	B	C	D
1	10	12	8	14
2	15	8	13	8
3	12	9	14	12

Based on a graphical analysis, is it apparent to you that the shift is relevant to the occurrence of a breakdown? Explain.

SUPPLEMENTARY EXERCISES

2.99 A training program on a new piece of production equipment was initiated for workers in a manufac- turing company. The training program culminates with both a written and a practical evaluation. The practical evaluation consists of six tasks that the trainee must complete correctly. The following data are the times (in seconds) needed to complete one of the six tasks for 78 trainees:*

Employee:	1	2	3	4	5	6	7	8	9	10
Time:	247	238	226	274	274	271	241	249	294	254

Employee:	11	12	13	14	15	16	17	18	19	20
Time:	263	244	259	256	292	210	210	225	213	318

Employee:	21	22	23	24	25	26	27	28	29	30
Time:	206	215	193	195	252	254	201	253	301	247

Employee:	31	32	33	34	35	36	37	38	39	40
Time:	271	270	219	229	294	274	195	222	264	258

Employee:	41	42	43	44	45	46	47	48	49	50
Time:	238	231	263	313	238	240	197	271	296	209

Employee:	51	52	53	54	55	56	57	58	59	60
Time:	217	198	228	309	286	244	262	217	324	224

Employee:	61	62	63	64	65	66	67	68	69	70
Time:	265	302	179	299	226	236	242	239	218	266

Employee:	71	72	73	74	75	76	77	78		
Time:	276	221	220	259	239	258	254	244		

(a) Determine the mean, median, and standard deviation.

(b) Construct a histogram and use it to explain the distribution of completion times.

(c) How might management use this distribution to improve the training program?

2.100 The following are the winning and losing scores of the past 56 National Football League championship games (the last 32 are the Super Bowls):

	1943	1944	1945	1946	1947	1948	1949
Winner:	41	14	15	24	28	7	14
Loser:	21	7	14	14	21	0	0

	1950	1951	1952	1953	1954	1955	1956
Winner:	30	24	17	17	56	38	47
Loser:	28	17	7	16	10	14	7

	1957	1958	1959	1960	1961	1962	1963
Winner:	59	23	31	17	37	16	14
Loser:	14	17	16	13	0	7	10

	1964	1965	1966	1967	1968	1969	1970
Winner:	27	23	34	35	33	16	23
Loser:	0	12	27	10	14	7	7

	1971	1972	1973	1974	1975	1976	1977
Winner:	16	24	14	24	16	21	32
Loser:	13	3	7	7	6	17	14

	1978	1979	1980	1981	1982	1983	1984
Winner:	27	35	31	27	26	27	38
Loser:	10	31	19	10	21	17	9

	1985	1986	1987	1988	1989	1990	1991
Winner:	38	46	39	42	20	55	20
Loser:	16	10	20	10	16	10	19

	1992	1993	1994	1995	1996	1997	1998
Winner:	37	52	30	49	27	35	31
Loser:	24	17	13	26	17	21	24

(a) Construct run charts for the winning and losing scores. Are any patterns discernible? Explain.

(b) Determine means, medians, and standard deviations for the winning and losing scores prior to the Super Bowl (1943–1966) and for the Super Bowls (1967–1998). In addition, construct dot diagrams for each period. Compare and explain your findings.

2.101 The following data consist of the number of individual federal income tax returns and the adjusted gross incomes reported in those returns for the 50 states and the District of Columbia in 1988:*

State	Number of Returns (in thousands)	Adjusted Gross Income (in million $)	State	Number of Returns (in thousands)	Adjusted Gross Income (in million $)
ME	560	13,613	NC	2,930	72,137
NH	551	16,986	SC	1,463	33,860
VT	262	6,719	GA	2,741	73,302
MA	2,958	93,776	FL	5,760	159,547
RI	473	13,237	KY	1,462	33,897
CT	1,676	62,073	TN	2,097	50,988
NY	8,066	262,846	AL	1,624	38,631
NJ	4,012	137,372	MS	970	19,463
PA	5,416	144,761	AR	932	19,932
OH	4,910	126,962	LA	1,625	36,696
IN	2,444	62,376	OK	1,261	29,224
IL	5,196	154,863	TX	7,005	179,977
MI	4,071	115,419	MT	341	6,994
WI	2,169	56,322	ID	391	8,632
MN	1,955	53,715	WY	199	4,870
IA	1,225	28,546	CO	1,493	39,650
MO	2,224	57,033	NM	623	13,548
ND	279	5,844	AZ	1,520	39,322
SD	299	5,987	UT	634	13,548
NE	707	16,680	NV	538	15,779
KS	1,077	28,071	WA	2,129	58,391
DE	316	9,222	OR	1,245	30,732
MD	2,281	72,437	CA	13,012	398,831
DC	324	9,766	AK	336	7,327
VA	2,775	82,543	HI	521	14,216
WV	679	15,439			

(a) Determine the average adjusted gross income for each state and the District of Columbia. Use these averages to determine the mean, median, standard deviation, the extremes, and the first and third quartiles.

(b) Use the information in part (a) to construct a box plot for the average adjusted gross income. Explain your finding.

(c) Rank the states and the District of Columbia by determining their Z-values.

2.102 In the manufacture of a nylon chip, additives are sprayed on the chip. The spraying process is monitored closely by taking a sample of chips every 2 hours and observing the concentration of copper in parts per million. The following concentrations were found in 3 days of test results:†

34	31	32	33	33	32	34	34	35
37	36	35	38	39	39	39	35	37
36	37	38	36	33	33	41	41	40
36	44	38	35	38	38	39	39	34

(a) Construct a run chart and determine whether the spraying process was stable with regard to copper concentration during these 3 days.

(b) Construct a stem-and-leaf diagram and a box plot for these concentrations and explain your findings.

(c) How useful would your results in part (b) be if you had concluded in part (a) that the process was not stable? Explain.

2.103 A random survey of voting citizens was conducted to determine whether there is a relationship between party affiliation and opinion on gun control. The survey data are as follows:

Party	Favor	Oppose	Undecided
Democrat	110	64	26
Republican	90	116	14
Independent	55	35	10

Based on graphical analysis, is it apparent to you that party affiliation and opinion on gun control are related?

2.104 *Business Week*, in its October 29, 1990, issue, reported its ranking of the top 20 business schools in the country. It also listed the corporate poll ranks and the graduates' poll ranks for a number of business schools, including the top 20. The ranks are given in the table.

School	*Business Week* Rank	Corporate Poll Rank	Graduates' Poll Rank
Northwestern	1	2	7
Pennsylvania	2	1	10
Harvard	3	3	9
Chicago	4	5	1
Stanford	5	7	3
Dartmouth	6	8	5
Michigan	7	4	14
Columbia	8	6	11
Carnegie-Mellon	9	11	4
UCLA	10	16	2
MIT	11	10	13
North Carolina	12	14	6
Duke	13	13	12
Virginia	14	12	16
Indiana	15	9	23
Cornell	16	19	15
NYU	17	20	18
Texas	18	28	8
Berkeley	19	23	19
Rochester	20	27	17

(a) Construct a scatter diagram between *Business Week*'s ranks and the corporate poll ranks. Is any relationship between these two rankings apparent to you? Explain.

(b) Repeat part (a) with the graduates' poll ranks replacing the corporate ranks. Is the association here weaker or stronger than that in part (a)? Explain.

(c) How might you explain any differences that are apparent to you in parts (a) and (b)?

2.105 In a sample of recent college graduates, two traits were recorded: grade point average and SAT score. The following information was obtained:

	SAT Score		
GPA	900–1100	1100–1300	1300–1500
>3.5	50	65	38
3.0–3.5	78	72	42
2.5–3.0	97	80	25
2.0–2.5	105	25	18

(a) Based on a graphical analysis, is it apparent to you that SAT scores and grade point averages are related?

(b) Can you think of other traits that should have been considered?

2.106 Refer to Exercise 2.31, concerning the study of the work process of associates at the law firm of Northup and Bauers. It was hypothesized that the number of years of experience might be a factor affecting the number of billable hours. The more experience, it was conjectured, the more billable hours. The following data are the number of billable hours over a 9-month period for each of 43 associates along with the associated number of years of experience.

Hours:	802	1,287	1,225	1,178	1,275	767	1,424	1,328
Years:	3	10	5	9	7	4	9	7
Hours:	1,223	790	1,399	1,434	1,050	796	1,308	1,464
Years:	2	4	4	7	3	5	5	8
Hours:	1,389	1,316	1,325	1,494	1,096	1,482	1,493	1,452
Years:	5	6	6	7	3	15	2	7
Hours:	1,060	1,407	1,067	934	901	1,400	1,320	1,132
Years:	3	12	5	5	4	6	4	10
Hours:	1,256	858	1,346	885	1,084	1,065	1,211	1,379
Years:	4	2	6	4	5	4	4	10
Hours:	1,340	1,098	1,407					
Years:	8	7	5					

(a) Construct a scatter diagram of billable hours versus years of experience.

(b) Describe the relationship between billable hours and years of experience.

(c) To what extent does knowledge of an associate's years of experience allow us to predict the associate's number of billable hours? To what extent does the variation among associates' billable hours remain unexplained by knowledge of the number of years of experience? (*Note:* Answers to these questions are subjective; you have not been introduced to methods for directly addressing them.)

2.107 It is commonly believed that most businesses fail in their first three years. The paper "The Misunderstood Role of Small Business" (*Business Economics,* July 1994) investigated rates of startups and rates of failures for businesses started in 1985. A failure is defined here to be a firm that has gone out of business. The study found that 69.7% of 1985 startups were still active in early 1994. The purpose of the study was to learn how the size (defined as the number of employees) of newly started firms affects the rate of failure. The following table shows the number of 1985 startups, number of survivors (through early 1994), and the proportion of survivors for these firms grouped by size.

Size (Number of employees)	Number of Startups	Number of Survivors	Survival Rate
1–4	166,708	123,729	74.2
5–9	46,612	30,085	64.5
10–14	14,297	8,496	59.4
15–19	6,051	3,427	56.6
20–49	11,162	5,950	53.3
50–99	3,882	1,998	51.5
100+	1,056	448	42.4
Total	249,768	174,133	69.7

(a) Develop a scatter diagram showing the relationship of the number of startups to size. (For plotting purposes, use the midpoint of the number of employees range to characterize each size group.) What does your scatter diagram say about this relationship?

(b) Develop a scatter diagram showing the relationship of survival rate to size. What does your scatter diagram say about this relationship?

2.1   Case Study
The Choice of a Copier Model and Price Plan

Copiers are often leased to a customer rather than sold outright. Each copier model can be leased with any of several price plans. For a given customer, the most cost-effective price plan is determined by his or her monthly copy volume and usage pattern.

The usage pattern of any copier can be described as a series of copying jobs occurring over a period of time and varying in the number of originals and run length. A job occurs when a person copies a document. Suppose a secretary makes 15 copies of a 10-page report. Then for this job, there are 10 originals and the run length is 15, resulting in a total of $10 \times 15 = 150$ copies being made.

This case study involves the selection of a copier model and price plan by an organization's purchasing agent. The brand of copier, copier model names, and specific price plan terms are disguised but are an essentially accurate depiction of a real situation.

The purchasing agent's task is to choose one of two copier models, the Model 3000 or the Model 5000, along with a specific price plan. In comparison to the Model 3000, the Model 5000 is appropriate for users who do a greater monthly copy volume. In comparison to price Plans A and C, Plans B and D are better for customers who run a larger proportion of jobs with longer run lengths. For Models 3000 and 5000, the price plan options are specified as follows:

Model	Price Plan	Terms
3000	A	$500.00 minimum monthly charge • $.03 per copy

Model	Price Plan	Terms
3000	B	$500.00 minimum monthly charge • $.04 per copy for jobs with run length 1–5 • $.02 per copy for jobs with run length 6–10 • $.01 per copy for jobs with run length of 11 or more
5000	C	$750.00 minimum monthly charge • $.025 per copy
5000	D	$750.00 minimum monthly charge • $.05 per copy for jobs with run length 1–5 • $.015 per copy for jobs with run length 6–10 • $.004 per copy for jobs with run length of 11 or more

It is known from billing records that the purchasing agent's organization currently makes an average of 40,000 copies per month on its current machine. To assist the agent in choosing an appropriate copier model and price plan, a record of all copying jobs on the current copier was maintained over a 1-week period (Monday through Friday). The record contains information for 232 jobs.

Your task is to explore and summarize the data to develop a recommendation of the least expensive choice for the customer. Along with your analysis and recommendation, include any associated concerns and/or limitations.

File Content

The data are contained in the file CASE0201. Each row of data contains observations for a specific job. The columns provide information about the jobs as follows:

$c1$ = job number (in order)
$c2$ = day (1 = Monday; 2 = Tuesday; etc.)
$c3$ = number of originals
$c4$ = run length
$c5$ = number of copies (originals × run length)

2.2

Case Study
Spokes-N-Wheels, Inc.

Spokes-N-Wheels, Inc.* markets bicycles and bicycle-related products through the mail. Their market consists of serious cyclists throughout the United States. They compete successfully by offering upscale specialized equipment at competitive prices and giving exceptional customer service.

Spokes-N-Wheels offers a complete line of cycling products. Complete bicycles are the largest contributor to both revenue and profit; however, they carry other cycling-related products in their catalog. Some items are carried even though they are marginally profitable since Spokes-N-Wheels wants to be able to meet all the customers' cycling needs. They do not want a customer to go to a competitor for a unique item because most mail-order customers prefer to deal with a single company. If customers order one item from a competitor, they are likely to order other items as well.

---

* Spokes-N-Wheels is a fictitious name used for confidentiality. This case deals with a real problem faced by a real company.

Spokes-N-Wheels' products are divided into four product lines:

- Bicycles: Complete bicycles
- Components: Frames, wheels, gears, etc., that customers use to construct, enhance, or maintain their own bicycles
- Accessories: Helmets, water bottles, etc.
- Clothing: Cycling apparel

Each product line has a product manager.

Spokes-N-Wheels publishes four catalogs per year. Each product manager wants to get as much display space (measured in square inches) in the catalog as possible. Although they have never analyzed it, they believe that the more display space devoted to an item, the more sales generated by the item. By coding orders, they are able to identify from which issue of the catalog the customer is ordering.

Recently, Spokes-N-Wheels' President and Chairman have become concerned about an apparent drop in sales. Sales from the last catalog were at a 3-year low. They do not know whether this is a one-time fluke or a trend. To boost sales, they have been increasing the amount of display space devoted to complete bicycles, their largest revenue line—but this does not seem to be enough.

The following table shows sales figures and the number of square inches devoted to each product line by catalog for the last 3 years. What conclusions can you draw? Do the data indicate only a one-time fluke, or do they suggest that a serious problem exists? Your task is to explain current market dynamics affecting Spokes-N-Wheels and to recommend possible marketing decisions based on an exploration of these data. Your recommendations should focus on the amount of advertising space that should be allocated to each product. Should some receive more space? Should some receive less?

Spokes-N-Wheels data

Period	Year	Catalog	Total Sales	Bikes sq. in.	Bikes Sales	Comp. sq. in.	Comp. Sales	Access. sq. in.	Access. Sales	Cloth. sq. in.	Cloth. Sales
1	1988	1	5,575	500	2,875	360	1,560	380	720	440	420
2	1988	2	6,140	460	2,530	630	2,700	320	660	270	250
3	1988	3	5,915	630	3,030	420	1,995	270	510	360	380
4	1988	4	6,925	680	4,290	340	1,580	470	880	190	175
5	1989	1	6,220	620	2,780	430	2,490	340	640	290	310
6	1989	2	5,980	570	2,370	430	2,590	360	680	320	340
7	1989	3	6,190	420	1,750	550	3,380	420	750	290	310
8	1989	4	6,710	720	3,550	370	2,300	230	550	360	310
9	1990	1	5,890	760	2,380	370	2,670	320	630	230	210
10	1990	2	5,780	690	2,560	420	2,370	350	640	220	210
11	1990	3	5,220	840	2,260	320	2,240	280	530	240	190
12	1990	4	4,840	920	1,800	300	2,380	240	430	220	230

The data are contained on the data disk in the file named CASE0202. They are organized in columns as follows:

c_1 = period index (1, 2, 3, . . .)
c_2 = year
c_3 = catalog (1 = Spring, 2 = Summer, 3 = Fall, 4 = Winter)
c_4 = total sales
c_5 = square inches for complete bikes (product line 1)
c_6 = sales for complete bikes (product line 1)
c_7 = square inches for components (product line 2)
c_8 = sales for components (product line 2)
c_9 = square inches for accessories (product line 3)
c_{10} = sales for accessories (product line 3)
c_{11} = square inches for clothing (product line 4)
c_{12} = sales for clothing (product line 4)

2.3

Case Study
Ford County Department of Social Services

The Ford County* Department of Social Services maintains a referral center that clients can call to seek information and register complaints. The volume of complaints had become enormous, generating still more complaints about the constantly busy telephone number. Typical complaints include:

- Why don't workers take calls on Wednesdays?
- This is an emergency!
- Can I come down there?
- Give me the number of my case worker's supervisor.
- Let me speak to the Commissioner.
- My case worker never answers the phone.

The large number of calls and complaints generated great stress within the department as many sought to assign blame.

The department was divided organizationally into seven geographic zones (Zones A, B, C, D, E, F, and G). The greatest number of complaints were related to Zone C, with Zone D a close second. These zones were receiving great pressure to reduce the number of complaints.

In an attempt to better understand the problem, data on the number of complaints were collected for the month of August, with the relevant zone recorded for each call. In addition to the number of calls per zone, other information of possible relevance includes the number of cases and the number of case workers for each zone. The data are as follows. They are also contained on the book data diskette under the name CASE0203, where c_1 = zone (1 = Zone A, 2 = Zone B, etc.); c_2 = complaints; c_3 = case workers; c_4 = cases.

---

* This is a fictitious name used for confidentiality. This case represents a real situation in a real county, and it uses real data.

Zone	Complaints	Case Workers	Cases
A	89	18	3,275
B	34	24	4,116
C	266	46	8,716
D	186	48	8,116
E	72	23	3,974
F	6	22	3,391
G	14	7	1,096
Unknown	38	—	—

Do the data suggest that Zones C and D deserve to be singled out for their high rates of complaint calls? Do the data suggest that any zones are performing poorly compared to the rest? Do the data suggest that any zones are performing better than the rest, thus providing the others an opportunity for improvement through the adoption of practices being used? Finally, describe the impact on the organization of the decision to gather data. That is, how do you suppose the environment within Ford County Department of Social Services has changed as a result of this action?

Appendix 2A

Computer Instructions for Using MINITAB, EXCEL, and JMP IN

MINITAB

Dot Diagrams

To generate a graph similar to Figure 2.1, a dot diagram for the 10 test grades, first enter the data into column c1 of the DATA window. Then choose GRAPH–DOTPLOT . . . and specify variable c1 in the dialogue box. Click OK.

If you wish to compare dot diagrams for several variables on a single graph, as in Figure 2.2, the data must be put into a stacked format. You may enter them directly in this format, or you may first enter them unstacked and then stack them as described in Appendix 1. Either way, the end result is that the 28 test grades comprise c1 and the subscripts indicating the sections (the values 1, 2, and 3) comprise column c2. Name columns c1 and c2 Grade and Section, respectively. To produce Figure 2.2, choose GRAPH–PLOT. In the dialogue box, specify c1 as Y (i.e., the vertical axis) and c2 as X (i.e., the horizontal axis). Then click OK.

Histograms

To produce the histogram in Figure 2.3, enter the data in c1. Choose GRAPH–HISTOGRAM . . . . In the dialogue box, specify column c1 in the GRAPH VARI-ABLES box. If you wish to define the classes, click the OPTIONS . . . button. Under TYPE OF INTERVALS, click the CUTPOINT button; under DEFINITION OF INTERVALS, click the MIDPOINT/CUTPOINT POSITIONS button and enter the "cutpoints" (Minitab's name for the class boundaries). Alternatively, you can specify class midpoints by clicking the MIDPOINT button and entering the desired midpoint values. Click OK twice.

Frequency Bar Charts and Pareto Diagrams

To produce a bar chart similar to Figure 2.4, you need a frequency table consisting of two columns of data, one containing the category names and another containing the frequencies. You can simply enter the category names into c1 and the corresponding frequencies into c2. If you are starting with the original categorical or ordinal data, Minitab can determine the frequencies for you. Enter the original data as c3. Although the data are categorical, they must be coded *numerically*. For example, to specify students' academic majors, you might use 1 for Finance, 2 for Accounting, etc. Choose STAT–TABLES–TALLY . . . . In the dialogue box, select c3, click the COUNTS button, and click OK. The desired frequency table will appear in the SESSION window. Now either type it into the DATA window or transfer it using the COPY and PASTE functions (select the lines in the SESSION window that contain the frequency table; choose EDIT–COPY; switch to the DATA window; select the first cell in column c1; and choose EDIT–PASTE). Once you have developed the frequency table in c1 and c2 of the DATA window, choose GRAPH–CHART . . . . In the dialogue box that appears, click the down arrow next to FUNCTION and select SUM; then select c2 (the frequencies) for the Y column and c1 (the majors) for the X column and click OK. Notice that Minitab automatically orders the categories alphabetically.

To develop a Pareto diagram, enter the original categorical data (the majors) into c1. Select STAT– QUALITY TOOLS–PARETO CHART . . . . In the dialogue box, click the CHART DEFECTS TABLE button; then enter c2 in the FREQUENCIES IN area and c1 in the LABELS IN area; and click OK.

Stem-and-Leaf Diagrams

To produce a stem-and-leaf diagram as in to Figure 2.5, enter the data into column c1. Choose GRAPH–STEM-AND-LEAF . . . ; in the resulting dialogue box, specify c1 and the desired increment (the desired difference between successive stem values). Notice that the desired increment for Figure 2.5 is 10 (50s, 60s, etc.).

Box Plots

To create a box plot as that in Figure 2.14 for the premium amounts in the insurance example, enter the data in c1. Choose GRAPH–BOXPLOT . . . . In the dialogue box, select c1 in the Y column and click OK. (Do not select any variable for the X column.)

To generate box plots for two or more variables on the same graph, you must arrange the data in stacked format. Suppose you want box plots for data in columns c1 and c2 on the same graph. Stack the two data sets into column c3; then place the subscripts (1s and 2s that identify the sample associated with each data value) into c4. Select GRAPH–BOXPLOT . . . and in the dialogue box enter c3 for Y and c4 for X.

Scatter Diagrams

To create a scatter diagram similar to Figure 2.15, depicting the relationship between test grade (data in c1) and study hours (data in c2), choose GRAPH–PLOT . . . . In the first row of the GRAPH VARIABLES area of the dialogue box, enter c1 for Y (the vertical axis) and c2 for X (the horizontal axis) and click OK.

Descriptive Statistics

It is very simple to compute numerical quantities such as means, medians, and standard deviations using Minitab. Select CALC–COLUMN STATISTICS . . . . In the dialogue box, click the desired statistic, enter the columns of data to be summarized in the INPUT VARIABLE box, and click OK.

If desired, you can compute most of the statistics of this chapter simultaneously. To produce an array of statistics like Table 2.2(a) for the insurance data (Example 2.4), enter the amounts and incomes into c1 and c2, respectively. Choose STAT–BASIC STATISTICS–DISPLAY DESCRIPTIVE STATISTICS . . . . In the VARIABLES part of the dialogue box, specify c1 c2. The output includes the mean, the median, the standard deviation, the extreme values, and the first and third quantiles, as well as some quantities not discussed in the chapter.

Sometimes you may want to determine the values of these statistics for subgroups of a sample. To produce an array of statistics like Table 2.2(c) for the insurance data, enter the gender data into c3. Choose STAT–BASIC STATISTICS–DISPLAY DE-SCRIPTIVE STATISTICS . . . . In the VARIABLES part of the dialogue box, specify c1 c2. In the BY VARIABLE box, enter c3.

You can develop dot diagrams, histograms, and box plots from this dialogue box. Click the GRAPHS . . . button; then click the buttons for the desired graphs.

EXCEL

Dot Diagrams

Excel does not provide a menu choice for dot diagrams. However, dot diagrams can be constructed by using INSERT–CHART as follows. To generate a graph similar to Figure 2.1, a dot diagram for the 10 test grades, first enter the data into cells a1:a10 (i.e., al through a10). Enter a column of 1s in b1:b10. Choose INSERT–CHART . . . . This activates the CHART WIZARD. Follow the four steps of the CHART WIZARD to produce the dot diagram: (1) Click the XY (SCATTER) chart type, then click the first chart subtypes option (scatter); (2) in the DATA RANGE box, enter the cell range containing the data (a1:b10) and click the SERIES IN COLUMNS button; (3) provide chart title and labels for the axes as desired; (4) indicate whether you wish the dot diagram to be placed on a new sheet or within the currently active sheet. This produces a dot diagram whose appearance you will want to improve by making adjustments to the scales of the axes and to the marker (i.e., plotting symbol) background. (Setting the background color to NONE makes nearly overlapping plotting symbols more distinct.) A limitation is that identical data values are all represented by only one plotting symbol. This can produce misleading dot diagrams for data sets containing some identical data values.

If you wish to compare dot diagrams for several variables on a single graph, as in Figure 2.2, enter the test grades for all three sections in b1:b28. Enter a column of 1s, 2s, and 3s in a1:a28 indicating the section for each grade. Choose INSERT–CHART . . . . Follow the four steps of the CHART WIZARD to produce the vertical dot diagram: (1) Click the XY (SCATTER) chart type, then click the first chart subtypes option (scatter); (2) in the DATA RANGE box, enter the cell range containing the data (a1:b28) and click the SERIES IN COLUMNS button; (3) provide chart title and labels for the axes as desired; (4) indicate whether you wish the dot diagram to be placed on a new sheet or within the currently active sheet. You will probably want to improve this dot diagram by adjusting the scales of the vertical and horizontal axes and the marker background.

Stem-and-Leaf Diagrams

Currently, Excel does not provide stem-and-leaf diagrams.

Box Plots

To create a box plot similar to that in Figure 2.14 for the premium amounts in the insurance example, enter the data in one column. Choose TOOLS–DATA ANALYSIS PLUS–BOXPLOT . . . . In the dialogue box, specify the range of cells containing the data. If you have included a column label (such as *amount*), do not include the cell containing the label.

Histograms

We use the example of the 20 test grades given in Section 2.3.2. To produce a histogram similar to Figure 2.3, enter the test grades into cells a1 through a20. Then enter the upper boundaries of the classes (60, 70, 80, 90, and 100) into cells b1 through b5. Choose TOOLS–DATA ANALYSIS . . . , click HISTOGRAM, and click OK. In the dialogue box, do the following: (1) In the INPUT RANGE box, indicate the cells containing the data by typing a1:a20 or by dragging over the cells al through a20; (2) in the BIN RANGE box, indicate the cells containing the upper bounds of the histogram classes by typing b1:b5 or dragging over the cells b1 through b5; (3) click CHART OUTPUT in the dialogue box. This produces a frequency table and, to its right, a histogram that needs to be improved. The problems are that adjacent rectangles are not contiguous (they should be); and the upper limits are placed in the center of the classes, making them appear to be midpoints. To make adjacent rectangles contiguous, first double-click any of the rectangular bars. In the dialogue box, click the OPTIONS tab; enter 0 in the "gap width" box; and click OK. Now, in the frequency table to the left of the histogram, replace the upper class limits with the class midpoints. The histogram adjusts itself so that the horizontal axis is scaled with properly placed midpoints.

Frequency Bar Charts and Pareto Diagrams

To produce a frequency bar chart like Figure 2.4, you need a frequency table consisting of two columns of data, one containing the category names and another containing the frequencies. Enter the names of the six majors into a1:a6, and enter the corresponding frequencies into b1:b6. Choose INSERT CHART . . . . In step 1 of the CHART WIZARD, click COLUMN chart type and click the upper left chart subtype (clustered column). In step 2, specify the range of cells containing the majors and their frequencies (a1:b6) and click the SERIES IN: COLUMNS button. In step 3, provide chart title and labels for the axes as desired. In step 4, indicate whether you wish the bar chart to be placed on a new sheet or within the currently active sheet.

If you are starting from the original sample data, Excel can determine the frequencies for you. Enter the data (i.e., the major for each of the 30 students) in c1:c30. Although the data are categorical, they must be coded *numerically*. For example, you might use 1 for Finance, 2 for Accounting, etc. Enter the six category codes 1, 2, . . . , 6 into d1:d6. Now use TOOLS–DATA ANALYSIS . . . –HISTOGRAM (described previously), where the data are the numerically coded students' majors in c1:c30 and the classes are the six categories in d1:d6. Also click the CHART OUTPUT button. This produces a frequency table and a frequency bar chart in which the categories are labeled by the category codes 1, 2, . . . , 6. To develop a Pareto diagram corresponding to the bar chart in Figure 2.4, click the button for PARETO (SORTED HISTOGRAM) in the dialogue box.

Scatter Diagrams

Consider the scatter diagram in Figure 2.15, depicting the relationship between test grades and hours studied. Enter the hours (the predictor variable) into a2:a21 and the grades (the response variable) into b2:b21. (The predictor variable *must* be in the first of two adjacent columns, with the response variable in the second column.) Enter the two variable names into a1 and b1. Select the range of cells containing the variable names and the data (a1:b21). Choose INSERT–CHART. In the CHART WIZARD, (1) click X-Y (SCATTER), then click the upper left chart subtype option (SCATTER); (2) in the DATA RANGE box, enter the cell range containing the data (a1:b10) and click the SERIES IN COLUMNS button; (3) provide chart title and labels for the axes as desired; (4) indicate whether you wish the scatter diagram to be placed on a new sheet or within the currently active sheet.

Descriptive Statistics

Numerical quantities such as means, medians, and standard deviations are easily determined in Excel as follows: (1) Select the cell where the statistic is to be placed; (2) type the appropriate function as follows: =*FUNCTION* (RANGE OF CELLS CONTAINING THE DATA). For the test grades example, the data were in cells a2 through a21. To place a statistic for these data into cell c1, select c1 and type the desired function command. The appropriate function commands for the mean, median, and standard deviation of these data are the following:

```
= average(a2:a21)
= median(a2:a21)
= stdev(a2:a21)
```

The range of data cells can be specified either by typing them or by dragging over the cells containing the data.

You can determine several important statistics simultaneously and for several variables at a time. Suppose we want to develop a numerical summary like Table 2.2(b) for the insurance data (Example 2.4), where the variables are AMOUNT and INCOME. First enter the data for AMOUNT into a2 through a52, and enter the data for INCOME into b2 through b52. Enter the variable names in cells a1 and b1. Select TOOLS–DATA-ANALYSIS . . . , click DESCRIPTIVE STATISTICS, and click OK. In the dialogue box, (1) specify the range of cells containing the variable names and the data (a1:b52); (2) click the GROUPED BY: COLUMNS button; (3) since variable names are in the first row, click LABELS IN FIRST ROW; (4) click SUMMARY STATISTICS (at the bottom of the dialogue box); and (5) click OK.

Sometimes you may want to determine the values of these statistics for subgroups of a sample. To produce an array of statistics similar to that in Table 2.2(c) that summarizes male and female customers separately, you need to rearrange the data into four columns: amounts for men, amounts for women, incomes for men, and incomes for women. Then proceed as in the previous paragraph.

JMP IN

The Role of a Variable in a Statistical Analysis When Using JMP IN

For any analysis you wish to perform using JMP IN, this software requires that you indicate how a particular column is to be treated in the analysis—that is, its *role*. This is done by clicking the COLUMN ROLE dialogue box (the small box above and to the right of the column name) and choosing either *None, X, Y,* or *Freq.* (There are also two other possible choices that are not used in this book.)

NONE indicates that the variable is not to be used in the analysis. *X* indicates that the variable is a predictor variable. *Y* indicates that the variable is a response variable. FREQ indicates that a variable is a frequency. For example, suppose your sample contains 112 women and 88 men. Then you might enter the labels FEMALE and MALE into the first two rows of a *Y* variable named GENDER and the values 112 and 88 into the first two rows of a FREQ variable named COUNT. Notice that this is easier than entering all 200 outcomes into a single column of a *Y* variable.

For analyses involving only one variable, the appropriate role is usually *Y.* The exception would be large samples where there are only a few different outcomes, as in the above example. In this case, you may find it more convenient to create a new variable (with role = FREQ) containing the frequencies for the different outcome categories.

In the chapter appendices, it is always assumed that you have set the role of a variable to *Y,* unless stated otherwise, and that the roles of all variables not involved in the analysis are set to NONE. Sometimes you may have a data table containing many variables. Before starting an analysis involving only a few variables, you can set the roles of all variables to NONE by choosing COLS–CLEAR ALL ROLES.

One of the unique features of JMP IN is that, based on your specification of the data type, the modeling type, and the role of each variable, it automatically provides appropriate analyses and graphs.

Dot Diagrams

JMP IN does not provide a menu choice for dot diagrams. Nevertheless, dot diagrams can be constructed as follows. To generate a graph similar to Figure 2.1, first enter the grades into COLUMN 1. Enter a column of 1s in COLUMN 2. For COLUMN

1 (the grades), set DATA TYPE to NUMERIC; set MODELING TYPE to CONTINUOUS; and set the role to Y. For COLUMN 2 (the 1s), set DATA TYPE to CHARACTER (this automatically sets the MODELING TYPE to NOMINAL); and set the role to X. Choose ANALYZE–FIT Y BY X. This produces a vertical dot diagram. If two or more values are identical or nearly so, then they will be represented by a single plotting symbol. To solve this problem, click the DISPLAY button beneath the graph and choose JITTER. This adjusts the location of the plotted points slightly so that each data value is uniquely represented.

If you wish to compare dot diagrams for several variables on a single graph, as in Figure 2.2, enter all the grades for all three sections in COLUMN 1. Enter a column of 1s, 2s, and 3s in COLUMN 2 indicating the section for each grade. [You may enter them directly in this stacked format, or you may first enter them in split columns and then stack them as described in Appendix 1. Either way, the end result is that the 28 test grades comprise COLUMN 1 and the subscripts indicating the sections (the values 1, 2, and 3) comprise COLUMN 2.] Set the role of COLUMN 2 to X. A graph similar to Figure 2.2 is produced by choosing ANALYZE–FIT Y BY X. As above, if two or more values are identical or nearly so, click the DISPLAY button beneath the graph and choose JITTER.

Histograms

To produce a histogram similar to Figure 2.3, enter the data into COLUMN 1. Choose ANALYZE–DISTRIBUTION OF Y. JMP IN automatically provides a histogram in the DISTRIBUTION window. If you wish to reshape the histogram, click anywhere on the graph. This produces a small sizing box in the lower right-hand portion of the graph; drag the sizing box to reshape as desired. If you wish to redefine the classes, click the vertical axis. In the dialogue box, specify the desired MINIMUM, MAXIMUM, and INCREMENT values.

Stem-and-Leaf Diagrams

To produce a stem-and-leaf diagram similar to Figure 2.5, enter the data into COLUMN 1 and choose ANALYZE–DISTRIBUTION OF Y. Click the popup option icon next to the variable name above the histogram and select STEM AND LEAF. JMP IN provides no way to adjust the division between stem and leaf.

Frequency Bar Charts and Pareto Diagrams

To produce a bar chart as in Figure 2.4, first set the data type for COLUMN 1 to CHARACTER and the modeling type to NOMINAL. Then enter the original data (the majors) into COLUMN 1. Choose ANALYZE–DISTRIBUTION OF Y. This produces the bar chart.

If you wish to develop a Pareto diagram, then choose GRAPH–PARETO CHARTS.

Box Plots

To create a box plot similar to Figure 2.14 for the premium amounts in the insurance example, enter the data in COLUMN 1. Choose ANALYZE–DISTRIBUTION OF Y. A box plot lies immediately to the right of the histogram. This box plot is a variation of the one discussed in Chapter 2. The lines above and below the box extend a distance of 1.5 times the *interquartile range* (that is, 1.5 times the difference between the third and first quartiles). Any data values that lie beyond these lines are plotted as dots. The diamond represents a *confidence interval* for the mean. (Confidence intervals are presented in Chapter 6.)

To generate box plots for two or more variables on the same graph, enter all the data in stacked format in COLUMN 1. Enter a column of 1s, 2s, etc., in COLUMN 2 indicating the sample for each data value. For COLUMN 2, set the data type to CHARACTER, the modeling type to NOMINAL, and the role to *X*. Choose ANALYZE–FIT Y BY X. Click the DISPLAY button beneath the graph and choose QUANTILE BOXES.

Scatter Diagrams

To create a scatter diagram as in Figure 2.15, put the test grades into COLUMN 1 and the study hours into COLUMN 2. Set the role of COLUMN 1 to *Y* and the role of COLUMN 2 to *X*. Choose ANALYZE–FIT Y BY X.

Descriptive Statistics

It is very simple to compute numerical quantities such as means, medians, and standard deviations using JMP IN. Consider Example 2.4. Enter the amounts and incomes into COLUMN 1 and COLUMN 2, respectively. Set the role of each column to *Y*: Choose ANALYZE–DISTRIBUTION OF Y. The quartile values for both variables are provided in the QUANTILES boxes below the histograms, and the mean and standard deviation are provided in the MOMENTS boxes below the QUANTILES boxes.

Sometimes you may want to determine the values of these statistics for subgroups of a sample. To produce an array of statistics similar to that in Table 2.2(c) for the insurance data, enter the gender data into COLUMN 3; set its data type to CHARACTER and its modeling type to NOMINAL; and set its role to *X*. Choose ANALYZE–FIT Y BY X. Click the ANALYSIS button below the graphs and select QUANTILES and MEANS, STD DEV, STD ERR. The minimum, maximum, and several quantile values (.10, .25, .5, .75, and .9) for male and female customers appear below the graph, and the means and standard deviations appear below the quantile values.

Appendix 2B

Your Turn to Perform a Statistical Study

At this point, you have learned a great deal about statistical thinking and statistical techniques for exploring and summarizing data. Although you have not yet learned the methods of statistical inference or how to develop statistical models, you know enough to plan a statistical study and to carry out an exploration of the data you obtain. As you learn more methods, you will be able to carry the analysis further. The following are directions for planning and carrying out a statistical study of a process or population of interest to you. You will find these directions quite explicit; the reason for this is to provide sufficient guidance to ensure that your first statistics project is a successful learning experience. Indeed these guidelines provide a model to follow for virtually all statistical projects you might plan in the future.

Project Directions

PLANNING

1. Identify a phenomenon that you want to learn about.

2. Is it a process or a population? You might wish to compare two or more processes, two or more populations, or two or more levels of a process factor.

3. Determine the statistical variables to be observed.

   - For each variable, identify its *role*. There are two possible roles: response variable and predictor variable. Response variables are those whose variation we wish to understand and explain. Predictor variables are those that help to explain variation of a response variable.

   - State whether each variable is quantitative or qualitative. To make the project work effectively as a learning experience for you, you should observe some variables that are quantitative (one of which should be a response variable) and some that are qualitative.

   - Provide operational definitions for all variables.

4. Define the sampled population or process.

5. Define the sampling units to be observed or measured (people, transactions, etc.). This is simple but seems to be a key step for students.

6. State what you wish to learn about the populations or processes in regard to the specific variables in the study.

   • For each response variable: its distribution and the value of the key parameter (usually means or proportions)

   • For relevant pairs of response and predictor variables: the relationship between them.

7. Assess your current knowledge by stating what you currently believe about the population or process (prior to observing your sample data). Here, you should state your expectation in regard to each item that you identified in step 6.

8. For recording and displaying your data, develop a tabular format in which each row will contain all the data observed for a given sampling unit, and each column will contain all the data for a given variable. Label the rows and columns. (Notice that this step occurs *prior to* collecting data.)

9. Develop a sampling (data-collection) plan. Identify the type of sampling procedure to be used (random samples, convenience samples, designed experiment), and describe its important details. State the planning sample size and justify it. Select the largest sample your resources allow. The only reasons to limit sample size are unavailability of data, limited resources (time, money, etc.), and limits on your ability to manage the data collection process.

10. Specify the measurement process for each variable (if applicable). Make sure that your operational definitions of the variables include specific measurement specifications for every variable.

11. Identify the statistical procedures you intend to use once you have obtained your data.

    • For each quantitative variable: With regard to each population or process studied, identify (a) the method of graphical description to characterize the distribution (we suggest dot diagrams for small samples, histograms for larger samples, box plots to compare several large samples), (b) descriptive statistics (mean, median, standard deviation, etc.), and (c) appropriate inference methods regarding means (estimation and/or hypothesis testing).

    • For each qualitative variable: With regard to each population or process studied, identify (a) the method of graphical description (frequency bar chart or Pareto diagram), (b) descriptive statistics (usually proportions of outcomes for each outcome category), and (c) appropriate inference methods regarding proportions (estimation and/or hypothesis testing).

    • For relationships between variables: (a) If both are quantitative, plan to develop a scatter diagram and a regression model (Regression is presented in Chapters 9 and 10.), and (b) if the response variable is qualitative, it may be possible to analyze it with a contingency table. (Analysis of contingency tables is presented in Chapter 11.)

DATA GATHERING

12. Collect data via direct observation of statistical variables for the selected sampling units. Record any unexpected problems or surprises in data collection.

DATA ANALYSIS AND MODELING

13. If your data were observed in time sequence, assess the stability of the underlying process over the observation period by developing run charts for all quantitative variables. If the purpose of the study is to predict future process performance, discuss why you think the process will or will not remain stable over the period of prediction.

14. Explore and summarize each variable individually.

15. Explore relationships between variables.

16. Interpret your findings in steps 14 and 15. What have you learned? What conclusions are suggested?

17. Assess how much you learned from your analysis: Use estimation, confidence intervals, hypothesis testing, two-sample T procedures, analysis of variance, and/or goodness-of-fit procedures as appropriate to check your beliefs about the populations or processes before you saw the data (see step 7). Use regression analysis and/or contingency table analysis to check your beliefs about relationships between variables (see step 7).

18. Identify sources of potential error in the study.

19. Identify any limitations that must be placed on your results, such as the time frame of the study and potential differences between the sampled population or process and the intended population or process.

20. Identify questions that have arisen that are worthy of study in the future.

REPORTING

21. Write a report. It should be long enough to explain the material in the outline and no longer. Your report should conform closely to these steps. It should conclude with a brief summary of what you have learned about the populations or processes.

22. Appendix. Place here a printed listing of your data and all your statistical outputs (computer outputs, tables, graphs) if they are not integrated into your report. *All of this material must be labeled (Exhibit 1, Exhibit 2, etc.) in the appendix and referenced in the text of your report.*

Getting Started

To develop an organized study plan, you should fill out the following planning worksheet. The workforce consists basically of the first 11 steps of the project guidelines.

PLANNING WORKSHEET

Take as much space as you need in filling in the blanks. Filling in most "blanks" requires a brief *paragraph*.

Planning Step

1. The phenomenon I plan to study is: (describe).

2. I will study a: (population or process—choose one).

3. The variables observed include: [list; for each, provide operational definitions, type (quantitative or qualitative), and role (response or predictor)].

4. The sampled population or process consists of: (describe or list the sampled population or process).

5. The sampling units consist of: (describe or list the sampling units).

6. With respect to these variables, I would like to learn: (specify).

7. I expect to observe the following results: (describe).

8. A tabular display of the data would have the following appearance: (Show detailed row and column headings but no data).

9. The sampling plan is as follows: (describe, and explain your decisions about selection method, sample size, etc.).

10. The measurement process is as follows: (describe in detail for each variable).

11. The statistical procedures I intend to use are: (detailed list).

Example of Tabular Format for Displaying Data

This is an example for a data set consisting of samples of $n = 40$ observations for each of two processes, where 3 variables are observed for each sampling unit.

	Process A				Process B		
Sampling Unit	Var 1	Var 2	Var 3	Sampling Unit	Var 1	Var 2	Var 3
1	x	x	x	1	x	x	x
2	x	x	x	2	x	x	x
3	x	x	x	3	x	x	x
4	x	x	x	4	x	x	x
5	x	x	x	5	x	x	x
•	•	•	•	•	•	•	•
•	•	•	•	•	•	•	•
•	•	•	•	•	•	•	•
40	x	x	x	40	x	x	x

Chapter 3

Probability, Random Variables, and Probability Distributions

3.1

Bridging to New Topics

In Chapter 2, we discussed various ways to explore and summarize sample data. Sample data provide us an opportunity to learn about the population or process from which they are taken. Since a sample is only part of a population or process, any inferences we make from the sample involve **uncertainty.** It is important to have some idea how much uncertainty is involved before we make important decisions. If uncertainty is too great, decisions suggested by sample data might be too risky to justify. In this chapter and Chapter 4, we introduce ways of dealing with uncertainty. To help you understand uncertainty, we often use simple examples such as coin flips or dice rolls because they are well defined and illustrate important principles.

Our entire world is filled with uncertainty. We make decisions affected by uncertainty virtually every day. For example, if the weather forecaster says that "there is a 40% chance of rain," should we take an umbrella with us? If a reliable stockbroker says that "chances are better than even" that a particular stock will go up in value during the next year, do we buy? A manager of a company's computing department may base a decision to upgrade a computer system on a forecast that "usage is likely to surpass 90% of capacity by the end of the year." Or you might have chosen the college or university you attend because you thought you had a good chance to succeed there. Often the words *chance* and *likelihood* occur when we discuss uncertainty. Each is essentially a synonym for the word *probability*. To think about and measure uncertainty, we turn to a branch of mathematics called **probability.** In this chapter, we discuss the basic ideas of probability and introduce two important statistical concepts: **random variables** and **probability distributions.** Probability provides structure to our thinking about uncertain events.

The following example illustrates the use of probability in a decision-making environment.

EXAMPLE 3.1

The periodic gauging of public opinion on a wide variety of social, economic, and political issues through the use of scientific polling has become a permanent fixture in our society. Such polls provide surprisingly accurate snapshots of public sentiment. And, of course, today's politicians would not dare conduct a political campaign without employing a professional pollster to gauge voter sentiment on important issues for possible adjustment of campaign strategies. This example illustrates how probability and statistics play a vital role in this kind of situation.

Two candidates, A and B, are vying for an elective office. With a month remaining before election day, the race is believed to be extremely close. It is important to know whether this belief is justified. If candidate A believes she is losing, she will change her campaign strategy for the final month. In a poll taken 1 month before the election, 1,000 persons who were likely to vote on election day were randomly selected and asked their preference. Of these, 400 said they would vote for candidate A. Based on this information, is it reasonable to continue to believe that the race is even? Should A change her strategy on the belief that she is now losing?

Solution

A way to think through this question is as follows. If the premise that the race is extremely close is correct, and if the 1,000 persons sampled are representative of the voting population, then we would expect a fairly even division of preferences among the 1,000 persons. The result, however, was that only 400 (and not about 500) indicated a preference for A. Now back to the original question: Is it reasonable to continue to believe that the race is even? We address the question by determining the chance or probability that, in a race in which the voting *population* is split 50–50 between A and B, a random *sample* of 1,000 voters divides as unevenly as 400–600. This probability turns out to be extremely small (considerably smaller than 1 chance in 1,000). Either a rare sampling quirk has occurred, or the original belief is untrue. Some uncertainty remains, but most people would agree that a decision to alter candidate A's campaign strategy is justified.

In the context of Example 3.1, it is most important to understand that the sample of 1,000 likely voters reflects the preference of the voting population *at the time the sample was taken*. Any shifts in preference that may occur after this sample was taken are likely to be detected only by subsequent samples. Therefore, the use of probability in a decision-making environment should be viewed as a continuing analytical process in which samples are taken periodically from a population or process of interest.

3.2 The Basic Elements of Probability

To understand probability sufficiently for your needs in learning statistical inference, it is necessary to understand some basic concepts and how they relate to one another. We begin with the concepts of random experiments, outcomes, events, and sample spaces.

When 1,000 persons were asked their voting preferences in Example 3.1, the purpose was to obtain information about an uncertain phenomenon—voter preference prior to an election. One way to obtain information about phenomena subject to uncertainty is to devise an experiment in which we observe or measure some characteristic of interest. A **random experiment** is the process of obtaining information through observation or measurement of a phenomenon whose outcome is not certain; that is, the outcome is not perfectly predictable.

Some typical examples of phenomena that might be studied by random experiments are:

- The number of no-shows for a scheduled flight
- The number of customers arriving at a service facility in one hour
- The length of life of an electrical component
- The daily sales volume of a retail establishment
- The length of time for a business telephone call
- The numerical grade received on a statistics test

When we perform an experiment, we observe an **outcome.** We say that the outcome is subject to chance because it may differ from a previous outcome if the experiment is repeated under identical conditions. For example, suppose the experiment is the toss of a coin. There are two possible outcomes each time we toss the coin (that is, each time we perform the experiment): either we observe *heads* or we observe *tails*.* Since we do not know which of these outcomes will occur when the coin is tossed, the outcome of the experiment is subject to chance.

Why can't we predict the outcome of a coin toss with certainty? An experimental outcome is always affected by some variables that cannot be controlled precisely. For a coin toss, such variables include the velocity of the rotation of the coin when tossed, the height to which it is tossed, and the location of the spot where it lands. No experiment can be repeated under absolutely identical conditions. We try to control the major factors, but we can never control *all* factors. The variation among experimental observations caused by the effects of minor, uncontrolled factors is usually lumped together and called **random variation.** It is assumed that these effects vary randomly and unpredictably from one repetition of an experiment to the next.

Let's return to the coin toss. We call heads and tails simple events because they are the most basic observations we can make when a coin is tossed. A **simple event** is the most basic possible observation of an experiment; it cannot be broken down into simpler occurrences. Suppose we observe heads when we toss a coin; then this rules

---

* It is reasonable to assume that an outcome such as the tossed coin landing on its edge is virtually impossible.

out tails for that toss. Thus, when an experiment is performed, one and only one of the possible simple events can occur.

For any random experiment, there is a set of possible simple events. The **sample space** for a random experiment consists of the entire set of possible simple events. When a coin is tossed, the sample space consists of two simple events: heads and tails. Identifying the sample space is an important step in determining the probabilities of various outcomes. We designate a sample space by the capital letter *S*.

For a more practical example, let's consider the following. Specialty retail stores such as trendy restaurants, gift shops, and so on, usually have relatively high failure rates—that is, they go out of business not long after they begin operation. Suppose two such stores open for business this year. Can you identify the sample space with regard to whether these two stores are still operating five years from now? It consists of the four simple events (labeled E_1, E_2, E_3, and E_4) listed in Table 3.1.

Table 3.1

The sample space for the success of two stores

Simple Event	Store 1	Store 2
E_1	Operating	Operating
E_2	Operating	Out of business
E_3	Out of business	Operating
E_4	Out of business	Out of business

We are often interested in the probability that an outcome is any one of a specified set of simple events. We define an **event** as the set of simple events that possess a specific, common characteristic. For the examples listed previously, we might be interested in the following events:

- *No more than five no-shows* for a scheduled flight
- *More than 15 requests* for service at a facility in one hour
- An electrical component failing *within 1 year of use*
- The sales volume of a retail establishment *exceeding $100,000 in a given day*
- A business telephone call lasting *no more than 30 minutes*
- Receiving a grade of *75 or better* on a statistics test

It is possible that an event could be satisfied by only one simple event, or an event could be satisfied by more than one simple event, or an event could be satisfied by no simple event (that is, it cannot happen), in which case it is known as the **empty event.**

We say that an event has occurred if the result of the experiment is one of the simple events that possesses the characteristic that defines the event. For example, "passing a statistics course" is a possible event of the random experiment "taking a statistics course." The sample space consists of the grades (simple events) A, B, C, D, and F. "Passing the course" occurs if any of the grades A, B, C, or D is achieved. In this context, the sample space is itself an event; we may think of it as the **certain event** because one of the simple events of the sample space is certain to occur when the experiment is performed.

Let's agree to use capital letters *A, B, C, . . .* , or capital letters with subscripts to denote different events. The following are examples of some possible events with regard to the success of two specialty stores (see Table 3.1):

A_1: the event "at least one store operating five years from now" (E_1, E_2, E_3)

A_2: the event "at least one store out of business five years from now" (E_2, E_3, E_4)

A_3: the event "no more than one store operating five years from now" (E_2, E_3, E_4)

A_4: the event "no more than one store out of business five years from now" (E_1, E_2, E_3)

Notice that events A_1 and A_4 are identical, as are events A_2 and A_3. They are simply two ways of saying the same thing. Notice also that the characteristic shared by the simple events of, say, event A_1 is that they all consist of outcomes in which one or both of the stores are still in operation five years from now.

EXAMPLE 3.2

Imagine an experiment involving couples with three children where we are interested in finding out the possible gender outcomes of the children. If a large number of such couples are involved, about half of these will have a girl first and about half will have a boy first. Of those couples who first have a girl, some will also have a girl for the second child, while the others will have a boy. We illustrate this branching with the tree diagram of Figure 3.1, where we use G and B to denote girl and boy, respectively. We see that

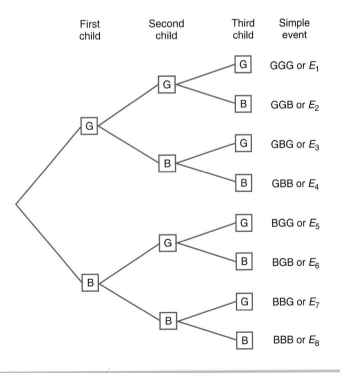

Figure 3.1

Possible gender configurations for three children

the sample space of this experiment consists of the eight simple events GGG, GGB, . . . , BBB, labeled $E_1, E_2, . . . , E_8$, respectively. The following are some examples of events of this sample space and their simple events that share the common characteristic:

> C: at least two girls (E_1, E_2, E_3, and E_5)
>
> D: exactly two girls (E_2, E_3, and E_5)
>
> E: all the same gender (E_1 and E_8)
>
> F: one or fewer girls (E_4, E_6, E_7, and E_8)

Complementary Events

With reference to Example 3.2, let's take a closer look at events C and F. Event C, *at least two girls*, consists of the simple events E_1, E_2, E_3, and E_5. Event F, *one or fewer girls*, consists of the simple events E_4, E_6, E_7, and E_8. When comparing these two events, we find two key features: The events contain no common simple events, and together they make up the entire sample space. (There are either at least two girls, or there is one girl or fewer.) Two such events are known as **complementary events.** So C is the complement event to F, and F is the complement event to C.

The complement of an event is an important concept that is used throughout the material in this text. Suppose A is any event of a sample space S. Then the **complement** of event A, indicated by $\bar{A}$, is the event containing all simple events in the sample space that are not in A.

Mutually Exclusive Events

Two events are **mutually exclusive** if the occurrence of one rules out the occurrence of the other—that is, they cannot *both* occur at the same time. For example, "heads" and "tails" are mutually exclusive events because they cannot both occur in a single coin toss. Notice that if we know that tails occurred, we can infer that heads did not occur. For further illustration, refer to Table 3.1. Are the events "at least one store still operating five years from now" and "at least one store out of business five years from now" mutually exclusive? The answer is *no*. In Table 3.1, we see that the simple event E_2 (as well as E_3) satisfies both events: It contains one store that is still operating five years from now and one store that is not. Both events "at least one store still operating five years from now" and "at least one store out of business five years from now" occur when E_2 occurs; therefore, they are not mutually exclusive. In general, any two events are said to be mutually exclusive if they have no simple events in common.

3.3 Interpretations and Fundamental Rules of Probabilities

Probability is a branch of mathematics that can be very helpful to us in dealing with uncertainty in the world we live in. A probability is a number that measures the degree of certainty associated with the occurrence of an event. Probabilities always lie between 0 and 1, inclusively. If an event cannot happen, the probability of the event is 0. If an event is certain to happen, its probability is 1. If an event is as likely to happen as not to happen, its probability is .5. The greater the likelihood that an event will happen, the greater the probability of that event. Consider the toss of a coin. If the coin is truly balanced, then the probability of heads is .5 because heads is just as likely as tails. So heads is as likely to occur as not to occur. These simple rules apply to all random phenomena. However, the way we interpret a probability depends on the nature of the random phenomenon.

3.3.1 Three Interpretations of Probability

The use of probability as a means of dealing with uncertainty goes back to the 16th century. The earliest applications involved the analysis of games of chance. Many games of chance were especially amenable to analysis because their properties and rules were well defined and their possible outcomes were equally likely to occur. This represented a favorable starting point for this new field of endeavor.

Consider the roll of a single die. If we assume that the die is perfectly balanced, then the six possible face values (1, 2, 3, 4, 5, 6) are equally likely to lie face up. Consequently, it is logical to expect that the probability of observing, say, an even number when the die is rolled is $\frac{3}{6}$, since there are three even numbers among the six equally likely and mutually exclusive outcomes.

This approach to probability which applies only when possible simple events are mutually exclusive and equally likely, came to be known as the **classical interpretation.** It states that, *if the simple events of an experiment are equally likely, the probability of any event equals the proportion of simple events that satisfy that event out of the set of all possible simple events.* Although the classical interpretation is quite useful in games of chance, it is seriously limited in other applications. The validity of a probability calculation based on the classical interpretation is only as good as the assumption of equally likely simple events. In real applications, such an assumption can rarely be verified with certainty.

There are many experiments to which the classical interpretation cannot be applied; these are experiments whose properties are not well known or whose simple events are not equally likely. For example, what is the probability that a defective unit is produced by a stable manufacturing process? There are two possible outcomes, "defective" or "nondefective." But we cannot apply the classical interpretation here because we have no assurance that the two outcomes are equally likely. Situations like this led to the *relative frequency interpretation* of probability.

The **relative frequency interpretation** is based on the assumption that a random experiment can be repeated many times under essentially identical conditions. Each time we perform the experiment, we observe an outcome. Sometimes a given event will be satisfied; sometimes it will not. But as we repeat the experiment many times, that event will be satisfied some proportion of the time. The probability of any event can be defined as *the proportion of the time (i.e., the relative frequency) with which the event occurs over an infinite number of repetitions of the experiment under identical conditions.*

Since an *infinite* number of repetitions is required, a probability can never be exactly determined because no experiment can be repeated an infinite number of times. But we can *approximate* the probability of a given event by observing the relative frequency with which the event has occurred over a finite number of repetitions of the experiment under nearly identical conditions. Such an approximation is called an **empirical probability** because it is based on the empirical observation of experimental outcomes. For example, consider the problem of determining the proportion of defective units produced by a stable manufacturing process. To do this, we sample a certain number of units, considering each selection of a unit as an experiment. The result of each experiment is determined by observing whether the unit is defective. Suppose we sample 200 units from this process and find five of these to be defective. Then the relative frequency (the empirical probability) of a defective unit is $\frac{5}{200}$. We can expect the relative frequency of defective units in a sample to approach the proportion of defective units produced by the process as the number of units sampled increases.

In many situations, we must make decisions involving uncertain phenomena that are unique and therefore unrepeatable under identical conditions. For example, when contemplating the purchase of stocks, one usually assesses the risk of such an investment. When a priceless painting or sculpture is insured against theft or damage, the insurer must assess the risk involved to determine an appropriate premium. In neither of these examples can we imagine a repetitive experiment being performed under nearly identical conditions.

Probabilities for these examples cannot be based on long-term relative frequencies. Rather, probabilities express a subjective **degree of belief** or conviction concerning the likelihood of occurrence of a proposition. In this context, probability represents an individual's judgment about a random phenomenon. This interpretation of probability is therefore known as **subjective assessment.** For example, petroleum engineers A and B are asked for their assessment of the likelihood of finding oil at a particular site. Neither has ever seen a site quite like this one, so past relative frequency information for such a site is unavailable. Engineer A responds by saying that he is 80% certain that oil will be discovered, while B says that she is 70% certain that oil will be discovered at this particular site. Each percentage cited is a measure of that engineer's degree of belief (or degree of certainty) that oil will be discovered. Thus, different measures of belief may be assigned to the same proposition by different people.

3.3.2 The Fundamental Rules of Probabilities

No matter how one approaches probability (the classical, relative frequency, or subjective assessment interpretation), a set of fundamental rules must be satisfied. To this end, let A and B represent events within a sample space S. The following rules govern probabilities:

Rule 1: $0 \le P(A) \le 1$, where $P(A)$ is read "probability of event A." This rule states that all probabilities are numbers between 0 and 1, inclusively.

Rule 2: $P(S) = 1$, where $P(S)$ is read "probability of the certain event." This rule states that one of the simple events of the sample space is certain to occur when the experiment is performed.

Rule 3: If two or more events, say A and B, are mutually exclusive, then

$$P(A \text{ or } B) = P(A) + P(B)$$

This rule states that the probability of occurrence of any one of two or more mutually exclusive events is the sum of their individual probabilities.

The ramifications of these simple rules are extremely important to master:

- The probability of an event could never equal a number like 1.7 or −.4. According to Rule 1, all probabilities must lie between 0 and 1.

- If an event *cannot* occur, its probability is 0; if an event is *certain* to occur, its probability is 1. If the probability of an event is near 0, the event has little chance of occurring; if the probability of an event is near 1, the event is very likely to occur.

- An extremely important result of Rules 2 and 3 is that *the probabilities of the simple events of a random experiment must sum to 1.* For example, in a coin toss, the probabilities of heads and tails must sum to 1. In one roll of a die, the probabilities of the face values of 1, 2, 3, 4, 5, and 6 must sum to 1. If the number of bicycles sold by a bicycle shop on any given day ranges from 0 to 25, then the probabilities of selling 0, 1, 2, 3, . . . , 25 bicycles in a day must sum to 1.

Let's return to the roll of a single balanced die. Because the simple events 1, 2, 3, 4, 5, 6 are equally likely, each face value must have a probability of $\frac{1}{6}$. Furthermore, because the simple events are also mutually exclusive, Rule 3 tells us we can add the individual probabilities of 2, 4, and 6 to determine the probability of, say, "even number" to be $\frac{3}{6}$; that is, $\frac{1}{6} + \frac{1}{6} + \frac{1}{6} = \frac{3}{6}$.

Here is another important application of Rule 3. Any event A and its complement event $\bar{A}$ are mutually exclusive by definition; the occurrence of $\bar{A}$ signifies that A did not occur, and vice versa. But one or the other must occur. Since it is certain that either A or $\bar{A}$ will occur, the probability that either A or $\bar{A}$ occurs equals 1. Now, Rule 3 states that the probability that either A or $\bar{A}$ occurs equals the sum of their individual probabilities. So, P(either A or $\bar{A}$) = $P(A) + P(\bar{A})$ = 1. Thus,

$$P(\bar{A}) = 1 - P(A) \qquad\qquad \textbf{(3.1)}$$

In other words, *the probability of the complement of an event equals 1 minus the probability of the event.* This relationship is known as the **probability rule for complementary events.**

A powerful consequence of this result is that, if we know the probability of any event, we can determine the probability that the event does *not* occur (that is, the probability of the complement of the event) by subtracting the probability of occurrence from 1. Suppose you assess subjectively the probability of your getting a grade of A or B in your statistics course to be .4. Then the probability that you make neither an A nor a B equals $1 - .4 = .6$.

Finally, notice that the three fundamental rules apply consistently to all three interpretations of probability. With the classical interpretation, the probability of an event is the proportion of simple events that satisfy an event out of the set of all possible, equally likely simple events. With the relative frequency approach, the probability of an event is the proportion of times the event occurs over repeated trials of a random experiment. In both cases, the probability is a *proportion;* thus, its value must lie between 0 and 1, inclusively. The fundamental rules are also consistent with the subjective assessment approach because a degree of belief is converted into a proportion.

Joint and Conditional Probabilities

We are often interested in the probability that two or more events of a random experiment occur jointly. Consider getting the ace of spades when you draw a card from a deck. This card represents the joint occurrence of two events: "drawing an ace" and "drawing a spade." A salesperson who carries two products might be interested in the probability that a potential customer buys *both* products. This outcome represents the joint occurrence of two events: "customer buys product A" and "customer buys product B." The probability of the joint occurrence of two or more events is called a **joint probability.** The joint probability of two events A and B is denoted by $P(A \text{ and } B)$.

Sometimes the probability of an event changes because we obtain additional information. Consider an example that arises from random sampling. Suppose we have just received a shipment of 100 automobile batteries. The shipment contains five defective batteries, but we do not know this. If one of the 100 batteries is randomly selected and tested, the probability that it is defective is $\frac{5}{100}$ (applying the classical interpretation). Now suppose that battery is found to be defective. If a second battery is randomly selected and tested, what is the probability that it is also defective? After the first battery is selected, there are 99 batteries remaining in the lot, only four of which are defective. Thus, the probability that the second battery is defective becomes $\frac{4}{99}$. On the other hand, if the first battery selected had been nondefective, all five defectives would have remained in the lot. In this case, the probability that the second battery selected is defective would be $\frac{5}{99}$. Thus, the probability that the second battery selected is defective depends on what we learn about the first battery selected. This is an example of what is known as a conditional probability. A **conditional probability** is the probability that one event occurs, given the information that another event occurred. The conditional probability of event A given the knowledge that event B occurred is denoted by $P(A, \text{given } B)$.

Statistically Independent Events

Suppose we have tossed a perfectly balanced coin once and observed tails. Now suppose we toss the coin a second time. Does the fact that we observed tails the first time alter the probability of tails on the second toss? What do you think? Do you believe that the probability of tails on the second toss, if tails occurred on the first toss, is going to be different from the probability of tails anytime we toss a balanced coin, which we know to be .5? The answer should be *no*. The events "tails the first time" and "tails the second time" are called statistically independent events. In general, any two events A and B are **statistically independent** if the probability of event B is not affected by the knowledge regarding the occurrence of A. Thus, if two events are statistically independent, the individual probability of B equals the conditional probability of B given the knowledge that A occurred. Alternatively, if the probability of event B *is* affected by the knowledge regarding the occurrence of A, then the events A and B are **statistically dependent.**

An easy way to decide whether two or more events are statistically independent is to examine whether there is a change to the sample space from one experiment to the next. If no, subsequent probabilities will not be affected by prior outcomes and the events will be statistically independent. If yes, subsequent probabilities will be affected by prior outcomes and the events will be dependent. Thus, in the battery example the events are dependent, since the sample space changed to 4 defectives and 95 good batteries after the first selection. But in the coin toss example, the fact that tails occurred the first time does not alter the sample space before the second toss. It still consists of the equally likely simple events tails and heads.

If events are statistically independent, their joint probability is easy to determine. Suppose we toss a balanced coin twice. What is the probability of getting tails on both tosses? Well, there are four possible sequences of outcomes: head–head, head–tail, tail–head, and tail–tail. If the probabilities on the second toss do not depend on the outcome of the first toss, then all four sequences are equally likely and each has probability $\frac{1}{4}$ of occurring. But there is another, very useful way to find this probability. The probability of tails on the first toss is $\frac{1}{2}$. Similarly, the probability of tails on the second toss is $\frac{1}{2}$. If the results of the two tosses are statistically independent, then the probability of tails on both tosses equals $\frac{1}{2} \times \frac{1}{2} = \frac{1}{4}$. In general, *we obtain the probability of the joint occurrence of two or more statistically independent events by multiplying their individual probabilities.* Thus, if events A and B are statistically independent, then their joint probability is the product of their individual probabilities:

$$P(A \text{ and } B) = P(A)P(B) \tag{3.2}$$

EXAMPLE 3.3

Refer to the example in Section 2.7.2 involving a random sample of 500 students enrolled in schools of business and arts and sciences. The breakdown of the 500 students with regard to gender and type of school, as given in Table 2.3, is repeated here.

	Schools of Business	Schools of Arts & Sciences	Total
Male	130	130	260
Female	70	170	240
Total	200	300	500

(a) Based on the relative frequency interpretation, what is the probability that a student is a female attending a school of business?

(b) Use the answer in part (a) to determine whether gender and type of school are independent.

Solution

(a) There are two events: gender and type of school. We seek the joint probability of female and school of business. Since there are 70 females out of the 500 students in the sample attending schools of business, the desired joint probability is

$$P(\text{female and school of business}) = \frac{70}{500} = .14$$

(b) If gender and type of school are independent, then from Expression (3.2)

$$P(\text{female and school of business}) = P(\text{female})P(\text{school of business})$$

Since there are 240 females out of the sample of 500 students, $P(\text{female}) = \frac{240}{500} = .48$. Similarly, since 200 out of the 500 students attend schools of business, $P(\text{school of business}) = \frac{200}{500} = .4$. Then

$$P(\text{female})P(\text{school of business}) = (.48)(.4) = .192 \neq .14$$

where .14 is the joint probability of female and school of business. Based on this information, therefore, gender and type of school are not independent.

EXAMPLE 3.4

Today, manufacturers of products that are part of crucial and expensive systems, such as airplanes, communication satellites, and sophisticated weapons, must assure their customers that the products are highly reliable. The manufacturers enhance the reliability of these products by using the principle of *redundancy*—that is, by designing backup parts into the product. This example illustrates this principle.

A manufacturer must be able to assure customers that a product's *failure rate* (the probability that the product fails any time it is used) does not exceed .0005 (5 chances in 10,000). The problem is that a key part is known to have a failure rate of .001. To lower the chance of failure of this part, the manufacturer designs a backup part into the product. If the original part fails, the product still functions unless the backup part also fails. The failure rate of the backup part is also .001. Assuming the failure of the backup part is statistically independent of the failure of the original part, determine the joint probability that *both* fail.

Solution

Since the failures of the two parts are statistically independent, the joint probability that they *both* fail is the product of their individual probabilities of failure:

$$P(\text{both fail}) = P(\text{original part fails}) \times P(\text{backup part fails})$$

$$= .001 \times .001 = .000001$$

Thus, the probability that both fail is only 1 chance in 1 million. Since the second part is not needed unless the original part fails, its presence is redundant under normal usage of the product.

Elements of Random Experiments and Fundamental Rules of Probabilities: A Summary

The following boxes summarize (1) the key elements of random experiments and (2) the fundamental rules of probabilities.

**DEFINITIONS FOR KEY ELEMENTS
OF RANDOM EXPERIMENTS**

1. A **random experiment** is the process of obtaining information through observation or measurement of a phenomenon whose outcome is subject to chance.
2. A **simple event** is the most basic possible outcome of an experiment; it cannot be broken down into simpler outcomes.
3. The **sample space** for a random experiment is the collection of all possible simple events.
4. An **event** is the set of simple events within a sample space that possess a common characteristic.
5. The **complement** of event A is the event containing all the simple events in the sample space that do *not* satisfy A.
6. Two or more events are **mutually exclusive** if they have no simple events in common.

> ## ESSENTIAL RULES OF PROBABILITIES
>
> 1. The probability of any event is always a number between 0 and 1, inclusively.
> 2. The probability of the certain event—that is, the sample space—is 1. In other words, one of the simple events of the sample space is certain to occur when a random experiment is performed.
> 3. If two events are mutually exclusive, then the probability that either or both occur is the sum of their individual probabilities:
>
> $$P(A \text{ or } B) = P(A) + P(B)$$
>
> 4. The probability that an event does not occur equals 1 minus the probability that the event does occur (the probability rule for complementary events):
>
> $$P(\overline{A}) = 1 - P(A)$$
>
> 5. If two events are statistically independent, then their joint probability of occurrence equals the product of their individual probabilities:
>
> $$P(A \text{ and } B) = P(A) \times P(B)$$

3.4   Discrete and Continuous Random Variables

We have introduced the fundamental aspects of probabilities of events that result from chance experiments. Now we focus on using numerical measures to study the outcomes of random experiments. This leads to the introduction of two key concepts: **random variable** and **probability distribution,** which form the backbone of statistical inference.

To understand what a random variable is, let's consider couples who plan to have two children. Suppose they are interested in the number of girls they might have. Before reading on, how many possibilities do you think there are? If you said three, you are right. The three mutually exclusive possibilities are no girls, one girl, and two girls. Now, let's examine these three possibilities in the context of all simple events with respect to gender for two children. The simple events representing all possible gender configurations for two children are: BB, BG, GB, and GG. In terms of the variable "number of girls," the four simple events yield outcomes as follows:

Simple Event	Number of Girls
BB	0
BG ⎫ GB ⎭	1
GG	2

Notice that we have transformed the four simple events of the experiment into corresponding numerical values, each representing a certain number of girls. Such a "mapping" of simple events into a numerical representation is the nature of a random variable. Thus, we define a **random variable** as the transformation of the simple events of a chance experiment into numerical quantities that represent all possible results for a phenomenon of interest.

It is customary to denote a random variable by using a capital letter such as X. Unless otherwise indicated, we adhere to this custom throughout the book. For the example under discussion, we define the random variable to be

X: the number of girls in a family of two children

We have just seen that the possible values of the random variable X are 0, 1, and 2. Therefore, X is a variable because it assumes numerical quantities as values. And the values of X are subject to uncertainty; that is why X is referred to as a random variable. This leads to a somewhat more informal definition: *A random variable is any numerical quantity whose values are determined by chance.*

Since the values of a random variable are associated with simple events, each of the values of X has a corresponding probability. For example, the value "0 girls" comes from the simple event BB. If we assume that the probability of having a boy is $\frac{1}{2}$ and assume statistical independence of gender from one child to the next, then the probability of having two boys in a row is $(\frac{1}{2})(\frac{1}{2}) = \frac{1}{4}$. Therefore,

$$P(X = 0) = \frac{1}{4}$$

This is read "the probability that the random variable X takes on the value 0 (no girls) is $\frac{1}{4}$." The value $X = 1$ stems from the two simple events BG and GB, each of which also has the probability $\frac{1}{4}$ of occurring. Thus, the probability that the random variable X takes on the value 1 is the sum of the probabilities of the two mutually exclusive simple events, BG and GB, that lead to exactly one girl; that is,

$$P(X = 1) = \frac{1}{4} + \frac{1}{4} = \frac{1}{2}$$

Finally, the value $X = 2$ stems from the simple event GG, which has the probability $\frac{1}{4}$ of occurring:

$$P(X = 2) = \frac{1}{4}$$

We remind you that for these quantities to be probabilities, they must adhere to the rules given in Section 3.3.2. Specifically, since with two children there must be either no girls, one girl, or two girls, the sum of the probabilities of these values must equal 1. For this example, we have

$$P(X = 0) + P(X = 1) + P(X = 2) = \frac{1}{4} + \frac{1}{2} + \frac{1}{4} = 1$$

EXAMPLE 3.5

There are 36 possible pairs of face values when two dice are rolled. Define X to be the random variable representing the sum of the two face values. Determine the possible values of X and the probability for each.

Solution

We know, of course, that each die has six sides, with 1, 2, 3, 4, 5, and 6 dots appearing on the six sides. The smallest value that the random variable X, the sum of the face values on two dice, can take on is 2, while the largest is 12. Therefore, the possible values of X are 2, 3, 4, ..., 12. To illustrate the determination of probabilities for these values, let's select the value "lucky 7." Table 3.2 displays all possible pairs of dice rolls, grouped according to their sums. One pair yields a sum of 2, two pairs yield sums of 3, and so on. Notice that exactly six pairs of face values lead to the value 7. Since the 36 pairs are mutually exclusive, with each having a probability $\frac{1}{36}$ of occurring, we have (using the classical interpretation)

$$P(X = 7) = \frac{6}{36}$$

The probabilities for the other values follow from a similar argument and are listed in the right-hand column of Table 3.2.

Table 3.2

Correspondence between face values when a pair of dice are rolled and a random variable representing the sum of the two face values

Face Values	Value of Random Variable	Number of Occurrences	Probability
(1, 1)	2	1	$\frac{1}{36}$
(1, 2), (2, 1)	3	2	$\frac{2}{36}$
(1, 3), (2, 2), (3, 1)	4	3	$\frac{3}{36}$
(1, 4), (2, 3), (3, 2), (4, 1)	5	4	$\frac{4}{36}$
(1, 5), (2, 4), (3, 3), (4, 2), (5, 1)	6	5	$\frac{5}{36}$
(1, 6), (2, 5), (3, 4), (4, 3), (5, 2), (6, 1)	7	6	$\frac{6}{36}$
(2, 6), (3, 5), (4, 4), (5, 3), (6, 2)	8	5	$\frac{5}{36}$
(3, 6), (4, 5), (5, 4), (6, 3)	9	4	$\frac{4}{36}$
(4, 6), (5, 5), (6, 4)	10	3	$\frac{3}{36}$
(5, 6), (6, 5)	11	2	$\frac{2}{36}$
(6, 6)	12	1	$\frac{1}{36}$
Total possible occurrences:		36	

Discrete and Continuous Random Variables

You may have noticed in the examples discussed so far that the number of values for the random variables has been finite in each case. In fact, we actually listed the possible values from smallest to largest. Values that can be listed are said to be **countable.** Countable values are not necessarily finite in number, however. For example, let X be the number of telephone calls made on a given day within a city. There could be no calls, one call, two calls, three calls, and so on, with (theoretically) no upper limit. Nevertheless, we can indicate the possible values with a list as follows: $X = 0, 1, 2, 3, \ldots$. The sequence of dots indicates that the list of possible values continues infinitely.

Now, suppose the random variable represents the diameters of pistons, measured in millimeters. Possible diameters of pistons range from 0 (or some minimum value) to infinity (or some maximum value). They include all values on some continuous line segment. Thus, between any two possible values lies another possible value. If we had a sensitive enough measuring device, the number of possible values would be infinite, and we would certainly not be able to list them. When possible values lie on a continuous line segment, they are said to be **uncountable.** When the possible values of a random variable are countable, the random variable is said to be **discrete.** If the values are uncountable, the random variable is said to be **continuous.**

The following are examples of discrete random variables:

X_1: The number of units of a product sold on a given day. If there are at most 50 units available, the possible values of X_1 are 0, 1, 2, . . . , 50.

X_2: The number of telephone calls received by a business office in a given hour. The possible values of X_2 are 0, 1, 2, 3, . . . on up to some conceivably very large (integer) number.

X_3: The number of persons arriving at a service facility (bank, repair shop, etc.) in a given day. The possible values of X_3 are 0, 1, 2, 3, . . . on up to some conceivably very large (integer) number.

The following are examples of continuous random variables:

X_4: The fill amount in a container. If we assume that the maximum amount possible for the container is 20 ounces, then the possible values of X_4 lie in the interval 0 to 20 ($0 \leq X_4 \leq 20$).

X_5: The percentage increase (or decrease) in profit of a company when compared to last year. The possible values of X_5 can be negative (a decrease) or positive (an increase) and are (theoretically) without bound ($-\infty < X_5 < \infty$).

X_6: The length of a business telephone conversation. The possible values of X_6 are in the interval 0 to (theoretically) infinity ($0 < X_6 < \infty$).

3.5 Probability Distributions of Discrete Random Variables

Consider the discrete random variable X. The **probability distribution** of X is a representation of the probabilities for all values that X can take on. The form of the representation can vary. Common forms are tables, graphs, and mathematical expressions. For example, let the discrete random variable X be the number of girls in a two-child family. We can represent the probability distribution in tabular form by simply listing each possible value of X along with its probability as in Figure 3.2.

We can also represent the probability distribution of X graphically by plotting the probability on the vertical axis for each value of X on the horizontal axis, as illustrated in Figure 3.2. Notice that for each value of X on the horizontal axis, the

Figure 3.2

Probability distribution
for the number
of girls in a two-child
family

Values of X	Probability
0	$P(X = 0) = \frac{1}{4}$
1	$P(X = 1) = \frac{1}{2}$
2	$P(X = 2) = \frac{1}{4}$

probability is shown by a vertical line that ends at the corresponding probability value on the vertical axis.

Probability distributions of discrete random variables are similar to relative frequency distributions, discussed in Chapter 2. But unlike the rectangles typically used to show relative frequencies, we use vertical lines here to show probabilities because, for the example at hand, the random variable X takes on only the values 0, 1, and 2. The intervals between these values represent events that cannot occur; therefore, they have zero probability of occurrence.

Using the information in Table 3.2 involving face values on a pair of dice, we can represent the probability distribution for this example graphically as in Figure 3.3.

Figure 3.3

The probability
distribution for the sum
of the two face val-
ues when rolling
a pair of dice

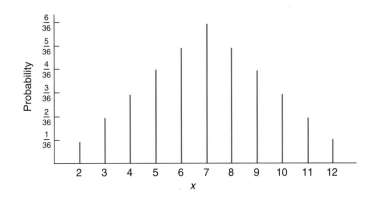

A probability distribution allows us to simultaneously observe and compare the probabilities for the possible values of the random variable. For example, in Figure 3.2, notice that the probability of having a boy and a girl in a two-child family is twice that of having two boys or two girls. From Figures 3.2 and 3.3, it is obvious that both of these distributions are symmetric. To describe the shapes of probability distributions, we use terminology similar to that used in Chapter 2. Most probability distributions are single peaked and either symmetric or skewed (left or right).

The probability distributions discussed in this chapter and in Chapter 4 are theoretical in the sense that they cannot really be observed. In a real application, we can regard a relative frequency table as a set of empirical probabilities, which we may use to approximate a theoretical probability distribution. We need to have a conceptual understanding of theoretical distributions to be in a better position to deal with empirical probabilities.

The Probability Function of a Discrete Random Variable

For many discrete random variables that are important in real applications, it is possible to find a mathematical function that gives the probability for any particular value of the random variable when that value is substituted into the function. This kind of function is known as the **probability function** of a discrete random variable; it is the expression we use to determine the probability for each value that a discrete random variable can take on. Let's agree to use the lowercase letter x to denote a particular (but unspecified) value that the random variable X can take on. Thus, the meaning of $P(x)$ is such that

$$P(x) = P(X = x)$$

The probability that the random variable X takes on the particular value x is determined by substituting the value x into the probability function.

To illustrate, let's see whether the following expression gives the probabilities for each possible value of the random variable X representing the number of girls in a two-child family:

$$P(x) = \frac{2!}{(2-x)!\, x!} \left(\frac{1}{2}\right)^x \left(\frac{1}{2}\right)^{2-x} \quad \text{where } x = 0, 1, \text{ or } 2$$

The number 2! is read "two factorial" and is the product of 2 times each preceding positive integer. So $2! = 2 \times 1 = 2$; $3! = 3 \times 2 \times 1 = 6$; $4! = 4 \times 3! = 24$; and so on. Generally, $n! = n \times (n-1)!$. Also $1! = 0! = 1$ by definition. In Chapter 4, you will see where this probability function comes from. At this time, we want only to show that this function gives the same probabilities that we obtained earlier. The idea is simply to substitute a particular value of X into the expression and then evaluate it; that is,

$$P(X = 0) = P(0) = \frac{2!}{(2-0)!\, 0!} \left(\frac{1}{2}\right)^0 \left(\frac{1}{2}\right)^2 = \left(\frac{1}{2}\right)^2 = \frac{1}{4}$$

$$P(X = 1) = P(1) = \frac{2!}{(2-1)!\, 1!} \left(\frac{1}{2}\right)^1 \left(\frac{1}{2}\right)^1 = (2)\left(\frac{1}{2}\right)\left(\frac{1}{2}\right) = \frac{1}{2}$$

and

$$P(X = 2) = P(2) = \frac{2!}{(2-2)!\, 2!} \left(\frac{1}{2}\right)^2 \left(\frac{1}{2}\right)^0 = \left(\frac{1}{2}\right)^2 = \frac{1}{4}$$

Because the function $P(x)$ yields probabilities, the result of evaluating $P(x)$ for any possible value of X must be a number in the interval 0 to 1, and the sum of these probabilities over all possible values of the random variable must be 1. (Note that these conditions are required by fundamental Rules 1 and 2 in Section 3.3.2.) Thus, a probability function of a discrete random variable must meet the following two conditions:

Let X be a discrete random variable. The function $P(x) = P(X = x)$ is called the **probability function** of the random variable X if the following two conditions are met:

1. $0 \le P(x) \le 1$ for all possible values x of X.
2. $\sum_{\text{all } x} P(x) = 1$.

The Cumulative Probability Distribution of a Discrete Random Variable

We now turn our attention to another important concept: the **cumulative probability distribution** of the discrete random variable X. To understand this concept, ponder for a moment how often you hear expressions similar to these: "The number of questions that I might have missed on this test is no more than three," "I expect to get at least two A's this semester," "I can give a ride to at most four persons on this trip." The phrases *no more than, at least,* and *at most* all suggest an accumulation. For example, if you have missed "no more than three questions" on a test, then you may have missed exactly zero questions, or exactly one, or exactly two, or exactly three. And if you expect to receive "at least two A's," then you expect to receive exactly two A's, or exactly three, or exactly four, and so on, up to the number of courses you are taking this term.

With reference to the two-child family example, we might ask: What is the probability of having at most one girl? The answer is the sum of the probabilities of the values of X that satisfy the event "at most one girl." These values are no girls ($X = 0$) and one girl ($X = 1$). The desired probability is

$$P(X \leq 1) = P(0) + P(1) = .25 + .50 = .75$$

where $P(X \leq 1)$ is read "the probability that the random variable X takes on a value less than or equal to 1" (or, equivalently, "at most 1," "1 or less," or "no more than 1"). This is an example of a cumulative probability in the sense that we accumulate the probabilities for individual values of X that satisfy the statement "at most one girl." We can determine the entire cumulative probability distribution for this example by accumulating the individual probabilities as we go successively from one possible value of X to another in increasing order, as follows:

Verbal phrase	Values of X	Cumulative Probability
At most zero girls	0	$P(X = 0) = .25$
At most one girl	0, 1	$P(X \leq 1) = P(0) + P(1) = .75$
At most two girls	0, 1, 2	$P(X \leq 2) = P(0) + P(1) + P(2) = 1$

Now, suppose we want to determine the probability of having *at least one girl*. Since the phrase "at least one girl" implies either exactly one girl or exactly two girls, we seek the sum of the probabilities of these values; that is,

$$P(X \geq 1) = P(1) + P(2) = .5 + .25 = .75$$

We can also determine this probability by first realizing that the event "at least one girl" is the complement of the event "no girls." Then by using the probability rule for complementary events, we determine that

$$P(X \geq 1) = 1 - P(X = 0) = 1 - .25 = .75$$

For another illustration, Table 3.3 provides the cumulative probability distribution of the sum of the two numbers that come up when a pair of dice are rolled. Notice that we can use the "at most" probabilities in Table 3.3 to determine probabilities of the "at least" variety. For example, the probability that the sum of the two numbers is at least 7 is equal to 1 minus the probability that the sum is at most 6, because

Table 3.3

Cumulative probability
distribution of the sum
of the face values when
a pair of dice are rolled

Verbal Phrase	Values of X	Probability
At most 2	2	$P(X \leq 2) = \frac{1}{36}$
At most 3	2, 3	$P(X \leq 3) = \frac{3}{36}$
At most 4	2, 3, 4	$P(X \leq 4) = \frac{6}{36}$
At most 5	2, 3, 4, 5	$P(X \leq 5) = \frac{10}{36}$
At most 6	2, 3, 4, 5, 6	$P(X \leq 6) = \frac{15}{36}$
At most 7	2, 3, 4, 5, 6, 7	$P(X \leq 7) = \frac{21}{36}$
At most 8	2, 3, 4, 5, 6, 7, 8	$P(X \leq 8) = \frac{26}{36}$
At most 9	2, 3, 4, 5, 6, 7, 8, 9	$P(X \leq 9) = \frac{30}{36}$
At most 10	2, 3, 4, 5, 6, 7, 8, 9, 10	$P(X \leq 10) = \frac{33}{36}$
At most 11	2, 3, 4, 5, 6, 7, 8, 9, 10, 11	$P(X \leq 11) = \frac{35}{36}$
At most 12	2, 3, 4, 5, 6, 7, 8, 9, 10, 11, 12	$P(X \leq 12) = 1$

"at most 6" and "at least 7" are complementary events. To see this, let's first list all 11 possible outcomes: 2, 3, 4, 5, 6, 7, 8, 9, 10, 11, and 12. Of these, the outcomes 7, 8, 9, 10, 11, and 12 are "at least 7." The remaining outcomes 2, 3, 4, 5, and 6 are "6 or fewer." So "at least 7" and "at most 6" ("6 or fewer") have no common outcomes, exhaust all possible outcomes, and thus are complementary events. So

$$P(X \geq 7) = 1 - P(X \leq 6) = 1 - \frac{15}{36} = \frac{21}{36}$$

Determining Individual Probabilities from Cumulative Probabilities

If the cumulative probabilities are known, we can "work backward" to determine individual probabilities. For example, suppose we want to find the probability that the sum of the numbers that come up when two dice are rolled is exactly 6. Of course, we know from Table 3.2 that the answer is $\frac{5}{36}$. But, let's see how to obtain the same result by using the appropriate cumulative probabilities from Table 3.3. The cumulative probability that the random variable X is at most 6, $P(X \leq 6)$, is the sum of the probabilities of the values 2, 3, 4, 5, and 6. Similarly, the cumulative probability of at most 5, $P(X \leq 5)$, is the sum of the probabilities of the values 2, 3, 4, and 5. Since the accumulation of probabilities is exactly the same up to and including the value 5, the difference between $P(X \leq 6)$ and $P(X \leq 5)$ must be the probability that X takes on the value 6. In other words,

$$P(X = 6) = P(X \leq 6) - P(X \leq 5) = \frac{15}{36} - \frac{10}{36} = \frac{5}{36}$$

Similarly, the probability that X takes on the value 9 is

$$P(X = 9) = P(X \leq 9) - P(X \leq 8) = \frac{30}{36} - \frac{26}{36} = \frac{4}{36}$$

We can generalize by saying that for any integer-valued discrete random variable X, the probability that X takes on any particular value x is given by

$$P(X = x) = P(X \le x) - P[X \le (x - 1)] \tag{3.3}$$

3.6   Probability Distributions of Continuous Random Variables

In this section, we examine probability distributions for continuous random variables. From Section 3.4, we know that a continuous random variable is one whose possible outcomes consist of all values on a line segment. The number of possible values for any continuous random variable is uncountable and infinite. Consequently, *the probability of a continuous random variable X taking on any specific value x is 0.*

To illustrate, suppose we are observing the length of time required to complete a transaction at a bank, where the measuring device can measure time only to within a tenth of a second. Then an observed length of, say, 83.4 seconds means that the true length of time is somewhere in the interval 83.35 to 83.45 seconds because all values in this interval round off to 83.4 seconds. On the other hand, a time length of *exactly* 83.4 seconds means 83.400000 . . . and not 83.400000001 or 83.3999999999. . . . To be truly exact, a number must be specified to an infinite number of decimal places. Thus, there are an infinite number of possible exact outcomes, each having a theoretical probability of 0. In fact, this is not a serious limitation because we would never be interested in such an exact outcome. All problems of practical interest deal with *ranges* of outcomes, such as "no more than 90 seconds" and "between 5 and 10 minutes." In summary, for continuous random variables, we are not concerned about probabilities that the random variable takes on particular values. Rather, we are concerned about the probability that a continuous random variable takes on values in a given interval. This is an important distinction between continuous and discrete random variables.

The Probability Density Function of a Continuous Random Variable

A continuous random variable X is characterized by a mathematical expression known as the **probability density function.** We label such a function as $f(x)$, where x is any particular value of X. The probability density function $f(x)$ does not have the same meaning as the probability function of a discrete random variable. The density function $f(x)$ does not represent the probability that X takes on a particular value. Rather, it provides the means by which the probability that X takes on values that lie in a given interval can be determined, as you will soon see.

To illustrate the notion of a probability density function, suppose we measured the service times of 100 customers at some facility and grouped the observations into ten 1-minute intervals, as given in Table 3.4. We can plot the relative frequencies for each interval by using rectangles (rather than vertical lines), as shown in part (a) of Figure 3.4, to indicate that the frequency refers to the entire interval rather than an individual point within the interval. Notice that the base of each rectangle equals 1. Thus, the area of each rectangle (base times height) equals the relative frequency (height) of the corresponding interval. Since the relative frequencies sum to 1, the sum of the areas of all rectangles also equals 1.

Table 3.4

Grouped service times of 100 customers at some facility

Time Interval	Number of Service Times	Relative Frequency
(0, 1)	21	.21
(1, 2)	17	.17
(2, 3)	16	.16
(3, 4)	12	.12
(4, 5)	13	.13
(5, 6)	7	.07
(6, 7)	5	.05
(7, 8)	6	.06
(8, 9)	2	.02
(9, 10)	1	.01
	100	1.00

Instead of observing the service times of 100 customers and grouping them into ten 1-minute intervals, suppose we observed the times of 1,000 customers and grouped them into 20 half-minute intervals. The graph of the relative frequencies for the 20 half-minute intervals is given in part (b) of Figure 3.4. A comparison of parts (a) and (b) of Figure 3.4 reveals that, although they are essentially the same, part (b) appears to be somewhat less irregular than part (a). By continuing this process of increasing the observed number of time intervals while decreasing the width of the intervals, we would find each succeeding relative frequency distribution to be less and less irregular while maintaining essentially the same essential shape with regard to frequency.

Figure 3.4

Relative frequencies of grouped service times for (a) 10 intervals and (b) 20 intervals

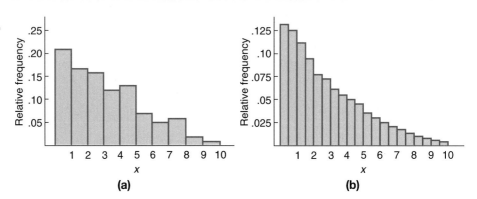

Eventually, we would arrive at a *limiting curve;* that is, as the observed number of time intervals becomes very large and the width of the intervals becomes very small, the relative frequency approaches a smooth curve. Based on Figure 3.4, we may speculate that the limiting curve for this illustration would appear as shown in Figure 3.5.

The function $f(x)$, whose graph is the limiting curve obtained as the number of intervals approaches infinity and the interval widths approach 0, is the probability density function of the continuous random variable X, provided that the vertical scale is chosen so that the total area under the curve equals 1.

In Appendix 3 at the end of this chapter, we provide the formal definition of a probability density function using integral calculus. For our purposes, however, the following definition is sufficient:

Figure 3.5

Limiting curve for the
relative frequency
of the service times

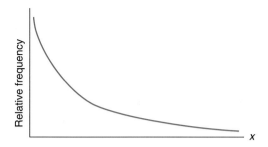

> A mathematical expression $f(x)$ (read as "f of x") is the **probability density function** of a continuous random variable X if the following two conditions are met:
>
> 1. For any value x of the random variable X in the interval over which X is defined, the function $f(x)$ yields a nonnegative quantity.
> 2. The total area under the graph of $f(x)$, bounded below by the horizontal axis and on the left and right by the minimum and maximum values of X, equals 1.

This definition tells us that a mathematical expression cannot serve as a probability density function of a continuous random variable unless the area under the graph of the expression equals 1. In substance, all this stems from the need to adhere to Rules 1 and 2 in Section 3.3.2; that is, if the total area equals 1 for the interval in which the continuous random variable is defined, then any portion of this area corresponding to a smaller interval must be a number between 0 and 1. The area for the smaller interval is the probability that the random variable X takes on values in the smaller interval.

To illustrate, recall the service times example. Let the continuous random variable X be the length of a service time at the facility. The possible values of X lie in the interval 0 to ∞ (theoretically). Thus, the area under the graph of the probability density function of X that is bounded below by the horizontal axis and on the left and right by the interval $(0, \infty)$ must equal 1. If, say, we wish to determine the probability that the service time is between 4 and 6 minutes—stated symbolically as $P(4 \leq X \leq 6)$—we would have to evaluate the portion of the total area under the graph of the density function of X that is bounded below by the horizontal axis and on the left and right by the values 4 and 6, respectively. This area, of course, must be less than 1; it corresponds to the probability that X takes on values in the interval $(4, 6)$ as illustrated in Figure 3.6.

Figure 3.6

The probability that a
service time is between
4 and 6 minutes

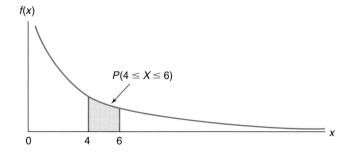

More generally, let's consider any continuous random variable X with the probability density function $f(x)$. The probability that X takes on values in the interval a to b is the portion of the total area under the graph of $f(x)$ that is bounded below by the horizontal axis and on the left and right by a and b, respectively. This interval probability is written symbolically as $P(a \leq x \leq b)$ and is illustrated in Figure 3.7.

Figure 3.7

A probability depicted as the area under the density function

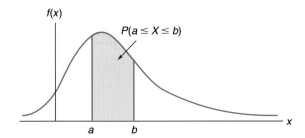

EXAMPLE 3.6

Suppose the probability density function of a continuous random variable X with values in the interval $(0, 1)$ is

$$f(x) = 2x \qquad 0 \leq x \leq 1$$

(a) Show that this is a probability density function.

(b) Determine the probability that X takes on values in the interval $(.25, .75)$.

(c) Determine the probability that X takes on values that exceed .75.

Solution

(a) Condition 1 in the definition of a probability density function is satisfied, because for any value x in the interval $(0, 1)$, $f(x) = 2x$ will indeed yield a nonnegative quantity. For the second condition, we need to show that the area under the graph of $f(x) = 2x$ that is bounded below by the horizontal axis and on the left and right by the interval $(0, 1)$ is equal to 1. We can do this for this density function without using calculus because $f(x) = 2x$ is the equation of a straight line with slope 2 and intercept 0. Although only two points are needed to graph this function, let's evaluate it for the values 0, .25, .50, .75, and 1 from the interval $(0, 1)$; then we have the following:

x	$f(x) = 2x$
0	$f(0) = 2(0) = 0$
.25	$f(.25) = 2(.25) = .50$
.50	$f(.50) = 2(.50) = 1$
.75	$f(.75) = 2(.75) = 1.50$
1	$f(1) = 2(1) = 2$

The graph of $f(x) = 2x$ is given in Figure 3.8(a). You should immediately notice that this figure is a triangle. Because the formula for finding the area of a triangle is: Area equals one-half the base times the height, we see from Figure 3.8(a) that the base is 1 and the height is 2, so the area is $(\frac{1}{2})(1)(2) = 1$. Thus, $f(x) = 2x$ is indeed a probability density function in the interval $(0, 1)$.

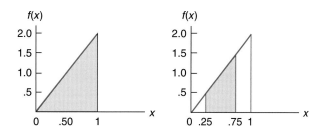

Figure 3.8

The probability density function of Example 3.6

Although $f(x) = 2x$ is a probability density function in the range 0 to 1, it is important to notice that $f(x)$ is certainly *not* a probability function in the same sense that we defined probability functions for discrete random variables. For example, $f(.75) = 1.50$ and $f(1) = 2$, which obviously violate the rule that any probability must be a number between 0 and 1.

(b) To determine the probability that X takes on values in the interval $(.25, .75)$, we graph the probability density function again, as in Figure 3.8(b), and shade the desired area. From this figure, you should see two triangles: the bigger triangle with base from 0 to .75, and the smaller triangle with base from 0 to .25. It should be apparent that the desired probability represented by the shaded area is the difference between the areas of the bigger and smaller triangles. Since their heights are 1.5 and .5, respectively, their areas are $(\frac{1}{2})(.75)(1.5) = .5625$ and $(\frac{1}{2})(.25)(.5) = .0625$. Thus, the desired probability is

$$P(.25 \leq X \leq .75) = P(X \leq .75) - P(X \leq .25) = .5625 - .0625 = .5$$

(c) To compute the probability that X takes on values in excess of .75, it is important to realize that "in excess of .75" and "at most .75" are complementary events. We have just seen that $P(X \leq .75) = .5625$. Thus, using the probability rule for complementary events, we have $P(X > .75) = 1 - P(X \leq .75) = 1 - .5625 = .4375$. Notice here that since X is a continuous random variable, $P(X = x) = 0$ for any unique value x. In other words, $P(X > .75) = P(X \geq .75)$ because $P(X = .75) = 0$.

The Cumulative Distribution Function of a Continuous Random Variable

In Example 3.6, we determined the probabilities that the random variable X took on values less than or equal to .25 and less than or equal to .75. In both cases, the probabilities were the areas under the graph of the density function, bounded below by the horizontal axis and on the right by the particular value of X (either .25 or .75). This kind of a probability—in which we compute the portion of the total area from the smallest value of X up to some particular value on the right—is used extensively in later chapters.

To generalize, let's consider a random variable X that can take on any value over the range $-\infty$ to $+\infty$. (For example, think of the random variable X_5—the percentage increase or decrease in a company's profit compared to the previous year—discussed in Section 3.4.) The probability that X takes on values less than or equal to some particular value x is given by the expression

$$F(x) = P(X \le x)$$

where $F(x)$ is known as the **cumulative distribution function** of the continuous random variable X and is read "the probability of X taking on values less than or equal to x." The cumulative distribution function $F(x)$ represents the portion of the area under the graph of the density function $f(x)$ that is bounded on the right by the value x, as illustrated in Figure 3.9. It is important to notice that the particular value x is a **quantile** value, since the area to the *left* of it represents the probability that the random variable takes on values less than or equal to x.

Figure 3.9

The cumulative distribution depicted as an area under the density function

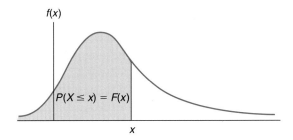

The use of calculus is beyond the scope of this text, but we point out that with calculus it is possible in some cases to determine the cumulative distribution function of a continuous random variable. To illustrate, the cumulative distribution function of Example 3.6, where $f(x) = 2x$, turns out to be (using calculus)

$$P(X \le x) = F(x) = x^2$$

Therefore, as we showed in Example 3.6,

$$P(X \le .25) = F(.25) = (.25)^2 = .0625$$

and

$$P(X \le .75) = F(.75) = (.75)^2 = .5625$$

From this illustration, it is possible to infer some important properties of a cumulative distribution function. Notice, for example, that since $.25 < .75$, $F(.25) < F(.75)$. In general, *as we move in a rightward direction, the quantile value increases and, thus, the portion of the total area to the left of the quantile value can never decrease.* Notice also that, as before,

$$P(.25 \le X \le .75) = F(.75) - F(.25) = .5625 - .0625 = .5$$

In general, suppose two points a and b define the interval of interest for a continuous random variable X such that $a < b$. Then the statements in the following box are essential properties of the cumulative distribution function of the continuous random variable X:

TWO ESSENTIAL PROPERTIES OF THE CUMULATIVE DISTRIBUTION FUNCTION $F(x)$

1.
$$F(a) \leq F(b) \quad \text{if } a < b \qquad (3.4)$$

That is, if a is less than b, then the probability that X takes on values that are less than a cannot be greater than the probability that X takes on values that are less than b.

2.
$$P(a \leq X \leq b) = F(b) - F(a) \qquad (3.5)$$

That is, the probability that X takes on values that lie between a and b is found by subtracting the probability that X takes on values that lie below a from the probability that X takes on values that lie below b.

3.7 Expected Values of Random Variables

In this section, we discuss numerical measures that summarize random variables and their probability distributions, much as we did in Chapter 2 to summarize data sets through numerical descriptions such as the mean, variance, and standard deviation.

When we consider random variables and their probability distributions, numerical measures such as the mean and variance are based on an important concept known as *expected value*. The notion of the expected value of a random variable has its roots in games of chance because gamblers wanted to know what they could "expect" to win, on average, upon repeated playing of a game. In this sense, the expected value means the average amount a gambler stands to win or lose per play over a very long series of plays. This meaning holds true with regard to any random variable. The **expected value** of a random variable is the mean of the values of the random variable over many repetitions of the experiment that defines the random variable. In other words, *the expected value is the long-run average value of the random variable*.

The concept of expected value is very useful as an aid to decision making. For example, let's analyze the following game of chance. Suppose you are given a balanced coin with which you have up to three chances to toss heads. The game ends as soon as you toss heads or after three attempts, whichever comes first. If the first, second, or third toss is heads, you receive $2, $4, or $8, respectively. However, if you fail to toss heads in three attempts, you lose $20. Would you like to play this game? How might you objectively determine whether you should play the game? One approach is to see how you would fare in the long run if you played the game many times—that is, find the expected value.

To determine the expected value, the long-run average gain or loss, let X represent the amount we win or lose any time we play the game. The possible values of X are $2, $4, $8, and –$20. The probability of the first value is the same as the probability of tossing heads, which is $\frac{1}{2}$. The probability of winning $4 is the same as the probability of tossing tails first and then tossing heads. These two events are statistically independent, so the probability of "tails and heads" is $(\frac{1}{2})(\frac{1}{2}) = \frac{1}{4}$. By continuing this approach, we determine the remaining two probabilities to be $\frac{1}{8}$ and $\frac{1}{8}$, respectively. Thus, the possible values of the random variable X and their probabilities are as follows:

Values of X	Sequences	Probabilities
2	H	$P(X = 2) \quad = \frac{1}{2}$
4	T, H	$P(X = 4) \quad = \frac{1}{4}$
8	T, T, H	$P(X = 8) \quad = \frac{1}{8}$
−20	T, T, T	$P(X = -20) = \frac{1}{8}$

Notice that the sum of these probabilities equals 1, as it must for any discrete probability distribution.

We can interpret this information in the following manner. First, recall from Section 3.3.1 that the probability of an event can be interpreted as the relative frequency with which the event occurs *in the long run.* Therefore, in the long run we expect to win $2 about once in every two tries, to win $4 about once in four tries, to win $8 about once in eight tries, and to lose $20 about once in eight tries.

The long-run average amount won or lost can be determined by weighting each amount we stand to win or lose by the corresponding probability and determining a *weighted average* of the possible values of X. That is precisely what the expected value of X is. By multiplying each amount we stand to win or lose by the probability of winning or losing that amount and adding the results, we obtain a weighted average. This weighted average represents the average amount that we win (or lose) in the long run. For the example, the expected value of X turns out to be

$$(\$2)\left(\frac{1}{2}\right) + (\$4)\left(\frac{1}{4}\right) + (\$8)\left(\frac{1}{8}\right) + (-\$20)\left(\frac{1}{8}\right) = \$.50$$

which means that *if we play this game many, many times, we expect to win $.50 per game, on the average.*

Notice that the expected value of $.50 is not one of the possible values of the random variable. It does not have to be because it represents the long-run *average* value of X. For this reason, "expected value" is somewhat of a misnomer, since it may actually be impossible for X to equal its *expected value* on any single observation of X!

In games of chance in which the random variable represents the amount won or lost, the game is said to be **fair** if the expected value of the random variable is 0. If the expected value is positive, you are assured to win in the long run. If it is negative, you will lose in the long run. Be assured that in gambling casinos, the players do not have positive expected values.

The preceding illustration suggests the following mathematical definition of the expected value of a discrete random variable:

> The **expected value** of a discrete random variable X, written as $E(X)$ and read as "the expected value of the random variable X," is given by the weighted average
>
> $$E(X) = \sum_{\text{all } x} xP(x) \tag{3.6}$$
>
> where the probability function $P(x)$ provides the weights associated with the possible values of X.

The preceding definition of expected value applies only to discrete random variables. What if X is continuous? The expected value of a *continuous* random variable is also the long-run average value of the random variable. In substance, the definition is the same as that for a discrete variable with an integral replacing the summation and the probability density function replacing the probability function. Because integral calculus is involved in the definition, we give the formal definition for the expected value of a continuous random variable in the appendix to this chapter. Since $E(X)$ is the long-run average value of any random variable X, it is also common to use the symbol μ to represent the expected value. Thus, the symbols μ and $E(X)$ are considered interchangeable.

The concept of expected value has applications in many industries and especially in the insurance industry. Have you ever wondered how an insurance premium is determined? Most likely you know that a young adult male has to pay so much more for automobile insurance because young adult males as a group have higher accident probabilities than other drivers. In simple terms, an insurance company determines the empirical probabilities of various claim amounts for a category of drivers (such as "young adult male"). Such probabilities are based on historical information, which is periodically updated. By letting the random variable X represent the gain or loss to the company over a given period of time, the company determines a break-even premium for which the expected value of X is 0 (making it a fair game). This means that the average gain or loss for a large number of customers is 0. Of course, the company adds fixed costs and a profit margin to the break-even premium to determine the final premium. The following two examples illustrate the use of the expected value in insurance and financial situations.

EXAMPLE 3.7

An insurance company wishes to determine the annual break-even premium for a $100,000 term life insurance policy for a 25-year-old man. From actuarial tables, the insurance company knows that about three out of 10,000 25-year-olds die before their 26th birthday. What is the break-even premium?

Solution

Let m be the desired break-even premium, and let X be the random variable representing the gain or loss to the company on an individual policy. There are two possible values of X: the premium m, which the company will gain if the person survives, and the loss $m - 100,000$, which the company will incur if the person dies. If three out of 10,000 die within the year, the probability of the loss $m - 100,000$ is .0003. Alternatively, if 9,997 out of 10,000 survive the year, the probability of the gain m is .9997. To determine the break-even premium m, we set the expected value of X to zero and solve for m:

$$E(X) = (m)(.9997) + [(m - 100,000)(.0003)] = 0$$

$$.9997m + .0003m - 30 = 0$$

$$m = \$30$$

Therefore, to break even, the company should charge such a person a $30 annual premium for $100,000 of term life insurance. To cover fixed costs and make a profit, the company must charge more than $30.

EXAMPLE 3.8

An investor has $100,000 available for a 1-year investment. The investor is weighing two options: a money market fund that guarantees a fixed annual rate of return of 6% and an investment plan with an annual rate of return that can be regarded as a random variable with values that depend on prevailing economic conditions. Based on the second plan's past history under a variety of economic conditions, a reliable analyst has subjectively determined the following probabilities associated with several possible rates of return:

Rate of Return:	.16	.12	.10	.08	.06	−.02	−.04
Probability:	.25	.20	.25	.10	.10	.05	.05

Which investment plan should be selected, if the choice is to be made based on the expected value of the rate of return?

Solution

If the money market fund is selected, the return on an investment of $100,000 will be $6,000, because the rate is fixed at 6%. For the second plan, let the random variable X be the rate of return. The possible values of X and their probabilities are listed in the table. The expected value works out to be

$$E(X) = (.16)(.25) + (.12)(.20) + (.10)(.25) + (.08)(.10) + (.06)(.10) +$$
$$(-.02)(.05) + (-.04)(.05) = .10$$

Thus, the second plan is the better choice because the expected rate of return is 10%, yielding to the investor an expected return of $(.10)(100,000) = \$10,000$. However, some risk is incurred with this option. The return of $10,000 is only an *expected value;* the investor has no guarantee that the actual return will exceed that of the money market fund. In fact, there is a .10 probability that a loss is incurred (the rate of return is negative).

The Variance and Standard Deviation of a Random Variable

In Example 3.8, we saw that the expected value of the second plan exceeded the guaranteed rate of return of a money market fund. Nevertheless, some investors would choose the money market fund because the return rate is entirely predictable. When there is risk involved, we need to know more than the expected value, because the expected value of a random variable measures only the central tendency of the values of the random variable and says nothing about the variation among the values. For that we need a measure of variation such as the variance. Our approach here parallels the discussion in Chapter 2 when we sought to measure the variation of the values in a data set. In this case, we seek to measure the variation of the values of a random variable that would occur in the long run. We define the variance of a discrete random variable X as follows:

The **variance** of X, written as Var(X), is the expected value of the squared difference between the random variable and its average μ. It is given by

$$\text{Var}(X) = E(X - \mu)^2 = \sum_{\text{all } x} (x - \mu)^2 P(x) \qquad \textbf{(3.7)}$$

where the probability function $P(x)$ provides the weights associated with the corresponding squared differences.

As indicated by this definition, the variance also involves the notion of expected value. The same holds true for the variance of a continuous random variable whose definition (given in the appendix to this chapter) is, in substance, the same. You can think of the variance as measuring the variation among the values of a random variable in the same way that the expected value is the long-run average of these values.

The variance is determined by computing a weighted average of the squared deviations of the values of X from the mean, where each squared deviation is weighted by its corresponding probability. You can also think of the variance of a random variable as a measure of the spread in the probability distribution of the random variable. For example, in the continuous case, if most of the area depicted by the probability density function lies close to the mean, the variance is small; if the area is spread out, the variance is large.

As in Chapter 2, *the square root of the variance is the standard deviation* σ. Although σ^2 and σ are nearly universal symbols for the variance and standard deviation of a random variable, respectively, we often use the designations **Var(X)** for the variance and **SD(X)** for the standard deviation of the random variable X.

EXAMPLE 3.9

With reference to Example 3.8, determine the variance and standard deviation of the second plan's rate of return.

Solution

Recall that the expected value of the rate of return is $\mu = .1$. The step-by-step determination of the variance is given in the following table:

Rate of Return, x	$x - \mu$	$(x - \mu)^2$	Probability, $P(x)$	$(x - \mu)^2 P(x)$
.16	$(.16 - .1) = .06$	.0036	.25	$(.0036)(.25) = .00090$
.12	$(.12 - .1) = .02$	.0004	.20	$(.0004)(.20) = .00008$
.10	$(.10 - .1) = .00$	.0000	.25	$(.0000)(.25) = .00000$
.08	$(.08 - .1) = -.02$	.0004	.10	$(.0004)(.10) = .00004$
.06	$(.06 - .1) = -.04$	.0016	.10	$(.0016)(.10) = .00016$
−.02	$(-.02 - .1) = -.12$	.0144	.05	$(.0144)(.05) = .00072$
−.04	$(-.04 - .1) = -.14$	.0196	.05	$(.0196)(.05) = .00098$
				$\overline{.00288}$

$$\sigma^2 = \text{Var}(X) = \sum (x - \mu)^2 P(x) = .00288$$

Since $\text{Var}(X) = .00288$, $\sigma = \text{SD}(X) = \sqrt{.00288} = .05367$.

EXAMPLE 3.10

With reference to Example 3.8, suppose there were a third investment plan with return rates and associated probabilities as follows:

Rate of Return:	.12	.10	.08	−.04
Probability:	.50	.30	.15	.05

Between the second and third investment plans, which would you select?

Solution

The expected value of the third plan works out to be the same as that for the second plan; that is,

$$E(X) = (.12)(.50) + (.10)(.30) + (.08)(.15) + (-.04)(.05) = .10$$

The step-by-step computation for the variance of the third plan using Expression (3.7) is given in the following table:

x	$x - \mu$	$(x - \mu)^2$	$P(x)$	$(x - \mu)^2 P(x)$
.12	$(.12 - .1) = .02$	.0004	.50	$(.0004)(.50) = .00020$
.10	$(.10 - .1) = .00$	.0000	.30	$(0)(.30) = 0$
.08	$(.08 - .1) = -.02$	.0004	.15	$(.0004)(.15) = .00006$
-.04	$(-.04 - .1) = -.14$	.0196	.05	$(.0196)(.05) = .00098$
				Sum = .00124

Thus for the third plan, $\text{Var}(X) = .00124$ and $\text{SD}(X) = .0352$. As a result, the third plan is a better choice, since its standard deviation is about one-third less than that for the second plan ($.05367$), while their expected values are the same. In other words, there is less variation and thus less risk for the third than for the second plan.

3.8

Summary

In this chapter, we explored the fundamental aspects of probability, random variables, and probability distributions.

A probability is a number between 0 and 1 that measures the likelihood of occurrence of a phenomenon whose outcomes are not perfectly predictable. The understanding of probability is important because it measures uncertainty. There are three interpretations of probability: classical, relative frequency, and subjective assessment. The classical interpretation is based on the idea that chance outcomes are equally likely and mutually exclusive. The relative frequency interpretation applies to phenomena that can be repeated many times under essentially the same conditions. The subjective assessment interpretation represents a subjective degree of belief about an unpredictable phenomenon.

A random variable is any numerical quantity whose value is determined by chance. There are two types of random variables: discrete (the possible values can be listed) and continuous (the possible values cannot be listed). The probability distribution of a random variable is a representation of the probabilities for all possible values of the random variable. If a random variable is discrete, there exists a probability function that is used to determine the probability for each possible value of the random variable. If a random variable is continuous, there exists a probability density function that provides the means to determine the probability that the random variable lies in a given interval.

Numerical quantities that are used to summarize random variables and their probability distributions are based on a concept known as expected value. The expected value of a random variable is the long-run mean of the values of the random variable. The variance of a random variable is the expected value of the squared difference between the random variable and its mean.

EXERCISES FOR SECTION 3.2

3.1 What is the purpose of a random experiment? Provide an example of a random experiment.

3.2 What do we call the set of all possible simple events of a random experiment? For your example in Exercise 3.1, list the possible simple events.

3.3 What do we call a set of simple events of a random experiment that possess a common characteristic? Identify such a set for your example in Exercise 3.1.

3.4 What do we call two events that contain no common simple events and together exhaust all possible simple events of a random experiment? Identify two such events for your example in Exercise 3.1.

3.5 For the following random experiments, identify the sample space and list the possible simple events.
   (a) A six-sided die is tossed.
   (b) Three coins are tossed.

3.6 With respect to part (b) of Exercise 3.5, list the simple events included in the following events:
   (a) At least one head
   (b) At most one tail

(c) At most one head
(d) Exactly two heads
(e) Exactly two tails

3.7 Shares of stock in three companies A, B, and C are purchased by an investor. Assume that after 1 year, the value of the stocks will be either higher or lower than the purchase price.
   (a) With regard to the price after 1 year, list all possible outcomes.
   (b) List the simple events of the event "exactly two stocks are higher."
   (c) List the simple events of the event "at least two stocks are higher."
   (d) List the simple events of the event "at most two stocks are higher."
   (e) List the simple events of the event "exactly one stock is higher."

3.8 With respect to Exercise 3.6, identify and list the simple events of:
   (a) The complement of the event in part (a)
   (b) The complement of the event in part (c)

EXERCISES FOR SECTION 3.3

3.9 Explain what a probability is.

3.10 Compare and contrast the three interpretations of probability.

3.11 Identify the interval that a probability must always lie within and interpret the extremes of this interval.

3.12 Explain why the probability of the certain event equals 1.

3.13 Explain the difference between statistically independent and statistically dependent events.

3.14 Explain the difference between sampling with replacement and sampling without replacement in the context of Exercise 3.13.

3.15 A balanced six-sided die is tossed.
   (a) What is the probability that the number 5 will come up?
   (b) What is the probability that the number that comes up will be even?
   (c) What approach to probability are you using in answering these questions? Why?

3.16 From a well-shuffled deck of playing cards, a card is drawn.
   (a) What is the probability that it is a spade?
   (b) What is the probability that it is a face card?
   (c) Is the approach being used to answer parts (a) and (b) the same as that used in Exercise 3.15? Explain.

3.17 On a typical day, an office manager observed that out of 80 telephone calls received by the office, 25 callers could not be helped immediately and were asked to hold.
   (a) Based on this information, what is the probability that you would be asked to hold if you were to call this office?
   (b) What approach to probability are you using in arriving at your answer? Explain.

3.18 In a typical week, a gift shop owner observed that out of 400 customers who entered the shop, 280 eventually bought something.
   (a) Based on this information, what is the probability that a person entering this shop will buy something?
   (b) What approach to probability did you use in part (a)? Explain.

3.19 You are advised by a stockbroker that the chances of a particular stock increasing in value during the next month are 3 in 5.
   (a) What is the probability that the stock will increase in value during the next month?
   (b) What approach to probability are you using to arrive at your answer in part (a)? Explain.

3.20 A famous odds-maker has established the chances of the San Francisco 49ers winning this year's Super Bowl as 3 in 10.

(a) What is the probability that this team will win the Super Bowl?

(b) What approach to probability are you using to arrive at your answer in part (a)? Explain.

3.21 Using a tree diagram, list the possible simple events with respect to gender of families with four children; then consider the following specific events:

A: at least three boys
B: all the same gender

(a) Name the complement of event *A* and determine its probability.

(b) Name the complement of event *B* and determine its probability.

3.22 This interesting probability question was posed in a letter written by a reader of *Parade* magazine ("Ask Marilyn," *Parade,* March 31, 1996). Suppose you have two pairs of shoes in your closet, one red pair and one black pair. If you select two shoes randomly, what is the probability that both will be the same color? The writer proposed a possible solution and asked whether it was correct: "There are four possible simple events, both red, both black, first red then black, first black then red. Since two of the four outcomes yield a pair of the same color, the answer is $\frac{2}{4} = \frac{1}{2}$."

(a) The proposed solution is incorrect. Why?

(b) What is your solution?

3.23 Two service stations cooperate by sharing their tow trucks. If one receives a request for towing while its tow truck is in service, it borrows the other's tow truck. Thus, each has the equivalent of two tow trucks as long as the other's tow truck is not being used. A study of the usage of the tow trucks indicates that each is in service one-fourth of the time and that demand is uniform throughout the day.

(a) Suppose a customer requests towing from service station A. What is the probability that that station's tow truck is available?

(b) What approach to probability did you use in part (a)?

(c) What is the probability that both tow trucks are available when a customer requests towing? Justify your answer.

(d) What is the probability that neither tow truck is available when a customer requests towing? Justify your answer.

(e) What is the probability that at least one of the tow trucks is available when a customer requests towing? Justify your answer.

(f) How much does the cooperative arrangement increase the probability that a tow truck will be available when a customer requests towing?

3.24 Clinical trials are carefully controlled medical experiments that enable researchers to learn about the effectiveness of various treatments. One study involved 668 patients who suffered from large-cell lymphoma. Out of 668 who received an aggressive type of chemotherapy, 455 survived at least 5 years.

(a) What does the study indicate is the probability of surviving more than 5 years for a patient with this form of disease who receives the aggressive chemotherapy treatment?

(b) What approach to probability did you use in part (a)?

(c) Is your answer to part (a) the true probability or an estimate? Explain.

(d) Suppose a person diagnosed with large-cell lymphoma has been told that the disease was detected unusually early. Does your probability in part (a) apply to this person?

3.25 In the 1990 World Series, odds-makers announced that the Oakland Athletics were 3-to-1 favorites to win the championship. (The winner is the first team to win four games.) However, the Cincinnati Reds won the first two games. In 86 previous World Series, one team jumped out to a 2–0 lead on 40 occasions. On 30 of those occasions, the team with the early lead went on to win. Use this information to answer the following questions:

(a) At the outset of the Series, what was the probability that the Reds would win, according to the odds-makers?

(b) What approach to probability was used by the odds-makers?

(c) Based on the information given, what is the estimated probability that one team wins the first two games of a World Series?

(d) What approach to probability is used in part (c)?

(e) After the Reds won the first two games, what was the estimated probability that they would go on to win the World Series?

(f) What approach to probability is used in part (e)?

3.26 In baseball, a .300 batting average has been a long-time standard of excellence for hitting. A ".300 hitter" averages 3 base hits per 10 official at-bats (i.e., not counting walks, sacrifices, and being hit by a pitch) in the long run. Thus, the probability of a base hit is .3 in any one at-bat.

(a) Determine the probability that a .300 hitter gets no hits if he bats four times (officially) in a game. Assume the outcomes of these times at bat are statistically independent.

(b) Suppose you are completely unfamiliar with a hitter. The first time you see him play, he goes hitless in four times at bat. Based on your result in part (a), can you be reasonably certain that he is less than a .300 hitter?

3.27 The following table provides the number of on-time and late arrivals by two airlines at each of two airports.

	Airline A			Airline B		
Location	On time	Late	Number of Flights	On time	Late	Number of Fllights
Atlanta	185	15	200	1,750	250	2,000
Seattle	1,650	350	2,000	150	50	200
Overall	1,835	365	2,200	1,900	300	2,200

(a) For each airline, determine the empirical probability that a randomly selected flight into Atlanta is on time. Repeat for Seattle. Based on these results, which airline appears to be more likely to get you to either one of these destinations on time?

(b) Between these two airlines, which one can claim to deliver the higher overall proportion of on-time flights?

(c) Explain the apparent contradiction between your results in parts (a) and (b).

3.28 The manager of a small insurance agency was considering the mailing of printed ads prior to calling to set appointments for insurance proposals. The potential customer base consisted of registered owners of boats in her county. To evaluate the effectiveness of the mailed ads, she performed an experiment as follows. She identified random samples of 50 boat owners whom she knew (warm contacts) and 50 whom she did not know (cold contacts). From each group, she sent an introductory mailed ad to 25 (selected randomly) and none to the other 25. She then called each person and attempted to set an appointment for an insurance proposal. The results* are given in the following table.

*Courtesy of Bernadette Hendrix.

	Warm Contact			Cold Contact		
	Appt.	No Appt.	Total	Appt.	No Appt.	Total
Mailer & Call	17	8	25	8	17	25
Call Only	11	14	25	4	21	25
Total	28	22	50	12	38	50

(a) Assuming these data accurately represent the population of boat owners, estimate the probability of getting an appointment from (1) warm contacts after sending an introductory mailer ad; (2) cold contacts after sending an introductory mailer ad; (3) warm contacts without sending an introductory mailer ad; (4) cold contacts without sending an introductory mailer ad.

(b) If she attempts to set up an appointment with a cold contact, is the probability of a success independent of whether she sends an introductory mailer ad?

(c) If she attempts to set up an appointment with a warm contact, is the probability of a success independent of whether she sends an introductory mailer ad? Justify your answer. If dependent, describe the nature of the dependence.

3.29 A study of high school sports injuries resulted in the following data for random sample of athletes from four sports.

	Number of Players Injured	Total Number of Players
Football	50	642
Soccer	36	558
Baseball	25	449
Basketball	42	588

(a) Determine the probability of being injured for a randomly selected player from each sport.

(b) Do these data show that being injured is statistically independent of the sport? Justify your answer.

EXERCISES FOR SECTION 3.4

3.30 Explain the difference between discrete and continuous random variables.

3.31 For your example of a random experiment in Exercise 3.1, define a random variable, state whether it is discrete or continuous, and identify its possible values.

3.32 For each of the following chance-related tasks, define an appropriate random variable, state whether the random variable is discrete or continuous, and identify the possible values that the random variable can take on.

(a) Selling insurance policies in a given time period

(b) Taking an examination consisting of 50 true–false questions

(c) How long you will study for this course next week

(d) The number of A's you may receive in the 42 courses needed for some undergraduate degree

(e) The proportion of students who are nonsmokers in this class

(f) The difference between one's weight and the average weight for that person's height (Assume the range is −50 to 150 pounds.)

3.33 Repeat Exercise 3.32 for the following tasks:

(a) Number of home runs a baseball player hits in a game (Assume five times at bat.)

(b) How long the water pump in one's new car will last

(c) How much gasoline will be pumped into a randomly selected automobile at a service station (Assume a 25-gallon maximum.)

(d) Number of tax returns that are found to contain errors among 500 randomly selected returns this year

(e) Proportion of units found to be defective in a production process

(f) Defective units found among 100 randomly selected units from a production process

EXERCISES FOR SECTION 3.5

3.34 What is the purpose of the probability function of a discrete random variable?

3.35 State and explain the conditions that a probability function must meet.

3.36 With reference to Example 3.2, define the random variable X to be the number of boys in a three-child family.

(a) Determine the possible values of X and their probabilities.

(b) What is the probability of at least one boy? At most two boys?

(c) Graph the probability distribution of X.

3.37 Explain whether each of the following is a probability distribution of the discrete random variable X.

(a)

x	$P(x)$
−2	.1
−1	.2
0	.4
1	.2
2	.1

(b)

x	$P(x)$
0	.4
1	.3
2	.1
3	.1

(c)

x	$P(x)$
−4	.2
0	1.2
4	−.4
8	0

(d)

x	$P(x)$
−2	.4
−1	.2
0	.1
1	.2
2	.1

3.38 An insurance salesperson normally sees five potential customers per day. Define the random variable X to be the number of persons who buy insurance in one day, and assume the probability function of X is

$$P(x) = \frac{5!}{(5-x)! \, x!} (.1)^x (.9)^{5-x}$$

where $x = 0, 1, 2, 3, 4, 5$

(a) Determine the probability for each value of X and graph the probability distribution.

(b) What is the probability that the salesperson will sell at least one policy in a day?

(c) What is the probability that the salesperson will sell at most one policy in a day?

(d) Use Expression (3.3) to determine the probability that the salesperson will make exactly one sale during the day.

3.39 Repeat Exercise 3.38 if the salesperson visits eight potential customers per day and the probability function is now

$$P(x) = \frac{8!}{(8-x)! \, x!} (.1)^x (.9)^{8-x}$$

where $x = 0, 1, \ldots, 8$

3.40 Based on extensive observation, the probability distribution of the number of customers who arrive at a convenience store in a 5-minute interval is as follows:

x:	0	1	2	3	4	5
$P(x)$:	.01	.04	.10	.12	.16	.20

x:	6	7	8	9	10
$P(x)$:	.17	.08	.07	.04	.01

(a) Graph the probability distribution.

(b) Determine the cumulative probability distribution.

(c) Determine the probability that at least three customers will arrive during a 5-minute interval.

(d) Use Expression (3.3) to verify that the probability of exactly four customers arriving in a 5-minute interval is .16.

3.41 Based on extensive observation, an airline has determined that the probability distribution of the number of seats it overbooks on a popular route is as follows:

x:	0	1	2	3	4	5	6
P(x):	.05	.10	.20	.25	.20	.15	.05

(a) Determine the cumulative probability distribution.
(b) What is the probability of overbooking at least four seats?
(c) What is the probability of no overbooking?
(d) Use Expression (3.3) to verify that the probability of exactly three seats overbooked is .25.

EXERCISES FOR SECTION 3.6

3.42 What is the probability of a continuous random variable taking on any specific value? Explain.

3.43 Explain the essential difference between a probability function of a discrete random variable and a probability density function of a continuous random variable.

3.44 Given the probability density function, explain how we view the probability that the random variable takes on values in a specific interval.

3.45 By using geometry, show whether the given functions are probability density functions of a continuous random variable X.
(a) $f(x) = x/4, \quad 0 \leq x \leq 2$
(b) $f(x) = x/50, 0 \leq x \leq 10$

3.46 Suppose the probability density function of a continuous random variable X is
$$f(x) = \frac{x}{2} \quad \text{where } 0 \leq x \leq 2$$
By using geometry, determine the following probabilities:
(a) The probability that X takes on values greater than 1
(b) The probability that X takes on values less than $\frac{1}{2}$
(c) The probability that X takes on values in the interval $\left(\frac{1}{2}, 1\right)$
(d) What is the probability that X is exactly equal to 1? Why?
(e) What is the probability that X takes on values greater than 3?

3.47 Suppose the probability density function of a continuous random variable X is
$$f(x) = \frac{1}{8} \quad \text{where } -2 \leq x \leq 6$$

By using geometry, answer the following questions:
(a) What is the probability that X takes on values less than 0?
(b) What is the probability that X takes on values greater than 4?
(c) What is the probability that X takes on values in the interval (0, 4)?

3.48 Suppose the probability density function of a continuous random variable X is
$$f(x) = \frac{1}{2} \quad \text{where } 0 \leq x \leq 2$$
By using geometry, determine the following probabilities:
(a) The probability that X takes on values in the interval $\left(\frac{1}{2}, \frac{3}{2}\right)$
(b) The probability that X takes on values less than $\frac{1}{2}$
(c) The probability that X takes on values greater than $\frac{3}{2}$

3.49 Suppose the cumulative distribution function of the random variable in Exercise 3.47 is
$$F(x) = \frac{x+2}{8} \quad \text{where } -2 \leq x \leq 6$$
Use the properties of the cumulative distribution function given at the end of Section 3.6 to affirm your answers to the questions in Exercise 3.47.

3.50 Suppose the cumulative distribution function of the random variable in Exercise 3.46 is
$$F(x) = \frac{x^2}{4} \quad \text{where } 0 \leq x \leq 2$$
Use the properties of the cumulative distribution function to affirm your answers to parts (a)–(c) of Exercise 3.46.

EXERCISES FOR SECTION 3.7

3.51 Explain what the expected value of a random variable represents.

3.52 Does knowledge of the expected value of a random

variable provide information about the variation of the values of the random variable? Explain.

3.53 With reference to Exercise 3.36, determine:

(a) The expected value of the number of boys in three-child families

(b) The variance and the standard deviation

3.54 With reference to Exercise 3.41, determine:

(a) The expected value of the number of over-booked seats

(b) The variance and the standard deviation

3.55 With reference to Exercise 3.38, determine:

(a) The expected value of the number of persons who buy insurance in one day

(b) The variance and the standard deviation

3.56 Based on historical records, the probability distribution for claims paid by an insurance company under the comprehensive auto insurance portion is as follows:

Claim	Probability
$ 0	.880
200	.050
500	.030
1,000	.020
2,000	.010
5,000	.005
10,000	.005

If the insurance company charges an annual premium of $200 for the comprehensive portion, what is the average profit to the company for the comprehensive portion based on the expected value criterion?

3.57 An insurance company that provides homeowners' coverage knows from historical records that for a $100,000 homeowner's policy in a certain area, there is a .001 probability of a total loss in a given year and a .003 probability of a 50% loss. Without regard to other partial losses, what should the company charge for an annual premium for this homeowner's policy to break even?

3.58 An investor has $10,000 available for a 1-year investment. The investor is considering the following three options:

• Option A: 30% return with probability .5
   no return with probability .1
   10% loss with probability .4

• Option B: 50% return with probability .2
   20% return with probability .5
   no return with probability .1
   40% loss with probability .2

• Option C: a guaranteed return of 9%

(a) Based on the expected return, which of these options should the investor choose?

(b) Compute the standard deviations for options A and B.

SUPPLEMENTARY EXERCISES

3.59 Two cards are drawn without replacement from an ordinary deck of playing cards. What is the probability that both are aces?

3.60 Suppose the probability of a share of stock rising in value at the end of a trading day is .5.

(a) If we assume a rise or a fall only and assume these to be independent, determine the probability that this stock will rise for five consecutive trading days.

(b) What do you see as fundamentally flawed here?

3.61 A balanced coin is tossed ten times and all ten tosses yield heads. What is the probability of such an occurrence? If the coin is indeed balanced, what is the probability that the 11th toss will be tails?

3.62 The probability that a certain electrical component will work is .9. A machine contains two such components. The machine will operate as long as at least one of these components works.

(a) Regarding whether these two components work or not, what are the possible simple events and their respective probabilities? (You may assume independence of operation between these components.)

(b) What is the probability that the machine will operate?

3.63 Let the random variable X be the number of phone calls received by an office during a 5-minute interval and assume that the probability function of X is

$$P(x) = \frac{e^{-3}(3)^x}{x!}$$

where $x = 0, 1, 2, \ldots$; $e = 2.7182 \ldots$

(a) Determine the probabilities that X takes on the values $0, 1, 2, \ldots, 7$.

(b) Graph the probability function for these values of X.

(c) Determine the cumulative probability distribution for these values.

3.64 Based on information obtained from a large number of insurance companies about term life insurance for 30-year-old men, it was determined that the annual premium for a $50,000 policy is a continuous random variable with probability density function

$$f(x) = \frac{1}{80} \quad \text{where } \$100 \le x \le \$180$$

By using geometry, answer the following questions:
(a) Show that $f(x)$ is indeed a probability density function.
(b) What is the probability that the annual premium is less than $120?
(c) What is the probability that the annual premium is between $120 and $160?
(d) What is the probability that the annual premium exceeds $160?

3.65 The market share (as a proportion of total) of a large corporation's main product fluctuates randomly. Let the continuous random variable X be the market share for this product and assume the probability density function is

$$f(x) = 2(1 - x) \quad \text{where } 0 \le x \le 1$$

By using geometry, answer the following questions:
(a) What is the probability that the market share is less than $\frac{1}{2}$?
(b) What is the probability that the market share exceeds $\frac{1}{2}$?
(c) What is the probability that the market share is in the interval $(\frac{1}{2}, \frac{3}{4})$?
(d) What is the probability that the market share is less than $\frac{1}{4}$?

3.66 Suppose the cumulative distribution function of the market share in Exercise 3.65 is

$$F(x) = x(2 - x) \quad \text{where } 0 \le x \le 1$$

Use the properties of the cumulative distribution function given at the end of Section 3.6 to affirm your answers to the questions in Exercise 3.65.

3.67 Consider the following game of chance. You randomly select a ball from a box that contains two red balls, four green balls, and four white balls. If the ball selected is red, you win $20; if it is green, you lose $10; and if it is white, you lose $2. If the random variable X is the amount you win or lose each time you play, determine the expected value of X. Should you play this game? Support your answer.

3.68 With reference to Exercise 3.67, how much should you win if a red ball is selected so that the game is fair?

3.69 A roulette wheel at a gambling casino has 18 red numbers, 18 black numbers, and 2 green numbers. Suppose you place a $100 bet on a red number. If a red number comes up, you win $100; if a black number comes up, you lose $100; and if a green number comes up, you lose half of your bet or $50. Define the random variable X to be the amount you win each time you play the game. Determine the expected value of X. Should you play this game? Support your answer.

3.70 Based on historical records, a rental establishment has determined that the probability distribution of the number of daily rentals (X) of a piece of equipment is as follows:

x	$P(x)$
0	.10
1	.25
2	.40
3	.20
4	.05

If the establishment charges $25 per rental, determine the expected daily income from the rentals of this equipment and the standard deviation.

3.71 Use a computer to simulate 500 plays of the roulette game in Exercise 3.69. How well does your result approximate the expected value of X?

3.72 An insurance company wishes to determine the annual break-even premium for a $500,000 term life insurance policy for a 45-year-old woman. From actuarial tables, the company knows that about 24 out of 10,000 nonsmoking 45-year-old women die before their 46th birthday, and that 48 out of 10,000 smoking 45-year-old women die before their 46th birthday. Determine the break-even premiums for nonsmoking and smoking 45-year-old women.

3.73 A system consists of three main components A, B, and C. The components could be electrical or mechanical or even three different divisions in an organization. These may be arranged in any one of the four configurations shown in the accompanying figure. If the three components operate independently, and if the probability of any one operating properly is .95, determine the probability of proper system operation for each of the four configurations, where system operation means that at least one path is open from beginning to end. Then determine which configuration is best with regard to proper system operation.

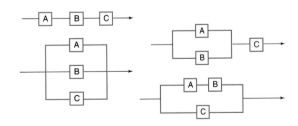

3.74 In the context of Exercise 3.73, suppose four independent components, each with .9 probability of proper operation, are arranged as shown in the figure. Determine the probability of proper system operation.

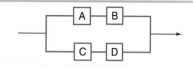

3.75 Suppose your company plans to introduce two new products, A and B. Based on test marketing results, it is believed that the probability of public acceptance for product A is .6 and that for B is .4. Assume that the acceptance of one is independent of the acceptance of the other. Determine the probability that both products fail in the marketplace.

Appendix 3

Calculus-Based Introduction to Probability Distributions for Continuous Random Variables

In this appendix, we define key concepts of Sections 3.6 and 3.7 involving *continuous* random variables using calculus. The formal definition of a probability density function of a continuous random variable is as follows:

> The function $f(x)$ is the **probability density function** of the continuous random variable X if the following conditions are true:
>
> 1. $f(x) \geq 0, \quad -\infty < x < \infty$
>
> 2. $\displaystyle\int_{-\infty}^{\infty} f(x)\, dx = 1$
>
> 3. $P(a \leq X \leq b) = \displaystyle\int_{a}^{b} f(x)\, dx \quad$ for any values a and b

As we discussed in Section 3.6, the interval $a \leq X \leq b$ is the area bounded by the density function and the points $X = a$ and $X = b$, as shown in Figure 3.7. This area represents the probability of the interval, since the total area under $f(x)$ is 1.

The cumulative distribution function of a continuous random variable X is the probability that X takes on values less than or equal to some particular x and is defined to be

$$P(X \leq x) = F(x) = \int_{-\infty}^{x} f(t)\, dt \tag{3.8}$$

where t is a dummy variable of integration. As before, the cumulative distribution function $F(x)$ is the area bounded above by the density function and on the right by the quantile value $X = x$, as illustrated in Figure 3.9. The cumulative distribution $F(x)$ is a nondecreasing function of the values of the random variable X with the following properties:

1. $F(-\infty) = 0$

2. $F(\infty) = 1$

3. $P(a < X < b) = F(b) - F(a)$

4. $\dfrac{dF(x)}{dx} = f(x)$

The property that the derivative of the cumulative distribution function is the probability density function stems from the fundamental theorem of integral calculus. We should note again that for any continuous random variable X,

$$P(X = x) = \int_x^x f(t)\, dt = 0$$

This is true because if the upper and lower limits of an integral are the same, then the value of the integral is 0. As a result,

$$P(X \le x) = P(X < x) = F(x)$$

To illustrate the preceding concepts, let's recall Example 3.6. The function $f(x) = 2x$, where $0 \le x \le 1$, is indeed a probability density function, since

$$\int_{-\infty}^{\infty} 2x\, dx = \int_0^1 2x\, dx = x^2 \Big|_0^1 = 1^2 - 0^2 = 1$$

The probability that the random variable X takes on values in the interval $(.25, .75)$ is

$$P(.25 < X < .75) = \int_{.25}^{.75} 2x\, dx = x^2 \Big|_{.25}^{.75} = (.75)^2 - (.25)^2 = .5$$

Similarly, the probability that X exceeds .75 is

$$P(X > .75) = \int_{.75}^1 2x\, dx = x^2 \Big|_{.75}^1 = 1^2 - (.75)^2 = .4375$$

Finally, the cumulative distribution function is evaluated to be

$$P(X \le x) = F(x) = \int_0^x 2t\, dt = t^2 \Big|_0^x = x^2$$

We now formally define the expected value and variance of a continuous random variable.

The **expected value** of a continuous random variable X is the average or mean value of X and is given by

$$E(X) = \int_{-\infty}^{\infty} xf(x)\,dx$$

(3.9)

where $f(x)$ is the probability density function.

The **variance** of a continuous random variable X is the expected value of the squared difference between X and its mean μ and is given by

$$Var(X) = E(X - \mu)^2 = \int_{-\infty}^{\infty} (x - \mu)^2 f(x)\,dx$$

(3.10)

To illustrate, let's again use the probability density function of Example 3.6. The expected or mean value turns out to be

$$E(X) = \int_{0}^{1} (x)(2x)\,dx = \frac{2x^3}{3}\Big|_{0}^{1} = \frac{2}{3}(1^3) - \frac{2}{3}(0^3) = \frac{2}{3}$$

The variance is determined as follows:

$$Var(X) = \int_{0}^{1} \left(x - \frac{2}{3}\right)^2 (2x)\,dx = \int_{0}^{1} \left(x^2 - \frac{4}{3}x + \frac{4}{9}\right)(2x)\,dx$$

$$= \int_{0}^{1} \left(2x^3 - \frac{8}{3}x^2 + \frac{8}{9}x\right)dx = \left[\frac{2}{4}x^4 - \frac{8}{9}x^3 + \frac{8}{18}x^2\right]\Big|_{0}^{1}$$

$$= \frac{1}{2} - \frac{8}{9} + \frac{8}{18} = \frac{9 - 16 + 8}{18} = \frac{1}{18}$$

Chapter 4

Some Important Probability Distributions

CHAPTER OUTLINE

4.1 Bridging to New Topics

In Chapter 3, we presented the basic principles of probability needed for an understanding of statistical inference. We used these principles to define the concepts of *random variable* and *probability distribution* and to develop their general properties. In this chapter, we examine two special probability distributions that have proven themselves useful in a broad range of business applications. For each distribution, we discuss the general characteristics that distinguish it from other distributions and present examples of its applications.

In Chapter 1, you learned that a population or process is usually characterized by one or more quantities known as parameters. Specifically, a parameter characterizes the probability distribution of an important variable for a population or process. In this regard, a **parameter** is a number whose particular value gives rise to a unique member of the probability distribution of interest. A parameter, therefore, is the numerical quantity that uniquely distinguishes the members of a probability distribution.

For example, recall from Section 3.5 that the probability function of the number of girls in a two-child family is

$$P(x) = \frac{2!}{(2-x)!\,x!} \left(\frac{1}{2}\right)^x \left(\frac{1}{2}\right)^{2-x} \qquad x = 0, 1, 2$$

If we assume a 50–50 chance of a girl at each birth, the probability function of the number of girls in a three-child family turns out to be

$$P(x) = \frac{3!}{(3-x)!\,x!} \left(\frac{1}{2}\right)^x \left(\frac{1}{2}\right)^{3-x} \qquad x = 0, 1, 2, 3$$

By closely comparing these two probability functions, we notice that the only difference between them is the total number of children—two in the first and three in the second. Thus, the number of children is a parameter of this probability distribution. Its value distinguishes among different members of this "family" of distributions.

Unless a parameter involves a count, we label parameters using lowercase Greek letter such as μ (mu), π (pi), and σ (sigma). For a count parameter, we use the Roman letter n. When the discussion is of a general nature with no specific probability distribution in mind, we use the Greek letter θ (theta) to designate a parameter.

The two special distributions that we discuss in this chapter are the *binomial* and *normal* distributions. The binomial is a discrete probability distribution, whereas the normal is continuous. The normal distribution is easily the most prominent distribution in the application of statistical inference.

4.2   The Binomial Distribution

The **binomial distribution** is one of the most useful discrete probability distributions. Its general areas of application include sales, marketing, opinion research, quality inspection, auditing, and many others. The binomial distribution is particularly useful in sampling when we observe a dichotomous qualitative variable—for example, male/female, sale/no sale, and so forth. For dichotomous qualitative variables, the parameter of interest is usually the proportion of elements in the population that are in one or the other category. In the insurance study (Example 1.1), for instance, two dichotomous qualitative variables were observed: gender and type of policy (universal or term). If the proportion of female customers is of interest or the proportion of term policies, then the binomial distribution becomes important in the analysis of the data.

The binomial distribution derives from the following general situation: Imagine a repetitive random experiment in which each outcome is either the occurrence or nonoccurrence of an event of interest. For example, if we toss a coin and the event of interest is heads, we either observe heads or we do not (if not heads, we observe tails). If we randomly select a unit from a production line and inspect it, we may observe the unit to be either defective or nondefective. If a sales representative makes a sales call, he either makes a sale or he does not.

In general, let's agree to label an event's occurrence a "success" and its nonoccurrence a "failure." Thus "failure" is the complement of "success." Repetitions of a random experiment under identical conditions are called **trials.** Suppose we perform an experiment n times independently and under identical conditions (that is, n independent trials). Since the sample space is precisely the same each time we perform the experiment, the probability of success is the same for every trial. Let this probability of success be denoted by π. For example, when we toss a balanced coin, the probability of heads (a "success") is $\pi = .5$ for every toss. Since the experiment can result only in a success or in a failure, it follows that the probability of failure on any trial is $1 - \pi$.

The random variable of interest, denoted by X, is the *number of successes* we observe among the n trials of the experiment. Under the conditions described, X has a binomial probability distribution. We can have no fewer than 0 successes, and we can have no more than n successes over the n trials of the experiment. Consequently, the possible values of X must be 0, 1, 2, 3, . . . , n—that is, 0 and all the integers from 1 up to the number of trials n. Suppose we toss a balanced coin $n = 10$ times and the random variable of interest is X = the number of heads we observe. The possible values of X are 0, 1, 2, . . . , 10. Since the possible values are countable, the binomial random variable X is discrete.

The characteristics that define when a random variable has a binomial distribution are summarized in the following box.

CONDITIONS UNDER WHICH A RANDOM VARIABLE HAS A BINOMIAL DISTRIBUTION

1. The experiment consists of n identical trials.
2. The outcome of each trial is either "success" or "failure."
3. The n trials are statistically independent of each other, with the probability of success π remaining the same from trial to trial.
4. The random variable X represents the number of successes.

In Chapter 3, we discussed several examples that meet the criteria for the binomial distribution. Consider the example of the two-child family. The birth of each child can be considered a trial. Each trial has only two possible outcomes: a boy or a girl. We usually assume the same probability of having a girl anytime a child is born; this probability is usually taken to be .5. In reality, it may not be exactly .5, but it is certainly very close to is. (Note that if the probability of having a girl is constant whenever a child is born, then the probability of having a boy is also constant.) For two-child families, suppose we define the random variable X to be the number of girls. Since we are counting the number of girls born, the birth of a girl is called a "success" and the birth of a boy is a "failure." The designation of "success" indicates occurrence of the outcome looked for but does not necessarily imply a *desired* outcome. The possible values of X are 0 girls, 1 girl, and 2 girls. Finally, it is reasonable to regard a couple as remaining biologically the same from the conception of one child to that of the next. If so, the gender of the first child and the gender of the second child are statistically independent. Under these conditions, X has a binomial distribution. Notice that our conclusion about the distribution of X is based on assumptions deriving from our knowledge of the subject matter—in this case, the human birth process and its relationship to gender.

Application of the Binomial Distribution in Sampling

There are many studies in which we observe the number of "successes" over a series of trials. The usual application involves sampling, either random sampling from a population or sampling consecutive items from an ongoing process. In such situations, the selection of each sampled item constitutes a trial in which the outcome is deemed either a "success" or a "failure." After the end of the trials, the variable of interest is the number of "successes." Because the number of "sucesses" follows a binomial distribution, the distribution comes into play when we wish to estimate the *proportion* of "successes" in the population. Some examples include the following:

- The proportion of customers who have purchased a particular product
- The proportion of consumers who prefer a particular brand
- The proportion of service calls attributed to a particular type of malfunction
- The proportion of college freshmen who plan to attend graduate school
- The proportion of registered voters who prefer a political candidate
- The proportion of customers who use credit to pay for purchases
- The proportion of consumers who mail in product rebates after a purchase

With respect to random sampling, the key concept of the binomial distribution is a scheme known as **sampling with replacement,** in which each item selected is returned to the population before the next item is selected. Sampling with replacement assures that the underlying sample space is precisely the same each time another outcome is observed. Consequently, the probability of success π is the same for each trial and is not affected by the outcomes of previous trials; that is, sampling with replacement leads to statistically independent events.

In practical applications, however, random sampling is done *without* replacement. **Sampling without replacement** leads to outcomes that are statistically dependent because the sample space changes from one selection to the next, thereby changing the probabilities to success with each additional selection. For example, suppose we select a sample of $n = 2$ items randomly from a population of 10 items in which 4 have the attribute of interest and 6 do not (that is, $\pi = .4$). The probability of a success on the first selection is $\frac{4}{10}$. If the first selection is a success, then the probability of a success on the second selection is $\frac{3}{9}$, because the sample space now consists of 9 remaining items, of which 3 have the attribute of interest. Alternatively, if the first selection is a failure, then the probability of a success on the second selection is $\frac{4}{9}$. This may appear to limit the practical usefulness of the binomial distribution, since it is based on sampling *with* replacement. However, most populations from which random samples are selected are large enough that changes in probability from one random selection to the next are insignificant. For example, suppose we are selecting a random sample of $n = 2$ items from a population of 1,000 items, of which 400 have the attribute of interest. Then the probability of a success on the first selection is .4 as in the previous example. On the second selection, the probability of success is either $\frac{399}{999}$ or $\frac{400}{999}$, depending on the first outcome. Such a small dependence is negligible. Using the binomial distribution in this case will result in probabilities that are correct to a very close approximation. In general, this means that *as long as the sample size n is small relative to the size of the population, the use of the binomial distribution is appropriate.* A common guideline is that the sample size n should be no more than 5% of the population size N.

Now let's consider the sampling of consecutive items from a process. The following are some examples for which the binomial distribution might be appropriate:

- We observe the number of items that fail to meet specification out of 20 consecutive items produced.
- We observe the number of successful sales calls out of the last 200 sales calls.
- We observe the number of invoices with errors out of the last 250 invoices processed.

In each of these cases, a crucial question is: Is the process that generates successes and failures stable over the period of observation? If not, then the probability of a success may not be constant over all trials or the trials may not be independent. For example, suppose a problem in generating invoices crops up halfway through the observation period. This increases the probability that an invoice will have an error, thus violating the "constant probability of success" requirement.

The probability of success π is an important quantity in many situations because it represents the proportion of items in the population or process that have an attribute of interest. But in most real applications, we do not know the value of π. For example, when we select a sample of n items from a production process, we do not know the actual proportion of defective items being produced by the process. In such a case, the purpose of sampling is to *estimate* π by observing how many of the n sampled items are defective. For instance, if 2 items were found to be defective in a sample of 10, our best estimate of π is $\frac{2}{10}$. *The estimate of π is p, the sample proportion defective,* where p equals the number of defective items (X) found in the sample divided by the total number of items (n) inspected. To understand how we make inferences about π based on p, we must first study the probability distribution of the binomial random variable (X) representing the number of defective items. The role of the binomial distribution in sampling applications is illustrated by Figure 4.1.

Figure 4.1

The role of the binomial distribution in sampling applications

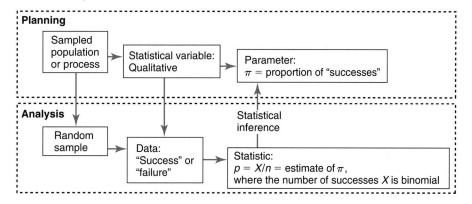

EXAMPLE 4.1

Consider the manufacture of a certain kind of automobile tire. Suppose, as a matter of routine inspection, ten tires are randomly selected, one after another without replacement, from each day's production to check for defective tires. Corrective action may be necessary if one or more of the ten tires inspected are found to be defective. Comment on the appropriateness of using the binomial distribution in this situation.

Solution

The selection of a random sample of ten tires constitutes a series of trials. If specifications are clearly defined and known in advance by the inspector, then any inspected tire can be judged to be either defective or good. The random variable of interest is the number of defective tires among the ten inspected. Any value of this random variable except 0 would cause concern. The sample proportion of defective tires provides an estimate of the proportion of defective tires produced during the entire day. Since sampling is done without replacement, there may be small changes in this proportion (probability) from one random selection to the next. But the application of the binomial distribution would be appropriate if the total number of tires produced each day is much larger than the number selected for inspection.

The Binomial Probability Function

We need to determine the probability function for the binomial distribution. Let X represent the number of successes during n independent trials such that the probability of success at each trial is π. We want to determine the probability of observing exactly x successes (and, by implication, exactly $n - x$ failures) during the n trials. Before we do this, notice that the two probability functions presented in Section 4.1, involving the number of girls in two- and three-child families, are specific examples of the binomial probability function. For convenience, we repeat the probability function for three-child families:

$$P(x) = \frac{3!}{(3 - x)!\, x!} \left(\frac{1}{2}\right)^x \left(1 - \frac{1}{2}\right)^{3-x} \qquad x = 0, 1, 2, 3$$

The parameter values are $n = 3$ and $\pi = .5$. (For two-child families, the parameter values are $n = 2$ and $\pi = .5$.) Notice that the probability $P(x)$ of having exactly x girls is the product of two factors: $\dfrac{3!}{(3 - x)!\, x!}$ and $\left(\dfrac{1}{2}\right)^x\left(1 - \dfrac{1}{2}\right)^{3-x}$. The first factor represents the number of different gender configurations that lead to exactly x girls. The second factor represents the probability of any specific gender configuration leading to exactly x girls. For example, consider the outcome "two girls among three children." The number of gender configurations with two girls and one boy among three children is $\dfrac{3!}{(3 - 2)!\, 2!} = 3$. Notice that this is the same result obtained in Figure 3.1, Section 3.2.

In general, we can infer from this example that the probability of getting exactly x successes and exactly $n - x$ failures over n trials is $P(x) = $ *the number of sequences for which the event "exactly x successes" occurs times the probability of any specific sequence resulting in exactly x successes*. How many such sequences are there? The answer is given by the expression for determining the number of permutations of n things (number of trials) in which x are alike (all are successes) and $n - x$ are alike (all are failures). This expression is as follows:

$$\frac{n!}{(n - x)!\, x!} \tag{4.1}$$

We are now ready to define the binomial probability function.

THE BINOMIAL PROBABILITY FUNCTION

Let the random variable X be the number of successes out of n independent trials such that the probability of success at each trial is π. Then X has a binomial distribution with the probability function

$$P(X = x) = P(x) = \frac{n!}{(n - x)!\, x!}\, \pi^x (1 - \pi)^{n-x} \tag{4.2}$$

$$x = 0, 1, 2, \ldots, n; \quad 0 \le \pi \le 1$$

Notice that the number of trials n and the probability of success π appear in the binomial probability function. *The quantities n and π are the parameters of the binomial distribution;* that is, when we specify values for n and π, a unique member of the binomial distribution is defined. For example, we have already indicated that the two probability functions given in Section 4.1 are binomial probability functions, the first with $n = 2$ and $\pi = \frac{1}{2}$, and the second with $n = 3$ and $\pi = \frac{1}{2}$.

To illustrate the determination of binomial probabilities, consider the following example. Suppose you are a life insurance salesperson who, during a normal day, visits $n = 5$ potential customers. Suppose further that 40% of all your sales calls result in the sale of a policy. If the sales process is stable, the probability of a customer buying a policy from you is $\pi = .4$. You are interested in the number of customers who will buy a policy from you during the next day. Let this be the random variable X. We can determine the probabilities for each possible value of X (0, 1, 2, 3, 4, and 5) by substituting each value in Expression (4.2), where $n = 5$ and $\pi = .4$. The far easier thing to do, however, is to use a computer.* In particular, the Minitab and Excel outputs for this example produce the following probabilities. These probabilities show that the most likely number of customers who buy during a given day is two. They also show that it is almost equally likely that one or three policies will be sold.

```
BINOMIAL WITH
n = 5 and
p = 0.400000
    X       P( X = x )
0.00      0.0778
1.00      0.2592
2.00      0.3456
3.00      0.2304
4.00      0.0768
5.00      0.0102
```

	A	B
1	x	P(X = x)
2	0	0.07776
3	1	0.25920
4	2	0.34560
5	3	0.23040
6	4	0.07680
7	5	0.01024

Cumulative Binomial Probabilities

In most real applications, the outcome of interest is a range of possible values such as "X takes on values that are at most 2" or "X takes on a value of at least 3." Suppose the life insurance salesperson can win a bonus by selling three or more policies in 1 day. What is the probability of winning a bonus? Recall from Section 3.5 that statements such as "at least" imply an accumulation of probabilities. So if X represents the number of persons who buy insurance out of the five visited, we want to determine the probability that X takes on one of the values from 3 to 5 inclusive. In other words, we seek $P(X \geq 3) = 1 - P(X \leq 2)$, where $P(X \leq 2)$ is the probability of the complementary event.

Cumulative binomial probabilities can be determined using the binomial probability function. Here we are interested in the binomial distribution with $n = 5$ and $\pi = .4$.

---

*Computer instructions for using Minitab, Excel, and JMP IN for the binomial and normal distributions are given in the chapter appendix.

From Expression (4.2), the probability that the binomial random variable X takes on integer values less than or equal to 2 is

$$P(X \leq 2) = P(X = 0) + P(X = 1) + P(X = 2) = .0778 + .2592 + .3456$$
$$= .6826$$

Therefore, the probability of winning a bonus is the same as the probability that X takes on integer values that are at least 3, which is

$$P(X \geq 3) = 1 - P(X \leq 2) = 1 - .6826 = .3174$$

In general, the probability that a binomial random variable X takes on an integer value that is less than or equal to some particular value x is as shown in the box.

THE CUMULATIVE BINOMIAL PROBABILITY FUNCTION

$$P(X \leq x) = F(x; n, \pi)$$
$$= P(X = 0) + P(X = 1) + \cdots + P(X = x) \qquad \textbf{(4.3)}$$

where $F(x; n, \pi)$ denotes the cumulative probability for values of X up to and including the particular value x.

Again, it is easy to use a computer to determine cumulative binomial probabilities as in Expression (4.3). The Minitab and Excel cumulative probabilities for this example are as follows:

```
BINOMIAL WITH
n = 5 and
p = 0.400000
     x      P( X <=x )
   0.00       0.0778
   1.00       0.3370
   2.00       0.6826
   3.00       0.9130
   4.00       0.9898
   5.00       1.0000
```

	A	B
1	x	P(X<=x)
2	0	0.07776
3	1	0.33696
4	2	0.68256
5	3	0.91296
6	4	0.98976
7	5	1.00000

Using the Computer

Statistical tables have long been a fixture in statistics books, but with the advent of sophisticated microcomputer software, statistical tables may become a thing of the past. As we have illustrated, Minitab and Excel can be used to determine individual probabilities [that is, $P(X = x)$] and cumulative probabilities [$P(X \leq x)$] for a binomial distribution. And in the chapter appendix you are given instructions how to use Minitab,

Excel, and JMP IN. We encourage you to use the computer for this purpose (when it is feasible) rather than the statistical tables of the book appendix.

EXAMPLE 4.2

We have all heard preference claims made about certain products on radio and television commercials. Federal laws require that claims be grounded in fact, based on scientific studies. This example illustrates how an advertised claim can be checked through the use of the binomial distribution.

An advertisement for a toothpaste claims that the toothpaste is preferred by 40% of adults in the United States. A random sample of 50 adults is selected by a competitor to check the claim. Assume for the moment that the claim is true and use the binomial distribution to determine the following probabilities:

(a) The probability that exactly 18 adults in the sample prefer the toothpaste

(b) The probability that at most 25 adults prefer the toothpaste

(c) The probability that the number of adults in the sample who prefer the toothpaste is between 12 and 30, inclusive

(d) Suppose 10 of the 50 adults in the sample prefer the toothpaste. In view of the answer to part (c), what might be a reasonable conclusion about the advertised claim based on the current random sample?

Solution

Let the random variable X be the number of adults in the sample who prefer this toothpaste. The parameter values of the binomial distribution are $n = 50$ and $\pi = .4$.

(a) We seek the probability that X takes on the value 18—that is, $P(X = 18)$. This probability (.0987) determined by Minitab is as follows:

```
BINOMIAL WITH n = 50 and p = 0.400000
          x          P( X=x )
        18.00        0.0987
```

(b) We seek the probability that X takes on integer values up to and including 25, or $P(X \leq 25)$. The desired probability (.9427) is as follows:

```
BINOMIAL WITH n = 50 and p = 0.400000
          x          P( X<=x )
        25.00        0.9427
```

(c) The desired probability is that X takes on integer values in the interval 12 to 30, inclusive; that is,

$$P(12 \leq X \leq 30) = P(X \leq 30) - P(X \leq 11)$$

The cumulative probabilities $P(X \leq 30)$ and $P(X \leq 11)$ are as follows:

```
BINOMIAL WITH n = 50 and p = 0.400000
          x          P( X<=x )
        30.00        0.9986
```
```
BINOMIAL WITH n = 50 and p = 0.400000
          x          P( X<=x )
        11.00        0.0057
```

As a result, the desired probability is

$$P(12 \leq X \leq 30) = .9986 - .0057 = .9929$$

(d) Since from part (c) the probability that X takes on integer values in the interval 12 to 30, inclusive, is .9929, the probability that X takes on values outside of this interval is only $1 - .9929 = .0071$. Consequently, the observed result of ten adults preferring this toothpaste would be a very unlikely outcome, if the claim that 40% of adults prefer the toothpaste were true. Therefore, a reasonable conclusion based on this random sample is that the claim is not true; the actual percentage appears to be lower than claimed.

Binomial Tables

If you do not have ready access to a statistical software package, you can use Table A of the Appendix at the end of the book to determine binomial probabilities. The binomial distribution has been extensively tabulated for various values of n and π by using either Expression (4.2) or (4.3) or both. In Table A, we evaluate the binomial *cumulative* probabilities [Expression (4.3)] for selected values of x, n, and π. It is important for you to understand that we can also determine individual probabilities using this table; because the binomial random variable is integer valued, the property given by Expression (3.3) in Chapter 3 applies. Specifically, the probability that the binomial random variable X takes on the particular value x is

$$P(X = x) = P(X \leq x) - P[X \leq (x - 1)] \qquad \textbf{(4.4)}$$

where $P(X \leq x)$ is the cumulative probability for values up to and including x and $P[X \leq (x - 1)]$ is the cumulative probability for values up to and including $x - 1$. For example, the probability that X takes on the value 3 equals the probability that X takes on values that are less than or equal to 3 minus the probability that X takes on values that are less than or equal to 2.

To illustrate the use of Table A, let $n = 10$ and $\pi = .3$. The probability that X takes on integer values that are less than or equal to 4 is

$$P(X \leq 4) = .8497$$

The probability that X takes on integer values that are greater than 2 is

$$P(X > 2) = P(X \geq 3) = 1 - P(X \leq 2) = 1 - .3828 = .6172$$

and the probability that X takes on the value 5 is

$$P(X = 5) = P(X \leq 5) - P(X \leq 4) = .9527 - .8497 = .1030$$

EXAMPLE 4.3

When units of many products such as TVs, VCRs, camcorders, and so on are mass-produced, there is bound to be a relatively small proportion of the units that will turn out to be defective, even if the manufacturing process is stable. Management must periodically monitor the manufacturing process that produces the units to make sure the proportion of defective units remains at a very small value. This example illustrates how the binomial distribution is an effective tool in this monitoring procedure.

In the manufacture of stereo speakers, 25 units are selected randomly each day from the production line for complete inspection. Based on recent historical information, it is believed that the proportion of defective stereo speakers produced by the current process is .01 under stable conditions.

(a) With respect to the binomial distribution, what is the probability that on a given day at least three sampled speakers are found to be defective?

(b) Suppose three or more speakers are indeed found to be defective on some day. In view of your answer to part (a), what might be a reasonable conclusion about the process that day?

Solution

(a) Let the random variable X be the number of defective speakers found among the selected 25. For $n = 25$ and $\pi = .01$, we find the probability that X takes on integer values greater than or equal to 3 to be

$$P(X \geq 3) = 1 - P(X \leq 2) = 1 - .9980 = .002$$

(b) Since the probability of finding three or more defective speakers is only .002 (i.e., this would occur only 2 times out of 1,000), we must regard this occurrence as highly unlikely if $\pi = .01$. A reasonable conclusion is that the quality of the speakers may have been compromised through some problem in the production line that day. An attempt should be made to identify a possible assignable cause of variation.

The Effect of the Value of π

By changing the value of the parameter π, we obtain binomial distributions whose graphs look distinctly different. For example, let's consider three binomial distributions with parameter values $n = 5$, $\pi = .2$; $n = 5$, $\pi = .5$; and $n = 5$, $\pi = .8$, respectively. The graphs of the corresponding probability distributions are given in Figure 4.2.

The three graphs of Figure 4.2 clearly look different. Since the number of trials ($n = 5$) is the same for all three, the differences must be caused by the different π values. Notice, for example, that when $\pi = .2$, the probabilities decrease considerably as the values of X increase from 2 up to 5. In other words, this distribution tails off to the right and cuts off rather abruptly to the left. The opposite effect is observed in part (c) when $\pi = .8$; the distribution tails off to the left with an abrupt cutoff to the right. When $\pi = .5$, the distribution is symmetric.

Figure 4.2

Graphs of the binomial probability function

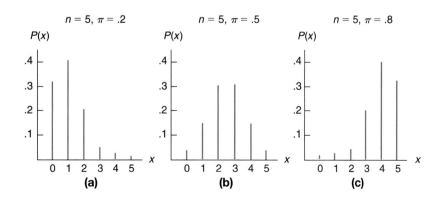

The parameter π affects the shape of the binomial distribution in such a way that it can yield positively skewed, negatively skewed, or symmetric distributions, depending on its value. In particular, for any n:

1. If $\pi < \frac{1}{2}$, the binomial distribution is skewed to the right (positively skewed).
2. If $\pi > \frac{1}{2}$, the binomial distribution is skewed to the left (negatively skewed).
3. If $\pi = \frac{1}{2}$, the binomial distribution is symmetric.

The skewness diminishes for values of π close to .5 and becomes more pronounced for values of π that are closer to either 0 or 1.

Summarizing the Binomial Distribution: Expected Value and Standard Deviation

Now we turn our attention to ways of summarizing a binomial distribution. Suppose that before you tossed a balanced coin 100 times, you were asked: How many heads do you *expect* to observe? Would you say 50? Did you arrive at this number by figuring that since the probability of heads any time you toss the coin is $\frac{1}{2}$, and since there will be 100 tosses, the product of 100 and $\frac{1}{2}$ must be the number of heads to expect? If so, you are absolutely correct.

If a discrete random variable X has a binomial distribution, then the expected (or long-run mean) value of X turns out to be the product of the number of trials n and the probability of success π, that is

$$E(X) = n\pi \tag{4.5}$$

In addition, the variance of X can be shown to be the product of the mean of X ($n\pi$) and the probability of failure $(1 - \pi)$:

$$\text{Var}(X) = n\pi(1 - \pi) \tag{4.6}$$

It follows, therefore, that the standard deviation of X is

$$\text{SD}(X) = \sqrt{n\pi(1 - \pi)} \tag{4.7}$$

As the following example illustrates, the standard deviation describes how much variation can be expected from a binomial random variable.

EXAMPLE 4.4

Life insurance agents are constantly trying to arrange visits with potential customers. The more persons they get a chance to visit, the more likely it is that at least one will buy a policy from the agent. Many agents set goals for themselves with regard to the number of persons they will try to see during, say, a month. This provides them the opportunity to estimate potential income by determining averages and standard deviations of the number of persons who actually buy insurance. This example illustrates the use of the binomial distribution for such a situation.

In a typical month, an insurance agent presents life insurance options to 20 potential customers. Historically, the sales process has been stable, with one in five such customers buying life insurance from this agent. Justify the use of the binomial distribution here and answer the following questions for next month's activity:

(a) Determine the mean, variance, and standard deviation of the number of customers that buy life insurance next month.

(b) Determine the probabilities that the actual number of customers who buy life insurance next month will lie within two and within three standard deviations of the mean.

Solution

We assume that the buy/do not buy decisions of the 20 customers visited by this agent next month constitute a set of independent trials such that the probability of a customer buying life insurance is $\pi = .2$ (one out of five). It seems reasonable to conclude that a customer's decision to buy life insurance is personal and therefore likely to be independent of the decisions of other customers. Since the same agent is involved, we may treat this group as a random sample of this agent's potential customers for which the buy probability is .2. (*Note:* If these assumptions are incorrect, then the answers that follow might be incorrect as well.)

To answer the questions, let's define the random variable X to be the actual number of customers who buy life insurance from this agent next month out of the $n = 20$ potential customers visited by the agent.

(a) Since $n = 20$ and $\pi = .2$, from Expressions (4.5)–(4.7) we have $\mu = E(X) = (20)(.2) = 4$; $\sigma^2 = \text{Var}(X) = (20)(.2)(.8) = 3.2$; and $\sigma = \text{SD}(X) = \sqrt{3.2} = 1.79$, respectively.

(b) Since $\mu = 4$ and $\sigma = 1.79$, the interval of values within two standard deviations of the mean is*

$$\mu \pm 2\sigma = 4 \pm (2)(1.79) = 4 \pm 3.58 = (.42, 7.58)$$

The possible values of X that are *included* in the interval (.42, 7.58) are 1, 2, 3, 4, 5, 6, and 7. Therefore, the desired probability is the probability that X takes on one of these values; that is,

$$P(1 \leq X \leq 7) = P(X \leq 7) - P(X = 0) = .9679 - .0115 = .9564$$

Thus, there is about a 96% chance that the actual number of customers who buy life insurance will be within two standard deviations of the mean.

In a similar manner, the interval of values within three standard deviations of the mean is

$$\mu \pm 3\sigma = 4 \pm (3)(1.79) = 4 \pm 5.37 = (-1.37, 9.37)$$

Since X cannot take on a negative value, the desired interval is (0, 9.37), and the possible values of X included in this interval are 0, 1, 2, ..., 9. Therefore, the desired probability is

---

Reminder: The symbol $\pm$ means "plus or minus." Thus, 4 ± 3.58 consists of the interval $4 - 3.58 = .42$ to $4 + 3.58 = 7.58$.

$$P(0 \leq X \leq 9) = P(X \leq 9) = .9974$$

Notice that these probabilities correspond closely to the probabilities of the empirical rule and are considerably greater than those of Tchebysheff's finding. This should not be too surprising, since we are dealing with a single-peaked distribution here [much like Figure 4.2(a)].

EXAMPLE 4.5

Periodically, national manufacturers and retailers buy large lots of products such as ball bearings, brake pads, CDs and stereo speakers—to name a few—from their suppliers. Since these products are used either as components in another product (bearings and brake pads) or are directly sold to consumers (CDs and stereo speakers), the buyers insist from their suppliers some assurance with regard to the quality of an incoming lot. Many buyers choose to select a small random sample of units from a lot and inspect the selected units to verify a supplier's claim. This example illustrates this kind of situation through the use of the binomial distribution.

A large retailer has purchased 10,000 high-quality videocassette tapes. The retailer is assured by the supplier that the shipment contains no more than 1% defective tapes (according to agreed specifications). To check the supplier's claim, the retailer randomly selects 100 tapes and finds six of the 100 to be defective.

(a) Assuming the supplier's claim is true and $\pi = .01$, compute the mean and the standard deviation of the number of defective tapes in the sample.

(b) Based on your answer to part (a), is it likely that as many as six tapes would be found to be defective, if the claim is correct?

(c) Suppose that six tapes are indeed found to be defective. Based on your answer to part (b), what might be a reasonable inference about the manufacturer's claim for this shipment of 10,000 tapes?

Solution

First, notice that the application of the binomial distribution is appropriate, since a tape is either defective or not and the sample size $n = 100$ is indeed a very small proportion of the total number of tapes purchased, thus assuring independence between sampled tapes.

(a) Let the random variable X be the number of defective tapes found in the sample. For $n = 100$ and the probability of a defective tape $\pi = .01$, the expected value of the number of defective tapes is

$$\mu = E(X) = n\pi = 100(.01) = 1$$

Thus, over many samples of 100 tapes, the average number of defective tapes is one. The standard deviation is

$$\sigma = SD(X) = \sqrt{n\pi(1 - \pi)} = \sqrt{100(.01)(1 - .01)} = .995$$

(b) To answer this question, notice that the observed number of defective tapes (six) is greater than the mean by more than three standard deviations; that is,

$$\mu + 3\sigma = 1 + 3(.995) = 3.985 < 6$$

In fact, the observed number of defective tapes is more than five standard deviations above the mean. If the claim is true, the occurrence of six defective tapes is extremely unlikely even in light of the very conservative Tchebysheff's finding.

(c) Based on the answer to part (b), a reasonable inference here may be that the claim is not true; that is, the shipment apparently contains more than 1% defective tapes.

Practical Implications for Example 4.5

The procedure in which a small sample of units is randomly selected for inspection from a large lot to verify the quality of the lot is known as **acceptance sampling.** Acceptance sampling is often used as a means by which a supplier and a customer can agree on whether a shipment is acceptable or not. Based on the number of units that are found to be defective in the sample, the usual procedure is either to accept the entire lot or to reject it and send it back to the supplier. With regard to Example 4.5, this would mean that the 10,000 tapes would be returned to the supplier, because the likelihood of finding six defective tapes out of 100 is very remote if π were indeed .01 or less.

On the surface, this procedure appears to be beneficial; however, it has drawbacks that probably overshadow its benefits. Inspection procedures do not fundamentally improve the quality of a product because they do not improve the process that produces the product. In fact, the existence of an "acceptable level of defectives" is a disincentive to continued improvement once the acceptable level has been achieved. The best way to improve the quality of a product is to design quality into the product and to strive continually to improve the process that produces it.

4.3 The Normal Distribution

The normal distribution is without doubt the most important and most widely used continuous probability distribution. As you will see in later chapters, it is the cornerstone in the application of statistical inference based on random samples of data. As illustrated in Figure 4.3, the graphical appearance of the normal probability density function is a symmetric, bell-shaped curve that has a dense concentration around the central value and tails off without bound to the left and to the right.

A substantial number of empirical studies have indicated that the normal distribution often provides an adequate representation of populations or processes in business environments and in other areas of endeavor. For example, the distribution of

Figure 4.3

A normal probability density curve

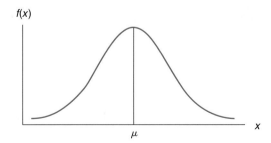

the weights of a product poured by a machine into a container is often approximated well by a normal distribution. So might be the weekly sales volume in a fast-food restaurant. In addition, the normal distribution often provides a useful model of subjective probabilities for the possible outcomes of a future event. For example, it might be used as a probability distribution model of possible annual rates of return for a common stock. Yet you should exercise some caution in assuming that the normal distribution serves as an adequate model without empirical verification. For example, it is widely known that the distribution of annual incomes is considerably skewed, so the normal distribution is certainly not an appropriate model in that case. If the normal distribution is the most widely used, it is also the most widely abused, partly because of the possible misinterpretation of the word *normal,* especially if its literal meaning of "accepted standard or pattern" is mistakenly applied.

The normal distribution is also known as the Gaussian distribution because the German mathematician Karl Friedrich Gauss considered it in his work during the early part of the 19th century. Throughout the 19th century it was used extensively by scientists who frequently observed that errors in physical measurements followed a pattern that suggested the normal distribution.

The Normal Probability Density Function

Recall that a probability density function of a continuous random variable does not provide the probability that the random variable takes on a particular value; that probability is in fact 0. Instead, we find the probability that a random variable lies in a given interval by finding the area *under* the density function and within the boundaries of that interval (using integral calculus). For the normal distribution, the probability density function is given by the mathematical expression

$$f(x) = \frac{1}{\sigma\sqrt{2\pi}}\, e^{(-1/2)[(x-\mu)/\sigma]^2} \qquad\qquad \textbf{(4.8)}$$

In this application, the symbols e and π represent constants; they are "natural numbers" that arise in many mathematical expressions. Their numerical values are $e = 2.71828\ldots$ and $\pi = 3.14159\ldots$.

You may be pleased to know that you will not actually work with Expression (4.8) because you can use computer software or statistical tables. However, it is important to notice in the expression that the parameters of the normal distribution are μ and σ. These parameters are the mean and standard deviation, respectively, of a normal distribution. So, if a random variable X is normally distributed, the expected value of X is μ and the standard deviation of X is σ.

By giving specific values for the mean μ and the standard deviation σ in Expression (4.8), we define a unique normal distribution. Graphs of the normal probability density function for different values of the mean μ with a fixed standard deviation σ, and for different values of σ with a fixed μ are given in Figure 4.4. From this figure, several important observations may be made:

- For every pair of values of μ and σ, the normal probability density function is bell shaped and symmetric.

- The point of symmetry with respect to the area under the graph of the density function is the mean μ; that is, half the area lies to the left of the mean and the other half lies to the right of the mean. This implies that it is as likely that an

Figure 4.4

Graphs of the normal density function for various values of μ and σ

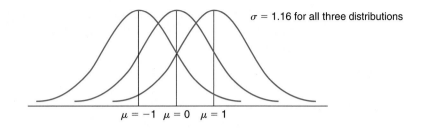

$\sigma = 1.16$ for all three distributions

$\mu = -1$ $\mu = 0$ $\mu = 1$

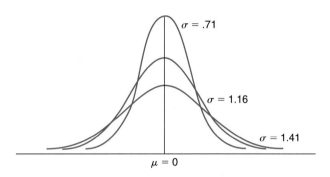

$\sigma = .71$

$\sigma = 1.16$

$\sigma = 1.41$

$\mu = 0$

individual outcome will lie below the mean as it is that it will lie above the mean. Thus, for any normal random variable X,

$$P(X \leq \mu) = P(X \geq \mu) = .5 \qquad \textbf{(4.9)}$$

- Since the normal distribution is symmetric, the median is exactly the same as the mean. In fact, the mode for the normal distribution is also the same as the mean and the median because the highest value of the probability density function occurs when $x = \mu$.
- The mean μ determines *location*—that is, the central location of the curve.
- The standard deviation σ determines the *spread* of the distribution—that is, the range of values that the random variable is likely to assume.

The Cumulative Normal Distribution

We can determine the probability that a normally distributed random variable X is less than or equal to some particular value x by using the cumulative distribution function

$$P(X \leq x) = F(x;\ \mu,\ \sigma) \qquad \textbf{(4.10)}$$

From Chapter 3, recall that a cumulative distribution function such as $F(x;\ \mu,\ \sigma)$ represents the portion of the area under the graph of the normal probability density function $f(x)$ that is bounded on the right by the particular value x. It is important to realize that the particular value x is a quantile value, since the cumulative function $F(x;\ \mu,\ \sigma)$ represents the area to the left of x. We saw in Section 3.6 how to use the cumulative distribution function of a continuous random variable to determine interval probabilities for that variable. Unfortunately, no one has yet been able to determine the cumulative normal distribution function $F(x;\ \mu,\ \sigma)$ in a mathematical form that we can easily use. However, statistical software can readily compute interval probabilities for normal distributions. Alternatively, one can use statistical tables (Table B in the Appendix) instead. First we illustrate the use of Minitab in this regard, then explain the use of Table B.

Using the Computer

We can bypass the use of statistical tables in determining interval probabilities for normal distributions and use instead statistical software. If a computer is available, we urge you to do this. The following example illustrates the use of Minitab. Interval probabilities for normal distributions can also be determined by using Excel or JMP IN, as described in Appendix 4.

EXAMPLE 4.6

As a matter of routine practice, organizations accumulate important data with regard to their business activities. Based on such historical data, they are able to determine the distribution that adequately depicts an activity of interest. Consequently, they are able to assess probabilities for future outcomes of such activities. This example illustrates the use of the normal distribution in such a situation.

In reviewing the historical records of a bank, a loan officer finds that the average dollar amount per quarter of customer defaults on loans has been $1.5 million over the last 4 years, with a standard deviation of $.4 million. Assume that the loan default process will remain stable for the near future and that the distribution of the total amounts defaulted per quarter is adequately approximated by a normal distribution.

(a) What is the probability that the total amount defaulted in a given quarter will be no more than $1.1 million?

(b) What is the probability that the current quarter's total amount defaulted will be greater than $2 million?

(c) What is the probability that one quarter's default amount is in the range $1.2 million to $2.2 million?

Solution

Let the random variable X be the total dollar amount defaulted during a given quarter. The parameter values of the assumed normal distribution are $\mu = 1.5$ and $\sigma = .4$.

(a) We seek the probability that the total amount is no more than $1.1 million, or $P(X \le 1.1)$. The desired probability is as follows:

```
Normal with mean = 1.50000 and
standard deviation = 0.400000
          x          P( X<=x )
      1.1000           0.1587
```

(b) We seek the probability that X takes on values greater than $2 million, or $P(X > 2)$. Using the rule for complementary events, we have

$$P(X > 2) = 1 - P(X \le 2)$$

where $P(X \le 2)$ is as follows:

```
Normal with mean = 1.50000 and
standard deviation = 0.400000
           x         P( X<=x )
        2.0000        0.8944
```

As a result, the desired probability is

$$P(X > 2) = 1 - .8944 = .1056$$

(c) We seek $P(1.2 \le X \le 2.2)$. From the second property of a cumulative distribution function (see the end of Section 3.6), we have

$$P(1.2 \le X \le 2.2) = P(X \le 2.2) - P(X \le 1.2)$$

The probabilities $P(X \le 2.2)$ and $P(X \le 1.2)$ are as follows:

```
Normal with mean = 1.50000 and
standard deviation = 0.400000
           x         P( X<=x )
        2.2000        0.9599
```

```
Normal with mean = 1.50000 and
standard deviation = 0.400000
           x         P( X<=x )
        1.2000        0.2266
```

The desired probability is

$$P(1.2 \le X \le 2.2) = .9599 - .2266 = .7333$$

Tabulating Normal Distributions: The Standard Normal Distribution

When a computer is not available, it is possible to determine interval probabilities for any normal distribution by referring to a table for only one normal distribution—a very important distribution known as the *standard normal distribution*. We now show how this is done.

The concept of the standardizing transformation via the Z-value (discussed in Section 2.6.3) comes into play here. Using Expression (2.10), we can say that if X is a normal random variable with any mean μ and any standard deviation σ, then the equation

$$Z = \frac{X - \mu}{\sigma} \qquad\qquad \textbf{(4.11)}$$

defines the relationship between X and Z, where Z is the normal random variable with mean 0 and standard deviation 1. In other words, the standardized random variable Z has that unique normal distribution with mean $\mu = 0$ and standard deviation $\sigma = 1$. This distribution is known as the **standard normal distribution.** A graph of its probability density function is a symmetric, bell-shaped curve that is centered around 0 and has most of the area contained within the range -3 to $+3$.

For example, if X is a normal random variable with $\mu = 10$ and $\sigma = 2$, then $Z = (X - 10)/2$ is a normal random variable with mean 0 and standard deviation 1.

Suppose we are interested in determining the probability that X takes on values that are less than or equal to, say, 13.5. The relationship given by Expression (4.11) allows us to convert the value 13.5 to the corresponding value of the standard normal random variable Z. The Z-value corresponding to $X = 13.5$ is $Z = (13.5 - 10)/2 = 1.75$. From our discussion of Z-values in Chapter 2, we can interpret the value $X = 13.5$ as being 1.75 standard deviations ($\sigma = 2$) above the mean ($\mu = 10$). Since the value of Z is determined by the value of X, the probability that X takes on values less than or equal to 13.5 is the same as the probability that Z takes on values less than or equal to 1.75. In other words, the interval probability $P(X \le 13.5)$ is exactly the same as the interval probability $P(Z \le 1.75)$ This also means that the values 13.5 and 1.75 are corresponding quantile values such that the respective areas to the left of each are exactly the same. Therefore,

$$P(X \le 13.5) = P\left(Z \le \frac{13.5 - 10}{2}\right) = P(Z \le 1.75)$$

This correspondence is illustrated graphically in Figure 4.5.

Figure 4.5

The correspondence between the normal (10, 2) distribution and the standard normal distribution

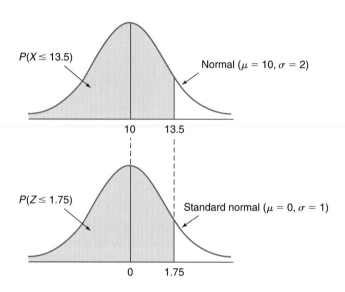

To generalize this correspondence, let X be a normally distributed random variable with any mean μ and any standard deviation σ. To find the probability that X takes on values that are less than or equal to some particular value x, we first convert the particular value x to the corresponding Z-value, denoted by z, using Expression (4.11). The probability that X takes on values less than or equal to the quantile value x is the same as the probability that Z takes on values less than or equal to the corresponding quantile value z. In other words, the quantile value x lies z standard deviations above (if z is positive) or below (if z is negative) the mean μ. Thus, the interval probability $P(X \le x)$ is exactly the same as the interval probability $P(Z \le z)$. So we can write

$$P(X \le x) = P\left(Z \le \frac{x - \mu}{\sigma}\right) = P(Z \le z) \qquad \textbf{(4.12)}$$

As a result, *we can determine interval probabilities involving any normal random variable X by using the standard normal cumulative distribution function.*

$$P(Z \leq z) = F(z; 0, 1) \qquad \textbf{(4.13)}$$

Using the Standard Normal Table

The tabulation of the cumulative distribution function $F(z; 0, 1)$ is given in Table B of the Appendix. For any particular value z, the entry in the table is the probability that the standard normal random variable Z takes on values less than or equal to z. The first column lists Z-values to one decimal place. The headings for the other columns specify the hundredths digit of the Z-value. To locate a probability corresponding to a Z-value specified to two decimal places, you must scan the column headings until you locate the desired hundredths digit.

Let's illustrate the use of Table B for several typical Z-values. Consider the quantile value .89. To find the probability that the standard normal random variable Z takes on values less than or equal to .89, we first locate .8 from the row headings (first column) and then find .09 from the column headings. Finally, we scan across the .8 row and down the .09 column to locate the desired probability of .8133. We follow the same procedure to determine the standard normal interval probabilities corresponding to other quantile values, such as those in the following table.

Quantile Value	Probability
−1.8	$P(Z \leq -1.8) = F(-1.8; 0, 1) = .0359$
−.45	$P(Z \leq -.45) = F(-.45; 0, 1) = .3264$
1.76	$P(Z \leq 1.76) = F(1.76; 0, 1) = .9608$

Now let's see how we can use Table B to determine interval probabilities for any normal random variable. Suppose X has a normal distribution with mean $\mu = 50$ and standard deviation $\sigma = 10$. Let's determine the probability that X takes on values in the interval (46, 58). To find this probability, we convert this interval to the corresponding interval of Z-values using Expression (4.11); that is, $(46 - 50)/10 = -.4$ and $(58 - 50)/10 = .8$. So the probability that X takes on values between 46 and 58 is the same as the probability that Z takes on values between −.4 and .8. From Expression (3.5) in Section 3.6, the probability that Z takes on values between −.4 and .8 equals the area (with respect to the probability density function of Z) to the left of .8 minus the area to the left of −.4; that is,

$$P(-.4 \leq Z \leq .8) = P(Z \leq .8) - P(Z \leq -.4) = .7881 - .3446 = .4435$$

Therefore,

$$P(46 \leq X \leq 58) = P(-.4 \leq Z \leq .8) = .4435$$

The equivalence of areas for this example is illustrated in Figure 4.6.

EXAMPLE 4.7

During the past 50–75 years, it has been common practice to measure human intelligence using IQ tests. Based on mounting empirical evidence, it is fairly certain that

Figure 4.6

Equivalence of areas
under the density func-
tions of X and Z

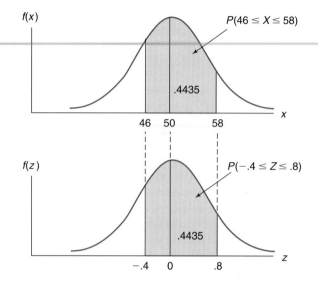

human intelligence conforms to a normal distribution. Given the mean and standard deviation of such a distribution, it is straightforward to determine the proportion of humans whose IQ falls within a given range. This example illustrates how to determine such proportions (probabilities) based on the normal distribution.

Let X be a random variable depicting human intelligence as measured by IQ tests. If X has a normal distribution with mean 100 and standard deviation 10, determine the probabilities that X takes on a value (a) greater than 100, (b) less than 85, (c) at most 112, (d) at least 108, (e) greater than 90, (f) between 86 and 98, and (g) between 104 and 112.

Solution

With this example we want to illustrate virtually all the different situations that may arise in determining probabilities using Table B. As before, our approach is to convert the X-values to the corresponding Z-values using Expression (4.11) and then use Table B. Notice that except in part (a), figures are provided to illustrate the equivalence of areas.

(a) Since any normal distribution is symmetric around the average, the probability that X takes on values greater than its mean of 100 is .5.

(b) $P(X < 85) = P(Z < -1.5)$
$\qquad\qquad\quad = .0668$

$f(x)$

.0668

85   100

x

$$Z = \frac{85 - 100}{10} = -1.5$$

(c) $P(X \le 112) = P(Z \le 1.2)$
     $= .8849$

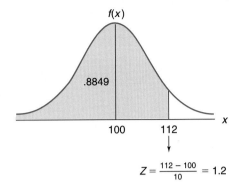

$Z = \frac{112 - 100}{10} = 1.2$

(d) $P(X \ge 108) = P(Z \ge .8)$
     $= 1 - P(Z < .8)$
     $= 1 - .7881$
     $= .2119$

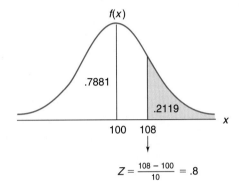

$Z = \frac{108 - 100}{10} = .8$

(e) $P(X > 90) = P(Z > -1)$
     $= 1 - P(Z \le -1)$
     $= 1 - .1587$
     $= .8413$

$Z = \frac{90 - 100}{10} = -1$

(f) $P(86 \le X \le 98) = P(-1.4 \le Z \le -.2)$
     $= P(Z \le -.2) - P(Z \le -1.4)$
     $= .4207 - .0808$
     $= .3399$

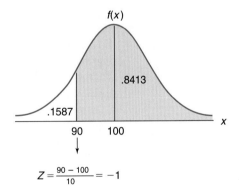

$Z = \frac{86 - 100}{10} = -1.4$ $Z = \frac{98 - 100}{10} = -.2$

(g) $P(104 \leq X \leq 112) = P(.4 \leq Z \leq 1.2)$
$\qquad\qquad\qquad\quad = P(Z \leq 1.2) - P(Z \leq .4)$
$\qquad\qquad\qquad\quad = .8849 - .6554$
$\qquad\qquad\qquad\quad = .2295$

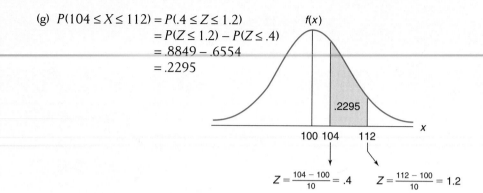

$$Z = \frac{104 - 100}{10} = .4 \qquad Z = \frac{112 - 100}{10} = 1.2$$

Recall the empirical rule introduced in Section 2.5. Since for the standard normal distribution $\mu = 0$ and $\sigma = 1$, the probabilities $P(-1 \leq Z \leq 1)$, $P(-2 \leq Z \leq 2)$, and $P(-3 \leq Z \leq 3)$ correspond to the probabilities that any normally distributed random variable X takes on values within one, two, and three standard deviations of its mean, respectively. Using either a computer or Table B, we can easily determine that these probabilities are .6826, .9544, and .9974, respectively. The probabilities associated with the empirical rule strongly indicate that for normal distributions, there is a high concentration of values around the mean. For example, more than two-thirds of the values are within one standard deviation of the mean.

EXAMPLE 4.8

In Example 4.3, we illustrated how the binomial distribution is an effective tool to monitor the proportion of mass-produced units that are defective. Alternatively, when the quality characteristic of a mass-produced product is a quantitative variable, such as diameter, width, length, weight, and so on, what is usually of interest is to ascertain whether the quality characteristic stays within an acceptable range of variation. The normal distribution is often useful in this kind of situation.

Suppose the outer diameter of certain ball bearings produced by a stable manufacturing process is adequately approximated by a normal distribution with mean equal to 3.5 centimeters and standard deviation equal to .02 centimeter. If the diameter of this type of bearing must be no smaller than 3.47 centimeters and no larger than 3.53 centimeters to be usable, what percentage of bearings produced by this process must be scrapped because the diameters are out of the acceptable range?

Solution

Let the random variable X be the diameter (in centimeters) of a bearing produced by this process. The distribution of X is assumed to be normal with $\mu = 3.5$ and $\sigma = .02$. This means that the probability distribution of possible values for the diameter of any one bearing produced by this process is a normal distribution with mean 3.5 cm and standard deviation .02 cm.

The probability that a bearing has a usable diameter is the same as the probability that its diameter X is between 3.47 cm and 3.53 cm. Thus, we first find the probability that a diameter is within the acceptable range. By subtracting this probability from 1, we will determine the percentage of diameters that are outside the acceptable range.

From the second property of cumulative distribution functions (see the end of Section 3.6), we have

$$P(3.47 \leq X \leq 3.53) = P(X \leq 3.53) - P(X \leq 3.47)$$

From Excel, the probabilities $P(X \leq 3.53)$ and $P(X \leq 3.47)$ are as follows:

	A	B	C	D
1	μ	σ	X	P(X <= x)
2	3.5	0.02	3.53	0.93319
3	3.5	0.02	3.47	0.06681

Therefore, $P(3.47 \leq X \leq 3.53) = .9332 - .0668 = .8664$. This result is illustrated by Figure 4.7.

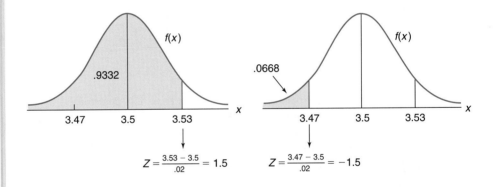

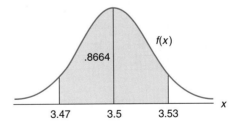

Figure 4.7

Illustration of the determination of probabilities for Example 4.8

Recall that the probability of an event was defined in Chapter 3 to be its long-run relative frequency of occurrence upon repeated experimentation under identical conditions. Therefore, about 86.64% of the bearings produced by this process will have usable diameters, if the process remains stable. It follows from the probability rule of complementary events that $1 - .8664 = .1336$, or about 13.36% of the bearings must be scrapped.

Process Improvement Considerations for Example 4.8

A process that produces as much as 13.36% scrap has considerable room for improvement through the reduction of process variation. Since this process is stable, the reduction of variation must come as a result of the redesign of the process to reduce common cause variation. For example, a 25% reduction in the process standard deviation (that is, from $\sigma = .02$ to $\sigma = .015$) will result in a reduction of the percentage of scrap from 13.36% to less than 5%. (You can verify this result by reworking Example 4.8 using $\sigma = .015$.)

Finding a Quantile Value x, Given F(x)

In statistical applications, we often need to determine a particular value x of a normally distributed random variable such that a given proportion of the area is to the left of this value. In other words, we are given a probability and wish to determine the corresponding quantile value x of the random variable. To illustrate, suppose it is known that grades on a statistics test are adequately approximated by a normal distribution with mean 75 and standard deviation 10. What particular grade must a student receive such that only 10% of the grades are higher than this grade?

If 10% of the grades exceed this grade, then 90% are less than or equal to it. Thus, this grade is the 90th percentile value for this distribution of test grades. Let's use the notation $x_{.90}$ to denote this grade.* Then

$$P(X \le x_{.90}) = .90$$

Using the Computer

A quantile value such as this can easily be determined by using Minitab or Excel. Statistical software packages usually refer to the process of finding a quantile value, given a probability, as "the inverse of a distribution." We use Excel and Minitab to illustrate quantile values, then explain the use of Table B in this regard. For example, the 90th percentile value for this distribution of test grades using Excel is as follows:

	A	B	C	D
1	μ	σ	$P(X \le x)$	x
2	75	10	0.9000	87.8155

Thus, the desired 90th percentile value is $x_{.90} = 87.8155$. This means that 10% of the grades exceed this value.

EXAMPLE 4.9

Let's return to Example 4.6, in which a bank loan officer has determined from historical records that the distribution of the total loan amounts defaulted per quarter is adequately approximated by a normal distribution with an average default amount of $1.5 million and a standard deviation of $.4 million.

---

*As introduced in Section 2.6, x_q is the quantile value such that $100q\%$ of the area under the density function of the random variable X lies to the left of x_q.

(a) What amount should the bank allow in its budget for a quarter's loan defaults, if it wishes the probability to be .01 that actual defaults in that quarter exceed this amount?

(b) Determine the first and third quartiles of the distribution of total loan amounts defaulted per quarter.

Solution

(a) We wish to determine the quantile value such that the probability of exceeding this value is .01; that is, the desired quantile value is the 99th percentile value. As a result,

$$P(X \leq x_{.99}) = .99$$

From the following Minitab output, the desired quantile value is $x_{.99} = \$2.4305$ million.

```
Normal with mean = 1.50000 and
standard deviation = 0.400000
     P( X <=x )           x
        0.9900         2.4305
```

(b) The first quartile is the same as the 25th percentile of the distribution; from the following Minitab output, it is $x_{.25} = \$1.2302$ million.

```
Normal with mean = 1.50000 and
standard deviation = 0.400000
     P( X <=x )           x
        0.2500         1.2302
```

The third quartile is the same as the 75th percentile of the distribution; it works out to be $x_{.75} = \$1.7698$ million from the following output.

```
Normal with mean = 1.50000 and
standard deviation = 0.400000
     P( X <=x )           x
        0.7500         1.7698
```

When a computer is not available, we can determine quantile values for normal distributions by using Table B. Let's return to the example of determining the 90th percentile value of the distribution of test grades. Since the desired quantile value $x_{.90}$ is such that $P(X \leq x_{.90}) = .90$, we can approximate the location of this value on the horizontal axis, as shown on the top graph of Figure 4.8. Notice that the grade $x_{.90}$ must be to the right of the mean grade of 75, because 90% of the grades are less than or equal to $x_{.90}$. Using Expression (4.11), we can convert the quantile value $x_{.90}$ to the corresponding quantile value $z_{.90}$, the 90th percentile value of the standard normal distribution; that is, $z_{.90} = (x_{.90} - 75)/10$. The correspondence between these quantile values is illustrated in Figure 4.8. If we knew the value $z_{.90}$, then we could use this equation to solve for the desired value $x_{.90}$.

To determine $z_{.90}$, we reverse the earlier process of using Table B and now look first in the body of this table to find the closest probability value to .90; then we match it with the corresponding Z-value—that is, the value from the row and column headings.

Figure 4.8

Correspondence between quantile values $x_{.90}$ and $z_{.90}$

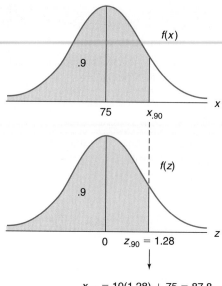

$$x_{.90} = 10(1.28) + 75 = 87.8$$

We first locate in the body of the table the number closest to .90; this is .8997. The row and column headings that correspond to .8997 are 1.2 (the row) and .08 (the column). So the desired 90th percentile value of the standard normal distribution is 1.28. This means that for all normal distributions, the 90th percentile value is 1.28 standard deviations above the mean. For the normal distribution with mean 75 and standard deviation 10, this means that

$$1.28 = \frac{x_{.90} - 75}{10}$$

and the 90th percentile value is

$$x_{.90} = (10)(1.28) + 75 = 87.8$$

Therefore, approximately 90% of the test grades will be less than 88.

As a further illustration, let's determine the minimum passing grade such that 5% of all students receive grades less than this minimum passing grade, and thus fail the test. This minimum passing grade is the 5th percentile value, $x_{.05}$, since

$$P(X < x_{.05}) = .05$$

Once again, we convert the minimum passing grade to the corresponding 5th percentile value, $z_{.05}$, of the standard normal distribution, as illustrated in Figure 4.9. In this case, notice that the quantile value $x_{.05}$ must lie to the left of the mean, because only 5% of the grades are less than $x_{.05}$. As before, we know from the equivalence of probabilities that the value $z_{.05}$ is such that

$$P(Z < z_{.05}) = .05$$

We scan the probability values in the body of Table B to find the value nearest to .05. This turns out to be exactly halfway between the values of .0505 and .0495. Since the

Figure 4.9

Correspondence between quantile values $x_{.05}$ and $z_{.05}$

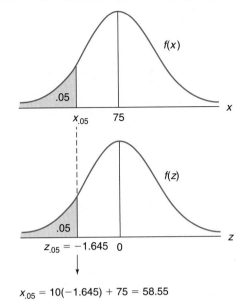

$$x_{.05} = 10(-1.645) + 75 = 58.55$$

Z-value corresponding to .0505 is -1.64 and that for .0495 is -1.65, we split the difference between -1.64 and -1.65 and settle on a Z-value of -1.645. This means that for all normal distributions, the 5th percentile value is 1.645 standard deviations *below* the average. Consequently,

$$-1.645 = \frac{x_{.05} - 75}{10}$$

and

$$x_{.05} = (10)(-1.645) + 75 = 58.55$$

Accordingly, a passing grade on this test is 59 or higher.

EXAMPLE 4.10

In any business establishment that deals with the sale of a tangible product, it is extremely important to control the inventory level of that product. On one hand, if inventory levels are too high, the establishment may be tying up too much of its capital on inventory, and inventory costs (housing, etc.) may become prohibitively high. On the other hand, if inventory levels are too low, stockouts are likely to occur. This means that the establishment does not have any units of the product to sell when demanded by customers; that is, the establishment loses the opportunity to make a sale of this product upon demand. The normal distribution plays an important role in the control of inventory levels, as illustrated by this example.

Suppose the monthly demand for a product is closely approximated by a normal distribution with mean 200 units and standard deviation 40 units. How large an inventory must we have available at the beginning of a month so that the probability of running out of the product (a stockout) during the month is no more than .05?

Solution

Let the random variable X represent monthly demand, where the distribution of X is normal with mean 200 units and standard deviation 40 units. We seek the particular beginning inventory level such that the probability of an actual month's demand exceeding it is .05. This is equivalent to saying that the probability is .95 that an actual month's demand is less than this level. Therefore, we seek the quantile value $x_{.95}$ such that 95% of the area of the demand distribution is to the left of it. In other words, $x_{.95}$ is the 95th percentile value.

From the following Excel output, the desired quantile value is seen to be $x_{.95} = 265.7941$ or 266 units.

	A	B	C	D
1	μ	σ	P(X <= x)	X
2	200	40	0.9500	265.7941

To determine the desired value using Table B, we know the area to the left of $x_{.95}$ is equal to the area to the left of the equivalent $z_{.95}$; that is,

$$P(X \le x_{.95}) = P(Z \le z_{.95}) = .95$$

where

$$z_{.95} = \frac{x_{.95} - 200}{40}$$

We scan the body of Table B for the probability nearest .95. This is seen to be exactly halfway between the table values of .9495 and .9505, which correspond to the Z-values of 1.64 and 1.65. As in the previous illustration, we split the difference between these two to obtain the value of 1.645. Thus, the 95th percentile value for all normal distributions is 1.645 standard deviations *above* the average. As a result,

$$1.645 = \frac{x_{.95} - 200}{40}$$

and

$$x_{.95} = (40)(1.645) + 200 = 265.8$$

(See Figure 4.10.) This means the beginning monthly inventory should be no less than 266 units if the probability of a stockout during the month is to be no more than .05. But heed this warning: Suppose a policy were established that set the beginning inventory at 266, based on this analysis. This policy makes sense only if one is willing to assume that the demand process of the future will remain well approximated by the normal distribution with mean 200 and standard deviation 40. The best way to affirm this is through periodic assessment of the demand distribution.

Figure 4.10

Correspondence between quantile values $x_{.95}$ and $z_{.95}$

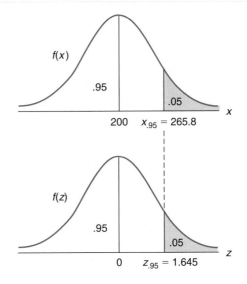

4.4 The Normal Distribution as an Approximation to the Binomial Distribution

The normal distribution can be used to approximate binomial probabilities when n is large. The correspondence between binomial probabilities and those determined by the appropriately chosen normal distribution is very close as long as $n\pi \geq 5$ and $n(1 - \pi) \geq 5$. In the past, this approximation was highly beneficial because it reduced the computational effort considerably. But with the prevalence of PCs and sophisticated statistical software packages, the normal approximation to the binomial distribution is less important today. We provide an opportunity to use the normal approximation in Chapters 5–7 in the context of statistical inference for the binomial parameter π.

Briefly, how does the approximation work? Consider a survey of 100 potential voters in which each is asked what political candidate he or she will vote for. Let the random variable X represent the number of respondents who prefer candidate A. Now suppose that the (unknown) proportion of potential voters who, at this time, intend to vote for candidate A is $\pi = .55$. Then X has a binomial distribution with mean $n\pi = 100(.55) = 55$ and standard deviation $\sqrt{n\pi(1 - \pi)} = \sqrt{100(.55)(.45)} = 4.97$. Notice that, according to the guideline given above, the sample size is large enough for a normal distribution to approximate this binomial distribution effectively. Both the expected number of successes, $n\pi = 55$, and the expected number of failures, $n(1 - \pi) = 45$, are much larger than 5. Which normal distribution should be used? *The normal distribution that provides a good approximation is the one with the same mean and standard deviation as the binomial distribution;* that is, we use the normal distribution with mean $\mu = 55$ and standard deviation $\sigma = 4.97$.

4.5 Summary

In this chapter, we presented two special probability distributions that have proven to be useful in decision making. These are the binomial and normal distributions.

The binomial distribution is an example of a discrete probability distribution. It is derived from a repetitive random experiment in which each outcome is classified as either a success or a failure. The random variable represents the number of successes out of n independent trials, where the probability of success is constant from trial to trial. The parameters of the binomial distribution are the constant probability of success and the number of trials. Depending on the value of the constant probability of success, a binomial distribution can be symmetric or skewed (to the right or to the left).

The normal distribution is an example of a continuous probability distribution. The graphical appearance of the normal probability density function is a symmetric, bell-shaped curve that has a dense concentration around the center and tails off without bound to the left and to the right. Approximately 68% of the values of a normal random variable are within a distance of one standard deviation from the mean, while 95% are within a distance of two standard deviations from the mean. The parameters of the normal distribution are its mean and its standard deviation. The standard normal distribution (that is, mean 0 and standard deviation 1) is used to determine interval probabilities for all other normally distributed random variables.

EXERCISES FOR SECTION 4.2

4.1 Explain the essence of what a binomial distribution represents.

4.2 In general, what does a binomial random variable represent? What possible values can this variable take on?

4.3 Is it sampling with replacement or sampling without replacement that characterizes a binomial distribution? Explain.

4.4 In practical applications, is random sampling done nearly always with or without replacement? Explain in the context of the binomial distribution.

4.5 Explain the purpose of the binomial probability function.

4.6 What are the parameters of a binomial distribution and what do they represent?

4.7 What controls the shape of a binomial distribution? Explain.

4.8 Explain what the expected value and variance of a binomial random variable are.

4.9 Suppose you are a real estate agent. Give an example of what you believe might be a binomial random variable in this context.

4.10 Suppose you own a retail shop that sells bicycles. Give an example of what you believe might be a binomial random variable in this context.

4.11 Suppose you are the manager of a plant that manufactures auto air bags. Give an example of what you believe might be a binomial random variable in this context.

4.12 Let X be a binomial random variable. Determine the probabilities for each value of X and graph the probability distribution for the following parameter values:

(a) $n = 4$, $\pi = .2$ (b) $n = 4$, $\pi = .5$
(c) $n = 4$, $\pi = .8$

4.13 Repeat Exercise 4.12 for the following parameter values:

(a) $n = 4$, $\pi = .3$ (b) $n = 5$, $\pi = .3$
(c) $n = 6$, $\pi = .3$

4.14 With reference to each part of Exercise 4.12, determine the following cumulative probabilities:

(a) $P(X \le 1)$ (b) $P(X \ge 2)$ (c) $P(X < 3)$
(d) $P(X \ge 3)$

4.15 With reference to each part of Exercise 4.13, repeat Exercise 4.14.

4.16 Let X be a binomial random variable with $n = 10$ and $\pi = .6$. Determine the following probabilities:

(a) $P(X < 4)$ (b) $P(X = 4)$ (c) $P(X \ge 6)$
(d) $P(X < 8)$ (e) $P(X > 2)$ (f) $P(X = 8)$

4.17 Repeat Exercise 4.16 for $n = 15$ and $\pi = .2$.

4.18 Let X be a binomial random variable with $n = 20$ and $\pi = .2$. Use Expressions (4.5) and (4.7) to determine the mean and standard deviation of X, respectively. Then determine the probability that X takes on a value that is within two standard deviations of the mean.

4.19 Twenty-five persons are randomly selected from a certain residential community and are sent a marketing questionnaire. Assume the response probability is .3 and the conditions of the binomial distribution are satisfied.

(a) What is the probability of no more than two responses?

(b) What is the probability of exactly four responses?

(c) What is the probability of at least ten responses?

(d) What are the mean and standard deviation of the number of responses?

4.20 A manufacturer of clothes washers knows from historical experience that 10% of the washers sold will require repair work under the product's warranty agreement. Assume that a retail establishment has sold 20 such washers in a given month. If the conditions of the binomial distribution are satisfied, answer the following questions:

(a) What is the probability that none of these washers will require repair work under the warranty period?

(b) What is the probability that at least three will require repair work during this period?

(c) Determine the mean and standard deviation of the number of washers that require warranty work and determine the probability that the actual number is within two standard deviations of the mean.

4.21 Two candidates, A and B, are running for sheriff in a small county. The prevailing belief is that the race is a dead heat. One week before the election, 25 registered voters from the county are randomly selected and asked for their choice between candidates A and B. Assume the conditions for the binomial distribution are satisfied.

(a) What is the probability that at least 14 will indicate a preference for candidate A?

(b) Determine the mean and standard deviation of the number of those polled who indicate a preference for candidate A and determine the probability that the actual number is within two standard deviations of the mean.

(c) Suppose seven out of the 25 persons polled indicated a preference for candidate A. In view of your answer to part (b), what do you now think of the race?

4.22 A manufacturer of pistons believes that the proportion that do not meet the specifications is no more than 5%. On a given day, 20 pistons are randomly selected and checked to see whether each meets the specifications. Assume the conditions of the binomial distribution are satisfied.

(a) What is the probability that no more than one piston is found to be substandard?

(b) Determine the mean and standard deviation of the number of pistons that do not meet the specifications and determine the probability that the actual number is within two standard deviations of the mean.

(c) Suppose on a given day you find three pistons out of the 20 that do not meet the specifications. In view of your answer to part (b), what do you now think of the manufacturer's belief?

4.23 An automobile manufacturer discovers that about 20% of all brake mechanisms that were installed in its 1996 sporty model are defective. Suppose the manufacturer sold 20,000 of these automobiles. Justify the use of the binomial distribution here and answer the following questions.

(a) On a particular day, 500 of these automobiles are brought to the manufacturer's network of service dealers for check and, if needed, repair. Determine the mean and standard deviation of the number of automobiles that would need repair that day.

(b) Suppose on that day, 140 of the 500 automobiles are found to have faulty brake mechanisms. In view of your answer to part (a), what do you think of the manufacturer's belief that 20% of all brake mechanisms are defective?

4.24 Based on historical records, the Internal Revenue Service (IRS) believes that about 70% of all audited taxpayers with adjusted annual incomes of at least $100,000 wind up owing the government $1,000 or more in additional taxes. In a current sample of 200 audits of this group, the IRS determines that 175 of the 200 audited taxpayers owe at least $1,000 in additional taxes. Should this sample information alter the IRS's historical belief? Support your answer.

4.25 A life insurance salesperson knows from past experience that she is successful in selling a universal life policy of at least $100,000 to about one out of 10 potential customers she contacts. For a given month, the salesperson's target number of potential customers to be visited is 25. Assume the conditions of a binomial distribution are satisfied.

(a) What is the probability that in a given month at least two persons buy a universal life policy of at least $100,000 from this salesperson?

(b) If during the first year the salesperson derives an income of $300 per month, on average, from every such policy sold, determine the income the salesperson expects to earn per month from this type of activity.

(c) Is it reasonable for the salesperson to count on a monthly income of, say, $2,000 from this activity? Support your answer.

4.26 A marketing research firm believes that 60% of the surrounding residents at some location would patronize a national chain restaurant if it located in this area.

(a) If the marketing firm selects 150 residents to survey from this area, determine the mean and standard deviation of the number of residents that would indicate support. Assume the conditions of the binomial distribution are satisfied.

(b) If in a survey of 150 residents randomly selected from this area the firm finds 70 that indicate support, what would be reasonable to conclude about the firm's initial belief? Support your answer.

4.27 Based on historical information, a home mortgage lender knows that about 5% of all outstanding home mortgages default within the first five years. The firm currently has 758 outstanding home mortgages that are less than five years old. Assume the conditions of the binomial distribution are satisfied.

(a) Determine the mean and standard deviation of the number of mortgages the firm holds that default within the first five years.

(b) Suppose that 19 such mortgages default within the first five years. Based on this result, would it be reasonable to conclude that the historical information is still valid? Explain.

4.28 Many of us are annoyed when we receive junk mail that tempts us to buy a certain product. The marketers of junk mail know that only a small proportion—about .01—actually respond to buy the product. To overcome this small proportion, the marketers send out an inordinately large number of solicitations. Suppose a marketer sends out 1,000,000 solicitations for a particular product. If each solicitation sent costs a total of 20 cents, what should the marketer's profit per sale be, on average, to break even? Assume the conditions of the binomial distribution are satisfied.

EXERCISES FOR SECTION 4.3

4.29 Describe the essential features of a normal distribution.

4.30 Identify the parameters of a normal distribution and explain what they represent.

4.31 Explain why a value of a normal random variable that is more than three standard deviations from the mean is regarded as unusual.

4.32 What do we call the normal distribution whose mean is 0 and whose standard deviation is 1? Explain why this distribution is important.

4.33 Explain why the probability of a normal random variable taking on a specific value is 0.

4.34 Consider the numerical grade distribution of an elective, senior-level course for business majors. Do you believe that this distribution would be adequately close to a normal distribution? Support your answer.

4.35 Suppose you are the manager of a plant that manufactures ball bearings. Give an example of what you believe might be a normal random variable in this context.

4.36 Suppose you are an investment analyst. Give an example of what you believe might be a normal random variable in this context.

4.37 Suppose you are a wholesaler who supplies staple goods to restaurants. Give an example of what you believe might be a normal random variable in this context.

4.38 Let Z be the standard normal random variable. Determine the following probabilities:
(a) $P(Z \leq -1.62)$ (b) $P(Z > .95)$
(c) $P(-1.42 \leq Z \leq .98)$ (d) $P(1.12 \leq Z \leq 2.84)$

4.39 Repeat Exercise 4.38 for the following probabilities:
(a) $P(-2.48 \leq Z \leq -.38)$ (b) $P(Z > -1.08)$

(c) $P(Z \leq 1.96)$ (d) $P(-1.96 \leq Z \leq 1.96)$

4.40 Let X be a normal random variable with mean 50 and standard deviation 10. Determine the following probabilities:
(a) $P(X < 40)$ (b) $P(X < 65)$ (c) $P(X > 55)$
(d) $P(X > 35)$ (e) $P(40 < X < 45)$
(f) $P(38 < X < 62)$

4.41 Let X be a normal random variable with mean 200 and standard deviation 20. Determine the following probabilities:
(a) $P(185 < X < 210)$ (b) $P(215 < X < 250)$
(c) $P(X > 240)$ (d) $P(X > 178)$

4.42 Let Z be the standard normal random variable. Find the indicated quantile values corresponding to the following probabilities:
(a) $P(Z < z_{.10}) = .10$ (b) $P(Z < z_{.98}) = .98$
(c) $P(Z < z_{.99}) = .99$ (d) $P(Z < z_{.01}) = .01$
(e) $P(Z < z_{.025}) = .025$ (f) $P(Z < z_{.975}) = .975$

4.43 Let Z be the standard normal random variable. Find the quantile values z corresponding to the following probabilities:
(a) $P(Z > z) = .1515$ (b) $P(Z > z) = .6700$
(c) $P(Z < z) = .0571$ (d) $P(Z < z) = .9788$

4.44 Let X be a normal random variable with mean 10 and standard deviation 5. Find the indicated quantile values corresponding to the following probabilities:
(a) $P(X < x_{.10}) = .10$ (b) $P(X < x_{.98}) = .98$
(c) $P(X < x_{.99}) = .99$ (d) $P(X < x_{.01}) = .01$
(e) $P(X < x_{.025}) = .025$ (f) $P(X < x_{.975}) = .975$

4.45 Let X be a normal random variable with mean -25 and standard deviation 10. Find the quantile values x corresponding to the following probabilities:

(a) $P(X < x) = .1251$ (b) $P(X < x) = .9382$
(c) $P(X > x) = .3859$ (d) $P(X > x) = .8340$

4.46 Suppose the grades on a statistics test are adequately described by a normal distribution with mean 72 and standard deviation 12.
  (a) If your grade on this test is 84, what percentage of the grades exceed your grade?
  (b) If your friend's grade is 62, what percentage of the grades are lower than this grade?

4.47 Suppose that a taxpayer whose income for a given year is between $40,000 and $50,000 claims $2,200 in deductions for charitable contributions for that year.
  (a) If the Internal Revenue Service knows that the amount claimed for charitable contributions by taxpayers in this income bracket is adequately approximated by a normal distribution with mean $1,200 and standard deviation $400, what is the probability that the amount claimed by some taxpayer in this income group will be at least $2,200?
  (b) Based solely on your answer to part (a), what do you think the IRS is likely to do with regard to this taxpayer?

4.48 Suppose the monthly rate of return for a growth mutual fund is adequately approximated by a normal distribution with mean 1.5% and standard deviation .95%. If at the beginning of a given month an investor has $10,000 in this fund, what is the probability that at the end of the month the amount will increase to at least $10,300 based on that month's return?

4.49 With reference to Exercise 4.46, suppose the professor decides that only the top 10% of the grades on this test will receive an A. What is the minimum numerical grade that one must get on this test in order to receive an A?

4.50 Two competing fast-food restaurants, M and W, have daily sales volumes that are adequately approximated by normal distributions. From past experience, it is determined that for M the mean is $5,000 and the standard deviation is $1,200, whereas for W they are $4,400 and $1,000, respectively. On a particular day, M does $6,500 worth of business. What must the sales volume of W be on that day in order to correspond relatively to that of M?

4.51 Determine the first and third quartiles of any normal distribution in terms of standard deviation units above or below the mean. Use these results to determine the first and third quartiles of the amount of charitable contributions in Exercise 4.47.

4.52 Determine the 10th and 90th percentiles of any normal distribution. Use these results to determine

the 10th and 90th percentiles of the monthly rate of return in Exercise 4.48.

4.53 Suppose the weekday sales volume at a popular bar is adequately represented by a normal distribution with mean $2,500 and standard deviation $250. Today (a weekday), the bar takes in $1,500. How would you describe today's sales volume in relative terms?

4.54 It is well known that common stock prices change because of many factors such as a company's economic well-being, investors' perception of the company, economic well-being of the industry, and many other factors. Suppose that for a well-established company, the annual change in its common stock price, as a percentage from the previous year, is adequately approximated by a normal distribution with average change of 12% and a standard deviation of 15%.
  (a) If you were to buy this company's stock, what is the probability that in one year the per-share price would increase by at least 20%?
  (b) What is the probability that in one year you would incur a loss?
  (c) If 5% of the time the change in one year exceeds this value, find this value.
  (d) If 5% of the time the change in one year is less than this value, find this value.

4.55 Health maintenance organizations (HMOs) are becoming the way of life with regard to health insurance. As a routine practice, HMOs determine their average annual costs per insured individual. Suppose the annual cost to an HMO for each insured individual is adequately approximated by a normal distribution with average cost of $2,000 and a standard deviation of $1,500.
  (a) What is the probability that the per-individual annual cost to the HMO will exceed $4,200?
  (b) Find the 98th percentile value of this distribution.
  (c) Do you see a problem with the supposition that the normal distribution adequately approximates the distribution of the annual cost for each insured individual? Explain.

4.56 Suppose that the daily revenue for weekdays of a popular fast-food chain in Virginia is adequately approximated by a normal distribution with average daily revenue of $5,000 and standard deviation of $1,000.
  (a) Find the percentage of weekdays that daily revenue will be between $2,500 and $6,500.
  (b) Find the daily revenue such that 6% of daily revenues exceed this value.
  (c) Do you see a problem with the supposition that the normal distribution adequately approxi-

mates the distribution of daily revenue for weekdays at this fast-food outlet? Explain.

4.57 In recent years, college-bound seniors in the United States had an average of about 500 and a standard deviation of about 100 for the math portion of the Scholastic Assessment Test. It has been established that the distribution of math SAT scores is adequately approximated by a normal distribution.

(a) What is the point difference between the 75th and 25th percentile values of this distribution? (This difference is commonly referred to as the *interquartile* range.)

(b) What is the point difference between the 90th and 10th percentile values of this distribution? (This difference is commonly referred to as the *interdecile* range.)

SUPPLEMENTARY EXERCISES

4.58 Let X be binomially distributed with $n = 10$ and $\pi = .5$.

(a) Determine the probabilities that X is within one standard deviation of the mean and within two standard deviations of the mean.

(b) What would be your answers to part (a) if $n = 15$ and $\pi = .4$?

4.59 Suppose the probability of a defective unit coming off an assembly line is .05. The process is stable and the units produced by this process constitute a set of independent trials.

(a) What is the probability that among 20 such units, exactly two are defective?

(b) At most two are defective?

(c) At least one is defective?

4.60 An electronics firm claims that the proportion of defective units of a certain component it produces is 5%. A buyer of large quantities of these components inspects 15 units that were randomly selected from a large lot and finds four defectives. If the claim is correct and the assumptions for the binomial distribution prevail, what is the probability of such an occurrence? Would you be inclined to conclude that the claim is not correct? Comment.

4.61 It is known from past surveys that consumer preference for two competing brands, A and B, of a given product is evenly divided. If we assume independence of choice between these two brands, what is the probability that out of 25 randomly selected persons, no more than ten will indicate a preference for brand A?

4.62 Suppose a test containing 15 true-or-false questions is given. A passing grade consists of at least nine correct answers. If one tosses a balanced coin to decide between true or false for each question, what is the probability of a passing grade?

4.63 A long-distance telephone company has begun a telephone drive to increase its long-distance market share. The company has determined from historical records that about one out of ten persons contacted decides to switch to this company.

(a) On a given day, 10,000 people are contacted.

Determine the mean and standard deviation of the number of individuals who switch to this company per day.

(b) The company needs at least 940 of the 10,000 contacted daily to switch to make this drive worthwhile. In view of your answer to part (a), what do you think the company's chances are for a successful drive?

4.64 A large university expects to receive 16,000 freshman student applications for the coming year. It can be safely assumed that the SAT scores of these applicants are adequately approximated by a normal distribution with mean 950 and standard deviation 100. If the university decides to admit the top 25% by SAT scores, what is the minimum SAT score that will be required for admission?

4.65 The diameters of pistons manufactured by a process are adequately approximated by a normal distribution with mean diameter 5 centimeters and standard deviation .001 centimeter. To be usable, the diameter of a piston has to be between 4.998 and 5.002 cm. If the diameter of a piston is less than 4.998, it must be scrapped; if it is greater than 5.002, the piston can be reworked. What percentage of pistons will be usable? What percentage will be scrapped? What percentage will be reworked?

4.66 Suppose that starting salaries for business graduates in a given year are adequately approximated by a normal distribution with mean $24,000 and standard deviation $2,000.

(a) If a graduate receives a starting salary that is in the top 5% of the starting salaries for that year, what is the person's salary?

(b) If one's starting salary corresponds to the 25th percentile, what is that person's salary?

4.67 Let X be a normal random variable. If it is known that the 40th percentile value of X is 50 and the 80th percentile value is 100, determine the mean and standard deviation of X.

4.68 An aircraft manufacturer wishes to procure rivets to use in mounting aircraft engines. The required minimum tensile strength of each rivet is 25,000 pounds. Three manufacturers of rivets (A, B, and C) are asked to provide pertinent information concerning the tensile strengths of such rivets. The three manufacturers respond that the tensile strengths of their rivets are adequately described by normal distributions with mean tensile strengths of 28,000, 30,000, and 29,000 pounds, respectively.

(a) Does the aircraft manufacturer have sufficient information to make a choice? Why?

(b) Suppose the standard deviations for A, B, and C are 1,000, 1,800, and 1,200 pounds, respectively. For each manufacturer, determine the probability of a rivet produced not meeting the minimum requirements.

(c) If you were the aircraft manufacturer, which would you choose among A, B, and C, based on your answer to part (b)? Why?

4.69 A manufacturer of automobile mufflers wishes to guarantee her mufflers for the life of the automobile. The manufacturer assumes that the life of her mufflers is a normally distributed random variable with an average of 3 years and a standard deviation of 6 months. If the unit replacement cost is $10, what would be the total replacement cost for the first 2 years if 1,000,000 such mufflers are installed?

4.70 The time required to assemble a certain unit is a normally distributed random variable with mean 30 minutes and standard deviation 2 minutes. Determine the time such that the probability of a unit's assembly time exceeding this value is .02.

4.71 The weight of cereal in a container is adequately approximated by a normal distribution with mean 600 grams. The filling process is designed so that the weight of no more than one container out of 100 lies outside the range 590–610 grams.

(a) What is the maximum value for the standard deviation necessary to meet this requirement?

(b) To reduce variation, the filling process is to be redesigned to shrink the range to 595–605 grams. What is the maximum value for the standard deviation of the redesigned filling process?

4.72 In Exercise 3.25, you estimated the probability that the Cincinnati Reds would go on to win the World Series after having won the first two games. The estimate was based on historical information. Another way to estimate this probability is to utilize the binomial distribution. Having won the first two games, the Reds needed only to win two more games out of five possible remaining games.

(a) Assuming the probability that the Reds win any single game is .5, determine the probability that the Reds go on to win the World Series.

(b) Compare your answer in part (a) to your answer in Exercise 3.25. Are they similar? Explain why they do not match exactly. Which is the "correct" answer?

Appendix 4

Computer Instructions for Using MINITAB, EXCEL, and JMP IN

MINITAB

Determining Binomial Distribution Probabilities

Consider Example 4.2, where we determine individual and cumulative binomial probabilities for $n = 50$ and $\pi = .4$. In part (a), you need to find the individual probability that $X = 18$. Choose CALC–PROBABILITY DISTRIBUTIONS–BINOMIAL.... In the dialogue box, (1) click the PROBABILITY button; (2) enter 50 in the NUMBER OF TRIALS box; (3) enter .4 in the PROBABILITY OF SUCCESS box; (4) click the INPUT CONSTANT button and enter 18 (the desired value of X) in the corresponding box; and click OK. You can also determine simultaneously the probabilities associated with several or all possible values of X. Enter the desired values of X into c1. In step 4 of the above procedure, click the INPUT COLUMN button and type or select c1 in the corresponding box.

In part (b), you need to obtain the cumulative probability that $X \leq 25$. Use the process just described, but click the CUMULATIVE PROBABILITY button in step 1.

Determining Normal Distribution Probabilities and Quantile Values

Consider Example 4.6, where we determine interval normal probabilities when $\mu = 1.5$ and $\sigma = .4$. In part (a), you need to find the interval probability that $X \leq 1.1$. Choose CALC–PROBABILITY DISTRIBUTIONS–NORMAL.... In the dialogue box, (1) click the CUMULATIVE PROBABILITY button; (2) enter 1.5 in the MEAN box; (3) enter .4 in the STANDARD DEVIATION box; (4) click the INPUT CONSTANT button and enter 1.1 (the desired value of X) in the corresponding box; and click OK.

You can also determine simultaneously the interval probabilities associated with several values of X. To work parts (a), (b), and (c), you must determine interval probabilities when $x = 1.1$, $x = 2$, $x = 1.2$, and $x = 2.2$, where in all cases $\mu = 1.5$ and $\sigma = .4$. Enter the values 1.1, 2, 1.2, and 2.2 in the first four rows of c1. In step 4 of the above procedure, click the INPUT COLUMN button and type or select c1 in the corresponding box. If you would like to store the interval probabilities, enter c2 in the OPTIONAL STORAGE box.

Now consider Example 4.9, where we determine the quantile value $x_{.99}$ for a normal distribution with $\mu = 1.5$ and $\sigma = .4$. Use the process just described, clicking the INVERSE CUMULATIVE PROBABILITY button in step 1, clicking the INPUT CONSTANT button, and entering .99 in the INPUT CONSTANT box. To set all three quantile values needed for parts (a) and (b) at once, enter .99, .25, and .75 into c1, click the INPUT COLUMN button, and enter c1 in the corresponding box.

EXCEL

Determining Binomial Distribution Probabilities

Consider Example 4.2, where we determine individual and cumulative binomial probabilities for $n = 50$ and $\pi = .4$. Enter 18, the value of X, into cell a1. Select b1, the cell where you will place the desired probability. Click the PASTE FUNCTION button on the toolbar (or choose INSERT–FUNCTION . . . from the menu). In the PASTE FUNCTION box, select the STATISTICAL function category and the function name BINOMDIST, and click OK. In the BINOMDIST dialogue box, enter a1 (the cell containing the value of X) in the first box; in the next three boxes, enter 50 (the number of trials), .4 (probability of success), and 0 (indicating that you want individual probabilities); then click OK.

You can also determine simultaneously the probabilities associated with several or all possible values of X. To determine the probabilities that $X = 0, 1, 2, \ldots, 50$, enter these values into cells a1:a51. Follow the PASTE FUNCTION procedure as just described. Then select cell b1 and fill down through cell b51. The desired probabilities will be in b1:b51.

Cumulative binomial probabilities are determined in the same manner, except that a 1 is entered in the last box of the BINOMDIST box.

Determining Normal Distribution Probabilities and Quantile Values

Consider Example 4.8, where we determine interval normal probabilities when $\mu = 3.5$ and $\sigma = .02$. You need to find the probabilities that $X \leq 3.47$ and $X \leq 3.53$. Enter 3.53 into a1 and 3.47 into a2. Select cell b1. Then click the PASTE FUNCTION button on the toolbar. In the PASTE FUNCTION box, select the STATISTICAL function category and the function name NORMDIST, and click OK. In the four boxes of the NORMDIST box, enter a1 (the cell containing the value $x = 3.53$), 1.5 (the mean μ), .4 (the standard deviation σ), and 1 (indicating that you want a cumulative area); then click FINISH. This places $P(X \leq 3.53)$ into b1. To put $P(X \leq 3.47)$ into b2, select cell b1 and fill down through b2.

You can determine normal distribution quantile values in similar fashion. To determine the .99 quantile value $(x_{.99})$ for Example 4.9(a), first enter .99 into cell a1. Select b1, then click the PASTE FUNCTION button. In the PASTE FUNCTION box, select the STATISTICAL function category and the function name NORMINV, and click OK. In the three boxes of the NORMINV box, enter c1 (the cell containing the given probability .99), 1.5 (the mean μ), .4 (the standard deviation σ); then click OK. To get the quantile values for part (b), $x_{.25}$, and $x_{.75}$ enter .25 and .75 in a2:a3. Then select cell b1 and fill down through cell b3. The desired quantile values will appear in b1:b3.

JMP IN

Determining Binomial Distribution Probabilities

Currently, JMP IN does not provide a way to determine probabilities for the binomial distribution.

Determining Normal Distribution Probabilities and Quantile Values

Consider Example 4.6. To work parts (a), (b), and (c), you must determine interval probabilities when $x = 1.1$, $x = 2$, $x = 1.2$, and $x = 2.2$, where in all cases $\mu = 1.5$ and $\sigma = .4$. Put the values 1.1, 2, 1.2, and 2.2 in the first four rows of COLUMN 1, and name this column X. You will first compute the z-values corresponding to these four x-values in COLUMN 2 and then compute the desired interval probabilities in COLUMN 3. Name these columns Z and PROB, respectively. Now you need to open the CALCULATOR window for Z (you may want to review the discussion of the CALCULATOR window in Appendix 1). In the CALCULATOR window for Z, calculate the expression $(x - 1.5)/.4$ by executing the following steps:

1. Click the left parenthesis key in the Keyboard area.
2. Select X from the Column Selector List.
3. Type -1.5 and press the ENTER key.
4. Click the right parenthesis key in the Keyboard area.
5. Type /.4 and press the ENTER key.
6. Close the CALCULATOR window.

This places the z-values in COLUMN 2 (Z).
    In the CALCULATOR window for PROB:

1. Select PROBABILITY—NORMAL DISTRIBUTION in the Function Browser area.
2. Select Z from the Column Selector List.
3. Close the CALCULATOR window.

This places the desired interval probabilities in COLUMN 3 (PROB).
    Now consider Example 4.9. In parts (a) and (b), you must determine the quantile values $x_{.99}$, $x_{.25}$, and, $x_{.75}$ for a normal distribution with $\mu = 1.5$ and $\sigma = .4$. In COLUMN 1, enter .99, .25, and .75 in the first three rows, and name this column PROBX. Add two columns and name them Z QUANTILE and X QUANTILE. In the CALCULATOR window for Z QUANTILE:

1. Select PROBABILITY–NORMAL QUANTILE in the Function Browser area.
2. Select PROBX from the Column Selector List.
3. Close the CALCULATOR window.

This places the Z quantile values in COLUMN 2 (Z QUANTILE).
In the CALCULATOR window for X QUANTILE:

1. Select Z QUANTILE from the Column Selector List.
2. Click the multiplication key on the keyboard.
3. Type *.4 and press the ENTER key.
4. Type +1.5 and press the ENTER key.
5. Close the CALCULATOR window.

This places the desired X quantile values in COLUMN 3 (X QUANTILE).

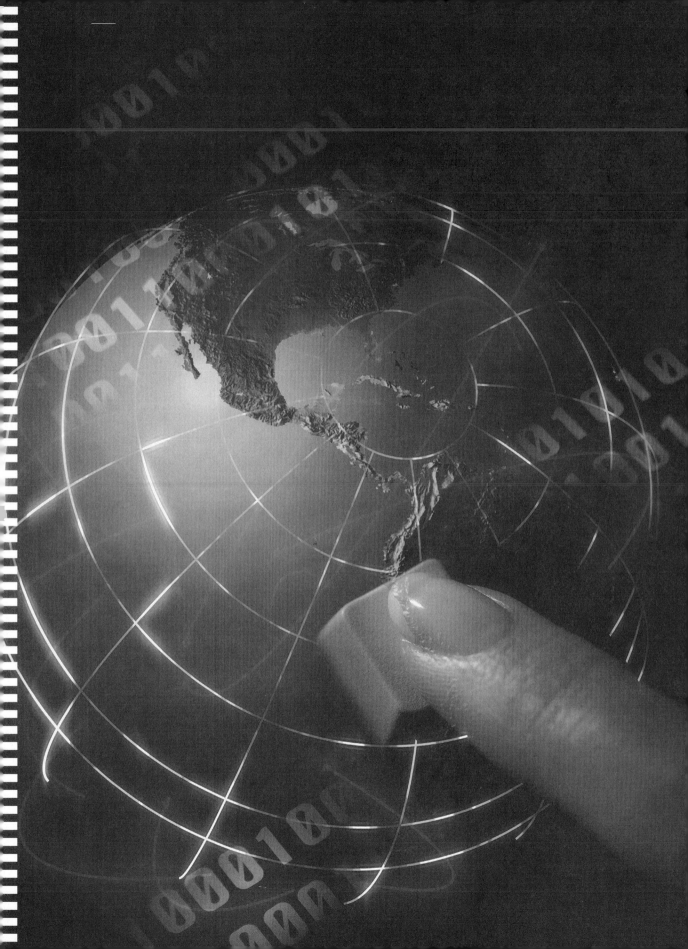

Chapter 5

Statistics and Sampling Distributions

CHAPTER OUTLINE

5.1   Bridging to New Topics

In Chapters 1 and 2, we introduced the analysis of data using simple, but quite useful, statistical methods to convert the data into information and thus increase knowledge about processes and populations. In Chapters 3 and 4, we have been studying probability. What is the difference between probability and statistics? In probability, we consider the distribution of a given population or process and ask what might happen when we select a random sample. For example, given a binomial distribution with $n = 100$ and $\pi = .4$, we might find the probability that X takes on values less than 35. In statistics, on the other hand, we obtain random sample data and ask what the data tell us about unknown features of the population or process from which the sample came. This is statistical inference. For example, suppose we have selected a random sample from a population whose distribution is binomial. Based on the sample data, what can we say about the value of the population proportion π? In general, statistical inference is simply a reversal of the direction of inquiry, as shown in the following figure.

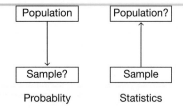

It is our goal to help you understand the methods and underlying thinking of statistical inference. For you to achieve this goal, an understanding of probability is essential. This is why you have been learning the fundamentals of probability, random variables, and probability distributions in the previous chapters. This chapter uses the concepts of probability to develop the framework for statistical inference. Therefore, it serves as a bridge between probability and statistical inference. For the remainder of the book, we deal with methods by which we use data to learn about populations or processes. It is important for you to realize that, if the data are outcomes of an unstable process, then results based on a single random sample are not sufficient for inferences. The following example illustrates the general nature of the problem of making inferences about populations and stable processes.

EXAMPLE 5.1

Suppose that you work for a company that uses a large number of part-time sales representatives to sell its products nationwide. Your responsibility is to develop the sales compensation plan (the formula by which sales reps are paid) for the coming year. As a starting point, you wish to know what the earnings have been *on the average* with the current compensation plan based on all part-time sales reps; that is, you wish to know the population mean μ. This knowledge will tell you whether the current compensation plan is rewarding the sales force adequately on average and, if not, suggest the direction of any adjustments that are needed.

Unfortunately, you have no record of the individual earnings of all sales reps. Therefore, it is not feasible to determine the population mean precisely. The alternative is to identify a random sample of sales reps, determine their earnings for the past year, and estimate μ based on the sample earnings. Now, suppose the average of your sample is $\bar{X} = \$22,500$. This is your most reasonable estimate of μ. But how reliable is it? That is, how far off might this estimate be from μ? If you could be confident that $\bar{X}$ is in error by no more than, say, $500, you would probably be willing to use it as a basis for planning. But if you knew that a value of the sample mean could be off by as much as $6,000, you might insist on more research (for example, a larger sample) before proceeding to develop the compensation plan.

The statistical problem in Example 5.1 is to specify the level of confidence when a sample statistic is used to estimate the corresponding population parameter. This problem lies at the core of virtually all applications of statistical inference. Notice that the key information must come from probability. The questions we really asked were: What is the probability that a value of the sample mean differs from the population mean by more than $500? By more than $6,000? In this chapter, we develop a basis for dealing with problems like this one. The same general approach is used to make inferences in a wide variety of situations, including inferences about means, proportions, variances, standard deviations, and other important parameters; inferences on some of these parameters will be introduced in later chapters.

5.2 Sampling Techniques

As we have already discussed in Chapter 1, sampling provides an attractive means of learning about a population or process. Compared to a census, sampling can be performed at a reduced cost, at greater speed, and can often achieve greater accuracy because, by limiting the scope of the effort, more careful supervision becomes possible. Simple random sampling is the most commonly used and most widely understood technique for selecting a random sample. In this section we elaborate further on simple random sampling and introduce several other techniques that provide opportunities for improved accuracy and/or practical advantages under certain conditions.

Simple Random Sampling

As discussed in Section 1.4.1, simple random sampling is a means of selecting a sample such that each member of the sampled population has an *equal* and *independent* chance of being selected. This approach is free of bias in that no population members are favored in the selection process (equal chance), and the selection of any population member is independent of the selection of any other member (independent chance). The approach provides the means by which the assessment of accuracy is made possible. It also makes possible the control of sampling error through the choice of sample size. (This is illustrated in detail in Section 6.3.2.) To select a simple random sample, the members of the population are numbered 1 through N. To select a sample manually, the numbers 1 through N are placed in a bowl and mixed thoroughly. Then n of these numbers are chosen one by one from the bowl. The population members corresponding to the chosen numbers become the sample. In practice, however, simple random samples are usually chosen with the aid of a computer. Minitab, Excel, and JMP IN have this capability; instructions are provided in the chapter appendix. For example, a sample of $n = 10$ items might be selected randomly from a population of 1,000 items with the following results:

$$17 \quad 896 \quad 112 \quad 940 \quad 129 \quad 179 \quad 300 \quad 350 \quad 60 \quad 822$$

Thus, the population items numbered 17, 896, 112, . . . , 822 are selected for the sample.

Random Sampling from a Process

We often wish to select a random sample from a process rather than a population. We cannot regard a process as a finite population of tangible objects from which a sample is selected. Rather, a process is essentially a continuous activity yielding outcomes over time. In this case, the "population" may be thought of as a collection of an infinite number of possible outcomes that would result if the process were to operate continually without change. In such a situation, it is usually of interest to sample outcomes of the process periodically with regard to some measurable characteristic such as weight, width, strength, length of time, and so on. If the process is stable, the outcomes are the product of essentially identical conditions that exist within the process and may be regarded as independent of each other. An appropriate sampling technique in such situations is to measure the characteristic of interest for a relatively small sample of process outcomes, impartially selected one after another, beginning at some (usually) preselected time and terminating shortly thereafter. Process stability should not be taken for granted. It is essential that we examine the stability of sample data collected over time using such tools as run charts.

Stratified Random Sampling

We are often interested not only in learning about a population but about various subpopulations as well. For example, marketing management may wish to learn not only about the population of business establishments in the United States, but also about the subpopulations of establishments in various regions. If a simple random sample were selected from the population of U.S. establishments, some regions might be underrepresented simply by the chance selection mechanism. A solution to this problem is to select a simple random sample from each region. Thus, instead of randomly selecting, say, 1,000 establishments nationally, we might select random samples of 200 establishments from each of five regions.

The regions of the country in this example are called *strata*. **Strata** are nonoverlapping subpopulations that together comprise an entire population. **Stratified random sampling** is a technique in which simple random samples are selected from each stratum. It offers the following potential advantages:

1. If knowledge is required for specific subpopulations as well as for the entire population, then it is best to treat each subpopulation as a population in its own right.

2. Stratified random sampling ensures that we obtain data for key subpopulations having relatively small sizes. For example, it may be essential to obtain an adequate sample of very large establishments, which may constitute only a small fraction of the population of all establishments.

3. Stratified random sampling may be more convenient administratively, especially if the data collection process is to be conducted by regional offices.

4. When subpopulations differ substantially from each other but are internally similar, stratified random sampling provides increased accuracy by ensuring that a small sample is obtained from each subpopulation. (Since the items within a subpopulation are similar, only a small sample is needed to characterize the subpopulation.)

The primary statistical issues that arise in planning a stratified random sample have to do with the identification of strata and the choice of stratum sample sizes. When there is a choice in the identification of strata, the idea is to construct the strata in such a way that the population items within a stratum are similar but between strata are likely to be quite different. For example, in sampling the waiting times of customers of a bank, the strata might consist of (1) all customers arriving between 11:45 A.M. and 1:30 P.M. (the busy period) and (2) all other customers. The choice of stratum sample sizes depends on several factors. In general, larger samples are appropriate for a stratum if (1) the stratum is larger; (2) the stratum exhibits more internal variation; and (3) the cost of sampling is lower within the stratum. If a certain level of precision is required for the individual strata, a sufficient sample size must be obtained for each stratum. In this case, the sample size is chosen by applying the theory of simple random sampling to each stratum [specifically, by applying Expression (6.5) in Section 6.3.2 or other similar expressions].

In subsequent discussions of statistical inference, we assume, unless otherwise noted, that the sampling process is simple random sampling.

5.3   Parameters, Statistics, and Fundamentals of Statistical Inference

Recall from Chapter 1 that a **parameter** is a number that summarizes some feature of a population or process, and a **statistic** is a quantity that summarizes some feature of a sample. In previous chapters, we have encountered parameters such as the mean μ, the variance σ^2, the standard deviation σ, and the proportion π. Corresponding to these parameters are the statistics $\bar{X}$ (the sample mean), S^2 (the sample variance), S (the sample standard deviation), and p (the sample proportion). As we mentioned in Chapter 1, statistics are usually denoted by uppercase Roman letters, and parameters are denoted by lowercase Greek letters. For the sample proportion p, we deviate from this tradition to avoid confusion with the use of capital P to denote a probability, as seen in the previous two chapters. As you will see in Section 5.4, the statistics $\bar{X}$ and p are deemed to be the "best statistics" for estimating μ and π, respectively. What do we mean by "best statistic"? The meaning of this term is explained in Section 5.4.

How do we characterize the amount by which an estimate might be in error? Consider the procedure suggested in Example 5.1. We select a random sample (of sales representatives) from a population (all sales representatives) and compute the value of the best statistic for estimating the parameter of interest (the mean earnings for the year). It is absolutely essential to understand that *every statistic fluctuates in value randomly from one sample to another, whereas parameters may be regarded as constants that are usually unknown*. The value we compute for a statistic from any one sample depends on the sample we happen to get. Therefore, *every statistic whose value is determined from a random sample is a random variable*. In Example 5.1, we used the statistic $\bar{X}$ because we were interested in μ. A variety of outcomes for $\bar{X}$ were possible: the specific value we got depended on the particular random sample we happened to obtain. No one random sample is more or less valid than any other random sample of the same size that might have been selected.

A Simulation

To illustrate the fact that statistics fluctuate from sample to sample, we use Minitab to simulate the outcomes of a stable process in which boxes are filled with a detergent. The variable of concern is the weight of the detergent in a given box. The process ordinarily fills boxes with an average of $\mu = 50$ ounces of detergent, and the detergent weights vary from box to box with a standard deviation of $\sigma = .5$ ounce. A production supervisor must check periodically whether the process has strayed from these values. To do this, random samples consisting of ten boxes are selected every hour. For each sample, the contents of each of the ten boxes are weighed; then the values for the statistics $\bar{X}$, S^2, and S are determined.

Suppose one of the hourly samples had a mean of $\overline{X} = 50.21$ ounces, and the supervisor used this value as an estimate of the current process mean. How far away from the process mean might this estimate be? Does the sample average of 50.21 ounces exceed the usual process average of 50.0 ounces by a large enough amount that the supervisor can safely conclude that the process mean has increased? Perhaps, but some caution is required because the difference from 50.0 might simply be the result of sampling error (i.e., random sampling variation).

For this simulation, the weights of the detergent in the boxes were generated randomly by a computer from a normal distribution with mean $\mu = 50$ ounces and standard deviation $\sigma = .5$ ounce. The weights for 40 samples, each sample consisting of $n = 10$ weights, are given in Table 5.1, along with the corresponding values of $\overline{X}$, S^2, and S. The simulation of 40 samples allows you to observe the fluctuation of various statistics over the possible samples that *could* be selected.

From Table 5.1, notice that, although all samples were taken from a stable process (the filling process) with constant mean and standard deviation ($\mu = 50$, $\sigma^2 = .25$, and $\sigma = .5$), the values of the sample mean, variance, and standard deviation vary from sample to sample. Over 40 samples, the values of the sample mean range from 49.68 to 50.26 ounces; the values of the sample variance range from .094 to .447 ounce squared; and the values of the sample standard deviation range from .306 to .669 ounce.

Now, let's think about what this simulation tells us. The 40 simulated samples indicate that the sample mean can easily lie anywhere between 49.68 and 50.26 ounces. Imagine that the next sample to be simulated (the 41st) is the *real* one—the one sample actually selected by the production supervisor. If the mean of this sample is between 49.68 and 50.26 ounces, there would be little reason to think that the process mean had shifted away from 50 ounces. But if the value is outside this range, there would be sufficient reason to think that the process mean had shifted away from 50 ounces.

Suppose we knew somehow that the values of $\overline{X}$ *over all possible samples of size 10* would range from 49.6 to 50.4 ounces. That is, assuming the process remained stable, none of the possible random samples of size 10 from the process would yield an $\overline{X}$ value that is more than .4 ounce above or below $\mu = 50$. Then we would know that the mean of the one sample of size 10 we happened to select at any one time could not be in error by more than .4 ounce from $\mu = 50$. This example suggests that *the key to understanding the usefulness of a statistic lies in understanding how much the statistic can vary from one random sample to another.* In other words, we need to understand the distribution of the possible values of the statistic over all possible random samples of the same size from the population.

The distribution of values of a statistic over all possible random samples is called a **sampling distribution.** The sampling distribution of a statistic has the properties of any probability distribution: for example, it has a mean, a standard deviation, and a certain shape. So a sampling distribution is simply a probability distribution that applies specifically to the outcomes of a statistic over all possible random samples of equal size taken from the population or process of interest.

A computer-generated histogram of the 40 values of $\overline{X}$ in Table 5.1 is given in Figure 5.1(a); it depicts the fluctuation of $\overline{X}$ over the 40 simulated samples and approximates the sampling distribution of $\overline{X}$ over all possible random samples of size $n = 10$. For comparison, Figure 5.1(b) depicts the fluctuation of $\overline{X}$ over 5,000

Table 5.1

Ten detergent weights for each of 40 samples

	Obs. 1	Obs. 2	Obs. 3	Obs. 4	Obs. 5	Obs. 6	Obs. 7	Obs. 8	Obs. 9	Obs. 10	$\bar{X}$	S^2	S
Sample													
1	49.794	50.100	49.770	49.544	49.854	50.804	50.086	50.113	50.710	49.470	50.025	.198	.445
2	49.446	50.091	49.298	49.935	49.724	49.822	49.996	50.065	49.621	50.423	49.842	.111	.333
3	49.428	50.621	49.584	49.782	49.064	50.223	50.278	49.627	49.368	49.086	49.706	.272	.521
4	50.101	50.069	49.268	50.612	49.773	49.584	50.251	50.245	49.577	49.372	49.885	.190	.436
5	49.358	49.325	50.583	50.379	49.995	49.868	50.227	50.418	49.168	49.626	49.895	.257	.507
6	50.559	49.860	49.571	49.880	49.432	49.407	50.151	50.636	50.299	50.203	50.000	.196	.443
7	48.697	50.170	50.293	49.866	49.430	49.727	50.819	50.051	49.401	49.975	49.843	.335	.579
8	50.327	50.453	49.245	50.668	50.354	49.577	50.379	49.901	50.249	50.467	50.162	.200	.448
9	50.391	50.800	49.606	50.204	50.051	50.752	49.527	50.397	50.211	50.095	50.203	.175	.419
10	50.625	50.125	50.483	50.665	49.474	50.443	49.999	50.367	50.153	50.311	50.265	.123	.351
11	50.278	50.040	49.602	49.180	49.616	49.947	49.118	49.747	50.167	49.143	49.684	.185	.430
12	49.108	50.903	49.302	49.688	50.922	50.105	49.234	50.386	50.216	49.799	49.966	.430	.656
13	50.472	49.756	50.583	49.571	50.600	51.141	49.898	50.265	49.704	50.476	50.247	.251	.501
14	48.900	50.042	50.180	50.317	49.640	49.995	49.983	49.669	51.007	49.722	49.946	.294	.542
15	50.751	50.998	49.730	50.029	50.546	49.791	50.494	50.345	49.857	49.622	50.216	.226	.475
16	50.086	49.634	50.286	49.315	50.259	50.808	49.692	49.666	49.338	49.974	49.906	.219	.468
17	50.027	50.091	49.940	49.989	50.314	51.112	49.908	49.983	49.799	50.386	50.155	.145	.381
18	50.761	49.496	49.307	49.853	49.468	50.067	50.017	50.773	50.298	50.267	50.031	.263	.513
19	49.913	49.383	49.537	49.997	50.654	50.182	50.606	50.195	49.653	49.838	49.996	.179	.424
20	49.348	50.173	49.908	49.637	49.628	49.350	49.883	50.184	50.074	49.841	49.803	.094	.306
21	49.504	50.157	50.430	50.209	51.131	49.776	49.398	49.829	49.987	50.364	50.079	.255	.505
22	49.470	50.242	49.667	49.642	49.751	50.449	49.036	49.501	49.706	49.945	49.741	.160	.400
23	50.019	50.542	49.652	49.626	49.849	50.119	50.647	50.742	49.358	49.669	50.022	.231	.481
24	50.322	49.400	50.132	50.102	49.540	50.306	49.805	49.624	49.746	50.672	49.965	.164	.406
25	50.086	49.694	49.364	50.467	49.893	50.757	48.933	49.019	49.467	49.970	49.765	.349	.591
26	49.824	50.734	49.623	50.508	50.700	49.732	50.300	49.436	49.713	50.946	50.125	.297	.545
27	50.037	50.495	49.800	49.658	50.041	50.149	49.617	49.798	49.438	50.089	49.912	.096	.309
28	50.652	50.655	50.075	49.578	50.027	49.445	49.937	49.803	50.576	49.983	50.073	.185	.431
29	49.725	50.271	50.140	49.658	49.983	49.709	50.620	49.864	50.403	50.353	50.073	.112	.335
30	49.706	49.862	49.685	50.512	49.627	50.163	50.071	49.354	49.975	50.108	49.906	.109	.330
31	50.215	50.199	50.669	49.616	49.389	50.228	49.854	50.383	49.559	50.001	50.011	.163	.404
32	49.484	49.667	49.743	49.938	49.983	49.861	50.353	51.050	49.458	49.814	49.935	.220	.469
33	49.638	49.427	49.641	50.330	49.799	49.785	49.773	48.981	50.365	49.829	49.757	.161	.401
34	50.541	50.666	50.161	50.006	49.538	50.439	49.230	49.933	50.497	49.868	50.088	.217	.466
35	50.075	49.937	50.014	50.640	50.936	50.188	49.935	48.973	50.375	49.859	50.093	.274	.523
36	49.264	50.355	49.252	51.005	49.129	50.111	49.945	50.366	50.032	49.888	49.935	.346	.588
37	49.995	50.146	50.822	49.454	49.794	50.418	49.101	50.123	49.639	50.592	50.008	.280	.529
38	49.476	48.954	49.875	49.642	49.765	49.861	49.468	49.715	49.829	50.418	49.700	.140	.374
39	50.815	49.390	50.403	50.891	50.197	48.884	50.635	49.511	50.341	50.476	50.154	.447	.669
40	49.851	50.239	49.711	50.395	50.202	50.030	49.789	49.050	50.557	50.305	50.013	.190	.436

simulated samples, each of size $n = 10$. Clearly, the histogram in Figure 5.1(b) more nearly resembles the sampling distribution of $\bar{X}$ over all possible samples of size $n = 10$.

Statistics serve as *estimators* of parameters. In this context, the standard deviation of a statistic—that is, the standard deviation of a statistic's sampling distribution—measures the statistic's precision. In other words, the standard deviation of a statistic indicates the degree to which values of the statistic can vary from the actual parameter value from one random sample to the next. Do you have some insight now into what constitutes the "best" statistic for a parameter of interest? It is desirable that a statistic have a small standard deviation, so that for any one sample it is not likely to vary much

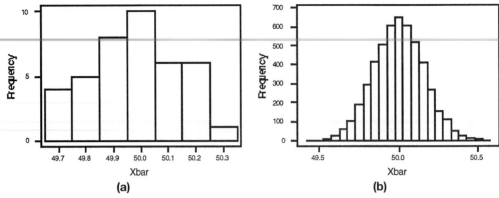

Figure 5.1

(a) Histogram of sample means for 40 random samples of $n = 10$
(b) Histogram of sample means for 5,000 random samples of $n = 10$

from the parameter value. The standard deviation of a statistic is often called the *standard error* because the variation of a value of the statistic for a particular sample from the parameter value represents the error by which this value of the statistic misestimates the parameter. A **standard error** is the standard deviation of a sampling distribution; and, thus, measures the variation of the values of a statistic over all possible random samples of the same size.

Using a computer, we determine that the average of the 40 values of $\overline{X}$ in Table 5.1 is 49.98 and the standard deviation (standard error) is .15484. You should understand that these are the approximate values for the mean and standard error of $\overline{X}$. To compute the actual mean and standard error of $\overline{X}$ requires that all possible random samples of the same size be included, which obviously would be an impossible task.

It is crucial to realize that, *in practice, we select only one sample at any one time and therefore observe only one of the possible values of a statistic.* Suppose we select a random sample from a population whose mean μ is unknown. Suppose further that, for this sample, we determine that $\overline{X} = 30$. This value becomes our best estimate of μ. Now, how far from μ is this estimate? We cannot know for sure, of course, since we do not know the value of μ; however, knowledge of the sampling distribution of the statistic tells us how much our one value *might* have deviated from the parameter value. For instance, if we knew that the value of $\overline{X}$ is within, say, 4 units (plus or minus) of μ for 95% of all possible equal-size random samples, we could be confident that for our sample the actual value of μ is no more than 4 units from 30. Therefore, we could be confident that the actual value of μ lies between 26 and 34. As this example suggests, *the key step in determining the usefulness of any statistic for making inferences about a parameter is to identify the sampling distribution of the statistic.*

This line of thinking presents an apparent dilemma: How can we determine the sampling distribution of a statistic (that is, its distribution over all possible samples of the same size) if we have obtained only one sample? One sample alone does not provide this information. We cannot perform a simulation because it would require knowledge of the population or process. However, by combining the information provided by a random sample with some statistical theory, we can usually determine the sampling distribution, at least approximately. In the remainder of this chapter, we develop the statistical concepts that allow us to determine the sampling distributions of two key statistics: the sample mean $\bar{X}$, and the sample proportion p. The sampling distributions of some other useful statistics are developed in later chapters, as we discuss the specific applications for which they are used.

In the context of using statistics to estimate parameters, we must also emphasize another crucial point: We have to understand that populations or processes change over time. For example, if the filling machines are not properly maintained in a filling process or workers are not properly trained, then the process average fill and standard deviation may drift considerably from their target values over time. Therefore, it is indeed important to recognize that a sample can reflect the characteristics of a population or process *only at the time the sample is taken.* An effective way to detect important shifts in key parameters is to institute an ongoing sampling procedure in which samples are taken periodically. Since each sample reflects the population or process at the time it was taken, a comparison among samples over time may indicate changes in the population or process. We elaborate further on this as we proceed through the application of statistical methods.

Fundamentals of Statistical Inference

Recall from Chapter 1 that the use of sample data to understand some important feature of a population or process of interest is called **statistical inference.** As we said in Chapter 1, we examine two types of statistical inference in this book. One type is called **estimation,** which can be subdivided into **point estimation** and **interval estimation.** In point estimation, the end result is a **point estimate,** which is a *single number* that serves as an intelligent guess of the value of a parameter. A point estimate is the value of a statistic determined from the particular sample. Consequently, a statistic is also known as an **estimator.** For example, we may observe that 14% of the invoices in a random sample have errors. Thus, "14%" is a point estimate of the percentage of invoices in the population that have errors. Until the next time we analyze a sample of invoices, we may proceed on the working assumption that the population error rate is 14%. In interval estimation, the estimate consists of a *range* of values. For the invoice error example, we realize that 14% is probably not precisely the population error rate. If we could determine with confidence that the population error rate say, lies between 12% and 16%, then we might use this interval as a working range for the population error rate until the next sample is selected. The range "12% to 16%" is an **interval estimate.**

The second type of statistical inference is called **hypothesis testing.** A statistical hypothesis is a claim or belief about an unknown parameter value. As we illustrate in subsequent chapters, hypothesis testing is closely related to estimation. In hypothesis testing, instead of estimating the unknown value of a parameter, we test the validity of a *claim* or *belief* about the value of the parameter; that is, we determine whether the sample data tend to support or contradict a certain claim or belief about the parameter value. For example, suppose the billing department of a company is committed to holding the percentage of invoices with errors to no more than 10%. Periodically, a random sample of invoices is analyzed by an audit team to test the claim that the population percentage of invoices with billing errors is no greater than 10%. If, based on periodic sampling, the claim is contradicted, then management may choose to institute corrective measures. Suppose that, for a given random sample, an interval estimate of the population error rate is determined to be 12% to 16%. Then the evidence provided by the random sample seems to indicate that the targeted 10% rate is being exceeded.

We summarize the important terms from the preceding discussion in the following box:

FUNDAMENTAL DEFINITIONS FOR STATISTICAL INFERENCE

1. A **sampling distribution** is the probability distribution of the values of a statistic over all possible random samples of the same size.
2. A **standard error** is the standard deviation of the values of a statistic over all possible random samples of the same size.
3. An **estimator** is any statistic used to estimate an unknown parameter value.
4. A **point estimate** is the value of a statistic that results from a specific sample; it provides a best guess of an unknown parameter value.
5. An **interval estimate** is a range of values thought to contain an unknown parameter value.
6. A **statistical hypothesis** is a claim or belief about an unknown parameter value.

5.4 Desirable Properties of Statistics

It is essential to understand that before any statistical inference is possible, two key issues must be resolved:

1. What is the "best" statistic to use to make inferences about a parameter of interest?
2. What is the sampling distribution of this best statistic?

In resolving the first issue, let's consider the following question: What characteristics should we look for in choosing a statistic to serve as the estimator of a parameter? At a general level, the answer is obvious. We want an estimator whose estimate based on a particular sample is likely to be as close as possible to the actual parameter value. However, the accuracy of a given estimator depends on the particular sample we happen to select at random. With some samples, the resulting estimate may be quite accurate; with others, it may be less accurate. The accuracy of an estimator varies from sample to sample, so there is no certainty of the accuracy achieved for the one sample we happen to obtain. Therefore, we must characterize the performance of an estimator by the accuracy it achieves *on average* over all possible random samples of the same size, even though we obtain only one sample at any given time. We wish to choose the estimator whose "average accuracy" is as good as possible. This is the general criterion we use in choosing an estimator. To apply this concept, we utilize two specific criteria: We prefer estimators that are **unbiased** and have **minimum standard error.**

Unbiased Estimators

For any given sample, the resulting estimate is likely to be above or below the unknown parameter value by some amount because of sampling error. It is desirable that the *average* of the estimates over all possible random samples equal the parameter value; that is, we want the expected value of the estimator to equal the parameter value. This means there is no tendency for the estimator to yield values that are either consistently too high or consistently too low. If this is the case, we say that the estimator is unbiased. In general, unbiased estimators are preferred over biased estimators.

> An estimator is **unbiased** if its expected value equals the parameter value.

Figure 5.2 illustrates this point by showing the sampling distributions of two possible statistics (called A and B) that may be considered for estimating a parameter θ (Greek letter theta). Assume that statistics A and B have the same standard error. Then statistic A is more likely than statistic B to yield an estimate close to θ because the expected value of A equals θ [$E(A) = \theta$], whereas the expected value of B does not [$E(B) \neq \theta$].

Figure 5.2

The sampling distributions of two statistics, one unbiased (A) and one biased (B)

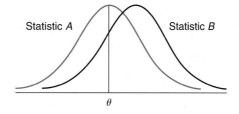

Estimators with Minimum Standard Error

Suppose two statistics are both unbiased. How should we choose between them as estimators? Consider Figure 5.3; it shows the sampling distributions of statistics A and C, which are being considered for estimation of the parameter θ. From these two unbiased statistics, which would you choose to estimate θ, A or C? Why? Stop here before reading on and think about your choice and especially the reason for your choice.

Figure 5.3

The sampling distributions of two unbiased statistics of parameter θ

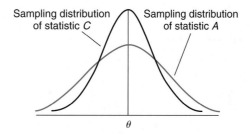

Statistic C is more likely than statistic A to provide an estimate that is close to θ for a given sample because it has the smaller standard error; that is, there is less variation in the sampling distribution of C. Over a large number of random samples, the estimates that result from C are more consistently near θ than are the estimates of statistic A. Statistic A tends to produce larger estimation errors both above and below θ. So the chance that a specific sample produces an estimate close to θ is better with estimator C than with estimator A.

It should be apparent to you now what we mean by a "best" statistic to estimate a parameter of interest. In this book, the phrase "best statistic for a parameter of interest" is defined as the statistic that meets the following two criteria:

CRITERIA FOR THE BEST STATISTIC

1. The statistic is an **unbiased estimator** of the parameter of interest.
2. The statistic has a **smaller standard error** than any other unbiased statistic for estimating the parameter of interest.

Two of the most important and most frequently estimated parameters are the mean μ, and the proportion π. Statistical theory indicates that the sample statistics $\overline{X}$ and p satisfy the indicated two criteria and, for our purposes, are deemed the best statistics for μ and π, respectively. In the remaining sections of this chapter, we deal with the identification of the sampling distributions of $\overline{X}$ and p.

5.5 The Sampling Distribution of the Sample Mean $\overline{X}$

In general, the sampling distribution of the sample mean $\overline{X}$ depends on the distribution of the population or process from which we are sampling. For example, if we are sampling from a population or process with a normal distribution, the sampling distribution of $\overline{X}$ is also normal. Even if the population or process distribution is not normal, the sampling distribution of $\overline{X}$ is approximately normal as long as the sample size is sufficiently large. The problem with either one of these situations is that the determination of the standard error of $\overline{X}$ requires knowledge of the population or process standard deviation σ. In practice, however, σ is rarely known. In the vast number of situations, σ has to be estimated by using the sample standard deviation S. When this happens, statistical theory has shown that the Student's T distribution, introduced later in this section, is the appropriate sampling distribution to use in making statistical inferences about μ based on $\overline{X}$. Thus, the T distribution plays the central role for inferences about μ based on $\overline{X}$, since in practice the population or process standard deviation σ is rarely known.

5.5.1 The Mean and Standard Error of $\overline{X}$

It is possible to determine the mean and standard error of $\overline{X}$ without knowing the population or process distribution. Suppose we are sampling from a large population or process with mean μ and standard deviation σ.* It can be shown mathematically that for a sample of size n, the expected value of $\overline{X}$ over all possible random samples from the population or process is

---

*Throughout our discussion of statistical inference, we assume that the size of the population is at least 20 times larger than the size of any random sample we happen to take. This ensures an acceptable amount of statistical independence among sampling outcomes.

$$E(\bar{X}) = \mu \qquad \textbf{(5.1)}$$

and the standard error of $\bar{X}$ over all equal-size random samples is

$$SE(\bar{X}) = \frac{\sigma}{\sqrt{n}} \qquad \textbf{(5.2)}$$

regardless of the distribution of the population or process.

Expression (5.2) says that for $n > 1$, the variation of the values of $\bar{X}$ is *less* than the variation of the values of the population or process. The simulated data in Table 5.1 can help you understand this important result. Recall that the 40 values of $\bar{X}$ vary from 49.68 to 50.26 ounces, a range of only .58 ounce. Now pick any one of the 40 samples and find the range of weights within that sample. The weights in the first sample range from 49.47 to 50.80 ounces, a range of 1.33 ounces. The weights in the second sample range from 49.30 to 50.42 ounces, a range of 1.12 ounces. The weights in the third sample range from 49.06 to 50.62 ounces, a range of 1.56 ounces, and so on. As you can see, the variation in the individual weights is greater than the variation among the $\bar{X}$ values.

To illustrate the determination of the standard error of $\bar{X}$, we turn again to the filling process example of Section 5.2, in which we randomly selected samples of size $n = 10$ from the process with $\mu = 50$ and $\sigma = .5$. From Expressions (5.1) and (5.2), the mean of the statistic $\bar{X}$ over all possible random samples of size $n = 10$ from this filling process is

$$E(\bar{X}) = 50$$

and the standard error of $\bar{X}$ over all possible samples of size $n = 10$ is

$$SE(\bar{X}) = \frac{.5}{\sqrt{10}} = .1581$$

Recall that, for the 40 simulated samples listed in Table 5.1, the average of the 40 values of $\bar{X}$ is 49.98, and the standard error is .15484. Clearly, the values of 49.98 and .15484 based on the 40 samples are close to the corresponding theoretical values 50 and .1581, respectively, over all possible random samples of size $n = 10$. The only reason they differ is that we simulated only 40 samples rather than an infinite number of samples.

It is important to understand the fundamental meaning of Expressions (5.1) and (5.2).

1. Expression (5.1) tells us that if we could list all possible samples of size n that could be taken from a population or process and compute the $\bar{X}$ value for each, then the average of these $\bar{X}$ values would be μ, the mean of the population. These $\bar{X}$ values tend to cluster around μ and are neither consistently too high nor too low. Since the mean of the possible values of $\bar{X}$ is μ, the statistic $\bar{X}$ is by definition an unbiased estimator of μ.

2. Expression (5.2) tells us that the standard error of $\bar{X}$ depends on both the population standard deviation σ and the sample size n. The standard error of $\bar{X}$ decreases in proportion to increases in the *square root* of n. For example, to halve

Figure 5.4

The effect of sample size on the standard error of the sample mean

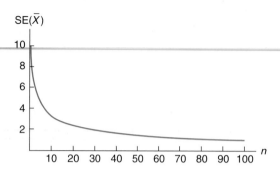

the standard error of $\bar{X}$, we have to increase the sample size by a factor of 4. Therefore, as the sample size increases, the precision of the sample mean for estimating the population mean improves. This is a highly advantageous property of $\bar{X}$ because it assures that for a large enough sample size, the value of $\bar{X}$ can be expected to approximate the population mean μ very closely.

To illustrate the nature of the standard error of $\bar{X}$ as a function of n, let's assume that we are sampling from a population with standard deviation $\sigma = 10$. We can determine SE($\bar{X}$) using Expression (5.2) for various values of n. For example, for $n = 5$, SE($\bar{X}$) = $10/\sqrt{5} = 4.47$; for $n = 10$, SE($\bar{X}$) = $10/\sqrt{10} = 3.16$; for $n = 20$, SE($\bar{X}$) = $10/\sqrt{20} = 2.24$; and so on. We graph these results in Figure 5.4. Notice that the decrease in the standard error of $\bar{X}$ is rather substantial as n takes on larger values, but beyond about $n = 30$, the drop tapers off considerably. This means that an extremely large sample size is not necessary for making inferences about μ based on $\bar{X}$. In fact, a large sample size is often not cost effective, and the additional work to obtain larger samples often leads to other kinds of errors, as discussed in Chapter 1.

5.5.2   The Sampling Distribution of $\bar{X}$ When the Population or Process Has a Normal Distribution

From the last section, we know that no matter what the population distribution is, the mean of $\bar{X}$ over all possible samples of equal size n is μ and the standard error of $\bar{X}$ is $\sigma/\sqrt{n}$. Suppose we assume that the population or process from which we are sampling has a normal distribution with mean μ and standard deviation σ. Then it can be shown mathematically that the sampling distribution of $\bar{X}$ is also normal with mean μ and standard error $\sigma/\sqrt{n}$. This result comes about because *any linear combination of normal random variables is also a normal random variable.* In particular, if the population or process has a normal distribution, the sampling distribution of $\bar{X}$ is also normal.

Notice that if the sampling distribution of $\bar{X}$ is normal with mean μ and standard error $\sigma/\sqrt{n}$, then the distribution of the standardized statistic Z, where

$$Z = \frac{\bar{X} - \mu}{\sigma/\sqrt{n}}$$

(5.3)

is the standard normal (see Section 4.3). As we pointed out in Chapter 4, the standard normal distribution provides a convenient way for determining probabilities involving any normal random variable, especially when a computer is not available. It serves precisely the same purpose for $\bar{X}$ when the sampling distribution of $\bar{X}$ is normal.

EXAMPLE 5.2

As we have indicated previously, periodic samples are taken from manufacturing processes to assess whether important process characteristics, such as average and standard deviation of outputs, appear to be at desired values. For each periodic sample selected, the value of the corresponding statistic is determined and, based on this value and the sampling distribution of the statistic, an assessment is made regarding whether it appears that the desired process value is being maintained. This example illustrates such a situation for a process average.

A manufacturing process produces ball bearings. Based on previous experimentation with the diameters of the bearings produced by this process, the supervisor is satisfied that, under stable conditions, (1) the process mean diameter is 5 centimeters, (2) the process standard deviation is .005 centimeter, and (3) the process distribution is normal. The supervisor is interested in maintaining the process mean diameter at 5 centimeters. To do this, she regularly selects random samples of nine ball bearings in an attempt to detect departures from indicated norms.

(a) What is the sampling distribution of $\overline{X}$?

(b) Suppose the supervisor selects a random sample of nine bearings, measures their diameters, and finds that $\overline{X} = 5.004$ centimeters. What is the likelihood that the average diameter of nine randomly selected bearings would be at least 5.004 centimeters, if the process mean remained at 5 centimeters and the process standard deviation continued to be .005 centimeter?

(c) What sample size would be needed to achieve a standard error of $\overline{X}$ equal to .001?

(d) In part (c), why might the inspector prefer that the standard error of $\overline{X}$ equal .001 rather than the value you obtain in part (a)?

Solution

(a) Since the process distribution is assumed to be normal with $\mu = 5$ and $\sigma = .005$, the sampling distribution of $\overline{X}$ is also normal with mean $\mu = 5$ and standard error (for $n = 9$) SE$(\overline{X}) = .005/\sqrt{9} = .001667$.

(b) This question is at the heart of statistical inference. A sample result has occurred (that is, $\overline{X} = 5.004$). What is the chance (probability) of such an outcome, if we assume the usual process ($\mu = 5$ centimeters and $\sigma = .005$ centimeter) is being maintained? If this probability is high, there is little reason to suspect that a shift away from the usual process mean has taken place. Changes to the system in this case would constitute tampering. On the other hand, if this probability is small, there may be good reason to believe a shift has occurred.

Since the sampling distribution of $\overline{X}$ is normal with $\mu = 5$ and SE$(\overline{X}) = .001667$, we can easily use a computer (instructions for using Minitab, Excel, and JMP IN in this regard are provided in the chapter appendix) to determine the desired probability that a value of $\overline{X}$ is at least 5.004. With Minitab, we first find the probability of the complementary event that a value of $\overline{X}$ is less than 5.004 given by the following output, then subtract this probability from 1. Thus, the desired probability is $P(\overline{X} \geq 5.004) = 1 - .9918 = .0082$.

```
Normal  with  mean = 5.00000  and
standard  deviation = 0.00166700
              x            P( X <= x)
          5.0040              0.9918
```

Alternatively, we can determine the desired probability by converting the value $\bar{X} = 5.004$ to the corresponding Z-value and use Table B, as illustrated in Figure 5.5.

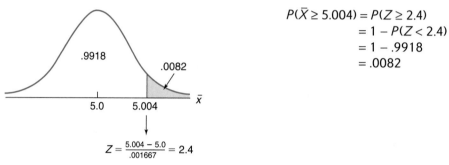

$$
\begin{aligned}
P(\bar{X} \ge 5.004) &= P(Z \ge 2.4) \\
&= 1 - P(Z < 2.4) \\
&= 1 - .9918 \\
&= .0082
\end{aligned}
$$

$$Z = \frac{5.004 - 5.0}{.001667} = 2.4$$

Figure 5.5

Correspondence between $\bar{X}$ and Z-values for Example 5.2

Clearly, a probability of less than 1% has to be deemed rather small. So there is good reason to believe that a shift from $\mu = 5$ has occurred. But the supervisor should be careful before deciding that corrective action on the process is needed. Further inquiry is warranted as to whether a problem truly exists and, if so, its cause.

(c) The needed sample size is determined simply by equating the expression for the standard error of $\bar{X}$ to the desired value and solving for n. Thus,

$$SE(\bar{X}) = \frac{.005}{\sqrt{n}} = .001$$

$$\sqrt{n} = \frac{.005}{.001}$$

$$n = 25$$

A sample size of $n = 25$ achieves the desired standard error.

(d) A standard error of .001 is smaller than .001667, the standard error found in part (a). If the standard error were .001, then inferences based on $\bar{X}$ would be more reliable and less subject to question. For example, let's rework part (b) using $SE(\bar{X}) = .001$. With Excel, we determine the probability that a random sample of 25 ball bearings from the process yields a mean diameter as large as 5.004 as follows:

	A	B
1	x	P(X<=x)
2	5.004	0.99997

Consequently, the desired probability is virtually zero: $P(\bar{X} \geq 5.004) = 1 - .99997 = .00003$. The probability of such an occurrence is now much smaller than before. Thus, a conclusion that the process mean has shifted would be even more convincing.

5.5.3 The Sampling Distribution of $\bar{X}$ When the Population or Process Has a Nonnormal Distribution

In many situations, the distribution of the population or process cannot be identified, so the sampling distribution of $\bar{X}$ cannot be determined. However, statisticians have been able to show that the sampling distribution of $\bar{X}$ is approximately normal for large sample sizes *no matter what the population distribution is.* This result is known as the **central limit theorem,** a statistical principle that can be summarized as follows: As the sample size n increases, the sampling distribution of $\bar{X}$ approaches a normal distribution regardless of the population distribution.

Since the central limit theorem states that, for large sample sizes, the sampling distribution of $\bar{X}$ is approximately normal with mean μ and standard error $\sigma/\sqrt{n}$, it follows that the distribution of

$$Z = \frac{\bar{X} - \mu}{\sigma/\sqrt{n}}$$

is approximately the standard normal distribution where μ and σ are the population mean and standard deviation, respectively.

How large must n be for $\bar{X}$ to have a normal distribution, at least approximately? The answer depends on how nearly normal the population or process distribution is. If the population distribution is single peaked and symmetric or only moderately skewed, the sampling distribution of $\bar{X}$ is approximately normal for sample sizes as small as 10 (or even smaller, in some cases). For population distributions that are distinctly nonnormal, the sampling distribution of $\bar{X}$ is approximately normal for sample sizes $n \geq 30$. It has been common practice to use $n = 30$ as a threshold value for assuming that the sampling distribution of $\bar{X}$ is approximately normal.

To illustrate the central limit theorem, we simulate 500 samples of size $n = 10$ from a population whose distribution is extremely skewed. Then we repeat the simulation of 500 samples using a sample size of $n = 40$. Part (a) of Figure 5.6, illustrates the population distribution; notice the severity of the skewness. In parts (b) and (c), the sampling distributions of $\bar{X}$ over the 500 samples are depicted for $n = 10$ and $n = 40$, respectively. In part (b), notice that for $n = 10$ the sampling distribution of $\bar{X}$ remains somewhat skewed. But in part (c), the sampling distribution of $\bar{X}$ for $n = 40$ is virtually symmetric and mound shaped. Notice also the decrease in the variation of

Figure 5.6

The simulated effect of sample size on the shape of the distribution of the sample mean when sampling from a skewed population

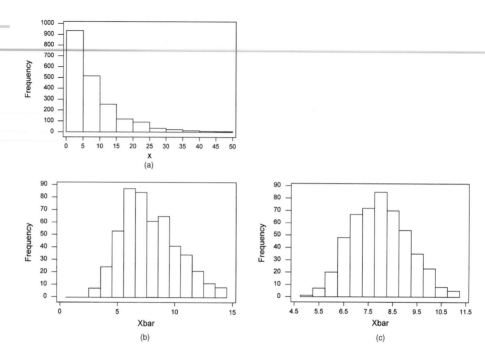

the sampling distribution as n increases from 10 to 40. For $n = 10$, values of $\bar{X}$ range from about 1 to 14, whereas for $n = 40$ they range from about 5 to 11.

EXAMPLE 5.3

For a certain aptitude test, it is known from past experience that the average score is $\mu = 1000$ and the standard deviation is $\sigma = 125$. If the test is administered to 100 randomly selected individuals, what is the probability that the value of $\bar{X}$ for this sample will lie in the interval 970 to 1030? Assume the current population distribution is identical to that of previous populations.

Solution

Although no mention is made about the shape of the population distribution, none is necessary, since the sample size of $n = 100$ is more than enough for the application of the central limit theorem. Assuming that $\mu = 1000$ and $\sigma = 125$ remain true for the individuals who are taking this test now, we find the sample mean $\bar{X}$ is (to an excellent approximation) a normal random variable with $E(\bar{X}) = 1000$ and $SE(\bar{X}) = 125/\sqrt{100} = 12.5$. The determination of the probability that a value of $\bar{X}$ lies between 970 and 1030 is illustrated in Figure 5.7.

5.5.4 Population or Process Standard Deviation σ Unknown; An Introduction to the T Distribution

In discussing the sampling distribution of $\bar{X}$ so far, we have proceeded as if the population standard deviation σ were known. For example, recall from Expression (5.3) that, if the sample mean $\bar{X}$ has a normal distribution, then

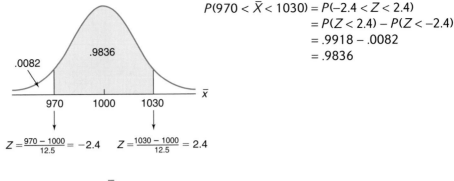

Figure 5.7

Probability deter-
mination for
Example 5.3

$$P(970 < \bar{X} < 1030) = P(-2.4 < Z < 2.4)$$
$$= P(Z < 2.4) - P(Z < -2.4)$$
$$= .9918 - .0082$$
$$= .9836$$

.9836

.0082

970   1000   1030 $\bar{x}$

$$Z = \frac{970 - 1000}{12.5} = -2.4 \qquad Z = \frac{1030 - 1000}{12.5} = 2.4$$

$$Z = \frac{\bar{X} - \mu}{\sigma/\sqrt{n}}$$

has the standard normal distribution. This result presupposes that σ is a known constant. But if σ is not known, then Z is a function of an *unknown* parameter and the value of Z for a specific sample cannot be determined. This appears to create a problem since, as we pointed out in the introduction to Section 5.5, the value of the population standard deviation σ is rarely known in real statistical applications. In all likelihood, your natural reaction at this point is to say: Why not replace σ with its estimator, the sample standard deviation S? Well, that is precisely what is done. The replacement of σ with S in Expression (5.3) leads to the quantity (called the "T statistic")

$$T = \frac{\bar{X} - \mu}{S/\sqrt{n}} \qquad \qquad \textbf{(5.4)}$$

Unfortunately, the sampling distribution of T is *not* the standard normal distribution, even if the population distribution is normal! To understand why this is so, compare the quantities

$$Z = \frac{\bar{X} - \mu}{\sigma/\sqrt{n}} \quad \text{and} \quad T = \frac{\bar{X} - \mu}{S/\sqrt{n}}$$

How many statistics do you see within each of these quantities? For Z, there is *one*—namely, $\bar{X}$ (remember that μ, σ, and n are constants). But T depends on *two* statistics—$\bar{X}$ and S. The introduction of the additional statistic S increases the variation of T from sample to sample compared to that of Z, so we should not expect the distributions of Z and T to be the same. The distribution of the T statistic when sampling is from a normally distributed population known as the **Student's T distribution,** which is often shortened to the simpler T distribution.*

The T distribution is similar to the standard normal distribution in that it is symmetric and centered around 0, but it has more variation because of the substitution of S for σ. How much variation is added because of this substitution? That

---

*The T distribution was developed in 1908 by W. S. Gosset, who published his work under the pen name "Student." Many authors use the lowercase t in referring to this distribution. We use the uppercase T to maintain our consistent practice of using uppercase letters to denote random variables and lowercase letters to denote values of random variables.

Figure 5.8

A comparison of
the *T* and standard nor-
mal distributions for
different sample sizes

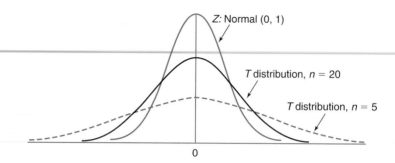

Figure 5.8

A comparison of
the *T* and standard nor-
mal distributions for
different sample sizes

depends on the sample size *n*. If *n* is quite large, then the value of *S* is a very accurate estimate of σ and little variation is added. If the sample size is quite small, the value of *S* is an imprecise estimate of σ and more variation is added. So the variation of the *T* distribution depends on the sample size *n*. This is illustrated in Figure 5.8.

Notice from Figure 5.8 that as *n* increases, the Student's *T* distribution exhibits less and less variation and becomes more and more like the standard normal distribution. In fact, they become identical in theory as *n* approaches infinity. This means that if *n* is large enough, the standard normal distribution approximates the *T* distribution quite closely and can be used in its place, if desired. A widely accepted rule of thumb is that the approximation is acceptable if $n \geq 30$. Notice that this guideline coincides conveniently with the guideline for application of the central limit theorem.

The Degrees of Freedom of the *T* Distribution

Actually, the key parameter of the *T* distribution is not the sample size *n* but a quantity that we introduced in Chapter 2 known as the **degrees of freedom.** This quantity is usually denoted by the lowercase Greek letter ν (nu). The degrees of freedom are determined by the sample size; for this application, $\nu = n - 1$. The greater the sample size, the greater the degrees of freedom. Generally, the degrees of freedom for the *T* distribution are precisely the same as the degrees of freedom associated with the sample variance S^2. Since for this application S^2 has $n - 1$ degrees of freedom,* the *T* distribution also has $\nu = n - 1$ degrees of freedom.

Using the Computer

Quantile values of the Student's *T* distribution can easily be determined using the computer by applying procedures similar to those for normal distributions; see the chapter appendix for instructions. Suppose that for $n = 16$, we wish to find $t_{.025,15}$ and $t_{.95,15}$,[†] the quantile values of a *T* distribution with 15 degrees of freedom corresponding to the probabilities (areas to the left of these values) of .025 and .95, respectively. These quantile values are illustrated in Figure 5.9 and are given by the following Minitab and Excel outputs.

---

*Recall from Chapter 2 that the quantity in the denominator of $S^2 = [\Sigma(X_i - \bar{X})^2]/(n - 1)$ is its degrees of freedom. In later applications, the denominator will be different from $n - 1$; correspondingly, the degrees of freedom will also be different.

†Notice that the degrees of freedom are also indicated in denoting quantile values of a *T* distribution.

Figure 5.9

Illustration of T quantile values for $\nu = 15$ degrees of freedom

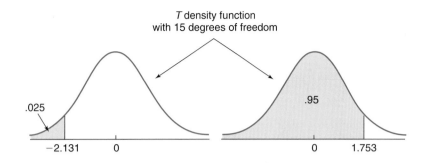

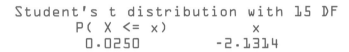

```
Student's t distribution with 15 DF
        P( X <= x)                 x
           0.0250             -2.1314
```

	A	B	C	D
1	df	P(X<=x)	2[P(X>x)]	x
2	15	0.95000	0.10000	1.753051

In other words, the probabilities that the T random variable with 15 degrees of freedom takes on values no more than −2.131 or 1.753 are .025 and .95, respectively.

The T Table and Its Use

The T distribution is widely tabulated. Table C in the Appendix gives quantile values of the T distribution associated with specific probabilities that represent areas to the left of the particular quantile value. To use this table, we first identify the appropriate number of degrees of freedom. This number is given in the first column of the table, under the heading "ν." Next, we choose the desired probability from the values in the column headings. For the given number of degrees of freedom and the selected probability, the table gives the corresponding quantile value.

Let's use the example in the computer application to illustrate the use of Table C. That is, for $n = 16$, we wish to find the T quantile values for which the probabilities are .025 and .95, respectively. For $\nu = 15$ degrees of freedom and under the .025 and .95 columns, we find the quantile values to be −2.131 and 1.753, respectively. Symbolically, we may write

$$P(T_{15} \leq -2.131) = .025$$

and

$$P(T_{15} \leq 1.753) = .95$$

A Comparison of the Standard Normal and Student's T Distributions

Because the standard normal and T distributions diverge considerably for small sample sizes n, a particular T-value can differ considerably from the corresponding Z-value for the same probability. Figure 5.10 illustrates this point for a T distribution with 5 degrees of freedom. This figure contrasts the Z- and T-values corresponding to .05 and

Figure 5.10

A comparison of the intervals encompassing 90% of a T distribution with 5 degrees of freedom and 90% of the standard normal distribution

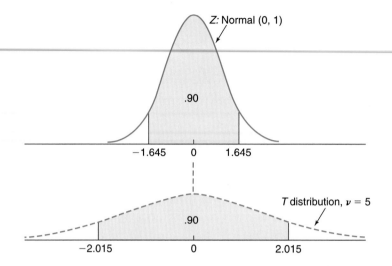

.95 probabilities. Notice that the Z-values are $z_{.05} = -1.645$ and $z_{.95} = 1.645$, whereas the T-values are $t_{.05,5} = -2.015$ and $t_{.95,5} = 2.015$. Therefore, since the T distribution with 5 degrees of freedom is much more spread out than the standard normal, we must go farther to the right and to the left of zero (the center of both distributions) to encompass 90% of the total area (the difference between .95 and .05).

The Normality Assumption with Regard to the T Distribution

We have said that the sampling distribution of the statistic

$$T = \frac{\bar{X} - \mu}{S/\sqrt{n}}$$

is the T distribution with $n - 1$ degrees of freedom, *if the population or process distribution is normal*. This assumption may appear to be somewhat restrictive. After all, we are not likely to know the population distribution. The concern is that, if this assumption of a normally distributed population is incorrect, the T probabilities associated with given T-values might not be correct. However, many studies over the years have shown the T distribution to be relatively **robust** to this assumption. That is, the T distribution is *approximately* the true distribution of the T statistic for sample sizes of about 15 or more, as long as the disparity from a normal distribution is not severe. For large enough sample sizes ($n \geq 30$), there should be virtually no concern about the possible violation of the normality assumption when using the T distribution. In such cases, the T probabilities are correct to a close approximation.

5.5.5 The Sampling Distribution of $\bar{X}$: A Summary

Let's summarize the two situations that determine which sampling distribution of $\bar{X}$ can be used to make statistical inferences about μ:

1. When the population or process standard deviation σ is known: This leads to the Z statistic. However, it is rare that we know σ.

2. When the population or process standard deviation σ is unknown: This leads to the T statistic. This is the usual situation in real statistical applications.

Since virtually all applications involve the second of these situations, the appropriate distribution in most analyses involving the population mean is the T distribution rather than the standard normal distribution. We summarize these two situations as follows:

SUMMARY: THE SAMPLING DISTRIBUTION FOR MAKING INFERENCES ABOUT μ BASED ON $\bar{X}$

1. If the value of the population standard deviation σ is known and either
   (a) the population distribution is normal, or
   (b) the population distribution is not normal but the sample size n is large enough ($n \geq 30$),
   then the sampling distribution of $\bar{X}$ is (at least approximately) the normal with mean μ and standard error $\sigma/\sqrt{n}$. Therefore, the sampling distribution of the Z statistic

$$Z = \frac{\bar{X} - \mu}{\sigma/\sqrt{n}}$$

   is (at least approximately) the standard normal distribution.
2. If the value of the population standard deviation σ is not known and either
   (a) the population distribution is approximately the normal distribution, or
   (b) the sample size n is large enough ($n \geq 30$),
   then the sampling distribution of the T statistic

$$T = \frac{\bar{X} - \mu}{s/\sqrt{n}}$$

   is (at least approximately) the T distribution with $n - 1$ degrees of freedom.

EXAMPLE 5.4

Many of the products we purchase today carry claims about, for example, how long they will last, on average (light bulbs), or average fuel efficiency (automobiles). It is not possible to verify or dispute such claims with absolute certainty. But it is possible to determine whether such claims are plausible by analyzing sample data using statistical inference. This example illustrates this kind of situation.

The Environmental Protection Agency gave an average highway miles-per-gallon rating of 45 to a particular model of subcompact car. An independent consumer organization purchased one of these cars and tested it to verify the EPA rating. Under controlled conditions, the car was driven for a distance of 100 miles on each of 25 different occasions. The actual miles per gallon achieved during the trip were recorded for each occasion. Over the 25 trials, the average and standard deviation turned out to be 43.5 and 2.5 miles per gallon, respectively. It is believed that the distribution of the actual highway miles per gallon for this car is close to a normal distribution.

(a) Assuming for the moment that the EPA rating of 45 miles per gallon is correct for this car, find the probability that the average miles per gallon over a random sample of 25 trials would be 43.5 or less.

(b) Based on the current sample information, is there good reason for the organization to doubt that the EPA average rating is correct for this car?

Solution

(a) The sample of $n = 25$ trials has yielded $\bar{X} = 43.5$ and $S = 2.5$ miles per gallon. The determination of whether this sample information supports the EPA rating should be based on probability; that is, we wish to answer the following question: If μ were really equal to 45 miles per gallon, what is the probability that by chance alone we would observe a value of $\bar{X}$ of 43.5 miles per gallon or less? Since the population standard deviation is unknown, the question may be addressed by computing the T-value that corresponds to $\bar{X} = 43.5$. In other words,

$$T = \frac{\bar{X} - \mu}{S/\sqrt{n}} = \frac{43.5 - 45}{2.5/\sqrt{25}} = -3.0$$

is a value of the Student's T distribution with $25 - 1 = 24$ degrees of freedom. The desired probability, $P(T_{24} \leq -3)$ (determined by Minitab), is as follows:

```
Student's t distribution with 24 DF
            x         P( X <= x)
      -3.0000           0.0031
```

This means that, if $\mu = 45$, the probability of observing a value of $\bar{X}$ of 43.5 or less, or, equivalently, a T-value of -3 or less, is .0031.

Alternatively, we can use Table C to approximate this probability. For 24 degrees of freedom, we see that $P(T_{24} \leq -3) < .005$. Thus, a sample mean as small as that actually observed ($\bar{X} = 43.5$ or, equivalently, $T = -3.0$) has a very small chance of occurrence if indeed μ is 45.

(b) Based on the answer to part (a), it is reasonable to doubt the EPA rating. Before blaming the EPA for false or improper ratings, however, further investigation is a good idea. For example, the observed discrepancy might simply be attributable to differences between the two organizations' methods of measuring mileage.

5.6

The Sampling Distribution of the Sample Proportion *p*

There are many situations in which the key parameter is a proportion. Examples are the proportion of invoices with errors, the proportion of service calls exceeding a standard (such as 4 hours), the proportion of customer checks that bounce, and the proportion of retail items returned by customers. Recall that we stated earlier in the chapter that the sample proportion *p* is the best statistic to use for inferences about the important proportion parameter π. In this section, we determine the mean, standard error, and sampling distribution of *p*.

5.6.1   The Mean and Standard Error of the Sample Proportion

The sampling distribution of the sample proportion arises in the context of a binomial distribution. Consider a situation where the binomial distribution is appropriate: Either we observe the number of successes X out of n independent trials, or X is the number of responses that are "successes" in a random sample of size n from a large population. Statistical theory shows that the mean of the sample proportion

$$p = \frac{X}{n} \qquad \qquad \textbf{(5.5)}$$

over all possible samples of size n is

$$E(p) = \pi \qquad \qquad \textbf{(5.6)}$$

and that the standard error of p over all possible samples of size n is

$$SE(p) = \sqrt{\frac{\pi(1 - \pi)}{n}} \qquad \qquad \textbf{(5.7)}$$

The implications of Expressions (5.6) and (5.7) are like those for the mean and standard error of $\bar{X}$, respectively. In particular, the sample proportion p is an unbiased estimator of π, and its standard error depends on both n and the usually unknown value of π. The larger the sample size n, the smaller the standard error of p. Thus, if we wish to estimate π with greater precision, we increase n. The key point is that the nature of $SE(p)$ as a function of n is identical to that of $SE(\bar{X})$: $SE(p)$ depends inversely on the square root of n. For example, *to halve the standard error of p, we have to increase the sample size by a factor of* 4.

How does the value of π affect the standard error of p? To explore this question, let's assume $n = 100$ and compare the standard errors of p when $\pi = .2$ and $\pi = .5$. For $n = 100$ and $\pi = .2$, we have

$$SE(p) = \sqrt{\frac{(.2)(.8)}{100}} = .040$$

For $n = 100$ and $\pi = .5$, we have

$$SE(p) = \sqrt{\frac{(.5)(.5)}{100}} = .050$$

Since the standard error when $\pi = .5$ is larger than that when $\pi = .2$, the precision of p as an estimator of π is worse when $\pi = .5$. In fact, the standard error of p is highest when $\pi = .5$; it improves as values of π are near 0 or near 1. This result is not surprising, since the binomial distribution exhibits the greatest variation when $\pi = .5$. You can demonstrate this for yourself easily by using Expression (4.6), which gives the variance of a binomial random variable.

EXAMPLE 5.5

We have commented before on the importance of scientific polls. For example, how does a marketing research firm determine the number of persons to survey with regard to an issue of interest? That is, does the number matter? The easy answer, of course, is that it does indeed matter! The more persons a marketing research firm surveys, the more expensive the operation is. So the firm first defines the accuracy it seeks, then determines the least number that satisfies that accuracy. This example illustrates how a sample size is determined with regard to the proportion parameter π of the binomial distribution.

Assume the greatest variation possible for a binomial distribution (i.e., $\pi = .5$). What sample size n is needed from this distribution so that the standard error of the sample proportion is .01?

Solution

The greatest variation for a binomial distribution occurs when $\pi = .5$. *The sample size needed to achieve a desired standard error of p is determined by equating the standard error expression to the desired value and solving for n.* Thus,

$$\text{SE}(p) = \sqrt{\frac{(.5)(.5)}{n}} = .01$$

$$\frac{.25}{n} = (.01)^2$$

$$n = \frac{.25}{(.01)^2} = 2{,}500$$

Therefore, the required sample size is $n = 2{,}500$.

5.6.2   The Type of Sampling Distribution for the Sample Proportion p

Although the exact sampling distribution of p has been determined by statisticians, it may not be practical to work with in most actual applications. It would serve our purpose equally well to opt for an approximation to the sampling distribution of p that works well when the sample size is fairly large. From Section 4.4, recall that the binomial distribution can be approximated by a normal distribution for large sample sizes. And since $p = (1/n)X$ is a linear function of the binomial random variable X, it turns out that the sampling distribution of p is also adequately approximated by a normal distribution for large sample sizes. In particular, recall that a binomial distribution is reasonably approximated by a normal distribution when $n\pi \geq 5$ and $n(1 - \pi) \geq 5$. *Under these same guidelines, the sampling distribution of p is closely approximated by a normal distribution* with mean $E(p) = \pi$ and standard deviation $\text{SE}(p) = \sqrt{\pi(1 - \pi)/n}$.

In an actual application, π is usually unknown (that is why we are interested in the sample proportion p in the first place). So how do we apply these guidelines if we do not know the value of π? Well, we can't! Instead, we use the value of p for a random sample as an estimate of π in the guidelines. When doing this, we should keep in mind the reason for these guidelines. The sampling distribution of p is symmetric only when $\pi = .5$. So when π is close to .5, the normal approximation is very good even for small sample sizes. But when π is near 0 or near 1, the sampling distribution of p is skewed (just like the binomial distribution). So when π is near the extremes of its range, the normal approximation to the sampling distribution of p is adequate only for very large sample sizes n. The following statement summarizes the sampling distribution of p:

SUMMARY: THE SAMPLING DISTRIBUTION FOR MAKING INFERENCES ABOUT π BASED ON p

The sampling distribution of p is adequately approximated by a normal distribution with

$$\text{mean} = \pi$$

and

$$\text{standard deviation} = \sqrt{\frac{\pi(1-\pi)}{n}}$$

if $n\pi \geq 5$ and $n(1-\pi) \geq 5$.

Therefore, if we standardize p, the sampling distribution of the Z statistic

$$Z = \frac{p - \pi}{\sqrt{\pi(1-\pi)/n}}$$

is approximately the standard normal distribution.

EXAMPLE 5.6

How does a retailer decide to open for business in a particular location? Large retailers usually spend a considerable amount of money on studies to identify the most desirable locations to open new stores. Even smaller retailers such as video outlets often conduct marketing surveys before deciding to open an outlet at a particular location. These studies are necessary to give the new outlet reasonable opportunity for success. This example illustrates this kind of situation with regard to inference about the proportion parameter.

A home video rental company has a policy that at least 65% of the area's residences must have a VCR before it will open a new outlet. A marketing executive claims that this is true for Farmville and proposes to establish an outlet there. A market research study reveals that only 54 Farmville residences have a VCR out of 100 residences sampled randomly.

(a) Assuming $\pi = .65$ (that is, the executive is correct), determine the probability that a value of p is no more than $\frac{54}{100} = .54$ for a random sample of $n = 100$ residences.

(b) Does this sample contradict the executive's claim?

Solution

(a) If $\pi = .65$, then $n\pi = (100)(.65) = 65$ and $n(1-\pi) = 100(.35) = 35$. Therefore, p has an approximately normal distribution with mean $\pi = .65$ and standard error $\sqrt{\pi(1-\pi)/n} = \sqrt{(.65)(1-.65)/100} = .0477$. The desired probability, $P(p \leq .54)$, is as follows:

```
Normal with mean = 0.650000 and
standard deviation = 0.0477000
          x         P( X <= x)
       0.5400        0.0106
```

Thus, $P(p \le .54) = .0106$. Alternatively, we can convert $p = .54$ to the corresponding Z-value and use Table B as illustrated in Figure 5.11. Notice that the slight discrepancy in the answers is due to the rounding of the Z-value.

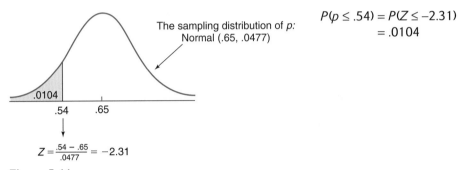

The sampling distribution of p:
Normal (.65, .0477)

$$P(p \le .54) = P(Z \le -2.31)$$
$$= .0104$$

$$Z = \frac{.54 - .65}{.0477} = -2.31$$

Figure 5.11

Correspondence between p- and Z-values

(b) Since the probability of obtaining a value of the sample proportion p of no more than .54 is only .0106, the actual market research result ($p = .54$) would be unlikely to occur if the claim were really correct. Because it did occur, the claim seems implausible, at least in regard to the situation in Farmville at the time of the market research study. But keep in mind that more and more people are buying VCRs, so a market research study done even 1 year later might reveal a result closer to the executive's claim.

5.7   Summary

In this chapter, we studied the fundamentals of statistical inference in using sample data to understand important features of a population or process. In particular, we studied two important statistics ($\overline{X}$ and p) and developed the basic methodology to use for making inferences about the corresponding population or process parameters (μ and π).

One type of statistical inference is estimation. In estimation, the end result is either a point estimate or an interval estimate of a parameter of interest. Another type of inference is hypothesis testing, in which we test the validity of a claim about the value of a parameter.

Every statistic fluctuates in value randomly from sample to sample. The key step in determining the usefulness of any statistic for making inferences is to identify its sampling distribution. The sampling distribution of a statistic is important because it reveals the pattern of variation of the values of the statistic over repeated samples. Generally, we deem a statistic to be the best statistic if its average accuracy over repeated random samples is as good as possible, and if its variation over repeated random samples is as small as possible. In this regard, the statistics $\bar{X}$ and p are the best statistics for μ and π, respectively.

The sampling distribution to use for inferences about μ based on $\bar{X}$ is either the standard normal (if the population standard deviation σ is known) or the Student's T distribution (if σ is not known). The T distribution is similar to the standard normal distribution except that it exhibits more variation. The sampling distribution to use for inferences about π based on p is well approximated by the normal distribution for large sample sizes.

EXERCISES FOR SECTIONS 5.3 AND 5.4

5.1 What is the purpose of a statistic?

5.2 Explain why a statistic is a random variable.

5.3 State in your own words what a sampling distribution is.

5.4 What is the distinction, if any, between a sampling distribution and a probability distribution?

5.5 What is the distinction, if any, between a relative frequency distribution for sample observations and the sampling distribution of the sample mean?

5.6 What is the distinction, if any, between a standard deviation and a standard error?

5.7 Suppose we wish to use the sample mean $\bar{X}$ to estimate the population mean μ. Why would it be useful to know the sampling distribution of $\bar{X}$?

5.8 The following data are 25 samples, each with five observations, taken from a process that produces a certain kind of yarn. The observations represent the measured tensile strengths of the yarn specimens, in pounds. Assume the process is producing yarn with an average tensile strength of 47.5 pounds and a standard deviation of 2.5 pounds.

Sample Number	Sample Values				
1	44	46	48	52	49
2	44	47	49	46	44
3	47	49	47	43	44
4	45	47	51	46	48
5	44	41	50	46	50
6	49	46	45	46	49
7	47	48	50	46	47
8	49	46	51	48	46
9	47	42	48	44	46
10	46	48	45	51	50
11	45	47	51	48	46
12	52	51	48	48	45
13	45	45	47	49	44
14	46	47	43	48	45
15	48	49	52	46	51
16	44	46	45	47	52
17	48	50	47	46	49
18	48	52	51	47	46

Sample Number	Sample Values				
19	47	51	50	46	49
20	45	46	48	47	49
21	45	48	46	45	49
22	46	49	50	46	48
23	49	48	46	52	45
24	47	49	45	46	50
25	44	51	50	48	46

(a) For each sample, determine the values of the sample mean $\bar{X}$ and the sample variance S^2.

(b) From your answer to part (a), what is apparent to you about the statistics $\bar{X}$ and S^2? Explain.

(c) Using the methods of Chapter 2, construct a histogram of the 25 values of $\bar{X}$. What does this histogram represent? Explain.

(d) Repeat part (c) for the 25 values of S^2.

5.9 Using the 25 values of $\bar{X}$ for the data in Exercise 5.8, construct a run chart. Do you detect an unexpected pattern in these values? Explain.

5.10 In a manufacturing process, 100 units are randomly selected from each day's production and inspected for defective units. The following is the number of defective units found in each day's sample for 25 days. Assume that the process is producing 2% defective units.

Day:	1	2	3	4	5	6	7	8	9
Number of Defectives:	2	1	4	3	2	2	0	2	3

Day:	10	11	12	13	14	15	16	17
Number of Defectives:	2	1	2	3	2	1	2	3

Day:	18	19	20	21	22	23	24	25
Number of Defectives:	3	4	3	5	5	6	5	7

(a) For each day's sample, determine the value of the sample proportion of defective units p.

(b) From your answer to part (a), what is apparent to you about the statistic p? Explain.

(c) Using the methods of Chapter 2, construct a histogram of the 25 values of p. What does this histogram represent? Explain.

5.11 Using the 25 values of p for the data in Exercise 5.10, construct a run chart. Do you detect an unexpected pattern in these values? Explain.

5.12 Explain the difference between a point estimate and an interval estimate.

5.13 Is there any difference between a statistic and an estimator? Explain.

5.14 What kind of inference are you interested in if you wish to assess the validity of a claim about the value of a parameter?

5.15 Identify the two key issues that have to be resolved before any statistical inference is possible.

5.16 For our purposes, explain what constitutes a best statistic.

5.17 Based on a random sample, a personnel manager estimates that the employees in a large sawmill use an average of 9.9 days of sick leave per year.
  (a) Is the number 9.9 an estimate or an estimator? Explain your answer.
  (b) What parameter is being estimated?
  (c) Suppose this sample estimate is to be used to support a proposal to implement a program designed to reduce absenteeism. Do you think the computation of an interval estimate would be better in this regard? Explain.

5.18 Explain:
  (a) What it means to say an estimator is biased.

  (b) The advantages of an unbiased estimator.
  (c) The reason it is desirable that an estimator have a small standard error.

5.19 Here is a question asked by a confused student: "We have learned that $\bar{X}$ is an unbiased estimator of μ. But for a given sample, it is almost certain that the value of $\bar{X}$ is either above μ or below μ by some amount. If it is below μ, for example, how can this statistic be unbiased?" Clarify the concept of unbiasedness for this student.

5.20 Statistic R has a mean of θ (where the value θ is unknown) and a standard error of 11.2. Statistic V has a mean of θ and a standard error of 14.7.
  (a) Which statistic is preferred as an estimator of θ? Why?
  (b) For a given sample, will the preferred estimator in part (a) necessarily provide the closer estimate of θ? Explain why it will or will not.

5.21 Suppose you have interviewed a random sample of shoppers leaving a supermarket. What sample statistic would you use to estimate:
  (a) The mean amount of money that shoppers spend for groceries at this supermarket?
  (b) The standard deviation of the ages of shoppers at this supermarket?
  (c) The proportion of senior citizens among shoppers at this supermarket?

5.22 What is the essential difference in purpose between the estimation of parameters and the testing of statistical hypotheses?

EXERCISES FOR SECTION 5.5

5.23 Is the standard deviation (standard error) of $\bar{X}$ the same as the standard deviation of the population or process? Explain.

5.24 In making inferences about μ based on $\bar{X}$:
  (a) What is the realistic situation with regard to knowledge of the population or process standard deviation σ?
  (b) Explain the difference between the standard normal and Student's T distributions.

5.25 With respect to the 40 samples listed in Table 5.1, form another statistic for estimating the population mean by averaging the minimum and maximum observations in each sample. Then use the 40 values of this new statistic to determine its average and its standard error. In comparison to the sample mean $\bar{X}$, which statistic has the smaller standard error over the 40 samples? Explain your finding.

5.26 For the data in Exercise 5.8, determine the mean and standard error of $\bar{X}$ over the 25 samples. How

do these values compare with the corresponding mean and standard error of $\bar{X}$ over all possible samples of $n = 5$ from this process?

5.27 Suppose a sample is to be taken randomly from a population whose distribution is the normal with $\mu = 1{,}400$ and $\sigma = 480$. For the given sample sizes, determine the mean and standard error of $\bar{X}$.
  (a) $n = 10$
  (b) $n = 40$
  (c) $n = 160$

5.28 In Exercise 5.27, does $\bar{X}$ have a normal sampling distribution in parts (a), (b), and (c)? Justify your answer for each part individually.

5.29 In Exercise 5.27, what sample size would be required to achieve $SE(\bar{X}) = 12.0$?

5.30 Suppose we select a random sample of $n = 40$ items from a population whose distribution is skewed to the left. Is it more likely that the value of the sample mean will lie above μ or below μ, or are these possibilities equally likely? Justify your answer.

5.31 A statistician has determined the standard error of $\bar{X}$ for a proposed market research sample of $n = 100$ consumers. Unfortunately, this standard error is twice the level that marketing management considers acceptable. What can be done to achieve an acceptable standard error for $\bar{X}$? Be as specific as you can.

5.32 Expression (5.2) $[SE(\bar{X}) = \sigma/\sqrt{n}]$ indicates that the standard error of $\bar{X}$ depends on both σ, the standard deviation of the population, and the sample size n.

(a) Explain why it makes sense that the standard error of $\bar{X}$ depends on the sample size.

(b) Explain why it makes sense that the standard error of $\bar{X}$ depends on the standard deviation of the population.

5.33 A contractor for a large office building is considering buying a large quantity of high-intensity lightbulbs from a certain manufacturer. The manufacturer assures the contractor that the bulbs have an average life of 1,000 hours and a standard deviation of 80 hours. The contractor, being prudent, decides to buy bulbs from this manufacturer only if a random sample of 64 such bulbs yields an average lifetime of at least 1,010 hours. Under this plan, what is the probability that the contractor will buy these bulbs from the manufacturer?

5.34 A federal inspector for weights and measures visits a packaging plant to affirm that the net weight of packages is as indicated on the packages. The plant manager assures the inspector that the packaging process results in an average weight of 750 grams and a standard deviation of 14 grams. The inspector selects 100 packages at random and finds their average weight to be 748.5 grams.

(a) For $n = 100$ (the inspector's sample size), specify the sampling distribution of $\bar{X}$ (assuming the manager's statement is accurate).

(b) If the manager's statement is correct, how likely is a sample mean of 748.5 grams or less?

(c) Based on your result in part (b), does the inspector have convincing evidence that the process is underfilling packages, on the average? Explain why the evidence is either convincing or not so convincing.

5.35 For each of the following cases, name the appropriate sampling distribution to use for inferences about μ and explain the reason for your choice.

(a) Population distribution is the normal with known $\sigma = 10$.

(b) A sample of $n = 15$ observations taken from a normal population distribution with unknown mean and standard deviation, where $\bar{X} = 48.2$ and $S = 8.3$.

(c) Population distribution is skewed with known $\sigma = 10$; for a sample of 40 observations, $\bar{X} = 48.2$.

(d) Population distribution is skewed; for a sample of 40 observations, $\bar{X} = 48.2$ and $S = 8.3$.

5.36 With reference to Exercise 5.35, could you name the appropriate sampling distribution in parts (a) and (b), if the population distribution were known to be skewed? Explain.

5.37 A nationwide study of graduate schools of business indicates that the average score on the Graduate Management Aptitude Test (GMAT) for successful 1996 applicants was 528. The Associate Dean for Graduate Studies at a business school wished to compare the recent admissions to his program to the national figures. A little research indicated that, for the 46 applicants accepted for 1996, the mean GMAT score was 544.8, and the standard deviation of GMAT scores was 34.6.

(a) Assuming that the population from which these 46 applicants were taken is identical to the population of applicants nationally, determine the probability of getting a sample mean of 544.8 or higher because of random sampling error.

(b) Based on your answer in part (a), can the associate dean claim convincingly that the mean GMAT score for his population of applicants exceeds the national mean?

5.38 An accounting firm's planning assumption is that, in the long run, their non-CPA members will average 1550 chargeable hours per year. Some members of the firm were concerned that chargeable hours were below plan in 1997. In 1997, the 16 non-CPA members charged an average of 1,531.4 hours, with a sample standard deviation of 239.6 hours.

(a) Assume that for 1997 the mean for chargeable hours was indeed 1,550 hours as planned. Determine the probability of observing a sample mean of 1,531.4 or lower due to random sampling error.

(b) Based on your result in part (a), do the data provide a convincing reason to believe that the mean was discernibly lower than planned?

5.39 The Environmental Protection Agency (EPA) has set a limit of 4 parts per billion, on average, of a certain toxic substance in a drinking water source. A recent random sample of 36 water specimens from this source yields an average level of 4.45 parts per billion for this substance and a standard deviation of .9 part per billion.

(a) Assuming the EPA limit is still being maintained, determine the probability that the average amount of this substance for a random sample of 36 water specimens would be 4.45 parts per billion or more.

(b) In view of your answer to part (a), should there be good reason for concern that the EPA average limit is being exceeded? Explain.

5.40 It is well known that cigarette smokers usually begin smoking at a young age. The longer a young person can resist the lure of cigarette smoking, the less likely it is that he or she will ever smoke. The historical average age at which smokers begin their habit is 15 years old. A current random sample of 36 young smokers yields an average starting age of 14.1 years and a standard deviation of 1.8 years.

(a) Assuming the historical starting age still holds, determine the probability that the average starting age of 36 randomly selected young smokers would be 14.1 years or less.

(b) In view of your answer to part (a), should epidemiologists, say, at the Centers for Disease Control be concerned that young smokers are taking up the habit at an earlier age? Explain.

5.41 The average completion time for a particular task in an assembly line operation has been 5 minutes. Because of the effect of completion time on later assembly operations, it is important that the 5-minute average not be exceeded. A current random sample of 25 completion times for this task yields a mean of 5.17 minutes and a standard deviation of 1 minute. Assume that the distribution of completion times is reasonably close to a normal distribution.

(a) Assuming the historical average time still holds, determine the probability that the average time for 25 randomly selected completion times would be 5.17 minutes or more.

(b) In view of your answer to part (a), should there be good reason for concern that the average completion time is longer than 5 minutes? Explain.

5.42 How well have equity mutual funds performed in the past compared with the Standard & Poor's 500 Stock Index? A random sample of 36 equity mutual funds averages a 16.9% annual investment return for 1993–97 with a standard deviation of 3.6% annual return. The Standard & Poor's 500 Stock Index grew at an annual average rate of 16.3% over the same period. Do these data show convincingly that, on the average, the mutual funds outperformed the Standard & Poor's 500 Stock Index during this period? Explain.

5.43 The average time required for students to complete the registration process at a university has been 40 minutes. A university administrator is trying a new procedure. Under this procedure, the registration times of 20 randomly selected students are recorded, resulting in a sample mean of 37.2 minutes and sample standard deviation of 4.5 minutes. It can be safely assumed that the distribution of registration times is reasonably close to a normal distribution.

(a) Assuming there has been no improvement in the average time with the new procedure, determine the probability that the mean time for 20 students would be 37.2 minutes or less.

(b) In view of your answer to part (a), is there good reason for the university administrator to believe that the new procedure reduces the average time for completing registration? Explain.

EXERCISES FOR SECTION 5.6

5.44 Determine the mean and standard error of the sample proportion p for each of the following situations:

(a) $n = 100$ items are selected from a population for which $\pi = .5$.

(b) $n = 20$ items are selected from a population for which $\pi = .5$.

(c) $n = 100$ items are selected from a population for which $\pi = .05$.

(d) $n = 20$ items are selected from a population for which $\pi = .05$.

5.45 Refer to Exercise 5.44

(a) Based on your results in parts (a) and (b), how does the sample size affect the mean and standard error of p (assuming $\pi = .5$)?

(b) Based on your results in parts (a) and (c), how does the value of π affect the mean and standard error of p (assuming the sample size n equals 100)?

5.46 Refer to Exercise 5.44. In parts (a)–(d), determine whether the sampling distribution of the sample proportion is adequately approximated by a normal distribution. Justify your answer in each case.

5.47 The results of political polls exert great influence on candidates' campaign strategies. A congressional candidate fears she is trailing her opponent and in desperation wishes to introduce more aggressive but risky campaign tactics. Her campaign manager thinks she is at least even with her opponent and advocates maintaining a less risky, more statesmanlike strategy. To shed light on the situation, the campaign manager commissions a poll based on a random sample of 250 voters. Assume for the moment that the campaign manager is correct, that 50% of all eligible voters favor the candidate and 50% favor the opponent.

(a) Specify the sampling distribution of the sample proportion.

(b) Find the probability that the poll indicates that no more than 48% favor the candidate (i.e., that $p \leq .48$ for the sample).

(c) Suppose the result of the poll is $p = .48$. Based on your answer in part (b), can it be concluded with confidence that the campaign manager is wrong and the candidate is in fact trailing her opponent? Explain your thinking.

5.48 Refer to Exercise 5.47. The candidate's campaign manager is concerned about the inconclusiveness of a poll result of $p = .48$.

(a) Determine the sample size needed to reduce the standard error of p to $SE(p) = .01$ (assuming $\pi = .50$ as in Exercise 5.47).

(b) Assuming the sample size you just computed in part (a) of this exercise were used, repeat Exercise 5.47, parts (b) and (c). Is your thinking the same as in part (c) of Exercise 5.47? Explain.

5.49 Companies that purchase parts from suppliers often specify the maximum allowable proportion of defective parts. Random sampling is used to decide whether this limit has been exceeded. Suppose the maximum allowable proportion defective for a purchase of computer chips is .03. An inspection plan has been devised, based on a random sample of 300 chips. If 3% or more defective chips are found (i.e., $p \geq .03$), the entire lot is deemed unacceptable and is inspected in its entirety at the suppliers' expense. Suppose a large batch actually contains 1.9% defective chips (this would be unknown to both supplier and purchaser, since the batch has not been inspected). Note that this is an acceptable proportion of defectives.

(a) Specify the sampling distribution of p.

(b) Find the probability that a value of the sample proportion exceeds .03, thus causing the lot to be deemed unacceptable.

5.50 Refer to Exercise 5.49. Now suppose a large batch contains 4% defective chips, an unacceptable level of defects. Determine the probability that a value of the sample proportion is less than .03, thus failing to detect the unacceptable defect level.

5.51 Over the last year, 40% of the properties listed with the ERI real estate agency have been sold within 2 months of the listing date.

(a) Suppose ERI receives 50 listings over the next few weeks. Find the probability that at least 60% of these listings sell within 2 months of the listing date. Assume that π, the underlying probability that a property is sold within 2 months, remains at .40.

(b) Suppose that 30 of the 50 listings actually do sell within 2 months of the listing. Based on your answer in part (a), would you conclude that π is now greater than .40, which would indicate that market conditions have changed? Justify your answer.

(c) Try to think of a decision or policy of ERI's management that might be affected by your answer in part (b).

5.52 A management instructor has used the same final exam for many years. Historically, 28% of his students have gotten an A or a B on the exam.

(a) This semester's class has 50 students. Assuming $\pi = .28$ as in prior years, find the probability that no more than 14% get a grade of B or better.

(b) Suppose that only 14% of this year's class get a grade of B or better. Based on your answer in part (a), what conclusion is justifiable?

5.53 The Tredegar Corporation in Sandston, Virginia, manufactures bottle caps for companies such as Pepsi and Coca-Cola.

(a) Suppose it is claimed that, for a large batch of bottle caps, the proportion π of defective bottle caps is .03. Assuming this claim is true, determine the probability that, for a random sample of 275 bottle caps, the proportion that are defective will be greater than .065.

(b) Suppose that you selected a random sample of 275 bottle caps from this batch and determined that the sample proportion of defective caps was indeed .065. In light of your answer in part (a), what conclusion would you reach about the claim that $\pi = .03$? Explain.

5.54 The marketing plan for a new product assumes that 50% of current customers will switch to the new product in the first year after its introduction.

(a) Suppose you were to survey a random sample of 200 current customers one year after the introduction. Assuming the plan is correct, determine the probability that 46% or fewer of the surveyed customers would report that they had switched to the new product in the first year.

(b) Suppose that you carried out the survey described in part (a), and found that indeed 46% of the surveyed customers had switched to the new product in the first year. In light of your answer in part (a), what would you conclude about the plan?

5.55 A manager in the invoice processing department periodically checks on the proportion of customers who are paying their bills late. Company policy dictates that this proportion should not exceed 20%.

(a) Suppose that the proportion of all invoices that were paid late is 20%. If you selected a random sample of 140 invoices, determine the probability that more than 28% of the sampled invoices were paid late.

(b) Suppose that you carried out the sample as described in part (a) and found that indeed 28% of the selected invoices had been paid late. Given your answer in part (a), what would you conclude about the current payment of invoices compared to company policy?

SUPPLEMENTARY EXERCISES

5.56 An automobile insurer has experienced over the last 2 years an average repair claim of $1,140 with a standard deviation of $880. At the beginning of the current year, new policies were put in place to reduce the average repair claim. So far this year, there have been 45 claims.

(a) Is it necessary to know the distribution for the population of repair claims to find probabilities concerning the sample mean? Justify your answer.

(b) Specify the sampling distribution of the sample mean, assuming for now that the new policy has had no effect. (Treat the 45 claims as if they were a random sample.)

(c) Using the sample distribution you obtained in part (b), find the probability that the sample of 45 claims would have a mean as low as $980.

(d) Was it reasonable to treat these 45 claims as if they were a random sample of the current year's claims (most of which are yet to come)? Why or why not?

5.57 Monthly revenues for a state lottery have historically been normally distributed with an average of $260,400 and a standard deviation of $18,500. Find the probability that the average monthly revenue for the entire coming year will fall short of $250,000 simply because of random sampling variation from month to month (that is, assuming that the underlying historical pattern does not change).

5.58 The assembly time for a difficult job is 2.25 minutes on average, with a standard deviation of .55 minute. The production plan calls for this task to be performed 50 times in a day.

(a) Specify the sampling distribution of the average assembly time in performing this job 50 times, assuming assembly times are independent from job to job.

(b) For the assumed conditions, what is the probability that, in a given day, the average assembly time exceeds 2.35 minutes?

5.59 A cigarette manufacturer claims that one of its brands has an average nicotine content of .6 milligram per cigarette. An independent testing organization has measured the nicotine content of 16 such cigarettes and determined the sample average and sample standard deviation to be .75 and .175 mg of nicotine, respectively. Assume the nicotine content in these cigarettes is adequately approximated by a normal distribution.

(a) Assuming the claim is correct, find the probability that the average nicotine content for 16 cigarettes is .75 mg or more.

(b) In view of your answer to part (a), would you say that the manufacturer's claim is plausible? Explain.

5.60 Historically, the daily sales of a fast-food restaurant have averaged $2,000. However, since a competitor opened for business nearby 25 days ago, daily sales have averaged $1,945, with a standard deviation of $300.

(a) Treating the 25 days as a random sample, find the probability of getting a sample mean of $1,945 or less over a 25-day period if the historical mean is still $2,000 (that is, if the competitor's presence has not affected business).

(b) Based on your result in part (a), is it plausible to conclude that the mean daily sales have dropped since the competitor's business opened? Explain.

(c) For your answers to parts (a) and (b), is it essential that the distribution of daily sales be normal? Explain.

5.61 Refer to Exercise 5.58. Historically, 12% of these assembly jobs have required some rework.

(a) Find the probability that, on a given day, more than 18% require rework.

(b) Suppose 18% of today's assembly jobs must be reworked. Based on your answer in part (a), is this a clear indication of a new problem, or is it plausible that the large proportion of reworked jobs today was a chance occurrence? Explain.

5.62 When functioning correctly, a machine produces switches with a .8% defect rate.

(a) Find the probability that a batch of 1,200 switches contains 15 or more defective switches.

(b) Suppose a batch of 1,200 switches were inspected when completed, and 15 defective switches were found. Based on your answer to part (a), can this result be attributed to random variation in the production process? (If not, it implies that the process needs adjustment.) Explain.

(c) Is the normal approximation you used in part (a) adequate? Explain.

5.63 After hearing numerous recent complaints, an accounting manager is investigating the incidence of errors in invoices. Historically, it is believed that errors have occurred on 8% of invoices. He inspects a random sample of 144 recent invoices.

(a) If the historical error rate still applies, find the probability that the proportion of invoices with errors in the sample is 10% or more.

(b) Suppose he actually found 10% defective in the sample. Do you find it plausible that this higher rate resulted from random sampling variation alone and that there has been no systematic change leading to a higher rate of error? Explain, based on your answer to part (a).

5.64 A sporting goods manufacturer buys string for tennis racquets from a supplier. The string varies somewhat in its resistance to breaking. If the breaking strength is too low, the string will not last long enough. If it is too great, this type of string is known to lose its playing quality. On a standard test of breaking strength, the manufacturer requires that the mean breaking strength be 81.5 units. For a random sample of 28 lengths of string, the following breaking strengths were recorded:

78.1	79.9	84.1	80.7	78.6	86.1	83.3
84.2	82.0	77.8	80.4	78.8	81.3	80.5
76.6	78.8	81.1	79.3	77.3	76.7	79.4
82.2	80.9	80.1	79.8	77.4	80.9	83.2

(a) Assume the mean breaking strength is as required, and the distribution of breaking strengths is the normal. Find the probability that a random sample of $n = 28$ breaking strengths would yield a mean value as small as or smaller than the value you determined from this sample.

(b) Based on your result in part (a), do you still find it plausible that the mean breaking strength for the entire lot is within the stated requirement? Explain.

5.65 Using either a computer or Tables B and C, complete the following table by inserting the quantile values of the Z and T statistics as indicated. Compare the Z and T quantile values as the number of degrees of freedom increases. Explain your findings.

	Probability					
Statistic	.005	.025	.05	.95	.975	.995
T_5						
T_{15}						
T_{30}						
T_{100}						
T_∞						
Z						

Appendix 5

Computer Instructions for Using MINITAB, EXCEL, and JMP IN

MINITAB

Selecting Simple Random Samples

Minitab can be used to select a simple random sample as in Section 5.2, as follows. To randomly select 10 items from a population of 1,000 items, first assign identification numbers 1 through 1,000 to the population items. Choose CALC–RANDOM DATA–INTEGER . . . . In the dialogue box, enter 10 in the GENERATE ROWS OF DATA box; enter c1 in the STORE IN COLUMN(S) box; enter 1 and 1000 in the MINIMUM VALUE and MAXIMUM VALUE boxes; and click OK. This places the identification numbers for the selected items in c1.

Determining *T* Distribution Probabilities and Quantile Values

Consider first Example 5.4(a). The desired probability, $P(T_{24} \leq -3)$ (where the T distribution has $\nu = 24$ degrees of freedom), is determined as follows: Choose CALC–PROBABILITY DISTRIBUTIONS–T . . . . In the dialogue box, (1) click the CUMULATIVE PROBABILITY button; (2) enter 24 in the DEGREES OF FREEDOM box; (3) click the INPUT CONSTANT button and enter −3.0 in the corresponding box; and click OK. You can determine simultaneously the probabilities associated with several values of T. Enter the desired T-values into c1. In step 3 of the above procedure, click the INPUT COLUMN button and type or select c1 in the corresponding box.

Now consider the example in the Using the Computer portion of Section 5.5.4, in which we determine the quantile values $x_{.025}$ and $x_{.95}$ for a T distribution with 15 degrees of freedom. Use the process just described, except (1) click the INVERSE CUMULATIVE PROBABILITY button and (2) click the INPUT CONSTANT button and enter .025 in the INPUT CONSTANT box. To get $x_{.95}$, repeat this process, entering .95 in the INPUT CONSTANT box.

EXCEL

Selecting Simple Random Samples

Excel can be used to select a random sample as in Section 5.2, as follows. To randomly select 10 items from a population of 1,000 items, first number the items 1 through 1,000. Select a1; it is the first cell of the intended column of random numbers. Click the PASTE FUNCTION button on the toolbar. In the dialogue box, click MATH & TRIG, then RANDOMBETWEEN, and click OK. In the dialogue box, enter 1 for the BOTTOM number and 1000 for the TOP number, and click OK. A random number between 1 and 1,000 will be placed in a1. With a1 selected, fill down through a10. Duplication of selected values is possible, so you might have to generate a few extra values.

Determining *T* Distribution Probabilities and Quantile Values

Excel handles probabilities for the *T* distribution a little differently. Rather than providing the area to the *left* of a *T*-value, it provides the area to the *right* of the *T*-value for *positive* *T*-values only. Consider Example 5.4(a), where we wish to determine $P(T_{24} \leq -3)$. First select the cell where the probability value is to be placed. Then click the PASTE FUNCTION button. In the dialogue box, click STATISTICAL, then TDIST, and click OK. In the dialogue box, enter +3.0 (the *positive* *T*-value of interest) for X; enter 24 for DEG FREEDOM; and enter 1 for TAILS. Then click OK. The result is the area to the right of +3.0 for the *T* distribution, which equals the desired area to the left of −3.0 because of the symmetry of the *T* distribution.

Now consider the example in the Using the Computer portion of Section 5.5.4, in which we determine the quantile value $x_{.95}$ for a *T* distribution with 15 degrees of freedom. First select the cell where the quantile value is to be placed. Then click the PASTE FUNCTION button. In the dialogue box, click STATISTICAL, then TINV, and click OK. In the next dialogue box, enter .10 for PROBABILITY. [This value is $2(1 − .95) = 2(.05) = .10$; Excel requires the *two-tail* probability that corresponds to the probability of interest.] Enter 15 for DEGREES-FREEDOM; and click OK.

JMP IN

Selecting Simple Random Samples

JMP IN can be used to select a simple random sample as in Section 5.2, as follows. To randomly select 10 items from a population of 1,000 items, first number the items 1 through 1,000. Enter the integers 1 through 1000 in COLUMN 1 and name this column POP ID. Create COLUMN 2 and name it RANDOM ID. In the CALCULA-TOR window for RANDOM ID:

1. Select CONDITIONS—IF in the Function Browser area.
2. Select POP ID from the Column Selector List.
3. Select TERMS—SUBSCRIPT in the Function Browser area.

4. Select RANDOM–SHUFFLE in the Function Browser area.

5. Select TERMS–I (ROW #) in the Function Browser area.

6. Select COMPARISONS–X < Y in the Function Browser area.

7. Type 10 and press the ENTER key (of your computer's keyboard).

8. Close the CALCULATOR window.

RANDOM ID now contains the identification numbers of the randomly selected items.

Determining *T* Distribution Probabilities and Quantile Values

Consider first Example 5.4(a), where we wish to determine $P(T_{24} \leq -3)$. Give the name T VALUE to COLUMN 1. In the CALCULATOR window for T VALUE:

1. Select PROBABILITY–STUDENT'S T DISTRIBUTION in the Function Browser area.

2. Highlight the first missing term and type 3; press your ENTER key; and click the ± button in the Keyboard area (to make the value negative).

3. Highlight the second missing term and type 24; press your ENTER key.

4. Close the CALCULATOR window.

This places the desired probability in COLUMN 1 (T VALUE).

Now consider the example in the Using the Computer portion of Section 5.5.4, in which we determine the quantile values $x_{.025}$ and $x_{.95}$ for a T distribution with 15 degrees of freedom. Enter .025 and .95 into the first two rows of COLUMN 1, and name this column CUM T PROB. Create COLUMN 2 and name it T QUANTILE. In the CALCULATOR window for T QUANTILE:

1. Select PROBABILITY—STUDENT'S T QUANTILE in the Function Browser area.

2. Highlight the first missing term and select CUM T PROB from the Column Selector List; then press your ENTER key.

3. Highlight the second missing term and type 15; then press your ENTER key.

4. Close the CALCULATOR window.

The desired quantile values are now in the first two rows of T QUANTILE.

Chapter 6

Statistical Inferences for a Single Population or Process

CHAPTER OUTLINE

6.1   Bridging to New Topics

In Chapter 2, you studied a variety of methods designed to provide insight into a set of data. In general, this is called *exploratory analysis*. In this chapter, we begin to apply the fundamentals of statistical inference that were introduced in Section 5.3. In particular, we show how to determine interval estimates for the important parameters μ and π based on a random sample of observations from the population or process of interest. The interval estimates are called **confidence intervals.** In addition, we develop procedures to test claims about the values of these parameters. This type of inference is called **hypothesis testing.** These methods of statistical inference are used to rigorously assess the insights resulting from exploratory analysis. Thus, they provide a ***confirmatory analysis.***

There is a strong association between confidence intervals and hypothesis testing. As you will see, we can, for the most part, utilize the former to carry out the latter. Also, we introduce another approach for testing statistical hypotheses, known as the **P-value,** which is especially useful when using a computer. Keep in mind that if sample data are the outcomes of an unstable process, then such data are not sufficient for meaningful inference, even if the data constitute a random sample.

Figure 6.1

Use of confidence
intervals and hypoth-
esis testing for μ
and π

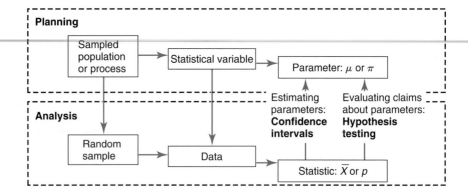

As you might expect, the statistics $\bar{X}$ and p and their sampling distributions are essential for inferences about the corresponding parameters μ and π. The use of confidence intervals and hypothesis testing for these two parameters is illustrated in Figure 6.1.

6.2   An Introduction to Confidence Intervals and Hypothesis Testing

In this section, we provide an overview of interval estimation (confidence intervals) and hypothesis testing. These two concepts are the primary means by which statistical inferences are made about unknown population or process parameters based on random samples. In other words, these are the primary inferential means by which we convert data (random sample) into useful information about populations or processes.

6.2.1   The Precision of Point Estimators: An Introduction to Confidence Intervals

In practical problems involving the estimation of a parameter, it is usually not sufficient to provide only a point estimate. Suppose you are a manager in the repair department of an office products retailer. A key factor in customer satisfaction is "response time"—the time it takes for a service representative to arrive at a customer's site after a request for service. One of the departments key service standards is that the response time is less than 4 hours for at least 80% of all service calls. You are held accountable for the department's meeting this standard. To evaluate the response time currently being achieved, a member of your staff determines the response times for a random sample of 100 recent service calls. Based on the sample response time data, the estimate of the proportion of response times below 4 hours is .75. Can you conclude with confidence that the standard for the proportion of response times is not being met?

The correct answer is that you cannot tell from the information given. The estimate of .75 is derived from a *sample*, so it is subject to sampling error. The process proportion of response times that meets the standard could be higher or lower than .75 by some amount. Indeed, it is conceivable that the current process proportion is greater than .80. To address this question, you need to know the *precision* of the statistic (the sample proportion in this case). Suppose you could be assured that the estimate of .75 is in error by no more than .03; that is, you are confident that π lies between .72 and .78. Then, you could assume that the current process proportion fails to met the standard. On the other hand, suppose you knew the estimate could be in error by as much as .09. Then π could be as large as .84 or as small as .66. In this case, you could not be confident that the current process proportion fails to meet the standard. Thus, a decision based on the point estimate .75 would be risky. As this example illustrates, *it is important to understand the precision of a statistic before relying on it to make a decision.*

In most practical situations, point estimates are insufficient for planning or decision making unless accompanied by a statement of possible error based on the sampling distribution of the statistic. In this example, it would be important that the statement "We estimate that $\pi = .75$" be accompanied by a statement such as "We believe that this estimate is in error by no more than .03." Notice that these two statements taken together say that we have reason to believe π lies within the interval $.75 \pm .03$. The resulting interval .72 to .78 is an *interval estimate* of π and implies that π is believed to lie within this interval.

It is also important to state *how confident* we are that the interval estimate actually contains the value of π. The phrase "We believe . . . " is too imprecise. Are we 75% confident in our belief? 90% confident? 99% confident? It is important that the degree of confidence in the statement be stated and that it be acceptable to the decision maker. In this example, a statement such as "We are 90% confident that π is between .72 and .78" gives the decision maker sufficient information either to act or to postpone a decision until more sample information is obtained.

To summarize: In estimating a parameter, it is important to provide (1) a point estimate, (2) the amount of possible error in the point estimate or, equivalently, an interval thought likely to contain the parameter value, and (3) the degree of confidence we can attach to the statement that the parameter value lies within the interval. A statement containing these three pieces of information is called a confidence interval. A **confidence interval,** therefore, is an interval estimate of a parameter accompanied by a statement of confidence that the interval contains the parameter value. In Section 6.3, we show how to develop a confidence interval.

6.2.2   The Testing of Statistical Hypotheses: An Introduction

A **statistical hypothesis** is a *claim* or *belief* about an unknown parameter value. Claims are often based on a belief (or an assumption) that a parameter has a given value. For example, a politician may plan a campaign strategy based on the belief that 60% of all taxpayers support lower taxes (that is, the politician believes that the proportion of all taxpayers who support lower taxes is $\pi = .6$). In the filling process example of Section 5.3, we might claim that the average amount of detergent poured into containers is the target value of 50 ounces (that is, we claim $\mu = 50$). Notice that in both of these examples we are not interested, per se, in estimating the value of π or μ. Rather, we wish to determine whether the claims "$\pi = .6$" and "$\mu = 50$" are supported or contradicted by the sample data. The use of sample data to assess such claims is called **hypothesis testing.**

There is a strong relationship between the methodologies of hypothesis testing and confidence intervals. Suppose the value claimed for a parameter lies within the confidence interval determined for that parameter based on a random sample. Then the value claimed for the parameter may be regarded as *plausible*. Otherwise, the value claimed is implausible. For example, recall the statement given at the end of the last section: "We are 90% confident that π is between .72 and .78." In the context of hypothesis testing, this means that any value claimed for π within the interval .72 to .78 is considered plausible, whereas any other is not.

The Null and Alternative Hypotheses

In hypothesis testing applications, there are actually two competing hypotheses under consideration: the *null hypothesis* and the *alternative hypothesis*. The **null hypothesis** is characterized by the fact that *we act as if it is true unless it is clearly contradicted by the sample data*. If the null hypothesis is not clearly contradicted by the sample data, we have insufficient reason to reject it. As its name implies, the **alternative hypothesis** provides an alternative to the null hypothesis. Its defining characteristic is that *it is regarded as true only if the null hypothesis is clearly contradicted by the sample data*. Thus, the philosophy of hypothesis testing rests on the notion of *proof by contradiction*. We tentatively assume the null hypothesis is true, so it becomes a sort of working assumption. Then we obtain a random sample of data from the population or process of interest. If the data seem compatible with our working assumption, we proceed as if the null hypothesis is true. But if the sample data are incompatible with the null hypothesis, we reject it and regard the alternative hypothesis as true. The rejection of a null hypothesis often provides a statistical basis for taking action or changing a plan.

An analogy is found in the familiar jury trial. One hypothesis is "not guilty"; the other is "guilty." A jury is instructed to assume the defendant is not guilty unless the prosecution presents evidence of guilt beyond a reasonable doubt. Can you identify the null and alternative hypotheses in this analogy? The ability to identify the null and alternative hypotheses is important. So take a moment now to identify these hypotheses in the jury trial analogy before reading ahead.

Because "not guilty" is the working assumption unless convincing contradictory evidence is presented, it is the null hypothesis. Because "guilty" must be established beyond a reasonable doubt, it is the alternative hypothesis. That is, only if the evidence is incompatible with "not guilty" does the jury reach a verdict of "guilty."

In the filling process example, the process is supposed to fill containers with a mean of 50 oz. of detergent. To avoid tampering with the process, management policy is to look for special causes of variation only if sample data strongly suggest that a change has occurred. Thus, we assume that the mean equals 50 oz. and state the null hypothesis, denoted by H_0, as

$$H_0: \quad \mu = 50$$

The alternative hypothesis, denoted by H_a, is that *the current process mean differs from* 50 *oz.;* it is stated as

$$H_a: \quad \mu \neq 50$$

This alternative hypothesis is **two-sided** because a potential problem may exist if the sample data indicate that the process mean μ is *either less than* 50 *ounces or greater than* 50 *ounces*.

In the political campaign example, the strategy is based on the politician's belief that the proportion of taxpayers who support lower taxes is (at least) .6. The politician does not wish to change strategy unless data from a poll clearly indicate that the proportion is *less* than .6. Thus, we express the null and alternative hypotheses as

$$H_0: \quad \pi = .6$$

$$H_a: \quad \pi < .6$$

This alternative hypothesis is **one-sided** because the politician would change his campaign strategy only if poll data indicate clearly that the proportion opposed to lowering taxes is *smaller* than .6 (i.e., $\pi < .6$) but not if $\pi \geq .6$. In other words, even if poll data indicate that the proportion is larger than .6, the campaign strategy would remain the same as if the proportion were equal to .6.

Notice that a one-sided alternative hypothesis provides a specific direction of departure from the parameter value claimed by the null hypothesis, but a two-sided alternative hypothesis does not. Generally, a reasonable philosophy in this regard is to formulate a one-sided alternative hypothesis *only if a parameter value that differs from the null hypothesis value in the other direction of the alternative hypothesis would not lead to an action or change of plan.*

An Overview of Hypothesis Testing Methodology

In subsequent sections, we consider hypothesis testing on the key parameters μ and π. There is a common thread in the method we use no matter what the particular parameter happens to be.

Let θ represent *any* unknown parameter and let θ_0 be the value claimed for θ in the null hypothesis. In testing hypotheses concerning θ, we focus on the best statistic for θ. Suppose A is the best statistic for inferences concerning the parameter θ. The test is based on a comparison of the value of A we happen to get from a random sample and the claimed value θ_0. The premise is simple: If the value of A differs from θ_0, there are only two possible explanations:

1. θ_0 is indeed the value of θ; so the value of A differs from θ_0 simply because of sampling error.

2. θ_0 is not the value of θ (therefore, the alternative hypothesis is true).

Recall that the null hypothesis is contradicted only if it is incompatible with the sample data. If the value of A based on a random sample is reasonably close to θ_0, the first explanation seems plausible. After all, some variation of A from θ is to be expected because of sampling error. But the more the value of A differs from θ_0, the less plausible it is that the difference is caused by random sampling variation alone. If the value of the best statistic A differs *sufficiently* from the claimed value θ_0, the null hypothesis is contradicted in favor of the alternative hypothesis. This is the basic philosophy of hypothesis testing.

6.3 Statistical Inferences for μ Based on $\bar{X}$

In this section, we discuss procedures to determine confidence intervals and to test hypotheses about the unknown value of the population or process mean μ. These procedures are based on $\bar{X}$, the best statistic for inferences concerning μ. From Section 5.5.5, recall the two situations that emerge with regard to the sampling distribution of $\bar{X}$: (1) The value of the population standard deviation σ is known, in which case the sampling distribution of $\bar{X}$ is essentially normal for large sample sizes and the statistic $Z = (\bar{X} - \mu)/(\sigma/\sqrt{n})$ has the standard normal distribution, and (2) the value of σ is not known, which leads to the T distribution for the statistic $T = (\bar{X} - \mu)/(S/\sqrt{n})$. In actual statistical applications, we rarely know the value of σ. Consequently, in virtually all instances we find ourselves dealing with case (2). But to introduce the thought process, it helps to discuss first case (1), in which σ is known, and then focus on case (2).

6.3.1 Confidence Intervals for μ When σ Is Known

To see how a confidence interval is developed, let's continue with the filling process example from Section 5.3. The process produces detergent box weights according to a normal distribution with a known standard deviation $\sigma = .5$ ounce. Suppose we wish to determine a 95% confidence interval for μ based on a random sample of the weights of $n = 10$ boxes.

The sampling distribution is the key to the determination of a confidence interval. We know from Chapter 5 that the sampling distribution of $\bar{X}$ is normal, since the process distribution is normal. The standard error of $\bar{X}$ is SE($\bar{X}$) $= .5/\sqrt{10} = .158$ ounce. Thus, *the sampling distribution of $\bar{X}$ is normal with unknown mean μ and standard error* .158. Now, based on this sampling distribution, how much might a value of $\bar{X}$ deviate from μ as a result of sampling error? Since the sampling distribution of $\bar{X}$ is normal, we know that a value of the sample mean $\bar{X}$ would lie within three standard errors of the process mean μ 99.74% of the time over a large number of random samples. Therefore, we can be almost certain that the value of $\bar{X}$ for a given sample lies within .474 ounce of μ (since $3 \times .158 = .474$). This result is illustrated in Figure 6.2.

Figure 6.2

An illustration of the probability that $\bar{X}$ lies within three standard errors of μ

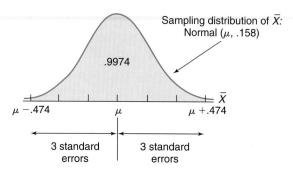

Suppose that when we select a random sample, we find that $\bar{X} = 50.025$. What can we reasonably conclude about the value of μ? Well, we have just seen that for 99.74% of all random samples, a value of $\bar{X}$ will not deviate from μ by more than .474 ounce. So it is reasonable to say that we are 99.74% *confident* that the value $\bar{X} = 50.025$ lies within .474 unit of μ (either above or below). If this conclusion is correct, then the population mean μ lies between 49.551 (50.025 − .474) and 50.499 (50.025 + .474). Notice that our level of confidence that μ lies between these two values is dictated by our confidence in the procedure we used; we know that intervals derived by this method include the value of μ for 99.74% of all random samples. The interval 50.025 ± .474 is called a **confidence interval,** and 99.74% is called the **level of confidence.** This interval suggests that the potential error in the point estimate $\bar{X} = 50.025$ is plus or minus .474 ounce. We refer to the potential error of a point estimate as the **margin of sampling error** associated with a given level of confidence. The boundaries of the confidence interval, 49.551 and 50.499, are called the **lower and upper confidence limits,** respectively.

Before proceeding, notice the individual elements of the interval $50.025 \pm .474$. The point estimate 50.025 is the value of the sample mean $\bar{X}$ for a particular sample. The margin of error, $.474$ represents three standard errors of $\bar{X}$, where $SE(\bar{X}) = .5/\sqrt{10} = .158$. We add and subtract $.474$ unit (the margin of error) from the particular value of $\bar{X}$ to determine the confidence limits. Thus, the 99.74% confidence interval is determined from the expression $\bar{X} \pm 3SE(\bar{X})$.

In this example, we first chose an interval whose margin of sampling error was $.474$ (three standard errors) and then found the corresponding level of confidence (99.74%). A more common practice is first to identify an acceptable level of confidence and then to determine the corresponding confidence interval. The determination of a confidence interval for a given confidence level is easily done by using a computer. We can also determine the confidence intervals using Table B in the Appendix, as we illustrate now. The following discussion benefits your understanding of confidence intervals even if you are using a computer.

Suppose you decided that a 95% level of confidence was appropriate. Let's now find the resulting confidence interval. The key is to determine the maximum number of standard errors by which values of $\bar{X}$ deviate from μ for 95% of all random samples of size n. Let's call this number of standard errors z. Since the sampling distribution of $\bar{X}$ is the normal distribution, 95% of all samples have $\bar{X}$-values within z standard errors of μ, and 5% have $\bar{X}$-values more than z standard errors from μ, with 2.5% lying below μ and 2.5% lying more than z standard errors above μ (because of the symmetry of normal distributions). According to Table B of the Appendix, we have $z_{.025} = -1.96$ and $z_{.975} = +1.96$. *Therefore, values of the sample mean $\bar{X}$ lie within 1.96 standard errors of μ for 95% of all random samples of size n.* The development of a 95% confidence interval for μ in the filling process example is illustrated in Figure 6.3.

Figure 6.3

The development of a 95% confidence interval for μ

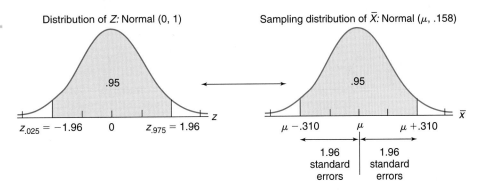

Since for this random sample the value of $\bar{X}$ turned out to be 50.025, a 95% confidence interval consists of this value plus or minus 1.96 standard errors—that is, $\bar{X} \pm 1.96(.158) = 50.025 \pm .310 = (49.715$ to $50.335)$. The quantity $.310$ is the margin of sampling error. The quantile values ± 1.96 correspond to a 95% level of confidence and are taken from the standard normal table. Notice that this 95% confidence interval, $(49.715$ to $50.335)$, is narrower than the 99.74% confidence interval, $(49.551$ to $50.499)$. Does this make sense to you? The rationale is that, for a wider interval, more of the area of the sampling distribution of $\bar{X}$ is involved and, consequently, there is greater confidence that the interval surrounds the unknown value of the population or process mean μ. Thus, the *higher* the level of confidence we require, the more area of the sampling distribution we encompass and the *wider* the interval must be, and vice versa.

This approach leads to a general expression for confidence intervals for μ when σ is known. Suppose the desired level of confidence is $100(1 - \alpha)\%$ where α (Greek letter alpha) represents the proportion of samples whose $\bar{X}$-values lie more than z standard errors from μ. For example, for a 95% confidence interval, $\alpha = .05$; for a 99% confidence interval, $\alpha = .01$; and so on. To develop the confidence interval, we let $1 - \alpha$ be an area of the sampling distribution of $\bar{X}$, where this area is centered around μ. The points that delineate the lower and upper limits of this centered area, expressed as Z-values, are **quantile values.** These quantile values indicate the maximum number of standard errors by which a value of $\bar{X}$ based on a particular sample can deviate from μ with probability $1 - \alpha$.

The general expression for a $100(1 - \alpha)\%$ confidence interval for μ when σ is known is as follows:

$$\bar{X} \pm z_{1-\alpha/2}\, SE(\bar{X}) \tag{6.1}$$

or

$$\bar{X} \pm z_{1-\alpha/2}\, \frac{\sigma}{\sqrt{n}} \tag{6.2}$$

where

$$\text{Margin of sampling error} = z_{1-\alpha/2}\, \frac{\sigma}{\sqrt{n}} \tag{6.3}$$

and $z_{1-\alpha/2}$ represents the standard normal quantile value needed to produce the desired level of confidence $1-\alpha$. Thus, for 95% confidence, $\alpha = .05$ and $z_{1-\alpha/2} = z_{.975} = 1.96$. Notice that the general structure of these expressions for a confidence interval (CI) is the following:

$$\text{CI} = \text{Point estimate} \pm \text{Margin of sampling error} \tag{6.4}$$

This general formulation provides a confidence interval whenever the statistic has a symmetric sampling distribution such as the normal distribution or the T distribution. You may find this general formulation useful as new applications are introduced in later sections. The essential statistical terms associated with confidence intervals are summarized as follows:

STATISTICAL TERMS ASSOCIATED WITH CONFIDENCE INTERVALS

1. A **confidence interval** consists of an interval estimate of a parameter accompanied by a level of confidence that the interval contains the parameter value.
2. **Confidence limits** are the lower and upper boundaries of a confidence interval.
3. The **level of confidence** is the long-term relative frequency with which random samples yield confidence intervals that include the value of the parameter being estimated.
4. The **margin of sampling error** characterizes the precision of a statistic. It is the maximum amount by which a value of the statistic can be in error for a given level of confidence. The width of a confidence interval is twice the margin of the sampling error.

The Proper Interpretation of Confidence Intervals

It is important for you to understand the proper interpretation of confidence intervals. Recall that the 95% confidence interval for the mean of the filling process was $\bar{X} \pm .310 = 50.025 \pm .310 = (49.715$ to $50.335)$. Since the statistic $\bar{X}$ is a random variable, the interval $(\bar{X} - .310, \bar{X} + .310)$ is a random interval, and the probability that this interval contains the value of μ is .95. That is, if we repeatedly drew random samples of $n = 10$ boxes from the filling process, and if each time a sample was selected we computed a particular interval $(\bar{X} - .310, \bar{X} + .310)$, then in the long run we would expect 95% of those intervals to contain the unknown mean μ. Notice that the random variable associated with this confidence interval is the sample mean $\bar{X}$. The margin of error remains constant at .310 from one sample to the next. Only the values of $\bar{X}$ vary among the samples. The key to the proper interpretation of confidence intervals is to realize that *it is incorrect to say that the probability of μ being contained in the interval* 49.715 *to* 50.335 *is* .95. No probability can be attached to the statement "49.715 $< \mu <$ 50.335" because μ is not a random variable; it is the fixed value of the unknown mean of the population. It either lies within the interval we determined, or it does not. However, the .95 probability for the random interval does suggest that our confidence should be high that the interval (49.715, 50.335) contains the fixed value of μ. It is in this sense that we assign the degree of confidence in the statement "49.715 $< \mu <$ 50.335" to be the same as the probability associated with the random interval $(\bar{X} - .310, \bar{X} + .310)$. Accordingly, the interval (49.715, 50.335) is called a 95% confidence interval for μ.

To demonstrate the fact that confidence intervals vary over repeated samples, let's continue with the 40 simulated samples from the filling process listed in Table 5.1. For the first sample, the mean is $\bar{X} = 50.025$, which results in the 95% confidence interval 49.715 to 50.335 that we just developed. For the second sample, the value of $\bar{X}$ is 49.842, which leads to a 95% confidence interval for μ of $49.842 \pm .310 = (49.532$ to $50.152)$. Obviously, this interval differs from the interval for the first sample because the value of $\bar{X}$ differs. Continuing in this fashion, we determine 95% confidence intervals for μ based on each of the 40 samples. The intervals are graphed in Figure 6.4 as horizontal lines indicating the spread of each interval.

In Figure 6.4, notice that one interval (for the 11th sample) does not contain the mean value $\mu = 50$ for the simulated filling process. Therefore, 97.5% (39 of the 40) of the intervals—rather than 95%—do contain the value $\mu = 50$. Remember that 95% is the theoretical proportion of random samples of size $n = 10$ that would contain μ *in the long run*. The 97.5% success rate experienced here differs from the theoretical value of 95% only because of the relatively small number (40) of samples in the simulation.

6.3.2 Choosing the Confidence Level and Sample Size

Consider this question: Why would we ever prefer a lower level of confidence like 95% to a higher level like 99%? From Expressions (6.2) and (6.3), it is not difficult to see that the greater the level or confidence we require, the larger the quantile value, thus producing a larger margin of sampling error, and a wider interval estimate for a given sample size. The width of an interval estimate is important because all values within the interval are considered plausible values of the population or process mean. Therefore, a decision maker's plans must be viable for all values within the confidence

Figure 6.4

An illustration of the sampling variation of confidence intervals for μ

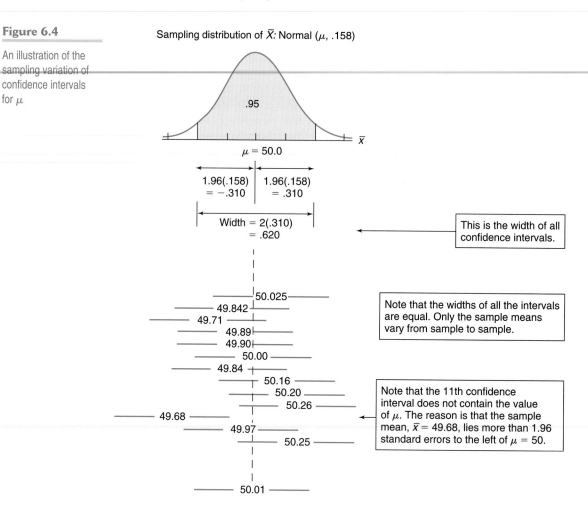

Sampling distribution of $\bar{X}$: Normal $(\mu, .158)$

interval. Because it is easier to make plans and decisions based on a narrow range of plausible values than for a wider range, narrower intervals are often desirable. In general, they are preferred as long as the level of confidence remains acceptable. A general guideline is to choose the *lowest acceptable* level of confidence to obtain an interval estimate that is as narrow as this level of confidence allows.

A key aspect of planning a statistical study is controlling the sampling error. Once we have chosen the desired level of confidence, we can achieve a desired margin of sampling error by choosing an adequate sample size. From Expression (6.3), it is again not difficult to see that the margin of error decreases as the sample size increases for a given confidence level. This is true because the sample size n is in the denominator of the expression for the margin of sampling error. To illustrate the determination of a sample size, let's consider the following example. Suppose a consumer product testing organization wishes to estimate, with 94% confidence, the average lifetime of a popular steel-belted tire. It is known that the lifetime mileage of this tire is adequately approximated by a normal distribution with a best guess value of $\sigma = 4{,}000$ miles. What sample size is needed such that the desired margin of sampling error for estimating the average lifetime is 1,000 miles, plus or minus?

For 94% confidence, $\alpha = .06$; thus, we center .94 of the area around μ and leave .03 of the area in each tail of the sampling distribution. Accordingly, the standard normal quantile value obtained by using a computer or Table B is $z_{.97} = 1.88$. Using Expression (6.3) with $\sigma = 4,000$, the margin of sampling error is $(1.88)(4,000/\sqrt{n})$. We equate this to 1,000, the desired margin of sampling error, and with a little algebra solve for the corresponding sample size n. Thus,

$$1.88 \frac{4,000}{\sqrt{n}} = 1,000$$

$$\sqrt{n} = \frac{(1.88)(4,000)}{1,000}$$

$$n = \left[\frac{(1.88)(4,000)}{1,000}\right]^2 = 56.55$$

or $n = 57$

We have rounded up to ensure that the desired margin of sampling error is achieved. Thus, a sample size of 57 tires is required to produce a margin of sampling error of 1,000 miles with 94% confidence.

The preceding steps can easily be generalized to develop an expression for determining the sample size n corresponding to any desired margin of sampling error or, equivalently, a confidence interval for μ of a desired width. To achieve a $100(1 - \alpha)\%$ confidence interval for μ with a desired width of $2E$, where E represents the desired margin of sampling error, we determine the sample size n using the following expression:

$$n = \left(\frac{z_{1 - \alpha/2}\sigma}{E}\right)^2 \qquad \textbf{(6.5)}$$

where $z_{1 - \alpha/2}$ is the corresponding quantile value of the standard normal distribution.

As you have seen, the determination of the sample size required to achieve a desired margin of sampling error is rather straightforward. A more difficult task for management is to determine an acceptable margin of sampling error because of the fact that the smaller the desired margin of error, the larger the sample size. This determination depends on an assessment of sampling costs, among other considerations.

EXAMPLE 6.1

In Example 5.5, we illustrated how to determine a sample size for scientific polls in the context of inferences about the proportion parameter π. As we have just discussed, it is equally important to be able to determine a sample size for inferences about the population or process mean μ, given a level of confidence. In this context, we will need a best-guess value for the population standard deviation σ, since we are not likely to know the actual value. In real applications, there are two ways of doing this: use judgment and subject-matter knowledge to arrive at a best-guess value, or determine a rough estimate by taking a relatively few measurements. This example illustrates such a situation.

The marketing department wants an interval estimate of the average age of current viewers of a TV show. Specifically, a 92% confidence interval is desired with a width of no more than 4 years. A market researcher must determine the number of viewers to include in a random sample to achieve an interval estimate of this width. Based on historical information, it is believed that the age of viewers of similar TV shows is adequately approximated by a normal distribution with a best-guess value of $\sigma = 8$ years. Assuming this belief to be correct, what is the required sample size?

Solution

If the width of the interval is to be 4 years, the desired margin of sampling error is $E = 2$ years. For a 92% level of confidence, we have $\alpha = .08$. Thus, the quantile value is $z_{.96} = 1.75$. Then from Expression (6.5), the required sample size is

$$n = \left[\frac{1.75(8)}{2}\right]^2 = 49 \text{ viewers}$$

Therefore, with 92% confidence, the actual average age of viewers should be within 2 years of the sample average for a random sample of 49 viewers.

6.3.3 Confidence Intervals for μ When σ Is Unknown

In most real statistical applications, the value of σ is unknown. Accordingly, we concentrate entirely on this case for the remainder of Section 6.3. Suppose we are interested in an interval estimate for μ based on a random sample of n observations from a population or process whose distribution is reasonably close to the normal distribution but with *unknown* standard deviation σ. From the discussion in Section 5.5.4 and the summary statement in Section 5.5.5, we know that the sampling distribution of the statistic

$$T = \frac{\bar{X} - \mu}{S/\sqrt{n}} \tag{6.6}$$

is the T distribution with $n - 1$ degrees of freedom. *The determination of a confidence interval for μ when σ is unknown mirrors the approach taken when σ is known, with T-values replacing Z-values, and the standard error of $\bar{X}$ being estimated by $S/\sqrt{n}$ rather than being $\sigma/\sqrt{n}$.*

Generally, therefore, a $100(1 - \alpha)\%$ confidence interval for μ when σ is unknown is

$$\bar{X} \pm t_{1 - \alpha/2, n - 1} \frac{S}{\sqrt{n}} \tag{6.7}$$

where

$$\text{Margin of sampling error} = t_{1 - \alpha/2, n - 1} \frac{S}{\sqrt{n}} \tag{6.8}$$

and $t_{1 - \alpha/2, n - 1}$ is the corresponding quantile value of the T distribution with $n - 1$ degrees of freedom.

It is important to recall from Section 5.5.4 that the T distribution is relatively robust to the assumption that the population or process distribution is the normal. Even for relatively small sample sizes (sometimes as few as 10 to 15), the procedure is still valid. Ultimately, the investigator's subject-matter knowledge can play an important role in deciding whether this assumption is warranted.

Using the Computer

Minitab, Excel, and JMP IN all have the capability of determining a confidence interval for μ when σ is unknown, with some differences among them. For example, Minitab and our Excel add-ins will provide a confidence interval for any given confidence level, whereas JMP IN provides only 95% confidence intervals. The following example illustrates the outputs.

EXAMPLE 6.2

In the production of synthetic fibers, the strengths should be monitored periodically to maintain and assure certain quality standard in the strength. The following example illustrates this kind of situation.

A manufacturer of a synthetic fiber takes periodic samples to estimate the mean breaking strength of the fiber. For each periodic sample, an experiment is devised in which the breaking strengths (in pounds) are observed for 16 strands randomly selected from the production process. The strengths of the current sample are: 20.8, 20.6, 21.0, 20.9, 19.9, 20.2, 19.8, 19.6, 20.9, 21.1, 20.4, 20.6, 19.7, 19.6, 20.3, and 20.7. It is assumed that the breaking strengths are adequately approximated by a normal distribution. Determine 90%, 95%, and 99% confidence intervals for the average breaking strength of the fiber.

Solution

The Minitab output for the 90% and 99% intervals is given first, followed by the JMP IN and Excel outputs given side-by-side for the 95% interval. Notice that essentially the same quantities are provided by Minitab and JMP IN; they include the sample size (16), the value of the sample mean (20.381), the value of the sample standard deviation (.523), the standard error of the sample mean (.131), and the confidence intervals (20.152 to 20.611 for the 90% confidence interval, 20.103 to 20.660 for the 95% interval, and 19.996 to 20.767 for the 99% interval). Minitab arranges them in a row, and JMP IN arranges in a column. Excel provides values of the sample mean and sample standard deviation and the confidence limits.

From these intervals, it is important to notice that the greater the level of confidence, the wider the interval because the magnitude of the quantile value is larger [see Expression (6.7)]. Also notice that since the T distribution is symmetric, the margin of sampling error is one-half the width of a confidence interval. To illustrate, for the 90% interval, the margin of sampling error is $(20.611 - 20.152)/2 = .2295$.

```
Variable   N    Mean StDev SE Mean     90.0 % CI
Strength  16 20.381 0.523   0.131 (20.152, 20.611)

Variable   N    Mean StDev SE Mean     99.0 % CI
Strength  16 20.381 0.523   0.131 (19.996, 20.767)
```

JMP IN

Moments

Mean	20.38125
Std Dev	0.52309
Std Error Mean	0.13077
Upper 95% Mean	20.65998
Lower 95% Mean	20.10252
N	16.00000
Sum Weights	16.00000

Excel

	A	B	C	D	E	F
1	0.95 Confidence Interval Estimate of MU (SIGMA Unknown)					
2	Data					
3	20.8	Sample mean = 20.3813				
4	20.6	Sample standard deviation = 0.5231				
5	21	Lower confidence limit = 20.1025				
6	20.9	Upper confidence limit = 20.66				

6.3.4   Hypothesis Testing: A Graphical Analysis

When possible, the initial analysis in hypothesis testing should be exploratory, consisting of a graph of the sample data. A graphical approach provides an opportunity to gain valuable insight into the plausibility of a null hypothesis. The graphical analysis complements the statistical inferential method (confirmatory analysis) because it provides an early, visual indication of the plausibility of the claim. Data visualization is very important because it gives an opportunity even for a novice to understand the inferential result. For testing hypotheses about a population or process mean, we illustrate graphical analysis with the following examples.

EXAMPLE 6.3

In an assembly process, it is important to monitor periodically the average time it takes to assemble a certain product because subsequent stages in the overall process may be adversely affected if a previous stage required more than the usual time. So, frequently a random sample of actual assembly times is obtained to assess the average assembly time. This example illustrates this kind of situation.

The historical average time required to assemble a unit in an assembly process has been 10 minutes. The current sample of 20 randomly selected units yields the following assembly times: 9.8, 10.4, 10.6, 9.6, 9.7, 9.9, 10.4, 9.8, 9.6, 10.2, 10.3, 9.6, 9.9, 10.5, 10.6, 9.8, 10.5, 10.1, 10.5, and 9.7 minutes. From historical data, it is believed that the process distribution of assembly times is adequately approximated by a normal distribution. Graph the 20 assembly times. Does the graph suggest that there has been a change in the average assembly time of 10 minutes?

Solution

We graph the 20 assembly times like a run chart, using the vertical axis for the assembly times and the horizontal axis for indicating observation numbers with integers from 1 up to the sample size, as illustrated in Figure 6.5. It is important to realize that, unlike a run chart, the horizontal axis here does not imply a time sequence because the sample of 20 assembly times is assumed to have been taken during the same time period. Now, what does the graph in Figure 6.5 indicate about the claim that $\mu = 10$? The sample assembly times appear to hover around the horizontal line corresponding to the claim. Thus, the graph does not reveal an obvious change in the average assembly time.

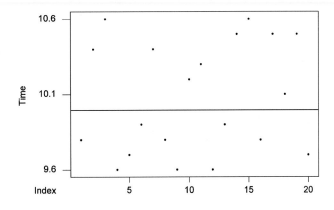

Figure 6.5

Minitab graph of the assembly times in Example 6.3

EXAMPLE 6.4

In a global marketplace, change is necessary in order to remain competitive. But before implementing a change, such as converting to a new method, management must evaluate the change to ensure that indeed it is an improvement. This example illustrates such an evaluation.

A manufacturer produces steel rods. As part of an ongoing quality improvement effort, management has decided to adopt a new manufacturing process if it produces steel rods that are superior to the current standard of 500 pounds for average breaking strength. A sample of 12 rods manufactured by the new process yields the following breaking strengths: 502, 496, 510, 508, 506, 498, 512, 497, 515, 503, 510, and 506 pounds. Assume that the distribution of the breaking strengths is reasonably close to the normal. Graph the sample data. Does the graph suggest an improvement in the average breaking strength?

Solution

Following the procedure outlined in Example 6.3, a graph of the sample data is given in Figure 6.6. In this figure, notice that most of the observations are above the horizontal line corresponding to the average strength of 500 pounds of the current process. This occurrence would not be expected if μ were equal to 500 and the distribution of breaking strengths were reasonably close to the normal distribution. Therefore, the sample data seem to suggest that an improvement in the average breaking strength (i.e., $\mu > 500$) has occurred with the new process.

6.3.5 **Testing Statistical Hypotheses on μ Using Confidence Intervals**

Recall from Section 6.2 that we can use confidence intervals to test the plausibility of claims about the unknown value of any parameter. For the population mean μ, suppose we wish to test the null hypothesis

$$H_0: \quad \mu = \mu_0$$

against the two-sided alternative

$$H_a: \quad \mu \neq \mu_0$$

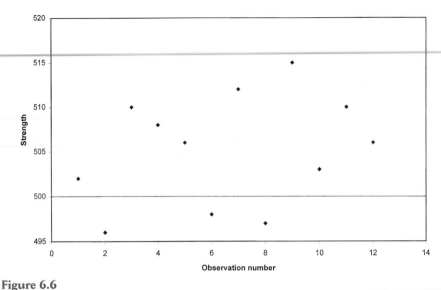

Figure 6.6

Excel graph of the breaking strengths in Example 6.4

where μ_0 is the value claimed for μ. The procedure for deciding on the claim as stated by the null hypothesis is as follows:

1. Determine a confidence interval for μ.

2. If the claimed value μ_0 lies within this confidence interval, then μ_0 is regarded as a plausible value for μ and the null hypothesis is not contradicted.

3. If the claimed value μ_0 does not lie within the confidence interval, then μ_0 is regarded as an implausible value for μ and the null hypothesis is contradicted in favor of the alternative hypothesis.

Generally, therefore, we can regard any confidence interval for μ as representing the range of plausible values that can be claimed for μ at the stated level of confidence.

The preceding use of confidence intervals in hypothesis testing is appropriate only with regard to a two-sided alternative hypothesis. If a one-sided alternative hypothesis is desired, we use the P-value approach discussed in the next section. One-sided confidence intervals can also be used to assess one-sided alternative hypotheses, but such a consideration is beyond the scope of this book.

EXAMPLE 6.5

With reference to Example 6.3, does the current sample suggest that there has been a change in the average assembly time based on a 95% confidence interval?

Solution

If there has been no change in the average assembly time, then the mean time μ is 10 minutes. If there has been a change, then μ is not equal to 10 minutes. That is, since the word "change" does not imply a direction, then μ is either less than 10 minutes or greater than 10 minutes. Thus, we state the null and alternative hypotheses as follows:

$$H_0: \quad \mu = 10$$

$$H_a: \quad \mu \neq 10$$

The following is the computer output (Minitab) for the desired confidence interval estimate of μ. Since the interval (9.9013, 10.2487) contains the value for μ claimed in the null hypothesis, we stay with H_0 and proceed as if there has been no change in the mean assembly time of the process. It is important to note that our initial conclusion based on the graph in Figure 6.5 is consistent with that based on this confidence interval.

```
Variable    N     Mean    StDev   SE Mean      95.0 % CI
time       20   10.0750   0.3712   0.0830   (9.9013, 10.2487)
```

6.3.6 Testing Statistical Hypotheses on μ Using *P*-Values

The *P*-value approach to hypothesis testing is designed to quantify the *extent* to which the sample data support or contradict the claim stated in the null hypothesis. This cannot be accomplished with confidence intervals because the final result is either that the parameter value claimed by the null hypothesis lies within the interval, or it lies outside the interval. Thus our conclusion is either yes, the data support the null hypothesis, or no, the data contradict it. But this approach does not reveal the *degree* to which the sample data support or contradict the null hypothesis. To illustrate, the null hypothesis in the filling process example of Section 5.3 is $H_0: \mu = 50$. Suppose the confidence interval for a given random sample turns out to be 49.99 to 50.79. This leads to the conclusion "the sample data do not contradict the nun hypothesis" because the value 50 lies (barely) inside the interval. If the almost identical interval 50.01 to 50.81 had resulted, the conclusion would have been "the sample data contradict the null hypothesis"—an opposite conclusion—because 50 now lies (just) outside the interval. In both cases, of course, the conclusion was a close call. But if the interval had been 52.11 to 52.91, a far different interval from either of the other two, the conclusion would still have been "the data contradict the null hypothesis" even though this conclusion is *not* a close call.

The "*P*" in *P*-value stands for *probability*. The idea of this approach is to assume temporarily that the claim of the null hypothesis is true, then determine the probability of getting a sample result like the one we have observed. The smaller this probability, the more precarious the assumption that the null hypothesis is true. In general, a **P-value** is *the probability of observing a value of a statistic that is more extreme (in the direction of the alternative hypothesis) than the value actually observed for a random sample, assuming the null hypothesis is true.*

To illustrate, suppose we wish to learn whether a coin is balanced or not. To start, we assume the coin is balanced (the null hypothesis). To gather sample data for this coin, we toss it 100 times. Suppose we observe 80 heads and 20 tails; does this result support or contradict the claim that the coin is balanced? If the coin is indeed balanced, we would expect approximately an even split between heads and tails. Acknowledging the presence of sampling error, we certainly would not doubt the claim if we observed nearly 50 heads—say, between 45 and 55 heads. But that is not what happened. The probability of observing 80 or more heads in 100 tosses is very small; in fact, it works out to be less than 0.0001. This probability is the *P*-value for our sample result. Because this *P*-value is extremely small, our sample data provide strong evidence that the coin is not balanced. In other words, it is highly unlikely that the sample result (80 heads and 20 tails) occurred by chance alone (i.e., due to sampling error) while flipping a balanced coin 100 times. *In general, the smaller the P-value, the less plausible the null hypothesis and the more plausible the alternative hypothesis. When the P-value is quite small, it is reasonable to conclude that the claim of the null hypothesis is not true.*

How do we interpret a *P*-value? A common rule of thumb is that if the *P*-value is .05 or smaller, the sample data contradict the null hypothesis and support the alternative hypothesis. Of course, the smaller the *P*-value, the greater the contradiction of the null hypothesis. For example, using .05 as a guideline:

- A *P*-value of .32 indicates that the data are consistent with the null hypothesis and are not close to contradicting it.
- *P*-values of .046 and .054 are borderline values, indicating the data marginally contradict or fail to contradict the null hypothesis.
- A *P*-value of .007 indicates that the data strongly contradict the null hypothesis.

The interpretation of *P*-values is illustrated in the following diagram using the statistic $\bar{X}$:

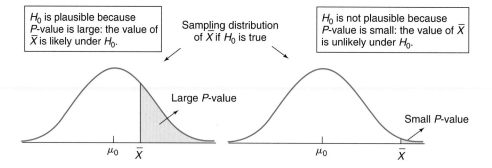

Evaluating and Controlling the Probability of Error in Hypothesis Testing

In some business applications of hypothesis testing, the participants agree in advance that the formal conclusion of the analysts is either "the null hypothesis will be regarded as true" (if the data do not contradict it) or "the alternate hypothesis is true" (if the data contradict the null hypothesis). For example, large-scale tests of proposed prescription drugs (called clinical trials) must demonstrate that the drug has the desired effect for it to be approved by the Food and Drug Administration (FDA). In these tests, the pharmaceutical company and the FDA agree to use a cutoff value of .05 for the *P*-value. That is, (1) if the *P*-value is less than or equal to .05, the conclusion is that the desired effect has been demonstrated; and (2) if the *P*-value exceeds .05, the conclusion is that the desired effect has not been demonstrated.

When a specific cutoff level for the *P*-value is agreed upon in advance as the basis for a formal conclusion, it is called the **level of statistical significance** and is denoted by α. The terminology has led some authors and the general media to use the phrase "statistically significant" to indicate a result in which a null hypothesis is contradicted. We believe that the phrase "the sample data contradict the null hypothesis" is more to the point because it avoids potential confusion with the literal meaning of the word "significant." The determination of whether a result is significant (using the literal meaning of the word) depends on subject-matter knowledge and is beyond the realm of statistics.

In hypothesis testing, we perform the analysis under the assumption that the null hypothesis is true. If this assumption is indeed true, and if by chance the data result in a sufficiently small *P*-value, then we conclude erroneously that the null hypothesis is not true. On the other hand, the null hypothesis may not be true. If this is the case, and if the data result in a sufficiently large *P*-value, then we conclude erroneously that the null hypothesis is true. Therefore, two types of error are possible in hypothesis testing. A **type 1 error** occurs if we conclude "the null hypothesis is not true" when in fact the null hypothesis is true. A **type 2 error** occurs if we conclude "the null hypothesis is true" when in fact the null hypothesis is not true. Of course, we would like the probabilities of these errors to be as small as possible.

If the null hypothesis is true, then a type 1 error occurs if (due to sampling error) the *P*-value is less than or equal to α. Suppose $\alpha = .05$. If the null hypothesis is indeed true, then the probability is .05 that sampling error alone produces a value of a statistic (for example, a value of $\bar{X}$) for which *P*-value $\leq .05$. This is illustrated by the following diagram. In general, the probability of a type 1 error is simply α, the chosen level of statistical significance.

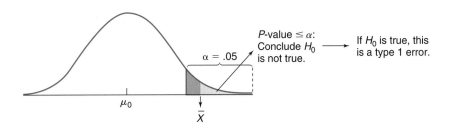

If the null hypothesis is *not* true, then a type 2 error occurs when the *P*-value exceeds the level of significance. The probability of a type 2 error is denoted by β. The determination of β is beyond the scope of this book. Nevertheless, two principles are important to understand. First, the value of β varies inversely with α. Thus, the larger the value of α, the smaller the value of β. This suggests that you should select the largest acceptable probability of type 1 error. Do not use $\alpha = .01$ if $\alpha = .05$ is acceptable because choosing $\alpha = .05$ provides a smaller probability of a type 2 error. Second, for a given value of α, β decreases as the sample size increases. In planning a formal test of hypothesis, the usual practice is first to agree upon an acceptable value of α, and second to determine the sample size needed to achieve an agreed-upon value of β.

We regard the use of hypothesis testing to reach a formal conclusion with respect to the null hypothesis as an atypical practice in business. Our purpose in discussing α and β has been primarily to acquaint you with the two possible errors in reaching a conclusion about a null hypothesis. Hereafter, we concentrate entirely on the determination and interpretation of *P*-values.

We concentrate on hypothesis testing situations for the population or process mean μ in which the value of the population or process standard deviation σ is unknown (since it is rare in practice that we know the value of σ). As you would expect, this situation leads to use of the *T* distribution. A *P*-value is part of the output of virtually all statistical software for hypothesis testing. Without the use of the computer, we can approximate *P*-values using Table C of the Appendix (the *T* table). We illustrate both approaches for determining *P*-values with Examples 6.3 and 6.4.

Using the Computer

We now use Examples 6.3 and 6.4 to illustrate the use of Minitab and Excel, respectively, for testing statistical hypotheses on μ when σ is unknown (see the appendix to this chapter for computer instructions).

For Example 6.3, we are interested in testing H_0: $\mu = 10$ versus H_a: $\mu \neq 10$. As we pointed out in Example 6.5, the alternative hypothesis is two-sided because we want to determine whether there has been a *change* in the average assembly time of 10 minutes. The Minitab output is as follows. Notice that it indicates the null and alternative hypotheses, and provides the sample size (20), the sample mean (10.075), the sample standard deviation (.3712), the standard error of the sample mean (.0830), the *T*-value from Expression (6.6) (.90), and the corresponding *P*-value (.38). A *P*-value of .38 is certainly not small enough to indicate convincing evidence against the null hypothesis. This is, of course, the same conclusion we reached based on data visualization in Figure 6.5 and the confidence interval in Example 6.5.

```
Test of mu = 10.0000 vs mu not = 10.0000
Variable    N      Mean    StDev   SE Mean      T      P
time       20   10.0750   0.3712   0.0830   0.90   0.38
```

For Example 6.4, we are interested in testing H_0: $\mu = 500$ versus H_a: $\mu > 500$. The alternative hypothesis is one-sided because we want to determine whether the new process produces steel rods that are better, in terms of average breaking strength, than those of the current process. The Excel output that follows includes the null and alternative hypotheses, the value of the sample standard deviation (6.1515), the value of the sample mean (505.25), the *T*-value from Expression (6.6) ($t = 2.9564$), and the corresponding one-sided *P*-value (.0065). The *P*-value of .0065 is quite small, thus confirming our initial inclination based on Figure 6.6 that an improvement in the average breaking strength has occurred with the new process.

	A	B	C	D	E	F
1	**Test of Hypothesis About MU (SIGMA Unknown)**					
2	*Data*					
3	502	*Test of MU = 500 Vs MU greater than 500*				
4	496	*Sample standard deviation = 6.1515*				
5	510	*Sample mean = 505.25*				
6	508	*Test Statistic: t = 2.9564*				
7	506	*P-Value = 0.0065*				
8	498					
9	512					

Determining *P*-values Using Table C

To approximate *P*-values using Table C, consider first Example 6.3. Since the alternative hypothesis is two-sided, we are concerned that the process mean is something other than the value claimed by the null hypothesis (i.e., $\mu = 10$) in either direction from this value. This means that the probability of observing a value of the statistic $\bar{X}$ more extreme than the value $\bar{X} = 10.075$, in the direction of the alternative hypothesis, involves both sides of the sampling distribution. Since the value $\bar{X} = 10.075$ corresponds to the *T*-value of .90 by means of Expression (6.6) [that is, $T = (10.075 - 10)/(.3712/\sqrt{20}) = .90$], and since the *T* distribution is symmetric,

$$P\text{-value} = P(|T| > .90)$$

$$= P(T < -.90) + P(T > .90)$$

$$= 2P(T < -.90)$$

where *T* has $n - 1 = 19$ degrees of freedom. This means that we can simply find the *P*-value using one side (preferably the lower side) of the *T* distribution and then double it. To approximate this *P*-value, we examine the row in Table C for 19 degrees of freedom and find the two quantile values that bracket $T = -.90$ to be $-.861$ and -1.328. We see that the area to the left of -1.328 is .100 and the area to the left of $-.861$ is .200. Thus, the probability that *T* is to the left of $-.90$ is between .100 and .200, and the desired *P*-value is between .200 and .400 (twice the range between .100 and .200). A *P*-value in the range .2 to .4 is clearly not small enough to provide convincing evidence against the null hypothesis. Consequently, we proceed as if there has not been a change in the average assembly time.

Now let's consider Example 6.4. Since the alternative hypothesis is one-sided, we are concerned that the process mean is something *greater* than the value claimed by the null hypothesis (i.e., in the direction indicated by the alternative hypothesis). Since the value $\bar{X} = 505.25$ corresponds to the *T*-value of 2.96 by means of Expression (6.6) [that is, $T = (505.25 - 500)/(6.151/\sqrt{12}) = 2.96$],

$$P\text{-value} = P(T > 2.96)$$

where there are $n - 1 = 11$ degrees of freedom. We can make things a bit easier for ourselves by taking advantage of the fact that the *T* distribution is symmetric around zero. This means that the area to the *right* of 2.96 is exactly the same as the area to the *left* of -2.96. In other words,

$$P\text{-value} = P(T < -2.96)$$

We approximate this *P*-value by examining the row in Table C for 11 degrees of freedom and finding the two quantile values that bracket -2.96 to be -2.718 and -3.106. We see that the area to the left of -2.718 is .010 and the area to the left of -3.106 is .005. Thus, the probability that *T* is to the left of -2.96 is between .005 and .010. A *P*-value this small provides convincing evidence against the null hypothesis. Consequently, the new process provides an improvement in the average breaking strength.

EXAMPLE 6.6

Recall Example 1.3, in which the management of a printing plant was concerned about the amount of scrap being accumulated after the plant had switched to water-based printing inks. Suppose that, subsequent to the sample of 23 consecutive printing runs discussed in Example 1.3, another sample was taken 1 week later in which the scrap (in pounds per 1,000 yards) was observed for 20 consecutive printing runs. The new sample data are as follows (sequenced from left to right in rows):

26	19	30	29	23
21	32	24	27	29
30	25	32	31	34
36	39	35	42	40

Management has determined that the amount of scrap being produced is acceptable as long as the process average per run is not exceeding 30 pounds per 1,000 yards. Do the new sample data suggest that the average level of scrap continues to be acceptable?

Solution

We wish to test the hypothesis H_0: $\mu = 30$ versus H_a: $\mu > 30$. We are selecting a one-sided alternative hypothesis here because $\mu > 30$ represents an unacceptable average amount of scrap that would signal action to be taken on the process, if the sample data were to contradict the null hypothesis. The following is a JMP IN output for this example. It includes the claimed value of the null hypothesis (Hypothesized Value = 30), the value of the sample mean (Actual Estimate = 30.2), the T-value from Expression (6.6) (Test Statistic = .1424), and—because of the direction of the alternative hypothesis—the upper, one-sided P-value (Prob > t = .4441). The rather large P-value of .4441 indicates that the null hypothesis is not contradicted.

   This analysis tempts one to conclude that the sample data are consistent with the null hypothesis that the average amount of scrap is 30 pounds. However, a graph of the sample data provides more insight into the current situation. Figure 6.7 is a run chart to which a horizontal line has been added to designate the maximum acceptable average amount of scrap of $\mu = 30$ pounds. Notice that, starting at about the 13th run, there is an increasing trend in the amount of scrap being accumulated. This strongly suggests that the printing process has become unstable and the average amount of scrap is now exceeding the acceptable limit. Consequently, the application of statistical inference alone is misleading; the apparent result that the process average remains 30 pounds is incorrect because of the clear indication that the process has become unstable.

Test Mean=value	
Hypothesized Value	30
Actual Estimate	30.2
t Test	
Test Statistic	0.1424
Prob > ItI	0.8882
Prob > t	0.4441
Prob < t	0.5559

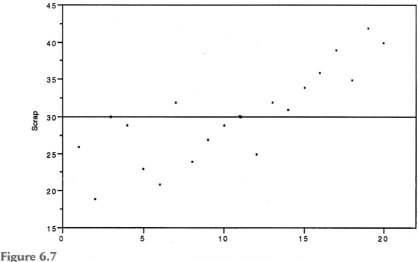

Figure 6.7

JMP IN run chart of scrap in Example 6.6

In the following box, we summarize the fundamental steps needed to test statistical hypotheses. These remain the same no matter what the particular application is. The only thing that changes from one application to the next is the appropriate statistic and its sampling distribution used to determine the P-value.

OVERVIEW OF STEPS IN HYPOTHESIS TESTING

1. State the null and alternative hypotheses based on subject-matter knowledge:
   - H_0 gets the benefit of the doubt.
   - H_a requires proof beyond reasonable doubt.
2. If a formal decision is to result directly from the test (an unusual situation in business): Choose the level of statistical significance α to be the largest acceptable probability of a type 1 error; this minimizes β, the probability of a type 2 error.
3. Assume that H_0 is true.
4. Determine the value of the best statistic and the corresponding P-value based on the sampling distribution.

   [For example, for inferences about μ, convert the value of $\bar{X}$ to $T = (\bar{X} - \mu_0)/(S/\sqrt{n})$ and determine the resulting P-value.]
5. Interpret results:
   - For most applications, simply report the P-value:
        The lower the P-value, the more strongly the data contradict H_0 in favor of H_a.
   - For formal conclusions:
        If P-value $\leq \alpha$, conclude H_0 is not true (H_a is true).
        If P-value $> \alpha$, conclude H_0 is true.

Statistical Inferences for π Based on p

The procedures introduced in Section 6.3 deal with inferences about the population mean μ. With a little adjustment, the same procedures can be used to carry out statistical inferences about the population proportion π.

Suppose we are selecting a random sample and observing for each sampling unit the presence or absence of some attribute (e.g., Was it a successful sale? Was it a female employee? Was it a defective item?). Our primary interest is to estimate the proportion of the members of the population that possess an attribute of interest. Let X represent the number of sampling units that possess the attribute of interest out of a random sample of n items. As you know from Chapter 4, X has a binomial distribution provided the population is large enough to assure independence among sampling trials. Furthermore, we know from Section 5.6 that the best statistic for inferences regarding the population proportion π is p, the sample proportion, where $p = X/n$. You also learned in Chapters 4 and 5 that, under certain common conditions, the sampling distribution of the sample proportion p is closely approximated by a normal distribution with mean $= \pi$ and standard deviation $= \sqrt{\pi(1 - \pi)/n}$. [The guideline is that both $n\pi$ and $n(1 - \pi)$ are at least 5.] Therefore, the sampling distribution of the statistic $Z = (p - \pi)/\sqrt{\pi(1 - \pi)/n}$ is approximately the standard normal distribution. This means that, if the necessary conditions are present, inferences about π involve the use of the now-familiar standard normal distribution.

6.4.1 Confidence Intervals for π

Recall that the sample proportion is $p = X/n$, where X is the observed number of sampling units that possess the attribute of interest in a random sample of size n. Suppose we desire a confidence interval for the unknown proportion π. Since the approximating sampling distribution is the standard normal distribution, the determination of an approximate $100(1 - \alpha)\%$ **confidence interval for π** is based on the general discussion from Section 6.3.1 and is given by

$$p \pm \text{Margin of sampling error}$$

or

$$p \pm z_{1 - \alpha/2} \sqrt{\frac{p(1 - p)}{n}} \qquad \textbf{(6.9)}$$

where

$$\text{Margin of sampling error} = z_{1 - \alpha/2} \sqrt{\frac{p(1 - p)}{n}} \qquad \textbf{(6.10)}$$

In Expressions (6.9) and (6.10), notice that we have estimated the standard error of p, $\text{SE}(p) = \sqrt{\pi(1 - \pi)/n}$, by substituting the value of the sample proportion p for the unknown value of π. Notice also that we have used the word *approximate* because the statistic $Z = (p - \pi)/\sqrt{p(1 - p)/n}$ is approximately the standard normal. (The substitution of p for π does not introduce enough additional variation to cause the standard normal approximation to be inadequate, as long as the guideline conditions are satisfied.)

Using the Computer

Recently, statistical software packages such as Minitab (Release 12) have added the capability for inferences about proportions involving a single sample as in this section (or two samples as in Section 7.5). We use Examples 6.7–6.9 to illustrate.

EXAMPLE 6.7

As we have noted before, modern political campaigns gauge voter sentiment frequently by using scientific polls. During a campaign, a candidate wishes to track the proportion of voters favoring him. It is not unusual for polls to be taken on a weekly basis with regard to this proportion. This example illustrates a statistical inference for the proportion parameter π based on a scientific poll.

Based on the current random sample of 200 registered voters, 92 indicate a preference for candidate Wheeler over his opponent.

(a) Determine an approximate 95% confidence interval for the proportion of all registered voters who favored Wheeler at the time the sample was taken.

(b) Would it be correct to say the probability is .95 that the value of π lies within the interval you determined in part (a)?

(c) Is it appropriate to say that we are 95% confident that the proportion who actually vote for Wheeler will lie within the interval you determined?

Solution

(a) For $X = 92$ and $n = 200$, the Minitab-generated confidence interval is as follows (disregard the last two columns on the right for now):

```
Sample   X    N   Sample p   95.0 % CI   Z-Value   P-Value
1        92  200  0.460000  (0.390927,    -1.13     0.258
                             0.529073)
```

Notice that the sample proportion is $p = .46$; the 95% confidence interval is given next. Therefore, we can say with approximately 95% confidence that the proportion who favored Wheeler *at the time the sample was taken* was between .391 and .529. You should know that when the news media qualify a result based on a political poll by saying that it has an error of plus or minus some number of percentage points, they are simply stating the margin of sampling error (which is one-half the width of the confidence interval) based on a 95% level of confidence.

(b) It would not be correct to say that the probability is .95 that the value of π lies within this interval! The proportion who favored Wheeler is an existing, fixed but unknown number, not a random variable. Ninety-five percent of all random samples of the same size that we might have selected at the same time would have yielded confidence intervals that contain this unknown value. So it makes sense to be 95% "confident" that our sample's interval estimate contains the proportion that we would observe for a 100% sample.

(c) It would not be appropriate. The proportion who favor Wheeler might change between the time the poll was taken and the election. Furthermore, the confidence interval deals only with sampling error; it does not deal with the other sources of error discussed in Chapter 1.

Alternatively, you can determine the confidence interval with a calculator as follows. The sample proportion is $p = 92/200 = .46$. For a 95% confidence level, we center .95 of the area and leave an area of .025 in each tail of the standard normal distribution. Thus, the quantile values obtained from Table B are ±1.96, and the 95% confidence interval for π is

$$.46 \pm 1.96 \sqrt{\frac{(.46)(1 - .46)}{200}} = .46 \pm .0691$$

or .391 to .529. The margin of sampling error is .0691.

Practical Implications for Example 6.7

It is most important to understand the need for the phrase "at the time the sample was taken." Statistical inferences are limited to the time during which the sample was taken. Example 6.7 illustrates this point very well. The sentiment of a population of voters can change rather quickly. What existed last week may no longer be valid. Generally, the best procedure to track shifts in a population or process is to analyze periodic samples.

6.4.2 Choosing an Adequate Sample Size

Let's return to Example 6.7, where we determined that an approximate 95% confidence interval for the population proportion of voters who favored candidate Wheeler is .391 to .529. This interval means that, if voter sentiment does not change, Wheeler could either lose the election (if π is any value less than .5 within the interval) or win the election (if π is any value greater than .5 within the interval). In other words, the outcome cannot be predicted based on this interval. This result stems directly from the rather large margin of sampling error of .0691. A smaller margin of error is needed to clarify the situation.

To achieve a desired margin of sampling error, we can determine the necessary sample size in the same manner used for a mean in Section 6.3.2. Suppose the desired margin of sampling error for Example 6.7 is .025 (plus or minus 2.5 percentage points). What sample size is needed? For a 95% level of confidence, we equate Expression (6.10) for the margin of sampling error to the desired value, as follows:

$$1.96 \sqrt{\frac{\pi(1 - \pi)}{n}} = .025 \qquad \textbf{(6.11)}$$

To solve for n in Expression (6.11), we must either know or estimate π. As we illustrated in Section 5.6, a reasonable procedure is to arbitrarily assume that $\pi = .5$. This produces a sample size that is somewhat larger than necessary because the standard error of p is never greater than when $\pi = .5$. But it is certain to achieve the desired margin of sampling error, regardless of the value of π. In other words, it might be wise to play it safe and assume $\pi = .5$.

Substituting $\pi = .5$, we can solve Expression (6.11) for n with a little algebra:

$$1.96 \sqrt{\frac{(.5)(.5)}{n}} = .025$$

$$\sqrt{\frac{.25}{n}} = \frac{.025}{1.96}$$

$$\frac{.25}{n} = \left(\frac{.025}{1.96}\right)^2$$

$$n = \frac{.25}{(.025/1.96)^2} = 1,536.64$$

or, rounding up,

$$n = 1,537$$

Therefore, if a random sample of 1,537 registered voters were selected, the margin of sampling error for 95% confidence would be not more than ±2.5 percentage points. If, for this larger sample, the same proportion favored Wheeler as in Example 6.7 (46%), then the 95% confidence interval would be $.46 \pm .025$ or (.435 to .485). Unlike the previous confidence interval, this result suggests that candidate Wheeler is currently losing. Accordingly, Wheeler may deem it appropriate to change his campaign strategy.

With algebra we can solve Expression (6.11) for n using any confidence level and any margin of sampling error. To achieve an approximate $100(1 - \alpha)$% confidence interval for π with a desired margin of sampling error, we determine the sample size n using the expression

$$n = \pi(1 - \pi)\left(\frac{z_{1 - \alpha/2}}{E}\right)^2 \tag{6.12}$$

where E denotes the desired margin of sampling error. It is often prudent to set $\pi = .5$.

6.4.3 Testing Statistical Hypotheses on π Using Confidence Intervals

The procedure for using confidence intervals to test hypotheses on the population proportion π is the same as that for μ (see Section 6.3.5). Suppose we wish to test the null hypothesis

$$H_0: \quad \pi = \pi_0$$

against the two-sided alternative

$$H_a: \quad \pi \neq \pi_0$$

where π_0 is the value claimed for π. Using Expression (6.9), we can determine an approximate $100(1 - \alpha)$% confidence interval for π. If the claimed value π_0 is inside this interval, then π_0 is regarded as a plausible value for the population proportion; otherwise, it is not. To illustrate, recall Example 6.7, in which we determined an approximate 95% confidence interval to be .391 to .529. Suppose we want to test the null hypothesis H_0: $\pi = .5$ versus the alternative hypothesis H_a: $\pi \neq .5$. Since the claimed value for π is inside this interval, this value is a plausible value for π and the null hypothesis cannot be contradicted.

When we use confidence intervals for hypothesis testing, a slight discrepancy arises because the confidence interval uses the value of the *sample* proportion, rather than the claimed value π_0, to estimate SE(p). For the most part—and especially if the value of p is reasonably close to π_0—this is of little concern.

6.4.4 Testing Statistical Hypotheses on π Using *P*-Values

As in Section 6.4.3, consider testing the null hypothesis H_0: $\pi = \pi_0$, where π_0 is the value claimed for π. To test this null hypothesis based on the *P*-value approach, we simply convert the value of the sample proportion p to its *Z*-value by means of the expression

$$Z = \frac{p - \pi_0}{\sqrt{\dfrac{\pi_0(1 - \pi_0)}{n}}}$$

and use the approximating standard normal distribution to determine the *P*-value.

We illustrate the use of the *P*-value approach for testing hypotheses on π with the following examples.

EXAMPLE 6.8

For banks, there is a need to have an independent confirmation of account balances that are routinely reported by a bank. For this purpose, banks hire auditing firms that usually select a random sample of a bank's customer balances to check for discrepancies. This example illustrates such a situation.

Historically, the proportion of accounts for which reporting discrepancies have been found is .1 (i.e., 10%) for a particular bank. The bank has been attempting to lower this proportion by improving its reporting. In a recent sample of 200 accounts from this bank, an auditing firm found 16 to have a discrepancy. To what extent does this sample suggest that the bank has decreased the proportion of discrepancies from the historical value?

Solution

Based on the current sample, the estimated proportion of discrepancies is 16/200 = .08. A true decrease of 2% would represent a valuable improvement in service quality for the bank. A test of hypotheses can be used to see whether the sample establishes that the bank has indeed improved. Since a direction is provided in the question asked (i.e., we want to know whether the proportion has decreased), we state the null and alternative hypotheses as follows:

$$H_0: \quad \pi = .1$$

$$H_a: \quad \pi < .1$$

For $X = 16$ and $n = 200$, the Excel output is as follows. In this case, the *P*-value is the probability that a sample proportion would be .08 *or less* (in the direction of the alternative hypothesis) if the proportion of discrepancies remained at $\pi = .10$. The P-value of .1729 means that there is a .1729 chance that a sample proportion would be .08 or lower due to sampling error alone, if indeed the null hypothesis is true. Most of us would say that this P-value does not offer convincing evidence of a decrease in the proportion of discrepancies from the historical value of .10.

	A	B	C	D	E	F
1	n	π_0	SE(p)	X	p	P-value
2	200	0.1	0.021213	16	0.08	0.172889276

Alternatively, we can convert $p = .08$ to the corresponding Z-value and use Table B as illustrated in Figure 6.8, where

$$\text{P-value} = P(p < .08) = P(Z < -.94) = .1736$$

The slight discrepancy in the answers is because of the rounding of the Z-value when using Table B. Notice in Figure 6.8 that in determining the standard error of p, we use the value claimed by the null hypothesis (i.e., $\pi = .1$).

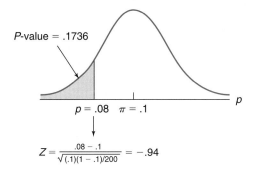

Figure 6.8

The P-value determination for Example 6.8 using Table B

EXAMPLE 6.9

The marketing department is advocating a new approach to sales called "team selling," in which telephone marketers screen potential customers prior to sales calls by regular salespersons. It claims that team selling would increase the proportion of successful sales calls over the 18% level currently achieved. Management intends to implement team selling, but first the proportion of successful sales calls must be shown to exceed the current rate convincingly. In a test, team selling is tried for a sample of 100 sales calls, of which 22 are successful. Does this sample adequately demonstrate improvement with team selling?

Solution

This is another example in which a direction is provided. Since convincing evidence that team selling *improves* the success rate is required, this becomes the alternative hypothesis. Thus, the null and alternative hypotheses are stated as H_0: $\pi = .18$ and H_a: $\pi > .18$. For $X = 22$ and $n = 100$, the Minitab output is as follows. The *P*-value is the probability that a sample proportion *exceeds* .22 (in the direction of the alternative hypothesis) if $\pi = .18$. From the output, the *P*-value is .149. This means there is a .149 chance that an apparent improvement as large as that seen in our sample would arise due to sampling error alone, if there were in fact no real improvement. Given a *P*-value as high as .149, it may not be prudent to implement team selling based on this sample.

```
Test of p = 0.18 vs p > 0.18
Sample  X    N    Sample p    95.0 % CI    Z-Value    P-Value
1       22   100  0.220000    (0.138809,    1.04       0.149
                               0.301191)
```

To determine the *P*-value using Table B, we first convert the value $p = .22$ to the corresponding *Z*-value and then determine the *P*-value as follows:

$$P\text{-value} = P(p > .22) = P\left(Z > \frac{.22 - .18}{\sqrt{(.18)(1 - .18)/100}}\right)$$
$$= P(Z > 1.04)$$
$$= 1 - .8508$$
$$= .1492$$

To determine *P*-values for two-sided alternative hypotheses using Table B (i.e., not using the computer), we have to consider the possibility that the population proportion departs from the claimed value of the null hypothesis in either direction. But since the sampling distribution involved (i.e., the standard normal) is symmetric around zero, we simply find the *P*-value for one side of the standard normal distribution as in Examples 6.8 and 6.9, and then double it.

6.5   Summary

In this chapter, we used the fundamental concepts discussed in Chapter 5 along with the standard normal and Student's *T* distributions to develop confidence intervals and test statistical hypotheses for the important parameters μ and π based on a random sample from a population or process.

A confidence interval consists of an interval estimate for a parameter accompanied by a statement of confidence that the interval contains the unknown parameter value. If the sampling distribution of the best statistic is symmetric, the confidence interval is the point estimate plus or minus the margin of sampling error, where the margin of sampling error characterizes the precision of the best statistic.

A statistical hypothesis is a claim or belief about an unknown parameter value. There are two competing hypotheses: the null hypothesis, which states the claim, and the alternative hypothesis, which states the opposite of the claim. The plausibility of the null hypothesis is tested using either confidence intervals or *P*-values. If the value claimed by the null hypothesis is covered by the corresponding confidence interval, the claim is regarded as a plausible value for the parameter; otherwise, it is not. The *P*-value approach quantifies the extent (in terms of probability) to which the sample contradicts the claim of the null hypothesis. The plausibility of a claim may also be tested by graphing the sample data. At the very least, the graphical approach provides an early indication of the plausibility of the claim.

EXERCISES FOR SECTION 6.2

6.1   Outline the important provisions in estimating a parameter of interest.

6.2   In determining the precision of an estimator, what must be known and why is this important?

6.3   Suppose an interval estimate for a parameter θ is of the form 10 ± 2.
   (a) What is the point estimate of θ?
   (b) What is the amount by which the point estimate could be in error?
   (c) What is the range of values thought likely to contain θ?

6.4   Discuss the essential difference in purpose between the estimation of parameters and the testing of statistical hypotheses.

6.5   Suppose a 95% confidence interval for a population mean μ is 110 to 160 units. Suppose further that someone claims μ to be 120 units. Based on this confidence interval, what conclusion is plausible about the claim? Explain.

6.6   Explain the nature of the null and alternative hypotheses.

6.7   When should a one-sided alternative hypothesis be used rather than a two-sided alternative hypothesis?

6.8   Historically, an appliance model has required an average of 1.5 service calls per year. A recent random sample of service calls for this model has shown an average of 2.3 service calls per appliance over the last year. There is some concern that the manufacturing quality has declined.
   (a) Set up the null and alternative hypotheses and justify your choices.
   (b) State what is to be compared in testing the claim of the null hypothesis, and outline the

possible explanations for any differences in what you are comparing.

6.9   Historically, the proportion of a state's adult residents who regularly play the lottery has been .4. A recent random sample has shown that 37% of adult residents regularly play the lottery. There is some concern that the proportion has changed from its historical value. Answer parts (a) and (b) of Exercise 6.8.

6.10 Historically, the average number of units of a product produced daily by workers in a plant has been 100 units. The plant manager has instituted an intensive training program for the workers to increase the average number of units produced per day by the plant. After the training program, a random sample yields a mean of 104.5 units. Answer parts (a) and (b) of Exercise 6.8.

6.11 Historically, the proportion of adults over 24 years old that smoke has been .3. Because of continuing revelations that smoking has considerable effect on one's health, it is believed that the proportion of adult smokers over 24 years old has now declined. A recent random sample revealed that 23% of adults over 24 years old are smokers. Answer parts (a) and (b) of Exercise 6.8.

6.12 Historically, the average time required to complete a transaction at a particular bank has been 3 minutes. The employees of this bank have recently undergone additional training to increase the efficiency of customer transactions. A recent random sample of transaction times at this bank revealed an average transaction time of 2.7 minutes. Answer parts (a) and (b) of Exercise 6.8.

EXERCISES FOR SECTION 6.3

6.13 Assume that the following random samples are taken from populations with normal distributions. In each case, find the margin of sampling error and a confidence interval for μ for the indicated level.
   (a) $n = 12$, $\bar{X} = 122$, $\sigma = 25$, 90% level of confidence

   (b) $n = 56$, $\bar{X} = 122$, $\sigma = 25$, 90% level of confidence
   (c) $n = 12$, $\bar{X} = 122$, $\sigma = 25$, 95% level of confidence
   (d) $n = 56$, $\bar{X} = 122$, $\sigma = 25$, 95% level of confidence

6.14   Refer to Exercise 6.13.
  (a) Describe how increasing the sample size while maintaining the same level of confidence affects the margin of sampling error and the confidence interval.
  (b) Describe how increasing the level of confidence while maintaining the same sample size affects the margin of sampling error and the confidence level.

6.15   A random sample of 44 items has a mean $\bar{X} = 16.8$. It is known that the population standard deviation is $\sigma = 9.9$.
  (a) Determine a 92% confidence interval for the population mean μ.
  (b) Is it necessary to know the population distribution for your answer to part (a) to be valid? Explain.
  (c) What sample size would be required to achieve a margin of sampling error of 1.5, plus or minus?

6.16   A manufacturer of a certain metal wishes to estimate the mean breaking strength of the metal. On a given day, 12 specimens of the metal are randomly selected from the production, and each specimen is subjected to stress until a crack is observed. The following are the breaking strengths of the specimens (in kilograms per square centimeter): 428, 419, 458, 439, 441, 456, 463, 429, 438, 445, 441, and 463. Assume the breaking strength of the metal is adequately approximated by a normal distribution.
  (a) Determine a 98% confidence interval for the average breaking strength of the metal.
  (b) If no other sample information is obtained, under what conditions would the interval estimate in part (a) be valid a year from now? Do you believe these conditions are realistic? Explain.

6.17   Referring to part (a) in Exercise 6.16, which of the following statements is correct for the interpretation of the confidence interval?
  (a) The probability that the average strength of the metal is between the confidence limits is .98.
  (b) Approximately 98% of the confidence intervals computed as a result of repeated samples of size 12 from the stable process that produces the metal would include the average strength of the metal.
  (c) The probability that the breaking strength of any such metal is outside the confidence limits is .02.

6.18   In Exercises 2.17 and 2.58, you estimated the total direct spending by out-of-town fans attending the 1994 Women's Final Four Basketball Tournament in Richmond, Virginia. The data were taken from a study whose purpose was to assist Virginia Commonwealth University and the City of Richmond in future decisions to host tournaments like this (see these exercises for source). They are contained on the book's data diskette, in the file named EX0217.
   Your estimate was based on estimates of the mean amounts spent in five distinct categories: lodging, meals, entertainment, shopping, and local transportation. Now, what level of accuracy can be expected of these estimates? For each spending category, determine and interpret a 95% confidence interval for the mean amount spent.

6.19   In Exercises 1.37 and 2.57, you used graphical analysis to learn about the visitation process at the Information Age Exhibit of the Smithsonian Institute in Washington, D.C. The data are produced by the Institute's computer tracking system and represent the 56-day period from September 30, 1995 to November 26, 1995, during which time 33,189 visitors passed through the exhibit (see these exercises for source). They are on the book's data diskette in the file named EX0137. Management wishes to estimate the mean visitation time and the distribution of visitors by gender.
  (a) Estimate the mean daily visitation time. Provide a point estimate of the process mean as well as a 95% confidence interval for the process mean.
  (b) Based on your results in part (a), is it plausible to claim that the mean visitation time is 35 minutes?
  (c) Estimate the mean daily proportion of visitors who are female. Provide a point estimate of the process mean as well as a 95% confidence interval for the process mean.
  (d) To what extent do the data contradict a null hypothesis that the mean percentage of females is 50%?

6.20   Fifteen sections of recently produced glass tubing were randomly selected in an investigation of "cord," a measure of brittleness. The observed cord levels are as follows: 7.28, 7.63, 7.89, 7.91, 8.20, 7.35, 8.07, 8.09, 6.71, 8.09, 7.74, 7.60, 6.93, 7.41, and 7.19. Assume that the cord level is adequately approximated by a normal distribution.
  (a) Determine a point estimate for the mean of the process currently producing the glass tubing.
  (b) For a 95% confidence level, determine the margin of sampling error for your point estimate.
  (c) Use an estimate of σ in Expression (6.5) to

determine the approximate sample size that would be required to achieve a margin of sampling error of .1, plus or minus.

6.21 The Virginia Department of Transportation monitors the weight of trucks on its interstate highways. A recent sample of 25 trucks revealed the following weights (in tons): 13.98, 21.58, 27.74, 21.49, 12.88, 20.01, 22.22, 19.10, 25.93, 17.43, 15.39, 24.05, 5.73, 16.35, 21.99, 18.86, 24.48, 19.93, 23.05, 26.94, 16.25, 26.48, 20.54, 29.84, and 28.51. Assume the weight is adequately approximated by a normal distribution.

(a) Determine a point estimate for the mean weight of trucks currently traveling on Virginia's interstate highways.

(b) Determine a 95% confidence interval for μ.

(c) In part (b), approximately how large a sample would be required to achieve a margin of sampling error of 1.5 tons, plus or minus? *Hint:* Use an estimate of σ in Expression (6.5).

(d) If the confidence interval in part (b) is appropriate to use 1 year from now without more sample information, discuss the conditions that must be in place.

6.22 The following are the lifetimes (in hours) of a random sample of a type of electrical component: 142.84, 97.04, 32.46, 69.14, 85.67, 114.43, 41.76, 163.07, 108.22, and 63.28. Assume the distribution of component lifetimes is reasonably close to a normal distribution.

(a) Determine a 98% confidence interval for μ.

(b) In part (a), approximately how large a sample would be required to achieve a margin of sampling error of 20 hours? *Hint:* Use an estimate of σ in Expression (6.5).

(c) Answer the same question as in part (b) of Exercise 6.16.

6.23 Refer to Exercise 6.16.

(a) Suppose the average breaking strength for this metal has been 450. Graph the data as in Example 6.3. Does the graph suggest that there has been a change in the average breaking strength? Is this in line with the confidence interval of part (a) in Exercise 6.16?

(b) Determine the P-value and discuss the extent to which this sample contradicts the claim of the null hypothesis in part (a).

6.24 Refer to Exercise 6.20.

(a) Suppose the average cord level for this process has been 7.7. Graph the data as in Example 6.3. Does the graph suggest that there has been a change in the average cord level? Is this in line with the confidence interval of part (b) in Exercise 6.20?

(b) Based on the confidence interval, what are the plausible values that we can claim for the average cord level?

(c) Determine the P-value and answer the same question as in part (b) of Exercise 6.23.

6.25 Consider the hypotheses H_0: $\mu = 100$ and H_a: $\mu < 100$. A random sample yields values for the statistics $\bar{X} = 85$ and $S = 50$. Assume the population distribution is the normal.

(a) Find the P-value if $n = 5$.

(b) Find the P-value if $n = 20$.

(c) Find the P-value if $n = 80$.

(d) Based on your results in parts (a)–(c), discuss how the strength of the sample in favor of H_a depends on the sample size for which the values $\bar{X} = 85$ and $S = 50$ were obtained.

6.26 Suppose you are testing the hypotheses H_0: $\mu = 100$ and H_a: $\mu > 100$. You observe for a random sample of $n = 36$, $\bar{X} = 115$ and $S = 38$.

(a) Determine the P-value.

(b) Based on the P-value you found in part (a), assess the strength of this sample against the null hypothesis.

(c) Is it necessary to know the population distribution in order for your answers to be valid? Explain.

6.27 A recent random sample of 15 automobile accident victims in a northeast city revealed the following costs for medical treatment: $582, 698, 1,029, 732, 2,436, 5,932, 242, 307, 862, 186, 643, 597, 761, 508, and 1,135. All victims were wearing seat belts at the time of the accident.

(a) Determine a 98% confidence interval for the average medical cost.

(b) Suppose the average medical cost has been $1,000. Graph the data. Does the graph suggest there has been a change in the average medical cost for accident victims? Explain.

(c) Determine the P-value and discuss the extent to which this sample contradicts the claim that the average cost is $1,000.

6.28 During a recent water shortage in a southern city, the water company randomly sampled residential water consumption on a daily basis. A random sample of 20 residences revealed the following consumptions (in gallons) on a particular day: 180, 220, 235, 195, 265, 245, 175, 196, 248, 212, 238, 252, 208, 214, 228, 236, 240, 218, 223, and 246.

(a) Determine a 95% confidence interval for the current daily average water consumption in this city.

(b) Suppose the average daily consumption before

the water shortage was 250 gallons. Graph the data. Does the graph suggest there has been a decrease in the average daily consumption since the water shortage? Explain.

(c) Determine the *P*-value and discuss the extent to which this sample contradicts the claim of no decrease in the average daily consumption.

6.29 A video rental company offered a special deal in which new members were allowed ten free video rentals the first year. The company estimated that the offer would be profitable the first year if the new members averaged 15 additional rentals for the year. They plan to continue the program unless it can be shown to have been unprofitable. To evaluate the policy after a year, a random sample of 36 new members was selected. The 36 members averaged 13.4 additional rentals for the year, with a standard deviation of 7.8 rentals. Set up the appropriate null and alternative hypotheses, and determine whether this sample shows that the target of 15 additional rentals, on average, for all new members is not being met in favor of a lower number.

6.30 In a study of the wages earned by auto mechanics in a city, 18 randomly selected auto mechanics were interviewed. Their hourly wages are as follows: $12.00, 12.50, 13.00, 10.50, 11.00, 12.50, 12.25, 9.75, 10.75, 13.25, 10.25, 8.75, 10.00, 10.75, 11.25, 10.25, 11.50, and 12.75. Assume the distribution of wages is adequately modeled by the normal distribution.

(a) For a 99% confidence level, determine the margin of sampling error.

(b) Determine a 99% confidence interval for the mean wages of all auto mechanics in this city.

(c) Should you use this interval estimate 1 year from now? Support your answer.

6.31 Referring to Exercise 6.30, suppose 6 months ago it was known that the average hourly wage for auto mechanics in this city was $11.75.

(a) Graph the data. Does the graph suggest that there has been a change in the average hourly wage? Is this in line with the confidence interval of part (b) in Exercise 6.30?

(b) Determine the *P*-value and discuss the extent to which the current sample contradicts the known average hourly wage of 6 months ago.

6.32 The Chamber of Commerce wishes to estimate the average amount of money spent by those who attend conventions in the city. Sixteen persons were randomly selected from various conventions taking place in the city and were asked to record their expenditures for a given day. The following dollar amounts were recorded: 150, 175, 163,

148, 142, 189, 135, 174, 168, 152, 158, 184, 134, 146, 155, and 163. Assuming expenditures are distributed normally, determine 90%, 95%, and 99% confidence intervals for the mean spending level.

6.33 Refer to Exercise 6.32. Suppose the claim is that the mean spending level is $165 per day.

(a) Graph the data. Does the graph suggest to you that there has been a change in the average spending level? Explain.

(b) Using the 95% confidence interval, is the claim supported by this sample? Explain.

(c) Test the null hypothesis that the average spending level is the lower limit of the 95% confidence interval against a two-sided alternative. Compute the *P*-value. Explain your findings.

(d) Repeat part (c) by using the upper limit of the 95% confidence interval.

6.34 A computer center manager wishes to understand the effect of new procedures on the average throughput time for jobs run on a mainframe computer. The throughput time of a job is the elapsed time from entry to output. The following are the throughput times (in minutes) for a random sample of 25 jobs run during the week after the change in procedures, listed in the order in which they were run.

15 18 16 14 14 22 21 16 14 8 18 14 8
14 10 8 7 8 10 5 11 6 5 10 6

With the previous procedures, the average throughput time was 8 minutes. The new procedures were expected to save money without increasing the average throughput time. Investigate statistically whether these sample data suggest that the average throughput time under the new procedures increased from that of the previous procedures.

6.35 The study "A Comparison of Women in Small and Large Companies" (*American Journal of Small Business,* Winter 1988, pp. 23–33) reported on biographical data of surveyed women who work for small companies—defined as those with fewer than 100 employees. Of particular interest was the age of female managers who work for small firms. The following data are simulated based on the summary information given in this study and represent the ages of 14 randomly selected female managers who work for small firms: 38, 29, 36, 44, 30, 41, 37, 28, 34, 30, 28, 41, 48, and 45.

(a) Suppose that studies from five years earlier indicated that the average age of female managers who work for small companies was 35 years at that time. Graph these data. Does the graph suggest that the average age has increased? Explain.

(b) Determine the extent to which this sample contradicts a claim that the average age remains 35 years and supports a claim that the average age is now higher.

6.36 The paper "Are Young Children Adaptive Decision Makers? A Study of Age Differences in Information Search Behavior" (*Journal of Consumer Research,* Vol. 21, Mar. 1995, pp. 567–580) explored the understanding of how young children make consumer choices. Children's search behavior was examined by having participating children play a game called "house of prizes." The game involved making a choice between two "houses," each "house" containing four different types of prizes, with each prize hidden behind a "curtain." The participating children were instructed that they could have as many "curtains" opened as they wished (maximum of eight) before making a choice. The following data are simulated based on the summary information given in this study and represent the number of "curtains" opened before choosing between the two "houses" for 17 randomly selected children 6 to 7 years old: 8, 8, 3, 4, 7, 6, 8, 2, 8, 4, 5, 3, 8, 3, 8, 2, 3.

(a) Determine a 95% confidence interval for the average number of "curtains" opened before making a choice for children of this age group.

(b) Notice that some children had a relatively small number of curtains opened before making a choice. Why might this be?

6.37 The paper "A Taxonomy of Business Start-Up Reasons and Their Impact on Firm Growth and Size" (*Journal of Business Venturing,* Vol. 9, 1994, pp. 7–31) studied the characteristics of new independent business in Great Britain. The study is based on a sample of 79 principal owner-managers of businesses that received their first order between January 1986 and December 1990. The number of employees and sales for these businesses are given in the table. Determine 95% confidence intervals for the mean number of employees and the mean sales amount for these new businesses.

Bus.	Sales	Employees	Bus.	Sales	Employees
1	118.1	5	41	28.3	16
2	456.2	3	42	68.7	18
3	43.1	1	43	164.0	1
4	131.0	8	44	192.8	1
5	124.3	4	45	28.8	4

Bus.	Sales	Employees	Bus.	Sales	Employees
6	119.2	1	46	723.1	1
7	93.3	16	47	29.3	8
8	157.5	3	48	177.6	1
9	215.8	3	49	48.6	7
10	96.5	1	50	110.2	1
11	86.5	4	51	359.1	17
12	138.0	6	52	227.8	9
13	399.2	3	53	46.5	15
14	25.3	1	54	66.6	28
15	24.2	1	55	52.8	6
16	128.5	16	56	173.9	2
17	75.9	0	57	52.3	2
18	59.5	0	58	36.8	11
19	63.8	5	59	164.6	18
20	170.8	2	60	39.1	3
21	20.0	9	61	88.6	2
22	300.3	4	62	79.8	10
23	926.7	10	63	141.1	7
24	35.7	8	64	183.1	30
25	209.6	4	65	217.0	9
26	36.5	0	66	195.3	5
27	58.0	16	67	151.5	3
28	127.2	14	68	178.8	2
29	172.5	1	69	89.9	1
30	14.4	7	70	178.9	7
31	19.8	1	71	79.1	19
32	78.7	5	72	771.6	2
33	52.7	1	73	15.9	10
34	271.0	6	74	415.8	1
35	6.4	3	75	111.6	1
36	145.4	8	76	169.8	3
37	136.2	8	77	11.6	17
38	59.7	6	78	70.8	9
39	36.3	9	79	116.7	5
40	66.6	9			

6.38 Historically, comparisons of women's and men's earnings have demonstrated a consistent and substantial gender inequality. The paper "Gender, Earnings, and Proportions of Women" (*Gender and Society,* Vol. 10, No. 2, Apr. 1996, pp. 168–184) investigated the reasons for such differences. The sample consisted of 420 computer processionals working in a western Canadian city. Data obtained included income and gender; they are on the book diskette in the file EX0638.

(a) Estimate the population mean incomes for men and for women.

(b) Determine 95% confidence intervals for the population mean incomes for men and for women.

(c) Based on the results in parts (a) and (b), do

these data seem to agree with previous findings concerning gender inequality?

(d) If indeed the population mean incomes differ for men and women, does this fact necessarily imply that gender is the basis for the difference? Explain.

6.39 The paper "Fair Values of Equity and Debt Securities and Share Prices and Property–Liability Insurers" (*The Journal of Risk and Insurance*, Vol. 62, No. 4, 1995, pp. 719–737) investigated the relationship between share prices of property–liability insurers with the fair values of their equity investments and their fixed-maturity debt securities. Of chief interest is whether their fair values affect their share prices beyond the effects of their historical costs. One aspect of the study involved a comparison of insurers' fair values of equity and fixed maturity investments with the corresponding historical (book) values. Do fair values differ enough from historical (book) values to have the potentially incremental effect on share prices? The sample for this exercise consists of 56 publicly held property–liability insurers operating during 1985 through 1991. The following data consist of (1) the 1991 differences between fair value of equity and the historical cost of equity (expressed as a percent of stockholders' equity) and (2) the 1991 differences between fair value and book value of fixed-maturity investments (also expressed as a percent of stockholders' equity) for each of the sample insurers.

Fair Value of Equity – Historical Cost of Equity

6.3	5.1	−3.4	27.4	38.5
2.7	−5.0	−13.8	−11.5	21.5
13.0	9.0	−24.5	−22.0	−8.9
13.1	−20.9	12.6	19.8	−19.0
−20.9	−26.0	20.6	−4.8	5.2

Fair Value of Equity – Historical Cost of Equity

9.7	15.1	−13.2	−14.1	40.3
.4	13.6	14.2	8.2	1.8
31.0	32.9	19.6	10.6	−15.3
−4.7	19.3	−10.2	−7.3	−.3
−20.2	−6.0	−10.5	27.5	18.7
−9.3	12.8	−12.2	−14.7	24.9
2.5				

Fixed-Maturity Investments:
Fair Value – Book Value

−32.7	6.5	26.2	−17.5	39.1
−3.9	−.4	−6.2	−3.8	13.5
−17.7	4.0	−21.2	−28.5	12.4
35.6	25.3	−31.1	11.9	8.4
−10.1	33.3	20.7	−13.4	9.0
30.2	−23.6	−24.3	14.6	−23.1
−11.9	−13.8	8.8	−2.7	−34.5
−15.2	57.5	−38.1	−5.8	43.9
−29.7	45.3	−28.9	32.0	5.3
−27.0	−6.4	21.3	24.0	−6.0
−17.9	64.7	−42.5	9.5	28.1
−9.9				

(a) Determine a 95% confidence interval for the mean difference of insurers' fair value from its historical cost of equity.

(b) Based on your result in part (a), do these data contradict a null hypothesis that the mean difference is zero?

(c) Determine a 95% confidence interval for the mean difference of an insurer's fair value from its book value of fixed-maturity investments.

(d) Based on your result in part (c), do these data contradict a null hypothesis that the mean difference is zero?

EXERCISES FOR SECTION 6.4

6.40 For the following samples, determine whether the necessary conditions are present for the sampling distribution of p to be approximated adequately by a normal distribution. For those cases where the normal distribution is appropriate, compute a 95% confidence interval for π.

(a) $n = 142$, π is unknown, $p = .05$
(b) $n = 142$, π is unknown, $p = .50$
(c) $n = 36$, π is unknown, $p = .05$
(d) $n = 36$, π is unknown, $p = .50$

6.41 Refer to Exercise 6.40. Based on your results in parts (a)–(d):

(a) Discuss how the margin of sampling error is related to the sample size.

(b) Discuss how the margin of sampling error is related to the sample proportion p.

(c) Are the confidence intervals you computed exact or approximate? Why?

6.42 Determine the sample size required to achieve a margin of sampling error of plus or minus .035

with a 95% level of confidence for the following situations, where the values of π are best-guess estimates.

(a) We estimate that $\pi = .12$.

(b) We estimate that $\pi = .40$.

(c) We estimate that $\pi = .60$.

(d) We arbitrarily assume that $\pi = .50$.

6.43 In parts (a)–(d) of Exercise 6.42, for which value of π is the sample size certain to produce the desired margin of sampling error? Explain.

6.44 One of the aftereffects of the 1994 Major League Baseball strike may have been a decrease in fan interest in baseball. There was concern this would translate into a long-term problem for professional baseball. To estimate the level of interest in the sport, the Gallup Organization randomly selected a sample of 1,010 adults over February 24–26, 1995. They asked the following question: "Thinking about sports, are you a fan of professional baseball, or not?" Three hundred seventy-four of the respondents answered "yes" (*Source: The Gallup Poll Monthly,* Mar. 1995). Based on this result, determine a 95% confidence interval for the population proportion of Americans who would have said they were fans at the time of the survey.

6.45 The minimum wage is an issue of obvious importance to the business community. In 1995, President Clinton supported an increase in the minimum wage from $4.25 to $5.15 (which was voted into law by Congress in 1996). Past increases to the minimum wage had always had the strong support of the American people. Therefore, the degree of current support for an increase was of great interest. To assess public opinion on this issue, the Gallup Organization (*Source: The Gallup Poll Monthly,* Mar. 1995) asked a random sample of adults whether they favored this proposal. In a sample of 1,010 adults, 732 said they favored the proposal. If this was an accurate estimate of public opinion, it represented stronger public support than existed for previous hikes. Determine and interpret a 95% confidence interval for the proportion of the population of American adults who, at the time of the survey, supported this proposal to increase the minimum wage.

6.46 There has been considerable concern over the economic well-being of Americans when they reach retirement age. In an extensive survey, the Gallup Organization (*Source: The Gallup Poll Monthly,* May 1995) asked a sample of adults a number of questions about their retirement plans. One of the results was that, for a random sample of 572 adults, 177 stated that they had saved nothing for retirement in the last year. Determine and interpret the 95% margin of error associated with this estimate.

6.47 In Exercise 6.18, you determined confidence intervals for the mean amounts spent in five spending categories by out-of-town fans attending the 1994 Women's Final Four Basketball Tournament in Richmond, Virginia. The economic impact of events like this is of interest to the entertainment industry. The relevant data are contained on the book's data diskette, in the file named EX0217. In the survey, each respondent was asked to identify the primary source of entertainment for his or her group while in Richmond. The most frequent responses were bars and museums. (On the diskette, code 1 is for bars, code 2 is for museums, and code 3 is for all others.)

(a) Use the data to estimate the proportions of out-of-town fans whose primary source of entertainment was (1) bars and (2) museums.

(b) Determine the 95% margins of error associated with your estimates in part (a).

6.48 The percent defective for parts produced by a manufacturing process is targeted at 4%. The process is monitored daily by taking samples of $n = 160$ units. Suppose today's sample contained 15 defectives.

(a) Determine a 95% confidence interval for π, the proportion defective for the process today.

(b) Based on your answer in part (a), is it still reasonable to think the overall proportion defective produced by today's process is actually the targeted 4%? Explain your reasoning.

(c) How likely is today's result if the percentage of defective parts for today is at its target value?

6.49 The final poll in a recent senatorial contest revealed that 1,400 out of 2,500 randomly selected individuals who are likely to vote on election day indicated a preference for candidate A over candidate B.

(a) Determine a 95% confidence interval for the population proportion of voters who favor A. Based on this result, would you say it is likely that A will win the election? Why?

(b) Suppose that 250 likely voters had been selected rather than 2,500 and the same proportion as in part (a) indicate a preference for A. Recompute a 95% confidence interval. Is your conclusion different this time? Why?

6.50 Refer to Exercise 6.49.

(a) Determine the sample size needed to achieve a margin of sampling error of 2.5%, plus or minus, for a 95% confidence level.

(b) Answer the same question as in part (a) for a margin of sampling error of 3.5%. (*Note:* Think of this problem the next time you hear a TV announcer refer to the margin of sampling error for a political poll.)

6.51 In a random sample of 100 adult consumers, 57 preferred a new soft drink flavor over the traditional flavor that had been used by the market leader for many years.

(a) Is this sample result sufficient to demonstrate that more than half of all adult consumers prefer the new flavor? Support your answer.

(b) Discuss what you believe are important criteria in the selection of these 100 adult consumers.

6.52 A manufacturer of washing machines claims that only 5% of all units sold will experience some malfunction during the first year of normal operation. A consumer organization has asked 150 randomly selected families who have bought these washers to report any malfunctions during the first year. By the end of the first year, 18 families have reported malfunctions.

(a) Determine a 95% confidence interval for the proportion of these washers that experience some malfunction during the first year of normal operation.

(b) Use the answer in part (a) to determine whether the sample contradicts the manufacturer's claim.

(c) To what extent does this sample contradict the claim that the proportion of washers experiencing some malfunction during the first year is .05 in favor of a higher value?

(d) With respect to the manufacturer's claim, help the consumer organization define the sampled population from which the random sample of families should be selected.

6.53 In a survey of taxpayers, 775 out of 1,320 polled said that they would prefer to set aside any budget surplus for Social Security rather than reduce federal taxes. The administration claims the proportion who support setting aside any budget surplus for Social Security is no less than .6. Determine the extent to which the current sample contradicts the administration's claim.

6.54 A vendor claims that no more than 8% of parts shipped to a manufacturer fail to meet specifications. The manufacturer selects at random 200 parts from a large batch just received from the vendor and finds 19 defective parts. Determine the extent to which the current sample contradicts the vendor's claim.

6.55 A study of small-scale retailers ("Planning Practices of Small-Scale Retailers," *American Journal of Small*

Business, Fall 1987, pp. 19–32), reported that 127 out of 177 retailers surveyed had annual sales of less than one million dollars.

(a) Assuming this constitutes a random sample of small-scale retailers, determine a 95% confidence interval for the proportion of all retailers with annual sales of less than one million dollars.

(b) Based on previous studies, suppose it was known that 75% of all small-scale retailers had annual sales of less than one million dollars. Based on this study, is there reason to believe the proportion has now changed? Support your answer.

6.56 The *Sunday Star-Ledger* (New Jersey, Mar. 17, 1996) reported a Barna Research survey of 1,004 adults with regard to religious involvement. Of these, 371 (37%) indicated that they had attended a worship service within the week prior to being polled. If in the past, 40% of adults attended worship services, is there good reason to believe based on the current survey that the proportion of all adults who attend worship services has now decreased? Support your answer.

6.57 A study of initial employment of physicians ("The Initial Employment Status of Physicians Completing Training in 1994," *Journal of the American Medical Association,* Vol. 275, No. 9, Mar. 6, 1996, pp. 708–712) reported that 799 out of 1,272 physicians surveyed who were completing residency in family practice in 1994 were going into group practice. Suppose that in recent years prior to 1994, 60% of physicians completing residency in family practice were going into group practice. Based on this study, is there reason to believe the proportion has now increased? Support your answer.

6.58 The paper "A Taxonomy of Business Start-Up Reasons and Their Impact on Firm Growth and Size" (*Journal of Business Venturing,* Vol. 9, 1994, pp. 7–31) studied the characteristics of new independent business in Great Britain. The study is based on a sample of 79 principal owner-managers of businesses that received their first order between January 1986 and December 1990. It was found that 71 of sample owner-managers were men; 52 of the new businesses had two or more partners or shareholders; 59 of the firms were in urban locations; and 46 had operated at a profit during the past fiscal year.

(a) Determine 95% confidence intervals for the corresponding population proportions.

(b) Was the sample size ($n = 79$) satisfactory? Determine the sample size that would be required to ensure that margins of error of not more than ±.03 are achieved based on 95% confidence.

6.59 The paper "Successor Origin, Initiating Force, and Managerial Tenure in Banking" (*Journal of Business Research*, Vol. 29, 1994, pp. 47–55) investigated successions of top managers in the banking industry and factors associated with that succession. The sample consisted of 150 banks that changed the highest ranking officer in 1985. All had less than $100 million in assets. These are "small" banks; the sample banks averaged 30 employees and $40 million in assets. Each completed a questionnaire regarding specific facts about the managerial succession. Of the 150 successor managers, 96 subsequently had tenures greater than 4 years; 73 were replacements from outside the organization; and for 86 of the banks, the succession was initiated by the bank's board of directors.

(a) Assume that these 150 banks represent a random sample of mid-1980s successions in "small" banks. Use these results to determine 95% confidence intervals for the population proportions of successions that (1) led to a tenure of more than 4 years for the successor manager; (2) involved a successor manager from outside the organization; and (3) were initiated by the bank's board of directors.

(b) Was the sample size ($n = 150$) satisfactory? Determine the sample size that would be required to ensure that margins of error of not more than ±.04 are achieved based on 95% confidence.

6.60 The pervasive use of historical-based accounting (HBA) standards is thought by many critics to have contributed to the savings and loan debacle of the 1980s and the banking problems of the 1990s. Market-value accounting (MVA) has been proposed as an alterative to avoid such future crises.

So is MVA the future of accounting for the banking industry? The paper "Market-Value Accounting Standards in the United States and Their Significance for the Global Banking Industry" (*International Journal of Accounting*, Vol. 30, 1995, pp. 208–221) reported the results of a survey of 120 bankers regarding their perceptions of market-value accounting. Respondents were asked whether they agreed or disagreed with the following statements.

Statement	Number in agreement (ignoring "no opinion")
1. "Historical cost system has failed to measure the economic reality of today's financial environment."	84
2. "Banks will benefit from a shift away from an historical cost system to a market-value system in the long run."	17
3. "MVA should be used for external financial reporting."	16
4. "MVA can be implemented successfully."	37

(a) Determine 95% confidence intervals for the population proportions who agree with each statement.

(b) Was the sample size ($n = 120$ satisfactory? Determine the sample size that would be required to ensure that margins of error of not more than ±.05 are achieved based on 95% confidence.

(c) What do the responses of the sample bankers suggest about their opinions of historical-based accounting and market-value accounting?

SUPPLEMENTARY EXERCISES

6.61 Describe the effect of the sample size on the margin of sampling error of point estimates of the population mean. Does the margin of sampling error of point estimates of π depend on the sample size in the same way?

6.62 A filling device fills bottles with a target mean of 12 ounces of a soft drink. For a random sample of 18 recently filled bottles, the following weights were observed: 11.84, 11.98, 11.91, 11.75, 12.06, 11.83, 11.95, 11.86, 11.97, 12.00, 11.96, 11.96, 11.95, 11.86, 12.03, 11.82, 11.85, and 11.92.

From historical information, it is known that the weight of each bottle is a normally distributed random variable.

(a) Graph the data. Does the graph suggest that there has been a change in the average fill amount? Explain.

(b) To what extent do these data contradict the claim that the target mean is being met in favor of a change in the average value?

6.63 A university admissions officer is interested in estimating the mean of grade point averages of seniors in the School of Business who had similar SAT scores when they applied for admission. A random sample of 20 such students revealed the following GPAs: 2.28, 2.62, 3.04, 2.81, 2.82, 2.50, 2.86, 2.88, 3.22, 2.68, 3.00, 2.50, 3.28, 2.79, 2.64, 2.49, 3.15, 2.84, 3.00, and 2.63. The admissions officer knows that the distribution of GPAs for such students is the normal.

(a) Determine 90%, 95%, and 99% confidence intervals for the population mean of all such students and comment on what happens to the intervals as the confidence level increases.

(b) Is it essential that the population distribution be the normal for the inference in part (a) to be valid? Explain.

6.64 In a study of television-viewing habits, a television station manager monitors all viewing done by a sample of 100 families for one week. Of particular interest was the station's 30-minute local news program. The sample revealed that 48% of all adults surveyed watched a news program at least once. Determine a 95% confidence interval for the proportion of viewers who watched some local news programming.

6.65 An insurance company manager wishes to keep abreast of recent trends involving claims for automobile accidents. In a survey of 81 recent claims, 55 of the accidents reported involved more than one vehicle.

(a) Determine a 95% confidence interval for the proportion of all recent claims that involved more than one automobile.

(b) What is the most conservative sample size that would be required to reduce the margin of sampling error in part (a) to .050?

6.66 In a recent survey, a radio station asked listeners to call in and state whether they favor the recall of a city councilman found guilty of corrupt practices. Of the 110 callers during the first hour, 77 favored the recall.

(a) Determine a 95% confidence interval for the proportion of listeners who favor the recall.

(b) Describe the population to which your confidence interval in part (a) is applicable.

(c) How useful do you find this effort to discern the public sentiment? Explain.

6.67 A manufacturing process is designed to produce cigarettes that contain on average no more than 3.5 milligrams of tar. The tar amounts of 12 recently produced cigarettes are as follows: 4.18, 3.36, 4.09, 4.10, 3.65, 3.77, 3.55, 3.60, 3.44, 4.16, 3.83, and 3.75.

(a) Graph the data. Does the graph suggest that the average tar content is greater than that claimed?

(b) Determine the extent to which the current sample contradicts the claim of 3.5 milligrams of tar in support of a higher tar amount, on average. Explain.

(c) What assumption is necessary for your answer to part (b)? Explain.

6.68 A production manager insists that total production be reasonably consistent from day to day. He has established a policy that the average daily production be 1,075 units for a particular product. For the last 12 days, daily totals have been: 1,010, 1,085, 1,054, 1,099, 1,066, 1,033, 1,057, 1,022, 1,044, 1,008, 1,038, and 1,075.

(a) Treating these data as a random sample, determine the extent to which the current sample contradicts the claim of 1,075 units in support of a lower average daily production.

(b) What assumption is required by your method in part (a)? Explain.

(c) When daily production quotas are established, what do you think can happen to the quality of the product being produced? Explain.

6.69 A food manufacturer has a machine that fills cans with kidney beans. The cans are labeled as containing 10 ounces, but the actual fill can vary somewhat. In a random sample of 12 cans just filled, the following fill amounts (in ounces) are observed: 9.78, 9.90, 9.67, 9.68, 10.06, 10.02, 9.61, 10.08, 9.77, 10.03, 10.17, and 9.82. From historical information, it is safe to assume that fill amount is a normally distributed random variable.

(a) Graph the sample data. Does the graph suggest a change in the average fill amount? Explain.

(b) Determine a 90% confidence interval for the mean fill for this machine.

(c) Based on your answer to part (b), should the manufacturer be concerned about truth in packaging? Explain.

6.70 A health organization is interested in updating its information about the proportion of men who smoke. Based on previous studies, the proportion has been 35% in the recent past. The organization commissions a poll in which 1,200 randomly selected men are questioned about whether they smoke. Of the 1,200, 372 are smokers.

(a) Determine the extent to which this sample contradicts the 35% claim in favor of a lower proportion.

(b) Do you believe that your answer to part (a) is

likely to be valid 1 year from now? Explain in the context of this particular example.

6.71 Suppose that in a random sample of 50 babies conceived by an *in vitro* fertilization process, 35 are girls.

(a) Does this sample show convincingly that the *in vitro* process favors the female gender? Explain.

(b) Is the normal approximation you used to answer part (a) valid? Explain.

6.72 A study of small retailers ("Planning Practices of Small-Scale Retailers," *American Journal of Small Business,* Fall 1987, pp. 19–32), reported that 160 out of 179 retailers surveyed employed no more than 50 persons in their retail establishments.

(a) Assuming this constitutes a random sample of small retailers, determine a 95% confidence interval for the proportion of retailers with no more than 50 employees and use the interval to determine whether the result of this survey is consistent with the assumed historical proportion of 86%.

(b) To what extent does the result of this survey contradict the historical proportion of 86%? Support your answer.

6.73 In a nationwide survey of 1,008 adults regarding the homeless conducted by the Gallup Organization and reported by the *Sunday Star-Ledger* (New Jersey, Mar. 17, 1996), 867 of those polled indicated either some or great sympathy for the homeless.

(a) Determine a 95% confidence interval on the proportion of all adults who feel this way for the homeless based on the results of this survey.

(b) Relative to your answer in part (a), what is the margin of sampling error?

6.74 The study "A Comparison of Women in Small and Large Companies" (*American Journal of Small Business,* Winter 1988, pp. 23–33) reported on biographical data of surveyed women who work for small companies, defined as those with fewer than 100 employees. Of particular interest were the annual salaries of female managers who work for small firms. The following data are simulated based on an update of the summary information given in this study and represent annual salaries in thousands of dollars of 14 randomly selected female managers who work for small firms: 44.2, 36.7, 29.8, 21.9, 30.6, 42.0, 17.8, 27.1, 41.4, 28.3, 37.8, 35.6, 36.6, and 17.6.

(a) Determine a 95% confidence interval for the average annual salary of all female managers who work for small firms.

(b) Based on your answer to part (a), what are the plausible values one could claim for the average annual salary of all female managers who work for small firms with 95% confidence?

6.75 The following are 20 consecutive samples, each consisting of five observations from a process that produces a certain type of ball bearing. The observations represent the outer diameters of the bearings in centimeters. The process is thought to be stable, adhering to a normal distribution with a mean diameter of 4 centimeters and a standard deviation of .02 centimeter.

1	2	3	4	5
4.00258	3.97996	4.02209	4.02989	3.98236
4.02584	3.95092	3.98708	4.01681	3.98255
3.98991	4.00480	4.05705	3.97959	4.02488
4.03457	4.05146	3.97456	3.98889	4.03544
3.97417	3.99159	3.98445	3.98674	3.99274

6	7	8	9	10
3.98849	4.02171	3.98672	3.98115	4.01446
4.02762	3.99723	4.02332	4.00576	3.99356
3.99876	4.00329	3.97479	3.99987	4.02164
3.98490	4.01103	4.00428	3.98316	3.98464
4.03967	4.00937	3.99450	3.98258	3.97290

11	12	13	14	15
4.02711	3.97749	3.99577	4.02203	4.03814
3.98199	4.02680	3.99339	3.98947	3.99283
4.02385	4.00468	4.02272	3.99834	4.00888
4.02527	3.99437	4.00683	4.04176	4.00598
4.02164	4.00535	3.97484	3.98683	4.00303

16	17	18	19	20
3.98455	3.99278	3.99447	3.94688	3.98233
4.00182	3.99118	3.97239	4.01361	3.98535
3.93662	4.00199	3.95850	4.02924	4.00453
3.98415	3.96247	3.98334	3.95708	4.01545
3.96441	4.00644	4.01080	3.95272	3.98772

(a) For each sample, determine a 95% confidence interval for the average diameter. Graph the intervals for the 20 samples as in Figure 6.4. Do you detect anything unusual? Explain.

(b) Construct a run chart for the average diameter of the ball bearings using the 20 samples. Do you detect assignable cause variation? Explain.

6.1

Case Study
Analysis of Income Tax Returns

This case involves the analysis of income tax returns. The population to be studied consists of all 1989 tax returns. In 1989, 112,201,751 income tax returns were filed. The data are obtained from simple random samples of each of five categories of tax returns from this population. The five categories represent the following ranges of adjusted gross income (AGI):

- $0–$10,000
- $20,000–$30,000
- $50,000–$100,000
- $100,000–$200,000
- $200,000–$500,000

For each category, a simple random sample of about 75 tax returns was selected. This sampling plan is an example of stratified random sampling, as discussed in Section 5.2. Stratified random sampling was used rather than simple random sampling from the entire population to assure that adequate data were obtained over the entire range of incomes up to $500,000.

The sample data are contained on the data diskette in a file named CASE0601. It consists of 379 rows, where each row provides information for a single tax return. The specific column variables on the file are:

$c1$ = stratum identification
$c2$ = adjusted gross income
$c3$ = deductions (0 = standard deduction; 1 = itemized)
$c4$ = total deductions (amount)
$c5$ = taxable income
$c6$ = total exemptions (self, spouse, dependents)
$c7$ = total credits (for child and dependent care, etc.)
$c8$ = total contributions
$c9$ = tax liability

This is primarily an exploratory study. Your task is to describe and compare the strata with respect to the variables for which you have data as well as any new variables you wish to create from the variables provided. Your analysis should rely on statistical concepts and methods covered thus far in this book, including graphical description and appropriate use of statistical inference. Discuss any concerns and/or limitations of your conclusions. Identify any additional data and/or follow-up analyses that might be of interest as a result of your analysis. As you think about your study of the five strata, notice that no claims have been asserted. Therefore, your use of inference procedures should focus upon estimation (both point and interval) of means and proportions, rather than on hypothesis testing. This case will be revisited in Chapter 8, at which point you will have learned methods for testing claims of equality among the means of the five strata (with respect to variables such as "taxes paid").

The number of 1989 returns in the population and the sample size for each stratum from which a sample was selected are provided in the table that follows.

AGI Category	Number Returns in Population	No. Returns in Sample
no income	823,653	
$1–under $10,000	31,794,949	75
$10,000–under $20,000	26,072,725	
$20,000–under $30,000	16,959,329	77
$30,000–under $50,000	20,694,936	
$50,000–under $100,000	12,988,660	74
$100,000–under $200,000	2,081,939	78
$200,000–under $500,000	612,697	75
>$500,000	172,863	
Population total	112,201,751	379

Appendix 6

Computer Instructions for Using MINITAB, EXCEL, and JMP IN

MINITAB

Confidence Intervals for a Population or Process Mean

To determine the confidence intervals in Example 6.2, first enter the 16 breaking strengths into c1 (in the DATA worksheet). Choose STAT–BASIC STATISTICS–1-SAMPLE T . . . . In the dialogue box, enter or select c1 in the VARIABLES: box; click the CONFIDENCE INTERVAL button; enter the desired confidence level (as a percentage) for LEVEL; and click OK.

Hypothesis Testing with *P*-values for the Population or Process Mean

Consider Example 6.3. Enter the 20 assembly times into column c1 of the DATA worksheet and name this column Time. To develop the graph in Figure 6.5, choose GRAPH–TIME SERIES PLOT . . . . In the dialogue box, enter or select c1 for the first line in the GRAPH VARIABLES box. Under TIME SCALE, click the INDEX button; under DATA DISPLAY, select SYMBOL under DISPLAY, select GRAPH under FOR EACH, and click OK. You must add the horizontal line at the null hypothesis value (10.0) manually.

To test the hypothesis H_0: $\mu = 10$ vs. H_a: $\mu \neq 10$ (see the Using the Computer discussion in Section 6.3.6), execute the T procedure by choosing STAT–BASIC STATISTICS–1-SAMPLE T . . . . In the dialogue box, specify column c1 in the VARIABLES: box; click the TEST MEAN button; enter the null hypothesis value 10.0; set the alternative to NOT EQUAL, and click OK.

Follow the same procedure for Example 6.4, with one exception. Because the alternative hypothesis is one-sided, the alternative GREATER THAN must be selected in the dialogue box.

Confidence Intervals and Hypothesis Testing for a Population Proportion

Consider Example 6.7, in which a 95% confidence interval for π is determined. Choose STAT–BASIC STATISTICS–1 PROPORTION . . . . In the dialogue box, click SUMMARIZED DATA and enter the NUMBER OF TRIALS (200) and the NUMBER OF SUCCESSES (92); and click the OPTIONS button. In the OPTIONS dialogue box: For CONFIDENCE LEVEL, specify the desired level of confidence as a percentage (95). For USE TEST AND INTERVAL BASED ON NORMAL DISTRIBUTION: click the box to indicate use of the normal approximation. Click OK twice and you have the desired output. (You will notice that the OPTIONS dialogue box also provides an opportunity to test hypotheses concerning π; if you ignore this, Minitab automatically provides output for H_0: $\pi = .5$ vs. H_a: $\pi \neq .5$.)

Now consider Example 6.9, a test of hypothesis with a one-sided (greater than) alternative hypothesis. Choose STAT–BASIC STATISTICS–1 PROPORTION . . . , as previously described. In the OPTIONS dialogue box: For TEST PROPORTIONS, specify the null hypothesis value (.18). For ALTERNATIVE, select GREATER THAN. For USE TEST AND INTERVAL BASED ON NORMAL DISTRIBUTION: click the box to indicate use of the normal approximation. (You will find that Minitab automatically provides a 95% confidence interval along with the hypothesis testing information.)

If your data file consists of the original data (that is, numerical indices representing successes and failures, with each observation coded numerically, e.g., 0 and 1), you can still use this procedure. In the STAT–BASIC STATISTICS–1 PROPORTION- . . . dialogue box, click SAMPLES IN COLUMNS and enter the column containing the data. All other selections are the same.

EXCEL

Confidence Intervals for a Population or Process Mean

To determine the 95% confidence interval in Example 6.2, first enter the 16 breaking strengths into a1:a16. Choose TOOLS–DATA ANALYSIS PLUS and select INFERENCE ABOUT A MEAN (SIGMA UNKNOWN). In the BLOCK COORDINATES dialogue box, enter the range of cells containing the data (a1:a16); and click OK. In the INFERENCE dialogue box, click INTERVAL ESTIMATE. In the CONFIDENCE LEVEL INPUT dialogue box, enter .95 (as a decimal fraction, not a percentage), and click OK.

Hypothesis Testing for a Population or Process Mean

To develop the graph in Figure 6.6 (Example 6.4), enter the data into cells a2 through a13 of the worksheet and enter the name STRENGTH in cell a1. The graph in Figure 6.6 can be developed as if it were a run chart. Choose INSERT–CHART . . . . Follow the four steps of the CHART WIZARD to produce the run chart: (1) Click the XY (SCATTER) chart type, then click the first chart subtype option; (2) in STEP 2 OF 4, enter the cell range containing the data (a1:a13) and click the SERIES IN COLUMNS button; (3) in STEP 3 OF 4, provide chart title and labels for the axes as desired; (4) in

STEP 4 OF 4, indicate whether you wish the run chart to be placed on a new sheet or within the currently active sheet.

Now consider hypothesis testing in Example 6.4 (see the Using the Computer discussion in Section 6.3.6). To test the hypothesis H_0: $\mu = 500$ vs. H_a: $\mu > 500$, execute the T procedure by choosing TOOLS–DATA ANALYSIS PLUS. In the BLOCK COORDINATES dialogue box, enter the range of cells containing the data (a2:a13). In the INFERENCE dialogue box, click TEST OF HYPOTHESES. In the NULL HYPOTHESIS INPUT dialogue box, enter 500. In the ALTERNATIVE HYPOTHESIS dialogue box, select HA: MU GREATER THAN 500.

Confidence Intervals and Hypothesis Testing for a Population or Process Proportion

The way that you can develop confidence intervals and test hypotheses concerning a proportion with Excel depends on whether you are working with (1) raw data (i.e., numerical values representing success and failure for a sample of data) or (2) summary data (i.e., the values of n and X). If you are starting with raw data, you can use add-ins from DATA ANALYSIS PLUS. If you are starting with summary data, you can use Excel formulas.

Consider Example 6.7, in which, starting with summary data, a 95% confidence interval for π is determined. Enter the value of n (200) in cell a1; enter the value of X (92) into b1. Put the value of p into c1 by typing the formula =b1/a1. Put the estimated standard error of p into d1 by typing the formula =(c1*(1−c1)/a1)$^\wedge$.5. Put the lower 95% confidence limit into e1 by typing the formula =c1−1.96*d1. Put the upper 95% confidence limit into f1 by typing the formula =c1 + 1.96*d1.

Now consider Example 6.8, in which, again starting with summary data, a test of hypothesis is performed. Enter the value of n (200) into cell a1; enter the null hypothesis value of π (.1) into b1. Enter the standard error of p (under H_0) into c1 by typing the formula =(b1*(1 − b1)/a1)$^\wedge$.5. Enter the value of X (16) into d1. Put the value of p into e1 by typing the formula =d1/a1. Put the P-value into f1 as follows. Select f1 and click the PASTE FUNCTION button on the toolbar. In the dialogue box, select STATISTICAL, then select NORMDIST. In the NORMDIST dialogue box, enter e1 for X; enter b1 for MEAN; enter c1 for STANDARD DEV; and enter 1 for CUMULATIVE.

Now suppose you were working these examples starting with raw data. To develop a confidence interval as in Example 6.7, enter the 200 numerical values indicating success and failure into a1:a200. For example, enter 92 1s into a1:a92 and enter 108 0s into a93:a200. Select TOOLS–DATA ANALYSIS PLUS. In the dialogue box, select INFERENCE ABOUT A PROPORTION. In the BLOCK COORDINATES DIALOGUE BOX, enter a1:a200. In the INFERENCE ABOUT A PROPORTION DIALOGUE BOX, enter 1 to specify the code representing "success." In the INFERENCE dialogue box, click INTERVAL ESTIMATE. In the CONFIDENCE LEVEL INPUT dialogue box, enter .95, and you are finished.

To carry out a test of hypothesis as in Example 6.8 starting with raw data, enter the 200 numerical values indicating success and failure into a1:a200. Proceed as described for confidence intervals until you get to the INFERENCE dialogue box. In the INFERENCE dialogue box, click TEST OF HYPOTHESES. In the PROPORTION VALUE dialogue box, enter the null hypothesis value of π (.10). In the ALTERNATIVE HYPOTHESIS dialogue box, select HA: P LESS THAN .1, and you are finished.

JMP IN

Confidence Intervals for a Population or Process Mean

JMP IN provides confidence intervals only for a 95% level of confidence. To determine the 95% confidence interval in Example 6.2, first enter the 16 breaking strengths into COLUMN 1 and name the column STRENGTH. Set its role to Y. Choose ANALYZE–DISTRIBUTION OF Y. The confidence limits are in the MOMENTS area of the output.

Hypothesis Testing for a Population or Process Mean

Consider Example 6.3. Enter the data into COLUMN 2, and name this column TIME. Set its role to Y. To develop a graph like Figure 6.5, choose GRAPH–BAR/PIE CHARTS. In the resulting CHART window, click the TIME button (immediately below the graph) and select LINE CHART and SHOW POINTS, but not CONNECT LINE. You will want to adjust the scaling of the vertical axis and to add a horizontal line at 10.0. To do so, double-click just to the left of the vertical axis. In the dialogue box, set the desired MINIMUM, MAXIMUM, and INCREMENT values. (We suggest 9.6, 10.7, and .5.) Click the REFERENCE LINES button and enter 10.0 in the resulting dialogue box.

To test the hypothesis H_0: $\mu = 10$ vs. H_a: $\mu \neq 10$, choose ANALYZE–DISTRIBUTION OF Y. Click the TIME check mark popup box and select TEST MEAN = VALUE . . . . In the dialogue box, enter 10.0 in the SPECIFY HYPOTHESIZED VALUE FOR MEAN box. The results appear in the TEST MEAN = VALUE area below the MOMENTS area. Since this is a two-sided alternative, the appropriate P-value corresponds to PROB > |t|.

Follow the same procedure for Example 6.4, with one exception. Because the alternative hypothesis is one-sided (greater than), use the P-value corresponding to PROB > t.

Confidence Intervals and Hypothesis Testing for a Population Proportion

JMP IN does not provide a confidence interval for a population or process proportion, but it does provide the standard error of the sample proportion, which is the key computational task in developing a confidence interval. Consider Example 6.7. Set the data type for COLUMN 1 to CHARACTER and the modeling type to NOMINAL. Enter WHEELER and OPPONENT into the first two rows of COLUMN 1, and name this column VOTER PREF. Enter 92 and 108 (the frequencies of votes for Wheeler and his opponent, respectively, in the sample) in COLUMN 2, and name this column VOTES. Set the role of VOTER PREF to Y, and the role of VOTES to *FREQ*. Choose ANALYZE–DISTRIBUTION OF Y. Click the FREQUENCIES check mark (below the graph) and select STDERR PROB. The FREQUENCIES output will now include the standard errors of the sample proportions for Wheeler and for his opponent.

JMP IN does perform hypothesis testing on a proportion. Consider Example 6.8. Enter DISCREP and OK into the first two rows of COLUMN 1, and name this column

OUTCOME. Enter 16 and 184 (the frequencies of discrepancies and OK accounts, respectively, in the sample) in COLUMN 2, and name this column FREQ. Set the roles, data types, and modeling types for OUTCOME and FREQ as described in the previous paragraph. Choose ANALYZE–DISTRIBUTION OF Y. Click the OUT-COME check mark popup box (above the graph) and select TEST PROBABILI-TIES . . . . In the TEST PROBABILITIES box, click the question mark (?) for DISCREP and enter .1 (the value claimed for π in the null hypothesis). Similarly, click the bullet for OK and enter .9 (i.e., .9 = 1 − .1), then click DONE. The appropriate *P*-value for a two-sided alternative hypothesis appears on the *Pearson* row under *Prob > Chisq*. Since the alternative hypothesis in this example is one-sided, the appropriate *P*-value is one-half the value provided here.

Chapter 7

Statistical Inferences for Two Populations or Processes

7.1   Bridging to New Topics

In this chapter, we present methods of statistical inference for comparing parameters of two populations or processes with regard to their means or their proportions. Such comparisons probably occur more commonly than problems involving a single population. Examples include studies to determine whether, on average, men receive higher wages than women for the same work, comparisons of the demands for a new product versus an older product, comparisons of the quality of materials from two suppliers, and comparisons of unemployment rates for two distinct geographic regions. In addition, we often compare averages in "before and after" situations. For example, we might compare sales levels before and after a marketing campaign to assess its effectiveness.

Statistically, the methods of this chapter are straightforward extensions of those in Chapters 5 and 6. In fact, the principles involved are identical; that is, we first define the parameters to be compared, and then we must resolve the same two key issues discussed in Section 5.4: *We must determine the best statistic for the desired comparison and the sampling distribution of that statistic.* It turns out that once we define the best statistic for comparing two means or two proportions, the resulting sampling distribution is either the T distribution or an approximation based on the normal distribution, respectively.

For the methods of this chapter and those presented in Chapter 8, the key feature is the approach used to acquire appropriate sample data. In fact, as we suggested in Section 1.6, *the data-collection plan is the most important aspect of any statistical study.* We begin this chapter with this issue and consider at greater length the design of experiments. This discussion leads to three basic principles for comparing two (or more) population or process parameters.

7.2   Planning a Comparison of Two Means

Suppose the manager of a property appraisal service wishes to compare the work of two appraisers, each of whom has been employed for a year. He would like to know whether their appraisals differ on average, if all other factors (such as the properties being appraised) are equal. He intends to observe some sample data (their actual appraisals of some properties) to compare the population mean appraisal values, μ_1 and μ_2, for appraisers 1 and 2, respectively. What might be an appropriate plan for obtaining sample data in this situation? Students have had strong and interesting opinions about this. Before reading ahead, take a few minutes to write down how you think this should be done and, especially, your reasoning.

We discuss two basic plans that are available for this purpose, called **independent samples** and **paired samples.** Our students have proposed many worthwhile variations on these two themes.

7.2.1   The Independent Samples Design

With the independent samples design, a sample of *similar* properties is selected and divided into two groups. Each group is appraised by only one person acting independently of the other. A key feature is that *the properties are allocated to the appraisers randomly.* This assures that there is no persistent bias against either appraiser. Suppose we identified a sample of ten similar properties. We would randomly assign five to be evaluated by appraiser 1 and five to be evaluated by appraiser 2. Thus, we regard the two appraisers as two distinct populations for which the appraisals of the five properties constitute an independent random sample from each population. In the language of designed experiments, appraiser is the *factor of interest* here. A **factor** is a variable that we deliberately control to observe its effect on the statistical variable of interest. Since we are comparing two appraisers, this factor has two *levels.* Thus, the values that are chosen for a factor are called **levels.** The ten properties are the **experimental (or sampling) units;** that is, the experimental units (properties) produce the observations of the experiment. Therefore, the appraisal value of a property is the *response variable*—that is, the statistical variable that represents the observation (outcome) of the experiment for any experimental unit.

Suppose properties numbered 4, 10, 1, 8, and 5 were randomly assigned to appraiser 1, and the others were assigned to appraiser 2. The resulting sample data would appear in the following form:

Sample 1			Sample 2	
Property	Appraiser 1		Property	Appraiser 2
4	x		7	x
10	x		2	x
1	x		9	x
8	x		6	x
5	x		3	x
	$\bar{X}_1$			$\bar{X}_2$

where

$$x = \text{An appraised property value}$$
$$\bar{X}_1 - \bar{X}_2 = \text{The difference between the mean appraisals of appraiser 1 and appraiser 2}$$

The idea with independent samples is to select similar properties and assign them at random to each appraiser. Some difference between the mean appraisal values for the two samples is expected due to random sampling variation. However, if the sample mean appraisals of appraisers 1 and 2 differ sufficiently, we may conclude that the appraisers differ, on average.

7.2.2 The Paired Samples Design

In a paired samples design, we identify a sample of properties. The sample properties could have similar values or they could differ substantially. Each appraiser would evaluate *every* selected property. This provides a series of direct, property-by-property comparisons between the appraisers, each unaffected by differences among property values. To assure impartiality, the order in which an appraiser evaluates the properties is determined randomly. Suppose a sample of $n = 5$ properties is identified. The sample data would have the following appearance:

	Appraiser		
Property	1	2	Difference
1	x	x	d
2	x	x	d
3	x	x	d
4	x	x	d
5	x	x	d
	$\bar{X}_1$	$\bar{X}_2$	$\bar{D} = \bar{X}_1 - \bar{X}_2$

where

$$x = \text{An appraised property value}$$
$$d = \text{The difference between the two appraisals of a property}$$
$$\bar{D} = \text{The mean of the differences} = \bar{X}_1 - \bar{X}_2$$

The idea with a paired samples design is to record the *differences* between the appraisals, property by property. This eliminates any blurring of the analysis due to distinct differences among the properties. In the language of designed experiments, property value is a *background variable* whose effect is controlled by *blocking*. There are usually many variables (such as properties) that can cause substantive variation in the response variable. These are called **background** or **blocking variables.** The difference between a blocking variable and a factor is that the effect of the blocking variable on the response is usually well known in advance by the investigator. Thus, for our example, the reason we choose to record the differences between the appraisals, property by property, is that we recognize that property values can be substantially different. Consequently, *the analysis focuses on the five appraisal differences.* If they are *consistently* greater than 0 or *consistently* less than 0, then we have reason to conclude that the two appraisers are not the same, on average.

7.2.3   Comparing the Two Sampling Designs

Each of the two sampling plans is technically sound and frequently used. But which is better? In virtually every case, the preferred method is paired samples, if it is feasible. Suppose the sample mean appraisal value for appraiser 1 is $\bar{X}_1 = \$100,000$ and for appraiser 2 is $\bar{X}_2 = \$90,000$. With either sampling plan, the basic concept of the analysis is to pose this question: Could the observed difference of $\$10,000$ between $\bar{X}_1$ and $\bar{X}_2$ have resulted simply from random sampling variation? That is, we must consider the possibility that the variation among property values is large enough that their random assignment to appraisers could have caused a difference this large, on average, when there is no difference between the appraisers themselves. If we can rule out this possibility, we can conclude with confidence that the appraisers' means are different. This philosophy is identical to that used in hypothesis testing for a single mean in Chapter 6.

Analyzing the Independent Samples Approach

In the context of the question posed, let's examine the independent samples approach. An observed difference of $\$10,000$ between $\bar{X}_1$ and $\bar{X}_2$ could have been caused by either or both of two reasons: (1) a difference between μ_1 and μ_2, and/or (2) sampling error, i.e., variation among the properties randomly assigned to the two appraisers. (One set of properties could, by chance, be worth more than the other set.) Let's consider the random sampling variation of $\bar{X}_1$ and $\bar{X}_2$ more carefully. You learned in Section 5.5 that the variation of a sample mean is measured by its standard error, where $\text{SE}(\bar{X}) = \sigma/\sqrt{n}$ [Expression (5.2)]. Thus, the variation of a sample mean depends on both σ, which characterizes the variation of the appraisal process for an individual appraiser, and n, the sample size. Now consider what factors cause variation among the appraisals of an individual appraiser. We can think of two:

1. *Property variation:*   Appraisals vary simply because the property values are different.

2. *Appraiser inconsistency:*   No person exhibits perfectly consistent judgment for a wide variety of reasons. Perhaps an appraiser is feeling ill on a given day, or perhaps the weather is particularly refreshing. Appraisals of virtually identical properties can vary somewhat because of appraiser inconsistency.

Consequently, a difference between the appraisers, on average, is but one of *three* possible causes of the observed difference of $10,000: (1) differences between μ_1 and μ_2, (2) differences among property values, and (3) appraiser inconsistency. The latter two factors, property differences and appraiser inconsistency, are both *random effects*. The effect of property differences is random because we assign properties to the appraisers randomly. And it seems reasonable to assume that the effect of appraiser inconsistency occurs in random fashion. Therefore, both of these factors contribute to random variation.

Analyzing the Paired Samples Approach

Let's turn now to the paired samples design. As before, the possible causes of an observed difference of $10,000 between the sample means are (1) a difference between the two appraisers, on average, and (2) random variation. Let's now reconsider the factors that cause random variation:

1. *Property differences:* Although property values vary, both appraisers evaluate the same set of properties. Since we analyze the difference between appraisals property by property, these comparisons are not affected by differences among the sample properties. Pairing *blocks out* the effect of differences among the properties. Therefore, property differences are eliminated as a possible explanation for the observed difference between $\bar{X}_1$ and $\bar{X}_2$.

2. *Appraiser inconsistency:* As before, a variety of minor, random factors could cause appraisers to be inconsistent and cause differences among the appraisals of the same appraiser.

The advantage of paired samples is simple. By getting appraisals in pairs and determining appraiser differences property by property, we eliminate property differences as a possible explanation of the observed difference between the sample means. This reduces random variation. As a result, it becomes less plausible to attribute an observed difference between two sample means to random factors. Therefore, if a paired samples design is used, an observed difference between the sample means constitutes stronger evidence of a difference between appraisers, on average, than if independent samples were used.

These design considerations are summarized in the following box.

A COMPARISON OF INDEPENDENT SAMPLES VERSUS PAIRED SAMPLES FOR THE APPRAISER PROBLEM

Possible causes of an observed difference between sample means:

Independent Samples	Paired Samples
1. Appraiser differences	1. Appraiser differences
2. Random sampling variation	2. Random sampling variation
• Property differences	• *No* property effect
• Appraiser inconsistency	• Appraiser inconsistency

7.2.4 The Fundamental Principles of Designed Experiments

The fundamental objective of a designed experiment is to acquire sample data in such a way as *to minimize random variation by controlling as much as possible the identifiable causes of variation (for example, property differences).* To the extent that this can be done, the effect of differences in the factor of interest (appraisers) can be directly observed. In carrying out this objective, we are guided by three specific principles:

1. *Randomization.* The sampling units (properties) to be observed are assigned *randomly* to each level of the factor under investigation. (Thus, properties are assigned randomly to the appraisers.) In addition, all other potential causes of variation (such as the scheduled appraisal times) that might affect the response variable should be allocated at random. This assures that no condition of the factor under investigation is systematically favored over another.

2. *Blocking.* When possible, background variables (such as properties) that may contribute substantial variation to the response variable should be *blocked.* This isolates the effect of background variables, thereby reducing random variation.

3. *Replication.* Random variation can be assessed by *repeatedly* observing the response variable for each level of the factor under investigation (within each block, if blocking is used). By measuring the observed variation among repeated observations under fixed experimental conditions, we can estimate the extent of random variation in the data.

In designing an experiment, one should list all background variables, both nontrivial and trivial. *To the extent possible, we want to control the variation of background variables as we carry out the experiment.* By controlling the levels of background variables, we can make "apples-to-apples" comparisons of the effects of the factors of interest on the response variable under essentially the same background conditions. There are three primary ways to control a background variable:

1. *Eliminate it as a variable.* One approach is to keep a background variable constant at one level for the entire experiment, so that it cannot cause the response variable to vary. A drawback to this strategy is that inferences from the experiment are limited to the conditions of the experiment. For example, in the appraiser problem, this would mean selecting only one property for the two appraisers to appraise—clearly, an unwise choice.

2. *Control the levels of the background variable.* The blocks (levels) of a background variable should span the range of values likely to be encountered in the process. In the appraiser example, this would mean that the values of the selected properties should span the range likely to be encountered by the appraisers in their normal work environment.

3. *Record its values.* Sometimes we cannot control the levels of a background variable. In this case, we should simply record its values. This might allow us to better understand the effects of the factors on the response variable when we analyze the results of the experiment.

If we cannot control a background variable in any of the three ways suggested, then we can mistakenly attribute its effect to one of the factors of the experiment. It is to guard against this possibility that we assign all experimental units at random after factor levels and background variable levels have been determined. This randomization ensures that the effects of all uncontrolled variables are distributed impartially to the levels of the factors under investigation. In other words, randomization prevents uncontrolled variables from *systematically* favoring one factor level over another.

EXAMPLE 7.1

A merchandiser wishes to test the effectiveness of two possible displays. She plans to try the displays in 28 shops that vary greatly in sales. She randomly selects 14 shops to use one of the displays. The other 14 shops are to use the other display. Her analysis is based on a comparison of the mean sales for these two independent samples.

(a) Can you suggest a more effective sampling design?

(b) Explain why your idea is better.

Solution

(a) Since the shops vary widely in sales, the sample means may differ substantially simply because of the random assignment of shops. Thus, "historical sales level" is an important background variable that, under her plan, will contribute substantially to variation in the response variable. The effect of shop differences can be virtually eliminated by pairing the shops according to their historical sales levels. Suppose shops A and B are the two with the highest historical sales levels. One display can be chosen randomly and used in shop A, and the other display can be used in shop B. The next two shops (according to historical sales levels) are then paired, with the assignment of displays again made randomly. Continuing in this manner, the merchandiser assigns the displays to the 28 shops. This is the paired samples design.

(b) By pairing shops with similar sales volumes, we have essentially isolated a substantial amount of variation caused by differences in historical sales levels. Any observed differences between the sample means could no longer be attributed to the differences among the historical sales levels of the shops. Thus, any observed difference in the sample means would be more truly indicative of a difference between the effects of the displays.

EXAMPLE 7.2

A marketing manager for the Hundley Company thinks that the average income of his customers is higher than that of his chief competitor's customers. He wishes to investigate with a market research survey. Is a sampling plan based on paired comparisons possible for this problem? Explain your thinking.

Solution

There are many instances in which blocking is not feasible; this is one of them. In this example, there is no natural way to observe sample data in pairs. The alternative is to use the independent samples approach by taking random samples independently from Hundley's customers and from the chief competitor's customers.

Statistical Inferences for Two Means Based on Independent Samples

Suppose we wish to compare the means of two populations or two stable processes. Let the means be denoted by μ_1 and μ_2, and let the standard deviations be denoted by σ_1 and σ_2, respectively. After careful consideration, we decide that blocking is not feasible. Therefore, we decide to select independent random samples of sizes n_1 and n_2 from the two populations or processes. Often, our goal is to determine whether it is plausible to regard the population or process means as equal. In this case, it is mathematically convenient to consider the parameter of interest to be the *difference* between μ_1 and μ_2—that is, $\mu_1 - \mu_2$. If the difference between μ_1 and μ_2 equals 0, then μ_1 and μ_2 are equal.

Since $\bar{X}_1$ is the best statistic for inferences regarding μ_1, and $\bar{X}_2$ is the best statistic for inferences regarding μ_2, you should not be surprised to find that the best statistic for $\mu_1 - \mu_2$ is $\bar{X}_1 - \bar{X}_2$. Is it correct to regard $\bar{X}_1 - \bar{X}_2$ as a statistic? Of course it is; $\bar{X}_1 - \bar{X}_2$ is a statistic because it is the difference between two statistics. Any two random samples result in values for $\bar{X}_1$ and $\bar{X}_2$; they in turn yield a value of $\bar{X}_1 - \bar{X}_2$. Since it is a statistic resulting from random sampling, $\bar{X}_1 - \bar{X}_2$ has a sampling distribution with a certain mean and a certain standard error. The fact that $\bar{X}_1 - \bar{X}_2$ is the best statistic for making inferences about $\mu_1 - \mu_2$ assures us that $\bar{X}_1 - \bar{X}_2$ *is unbiased and has a smaller standard error than any other unbiased statistic for $\mu_1 - \mu_2$.* (See Section 5.4 if you wish to review these concepts.)

In this section, we discuss procedures used to determine confidence intervals and to test statistical hypotheses for $\mu_1 - \mu_2$ based on $\bar{X}_1 - \bar{X}_2$. Our approach is very similar to that of Section 6.3. Before proceeding, you might want to review briefly that section as well as Section 5.5.

7.3.1 The Mean and Standard Error of $\bar{X}_1 - \bar{X}_2$

It is possible to determine the mean and standard error of $\bar{X}_1 - \bar{X}_2$ without knowing the distributions of the two populations or processes. This is done in a manner similar to that of the one-population case discussed in Section 5.5. The expected value of $\bar{X}_1 - \bar{X}_2$ is not a surprise. It can be shown that *the expected value of the difference between two random variables is the difference between their expected values.* Since $E(\bar{X}_1) = \mu_1$ and $E(\bar{X}_2) = \mu_2$, we have

$$E(\bar{X}_1 - \bar{X}_2) = E(\bar{X}_1) - E(\bar{X}_2) = \mu_1 - \mu_2 \tag{7.1}$$

Expression (7.1) tells us that the statistic $\bar{X}_1 - \bar{X}_2$ is indeed an unbiased estimator of $\mu_1 - \mu_2$.

To determine the standard error of $\bar{X}_1 - \bar{X}_2$, we first determine its variance. It can also be shown that, *if two random variables are independent, the variance of their difference equals the sum of their variances.* This rule applies here because we are selecting two independent random samples. Since $\text{Var}(\bar{X}_1) = \sigma_1^2/n_1$ and $\text{Var}(\bar{X}_2) = \sigma_2^2/n_2$, we have

$$\text{Var}(\bar{X}_1 - \bar{X}_2) = \text{Var}(\bar{X}_1) + \text{Var}(\bar{X}_2) = \frac{\sigma_1^2}{n_1} + \frac{\sigma_2^2}{n_2} \tag{7.2}$$

Thus, the standard error of $\bar{X}_1 - \bar{X}_2$ is

$$\text{SE}(\bar{X}_1 - \bar{X}_2) = \sqrt{\frac{\sigma_1^2}{n_1} + \frac{\sigma_2^2}{n_2}} \qquad \textbf{(7.3)}$$

The general meaning of Expressions (7.1) and (7.3) is the same as that for the one-population case in Section 5.5.1. If we could list all possible independent samples of sizes n_1 and n_2 from the two populations or processes, we could construct a list of the corresponding possible outcomes of $\bar{X}_1 - \bar{X}_2$. These possible values of $\bar{X}_1 - \bar{X}_2$ would tend to cluster around the difference $\mu_1 - \mu_2$. Some would be higher than $\mu_1 - \mu_2$ and some would be lower, but over all possible samples they would tend to be neither consistently too high nor too low. In addition, as one or both sample sizes increase, the standard error of the statistic $\bar{X}_1 - \bar{X}_2$ decreases and, therefore, its precision as an estimator of the difference $\mu_1 - \mu_2$ improves. In fact, if the sample sizes are equal, the standard error is inversely proportional to the square root of the common sample size. This is the same property as in the one-population case.

Because we regard knowledge of the population or process standard deviations as rare in statistical applications, we do not consider this situation in this chapter. Rather, we concentrate on the realistic situation when the population or process standard deviations are unknown.

7.3.2 The Sampling Distribution of $\bar{X}_1 - \bar{X}_2$ When σ_1 and σ_2 Are Unknown

In virtually every real application of statistics, the values of the population standard deviations are unknown. Consequently, σ_1^2 and σ_2^2 must be estimated in Expression (7.3) using the sample variances S_1^2 and S_2^2. When we do this, the ensuing sampling distribution does not have a normal distribution, even if we are sampling from two populations with normal distributions. The reason for this is, in substance, identical to that for the single-population case. You may not be surprised to learn that the sampling distribution of interest turns out to be (at least approximately) a T distribution.

In determining this sampling distribution, we can simplify things if we assume that the population variances are equal. However, if this assumption seems inappropriate, especially after a graphical analysis of the sample data suggests differences in variation, then another procedure can be used that does not require the equal variance assumption. The presentation of these two procedures follows. We encourage you to rely on statistical software for either procedure, as we illustrate shortly.

A. Population Variances Unknown but Equal

Assume that the two population variances are equal; let's use the symbol σ^2 to represent their common but unknown value. Thus, $\sigma^2 = \sigma_1^2 = \sigma_2^2$. When both σ_1^2 and σ_2^2 are replaced with σ^2 in Expression (7.3), the standard error of $\bar{X}_1 - \bar{X}_2$ simplifies to

$$\text{SE}(\bar{X}_1 - \bar{X}_2) = \sqrt{\frac{\sigma^2}{n_1} + \frac{\sigma^2}{n_2}} = \sqrt{\sigma^2 \left(\frac{1}{n_1} + \frac{1}{n_2} \right)} \qquad \textbf{(7.4)}$$

How should we estimate the common variance σ^2? We use the sample variances S_1^2 and S_2^2 in combination [as shown in Expression (7.5)]. Since the two populations have equal variances, each sample provides an independent estimate of the common population variance.

Although we rely on the computer for statistical inferences involving these procedures, nevertheless it is beneficial to understand the fundamental thinking in the determination of Expression (7.5) with the following example. Suppose the sample variances of two independent samples are $S_1^2 = 88.36$ and $S_2^2 = 72.25$, with sample sizes $n_1 = 10$ and $n_2 = 20$.

For the independent samples approach, we have two independent estimates of σ^2, the common variance: $S_1^2 = 88.36$ and $S_2^2 = 72.25$. We wish to combine these estimates into a single estimate by averaging them. Notice, however, that the value of S_2^2 is the more reliable estimate because it is based on a larger sample ($n_2 = 20$, whereas $n_1 = 10$). Therefore, the desired variance estimate is a *weighted* average of the values of S_1^2 and S_2^2, in which the weights are based on the sample sizes. But, for the single variance estimator to be an unbiased statistic for σ^2, it turns out that we must use the degrees of freedom $n_1 - 1$ and $n_2 - 1$ as the weights, rather than using the sample sizes n_1 and n_2 directly. Accordingly, the estimator for the common variance σ^2 is given by

$$S_p^2 = \frac{(n_1 - 1)S_1^2 + (n_2 - 1)S_2^2}{(n_1 - 1) + (n_2 - 1)} = \frac{(n_1 - 1)S_1^2 + (n_2 - 1)S_2^2}{n_1 + n_2 - 2} \tag{7.5}$$

The statistic S_p^2 is called the **pooled sample variance** because it is formed by pooling the information from the two samples. As in previous discussions of sample variances, the denominator of S_p^2 is its degrees of freedom. Notice that the degrees of freedom for S_p^2 equals the sum of the degrees of freedom for S_1^2 and S_2^2. Notice also that, when the sample sizes n_1 and n_2 are equal, the value of S_p^2 turns out to be the simple arithmetic average of the values of S_1^2 and S_2^2.

For the example, the value of the pooled sample variance is

$$S_p^2 = \frac{(10 - 1)(88.36) + (20 - 1)(72.25)}{10 + 20 - 2} = 77.4282$$

Notice that the weighted average $S_p^2 = 77.4282$ lies between the values being averaged—that is, between $S_1^2 = 88.36$ and $S_2^2 = 72.25$. This is always true; the pooled variance always lies between the two individual sample variances. Notice also that the value $S_p^2 = 77.4282$ is closer to $S_2^2 = 72.25$ than to $S_1^2 = 88.36$ because the sample size $n_2 = 20$ is larger than $n_1 = 10$.

Replacing σ^2 with S_p^2 in Expression (7.4), we estimate the standard error of $\overline{X}_1 - \overline{X}_2$ to be

$$SE(\overline{X}_1 - \overline{X}_2) \approx \sqrt{S_p^2 \left(\frac{1}{n_1} + \frac{1}{n_2} \right)} \tag{7.6}$$

Following the same thinking as in the one-population case, we can standardize the statistic $\overline{X}_1 - \overline{X}_2$ by subtracting its mean ($\mu_1 - \mu_2$) and dividing the difference by its standard error [given by Expression (7.6)]. This defines the following T statistic:

$$T = \frac{(\bar{X}_1 - \bar{X}_2) - (\mu_1 - \mu_2)}{\sqrt{S_p^2 \left(\dfrac{1}{n_1} + \dfrac{1}{n_2} \right)}} \tag{7.7}$$

It should come as no surprise to you that *the sampling distribution of the T statistic in Expression (7.7) is well approximated by the T distribution with $n_1 + n_2 - 2$ degrees of freedom, as long as either (1) the two population distributions do not deviate substantially from normal distributions, or (2) both sample sizes are large (at least 30).* Because of the pooling of the sample variances, the T statistic of Expression (7.7) is often referred to as the *pooled T* procedure.

B. Population Variances Not Necessarily Equal

If the equal variance assumption does not appear to be reasonable, we may estimate the standard error of the statistic $\bar{X}_1 - \bar{X}_2$ by substituting the corresponding sample variances S_1^2 and S_2^2 for σ_1^2 and σ_2^2, respectively, in Expression (7.3). That is, an estimate of the standard error of $\bar{X}_1 - \bar{X}_2$ is determined by using

$$\text{SE}(\bar{X}_1 - \bar{X}_2) \approx \sqrt{\frac{S_1^2}{n_1} + \frac{S_2^2}{n_2}} \tag{7.8}$$

By the same argument as in the determination of Expression (7.7), the appropriate statistic here is given by

$$T = \frac{(\bar{X}_1 - \bar{X}_2) - (\mu_1 - \mu_2)}{\sqrt{\dfrac{S_1^2}{n_1} + \dfrac{S_2^2}{n_2}}} \tag{7.9}$$

The sampling distribution of the T statistic in Expression (7.9) is *approximately* a Student's T distribution with degrees of freedom given by a rather complex expression, which is not given here because the computer should be used to carry out this procedure. The number we get for the degrees of freedom in this procedure is less than that obtained under the assumption of equal population or process variances.

The pertinent information for inferences about $\mu_1 - \mu_2$ based on independent samples and unknown population or process variances is summarized in the box on the top of page 298. As we mentioned earlier, it is best that you rely on statistical software in using either procedure.

7.3.3 Confidence Intervals and Hypothesis Testing for $\mu_1 - \mu_2$ When σ_1 and σ_2 Are Unknown

Since the T distribution is involved for inferences about $\mu_1 - \mu_2$ when σ_1 and σ_2 are unknown, the determination of confidence intervals and the testing of statistical hypotheses parallels the discussion in Section 6.3.

SUMMARY: THE SAMPLING DISTRIBUTION FOR INFERENCES ABOUT $\mu_1 - \mu_2$ BASED ON INDEPENDENT SAMPLES AND UNKNOWN POPULATION OR PROCESS VARIANCES

A. If the unknown population standard deviations (or variances) are assumed equal and either (1) the population distributions do not differ substantially from normal distributions, or (2) the sample sizes are large enough ($n_1 \geq 30$ and $n_2 \geq 30$), then the sampling distribution of the T statistic

$$T = \frac{(\bar{X}_1 - \bar{X}_2) - (\mu_1 - \mu_2)}{\sqrt{S_p^2 \left(\dfrac{1}{n_1} + \dfrac{1}{n_2} \right)}}$$

is (at least approximately) the T distribution with $n_1 + n_2 - 2$ degrees of freedom, where S_p^2 is the pooled estimator of the assumed common variance $\sigma^2 = \sigma_1^2 = \sigma_2^2$.

B. If the unknown population standard deviations are not necessarily equal and either (1) the population distributions do not differ substantially from normal distributions, or (2) the sample sizes are large enough ($n_1 \geq 30$ and $n_2 \geq 30$), then the sampling distribution of the statistic

$$T = \frac{(\bar{X}_1 - \bar{X}_2) - (\mu_1 - \mu_2)}{\sqrt{\dfrac{S_1^2}{n_1} + \dfrac{S_2^2}{n_2}}}$$

is approximately the T distribution with degrees of freedom as provided by a computer.

Confidence Intervals

Given a value of the statistic $\bar{X}_1 - \bar{X}_2$, an approximately $100(1 - \alpha)\%$ confidence interval for $\mu_1 - \mu_2$ is

$$(\bar{X}_1 - \bar{X}_2) \pm t_{1 - \alpha/2, df} \, SE(\bar{X}_1 - \bar{X}_2) \tag{7.10}$$

where, if the population variances are assumed equal,

$$SE(\bar{X}_1 - \bar{X}_2) \approx \sqrt{S_p^2 \left(\frac{1}{n_1} + \frac{1}{n_2} \right)} \tag{7.11}$$

or where, if the population variances are *not* necessarily equal,

$$SE(\bar{X}_1 - \bar{X}_2) \approx \sqrt{\frac{S_1^2}{n_1} + \frac{S_2^2}{n_2}} \tag{7.12}$$

The quantity $t_{1 - \alpha/2, df}$ is the corresponding quantile value of the T distribution with $df = n_1 + n_2 - 2$ if the population variances are assumed equal, or with degrees of freedom as determined by a computer if the population variances are not necessarily equal.

Hypothesis Testing for $\mu_1 - \mu_2$

As we illustrated in Chapter 6, we may test hypotheses on $\mu_1 - \mu_2$ using either confidence intervals or P-values. The testing of statistical hypotheses on $\mu_1 - \mu_2$ using confidence intervals follows precisely the same line of reasoning as in the single-population case discussed in Section 6.3.5. For example, suppose we claim that the difference $\mu_1 - \mu_2$ is some amount denoted by D_0. In most situations, D_0 is simply 0—that is, no difference. To test the null hypothesis

$$H_0: \quad \mu_1 - \mu_2 = D_0$$

against the two-sided alternative

$$H_a: \quad \mu_1 - \mu_2 \neq D_0$$

we determine the corresponding confidence interval for $\mu_1 - \mu_2$ using the appropriate T statistic. If the claimed difference D_0 lies within this confidence interval, then D_0 is regarded as a plausible value for the difference $\mu_1 - \mu_2$, and there is no good reason to contradict the null hypothesis. Otherwise D_0 is not a plausible value for $\mu_1 - \mu_2$, and there is good reason to contradict the null hypothesis.

The testing of statistical hypotheses on $\mu_1 - \mu_2$ using P-values also follows precisely the same line of reasoning as in the single-population case discussed in Section 6.3.6. The P-value is the probability of observing a value of the statistic $\overline{X}_1 - \overline{X}_2$ that is more extreme than the value actually observed for the current sample, in the direction specified by the alternative hypothesis. As in the single-population case, this requires that we transform the observed value of $\overline{X}_1 - \overline{X}_2$ to a T-value using either Expression (7.7) or (7.9) and then determine the corresponding probability.

Using the Computer

We illustrate the use of Minitab, Excel, and JMP IN to carry out a comparison of two population or process means based on independent samples with the following three examples. Computer instructions for generating figures and output are given in the appendix to this chapter.

EXAMPLE 7.3

Family incomes in residential neighborhoods can vary substantially from neighborhood to neighborhood, on average. Because family income dictates to a large degree the value of the house that a family can afford to live in, real estate agencies need to have concrete information in this regard to better serve their customers. This example illustrates this kind of situation.

A real estate agency is interested in comparing the average family incomes in two residential neighborhoods. Independent random samples consisting of 14 families from each neighborhood were selected. The following sample data represent family income in thousands of dollars:

Neighborhood

1	86.5	49.2	54	47	60.6	57.1	29.3	51.4	39.8	34.4	60	66.7	75.2	65.9
2	58.8	30.4	38	48.5	46	32.7	34.5	48.4	41.7	60.5	44	40.4	41.5	34.9

Based on these data, is there good reason to believe that the average family incomes differ between these two neighborhoods?

Solution

Before we use any statistical method, it is advisable to graph the data. An examination of an appropriate graph may put us well on the way to answering the question. In addition, we can use the graph to decide on which of the two procedures to use. To graph these data, we use the horizontal axis for the two neighborhoods and the vertical axis for the observed incomes, as illustrated in Figure 7.1. The Minitab instructions for generating this figure are given in the appendix to this chapter. From this figure, it should be clear that the vertical spreads are not the same. There appears to be considerably greater variation in the family incomes of the first neighborhood than in those of the second. Accordingly, we should use the T statistic given by Expression (7.9), which does not require the assumption of equal variances. In Figure 7.1, notice also that, despite the apparent differences in variation, the family incomes in the first neighborhood tend to be greater than those in the second neighborhood. This suggests that the average family incomes are not likely to be the same in these two neighborhoods.

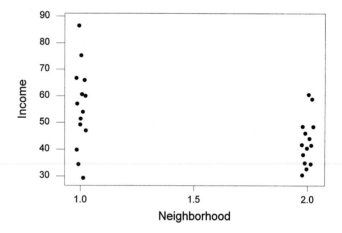

Figure 7.1

Minitab graph of income versus neighborhood for Example 7.3

The Minitab output for testing the null hypothesis H_0: $\mu_1 - \mu_2 = 0$ against the alternative H_a: $\mu_1 - \mu_2 \neq 0$ is shown here. The alternative hypothesis is two-sided because we want to determine whether the average family incomes *differ* between the two neighborhoods.:

```
Two sample T for income
neighborhood       N          Mean          StDev          SE Mean
1                 14          55.5          15.5              4.2
2                 14          42.88          9.04             2.4

95% CI for mu (1) - mu (2): (2.6, 22.7)

T-Test mu (1) = mu (2) (vs not =): T = 2.63 P = 0.016 DF = 20
```

Notice that the output includes the T-value (2.63), the P-value (.016), and a 95% confidence interval for $\mu_1 - \mu_2$ (2.6, 22.7). Notice also that the number of degrees of freedom (20) is smaller than that if equal variances were assumed (i.e., $14 + 14 - 2 = 26$). Since the P-value is sufficiently small and the 95% confidence interval does not contain zero, our initial conclusion based on graphical analysis is affirmed: Based on this sample evidence, the average family incomes of the two neighborhoods cannot be regarded to be the same.

EXAMPLE 7.4

Many organizations commit considerable resources to improving the work environment by eliminating as much as possible potential distractions that can have an adverse effect on productivity. A continuing potential distraction in work environments is offensive background noise. This example illustrates the study of the effect of offensive background noise in a work environment.

There has been continued interest in assessing the effect of offensive noise on one's ability to perform a given task. A researcher has devised an experiment in which a number of subjects are asked to perform a task in a controlled environment under two levels of background noise. To reduce random variation, the researcher selects 32 persons who are capable of performing the task in about the same time. Of these, 16 are selected at random and are asked to perform the task under a modest level of background noise (level 1). The remaining 16 perform the task under level 2, a more severe level of offensive noise than level 1. The following sample data represent the observed times (in minutes) required to complete the task by the 16 persons for each level:

Level 1:   14   12   15   15   11   16   17   12   14   13   18   13   18   15   16   11
Level 2:   20   22   18   18   19   15   18   15   22   18   19   15   21   22   18   16

Assume that these data constitute independent random samples from two normal distributions. Is there good reason to believe that the average time for level 2 exceeds that for level 1?

Solution

The independent samples approach is used here; the 32 persons selected for the study were randomly divided into two groups and all 32 were equally capable of completing the task in about the same time. If the researcher had good reason to believe that the capabilities were not the same, the better approach would have been to have each person selected complete the task under each level of background noise, using randomization to determine which level a person experiences first.

The JMP IN graph of the data is given in Figure 7.2. From this figure, it is clear that the vertical spreads are about the same; thus, we use the T statistic given by Expression (7.7) based on the pooling procedure. In addition, it is apparent from this figure that the completion times for level 2 tend to be higher than those for level 1. That is, the average completion time for level 2 is noticeably higher than that for level 1. As shown in Figure 7.2, JMP IN allows a user to connect the sample averages with a line. The more distinctly nonhorizontal this line is, the more likely the population or process means differ, as in this case.

The JMP IN output for testing H_0: $\mu_1 - \mu_2 = 0$ against H_a: $\mu_1 - \mu_2 < 0$ follows Figure 7.2 on page 302. The alternative hypothesis is one-sided because we want to determine whether the average completion time for level 1 is less than that for level 2. Since the alternative hypothesis is one-sided, it would not be appropriate to use the two-sided confidence interval provided by the JMP IN output for this test.

Similar to Minitab, the JMP IN output includes the values of the sample means (14.375 and 18.5), the sample standard deviations (2.27669 and 2.44949), the

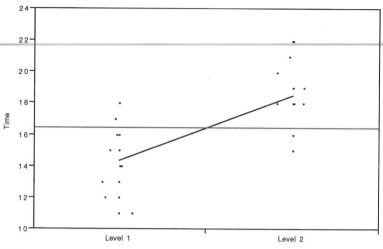

Figure 7.2

JMP IN graph of completion times for Example 7.4

Means and Std Deviations

Level	Number	Mean	Std Dev	Std Err Mean
Level 1	16	14.3750	2.27669	0.56917
Level 2	16	18.5000	2.44949	0.61237

t-Test

	Difference	t-Test	DF	Prob>|t|
Estimate	-4.12500	-4.934	30	<.0001
Std Error	0.83604			
Lower 95%	-5.83240			
Upper 95%	-2.41760			
Assuming equal variances				

difference between the two sample means (−4.125), the standard error as determined by Expression (7.6) (.83604), the T-value (−4.934), and the corresponding *two-sided* P-value (Prob > |t| < .0001). (JMP IN provides only a two-sided P-value in this application.) Since in this example the alternative hypothesis is one-sided, the *one-sided* P-value is one-half of .0001 or .00005, an extremely small P-value. Consequently, the results affirm what we already suspected from Figure 7.2. The one-sided P-value is so small that it leaves very little doubt that μ_1 is indeed less than μ_2.

EXAMPLE 7.5

In a manufacturing process, it is important to maintain the same production and quality levels across different shifts. Management needs to identify corrective actions that may be appropriate to reduce unacceptable differences. For example, often employees in the overnight shift are less experienced than those in the morning shift, who usually have greater seniority. If the overnight shift is less productive and the product it produces is of inferior quality in comparison with the process standard, then additional training is warranted.

A production manager is checking to see whether a difference exists between the average production levels of the day and night shifts. For the two shifts, he selects independent random samples of 15 days' production. The numbers of units produced by each shift per day are as follows:

Shift 1 (day):   250 269 264 246 252 253 244 255 245 255 244 245 249 256 257
Shift 2 (night): 252 241 251 239 251 259 243 258 261 251 253 248 233 251 241

Assume that sampling is from two independent normal populations. Based on these sample data, is there good reason for the production manager to believe that there is a difference in mean production levels between the two shifts?

Solution

Before we proceed with the solution, consider what might have led us to use a pairing approach in this problem. If the production manager knows that production levels vary sufficiently from day to day, then daily differences are a potential source of substantial production variation. When a background variable can be identified that may account for substantial variation, pairing with respect to that variable should be used, if feasible. Therefore, the sample production levels for the two shifts should be paired with respect to days if there is sufficient day-to-day difference.

As in Examples 7.3 and 7.4, much can be revealed by graphing the sample data. From Figure 7.3, notice that, although the production levels for the day shift appear to be somewhat higher than those for the night shift, it is certainly not crystal clear that the average production levels are really different. In addition, the spreads do not appear to be different; thus, the pooling procedure is used.

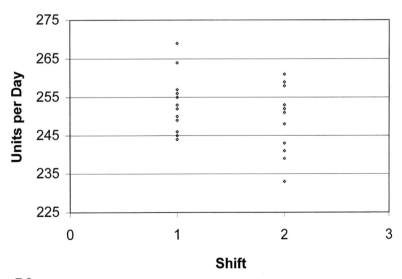

Figure 7.3

Excel graph of the number of units produced for Example 7.5

The Excel output for determining whether the sample data contradict a claim of no difference between μ_1 and μ_2 against a two-sided alterantive hypothesis (we want to know whether there is a *difference* in mean production levels) is as follows:

	A	B	C
1	t-Test: Two-Sample Assuming Equal Variances		
2			
3		*Day Shift*	*Night Shift*
4	Mean	252.2667	248.8
5	Variance	54.7810	63.3143
6	Observations	15	15
7	Pooled Variance	59.0476	
8	Hypothesized Mean Difference	0	
9	df	28	
10	t Stat	1.2355	
11	P(T<=t) one-tail	0.1135	
12	t Critical one-tail	1.7011	
13	P(T<=t) two-tail	0.2269	
14	t Critical two-tail	2.0484	

Similar to Minitab and JMP IN outputs, Excel output includes the values of the sample means (252.2667 and 248.8), the values of the sample variances (54.781 and 63.3143), the value of the pooled variance as determined by Expression (7.5) (59.0476), the value of the T statistic as determined by Expression (7.7) (1.2355), and the P-value for a two-sided alternative hypothesis [P(T < = t) two-tail = .2269]. These results support our indecision in our examination of Figure 7.3. The P-value of .2269 is certainly not small enough to conclude with great confidence that there is a difference between the average production levels for the two shifts. In other words, these data do not show a difference between the average production levels of the two shifts.

7.3.4   The Assumptions and Their Importance

One assumption that is necessary for all inferences of this section is that the population distributions are normal. Another assumption that may be made is that the population variances are equal.

The Assumption of Populations with Normal Distributions

Although this assumption is necessary for the mathematical development of the inferential methods, it is not crucial in an actual situation. The sampling distributions for sample means are approximately normal for moderate-sized samples. If the distributions of the populations are only moderately skewed, the inferential procedures in this section are adequate for all but the situations that involve very small sample sizes.

The Assumption of Equal Variances

The T statistic based on the equal variance assumption may be used if the graph of the sample data reveals that the spreads of the two samples are about the same, thus giving credence to the belief that the population variances are the same. On the other hand, if such a graph reveals distinct differences in the spreads, the T statistic that is not based on the equal variance assumption should be used. At any rate, it is a very good idea to choose equal sample sizes in applying either one of these procedures.

7.4 Statistical Inferences for Two Means Based on Paired Samples

Let's return to the appraiser problem introduced at the beginning of Section 7.2, in which the manager of a property appraisal service wishes to compare two appraisers. Recall that the reason for pairing by properties is to isolate differences that may exist among the properties and prevent differences in property values from blurring the comparison of sample means.

According to the plan outlined in Section 7.2, suppose the appraisals (in thousands of dollars) for the five properties evaluated by both appraisers 1 and 2 are as follows:

Property	Appraiser 1	Appraiser 2	Difference
1	90	93	−3
2	94	96	−2
3	91	92	−1
4	85	88	−3
5	88	90	−2
Means	89.6	91.8	−2.2
Standard deviations	3.3615	3.0332	.83666

Take a moment to inspect the data before reading ahead. Do you think the data indicate a difference between the appraisers? Be sure you know what aspects of the data lead you to your conclusion. This is important because it illustrates the specific advantage of using paired comparisons instead of independent samples.

An examination of the data shows that, although the differences between the appraisers are never great, the appraisals of appraiser 1 are consistently lower than those of appraiser 2. We may conjecture, therefore, that a formal statistical analysis would indicate that the means of the two appraisers are different. This observation is made possible by pairing the data. With two independent samples, the opportunity for this sort of direct comparison between appraisers, free of property differences, is not available.

The analysis is based on the pairwise differences between appraisals. In essence, we have a sample of five differences taken from a population of differences for all possible properties. Thus, *the paired comparisons analysis reduces to a one-sample analysis of the mean of the differences between appraisals.*

Let μ_D be the mean of the population of differences for all possible properties. We seek the best statistic for inferences involving μ_D and its sampling distribution. You should not be surprised that the best statistic for μ_D is $\bar{D}$, the average of the sample differences.

7.4.1   The Mean and the Standard Error of $\bar{D}$

It should also not come as a surprise to you to learn that the best statistic for μ_D is an unbiased estimator of μ_D; that is,

$$E(\bar{D}) = \mu_D \tag{7.13}$$

Let σ_D^2 be the variance of the population of differences. In virtually all instances, we would not know the value of σ_D^2. An unbiased estimator of σ_D^2 is S_D^2, the variance of the sample differences. Since the statistic $\bar{D}$ is an average, the standard error of $\bar{D}$ is estimated to be

$$SE(\bar{D}) \approx \frac{S_D}{\sqrt{n}} \tag{7.14}$$

where n is the number of pairs (that is, $n = 5$ properties for the appraiser problem).

7.4.2   The Sampling Distribution of $\bar{D}$

Since the standard deviation of the population of differences is unknown, we would expect from previous discussions that statistical inferences about μ_D based on $\bar{D}$ would involve the T distribution rather than the standard normal distribution. That is precisely the case. In a manner analogous to $\bar{X}$, standardizing the statistic $\bar{D}$ leads to the T statistic

$$T = \frac{\bar{D} - \mu_D}{S_D/\sqrt{n}} \tag{7.15}$$

which (at least approximately) has a Student's T distribution with $n - 1$ degrees of freedom. Keep in mind that n represents the number of differences (that is, the number of pairs).

Therefore, statistical inferences on the means of two populations when the samples are paired are made by treating the pairwise differences as a single random sample and applying the methods of Section 6.3.

7.4.3   Confidence Intervals and Hypothesis Testing for μ_D

From the preceding discussion, we can surmise that statistical inferences on the means of two populations for paired samples are made by treating the pairwise differences as a single random sample and using the T statistic of Expression (7.15) in conjunction with the methods of Section 6.3.

Confidence Intervals for μ_D

Based on the discussion of Section 6.3, and in particular Section 6.3.3, a $100(1 - \alpha)\%$ confidence interval for μ_D is

$$\bar{D} \pm t_{1 - \alpha/2, n - 1} \frac{s_D}{\sqrt{n}} \tag{7.16}$$

where

$$\text{Margin of sampling error} = t_{1 - \alpha/2, n - 1} \frac{s_D}{\sqrt{n}} \tag{7.17}$$

and $t_{1 - \alpha/2, n - 1}$ is the corresponding T quantile value with $n - 1$ degrees of freedom.

Hypothesis Testing for μ_D

We may test hypotheses on μ_D using either confidence intervals or P-values.

For confidence intervals, we follow precisely the same line of reasoning as in the single-population case discussion in Section 6.3.5. For a two-sided alternative hypothesis, we determine the confidence interval using Expression (7.16). If the claimed value of the null hypothesis, $\mu_D = 0$, lies within the confidence interval, then zero is regarded as a plausible value for μ_D, and the null hypothesis is not contradicted. Otherwise, zero is not a plausible value for μ_D, and the null hypothesis is contradicted.

To test hypotheses on μ_D using P-values, we follow precisely the same line of thinking as in Section 6.3.6. The P-value in this application is the probability of a value of the statistic $\bar{D}$ that is more extreme than the value determined from the current sample in the direction specified by the alterantive hypothesis, if in fact the null hypothesis is true. As before, we convert the value of $\bar{D}$ from the current sample to a T-value using Expression (7.15) and then determine the corresponding P-value.

Using the Computer

With the following two examples, we illustrate the use of Minitab, Excel, and JMP IN for a paired samples situation. Computer instructions are given in the chapter appendix.

EXAMPLE 7.6

Let's continue with the appraiser example. Do the paired data given at the beginning of this section provide sufficient evidence to contradict a claim of no difference between the two appraisers, on average?

Solution

As before, we can gain valuable insight into the answer to this question by graphing the sample data. The Minitab graph is given in Figure 7.4, where we use the horizontal axis for the five properties, the vertical axis for the appraisal values, and the symbols "○" and "+" for appraisers 1 and 2, respectively. In this figure, notice that the appraisals of the second appraiser are always higher than those of the first. Such consistency strongly implies that the two appraisers cannot be regarded as the same, on average.

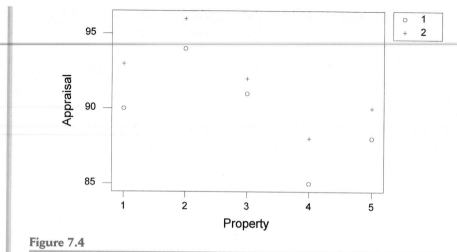

Figure 7.4

Minitab graph of the appraisals for Example 7.6

Because we want to detect whether there is a difference between the two appraisers, on average, we want a two-sided alternative hypothesis. If there is no difference, then $\mu_D = 0$; thus, the null and alternative hypotheses may be stated as H_0: $\mu_D = 0$ and H_a: $\mu_D \neq 0$. The column of differences between the two appraisers is created by subtracting the appraisals of 2 from those of 1. The Minitab output is as follows:

```
Test of mu = 0.000 vs mu not = 0.000
Variable    N    Mean  StDev  SE Mean       T        P
difference  5  -2.200  0.837   0.374   -5.88  0.0042
```

Notice that the P-value is quite small (.0042). Consequently, the current sample data strongly contradict the null hypothesis of no difference between the two appraisers, on average, and support the alternative hypothesis. Of course, this is the same conclusion we reached based on data visualization in Figure 7.4.

EXAMPLE 7.7

It is wise for any organization to commit appropriate resources to maintain a healthy work force because that kind of policy not only reduces the total number of sick leave days and thus increases productivity, but also reduces the health insurance costs of the organization for its employees. This example illustrates that kind of situation.

A corporate personnel manager is charged with promoting the "wellness" of employees. One area of opportunity is lowering blood pressure for employees who are reacting to severe stress. He devises a test of a stress-reduction program with the goal of lowering systolic blood pressure levels that are too high. Ten employees with high blood pressure are identified. Their blood pressures before and after participating in the stress-reduction program are as follows:

Employee	1	2	3	4	5	6	7	8	9	10
Before	158	176	150	179	183	206	177	165	175	186
After	148	133	152	170	155	178	185	151	180	144

Do these sample data contradict a claim that the stress-reduction program does not reduce systolic blood pressure, on average?

Solution

Since blood pressure is measured before and after the stress-reduction program for *each* employee in the sample, this is a paired samples design in which employees serve as a background variable. Because we believe that there may be appreciable differences in systolic blood pressures among the employees, we want to set aside those differences so that we can more precisely determine the effect of the stress-reduction program.

The sample data are graphed by using Excel to produce Figure 7.5. The format of this figure is the same as that in Figure 7.4. Notice that Excel distinguishes between the "before" and "after" blood pressures by using the symbols "♦" and "□", respectively. From this figure, most of the "before" blood pressures are higher; thus, the stress-reduction program appears to have been beneficial.

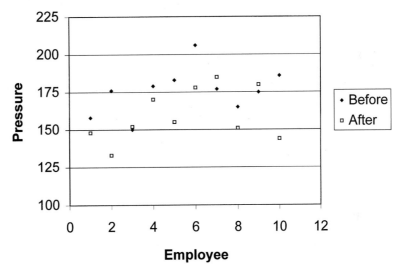

Figure 7.5

Excel graph of the blood pressures for Example 7.7

Let's find the differences by subtracting the after pressure from the before pressure for each employee. If there has been a lowering of the average systolic blood pressure as a result of the stress-reduction program, the mean of the differences over all employees should be greater than 0. So we state the hypotheses as H_0: $\mu_D = 0$ and H_a: $\mu_D > 0$ and obtain the side-by-side outputs from JMP IN and Excel, respectively, appearing on the top of page 310.

Notice that the outputs include the value of the T statistic (2.6992)—Test Statistic for JMP IN, t Stat for Excel—and the corresponding one-sided P-value (.0122)—Prob > t for JMP IN, and P(T <= t) one-tail for Excel. Because the P-value is sufficiently small, the sample data contradict the null hypothesis that the stress-reduction program is not beneficial. Therefore, based on these data, there is good reason to believe that the stress-reduction program has been beneficial. Again, we reach the same conclusion as that when the data are graphed.

Moments

Mean	15.90000
Std Dev	18.62764
Std Error Mean	5.89058
Upper 95% Mean	29.22552
Lower 95% Mean	2.57448
N	10.00000
Sum Weights	10.00000

Test Mean=value

Hypothesized Value	0
Actual Estimate	15.9
	t Test
Test Statistic	2.6992
Prob > Itl	0.0244
Prob > t	0.0122
Prob < t	0.9878

	A	B	C
1	t-Test: Paired Two Sample for Means		
2			
3		*Before*	*After*
4	Mean	175.5	159.6
5	Variance	242.0556	305.1556
6	Observations	10	10
7	Pearson Correlation	0.3684	
8	Hypothesized Mean Difference	0	
9	df	9	
10	t Stat	2.6992	
11	P(T<=t) one-tail	0.0122	
12	t Critical one-tail	1.8331	
13	P(T<=t) two-tail	0.0244	
14	t Critical two-tail	2.2622	

7.4.4 The Assumption for the Paired *T* Analysis and Its Importance

As discussed earlier, a paired samples analysis involves, in a sense, only one sample—the sample of pairwise differences. The assumption that we are sampling from a population whose distribution is the normal is the same as that required in single-population *T* inferences (see Section 5.5.4). The only change here is that this assumption applies to the population of pairwise differences. But we have already mentioned that the *T* distribution is largely insensitive to the violation of the normality assumption as long as the sample size (that is, the number of differences) is fairly large. Thus, as in Section 7.3, the inferential procedures presented in this section are valid in general for all but very small sample sizes. They are valid even for small sample sizes if the populations are very close to being normally distributed.

7.5 Statistical Inferences for Two Proportions Based on Independent Samples

In Section 6.4, we discussed procedures for making inferences about the proportion parameter π. We are often interested in comparing the proportions of two distinct groups relative to some attribute. For example, we may be interested in comparing the proportions of defective units of a given product produced by two competing manufacturers. Consequently, we need to extend the methods presented in Section 6.4 to comparisons of the proportion parameters π_1 and π_2.

Suppose an accounting manager wishes to compare the proportions of billing errors in two districts of his company. More specifically, he is interested in determining whether there is any difference between π_1, the proportion of bills with errors for district 1, and π_2, the proportion with errors for district 2. As in the case involving comparisons of two population means, it is best to consider the parameter of interest to be the difference between π_1 and π_2—that is, $\pi_1 - \pi_2$. If this difference equals 0, then π_1 and π_2 are equal. What do you think is the best statistic for inferences about $\pi_1 - \pi_2$? It is, of course, the difference between the two sample proportions, $p_1 - p_2$, since p_1 is the best statistic for π_1 and p_2 is the best statistic for π_2.

In this section, we discuss inferential procedures for $\pi_1 - \pi_2$ based on the best statistic $p_1 - p_2$. Our approach is the same as for inferences about π based on the sample proportion p. Therefore, we begin by identifying the mean, standard error, and sampling distribution of $p_1 - p_2$. The procedures for confidence intervals and hypothesis testing are based on the normal distribution, as in the single-population case discussed in Section 6.4.

7.5.1 The Mean and Standard Error of $p_1 - p_2$

Let's return to the example involving the billing errors for two districts of a company. Suppose we randomly and independently select samples of n_1 accounts from district 1 and n_2 accounts from district 2 and find that the numbers of accounts with billing errors are X_1 and X_2, respectively. We already know that the sample proportions $p_1 = X_1/n_1$ and $p_2 = X_2/n_2$ are unbiased statistics and that their standard errors are $SE(p_1) = \sqrt{\pi_1(1 - \pi_1)/n_1}$ and $SE(p_2) = \sqrt{\pi_2(1 - \pi_2)/n_2}$, respectively. It can be shown that the statistic $p_1 - p_2$ is an unbiased estimator of $\pi_1 - \pi_2$; that is,

$$E(p_1 - p_2) = \pi_1 - \pi_2 \qquad \textbf{(7.18)}$$

Furthermore, its variance is the sum of the variances of p_1 and p_2:

$$Var(p_1 - p_2) = \frac{\pi_1(1 - \pi_1)}{n_1} + \frac{\pi_2(1 - \pi_2)}{n_2} \qquad \textbf{(7.19)}$$

So, the standard error of $p_1 - p_2$ is

$$SE(p_1 - p_2) = \sqrt{\frac{\pi_1(1 - \pi_1)}{n_1} + \frac{\pi_2(1 - \pi_2)}{n_2}} \qquad \textbf{(7.20)}$$

In Expression (7.20), notice that the standard error of $p_1 - p_2$ cannot be determined, because π_1 and π_2 are unknown. (If they were known, the study would not be needed.) In practice, we replace π_1 and π_2 with the sample proportions p_1 and p_2 to estimate $SE(p_1 - p_2)$. Thus, the estimated standard error of $p_1 - p_2$ is

$$SE(p_1 - p_2) \approx \sqrt{\frac{p_1(1 - p_1)}{n_1} + \frac{p_2(1 - p_2)}{n_2}} \qquad \textbf{(7.21)}$$

Surprisingly, little error is introduced by the substitution of p_1 and p_2 for π_1 and π_2. The reason is that any error caused by using a value of p_1 as an estimate of π_1 is compensated for by an error in the opposite direction when we estimate $1 - \pi_1$ with $1 - p_1$. The same situation holds for π_2 and p_2.

7.5.2 The Sampling Distribution of $p_1 - p_2$

From Section 5.6, recall that the sampling distribution of a sample proportion is closely approximated by a normal distribution for large sample sizes. Since the best statistic $p_1 - p_2$ is simply the difference between two sample proportions, it follows that the sampling distribution of $p_1 - p_2$ is also closely approximated by a normal distribution for large enough sample sizes.* Its mean and standard deviation are given by Expressions (7.18) and (7.21). Therefore, the statistic $p_1 - p_2$ can be transformed to a Z statistic as follows:

$$Z = \frac{(p_1 - p_2) - (\pi_1 - \pi_2)}{\sqrt{\dfrac{p_1(1 - p_1)}{n_1} + \dfrac{p_2(1 - p_2)}{n_2}}} \tag{7.22}$$

The sampling distribution of this Z statistic is the standard normal distribution to a close approximation—subject to the application of the usual guidelines. Therefore, statistical inferences for $\pi_1 - \pi_2$ can be based on the standard normal distribution. The use of this distribution should be very familiar to you by now.

7.5.3 Confidence Intervals and Hypothesis Testing for $\pi_1 - \pi_2$

Because the standard normal distribution provides a close approximation for large sample sizes, the procedures for confidence intervals and hypothesis testing on $\pi_1 - \pi_2$ are essentially the same as those in Section 6.4.

Confidence Intervals for $\pi_1 - \pi_2$

An approximate $100(1 - \alpha)\%$ confidence interval for $\pi_1 - \pi_2$ is given by

$$(p_1 - p_2) \pm z_{1 - \alpha/2} \sqrt{\frac{p_1(1 - p_1)}{n_1} + \frac{p_2(1 - p_2)}{n_2}} \tag{7.23}$$

where

$$\text{Margin of sampling error} = z_{1 - \alpha/2} \sqrt{\frac{p_1(1 - p_1)}{n_1} + \frac{p_2(1 - p_2)}{n_2}} \tag{7.24}$$

To illustrate, let's return to the problem of the accounting manager. Suppose he samples $n_1 = 400$ bills from district 1 and $n_2 = 400$ bills from district 2 and finds that $X_1 = 30$ and $X_2 = 10$ contain errors. For these samples, the values for the sample proportions are $p_1 = \frac{30}{400} = .075$ and $p_2 = \frac{10}{400} = .025$. Then, an approximate 95% confidence interval for the difference, $\pi_1 - \pi_2$, between the proportion of bills with errors for district 1 and the proportion of those for district 2 is

$$(.075 - .025) \pm 1.96 \sqrt{\frac{(.075)(1 - .075)}{400} + \frac{(.025)(1 - .025)}{400}} = .05 \pm .03$$

or .02 to .08.

---

* The rule of thumb for adequate approximation is that both the expected number of "successes" and the expected number of "failures" must be at least five—that is, $n_1\pi_1 \geq 5$, $n_1(1 - \pi_1) \geq 5$ and $n_2\pi_2 \geq 5$, $n_2(1 - \pi_2) \geq 5$.

Based on these sample data, do you think that there is a difference between the proportions of billing errors for these two districts? The answer is yes, because the interval .02 to .08 does not contain 0. Apparently, the proportion of billing errors for district 1 is higher than that for district 2 (notice that the interval is entirely to the right of 0).

Hypothesis Testing for $\pi_1 - \pi_2$

Suppose the accounting manager wants to test a claim that there is no difference between the proportions of billing errors for the two districts; that is, he wants to test the null hypothesis

$$H_0: \quad \pi_1 - \pi_2 = 0$$

against the alternative

$$H_a: \quad \pi_1 - \pi_2 \neq 0$$

Of course, we have a pretty good idea about this test, since the confidence interval .02 to .08 does not include "$\pi_1 - \pi_2 = 0$" as a plausible claim.

In essence, the same result can be achieved by the P-value approach. Notice that if the null hypothesis is true, then $\pi_1 = \pi_2$. Let's use the symbol π to represent their common but unknown value. In other words, $\pi = \pi_1 = \pi_2$ if the null hypothesis is true. In this approach, we pool the information from the two independent samples to estimate π much as we pooled sample information to estimate the common variance σ^2 in Section 7.3.2. Pooling creates only a very slight discrepancy between the confidence interval and the P-value approaches for testing the null hypothesis of no difference between π_1 and π_2.

When $\pi_1 = \pi_2$, the standard error of the statistic $p_1 - p_2$ given by Expression (7.20) becomes

$$\text{SE}(p_1 - p_2) = \sqrt{\frac{\pi(1-\pi)}{n_1} + \frac{\pi(1-\pi)}{n_2}} = \sqrt{\pi(1-\pi)\left(\frac{1}{n_1} + \frac{1}{n_2}\right)} \quad \textbf{(7.25)}$$

Let's use the symbol p for the pooled estimator of π. *The pooled sample proportion p is a weighted average of the sample proportions p_1 and p_2, where the weights are proportional to the respective sample sizes.* Accordingly, the estimator p is defined as

$$p = \frac{n_1 p_1 + n_2 p_2}{n_1 + n_2} \quad \textbf{(7.26)}$$

or, equivalently,

$$p = \frac{X_1 + X_2}{n_1 + n_2} \quad \textbf{(7.27)}$$

Expression (7.27) tells us that the pooled proportion p is simply the combined number of "successes" in both samples divided by the combined sample sizes. When $H_0: \pi_1 - \pi_2 = 0$ is true, the estimated standard error of $p_1 - p_2$ is obtained by substituting the pooled sample proportion p for π in Expression (7.25); that is,

$$SE(p_1 - p_2) \approx \sqrt{p(1-p)\left(\frac{1}{n_1} + \frac{1}{n_2}\right)} \qquad\qquad \textbf{(7.28)}$$

From previous discussion, it follows that the statistic

$$Z = \frac{(p_1 - p_2) - 0}{\sqrt{p(1-p)\left(\frac{1}{n_1} + \frac{1}{n_2}\right)}} \qquad\qquad \textbf{(7.29)}$$

is the standard normal to a close approximation.

Using the Computer

We use the problem of the accounting manager and Example 7.8 to illustrate the use of a computer for inferences involving two proportions based on independent samples.

In the problem of the accounting manager, we had $n = n_2 = 400$, $X_1 = 30$, and $X_2 = 10$. The Minitab output for testing the null hypothesis of no difference between the two proportions of billing errors against a two-sided alternative hypothesis is as follows. The Minitab output includes the values of the two sample proportions, a 95% confidence interval on $\pi_1 - \pi_2$ as given by Expression (7.23), the Z-value as given by Expression (7.29), and the P-value. The P-value is seen to be .001. Since this value is quite small, the current sample data contradict the claim of no difference between the proportions of billing errors for the districts. Apparently, a difference exists.

```
Sample           X              N           Sample p
1               30             400          0.075000
2               10             400          0.025000


Estimate for p(1) - p(2): 0.05
95% CI for p(1) - p(2): (0.0199943, 0.0800057)
Test for p(1) - p(2) = 0 (vs not = 0): Z = 3.24
P-Value = 0.001
```

Alternatively, we can use a calculator and Table B to determine the P-value by first converting the value $p_1 - p_2 = .05$ to the corresponding Z-value—Expression (7.29)—as follows. Since $n_1 = n_2 = 400$, $X_1 = 30$, and $X_2 = 10$, the value of the pooled sample proportion is

$$p = \frac{30 + 10}{400 + 400} = .05$$

Assuming that $H_0: \pi_1 - \pi_2 = 0$ is true, the estimated standard error of $p_1 - p_2$ from Expression (7.28) is

$$SE(p_1 - p_2) \approx \sqrt{(.05)(1 - .05)\left(\frac{1}{400} + \frac{1}{400}\right)} = .015411$$

Then,

$$Z = \frac{(.075 - .025) - 0}{.015411} = 3.24$$

The P-value for a two-sided alternative hypothesis is twice the probability that a Z statistic takes on a value greater than 3.24 or, equivalently, twice the probability that a Z statistic takes on a value less than -3.24. From Table B, this probability is .0006. Therefore, the P-value is $(2)(.0006) = .0012$.

EXAMPLE 7.8

How should a firm choose its suppliers? Should the choice be based solely on price? Or should other considerations such as quality of product, timely delivery, and dependability be factored in the choice decision? Most firms opt to do business not based on price alone. This example illustrates quality considerations of incoming materials.

A user of large quantities of electrical components is considering reducing the number of suppliers used in order to improve the quality of incoming materials. She has purchased electric components primarily from two suppliers, A and B, and she wants to compare their rates of defective product. From two large lots, she randomly selects 125 units of A's components and 100 units of B's. She inspects the selected units and finds seven defective units in each sample.

(a) Determine a 95% confidence interval for the difference between π_A and π_B, the proportions of defectives for A and B, respectively.

(b) Determine the P-value and, based on this value, comment on whether there is ample evidence that the proportions of defectives differ.

Solution

Since we wish to determine whether there is a difference between the two proportions, the null and alternative hypotheses may be stated as follows:

$$H_0: \quad \pi_A - \pi_B = 0$$

$$H_a: \quad \pi_A - \pi_B \neq 0$$

For $X_A = X_B = 7$, $n_A = 125$, and $n_B = 100$, the Excel output is as follows. The confidence interval is $-.078$ to .05; since it includes zero, the null hypothesis cannot be contradicted. The P-value is .6658. For this large P-value, there is no evidence to contradict the null hypothesis. Therefore, the user should not favor either supplier with regard to proportion defectives on the basis of this study.

	A	B	C	D	E	F	G	H	I	J
									Lower confidence limit	Upper confidence limit
1	n_A	X_A	p_A	n_B	X_B	p_B	$p_A - p_B$	$SE(p_A - p_B)$		
2	125	7	0.0560	100	7	0.0700	-0.0140	0.032771	-0.078230	0.050230
3										
4	$\pi_1 - \pi_2$	p	SE under null hypothesis	P-value						
5	0	0.0622	0.03241	0.6658						

(a) Alternatively, we can use a calculator and Table B to determine a 95% confidence interval and the P-value. Since the sample proportions are $p_A = 7/125 = .056$ and $p_B = 7/100 = .07$, an approximate 95% confidence interval for $\pi_A - \pi_B$ using Expression (7.23) is given by

$$(.056 - .07) \pm 1.96 \sqrt{\frac{(.056)(1 - .056)}{125} + \frac{(.07)(1 - .07)}{100}}$$

$$= -.014 \pm .0642$$

or $-.0782$ to $.0502$. Since this interval contains the value 0, there is little evidence of a difference between π_A and π_B.

(b) The determination of the P-value is as follows. Assuming $\pi_A = \pi_B = \pi$ is true as stated by the null hypothesis, we find the value of the pooled estimator of π from Expression (7.27):

$$p = \frac{7 + 7}{125 + 100} = .0622$$

Consequently, the estimated standard error of $p_A - p_B$ is determined from Expression (7.28) to be

$$SE(p_A - p_B) \approx \sqrt{(.0622)(1 - .0622)\left(\frac{1}{125} + \frac{1}{100}\right)}$$

$$= .032403$$

Since $p_A - p_B = -.014$ and the statistic has an approximately normal distribution with mean 0 and standard deviation $.032403$, the corresponding Z-value using Expression (7.29) is

$$Z = \frac{(.056 - .07) - 0}{.032403} = -.43$$

From Table B, the probability that the Z statistic takes on a value less than $-.43$ is $.3336$. Since the alternative hypothesis is two-sided, the P-value is twice this probability, or $.6672$. Again, the small discrepancy results from the rounding in the Z-value when using Table B.

Practical Implications for Example 7.8

Example 7.8 illustrates again the futility of using random sampling to discern very small proportions of defective products. The sample sizes required to do so with sufficient accuracy are simply too large to be practical in most situations. For this reason, many companies are abandoning inspection as a way to ensure the quality of incoming or outgoing product. A more effective approach is *total quality management,* emphasizing quality at every step in the process.

Statistical Inferences for Two Populations or Processes: A Comprehensive Example

7.6

A bank hires management trainees on a regular basis. Twice a year, a new group of trainees go through a training program where they are introduced to some fundamental concepts of banking, including monetary policy, finance, marketing, management, and economics. One way the success of the program is measured in the short term is by a comparison and evaluation of trainees' pretest and posttest scores on their knowledge of the academic portion of the program; that is, each trainee is given a test both before and after participation in the program. The effectiveness of the course is characterized by the amount of improvement on these tests.

The trainees are graduates of various colleges and universities. Their degrees are from diverse fields. The hiring process does not concentrate on grade point average. The trainees' numbers of years of work experience vary substantially, with lengths of service to the bank ranging from 0 to 15 years. Their age range is also wide, ranging from 21 to 52 years. Thus, differences among the trainees' degree fields, grade point averages, work experiences, and ages are all likely sources of variation in their pretest and posttest scores.

A bank personnel manager is responsible for tracking the effectiveness of the training program. She studied the pretest and posttest scores of a sample of 28 trainees who recently went through the program. She was interested primarily in two questions: (1) What degree of learning was indicated by the test results? (2) Did trainees with business degrees perform better on these tests than those with other degrees? The second question had implications for the hiring process. She also would have been interested in the effects of grade point averages, experience, and age, but this information was not available at the time of the study. The pretest and posttest scores of the 28 trainees, the trainees' increases in score, and their degree disciplines (business or other) are given in Table 7.1.*

The graph in Figure 7.6 indicates that the posttest scores are consistently higher than the pretest scores. The pairs of scores are plotted in sequence and connected by a vertical line.

Table 7.2 is a descriptive analysis of the pretest and posttest scores and the changes in scores for the participants. The average pretest and posttest scores were 40.07 and 59.39, respectively. Thus, the average test score improved about 19.3 points as a result of the training program (a 48% increase).

How precisely has the population mean change been estimated? Might the estimated 19-point improvement simply reflect random variation in testing rather than true learning? Since the data were collected in pairs, with two scores for each trainee, a paired samples analysis focusing on the *pairwise differences* between the test scores of the trainees is appropriate.

Table 7.3 provides a 95% confidence interval for the mean change in test scores for the relevant population (i.e., all current and future trainees if the hiring/training process continued unchanged). With 95% confidence, it can be said that the population mean improvement lies within the confidence limits (17.410, 21.233).

---

* Courtesy of Denise Rimes.

Table 7.1

Pretest and posttest results for management trainees by degree type

Trainee	Degree	Pretest Score	Posttest Score	Change
1	Business	35	44	9
2	Business	49	66	17
3	Business	38	51	13
4	Business	41	63	22
5	Business	45	62	17
6	Business	51	66	15
7	Business	36	57	21
8	Business	41	63	22
9	Business	41	60	19
10	Business	43	63	20
11	Business	38	60	22
12	Business	43	58	15
13	Business	31	55	24
14	Business	33	52	19
15	Business	46	75	29
16	Business	33	50	17
17	Other	44	55	11
18	Other	33	54	21
19	Other	44	58	14
20	Other	42	63	21
21	Other	38	58	20
22	Other	47	65	18
23	Other	41	63	22
24	Other	38	67	29
25	Other	41	64	23
26	Other	42	57	15
27	Other	34	62	28
28	Other	34	52	18

Figure 7.6

Graph of pretest and posttest scores for 28 management trainees

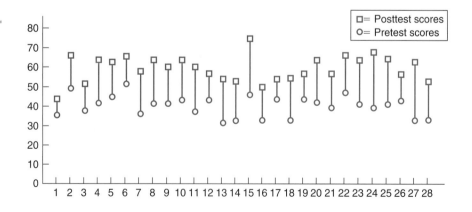

That is, with 95% confidence, the population mean improvement is no less than 17.410 points and no greater than 21.233 points. Since these limits do not include 0, it is not plausible to claim that no real improvement took place. Of course, the mean improvement could move outside these limits if there were significant changes in the hiring/training process.

Table 7.2

Descriptive summary of pretest scores, post-test scores, and increases in score

	N	MEAN	MEDIAN	TRMEAN	STDEV	SEMEAN
pre-test	28	40.071	41.000	40.000	5.206	0.984
posttest	28	59.39	60.00	59.38	6.41	1.21
change	28	19.321	19.500	19.346	4.930	0.932

	MIN	MAX	Q1	Q3
pre-test	31.000	51.000	35.250	43.750
posttest	44.00	75.00	55.00	63.00
change	9.000	29.000	15.500	22.000

Table 7.3

Minitab-generated 95% confidence interval for the mean change in test scores

	N	MEAN	STDEV	SEMEAN	95.0 PERCENT C.I.
change	28	19.321	4.930	0.932	(17.410, 21.233)

Now, what about the effect of degree discipline? Table 7.4 provides a descriptive analysis of test scores for business students versus those with degrees in other fields (1 = business, 0 = other). It suggests little, if any, difference between the groups.

Table 7.4

Descriptive summary of pretest and posttest scores by degree

	Degree	N	MEAN	MEDIAN	TRMEAN	STDEV	SEMEAN
pre-test	0	12	39.83	41.00	39.80	4.47	1.29
	1	16	40.25	41.00	40.14	5.84	1.46
posttest	0	12	59.83	60.00	59.90	4.80	1.39
	1	16	59.06	60.00	59.00	7.54	1.89
change	0	12	20.00	20.50	20.00	5.31	1.53
	1	16	18.81	19.00	18.79	4.74	1.18

	Degree	MIN	MAX	Q1	Q3
pre-test	0	33.00	47.00	35.00	43.50
	1	31.00	51.00	35.25	44.50
posttest	0	52.00	67.00	55.50	63.75
	1	44.00	75.00	52.75	63.00
change	0	11.00	29.00	15.75	22.75
	1	9.00	29.00	15.50	22.00

A pooled T procedure was performed to follow up on the preliminary conclusions drawn from the descriptive analysis. Since having a business degree seems most likely to create a difference in the pretest scores, the pooled T analysis focused on this variable. The result is provided in Table 7.5. The 95% confidence interval for the difference between the two group means is (–3.7, 4.6), easily overlapping a null hypothesis value of 0 difference. The P-value of .84 is so large that there is virtually *no* reason to suspect any difference between the group means. This study offers no reason to prefer business majors over students from other disciplines in hiring decisions.

Table 7.5

Pooled *T* analysis of mean pretest scores, business versus nonbusiness

```
Two sample T for Pre-test
Degree      N        Mean       StDev      SE Mean
    1      16       40.25       5.84         1.5
    0      12       39.83       4.47         1.3

95% C.I. for mu 1 - mu 0: ( -3.7, 4.6)
T-Test mu 1 = mu 0 (vs not =): T = 0.21 P = 0.84 DF = 26
Both use Pooled StDev = 5.30
```

7.7   Summary

In this chapter, we examined statistical methods for comparing the parameters of two populations or processes with regard to their means and proportions. The validity of these comparisons depends on the data-collection plan, which is the most important aspect of any statistical study. The general principle of a designed experiment is to acquire sample data in such a way as to minimize random variation by controlling as much as possible the identifiable causes of variation.

For comparing two means, we regard the two populations or processes as representing two distinct levels of a factor of interest. There are two basic plans available for data acquisition: independent samples and samples in pairs. The difference between these plans is that with the second plan, a background variable's effect is controlled by pairing (blocking). In virtually all real applications, statistical inferences for the two population means are based on the Student's *T* distribution. As in Chapter 6, we use a graphical analysis as a first step in hypothesis testing.

The comparison of two proportions is based on independent random samples from two populations. The procedures for confidence intervals and hypothesis testing are based on the normal distribution, as in the single-population situations discussed in Chapter 6.

EXERCISES FOR SECTION 7.2

7.1 What advantage is gained by observing data in paired samples rather than independent random samples?

7.2 Describe a situation in which it would not be feasible to use the paired samples design.

7.3 Identify and explain the fundamental principle of designed experiments.

7.4 Identify and explain the primary ways of controlling a background variable.

7.5 Explain how the following components of designed experiments affect the accuracy of statistical analysis:
(a) Randomization
(b) Blocking
(c) Replication (repetition)

7.6 In an independent random samples approach, to what do we attribute the variation of the sample data within each sample? Should we use the independent samples approach if we suspect that substantial variation of the data within a sample can be caused by some identifiable factor? What should we do in this case? Explain.

7.7 A mail order house plans to perform an experiment to help in choosing between the U.S. Postal Service and a private mail delivery service. Its experimental design is as follows: Twenty locations of widely varying distances will be identified. Packages will be sent to ten locations, selected randomly, via U.S. mail. Identical packages will be sent to the other ten locations via the private carrier. The delivery times for all 20 packages will be recorded. The mean delivery time for the U.S. Postal Service will then be compared to the mean for the private service.
(a) Can you suggest a better plan?
(b) Explain how your plan is an improvement.

7.8 A health director for a corporation wishes to perform an experiment to determine the average amount of improvement in the lung capacity of executives who participate in an exercise program.

The subjects of the experiment are a group of executives who have not previously exercised regularly; they will participate in a supervised exercise program for 3 months. Describe how you would design this experiment.

(a) What variable is to be observed for each person in the experiment?

(b) In what way or ways would you use blocking (i.e., pairing)?

(c) Why would blocking help? Answer for each kind of blocking mentioned in part (b).

(d) List the factors you can think of that might contribute to random variation in the experiment.

7.9 A corporate advertising manager is choosing between two television shows on which to buy commercial time. To aid in choosing, she wishes to perform a statistical comparison of two means to see whether the ages of the viewers of the shows differ on average. Which sampling plan is appropriate or better here, independent samples or paired samples? Explain.

EXERCISES FOR SECTION 7.3

7.10 For inferences about two population or process means, what is the realistic situation with regard to the population or process standard deviations? Consequently, what is the appropriate sampling distribution to use?

7.11 In comparing two population means, when is the pooled variance S_p^2 used?

7.12 When you use a T statistic for independent samples inferences about two population means, what assumptions are necessary concerning the two populations? Are these assumptions crucial in all cases? Explain.

7.13 Suppose we wish to compare the means of two production shifts relative to the number of sick leave days taken by the employees of each shift per year. Twelve employees were randomly selected from each shift, and the number of sick leave days taken by each selected employee during the past year was recorded. The following sample information was obtained:

Number of Sick Leave Days

Shift 1: 3 7 2 4 5 4 8 3 2 5 7 3
Shift 2: 5 4 7 9 6 5 3 8 10 4 8 6

(a) Graph the data. Is it apparent to you that a difference exists for these two shifts in their average number of sick leave days? Explain.

(b) Based on the Excel output in the next column, determine whether these data provide sufficient evidence to conclude that a difference exists in the average number of sick leave days for these two shifts. (*Hint:* Use the *P*-value approach.)

7.14 A manufacturer wishes to compare the average strength of a proposed yarn with that of a currently popular yarn. Independent samples of 25 specimens of each type of yarn are taken; for each sample, the yarn strength is measured. The following sample information is obtained:

	A	B	C
1	t-Test: Two-Sample Assuming Equal Variances		
2			
3		*Shift 1*	*Shift 2*
4	Mean	4.417	6.25
5	Variance	4.083	4.75
6	Observations	12	12
7	Pooled Variance	4.417	
8	Hypothesized Mean Difference	0	
9	df	22	
10	t Stat	-2.137	
11	P(T<=t) one-tail	0.022	
12	t Critical one-tail	1.717	
13	P(T<=t) two-tail	0.044	
14	t Critical two-tail	2.074	

Popular 104 108 90 106 108 113 114 82 113 91 79 99 116
yarn: 99 101 122 100 102 127 104 103 103 94 103 102

New   127 109 113 98 98 95 86 108 100 119 109 122 96
yarn: 101 97 125 126 92 118 100 110 107 106 118 94

(a) Graph the data. Is it apparent to you that the strength of the new yarn exceeds that of the popular yarn, on average? Explain.

(b) Based on the following Minitab output, use the *P*-value approach to determine whether the sample data provide sufficient evidence to conclude that the strength of the new yarn exceeds that of the popular yarn, on average.

```
Two Sample T-Test and Confidence Interval

Two sample  T    for      Strength
Yarn        N    Mean     StDev      SE Mean
1           25   103.3    11.1       2.2
2           25   107.0    11.6       2.3

95% C.I. For mu 1 - mu 2: (-10.1, 2.8)
T-Test mu 1 = mu 2 (vs <): T = 1.13 P = 0.13 DF = 48
Pooled StDev = 11.4
```

7.15 Exercise 2.60 involved a comparison of for-profit and not-for-profit Virginia hospitals with respect to efficiency of management as characterized by return on assets (ROA), a commonly accepted indicator of efficiency. A belief that competition is the best way to control costs has resulted in a proliferation of for-profit providers. But are they really more efficient? The data for this exercise represent 1993 ROA for samples of 76 not-for-profit hospitals and 14 for-profit hospitals in Virginia *(Source: 1994 Annual Report of the Virginia Health Services Cost Review Council)*. The data are on the book's data diskette, in the file named EX0260.

   (a) In Exercise 2.60, you compared these two groups based on graphs of their distributions and summary statistics. Now, determine whether statistical inference confirms your previous conclusions. Do these data provide convincing evidence that the 1993 mean ROA is greater for the for-profit hospitals than for the not-for-profit hospitals? Base your analysis on an independent samples *T* procedure.

   (b) State any concerns or limitations regarding your analysis in part (a).

7.16 A manager is responsible for testing a new marketing proposal to include 3 months of free service with every purchase of a particular product. To test the effect on sales, 30 sales territories are randomly selected. The proposal is implemented in 15 test territories chosen randomly, while the other 15 control territories continue business as usual for the sake of comparison. Two months are allowed to pass so that the sales process in the test territories can stabilize. Over the following 3 months, the sales per territory for the test territories are as follows (in thousands of dollars): 32.8, 39.9, 24.8, 25.3, 27.1, 28.4, 29.5, 41.2, 31.9, 28.7, 19.2, 26.2, 27.2, 27.6, and 31.8. For the control territories, the sales are as follows: 28.6, 19.9, 22.7, 24.2, 23.9, 34.7, 22.8, 29.9, 27.6, 18.4, 22.5, 19.3, 22.8, 18.7, and 18.6. Assume the two samples were taken randomly and independently from two populations with normal distributions.

   (a) Graph the data for the test and control territories. Is it apparent to you that the new marketing scheme has increased sales, on average? Explain.

   (b) To what extent do these data contradict the claim of no difference in average sales in favor of an increase for the test territories?

7.17 A certain metal is currently manufactured by a standard process. A new process has been developed in which an alloy is added. The manufacturer believes the alloy will increase the average breaking strength of the metal. Sixteen specimens of the metal are randomly selected from each of the two production methods, and each specimen is subjected to stress until a crack is observed. The following are the breaking strengths of the sample specimens (in kilograms per square centimeter). Assume that sampling is from two independent normal distributions.

Standard process:
50 38 50 58 46 51 50 45 35 51 51 45 41 40 56 42
New process:
45 27 42 84 40 43 45 49 44 51 54 58 65 76 25 38

   (a) Graph the data. Do these data lend credibility to the manufacturer's belief? Explain.

   (b) Do these data provide sufficient evidence to conclude that the new process increases the mean breaking strength?

7.18 An employee is interested in which is the faster way to get to work, riding the local commuter train or driving her automobile. In a test, she used each mode of transportation for 10 days. The days in which each mode was used were chosen randomly. She left home at the same time every day and recorded the elapsed time until she arrived at her workplace. With the commuter train her times were: 48, 47, 44, 45, 46, 47, 43, 47, 42, and 48 minutes. With the automobile, her times were 36, 45, 47, 38, 39, 42, 36, 42, 46, and 35 minutes. Assume the sample information constitutes independent random samples from two normal distributions.

   (a) Graph these data. Is it apparent to you that there is a difference in the time needed to get to work, on average? Explain.

   (b) Do these data provide sufficient evidence to conclude that driving is faster on the average?

   (c) Can you think of a better design for this experiment? Specifically, how could blocking have been utilized to reduce the amount of random variation in this experiment?

7.19 A purchasing manager wants to compare the average amount of downtime per service call for two copier models his company uses. They have eight Suny 1000 copiers and ten Saban XL100 copiers. He compiles the total downtime in hours for all service calls over the last 6 months with each copier, obtaining the following results:

Model	Downtime (hours)
Suny 1000	7.2 3.6 5.5 4.6 3.7 3.1 2.6 7.2
Saban XL100	4.4 3.3 5.6 6.1 4.2 3.6 3.4 4.2 5.0 3.0

Assume these samples are independently taken from normal distributions.

    (a) Graph the downtimes per service call for each model. Based on this graph, do you perceive that there is a difference in the average downtimes per service call for these two copiers? Explain.

    (b) To what extent do these data contradict the claim of no difference in average downtimes in favor of a difference?

7.20 A large manufacturing plant requires all new employees to be trained with regard to the quality of assembly of a product before assuming responsibility on an assembly line. Sixteen newly hired employees were randomly divided into two groups. One group of eight employees was assigned to the standard method of training, while the other group was assigned to a new method of training with greater emphasis on efficiency of assembly. At the end of the training period, the length of time in minutes required by each employee to assemble the product to a satisfactory quality level was observed to be as follows:

Standard method: 42 38 41 37 43 44 45 36
New method: 34 35 35 36 39 37 38 34

Assume the samples are independently taken from normal distributions.

    (a) Graph the assembly times for each method. Is it apparent to you that the average assembly time for the new method is less than that for the standard method? Explain.

    (b) To what extent do these data contradict the claim of no difference in average assembly times in favor of a smaller average assembly time for the new method?

    (c) For the 16 new employees, is it possible to have considered a paired samples approach to compare the two methods? Explain.

7.21 In the production of lightbulbs, a large number of bulbs are broken. A production manager plans to test a new type of conveyor system in hopes of reducing the percentage of bulbs lost each day, on the average. For 10 days prior to installing the new system, he monitors bulb breakage. He then records bulb breakage for 10 days with the new system, after allowing sufficient time for the new system to stabilize. His data are as follows:

Conveyor System	Daily Percentage of Bulbs Broken									
Old	8.7	11.1	4.4	3.7	9.2	6.6	7.8	4.9	6.9	8.3
New	7.8	6.2	3.2	4.6	5.3	6.5	4.6	7.1	4.9	7.2

Assume the samples are taken independently from normal distributions. Answer questions similar to parts (a)–(c) of Exercise 7.20.

7.22 In Exercises 2.15, 2.62, and 2.92, you studied data for samples of 37 Turkish banks and 8 foreign banks (see Exercise 2.15 for source). Five comparisons were made, using the five CAMEL characteristics of bank performance. In comparing the means of the two groups for each characteristic, is it possible that the observed differences between the sample means derived entirely from sampling error? For each CAMEL variable, use an independent samples T procedure to assess the extent to which the data contradict a claim of no difference between the group means. State your conclusion clearly. Assume that these are independent random samples taken from the populations of Turkish banks and southern-tier European banks, respectively. The data for this exercise are on the book's data diskette, in the file named EX0215.

7.23 The profits earned by most banks increased in 1995 over the previous year. But was this overall increase uniform over the regions of the country? The following data (*Source: Wall Street Journal,* Nov. 6, 1995) are the profits reported for the third quarters of 1994 and 1995 and the percentage change for random samples of 11 southern banks and 7 western banks. They are stored in the book's data diskette under file name EX0723. Do these sample data provide convincing evidence that the mean percentage changes differed for the two regions? Support your answer.

Southern Banks	% Change	Western Banks	% Change
Am South Bancorp	4.62	Bancorp Hawaii	3.00
Barnett Banks, Inc.	8.67	1st Hawaiian Inc.	−0.54
Crestar Financial	11.01	First Security Corp.	6.79
1st Tennessee	16.57	U.S. Bancorp	29.41
First Union Corp.	5.49	Wells Fargo & Co.	20.28
NationsBank	22.97	West One	21.47
Regions Fin'l.	17.55	Zion Bancorp	26.19
South Trust Corp.	13.57		
Sun Trust Banks	8.95		
Synovus Financial	22.67		
Wachovia Corp.	9.63		

7.24 The study "Physical and Performance Characteristics of NCAA Division I Football Players" (*Research Quarterly for Exercise and Sport,* Vol. 61, No. 4, 1990, pp. 395–401) reported on various physical measurements of Division I football players for the 1987 season. One measurement of interest was the ratio of bench press to weight (as a percentage).

The following data are simulated based on the summary information given in this study and represent independent random samples of bench press to weight percentage of football players in top 20 teams and players in non–top-20 teams.

Bench press/weight (%)

Top 20: 144.8 144.0 137.7 151.2 151.4 150.3 150.5 177.9
151.6 183.2 182.1 167.3 151.7 124.8 133.7

Non–
top-20: 155.8 156.7 147.3 164.4 127.5 184.1 143.1
159.9 134.1 150.4 147.2 120.0 143.8 182.9
175.8 148.9 142.8 131.0 137.5 159.9

(a) Graph the data for the top 20 and non–top-20 players. On average, are any differences in bench press to weight ratios apparent to you between top 20 and non–top-20 players?

(b) To what extent do these data contradict the claim of no difference in average bench press to weight ratios for top 20 and non top-20 players in 1987?

7.25. The study "Accepted Risk and Alcohol Use During Pregnancy" (*Journal of Consumer Research*, Vol. 21, June 1994, pp. 135–144) reported on demographic information, views, beliefs, and behaviors of surveyed pregnant women. One demographic variable of interest was the annual family income for the women who were surveyed. It was of particular interest to compare two groups: nondrinkers and abstainers, the latter defined as women who normally consumed alcoholic beverages but who abstained from drinking during pregnancy. The following data are simulated based on the summary information given in this study and represent independent samples of annual incomes (in thousands of dollars) of 15 randomly selected pregnant women from each group.

Nondrinkers: 29.1 29.5 26.8 27.9 25.5 29.3 29.6 34.8
31.2 32.8 26.8 26.8 31.0 36.0 32.6

Abstainers: 35.1 26.3 36.5 38.6 33.8 28.7 29.2 33.2
41.3 31.6 28.7 33.8 31.8 37.4 37.9

(a) Graph the data for the two groups. On average, are any differences in annual incomes apparent to you?

(b) To what extent do these data contradict a claim of no difference in average annual incomes between these two groups? Explain.

7.26. The study "A Comparison of Women in Small and Large Companies" (*American Journal of Small Business*, Winter 1988, pp. 23–33) reported on biographical data of surveyed female managers who work for small or large firms. The following data are simulated based on the summary information given in this study and represent the ages of

randomly selected female managers from each type of firm.

Small firms: 38 29 36 44 30 41 37 28 34 30 28 41 48 45

Large firms: 40 33 24 27 39 38 30 24 51 34 19 23 42 44

(a) Graph the data. On average, are any differences in ages apparent to you?

(b) To what extent do these data contradict a claim of no difference in average age of female managers in these two types of firms?

7.27. The paper "Are Young Children Adaptive Decision Makers? A Study of Age Differences in Information Search Behavior" (*Journal of Consumer Research*, Vol. 21, Mar. 1995, pp. 567–580) explored the understanding of how young children make consumer choices. Children's search behavior was examined by having participating children play a game called "house of prizes." The games involved making a choice between two "houses," each "house" containing four different types of prizes, with each prize hidden behind a "curtain." The participating children were instructed that they could have as many "curtains" opened as they wished (maximum of eight) before making a choice. The following data are simulated based on the summary information given in this study and represent the number of "curtains" opened before a choice is made of randomly selected children from two age groups: 4 to 5 and 6 to 7 years old.

4–5 years: 6 4 6 6 2 0 4 3
5 8 0 4 5 5 8

6–7 years: 8 8 3 4 7 6 8 2 8
5 3 8 3 8 2 3 4

(a) Graph the data. On average, are any differences in the number of "curtains" opened for these two age groups apparent to you?

(b) To what extent do these data contradict a claim of no difference in the average number of "curtains" opened for these two groups in favor of a higher average for the older group?

7.28. The paper "Validation of the Rockport Fitness Walking Test in College Males and Females" (*Research Quarterly for Exercise and Sport*, Vol. 65, No. 2, 1994, pp. 152–158) examined aerobic capacity of college males and females using a test procedure known as the Rockport Fitness Walking Test (RFWT). One measure of aerobic capacity is maximum heart rate achieved (in beats per minute). The following data are simulated based on the summary information provided in this study and represent maximum heart rates of selected female and male college students who undergo this test.

Female: 200 190 204 205 196 204 191 193 212 207
Male: 189 214 188 197 198 196 201 207 199

(a) Graph the data. On average, are any differences in maximum heart rates achieved by females and males apparent to you?

(b) Determine the extent to which these data indicate differences between the two genders, on average.

7.29. The study "Exploring Group Maturity in the Classroom" (*Small Group Behavior,* Vol. 19, No. 2, 1988, pp. 259–272) examined differences in behavioral and performance outcomes between mature and immature groups. Groups are often formed to enhance learning in classroom settings. According to the study, a mature group is able to function independently of the leader, is active, organized, and brings an extended time perspective to its activities. An immature group is dependent on its leader for proper functioning, is passive, disorganized, and brings short time perspective to its activities. The study investigated groups of students taking a variety of undergraduate courses. The measure of interest was the number of voluntary meetings held by mature and immature groups. The following data are simulated based on the summary information provided in the study and represent independent random samples of the number of voluntary meetings of the two groups.

Mature:	3	5	6	5	2	6	8
	3	6	1	5	4	5	1
Immature:	0	1	2	0	3	4	0	0
	2	2	4	3	1	6	0

(a) Graph the data. On average, are any differences in the number of meetings held by each group apparent to you?

(b) Determine the extent to which these data provide convincing evidence that the average number of meetings of mature groups exceeds that of immature groups.

7.30 When a top manager is replaced, does the success of the company under the new manager depend on whether the change is initiated by the board of directors or not? Does success depend on whether the new manager is hired from within or from outside the company? The article "Successor Origin, Initiating Force, and Managerial Tenure in Banking" (*Journal of Business Research,* Vol. 29, 1994, pp. 47–55) investigated successions of top managers in the banking industry. The total sample consisted of 150 relatively small banks (having less than $100 million in assets) that changed the highest ranking officer in 1985. One aspect of the study was a comparison of performance changes that take place

after a succession for (1) successions that were board-initiated and the new manager was hired from outside the bank ($n_1 = 40$) and (2) successions that were not board-initiated and the new manager was hired from within the bank ($n_2 = 34$). A key measure of performance under the new manager was the percentage change in total assets over the 3 years following the succession. The data for this exercise were simulated to match the characteristics of the actual data as described in the paper; they are on the book's data diskette, in the file named EX0730.

(a) Graph the data. Do the two types of successions appear to differ with respect to the mean change in assets?

(b) To what extent do these data provide convincing evidence that the two types of successions differ with respect to the mean change in assets that occurs?

7.31 Distance learning is increasingly being used as a strategy to offer courses to large numbers of geographically dispersed students. But do they facilitate learning as well as standard in-class instruction? The paper "Perspectives on an Interactive Satellite-based Japanese Language Course" (*The American Journal of Distance Learning,* Vol. 7, No. 3, 1993) evaluated the effectiveness of an interactive, television-based distance learning course in introductory high school Japanese. Originating in Nebraska, the course was first offered in 1990 to students in 170 schools in 20 states. To evaluate the course, tests of Japanese listening and writing ability were given to 771 students in this course and to a sample of 198 students who took a standard classroom-based course. The data for this exercise have been created to match the characteristics of the data reported in the paper. They are on the book diskette in the file EX0731.

(a) Graph the listening data for the two samples. What does your graph suggest about the relative effectiveness of the distance learning course in teaching listening skills?

(b) Determine a 95% confidence interval for the difference between the mean listening scores for the two courses. Based on this interval, is a difference between the means discernible?

(c) Graph the writing data for the two samples. What does your graph suggest about the relative effectiveness of the distance learning course in teaching writing skills?

(d) Determine a 95% confidence interval for the difference between the mean writing scores for the two courses. Based on this interval, is a difference between the means discernible?

7.32 Economists have not had as great an effect on

health-care reform as many might expect. The paper "Economics, Values, and Health Care Reform" (Presidential Address delivered at the 108th meeting of the American Economic Association, Jan. 6, 1996, and published in *The American Economic Review,* Vol. 86, No. 1, Mar. 1996) addressed the reasons for this via a survey of 46 leading health economists. The respondents indicated whether they agreed or disagreed with 20 relatively short statements concerning health-care policy. Seven of the twenty questions were considered to be relatively value-free (questions whose answers do not depend on one's values), whereas 13 questions had substantial value-based aspects. Of great interest was the extent to which health economists were in agreement with each other on the questions. For a given statement, maximum agreement among economists would be reflected by proportions of either 1.00 or 0.00 agreeing with the statement, whereas minimum agreement would be reflected by proportions of .50 in agreement and .50 in disagreement with the statement. Thus, the amount of disagreement among economists can be measured by the absolute value of the difference between the proportion in agreement with a statement and the proportion in disagreement with the statement. The data are as follows.

Value-Free Statements	% Agreed	% Disagreed	Absolute Value of Difference
1	9	91	82
2	84	16	68
3	68	32	36
4	11	89	78
5	81	19	62
6	0	100	100
7	13	87	74

Value-Based Questions	% Agreed	% Disagreed	Absolute Value of Difference
8	62	38	24
9	54	46	8
10	38	62	24
11	36	64	28
12	51	49	2
13	71	29	42
14	14	86	72
15	62	38	24
16	12	88	76
17	42	58	16
18	66	34	32
19	27	73	46
20	30	70	40

(a) Graph the absolute differences between the proportions agreeing and disagreeing with each of the 7 value-free statements and with each of the 13 value-based questions. What does the graph suggest about the effect of values on the amount of agreement among health economists with respect to their policy opinions?

(b) To what extent do these data provide convincing evidence that the mean amount of policy agreement among health economists (as measured by the absolute differences between the proportion who agree and the proportion who disagree to a statement) is greater for statements that are value-free than for statements that are value-based?

7.33 The paper "Consumers' Perception of Risk and the Purchase of Apparel from Catalogs" (*Journal of Direct Marketing,* Vol. 8, No. 2, Spring 1994) examined the role that a consumer's gender plays in purchases of apparel from catalogs. Samples of 64 male college students and 155 female college students were given a questionnaire. Each respondent was asked to provide the number of orders for apparel from a catalog placed in the past 12 months (ORDERS) and the approximate amount spent on apparel bought by catalog over the past 12 months (DOLLARS). The data for this exercise have been simulated to match the characteristics described in the paper; they are on the book diskette in the file named EX0733.

(a) Graph the ORDERS data. What does the graph suggest about possible differences between male and female college students with respect to the average number of catalog orders placed in the past 12 months?

(b) To what extent do these data provide convincing evidence that a difference exists between the average numbers of catalog orders placed in the past 12 months for the populations of male and female college students?

(c) Repeat parts (a) and (b) for the DOLLARS data.

7.34 A belief that gender equity has not occurred in the home is widespread among gender researchers. The paper "Gender and Family Effects on the 'Second Shift' Domestic Activity of College-Educated Young Adults" (*Gender and Society,* Vol. 10, No. 1, Feb. 1996, pp. 78–93) examined gender differences in the extent and type of household activity within a sample of young college-educated adults. The sample consists of 1,151 graduates (621 men and 530 women) of a northeastern liberal arts college with an upper-middle-class student body. All graduated between 1979 and 1989, and all were employed. The men entering this college are similar to male collegians in general in their attitudes toward gender, but the women are typically more feminist in their values than are undergraduate females nationwide. The respondents reported the number of hours per week they devoted to household activities and the number of hours per week they usually devoted to their jobs. The data for this exercise have been simulated to match the characteristics of the actual sample data as described in the paper; they are on the book diskette in the file EX0734.

(a) Graph the data for hours devoted to household activities by men and women. What do they suggest about possible gender differences, on average?

(b) To what extent do these data contradict a null hypothesis that, for the populations studied, men and women graduates devote an equal number of hours to homemaking or household activities, on average?

(c) Graph the data for hours devoted to their jobs by men and women. What do they suggest about possible gender differences, on average?

(d) To what extent to these data contradict a null hypothesis that, for the populations studied, men and women graduates devote an equal number of hours to their jobs, on average?

(e) Based on these data, would you say that gender equity has not occurred in the home?

7.35 Comparisons of women's and men's earnings have consistently demonstrated a substantial gender inequality. The paper "Gender, Earnings, and Proportions of Women" (*Gender and Society,* Vol. 10, No. 2, Apr. 1996, pp. 168–184) investigated the reasons for such differences. The sample consisted of 420 computer professionals working in 14 organizations in a western Canadian city. These organizations were chosen because they seemed to best represent the nature of computer work available in the city. A questionnaire was completed by each professional (or, for some items, his or her manager). Information obtained included the professional's income, gender, position, years of work experience, and level of education. Position was coded on a 1–3 scale reflecting increasing levels of responsibility. Education was coded on a 1–6 scale reflecting increasing levels of education. An additional suspected factor was the percentage of female employees in the organization. The literature is divided over the effect of this factor. It has been argued that women fare better in terms of income in organizations with greater percentages of women. Others have argued that women do less well in such environments. To investigate, the sample was broken into four groups: men in organizations with more than 35% women, men in organizations with

less than 35% women, women in organizations with more than 35% women, and women in organizations with less than 35% women. The incomes, positions, years of experience, and education levels for the employees in each group are on the book diskette in the file EX0735.

(a) Graph the income data for the four groups. For organizations employing less than 35% women, do you see a difference in the mean incomes of men and women? For organizations employing greater than 35% women, do you see a difference in the mean incomes of men and women?

(b) To what extent do these data contradict a null hypothesis that the mean income for women in organizations employing less than 35% women differs from the mean income for men in such organizations?

(c) To what extent do these data contradict a null hypothesis that the mean income for women in organizations employing greater than 35% women differs from the mean income for men in such organizations?

7.36 Firms in the same industry tend to use the same accounting methods. At times, a firm will adopt an accounting method not commonly used by other firms, whereas others may switch toward the commonly used method. The paper "Differential Market Reactions to Accounting Changes Away-From Versus Towards Common Accounting Practices" (*Journal of Accounting and Public Policy,* Vol. 15, 1996, pp. 29–53) examined whether the *direction* of such changes has any stock price implications. When firms change to or away from common accounting practices for their industry, they often do not disclose the motive. Thus, it is difficult for the market to assess the implications of the decision to change. The sample for this study consists of 102 firms, of which 63 changed away from common accounting practices and 39 changed toward common practices. It was drawn from New York Stock Exchange, American Stock Exchange, and over-the-counter firms that had accounting changes over the period June 1979 to May 1987. The statistical variable that was used was the daily return for the day the accounting change was announced. The data for each group (AWAY and TOWARD) have been simulated to reflect the characteristics of the data as reported in the paper; they are on the book diskette in the file EX0736.

(a) Graph the data for the two groups. What does your graph suggest about daily returns for changes toward and away from common accounting practices, on average?

(b) To what extent do these data provide convincing evidence that the mean daily return for changes away from common practices exceeds that for changes toward common practices?

(c) Interpret what your analysis in parts (a) and (b) tells us about the stock market reaction to changes toward and away from common accounting practices.

7.37 A puzzling finding of empirical studies of stock returns is the presence of abnormally high returns on the day before holidays. The paper "Holiday Effects and Stock Returns: Further Evidence" (*Journal of Finance and Quantitative Analysis*, Vol. 29, No. 1, Mar. 1994) sought to determine whether this holiday effect persists across stock exchanges regardless of differences in their trading mechanism. The data for this exercise consist of the weighted mean daily returns (expressed as percentages) for the New York Stock Exchange over 1963–1986. The data are on the book diskette in the file EX0737; they have been simulated to reflect the characteristics of the actual data as reported in the paper. There are two samples: (1) ordinary days ($n_1 = 1,000$) and (2) preholidays, i.e., the day before a holiday ($n_2 = 186$).

(a) Graph the data. What does your graph suggest about a possible difference between the mean returns for preholidays versus ordinary days?

(b) Determine the extent to which these data provide convincing evidence that, for New York Stock Exchange firms, the mean daily return for preholidays exceeds that for ordinary days.

EXERCISES FOR SECTION 7.4

7.38 A sales manager of a chain of retail stores wishes to compare the sales performances of the women's fashion departments of its two major locations. A staff analyst has compiled the following monthly sales totals (in thousands of dollars) for each location:

	Jan.	Feb.	Mar.	Apr.	May	June
Northside	35	29	39	44	41	49
Southside	28	22	33	44	38	47

(a) Inspect the sample data without doing any formal analysis. Do you think these data indicate clearly that the mean sales levels of the two locations are different? Why?

(b) Graph the data. Is your interpretation of the graph consistent with your answer to part (a)?

(c) Based on the following Excel output (on the left), to what extent do these data contradict a claim of no difference in mean sales between these two locations? Justify your answer.

(d) In answering part (c), why was it necessary to block out the months?

(e) Suppose the observed sales levels for these two stores were regarded as independent samples from normal distributions with equal variances. (This is purely an academic question; the samples are not independent because blocking was used.) Use the following Excel output (on the right) to answer part (c) based on independent samples, and explain why your results differ.

7.39 Document retrieval systems are computer programs that identify articles, books, and other resources that might pertain to a topic of interest. The manager of a corporate technical library wishes to compare two document retrieval systems being considered for adoption. Each system is used to

	A	B	C	D	E	F	G
1	t-Test: Paired Two Sample for Means				t-Test: Two-Sample Assuming Equal Variances		
2							
3		*Northside*	*Southside*			*Northside*	*Southside*
4	Mean	39.5	35.333		Mean	39.5	35.333
5	Variance	48.7	91.067		Variance	48.7	91.067
6	Observations	6	6		Observations	6	6
7	Pearson Correlation	0.985			Pooled Variance	69.883	
8	Hypothesized Mean Difference	0			Hypothesized Mean Difference	0	
9	df	5			df	10	
10	t Stat	3.487			t Stat	0.863	
11	P(T<=t) one-tail	0.009			P(T<=t) one-tail	0.204	
12	t Critical one-tail	2.015			t Critical one-tail	1.812	
13	P(T<=t) two-tail	0.018			P(T<=t) two-tail	0.408	
14	t Critical two-tail	2.571			t Critical two-tail	2.228	

identify potentially relevant articles for a test set of ten requests. Responses to requests are evaluated on two criteria: the number of relevant documents found (more is better) and the number of irrelevant documents found (fewer is better). The results are as follows:

	Relevant Documents Found		Irrelevant Documents Found	
Request	System A	System B	System A	System B
1	8	11	12	16
2	5	8	7	9
3	11	16	5	2
4	22	29	16	20
5	14	12	11	17
6	10	15	7	13
7	12	11	14	13
8	15	22	13	13
9	6	11	8	11
10	18	27	5	16

(a) Why is there a need to use blocking with regard to the requests?

(b) Determine a 98% confidence interval for the mean difference in the numbers of relevant documents identified by the two systems. Does this interval suggest a difference between the means for the two systems? Explain.

(c) Answer part (b) with regard to the irrelevant documents identified by the two systems.

(d) Based on your answers to parts (b) and (c), which document retrieval system should management consider selecting? What nonstatistical considerations should management address before making a selection?

7.40 The Lawford Manufacturing Company produces pillows and pads and sells them wholesale. Pillow and pad upholstery are sewed manually. Two trained operators are expected to produce, on the average, the same number of finished units over time. The following are the observed numbers of finished units per day for the two workers during 1 week:

	M	T	W	Th	F
Operator 1:	108	115	118	116	110
Operator 2:	110	118	120	117	113

(a) Graph the sample data. Does the graph support the belief that operator 2 is doing better, on average?

(b) Why is there a need to block out the days? Explain.

(c) To what extent do these data contradict the

claim of no difference in the average number of finished units and support the belief that operator 2 is producing more, on average? Explain.

(d) Do these data indicate necessarily that operator 2 is *outperforming* operator 1? Do the data indicate that operator 2 will produce more than operator 1 next week? What action might be appropriate, based on these data? Explain your thinking.

(e) Suppose these data were considered as independent samples from normal distributions with equal variances. (This is purely an academic question. The samples are not independent because blocking was used.) Is your answer to part (c) different now? Explain.

7.41 An office manager has hired a consultant to evaluate a proposed new computer system. If the consultant says the new system uses less processing time than the current system and can back up this claim, it will be adopted. The consultant selects a sample of eight representative jobs and runs them on both systems. The processing times (in seconds) are as follows for each trial:

	Job							
	1	2	3	4	5	6	7	8
Old system:	7	8	11	8	14	15	6	10
New system:	5	7	8	7	11	10	9	6

(a) Graph the data. What is your initial conclusion?

(b) Based on the following Minitab output, to what extent do the data contradict the claim of no improvement in mean processing time in favor of an improvement (i.e., smaller processing time) by the new computer systems?

(c) Why is it necessary to block out the jobs?

```
T-Test of the Mean
Test of mu = 0.000 vs mu > 0.000
Variable   N   Mean   StDev   SE Mean    T      P
diff       8  2.000  2.449   0.866    2.31  0.027
```

7.42 A computerized sales forecasting system is being tested. Forecasts of the current year's sales have been made for five products, using only the data through the end of the previous year. For each product, the forecasted sales and the actual sales (in thousands of dollars) for the current year are as follows:

	Product				
	1	2	3	4	5
Forecast:	110	55	230	22	314
Actual:	185	75	168	17	311

(a) Graph the data. What is your preliminary conclusion?

(b) To what extent do these data contradict the claim of no difference between forecast and actual sales, on average? Explain.

(c) Why is there a need to block out the products?

7.43 A sample of ten randomly selected faculty members of a business school were asked to rate the overall performance of two administrators on a scale ranging from 1 (lowest rating) to 5. Their ratings are given here:

Faculty member: 1 2 3 4 5 6 7 8 9 10

Rating for

Dr. Williams: 3.7 4.1 4.2 3.8 3.1 3.6 3.9 4.4 2.9 4.0

Dr. Knox: 3.9 4.3 4.3 3.9 3.4 3.5 3.9 4.6 3.1 4.4

The dean wants to use this information in her evaluation of Dr. Williams's and Dr. Knox's performances.

(a) Graph the ratings of Williams and Knox by faculty rater. What is your preliminary conclusion?

(b) Use a 95% confidence interval to determine whether the data reveal a discernible difference between the mean performance ratings in the eyes of the faculty.

(c) To what extent do the data contradict the claim of no difference between the average ratings? Explain.

(d) Was it important to use blocking here? Why (or why not)?

(e) What reservations might you have with regard to the method you used?

7.44 The food service manager for the headquarters of a Fortune 500 manufacturer located in Richmond, Virginia, wished to understand spending behaviors of employees who eat lunch on site. One variable of interest was the average dollar amount spent at two different product areas that operate as distinct profit centers (other than the Main dining room): the Deli and Cart areas. The data* for this exercise consist of the daily average amounts spent per customer at each product area for all work days in May, June, and July 1997; they are on the book diskette in the file EX0744.

(a) Develop a run chart of the data for each product area, with both areas on the same graph. Are these data stable over the period of observation? What do these run charts suggest about the need to use days as a background variable (i.e., to consider these data as being paired by day)? What do they suggest about

possible differences between the two product areas in the mean amount spent per customer?

(b) Determine the extent to which these sample data contradict a null hypothesis of no differences in the mean daily amounts spent per customer for the two product areas.

7.45 When governments attempt to reform tax systems, often the goal is to increase efficiency while remaining revenue-neutral. The paper "Is Revenue-Neutral Tax Reform Revenue Neutral?" (*Public Financial Quarterly*, Vol. 22, No. 1, Jan. 1994, pp. 65–85) explored the revenue-neutrality of tax reform by analyzing the effect on revenues of nine European tax reforms implemented between 1967 and 1973. Each involved the introduction of a value-added tax (VAT) to conform to the then European Economic Community guidelines. These countries had widely differing tax structures before their tax reforms, and each implemented VAT differently. Of the nine tax reforms, seven were intended to be revenue-neutral, one was intended to increase revenue, and one was intended to decrease revenue. The following data show the primary tax rate (tax revenue as a percentage of gross domestic product, or GDP) for each country at the time of the adoption of VAT and in July 1989.

Country	Date Introduced	Intended Effect on Revenue	Primary Tax Rate	
			At Adoption	July 1989
Belgium	Jan. 1971	Neutral	18	19
Denmark	July 1967	Increase	10	22
France	Jan. 1968	Neutral	13.6	18.6
Germany	Jan. 1968	Neutral	10	14
Ireland	Nov. 1972	Neutral	16.37	25
Italy	Jan. 1973	Neutral	12	19
Luxembourg	Jan. 1970	Neutral	8	12
The Netherlands	Jan. 1969	Neutral	12	18.5
United Kingdom	Apr. 1973	Decrease	10	15

(a) Graph the data. What does your graph suggest about the effect of the VAT tax reform on revenues?

(b) To what extent do these data contradict a claim that primary tax rates do not change when tax reforms like these are implemented, in favor of a claim that they increase? (Make the necessary statistical assumptions and assume that no factors other than tax reform account for the changes observed.)

7.46 The paper "Key Issues Facing European Car Manufacturers and Their Strategic Responses" (*Business Economics*, Oct. 1994) claimed that a " . . . severe drop in demand for European cars in 1993 forced

---

* Courtesy of Lewis Broome.

the auto industry to face underlying structural problems that had been growing for several years . . . ." The paper focused on reduced utilization of production capacity as a key area of weakness. The following data represent percentage utilizations for six European automobile manufacturers for 1992 and 1993.

Manufacturer	% Utilization	
	1992	1993
PSA	69	57
Renault	79	65
GM Europe	93	73
Ford Europe	75	63
VW Group	91	61
Fiat Auto	78	51

(a) Graph the data. What does your graph suggest about the overall average change in utilization of production capacity from 1992 to 1993?

(b) To what extent do these data provide convincing evidence of a change in the mean utilization percentage from 1992 to 1993 for these manufacturers?

7.47 Studies have indicated that caffeine increases performance time during continuous exercise such as distance running. The paper "Effects of Caffeine Ingestion on Exercise-Induced Changes During High-Intensity, Intermittent Exercise" (*International Journal of Sport Nutrition*, Vol. 5, 1995, pp. 37–44) reported the results of an experiment regarding the effects of caffeine on performance during intense, intermittent cycling exercise. Eight trained male volunteers were recruited from the Florida State University Rugby Club to participate. In preliminary testing, the maximum cycling workload was established for each subject. The experiment was conducted in two phases 7 days apart. In each phase, the subjects were encouraged to complete three 30-minute cycling sets, with a 5-minute break between sets. Each set consisted of alternating 1-minute cycling and rest intervals. When cycling, subjects were instructed to maintain 70 RPM at 85%–90% of the maximum workload established in the preliminary test. Time to exhaustion was defined as the number of minutes until a subject stopped or failed to maintain 70 RPM for at least 15 consecutive seconds. The first 30-minute set was begun 1 hour after ingestion of either a coffee solution or a placebo (an indistinguishable decaf solution). Half the subjects (selected randomly) received the coffee solution; the other half got decaf. Seven days later, the experiment was re-

peated, switching the treatment for each participant. The time-to-exhaustion data are as follows.

Subject	Caffeine	Placebo
1	77.6	59.7
2	86.2	65.5
3	76.9	61.9
4	78.7	60.8
5	77.2	62.5
6	76.8	58.3
7	82.0	63.8
8	64.2	58.2

(a) Graph the sample data. What does the graph suggest about the effect of caffeine?

(b) To what extent do these data provide convincing evidence that the mean time to exhaustion is greater with caffeine than without?

(c) Suppose the experiment were replicated using your class as subjects. Should we expect similar results? Explain.

7.48 Numerical goal setting is often a component of business planning, but does it really promote greater achievement? The paper "Effects of a Seasonal Goal-setting Program on Lacrosse Performance" (*The Sport Psychologist*, Vol. 8, 1994, pp. 166–175) examined the effect of goal setting in enhancing players' productivity in lacrosse. An experiment was conducted using 24 members of an NCAA Division III men's lacrosse team. Performance was measured on four statistics that were emphasized by the coaches: assists (passes that led to goals), defensive ground balls (gaining possession of a free ball in the defensive half of the field), offensive ground balls (gaining possession of a free ball in the offensive half of the field), and defensive clears (passing a ball out of the defensive half of the field to a teammate in the offensive half). The 24 subjects, all regular players, were matched in pairs by the coaches according to ability and position played. For each matched pair, one player was randomly assigned to a "goal-setting" group, while the other was assigned to a "best-effort" group. The players in the goal-setting group established with their coaches individual numerical goals for their season's statistics in each category. These players met with a sports psychologist regularly during the season to review progress toward their goals. The players in the best-effort group were exhorted by their coaches to give their best overall effort at all times, but they were not given numerical goals. These players also met regularly with the sports psychologist; they reviewed their statistics and were again exhorted to give best efforts. The data represent the average per-game achievements of each subject for the season in all four categories of performance. The data are on the book diskette in the file EX0748; they have been simulated to reflect the characteristics of the actual data as reported in the paper.

(a) Graph the data for each performance characteristic. What do your graphs suggest about the differences in achievement between the two groups, if any?

(b) For each performance characteristic, to what extent do these data provide convincing evidence that the goal-setting process produces a greater mean achievement than does the best-effort process?

(c) Do you think this study offers any insight about goal setting in a business environment? Explain.

EXERCISES FOR SECTION 7.5

7.49 In developing a confidence interval for the difference between two proportions, the standard error computation uses the values of p_1 and p_2 to estimate π_1 and π_2, respectively. But when testing hypotheses, we use the value of the pooled estimator p in the standard error computation. Explain this difference in methodology.

7.50 What conditions regarding the populations and sampling procedure are required in using the normal distribution to develop confidence intervals and to test hypotheses about the difference between two proportions?

7.51 Why is it necessary to know or to approximate closely the sampling distribution of $p_1 - p_2$?

7.52 Suppose we selected samples of $n_1 = 150$ and $n_2 = 100$ from populations 1 and 2 and observed 12 and 15 "successes," respectively.

(a) Determine estimates of the population proportions π_1 and π_2.

(b) Determine as closely as possible the sampling distribution of $p_1 - p_2$.

(c) Compute a 95% confidence interval for $\pi_1 - \pi_2$. Does this interval suggest a difference between π_1 and π_2? Explain.

(d) For the hypotheses H_0: $\pi_1 - \pi_2 = 0$ versus H_a: $\pi_1 - \pi_2 \neq 0$, determine the P-value.

7.53 Refer to Exercise 7.52. In testing hypotheses, how much difference does it make to use the value of the pooled proportion p in computing the standard error [as in Expression (7.28)] rather than using the values of p_1 and p_2 to estimate π_1 and π_2, respectively [as in Expression (7.21)]? Compare your standard error computations in parts (c) and (d), and comment.

7.54 Refer to Exercise 7.52. Suppose the sample sizes were $n_1 = 40$ and $n_2 = 20$ and the numbers of successes were 3 and 4, respectively. To rework the questions in that exercise, would the same methodology be appropriate? Explain.

7.55 A major copier manufacturer conducts a quarterly survey of its customers in an effort to monitor their perceptions of service and copy quality. In the

fourth quarter, 42 customers in a random sample of 150 customers perceived the average response time to service calls to be too slow. As a result, some changes in service policy were implemented to reduce the average response time. In the quarter following the implementation, 32 customers in a random sample of 177 customers perceived the response time to be too slow.

(a) Compute a 95% confidence interval for the difference between the population proportions before and after the policy change.

(b) Determine whether the confidence interval in part (a) suggests a difference in the proportion of customers who find the response time to be too slow.

(c) Do these sample data show convincingly that the proportion of unsatisfied customers following the implementation has decreased? Explain.

7.56 This exercise refers to Exercise 6.44, in which, based on a Gallup poll, 374 out of 1,010 American adults said that they were fans of professional baseball. The same question had been asked two years previously, in February 1993. At that time, 444 out of 1,010 persons sampled said that they were fans of professional baseball. Do these two sample results provide convincing evidence that fan interest in professional baseball declined over this period? Justify your answer.

7.57 This exercise refers to Exercise 6.45. To assess public opinion on an increase to the minimum wage proposed by the president, the Gallup Organization asked a random sample of 1,010 adults whether they favored this proposal. Of 497 males in the sample, 358 stated support for the proposal. Of 513 females, 426 stated support for the proposal (*Source: The Gallup Poll Monthly*, Mar. 1995). Do these data provide convincing evidence that the proportions of men and women who support the proposed increase differ? Support your answer.

7.58 This exercise refers to Exercise 6.46. In an extensive

survey, the Gallup Organization asked a sample of adults a number of questions about their retirement plans. Overall, only 31% said they had saved nothing for retirement in the last year. Among the 424 respondents in the 30–49 years age group, 123 said they had not saved. Among the 148 respondents in the 50 years and older age group, 56 said they had not saved (*Source: The Gallup Poll Monthly,* May 1995). To what extent do these data contradict a null hypothesis that the proportions of these two age groups who have not saved for retirement are equal? Support your answer.

7.59 Are drivers who use cellular telephones while driving more likely to have an accident than those who do not use them? A professor at Rochester Institute of Technology studied accident reports for a sample of 124 motorists, based on records of the New York State Department of Motor Vehicles (*Source: Rochester Democrat and Chronicle,* Mar. 22, 1995). Of these motorists, 17 had cellular telephones. The professor also surveyed 132 motorists who had never been in an accident and found that 14 had cellular telephones. Based on these findings, the professor was reported to have concluded that there was greater risk of having an auto accident for those who use cellular telephones while driving.

(a) Is it plausible that the observed differences between the proportions that had cellular telephones for these two samples resulted from random sampling error alone? To what extent do the sample data contradict a claim of no difference between the population proportions in favor of a greater proportion for those with cellular telephones? Support your answer.

(b) Suppose that the proportion with cellular phones among the population of motorists who have had accidents were in fact greater than the corresponding proportion for the population of motorists who have had no accidents. Would this necessarily mean that the use of cellular phones increases the risk of accidents? Explain.

7.60 A poll of eligible voters in a state suggests that women differ sharply from men in their preferences for a gubernatorial candidate. Specifically, 640 of 1,000 women preferred the Democratic candidate, whereas 416 of 800 men preferred that candidate.

(a) Compute a 95% confidence interval for the difference between the proportions of women and men who prefer the Democratic candidate.

(b) Based on the interval in part (a), do you detect a difference between the populations of male and female voters? Explain.

(c) Do these sample data show convincingly that the proportions of women and men who prefer the Democratic candidate are different?

7.61 An advertising agency monitors the effectiveness of its television commercials by conducting surveys of random samples of viewers. In one survey, 188 of 418 viewers of the Channel 12 local news program recalled seeing a commercial. The same commercial run on Channel 5's local news program was recalled by 172 of 338 viewers.

(a) Compute a 95% confidence interval for the difference between the proportions of viewers of the two channels' news programs who would recall seeing the commercial if asked. Does this interval suggest that a difference exists? Explain.

(b) To what extent do these data contradict the claim of no difference between the proportions in favor of a difference?

(c) Regardless of your answers to parts (a) and (b), why should the advertising agency continue to monitor the effectiveness of its commercials? Explain.

7.62 The study by W. Douglas Weaver et al. of the Henry Ford Health System in Detroit, Michigan, published in the December 17, 1997 issue of *The Journal of the American Medical Association,* reported that angioplasty—threading a tiny balloon into clogged arteries to open them—worked better than clot-busting drugs in treating heart attack victims. The study involved 2,606 heart attack patients. In 30 days of follow-up, 57 of the 1,290 patients treated with angioplasty died, while 86 of the 1,316 patients treated with clot-busters died. Under suitable assumptions, to what extent do these data contradict a claim of no difference between the two death rates in favor of a lower death rate for those heart attack patients who receive angioplasty?

7.63 A study of initial employment of physicians ("The Initial Employment Status of Physicians Completing Training in 1994," *Journal of the American Medical Association,* Vol. 275, No. 9, Mar. 6, 1996, pp. 708–712) reported that 212 out of 1,014 surveyed physicians completing residency in internal medicine in 1994 were locating in cities with less than 50,000 population, whereas 113 out of 644 physicians completing residency in pediatrics in 1994 were locating in cities of this size.

(a) Assuming these constitute independent random samples, determine a 95% confidence interval for the difference between the proportions of physicians in internal medicine and in pediatrics located in cities of this size. Does this interval suggest that a difference exists? Explain.

(b) If the claim is that there is no difference

between the two proportions, to what extent do these data contradict the claim of no difference?

7.64   A purchasing manager for a Fortune 500 manufacturer wished to investigate a perceived high level of invoice discrepancies. When a service or material is ordered from a vendor, the vendor submits an invoice, which is then paid by the purchasing department. It was of particular interest to estimate and compare the proportions of invoices with errors generated at two locations. The data* for this exercise consist of all invoices posted between October 6 and October 10, 1997 at two locations: Richmond, Virginia, and Louisville, Kentucky. The data are on the book diskette in the file EX0764.

(a) Estimate the proportion of invoices with errors generated at each location.

(b) To what extent do these data contradict a null hypothesis that the proportions of invoices with errors are the same at these two locations? Support your answer.

7.65.   The March 11, 1996 issue of *Business Week* reported on a Harris poll of 1,004 adults conducted in February 1996 on how Americans feel about certain issues. Of those polled in 1996, 502 indicated that they expected their children to have a better life than they did. In a similar poll of 1,250 adults conducted in August 1989, 738 indicated an expectation of a better life for their children. Based on these polls, is there reason to believe that the proportion of adults in 1996 who expect a better life for their children is less than that in 1989? Support your answer.

7.66   The Home Mortgage Disclosure Act was enacted to monitor minority and low-income access to the mortgage market. The paper "Mortgage Lending in Boston: Interpreting the HMDA Data" (*The American Economic Review*, Vol. 86, No. 1, Mar. 1996) analyzed the role of race in decisions to grant a mortgage in the Boston, Massachusetts, area. The paper is based on 1990 mortgage application data for samples of 1,200 African-Americans and Hispanics and 3,300 white applicants. The data revealed that 330 applications by whites were rejected, while 336 applications by African-Americans and Hispanics were rejected.

(a) To what extent do these data provide convincing evidence that the population proportion rejection rate was higher for African-Americans and Hispanics than for whites?

(b) If you concluded that the population propor-

tion was indeed greater for African-Americans and Hispanics, does this necessarily mean that the cause was racial discrimination? Explain.

7.67   The paper "Economic Conditions and Ideologies of Crime in the Media: A Content Analysis of Crime News" (*Crime and Delinquency*, Vol. 41, January 1995) explored the relationship between the media's portrayal of crime with actual conditions. The analysis was based on a review of the content of 175 *Time* articles about crime, criminals, or the criminal justice system during the years 1953, 1958, 1975, 1979, and 1982. These results were compared to official arrest statistics (*Source*: U.S. Department of Commerce, *Statistical Abstracts*). Offender characteristics studied included race and gender. Of interest is whether *Time's* portrayal of these characteristics is consistent with actual arrest statistics. The following table shows the distribution of mentions in the *Time* articles for each characteristic and the actual distributions according to the official arrest statistics.

Characteristic	Proportion of Mentions in Articles	Proportion of Actual Arrests	Characteristic	Proportion of Mention in Articles	Proportion of Actual Arrests
Race			Gender		
White	.26	.72	Male	.66	.84
Non-white	.74	.28	Female	.34	.16
n	100	31,744	n	423	31,744

(a) Determine whether the data provide convincing evidence that, when an offender's race is mentioned, the proportion of mentions of offender race being white differs from the proportion of offenders who are white.

(b) Determine whether the data provide convincing evidence that, when an offender's gender is mentioned, the proportion of mentions of males differs from the proportion of offenders who are male.

(c) Based on the data and your answers in parts (a) and (b), how would you describe *Time's* portrayal of crime in comparison to actual arrest statistics?

7.68   One of the crucial issues in the debate over national health insurance is its likely impact on the quality of health care. The paper "Canadian National Health Insurance and Infant Health" (*The American Economic Review*, Vol. 89, No. 1, Mar. 1996, pp. 276–284) estimated the impact on infant health outcomes when Quebec implemented its national health insurance program in November 1970. Of immediate interest was whether (1) the proportion of women who received a first trimester doctor visit

---
* Courtesy of Holly Killius.

and (2) the proportion of infants who received a doctor's exam after returning home increased after the implementation of national health care. In a random sample of 272 Montreal women who reported a birth in 1969–1970, immediately prior to implementation, 102 reported a first trimester doctor visit and 201 reported an infant exam upon returning home. In a random sample of 215 Montreal women who reported a birth in 1971–1972, immediately after implementation, 113 reported a first trimester doctor visit and 175 reported an infant exam upon returning home.

(a) Determine point estimates for the change in the proportions of (1) women who had a first trimester doctor visit and (2) infants who had a doctor's exam upon returning home.

(b) To what extent do these data provide convincing evidence that the population proportion (of pregnant Montreal women) who received a first trimester doctor visit increased after national health care was introduced?

(c) To what extent do these data provide convincing evidence that the population proportion (of pregnant Montreal women) whose infants received a doctor's exam after returning home increased after national health care was introduced?

(d) Based on your answers in parts (a)–(c), discuss the apparent impact of national health insurance on pregnant Montreal women.

SUPPLEMENTARY EXERCISES

7.69 Refer to Exercise 6.27. In addition to the medical costs for accident victims who were wearing a seat belt (the costs were $582, 698, 1,029, 732, 2,436, 5,932, 242, 307, 862, 186, 643, 597, 761, 508, and 1,135), another random sample of 15 accident victims who were not wearing a seat belt revealed the following costs: $2,938, 819, 1,845, 649, 1,438, 3,946, 8,629, 548, 1,631, 2,207, 973, 1,593, 694, 6,924, and 950. Assume independent random samples.

(a) Graph the data. Is it apparent to you that wearing seat belts makes a difference in the cost for medical treatment, on average? Explain.

(b) Do these sample data contradict the claim that there is no difference? Support your answer.

(c) What do you suggest should be done to reduce the variation of the data in this problem?

7.70 Refer to Exercise 6.28. The water company took another random sample of 20 residences on a different day during the shortage and obtained the following consumptions (in gallons): 192, 206, 213, 224, 175, 249, 262, 236, 228, 196, 189, 214, 219, 243, 237, 206, 194, 229, 234, and 187. The consumptions on the other day, as given in Exercise 6.28, were as follows: 180, 220, 235, 195, 265, 245, 175, 196, 248, 212, 238, 252, 208, 214, 228, 236, 240, 218, 223, and 246. Assume that these constitute independent random samples.

(a) Graph the data. Is it apparent to you that the water consumption on these two days is the same, on average? Explain.

(b) Answer part (b) of Exercise 7.69.

7.71 A manager responsible for computer equipment must allocate a shipment of personal computers between two departments, Marketing Analysis and Market Research. Her policy is to base such allocations on the departments' prior-year usage of computer time. For the past 12 months, the departments' computer charges have been as follows (in dollars):

Month	Analysis	Research
1	1,780	2,440
2	2,120	2,010
3	2,440	2,780
4	1,860	2,290
5	2,760	3,190
6	2,020	2,240
7	1,680	1,550
8	1,550	1,530
9	2,780	2,790
10	2,660	3,000
11	2,540	2,710
12	1,930	2,090

(a) Graph the data. Based on this graph, do you see a difference in the mean levels of computer expenditures for the analysis and research departments? Explain.

(b) Do these sample data contradict the claim that there is no difference between the mean levels of computer expenditures? Justify with an appropriate analysis.

7.72 A manufacturing company produces its product at two plants. The Baltimore plant is thought to have become less productive (that is, longer average assembly time) than the Kansas City plant. As part of an effort to investigate this suspicion, the assembly times were recorded for random samples of 16 items produced at each plant. The data (in hours) are summarized as follows:

Baltimore:	6.1	5.4	6.2	6.1	6.4	6.8	6.7	6.4
	6.8	6.9	5.6	5.7	6.9	6.8	6.4	7.2
Kansas City:	5.1	6.2	5.8	6.3	4.9	5.7	5.6	4.8
	4.9	6.1	5.9	5.8	5.4	6.2	5.7	6.8

(a) Graph the data. Do you see a difference in productivity between these two plants, on average? Explain.

(b) Do these sample data convincingly confirm the suspicion? Support your answer.

7.73 A sample survey was conducted in two adjacent counties for a study of the proportions of their high school graduates who went on to attend college. In Sullivan County, 88 of 171 graduates in a recent year attended college. In Montgomery County, 131 of 220 such graduates attended college.

(a) Do these data indicate a discernible difference between the two counties in the proportions who attend college? Support your answer.

(b) Suppose the samples of 171 and 220 graduates represented *all* the graduates in the two counties for that year. Would your inference in part (a) make sense? Specifically, to what *populations* or *processes* would your inference in part (a) apply, and what conditions are necessary for the analysis to be valid?

7.74 A consumer group is investigating the repair costs of two automobile models. The repair cost is recorded for the most recent repair performed on each vehicle in random samples of eight automobiles for each model. The sample data (in dollars) are as follows:

Model X: 88 221 149   44 310 720 121 310
Model Y: 339 101 189 181 244 388 199 479

(a) Graph the data. Based on this graph, do you see a difference in the mean costs for models X and Y? What other concerns might you have, based on this graph? Explain.

(b) Assuming that samples are taken randomly and independently from two normal distributions, determine the extent to which these data support the claim that there is no difference in mean costs for these two models.

7.75 A restaurant manager is considering using a different menu in hopes of increasing customers' expenditures on appetizers, which are especially profitable. It involves only a change of design; the specific items offered would not change. In a test conducted on a Saturday evening, 100 persons were given the current menu and 100 were given the menu with the proposed new format. The results were summarized by determining the proportion of persons who ordered an appetizer.

	Current Menu	Proposed Menu
Proportion ordering appetizers	$p_1 = .52$	$p_2 = .66$

Do the sample data provide sufficient evidence to say that the proportion ordering appetizers is greater with the new menu? Support your answer.

7.76 *Business Week*, in its October 29, 1990, issue, reported the following starting annual salaries for men and women MBA graduates from some of the best business schools in the country:

School	Men	Women
MIT	$77,539	$58,500
Columbia	65,009	54,817
Dartmouth	57,393	54,643
Rochester	46,521	40,367
Cornell	53,762	54,433
Virginia	67,397	54,306
UCLA	62,785	51,147
Stanford	80,412	74,925
Berkeley	54,322	52,934
Michigan	54,058	51,702

(a) Graph the data. Do you see a difference in salaries between men and women, on average?

(b) Suppose these data are treated as random samples; to what extent do these data contradict the claim of no difference in starting salaries, on average?

(c) To what extent do these sample data contradict the claim of a $5,000 difference between starting salaries for men and women, on average, in favor of a higher amount?

7.77 A corporate personnel analyst wishes to study employee absenteeism at each of two large plants. Specifically, he wishes to compare the average numbers of absences over a 3-year period for these two plants. He believes that an individual's number of years of employment is an influencing factor in this regard.

(a) Help the analyst design his sampling procedure.

(b) Can you think of other factors that might have an influence on the number of absences? Explain.

7.78 A marketing student conducted telephone interviews* with 16 randomly selected pizza restaurants in Richmond and 16 in the Virginia Tidewater area. She observed that 7 of the Richmond and 10 of the Tidewater restaurants provided free delivery.

   (a) Do these sample data provide sufficient evidence to say that the proportion of pizza restaurants in Richmond that provide free delivery is less than that in Tidewater? Support your answer.

   (b) What assumption is necessary for your analysis in part (a), and does it hold here? Support your answer.

7.79 A professor studied the performances of sophomores and juniors in an information systems class. The following sample data† show the grades on the first two tests:

Juniors			Sophomores		
Student	Test 1	Test 2	Student	Test 1	Test 2
1	62	75	1	60	53
2	68	60	2	62	52
3	68	82	3	62	68
4	70	63	4	64	63
5	70	72	5	64	73
6	72	75	6	66	62
7	72	78	7	68	58
8	76	65	8	70	53
9	76	78	9	70	52
10	76	65	10	72	58
11	78	67	11	72	60
12	80	93	12	74	72
13	82	70	13	76	60
14	84	67	14	78	68
15	86	82	15	80	68
16	88	62	16	84	80
17	90	78	17	86	88
18	94	78	18	88	75
19	94	85			

   (a) Graph the grades for the juniors and sophomores (separately). Do this for test 1 grades; then repeat for test 2. Is it apparent to you that juniors perform better in this class than sophomores? Explain.

   (b) To what extent do these data contradict a claim that the mean performance is the same for juniors and sophomores in favor of a higher average for juniors? Perform an appropriate analysis for test 1; then repeat for test 2.

   (c) For the juniors, do the sample data provide sufficient evidence to say that there is a difference in the mean level of difficulty for the two tests? Support your answer.

   (d) For the sophomores, do the sample data provide sufficient evidence to say that there is a difference in the mean level of difficulty for the two tests? Support your answer.

   (e) Affirm your answers in parts (c) and (d) by determining 95% confidence intervals.

7.80 This exercise is a study of response times at the Farrington, Virginia, Fire Station. Response time is defined as the number of minutes elapsed from the time the call was dispatched until the fire engine had left the station. The data‡ are the response times for all calls over a 6-month period. Each call is classified as fire (a response to a fire) or non-fire.

Fire:
```
10  0  7 11  9  5 11 15  7  5 12 14
11 10 24 14 13  8 12  6 10  8 15  9
13  3 12  6 14  5  5 13  4  9  9  3
 4 13 12  4  6  7  6  4  0  9  7 13
20  7  6 11  3
```

Non-fire:
```
15 11 23  0  9  5  7  5  7 10  5  8
 9  9  4 10  8 12  3  8  7  2  4  6
 8 13 23  3 13  5
```

   (a) Graph the response times for fire calls and for non-fire calls. Describe any differences you see between the distributions of response time for the two types of calls.

   (b) Based on the graph in part (a), use an appropriate procedure to determine whether these data contradict the claim that there is no difference in mean response times for these two types of calls.

7.81 A corporate personnel analyst wished to study employee absenteeism at each of two plants, Richmond and Louisville. For samples of 30 employees at each plant, the cumulative numbers of absences over a 3-year period were recorded. The sample data§ follow:

Richmond:
```
18 14 24  5  7  0  8 13  2  0  5 11 10  1  7
 2 21 18  2 12  9  5  9 13 16 11  9 23  5 13
```

Louisville:
```
24  0 18 28 30 51 48  3 14 19 50  9 13 9  4
50 49 15 11 15  9 13  5  6 33 64 12  8 0  3
```

---

* Courtesy of Kim Ogle.

† Courtesy of Tony Woo.

‡ Courtesy of Martha Mitchell and Greg Martin.

§ Courtesy of Chalmers Ward.

(a) Graph the data for the two plants. Does your graph seem to indicate that the average number of days absent differs between the two plants?

(b) Based on the graph in part (a), use an appropriate procedure to determine whether these data provide sufficient support to show that the mean levels of absenteeism differ.

7.82 The professor of a literature class at a university provided a voluntary study session prior to tests. In an attempt to evaluate the effectiveness of the study sessions, the grade on the first test was recorded for students who attended the study session and for those who did not attend. The data* are provided here for the class of 91 students.

```
75  88  75  95  95  75  75  75  85  65  75  95
 1   1   0   1   0   0   0   1   0   0   0   0

85  88  72  82  82  82  85  92  98  78  85  78
 1   1   0   0   0   0   0   0   1   1   1   0

95  95  85  75  72  78  65  75  72  95  98  88
 1   1   0   0   0   0   0   0   0   1   1   1

75  82  85  78  88  92  65  78  88  82  88  78
 1   0   0   1   1   1   0   0   1   1   0   0

75  75  85  95  92  75  95  75  88  85  82  95
 0   0   0   1   0   0   1   0   1   1   0   0

85  95  65  82  75  98  65  98  75  85  85  78
 0   0   0   0   0   0   0   1   0   0   0   1

85  85  75  88  95  92  95  92  88  78  72  75
 1   0   1   0   1   0   1   1   0   0   0   1

92  72  78  92  92  82
 0   0   0   1   1   1
```

Note: 1 = attended the study session;
0 = did not attend.

(a) Describe the designed experiment of this study.

(b) Suggest other factors that might explain some of the random variation present in these data.

(c) Graph the data. Does your graph suggest that a difference exists, on average, between the test scores of the students who attended the study session and those of the students who did not attend?

(d) Does a formal analysis establish that, on average, students make higher test scores if they attend the study session?

7.83 The study "Physical and Performance Characteristics of NCAA Division I Football Players" (*Research Quarterly for Exercise and Sport*, Vol. 61, No. 4, 1990,

pp. 395–401) reported on various performance characteristics of Division I football players for the 1987 season. One performance characteristic of interest was the time for the 40-yard dash. The following data are simulated based on the summary information given in this study and represent independent random samples of running times (in seconds) of football players in top 20 teams and players in non–top-20 teams.

Time (in seconds)

Top 20:	5.08	4.54	4.64	4.59	4.91	5.27	4.76	4.56	
	4.62	5.08	4.89	4.86	4.87	4.65	4.26		
Non–top-20:	4.64	4.61	4.41	5.10	4.63	4.86	4.79	4.36	4.84	4.84
	4.81	5.20	5.11	5.15	4.65	5.44	4.89	5.04	4.84	

(a) Graph the data for the top 20 and non–top-20 players. On average, are any differences in running times apparent to you?

(b) To what extent do these data contradict a claim of no difference in average running time for the 40-yard dash for top 20 and non–top-20 players, on average?

(c) Can you suggest a way to improve the sampling plan to make it more likely that a difference between the two population means would be detected if one exists?

7.84 The study "A Comparison of Women in Small and Large Companies" (*American Journal of Small Business*, Winter 1988, pp. 23–33) reported on biographical data of surveyed women who work for small (fewer than 100 employees) and large companies. Of particular interest were the annual salaries of female managers in small firms and in large firms. The following data are simulated based on updating the summary information given in this study and represent annual salaries (in thousands of dollars) of randomly selected female managers from each type of firm.

Small firms:	44.2	36.7	29.8	21.9	30.6	42.0	17.8
	28.3	37.8	35.6	36.6	17.6	27.1	41.4
Large firms:	28.0	23.8	25.9	29.3	24.3	27.0	35.2
	28.8	17.8	34.2	29.1	34.7	30.0	32.7

(a) Graph the data. On average, are any differences in salaries apparent to you?

(b) To what extend do these data contradict a claim of no difference in average annual salaries of female managers in these two types of companies?

7.85 The paper "Validation of the Rockport Fitness Walking Test in College Males and Females" (*Research Quarterly for Exercise and Sport*, Vol. 65, No. 2, 1994, pp. 152–158) examined aerobic capacity of

---

* Courtesy of Heather Burke.

college males and females using a test procedure known as a Rockport Fitness Walking Test (RFWT). One measure of aerobic capacity is maximal oxygen uptake (VO_2 max in liters per minute). The following data are simulated based on the summary information provided in this study and represent maximal oxygen uptake of randomly selected female and male college students who undergo this test.

Female: 2.22 1.45 1.55 1.96 2.53 2.38 2.43 2.22 2.28 2.45
Male: 4.36 3.41 4.27 2.74 4.12 3.67 2.55 3.35 2.84

(a) Graph the data. On average, are any differences in maximal oxygen uptake for females and males apparent to you?

(b) Determine the extent to which these data indicate higher maximal oxygen uptake for males, on average.

7.86 The March 11, 1996 issue of *Business Week* reported on a Harris poll of 1,004 adults conducted in February 1996 on how Americans feel about certain issues. Of those polled in 1996, 120 indicated a great deal of confidence in the people running big business. In a similar poll of 1,249 adults conducted a year earlier, 237 indicated a great deal of confidence in the people running big business. Based on these polls, is there reason to believe that the proportion of adults in 1996 who have a great deal of confidence in the people running big business is less than that in 1995? Explain.

Case Study 7.1: The Impact of Air Bags on Automobile Safety

The addition of air bags to many automobile models constitutes the most touted effort of manufacturers in recent years to improve automotive safety. One would expect that accident frequency is unaffected, but the severity of injury should decline as a result of the air bag. Some researchers such as Sam Peltzman,* however, have argued that, while the severity of injury might indeed decrease due to mandated safety features, it is accompanied by an offsetting increase in frequency of accidents. This is a serious issue because of its implications regarding the efficacy of governmental safety regulation and insurance rating policies. For example, most insurers offer premium discounts for air-bag-equipped cars on the presumption that insurance claims will be lower in the aggregate. Steve Peterson and George Hoffer† studied data regarding changes in personal injury claims and collision insurance claims attributable to the inclusion of air bags in automobile models. Their conclusion, supporting the findings of Peltzman, was that the effect of adding air bags was to increase the relative frequency of claims filed for personal injury. They offered several possible explanations of the cause of the increase. However, Howard O'Neill, president of the Highway Loss Data Institute (HLDI), responded that Hoffer "either misinterprets our data or he doesn't understand our data. He draws conclusions that are totally invalid."‡

In this case study, you are to analyze the data used by Peterson and Hoffer to decide whether their conclusions seem justified. If you think this is indeed the case, then provide several alternative possible explanations for the changes that accompanied the addition of air bags. State any concerns you have about your conclusions and any limitations of your study.

The data consist of relative personal injury claim frequencies and average collision loss payments for all of the automotive models contained in the HLDI reports for the

---

* Peltzman, Sam, "The Effects of Automobile Safety Regulation," *Journal of Political Economy,* 83 (August 1975).

† Peterson, S. P. and Hoffer, G. E., "The Impact of Airbag Adoption on Relative Personal Injury and Absolute Collision Insurance Claims," *Journal of Consumer Research* 20 (March 1994).

‡ *Source: The Richmond Times-Dispatch,* December 21, 1993.

years 1989, 1990, 1991, and 1992. Relative personal injury claim frequency is a *relative* measure developed by HLDI such that a value of 100 represents the average frequency of personal injury claims for all cars in a given year, after the original data are adjusted for "exposure" (based on number of miles driven) and operator age group. For example, a rating of 150 represents a model for which the personal injury claim frequency is 50% higher than the average for all models in that year. Average collision loss payments are the average dollar amounts of collision claim losses for all vehicles of a given model in a given year. The data appear on the data diskette in a file named CASE0701. This file contains 87 observations (rows) and 13 variables (columns). Each row provides data for one automobile model. The variables are:

c_1 = model name
c_2 = presence of air bag in 1989 (1 = yes; 0 = no)
c_3 = 1989 relative personal injury claim frequency
c_4 = 1989 average collision loss payment
c_5 = presence of air bag in 1990 (1 = yes; 0 = no)
c_6 = 1990 relative personal injury claim frequency
c_7 = 1990 average collision loss payment
c_8 = presence of air bag in 1991 (1 = yes; 0 = no)
c_9 = 1991 relative personal injury claim frequency
c_{10} = 1991 average collision loss payment
c_{11} = presence of air bag in 1992 (1 = yes; 0 = no)
c_{12} = 1992 relative personal injury claim frequency
c_{13} = 1992 average collision loss payment

We suggest that you use separate analyses to address the changes that occurred in relative personal injury frequencies from 1989 to 1990, from 1990 to 1991, and from 1991 to 1992. In like fashion, we suggest that you use separate analyses for studying average collision loss payment data.

Appendix 7

Computer Instructions for Using MINITAB, EXCEL, and JMP IN

MINITAB

Independent Samples: Confidence Intervals and Tests of Hypotheses for the Difference Between Two Population or Process Means

Consider Example 7.3, in which the mean incomes of families from two neighborhoods are compared. To produce the graph in Figure 7.1, first enter the data in a stacked format, with the 28 sample incomes in c1 and the "subscripts" (1s and 2s) to indicate the two neighborhoods in c2. Name c1 and c2 Income and Neighborhood, respectively. Choose GRAPH–PLOT .... In the resulting dialogue box, under GRAPH VARIABLES: specify c1 as Y (the vertical axis) and c2 as X (the horizontal axis). Now click the OPTIONS ... button; in its dialogue box, click the ADD JITTER TO DIRECTION button and click OK twice. (Adding "jitter" helps to distinguish overlapping plotting symbols.)

To obtain the output of the independent samples T procedure for this example, choose STAT–BASIC STATISTICS–2 SAMPLE T .... In the dialogue box, click the SAMPLES IN ONE COLUMN button and enter c1 for SAMPLES and c2 for SUBSCRIPTS; then select NOT EQUAL for the ALTERNATIVE hypothesis and enter the desired CONFIDENCE LEVEL (Minitab's default value is 95 percent). Do not click the ASSUME EQUAL VARIANCES button.

In Example 7.4, we proceed in the same manner as for Example 7.3, with two important exceptions: (1) Since the alternative hypothesis is one-sided, select the alternative LESS THAN; and (2) since the assumption that the population variances are equal is reasonable, click the ASSUME EQUAL VARIANCES button to indicate the use of the pooled T statistic.

Paired Samples: Confidence Intervals and Tests of Hypotheses for the Difference Between Two Population or Process Means

Consider Example 7.7, in which the mean blood pressures of employees before and after participating in a stress-reduction program are compared. To produce a graph like Figure 7.5, first enter subscripts (1s and 2s) indicating "before" and "after" into c1, subscripts to identify the employee (1 through 10) into c2, and the 20 blood pressures into c3. Name c1, c2, and c3 When, Employee, and Pressure, respectively. Choose GRAPH–PLOT . . . . In the dialogue box, (1) enter c3 for Y (the vertical axis); (2) enter c2 for X (the horizontal axis); (3) select FOR EACH–GROUP; (4) enter c1 in the first cell under GROUP VARIABLES . . . ; then click OK. (Steps 3 and 4 make the plotting symbols correspond to the values of c1 for the plotted points.)

To carry out the paired T procedure for Example 7.7, you must first unstack the blood pressure data, placing the resulting two samples ("before" and "after") into c4 and c5, respectively, as described in Appendix 1. Then choose STAT–BASIC STATISTICS–PAIRED T . . . . In the dialogue box, enter c4 for FIRST SAMPLE and c5 for SECOND SAMPLE. Then click the OPTIONS button. In the resulting dialogue box, enter the desired CONFIDENCE LEVEL, specify the null hypothesis value of the population or process mean difference (Minitab's default value is zero), choose the GREATER THAN alternative, and click OK. This produces a paired T test of hypothesis and a confidence interval for the mean difference.

Independent Samples: Confidence Intervals and Tests of Hypotheses for the Difference Between Two Population or Process Proportions

Consider Example 7.8, which calls for a 95% confidence interval for $\pi_1 - \pi_2$ and a test of hypothesis with a two-sided alternative hypothesis. Choose STAT–BASIC STATISTICS–2 PROPORTIONS . . . . In the dialogue box, click SUMMARIZED DATA and enter (1) for FIRST SAMPLE, the number of TRIALS (125) and the number of SUCCESSES (7); (2) for SECOND SAMPLE, the number of TRIALS (100) and the number of SUCCESSES (7); and then click the OPTIONS button. In the OPTIONS dialogue box: For CONFIDENCE LEVEL, specify the desired level of confidence as a percentage. (Minitab's default value is 95 percent.) For TEST DIFFERENCE, specify the null hypothesis value (0). For ALTERNATIVE, specify NOT EQUAL. For USE POOLED ESTIMATE OF P FOR TEST: click to indicate use of the pooled proportion. Click OK twice and you have the desired output.

If your data file consists of the original data (successes and failures, with each observation coded numerically, e.g., 1 and 0), you can still use this procedure. If your data are in two columns, then in the STAT–BASIC STATISTICS–2 PROPORTIONS . . . dialogue box, click SAMPLES IN DIFFERENT COLUMNS and enter the two columns containing the raw data. If your data are in one (stacked) column, with a second column containing numerical indicators of the sample for each observation, then in the STAT–BASIC STATISTICS–2 PROPORTIONS . . . dialogue box, click SAMPLES IN ONE COLUMN; then for SAMPLES, enter the column containing the data and for SUBSCRIPTS, enter the column containing the sample indicators. All other selections are the same as for using summarized data.

EXCEL

Independent Samples: Confidence Intervals and Tests of Hypotheses for the Difference Between Two Population or Process Means

Consider Example 7.3, in which the mean incomes of families from two neighborhoods are compared. To produce a graph like Figure 7.1, enter the income data into a single column by putting the data for the first neighborhood in cells b2 through b15, and the data for the second neighborhood in cells b16 through b29. Now enter 1s in cells a2 through a15 (indicating neighborhood 1) and 2s in cells a16 through a29 (indicating neighborhood 2). Put variable names Neighborhood and Income in cells a1 and b1, respectively. Select the range of cells containing the variable names and the data (a1:b29). Then choose INSERT—CHART . . . . In the CHART WIZARD, (1) click X-Y (SCATTER), then click the upper-left chart subtype option (SCATTER); (2) in the DATA RANGE box, enter the cell range containing the data (a1:b29) and click the SERIES IN COLUMNS button; (3) provide chart title and labels for the axes as desired; (4) indicate whether you wish the scatter diagram to be placed on a new sheet or within the currently active sheet.

To obtain the output of the independent samples T procedure for this example, rearrange the income data into two columns. Use cells a2:a15 for the incomes of the first neighborhood and b2:b15 for the incomes of the second neighborhood. Enter the names Neighborhood 1 and Neighborhood 2 in cells a1 and b1, respectively. To test the hypothesis H_0: $\mu_1 - \mu_2 = 0$ vs. H_a:$\mu_1 - \mu_2 \neq 0$, choose TOOLS—DATA ANALYSIS . . . and select T TEST: TWO-SAMPLE ASSUMING UNEQUAL VARIANCES. In the dialogue box, indicate in the VARIABLE 1 RANGE box the range of cells containing the variable name and the data for the first sample (a1:a15); indicate in the VARIABLE 2 RANGE box the range of cells containing the variable name and the data for the second sample (b1:b15); specify the HYPOTHESIZED MEAN DIFFERENCE to be 0; and click the LABELS button. The output includes the P-values for both one-sided lower-tailed, one-sided upper-tailed, and two-sided alternative hypotheses. In this case, the two-sided P-value is the appropriate choice.

In Example 7.4, we proceed in the same manner as for Example 7.3 except for two differences: (1) after choosing TOOLS—DATA ANALYSIS . . . , select T TEST: TWO-SAMPLE ASSUMING EQUAL VARIANCES (since this time equal population variances were assumed); and (2) the appropriate P-value to use is the $P(T <= t)$ ONE-TAIL value.

Paired Samples: Confidence Intervals and Tests of Hypotheses for the Difference Between Two Population or Process Means

Consider Example 7.7, in which the mean blood pressures of employees before and after participating in a stress-reduction program are compared. To produce the graph in Figure 7.5, enter the employee IDs (1 through 10) in cells a2:a11, place the "before" blood pressures in cells b2:b11, and place the "after" blood pressures in cells c2:c11. Put variable names Employee, Before, and After in cells a1, b1, and c1, respectively.

Select the range of cells containing the variable names and the data (a1:c11). Choose INSERT—CHART. In the CHART WIZARD, (1) click X-Y (SCATTER), then click the upper-left chart subtype option (SCATTER); (2) in the DATA RANGE box, enter the cell range containing the data (a1:c11) and click the SERIES IN COLUMNS button; (3) provide chart title and labels for the axes as desired; (4) indicate whether you wish the scatter diagram to be placed on a new sheet or within the currently active sheet.

To carry out the paired T procedure, choose TOOLS—DATA ANALYSIS . . . and select T-TEST: PAIRED TWO SAMPLE FOR MEANS. In the dialogue box, indicate in the VARIABLE 1 RANGE box the range of cells containing the variable name and the data for the "Before" sample (b1:b11); indicate in the VARIABLE 2 RANGE box the range of cells containing the variable name and the data for the "After" sample (c1:c11), specify the HYPOTHESIZED MEAN DIFFERENCE to be 0, and click the LABELS button. The output includes the P-values for both one-sided and two-sided alternative hypotheses. In this case, the one-sided P-value is the appropriate choice.

To develop a confidence interval for the population mean of the paired differences, you must first create the column of pairwise differences in cells d1:d11. Enter the variable name DIFF in cell d1. Type into cell d2: = b2 − c2; then drag the fill handle for d2 down through d11. Following the procedure described in Appendix 6, choose TOOLS   DATA ANALYSIS PLUS and select INFERENCE ABOUT A MEAN (SIGMA UNKNOWN). In the BLOCK COORDINATES dialogue box, enter the range of cells containing the pairwise differences (d2:d11); and click OK. In the INFERENCE dialogue box, click INTERVAL ESTIMATE. In the CONFIDENCE LEVEL INPUT dialogue box, enter .95 (as a decimal fraction, not a percentage), and click OK.

Independent Samples: Confidence Intervals and Tests of Hypotheses for the Difference Between Two Population or Process Proportions

Consider Example 7.8, which calls for a 95% confidence interval for $\pi_1 - \pi_2$ and a test of hypotheses with a two-sided alternative hypothesis. If the data are in summarized form, as in Example 7.8, you must use Excel's formulas. For sample 1, enter the sample size and the number of defectives (i.e., successes) in cells a2 and b2. Put the proportion of defectives in c2 by typing =b2/a2. Similarly, put the sample size, number of defectives, and proportion of defectives for the second sample into d2, e2, and f2, respectively. Put the difference between the sample proportions into g2 by typing =c2−f2. Put the standard error of $p_1 - p_2$ into h2 by typing =(c2*(1−c2)/a2 + f2*(1−f2)/d2)^.5. Put the lower 95% confidence limit into i2 by typing =g2−1.96*h2. Put the upper 95% confidence limit into j2 by typing =g2 + 1.96*h2. If desired, place labels for these values in cells a1 through j1.

To test the null hypothesis that the two population proportions are equal versus a two-sided alternative hypothesis, enter 0 in cell a5. Enter the pooled proportion into b5 by typing =(b2 + e2)/(a2 + d2). Put the standard error of $p_1 - p_2$ under the null hypothesis into c5 by typing =(b5*(1 − b5)*(1/a2 + 1/d2))^.5. Put the P-value into d5 by typing =2*NORMDIST(g2, 0, c5, 1). If desired, place labels for these values into cells a4 through d4.

If your data consist of the original values (successes and failures, with each observation coded numerically, e.g., 1 and 0), you can still use Excel. Enter the first sample into cells a1 through a125 and the second sample into cells b1 through b100. Do not label the columns. Choose TOOLS–DATA ANALYSIS PLUS . . . , then select INFERENCE ABOUT TWO PROPORTIONS. For BLOCK COORDINATES, enter a1:b125. Next, specify the code representing 'success' to be 1. Next, click INTERVAL ESTIMATE. Finally, enter .95 to specify the confidence level. In order to test hypotheses, follow the same sequence, except that in the INFERENCE dialogue box, click TEST OF HYPOTHESES (CASE 1) rather than INTERVAL ESTIMATE.

JMP IN

Independent Samples: Confidence Intervals and Tests of Hypotheses for the Difference Between Two Population or Process Means

First consider Example 7.4, in which the times to complete a task for two samples of subjects working under two levels of noise are compared. To produce the graph in Figure 7.2, enter the data in a stacked format, with the 32 sample times in COLUMN 1 and the indices (1s and 2s) to indicate the two samples in COLUMN 2. Name these columns TIME and LEVEL, respectively. Set the role of TIME to Y and the role of LEVEL to X. Choose ANALYZE–FIT Y BY X. You can enhance the comparison of the two sample means by clicking the DISPLAY check mark box and selecting CON-NECT MEANS and JITTER.

To produce the output of the independent samples T procedure for this example, click the ANALYSIS check mark box and select MEANS, ANOVA/t-TEST The output of interest here is found in the t-TEST area.

In Example 7.3, we proceed in the same manner as for Example 7.4, with two important exceptions: (1) Because the assumption that the population variances are equal is not reasonable here, click the ANALYSIS check mark box and select UNEQUAL VARIANCES (instead of MEANS, ANOVA/t-TEST). This produces a set of output called TESTS THAT THE VARIANCES ARE EQUAL. In the lower part of this output is an enclosed output called WELCH ANOVA TESTING MEANS EQUAL, ALLOWING STD'S NOT EQUAL. Here you will find the appropriate T-value (under t-TEST) and P-value (under PROB > F) for a two-sided alternative. (2) Since the alternative hypothesis is one-sided, the correct P-value is one-half the value provided in (1) under Prob > |t|.

Paired Samples: Confidence Intervals and Tests of Hypotheses for the Difference Between Two Population or Process Means

Consider Example 7.7, in which the mean blood pressures of employees before and after participating in a stress-reduction program are compared. To produce a graph like Figure 7.5, first enter indices identifying the employee (1 through 10) into COLUMN 1, the "before" blood pressures into COLUMN 2, and the "after" blood pressures into COLUMN 3. Name these columns EMPLOYEE, BEFORE, and AFTER, respectively. Set the role of EMPLOYEE to X and the other roles to Y. Choose GRAPH–OVERLAY PLOTS. Click each check mark box and click CONNECT (this "unselects" the

CONNECT option, which starts out selected by default). Also click each check mark box, select OVERLAY MARKERS, and choose the desired plotting symbol.

To carry out the paired T procedure for Example 7.7, you must first compute the differences between all 10 pairs of blood pressures. Add COLUMN 4 and name it DIFF. Set its role to Y and set all other variables' roles to *NONE*. In the CALCULATOR window for DIFF:

1. Select BEFORE from the *column selector list.*
2. Type – (the minus key on your computer's keyboard) and press the ENTER key.
3. Select AFTER from the *column selector list.*
4. Close the CALCULATOR window.

Choose ANALYZE–DISTRIBUTION OF Y. In the DIFF check mark box, select TEST MEAN = VALUE . . . . In the dialogue box that appears, enter 0 in the SPECIFY HYPOTHESIZED VALUE FOR MEAN box. The desired output appears in the TEST MEAN = VALUE area, below MOMENTS. Notice that a 95% confidence interval for the mean difference also appears in the MOMENTS area of the output.

Independent Samples: Confidence Intervals and Tests of Hypotheses for the Difference Between Two Population or Process Proportions

JMP IN does not provide a confidence interval for the difference between two population or process proportions, but does perform hypothesis testing on the difference between two proportions. Consider Example 7.8, which calls for a test of hypothesis with a two-sided alternative hypothesis. Enter the frequencies (counts) of successes and failures for both samples in COLUMN 1; (i.e., enter 125, 7, 100, 7, in order) and set the data type and role to CONTINUOUS and FREQ, respectively. Enter the corresponding sample IDs in COLUMN 2 (i.e., enter 1, 1, 2, 2, in order) and set the data type and role to NOMINAL and X, respectively. Enter the outcomes represented by the COLUMN 1 values into COLUMN 3 (i.e., enter S, F, S, F), and set the data type and role to NOMINAL and Y, respectively. Select ANALYZE—FIT Y BY X. The P-value for a two-sided alternative hypothesis appears in the row named PEARSON under the heading Prob > Chisq. (This value differs slightly from the P-value in Example 7.8 because of a minor difference in methodology.) If your alternative hypothesis is one-sided, divide the printed value by 2. If your data file consists of the original data (successes and failures), you can still use JMP IN. Enter your raw data for both samples in COLUMN 1 as one (stacked) column, and set the data type and role to NOMINAL and Y, respectively. In COLUMN 2, enter indicators (such as 0s and 1s) of the sample for each observation and set the data type and role to NOMINAL and X, respectively. Select ANALYZE—FIT Y BY X, and the output will be the same as for summarized data.

Chapter 8

Analysis of Variance

8.1 Bridging to New Topics

In Chapters 1 and 7, you were introduced to some fundamental principles of designed experiments. In Chapter 7, you saw how these principles can be used to compare two levels of a single factor (that is, two population or process means) using either independent random samples or paired random samples. The need often arises to understand differences among more than two levels of a factor. The **statistical design of experiments** is a powerful tool for this purpose. It has become an especially important tool for understanding the effects on a response variable of different levels of a factor or factors, thereby providing a basis for process improvement.

As we showed in Chapter 7, simple graphical techniques can be helpful in understanding differences. In many applications, however, it is not obvious from graphs alone whether the levels of a factor truly differ in their effects on a response variable. This is especially true in studies that involve more than one factor. In such situations, a more rigorous method of analysis via statistical inference is required. In this chapter, we introduce a procedure called **analysis of variance** (abbreviated **ANOVA**) that serves this purpose. As in Chapter 7, the statistical designs of this chapter deal with independent random samples and random samples selected in blocks, where blocking is a direct extension of the concept of pairing.

8.2   Comparing More Than Two Population or Process Means with Independent Samples

To extend the idea of comparing two population or process means to any number of population or process means, let's revisit the example from Chapter 7 involving two property appraisers. Recall that the manager of an appraisal service suspected that differences between individual appraisers were causing undesirable variation in appraisal amounts. He wanted to conduct an experiment to determine whether his suspicion was true. If his suspicion were confirmed, he would initiate a training program to standardize the appraisers' outputs. Let's now extend this example by assuming that there are three appraisers, A, B, and C, and that the manager has identified 15 similar properties to be used in the experiment. Five properties are to be assigned randomly to each appraiser. Notice that this is a direct extension of the independent samples design discussed in Chapter 7.

Suppose the experiment yields the data shown in Table 8.1 (where the units are thousands of dollars). First, let's examine the summary data. We see sample means of 89.6, 91.8, and 86.8 for the three appraisers. The manager should first ask himself whether these differences are large enough to warrant the initiation of a training program. If the answer is yes, he should first consider the possibility that the appraisers do not really differ on average and that the observed differences simply reflect random sampling variation. To address this issue in Chapter 7, we utilized the pooled T procedure (the one based on the assumption that the population variances are equal). Now that we have three appraisers, however, a different method of analysis is needed: the analysis of variance.

Table 8.1

Sample data for three appraisers

A	B	C
90	93	92
94	96	88
91	92	84
85	88	83
88	90	87
$\bar{X}_A = 89.6$	$\bar{X}_B = 91.8$	$\bar{X}_C = 86.8$
$S_A^2 = 11.3$	$S_B^2 = 9.2$	$S_C^2 = 12.7$
$n_A = 5$	$n_B = 5$	$n_C = 5$

The basic assumptions of the analysis of variance are the same as those for the pooled T procedure:

1. *Independent samples.*   The three random samples are selected so that they are independent of one another.

2. *Normal distributions.* The distribution of appraisal values for all properties evaluated by an individual appraiser is assumed to be adequately represented by a normal distribution.

3. *Equal population or process variances.* The normal distributions of appraisal values are assumed to have equal variances; that is, $\sigma_A^2 = \sigma_B^2 = \sigma_C^2 = \sigma^2$, where σ^2 denotes the common variance. The variances σ_A^2, σ_B^2, and σ_C^2 measure the inherent variation within each respective population or process.

4. *Stable processes.* In process studies, we often wish to compare the means of several processes. In general, the processes that are being compared are assumed to be stable—that is, free from assignable causes of variation.

Simply stating these assumptions does not guarantee that they are valid. It is important in any statistical analysis to check the validity of the assumptions. A careful examination of a graph of the sample data is usually sufficient for this purpose.

We wish to test the null hypothesis

$$H_0: \quad \mu_A = \mu_B = \mu_C$$

(where μ_A, μ_B, and μ_C represent the unknown process means for appraisers A, B, and C, respectively, for properties such as those in the samples) against the alternative hypothesis

$$H_a: \quad \text{At least one of these means is different from the rest}$$

If the data contradict the null hypothesis sufficiently, thus indicating that the appraisers differ on average, then these results constitute a sound basis for managerial action.

8.2.1 Partitioning the Variation in the Sample Data

Obviously, there are differences among the values of $\bar{X}_A$, $\bar{X}_B$, and $\bar{X}_C$ as given in Table 8.1. There will always be differences among the sample means because of random sampling variation, even if the three samples were taken from appraisal processes with identical means. The crucial question is whether the observed differences are large enough (i.e., beyond sampling error) to warrant the contradiction of the null hypothesis. If the sample means differ by a larger amount than can be reasonably attributed to random sampling variation, then we conclude that there are differences among the means of the three appraisal processes (μ_A, μ_B, and μ_C).

Before attempting to answer this question, we need to review the factors that might account for the observed differences among the sample means. In other words, we need to examine the *potential sources of variation in the sample data*.

1. One potential source of variation is the *appraisers.* Differences among their process means, if they exist, would cause differences among the sample means. Indeed, the existence of differences among the appraisers' process means is precisely what we are trying to detect.

2. As in Chapter 7, the other sources of variation in the sample data are differences among property values and appraiser inconsistency. We may regard both to be *random* sources of variation. The variation caused by property differences is random because of the random allocation of the 15 properties to

the three appraisers. And it seems reasonable to assume that the inconsistency of a single appraiser affects his or her appraisal outcomes in random fashion. The variation in the data due to the combined effects of all other factors is called *random variation,* or *random error.* It is highly desirable that random variation in sample data be minor. For example, if the differences among the property values are not minor or if appraiser inconsistency is appreciable, then differences among the appraisers, even if they exist, may not be discernible.

Let's examine graphically these sources of variation in the appraiser data, illustrated in Figure 8.1. The first source, appraiser differences, can be seen by comparing the sample observations for each appraiser, as a group, with those of the other appraisers. Notice that the group of observations for the second appraiser tends to be higher than those for the first and third appraisers. Suppose we were to visually locate the center of each group of sample observations and connect the centers with a line. If the line is essentially parallel to the *x*-axis, there would be no evidence that differences exist among the three appraisers, on average. At first glance, that does not appear to be the case here, but we should be careful and avoid reaching a hasty conclusion. Unless the result is obvious, a more formal analysis should be carried out to confirm this tentative conclusion.

Figure 8.1

Graphical analysis of the appraiser data

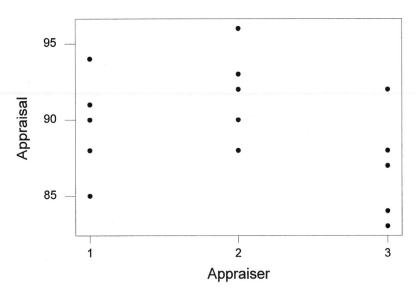

Now let's examine the second source of variation, random error. It is characterized by the spread within the group of observations associated with each appraiser. Visually, the spread is roughly the range of the sample data, the vertical distance from the largest observation to the smallest. This within-sample variation should be minor, since it represents random error. The greater the within-sample variation, the more difficult it is to detect differences among the appraisers.

In comparison to differences among the three appraisers, the spread within each appraiser's values appears to be fairly appreciable. Consequently, the graph in Figure 8.1 does not make it obvious whether there are differences among the appraisers, on average. Therefore, we must rely on a more formal inferential procedure for this purpose. It is also important to notice that the spreads within each of the three samples

Figure 8.2

An illustration of the graphical interpretation of within-sample variation versus among-sample variation

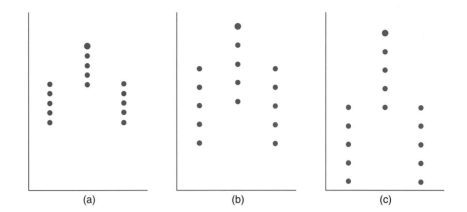

appear to be about the same. Large differences in the within-sample spreads would suggest that the assumption of equal variances might be unrealistic.

As suggested by Figure 8.1, *the key to determining graphically the existence of differences among the appraisers, on average, is the amount of variation among the samples relative to the amount of variation within the samples.* Figure 8.2 illustrates this point. In Figure 8.2(a), the population or process means appear to differ. It is more difficult to reach this conclusion with confidence from Figure 8.2(b) because the within-sample variation is considerably greater than that in part (a). Now consider part (c). It is once again clear that the population or process means differ because the center of the second sample group is much higher than those of the other two groups, even though the within-sample variations are about the same as those in part (b).

8.2.2 The Analysis of Variance Approach: Partitioning the Total Variation in the Data

While the graphical approach is a key first step in our overall analysis, at the same time we need a rigorous method of inference such as the **analysis of variance** procedure. *Analysis of variance is an inferential procedure based on the notion that the total variation in the sample data can be partitioned in such a way that we can estimate the contributions of factors that may cause variation.* The aim of analysis of variance is to discern which factors truly account for the variation in the sample data.

Since the analysis of variance is an inferential procedure, we have to resolve the two issues that are key to any method of inference (as presented in Section 5.4). That is, we must identify the best statistic for testing the equality of several population or process means, and we must determine the sampling distribution of that statistic. In analysis of variance, we develop a statistic to assess the amount of variation in the data *among the samples,* and we develop a statistic to assess the amount of variation *within the samples.* The ratio of these two statistics (the statistic for among-sample variation divided by the statistic for within-sample variation) is the best statistic for analysis of variance inferences. If the ratio is sufficiently large, then the variation among the samples is sufficiently larger than the variation within the samples. As in the graphical analysis, this would indicate that differences exist among the means of the population or processes being compared.

In general, we call the populations or processes being studied the **treatments.** If we are studying the effect of a factor on the response variable at different levels, these levels are the treatments. The treatments in our example are the three appraisers. Figure 8.3 illustrates the partitioning of the total variation in the sample data into two components: variation because of differences among the treatment means (i.e., variation among the samples, or among the three appraisers in our example), and variation due to random error (i.e., variation within the samples).

Figure 8.3

The partitioning of total variation

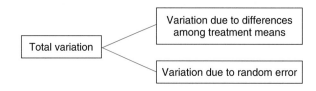

In the following sections, we show how to quantify these components of variation. After developing expressions for each component of variation, we return to the development of the best statistic.

Quantifying the Total Variation

We use the computer to carry out analysis of variance computations. However, you need to understand the basic formulation for each component of variation; we illustrate with simple data sets. As you learned in Chapter 2, the total variation within any data set can be determined by computing the squared deviations of the sample observations from the mean of the sample observations and then summing them. As in Chapter 2, this sum of squared deviations is called the **total sum of squares** and is denoted by **SST.** For the appraiser example, the average of all observations is $\bar{X} = (90 + 94 + \cdots + 83 + 87)/15 = 89.4$. Then the total sum of squares for these sample data is

$$\text{SST} = (90 - 89.4)^2 + (94 - 89.4)^2 + \cdots + (83 - 89.4)^2 + (87 - 89.4)^2 = 195.6$$

What do you think the total sum of squares would be if, as unlikely as it may seem, all of the sample observations were identical? The answer is 0, since there would be no deviation of the observations from their average value. So, the larger the value of SST, the greater the variation over the entire set of sample data.

Quantifying the Total Variation Among Sample Means

One of the components of SST accounts for the differences among the sample means for the treatments (the three appraisers). This component is determined by computing the squared deviation of each sample mean from the overall mean, multiplying each of these squared deviations by the corresponding sample size, and summing over all treatments. The resulting quantity is called the **sum of squares for treatments** (or **treatment sum of squares**) and is denoted **SSTR.** For the sample data in Table 8.1, the treatment sum of squares is

$$\begin{aligned} \text{SSTR} &= n_A(\bar{X}_A - \bar{X})^2 + n_B(\bar{X}_B - \bar{X})^2 + n_C(\bar{X}_C - \bar{X})^2 \\ &= 5(89.6 - 89.4)^2 + 5(91.8 - 89.4)^2 + 5(86.8 - 89.4)^2 \\ &= 62.8 \end{aligned}$$

What do you think the treatment sum of squares would be if the sample means were identical? The answer is 0 because the overall mean would have the same value. So, the larger the value of SSTR, the greater the differences among the sample means. Now, suppose the sample means differ. Does this necessarily imply that the process means for the three appraisers are different? Not necessarily. If there were no differences among the appraisers, on average, the *sample* means would still differ to some degree because of variation among the properties the appraisers were randomly assigned to appraise and the appraisers' inconsistencies. Thus, *the treatment sum of squares measures the variation among the sample means caused by treatment differences and random error.*

Quantifying the Variation Due to Random Error

Recall that the spreads of the observations within the samples reflect random error variation. The random error component of SST is determined by computing the squared deviations of the individual observations in a given sample from the mean of that sample, and then summing these deviations over *all* observations in the entire data set. Since this quantity represents the contribution of random error, it is called the **sum of squares for error** (or **error sum of squares**) and is denoted by **SSE.** For the sample data in Table 8.1, the sum of squares for error is

$$SSE = (X_{1A} - \bar{X}_A)^2 + \cdots + (X_{5A} - \bar{X}_A)^2$$

$$(90 - 89.6)^2 + \cdots + (88 - 89.6)^2 \quad \text{First appraiser's sample}$$

$$+ (X_{1B} - \bar{X}_B)^2 + \cdots + (X_{5B} - \bar{X}_B)^2$$

$$(93 - 91.8)^2 + \cdots + (90 - 91.8)^2 \quad \text{Second appraiser's sample}$$

$$+ (X_{1C} - \bar{X}_C)^2 + \cdots + (X_{5C} - \bar{X}_C)^2$$

$$(92 - 86.8)^2 + \cdots + (87 - 86.8)^2 \quad \text{Third appraiser's sample}$$

$$= 132.8$$

What do you think the error sum of squares would be if all the observations within each appraiser's sample were the same (but were not necessarily equal to those for the other appraisers)? Once again, the answer is 0; there would be no variation of an appraiser's individual observations from the average of his or her sample. The larger the value of SSE, the greater the variation among the data values within each sample.

For the appraiser data, we have determined the total sum of squares, the treatment sum of squares, and the error sum of squares to be SST = 195.6, SSTR = 62.8, and SSE = 132.8. Notice that adding the treatment sum of squares and the error sum of squares results in the total sum of squares: 62.8 + 132.8 = 195.6. This example illustrates the *partitioning* of the total sum of squares, as shown in Figure 8.3. Therefore, the partitioning of the total sum of squares yields the important general relationship

$$SST = SSTR + SSE \tag{8.1}$$

Expression (8.1) states that *the total sum of squares equals the treatment sum of squares plus the error sum of squares.* This relationship is true in general for any number of treatments, resulting in a corresponding number of independent samples.

We discussed a graphical way to analyze data to determine whether population or process means differ. This analysis was based on a visual comparison of the variation of data *among* the samples to the variation *within* the samples. We have now developed a way to quantify the total among-sample variation (SSTR) and the total within-sample variation (SSE). It would not be proper to compare the values of SSTR and SSE directly, however, because each is a *total*. Thus, the greater the number of treatments under consideration, the greater the value of SSTR tends to be. The mere fact that we are comparing, say, ten treatments rather than three treatments should not affect a consideration of whether treatment differences exist. Similarly, the greater the number of observations within each sample, the greater the value of SSE tends to be. Before these quantities can be compared in a meaningful way, we need to transform them into *averages*; that is, we must convert SSTR to the *average* variation among the samples and SSE to the *average* variation within the samples.

Quantifying the Average Variations Among and Within Samples: Mean Squares

In Chapter 2, you learned that the value of the sample variance S^2 of any sample data provides an estimate of the average squared deviation of population or process observations from the population or process mean; it is obtained by dividing the total sum of squares SST by the associated degrees of freedom $(n-1)$. In similar fashion, the average variation among the sample means is obtained by dividing the treatment sum of squares SSTR by the degrees of freedom for treatments. This quantity is known as the **mean square for treatments** (or treatment mean square) and is denoted by **MSTR.**

In general, if there are k treatments, the treatment sum of squares has $k-1$ degrees of freedom. So, for the appraiser example, SSTR has $k-1=3-1=2$ degrees of freedom, because there are $k=3$ appraisers. Thus, the among-sample variance (i.e., variation attributed to differences among the appraisers, on average) is

$$MSTR = \frac{SSTR}{k-1} = \frac{62.8}{3-1} = 31.4$$

Now we need to determine the average variation within the samples (i.e., variation due to random error). The within-sample variance is obtained by dividing the error sum of squares SSE by its associated degrees of freedom. *The degrees of freedom for the error sum of squares is the sum of the degrees of freedom for each independent sample.* For the appraiser example, there are $5-1=4$ degrees of freedom for each of the three independent samples. Thus, the degrees of freedom for the within-sample variance is 12. In general, the number of degrees of freedom for error works out to be the total number of observations in the sample data (n) minus the number of treatments (k). The quantity SSE divided by its degrees of freedom is known as the **mean square for error** (or error mean square) and is denoted by **MSE.** Therefore, the within-sample variance for the appraiser example is

$$MSE = \frac{SSE}{n-k} = \frac{132.8}{12} = 11.0667$$

The mean square for error is actually a direct extension of the pooled variance S_p^2 used in Chapter 7 for the comparison of means based on two independent random samples. Recall that the unknown population variances σ_A^2, σ_B^2, and σ_C^2 characterize the variation within each appraiser's process. So the corresponding sample variances S_A^2, S_B^2, and S_C^2 characterize the variation within each appraiser's sample. Since population or process variances are assumed to be equal, their common value σ^2 can be estimated by pooling the sample variances, taking into account their respective sample sizes as we did for two independent samples. With the appraiser example used as an illustration, this means that

$$MSE = \frac{(n_A - 1)S_A^2 + (n_B - 1)S_B^2 + (n_C - 1)S_C^2}{(n_A - 1) + (n_B - 1) + (n_C - 1)}$$

$$= \frac{(5 - 1)(11.3) + (5 - 1)(9.2) + (5 - 1)(12.7)}{4 + 4 + 4}$$

$$= \frac{132.8}{12}$$

$$= 11.0667$$

which is precisely the same as the value we already computed for MSE. Notice also that the numerator, 132.8, is the value we computed previously for SSE.

Figure 8.4 illustrates these quantities in the context of the graphical analysis of Figure 8.1. We now use these quantities to develop a more rigorous procedure for discerning differences among treatments, on average.

Figure 8.4

The correspondence of the quantities MSTR and MSE with the graphical ANOVA display of Figure 8.1

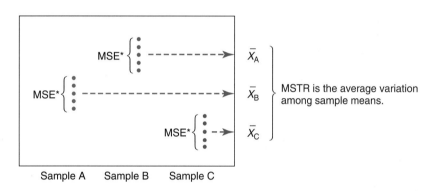

*MSE is the average within-sample variation.

The Best Statistic for the ANOVA Procedure

We now have developed statistics that quantify the amount of among-sample variation (MSTR) and the amount of within-sample variation (MSE). *The key statistic in the analysis of variance procedure is the ratio* MSTR/MSE. The larger this ratio, the greater the variation among the samples in comparison to the variation within the samples, and therefore the stronger the evidence against the null hypothesis of no differences among the population or process means.

The F Distribution

You should now realize that the testing of statistical hypotheses requires that we know the sampling distribution of the statistic being used under the (tentative) assumption that the null hypothesis is true. The sampling distribution of the ratio MSTR/MSE is the **F distribution** with $k - 1$ numerator degrees of freedom and $n - k$ denominator degrees of freedom, *if the null hypothesis is true.* The best statistic for the analysis of variance procedure is

$$F = \frac{MSTR}{MSE} \tag{8.2}$$

Like the T distribution, an F distribution is a function of its degrees of freedom. But unlike the T distribution, an F distribution has two kinds of degrees of freedom: the degrees of freedom associated with MSTR (the numerator degrees of freedom), and the degrees of freedom associated with MSE (the denominator degrees of freedom). The degrees of freedom are denoted by v_1 and v_2, respectively.

A random variable with an F distribution cannot take on negative values. This is clear from Expression (8.2); notice that neither of its components can be negative. An F distribution is centered about the value 1, is skewed to the right, and its theoretical range of values is from 0 to infinity. The shape of the F distribution is illustrated in Figure 8.5.

Figure 8.5

The shape of the F distribution

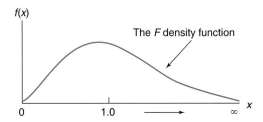

Like the normal and T distributions, the F distribution is included in most statistical software packages, in addition to being widely tabulated. Since an F distribution depends on two degrees of freedom values, reasonably complete F tables exist only as an entire volume. In this book, you can find quantile F values for various combinations of degrees of freedom corresponding to the probabilities of .01, .025, .05, .1, .9, .95, .975, and .99 in Table D of the Appendix. A separate table is given for each of these probabilities.

To use this table, first find the desired probability (identified as area "A," which represents the area to the left of the corresponding quantile value). Then find the numerator degrees of freedom v_1 from the column headings and the denominator degrees of freedom v_2 from the row headings. The F value corresponding to the degrees of freedom v_1 and v_2 is a quantile value, since the area to the left of it is the desired probability.

For the appraiser example, if the null hypothesis is correct, the sampling distribution of this statistic is the F distribution with $v_1 = k - 1 = 2$ and $v_2 = n - k = 12$ degrees of freedom. Notice that large values of this ratio indicate considerable variation among the samples compared to the variation within the samples. In fact, if H_0 is indeed correct, we expect MSTR $\approx$ MSE so that MSTR/MSE $\approx$ 1. If MSTR is much larger than MSE (or equivalently, MSTR/MSE is much greater than 1), it is reasonable to attribute the much larger variation among the samples to differences among the population or process means. Therefore, *the sample data contradict the null hypothesis only for large values of F = MSTR/MSE. As a result, the analysis of variance is an upper one-sided procedure.* As usual, the smaller the P-value, the less plausible the null hypothesis and the more certain we can be that the population or process means differ.

Let's complete the analysis of variance procedure for the appraiser example. The value of the F statistic is

$$F = \frac{31.4}{11.0667} = 2.84$$

The P-value for $F = 2.84$ is determined by computer to be .098; that is, there is a .098 probability of observing an F value of 2.84 or larger if the null hypothesis of no treatment differences is true. Therefore, although there is some evidence of differences among the three appraisers, on average, the evidence is not overwhelming. If there are differences among the appraisers, on average, the random variation within samples has been too great for the procedure to detect the differences with great confidence.

Notice that the P-value for $F = 2.84$ cannot be obtained directly from Table D of the Appendix. For 2 and 12 degrees of freedom, we find $f_{.90,2,12} = 2.81$ and $f_{.95,2,12} = 3.89$. Since 2.84 lies between these two values, we know the P-value must be between .05 and .10 (and, as indicated, it is actually .098).

Practical Implications for the Appraiser Example

What should the manager do since the results are not clear-cut? If the differences among the appraisers' sample means were large enough to concern the manager, then he should attempt to reduce the amount of random variation in the data. For example, this could be achieved by blocking with respect to properties. The appraisers could evaluate the same set of properties. In this case, each property would provide a block of data. Blocking is discussed in Section 8.3. If the observed differences among the appraisers are considered negligible, then there is no need to enlarge the study.

The determination of the sums of squares (SST, SSTR, SSE), degrees of freedom, mean squares (MSTR, MSE), the value of the F statistic (hereafter referred to as the F-value), and the corresponding P-value constitutes the analysis of variance procedure. These results are usually collected and displayed in what is known as an **analysis of variance table.** The ANOVA table provides a convenient way for testing the null hypothesis. Table 8.2 is the analysis of variance table for the appraiser example. Notice that the sources contributing to the variation in the sample data are listed in the column "Sources of Variation," the degrees of freedom are displayed in the column "df," the sums of squares are displayed in the column "SS," the mean squares are displayed in the column "MS" and the F-value and P-value are given. An ANOVA table is readily obtained by using virtually any statistical software, as we will shortly illustrate.

Table 8.2

The ANOVA table for the appraiser example

Source of Variation	df	SS	MS	F-value	P-value
Appraisers	2	62.8	31.4	2.84	.098
Error	12	132.8	11.0667		
Total variation	14	195.6			

In Table 8.2, notice that the total degrees of freedom is $n - 1 = 15 - 1 = 14$. The total degrees of freedom is simply the degrees of freedom associated with the variance of the entire sample of $n = 15$ observations. Notice also that the degrees of freedom associated with appraisers and the degrees of freedom associated with random error sum to the total degrees of freedom: $2 + 12 = 14$. This is true in general. Therefore, not only can the total sum of squares be partitioned into sums of squares for treatments and random error, but the total degrees of freedom can be partitioned in the same way.

8.2.3 Generalizing the Analysis of Variance Procedure to k Independent Samples

We rely on the use of a computer to determine an analysis of variance table. Before we illustrate computer usage, you need to understand how to generalize the preceding analysis to any number of independent samples with respect to degrees of freedom, mean squares, and the ANOVA table.

Degrees of Freedom

There are $k - 1$ degrees of freedom associated with SSTR, there are $n - k$ degrees of freedom associated with SSE, and there are $n - 1$ degrees of freedom for SST. As we pointed out for the appraiser example, the degrees of freedom are additive; that is,

$$n - 1 \;\; = \;\; (k - 1) \;\; + \;\; (n - k) \tag{8.3}$$

$$\text{Total df} \;\; = \;\; \text{treatments df} \;\; + \;\; \text{random error df}$$

where n is the total number of observations in the entire sample data array, and k is the number of treatments.

It is quite helpful to remember that, in general, the degrees of freedom for SST is 1 less than the total number of observations in the data array, and the degrees of freedom for SSTR is 1 less than the number of treatments. The degrees of freedom for SSE can be determined by subtraction.

Mean Squares

As we have illustrated, the mean squares are determined by dividing each component's sum of squares by its corresponding degrees of freedom. The mean squares are

$$\text{MSTR} = \frac{\text{SSTR}}{k - 1} \tag{8.4}$$

and

$$\text{MSE} = \frac{\text{SSE}}{n - k} \tag{8.5}$$

The Analysis of Variance Procedure

To test the null hypothesis

$$H_0: \quad \mu_1 = \mu_2 = \cdots = \mu_k$$

against the alternative

$$H_a: \quad \text{At least one of these means is different from the rest}$$

we compare the among-sample variance to the within-sample variance by forming the ratio $F = \text{MSTR}/\text{MSE}$. If the null hypothesis is true, then the sampling distribution is the F distribution with $k - 1$ and $n - k$ degrees of freedom. The analysis of variance is an upper one-sided procedure because evidence against the null hypothesis exists only when the among-sample variance MSTR is large in comparison to the within-sample variance MSE. The smaller the P-value corresponding to the determined F-value, the

Table 8.3

General ANOVA table for k independent samples

Source of Variation	df	SS	MS	F-value	P-value
Treatments Error	$k - 1$ $n - k$	SSTR SSE	MSTR MSE	MSTR/MSE	$P(F^* > \text{MSTR/MSE})$
Total variation	$n - 1$	SST			

*Statistic has an F distribution with $k - 1$ and $n - k$ degrees of freedom.

stronger the sample evidence against the null hypothesis. The general ANOVA table that consolidates the analysis of variance information for k treatments (k independent samples) is shown in Table 8.3.

Using the Computer

Although different software may use different labels, virtually all provide an ANOVA table containing the pertinent quantities that we have presented.

We now illustrate computer output from Minitab, Excel, and JMP IN; instructions are provided in the chapter appendix.

EXAMPLE 8.1

Does it pay to use more ceiling insulation in residential houses? Obviously, the cost of ceiling insulation is related to the amount used. Since the ceiling insulation is regarded as an important factor in heating a home, the amount to use becomes an important consideration. The following example illustrates this kind of situation.

The sample data that follow are the kilowatt-hours (in hundreds) used in a given month by a heating systems of a sample of similar houses as a function of five different amount of ceiling insulation (in inches).

4 in.	6 in.	8 in.	10 in.	12 in.
14.4	14.5	13.8	13.0	13.1
14.8	14.1	14.1	13.4	12.8
15.2	14.6	13.7	13.2	12.9
14.3	14.2	13.6		13.2
14.6		14.0		13.3
				12.7

(a) Based on a graphical analysis, what do these data indicate about the effect of the thickness of ceiling insulation on energy consumption?

(b) Apply the analysis of variance procedure to these sample data. Is your tentative conclusion from part (a) confirmed?

Solution

We assume that each amount of ceiling insulation (the treatments in this example) represents a population of energy consumption from which the indicated sample has been obtained. Also, we assume that the distributions of the populations for each amount of ceiling insulation are normal with equal variances. The use of very similar houses means that all houses are essentially the same size, have the same type of heating system, have the same amount of wall insulation, have the same type of

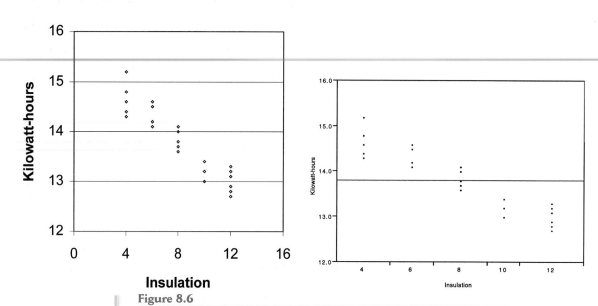

Figure 8.6

Excel and JMP IN graphs of sample data for Example 8.1

weather stripping, and are located in the same geographic area. This assures that the variation in energy consumption caused by differences among the houses within each amount of ceiling insulation is attributed to random error. Accordingly, the total variation is made up of the variation caused by differences among the amounts of ceiling insulation (the treatments) and random error variation.

(a) The variations within the samples and among the samples are illustrated graphically in Figure 8.6. Notice that the number of kilowatt-hours per month decreases steadily as the amount of ceiling insulation increases. It is apparent from this figure that differences exist in the population mean numbers of kilowatt-hours used over the five amounts of ceiling insulation considered. In addition, the spreads in the samples for the five levels do not appear to differ enough to cause concern about the equal variance assumption.

(b) Minitab, Excel, and JMP IN analysis of variance tables, in that order, are given in Table 8.4. The important quantities are easily found in these tables. Notice that in the "Source" column of Minitab, the treatments source of variation uses the user-supplied label "thickness." Excel gives the sums of squares first, then the degrees of freedom. Excel identifies the treatments source as "Between Groups" and the error source as "Within Groups." JMP IN identifies the treatments source as "Model" and the total source as "C Total." The *P*-value (given to the right of the *F*-value by Minitab and Excel, and under the *F*-ratio by JMP IN) is extremely small (<.0001). With such a small *P*-value, the null hypothesis of no differences, on average, among the five levels of ceiling insulation is easily contradicted. Thus, the analysis of variance procedure confirms the initial conclusion we reached from the graphical analysis: The mean energy consumptions are not the same for the five amounts of ceiling insulation considered.

Table 8.4

Minitab, Excel, and JMP IN analysis of variance output for Example 8.1

```
Analysis of Variance for kilowatt
Source        DF         SS         MS          F          P
thickness      4     9.8356     2.4589      36.46      0.000
Error         18     1.2140     0.0674
Total         22    11.0496
```

	A	B	C	D	E	F
1	Anova: Single Factor					
2						
3	ANOVA					
4	*Source of Variation*	*SS*	*df*	*MS*	*F*	*P-value*
5	Between Groups	9.8356	4	2.4589	36.4580	0.0000
6	Within Groups	1.214	18	0.0674		
7						
8	Total	11.0496	22			

Analysis of Variance

Source	DF	Sum of Squares	Mean Square	F Ratio
Model	4	9.835565	2.45889	36.4580
Error	18	1.214000	0.06744	**Prob>F**
C Total	22	11.049565	0.50225	<.0001

8.3 Comparing More Than Two Treatments with Samples Selected in Blocks

In this section, we extend the paired samples procedure of Chapter 7, which involved the comparison of two means based on paired samples, to comparison of *more than two means* based on sample data that have been collected in blocks. To discuss the extension to more than two population or process means, let's first revisit the appraiser example. In the previous section, we emphasized that the differences among the 15 selected properties must be relatively minor. In reality, differences among any set of properties are likely to be large, causing the within-sample variation to be so large that any differences among population or process means cannot be detected. A more effective approach is to have each appraiser provide an appraisal of *all* selected properties. Each set of three appraisals for a given property would constitute a **block** of sample data. Thus, blocking is an extension of the idea of pairing used in Chapter 7. Blocking provides the opportunity for apples-to-apples comparisons of the appraisers, where any observed differences cannot be attributed to differences among the properties. The properties in this example, therefore, are a blocking variable.

Suppose we select five properties and instruct each appraiser to evaluate all five. Suppose further that the sample data are exactly the same as those given in Table 8.1. (We are using the same data to more dramatically illustrate the benefit of blocking.)

We repeat the sample data in Table 8.5, with the additional indication that the appraisers have evaluated the same set of five properties rather than three independent samples of five properties each. Totals and averages are provided for the rows of data as well as for the columns—that is, for the properties as well as the appraisers.

Table 8.5

Data for three appraisers and five properties

| Property | Appraiser | | | Totals | Averages |
	A	B	C		
1	90	93	92	275	91.67
2	94	96	88	278	92.67
3	91	92	84	267	89.00
4	85	88	83	256	85.33
5	88	90	87	265	88.33
Totals	448	459	434	1,341	89.40
Averages	89.6	91.8	86.8		

Our primary concern is to compare the three appraisers to determine whether their appraisals can be considered the same, on average; that is, we are still interested in testing the null hypothesis

$$H_0: \quad \mu_A = \mu_B = \mu_C$$

against the alternative hypothesis

$$H_a: \quad \text{At least one of these means differs from the rest}$$

But our approach to the use of selected properties is different now. Since we believe that differences among property values may be appreciable, we want to account for them and set them aside so that our comparison of the three appraisers is not blurred by the differences among the properties selected for the study.

8.3.1 Analysis of Variance with Blocked Data: Partitioning the Total Sum of Squares

As was the case with independent samples, the total variation measures the overall variation of the entire data set, regardless of the cause. As Figure 8.7 illustrates, the total variation can now be partitioned into *three* components: variation due to differences among the five properties (the blocking factor), variation due to differences among the three appraisers (the treatments), and variation due to random causes (random error).

The primary objective is to compare the treatment means. Thus, when we determine the block variation (or the effect due to differences among the blocks), *we set it aside and proceed precisely as we did with independent samples.* In other words, after the block variation is set aside, the analysis of variance procedure for this case also boils down to comparing the treatment variation to the random error variation.

Figure 8.8 provides a graphical display of the sample data of Table 8.5. The sample appraisals for each of the three appraisers (the treatments) are plotted on the vertical axis corresponding to the appropriate properties (the blocks) on the horizontal axis.

Figure 8.7

The partitioning of
total variation

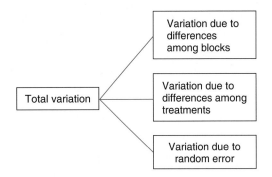

Figure 8.8

Minitab graph of the
appraiser data with
properties as blocks

Notice that the appraisals for appraiser B are the highest in every case and that C's appraisals are, with one exception, consistently the lowest. The consistency of the ordering among A, B, and C suggests that there are differences, on average, among the three appraisers. Could such a consistent ordering of the treatments have resulted from random factors alone? Perhaps. We use the analysis of variance procedure to confirm our initial conclusion from the graphical analysis.

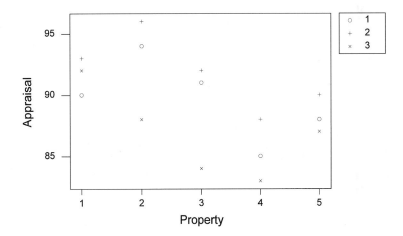

The Sums of Squares

As with independent samples, the first step in the analysis of variance procedure is to determine the various sums of squares. As illustrated by Figure 8.7, the total sum of squares (SST) is partitioned into the block sum of squares (SSBL), the treatment sum of squares (SSTR), and the error sum of squares (SSE). Thus,

$$SST = SSBL + SSTR + SSE \qquad\qquad (8.6)$$

All these sums of squares except SSBL are defined exactly as in the previous section. SSBL is the component of SST that accounts for differences among the blocks—that is, the properties. Shortly, we will use the computer to determine these sums of squares. At this time, it suffices to say that SSBL is determined in a manner fundamentally similar to the determination of SSTR. We compute the squared deviation of the mean for each block (property) from the overall mean, we sum these squared deviations over all blocks (all five properties), and then we multiply this sum by the number of treatments (i.e., three appraisers).

For the sample data in Table 8.5,

$$SSBL = 3[(91.67 - 89.4)^2 + (92.67 - 89.4)^2 + (89.00 - 89.4)^2$$
$$+ (85.33 - 89.4)^2 + (88.33 - 89.4)^2]$$
$$= 100.93$$

Since the observations in Table 8.5 are identical to those in Table 8.1, SST and SSTR have the same values that were computed previously—namely, $SST = 195.6$ and $SSTR = 62.8$. From Expression (8.6), we can determine the error sum of squares by subtracting SSBL and SSTR from SST; that is,

$$SSE = SST - SSBL - SSTR = 195.6 - 100.93 - 62.8 = 31.87$$

It is instructive to compare this value of SSE to the value we obtained with the independent samples example. (This comparison is meaningful only because we have used the same data in both examples.) This new value of SSE turns out to be the difference between the error sum of squares for independent samples, $SSE = 132.8$ (see Table 8.2), and the sum of squares for blocks in this example, $SSBL = 100.93$; that is, $31.87 = 132.8 - 100.93$. What is the significance of this? With independent samples, the error sum of squares measures the variation that results from all random causes, including differences in property values. When blocking is used, the variation attributed to property differences is isolated from random error. The sum of squares for blocks, $SSBL = 100.93$, represents the effect of property differences that has been removed from the error sum of squares. The new value of the error sum of squares, $SSE = 31.87$, represents the effect of the remaining random causes. Hence, *blocking provides a way to isolate the variation in the sample data caused by the blocking factor, thereby reducing the amount of random error. By reducing random error, we are better able to detect differences among population or process means when they do exist.*

Degrees of Freedom and the Best Statistic for ANOVA with Blocking

Since there are 15 observations in the sample data array, SST still has 14 degrees of freedom. Since there are three appraisers, SSTR still has 2 degrees of freedom. Similarly, since there are five properties (blocks), SSBL has 4 degrees of freedom—that is, 1 less than the number of properties (blocks). Recall that the degrees of freedom are additive, so we can obtain the degrees of freedom for SSE by subtracting the degrees of freedom for SSBL and SSTR from the total degrees of freedom; that is, $14 - 4 - 2 = 8$. The mean squares for treatments (MSTR) and error (MSE) are defined as before; that is, each sum of squares is divided by the corresponding degrees of freedom.

As before, we wish to compare the variation among sample treatment means (MSTR) to the variation due to random error (MSE). The best statistic for the ANOVA is again the ratio of MSTR to MSE. Following the same argument as in the previous section, we know that if $F = MSTR/MSE$ is sufficiently greater than 1, then it is reasonable to conclude with confidence that differences exist among the means of the treatment populations or processes. Consequently, the null hypothesis of equal population or process means is contradicted by the sample data when the P-value is sufficiently small.

Table 8.6

ANOVA table for the appraiser example with properties as blocks

Source of Variation	df	SS	MS	F-value	P-value
Properties	4	100.93			
Appraisers	2	62.80	62.8/2 = 31.4	31.4/3.98 = 7.89	.0128
Error	8	31.87	31.87/8 = 3.98		
Total variation	14	195.60			

The ANOVA table for the appraiser example with the five properties as blocks is provided in Table 8.6. Since the P-value is quite small, the null hypothesis is indeed contradicted by the sample data. Thus, the appraisers cannot be considered the same, on average.

8.3.2 Generalizing the Analysis of Variance Procedure to k Treatments in b Blocks

Before we illustrate computer output, let's generalize the preceding analysis of the appraiser example to the analysis of variance involving k treatment in b blocks. By "k treatments in b blocks," we mean that each of the b blocks contains sample observations for all k treatments (for example, each property was evaluated by all three appraisers). The observations in the sample data array for the k treatments in b blocks are usually displayed so that each treatment sample is a column and each block is a row.

There are $bk - 1$ degrees of freedom associated with SST, $b - 1$ degrees of freedom associated with SSBL, and $k - 1$ degrees of freedom associated with SSTR. As was the case with independent samples, the degrees of freedom are additive. Therefore, the error degrees of freedom may be determined by subtracting the degrees of freedom for blocks and the degrees of freedom for treatments from the total degrees of freedom. Accordingly, the degrees of freedom for error is:

$$
\begin{aligned}
df(error) &= (bk - 1) - (b - 1) - (k - 1) \\
&= bk - 1 - b + 1 - k + 1 \\
&= bk - b - k + 1 \\
&= (b - 1)(k - 1)
\end{aligned}
\tag{8.7}
$$

That is, *the error degrees of freedom is the product of the degrees of freedom for blocks and the degrees of freedom for treatments.*

The mean square for treatments and the mean square for error are once again determined by dividing the sums of squares by their respective degrees of freedom. Accordingly,

$$
MSTR = \frac{SSTR}{k - 1}
\tag{8.8}
$$

and

$$
MSE = \frac{SSE}{(b - 1)(k - 1)}
\tag{8.9}
$$

Let $\mu_1, \mu_2, \ldots, \mu_k$ be the population or process means corresponding to the k treatments. To test the null hypothesis

$$H_0: \quad \mu_1 = \mu_2 = \cdots = \mu_k$$

against the alternative hypothesis

$$H_a: \quad \text{At least one of these population means is different from the rest}$$

we again form the ratio of MSTR to MSE. Its sampling distribution is the F distribution with $k - 1$ numerator degrees of freedom and $(b - 1)(k - 1)$ denominator degrees of freedom. The P-value is either determined with the use of a computer or approximated with the F distribution table in the Appendix. If the value of the F statistic is sufficiently greater than 1, resulting in a small P-value, then the procedure indicates that differences among the population means do exist. The general ANOVA table for k treatments in b blocks is shown in Table 8.7.

Table 8.7

General ANOVA table for k treatments in b blocks

Source of Variation	df	SS	MS	F-value	P-value
Blocks	$b - 1$	SSBL			
Treatments	$k - 1$	SSTR	MSTR	MSTR/MSE	(by computer)
Error	$(b - 1)(k - 1)$	SSE	MSE		
Total variation	$bk - 1$	SST			

Most statistical software packages also provide in their output a similar analysis to determine whether the blocks differ, on average. However, this analysis should not be an integral part of the ANOVA procedure. After all, we choose a blocking arrangement to account for and set aside a potentially appreciable blocking effect. It is *assumed* based on subject-matter knowledge that there are differences among the blocks when this statistical design is chosen. Whether this assumption is statistically supported later by the ANOVA procedure is usually of little concern.

Using the Computer

In the following example, we illustrate computer output from Minitab, Excel, and JMP IN to carry out the ANOVA procedure.

EXAMPLE 8.2

Appropriate federal and state agencies are charged with the responsibility of providing useful information to consumers. Although the agencies themselves use designed experiments for evaluation, there are independent organizations that from time to time also use designed experiments to confirm the findings of the government agencies. This example illustrates that kind of situation.

The Environmental Protection Agency (EPA) annually rates every automobile available for purchase in the United States for fuel efficiency. An independent testing organization wants to determine whether differences exist among the average fuel efficiencies under actual road conditions for five different subcompacts that have virtually identical EPA ratings. The testing firm will use a 400-mile course that includes both city and highway driving. Four drivers will participate in the experiment. Potential differences in fuel efficiency attributable to the drivers themselves are believed to be appreciable. Therefore, the drivers are treated as blocks. Each driver will drive every car once over the 400-mile course. The order in which each driver drives the five cars will be determined by random draw, so that the effect of learning about the course, if any, will be considered random variation. The experiment results in the following sample data (miles per gallon).

| | Automobile | | | | |
Driver	1	2	3	4	5
1	33.6	32.8	31.9	27.2	30.6
2	36.9	36.1	32.1	34.4	35.3
3	34.2	35.3	33.7	31.3	34.6
4	34.8	37.1	34.8	32.9	32.8

(a) Depict the sample data graphically and state any initial conclusions that are suggested.

(b) Use a computer to perform the analysis of variance procedure and confirm your initial conclusions from the graphical analysis.

Solution

(a) The sample means for the five automobiles are $\bar{X}_1 = 34.875$, $\bar{X}_2 = 35.325$, $\bar{X}_3 = 33.125$, $\bar{X}_4 = 31.45$, and $\bar{X}_5 = 33.325$. These differences may be considered large enough to be of interest to consumers, especially since the EPA has previously reported the fuel efficiencies as being equal. Do these differences represent random sampling variation or genuine differences in fuel efficiencies? As in previous examples, we graph (see Figure 8.9) the fuel efficiencies of the five automobiles on the vertical axis against the drivers on the horizontal axis for an initial assessment of possible differences in the fuel efficiencies of the five automobiles. An examination of the graph suggests the existence of

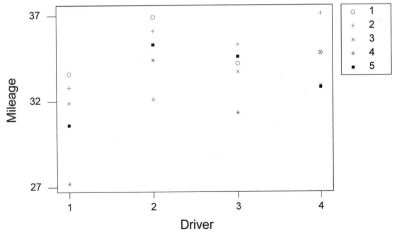

Figure 8.9

Minitab graph of automobile fuel efficiencies by driver

differences in the fuel efficiencies of the automobiles. For every driver, automobiles 1 and 2 rank at or near the top in mileage, whereas automobile 4's mileage was in every case either fourth or fifth. It seems unlikely that random error could produce such consistent results, but we use the ANOVA procedure to confirm this initial assessment.

(b) Notice that in this example the $k = 5$ automobiles are the treatments and the $b = 4$ drivers are the blocks. The null hypothesis concerns the population means of the five automobiles:

$$H_0: \quad \mu_1 = \mu_2 = \mu_3 = \mu_4 = \mu_5$$

The Minitab, Excel, and JMP IN analysis of variance tables are given in Table 8.8 in that order. As before, Minitab identifies the blocks source by the user-supplied label "Driver," and the treatments source by the user-supplied label "Auto." Excel identifies the blocks by "Rows" and the treatments by "Columns." JMP IN arranges the information a bit differently. Under the "Source" heading, it lists the term "Model." In this manner, "Model" combines the effects of blocks (drivers) and treatments (automobiles). Thus, the sum of squares listed for "Model" equals SSBL plus SSTR, and the degrees of freedom for "Model" are those of SSBL plus those of SSTR. JMP IN gives the corresponding information to Minitab and Excel under the heading "Effect Test," with the blocks source listed first, followed by the treatments. Since we are interested only in the treatments (the five automobiles), the F-value is seen to be 5.09 and the corresponding P-value is .0124, a sufficiently small value to contradict the null hypothesis. As in our initial conclusion based on Figure 8.9, these sample data suggest that differences exist in the average fuel efficiencies of these five automobiles.

Table 8.8

Minitab, Excel, and JMP IN analysis of variance tables for Example 8.2

Analysis of Variance for Mileage

Source	DF	SS	MS	F	P
Driver	3	41.676	13.892	7.43	0.005
Auto	4	38.092	9.523	5.09	0.012
Error	12	22.444	1.870		
Total	19	102.212			

	A	B	C	D	E	F
1	Anova: Two-Factor Without Replication					
2						
3	ANOVA					
4	Source of Variation	SS	df	MS	F	P-value
5	Rows	41.676	3	13.892	7.4276	0.0045
6	Columns	38.092	4	9.523	5.0916	0.0124
7	Error	22.444	12	1.8703		
8						
9	Total	102.212	19			

Analysis of Variance

Source	DF	Sum of Squares	Mean Square	F Ratio
Model	7	79.76800	11.3954	6.0927
Error	12	22.44400	1.8703	**Prob>F**
C Total	19	102.21200		0.0033

Effect Test

Source	Nparm	DF	Sum of Squares	F Ratio	Prob>F
Driver	3	3	41.676000	7.4276	0.0045
Auto	4	4	38.092000	5.0916	0.0124

8.4 Analysis of Variance: A Comprehensive Example

The administrator of a large state hospital wished to learn more about emergency room admissions patterns in an effort to optimize staffing assignments. The key question addressed by this study was whether staffing levels should vary with the day of the week. Since the appropriate level of staffing depends on the number of admissions, the response variable for this study was the daily number of emergency room admissions. The factor of primary interest was day of the week. Data were taken from the Daily Emergency Room Log kept routinely by the hospital.* The period of observation was the six months from May 1, 1991, through October 31, 1991.

Since this is a time-dependent study, it was important to check the stability of the admissions process over time. The run chart of daily admissions in Figure 8.10 shows that admissions were quite stable over the period of observation, except for a possible day-of-the-week pattern. One particularly low data value is possibly an outlier.

Figure 8.10

Run chart of total daily admissions over time

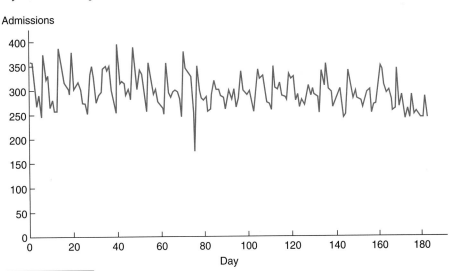

*Courtesy of Emily E. Dille.

The director looked at total daily admissions broken out by day of the week. Figure 8.11 provides histograms of total daily admissions for each day of the week. Each histogram appears on a vertical axis; the "M" designates the mean for a given day of the week. Although the ranges of the distributions overlap, the among-sample variation seems fairly large compared to the within-sample variation. This suggested to the director that total admissions did vary by the day of the week. It appears that the greatest demand occurs on Mondays. Admissions on Tuesdays, Wednesdays, and Thursdays seem about the same and lower than on Mondays. Admissions seem to decline again each day from Friday through Sunday. The low value mentioned earlier occurred on a Saturday. Upon investigation, it was found to be a legitimate figure, with no apparent special cause of variation. Thus, it seems to represent the extreme low end of the usual (common cause) distribution of Saturday admission totals.

Figure 8.11

Histograms of total admissions for the days of the week

```
             Monday   Tuesday   Wednesday  Thursday  Friday      Saturday   Sunday
Midpoints .............+.............+.............+.............+.............+.............+.............+
420.000)
408.000)
396.000) *
384.000) ****
372.000) ***
360.000) ***      **        ***          *
348.000) M****    ***
336.000) **       *         *****         *         *
324.000) *        *******   ***           ********  *
312.000)          M*****     M***          M*****    ***         **
300.000) **       **        *******       ****      *******     ***        *
288.000) *        *         **            ***       M*****      ******     ********
276.000) *        ***       **            *         **          M********  ***
264.000)          *                       **        ***         ***        M****
252.000) *                                          *           **         *******
240.000)                    *                       *                      **
228.000)
216.000)
204.000)
192.000)
180.000)
168.000)
```

Legend for group means: M - Mean coincides with an asterisk
                          N - Mean does not coincide with an asterisk

Table 8.9 provides a numerical summary of total admissions by day of the week. The means vary in a manner consistent with the observations made from the histograms. The means range from a high of 345.3 on Mondays to a low of 268.8 on Sundays. Thus, the average number of admissions on Mondays is about 28% higher than on Sundays. A difference of this magnitude, if real, would be sufficient to warrant the adjustment of staffing levels by the day of the week.

Table 8.9

Summary statistics for total daily admissions by day of the week

	Monday	Tuesday	Wednesday	Thursday	Friday	Saturday	Sunday
Mean	345.292	316.038	313.074	308.923	291.560	277.269	268.846
Std. dev.	37.072	25.629	27.237	22.269	21.900	25.209	16.856
SE of mean	7.567	5.026	5.242	4.367	4.380	4.944	3.306
Maximum	398.000	357.000	366.000	357.000	338.000	310.000	297.000
Minimum	255.000	267.000	244.000	262.000	246.000	180.000	240.000
n	24	26	27	26	25	26	26

An analysis of variance procedure based on independent samples was performed to check whether the among-sample variation observed in Figure 8.11 could have resulted from random sampling error alone, in the absence of any day-of-the-week effect. The treatments were the seven days of the week. The results are given in Table 8.10. For a test of the null hypothesis that there are no differences among the daily admissions means, the F-value is 25.70; the associated P-value is .000. Thus, if the daily means for the admissions process were equal, there would be virtually *no* chance of observing differences as great as those of this study. Accordingly, the null hypothesis is strongly contradicted by the data. The evidence overwhelmingly supports the existence of differences among the day-of-the-week means.

Table 8.10

ANOVA table for total daily admissions by day of the week

```
Analysis of Variance for admits
Source    DF         SS        MS       F       p
Day        6   101790.67  16965.11   25.70   0.000
Error    173   114216.28    660.21
Total    179   216006.95
```

This study provided a firm basis for adjusting staffing assignments. It is clear that staffing needs differ by day of the week, that the pattern of day-of-the-week variation is discernible and stable. One limitation is that the study covered the months of May through October. Therefore, there is no statistical basis to suggest that the observed pattern of admissions would persist for the other months. Any conclusion in this regard must be rooted in experience.

8.5 Summary

In this chapter, we extended the methods of Chapter 7 by introducing a statistical procedure called analysis of variance. Like the T procedures in Chapter 7, analysis of variance is an inferential procedure for assessing differences among the means of a number of populations or processes by partitioning the total variation in a sample data array in such a way that we can estimate the contribution of the factors that cause variation. The F distribution is used in the analysis of variance procedure.

In general, we call the populations, processes, or levels of a process factor being studied the *treatments*. The plans for acquiring data in this chapter are also extensions of the two basic plans introduced in Chapter 7—that is, independent samples and samples selected in blocks, where the blocks represent controlled levels of a background variable. As in Chapter 7, graphical analysis of the sample data remains an important first step in assessing differences among the treatments.

EXERCISES FOR SECTION 8.2

8.1 Explain what the treatments represent.

8.2 Explain the purpose of analysis of variance for $k = 5$ treatments.

8.3 Suppose there are $k = 4$ treatments. For each treatment, a sample of six observations is taken.

(a) Identify the potential sources of variation in the sample data.

(b) With regard to the sample data, explain what characterizes each source of variation.

8.4 Discuss whether the graphical analysis can be a

substitute for the analysis of variance procedure.

8.5 Discuss the relevant statistics in the analysis of variance procedure.

8.6 Suppose there are $k = 3$ treatments. For each treatment, a sample of five observations is taken. Suppose further that for any one treatment, the values of the sample observations are identical to each other, but not the same as those of another treatment.

(a) Without knowing the values of observations, what would be the value of SSE?

(b) In general, explain what SSE, SSTR, and SST measure.

8.7 It is believed that the sales volumes of a particular product when the items are placed near the checkout counters, in addition to their usual location, differ from the volumes when the items are placed only in their usual location. The following are random samples of 12 daily sales volumes for the items:

One location: 98 110 112   96 94   89 106 112   92   96 108 104
Two locations: 112   99 125 132 98 116 124   99 128 124 116 119

Assume that these are two independent random samples from normal populations with equal variances.

(a) Use the appropriate procedure from Chapter 7 to determine the extent to which these data contradict a claim that there is no difference in daily sales volumes, on average. Support your answer.

(b) Use an analysis of variance approach to answer the question in part (a), and compare your results.

8.8 In a recent study at a small liberal arts college, a professor compared the final numerical grades attained by her students in an accounting class during two different semesters.* In one semester (Fall 1990), the professor used multiple-choice exams; in the other semester (Fall 1991), she used problem-oriented exams. Because of the relatively small size of the college, the professor had no reason to believe that there are appreciable differences in the abilities of her students. The final grades for the two semesters are as follows:

Fall 90:   85.0 87.5 79.3 86.5   75.3 68.0 66.5 83.0 60.5
           77.5 73.5 73.0 78.5   92.5 76.5 70.8 91.5 88.5
           77.8 75.0 63.0 83.0   91.0 65.8 91.5

Fall 91: 102.0 84.5 68.7 78.5   100.0 93.3 92.7 69.7 75.3
           85.7 82.7 95.2 69.0   91.0 83.0 83.0 91.7 76.2
           79.7 78.3 79.7 88.3   88.7 65.2 92.0 87.3 85.7
           76.0

* Courtesy of Patricia Douglas.

Assume that these are two independent random samples from normal populations with equal variances.

(a) Graph the data. Do you see a difference in grades, on average, between these two examination formats? Explain.

(b) Based on this graph, should you be concerned about the equal variance assumption?

(c) Use an analysis of variance approach to determine the extent to which these data contradict a claim that there is no difference in performance, on average.

8.9 The following data are independent samples of cereal box fills (in ounces) for three identical filling machines:

Machine 1	Machine 2	Machine 3
20.25	20.90	20.18
20.20	20.99	20.26
20.45	21.08	20.38
20.38		20.32
		20.36

(a) Graph the sample data as in Example 8.1. Do you see differences among the average fills for these machines? Explain.

(b) Identify the sources that contribute to the variation in these sample data.

(c) Use the following Minitab analysis of variance output to determine the extent to which these sample data contradict a claim that there is no difference in average fills for the three machines. Support your answer.

```
Analysis of Variance on Ounces
Source   DF  SS        MS       F       p
Machine   2  1.04469   0.52235  57.05   0.000
Error     9  0.08240   0.00916
Total    11  1.12709
```

(d) What assumptions are necessary for your analysis in part (c)? Does the graph in part (a) help you to investigate any of these assumptions? Explain.

8.10 The following is a partial ANOVA table for $k = 5$ treatments and a total of $n = 28$ observations. Complete the table. To what extent does this analysis contradict the claim of no treatment differences, on average? Support your answer.

Source	df	SS	MS	F-value
Treatments			10	
Error				
Total		100		

8.11 Given that $k = 4$, $n_1 = n_2 = 6$, $n_3 = 5$, $n_4 = 4$, $SST = 200$, and $SSE = 50$, to what extent does this information contradict the claim of no treatment differences, on average? Support your answer.

8.12 Independent random samples from four different brands of recently produced alkaline batteries were placed on a life test. The following lifetimes (in hours) were observed:

Brand A	Brand B	Brand C	Brand D
110	118	108	117
113	116	107	116
108	112	112	116
115	117	108	119

(a) Graph the sample data as in Example 8.1. Do you see a difference in the average lifetimes for these four brands? Explain.

(b) Identify the sources that contribute to the variation of these sample data.

(c) Use the following Excel analysis of variance output to determine the extent to which these sample data contradict the claim that there are no differences in the average lifetimes for these four brands. Support your answer.

	A	B	C	D	E	F
1	Anova: Single Factor					
2						
3	ANOVA					
4	Source of Variation	SS	df	MS	F	P-value
5	Between Groups	174.5	3	58.167	9.901	0.001
6	Within Groups	70.5	12	5.875		
7						
8	Total	245	15			

(d) What assumptions are necessary for your analysis in part (c)? Does the graph in part (a) help you to investigate any of these assumptions? Explain.

8.13 Given that $k = 5$, $n_1 = n_2 = \cdots = n_5 = 6$, $SST = 400$, and $MSE = 6$, to what extent does this information support the claim of no treatment differences, on average? Support your answer.

8.14 A builder has built a considerable number of similar houses using the same design plan with only cosmetic changes at three different residential areas. The following data are samples of the selling prices (in thousands of dollars) of these houses that sold during the past year:

Area 1	Area 2	Area 3
125	129	143
132	138	139
129	142	140
136	134	144

Assume that these are three independent random samples from normal populations with equal variances.

(a) Graph the data. Is it apparent to you that differences in selling prices exist among these three areas, on average? Explain.

(b) Since these are essentially the same houses, to what might you attribute the differences in the selling prices within each residential area? Be specific in your answer.

(c) Based on the graph in part (a), should you be concerned about the equal variance assumption? Explain.

(d) Use the ANOVA procedure to determine the extent to which these data contradict a claim of no difference in selling prices for these three areas, on average.

8.15 In Exercises 1.37, 2.57, and 6.19, you used graphical analysis to learn about the visitation process at the Information Age Exhibit of the Smithsonian Institute in Washington, D.C. The data are produced by the Institute's computer tracking system and represent the 56-day period from September 30, 1995, to November 26, 1995, during which time 33,189 visitors passed through the exhibit (see these exercises for source). They are on the book's data diskette in the file named EX0815.

Exploratory analysis (graphical and numerical summaries) in the earlier exercises suggested that the number of visitors per day varies by the day of the week. Does the analysis of variance procedure support such a conclusion? Use the ANOVA procedure to determine the extent to which the data contradict a null hypothesis of no differences among the mean numbers of visitors per day for the seven days of the week.

8.16 In Exercise 2.59, you studied the distribution of 1994 major-league baseball players' salaries. Now the question is whether variation in salaries is related to the defensive positions played. That is, do players who play certain positions have higher salaries, on average, than those who play other positions? The salaries and positions for all major-league baseball players in 1994 are contained on the data diskette that accompanies this book in a file named EX0259 (*Source: USA Today*, Apr. 5, 1994).

(a) Construct a dot diagram of the 1994 salaries for each position in a single graph. Interpret the graph; that is, describe how the distribution of salaries depends on the position played.

(b) If we regard the 1994 baseball salaries as typical for the various defensive positions, could the differences observed in part (a) have occurred by chance? Use the analysis of variance procedure to determine the extent to which these data contradict a null hypothesis of no differences among the mean salaries for the nine positions. Support your answer.

8.17 One consideration in purchasing an automobile is safety. Many people believe that large cars are safer than small cars. Here is a chance to investigate this belief. The Highway Loss Data Institute tracks insurance claims and reports on the performances of virtually all automobile models sold in the United States. The sample for this exercise consists of 65 small car models, 101 midsize models, and 55 large models of various body styles. The data are contained on the data diskette that accompanies this book in a file named EX0817. For each model, the variables recorded are (1) personal injury claim frequency—these data have been adjusted in such a way that the average equals 100, making the results easier to compare, and (2) size/body style category: sizes are small, midsize, and large; body styles are 2-door, 4-door, wagon/van, sport, and luxury (*Source:* "Insurance Injury Report," Highway Loss Data Institute, Sept. 1995).

(a) Construct and interpret an appropriate graph of the data to determine whether the mean relative personal injury claim frequency seems to depend on the size/body style category of the automobile.

(b) Apply the analysis of variance procedure to these data and interpret its output. Do these results confirm your initial conclusion in part (a)?

8.18 The study "Physical and Performance Characteristics of NCAA Division I Football Players" (*Research Quarterly for Exercise and Sport,* Vol. 61, No. 4, 1990, pp. 395–401) reported on various performance characteristics of Division I football players for the 1987 season. The following data are simulated based on the summary information given in this study and represent independent samples of running times (in seconds) of eight randomly selected players in each of four distinct positions: quarterbacks, running backs, wide receivers, and defensive backs.

Quarterbacks	Running backs	Wide receivers	Defensive backs
4.77	4.73	4.72	4.66
5.07	4.30	4.68	4.46

Quarterbacks	Running backs	Wide receivers	Defensive backs
4.62	4.68	4.40	4.46
4.84	4.51	4.68	4.63
4.94	4.37	4.54	4.66
4.79	4.50	4.46	4.59
4.67	4.30	4.57	4.77
4.70	4.60	4.62	4.49

(a) Graph the data. Is it apparent to you that, on average, differences in running times exist for these four positions? Explain.

(b) Use the analysis of variance procedure to determine the extent to which these sample data contradict a claim of no difference in running times, on average, for these positions.

8.19 The study "Accepted Risk and Alcohol Use During Pregnancy" (*Journal of Consumer Research,* Vol. 21, June 1994, pp. 135–144) reported on demographic information, views, beliefs, and behaviors of surveyed pregnant women. The pregnant women were divided into three groups: nondrinkers—no alcoholic beverages during pregnancy and 6 months before, abstainers—no alcoholic beverages during pregnancy but some intake of alcoholic drinks during 6 months before, and drinkers—consumption of alcoholic beverages during and before pregnancy. It was of interest to know whether decisions about drinking were related to the ages of the pregnant women. The following data are simulated based on the summary information given in this study and represent the ages of randomly selected pregnant women from each group.

Nondrinkers	Abstainers	Drinkers
27	31	27
30	27	32
25	36	36
36	27	29
31	24	34
24	28	
26	33	
28	30	

(a) Graph the data for the three groups. On average, are any differences in ages apparent to you?

(b) Use the analysis of variance procedure to determine the extent to which these sample data contradict a claim of no difference in age, on average, for these three groups.

8.20 The paper "Work-related Consequences of Smoking Cessation" (*Academy of Management Journal,* Vol. 32, No. 3, 1989, pp. 606–621) examined the effects of smoking cessation on employee absenteeism, among other considerations. The study conducted a survey of blue- and white-collar employees. They were categorized into four groups in terms of their smoking behavior: continuous smokers, recent ex-smokers, long-term ex-smokers, and persons who never smoked. One variable of interest was short-term absenteeism in hours per month. The following data are simulated based on the summary information given in this study and represent absenteeism rates of randomly selected employees from each group.

Continuous Smokers	Recent Ex-smokers	Long-term Ex-smokers	Non-smokers
2.2	4.2	.6	.5
4.8	1.5	.5	5.2
3.8	2.5	4.1	.6
1.5	3.0	3.4	2.4
4.2	2.3	.8	3.2
2.2	5.5	1.4	.5
2.8	2.8	1.9	.5
2.3	1.4	.5	1.2
4.5	2.3	1.6	2.4
1.4	3.8	.6	1.6

(a) Graph the data for these four groups. On average, are any differences in absenteeism rates apparent to you?

(b) Use the analysis of variance procedure to determine the extent to which these sample data contradict a claim of no difference in absenteeism rates, on average, for these four groups.

8.21 The paper "A Pricing Study of Women's Apparel in Off-Price and Department Stores" (*Journal of Retailing,* Vol. 62, No. 3, 1986, pp. 321–330) investigated apparel price variations in off-price stores and department stores. The investigation was based on a survey of three off-price stores and three department stores with regard to three categories of women's apparel: separates, coordinates, and dresses/suits. For the surveyed items within each category, the following price relatives (department store price divided by off-price store price) were noted:

Separates	Coordinates	Dresses/Suits
1.27	1.47	1.41
1.20	1.73	1.60
1.39	1.39	1.29
1.49	1.61	1.44
1.34	1.21	1.46
1.14	1.22	
1.35		
1.35		
1.30		

(a) Graph the data. On average, are any differences in price relatives among the three categories apparent to you?

(b) Use the analysis of variance procedure to determine the extent to which these sample data contradict a claim of no difference in price relatives, on average, for the three categories of women's apparel

8.22 There are several common methods for controlling a computer cursor. The paper "A Comparison of Three Computer Cursor Control Devices: Pen on Horizontal Tablet, Mouse, and Keyboard" (*Information and Management,* No. 27, 1994, pp. 329–339) reported the results of an experiment comparing the electronic pen to two more familiar methods, a keyboard and a mouse. Sixty-three subjects (college students at a university) performed several cursor-control tasks. In one of the tasks, the subjects superimposed the red cursor onto small, white, randomly positioned square targets on a computer screen. The 63 subjects were allocated randomly to the three devices, so that each device was used by 21 subjects. Each subject performed the task six times over two days. The performance measures recorded for each subject were the average speed of use (in seconds) and the average number of errors over the six replications. The data are included on the book's data disk in the file EX0822.

(a) Graph the speed data by cursor-control device. Do these data suggest differences among the mean speeds for the three devices? Describe the apparent differences, if any. Which devices appear to perform best and worst?

(b) Do these data provide convincing evidence that the three cursor-control devices differ with respect to the mean speed for performing the experimental task?

(c) Graph the error count data by cursor-control device. Do these data suggest differences among the mean error counts for the three devices? Describe the apparent differences, if any. Which devices appear to perform best and worst?

(d) Do these data provide convincing evidence that the three cursor-control devices differ with respect to the mean error counts for performing the experimental task?

(e) Based on your work in parts (a)–(d), which device is most effective for controlling the cursor?

8.23 A 24-hours-a-day drop-in medical center in Richmond, Virginia, has four locations. A reputation for good customer service is essential to the growth of the center's customer base. Consequently, the management of the center was interested in the average waiting time experienced by patients. The data* for this exercise consist of the daily average waiting times at each of the four locations for each day in June 1997. They are on the book diskette in the file EX0823.

(a) Develop run charts for the daily average waiting times at each location. Do these run charts suggest a stable waiting-time process for each location over the period observed?

(b) Plot the waiting-time data for the four locations (vertical dot diagrams on the same graph). Do the data suggest differences among the mean waiting times at the four locations? Describe the apparent differences, if any.

(c) Do these data provide convincing evidence that the four locations differ with respect to the mean waiting time?

8.24 Video conferencing systems combine video, audio, and graphics to support two or more groups who are meeting together in geographically dispersed locations at the same time. The paper "Video Conferencing Human Machine Interface: A Field Study" (*Information and Management*, No. 27, 1994, pp. 341–356) examined the use of a video conferencing system at General Electric in Wilmington, North Carolina. One of the purposes of the study was to compare the uses of the system for three types of task: operational tasks (production control, scheduling, purchasing, etc.), tactical tasks (new product development, process development, contract negotiations, etc.), and strategic tasks (upper management planning and decision making). For 426 meetings that took place over a 10-month period, the task type and the length of the meeting were recorded. The data are included on the book data diskette in the file EX0824; they were simulated to match the characteristics of the data summarized in the study.

(a) Graph the meeting time data by task type. Do these data suggest differences among the mean meeting length for the three task types? Describe the apparent differences, if any.

(b) Do these data provide convincing evidence that the three task types differ with respect to the mean meeting length?

8.25 The paper "Consumers' Perception of Risk and the Purchase of Apparel from Catalogs" (*Journal of Direct Marketing*, Vol. 8, No. 2, Spring 1994) examined the role that a college student's major plays in his or her decisions to purchase apparel from catalogs. In response to a questionnaire, a sample of college students provided the number of orders for apparel from a catalog placed in the past 12 months (ORDERS) and the approximate amount spent on apparel bought by catalog over the past 12 months (DOLLARS). The sample included 62 Retailing and Consumer Science majors, 70 Business majors, and 86 Other majors. The data for this exercise have been simulated to match the characteristics described in the paper; they are on the book diskette in the file named EX0825.

(a) Graph the ORDERS data. What does the graph suggest about possible differences among the three majors with respect to the mean number of catalog orders placed in the past 12 months?

(b) To what extent do these data provide convincing evidence that differences exist among the mean numbers of catalog orders placed in the past 12 months for the populations of students in the three majors?

(c) Repeat parts (b) and (c) for the DOLLARS data.

8.26 Industries have different auditing standards, and audit firms specialize by industry. Yet little is known about industry differences in their propensities to make errors in financial statements. The paper "Audit Evidence Planning: An Examination of Industry Error Characteristics" (*Auditing: A Journal of Practice and Theory*, Vol. 15, No. 1, Spring 1996, pp. 71–85) investigated differences over a broad base of industries with regard to the incidence, magnitude, income effect cause, and method of detection of large financial statement errors. Data were obtained for 159 audit engagements from the U.S. practice of KPMG Peat Marwick across six industries: Manufacturing (36 companies), Merchandising (18 companies), Natural Resources (19 companies), Banking (36 companies), Insurance (36 companies), and Savings and Loans (14 companies). The data represent the total number of

---

* Courtesy of Charles Blottner.

reporting errors discovered for each of the 159 sample audit engagements. They have been simulated to match the characteristics of the data reported in the paper; they can be found on the book data diskette in the file EX0826.

(a) Graph the data. What does your graph suggest

about differences, on average, among error rates across the six industries?

(b) To what extent do these data provide convincing evidence that the average numbers of errors per audit engagement differ over the six industries?

EXERCISES FOR SECTION 8.3

8.27 Explain why on many occasions it is important to consider blocking when we wish to compare the means for a number of treatments.

8.28 Discuss the components of total variation when samples are selected in blocks.

8.29 If blocking should have been considered in a specific study but was not, what do you believe is the likely consequence in the analysis of variance procedure with regard to conclusions about the treatments?

8.30 The following is a partial ANOVA table for $k = 4$ treatments arranged in $b = 6$ blocks. Complete the ANOVA table and determine the extent to which this information supports the claim that there are no treatment differences, on average.

Source	df	SS	MS	F-value
Blocks		75		
Treatments				
Error			3	
Total		200		

8.31 The following data are the result of an experiment to compare the effects of three treatments arranged in four blocks:

	Treatment		
Block	A	B	C
1	8	10	9
2	12	16	15
3	15	18	14
4	6	10	7

(a) Graph the data as in Example 8.2. Do you see a treatment effect? Explain.

(b) Use the following Excel analysis of variance output to determine the extent to which these sample data contradict a claim of no treatment effect. Explain.

	A	B	C	D	E	F
1	Anova: Two-Factor Without Replication					
2						
3	ANOVA					
4	Source of Variation	SS	df	MS	F	P-value
5	Rows	138.667	3	46.222	47.543	0.000
6	Columns	22.167	2	11.083	11.4	0.009
7	Error	5.833	6	0.972		
8						
9	Total	166.667	11			

8.32 A leading energy company claims that its top-grade motor oil improves gasoline mileage. An independent testing organization conducts an experiment in which the company's brand (A) is compared to three other competing brands (B, C, and D). To conduct the experiment, the testing organization will use these four motor oils in each of four different-size automobiles (subcompact, compact, intermediate, and full size). The automobiles will serve as blocks because of obvious differences in gasoline mileage among them. The data of the experiment consist of the miles per gallon observed for a combination of city and highway travel, as follows:

	Brand			
Size	A	B	C	D
Subcompact	36	34	33	35
Compact	29	26	28	27
Intermediate	25	24	25	23
Full size	19	20	18	18

(a) Graph the data. Do you see differences in mileage, on average, for these four brands? Explain.

(b) Identify the sources that cause variation in the sample data.

(c) Based on the following Minitab ANOVA output, determine the extent to which these sample data indicate the existence of a treatment effect. Explain.

```
Analysis of Variance for MPG
Source DF      SS       MS       F       P
Size     3 519.500 173.167 155.85 0.000
Brand    3   5.500   1.833   1.65 0.246
Error    9  10.000   1.111
Total   15 535.000
```

8.33 Given $k = 5$ treatments arranged in $b = 4$ blocks, and given that SST = 500, SSBL = 240, and MSE = 5, to what extent does this information contradict the claim of no treatment effect? Explain.

8.34 Given $k = 4$ treatments arranged in $b = 6$ blocks, and given that SST = 725, SSBL = 200, and MSTR = 50, to what extent does this information contradict the claim of no treatment effect? Explain.

8.35 A marketing research firm has been asked to compare the percentage increases in sales in a large city over the past year for three competing brands of no-cholesterol margarine. Six supermarkets are selected from throughout the city to serve as blocks and account for variation in sales that result from demographic and socioeconomic differences among the customers. The percentage increases in sales for the three brands (A, B, and C) in the six supermarkets are shown in the table:

Supermarket	Brand		
	A	B	C
1	4.2	2.8	3.4
2	9.5	8.2	7.8
3	8.2	6.3	5.2
4	2.4	1.8	2.1
5	9.8	8.9	9.8
6	6.5	6.4	6.8

(a) Graph the data. Do you see differences in percentage increases, on average, for these three brands? Explain.
(b) Identify the sources that cause variation in the sample data.
(c) Use the ANOVA procedure to determine the extent to which these sample data indicate the existence of a treatment effect. Explain.

8.36 In Exercise 8.35, suppose the marketing research firm ignored the possible differences among the customers of the six supermarkets and treated the data as if they represented three independent samples. Use analysis of variance without blocking to see whether your conclusion would be different from that in Exercise 8.35.

8.37 The management of a large industrial plant wishes to reduce the number of machine breakdowns. As one aspect of their investigation, they wish to determine whether the three shifts of the plant differ in their numbers of machine breakdowns, on average. A week that is expected to be typical is selected for collecting data. During that week, the number of machine breakdowns is observed for each shift. Management is fairly certain that, at least for some days, daily differences in the numbers of machine breakdowns can be appreciable. Accordingly, the five working days are regarded as blocks.
(a) Graph the following sample data. What conclusion is suggested about the daily numbers of breakdowns for the three shifts?
(b) Perform the ANOVA procedure for data collected in blocks to confirm your conclusion from part (a). Is there good reason to believe that differences exist in the mean numbers of machine breakdowns for the three shifts?
(c) Does your conclusion apply to future rates of breakdown for the three shifts? Discuss.

Day	Shift		
	A	B	C
Monday	13	14	15
Tuesday	11	12	12
Wednesday	11	13	12
Thursday	10	12	13
Friday	13	14	14

8.38 The food service manager for the headquarters of a Fortune 500 manufacturer located in Richmond, Virginia, wished to understand spending behaviors of employees who eat lunch on site. One interest was the main dining area—in particular, the degree to which the daily number of customers varies by the day of the week. Currently, staffing levels are the same for all five days. The manager is considering varying the staffing levels by day of the week if this is supported by sample data. The data* for this exercise consist of the total number of customers at the main dining room for each day of the work week (Monday through Friday), and for each of three months (May through July, 1997). The data cover the first four weeks of each month; they are on the book disk in the file EX0838.
(a) Graph the data using the three months as

---

*Courtesy of Lewis Broome.

blocks. What does the graph suggest about the possible day-of-the-week effect on the mean number of customers in a day?

(b) Determine the extent to which these sample data contradict a null hypothesis of no differences in the average numbers of customers for the five work days.

(c) Based on your answer in part (c), do these data justify scheduling different numbers of workers in the main dining area each day of the week?

8.39 In the study "Anticipating the Future High-Tech Competitiveness of Nations: Indicators for Twenty-Eight Countries" (*Technological Forecasting and Social Change,* Vol. 51, No. 2, Feb. 1996, pp. 133–149), the following data were reported on 1993 indicators of competitiveness for the G7 countries, among others. The indicator values (ranging from 0 to 100) are with regard to four input indicators: national orientation (NO), which is the evidence

that a nation is undertaking directed action to achieve technological competitiveness, socioeconomic infrastructure (SE), technological infrastructure (TI), and productive capacity (PC).

Ind.	USA	Japan	Germany	UK	France	Italy	Canada
NO	69.95	85.32	75.23	63.17	74.22	59.19	60.14
SE	84.02	72.65	69.77	65.62	63.80	53.64	78.33
TI	87.51	83.67	66.61	57.53	59.96	50.51	49.52
PC	89.81	92.74	65.04	48.95	56.12	51.78	48.06

(a) Treating the four input indicators as blocks, graph the data. Do you see any differences in the 1993 indicator values, on average, for the G7 counties? Explain.

(b) Determine the extent to which these data suggest differences in the 1993 indicator values, on average, among the G7 countries.

SUPPLEMENTARY EXERCISES

8.40 Accident statistics indicate that about two-thirds of automobile fatalities in the United States are caused by drunken drivers. You have been hired to investigate the degree to which alcohol impairs one's ability to perform routine functions in driving an automobile. Fully describe a sampling plan to accomplish this task and indicate how this experiment should be carried out.

8.41 An insurance company wants to determine whether there are discernible differences in the average numbers of days that patients suffering from the same illness stay at an area's four major hospitals. Fully describe a statistical design to accomplish this objective.

8.42 A filling operation consists of three identical machines that are set to pour a specified amount of a product into equal-size containers. Random samples are taken periodically from the machines to check the equality of the average amounts poured by the machines. For a particular time period, the sample data in the following table were recorded:

Machine		
A	B	C
16	18	19
15	19	20
15	19	18
14	20	20

Machine		
A	B	C
	19	19
	19	

(a) Graph the data. Are any differences in the mean fills for these machines apparent to you? Explain.

(b) Use the analysis of variance procedure to determine the extent to which these sample data indicate that there are differences in mean fills. Support your answer.

8.43 Recently, a graduate student studied the length of time that it took to travel by car from a designated starting point to a designated finishing point using three different routes.* The routes are all within a large metropolitan area. The times of observation were essentially the same, as were the weather conditions. The observed data (in minutes) are as follows:

Route 1	Route 2	Route 3
18.63	18.30	20.53
23.17	18.77	21.92
20.25	21.93	17.43

*Courtesy of Melissa Gorman.

Route 1	Route 2	Route 3
18.08	22.32	18.22
18.10	21.00	19.20
16.83	18.30	16.13
17.47	18.77	18.30
19.88	21.00	17.60
16.37	22.32	16.40
18.67	21.00	19.65
18.08	21.93	18.23

Assume that these are three independent samples from normal populations with equal variances.

(a) Graph the data. Is it apparent to you that differences exist among these routes with regard to the average length of time? Explain.

(b) Based on this graph, should you be concerned about any assumptions that were made? Explain.

(c) Explain why there is variation in the lengths of times on each route.

(d) Use the ANOVA procedure to determine the extent to which these sample data contradict the claim of no difference in the lengths of times for these routes, on average.

8.44 An independent testing laboratory is asked to compare the durability of four different brands of golf balls. The laboratory sets up an experiment in which eight balls from each manufacturer are randomly selected and subjected to a machine set to hit the ball with a constant force. The measurement of interest is the number of times each ball is hit before its outside cover cracks. The information in the following table is obtained:

Brand

A	B	C	D
205	242	237	212
229	253	259	244
238	226	265	229
214	219	229	272
242	251	218	255
225	212	262	233
209	224	242	224
204	247	234	245

(a) Graph the data. Are any differences among the means for the four brands apparent to you? Explain.

(b) Use analysis of variance to determine the extent to which these sample data contradict a claim that there are no differences among

the means for the four brands. Support your answer.

8.45 We wish to determine whether the amount of carbon used in the manufacture of steel has an effect on the tensile strength of the steel. Five different percentages of carbon are investigated: .2%, .3%, .4%, .5%, and .6%. For each percentage of carbon, five steel specimens are randomly selected from the same batch and their strengths are measured. The sample information in the following table is obtained, where the strength is in kilograms per square centimeter:

Carbon Content

.2%	.3%	.4%	.5%	.6%
1,240	1,420	1,480	1,610	1,700
1,350	1,510	1,470	1,590	1,790
1,390	1,410	1,520	1,580	1,740
1,280	1,530	1,540	1,630	1,810
1,320	1,470	1,510	1,560	1,730

(a) Graph the data. Are any differences in mean tensile strengths apparent to you? Explain.

(b) Use analysis of variance to determine the extent to which these sample data contradict a claim that there is no carbon-content effect on the tensile strength of steel. Explain.

8.46 To determine whether there are differences in the average yields of three varieties of corn, a large homogeneous farm area is divided into three equal-size plots. Each plot is then divided into five equal subplots and planted with one variety of corn. At harvest time, the measurement of interest is the yield (in bushels per acre). The following is a partial analysis of variance table for this problem:

Source	df	SS	MS	F-value
Treatments		32		
Error				
Total		100		

Complete the ANOVA table and determine the strength of this information against the claim of no differences in average yields. Support your answer.

8.47 A number of company presidents were randomly sampled from four distinct geographic areas in the United States to determine whether area has a discernible effect on the annual average salaries of company presidents. The following annual salaries (in thousands of dollars) were observed:

Northeast	Midwest	Southeast	West
210	75	110	90
125	195	235	265
95	120	85	350
345	240	150	140
80	90	95	170

Graph the data. Based on what you see, can you think of any key points that may not have been considered in taking this sample information? In other words, provide an argument for or against whether we should even utilize the analysis of variance technique to determine whether area has an effect on average salaries based on the given data. Be sure to give substantive support in either case.

8.48 In a large plant, we wish to determine whether different workers with the same skill level have any effect on the number of units that are expected to be produced in a fixed period of time. An experiment is conducted in which five workers are randomly selected and the number of units produced by each worker for six equal-length time periods is recorded as follows:

Worker

1	2	3	4	5
45	52	39	57	48
47	55	37	49	44
43	58	46	52	55
48	49	45	50	53
50	47	42	48	49
44	57	41	55	52

(a) Graph the data. Are any differences in the average numbers of units produced by these workers apparent to you? Explain.

(b) To what extent do these sample data contradict the claim of no differences, on average? Support your answer.

(c) What assumptions are necessary for your analysis in part (b)? Does the graph in part (a) help you out with one of these assumptions? Explain.

8.49 Several devices have been developed that purport to increase the average mileage of automobiles when these devices are installed. A testing organization has selected three of the most popular devices for testing. The organization would like to compare the mileage of automobiles that contain these devices with the mileage of automobiles without the devices. The organization has selected five types of automobiles for the test. To control variation, it plans to use the same driver for the entire experiment. The following sample information (in miles per gallon) has been obtained:

Auto	No Device	Device A	Device B	Device C
1	18.2	18.9	19.1	20.4
2	27.4	27.9	28.1	29.9
3	35.2	34.9	35.8	38.2
4	14.8	15.2	14.9	17.3
5	25.4	24.8	25.6	26.9

(a) Graph the data. Are any differences in average mileage apparent to you? Explain.

(b) Why is there a need to block the automobiles here? Explain.

(c) Use an analysis of variance approach to determine the strength of the sample data against the claim that there is no difference in average mileage, with or without these devices.

8.50 In Exercise 8.49, suppose you had not considered the automobile a viable source of the variation in the observed mileage. Show whether this omission would have any effect on your answer to part (c) in Exercise 8.49.

8.51 Burning cigarettes produce appreciable quantities of carbon monoxide. When cigarette smoke is inhaled, carbon monoxide combines with hemoglobin to form carboxyhemoglobin. In a pertinent study, researchers wanted to determine whether an appreciable concentration of carboxyhemoglobin reduces the exercise tolerance of patients suffering from chronic bronchitis and emphysema. Seven such patients were selected and, in a controlled environment, they were asked to walk for 12 minutes, breathing one of four gas mixtures: air, oxygen, air plus carbon monoxide (CO), or oxygen plus carbon monoxide. The amount of carbon monoxide breathed was sufficient to raise the carboxyhemoglobin concentration of each subject by 9%. To control the intake of carbon monoxide, all smokers in the group of seven were asked to stop smoking 12 hours prior to the experiment. The data* in the following table represent the distances (in meters) walked by the subjects under each condition in 12 minutes:

---

*P. M. A. Calverly, R. J. E. Leggett, and D. C. Flenley, "Carbon Monoxide and Exercise in Chronic Bronchitis and Emphysema," *Brit. Med. J. 283* (1981), 877–880.

	Gas Mixture			
Subject	Air	Oxygen	Air + CO	Oxygen + CO
1	835	874	750	854
2	787	827	755	829
3	724	738	698	726
4	336	378	210	279
5	252	315	168	336
6	560	672	558	642
7	336	341	260	336

(a) Graph the data. Are any differences in the average distances walked for these four gas mixtures apparent to you? Explain.

(b) Why is there a need to block the subjects? Explain.

(c) Use an analysis of variance approach to determine the extent to which the sample data contradict the claim that there is no gas mixture effect on the distance walked. Support your answer.

8.52 We wish to determine whether there are appreciable differences in the average prices among four major supermarkets in a given city. From the regularly bought brand items, ten are randomly selected and their unit prices are observed at each supermarket. The following information is obtained:

	Supermarket			
Item	A	B	C	D
1	3.29	3.42	3.27	3.35
2	.59	.65	.59	.60
3	1.25	1.29	1.25	1.27
4	4.35	4.59	4.29	4.49
5	.89	.95	.89	.89
6	1.85	1.79	1.89	1.89
7	.95	.89	.89	.90
8	.75	.79	.69	.79
9	2.35	2.35	2.39	2.39
10	1.49	1.55	1.55	1.49

(a) Graph the data. Are any differences in the average prices for the four supermarkets apparent to you? Explain.

(b) Why is there a need to block the items? Explain.

(c) Use an analysis of variance approach to determine the extent to which the sample data contradict the claim that there is no supermarket effect on the unit prices of the brand items. Support your answer.

8.53 Exercises 2.30, 2.48, and 2.84 involved Educational Services, Inc., a small firm that provides tutoring to middle school and high school students. Clients are obtained through three sources: the Yellow Pages, professional referral, or referral from a previous client. The data, repeated here, represent sales revenues for a sample of 143 clients, broken out by source.[*]

Client Referrals:

40	300	100	120	160	140	80	110	160	180
80	710	120	220	100	250	120	20	160	120
1,340	160	280	200	560	3,940	60	600	140	840
230	160	530	200	140	480	140	120	560	120
38	180	100	220	100	220	1,040			

Yellow Pages Referrals:

950	120	75	200	100	620	320	120	140	80
130	830	180	320	90	1,220	380	60	70	1,600
80	120	160	760	850	420	150	140	20	520
260	100	100	840	480	150	230	220	220	

Professional Referrals:

2,200	140	480	480	150	2,840	560	530	2,470	140
160	320	80	320	180	940	580	900	1,730	100
900	360	1,560	1,050	680	4,160	200	165	300	60
1,870	390	1,920	740	140	60	140	40	540	8,320
1,020	175	1,260	710	720	1,540	4,680	1,460	400	1,120
240	360	540	1,500	3,280	880	1,120			

(a) Graph the data. Is it apparent that differences exist among the mean sales amounts for the three referral sources?

(b) Use the ANOVA procedure to determine the extent to which these sample data contradict a claim of no difference in sales revenues for these three sources, on average.

8.54 This exercise is an extension of Exercises 2.31, 2.49, 2.85, and 2.106, which deal with a study of the work process of associates at the law firm Northup and Bauers. It was hypothesized that the number of billable hours may depend on the department within the firm to which an associate is assigned. The following data[†] are the numbers of billable hours over a 9-month period for each of 43 associates, along with his or her department.

Hrs.:	802	1,287	1,255	1,178	1,275	767	1,424	1,328	1,223
Dept.:	1	1	1	2	1	1	3	2	1
Hrs.:	790	1,399	1,434	1,050	796	1,308	1,464	1,389	1,316
Dept.:	1	4	4	5	6	6	6	7	4
Hrs.:	1,325	1,494	1,096	1,482	1,493	1,452	1,060	1,407	1,067
Dept.:	8	1	1	3	7	3	6	6	8

---

*Courtesy of Douglas Haag and Timothy Geer.

†Courtesy of Alexis Campbell.

Hrs.:	934	901	1,400	1,320	1,132	1,256	858	1,346	885
Dept.:	3	1	1	7	1	3	1	8	1

Hrs.:	1,084	1,065	1,211	1,379	1,340	1,098	1,407
Dept.:	5	5	1	3	6	5	1

Dept. Code: 1 = Business/commercial litigation
2 = Labor relations
3 = Real estate
4 = Banking/finance
5 = Administrative
6 = Corporate
7 = Insurance/product liability
8 = Trusts/estates

(a) Graph the data. Is it apparent that the mean numbers of billable hours differ among the eight departments? If so, describe the differences.

(b) Use the ANOVA procedure to determine the extent to which the sample data contradict a claim of no differences among the departments in the mean number of billable hours for associates.

8.55 In the study "Anticipating the Future High-Tech Competitiveness of Nations: Indicators for Twenty-Eight Countries" (*Technological Forecasting and Social Change*, Vol. 51, No. 2, Feb. 1996, pp. 133–149), the following data were reported on 1993 indicators of competitiveness for Brazil, Mexico, and Argentina. The indicator values are with regard to four input indicators: national orientation (NO), which is the evidence that a nation is undertaking directed action to achieve technological competitiveness, socioeconomic infrastructure (SE), technological infrastructure (TI), and productive capacity (PC).

	Brazil	**Mexico**	**Argentina**
NO	63.60	47.87	44.96
SE	55.12	47.71	63.17
TI	41.59	25.23	25.49
PC	48.12	27.16	32.19

(a) Treating the four input indicators as blocks, graph the data and determine whether any differences in the 1993 values, on average, among these countries are apparent to you. Explain.

(b) Use an analysis of variance approach to determine whether these data suggest differences among Brazil, Mexico, and Argentina, on average.

8.56 The paper "Work-Related Consequences of Smoking Cessation" (*Academy of Management Journal*, Vol. 32, No. 3, 1989, pp. 606–621) examined the effects of smoking cessation on the weight of employees, among other considerations. The study was based on a survey of blue- and white-collar employees. They were categorized into four groups in terms of their smoking behavior: continuous smokers, recent ex-smokers, long-term ex-smokers, and nonsmokers. One variable of interest was the ratio of an employee's weight to the ideal weight for that employee's height. The following data are simulated based on the summary information given in this study and represent weight ratios of randomly selected employees from each group.

Continuous Smokers	Recent Ex-smokers	Long-term Ex-smokers	Nonsmokers
1.56	.77	1.27	.85
1.37	1.19	1.10	.94
.80	1.46	.99	1.41
.75	1.24	1.46	1.31
1.14	1.39	1.25	1.12
.83	1.52	1.38	.96
1.20	1.76	1.47	1.60
1.29	1.64	1.16	1.53
1.06	1.19	1.59	.98
1.10	.87	.77	1.09

(a) Graph the data for these four groups. On average, are any differences in weight ratios apparent to you?

(b) Use the appropriate analysis of variance procedure to determine the extent to which these sample data contradict a claim of no difference in weight ratios, on average, for these four groups.

8.1 Case Study
Analysis of Income Tax Returns

Case Study 6.1 involved an analysis of income tax returns. The population consisted of the 112,201,751 income tax returns filed in 1989. The data derived from simple random samples of about 75 returns from each of five categories of tax returns from this population, representing the following ranges of adjusted gross income (AGI):

- $0–$10,000
- $20,000–$30,000
- $50,000–$100,000
- $100,000–$200,000
- $200,000–$500,000

The sample data are contained on the data diskette in a file named CASE0601. It consists of 379 rows, where each row provides information for a single tax return. The specific column variables on the file are:

c1:   stratum identification
c2:   adjusted gross income
c3:   deductions (0 = standard deduction; 1 = itemized)
c4:   total deductions (amount)
c5:   taxable income
c6:   total exemptions (self, spouse, dependents)
c7:   total credits (for child and dependent care, etc.)
c8:   total contributions
c9:   tax liability

In Case Study 6.1, you performed an exploratory study. Inferences involved individual strata; no formal inferences were required with respect to comparisons of strata because you had not yet studied analysis of variance. Your task in this continuation of Case Study 6.1 is to extend your previous discussion involving comparisons of the strata by applying the methods of Chapter 8. If there are other variables for which you now wish to compare the strata, then that analysis should also be included here.

Appendix 8

Computer Instructions for Using MINITAB, EXCEL, and JMP IN

MINITAB

Analysis of Variance for Independent Samples

To produce the Minitab output for Example 8.1, enter the data in a stacked format. Let the subscripts indicating insulation thickness comprise c1 (you can use either 1, 2, 3, 4, 5 or 4, 6, 8, 10, 12), and let the 23 kilowatt-hours values comprise c2. Name columns c1 and c2 Insulation and Kilowatt-hours, respectively. To produce a graph like Figure 8.6, choose GRAPH–PLOT .... In the dialogue box, specify c2 as Y (the vertical axis) and c1 as X (the horizontal axis); then click OK.

To produce analysis of variance output corresponding to Table 8.4, choose STAT–ANOVA–BALANCED ANOVA .... In the dialogue box, specify c2 for RESPONSES; specify c1 for MODEL (i.e., the treatments); and click OK.

Analysis of Variance with Samples Selected in Blocks

Now consider Example 8.2. First, enter the data in stacked format, putting the 20 mileage values into c3 and the subscripts indicating the automobile and the driver into c1 and c2, respectively. Name c1, c2, and c3 Auto, Driver, and Mileage, respectively. To produce Figure 8.9, choose GRAPH–PLOT .... In the dialogue box, do the following: (1) enter c3 for Y (the vertical axis); (2) enter c2 for X (the horizontal axis); (3) select FOR EACH–GROUP; (4) enter c1 in the first cell under GROUP VARIABLES .... To add jitter (to better distinguish plotted data points), click the OPTIONS button; in the PLOT OPTIONS dialogue box, click ADD JITTER TO DIRECTION; then click OK twice.

To produce analysis of variance output like that in Table 8.8, choose STAT–ANOVA–BALANCED ANOVA .... In the dialogue box, specify c3 for RESPONSES; specify c2 c1 for MODEL (i.e., the blocks and treatments); and click OK.

EXCEL

Analysis of Variance for Independent Samples

To produce a vertical dot diagram as in Figure 8.6 for Example 8.1, enter the kilowatt-hours data into a single column by putting the data for 4 inches of insulation in cells b2 through b6; the data for 6 inches in cells b7 through b10; the data for 8 inches in cells b11 through b15; the data for 10 inches in cells b16 through b18; and the data for 12 inches in cells b19 through b24. Now enter 4s in cells a2 through a6 (indicating 4 inches of insulation), 6s in cells a7 through a10, 8s in cells a11 through a15, 10s in cells a16 through a18, and 12s in cells a19 through a24. Put variable names Insulation and Kilowatt-hours in cells a1 and b1. Select the range of cells containing the variable names and the data (a1:b24). Then choose INSERT–CHART . . . . In the CHART WIZARD, (1) click X-Y (SCATTER), then click the upper-left chart subtype option (SCATTER); (2) in the DATA RANGE box, enter the cell range containing the data (a1:b24) and click the SERIES IN COLUMNS button; (3) provide chart title and labels for the axes as desired; (4) indicate whether you wish the scatter diagram to be placed on a new sheet or within the currently active sheet.

To produce the analysis of variance output in Table 8.4, put the kilowatt-hours data in five columns. Use the range a2:a6 for the first sample (4 inches of insulation); b2:b5 for the second sample; c2:c6 for the third sample; d2:d4 for the fourth sample; and e2:e7 for the fifth sample. Enter the names 4 Inches, 6 Inches, 8 Inches, 10 Inches, and 12 Inches in cells a1, b1, c1, d1, and e1, respectively. Choose TOOLS–DATA ANALYSIS . . . and select ANOVA: SINGLE FACTOR. In the dialogue box, indicate in the INPUT RANGE box the range of cells containing the variable names and the data (a1:e7); click the LABELS IN THE FIRST ROW button. The output also includes the sample means and variances (not shown in Table 8.4).

Analysis of Variance with Samples Selected in Blocks

Now let's look at Example 8.2. To produce a graph like Figure 8.9, the data must be entered in five columns as shown in the text. Enter the miles-per-hour data for automobile 1 in cells b2:b5; the data for automobile 2 in cells c2:c5; the data for automobile 3 in cells d2:d5; the data for automobile 4 in cells e2:e5; and the data for automobile 5 in cells f2:f5. Now enter driver IDs 1, 2, 3, and 4 in cells a2 through a5, respectively. Put variable names Driver, Auto 1, Auto 2, Auto 3, Auto 4, and Auto 5 in cells a1 through f1, respectively. Select the range of cells containing the driver IDs and the data (a2:f5). (Notice that the auto IDs are not selected.) Then choose INSERT–CHART . . . . In the CHART WIZARD, (1) click X-Y (SCATTER), then click the upper-left chart subtype option (SCATTER); (2) in the DATA RANGE box, enter the cell range containing driver IDs and the data (a2:f5) and click the SERIES IN COLUMNS button; (3) provide chart title and labels for the axes as desired; (4) indicate whether you wish the scatter diagram to be placed on a new sheet or within the currently active sheet.

To produce the analysis of variance output in Table 8.8, arrange the data, auto IDs, and driver IDs in the format described in the preceding paragraph. Choose TOOLS–DATA ANALYSIS . . . and select ANOVA: TWO FACTOR WITHOUT REPLICATION. In the dialogue box, indicate in the INPUT RANGE box the range of cells containing the variable names and data (a1:f5). (Notice that now the auto IDs are included in the selection.) Click the LABELS button, and click OK.

JMP IN

Analysis of Variance for Independent Samples

To produce the JMP IN output for Example 8.1, enter the 23 kilowatt-hours values into COLUMN 1, and name this column KILOWATT-HRS. Set its role to be Y. Enter the corresponding insulation thicknesses in COLUMN 2, and name this column INSULATION. Set INSULATION to data type NUMERIC and modeling type NOMINAL, and set its role to be X. The JMP IN graph in Figure 8.6 is produced by choosing ANALYZE—FIT Y BY X.

To produce the analysis of variance output in Table 8.4, click the ANALYSIS check mark box and select MEANS, ANOVA/t-TESTS. The desired output is in the Analysis of Variance portion of the output, below the graph.

Analysis of Variance with Samples Selected in Blocks

Now consider Example 8.2. First, enter indices identifying the drivers (1 through 4) into COLUMN 1, and enter the mileage data into columns 2, 3, 4, 5, and 6. Name these columns DRIVER, AUTO1, AUTO2, AUTO3, AUTO4, and AUTO5, respectively. Set the role of DRIVER to X and set its data type and modeling type to NUMERIC and NOMINAL, respectively. Set the roles of the other variables to Y. Choose GRAPH—OVERLAY PLOTS. Click each check mark box and deselect CONNECT. Also click each check mark box, select OVERLAY MARKERS, and choose the desired plotting symbol.

To produce the analysis of variance output in Table 8.8, put the mileage data into one column (enter it or stack the data from the previous paragraph) and name it MILEAGE. Put indices (1, 2, . . .) identifying the driver and automobile corresponding to each mileage in two other columns, and name these columns DRIVER and AUTO. Set the roles of DRIVER and AUTO to X and set their data type and modeling type to NUMERIC and NOMINAL, respectively. Set the role of MILEAGE to Y. Choose ANALYZE—FIT MODEL. In the dialogue box, make sure that MILEAGE is listed in the upper right-hand box (the Y box) and that DRIVER and AUTO are listed in the EFFECTS box, and click RUN MODEL. The desired analysis of variance output is below the graph.

Chapter 9

Simple Linear Regression Analysis

CHAPTER OUTLINE

9.1 Bridging to New Topics

In this chapter, we introduce methods for studying statistical relationships between variables. As defined in Chapter 1, a **statistical model** is a mathematical equation that shows how a variable of interest is related to one or more variables. By identifying other variables that contribute to the variation of the variable of interest, statistical models provide a mechanism for prediction. In other words, with statistical models we can predict a value of the variable of interest based on known values of other variables. In this manner, statistical models can suggest changes that could lead to improvement.

Suppose a property tax assessor must estimate the market value of a home. (The market value is the expected selling price of the home, if it were sold.) He has information on a sample of comparable homes recently sold in the same neighborhood. As we pointed out in Chapter 1, such information constitutes *convenience data*—data that are not truly a random sample but instead represent all the relevant information available to the investigator. The assessor considers the sample homes to be comparable to the home to be assessed, and he treats them as if they were a random sample. The statistical problem is the following: Based on the sample data, what should be the predicted selling price for the particular home of interest?

If the only information known about the group of comparable homes were their selling prices, then the best predictor of the selling price of the home to be assessed would be $\bar{X}$, the mean selling price for the sample of comparable homes. Suppose, however, that this house were larger than the average for the sample. Wouldn't this suggest that its selling price is likely to be above average as well, if all other features are about the same? Indeed it would! The sample mean $\bar{X}$ is the best predictor only if we consider no other information except selling price. By estimating the relationship of the selling price of a house to its size, we can improve the prediction considerably.

As this example illustrates, the essence of this approach to improved prediction is an investigation of the degree to which one variable may be associated with another variable. **Regression analysis** is a method for establishing the association between one variable (selling price) and one or more other variables (e.g., size). If only one other variable is considered, the procedure is called **simple linear regression analysis,** the subject of this chapter. If more than one other variable is used, the procedure is called **multiple linear regression analysis,** covered in Chapter 10. The concepts of multiple linear regression are, for the most part, extensions of simple linear regression. Consequently, it is especially important that you learn well the concepts of this chapter.

The primary objective of a regression analysis is the development of a regression model to characterize the association between variables. A **regression model** is a mathematical equation that provides predictions of the values of one variable based on the known values of one or more other variables. Regression analysis is often used for the assessment of property values. Consequently, we use this example throughout the chapter to illustrate the statistical topics that arise. Other applications of regression analysis are introduced in numbered examples.

The computations involved in regression analysis are considerably more tedious than those encountered in Chapters 5–8. In fact, for most applications of multiple linear regression, it is virtually impossible to carry out the analysis without the use of a computer. For this reason, we rely heavily on the use of a computer to perform the analysis.

9.2 Relationships Between Two Variables: The Simple Linear Regression Model

Suppose we wish to predict the selling price for an individual house in a population of houses, taking into account the size of the house. Let Y represent the selling price and X the enclosed area in square feet. We refer to Y as the **response variable** (the variable to be predicted) and X as the **predictor variable** (the variable on which predictions are based).

9.2.1 Associative Relationships Versus Cause-and-Effect Relationships

If the knowledge of the value of X is useful in predicting the value of Y, then we say there is an **association** between X and Y. But the existence of an association between two variables does not assure that they have a cause-and-effect relationship. Causation implies that a change in X *causes* a corresponding change in Y if all other factors that affect Y remain unchanged. Establishing causation is crucial when the purpose of a regression model is to provide a basis for improvement. Perhaps there is a cause-and-effect relationship between house size and selling price; increasing the size of a house does increase its value if all other factors remain the same. But this is not the case for many other regression relationships. For example, a statistical study once revealed the existence of a strong association between the sale of scotch in New York City in the early 1800s and the number of ministers. Does this suggest that sales of scotch could be increased by increasing the number of ministers? Or that the sale of scotch could be eliminated by banishing all ministers? Of course not. Both scotch sales and the number of ministers reflected the population of the city in a given year. As the population grew, both scotch sales and the number of ministers grew as well, thus producing the association between these variables. On the other hand, the absence of causality does not necessarily mean that knowing the number of ministers is of no value in predicting scotch sales. If we knew that the number of ministers in a given year was very high, we could infer that the population was large that year. In turn, therefore, we could infer that scotch sales were also high that year.

How then can we establish that a regression relationship is causal? Our subject-matter knowledge might be sufficient to justify such a belief; this is the basis we used for suggesting that the relationship between the size of a house and its selling price is causal. Otherwise, the key is a carefully designed experiment in which we hold other factors and background variables constant while changing the value of the potential predictor variable. If the values of the response variable change in a manner consistent with our prior knowledge, this is evidence of a causal relationship.

Graphing the Relationship: Scatter Diagrams

We seek to develop a model of the association, if any, between Y and X. We begin by considering the population to which inferences are to be made. Suppose we could observe the selling price and size of every house in the population of comparable houses. (This is strictly a "what-if" supposition; we cannot actually do this because most houses have not been recently sold.) By graphing the observational data, we might gain insight into the nature of the relationship between Y and X.

Suppose the graph of selling price Y and size X is as given in Figure 9.1. Such a graph, in which each point represents the selling price and size of one house, is called a **scatter diagram.** Scatter diagrams were introduced in Chapter 2 as a means to investigate graphically the nature of the relationship between two variables. To amplify the type of relationship that may exist between Y and X, consider Figure 9.2. In part (a), notice that the larger houses (those with larger X-values) tend to have higher selling prices (larger Y-values). In part (b), notice that the relationship is not perfect because, among houses of the same size, selling prices vary. This happens because houses of the same size differ with regard to many other factors, such as overall condition, number

Figure 9.1

A scatter diagram of *Y* versus *X*

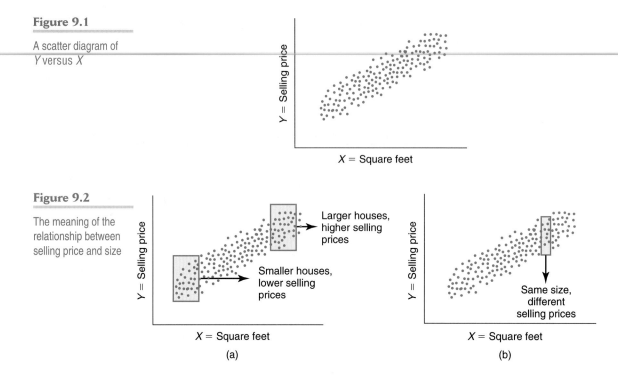

Figure 9.2

The meaning of the relationship between selling price and size

of bathrooms, and the presence of a fireplace. Thus, there appears to be an association between *Y* and *X*, but it is certainly not perfect.

9.2.2 The Regression Model

Our approach in regression analysis is to identify a **regression model**—a mathematical equation that seems to characterize the association between *Y* and *X* for the population. When only one predictor variable is being considered, a scatter diagram provides an important first step in determining an appropriate regression model. What kind of an approximate relationship does the scatter diagram of Figure 9.1 suggest to you? It appears that a straight-line model characterizes the relationship appropriately, as illustrated in Figure 9.3. The line serves as the regression model for the population.

Figure 9.3

The regression model: A line depicting the mean *Y* for any given *X*

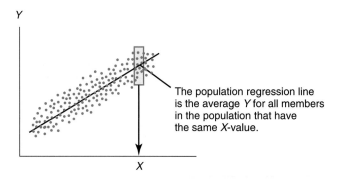

Notice that most data points do not fall on this line, because of effects with regard to variables other than *X*. Thus, the regression model does not represent each point perfectly, but the values of Y tend to increase in direct proportion to increases in the values of X. For example, larger houses tend to sell for higher prices. Consequently, the regression model depicts the *average* selling price Y for any given size X in the population. This is the essence of a linear association between Y and X.

It is important to be able to express a regression relationship between the variables Y and X as a mathematical model. In our example, the scatter diagram indicates that the appropriate regression model for the population is a straight line. Recall that a straight line can be expressed in the form

$$Y = \beta_0 + \beta_1 X \qquad \qquad \text{(9.1)}$$

where β_0 represents the Y-intercept (the value of Y when $X = 0$) and β_1 represents the slope (the change in Y per unit change in X). Greek letters are used to denote these quantities because they characterize a population. The intercept β_0 and the slope β_1 are the parameters of this regression model. Their values are not likely to be known, but they can be estimated with sample data, as explained in the next section.

To illustrate a straight-line relationship, suppose we knew that the population regression equation for Y = selling price and X = size in square feet is $Y = 60,000 + 30X$. The Y-intercept is $\beta_0 = 60,000$ and the slope is $\beta_1 = 30$. This equation may be interpreted as follows:

1. For houses of 3,000 square feet ($X = 3,000$), the average selling price is $150,000.

2. If $X = 0$, the average selling price is $60,000. This might be interpreted as the average selling price of an empty lot. (As we explain later, such an interpretation would be valid only if the data include values of $X = 0$.)

3. The change in Y as X changes from 0 to 3,000 is $150,000 - $60,000 = $90,000. This confirms that the slope is $\beta_1 = 90,000/3,000 = 30$.

4. Since the slope is 30, the average selling price increases by $30 for each additional square foot of space.

Suppose we wished to predict the selling price of a house with 2,800 square feet. Suppose further that the mean selling price for the population of comparable houses was $120,000 and that the average size of these homes was 2,000 square feet. If the size of this home is not considered, the best prediction of the selling price of any home would be the mean selling price for the population—$120,000. But the regression model allows us to use knowledge of size in predicting the selling price. This regression model indicates that the *average* selling price of all homes with $X = 2,800$ square feet is $60,000 + 30(2,800) = $144,000. This is the predicted selling price for the home of interest. Instead of using the mean of the entire population as the predictor, we are now able to use the mean for only those homes of size 2,800 square feet. The predicted selling price is above the average selling price of $120,000 apparently because a house with 2,800 square feet is larger than the average of 2,000 square feet for the population of comparable homes.

In reality, we are not able to determine the values of β_0 and β_1 because we cannot observe the entire population. If we can obtain a representative sample, however, we can estimate β_0 and β_1. This allows us to develop an estimated regression model that can be used for prediction. We show how this is done in a later section.

The mere existence of a regression model of the association between Y and X does not necessarily mean that the model is adequate. For this to be true, the model's predictions would have to be relatively close to the corresponding actual values of Y.

In other words, the **fit** of the regression model to the sample data has to be good. To illustrate, suppose we had representative housing data from two different neighborhoods with regression equations that were identical, as illustrated in Figure 9.4. Notice that, although the equations are identical, the data from the first neighborhood fit the regression line more closely than do the data from the second neighborhood; in other words, the individual Y values differ less from the average Y at any value of X. As a result, the prediction errors would tend to be smaller for homes in the first neighborhood than for those in the second.

Figure 9.4

An illustration of the variation of data about two identical regression lines

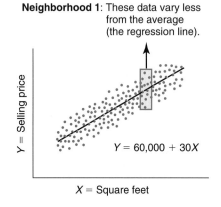

Neighborhood 1: These data vary less from the average (the regression line).

$Y = 60,000 + 30X$

Y = Selling price

X = Square feet

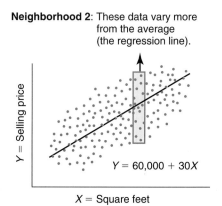

Neighborhood 2: These data vary more from the average (the regression line).

$Y = 60,000 + 30X$

Y = Selling price

X = Square feet

We need to be able to assess the degree to which the data vary from the regression line. For a given X, the deviation of a Y-value from the population regression line is called an **error**; it is denoted by the Greek letter ϵ (epsilon). This deviation is the error that would be made if the regression line were used to predict an individual Y-value. To account for these deviations from the regression line, a complete regression model for a linear relationship between the variables Y and X must include an **error term** as follows:

$$Y = \underbrace{\beta_0 \; + \; \beta_1 X}\; + \; \underbrace{\epsilon} \qquad\qquad \textbf{(9.2)}$$

The deterministic component:
Mean Y, given X

The random component: Unpredictable deviation of Y from the population regression line

Expression (9.2) is known as the **simple linear regression model.** It states that the value of Y for an individual member of the population consists of two components: (1) $\beta_0 + \beta_1 X$, the mean for all population members that have the same value of X; and (2) ϵ, the amount by which the individual Y-value departs from the population regression line. The first component, $\beta_0 + \beta_1 X$, is said to be *deterministic* because it is completely determined by the value of X. The deterministic component $\beta_0 + \beta_1 X$ is what we have called the **population regression line.** The error term, ϵ, is called the *random* component because its value for an individual population member is assumed to vary unpredictably for all members that have the same value of X. For this reason, it is often referred to as **random error.**

The extent of the random error for a given value of X is measured by the error variance, denoted by σ_ϵ^2. This is the variance of the prediction errors associated with the population. Equivalently, σ_ϵ^2 is the variance of Y for all population members that have a common value of X. Like β_0 and β_1, σ_ϵ^2 is an unknown parameter that must be estimated based on a representative sample of data. As suggested in Figure 9.4, the magnitude of σ_ϵ^2 governs the closeness of fit of the model to a sample of data. If the relationship between Y and X is indeed linear, the fit of Expression (9.2) to a representative sample should be good because the magnitude of σ_ϵ^2 is relatively small. But if the fit is not so good, the magnitude of σ_ϵ^2 is large and the error in Expression (9.2) is a significant component. In broad terms, *the fundamental goal in regression analysis is to determine a regression equation that makes sense and fits the representative data such that the error variance is as small as possible.* That is to say, the regression equation is deemed adequate for prediction. It is not sufficient simply to fit an assumed model to a representative sample. We must (1) select the proper form of the model (i.e., use a scatter diagram to ensure that a linear equation seems appropriate), (2) evaluate the model thoroughly, and (3) consider adding other predictor variables to the model to further reduce the error variance. (This is the subject of Chapter 10.)

EXAMPLE 9.1

Typically, power companies need to evaluate periodically the anticipated demands for power by the customers they serve. One way of doing this is to establish statistical relationships between power consumption and potentially important variables such as severity of the weather (for example, very hot summers or very cold winters), expanding customer base, and so on. This example illustrates that kind of situation.

A typical residential house was selected by the local power company to use in developing an empirical model for energy consumption (in kilowatts per day) as a function of the daily high temperature during the winter months in a given geographic region. For 18 days, the following information was obtained:

Temperature °C:	−1	1.5	3.5	−3	.5	2.5	4	5	−5
Energy use:	94	81	79	97	88	75	74	67	107

Temperature °C:	−.5	9	9.5	7	3	−2	6	8	10
Energy use:	86	58	55	65	73	91	65	58	52

(a) Identify the response and predictor variables for this application, based on the power company's purpose for developing a regression model.

(b) Graph the data. Based on this scatter diagram, does there seem to be a relationship between energy consumption and the daily high temperature? Do you believe that a straight-line fit to these data (i.e., a linear model) is going to be adequate? Explain.

(c) If the approximate relationship between energy consumption and high temperature is a straight line, what sign does the scatter diagram suggest for the slope of the line? Is your answer consistent with your knowledge of the relationship between energy consumption and temperature?

Solution

(a) Since the power company wants to predict energy consumption, that is the response variable. The predictor variable is the daily high temperature because the power company suspects that it explains to some degree the daily variation in energy consumption.

(b) The scatter diagram is given in Figure 9.5. This figure clearly illustrates the expected nature of the relationship between energy consumption and the daily high temperature. As the daily high temperature increases, energy consumption decreases. In fact, we can "eyeball" a straight line that would be close to virtually all of the data points. So a straight-line fit to these data seems appropriate, and the random error component appears to be very small.

(c) Since energy consumption seems to decrease in a linear fashion as winter high temperatures increase, we expect the slope to be negative. This is consistent with our prior understanding of the effect of temperature on energy consumption.

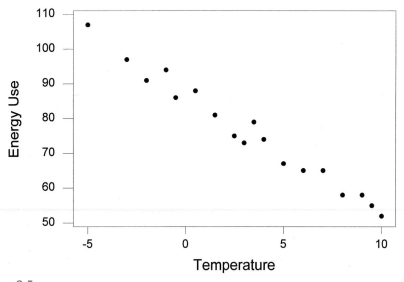

Figure 9.5

Minitab scatter diagram of energy use versus temperature

EXAMPLE 9.2

Salary administration is a very important task for any organization. For example, employees must feel that they are being rewarded financially for good job performance. Typically, the longer a person has been working for an organization, the higher the person's salary tends to be. What might be the relationship between salary and years of experience? This example addresses such a question.

A study was conducted to examine the relationship between the number of years of experience and the annual salary for individuals in a particular profession and geographic region. The following information is obtained for a representative sample of 16 such professionals (salary is in thousands of dollars):

Years (X):	1	2	4	5	6	9	11	14	16	20	22	24	25	27	29	30
Salary (Y):	23	27	29	34	38	46	48	54	54	59	58	59	61	63	59	60

Construct a scatter diagram. Does there appear to be a relationship between Y and X? If so, does it appear to be linear? Explain.

Solution

The scatter diagram is shown in Figure 9.6. Based on this figure, there is virtually no doubt that there exists a relationship between salary and years of experience, but there is substantial doubt whether the relationship is best described by a straight line. For example, notice that as years of experience increase, salary does indeed increase. But the *rate* of increase in salary slows as the number of years of experience increases. The scatter diagram strongly suggests curvature in the relationship. A straight line does not appear to be the most appropriate fit. (We show how to deal with curvature in Chapter 10.)

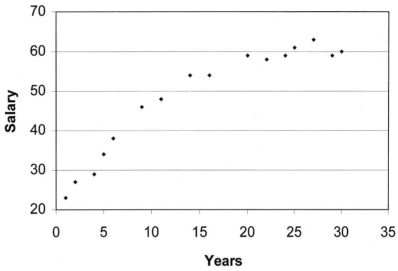

Figure 9.6

Excel scatter diagram of salary versus years of experience

EXAMPLE 9.3

A university administrator wishes to examine the relationship between grade point average (GPA) and age of undergraduate students in the business school. The following information is obtained for a representative sample of 15 students:

Age (*X*): 20   21   19   19   20   21   18   22   23   19   22   24   23   19   21
GPA (*Y*): 2.13 3.38 2.07 2.63 2.85 2.16 3.15 3.12 2.97 2.52 2.17 2.95 2.25 3.17 2.85

Construct a scatter diagram. Describe the relationship between grade point average and age, if one appears to exist.

Solution

The scatter diagram is given in Figure 9.7. From this figure, there appears to be no discernible relationship between grade point average and age. The average GPA of younger students is about equal to the average GPA of older students. About the best we can do here is to "eyeball" a straight line that is parallel to the *x*-axis and intersects the *y*-axis at about 2.7. Any straight line that is parallel to the *x*-axis has *zero* slope,

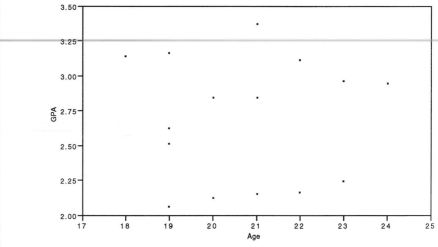

Figure 9.7

JMP IN scatter diagram of grade point average versus age

which means there is no linear relationship between Y and X. Thus, knowledge of a student's age appears to be of little value in predicting his or her grade point average.

9.2.3 Uses of Regression Models

Regression models can be very useful tools in the management of business processes. In general, there are two basic and overlapping ways in which regression models are used: (1) to provide insight into relationships and (2) for prediction and estimation.

Insight into Relationships

A regression model is used to represent a complex system in a simple, manageable form, thereby providing a better understanding of the system's characteristics. This understanding is among the greatest assets a professional can possess. To illustrate, suppose the estimated regression line for Example 9.1 (energy consumption versus daily high temperature in degrees Celsius) is

$$\hat{Y} = 87 - 3.46X$$

The "hat" symbol $\hat{}$ indicates estimation; thus, $\hat{Y}$ ("Y-hat") represents an estimator of Y for a given value of X. This equation suggests that daily energy consumption decreases *on average* by approximately 3.46 kilowatts for each degree (Celsius) increase in the daily high temperature. This is the interpretation of the slope estimate. It is important to keep in mind that *the slope is the key to describing a linear relationship between two variables*. If Y and X are linearly related, the slope *cannot* be 0. If the slope is 0, there is no linear relationship between Y and X.

We have a statistical basis for interpreting a regression model for only those values of the predictor variable X within the range of the sample data. It would be a mistake to interpret the model for X-values outside this range unless there is a theoretical (nonstatistical) basis for doing so. For the energy consumption model, notice that the range of temperatures is from -5 to 10 degrees Celsius. Therefore, the model should be used to predict energy consumption only for temperatures in this range. As an illustration, suppose we used this model to predict energy consumption for a summer day with a high temperature of 30 degrees Celsius. The model's prediction is $\hat{Y} = 87 - 3.46(30) = -16.8$ kilowatts! This is clearly a ludicrous result. In fact, experience tells us that daily energy usage eventually begins to increase as temperatures rise in the summer because of air conditioning. The folly of extrapolating outside the range of the sample data is illustrated in Figure 9.8.

Figure 9.8

The effect of extrapolation in the energy versus temperature example

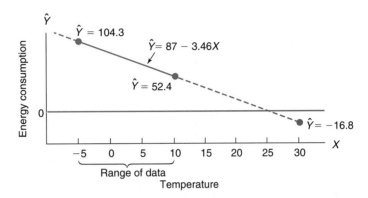

What about the interpretation of the Y-intercept? The regression equation suggests that the *average* energy consumption per day is 87 kilowatts when the daily high temperature is $X = 0$ degrees Celsius. This is the proper interpretation of the estimate of β_0. In some applications, however, such an interpretation might not make sense. The key is to see whether $X = 0$ lies within the range of the sample data. If it does, then this interpretation is valid. But if $X = 0$ lies outside the range of the sample data, we should not expect this interpretation to be meaningful or even realistic. In the energy consumption example, the range of X-values is from -5 to 10 degrees Celsius. Since this range includes the value $X = 0$, the interpretation of the intercept is meaningful here.

In summary, the interpretation of an estimated regression model applies only within the range of the sample values of X. Within this range, the key to interpretation is the estimated slope. It explains the amount of change in Y that corresponds to a change in X. The interpretation of an estimated regression model is important because it provides insight into the system being studied, ensures that the model makes sense, and increases the confidence of those who are not so familiar with statistics.

Prediction and Estimation

Once we gain insight into a relationship, understand it, and believe the estimated regression model adequately represents the relationship, we often want to use the model to predict values of the response variable. For the property assessment example, the property tax assessor can estimate the market value of a home merely by substituting the size of the home, among other possible considerations, into the estimated regression equation. In this context, there are actually two distinct ways in which a regression model may be used.

Estimation. An estimated regression model may be used to estimate the *average* value of the response variable Y, given a specific value of the predictor variable X. Suppose an investment firm wishes to compare the real estate values for comparable properties in two locales. Regression analysis can be used to compare the average selling prices of comparable properties in cities A and B. Samples of comparable properties in each city would be identified, and regression models relating Y = selling price (in $10,000) to X = square feet (in thousands) would be developed. Suppose the resulting models were as follows:

City A: $\hat{Y} = .8 + 6.0X$ X-values in (2.0, 3.2)
City B: $\hat{Y} = 1.1 + 5.2X$ X-values in (2.0, 3.2)

Notice that the models are applicable for X-values between 2.0 and 3.2. For houses with, say, 2,200 square feet (i.e., $X = 2.2$), these models estimate the *mean* selling prices to be $140,000 for city A and $125,400 for B. (These estimates are obtained by substituting $X = 2.2$ into each equation.) The important point here is that the investment firm is interested in the *mean* value of Y, given X. It has no particular interest in predicting the selling price of any individual house with 2,200 square feet.

Prediction.   An estimated regression model may be used to predict the value of Y for an *individual* member of the population, given a specific value of X. Let's now look at the property values example from the point of view of the assessor. Consider the estimated regression line for city A: $\hat{Y} = .8 + 6.0X$. It is not enough for a property assessor to estimate the average selling price; he must predict the selling price for each *individual* member of the population. This prediction is obtained in the same way that we estimate the mean value of Y, given a value of X: We simply substitute the value of X into the equation. Thus, the predicted selling price of a 2,200-square-foot house ($X = 2.2$) is $\hat{Y} = .8 + 6.0(2.2) = 14$, or $140,000. You may wonder why we differentiate between the estimation of means and the prediction of individual Y-values if they provide the same result for a given value of X. The reason has to do with accuracy. If we wish to use an estimated regression model for estimation and prediction, it is important to know how much in error its estimates and predictions may be. As you will see in Section 9.5, the potential for error is much greater in predicting Y for an *individual* member of the population than in estimating the *mean* of Y for all members of the population that have a given value of X.

9.3   Estimating the Parameters of the Simple Linear Regression Model

To fit the assumed regression model to representative sample data, the first step is to estimate the parameters of the model (β_0 and β_1 for the simple linear model). As a consequence of determining estimates of β_0 and β_1, we are in a position to estimate the error variance σ_ϵ^2. But first we need to consider the ways in which sample data may be obtained.

9.3.1   Obtaining Sample Data

There are three ways in which sample data may be obtained:

1. *Simple random sampling.*   Sometimes a simple random sample is selected in which both Y and X are regarded as random variables.

2. *Random sampling for selected X-values.* A random sample of Y-values is taken for a predetermined set of X-values. For example, suppose we are interested in the selling prices (Y) of houses with sizes ranging from 1,500 to 2,500 square feet. We may choose the sizes 1,500, 2,000, and 2,500 and select a random sample of homes for each category, ignoring homes of other sizes. The ability to select the range of X-values is highly desirable not only because it allows us to observe Y-values within a range of interest for X, but also because it provides an opportunity to increase the reliability of inferences, as discussed in Section 9.6.

3. *Convenience data.* Often random sampling is not feasible; we can obtain only data that happen to be available. In the property appraisal example, the only available data represented homes that had already been sold. These were determined by homeowners and not by random selection. In performing a regression analysis, we must be willing to assume that the "homeowner selection process" essentially represents the population with regard to the relationship between selling price and house size. In some cases, it would be a mistake to make this assumption. Suppose most of the homes in the convenience data were the older, more run-down homes in the neighborhood. A model developed from these data might not reflect the true association between selling price and house size for all homes in the neighborhood.

As long as the sample values of X are observed without error, regression analysis is appropriate for all three of these situations. There are two important points for you to understand: (1) By predetermining the range of X, you may be able to improve inferences (this is demonstrated in Section 9.6), and (2) if you wish to use convenience data, you must decide whether the data sufficiently represent the environment about which you wish to make generalizations. If not, conclusions based on regression analysis could be in error by an appreciable amount.

9.3.2 The Method of Least Squares

With regard to Expression (9.2), how do we estimate β_0, β_1, and, eventually, σ_ϵ^2 with sample data? Suppose the property appraiser has obtained the following data for five homes. In the table, Y represents selling price (in $10,000); thus, $Y = 10$ represents a home that sold for $100,000. The value for X represents the enclosed area (in thousands of square feet). The data are greatly rounded to simplify presentation.

Property	X	Y
1	1.0	6
2	1.5	12
3	2.0	10
4	2.5	18
5	3.0	18
Mean	$\bar{X} = 2.0$	$\bar{Y} = 12.8$

Take a minute to examine the data. Assuming these data are representative, would you be convinced that an association exists between selling price (Y) and size (X) in the population? A scatter diagram usually makes it much easier to see whether there is a relationship. Figure 9.9 is the scatter diagram for these data. Notice that selling price tends to increase as size increases, but the relationship is not perfect, as evidenced by the second and third points, for which Y decreased from 12 to 10 as X increased from 1.5 to 2.0. Similarly, Y remained at 18 as X increased from 2.5 to 3. The explanation is that other factors besides size also affect selling prices.

Figure 9.9

A scatter diagram for the property assessment example

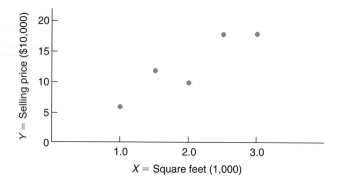

We estimate the population regression line by drawing a straight line through the sample data. This could be done with "eyeball judgment," but to get the best line, an appropriate procedure must be used. First, however, we must specify what we mean by the phrase "the best line." From Figure 9.9, you can see that no straight line will pass through all five data points. We wish to determine the one line for which the vertical distances from the data points to the line are as small as possible. These vertical distances represent, in a sense, sample errors that would occur if this particular line were used to estimate the mean of Y for each value of X in the sample. These sample errors are called **residuals** and are denoted by the symbol e. The residuals for this example are illustrated in Figure 9.10.

Figure 9.10

Residuals for the property assessment example

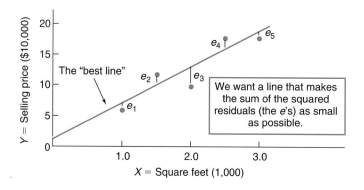

Since there are five residuals, we must summarize them in some way. A tempting idea might be to choose the line that minimizes the sum of the residuals. This does not work. Indeed, there are many lines for which the sum of the residuals is 0, and some do not fit the data well at all. For example, the sum of the residuals is 0 for the flat line $Y = \bar{Y}$. Even though the residuals for this line are large, the positive residuals balance the negative residuals, with a net result of 0. Instead, the preferred method is to minimize the sum of the *squared* residuals. The line that minimizes the sum of the squared residuals (Σe_i^2) is called the **least squares line,** or the **estimated regression line.** For this line, the sum of the *squares* of the residuals is the *least* it can be for any straight line. The following procedure for determining the least squares line is called the **method of least squares.**

To determine the least squares line, we must determine estimates of β_0 and β_1. These estimates represent the Y-intercept and the slope, respectively, of the estimated regression line and are determined by the following expressions, called the least squares equations. These equations define the statistics b_0 and b_1, which are known as the least squares estimators of β_0 and β_1, respectively.[*] The equations are determined by using differential calculus, which is beyond the mathematical scope of this book.

$$b_1 = \frac{SP(XY)}{SS(X)} \qquad \textbf{(9.3)}$$

$$b_0 = \bar{Y} - b_1 \bar{X} \qquad \textbf{(9.4)}$$

where

$$SP(XY) = \Sigma(X_i - \bar{X})(Y_i - \bar{Y}) = \Sigma X_i Y_i - \frac{(\Sigma X_i)(\Sigma Y_i)}{n} \qquad \textbf{(9.5)}$$

and

$$SS(X) = \Sigma(X_i - \bar{X})^2 = \Sigma X_i^2 - \frac{(\Sigma X_i)^2}{n} \qquad \textbf{(9.6)}$$

Using Expressions (9.3)–(9.6) and the sample data in the preceding table, we can determine that $b_0 = .8$ and $b_1 = 6.0$.[†] For the most part, however, the least squares estimates are determined by a computer. The Minitab and Excel regression outputs for the property assessment example are given in Table 9.1.

Table 9.1

Minitab and Excel Regression Outputs for the Property Assessment Example

```
MINITAB   The regression equation is

          Price = 0.80 + 6.00 Size

          Predictor    Coef     Stdev     t-ratio    p
          Constant     0.800    3.359     0.24       0.827
          Size         6.000    1.583     3.79       0.032

          s = 2.503    R-sq = 82.7%    R-sq(adj) = 77.0%

          Analysis of Variance

          SOURCE       DF       SS        MS         F        p
          Regression   1        90.000    90.000     14.36    0.032
          Error        3        18.800    6.267
          Total        4        108.800
```

---

[*] We depart from our usual practice of using capital letters to denote statistics because a lowercase b is used almost universally to denote least squares estimates.

[†] In Appendix 9B, we illustrate the determination of the least squares estimates of the slope and intercept using a calculator.

Table 9.1 (continued)

EXCEL

	A	B	C	D	E	F	G
1	SUMMARY OUTPUT						
2							
3	*Regression Statistics*						
4	Multiple R	0.9095					
5	R Square	0.8272					
6	Adjusted R Squar	0.7696					
7	Standard Error	2.5033					
8	Observations	5					
9							
10	ANOVA						
11		*df*	*SS*	*MS*	*F*	*Significance F*	
12	Regression	1	90	90	14.362	0.0322	
13	Residual	3	18.8	6.267			
14	Total	4	108.8				
15							
16		*Coefficients*	*Standard Error*	*t Stat*	*P-value*	*Lower 95%*	*Upper 95%*
17	Intercept	0.8	3.3586	0.2382	0.8271	-9.8885	11.4885
18	Size	6	1.5832	3.7897	0.0322	0.9614	11.0386
19							
20	RESIDUAL OUTPUT						
21							
22	*Observation*	*Predicted Price*	*Residuals*				
23	1	6.8	-0.8				
24	2	9.8	2.2				
25	3	12.8	-2.8				
26	4	15.8	2.2				
27	5	18.8	-0.8				

The least squares estimates of the intercept and slope are found under the column heading "Coef" for Minitab and "Coefficients" for Excel. Thus, $b_0 = .8$ and $b_1 = 6.0$. Accordingly, the least squares line is

$$\hat{Y} = .8 + 6.0X$$

Notice that Minitab explicitly provides the least squares line "Price = 0.80 + 6.00 Size" at the top of the output using user-supplied labels for the response and predictor variables.

The other information in the outputs will be explained as we introduce the relevant topics.

Remember that the least squares line minimizes the sum of the squared residuals. Let's obtain the sum of the squared residuals for the property assessment example. First recall that, for any sample data point, the residual is the difference between the sample Y-value and the Y-value predicted by the least squares line; that is, $e_i = Y_i - \hat{Y}_i$. The residuals are given in the Excel output in Table 9.1 in the "RESIDUAL OUTPUT" portion under the column heading "Residuals." They are determined as follows:

X (size)	Sample Y (price)	Predicted $\hat{Y} = .8 + 6.0X$	Residual $e = (Y - \hat{Y})$	Square Residual $e^2 = (Y - \hat{Y})^2$
1.0	6	6.8	−.8	.64
1.5	12	9.8	2.2	4.84
2.0	10	12.8	−2.8	7.84
2.5	18	15.8	2.2	4.84
3.0	18	18.8	−.8	.64
			$\Sigma(Y_i - \hat{Y}_i) = 0.0$	$\Sigma(Y_i - \hat{Y}_i)^2 = \Sigma e_i^2 = 18.8$

The sum of squared residuals for the least squares line is abbreviated as SSE. For the least squares line $\hat{Y} = .8 + 6.0X$, the sum of squared residuals is SSE = 18.8; it is found under the "SS" column and across the "Error" row in Minitab, and under the "SS" column and across the "Residual" row in Excel. Given these data, the sum of squared residuals would be larger for any other line. Note also that the sum of the residuals is 0. This means that, with regard to the residuals, the data points below the least squares line are offset perfectly by the data points above the line. The least squares line $\hat{Y} = .8 + 6.0X$ and the residuals are illustrated in Figure 9.11.

Figure 9.11

The least squares line and residuals for the property assess-ment data

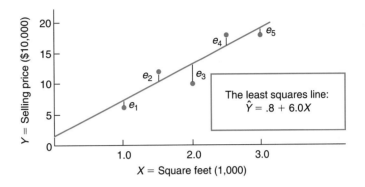

9.3.3 Estimating the Error Variance σ_ϵ^2

Now, we turn our attention to estimating the error variance σ_ϵ^2, which characterizes the closeness of the fit of the regression model to the data. To do this, we develop the estimator S_e^2 of σ_ϵ^2 in a fashion similar to that for estimating a population variance, as in Chapter 2.

The expression for the estimator S_e^2 is similar to Expression (2.7) for a sample variance given in Chapter 2. Remember that the population regression line is unknown. This means that S_e^2 must be based on the deviations of the sample observations (the Y-values) from the estimated regression line (the $\hat{Y}$-values). These deviations are the residuals: $e_i = Y_i - \hat{Y}_i$. Accordingly, *the numerator of S_e^2 is the sum of the squares of the residuals*: SSE = $\Sigma(Y_i - \hat{Y}_i)^2$. What about the denominator (i.e., the degrees of freedom)? To determine the $\hat{Y}$-values, we had to estimate two parameters, β_0 and β_1. So, to make S_e^2 an unbiased estimator of the error variance σ_ϵ^2, we must subtract 2 from n; thus, *the denominator is $n - 2$*. In general, the denominator is the degrees of freedom and is determined by subtracting from n the number of parameters that were estimated in determining the least squares equation. The estimator S_e^2 is defined by Expression (9.7):

$$S_e^2 = \frac{SSE}{n - 2}$$ **(9.7)**

where

$$SSE = \Sigma(Y_i - \hat{Y}_i)^2$$ **(9.8)**

is the sum of the squares of the residuals. Consequently, the error standard deviation σ_ϵ is estimated by

$$S_e = \sqrt{S_e^2}$$ **(9.9)**

It is extremely important to understand what S_e^2 measures. Since the residuals represent the amounts by which the $\hat{Y}$-values "miss" the sample Y-values, S_e^2 measures how well the least squares line fits the sample Y-values. If the fit were perfect, all residuals would equal 0 and therefore S_e^2 would equal 0. The larger the residuals are, the larger S_e^2 is and the worse the fit is. In this sense, S_e^2 may be regarded as an *absolute measure* of how good the fit is—absolute in the sense that if the fit were perfect, S_e^2 would be 0. The statistic S_e^2 is called the **residual variance,** or, equivalently, the **mean square for error (MSE).** The latter term has ties to the analysis of variance procedure of Chapter 8, as you will see later in this chapter. Similarly, the statistic S_e is called the **residual standard deviation,** or, equivalently, the **root mean square for error (RMSE).**

For the property assessment example, the residual variance is $S_e^2 = 6.267$. In Table 9.1, it is found under the "MS" column and across the "Error" row in the Minitab output, and in the "MS" column and "Residual" row in Excel. The residual standard deviation is $S_e = 2.503$; it is identified as "s = 2.503" in Minitab, and as "Standard Error" in the "Regression Statistics" portion of Excel.

9.3.4 The Coefficient of Determination: Partitioning the Total Variation

The primary purpose of regression analysis is to develop a model that fits the data as well as possible and is consistent with theoretical, nonstatistical knowledge of the system. Therefore, in developing a straight-line model, we emphasize the closeness of its fit to the data. As we have discussed, the residual variance (S_e^2 or MSE) provides a measure of the closeness of fit. Our objective in seeking the best fit is to make the value of S_e^2 as small as possible; this becomes especially important as we consider the addition of more predictor variables, as you will see in Chapter 10. But S_e^2 has one drawback as a measure of fit: Its value depends on the scale with which the sample Y-values are measured. This detracts from the ease of interpretation because we cannot interpret S_e^2 unless we first consider the units in which the Y-values are measured. Accordingly, we seek another measure of fit that is not influenced by the scale with which the sample values are measured. The **coefficient of determination,** denoted by r^2, is such a measure.

In defining r^2, we can gain a helpful perspective by taking the point of view of analysis of variance presented in Chapter 8. In analysis of variance, the basic idea is that the total variation for a sample (SST) can be partitioned into two components: (1) the variation attributable to differences among treatment means (SSTR), and (2) the variation attributable to random factors (SSE), where SST = SSTR + SSE.

This concept can be applied to regression analysis as well. Notice that if the Y-values for a population never varied (i.e., if they were constant), they would be perfectly predictable. The difficulty of prediction lies in the fact that Y-values do vary from one member of a population to another. Suppose we have sample data for which the least squares regression line has been determined. We ask the simple question: Why do the sample Y-values vary? There are two possible sources of variation. These are the same sources that are depicted in Expression (9.2) (the simple linear model):

1. *Y-values vary because of the relationship with X.* We know that Y is related to X, and the sample X-values vary. So, as X changes, the Y-values tend to change.

For example, larger homes tend to sell at higher prices than smaller homes, all other factors being equal.

2. *Y-values vary because of random factors.* Other factors also affect Y, and it is assumed they vary randomly. For instance, two homes of the same size may sell for different prices because of differences in location, kitchens, type of construction, and other factors.

Now, how do we measure these two sources of variation? The method for determining the total variation of any variable was introduced in Chapter 2, illustrated extensively in Chapter 8, and used earlier in this section to determine the total variation of the X-values [see Expression (9.6)]. It follows therefore that the total variation of the sample Y-values is determined in the same manner:

$$SS(Y) = \Sigma(Y_i - \bar{Y})^2 = \Sigma Y_i^2 - \frac{(\Sigma Y_i)^2}{n} \tag{9.10}$$

Expression (9.10) is identical to the expression for SST in Chapter 8. To be consistent with the analysis of variance notation of Chapter 8, we use the notation SST to represent this total variation. Thus, $SS(Y)$ and SST represent the same quantity and are equivalent. The variation due to random factors is simply the unexplained variation of the sample Y-values from the least squares line. It is represented by SSE, the sum of squared residuals. The difference between SST, the total variation, and SSE, the variation unexplained by the regression model, is called the **regression sum of squares** and is denoted by **SSR**; that is, $SSR = SST - SSE$. Therefore, *the regression sum of squares represents the variation of sample Y-values that can be explained by the variation among sample X-values.* This leads to a partitioning of total variation much like that seen in Chapter 8:

$$SST \quad = \quad SSR \quad + \quad SSE$$
$$\Downarrow \qquad\qquad \Downarrow \qquad\qquad \Downarrow$$

Total	Regression	Error
sum of	sum of	sum of
squares	squares	squares

For the property assessment example, the total variation of the sample Y-values is $SST = 108.8$. Since the sum of the squared residuals is $SSE = 18.8$, the regression sum of squares is $SSR = SST - SSE = 108.8 - 18.8 = 90.0$. In the Minitab and Excel outputs in Table 9.1, the values of SSR and SST are found under the "SS" column in the "Regression" and "Total" rows, respectively.

The fit of the estimated regression equation can be characterized by comparing the regression sum of squares SSR to the total sum of squares SST. *The coefficient of determination r^2 is the ratio of the regression sum of squares to the total sum of squares;* it is given by the expression

$$r^2 = \frac{SSR}{SST} = \frac{SST - SSE}{SST} \tag{9.11}$$

For the property assessment data, the coefficient of determination is $r^2 = \frac{90}{108.8} = .8272$; it is identified as "R-sq" and given as a percentage (82.7%) by Minitab, and identified as "R Square" and listed under "Regression Statistics" by Excel.

The Meaning and Interpretation of r^2

The coefficient of determination is a descriptive statistic that indicates the fraction of the total variation of the sample Y-values that has been explained by the linear relationship with X. This is relevant because the greater the variation among the sample Y-values, the more difficult they are to predict. To the extent that the total variation in the sample Y-values can be explained with the estimated regression equation, we should be able to predict Y.

The coefficient of determination is a scale-free statistic that always lies between 0 and 1. An r^2 value near 0 indicates that the estimated regression equation explains little of the variation in the sample Y-values. An r^2 value near 1 indicates that the estimated regression equation explains most of the variation in the sample Y-values. The greater the value of r^2, the better the fit and the more effective the estimated regression equation (the least squares line) is in predicting Y. Since r^2 is scale-free, its interpretation is not dependent on the measurement scale of the Y-values. Because r^2 is often misinterpreted, however, you should understand what r^2 does not measure. It does *not* measure the validity of the assumed regression model; that is, the value of r^2 cannot indicate that the population regression equation for Y and X is a straight line. It can only measure how much of the total variation in the sample Y-values is explained by the estimated regression equation. It is not uncommon, for example, to discover that the coefficient of determination for a least squares line is, say, $r^2 = .90$, but that another model fits even better. These issues are examined further in Chapter 10.

9.4 Statistical Inferences for the Simple Linear Regression Model

So far we have discussed the residual variance S_e^2 and the coefficient of determination r^2 as measures of how closely a least squares line fits the Y-values of a representative sample. Before using a regression model for estimation and prediction, however, it is important to ascertain whether the model is adequate for the intended use. The assessment of model performance involves all of the following issues:

1. *Do the sample data indicate convincingly that a linear association exists between Y and X in the population?* It is possible that there is no association at all or that the association is not linear. If so, the relationship suggested by the least squares line could simply be the result of random sampling variation. A scatter diagram provides initial insight into this question. The population slope β_1 is the key parameter here. If β_1 is 0, then there is no linear association between Y and X. Therefore, if the sample data do not support the existence of a linear relationship between Y and X in the population, it would be foolish to base serious decisions on the least squares line.

2. *How accurate are the estimates and/or predictions that result from using the least squares line?* If you wish to base decisions on these estimates and/or predictions, it is important to understand how far off they might be.

3. *Are the conditions necessary for regression analysis present in this application?* As you will soon see, the regression inferences to address the first two issues listed here

are based on certain assumptions about the population. If these assumptions are incorrect, some misleading or even ridiculous findings may result.

4. *Is it possible to extend the assumed regression model to include other potential predictor variables?* For example, in the property assessment problem, is it possible that variables such as the number of bathrooms, presence of a fireplace, or age of the house have a meaningful influence on selling price? This is, of course, quite possible; this task is examined in detail in Chapter 10.

After discussing model assumptions, we present the fundamental regression inferences for the simple linear model. Then we revisit the property assessment example to point out the appropriate quantities in Table 9.1 relative to these inferences.

9.4.1   Model Assumptions

The procedures involved in regression inferences are valid only if certain conditions exist for the population. Since we cannot observe the entire population, we must be willing to assume that these conditions exist. Later we provide ways to use the sample data to investigate the credibility of these assumptions. Regression inferences are based on the following four assumptions about the association between Y and X in the population. They refer specifically to the simple linear model given by Expression (9.2):

1. *The simple linear model correctly depicts the association between the response and predictor variables.* This means that for all values of X within the range of the sample data, the mean value of the response variable Y is given by the population regression line for each value of X. In other words, for any value X, there is a population of Y-values for which $E(Y) = \beta_0 + \beta_1 X$, and the mean of the random error equals 0.

2. *The error variance σ_ϵ^2 is constant.* A constant error variance means that the variation of the Y-values around the population regression line is the same for all values of X within the range of the sample data. If the variation of the Y-values around the regression equation depends on the value of X, then σ_ϵ^2 is not constant for all X-values. This necessitates the use of an alternative regression procedure known as *weighted least squares*, which is beyond the scope of this text.

3. *The random errors are independent.* This assumption implies that the errors associated with any two Y-values are independent. For example, knowing whether one Y-value is above or below the population regression line tells us nothing about whether another value is above or below the regression line.

4. *The random errors are normally distributed.* This assumption implies that the Y-values are normally distributed around the population regression line. So we assume that ϵ is a normal random variable with mean 0 and standard deviation σ_ϵ, and therefore for any value of X, Y is a normal random variable with mean $\beta_0 + \beta_1 X$ and standard deviation σ_ϵ.

These assumptions are illustrated in Figure 9.12.

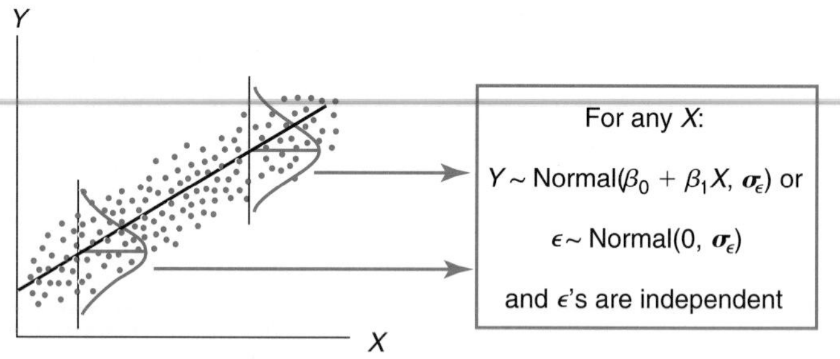

Figure 9.12

Assumptions for regression inferences

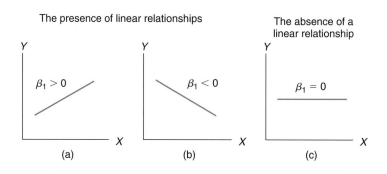

For any X:

$Y \sim \text{Normal}(\beta_0 + \beta_1 X, \sigma_\epsilon)$ or

$\epsilon \sim \text{Normal}(0, \sigma_\epsilon)$

and ϵ's are independent

Checking the Regression Assumptions

The first three assumptions are more important than the last one. Regression inferences are to a reasonable degree insensitive to the violation of the normality assumption. On the other hand, no regression analysis is complete without assurance of the validity of the first three assumptions. To do this, *we visually examine a plot of the residuals associated with the least squares line.* Our purpose is to detect a pattern among the residuals that would suggest a possible violation of an assumption. Since residuals represent random errors, they should exhibit no discernible pattern. An introduction to the analysis of residuals is given in Section 9.4.7.

9.4.2 The Mean and Standard Error of b_1 and b_0

The least squares estimators b_1 and b_0 are the best statistics for inferences concerning the population slope β_1 and intercept β_0, respectively. Recall that if β_1 is 0, there is no linear association between Y and X in the population. In other words, a linear relationship between Y and X exists for the population only if the slope β_1 is not 0. Figure 9.13 illustrates the nature of the population regression line $E(Y) = \beta_0 + \beta_1 X$ for the presence of a linear association, parts (a) and (b), and the absence of a linear relationship between Y and X, part (c). Inferences that involve the slope β_1 are far more important than inferences about the intercept β_0.

Figure 9.13

The presence or absence of linear relationships between Y and X

The presence of linear relationships

The absence of a linear relationship

$\beta_1 > 0$ (a)

$\beta_1 < 0$ (b)

$\beta_1 = 0$ (c)

You may recall from Chapters 5–8 that *the key to statistical inference is to determine the sampling distribution of the best statistic for the inference.* Since b_1 is the best statistic for establishing the existence of a linear relationship, we must determine its sampling distribution. At first, you may have difficulty thinking of b_1 as a random variable. It is, of course, because b_1 is a sample statistic; for that matter, so is b_0. Their values in a given application depend on the specific sample we happen to select.

We first determine the mean and standard error of b_1; then we determine its sampling distribution. It has been shown that the mean and standard error of b_1 are as follows:

$$E(b_1) = \beta_1 \tag{9.12}$$

$$SE(b_1) = \sqrt{\frac{\sigma_\epsilon^2}{SS(X)}} \tag{9.13}$$

where $SS(X)$ is the total sum of squares for the predictor variable X as defined by Expression (9.6). Recall that the unknown error variance σ_ϵ^2 is estimated by the residual variance S_e^2. Thus, the estimated standard error of b_1 is

$$SE(b_1) \approx \sqrt{\frac{S_e^2}{SS(X)}} \tag{9.14}$$

It has also been shown that the mean and estimated standard error of b_0 are given by

$$E(b_0) = \beta_0 \tag{9.15}$$

$$SE(b_0) \approx \sqrt{\frac{S_e^2 \Sigma X_i^2}{nSS(X)}} \tag{9.16}$$

respectively. So the least squares statistic b_1 is an unbiased estimator of the population slope β_1, as is the statistic b_0 for the intercept β_0.

9.4.3 The Sampling Distribution of b_1

If the necessary assumptions about the population are true, then it can be shown that the sampling distribution of the least squares statistic b_1 is the normal distribution with mean and standard error as given by Expressions (9.12) and (9.13), respectively. Since b_1 is normally distributed, we could easily standardize it to the Z statistic if we knew the error variance σ_ϵ^2. We could then use the standard normal distribution for inferences about the slope β_1. But since σ_ϵ^2 is not known, we must estimate σ_ϵ^2 in Expression (9.13) with the residual variance S_e^2. As you would suspect, standardizing b_1 in this way leads to the following T statistic:

$$T = \frac{b_1 - \beta_1}{SE(b_1)} \tag{9.17}$$

This statistic has a T distribution with $n - 2$ degrees of freedom. [There are $n - 2$ degrees of freedom here because the denominator of Expression (9.7) for the residual variance S_e^2 is $n - 2$.] Therefore, *statistical inferences concerning the slope β_1 are based on the least squares statistic b_1 and involve the T distribution with $n - 2$ degrees of freedom.*

9.4.4 Confidence Intervals and Hypothesis Testing for β_1

The use of the T distribution for making statistical inferences should be familiar to you by now. With regard to inferences about the slope β_1, the procedure remains the same in substance. (You may wish to review Sections 5.5.4 and 6.3.3–6.3.5 in this regard.)

Confidence Intervals for β_1

Since the key to understanding the association between Y and X is the slope β_1 of the population regression line, it is essential that we understand the precision with which β_1 is being estimated. As is always the case in estimation, *we characterize the precision of an estimator by computing its margin of sampling error and the resulting confidence interval.* Based on the discussion of confidence intervals in Section 6.3.3, a $100(1 - \alpha)\%$ confidence interval for the slope β_1 is given by

$$b_1 \pm t_{1 - \alpha/2, n - 2}\, \text{SE}(b_1) \qquad\qquad \textbf{(9.18)}$$

where

$$\text{Margin of sampling error} = t_{1 - \alpha/2, n - 2}\, \text{SE}(b_1) \qquad\qquad \textbf{(9.19)}$$

and $t_{1 - \alpha/2, n - 2}$ is the appropriate quantile value of the T distribution.

Hypothesis Testing for β_1

In the property assessment example, suppose we want to test a null hypothesis of no linear association between selling price (Y) and size (X) against the alternative hypothesis that there is a linear association. With respect to the simple linear model, Expression (9.2), these hypotheses may be stated as follows:

$$H_0: \quad \beta_1 = 0 \qquad\qquad \textbf{(9.20)}$$
$$H_a: \quad \beta_1 \neq 0$$

As we have already done, we can use confidence intervals to determine whether the sample evidence contradicts the claim of H_0 of no linear association between Y and X. If 0 is not included in an interval with a high level of confidence, then the sample data contradict the claim of no linear association between Y and X and support the presence of a linear association (the alternative hypothesis). The same result can be reached by using the P-value approach. The P-value reveals the extent to which the sample data contradict the claim of no linear association between Y and X. As before, the smaller the P-value, the stronger the evidence against H_0, or in favor of H_a.

Let's return to the computer output in Table 9.1 to point out regression inference quantities for the property assessment example. The estimated standard errors of the least squares statistics b_0 and b_1 are found under the column heading "Stdev" in Minitab and under the column heading "Standard Error" in Excel. Thus, SE $(b_0) = 3.359$ and SE $(b_1) = 1.583$. The 95% confidence limits for β_0 and β_1 are found under the columns "Lower 95%" and "Upper 95%," respectively, in the Excel output. (Minitab does not explicitly provide confidence limits for population coefficients, but they can be determined from the Minitab output.) Thus, the 95% confidence interval for β_1 is (.9614, 11.0386). The T-value [Expression (9.17)] for testing the null hypothesis of no linear association between price and size [Expression (9.20)] is found under the column heading "t-ratio" (or "T") and across the "size" row in Minitab, and under the column heading "t Stat" in the "Size" row in Excel. The corresponding P-value is found immediately to the right of the T-value. Thus, $T = 3.79$ and P-value = .032. Since this P-value is sufficiently small, the null hypothesis of no linear association is contradicted. Consequently, there appears to be a discernible linear association between selling price and size.

9.4.5 An Analysis of Variance Approach in Simple Linear Regression

In defining the coefficient of determination r^2 in Section 9.3.4, we took an analysis of variance perspective by partitioning the total variation in the sample Y-values (SST) into two components: the regression sum of squares (SSR), which accounts for the variation in the sample Y-values that can be explained by the variation in the sample X-values, and the error sum of squares (SSE), which accounts for the variation in the Y-values that remains unexplained by the variation in the X-values—that is, the variation due to random causes.

As an alternative to the T procedure of the previous section, we may use an analysis of variance procedure to test the null hypothesis

$$H_0: \quad \beta_1 = 0$$

against the two-sided alternative hypothesis

$$H_a: \quad \beta_1 \neq 0$$

The analysis of variance procedure is equivalent to the T statistic procedure if the alternative hypothesis is two-sided. This means that the P-values are identical and therefore the conclusion is the same. However, the analysis of variance procedure provides an insight into the possible sources of variation that becomes especially useful if more complicated models are considered (as discussed in Chapter 10). In addition, the outputs of most computer statistical packages include the pertinent information for both the T statistic and the analysis of variance procedure. If you learn both procedures, virtually all of this output will be meaningful to you, and you will be better prepared to study the development of more complex models.

Recall that in analysis of variance, each sum of squares has associated with it a certain number of degrees of freedom. The total sum of squares SST has $n - 1$ degrees of freedom. The number of degrees of freedom for the error sum of squares SSE is $n - 2$, since there are two parameters being estimated (β_0 and β_1) in the expression for SSE. Because the degrees of freedom are additive (df for SST = df for SSR + df for SSE), this leaves a single degree of freedom for SSR. It is always true that *the number of degrees of freedom for SSR corresponds to the number of terms in the assumed regression model that involve predictor variables.* Since there is only one such term for the simple linear model (that term is $\beta_1 X$), there is 1 degree of freedom for the regression sum of squares SSR.

Now recall from Chapter 8 that a mean square is defined as a sum of squares divided by its degrees of freedom. Consequently, the mean square for regression is

$$\text{MSR} = \frac{\text{SSR}}{1} \tag{9.21}$$

whereas the mean square for error (the residual variance) is

$$\text{MSE} = S_e^2 = \frac{\text{SSE}}{n - 2} \tag{9.22}$$

To test the null hypothesis that there is no linear association between Y and X, we compare the mean square for regression to the mean square for error. Thus, the statistic in the analysis of variance procedure is the ratio

$$F = \frac{MSR}{MSE} \qquad\qquad \textbf{(9.23)}$$

If the null hypothesis of no linear association between Y and X is true, the sampling distribution of this ratio is the F distribution with 1 and $n - 2$ degrees of freedom.

Let's use intuition to consider what values of the F ratio would lead us to conclude that a linear relationship does exist between Y and X. If Y is linearly related to X, then SSR, the variation of the sample Y-values that is explained by the variation in the X-values, should be relatively large. In comparison, the unexplained variation in Y, SSE, should be relatively small. To the extent that SSR is large and SSE is small, the sample data suggest that a linear association exists. Therefore, *the larger the F value, the stronger the evidence of a linear association between Y and X, and the smaller the P-value.*

Let's return again to the computer output in Table 9.1 to illustrate the analysis of variance procedure for the property assessment example. From the analysis of variance tables given by both Minitab and Excel, SSR = 90, SSE = 18.8, SST = 108.8, MSR = 90, MSE = 6.267, and the F-value is 90/6.267 = 14.362. Since the corresponding P-value is .032 (given under the column "p" in Minitab and "Significance F" in Excel) is sufficiently small, the null hypothesis of no linear association is contradicted.

As we have said, the analysis of variance and T procedures are equivalent. In fact, it can be demonstrated mathematically that the square of a T random variable with ν degrees of freedom is an F random variable with 1 numerator and ν denominator degrees of freedom; that is,

$$T_\nu^2 = F_{1,\nu} \qquad\qquad \textbf{(9.24)}$$

This means that, for a particular application, the square of the T-value equals the F-value, and the P-values of the T and F statistics are exactly the same. For the property assessment example, $T^2 = (3.79)^2 = F = 14.36$, and P-value = .032. Therefore, the T statistic [Expression (9.17)] and the analysis of variance F statistic [Expression (9.23)] are equivalent.

Using the Computer

In Tables 9.2 and 9.3, we provide further illustration of regression output using Excel and JMP IN for Example 9.1 (energy versus temperature) and Example 9.2 (salary versus years of experience), respectively.

From the output in Table 9.2, there is very little doubt that a linear relationship exists between energy consumption and a day's high temperature in the population (the sample data easily contradict the null hypothesis $H_0: \beta_1 = 0$ using either the T or F statistic). In addition, 97.5% of the variation in the sample energy values is explained by the variation in temperatures. This finding, along with the important fact that the slope β_1 is being estimated with considerable accuracy (as we explain in the following subsection), leads us to believe (at least tentatively) that the least squares line "energy = 87.0 − 3.46 temp" is indeed adequate for estimation and prediction within the range of high temperatures used to determine this line.

Table 9.2

Excel output for
Example 9.1

	A	B	C	D	E	F	G
1	SUMMARY OUTPUT						
2							
3	*Regression Statistics*						
4	Multiple R	0.9873					
5	R Square	0.9747					
6	Adjusted R Square	0.9731					
7	Standard Error	2.5856					
8	Observations	18					
9							
10	ANOVA						
11		*df*	*SS*	*MS*	*F*	*Significance F*	
12	Regression	1	4123.538	4123.538	616.822	0.000	
13	Residual	16	106.962	6.685			
14	Total	17	4230.5				
15							
16		*Coefficients*	*Standard Error*	*t Stat*	*P-value*	*Lower 95%*	*Upper 95%*
17	Intercept	86.996	0.757	114.887	0.000	85.390	88.601
18	Temperature	-3.464	0.139	-24.836	0.000	-3.760	-3.168

Table 9.3

JMP IN output for
Example 9.2

Linear Fit

Salary = 28.9457 + 1.26069 Years

Summary of Fit

RSquare	0.874126
RSquare Adj	0.865135
Root Mean Square Error	5.016546
Mean of Response	48.25
Observations (or Sum Wgts)	16

Analysis of Variance

Source	DF	Sum of Squares	Mean Square	F Ratio
Model	1	2446.6798	2446.68	97.2227
Error	14	352.3202	25.17	Prob>F
C Total	15	2799.0000		<.0001

Parameter Estimates

Term	Estimate	Std Error	t Ratio	Prob>|t|
Intercept	28.945719	2.325052	12.45	<.0001
Years	1.2606878	0.127857	9.86	<.0001

For the sample data of Example 9.2, the format of the JMP IN output is quite similar to those of Minitab and Excel. The analysis of variance table is given, followed by the least squares estimates, standard errors, and so on. The output in Table 9.3 reveals that there is virtually no doubt a relationship exists between salary and years of experience. Although this analysis easily detects a linear association between salary and years of experience (T-value = 9.86, F-value = 97.2227, and P-value < .0001), it remains to be seen whether this relationship is *best* described by a straight line. We say this because in the scatter diagram (Figure 9.6), we see a leveling off after about 20 years. Therefore, the least squares line "Salary = 28.95 + 1.26 Years" should not be used for estimation or prediction until we explore the possibility that a model with curvature better characterizes the nature of the association. (Such models are discussed in Chapter 10.)

9.4.6 Using the Precision of b_1 in Assessing the Linear Relationship Between Y and X

The slope β_1 of the population regression line is the key determinant of the linear relationship between Y and X. As we pointed out in the second item at the beginning of Section 9.4, it is important to know the accuracy or precision of b_1, the best statistic for inferences about the population slope. As an alternative to computer use, let's determine a 95% confidence interval for the population slope β_1 using the property assessment example. For $n - 2 = 3$ degrees of freedom and a 95% confidence level, the T quantile value is $t_{.975,3} = 3.182$. Since $b_1 = 6$ and $SE(b_1) = 1.583$ (from Table 9.1), a 95% confidence interval for β_1 is [using Expression (9.18)]

$$6 \pm (3.182)(1.583) = 6 \pm 5.04$$

or (.96, 11.04). Notice that the value $\beta_1 = 0$ is not included in this interval, thus indicating the presence of a linear association between Y and X. At the same time, though, this interval shows that the slope β_1 is not being estimated very accurately. When X increases by one unit (1,000 square feet), the corresponding increase in the mean selling price could be as little as $9,600 (if $\beta_1 = .96$) or as much as $110,400 (if $\beta_1 = 11.04$), with 95% confidence. This large spread indicates a lack of meaningful precision in the estimation of β_1. Without doubt, the small sample size ($n = 5$) has contributed to this. Therefore, the range of plausible values of β_1 is unacceptably wide. This lack of precision resulted directly from a large standard error for b_1. The point is that the larger the standard error, the larger the margin of sampling error, and the greater the range of plausible values of β_1.

For any meaningful precision in estimating β_1, the standard error of b_1 should be much smaller than the magnitude of the b_1 value. In other words, the ratio of the b_1 value to its standard error should be quite large in magnitude. But notice that this ratio is simply the T-value $[T = b_1/SE(b_1)]$ for the null hypothesis H_0: $\beta_1 = 0$. Therefore, the larger the magnitude of the T-value, the better the precision in estimating the population slope β_1.

In Table 9.4, we provide the values of b_1, their standard errors, and their T-values for the three examples analyzed so far in this chapter. Notice that the best precision by far in estimating the slope β_1 is achieved in the energy versus temperature problem because the T-value has the greatest magnitude ($T = -24.84$). This should not be too

Table 9.4

Comparison of standard errors and *T*-values for three examples

Example	Value of b_1	Standard Error	*T*-value
Property assessment	6.0	1.5832	3.79
Salary versus experience	1.2607	.1279	9.86
Energy versus temperature	−3.4642	.1395	−24.84

surprising if we compare the scatter diagram for the energy versus temperature example (Figure 9.5) with those of the other two examples (Figures 9.6 and 9.9).

As you know, confidence intervals can be used to characterize the precision of estimators. For the least squares statistic b_1, a $100(1 - \alpha)\%$ confidence interval for β_1 was given by Expression (9.18) and the margin of sampling error was given by Expression (9.19). For the salary versus experience example, a 95% confidence interval for β_1 is (the quantile value is $t_{.975,14} = 2.145$)

$$1.2607 \pm (2.145)(.1279) = 1.2607 \pm .2743$$

or (.99, 1.54). This interval means that when the number of years of experience increases by 1, the average salary may increase by as little as \$990 (if $\beta_1 = .99$) or by as much as \$1,540 (if $\beta_1 = 1.54$), with 95% confidence. In relative terms, the spread of this interval is considerably less than that in the property assessment example.

For the energy versus temperature example, a 95% confidence interval for β_1 is (the quantile value is $t_{.975,16} = 2.120$)

$$-3.4642 \pm (2.120)(.1395) = -3.4642 \pm .2957$$

or $(-3.76, -3.17)$. (See also Table 9.2.) This interval means that when the daily high temperature increases by 1 degree Celsius, the average energy usage might decrease by as much as 3.76 kilowatts (if $\beta_1 = -3.76$) or by as little as 3.17 kilowatts (if $\beta_1 = -3.17$), with 95% confidence. The narrowness of this interval when compared to those of the other two examples makes it clear that the population slope β_1 for the energy versus temperature example is being estimated with the best precision.

9.4.7   An Introduction to the Analysis of Residuals

In this section, we introduce the analysis of residuals by using Examples 9.1 and 9.2 as illustrations. The analysis of residuals is an important tool in attempting to improve an estimated regression equation. We introduce analysis of residuals here and explore the topic in greater depth in Chapter 10.

In Section 9.4.1, we discussed the assumptions essential to regression inferences. The first assumption was that the simple linear model correctly represents the association between the response and predictor variables. If this assumption is true, then the graph of the residuals (on the vertical axis) against the corresponding X-values (on the horizontal axis) should reveal no discernible pattern. The reason for this is simple enough: If the model is correct, the residuals represent pure random errors; thus, the residuals should exhibit no pattern whatsoever when graphed against any variable. If a pattern is revealed, the residuals may not represent purely random errors. Consequently, this key assumption may not be correct.

In Figure 9.14, the residuals for the least squares line of Example 9.1 (daily energy usage versus daily high temperature) are plotted against the corresponding temperatures. Similarly, in Figure 9.15, the residuals for Example 9.2 (salary versus years of experience) are plotted against the corresponding years of experience. Let's start with Figure 9.14. There appears to be no discernible pattern with regard to the temperature values. In other words, there seems to be no association between the residuals and the temperature values. But now examine the residuals in Figure 9.15. It should be clear to you that the same thing cannot be said here. There appears to be a distinct pattern for the residuals with regard to the number of years of experience. Notice that the

Figure 9.14

Residuals versus temperature for Example 9.1 using Excel

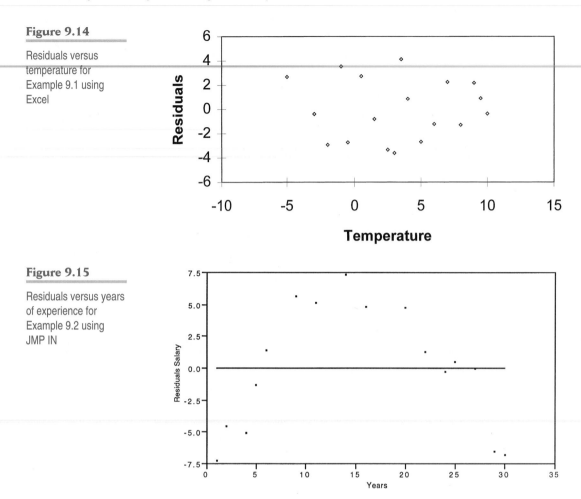

Figure 9.15

Residuals versus years of experience for Example 9.2 using JMP IN

residuals at the low end of the range of years of experience are negative, at mid-range they are positive, and at the high end they are negative again. Such an inverted U-shaped pattern suggests the presence of curvature in the response with regard to increasing years of experience. We need to consider a model that incorporates curvature in the relationship.

9.5   The Reliability of Estimates and Predictions

Generally, if the T statistic (or, equivalently, the analysis of variance F statistic) fails to indicate that Y is linearly related to X, then we would not use the least squares line for estimation or prediction. But even if these procedures support the existence of a linear relationship, the least squares line is not likely to be satisfactory for estimation or prediction, if the estimates or predictions are not very accurate.

Recall that the fundamental goal in regression analysis is to develop a model that makes sense and fits the representative data such that the error variance is as small as possible. Such a model provides acceptable accuracy when used for estimation or prediction. In other words, the goal is to develop a model that makes sense and provides satisfactory accuracy (precision) in its estimates and predictions.

9.5.1 Estimating the Mean of Y, Given X

As we discussed in Section 9.2.3, there are two primary uses of regression models: (1) to gain insight into potential relationships and (2) to estimate and predict. The latter use consists of either of two cases. In one case, we wish to estimate the *average* value of Y given the knowledge that X equals some particular value, which we denote as x. In the other case, we wish to predict an *individual* Y-value given that X equals x. To better distinguish between these two uses, we use the term *estimation* to refer to the estimation of an average value of Y and *prediction* to refer to predictions for individual Y-values.

It is the need to estimate means that we now address. For the property assessment example, suppose we want to estimate average selling price for all comparable houses with 2,200 square feet of space. We simply substitute $X = 2.2$ into the estimated regression equation $\hat{Y} = .8 + 6.0X$. Thus, we determine the estimated average selling price to be $\hat{Y} = .8 + (6.0)(2.2) = 14.0$—that is, $140,000. It is essential to understand the precision of an estimate before using it to make important decisions. Let's examine the accuracy that can be expected of the estimate of $140,000 for the average selling price of comparable 2,200-square-foot houses. The precision of any estimate is characterized by its margin of sampling error or, equivalently, the associated confidence interval. In either case, the first step is to determine the standard error of the estimator.

It can be demonstrated with algebra that the standard error of $\hat{Y}$, given that $X = x$, works out to be

$$SE(\hat{Y}) = \sqrt{\sigma_\epsilon^2 \left[\frac{1}{n} + \frac{(x - \bar{X})^2}{SS(X)} \right]} \tag{9.25}$$

Since the error variance σ_ϵ^2 is unknown, it is estimated by the residual variance S_e^2. *Thus, the estimated standard error of $\hat{Y}$, given that $X = x$, is*

$$SE(\hat{Y}) \approx \sqrt{S_e^2 \left[\frac{1}{n} + \frac{(x - \bar{X})^2}{SS(X)} \right]} \tag{9.26}$$

Now, the estimator $\hat{Y} = b_0 + b_1 X$ can be shown to be a normally distributed random variable. And since we have estimated σ_ϵ^2 with S_e^2 inferences about the population mean of Y when $X = x$ are based on the T distribution with $n - 2$ degrees of freedom. Consequently, a $100(1 - \alpha)\%$ confidence interval for the mean of Y when $X = x$ is as follows:

$$\hat{Y} \pm t_{1 - \alpha/2, n - 2} \sqrt{S_e^2 \left[\frac{1}{n} + \frac{(x - \bar{X})^2}{SS(X)} \right]} \tag{9.27}$$

where

$$\text{Margin of error} = t_{1 - \alpha/2, n - 2} \sqrt{S_e^2 \left[\frac{1}{n} + \frac{(x - \bar{X})^2}{SS(X)} \right]} \tag{9.28}$$

Shortly, we use the computer to determine SE($\hat{Y}$) and a 95% confidence interval for the mean of Y when $X = x$.

9.5.2 Predicting an Individual Y-Value, Given X

Given an X-value, predictions of *individual Y-values* are identical to estimates of the average value of Y corresponding to the value of X. Both are determined by substituting the X-value into the estimated regression equation $\hat{Y} = b_0 + b_1 X$. However, *prediction errors for individual Y-values are larger than those for the mean.* The reason is not difficult to understand. In both cases, the prediction or estimate is the $\hat{Y}$-value of the least squares line corresponding to the given X-value. Since the least squares line is not likely to match the population regression line perfectly, this results in error. This error is the same for predictions of individual Y-values as for estimates of the population average value. But predictions for individual Y-values are subject to an additional error as well, because an *individual Y-value* is not likely to lie directly on the population regression line. If we knew the regression line perfectly, we would estimate the mean of Y for that value of X without error, but we would not be able to predict an individual Y-value perfectly. This is the reason that errors are larger when we predict *individual Y-values* than when we estimate the population *mean* of Y, given the particular X-value. Figure 9.16 illustrates this point.

Figure 9.16

The two components of prediction errors: (1) Incorrect estimation of the population regression line and (2) deviation of an individual data point from the population regression line

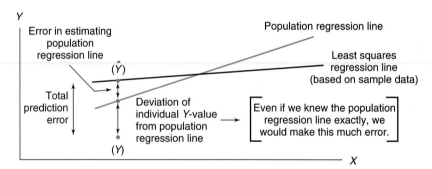

Let's see how the additional source of error affects the standard error of predictions of individual Y-values. We learned in Section 9.5.1 that the variance of the estimated *mean* of Y, given $X = x$, is

$$\text{Var}(\hat{Y}) = \sigma_\epsilon^2 \left[\frac{1}{n} + \frac{(x - \bar{X})^2}{\text{SS}(X)} \right]$$

We also know from item 4 in Section 9.4.1 that the variance of the individual Y-values about the population regression line is

$$\text{Var}(Y) = \sigma_\epsilon^2$$

It can be shown mathematically that *the variance of prediction errors for individual Y-values is the sum of these two variances*—that is,

$$\sigma_\epsilon^2 + \sigma_\epsilon^2 \left[\frac{1}{n} + \frac{(x - \bar{X})^2}{\text{SS}(X)} \right]$$

By factoring out σ_ϵ^2, we can simplify this to

$$\sigma_\epsilon^2\left[1 + \frac{1}{n} + \frac{(x - \bar{X})^2}{SS(X)}\right] \tag{9.29}$$

The standard error of predictions for individual Y-values, when $X = x$, is found by taking the square root of Expression (9.29). To distinguish it from the standard error of estimates of the mean of Y given $X = x$ [which was denoted by $SE(\hat{Y})$], this standard error is denoted by $SE_p(\hat{Y})$. The subscript p indicates "prediction for an individual Y-value." So,

$$SE_p(\hat{Y}) = \sqrt{\sigma_\epsilon^2\left[1 + \frac{1}{n} + \frac{(x - \bar{X})^2}{SS(X)}\right]} \tag{9.30}$$

As before, the error variance σ_ϵ^2 is estimated by the residual variance S_e^2. Thus, the estimated standard error is

$$SE_p(\hat{Y}) \approx \sqrt{S_e^2\left[1 + \frac{1}{n} + \frac{(x - \bar{X})^2}{SS(X)}\right]} \tag{9.31}$$

By comparing Expressions (9.26) and (9.31), you should see that the standard error for predictions of individual Y-values is larger than the standard error for estimating the mean of Y, given a particular value of X. This suggests that we expect less precision in predicting individual Y-values than in estimating the mean of Y, given that $X = x$.

To measure the precision of predictions, we determine an interval estimate based on $SE_p(\hat{Y})$. We call this interval a *prediction interval* to distinguish it clearly from the confidence interval for the mean of Y, given in Expression (9.27). A $100(1 - \alpha)\%$ prediction interval for an *individual Y-value*, given $X = x$, is as follows:

$$\hat{Y} \pm t_{1 - \alpha/2, n - 2}\sqrt{S_e^2\left[1 + \frac{1}{n} + \frac{(x - \bar{X})^2}{SS(X)}\right]} \tag{9.32}$$

We now use the property assessment example to illustrate the relationship between prediction intervals for individual Y-values and confidence intervals for the mean Y-value, given particular values of X, as seen in Figure 9.17. The "confidence

Figure 9.17

A comparison of confidence intervals for the mean of Y, given $X = x$, and prediction intervals for an individual Y-value, given $X = x$ over a range of X-values

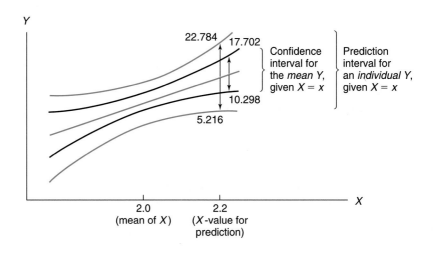

bands," determined by computer, represent the intervals that correspond to a range of X-values. The two intervals for $X = 2.2$ are indicated on the graph. Notice that (1) the prediction interval is always wider than the corresponding confidence interval for the mean, and (2) the intervals become wider as we consider X-values farther from the center. The reason for this is provided in Section 9.6.

Using the Computer

We can use a computer to determine estimates and predictions as well as confidence and prediction intervals. Minitab and JMP IN have this capability, but Excel currently does not.

We use the three examples that we have discussed at length in this chapter to illustrate JMP IN output in this regard. The Minitab output is very similar in format. For each problem, we identify three values of X: one near the center of the X range and the other two near the extremes (for property assessment, $X = 1$, 2, and 3; for salary, $X = 3$, 15, and 27; and for energy, $X = -4$, 3, and 9). The outputs are given in Tables 9.5–9.7, respectively. For each X-value, they consist of the estimated average Y-value (under the column "Predicted"), the standard error for the average Y-value as given by Expression (9.26) (under the column "StdErr Predicted"), a 95% confidence interval for the average Y-value as given by Expression (9.27) (the range is found under the columns "Lower 95%" and "Upper 95%"), the standard error for an individual Y-value as given by Expression (9.31) (under the column "StdErr Indiv"), and a 95% prediction interval for an individual Y-value as given by Expression (9.32) (the range is found under the columns "Lower 95% Indiv" and "Upper 95% Indiv"). From these results, it is important to notice that the best accuracy in estimation and prediction is achieved when the desired X-value is near the average of the X-values used to determine the regression equation. As the X-value moves away from the average X-value, the accuracy in estimation and prediction decreases. This result is illustrated in Figure 9.17. Finally, the accuracy of estimation and prediction is clearly the best, in relative terms, for the energy consumption example.

Table 9.5

Confidence and prediction intervals for the property assessment example when $X = 1$, 2, and 3

Size	Predicted Price	StdErr Predicted Price	Lower 95% Pred Price	Upper 95% Pred Price	StdErr Indiv Price	Lower 95% Indiv Price	Upper 95% Indiv Price
1	6.8	1.939072	0.628904	12.9711	3.166491	-3.27736	16.87736
2	12.8	1.119524	9.237116	16.36288	2.742262	4.072752	21.52725
3	18.8	1.939072	12.6289	24.9711	3.166491	8.722642	28.87736

9.6

Factors That Affect Regression Standard Errors: Some Design Considerations

If we had the opportunity to plan the collection of sample data, is there anything we could do to assure better accuracy for the various least squares estimates? To answer this question, we need to examine the factors that affect the standard errors

Table 9.6

Confidence and prediction intervals for the salary example when $X = 3$, 15, and 27

Years	Predicted Salary	StdErr Predicted Salary	Lower 95% Pred Salary	Upper 95% Pred Salary	StdErr Indiv Salary	Lower 95% Indiv Salary	Upper 95% Indiv Salary
3	32.72778	2.012729	28.41092	37.04465	5.405258	21.13468	44.32088
15	47.85604	1.254773	45.16482	50.54725	5.171091	36.76517	58.9469
27	62.98429	1.950864	58.80011	67.16846	5.382527	51.43994	74.52863

Table 9.7

Confidence and prediction intervals for the energy example when $X = -4$, 3, and 9

Temper- ature	Predicted Energy use	StdErr Predicted Energy use	Lower 95% Pred Energy use	Upper 95% Pred Energy use	StdErr Indiv Energy use	Lower 95% Indiv Energy use	Upper 95% Indiv Energy use
-4	100.8525	1.177372	98.35656	103.3484	2.84101	94.82982	106.8751
3	76.60315	0.610211	75.30957	77.89673	2.656593	70.97145	82.23485
9	55.81803	1.010383	53.67612	57.95993	2.775969	49.93327	61.70279

of the least squares estimators. Of particular interest are the standard errors of the slope estimator b_1, the estimated average value of Y, given $X = x$, and the predicted value of an individual Y, given $X = x$. The expressions for these standard errors are repeated here:

$$SE(b_1) = \sqrt{\frac{\sigma_\epsilon^2}{SS(X)}}$$

$$SE(\hat{Y}) = \sqrt{\sigma_\epsilon^2 \left[\frac{1}{n} + \frac{(x - \bar{X})^2}{SS(X)} \right]}$$

$$SE_p(\hat{Y}) = \sqrt{\sigma_\epsilon^2 \left[1 + \frac{1}{n} + \frac{(x - \bar{X})^2}{SS(X)} \right]}$$

Take a close look at these expressions. Do these standard errors have anything in common? The answer, of course, is yes. All three depend on the error variance σ_ϵ^2. They also depend on $SS(X)$, which measures the variation in the X-values. Finally, the last two standard errors depend directly on the sample size n and the quantity $(x - \bar{X})^2$. This quantity represents the square of the distance of the particular value x from the value of the sample mean $\bar{X}$.

Let's examine these factors with regard to how they affect the accuracy of estimation or prediction and what this suggests about the selection of sample data.

1. *The error variance.* Recall that σ_ϵ^2 measures how closely the Y-values cluster around the population regression line. Thus, the larger the error variance is, the less reliable the estimates and predictions are. Keep in mind, however, that ideally the error variance is not large because true random errors are relatively

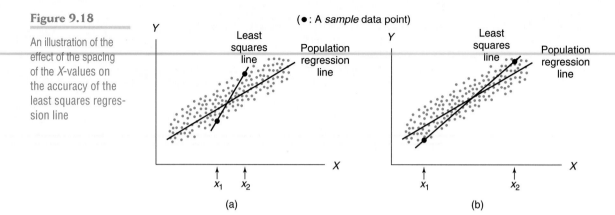

(a) (b)

small. Since the error variance σ_ϵ^2 is estimated by the residual variance S_e^2 it is always advisable to make sure that the value of S_e^2 is not large because of the omission of other terms or predictor variables that need to be incorporated in the regression model to improve it.

2. *The variation in the sample values of the predictor variable.*   The larger SS(X) is, the more accurate the estimates and predictions tend to be. Recall that SS(X) measures the total variation of the X-values in the sample. Thus, the larger the range of values in our sample data for the predictor variable X, the more accurate our estimates are expected to be. Let's think about why this is true. Suppose we wished to determine a regression line with a sample of only $n = 2$ observations. Consider doing this in two different ways. For the first way, we choose the two X-values very close together. For the second way, we choose the two X-values farther apart (the latter case involves more variation for X). Suppose in each case that the first observed Y-value happens to be smaller than expected (in other words, below the population regression line), and the second happens to be larger than expected. This situation is illustrated in Figure 9.18. Notice what happens when we develop the least squares lines. The selected data points are indicated by large, black dots. In Figure 9.18(a), where the two X-values are close together, the least squares line is much steeper than the population regression line. In Figure 9.18(b), on the other hand, when the two X-values are much farther apart, the least squares line is much closer to the population regression line. This simple example illustrates why the precision of estimates and predictions improves when we choose greater variation among the X-values. This great benefit is possible only if we have the flexibility of choosing the X-values for which to observe a sample of Y-values. And if we can do so, we should choose those X-values that result in the greatest variation over a desired range of interest.

3. *The sample size.*   The term $1/n$ in $SE(\hat{Y})$ and $SE_p(\hat{Y})$ indicates that these standard errors decrease as n increases. This should not be a surprising result, since increasing the sample size makes estimates more reliable, as one would expect.

4. *The proximity of the desired X-value to $\bar{X}$.*   The term $(x - \bar{X})^2$ in $SE(\hat{Y})$ and $SE_p(\hat{Y})$ indicates that the farther the particular x is from $\bar{X}$, the larger these standard errors will be. Thus, the sample X-values should be chosen so that a

desired X-value for estimation and prediction is near the average of the sample X-values. Does the effect of this factor make sense to you intuitively? Consider the following explanation. The least squares statistic b_1 is, by definition, only an estimator of the population slope β_1, so the value of b_1 based on a particular sample will surely be in error by some amount. Since the slope of the least squares line will differ somewhat from the slope of the population regression line, the lines will not be parallel. This is illustrated in Figure 9.19. The lines usually cross near the center of the range of X-values—that is, near $x = \bar{X}$. The farther the particular value x is from $\bar{X}$, the more the lines diverge. The difference between the lines represents the estimation error that occurs for any particular X-value. Therefore, the estimation error tends to increase as we consider X-values farther away from $\bar{X}$.

Figure 9.19

An illustration of the divergence of the least squares line from the population regression line

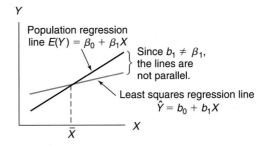

9.7 Correlation: Measuring the Linear Association Between *Y* and *X*

In the preceding sections, we assumed a linear association between the variables Y and X. By determining the least squares line based on a representative sample, we were able to model the nature of this linear relationship. In fact, we were able to determine whether a linear association between Y and X can be regarded as plausible by testing the null hypothesis $H_0: \beta_1 = 0$. In addition, we defined the coefficient of determination r^2, which is a relative measure of how well a straight line fits the sample Y-values. Closely related to these ideas is a descriptive statistic known as the **sample correlation coefficient.** In fact, the magnitude of the correlation coefficient is the square root of the coefficient of determination. *The sample correlation coefficient, denoted by r, measures the **degree of linear association** between two variables Y and X based on a sample of observations.* Like r^2, r is scale-free; thus, its interpretation is independent of the units with which the Y- and X-values are measured. We introduce the expression for determining the correlation coefficient; then we focus more specifically on its interpretation.

Determining the Correlation Coefficient

The expression for determining the sample correlation coefficient (whose development is beyond the scope of this text) is as follows:

$$r = \frac{SP(XY)}{\sqrt{SS(X)SS(Y)}}$$

(9.33)

For the property assessment example, the sample correlation coefficient is $r = .9095$. We can determine this value with a calculator or with the use of a computer—see the chapter appendix for instructions.

Interpreting the Correlation Coefficient

Now, what does this result mean? First, *r always lies between* -1 *and* $+1$. This is true for any data, regardless of the original units. For the purpose of discussion, consider the values $r = +1$, $r = -1$, and $r = 0$.

1. $r = +1$ indicates a perfect linear relationship between Y and X, with a positive slope.
2. $r = -1$ also indicates a perfect linear relationship between Y and X, but with a negative slope.
3. $r = 0$ indicates no linear relationship between Y and X. As we have seen, this implies that the slope of the population regression line is 0.

In practice, r is virtually always some nonzero value between -1 and $+1$. The value of r depends on both the value of the slope b_1 and the variation of the sample data about the least squares line. In general, *r is directly proportional to the slope b_1 and inversely proportional to the residual standard deviation, S_e.* Typical examples of values of r for the exhibited relationships are illustrated in Figure 9.20.

From Figure 9.20 we can conclude that the closer a value of r is to either $+1$ or -1, the stronger is the linear association between Y and X. On the other hand, the closer a value of r is to 0, the weaker the linear association between Y and X appears to be.

Figure 9.20

Examples of correlation coefficients for three typical samples of data

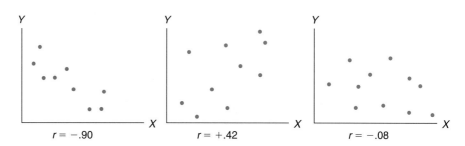

$r = -.90$ $r = +.42$ $r = -.08$

A Comparison of b_1, r, and r^2 in Describing a Linear Association

Recall that the least squares statistic b_1 provides detailed information about a linear relationship because it estimates the change in Y corresponding to a change in X. The coefficient of determination also provides detailed information about a linear relationship because it is a scale-free measure of how closely a straight line fits the sample Y-values. Since the sample correlation coefficient r measures the degree of linear association between Y and X, it is not surprising that these three quantities are closely related.

As we have mentioned, the coefficient of determination is the square of the correlation coefficient. For the property assessment example, we found $r = .9095$, so the coefficient of determination is $r^2 = .9095^2 = .827$, as we already know. If one of these quantities can be determined from the other, why are both commonly used? The reason is simple: They lend themselves to somewhat different interpretations.

Since $b_1 = \text{SP}(XY)/\text{SS}(X)$ and $r = \text{SP}(XY)/\sqrt{\text{SS}(Y)\text{SS}(X)}$, it can be shown mathematically that the least squares statistic b_1 and the sample correlation coefficient r are related by

$$b_1 = r\sqrt{\frac{\text{SS}(Y)}{\text{SS}(X)}} \qquad\qquad \textbf{(9.34)}$$

Notice that if $r = 0$, then $b_1 = 0$, and vice versa. Furthermore, the sign of b_1 is always the same as the sign of r. In other words, if the values of r^2 and b_1 are known, then r and its sign are known, since $r = \sqrt{r^2}$ and the sign of r is the same as the sign of b_1.

EXAMPLE 9.4

For the energy versus temperature example, determine and interpret the correlation coefficient using the computer output given in Table 9.2.

Solution

From the computer output, we see that $b_1 = -3.464$ and $r^2 = .9747$. Therefore, the magnitude of r equals $\sqrt{.9747}$ (the *magnitude* of r is given by Excel as "Multiple R"), and since the value of b_1 is negative, $r = -\sqrt{.9747} = -.9873$. A correlation coefficient of $-.9873$ is near -1; this indicates a strong linear association between energy and temperature. Since r is negative, the relationship is inverse: As winter daily high temperature increases, the amount of energy used decreases.

The Correlation Coefficient When the Y Versus X Relationship Is Not Linear

Finally, it is important to emphasize once again that r measures only the degree of *linear* association between Y and X. It is indeed possible for Y and X to be related in a nonlinear way. To illustrate, consider the graph in Figure 9.21, where Y is perfectly related to X, but not at all linearly. In such a case, the correlation coefficient is 0. It is for this reason that, in explaining what r^2 measures in Section 9.3.4, we said that it cannot measure the validity of the assumed regression model.

Figure 9.21

A perfect nonlinear relationship between Y and X, for which the correlation coefficient is 0

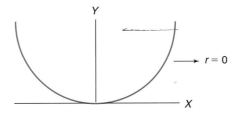

9.8

Simple Linear Regression: A Comprehensive Example

This example is based on an actual application at Xerox Corporation. The only departure from reality is a change in the data. The original data are proprietary, and the example has been made simpler by introducing a small sample of fabricated data. The business circumstances, issues, and statistical principles involved are identical to those of the actual situation. The computations have been carried out using a computer.

At Xerox, an extensive market research study was performed. A sample of 500 small establishments was taken from a list of 900,000 small establishments in the United States, obtained from the Dun & Bradstreet Company. The population of interest consisted of all small establishments in the United States. The sampled population consisted of the Dun & Bradstreet list. A "small establishment" was defined to be an establishment with 50 or fewer employees. Some descriptive information was provided by Dun & Bradstreet for each establishment in the population. The key predictor variable for the study was the number of employees in each establishment.

Each establishment in the sample was visited, and a great deal of information regarding copying habits was obtained. A key item of information for this study was the average number of copies an establishment makes in a day. This variable is called "copy volume." Xerox management believed that the copy volume of establishments tends to increase as the number of employees increases—the more employees, the more copies, on average. They also believed that the copying habits of establishments depend somewhat on the type of establishment—that is, the industry it belongs to. This is indicated by an establishment's Standard Industrial Classification (SIC) code, also provided by Dun & Bradstreet. Examples are "Colleges and Universities," "Banking," and "Manufacturing." In this example, we examine the data pertaining to *banking* establishments.

With regard to the banks to be selected for the study, the range of interest for the number of employees was 8 to 50. To assure acceptable precision in predictions and estimates, the investigative team wanted to create the greatest variation among the X-values (number of employees) within the range of interest. Initially, the team wished to sample the copy volumes (Y-values) of five banks with 8–10 employees each and five banks with 48–50 employees each (the extremes in the X range). But someone on the investigative team reported that the market planning department wanted to estimate the total copy volume of banks with 30 employees. In addition, it was realized that if there were curvature in the relationship between copy volume and number of employees, it could not be detected using only the extremes in the X range. Therefore, five banks were selected in the mid-range with 28–30 employees each, in addition to the extremes in the X range. As a result, the following sample data were obtained:

Number of employees (X): 8   9   9   10   10   28   29   29   30   30   48   48   49   50   50
Daily copy volume (Y):   80 130 170 150 230 560 460 600 520 650 860 900 950 990 880

Two organizations within Xerox wished to use the information of this study:

1. The market planning department wanted to estimate the total copy volume of banks with 30 employees (30 was one of several benchmark figures in their planning process). They knew from the Dun & Bradstreet information that there were 800 banking establishments that had approximately 30 employees, so they needed to estimate the *average* copy volume for these establishments.

2. The sales organization wanted a model to predict the copy volume of *individual* banks, given the number of employees. Sales representatives could use this prediction in preparing their presentations for initial sales calls with regard to the size of copier appropriate for a customer.

The purpose of regression analysis in this example is to provide a model that satisfies the needs of both the market planning department and the sales organization.

Relevant Questions for This Study

1. How does the copy volume Y seem to depend on the number of employees X? Here we must estimate the Y versus X relationship with the sample data.

2. Does the Y versus X relationship in the sample provide strong evidence of an association between Y and X in the population? Or, on the other hand, could the sample relationship be due simply to random sampling from a population in which there is no association between Y and X?

3. Suppose the sample does indicate convincingly that copy volume is related to the number of employees. How accurately does the least squares regression model portray the Y versus X relationship? Does this level of accuracy justify the use of the estimated regression equation by either sales or market planning? Is there any noticeable violation of the necessary regression assumptions?

4. Suppose market planning were to use the least squares regression equation to estimate the average copy volume of establishments in the population with 30 employees.
   (a) What is their estimate?
   (b) How accurate could they expect the estimate to be? (That is, how far off might it be?)

5. Suppose the sales organization were to use the least squares regression equation to predict the copy volume of a new banking establishment (not in the sample) with 30 employees.
   (a) What is their prediction?
   (b) How accurate could they expect the prediction to be?

Answers to Questions 1 and 2

The scatter diagram provides the clearest initial indication of the Y versus X relationship. The Minitab scatter diagram is shown in Figure 9.22. From this figure, there appears to be a strong linear association between copy volume and number of employees. In addition, no curvature is discernible in this relationship; thus, a straight-line fit should be quite adequate. The least squares line and other important

Figure 9.22

Minitab scatter diagram for copy volume versus number of employees

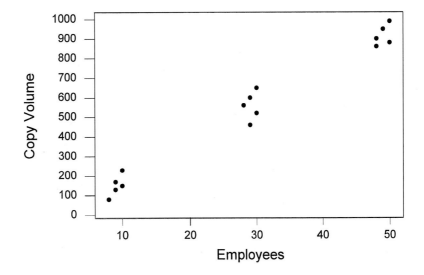

Table 9.8

Minitab output for the comprehensive example

```
The regression equation is
volume = -18.2 + 19.2 number

Predictor       Coef        Stdev        t-ratio      p
Constant       -18.22       28.61        -0.64        0.535
number          19.2295      0.8574       22.43        0.000

s = 54.02    R - sq = 97.5%    R - sq(adj) = 97.3%

Analysis of Variance

SOURCE         DF          SS           MS           F           p
Regression      1          1467903      1467903      503.02      0.000
Error          13          37937        2918
Total          14          1505840

Fit             Stdev.Fit         95% C.I.            95% P.I.
558.7           14.0          (528.5, 588.8)      (438.1, 679.2)

ROW            number        volume       yhat         residual
  1              8           80           135.617      -55.6165
  2              9           130          154.846      -24.8460
  3              9           170          154.846       15.1540
  4             10           150          174.076      -24.0755
  5             10           230          174.076       55.9245
  6             28           560          520.207       39.7935
  7             29           460          539.436      -79.4361
  8             29           600          539.436       60.5639
  9             30           520          558.666      -38.6656
 10             30           650          558.666       91.3344
 11             48           860          904.797      -44.7966
 12             48           900          904.797       -4.7966
 13             49           950          924.026       25.9739
 14             50           990          943.256       46.7444
 15             50           880          943.256      -63.2556
```

information are obtained by using Minitab. The computer output is given in Table 9.8.

Based on this sample, we estimate the average copy volume Y, given a number of employees X, by the least squares line

$$\hat{Y} = -18.2 + 19.2X$$

Since the X range does not include 0, the estimate of the intercept has no real meaning to the problem. But the slope estimate $b_1 = 19.2$ indeed does! It means that one additional employee creates 19.2 additional copies per day, on average.

Answers to Question 3

Based on the computer output, it should be clear to you from the T- or F-value ($T = 22.43$ or $F = 503.02$) that the null hypothesis of no linear association between Y and X (H_0: $\beta_1 = 0$) is strongly contradicted by the sample data (P-value is virtually 0). More important, the slope of the population regression line is estimated with considerable accuracy. The clear evidence for this is the fact that the estimated standard error of b_1 is quite small [$SE(b_1) = .8574$] in relation to the least squares slope $b_1 = 19.2295$. In other words, the T-value ($T = 22.43$) is quite large. As a result, a confidence interval for the slope β_1 is expected to be narrow. For example, a 95% confidence interval for β_1 is ($t_{.975,13} = 2.160$):

$$19.2295 \pm (2.160)(.8574) = 19.2295 \pm 1.852$$

or (17.38, 21.08). With 95% confidence, this interval means that an additional employee can create as few as 17.38 additional copies per day or as many as 21.08 additional copies per day, on average. The narrowness of this interval illustrates that the slope β_1 is estimated with considerable precision.

Notice also that the value of the coefficient of determination is very near 1 ($r^2 = .975$). This means that 97.5% of the total variation in the sample copy volumes is explained by the least squares line $\hat{Y} = -18.2 + 19.2X$.

Finally, when we graph the residuals in Figure 9.23, we see no discernible pattern. This means that we do not detect any noticeable violations of the assumptions. Therefore, the straight-line fit appears to be quite adequate and should be used for estimation and prediction within the range of interest.

Figure 9.23

Plot of residuals for copy volume versus number of employees

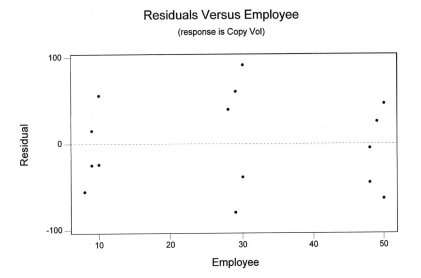

Answers to Questions 4 and 5

From Table 9.8 we see that if market planning uses the model when $X = 30$, the estimated average copy volume is $\hat{Y} = 558.7$ and the 95% confidence interval is (528.5, 588.8). So, for $X = 30$ employees, the average number of copies can be as small as 528.5 or as large as 588.8, with 95% confidence.

If the sales organization uses the model when $X = 30$, the predicted copy volume for a banking establishment with 30 employees is also $\hat{Y} = 558.7$. But, as we expect, the 95% prediction interval (438.1, 679.2) is wider than the corresponding confidence interval for the *average* copy volume for 30 employees. The prediction interval (438.1, 679.2) means that a new bank with 30 employees can create as few as 438.1 copies per day or as many as 679.2, with 95% confidence. Both the confidence and prediction intervals should be quite useful to market planning and sales, respectively, because they are relatively narrow.

9.9   Summary

In this chapter, we developed the fundamental aspects of simple linear regression analysis for establishing the association between a response variable and a potential predictor variable. We assumed the relationship between these variables is that of a straight line and used regression analysis to estimate and assess the extent of the assumed linear relationship.

A regression model is used to represent a complex system in a simple, manageable form that provides a better understanding of the system's characteristics. In addition, the regression model is used to estimate and predict values of the response variable. Consequently, it is important to ascertain whether the regression model performs adequately for the intended use. In this regard, three important questions arise: (1) Do the sample data indicate that there exists a linear association between the two variables? (2) How accurate are the estimates and/or predictions? (3) Can the assumed regression model be improved by considering other potential predictor variables? These questions are answered by a combination of graphical techniques and statistical inferences on the important parameters of the assumed model.

EXERCISES FOR SECTION 9.2

9.1 In regression studies, what is the distinction between a response variable and a predictor variable?

9.2 In regression studies, what do we seek to determine with regard to a response variable and a predictor variable?

9.3 Explain what is required to establish evidence of a cause-and-effect relationship between Y and X with regression analysis.

9.4 Describe the purpose of a regression model.

9.5 What technique is used initially to identify the kind of regression model that may be appropriate?

9.6 Suppose the estimated regression model for selling price versus house size in a particular neighborhood of a city is $\hat{Y} = .5 + 6.8X$.

(a) Interpret the meaning of the number .5 in this relationship.

(b) Interpret the meaning of the number 6.8 in this relationship.

(c) Does the determination of this equation necessarily mean that it adequately characterizes the relationship between selling price and size of house? Explain.

(d) If your answer in part (c) was "no," what information or further analysis would be needed to establish that the regression model does or does not adequately characterize the relationship between selling price and size of house?

9.7 Suppose the estimated regression model for the salary versus years of experience problem (Example 9.2) were $\hat{Y} = 28.9 + 1.26X$.

(a) Interpret the meaning of the number 28.9 in this relationship.

(b) Interpret the meaning of the number 1.26 in this relationship.

(c) Does the determination of this equation necessarily mean that it adequately describes the relationship between salary and years of experience? Explain.

(d) If your answer in part (c) was "no," what

information or further analysis would be needed to establish that the regression model does or does not adequately characterize the relationship between salary and years of experience?

9.8 Identify the two components of the simple linear model $Y = \beta_0 + \beta_1 X + \epsilon$, and explain their meaning.

9.9 State and explain the two types of uses of regression models.

9.10 An insurance analyst wants to determine the extent of the association between family income and amount of life insurance on the head of household. If the association is strong, income may serve as a good indicator of the amount of life insurance a customer may purchase. Based on a random sample of 18 families, the following information was obtained (data are in thousands of dollars):

Income:	45	20	40	40	47	30	25	20	15
Insurance amount:	70	50	60	50	90	55	55	35	40

Income:	35	40	55	50	60	15	30	35	45
Insurance amount:	65	75	105	110	120	30	40	65	80

(a) Construct a scatter diagram for these data. Do you detect a relationship? If so, what type of relationship is suggested?

(b) If the association were strictly linear, would you expect the sign of the slope to be positive or negative? Explain.

9.11 University students learn rather quickly that the better their grade point averages (GPA), the better their chances of landing good jobs upon graduation. Suppose the following data represent the grade point averages of 15 recent graduates of a university and their starting salaries (in thousands of dollars):

GPA:	2.95	3.20	3.40	3.60	3.20	2.85	3.10	2.85
Salary:	23.5	25.0	26.1	27.4	26.2	20.0	23.0	23.8

GPA:	3.05	2.70	2.75	3.10	3.15	2.95	2.75
Salary:	20.7	19.4	20.5	22.2	24.0	22.2	21.8

(a) Construct a scatter diagram for these data. Do you detect a relationship? If so, what type of relationship is suggested?

(b) If the association were strictly linear, would you expect the sign of the slope to be positive or negative? Explain.

9.12 The following data are the heights X and the weights Y of a random sample of ten female employees of a large company:

Height (inches):	68	67	65	68	64	67	66	65	64	66
Weight (pounds):	119	118	129	135	123	140	125	132	118	130

(a) Construct a scatter diagram for these data. Do you detect a relationship? If so, what type of relationship is suggested?

(b) If the association were strictly linear, would you expect the sign of the slope to be positive or negative? Explain.

9.13 How is alcohol consumption affected by the price of alcohol? The following data* are the relative prices (in cents) of alcohol and the per capita consumptions (in liters) of alcohol for the period 1948–1967 in Ontario, Canada:

Year	Relative Price (X)	Per Capita Consumption (Y)	Year	Relative Price (X)	Per Capita Consumption (Y)
1948	5.7	7.09	1958	4.3	7.96
1949	5.8	7.18	1959	4.3	7.77
1950	5.5	7.23	1960	4.3	8.14
1951	5.2	7.23	1961	4.3	8.14
1952	5.1	7.32	1962	4.1	8.23
1953	5.5	7.64	1963	4.0	8.46
1954	5.6	7.73	1964	3.9	8.73
1955	4.7	7.55	1965	3.8	8.77
1956	4.5	7.91	1966	3.9	9.18
1957	4.4	7.86	1967	3.5	8.91

(a) Construct a scatter diagram for these data. Do you detect a relationship? If so, what type of relationship is suggested?

(b) If the association were strictly linear, would you expect the sign of the slope to be positive or negative? Explain.

9.14 How well can a taxpayer's taxes, as a percentage of gross income, be predicted by knowledge of his or her gross income? The following information represents a random sample of 14 federal income tax returns in a given year:

---

* R. E. Popham, W. Schmidt, and J. de Lint, "The Prevention of Alcoholism: Epidemiological Studies of the Effect of Government Control Measures," *Brit. J. of Addiction 70* (1975), 125–144.

Gross income ($000):	25.6	42.2	57.6	98.8	10.4	30.1	40.0
Percent taxes paid:	15.4	16.8	19.7	21.7	10.8	15.2	18.9

Gross income ($000):	29.3	16.1	18.0	88.2	34.0	22.1	70.0
Percent taxes paid:	15.9	12.0	14.1	21.1	17.6	14.8	21.6

(a) Construct a scatter diagram for these data. Do you detect a relationship? If so, what type of relationship is suggested?

(b) If the association were strictly linear, would you expect the sign of the slope to be positive or negative? Explain.

EXERCISES FOR SECTION 9.3

9.15 Consider the following sample data:

X:	2	6	8	10	15
Y:	50	35	30	44	20

(a) Construct a scatter diagram.

(b) Draw a straight line on the scatter diagram that, to your eye, best represents the linear relationship between Y and X.

(c) Indicate the five residuals (deviations of the sample Y-values from your plotted line) on the scatter diagram.

(d) Determine the values of the five residuals by measuring them with a ruler.

(e) Compute the sum of the squared residuals from part (d).

9.16 Refer to Exercise 9.15.

(a) Determine the least squares line and interpret the estimates of the slope and intercept.

(b) Plot your least squares regression line from part (a) as an overlay on your previous scatter diagram.

(c) Determine the values of the five residuals and indicate them on the scatter diagram.

(d) Determine the sum of the squared residuals and compare this sum to the sum of the squared residuals you achieved in part (e) of Exercise 9.15. Which is smaller? What does this indicate about the relative fits of the two lines?

9.17 Refer to Exercise 9.16.

(a) Determine the value of the residual variance S_e^2 and explain its meaning.

(b) Determine the values of SST, SSE, and SSR. Explain what aspect of the data is characterized by each of these quantities.

(c) Determine the value of the coefficient of determination r^2 and explain its meaning.

9.18 Consider the following sample data:

X:	1	2	3	4	5	6
Y:	2	4	4	6	9	10

(a) Construct a scatter diagram for these data. Does a linear relationship seem plausible?

(b) Assuming a linear fit is appropriate, determine the least squares line and interpret its slope and intercept.

(c) Determine the values of the residual variance S_e^2 and the coefficient of determination r^2 and explain their meanings.

9.19 Consider the following sample data:

X:	2	3	4
Y:	4	6	11

(a) Construct a scatter diagram for these data.

(b) Assuming a linear fit is appropriate, determine the least squares line.

(c) Graph the least squares line and each of the following other lines on your scatter diagram from part (a): $\hat{Y} = 1 + 2X$ and $\hat{Y} = 7$. Which of these lines best represents the sample Y-values? Why?

(d) For each line in part (c), determine the residuals.

(e) For each line in part (c), determine the sum of the residuals. What do your results indicate about the usefulness of the sum of the residuals as an indicator of the fit of a line?

(f) For each line in part (c), determine the sum of the squared residuals. For which line is SSE the smallest?

9.20 Consider the following sample data:

X:	3	5	5	7	9	9
Y:	6	2	1	−1	−4	−8

(a) Construct a scatter diagram for these data. Does a linear relationship seem plausible?

(b) Assuming a linear fit is appropriate, determine the least squares line and interpret its slope and intercept.

(c) Determine the values of the residual variance S_e^2 and the coefficient of determination r^2 and explain their meanings.

EXERCISES FOR SECTION 9.4

9.21 Why is it beneficial to be able to select the range of X-values to use in a regression situation?

9.22 With regard to statistical inference for the simple linear model, what is the important parameter and why is this parameter important?

9.23 Why is the assumption of a representative sample of data important?

9.24 Can the assumption of a simple linear model to represent the association between Y and X be verified by knowing the coefficient of determination r^2? Explain.

9.25 For some sample data, suppose the least squares estimate of the slope is $b_1 = 6.5$ and its estimated standard error is $SE(b_1) = 1.5$.
  (a) Without any other information, what might be reasonable to conclude about the population slope β_1 in this case? Explain your thinking.
  (b) What does your answer to part (a) mean about a linear relationship between Y and X?

9.26 Answer the same questions as in Exercise 9.25 if $b_1 = -2.4$ and $SE(b_1) = 2.6$.

9.27 Answer the same questions as in Exercise 9.25 if $b_1 = 12.6$ and $SE(b_1) = 7.0$

9.28 For the following exercises, determine the least squares line, interpret the estimates of the slope and intercept, and decide whether the sample data contradict the claim of no linear association between Y and X.
  (a) (Refers to Exercise 9.18) Use the following Minitab regression output to answer the questions.

```
Regression Analysis
The regression equation is
Y = 0.133 + 1.63 X
Predictor   Coef    Stdev   t-ratio p
Constant    0.1333  0.7240  0.18    0.863
X           1.6286  0.1859  8.76    0.001
s = 0.7777    R-sq = 95.0%
R-sq(adj) = 93.8%
Analysis of Variance
SOURCE      DF   SS      MS     F      p
Regression  1    46.414  46.414 76.75  0.001
Error       4    2.419   0.605
Total       5    48.833
```

  (b) (Refers to Exercise 9.20) Use the following Excel regression output to answer the questions.

```
Regression Statistics
Multiple R            0.958
R Square              0.917
Adjusted R Square     0.897
Standard Error        1.570
Observations          6
```

ANOVA

	df	SS	MS	F	Signifi- cance F
Regression	1	109.469	109.470	44.393	0.003
Residual	4	9.864	2.466		
Total	5	119.333			

	Coeffi- cients	Standard Error	t Stat	P-value
Intercept	11.568	1.945	5.948	0.004
X	-1.932	0.290	-6.663	0.003

9.29 Repeat Exercise 9.28 for the following exercises:
  (a) Exercise 9.15

```
Regression Analysis
The regression equation is
Y = 51.5 - 1.92 X
Predictor   Coef    StDev   T      P
Constant    51.511  8.086   6.37   0.008
X           -1.9159 0.8729  -2.19  0.116
s = 8.409    R-Sq = 61.6%    R-Sq(adj) = 48.8%
Analysis of Variance
Source      DF   SS      MS     F     P
Regression  1    340.66  340.66 4.82  0.116
Error       3    212.14  70.71
Total       4    552.80
```

  (b) Exercise 9.19.

	A	B	C	D	E	F
1	Regression Statistics					
2	Multiple R	0.971				
3	R Square	0.942				
4	Adjusted R Square	0.885				
5	Standard Error	1.225				
6	Observations	3				
7						
8	ANOVA					
9		df	SS	MS	F	Significance F
10	Regression	1	24.5	24.5	16.333	0.154
11	Residual	1	1.5	1.5		
12	Total	2	26			
13						
14		Coefficients	Standard Err	t Stat	P-value	
15	Intercept	-3.5	2.693	-1.300	0.417	
16	X	3.5	0.866	4.041	0.154	

9.30 Refer to Exercise 9.10.
  (a) Assuming a linear relationship between amount of life insurance and income, deter-

mine the least squares line and interpret the estimates of the slope and intercept.

(b) Based on a 95% confidence interval for the slope β_1, is β_1 being estimated with considerable accuracy? Explain.

(c) Do the sample data contradict the claim of no linear association between amount of life insurance and income?

(d) Using an analysis of residuals, do you detect any noticeable violations of the assumptions? Explain.

9.31 Refer to Exercise 9.11. Answer questions similar to those in Exercise 9.30.

9.32 Refer to Exercise 9.13. Answer questions similar to those in Exercise 9.30.

9.33 Refer to Exercises 9.14.

(a) Based on a 95% confidence interval for β_1, is β_1 being estimated with considerable accuracy? Explain.

(b) To what extent do the sample data contradict the claim of no linear association between percent of taxes paid and gross annual income?

(c) Using an analysis of residuals, do you detect any noticeable pattern? Explain.

(d) Can you conclude from your answers to parts (a)–(c) that the least squares line is adequate for estimation and prediction? Explain.

9.34 In Exercise 2.93, you used scatter diagrams to examine the relationship between the proportion of a hospital's number of Medicaid patient-days and five indicators of its resource utilization and financial performance.

The data for this exercise are provided by the Virginia Health Services Cost Review Council *(1994 Annual Report: Efficiency and Productivity– Performance Profiles of Hospitals)* and are stored on the book data diskette, under file name EX0293. The sample consists of all Virginia acute-care hospitals that provided usable data for 1993 (67 of 100). The variables reported by the Review Council are:

Medicaid Participation Variables
- M/TRatio: Proportion of Medicaid patient-days (ratio of Medicaid patient-days to total patient-days)
- McaidDys: Medicaid patient-days
- TPatDys: Total patient-days

Resource Utilization Variables
- Hrs/Adm: Paid hours per adjusted admission— the number of hours for which employees were paid divided by the number of patients admitted
- ALoS: Average length of stay—total patient-days divided by the number of admissions

Financial Performance Indicators
- Debt: Cash debt coverage—cash flow from operations plus interest paid/current debt service; this indicates the ability to repay long-term debt. (Higher is better.)
- TotMargn: Total profit margin—operating and non-operating profit
- ROA: Return on assets—financial return on investment in assets plus cash flow from operations and total unrestricted assets

(a) Use simple linear regression analysis to confirm your tentative conclusions. That is, develop a simple linear regression model of the relationship between the proportion of Medicaid patient-days (as a predictor variable) vs. each of the five measures of resource utilization and financial performance (as response variables).

(b) For each least squares equation, determine whether it is adequate for estimation and prediction.

(c) Based on the models you developed in part (a), do you think that having a large proportion of Medicaid patient-days has a substantial negative impact on a hospital's resource allocation and financial performance?

9.35 In Exercise 2.94, you developed a scatter diagram for annual before-tax profits (the response variable) and annual sales (the predictor variable) of U.S. manufacturing corporations over the period 1980–1989. The data are repeated here. They are also on the book data diskette in the file named EX0294.

Year	1980	1981	1982	1983	1984
Sales	1,897	2,145	2,039	2,114	2,335
Before-tax profits	145	159	108	133	166

Year	1985	1986	1987	1988	1989
Sales	2,331	2,221	2,378	2,596	2,745
Before-tax profits	137	129	173	216	189

(a) Determine the equation of the least squares regression line and interpret its slope and intercept.

(b) If it were reported that U.S. manufacturing corporations had total sales of $2,450 billion, in 1990, what would you estimate to be their 1990 total before-tax profits? (Assume that the relationship between sales and before-tax profits holds for 1990.)

(c) Do the data provide convincing evidence of a linear relationship between annual before-tax profits (the response variable) and annual sales (the predictor variable)? Justify your answer.

(d) Determine a 95% confidence interval for the population slope β_1.

(e) Based on an analysis of the residuals, do you see any significant violations of the assumptions that underlie your inferences in parts (c) and (d)? Explain.

9.36 This exercise refers to Exercise 2.95, which dealt with the testing of the performance characteristics of engine oils. These data are used by manufacturers of engine oil additives to calibrate their testing facilities and to evaluate the performance properties of a proposed additive. The data for this exercise represent 64 test runs for reference oil 1002 over the period 1993–1995; they are stored on the book's data diskette under the file name EX0295. The performance characteristics of interest here are the rate of sludge formation (SLUDGE) and the average amount of wear on the eight lobes of a camshaft (CAMWEAR). The manufacturer was interested in learning whether sludge formation leads to camshaft wear. A scatter diagram in Exercise 2.95 did not suggest the existence of a relationship.

(a) Determine the least squares line that relates CAMWEAR to SLUDGE.

(b) To what extent do these data contradict a null hypothesis of no linear relationship between CAMWEAR and SLUDGE?

9.37 The following data (*Statistical Abstract of the United States,* 1995) depict the percentage of the population with a bachelor's degree (X) and the infant mortality rate per 1,000 births (Y) for a sample of 20 states.

Degree	16.4	13.2	16	11.1	12.1
IM rate	5.9	8.8	8.4	9.4	7.2
Degree	15.6	11.7	13.1	15.6	15.4
IM rate	7.1	8.5	7.4	9.8	9.5
Degree	12	9.7	10.5	13.9	12.4
IM rate	10.6	12.1	11.1	8.1	8.7
Degree	15.4	15.9	11.2	10.5	15.4
IM rate	5.9	7.8	10.4	10.3	7.2

(a) Graph the data; is a linear relationship between X and Y apparent to you? Explain.

(b) Assuming a linear relationship, determine the least squares line and interpret the estimate of the slope.

(c) Does this sample information contradict the claim of no linear relationship between X and Y? How would you explain any linear relationship between these two quantities?

9.38 This exercise relates to Exercise 8.17, in which you investigated the relationship between the size of an automobile and the frequency of personal injury claims. Another possible factor affecting an automobile model's personal injury claim frequency is the frequency of collision insurance claims for that model. The data for this exercise pertain to midsize cars; they are contained on the book's data diskette in a file named EX0938 (*Source:* "Insurance Injury Report" and "Insurance Collision Report," Highway Loss Data Institute, September 1995). The variables are (1) relative frequency of collision claims—where these data have been adjusted in such a way that the average is 100, thus making the results easier to compare; and (2) average loss payment per collision claim—also adjusted so that the average is 100.

(a) Construct and interpret a scatter diagram of the relationship between the average loss payment per claim (response variable) and the relative frequency of claims (predictor variable).

(b) Determine the least squares regression equation for predicting a midsize model's average loss payment per claim, given its relative frequency of collision claims, and interpret the coefficients of the model.

(c) To what extent do these data establish the existence of a positive linear relationship between average loss payment per claim and relative frequency of collision claims?

(d) Determine a plot of the residuals. Based on this plot, do the data seem to conform to the assumptions required to justify inference? Explain.

9.39 A personnel manager administers an aptitude test to all new sales representatives. Sales management is interested in the extent to which the test is able to predict eventual sales success. The following are the test scores and the weekly sales (in thousands of dollars) for eight sales representatives:

Sales	8	12	28	24	18	16	15	12
Test Scores	55	60	85	75	80	85	65	55

(a) Specify the response and predictor variables and justify your choices.

(b) Construct a scatter diagram and determine whether a linear association is apparent.

(c) Assuming a linear association, determine the least squares line, interpret the estimates of the slope and intercept, and decide whether the sample data contradict the claim of no linear relationship between the response and predictor variables.

(d) Based on a 95% confidence interval for β_1, would you say that β_1 is estimated with considerable accuracy? Explain.

9.40 Express Graphics is a printing firm. Express prints a wide variety of packaging, including flip-top boxes for cigarettes, detergent boxes, and boxes for cosmetics, pharmaceuticals, and fast foods. The jobs vary in size, configuration, print quality, and type of paper used. Express completes about 200 jobs per month. A manager is interested in the degree of correspondence between the target price (X) of a job and the eventual billed amount (Y). Data for a random sample of 15 jobs are as follows:*

Billed Amount (Y)	Target Price (X)	Billed Amount (Y)	Target Price (X)
$6,417	$5,295	328	551
85	83	543	469
2,178	2,336	2,577	1,882
127	123	404	545
4,349	4,285	15,090	13,596
115	76	292	929
381	125	1,045	633
122	44		

(a) Construct the scatter diagram. Is there a relationship between billed amount and target price, and is the relationship that of a straight line? Explain.

(b) Assuming a linear relationship, determine the least squares line, interpret the estimates of the slope and intercept, and decide whether the sample data contradict the claim of no linear relationship between the response and predictor variables.

(c) Determine a 95% confidence interval for the slope β_1. Do you believe that the estimated slope in part (b) is precise enough? Explain.

(d) What does a residual analysis tell you for this problem? Explain.

9.41 A concern at Express Graphics is developing a target price for a potential job that can be quoted to a customer. A key variable that affects the cost of production is the speed of the printing press for the job. In the past, press speed has been estimated subjectively in weekly quote meetings. This estimate, along with several others, served as input to a computer program that generated the estimated cost of production. A marketing analyst sought to determine whether better estimates of press speed could be obtained by using a regression model. In a preliminary analysis, he compiled the following data for a sample of 15 jobs. For each job, the press speed (hundreds of images per second) and the registration difficulty in printing the box (a rating of 1 = hard, 2 = regular, 3 = easy; assigned judgmentally) were recorded.†

Press Speed	Registration Difficulty	Press Speed	Registration Difficulty
74	1	107	3
69	2	95	3
71	2	104	3
67	3	45	3
109	3	69	2
114	3	100	2
94	3	99	2
120	3		

(a) Answer parts (a)–(c) of Exercise 9.40.

(b) What does your estimated equation suggest is the difference in printing speed between jobs rated 1 (hard) and jobs rated 2 (regular), on average?

9.42 A plant manager wishes to determine the effect of various lengths of time on the number of units assembled by assembly line operators before the operators take a break. He suspects that longer work intervals before a break tend to decrease productivity. In an experiment, work intervals of 1, 2, 3, and 4 hours are tried. For each interval, the number of units assembled is observed for four operators. The following results were observed:

Hours before a break:	1	2	3	4
Units assembled:	25, 29, 23, 31	55, 65, 63, 59	73, 75, 74, 71	90, 88, 91, 87

(a) Answer parts (a)–(d) of Exercise 9.39.

(b) Using an analysis of residuals, do you detect any noticeable pattern? Explain.

(c) Do you think that these sample data establish clearly that assembly line productivity really does depend on the length of time before operators take a break? Explain your thinking.

9.43 In the March 4, 1996 issue of *Fortune*, America's most admired companies for 1995 were reported. The scores were determined by surveying more than 11,000 executives, outside directors, and financial analysts. Nine of the top ten most admired companies in 1995, their scores, and their com-

---

* Courtesy of Jared Bjarnason.

† Courtesy of John Murphy.

pounded annual return rates for the years 1985–1995 are as follows:

Rank	Company	Score	Annual return (1985–1995)
1	Coca-Cola	8.70	29.3%
2	Procter & Gamble	8.55	20.0
3	Rubbermaid	8.35	13.0
4	Johnson & Johnson	8.32	23.1
5	Intel	8.30	27.9
6	Merck	8.26	27.1
7	Mirage Resorts	8.23	22.2
8	Hewlett-Packard	8.19	17.4
9	Motorola	8.19	20.7

(a) Is there an association between score (response) and annual return (predictor)? Construct a scatter diagram for these data. If you detect a relationship, what type of relationship is it?

(b) Assuming a linear association, determine the least squares line and interpret the estimate of the slope.

(c) Is there a discernible evidence of a linear association between a company's admiration score and its compounded annual return rate? Are you surprised by the result? Explain.

9.44 In the study "Trimmed Least Squares Estimation" (*Journal of the American Statistical Association*, 1980, pp. 828–838), the following data were reported on periodic measurements of water salinity (response) in North Carolina's Pamlico Sound and river discharge flow (predictor).

River flow	23.0	23.9	26.4	24.9	29.9	24.2
Salinity	7.6	7.7	4.3	5.9	5.0	6.5

River flow	23.2	21.9	22.3	23.8	25.1	
Salinity	8.3	8.2	13.2	12.6	10.4	

River flow	22.4	21.8	22.4	23.9	33.4	24.9
Salinity	10.8	13.1	12.3	10.4	10.5	7.7

River flow	22.7	21.8	22.0	21.0	21.0	25.9
Salinity	9.5	12.0	12.6	13.6	14.1	13.5

River flow	26.3	22.9	21.3	20.8	21.4	
Salinity	11.5	12.0	13.0	14.1	15.1	

(a) Construct a scatter diagram and determine whether there is a linear relationship between salinity and river flow.

(b) Assuming a linear association, determine the least squares line and interpret the estimate of the slope.

(c) Based on a 95% confidence interval for the population slope, would you say that it estimated with considerable accuracy? Explain.

(d) Do the sample data contradict the claim of no linear association between salinity and river flow? Support your answer.

9.45 The paper "Validity of the Physical Activity Interview and Caltrac with Preadolescent Children" (*Research Quarterly for Exercise and Sport*, Vol. 65, No. 1, 1994, pp. 84–88) reported on the physical activities of third and fifth graders and assessed the validity of the Caltrac, an electronic accelerometer, as a field measure of physical activity. Of particular interest was the relationship between vigorous physical activity (Y)—defined as 200% of resting heart rate—and the Caltrac counts (X). The following data depict 200% resting heart rates and Caltrac counts for a sample of third graders and are derived from Figure 2 of this study.

Caltrac count	52	63	63	64	67	70	72	75	76	83
Heart rate	15	22	24	30	22	25	19	25	19	26

Caltract count	84	104	110	111	112	122	125	160
Heart rate	34	49	44	60	43	50	75	106

(a) Graph the data. Is there an association between 200% of resting heart rate and Caltrac count? If so, what type of relationship is it?

(b) Determine the least squares equation for the association suggested in part (a) and interpret the estimate of the slope.

(c) Is there a discernible evidence of a linear association between 200% of resting heart rate and Caltrac count? Support your answer.

9.46 The article "A Textbook Case of Hype: Despite the Talk, Our Schools Aren't Failing" (*Washington Post*, Apr. 7, 1996) discussed the common belief that "American schools are deteriorating, academic test scores are plummeting, and billions of dollars are disappearing down the educational drain." They agreed that SAT scores have fallen over the years, but they argued that the proportion of high school graduates taking the test increased dramatically over the same period. "If you test only the top few students in a classroom, the scores will be higher than if you test the top half of the class," they stated. The data consist of mean 1990 SAT scores (*Richmond Times-Dispatch*, Mar. 22, 1993) and the proportion of students who took the SAT test for each of the 50 states. They can be found on the book data diskette in the file EX0946.

(a) Scan the states' mean SAT values. If mean SAT score is the measure of an effective educational system, which states are doing the best job?

(b) Develop a simple linear regression model of the relationship between mean SAT score and the percentage of students tested, and interpret the estimate of the slope.

(c) To what extent do these data contradict a null hypothesis of no linear relationship between mean SAT scores and percentage of students tested?

(d) What percentage of the variation among the states' mean SAT scores is explained by the variation in their percentages of students tested?

(e) A positive residual indicates that a state achieved a greater mean SAT than would be predicted based on its percentage of students tested. Thus, the residuals could be considered to be measures of the effectiveness of the states' educational systems after adjusting for their percentages of students tested. Using residuals in this way, which states now appear to have the most effective educational systems?

(f) Based on a graph of the residuals, comment on the appropriateness of the linear regression model you developed in part (b).

9.47 The paper "Key Issues Facing European Car Manufacturers and Their Strategic Responses" (*Business Economics,* Oct. 1994) claimed that a "... severe drop in demand for European cars in 1993 forced the auto industry to face underlying structural problems that had been growing for several years ...." Based on the following data, the paper claimed that reduced utilization of production capacity in 1993 led to (or closer to) loss positions.

Manufacturer	Year	Utilization (%)	Net Increase to Sales, %
PSA	1992	69	2.16
PSA	1993	57	−.97
Renault	1992	79	3.2
Renault	1993	65	.6
GM Europe	1992	93	5.29
GM Europe	1993	73	2.09
Ford Europe	1992	75	−2.99
Ford Europe	1993	63	−2.19
VW Group	1992	91	.002
VW Group	1993	61	−2.52
Fiat Auto	1992	78	.016
Fiat Auto	1993	51	−3.22

(a) Construct a scatter diagram for percent net increase to sales (response) vs. percent utilization of capacity (predictor). What does your graph suggest about the relationship between these two variables?

(b) Develop a simple linear regression model of the relationship between a manufacturer's net increase to sales and its percent utilization of capacity; interpret the estimate of the slope.

(c) Do these data provide convincing evidence that there is a positive linear relationship between net increase to sales and percent utilization?

(d) What percentage of the variation in these net increase to sales data is explained by the variation in their utilization of capacity?

EXERCISES FOR SECTIONS 9.5 AND 9.6

9.48 Refer to Exercise 9.15.

(a) Use the least squares line to estimate the mean of Y when $X = 7$.

(b) Based on a 95% confidence interval for the mean of Y, is this mean being estimated with considerable accuracy? Explain.

(c) Use the least squares line to predict the value of Y when $X = 7$. Is your answer different from that in part (a)? Explain.

(d) Based on a 95% prediction interval for the individual Y-value when $X = 7$, is this value estimated with considerable accuracy? Explain.

(e) Compare your answers for the intervals in parts (b) and (d). Which interval is wider and why is it wider?

9.49 Refer to Exercise 9.18. Answer all parts of Exercise 9.48 when $X = 4$.

9.50 Refer to Exercise 9.20. Answer all parts of Exercise 9.48 when $X = 8$.

9.51 Refer to Exercise 9.12. Answer all parts of Exercise 9.48 when $X = 67$.

9.52 Refer to Exercises 9.10 and 9.30. These involve the relationship between amount of life insurance (Y) and family income (X).

(a) Estimate the average amount of insurance when family incomes are $X = 15$, 35, and 60 (thousand dollars).

(b) For each X-value in part (a), determine a 95% confidence interval for the average amount of life insurance. For which X-value is the accuracy of estimation best and why?

(c) For each X-value in part (a), determine a 95% prediction interval for an individual's amount of life insurance and answer the same question as in part (b).

(d) Considering your answers to this exercise as well as those to Exercises 9.10 and 9.30, do you now believe that this least squares line is adequate for estimation and prediction? Explain your answer.

9.53 Refer to Exercises 9.11 and 9.31. These involve the relationship between starting salary (Y) and grade point average (X). Answer questions similar to those in Exercise 9.52 when the grade point averages are $X = 2.70$, 3.00, and 3.30.

9.54 Refer to Exercises 9.13 and 9.32. These involve the relationship between per capita alcohol consumption (Y) and the relative price of alcohol (X). Answer questions similar to those in Exercise 9.52 when the relative prices are $X = 3.5$, 4.6, and 5.8 cents.

9.55 Refer to Exercises 9.14, and 9.33. These involve the relationship between percent taxes paid (Y) and gross income (X). Answer questions similar to those in Exercise 9.52 when the gross incomes are $X = 11$, 42, and 98 (thousand dollars).

9.56 Refer to Exercise 9.40, which involves the relationship between billed amount (Y) and target price (X) for Express Graphics.
(a) Estimate the average billed amount of jobs whose target price is $5,000.
(b) Determine a 95% confidence interval for the average Y-value when the target price is $5,000.
(c) What do your answers to parts (a) and (b) suggest to management about the credibility of the target price? Explain your answer.
(d) Suppose you were asked to determine a prediction interval for the actual billed amount of an individual job whose target price was $5,000. Without computing anything, would this prediction interval be smaller than, the same as, or larger than the confidence interval in part (b), and why?

9.57 Refer to Exercise 9.41, which involves the relationship between press speed (Y) and registration difficulty (X) for Express Graphics.
(a) Predict the press speed of a job rated 1 ("hard").
(b) Determine a 95% prediction interval for the press speed when $X = 1$.
(c) If you were a manager, how would you characterize the usefulness of the prediction in part (a) based on your answer for part (b)?

9.58 Refer to Exercise 9.12, in which the relationship between the height (X) and weight (Y) of female employees in a large company was desired. Suppose further that the flexibility exists to select a number of female employees with heights in the range 62 to 70 inches. If it were known that the relationship is strictly linear, for what heights should we choose to observe the weights? Why should these heights be chosen?

9.59 Refer to Exercise 9.10, in which an insurance analyst wanted to determine the relationship between family income (X) and amount of life insurance (Y). Suppose the analyst wants to determine this relationship for family incomes in the range of $20,000 to $100,000. Suppose further that the analyst has the flexibility of selecting the family incomes (the X-values) to observe the amounts of life insurance.
(a) If it were known that the relationship is strictly linear, for what family incomes should the analyst observe the amounts of life insurance and why?
(b) Suppose some curvature in this relationship is suspected. Would your answer be the same as that in part (a)? Explain.

9.60 In Exercise 9.34, you determined simple linear regression models to examine the relationship between the hospital's proportion of Medicaid patient-days (the predictor variable) and five indicators of its resource utilization and financial performance (the response variables)—see that exercise for source.
One of the models for which the proportion of Medicaid patient-days seemed to be a contributing factor was the one involving the average length of stay (ALoS).
(a) Use this equation to predict ALoS for hospitals whose proportions of Medicaid patient-days are .04, .10, and .16, respectively.
(b) Determine a 95% prediction interval for each prediction in part (a).
(c) Compare the widths of the three prediction intervals in part (b), and explain why they vary.

9.61 In Exercise 9.35, you determined a simple linear regression model of the relationship between annual before-tax profits (response) and annual sales (predictor) of U.S. manufacturing corporations over the period 1980–1989. The data are repeated here—see that exercise for source.

Year	1980	1981	1982	1983	1984
Sales	1,897	2,145	2,039	2,114	2,335
Before-tax profits	145	159	108	133	166

Year	1985	1986	1987	1988	1989
Sales	2,331	2,221	2,378	2,596	2,745
Before-tax profits	137	129	173	216	189

(a) Assume that the relationship between these variables continued through 1990. Use the model to determine a prediction for before-tax profits if annual sales are $2,850 billion.

(b) Determine a 95% prediction interval for before-tax profits if annual sales are $2,850 billion.

(c) Do you have any concerns over the validity of your prediction in part (a)? Explain.

9.62 In Exercise 9.36, you determined a simple linear regression model of the relationship between the rate of sludge formation (SLUDGE) and the average amount of wear on the eight lobes of a camshaft (CAMWEAR) in tests of engine oils—see that exercise for source.

(a) Use the model to estimate the mean wear on a camshaft when the amount of sludge formation is 9.5.

(b) Determine a 95% confidence interval for the mean wear on a camshaft when sludge formation is 9.5.

(c) What is the margin of sampling error in part (b)?

9.63 In Exercise 9.37, you determined a least squares line for the relationship between infant mortality rate and the percentage of the population with a bachelor's degree.

(a) Estimate the average infant mortality rate per 1,000 births for the following percentages of population with a bachelor's degree: 10.8 and 15.8.

(b) For each percentage in part (a), determine a 95% confidence interval for the average infant mortality rate.

9.64 In Exercise 9.38, you determined a simple linear regression model of the relationship between the average loss payment per claim (response) and the frequency of collision claims (predictor) for midsize automobile models—see that exercise for source.

(a) Use the model to estimate the mean loss payment per claim for automobiles whose frequency of collision claims is 80. Repeat for frequency of collision claims of 100 and 140, respectively.

(b) Determine a 95% confidence interval for mean loss payment per claim for each value given in part (a).

(c) If you had determined prediction intervals for *individual* values of the response variable, would they have been narrower, about the same, or wider than the intervals you determined in part (b)? Explain.

EXERCISES FOR SECTION 9.7

9.65 Explain the meaning of the following hypothetical correlation coefficients.
(a) $r = -1$
(b) $r = 0$
(c) $r = +1$

9.66 In developing a linear regression model, it is found that $SS(Y) = 129$, $SS(X) = 9.5$, and $SP(XY) = 21.4$. Determine the correlation coefficient.

9.67 In developing a linear regression model, it is found that $b_1 = -2.58$ and $r^2 = .8238$. Determine the correlation coefficient.

9.68 In developing a linear regression model, it is found that $SS(Y) = 98$, $SS(X) = 38.6$, and $r = .6525$. Determine the least squares estimate of the slope.

9.69 If we substitute the X-values $-4, -3, -2, -1, 0, 1, 2, 3$, and 4 into the mathematical relationship $Y = X^2$, we obtain the corresponding Y-values 16, 9, 4, 1, 0, 1, 4, 9, and 16.
(a) Graph the Y versus X relationship.
(b) Determine the correlation coefficient using these Y- and X-values. Are you surprised by your result? Explain.

9.70 Using the information already available to you, determine the correlation coefficient for the following exercises:

(a) Exercise 9.15
(b) Exercise 9.39
(c) Exercise 9.40

9.71 A study showed that the correlation coefficient between a sales representative's earnings (Y) and the number of sales calls attempted (X_1) is .44. The same study also showed that the correlation coefficient between earnings (Y) and the number of hours spent on administrative tasks (X_2) is $-.55$. Which factor, X_1 or X_2, appears to be more strongly linearly related to earnings? Justify your answer.

9.72 A university admissions office is studying indicators of high school students' eventual college performance, measured by their grade point averages. Complete high school and college performance data are available for a sample of 498 recent students. The correlation coefficient between college GPA and high school GPA is found to equal .42. The correlation coefficient between college GPA and high school class rank is found to equal .36.
(a) Based on a linear relationship, which seems to be the stronger indicator of college performance? Explain.
(b) In predicting college performance, to what

extent does it help to know students' high school GPAs (as opposed to having no high school information at all)?

9.73 In Exercise 9.72, what fraction of the variation among college students' GPAs is explained by the variation among their high school GPAs? Explain your answer.

SUPPLEMENTARY EXERCISES

For the following exercises, your ultimate goal is to determine whether the least squares line makes sense and is adequate for estimation and prediction by determining the strength of the linear relationship between the response and the predictor variables. Your analysis should include the following: a scatter diagram, the determination and interpretation of the least squares line, the application and interpretation of the T and F statistics, the determination and interpretation of a 95% confidence interval for the population slope β_1, the determination and interpretation of r^2, and an analysis of the residuals.

9.74 A hospital staff analyst wishes to investigate the degree to which the length of a Medicare patient's hospital stay is determined by the age of the patient. Data for a sample of 24 patients are as follows:*

Age:	63	66	67	68	68	69	69	69	70	70	72	73
Length of stay (days):	3	16	6	9	3	4	8	19	9	6	7	10

Age:	74	83	84	85	88	66	70	72	77	77	78	78
Length of stay (days):	7	16	21	8	10	9	8	10	17	18	12	9

9.75 An analyst for a public school system wishes to investigate how well grade point averages reflect SAT scores of graduates from a city high school for outstanding underprivileged students. Data for a sample of 30 graduating seniors are as follows:†

GPA:	4.9	4.7	4.0	3.7	4.3	3.5	3.4
SAT:	1235	1105	1020	1000	1190	1010	1125

GPA:	3.8	3.2	5.0	4.4	4.5	4.8	4.6
SAT:	1020	975	1390	1050	1205	1300	1100

GPA:	3.6	3.7	4.5	4.6	3.8	3.7	3.5
SAT:	970	1110	1290	1250	1010	1310	1000

GPA:	4.0	4.5	4.1	3.4	3.0	2.8	2.9
SAT:	950	1275	950	990	895	890	920

GPA:	3.4	3.4
SAT:	1270	1210

9.76 A personnel manager for a bank is interested in evaluating the learning that takes place in the academic portion of a management trainee program. Learning is evaluated for a sample of 28 trainees on the basis of their scores on tests taken both before and after participation in the training program. Of interest is the ability to predict the post-program score based on the corresponding pre-program score. The following sample information is obtained:‡

Trainee:	1	2	3	4	5	6	7	8	9	10	11	12	13	14
Before:	35	39	38	41	45	51	36	41	41	43	38	43	31	33
After:	44	66	51	63	62	66	57	63	60	63	60	58	55	52

Trainee:	15	16	17	18	19	20	21	22	23	24	25	26	27	28
Before:	46	33	44	33	44	42	38	47	41	38	41	42	34	34
After:	75	50	55	54	58	63	58	65	63	67	64	57	62	52

9.77 In response to pressure to reduce the emissions of volatile compounds caused by the use of solvent-based printing inks, a printing plant switched to water-based, solvent-free ink. As a result of the change, both productivity and the amount of scrap were of concern. One question of interest was whether the amount of scrap per 1,000 yards produced is closely related to productivity as measured by the number of yards printed per shift. Productivity and scrap data for a sample of 23 runs using water-based inks are as follows:§

Yards per shift:	20,000	21,882	20,800	23,273
Scrap per 1,000 yards:	35.76	31.15	45.09	14.31

Yards per shift:	21,714	18,759	18,000	18,065
Scrap per 1,000 yards:	29.81	21.38	27.71	24.40

Yards per shift:	21,429	38,261	33,333	33,500
Scrap per 1,000 yards:	19.05	10.40	22.49	44.36

Yards per shift:	44,387	37,576	48,000	20,500
Scrap per 1,000 yards:	14.65	15.31	24.60	45.63

Yards per shift:	19,429	9,143	24,000	38,316
Scrap per 1,000 yards:	50.62	63.54	51.11	12.31

Yards per shift:	40,000	23,273	17,524
Scrap per 1,000 yards:	17.31	35.94	41.04

---

* Courtesy of Trent Crable.

† Courtesy of Spurgeon James.

‡ Courtesy of Denise Rimes.

§ Courtesy of Michael Roeder.

9.78 A corporate personnel analyst wishes to study employee absenteeism at each of two plants, Richmond and Louisville. For a sample of 30 employees at each plant, the number of absences over a 3-year period and the employee's years of service are recorded. It is believed that the number of absences is influenced by the years of service. The sample data are given here. Analyze each plant separately and compare your results.*

Richmond

Absences:	18	14	24	5	7	0	8	13	2	0
Years of service:	9	9	21	15	15	15	17	21	18	16

Absences:	5	11	10	1	7	2	21	18	2	12
Years of service:	15	9	14	8	10	15	9	12	15	16

Absences:	9	5	9	13	16	11	9	23	5	13
Years of service:	14	14	14	8	8	15	13	10	8	14

Louisville

Absences:	24	0	18	28	30	51	48	3	14	19
Years of service:	9	31	17	19	19	16	24	30	17	19

Absences:	50	9	13	9	4	50	49	15	11	15
Years of service:	7	13	7	7	20	16	9	12	11	18

Absences:	9	13	5	6	33	64	12	8	0	3
Years of service:	7	24	18	12	7	7	16	14	15	17

9.79 An investment analyst wishes to investigate whether the 52-week-low prices influence the 52-week-high prices for corporations headquartered in Virginia in 1990. The sample information for 15 Virginia companies is as follows:

Stock	52-Week High	52-Week Low
Best Products	$16.38	$9.00
CFB	36.50	24.25
Circuit City	33.38	11.75
CSX	37.50	25.63

Stock	52-Week High	52-Week Low
Dominion Resources	25.19	17.38
DuPont	90.88	59.50
Ethyl	22.75	13.31
James River	35.00	22.00
MCI	13.13	6.13
Robins	15.63	7.75
Philip Morris	78.00	39.25
Jefferson Bank	39.50	29.00
United Virginia Bank	35.38	22.63
Bassett Furniture	50.25	33.50
Sovran	44.25	29.38

9.80 A professor is interested in determining how well a student's score on one test can predict his or her score on the following test. The following data represent scores on the first two tests in an information systems class by 25 sophomores and 25 juniors:†

Juniors				Sophomores			
Test 1	Test 2	Test 1	Test 2	Test 1	Test 2	Test 1	Test 2
62	75	80	93	60	53	76	53
68	60	82	82	62	52	76	60
68	82	82	70	62	68	76	68
70	63	84	67	64	63	78	58
70	72	84	77	64	73	78	68
72	75	84	75	66	62	78	62
72	78	86	82	68	58	80	68
76	65	88	62	70	53	80	75
76	78	90	78	70	52	84	80
76	65	92	87	72	58	86	88
78	67	94	78	72	60	86	80
78	53	94	85	74	72	88	78
78	85			76	73		

Analyze each academic year separately and compare your results.

---

* Courtesy of Chalmers Ward.

† Courtesy of Tony Woo.

Case Study
Analysis of Environmental Characteristics of Water in Nomini Creek

A group of local citizens are the first to serve as water quality monitors representing the Potomac River watershed in a joint effort with the Alliance for the Chesapeake Bay. The purpose of their observations is to provide baseline data on water quality that can be used in the future to determine how land use affects water quality.

The object of this case study is to explore and develop a model of the relationships between water temperature and two important environmental variables, the level of dissolved oxygen (DO) and the secchi depth (SD)—the depth of water clarity. Both DO and SD are considered quality characteristics of water in regard to environmental concerns. Temperature is a suspected factor that must be considered in future analyses of the effects of land use. The data are provided by one of the local citizens* involved in the project. They consist of 151 weekly observations of water temperature, DO, and SD for Nomini Creek (which feeds the Potomac River) over a 3-year period. Water temperature was measured in degrees Celsius with a thermometer. Dissolved oxygen is specified in parts per million and was determined by performing a detailed experiment each week. Secchi depth was measured in meters by using a secchi depth disk, which is round and divided into quadrants painted alternately black and white. A rope measured in meters is attached and the secchi disk is lowered into the water to get the clarity (secchi depth) reading.

In this case study, you are to examine the variation of the level of dissolved oxygen and secchi depth over time, and the relationships between the level of dissolved oxygen and water temperature and between secchi depth and water temperature. Use statistical thinking and the methods and concepts of this chapter, as well as those of previous chapters. Your report should include a thorough discussion of the nature of these relationships, a statement of the degree of confidence that is appropriate for each model developed, the range of variation of dissolved oxygen and secchi depth to be expected in the future, if there are no adverse effects of land use, and any reservations you have about the appropriateness of any methods you have used.

The data are contained on the data disk in a file named CASE0901. The column indicators are c_1 = week; c_2 = the level of dissolved oxygen (DO); c_3 = secchi depth (SD); c_4 = water temperature.

---

* Courtesy of Rebecca France.

Appendix 9A

Computer Instructions for Using MINITAB, EXCEL, and JMP IN

MINITAB

Regression Output

To produce the Minitab regression output for Example 9.1, enter the temperature data into c1 and the energy use data into c2. Name c1 Temperature and c2 Energy Use. Choose STAT–REGRESSION–REGRESSION . . . . In the dialogue box, specify c2 as the RESPONSE variable and c1 as the PREDICTORS variable.

Residual Plots

You can specify that a Minitab residual plot similar to Figure 9.14 be produced as part of the regression analysis described above. In the STAT–REGRESSION– REGRESSION . . . dialogue box, click the GRAPHS . . . button. In the GRAPHS dialogue box, enter c1 (the predictor variable Temperature) in the RESIDUALS VERSUS THE VARIABLES box, and click OK.

Estimation and Prediction

Consider Table 9.7, which provides the estimated mean of Y and the predicted value of Y corresponding to three specific values of X, along with the associated standard error, confidence interval (for the mean), and prediction interval (for the predicted individual Y-value) for Example 9.1. To develop these results with Minitab, enter the temperature and energy use values in c1 and c2, respectively. Choose STAT– REGRESSION–REGRESSION . . . . Complete the dialogue box as described previously. Additionally, click the OPTIONS . . . button. In the OPTIONS dialogue box, enter the value of X for which an estimate of the mean of Y and/or a prediction of Y is desired in the PREDICTION INTERVALS FOR NEW OBSERVATIONS: box. (You can do this for only one value at a time.) To store the results, click the buttons for FITS (the estimated mean value and the predicted value), SDs OF FITS (the standard error of the estimated mean value), CONFIDENCE LIMITS, and PREDICTION LIMITS, and click OK.

Correlation Coefficient

To obtain the correlation coefficient for Example 9.1 (see Example 9.4), choose STAT–BASIC STATISTICS–CORRELATION .... In the dialogue box, enter (or select) c1 c2 and click OK.

EXCEL

Regression Output and Residual Plots

To obtain regression output like that in Table 9.2 and a residual plot like Figure 9.14 for Example 9.1, enter the data in two columns. Put the temperature data in cells a2 through a19, and put the energy data in cells b2 through b19. Enter the names Temperature and Energy in cells a1 and b1, respectively. Select TOOLS–DATA ANALYSIS . . . and click REGRESSION. In the dialogue box, specify in the INPUT Y RANGE: box the range of cells containing the variable name and data for energy use (b1:b19); in the INPUT X RANGE: box, specify the range of cells containing the variable name and data for temperature (a1:a19); and click the LABELS, RESIDUALS, and RESIDUAL PLOTS boxes. The output includes not only the regression output shown in Table 9.2, but also the predicted values, the residuals, and a residual plot versus temperature like Figure 9.14.

Estimation and Prediction

Consider Table 9.7, which provides the estimated mean of Y and the predicted value of Y (as well as other outputs) for Example 9.1. To develop these results with Excel, start with the data in cells a1:b19, as described in the preceding paragraph. Enter the temperature values for which you want predictions (–4, 3, and 9) into cells b20:b22. Select cell c20, and click the PASTE FUNCTION button. In the dialogue box, select the STATISTICAL function category and the function name TREND. In the TREND dialogue box, enter \$a\$2:\$a\$19 for KNOWN Y'S; enter \$b\$2:\$b\$19 for KNOWN X'S; enter b20 for NEW X'S; and enter 1 for CONST. Select cell c20 and fill down through cell c22. This places the predicted Y-values into cells c20:c22.

Correlation Coefficient

To obtain the correlation coefficient for Example 9.1 (see Example 9.4), arrange the data as described in the previous paragraph. Select TOOLS–DATA ANALYSIS . . . and click CORRELATION. In the dialogue box, specify in the INPUT Y RANGE: box the range of cells containing the variable names and data for energy use and temperature (a1:b19); and click the LABELS IN FIRST ROW box.

JMP IN

Regression Output

To produce the JMP IN regression output in Table 9.3 for Example 9.2, enter the years of experience into COLUMN 1 and the salaries into COLUMN 2. Name these columns YEARS and SALARY and set their roles to X and Y, respectively. Choose ANALYZE–FIT Y BY X. Click the FITTING check mark box and select FIT LINE. The regression output is below the graph.

Residual Plots

After choosing ANALYZE–FIT Y BY X, clicking the FITTING check mark box, and selecting FIT LINE, click the LINEAR FIT check mark box and select PLOT RESIDUALS. The residual plot, as given in Figure 9.15, appears below the regression output.

Estimation and Prediction

Consider Table 9.6 which provides the estimated mean of Y and the predicted value of Y corresponding to three specific values of X, along with the associated standard error, confidence interval (for the mean), and prediction interval (for the predicted individual Y-value) for Example 9.2. To develop these results with JMP IN, enter the salary and years of experience values and name them as described previously. Add three additional rows. Enter the values of Years (3, 15, and 27) for which you wish to predict Salary. Do not enter corresponding Salary values. Choose ANALYZE–FIT MODEL. In the MODEL dialogue box, click SALARY in the left-side box; then click the >Y> button at center top. Click YEARS in the left-side box; then click the >ADD> button. Then click the RUN MODEL button (lower right). In the resulting MODEL FIT window, click the $ button at the lower left corner of the window and click SAVE PREDICTED VALUES. Repeat sequentially for SAVE PREDICTION CONFIDENCE, SAVE INDIV CONFIDENCE, SAVE STD ERROR OF PREDICTED, and SAVE STD ERROR OF INDIVIDUAL. This adds the desired values to the data window.

Correlation Coefficient

To obtain the correlation coefficient for Example 9.2, change the role of YEARS to Y. Then choose ANALYZE–CORRELATION OF Y'S.

Appendix 9B

Determining Least Squares Estimates Using a Calculator

Using the data of the property assessment example, the following are step-by-step instructions for computing the least squares estimates of the slope and intercept using a hand-held calculator.

X	Y	XY	X^2
1.0	6	6	1.0
1.5	12	18	2.25
2.0	10	20	4.0
2.5	18	45	6.25
3.0	18	54	9.0
$\Sigma X_i = 10.0$	$\Sigma Y_i = 64$	$\Sigma X_i Y_i = 143$	$\Sigma X_i^2 = 22.5$

We have

$$\bar{Y} = \frac{64}{5} = 12.8 \quad \text{and} \quad \bar{X} = \frac{10.0}{5} = 2.0$$

Consequently, the sum of products is

$$SP(XY) = 143 - \frac{(10.0)(64)}{5} = 15$$

and the sum of squares for X is

$$SS(X) = 22.5 - \frac{10.0^2}{5} = 2.5$$

Substituting these quantities into Expressions (9.3) and (9.4), we obtain the following least squares estimates of the slope and intercept:

$$b_1 = \frac{15}{2.5} = 6.0 \quad \text{and} \quad b_0 = 12.8 - 6.0(2.0) = .8$$

Therefore, the estimated regression line is $\hat{Y} = .8 + 6.0X$.

Chapter 10

Multiple Linear Regression

10.1 Bridging to New Topics

In this chapter, we extend greatly the concepts of simple linear regression. Specifically, we deal with (1) having more than one predictor variable in a regression model, (2) including qualitative information in a regression model, (3) using regression analysis to model relationships that are not linear, and (4) avoiding common pitfalls in the application of regression analysis. The chapter concludes with a step-by-step framework for developing a regression model. The fundamental goal remains the determination of the most appropriate model that makes sense and fits the representative data such that the random error component is as small as possible. Since estimation and prediction remain primary reasons for using regression models, an appropriate model is one that provides sufficient precision when used for estimation and prediction.

A regression model with more than one predictor variable is called a **multiple linear regression model.** Multiple linear regression concepts are in many ways straightforward extensions of simple linear regression. However, the pertinent mathematical expressions are more complex; they involve matrix algebra, which is beyond the mathematical background assumed for this book. Multiple linear regression computations are too laborious to be performed with a hand calculator. Therefore, virtually all computations in this chapter are done by a computer.

Regression analysis can be a powerful tool for identifying the causes of variation of process outcomes and, more generally, for understanding better the decision-making environment. It is particularly useful when we have been unable to control the levels of key variables to conduct a designed experiment. Thus, we often apply regression analysis when using convenience data. Too often regression analysis is badly misused. It is very important for you to learn to use it properly, to understand its limitations, and to recognize its misuse. In addition to understanding the principles of regression analysis introduced in Chapter 9, your objectives for this chapter should include learning a sound procedure for developing a regression model and learning techniques for identifying the misapplications of regression.

10.2 The Multiple Linear Regression Model

Let's construct a model of the relationship of a response variable Y to more than one predictor variable. Let k represent the number of predictor variables involved. A multiple linear regression model may be expressed by extending the simple linear regression model as follows, where $X_1, X_2, \ldots, X_k$ are the k predictor variables:

$$Y = \underbrace{\beta_0 + \beta_1 X_1 + \beta_2 X_2 + \cdots + \beta_k X_k}_{\substack{\text{Mean of } Y \text{, given particular} \\ \text{values of } X_1, X_2, \ldots, X_k \\ \text{(the } \textit{deterministic} \\ \textit{component}\text{)}} } + \underbrace{\epsilon}_{\substack{\text{Random error: Unpredictable} \\ \text{deviations of } Y \text{ from the} \\ \text{population regression model} \\ \text{(the } \textit{random component}\text{)}}} \qquad \textbf{(10.1)}$$

As in simple linear regression, the multiple linear regression model consists of two components: the deterministic component $\beta_0 + \beta_1 X_1 + \cdots + \beta_k X_k$ and the random component ϵ. The component $\beta_0 + \beta_1 X_1 + \cdots + \beta_k X_k$ is known as the **population regression model** and is assumed to be the mean of Y, given particular values for X_1, $X_2, \ldots, X_k$. The component ϵ is the random error associated with any member of the population; it represents the unpredictable variation of Y-values from the population regression model. As in Chapter 9, the extent of random error is measured by the error variance σ_ϵ^2. Like the parameters $\beta_0, \beta_1, \ldots, \beta_k$, σ_ϵ^2 is an unknown parameter that must be estimated based on a representative sample. Again, the magnitude of σ_ϵ^2 measures the closeness of the fit. The smaller the estimated value of σ_ϵ^2 (the residual variance), the better the fit.

Recall from Chapter 9 that a scatter diagram provides an initial means of identifying the type of relationship that may exist between the response variable Y and a single predictor variable X. Unfortunately, when more than one predictor variable is involved, the graphing of Y versus each predictor variable does not help much in identifying the type of relationship that may exist between Y and the *set* of predictor variables. There are procedures, however, that can help us in this regard. These are presented in subsequent sections.

It is also important to understand that when we describe the population regression model given by Expression (10.1) as **linear,** this means "linear with regard to the parameters $\beta_0, \beta_1, \beta_2, \ldots, \beta_k$." This phrase means that all parameters (the β's) appear in the model with a power of 1. No parameter is itself used as a power (an exponent) or is multiplied by or divided by another parameter. For example, a model of the form

$$Y = \beta_0 + \beta_1 X_1 + \beta_2 X_2 + \beta_3 X_1^2 + \beta_4 X_2^2 + \epsilon \qquad \textbf{(10.2)}$$

is linear with regard to the parameters $\beta_0, \beta_1, \beta_2, \beta_3,$ and β_4, even though the model states that the relationship between the response variable Y and the predictor variables X_1 and X_2 is nonlinear. So when we say "multiple linear regression model," the word *linear* refers to the parameters of the model and not to the predictor variables in the model.

To illustrate a multiple linear regression model, let's consider an example in which the response variable Y is the daily sales of an ice cream parlor (in ounces of ice cream sold) and the two predictor variables are $X_1 =$ price (in cents per ounce) and $X_2 =$ daily high temperature (in degrees Fahrenheit). In this relationship, we would expect sales to increase if the price were lowered or if the temperature increased. Thus, we expect a negative sales–price relationship and a positive sales–temperature relationship.

Interpreting the Population Regression Equation

Suppose the population regression model for the ice cream parlor example were

$$Y = 0 - 1.6 X_1 + 4 X_2$$

Of course, in a real application this regression model would not be known; it would be estimated using a representative sample of data. But let's interpret the values of the parameters as if we knew them.

1. $\beta_0 = 0$ represents the mean daily sales if both X_1 and X_2 equal 0. In the unlikely event that the price is 0 (the ice cream is given free) and the temperature were $0°$ Fahrenheit, the model says the average daily sales would be 0.

2. The coefficient of price is $\beta_1 = -1.6$. Thus, the average daily sales decrease by 1.6 ounces for each cent that the price per ounce is increased, *if temperature remains constant.* As an illustration, consider a day for which $X_1 = 50¢$ and $X_2 = 85°$. The expected value of sales is $0 - 1.6(50) + 4(85) = 260$ ounces. But if X_1 is increased to $60¢$ and X_2 stays at $85°$, then the expected value of sales becomes $0 - 1.60(60) + 4(85) = 244$ ounces. The expected value of sales decreases by $260 - 244 = 16$ ounces, or 1.6 ounces for each cent that the price is increased.

3. Similarly, the coefficient of temperature is $\beta_2 = 4$. This indicates that the average daily sales increase by 4 ounces for every degree increase in the daily high temperature, *if price remains constant.*

To illustrate the model further, consider the following table of mean sales values corresponding to nine combinations of price and temperature:

Temperature (X_2)	Price (X_1)		
	65	50	35
75	196	220	244
85	236	260	284
95	276	300	324

In Figure 10.1(a), the relationship between mean daily sales and price is illustrated, when temperature is held constant. In Figure 10.1(b), the relationship between mean daily sales and temperature is illustrated, when price is held constant.

Figure 10.1

(a) Mean sales versus price at three levels of temperature, and (b) mean sales versus temperature at three levels of price

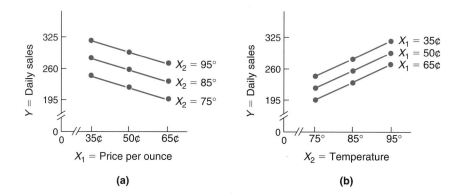

From Figure 10.1, notice that the linear relationship between the mean of Y and X_1 has the same slope for any value of X_1, as long as X_2 remains constant. The same statement is true for the linear relationship between the mean of Y and X_2 for any value of X_2, as long as X_1 remains constant. Thus, the lines are parallel. Consequently:

1. Given a particular temperature (X_2), the difference between two lines involving price (X_1) is constant. For example, the $X_1 = 35¢$ and $X_1 = 50¢$ lines are always 24 units apart. Thus, the mean of Y decreases by 24 units as X_1 increases by 15¢, provided X_2 remains constant. This is a decrease in Y of 1.6 ounces for every one-cent increase in price.

2. Given a particular price (X_1), the difference between any two lines involving temperature is constant. For example, the $X_2 = 85°$ and $X_2 = 95°$ lines are always 40 units apart. Thus, the mean of Y increases by 40 units as X_2 increases by 10°, provided X_1 remains constant. This is an increase in the mean of Y of 4 ounces for every degree increase in temperature.

10.3 Estimating the Parameters of the Multiple Linear Regression Model

To estimate the population regression model, we use sample data to estimate the parameters of the model: $\beta_0, \beta_1, \beta_2, \ldots, \beta_k$, and the error variance σ_ϵ^2. The methods for obtaining sample data are the same as those outlined in Section 9.3. For the most part, these involve either observing Y-values for predetermined values of the predictor variables $X_1, X_2, \ldots, X_k$ or simply using convenience data. It is indeed preferable to carefully select the values of the predictor variables, but in many cases we have no choice in the selection of data. We must keep in mind that the sample data used to estimate the parameters of the model must be representative of the environment about which we wish to learn.

10.3.1 The Method of Least Squares

As in Chapter 9, we use the least squares criterion to determine the best statistics for estimating the parameters $\beta_0, \beta_1, \beta_2, \ldots, \beta_k$. We use as estimates *the values for which the sum of the squared residuals is smallest for our sample of data*. The least squares estimators of $\beta_0, \beta_1, \ldots, \beta_k$ are denoted by $b_0, b_1, \ldots, b_k$, respectively. Just as in simple linear regression, we determine the values of $b_0, b_1, \ldots, b_k$ that minimize the sum of the squared errors. Given these values, the least squares regression equation may be written as

$$\hat{Y} = b_0 + b_1 X_1 + \cdots + b_k X_k \qquad\qquad \textbf{(10.3)}$$

The least squares expressions for $b_0, b_1, \ldots, b_k$ are not presented here because they involve matrix algebra. Consequently, *we rely entirely on the use of a computer for determining the least squares estimates of the model parameters based on a sample of data.*

For the ice cream parlor example, suppose we obtained the following data for a representative sample of 10 days:

Y (daily sales)	X_1 (price)	X_2 (high temperature)
374	35	74
386	35	82
472	35	94
429	50	93
391	50	82
475	50	96
428	50	91
412	65	93
405	65	88
341	65	78

Minitab, Excel, and JMP IN regression outputs are given in Table 10.1, in that order. The corresponding portions of these outputs are straightforward extensions of those from simple linear regression as provided in Chapter 9. As in Chapter 9, all information in the outputs will be explained as we present the relevant topics. [In the Minitab output we also list the sample Y-values (Sales), the $\hat{Y}$-values (Fit), and the residuals (Residual). Minitab also provides additional output that is not pertinent to our discussion now.] Thus, the least squares estimates are $b_0 = 25.88$, $b_1 = -1.3418$, and $b_2 = 5.1953$ for the model $Y = \beta_0 + \beta_1 X_1 + \beta_2 X_2 + \epsilon$, and the least squares equation is

$$\hat{Y} = 25.88 - 1.3418X_1 + 5.1953X_2$$

10.3.2 Estimating the Error Variance σ_ϵ^2

The procedure for estimating the error variance σ_ϵ^2 parallels that of Chapter 9. This means that the estimator S_e^2 must be based on the extent to which the sample observations (the Y-values) deviate from the corresponding predicted values (the $\hat{Y}$-values) determined from the least squares equation. These deviations are the residuals, so the numerator of S_e^2 is still the sum of the squares of the residuals, as

Table 10.1

Minitab, Excel, and JMP IN regression outputs for the ice cream example

Minitab

```
The regression equation is
Sales = 25.9 - 1.34 Price + 5.20 Temp

Predictor             Coef         StDev            T          P
Constant             25.88         51.33         0.50      0.630
Price              -1.3418        0.3620        -3.71      0.008
Temp                5.1953        0.5839         8.90      0.000

S = 13.13    R-Sq = 92.3%    R-Sq(adj) = 90.2%

Analysis of Variance

Source            DF         SS           MS         F          P
Regression         2     14553.9       7277.0     42.23      0.000
Residual Error     7      1206.2        172.3
Total              9     15760.1

Source     DF     Seq SS
Price       1      912.7
Temp        1    13641.3

Obs    Price    Sales       Fit    StDev Fit    Residual    St Resid
  1    35.0    374.00    363.37        9.58       10.63        1.19
  2    35.0    386.00    404.93        7.10      -18.93       -1.71
  3    35.0    472.00    467.27        8.37        4.73        0.47
  4    50.0    429.00    441.95        5.39      -12.95       -1.08
  5    50.0    391.00    384.80        5.11        6.20        0.51
  6    50.0    475.00    457.54        6.65       17.46        1.54
  7    50.0    428.00    431.56        4.73       -3.56       -0.29
  8    65.0    412.00    421.83        7.25       -9.83       -0.90
  9    65.0    405.00    395.85        6.79        9.15        0.81
 10    65.0    341.00    343.90        9.18       -2.90       -0.31
```

Excel

	A	B	C	D	E	F	G
1	SUMMARY OUTPUT						
2							
3	*Regression Statistics*						
4	Multiple R	0.961					
5	R Square	0.923					
6	Adjusted R Square	0.902					
7	Standard Error	13.127					
8	Observations	10					
9							
10	ANOVA						
11		*df*	*SS*	*MS*	*F*	*Significance F*	
12	Regression	2	14553.942	7276.971	42.232	0.000	
13	Residual	7	1206.158	172.308			
14	Total	9	15760.1				
15							
16		*Coefficients*	*Standard Error*	*t Stat*	*P-value*	*Lower 95%*	*Upper 95%*
17	Intercept	25.878	51.326	0.504	0.630	-95.489	147.244
18	Price	-1.342	0.362	-3.706	0.008	-2.198	-0.486
19	Temp	5.195	0.584	8.898	0.000	3.815	6.576

Table 10.1 (continued)

Minitab, Excel, and JMP IN regression outputs for the ice cream example

JMP IN

Response: Sales

Summary of Fit

RSquare	0.923468
RSquare Adj	0.901601
Root Mean Square Error	13.12663
Mean of Response	411.3
Observations (or Sum Wgts)	10

Parameter Estimates

Term	Estimate	Std Error	t Ratio	Prob>ltl	Lower 95%	Upper 95%
Intercept	25.877732	51.326	0.50	0.6296	-95.48996	147.24542
Price	-1.341751	0.362002	-3.71	0.0076	-2.197756	-0.485747
Temp-1	5.1952909	0.583896	8.90	<.0001	3.8145852	6.5759965

Analysis of Variance

Source	DF	Sum of Squares	Mean Square	F Ratio
Model	2	14553.942	7276.97	42.2323
Error	7	1206.158	172.31	Prob>F
C Total	9	15760.100		0.0001

Sequential (Type 1) Tests

Source	Nparm	DF	Seq SS	F Ratio	Prob>F
Price	1	1	912.667	5.2967	0.0549
Temp	1	1	13641.275	79.1678	<.0001

in simple linear regression. The denominator of S_e^2 in simple linear regression was $n - 2$. Now, what would you expect the denominator of S_e^2 to be for multiple linear regression? Keep in mind that in determining the $\hat{Y}$-values, we have estimated $k + 1$ parameters ($\beta_0, \beta_1, \ldots, \beta_k$) for the model $Y = \beta_0 + \beta_1 X_1 + \cdots + \beta_k X_k + \epsilon$. Therefore, to make the residual variance S_e^2 an unbiased estimator of σ_ϵ^2, we have to subtract $k + 1$ from n in the denominator of S_e^2. Accordingly, the residual variance S_e^2 is defined by

$$S_e^2 = \frac{SSE}{n - (k + 1)}$$

(10.4)

where

$$SSE = \Sigma(Y_i - \hat{Y}_i)^2$$

(10.5)

is the sum of the squares of the residuals. As before, the error standard deviation σ_ϵ is estimated by the residual standard deviation

$$S_e = \sqrt{S_e^2}$$

(10.6)

The residual variance S_e^2 remains an absolute measure of how well the least squares equation fits the sample Y-values. If a fit were perfect, all residuals would equal 0 and therefore S_e^2 would equal 0.

From the computer outputs in Table 10.1, the value of the residual variance is found in the same location of the output as in Chapter 9. Thus, for the ice cream example, the residual variance is $S_e^2 = 172.3$, the residual standard deviation is $S_e = 13.13$, and the error sum of squares is SSE = 1,206.2.

In evaluating a regression equation or several competing equations, the value of the residual variance S_e^2 is a very important criterion of goodness of fit. This is explored in detail later. As in the simple linear model, the residual variance is again known as the **mean square for error (MSE),** and the residual standard deviation is often referred to as the **root mean square for error (RMSE).**

10.3.3 The Coefficient of Determination

The coefficient of determination in multiple linear regression has precisely the same interpretation as in simple linear regression. It represents *the fraction of the total variation in the sample Y-values that has been explained by the predictor variables in the least squares equation.*

Suppose we have a sample for which the least squares equation has been determined. We ask the same simple question that we asked in Chapter 9: Why do the sample Y-values vary? Again there are two possible sources of variation:

1. *Regression:* The sample Y-values vary because the response variable Y is related to the predictor variables $X_1, X_2, \ldots, X_k$. As the values of the predictor variables change, the Y-values tend to change. For the ice cream parlor example, as the price changes and/or temperature changes, the daily sales volume tends to change.

2. *Random error:* The Y-values also vary because of factors other than the predictor variables in the model. For example, if the price and temperature did not change for several days, the daily sales volume still would vary for other reasons. The causes of additional variation are assumed to affect the response variable in a random fashion.

As in Chapter 9, the total variation in the sample Y-values is measured by SST, the total sum of squares. In addition, the unexplained variation in the sample Y-values is again measured by SSE, the sum of the squared residuals. Finally, the difference between SST and SSE is once again the regression sum of squares SSR, which measures the variation in the sample Y-values that is attributed to the changes among the sample values of the predictor variables in the model. So, as before,

$$SST = SSR + SSE \tag{10.7}$$

and the coefficient of determination is the ratio of the regression sum of squares to the total sum of squares. Thus,

$$R^2 = \frac{SSR}{SST} = \frac{SST - SSE}{SST} = 1 - \frac{SSE}{SST} \tag{10.8}$$

A capital R is generally the symbol for the coefficient of determination in multiple linear regression, whereas a lowercase r is generally used in simple linear regression.

From the computer output in Table 10.1 for the ice cream parlor example, SST = 15,760.1, SSR = 14,553.9, and $R^2 = .923$. This value for the coefficient of determination means that 92.3% of the total variation in the sample Y-values is attributed to the variation in the values of X_1 (price) and X_2 (temperature).

Misapplication of R^2

In the context of multiple linear regression analysis, R^2 is often misunderstood and misused. It is important for you to know that R^2 *does not decrease when a new term (either a new predictor variable or a term involving an existing predictor variable) is added to the regression model, even if the new term adds no useful information for predicting Y.* This is true because the unexplained variation in the sample Y-values, as measured by SSE, decreases at least slightly when an additional term is added to the regression model, whereas the total sum of squares SST remains constant no matter how many terms are in the model (because SST is determined completely by the sample Y-values). Therefore, the regression sum of squares SSR (the explained variation) must increase at least slightly when an additional term is added to the model.

If R^2 is used to determine whether a new term should be added to the model, then the question is not whether R^2 increases when the term is added, but by *how much R^2* increases. A higher R^2 value does not necessarily imply a better model. In fact, a sufficiently high R^2 value can be achieved by simply including enough predictor variables, some of which may actually contribute little in explaining the variation in the sample Y-values. In the ice cream parlor problem, for example, the addition of temperature to a model containing price alone is beneficial only if the addition substantially increases the regression sum of squares and thus increases the R^2 value by an appreciable amount. Some analysts often make the mistake of including too many predictor variables in the model on the basis of a high R^2 value.

Another common misuse is to assume that a model is good if R^2 is "high" and bad if R^2 is "low." A model with $R^2 = .60$ may be good if the goal is to establish the existence of some relationship between the sample Y-values and the predictor variables in the model. Conversely, a model with $R^2 = .9$ is not good if $R^2 = .99$ could be achieved by considering and including more meaningful predictor variables.

The Adjusted Coefficient of Determination

As we have said, R^2 can increase as more terms are added to a regression model. But an R^2 value of .95 is more impressive for a model with only four terms than for a model with 30 terms. For this reason, an alternative relative measure of goodness of fit has been suggested that takes into account the number of terms in the model. This measure is called the **adjusted coefficient of determination** and is defined by

$$R_a^2 = 1 - \left(\frac{n-1}{n-p}\right)\frac{\text{SSE}}{\text{SST}} \qquad \textbf{(10.9)}$$

where p denotes the number of terms in the model, including the intercept. In other words, p is the number of β parameters in the model. Notice that the expression for R_a^2 differs from that for R^2 only by the factor $(n-1)/(n-p)$. Since this factor always exceeds 1 (i.e., $p > 1$), the adjusted R^2 value is always less than the R^2 value. It is possible for the value of R_a^2 to decrease by an appreciable amount when an irrelevant predictor variable is added to a regression model. Therefore, the adjusted coefficient of determination R_a^2 is preferred to R^2 as a descriptive statistic for comparing competing regression models. In Section 10.5, we present an inferential (hypothesis testing) procedure for deciding whether the contribution of an additional term in the regression model is sufficient to justify keeping it in the model. A relatively high value for the coefficient of determination (or even for R_a^2) without additional regression analysis is *not* sufficient to determine whether a least squares equation is adequate for estimation and prediction. Notice that for the ice cream parlor example, the adjusted coefficient of determination is $R_a^2 = .902$.

EXAMPLE 10.1

For the ice cream parlor example, we found that the coefficient of determination is $R^2 = .923$ and the adjusted coefficient of determination is $R_a^2 = .902$ for the two predictor variables price and temperature. Suppose there were a third predictor variable, say X_3. When this variable is added along with price and temperature, the regression equation yields $R^2 = .931$ and $R_a^2 = .885$. Does the increase in R^2 indicate that the inclusion of X_3 results in a better model?

Solution

The answer is a resounding "no." The inclusion of any new predictor variable (or new term involving an existing predictor variable), however irrelevant, tends to increase R^2 by a small amount. The small increase from .923 to .931 when X_3 is added to the model is certainly not impressive. This conclusion is clearly supported by the decrease in the R_a^2 value from .902 to .885; thus, the inclusion of X_3 is not warranted on statistical grounds.

10.4 How Good Is the Model? Statistical Inference for Multiple Linear Regression

A multiple linear regression model is used in the same way that a simple linear regression model is used: for aiding the understanding of relationships among variables of interest and for estimating the mean of Y or for predicting an individual value of Y given a set of values for the predictor variables in the model. To illustrate, we consider the ice cream parlor example. The least squares equation $\hat{Y} = 25.88 - 1.3418X_1 + 5.1953X_2$ helps us understand the sensitivity of sales (Y) to changes in price (X_1) and temperature (X_2). The model also provides us the opportunity to estimate the average sales and to predict an individual day's sales for a given price and a given temperature. But no least squares model should be used unless it has been properly evaluated.

The issues with regard to the evaluation of a least squares model are the same as those outlined in Section 9.4. We repeat them here.

1. Do the sample data indicate convincingly that a relationship exists between Y and the predictor variables as specified by the regression model?

2. How accurate are the estimates and predictions of the least squares regression equation? Accuracy considerations include estimates of the β parameters and estimates and predictions for the response variable Y.

3. Are there any discernible violations of the assumptions necessary for statistical inferences? Even more than in Chapter 9, the analysis of residuals plays a major role in this regard for multiple linear regression.

Generally, these issues are resolved by appropriate statistical inferences on the least squares equation, including confidence intervals and hypothesis testing about the parameters $\beta_1, \beta_2, \ldots, \beta_k$. These inferences are extensions of those that you encountered in Chapter 9 for the simple linear model. As such, the inference methods are based on the assumptions presented in Section 9.4.1. We repeat them here.

Summary of Assumptions for Inferences in Multiple Linear Regression

1. *The specified regression model has the correct form.* The regression model $Y = \beta_0 + \beta_1 X_1 + \cdots + \beta_k X_k + \epsilon$ correctly represents the form of the association between the response variable and the predictor variables. Thus, for given values of the predictor variables $X_1, X_2, \ldots, X_k$, $E(Y) = \beta_0 + \beta_1 X_1 + \cdots + \beta_k X_k$ and the mean of the random errors is 0. This implies that when the least squares estimates are determined, the least squares equation $\hat{Y} = b_0 + b_1 X_1 + \cdots + b_k X_k$ estimates the *average* value of Y, given a set of values for the predictor variables.

2. *The error variance is constant.* The error variance σ_ϵ^2 is constant over all values of the predictor variables. Thus, the range of deviations of the Y-values from the regression model is the same regardless of the values of $X_1, X_2, \ldots, X_k$.

3. *Random errors are independent and normally distributed.* The random errors associated with the Y-values are statistically independent of one another and normally distributed.

10.4.1 Statistical Inferences on the Overall Model: An Analysis of Variance Approach

It is possible that some or all of the predictor variables in a least squares equation are not helpful in explaining the variation of the sample Y-values. One of the primary purposes of model evaluation is to determine which predictor variables, if any, should be included in the regression equation. But first we consider whether a relationship exists between Y and *any* of the identified predictor variables. For this we use the analysis of variance procedure.

For the ice cream parlor example, we may ask whether there is a discernible relationship between sales (Y) and either one or both of the predictor variables price (X_1) and daily high temperature (X_2). Suppose we assume tentatively that there is *no* relationship between Y and X_1 and X_2. This would mean that the coefficients β_1 and β_2 in the population regression model equal 0. We take this to be the null hypothesis. If there is a discernible relationship, then *at least one* of the parameters β_1 and β_2 cannot be 0. This becomes the alternative hypothesis.

For the regression model $Y = \beta_0 + \beta_1 X_1 + \cdots + \beta_k X_k + \epsilon$, an analysis of variance procedure similar to that of Chapter 9 is appropriate for testing the null hypothesis

$$H_0: \quad \beta_1 = \beta_2 = \cdots = \beta_k = 0$$

against the alternative

$$H_a: \quad \text{At least one of the parameters } \beta_1, \beta_2, \ldots, \beta_k \text{ is not } 0$$

Recall that the population regression model consists of two components: deterministic and random error. In the same manner as analysis of variance in Chapter 9, the total variation in the sample Y-values can be partitioned into two components that represent these two parts of the regression model. Thus, we partition the total variation among sample Y-values into two components: (1) variation attributable to change in the values of the predictor variables in the model, and (2) variation attributable to random error. In terms of sums of squares, $SST = SSR + SSE$. These quantities were explained in Section 10.3.3.

It is important to understand that SSE and SSR have a complementary relationship. SST remains constant for a given sample of data, regardless of which predictor variables are included in the model because it depends only on the sample Y-values. But SSE and SSR must sum to SST. Therefore, if one increases, the other decreases. The better a least squares equation fits the sample Y-values, the smaller the value of SSE and the larger the value of SSR. In the extreme case, a least squares equation that fits the sample Y-values perfectly has $SSE = 0$ and $SSR = SST$. A least squares equation that does not fit the sample Y-values at all has $SSR = 0$ and $SSE = SST$.

The best statistic for the analysis of variance procedure is the ratio of the mean squares for regression and error—that is, MSR/MSE. As in Chapter 9, these mean squares are developed by dividing the sums of squares by their degrees of freedom. Recall from Section 9.4.5 that the number of degrees of freedom for SSR is the number of terms in the regression model that involve predictor variables. For the model $Y = \beta_0 + \beta_1 X_1 + \cdots + \beta_k X_k + \epsilon$, there are k such terms; thus, k degrees of freedom are associated with SSR. In Section 10.3.2, we explained that since $k + 1$ "β" parameters must be estimated, the denominator for determining the mean square for error (the residual variance S_e^2) is $n - (k + 1)$. Accordingly, there are $n - (k + 1)$ degrees of freedom associated with SSE. Therefore, the mean squares for regression and error are

$$MSR = \frac{SSR}{k} \qquad \text{(10.10)}$$

and

$$MSE = \frac{SSE}{n - (k + 1)} \qquad \text{(10.11)}$$

respectively, and the F statistic is the ratio of the mean squares:

$$F = \frac{MSR}{MSE} \qquad \text{(10.12)}$$

If the null hypothesis of no association between Y and the predictor variables X_1, $X_2, \ldots, X_k$ is true, then the sampling distribution of this ratio is the F distribution with k numerator degrees of freedom and $n - (k + 1)$ denominator degrees of freedom. As before, the larger the F value, the smaller the P-value and the stronger the evidence against the null hypothesis of no association between Y and any of the predictor variables.

For the ice cream parlor example, recall from Table 10.1 that we had sample size $n = 10$, $k = 2$ terms involving predictor variables, error sum of squares SSE = 1,206.2, regression sum of squares SSR = 14,553.9, and total sum of squares SST = 15,760.1. Then for the hypotheses

$$H_0: \quad \beta_1 = \beta_2 = 0$$

$$H_a: \quad \text{At least one of the parameters } \beta_1 \text{ and } \beta_2 \text{ is not } 0$$

the F-value from the analysis of variance table is 42.23, for which the P-value is .000. Since the P-value is virtually 0, the sample data strongly contradict the null hypothesis of no relationship between Y and either X_1 or X_2. Therefore, we conclude that an association exists between sales and *at least one* of the predictor variables price (X_1) and temperature (X_2).

10.4.2 Evaluating the Contribution of an Individual Predictor Variable: The T Statistic

Suppose the analysis of variance procedure for the overall model supports the existence of a relationship between Y and at least one of the predictor variables. A logical next step is to determine which predictor variables appear to contribute to the explanation of the variation in the sample Y-values and which do not. This can be accomplished by testing individual hypotheses for each β coefficient that involves a predictor variable.

With regard to the assumed regression model $Y = \beta_0 + \beta_1 X_1 + \cdots + \beta_k X_k + \epsilon$, the null hypothesis for testing the contribution of an individual predictor variable X_i is H_0: $\beta_i = 0$, for $i = 1, 2, \ldots, k$. This hypothesis states that, *as the predictor variable X_i changes, the average value of Y remains constant as long as the other predictor variables in the model all remain unchanged.* An important equivalent interpretation of this null hypothesis is that *adding X_i to a model that already contains the other predictor variables does not explain further the variation in the sample Y*-values. That is, if H_0: $\beta_i = 0$ is true, then X_i provides no useful information for estimating Y beyond the information already provided by the other predictor variables. Thus, $\beta_i = 0$ means that the *marginal* or *incremental* contribution of X_i to the prediction of Y, *in the presence of all other predictor variables in the model,* is 0. The alternative hypothesis may be either two-sided or one-sided, depending on whether a particular direction is conjectured for the X_i versus Y relationship. Most computer software packages assume a two-sided alternative hypothesis. For this reason, we do the same.

You should not be surprised that the T statistic is the appropriate statistic for inferences about the marginal contribution of a predictor variable in the presence of all other predictor variables in the model. Given the value of the least squares estimator b_i and the standard error of b_i, the null hypothesis H_0: $\beta_i = 0$ can be tested either by computing the T-value

$$T_i = \frac{b_i - 0}{SE(b_i)} \tag{10.13}$$

and determining the resulting P-value (we get all these quantities from a computer), or by constructing a confidence interval for β_i. As always, a small P-value contradicts the null hypothesis and suggests that X_i provides a discernible contribution to explaining the variation in the sample Y-values. Alternatively, if a confidence interval for β_i does not include 0, the null hypothesis is not plausible and there is compelling evidence that X_i adds a discernible contribution to explaining the variation in the sample Y-values. In either case, the sampling distribution of the T statistic is the T distribution with $n - (k + 1)$ degrees of freedom (the number of degrees of freedom associated with SSE). Therefore, a $100(1 - \alpha)\%$ confidence interval for the parameter β_i is

$$b_i \pm t_{1 - \alpha/2, n - (k + 1)} \text{ SE}(b_i) \qquad\qquad \textbf{(10.14)}$$

where $t_{1 - \alpha/2, n - (k + 1)}$ is the appropriate quantile value of the T distribution.

From the computer outputs for the ice cream parlor example in Table 10.1, the standard errors of the least squares coefficients for price and temperature are .362 and .584 (found under the column heading "StDev" in Minitab, under the column heading "Standard Error" in Excel, and under the column heading "Std Error" in the "Parameter Estimates" portion of JMP IN). The T-values for the marginal contributions of price and temperature are found in the next column to the right and are $T_1 = -1.3418/.362 = -3.71$ and $T_2 = 5.1953/.584 = 8.9$, and the P-values are found in the next column on the right and are .008 and .000, respectively. The 95% confidence limits for the population coefficients of price and temperature are $(-2.198, -.486)$ and $(3.815, 6.576)$, respectively. They are found under "Lower 95%" and "Upper 95%," respectively, for both Excel and JMP IN. Currently, Minitab does not provide them explicitly in its output.

Interim Summary of the Regression Analysis for the Ice Cream Parlor Example

To evaluate how well the least squares equation fits the sample Y-values for the ice cream parlor example based on the information that we have discussed so far in Table 10.1, the following conclusions are appropriate.

1. *Analysis of the overall model.*   For the overall model, the null hypothesis H_0: $\beta_1 = \beta_2 = 0$ is strongly contradicted by the sample evidence because the P-value corresponding to the F value of 42.23 is very small (.000). So we know that either price or temperature or both help to explain the variation in the sample Y-values.

2. *Analysis of marginal contributions of individual predictors.*   We now evaluate the marginal contributions of price in the presence of temperature, and temperature in the presence of price. We note that the individual null hypotheses H_0: $\beta_1 = 0$ and H_0: $\beta_2 = 0$ are contradicted by the sample evidence because the corresponding P-values are very small. For price, the T-value is $T_1 = -3.71$, for which the P-value is .008. For temperature, $T_2 = 8.90$, for which the P-value is .000. Therefore, we conclude that price provides useful incremental information beyond that already provided by temperature, and temperature provides useful incremental information beyond that already provided by price. Consequently, the least squares equation that includes both price and temperature is indeed better for explaining the variation in the sample Y-values than a model that contains only one of these variables.

3. *Analysis of precision of estimated regression coefficients.*   The precision with which the parameters β_1 and β_2 are estimated is reasonably good, because the standard errors for the least squares estimates are considerably smaller than the

magnitudes of the estimates. This is evidenced by the T-values. In fact, by comparing the magnitudes of the T-values ($T_1 = -3.71$ and $T_2 = 8.90$), we conclude that β_2 is estimated with greater relative precision than is β_1. We can use Expression (10.14) directly to construct confidence intervals for β_1 and β_2. For example, a 95% confidence interval for β_1 is ($t_{.975,7} = 2.365$):

$$-1.3418 \pm (2.365)(.3620) = -1.3428 \pm .8561$$

or (-2.1979, $-.4857$). This means that, if temperature remains constant, average sales may decrease by as much as 2.2 ounces or by as little as .49 ounce for each one-cent increase in price, with 95% confidence. A 95% confidence interval for β_2 is

$$5.1953 \pm (2.365)(.5839) = 5.1953 \pm 1.3809$$

or (3.8144, 6.5762). This means that, if price remains constant, average sales may increase by as much as 6.58 ounces or by as little as 3.81 ounces for a one-degree increase in a day's high temperature, with 95% confidence.

4. *Analysis of coefficient of determination.* Both the R^2 value (.923) and the adjusted R^2 value (.902) are reasonably high. This suggests that most of the variation in the sample Y-values is explained by the least squares equation that includes price and temperature. It does *not* mean the model could not be improved by the addition of other predictor variables.

It is reasonable to be optimistic that the least squares equation $\hat{Y} = 25.88 - 1.3418X_1 + 5.1953X_2$ is adequate for estimation and prediction within the price and temperature ranges of the sample data. A residual analysis remains to be performed to check the validity of the model assumptions.

10.4.3 Further Examination of the Contributions of Individual Predictor Variables: The Extra Sum of Squares Principle

In the previous section, you learned that the T statistic can be used to investigate the marginal contribution of a specific predictor variable if all other predictor variables are included in the least squares equation. In this section, we introduce a concept known as the **extra sum of squares principle** to further investigate the marginal contribution of a predictor variable. The procedure that follows helps us to better understand the idea of "marginal contribution" and the problem of *collinearity*, to be discussed in Section 10.7. The pertinent information with regard to the extra sum of squares principle is provided by many computer packages, including Minitab and JMP IN, but not Excel. (The portions of the Minitab and JMP IN outputs that we did not explain for the ice cream parlor example deal specifically with this issue.)

In some regression applications, a predictor variable may provide no useful incremental information in a model that includes other predictor variables, even though it is useful for predicting the response when it is the only predictor variable considered. In some other applications, a predictor variable might provide useful incremental information in a model that contains other predictor variables, even though it does not when considered by itself. Subtle issues like these can be sorted out with the extra sum of squares principle. This principle is fundamentally based on the natures of the total, regression, and error sums of squares (SST, SSR, and SSE), which are worth repeating here:

1. Given a sample of Y-values, the total sum of squares SST is not affected (i.e., it stays the same) when additional terms involving predictor variables are introduced to a regression model.

2. The error sum of squares SSE decreases by at least a small amount when any additional term is added to the model.

3. The regression sum of squares SSR increases by at least a small amount when any additional term is added to the model. The increase in the regression sum of squares matches the decrease in the error sum of squares.

Consequently, a logical strategy in multiple linear regression is to consider adding terms to a model only if the addition of those terms *substantially* decreases SSE and thus *substantially* increases SSR.

We illustrate this principle with the ice cream parlor example. Recall that we have $SST = 15,760.1$, $SSR(X_1, X_2) = 14,553.9$, $SSE(X_1, X_2) = 1,206.2$, and $MSE(X_1, X_2) = 172.3$. To help you be aware of the predictor variables that have been included in the least squares equation, we have identified them in parentheses. Thus, $SSR(X_1, X_2)$ denotes "SSR for a model in which the predictor variables are X_1 and X_2." To locate the "extra sum of squares," refer to the last portions of the Minitab and JMP IN outputs in Table 10.1; they are reproduced here for convenience. Of particular interest are the two entries under the column heading "SEQ SS" in both Minitab and JMP IN outputs. We return to explain the meaning of these two quantities after a brief introduction of the fundamental issues involving such quantities.

MINITAB

SOURCE	DF	SEQ SS
Price	1	912.7
Temp	1	13641.3

JMP IN

Sequential (Type 1) Tests

Source	Nparm	DF	Seq SS	F Ratio	Prob>F
Price	1	1	912.667	5.2967	0.0549
Temp	1	1	13641.275	79.1678	<.0001

Marginal F Statistics for the Last Variable Entered: Sequential Sums of Squares

The extra sum of squares principle can be applied usefully in the following way: Suppose we are considering four predictor variables for inclusion in a regression model: X_1, X_2, X_3, and X_4. We wish to examine the effects of adding one variable at a time; that is, we actually fit four models, one with X_1 as the only predictor variable, the second with X_1 and X_2, the third with X_1, X_2, and X_3, and the fourth with X_1, X_2, X_3, and X_4. In each case, we observe how much the addition of a predictor variable reduces the error sum of squares (or, equivalently, how much it increases the regression sum of squares). These changes in the error sum of squares are called "sequential sums of squares." We use the following notation:

$SSR(X_1) =$ The regression sum of squares when X_1 is the only predictor variable in the model

$SSR(X_2|X_1) =$ The extra sum of squares when X_2 is added to the model, compared to the regression sum of squares for a model with X_1 alone

$$SSR(X_3|X_1, X_2) = \text{The extra sum of squares when } X_3 \text{ is added to the model, compared to the regression sum of squares for a model with only } X_1 \text{ and } X_2$$

$$SSR(X_4|X_1, X_2, X_3) = \text{The extra sum of squares when } X_4 \text{ is added to the model, compared to the regression sum of squares for a model with only } X_1, X_2, \text{ and } X_3$$

For example, suppose the error and regression sums of squares are as follows for these four models:

Model	SST	SSE	SSR	Seq. SS
$\hat{Y} = b_0 + b_1X_1$	100	50	50	50
$\hat{Y} = b_0 + b_1X_1 + b_2X_2$	100	40	60	10
$\hat{Y} = b_0 + b_1X_1 + b_2X_2 + b_3X_3$	100	25	75	15
$\hat{Y} = b_0 + b_1X_1 + b_2X_2 + b_3X_3 + b_4X_4$	100	5	95	20
Total				95

The **sequential sums of squares** therefore are the sequential increases in the regression sum of squares as predictor variables are added to the model one at a time. Notice that the total of the sequential sums of squares in the table is 95, the same as the value of the regression sum of squares for the final model that includes all predictor variables X_1, X_2, X_3, and X_4. This is true in general. Sequential sums of squares represent a *partitioning* of the regression sum of squares for the model that includes all predictor variables. For any model with four predictor variables,

$$SSR(X_1, X_2, X_3, X_4) = SSR(X_1) + SSR(X_2|X_1) \\ + SSR(X_3|X_1, X_2) + SSR(X_4|X_1, X_2, X_3) \quad \textbf{(10.15)}$$

Each sequential sum of squares has 1 degree of freedom because it represents the contribution of only one additional term involving a predictor variable. When using Minitab or JMP IN, we do not actually have to fit four distinct models. Instead, Minitab and JMP IN provide all the sequential sums of squares automatically when we fit the complete model containing all the predictor variables. They are listed under the column "SEQ SS."

For example, since there are two predictor variables in the ice cream parlor problem, it is possible to partition the regression sum of squares when both price (X_1) and temperature (X_2) are in the model into two components, each of which is a sequential sum of squares with a single degree of freedom. If we assume that the order of entry of predictor variables into the model is price first and then temperature, the partitioning of the regression sum of squares into components that can be attributed to the order of entry of each predictor variable is

$$SSR(\text{Price, Temperature}) = SSR(\text{Price}) + SSR(\text{Temperature}|\text{Price}) \quad \textbf{(10.16)}$$

The regression sum of squares for the model that includes both price and temperature was given in Table 10.1 to be 14,553.9. The values of the components $SSR(X_1)$ and $SSR(X_2|X_1)$ are found in the column SEQ SS in the Minitab and JMP IN outputs. $SSR(X_1) = 912.7$ represents the regression sum of squares that occurs when price is the only predictor variable in the model. $SSR(X_2|X_1) = 13{,}641.3$

represents the reduction in the error sum of squares that occurs when X_2 is added to the model that previously contained only X_1. To confirm the partitioning, notice that $SSR(X_1, X_2) = 14,553.9 = 912.7 + 13,641.3$ (save roundoff error).

We want to be able to assess the incremental contributions of the predictor variables as they are added sequentially to the regression equation. For a given predictor variable, is its contribution more than could be expected from adding an unrelated variable to the model? To carry out the assessment, we form an F statistic for each predictor variable based on its sequential sum of squares value. The numerator for the F statistic is the sequential sum of squares divided by its 1 degree of freedom. The denominator is the mean square for error for the overall model, $MSE(X_1, X_2)$. These ratios are known as **marginal** or **partial F statistics** for testing the hypotheses $H_0: \beta_1 = 0$ and $H_0: \beta_2 = 0$, where for the second hypothesis X_1 is already in the model. Thus, the F-value for the contribution of X_1 alone is

$$F_1 = \frac{SSR(X_1)/1}{MSE(X_1, X_2)} = \frac{912.7}{172.3} = 5.30$$

and the F-value for the incremental contribution of X_2 when it is added to a model that already includes X_1 is

$$F_2 = \frac{SSR(X_2|X_1)/1}{MSE(X_1, X_2)} = \frac{13,641.3}{172.3} = 79.17$$

These F-values and their associated P-values are not given by Minitab but are given by JMP IN; they are found to the right of the Seq SS column.

The P-value for the contribution of price is small but not negligible (.0549). This implies that if price were the only predictor variable in the model, then its contribution to the variation in the sample Y-values would be somewhat uncertain. It is interesting to compare this P-value to that associated with the T statistic for price, which was much smaller (.008). The latter P-value indicated that we can be quite certain that price, *in the presence of temperature,* helps to explain daily sales variation. What is the reason for the difference? Such a difference is usually the result of a relationship between predictor variables. This means that price and temperature might be related somehow. When there is a relationship between or among the predictor variables, a conflict will arise based on the P-values for sequential sum of squares and the corresponding T statistic. When the conflict is severe (that is, the P-values are distinctly different), it usually implies the existence of what is known as *collinearity* between or among the predictor variables. Collinearity is a serious concern in multiple regression applications. It is defined and examined closely in Section 10.7.

We should point out that the order of entry of the predictor variables into the model is identified by the user when requesting a regression analysis of the software package. If, for example, in the ice cream parlor problem, temperature (X_2) is identified first, followed by price (X_1), then the two components of $SSR(X_1, X_2) = 14,553.9$ would be

$$SSR(X_1, X_2) = SSR(X_2) + SSR(X_1|X_2) \qquad \textbf{(10.17)}$$

In this context, $SSR(X_2)$ is the regression sum of squares when only X_2 (temperature) is included in the model, and $SSR(X_1|X_2)$ is the additional sum of squares removed from SSE when X_1 (price) is added. By interchanging the order of entry to the model for the predictor variables, it is possible to partition the regression sum of squares in several ways, as illustrated by Expressions (10.16) and (10.17).

EXAMPLE 10.2

Suppose the three predictor variables X_1, X_2, and X_3 are considered for inclusion in a model to explain the variation of a response variable Y. Based on a representative sample, assume some statistical software (such as Minitab and JMP IN) is used to determine the least squares equation $\hat{Y} = b_0 + b_1 X_1 + b_2 X_2 + b_3 X_3$.

(a) If the entry order is X_1, then X_2, and then X_3, determine the proper notation for the three components of SSR(X_1, X_2, X_3).

(b) Answer the same question as in part (a) if the entry order is X_2, then X_1, and then X_3.

(c) Answer the same question as in part (a) if the entry order is X_3, then X_2, and then X_1.

Solution

The answers for the three parts are the sequential sums of squares relative to the order in which the variables are entered.

(a) SSR(X_1, X_2, X_3) = SSR(X_1) + SSR($X_2|X_1$) + SSR($X_3|X_1$, X_2), where
- SSR(X_1) is the reduction in the error sum of squares when X_1 is the first variable to enter the model.
- SSR($X_2|X_1$) is the additional reduction in SSE when X_2 is added to the model that already contains X_1.
- SSR($X_3|X_1$, X_2) is the additional reduction in SSE when X_3 is added to the model that already contains X_1 and X_2.

(b) SSR(X_1, X_2, X_3) = SSR(X_2) + SSR($X_1|X_2$) + SSR($X_3|X_2$, X_1)

(c) SSR(X_1, X_2, X_3) = SSR(X_3) + SSR($X_2|X_3$) + SSR($X_1|X_3$, X_2)

The components in parts (b) and (c) have similar meanings to those in part (a).

10.4.4 Using the Least Squares Model for Estimation and Prediction

Once we have gained insight into the relationship between a response variable and a set of predictor variables, we often want to use the least squares equation for estimation and prediction. In particular, we want either to estimate the average value of Y or to predict an individual value of Y, given a set of values for the predictor variables in the least squares equation.

To illustrate, let's return to the ice cream parlor example. Suppose we wish to estimate the average daily sales when $X_1 = 40$ cents and $X_2 = 75$ degrees. Substituting into the least squares equation, we obtain $\hat{Y} = 25.88 - 1.3418(40) + 5.1953(75) = 361.85$. Thus, the estimated *average* daily sales for this situation is 361.85 oz. The predicted sales for an *individual* day for these values of the predictor variables is also 361.85 oz. But, given a set of X-values, the precision for estimating an average Y-value is better than that for predicting an individual Y-value. We know that accuracy (precision) is determined by the standard error associated with the estimate or prediction. The mathematical expressions for these standard errors involve matrix algebra and are not presented here. However, statistical software such as Minitab and JMP IN can provide confidence intervals for an average Y-value and prediction intervals for an individual Y-value, given a set of values for the predictor variables in the least squares equation.

The following are JMP IN 95% confidence and prediction intervals for the indicated combinations of price and temperature. Let's explain the meaning of one of these. When price = 60 cents and temperature = 90 degrees, we estimate the average daily sales to be 412.95 oz. The 95% confidence interval (399.74, 426.16) means that the average daily sales could be as low as 399.74 oz. to as high as 426.16 oz., with 95% confidence. For the same price–temperature combination, we predict that the sales for an individual day is 412.95 oz., but the 95% prediction interval (379.21, 446.68) means that the sales that day could be a low as 379.21 oz. to as high as 446.68 oz., with 95% confidence.

Price	Temp	Predicted Sales	Lower 95% Pred Sales	Upper 95% Pred Sales	Lower 95% Indiv Sales	Upper 95% Indiv Sales
40	75	361.85	341.79	381.92	324.89	398.81
50	75	348.44	329.06	367.81	311.85	385.03
60	75	335.02	312.77	357.27	296.83	373.21
40	90	439.78	425.76	453.81	405.72	473.85
50	90	426.37	415.77	436.97	393.57	459.17
60	90	412.95	399.74	426.16	379.21	446.68

10.5 Incorporating Qualitative Variables in Multiple Linear Regression: Dummy Variables

So far we have established a foundation for developing and analyzing multiple linear regression models. We are now in a position to consider some ways to extend the usefulness of regression models. In this section, we introduce a method for including qualitative information in a regression model.

In the problems we have considered up to now, the predictor variables such as price and temperature have been quantitative. Often, however, qualitative variables such as marital status, gender, and academic major are important factors that need to be incorporated in a regression model. But for a qualitative variable, a numerically meaningful scale does not exist. For example, marital status is an attribute: A person either is married or is not. Academic major is also an attribute: A student's major may be managment, accounting, finance, and so on.

How then do we include qualitative predictor variables in a regression equation? We use **dummy variables;** these are artificial variables that are always assigned a value of 0 or 1. The value "1" indicates the presence of a characteristic (say, "female") and "0" indicates the absence of that characteristic (that is, "not female" or "male").

To illustrate, let's return to the ice cream parlor example. Recall that a key purpose of regression analysis is to gain insight into processes so that better decisions can be made. Thus, we ask what factors other than price and temperature might account for variation in daily ice cream sales. One possibility is that the demand is greater on weekends than on weekdays. If this is true, then we might choose to lower the price on weekdays or increase the price on weekends. The "type of day" is qualitative information that can be incorporated into the regression model by creating a dummy variable. We may define the dummy variable X_3 as follows:

$$X_3 = \begin{cases} 1 & \text{for weekend days} \\ 0 & \text{for weekdays} \end{cases}$$

The sample data for the ice cream parlor example with the "type of day" included are as follows:

Day	Y (sales)	X_1 (price)	X_2 (temperature)	X_3 (type of day)
1	374	35	74	1
2	386	35	82	0
3	472	35	94	1
4	429	50	93	0
5	391	50	82	1
6	475	50	96	1
7	428	50	91	1
8	412	65	93	0
9	405	65	88	1
10	341	65	78	0

We now consider the regression model

$$Y = \beta_0 + \beta_1 X_1 + \beta_2 X_2 + \beta_3 X_3 + \epsilon$$

If the type of day does not matter, then $\beta_3 = 0$. So an additional hypothesis we wish to test is $H_0: \beta_3 = 0$ in the presence of price and temperature. The Minitab output for this model is given in Table 10.2. The following conclusions are apparent from this output:

Table 10.2

Minitab output for the ice cream parlor example including type of day dummy variable

```
The regression equation is
Sales = 15.3 - 1.10 Price + 5.04 Temp + 20.2 Day

Predictor         Coef       Stdev     t-ratio          p
Constant         15.31       27.90        0.55      0.603
Price          -1.1012      0.2041       -5.40      0.002
Temp            5.0391      0.3183       15.83      0.000
Day             20.245       4.789        4.23      0.006

S = 7.108    R-sq = 98.1%    R-sq(adj) = 97.1%

Analysis of Variance

Source         DF          SS         MS          F          P
Regression      3     15457.0     5152.3     101.99      0.000
Error           6       303.1       50.5
Total           9     15760.1

Source     DF      SEQ SS
Price       1       912.7
Temp        1     13641.3
Day         1       903.0
```

Figure 10.2

(a) Graph of $\hat{Y}$ versus X_2 when $X_1 = 50$, and (b) $\hat{Y}$ versus X_1 when $X_2 = 85$ for weekends and weekdays

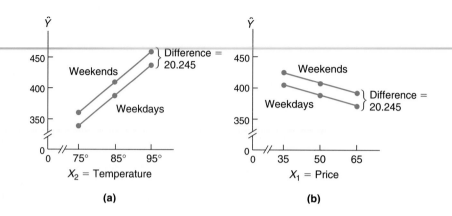

1. The least squares equation is

$$\hat{Y} = 15.31 - 1.1012X_1 + 5.0391X_2 + 20.245X_3$$

The least squares estimate $b_3 = 20.245$ represents the difference between the average daily sales when $X_3 = 1$ (a weekend day) and the average sales when $X_3 = 0$ (a weekday), if price and temperature remain constant. This can be seen by expressing the least squares equation for the two conditions, weekends and weekdays, separately as follows:

If $X_3 = 1$: $\hat{Y} = 15.31 - 1.1012X_1 + 5.0391X_2 + 20.245$
If $X_3 = 0$: $\hat{Y} = 15.31 - 1.1012X_1 + 5.0391X_2 + 0$

These two equations are identical except that the constant amount $b_3 = 20.245$ is added to the estimated average sales for weekend days. The nature of these two equations is illustrated further in Figure 10.2, the graphs of $\hat{Y}$ versus X_2 assuming $X_1 = 50$ and $\hat{Y}$ versus X_1 assuming $X_2 = 85$.

2. The null hypothesis H_0: $\beta_3 = 0$ is contradicted strongly by the sample data, since the P-value, based on the T statistic, is quite small (.006). This means that knowing the type of day is helpful in explaining the variation in the sample Y-values (sales) if price and temperature are known, with weekend sales averaging an estimated 20.245 ounces per day more than weekday sales.

3. The least squares model that includes the type of day is considerably better for estimation and prediction than the one that did not include type of day. This is true because the residual variance S_e^2 is considerably smaller than before (50.5 now versus 172.3 before). In addition, the standard errors of the least squares estimates for the coefficients of price and temperature are considerably smaller than before relative to the magnitudes of the estimates (T-values of -5.4 and 15.83 now versus T-values of -3.71 and 8.90 before for price and temperature, respectively).

Assignment of the 0, 1 Values for a Dummy Variable

In including the qualitative variable "type of day" in the ice cream parlor example, suppose we had assigned the values 0 and 1 to X_3 in a reversed fashion:

$$X_3 = \begin{cases} 0 & \text{for weekend days} \\ 1 & \text{for weekdays} \end{cases}$$

Would this make a difference? In substance, the answer is no. The least squares coefficients would be precisely the same except that the value of b_3 would change only in sign—that is, from $b_3 = 20.245$ to $b_3 = -20.245$. The interpretation would be that the average sales for weekdays are 20.245 *lower* than those for weekend days. Of course, this is the same interpretation as before. Thus, the assignment of the 0, 1 values for a dummy variable is purely arbitrary. You need only to remember that the coefficient of the dummy variable in the regression equation always represents the difference between the "1" condition and the "0" condition.

What If There Are More Than Two Conditions for a Qualitative Variable?

What if a qualitative predictor variable has more than two possible conditions? Another factor that might affect ice cream sales is how clear the sky is—that is, whether the day is sunny, overcast, or rainy. Therefore, we may want to consider the qualitative variable "sky condition" in the ice cream parlor example, with the three possible conditions: sunny, overcast, and rainy. The *three* sky conditions could be included by defining the following *two* dummy variables as follows:

$$X_4 = \begin{cases} 1 & \text{if sunny} \\ 0 & \text{otherwise} \end{cases}$$

$$X_5 = \begin{cases} 1 & \text{if overcast} \\ 0 & \text{otherwise} \end{cases}$$

These two dummy variables, observed in tandem, can specify any of the three sky conditions as follows:

	X_4	X_5
A sunny day	1	0
An overcast day	0	1
A rainy day	0	0

In general, *the number of dummy variables needed is 1 less than the number of possible conditions of a qualitative variable.* Notice that one of the conditions is a "default" condition; it is the condition for which all dummy variables equal 0. Thus, the default condition in the ice cream parlor example is a rainy day.

If we include the qualitative variable "sky condition" in the ice cream parlor example, then we can interpret the least squares coefficients for X_4 and X_5 by examining the least squares equation separately for each condition as follows:

If $X_4 = 1, X_5 = 0$ (sunny): $\quad \hat{Y} = b_0 + b_1X_1 + b_2X_2 + b_3X_3 + b_4$

If $X_4 = 0, X_5 = 1$ (overcast): $\quad \hat{Y} = b_0 + b_1X_1 + b_2X_2 + b_3X_3 + b_5$

If $X_4 = 0, X_5 = 0$ (rainy): $\quad \hat{Y} = b_0 + b_1X_1 + b_2X_2 + b_3X_3$

As a result, b_4 estimates the difference in average sales between sunny days ($X_4 = 1$) and rainy days (the default condition), and b_5 estimates the difference in average sales between overcast days ($X_5 = 1$) and rainy days. Finally, $b_4 - b_5$ estimates the difference in average sales between sunny days and overcast days. In general, the coefficient of any dummy variable estimates the difference between the average response (Y) when the dummy variable equals 1 and the average response for the default condition.

EXAMPLE 10.3

What factors affect starting salaries of business school graduates? The identification of such factors is valuable to both industry and students. Industry can build a statistical model that can easily provide a quantitative assessment of a potential employee's qualifications. And students will know in advance what factors count with regard to starting salaries. This example illustrates such a situation.

A personnel recruiter for industry wishes to identify the factors that explain the starting salaries for business school graduates. He believes that a student's grade point average (GPA) and academic major are both predictive. The following is a representative sample of 15 graduates from a business school, where Y is the starting salary (in thousands of dollars) and X_1 is the GPA:

Graduate	Y	X_1	Major	Graduate	Y	X_1	Major
1	21.5	2.95	Management	9	24.7	3.05	Accounting
2	23.0	3.20	Management	10	23.4	2.70	Accounting
3	24.1	3.40	Management	11	20.5	2.75	Finance
4	25.4	3.60	Management	12	22.2	3.10	Finance
5	24.2	3.20	Management	13	24.0	3.15	Finance
6	24.0	2.85	Accounting	14	22.2	2.95	Finance
7	27.0	3.10	Accounting	15	21.8	2.75	Finance
8	27.8	2.85	Accounting				

Fit an appropriate model to these data, evaluate it, and interpret it.

Solution

Since the qualitative variable "academic major" consists of three conditions, we need to define two dummy variables as follows:

$$X_2 = \begin{cases} 1 & \text{if a student's major is management} \\ 0 & \text{otherwise} \end{cases}$$

$$X_3 = \begin{cases} 1 & \text{if a student's major is accounting} \\ 0 & \text{otherwise} \end{cases}$$

Thus, the following configurations of these two dummy variables specify any of the three majors, where the finance major is the default condition (i.e., $X_2 = X_3 = 0$ indicates a finance major):

Major	X_2	X_3
Management	1	0
Accounting	0	1
Finance	0	0

For the model $Y = \beta_0 + \beta_1 X_1 + \beta_2 X_2 + \beta_3 X_3 + \epsilon$, the Excel output is given in Table 10.3. From this output, the following conclusions are apparent:

Table 10.3

Excel output for Example 10.3

	A	B	C	D	E	F	G
1	SUMMARY OUTPUT						
2							
3	*Regression Statistics*						
4	Multiple R	0.8558					
5	R Square	0.7324					
6	Adjusted R Square	0.6594					
7	Standard Error	1.1666					
8	Observations	15					
9							
10	ANOVA						
11		*df*	*SS*	*MS*	*F*	*Significance F*	
12	Regression	3	40.9743	13.6581	10.0362	0.0018	
13	Residual	11	14.9697	1.3609			
14	Total	14	55.944				
15							
16		*Coefficients*	*Standard Error*	*t Stat*	*P-value*	*Lower 95%*	*Upper 95%*
17	Intercept	5.9972	4.9423	1.2134	0.2504	-4.8807	16.8750
18	X1	5.4908	1.6717	3.2846	0.0073	1.8115	9.1700
19	X2	-0.3120	0.9212	-0.3386	0.7413	-2.3396	1.7157
20	X3	3.4047	0.7395	4.6041	0.0008	1.7771	5.0324

1. The least squares equation is

$$\hat{Y} = 5.997 + 5.491X_1 - .312X_2 + 3.405X_3$$

   The least squares estimate $b_2 = -.312$ means that, on average, a management major earns \$312 less than a finance major. Similarly, the least squares estimate $b_3 = 3.405$ means that, on average, an accounting major earns \$3,405 more than a finance major.

2. The adjusted R^2 is 65.9% and for the hypothesis H_0: $\beta_1 = \beta_2 = \beta_3 = 0$, the *P*-value for $F = 10.036$ is .0018. So, GPA and/or the two dummy variables appear to explain the variation in the sample starting salaries, at least to some degree.

3. The hypotheses H_0: $\beta_1 = 0$ and H_0: $\beta_3 = 0$ for individual contributions based on the *T* statistic are contradicted by the sample data (the *P*-values are .007 and .0018, respectively). This means that the distinction between accounting ($X_3 = 1$) and finance ($X_3 = 0$) is indeed useful. But the hypothesis H_0: $\beta_2 = 0$ is not contradicted by the sample data (*P*-value = .741). It appears, therefore, that the distinction between management ($X_2 = 1$) and finance ($X_2 = 0$) may not be useful. Consequently, we could drop X_2 from the model and refit it with only X_1 (GPA) and the dummy variable X_3, where $X_3 = 1$ indicates an accounting major and $X_3 = 0$ indicates either a management or a finance major.

   The Excel output for the model

$$Y = \beta_0 + \beta_1 X_1 + \beta_3 X_3 + \epsilon$$

   is given in Table 10.4. From this output, notice that the least squares equation $\hat{Y} = 6.894 + 5.152X_1 + 3.495X_3$ is better in explaining the variation in the sample starting salaries than before. The adjusted R^2 value has increased from

Table 10.4

Revised output for Example 10.3

	A	B	C	D	E	F	G
1	SUMMARY OUTPUT						
2							
3	*Regression Statistics*						
4	Multiple R	0.8542					
5	R Square	0.7296					
6	Adjusted R Square	0.6846					
7	Standard Error	1.1227					
8	Observations	15					
9							
10	ANOVA						
11		*df*	*SS*	*MS*	*F*	*Significance F*	
12	Regression	2	40.8182	20.4091	16.1916	0.0004	
13	Residual	12	15.1258	1.2605			
14	Total	14	55.9440				
15							
16		*Coefficients*	*Standard Error*	*t Stat*	*P-value*	*Lower 95%*	*Upper 95%*
17	Intercept	6.8937	4.0164	1.7164	0.1118	-1.8574	15.6447
18	X1	5.1518	1.2885	3.9984	0.0018	2.3445	7.9591
19	X3	3.4946	0.6643	5.2607	0.0002	2.0473	4.9419

65.9% to 68.5%, the residual variance S_e^2 has decreased from 1.3609 to 1.2605, and the standard errors of b_1 and b_3 are smaller than before.

10.6 Curvilinear Regression Models

In many applications, the relationship between a response variable Y and one or more predictor variables may exhibit curvature and thus is nonlinear. For example, a regression model may involve a *polynomial* such as quadratic (in which the highest power of a predictor variable is 2), cubic (in which the highest power is 3), and so on. To illustrate, recall Example 9.2 (salary versus years of experience). In particular, look again at Figures 9.6 and 9.15. Both figures strongly suggest that the inclusion of a quadratic term (that is, one involving X^2) in the regression model would improve the fit considerably.

We can incorporate a quadratic term involving a predictor variable by assuming the regression model

$$Y = \beta_0 + \beta_1 X + \beta_2 X^2 + \epsilon$$

where $\beta_2 X^2$ is the desired quadratic term. This relationship is nonlinear because of the inclusion of the quadratic term; it is still a multiple *linear* regression model, since it is linear with regard to the parameters β_0, β_1, and β_2. We simply treat X (years of experience) and X^2 (years of experience squared) as two predictor variables. Notice that if the quadratic term is indeed helpful, then β_2 would *not* equal 0. The JMP IN output for this model using the salary versus years of experience data is given in Table 10.5. The following conclusions are apparent from this output:

Table 10.5

JMP IN output for a quadratic fit for salary versus years of experience example

Response: Salary

Summary of Fit

RSquare	0.988424
RSquare Adj	0.986643
Root Mean Square Error	1.578742
Mean of Response	48.25
Observations (or Sum Wgts)	16

Parameter Estimates

Term	Estimate	Std Error	t Ratio	Prob>ltl	Lower 95%	Upper 95%
Intercept	19.980076	1.077797	18.54	<.0001	17.651638	22.308514
Years	3.2151887	0.177146	18.15	<.0001	2.8324893	3.5978881
Years*Years	-0.063391	0.005595	-11.33	<.0001	-0.075479	-0.051303

Analysis of Variance

Source	DF	Sum of Squares	Mean Square	F Ratio
Model	2	2766.5984	1383.30	555.0009
Error	13	32.4016	2.49	Prob>F
C Total	15	2799.0000		<.0001

Sequential (Type 1) Tests

Source	Nparm	DF	Seq SS	F Ratio	Prob>F
Years	1	1	2446.6798	981.6454	<.0001
Years*Years	1	1	319.9187	128.3563	<.0001

1. The least squares equation is

$$\hat{Y} = 19.98 + 3.2152X - .0634X^2$$

The sign of the coefficient of the quadratic term is negative ($b_2 = -.0634$). This means that the least squares curve flattens as X increases. This is consistent with the scatter diagram in Figure 9.6.

2. The inclusion of the quadratic term is useful in that the hypothesis $H_0: \beta_2 = 0$ is contradicted by the sample data (P-value < .0001 based on the T statistic).

3. The least squares equation that includes the quadratic term is considerably better for estimation and prediction than the straight-line model (see Table 9.3). The residual variance S_e^2 is less than one-tenth its previous value (2.49 versus 25.17); the adjusted R^2 value has increased from .865 to .987; and the parameter β_1 of the linear term $\beta_1 X$ is estimated with considerably better precision than before (a T-value of 18.15 now versus a T-value of 9.86 for the straight-line fit). Without a doubt, therefore, the quadratic least squares equation is much better for estimation and prediction than the straight-line equation *within the given range of the sample data for years of experience.*

10.7 Detecting Model Deficiencies and Avoiding Pitfalls: Residual Analysis and Collinearity

The T and marginal F statistics are important for detecting useful contributions of individual terms, but they are not sufficient to show that a least squares model is sound. No regression analysis is complete unless we check for possible deficiencies in the model, or problems that may still exist, even though the results based on the T and marginal F statistics appear to be good. Two notable problems that always need to be addressed involve the possible violations of assumptions and **collinearity,** which may occur when some of the predictor variables are highly correlated with each other. We explore these topics in this section.

10.7.1   The Analysis of Residuals

The best way to check for violations of the assumptions is through residual analysis. In addition, residual analysis can identify unusual problems in the sample data and can suggest ways to improve the model. In particular, we examine three common deficiencies: (1) the relationship between the response and one or more of the predictor variables may not be linear; (2) the error variance σ_ϵ^2 may not be constant; and (3) one or more influential predictor variables may not have been included in the model. We also look at the problem of *outlier* observations—that is, observations whose values are distinctly out of line with the rest of the sample data.

Residual analysis means an analysis of the graphs of the residuals. If a least squares equation is good and no deficiencies exist, then a graph of the residuals against the corresponding values of each predictor variable or against the $\hat{Y}$-values should reveal no discernible pattern. In other words, there should be no relationship between the residuals and the values of predictor variables, or between the residuals and the estimated Y-values. But if a pattern can be discerned, there may be a deficiency in the least squares equation.

To uncover the three common deficiencies, we proceed as follows:

1. *Detecting curvature.*   To determine whether the relationship of the response variable has curvature with regard to some of the predictor variables, we graph the residuals against the corresponding values of each predictor variable in the least squares equation.

2. *Detecting nonconstant error variation.*   To determine whether the error variance is constant, we graph the residuals against the $\hat{Y}$-values.

3. *Detecting the omission of an important predictor variable.*   To determine whether a potentially important predictor variable should have been included in the regression model (but was not included), we graph the residuals against the corresponding values of that variable.

If a least squares regression equation is practically free of any deficiencies, then the residuals tend to lie within a horizontal band centered around 0, with no systematic tendencies to be positive or negative. Any discernible deviation from this behavior would suggest some deficiency.

Figure 10.3 depicts typical residual plots when (a) the least squares model is free of deficiencies, (b) a quadratic effect of a predictor variable is present and ought to be included in the model, (c) the error variance is not constant (in which case a method called *weighted least squares* can be used as a remedy; the details of this method are beyond the scope of this book), and (d) an omitted predictor variable shows a strong, linear association with the residuals and ought to be included in the regression model.

Figure 10.3

Typical residual plots
for (a) a model
with no deficiencies,
(b) a quadratic effect,
(c) nonconstant er-
ror variance, and
(d) a linear effect of
an omitted variable

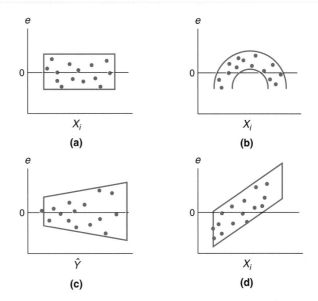

Residual plots also help in detecting extreme observations known as **outliers.** The residuals associated with outliers are usually very large in magnitude relative to the other residuals. Outliers can create difficulty because they have a dispro-portionate effect on the values of the least squares coefficients. Indeed, they can cause the estimated regression equation to be a poor, or even ridiculous, model of the relationship of interest. When an observation has been determined to be an outlier, it should be excluded from the sample data used to develop the estimated regression equation. (Recall that the sample data must be representative of the situation for which we are attempting to determine a good prediction equation.) If all sample data are truly representative, the removal of any one observation from the sample data should have little effect on the least squares equation. We caution, however, that even if a sample observation *looks* like an outlier, you have no valid reason to remove it unless there is corroborated evidence that the observation is unrepresentative of the situation. Examples of outliers include recording errors and data for unusual events such as strikes, natural disasters, the unexpected failure of equipment, or the unanticipated departure of a key employee.

EXAMPLE 10.4

In manufacturing environments, considerable effort is constantly exerted to keep unit costs to a minimum for a given standard of quality. In carrying out this task, it is important to identify explicit factors that affect unit cost and to develop statistical models that predict unit cost, given a set of conditions for these factors. This example illustrates such a situation.

A manufacturing firm wishes to be able to predict the manufacturing unit cost Y (in dollars) of one of its products as a function of fluctuating production rate X_1 and material and labor costs X_2. (X_1 is measured as a percentage of rated capacity, and X_2 is a standard index that combines the costs of materials and labor.) Data were collected over a 20-month span during which the production rate and labor costs fluctuated a great deal. Using the following sample data, determine the best least squares equation to predict unit cost.

Y	X_1	X_2	Y	X_1	X_2
13.59	87	80	15.93	102	116
15.71	78	95	16.45	82	117
15.97	81	106	19.02	74	127
20.21	65	115	18.16	85	133
24.64	51	128	18.57	86	135
21.25	62	128	17.01	90	136
18.94	70	115	18.03	93	140
14.85	91	92	19.22	81	142
15.18	94	93	21.12	72	148
16.30	100	111	23.32	60	150

Table 10.6

Minitab output for Example 10.4

```
The regression equation is
Cost = 20.3 - 0.138 Rate + 0.0742 Labor

Predictor          Coef       Stdev     t-ratio          p
Constant         20.281       2.125        9.54      0.000
Rate           -0.13770     0.01585       -8.69      0.000
Labor           0.07425     0.01096        6.77      0.000

S = 0.8942    R-sq = 91.4%    R-sq(adj) = 90.4%

Analysis of Variance

SOURCE            DF          SS          MS          F          p
Regression         2     144.387      72.194      90.29      0.000
Error             17      13.593       0.800
Total             19     157.980

SOURCE       DF       SEQ SS
Rate          1      107.726
Labor         1       36.662
```

Solution

To start, we tentatively assume the linear model

$$Y = \beta_0 + \beta_1 X_1 + \beta_2 X_2 + \epsilon$$

The Minitab output for this model is given in Table 10.6. From this output, notice that the estimates $b_1 = -.1377$ and $b_2 = .0742$ make sense (a negative value for the coefficient of X_1 and a positive value for the coefficient of X_2). The standard errors of these estimates are small relative to the values of the coefficients themselves. Thus, β_1 and β_2 are being estimated with considerable precision; the value of the adjusted $R^2 = .904$ is relatively high; and the incremental effect of each predictor variable in the presence of the other is quite discernible, since the P-values for the T tests are very small (both equal .000). The temptation is to conclude that we have determined a good prediction equation. Would you agree? But wait! How about the residual plots? Figure 10.4 shows the residual plots. Part (a) depicts the residuals plotted against X_1 (rate) and part (b) shows the residuals plotted against X_2 (labor). Although no pattern is apparent with regard to X_2, a definite quadratic pattern is revealed with regard to X_1. This suggests that we should include a quadratic term involving X_1 in the regression model.

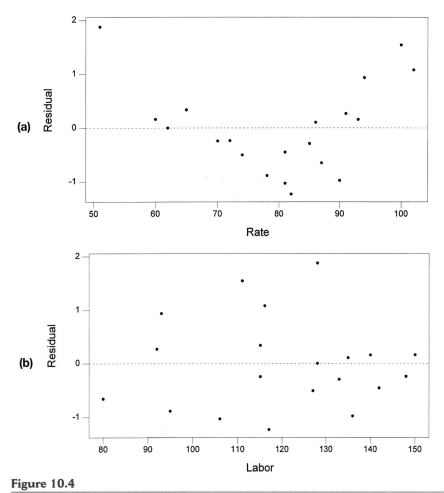

Figure 10.4

Minitab graphs of residuals versus rate (a) and versus labor (b) for Example 10.4

We now attempt to improve the model by adding a quadratic term for X_1, thus fitting the model

$$Y = \beta_0 + \beta_1 X_1 + \beta_2 X_2 + \beta_3 X_1^2 + \epsilon$$

We obtain the Minitab output given in Table 10.7. Based on these new results, can you see that the inclusion of a quadratic term involving X_1 has greatly improved the fit of the least squares equation? The null hypothesis H_0: $\beta_3 = 0$ is easily contradicted (P-value = .000); the parameters β_1 and β_2 are being estimated with better precision than before because the magnitudes of the corresponding T-values are larger; the residual variance S_e^2 is less than one-fourth its previous value (.191

Table 10.7

Revised Minitab output for Example 10.4

```
The regression equation is
Cost = 41.6 - 0.700 Rate + 0.0733 Labor
+ 0.00362 Ratesqrd

Predictor            Coef         StDev    t-ratio         p
Constant           41.551         3.047      13.64     0.000
Rate             -0.70027       0.07615      -9.20     0.000
Labor             0.073348      0.005361     13.68     0.000
Ratesqrd         0.0036237     0.0004880      7.43     0.000

s = 0.4371    R-sq = 98.1%    R-sq(adj) = 97.7%

Analysis of Variance

SOURCE         DF          SS         MS          F         p
Regression      3     154.923     51.641     270.29     0.000
Error          16       3.057      0.191
Total          19     157.980

SOURCE       DF      SEQ SS
Rate          1     107.726
Labor         1      36.662
Ratesqrd      1      10.536
```

for this model versus .800 for the previous model); and the adjusted R^2 value has increased substantially, from .904 to .977. Finally, the new residual plot involving rate in Figure 10.5 shows no discernible pattern. Although not shown, the new residual plot versus labor again shows no discernible pattern.

10.7.2   The Problem of Collinearity

A frequent problem in multiple linear regression is that some of the predictor variables are correlated; that is, they are linearly related. If the correlation is slight, the consequences are minor. But if two or more predictor variables are highly correlated, the consequences can be severe. This means, in effect, that such predictor variables offer redundant information. Consequently, the regression results can be very ambiguous, especially with regard to the values of the least squares estimators.

A very high correlation between two (or more) predictor variables creates the condition called **collinearity** (also known as *multicollinearity*). The problem of collinearity stems from deficient data. This is the price we pay at times when we cannot use a designed experiment to obtain data and have to rely on convenience data instead.

Recall that a least squares equation should make sense and provide the ability to estimate the average response or predict an individual response with reasonable accuracy, given a set of values for the predictor variables. Collinearity does not preclude a good fit, nor does it prevent the response from being adequately estimated or predicted within the range of the values of the predictor variables. However, collinearity can severely lower the precision of the least squares estimates. When two

Figure 10.5

Revised Minitab graph
of residuals versus
rate for Example 10.4

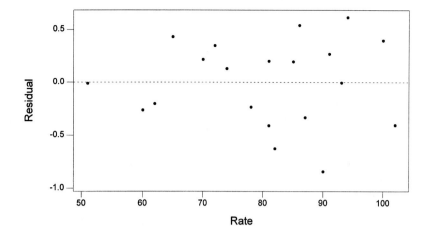

predictor variables are collinear, the least squares coefficients do not measure their individual effects on the response variable. Rather, they reflect an effect on the response that is dependent on the predictor variables that happen to be in the least squares equation. Therefore, when a predictor variable is added to or deleted from the least squares equation, the estimated effect of the correlated predictor variable may change dramatically. Moreover, the estimated effect of the correlated predictor variable may change substantially from one sample data set to another.

To illustrate, suppose we include the predictor variable "humidity" in the ice cream parlor example in addition to price and temperature (we are dropping the type of day dummy variable for the moment to illustrate more clearly the effect of collinearity). It is possible that temperature and humidity are highly correlated, so that they both simply indicate the comfort level on a given day (hot and humid at one extreme, cool and dry at the other). The sample data we have been working with, augmented by the daily relative humidity, are as follows:

Day	Daily Sales	Price	Temperature	Relative Humidity
1	374	35	74	50
2	386	35	82	72
3	472	35	94	92
4	429	50	93	88
5	391	50	82	70
6	475	50	96	94
7	428	50	91	85
8	412	65	93	89
9	405	65	88	80
10	341	65	78	60

Notice that on days when the temperature is rather low, the relative humidity is also low. And when temperature is high, so is relative humidity. For these data, there are no days for which temperature is high but relative humidity is low, or for which temperature is low but relative humidity is high. This kind of situation is the essence of collinearity—that is, a strong linear association between two predictor variables. A regression model that includes temperature and humidity as predictor variables is likely to exhibit the following two problems caused by collinearity:

Table 10.8

JMP IN output of ice
cream parlor example
with price, temperature,
and relative humidity
as predictor variables

Response: Sales

Summary of Fit

RSquare	0.937528
RSquare Adj	0.906292
Root Mean Square Error	12.8099
Mean of Response	411.3
Observations (or Sum Wgts)	10

Parameter Estimates

Term	Estimate	Std Error	t Ratio	Prob>ItI	Lower 95%	Upper 95%
Intercept	-217.607	215.4286	-1.01	0.3514	-744.7423	309.52821
Price	-1.412345	0.358452	-3.94	0.0076	-2.289447	-0.535244
Temp	10.504879	4.604433	2.28	0.0627	-0.761771	21.77153
Humid	-2.762188	2.376935	-1.16	0.2893	-8.578344	3.0539671

Analysis of Variance

Source	DF	Sum of Squares	Mean Square	F Ratio
Model	3	14775.539	4925.18	30.0145
Error	6	984.561	164.09	Prob>F
C Total	9	15760.100		0.0005

Sequential (Type 1) Tests

Source	Nparm	DF	Seq SS	F Ratio	Prob>F
Price	1	1	912.667	5.5619	0.0564
Temp	1	1	13641.275	83.1311	<.0001
Humid	1	1	221.597	1.3504	0.2893

1. If two predictor variables are highly correlated, then neither provides substantial incremental information that is not already provided by the other. Therefore, the individual effect may not be discernible for *either* variable, even though each variable by itself is helpful in explaining the variation in the sample Y-values. The P-values of the marginal F statistics for the last variable entered (sequential sums of squares) may be in considerable conflict with the P-values for the incremental effect of a predictor variable in the presence of all other predictor variables in the model (the T statistics). This behavior is illustrated by considering the JMP IN output in Table 10.8 for the ice cream parlor example with price, temperature, and relative humidity as the predictor variables. Notice that the P-values of the T statistics for the incremental effect of temperature or for that of humidity in the presence of the other two variables are .0627 and .2893, respectively. This suggests that neither effect can be regarded as especially helpful in explaining the variation in the sample Y-values. But when we look at the marginal F statistic for temperature in the presence of price only (sequential sum of squares), we find the P-value to be <.0001. This suggests that temperature, in the presence of price only, is quite helpful in explaining the variation in the sample Y-values. This kind of conflict is caused by the association between temperature and relative humidity.

2. The least squares coefficients of collinear variables are highly volatile and have inflated standard errors. This means that even slight changes in the sample data can cause large changes in a coefficient. Consequently, the least squares coefficients of collinear variables are unreliable for the purpose of interpreting model

relationships. On the other hand, they tend to compensate for each other. If a coefficient is relatively large for a given representative sample, then the coefficient of a collinear variable is likely to compensate by being relatively small. As a result, the overall effect of collinear variables (as a group) on estimation or prediction is usually fairly stable. To illustrate with the ice cream parlor example, the least squares coefficient of temperature is $b_2 = 5.1953$ and the standard error is $SE(b_2) = .5839$ when relative humidity is not included in the model (see Table 10.1). But this coefficient becomes $b_2 = 10.505$ with standard error $SE(b_2) = 4.6044$ when relative humidity is added to the model (see Table 10.8). The least squares coefficient of humidity compensates by being negative (-2.762). It is common for a coefficient of a collinear variable to have the wrong sign, as in this case, so that the least squares equation seems nonsensical. The message is that collinearity can cause the corresponding least squares coefficients to seem unrealistic and to be useless for the purpose of interpretation, even though predictions may remain fairly stable.

To illustrate further how sequential sums of squares can expose collinearity, let's run the ice cream parlor example data with relative humidity preceding temperature in the order of entry. the new "Sequential Tests" portion of the JMP IN output is given in Table 10.9 (the other portions are identical to those in Table 10.8). Notice now that the sequential sum of squares for relative humidity, in the presence of price only, is quite large: $SS(X_3|X_1) = 13,008.75$, for which the value of the marginal F statistic is 79.28 and the P-value is .0001. So now relative humidity, in the presence of price only, is quite helpful in explaining the variation in the sample Y-values. But this is in direct conflict with the P-value $= .2893$ of the T statistic for relative humidity (i.e., in the presence of both price and temperature) from Table 10.8.

Table 10.9

Sequential sums of squares with humidity preceding temperature—ice cream example

Sequential (Type 1) Tests					
Source	Nparm	DF	Seq SS	F Ratio	Prob>F
Price	1	1	912.667	5.5619	0.0564
Humid	1	1	13008.747	79.2764	0.0001
Temp	1	1	854.125	5.2051	0.0627

Complex statistical methods have been developed to detect the presence of collinearity, but simple ones such as noticing conflicting results between the T and marginal F statistics or noticing coefficient volatility can help immensely in this regard. The best solution is to avoid collinearity altogether. This can be accomplished by using a well-designed experiment to obtain sample data—that is, to select values of the predictor variables that assure the absence of collinearity. For the ice cream parlor example, this would mean that we would observe sales for days with high temperature and low humidity or low temperature and high humidity, in addition to days in which both are high or both are low. Unfortunately, when convenience data are the only source of information, this approach is usually not feasible.

How then do we remedy the situation when collinearity is uncovered? The following straightforward approaches are available:

1. If possible, add to the sample data values of the collinear variables that tend to lessen the severity of the correlation. For the ice cream parlor example, this

would mean adding observed sales for days with high temperature and low humidity or for days with low temperature and high humidity.

2. Discard one or more of the collinear variables. For the ice cream parlor example, it turns out (see the next section) that by eliminating relative humidity and including only price, temperature, and type of day, we get the least squares equation that is best for estimation and prediction.

3. Form a new predictor variable that serves as an index of the collinear variables. In the ice cream parlor example, we might create a new variable that is the average of the variables temperature and relative humidity. By using this new variable in the model instead of temperature and relative humidity, we eliminate collinearity while retaining information on both temperature and humidity.

10.8   Criteria for Selecting the Best Set of Predictor Variables

As we have strongly suggested, a very important problem in regression analysis is to determine which of the predictor variables in the original list ought to be included in the regression model. We believe it is prudent for every investigator to decide on an initial list of predictor variables that are thought to be influential for explaining the variation of the response variable. What is needed is a way of determining from the initial list those predictor variables that appear to be the best set for explaining most of the variation in the sample Y-values. The word *best* here means only that the resulting least squares equation provides sufficient accuracy for estimation and prediction within the range of the predictor variables and without any discernible deficiencies.

In determining how good a least squares equation is, two of the most useful criteria are the residual variance (or, equivalently, the adjusted R^2 value) and the standard errors of the least squares estimators. You may have noticed that these two criteria have guided our analyses so far in this chapter.

1. *The residual variance S_e^2.*   Recall that the residual variance is the same as the error mean square (MSE). Since MSE is the sum of the squares of the residuals divided by the degrees of freedom for SSE, MSE *does* take into account the number of terms in the model through the degrees of freedom. Whereas SSE cannot increase if more predictor variables are allowed into the model, S_e^2 can increase if the reduction in SSE is so small that it cannot offset the loss of additional degrees of freedom. For example, see Tables 10.3 and 10.4, in which a least squares equation with two predictor variables (Table 10.4) has a smaller residual variance (1.2605) than one with three predictor variables (1.3609, Table 10.3). With the residual variance criterion, we determine the set of predictor variables that either minimizes S_e^2 or nearly minimizes it to the point where the inclusion of additional predictor variables to the regression model is not beneficial.

   Recall from Section 10.3.3 that the adjusted R^2 value also takes into account the number of terms in the model. For this reason, it is regarded as an equivalent criterion to the residual variance. Using the adjusted R^2 value, we determine the set of predictor variables that either maximizes R_a^2 or nearly maximizes it to the point where the inclusion of additional predictor variables is not useful.

2. *The standard errors of the least squares estimators.* The precision with which the parameters of the assumed regression model are being estimated is one of the most important considerations in determining the best set of predictor variables. The smaller the standard errors of the least squares estimators, the better the precision, and the better the least squares equation for estimation and prediction. This means that the smaller the standard errors are relative to the corresponding least squares estimates, the larger are the magnitudes of the T-values. And when the magnitudes of the T-values are large, the corresponding P-values are small. As a result, the incremental effect of each predictor variable in the presence of all other predictor variables in the best set is quite helpful in explaining the variation in the sample Y-values.

Using these criteria, we can find the best set of predictor variables by determining and evaluating all possible linear least squares equations involving the initial list of predictor variables. If there are two predictor variables in the initial list, this would mean a total of three equations: two equations each containing one of the two variables, and one equation containing both. If there are three predictor variables, there would be a total of seven least squares equations: three equations each containing one of the three variables, three equations each containing two variables, and one equation containing all three. In general, if the initial list contains k predictor variables, there are a total of $2^k - 1$ possible linear least squares equations, each containing at least one predictor variable.

Variable Selection Techniques

When k is large (say, $k \geq 5$), the determination and evaluation of all possible linear least squares equations may not be practical. For such cases, **variable selection techniques** have been developed that provide useful information without an evaluation of all possible equations. In general, however, these techniques should not be regarded as equal to the evaluation of all possible equations using the indicated criteria. The most common variable selection technique uses a **stepwise regression** procedure to determine the best set of predictor variables. There are two main versions of this technique: forward selection and backward elimination.

Forward Selection Procedure

The forward selection procedure begins with the equation that contains no predictor variables (that is, $\hat{Y} = \bar{Y}$). The first predictor variable introduced to the model is the one that produces the greatest reduction in the error sum of squares. If, based on the P-value, this variable is helpful in explaining the variation in the sample Y-values, then it is retained in the model and a search begins for a second variable. The second variable to enter the equation is the one that produces the greatest reduction in the error sum of squares, given the presence of the first variable. If the incremental effect of the second variable is deemed helpful via the P-value, then the second variable is retained and a search begins for a third predictor variable. The process continues in this manner until the incremental effect of the last predictor variable that has entered the model is not deemed helpful.

The forward selection procedure has been modified so that the possibility of deleting a variable is considered at each stage. This modification produces what is usually identified in statistical software packages as a stepwise regression procedure. With this method, a predictor variable that has entered the model at an earlier stage may be removed at a later stage. The decision process is once again based on the extent of reduction in the error sum of squares and depends on the particular mix of variables in the regression model.

Backward Elimination Procedure

The backward elimination procedure begins with the regression model that contains all the predictor variables in the initial list. Then it eliminates, one at a time, the least important variables based on the extent of their contributions to the reduction in the error sum of squares. For example, the first variable deleted is the one that produces the smallest reduction in the error sum of squares, given the presence of the other variables. The procedure is terminated when the incremental effects of all remaining variables are helpful based on appropriate P-values.

Many statistical software packages, including Minitab and JMP IN, provide variable selection procedures, but Excel does not. You need to understand, however, that none of these procedures should be regarded as substitutes for model evaluation. Many aspects of the evaluation process including residual analysis and model deficiencies remain your responsibility.

EXAMPLE 10.5

With reference to the ice cream parlor example, suppose the initial list of predictor variables consists of price, temperature, type of day, and relative humidity. Use the modified forward variable selection procedure to determine the best set of predictor variables.

Solution

The Minitab output for the modified forward selection procedure is given in Table 10.10. The final solution containing temperature, price, and type of day is reached in three steps. In step 1, temperature is the first predictor variable to enter the

Table 10.10

Minitab output for the ice cream parlor example using the modified forward selection procedure

```
F-to-Enter:    4.00    F-to-Remove:    4.00
Response is Sales on 4 predictors, with N = 10
       Step          1         2         3
    Constant     -10.81     25.88     15.31

    Temp           4.85      5.20      5.04
    T-Value        5.22      8.90     15.83

    Price                   -1.34     -1.10
    T-Value                 -3.71     -5.40

    Day                                20.2
    T-Value                            4.23

    S             21.1      13.1       7.11
    R-Sq         77.33     92.35      98.08
```

regression equation. The least squares estimate of its coefficient is 4.85, the value of the T statistic for temperature is 5.22, the residual standard deviation is 21.1, the R^2 value is 77.33%, and the estimate of the intercept (constant) is -10.81. In step 2, price joins temperature in the equation, and in step 3, type of day is the last predictor variable to enter, while temperature and price are kept in the equation. Thus, as in Table 10.2, and best least squares regression equation is

$$\hat{Y} = 15.31 + 5.04\text{Temp} - 1.10\text{Price} + 20.2\text{Day}$$

10.9   Multiple Linear Regression: A Comprehensive Example

From the issues we have examined in this chapter, there are a certain number of necessary steps that we should follow in developing a multiple linear regression model. These steps are listed in the following box:

STEPS IN DEVELOPING A REGRESSION MODEL

1. Determine an initial list of potential predictor variables to be considered for inclusion in the model.
2. Obtain sample data and decide whether the data are representative of the environment of interest.
3. At least initially, assume that the relationship between the response variable and the predictor variables is represented by the multiple linear regression model as given by Expression (10.1).
4. Fit this model to the sample data and evaluate the least squares coefficients. Are their signs consistent with relationships that make sense?
5. Evaluate the least squares equation. The evaluation should include at a minimum consideration of model deficiencies (residual analysis) and pitfalls (collinearity) and determination of the best set of predictor variables. Then improve the model as suggested by the evaluation.

To illustrate these steps, consider the following example: A manager in a utility company wishes to develop a model of the factors that influence the use of electricity in residential homes during the heating season (defined as November through April for the geographic area of interest).

List Potential Predictor Variables

The manager proposes that the amount of electricity used by a house should depend on (1) the size of the heated area, (2) how well the house is insulated, (3) the type of the house's heating system, (4) how cold the weather is, and (5) the average thermostat setting. The manager defines the following operational variables: Y = kilowatt-hours per month; X_1 = number of square feet of heated space; X_2 = the R value of roof insulation; X_3 = 1 if a house has insulated windows, 0 if it does not; X_4 = average temperature; X_5 = 1 if a heat pump is used, 0 if electric forced air is used;

and X_6 = average number of hours of sunlight per day. The manager can obtain information for these variables but cannot obtain thermostat settings.

Obtain Sample Data

The manager selects a representative sample of 25 monthly customer bills taken from several recent heating seasons. The manager obtains information for variables X_1 through X_6 from the bills selected and from company records by performing a survey of the homes selected and from National Weather Service information. The sample data are as follows:

Y	X_1	X_2	X_3	X_4	X_5	X_6
2,405	1,400	0	0	40	0	11.0
1,064	1,650	11	1	41	1	11.3
2,203	1,680	19	0	41	0	10.9
2,535	1,820	14	0	36	1	10.5
1,801	1,750	0	0	43	1	11.7
1,068	1,900	30	1	38	1	11.0
2,972	1,880	11	0	38	1	10.8
1,545	1,600	0	1	40	1	10.9
2,141	2,000	25	0	42	0	10.8
1,670	1,850	11	0	43	0	11.2
1,236	2,050	19	1	48	0	11.7
1,912	2,080	14	0	47	0	11.5
1,825	2,140	25	1	39	0	10.7
1,988	2,150	0	0	50	0	12.0
788	2,200	22	0	45	1	11.4
400	2,310	11	0	33	0	9.7
2,072	2,420	19	1	45	0	11.6
2,644	2,480	11	0	38	0	10.4
2,786	2,130	19	1	34	0	9.8
2,704	2,500	24	0	34	1	9.7
3,073	2,300	19	0	33	0	10.2
2,263	2,750	19	1	36	1	9.9
4,075	3,000	11	0	32	0	9.7
1,665	3,100	24	0	41	1	11.1
3,480	3,400	11	1	38	0	10.5

Y = Kilowatt-hours per month
X_1 = Square feet of heated space
X_2 = R Value of roof insulation
X_3 = Presence/absence of insulated windows
X_4 = Mean temperature
X_5 = Heat pump/electric forced air
X_6 = Mean hours of sunlight per day

Use the Multiple Linear Regression Model

Initially, the manager assumes the model

$$Y = \beta_0 + \beta_1 X_1 + \beta_2 X_2 + \beta_3 X_3 + \beta_4 X_4 + \beta_5 X_5 + \beta_6 X_6 + \epsilon$$

correctly represents the relationship between the response variable Y and the potential predictor variables X_1–X_6.

Fit the Model to the Sample Data and Evaluate the Least Squares Coefficients

The JMP IN output is given in Table 10.11. From this output, the least squares equation is

$$\hat{Y} = 2{,}268.7 + .6372X_1 - 21.898X_2 - 192.8893X_3 - 111.5655X_4 \\ - 437.0679X_5 + 318.6621X_6$$

The signs of the least squares coefficients for predictor variables X_1, X_2, X_3, X_4, and X_5 are consistent with the manager's expectations; that is, the manager expects a positive relationship between Y and X_1, and negative relationships between Y and X_2, X_3, X_4, and X_5. The positive sign of the least squares coefficient for X_6 is not expected. This implies the unrealistic result that electricity consumption increases as the mean hours of sunlight increases, with all other variables being held constant.

Table 10.11

Initial JMP IN output for the comprehensive example

Response: K-W Hrs

Summary of Fit

RSquare	0.41724
RSquare Adj	0.222987
Root Mean Square Error	749.5901
Mean of Response	2092.6
Observations (or Sum Wgts)	25

Parameter   Estimates

Term	Estimate	Std Error	t Ratio	Prob>ltl	Lower 95%	Upper 95%
Intercept	2268.6957	4786.265	0.47	0.6412	-7786.808	12324.199
Heated SF	0.6372122	0.359756	1.77	0.0935	-0.118601	1.3930255
Insulation	-21.89799	19.5124	-1.12	0.2765	-62.89176	19.095777
Insul Win	-192.8893	320.9086	-0.60	0.5553	-867.0888	481.31016
Mean Temp	-111.5655	100.3004	-1.11	0.2806	-322.2874	99.15645
Heat Type	-437.0679	336.0028	-1.30	0.2097	-1142.979	268.84308
Sun Hrs	318.66211	740.3865	0.43	0.6720	-1236.822	1874.1462

Analysis of Variance

Source	DF	Sum of Squares	Mean Square	F Ratio
Model	6	7241299	1206883	2.1479
Error	18	10113935	561885	Prob>F
C Total	24	17355234		0.0976

Sequential (Type 1) Tests

Source	Nparm	DF	Seq SS	F Ratio	Prob>F
Heated SF	1	1	2843552.2	5.0607	0.0372
Insulation	1	1	907324.2	1.6148	0.2200
Insul Win	1	1	328823.3	0.5852	0.4542
Mean Temp	1	1	2209825.0	3.9329	0.0628
Heat Type	1	1	847688.1	1.5086	0.2352
Sun Hrs	1	1	104085.8	0.1852	0.6720

Evaluate the Least Squares Equation

From the information in Table 10.11, the least squares equation is clearly unimpressive. The P-value for the null hypothesis $H_0: \beta_1 = \beta_2 = \cdots = \beta_6 = 0$ is .0976, which implies that the evidence against this null hypothesis is *not* convincing. Of course, this means that none of the six predictor variables is truly helping to explain the variation in the sample Y-values. The same conclusion is reached by examining the P-values corresponding to the T statistics or the marginal F statistics. In fact, the only predictor variable that seems to be helping is X_1 when it is the only predictor variable in the model (P-value = .0372 from Sequential Tests).

To find out what is wrong, the manager graphs the residuals against each of the six predictor variables and discovers that the sample data contain an unusual observation. The unusual observation is clearly seen by examining the residual graph involving X_1 (square feet of heated space) provided in Figure 10.6. It is found at the bottom of the graph. The sample data reveal one house that used only 400 kilowatt-hours of electricity. The manager found out that the family had been away virtually the entire month. Because the manager believes that this observation does not represent the environment of interest, the manager removes it and refits the model with $n = 24$ observations. The new JMP IN output is given in Table 10.12.

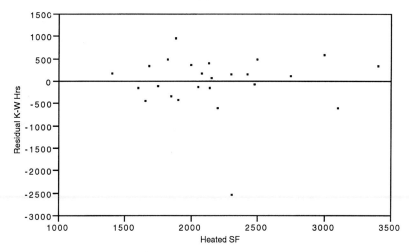

Now the least squares equation looks promising. The signs of the least squares coefficients are as expected. The null hypothesis $H_0: \beta_1 = \beta_2 = \cdots = \beta_6 = 0$ is clearly contradicted (P-value < .0001). The incremental effects of X_1, X_2, and X_5 in the presence of all other predictor variables are helpful in explaining the variation in the sample Y-values (P-values for T statistics of .0059, .0033, and .0017, respectively). The incremental effect of X_6 in the presence of all others is negligible (P-value < .6824). Those of X_3 and X_4 are in the gray area (P-values of .0491 and .0612, respectively). There may be some collinearity involving X_4 because the incremental effect of X_4 in the presence of only X_1, X_2, and X_3 is quite helpful (P-value < .0001 based on the sequential sum of squares), but the effect of X_4 in the presence of all predictor variables is not so convincing (P-value = .0612).

The manager believes that a variable selection procedure might be helpful in resolving the situation with respect to X_3, X_4, and X_6. The manager decides to use the backward elimination procedure. The final JMP IN output is given in Table 10.13. From the information in this table, a definite improvement has taken place. The variable X_6 has been removed from the model. The standard errors of the least squares coefficients are smaller than before. The residual variance has been reduced to $S_e^2 = 120,337$ from the previous value of $S_e^2 = 126,129$. The incremental effect of X_4 in the presence of all other variables is now quite helpful (P-value < .0001 based on the I Statistics). Apparently X_4 and X_6 were somewhat collinear, so the presence of X_6 in the model diminished the incremental effect of X_4. Now that X_6 has been

Table 10.12

Revised JMP IN output for the comprehensive example

Response: K-W Hrs

Summary of Fit

RSquare	0.850796
RSquare Adj	0.798136
Root Mean Square Error	355.1471
Mean of Response	2163.125
Observations (or Sum Wgts)	24

Parameter Estimates

Term	Estimate	Std Error	t Ratio	Prob>|t|	Lower 95%	Upper 95%
Intercept	7268.3992	2353.288	3.09	0.0067	2303.4255	12233.373
Heated SF	0.5375482	0.170909	3.15	0.0059	0.1769648	0.8981315
Insulation	-31.91995	9.330326	-3.42	0.0033	-51.6051	-12.2348
Insul Win	-324.0984	152.9361	-2.12	0.0491	-646.7636	-1.433272
Mean Temp	-95.34441	47.56497	-2.00	0.0612	-195.6971	5.0083037
Heat Type	-599.217	160.4958	-3.73	0.0017	-937.8315	-260.6024
Sun Hrs	-148.0791	355.6668	-0.42	0.6824	-898.4661	602.30778

Analysis of Variance

Source	DF	Sum of Squares	Mean Square	F Ratio
Model	6	12226768	2037795	16.1564
Error	17	2144201	126129	Prob>F
C Total	23	14370969		<.0001

Sequential (Type 1) Tests

Source	Nparm	DF	Seq SS	F Ratio	Prob>F
Heated SF	1	1	3180503.8	25.2162	0.0001
Insulation	1	1	1355656.0	10.7481	0.0044
Insul Win	1	1	727758.2	5.7699	0.0280
Mean Temp	1	1	4814280.3	38.1694	<.0001
Heat Type	1	1	2126706.3	16.8613	0.0007
Sun Hrs	1	1	21863.4	0.1733	0.6824

removed, the importance of X_4 is clear. Though not shown, all residual graphs with the predictor variables X_1–X_5 reveal no further deficiencies. Therefore, the final least squares equation

$$\hat{Y} = 6,356.174 + .5604X_1 - 31.2077X_2 - 327.503X_3$$
$$- 113.8952X_4 - 621.4582X_5$$

is deemed adequate for estimation and prediction.

10.10 Summary

In this chapter, we extended the statistical methods presented in Chapter 9 for the consideration of more than one predictor variable in a regression model.

In a multiple linear regression model, we can include predictor variables that are qualitative or we can consider predictor variables in a nonlinear form. The key questions that need to be answered are the same as those in Chapter 9, but the presence of several predictor variables in a model can complicate the statistical inferences somewhat. This is largely because of the potential problem that some of the predictor variables may be linearly related. The linear association between or among

Table 10.13

Final JMP IN output based on backward elimination method for the comprehensive example

Response: K-W Hrs

Summary of Fit

RSquare	0.849275
RSquare Adj	0.807407
Root Mean Square Error	346.8961
Mean of Response	2163.125
Observations (or Sum Wgts)	24

Parameter Estimates

Term	Estimate	Std Error	t Ratio	Prob>ltl	Lower 95%	Upper 95%
Intercept	6356.174	838.7014	7.58	<.0001	4594.1393	8118.2087
Heated SF	0.5603773	0.158113	3.54	0.0023	0.2281964	0.8925582
Insulation	-31.20768	8.959047	-3.48	0.0027	-50.02981	-12.38554
Insul Win	-327.503	149.1693	-2.20	0.0415	-640.8941	-14.11191
Mean Temp	-113.8952	16.2604	-7.00	<.0001	-148.0569	-79.73363
Heat Type	-621.4582	147.8283	-4.20	0.0005	-932.0319	-310.8845

Analysis of Variance

Source	DF	Sum of Squares	Mean Square	F Ratio
Model	5	12204904	2440981	20.2846
Error	18	2166064	120337	Prob>F
C Total	23	14370969		<.0001

Sequential (Type 1) Tests

Source	Nparm	DF	Seq SS	F Ratio	Prob>F
Heated SF	1	1	3180503.8	26.4300	<.0001
Insulation	1	1	1355656.0	11.2655	0.0035
Insul Win	1	1	727758.2	6.0477	0.0243
Mean Temp	1	1	4814280.3	40.0067	<.0001
Heat Type	1	1	2126706.3	17.6729	0.0005

predictor variables is known as *collinearity*. The essence of multiple linear regression analysis is to uncover model deficiencies such as collinearity, and to establish criteria for selecting the best set of predictor variables to use in a regression model.

EXERCISES FOR SECTION 10.2

10.1 Suppose the model $Y = 1.5 + 1.2X_1 + .15X_2$ is used by an automobile rental agency for assessing the annual maintenance cost Y (in thousands of dollars) as a function of the number of automobiles rented X_1 and the average number of miles each car is driven X_2 (in thousands of miles).

(a) Explain the meaning of each coefficient value.

(b) Determine the annual maintenance costs for all possible combinations of the following values of X_1 and X_2: $X_1 = 200, 400,$ and 600 and $X_2 = 20, 30,$ and 40. (*Note:* There will be nine combinations.)

(c) Use the results in part (b) to graph the relationship between Y and X_1, holding X_2 constant. Then graph the relationship between Y and X_2, holding X_1 constant.

10.2 Suppose the model depicting the average response variable Y as a function of two predictor variables X_1 and X_2 is $Y = 15 + 6X_1 - 2X_2 - 1.5X_2^2$.

(a) Graph the relationship between Y and X_1 when $X_2 = 2$.

(b) Graph the relationship between Y and X_2 when $X_1 = 1$.

10.3 Determine which of the following regression models are linear with regard to the indicated parameters. Explain your answer.

(a) $Y = \beta_0 + \beta_1 X + \beta_2 X^2 + \epsilon$

(b) $Y = \beta_0 + \beta_1 \log X_1 + \beta_2 X_2 + \epsilon$

(c) $Y = \beta_0 e^{\beta_1 X} + \epsilon$

(d) $Y = \beta_0 + \beta_1 X_1^{\beta_2} + \beta_3 X_2 + \epsilon$

EXERCISES FOR SECTION 10.3

10.4 For the following sample data, use the Excel output that is provided to answer parts (a)–(e).

Y	X_1	X_2
75	100	22
58	66	75
50	88	44
100	150	33
60	75	100

	A	B	C	D	E	F	G
1	SUMMARY OUTPUT						
2							
3	Regression Statistics						
4	Multiple R	0.918					
5	R Square	0.843					
6	Adjusted R Square	0.686					
7	Standard Error	11.063					
8	Observations	5					
9							
10	ANOVA						
11		df	SS	MS	F	Significance F	
12	Regression	2	1314.399	657.199	5.369	0.157	
13	Residual	2	244.801	122.401			
14	Total	4	1559.2				
15							
16		Coefficients	Standard Error	t Stat	P-value	Lower 95%	Upper 95%
17	Intercept	5.339	31.449	0.170	0.881	-129.977	140.655
18	X1	0.606	0.223	2.721	0.113	-0.352	1.565
19	X2	0.094	0.229	0.412	0.720	-0.890	1.078

(a) Does the estimated intercept value have real significance? Give reasons for your answer.

(b) Estimate the mean of Y when $X_1 = 90$ and $X_2 = 65$.

(c) Determine SSE and the values of the residual variance S_e^2. Interpret your results.

(d) Determine the coefficient of determination R^2 and interpret your result for this problem.

(e) Determine the value of the adjusted coefficient of determination. Explain why R_a^2 is much smaller than R^2 for this problem.

10.5 With reference to Exercise 10.4, fit a straight line to the sample data using only X_1. Excel regression output for this model follows.

	A	B	C	D	E	F	G
1	SUMMARY OUTPUT						
2							
3	Regression Statistics						
4	Multiple R	0.911					
5	R Square	0.830					
6	Adjusted R Square	0.773					
7	Standard Error	9.408					
8	Observations	5					
9							
10	ANOVA						
11		df	SS	MS	F	Significance F	
12	Regression	1	1293.642	1293.642	14.614	0.032	
13	Residual	3	265.558	88.519			
14	Total	4	1559.2				
15							
16		Coefficients	Standard Error	t Stat	P-value	Lower 95%	Upper 95%
17	Intercept	16.278	14.319	1.137	0.338	-29.292	61.847
18	X1	0.546	0.143	3.823	0.032	0.091	1.001

(a) Compare your results with those in part (c) of Exercise 10.4. Explain your findings.

(b) Compare your results with those in parts (d) and (e) of Exercise 10.4. Explain your findings.

(c) In view of your answers to parts (a) and (b) of this problem, what reasonable conclusion can you make about X_2?

10.6 Suppose the regression model $Y = \beta_0 + \beta_1 X_1 + \beta_2 X_2 + \epsilon$ is fitted to a sample of $n = 10$ observations, resulting in SSE = 121.2 and $R^2 = .927$. Subsequently, X_3 is added to the set of predictor variables. The model $Y = \beta_0 + \beta_1 X_1 + \beta_2 X_2 + \beta_3 X_3 + \epsilon$ is fitted to the same data, resulting in SSE = 116.2 and $R^2 = .930$.

(a) For the first model, R^2 equals .927, a rather high value. Does this indicate that the first model is good for predicting Y? Explain your answer.

(b) When X_3 was added to the model, SSE decreased and R^2 increased. Do these results indicate that the second model is an improvement over the earlier model? Explain why or why not.

(c) Determine the residual variance S_e^2 and the adjusted coefficient of determination R_a^2 for each model. (*Hint:* First use SSE and R^2 to determine SST.) What can be concluded from this information about the relative merits of the two models?

10.7 A regression model of Y versus four predictor variables is developed from a sample of $n = 22$ observations. For this model, SSE = 1,225 and SST = 14,570.

(a) Determine R^2 and explain its meaning.

(b) Based on the R^2 value determined in part (a), would you say the regression model is good for predicting Y? Explain your answer.

(c) Determine R_a^2.

(d) Why might one cite R_a^2 rather than R^2 in describing the fit of an estimated regression model?

10.8 Suppose you develop the following least squares model:

$$\hat{Y} = 22.0 + 5.2X_1 - .32X_2 + 2.7X_3 - 9.6X_4$$

with a sample of $n = 28$ observations. For this model, $R^2 = .65$ and SSE = 15.22.

(a) Do SSE and R^2 suggest that this model is a good predictor of Y? Explain your answer.

(b) Determine SST, SSR, and R_a^2. Explain why the value of R_a^2 is smaller than that of R^2.

10.9 Suppose you develop the following least squares model:

$$\hat{Y} = 3.06 - .22X_1 + 8.44X_2 - 2.44X_3$$

based on a sample of $n = 100$ observations. For this model, SSE = 144.3 and SST = 855.1. Determine R^2 and R_a^2. Would you say that this model is a good predictor of Y? Explain your answer.

10.10   For the following sample data, use the Minitab output that is provided to answer parts (a)–(d).

Y	X_1	X_2
158	2.2	5
165	2.1	3
145	1.9	8
172	2.4	6
179	2.8	2
152	2.3	10
154	2.6	12

The regression equation is
Y = 121 + 23.5 X1 - 2.26 X2

Predictor	Coef	Stdev	t-ratio	p
Constant	120.86	16.31	7.41	0.002
X1	23.492	6.680	3.52	0.025
X2	-2.2596	0.5570	-4.06	0.015

s = 4.964   R-sq = 88.5%   R-sq(adj) = 82.7%

Analysis of Variance

SOURCE	DF	SS	MS	F	p
Regression	2	756.88	378.44	15.36	0.013
Error	4	98.55	24.64		
Total	6	855.43			

SOURCE	DF	SEQ SS
X1	1	351.45
X2	1	405.43

(a) For these data, does the estimated intercept value have real significance? Explain.

(b) Estimate the mean of Y when $X_1 = 2.5$ and $X_2 = 4$.

(c) Determine and interpret S_e^2.

(d) Determine and interpret R^2 and R_a^2. Would you say that this least squares model is a good predictor of Y? Explain.

10.11   Refer to Exercise 10.10. Determine two simple linear regression equations, one using only X_1

and the other using only X_2. The Minitab regression output for these two models follows.

The regression equation is
Y = 102 + 25.2 X1

Predictor	Coef	Stdev	t-ratio	p
Constant	102.08	31.63	3.23	0.023
X1	25.18	13.49	1.87	0.121

s = 10.04   R-sq = 41.1%   R-sq(adj) = 29.3%

Analysis of Variance

SOURCE	DF	SS	MS	F	p
Regression	1	351.4	351.4	3.49	0.121
Error	5	504.0	100.8		
Total	6	855.4			

The regression equation is
Y = 176 - 2.38 X2

Predictor	Coef	Stdev	t-ratio	p
Constant	176.366	7.430	23.74	0.000
X2	-2.382	1.006	-2.37	0.064

s = 8.980   R-sq = 52.9%   R-sq(adj) = 43.4%

Analysis of Variance

SOURCE	DF	SS	MS	F	p
Regression	1	452.19	452.19	5.61	0.064
Error	5	403.24	80.65		
Total	6	855.43			

(a) Determine SSE and S_e^2 for the simple linear regression models and compare your results with those in part (c) of Exercise 10.10. Explain your findings.

(b) Determine R^2 and R_a^2 for the simple linear regression models and compare your results with those in part (d) of Exercise 10.10. Explain your findings.

(c) Graph the residuals of the simple linear regression model involving X_1 against the corresponding values of X_2. Do the same for the simple linear regression model involving X_2 against the corresponding values of X_1. Explain your findings.

(d) In view of your answers to parts (a)–(c) of this problem, what is the reasonable conclusion that you can make about X_1 and X_2?

EXERCISES FOR SECTION 10.4

10.12   When the model $Y = \beta_0 + \beta_1 X_1 + \beta_2 X_2 + \epsilon$ is fit to a sample of $n = 15$ observations, the following quantities are determined: SST = 200, SSR(X_1, X_2) = 140, SSR(X_1) = 90, and SSR($X_1 | X_2$) = 80.

(a) Do you detect an association between the sample Y-values and X_1 and X_2? (*Hint:* Test the null hypothesis H_0: $\beta_1 = \beta_2 = 0$.)

(b) Is the contribution of X_1 helpful in explaining the variation in the sample Y-values when X_1

is the only predictor variable in the model?

(c) Is the incremental contribution of X_1 helpful in explaining the variation in the sample Y-values in the presence of X_2?

(d) Is the incremental contribution of X_2 helpful in the presence of X_1?

(e) Is the contribution of X_2 helpful when X_2 is the only predictor variable in the model?

(f) Based on your answers to the previous parts

of this exercise, what can you conclude about the predictor variables X_1 and X_2?

10.13 With reference to Exercise 10.12, determine the value of R_a^2 for the model that contains both X_1 and X_2 and explain its meaning.

10.14 When the model $Y = \beta_0 + \beta_1 X_1 + \beta_2 X_2 + \epsilon$ is fit to a sample of $n = 23$ observations, the following quantities are obtained: $SST = 500$, $SSE(X_1, X_2) = 200$, $SSR(X_2) = 200$, and $SSR(X_2 | X_1) = 275$. Answer all parts of Exercise 10.12.

10.15 When the model $Y = \beta_0 + \beta_1 X_1 + \beta_2 X_2 + \beta_3 X_3 + \epsilon$ is fit to a sample of $n = 14$ observations, the following quantities are determined: $SST = 800$, $SSE(X_1, X_2, X_3) = 100$, $SSR(X_1) = 200$, and $SSR(X_2 | X_1) = 470$.
   (a) Do you detect an association between the sample Y-values and X_1, X_2, and X_3?
   (b) What is the adjusted R^2 value for the equation that includes all three predictor variables? Does this value indicate that the model is useful for prediction? Explain.
   (c) Is the contribution of X_1 helpful in explaining the variation in the sample Y-values when X_1 is the only predictor variable in the model?
   (d) Is the incremental contribution of X_2 helpful in the presence of X_1?
   (e) Is the incremental contribution of X_3 helpful in the presence of X_1 and X_2?

10.16 Refer to Exercise 10.15. Suppose that $SSR(X_2) = 350$.
   (a) Is the contribution of X_2 helpful when X_2 is the only predictor variable in the model?
   (b) Is the incremental contribution of X_1 helpful in the presence of X_2?

10.17 A university placement office conducted a study to determine whether there is an association between starting salaries Y (in thousands of dollars), and grade point average X_1 and student's age upon graduation X_2 for students in the school of business. The placement office obtained the following sample data:

Starting Salary	GPA	Age	Starting Salary	GPA	Age
25.5	2.95	22	22.7	3.05	23
27.0	3.20	23	21.4	2.70	22
28.1	3.40	23	22.5	2.75	28
29.4	3.60	23	24.2	3.10	22
28.2	3.20	27	26.0	3.15	26
22.0	2.85	22	24.2	2.95	23
25.0	3.10	25	23.8	2.75	26
25.8	2.85	28			

Determine whether grade point average and age contribute substantially in explaining the variation in the sample of starting salaries.

10.18 Suppose the least squares equation $\hat{Y} = -50 + .04X_1 + 25X_2 + 8X_3$ is determined based on a representative sample of the prices (Y) of 20 room air conditioners as a potential function of BTU-per-hour rating (X_1), energy efficiency ratio (X_2), and number of settings (X_3). Suppose further that $SST = 1{,}200$, $SSE(X_1, X_2, X_3) = 200$, $SE(b_1) = .005$, $SE(b_2) = 2.5$, and $SE(b_3) = 6.5$.
   (a) Do the signs of the least squares coefficients for X_1, X_2, and X_3 make sense? Explain.
   (b) Do you detect an association between price and X_1, X_2, and X_3? Support your answer.
   (c) Determine 95% confidence intervals for the parameters β_1, β_2, and β_3. Based on these intervals, what can you conclude about the incremental contribution of each predictor variable in the presence of the other two? Explain.

10.19 Suppose the least squares equation $\hat{Y} = 2.8 + 6.5X_1 - 3.2X_2$ is determined from the annual records of 15 districts of a chain of computer retail stores, where Y represents the number of PCs sold in the district (in thousands of units) as a potential function of each district's promotional expenditures X_1 (in thousands of dollars) and the number of competing computer stores in each district X_2. Suppose further that $SST = 800$, $SSR(X_1, X_2) = 750$, $SE(b_1) = .62$, and $SE(b_2) = .4$.
   (a) Do the signs of the least squares coefficients for X_1 and X_2 make sense? Explain.
   (b) Do you detect an association between sales and X_1 and X_2? Support your answer.
   (c) Determine 95% confidence intervals for the parameters β_1 and β_2. Based on these intervals, what can you conclude about the incremental contributions of each predictor variable in the presence of the other? Explain.

10.20 In Exercises 2.12 and 2.89, a commercial real estate developer wished to evaluate 17 Virginia localities as potential locations for a business expansion. To support the choice of a location, you studied the size and wealth of these locations and the relationships between wealth and several demographic characteristics of a locality pertaining to real estate. Now the developer wishes to determine a model of the relationship between wealth (as measured by the median income for all occupied housing units) and (1) size (as measured by the number of occupied housing units), (2) the proportion of housing units that are renter-occupied, (3) the proportion of housing units with incomes below the poverty line, and (4) the proportion of housing units that have a telephone. The data (see Exercise 2.12 for source) are contained in the file EX0212 on the book's data diskette.

(a) Determine the least squares equation for predicting wealth based on these four predictor variables; interpret the model coefficients in terms that are meaningful to the developer.

(b) Do these data provide convincing evidence that the four predictor variables as a group are helpful in predicting the wealth of a location? Justify your answer.

(c) Evaluate the marginal contribution of each predictor variable for explaining the variation of these data for wealth.

10.21 In Exercises 1.37, 2.57, 6.19, and 8.15, you studied several aspects of the visitation process at the Information Age Exhibit of the Smithsonian Institute in Washington, D.C. The data for these exercises were produced by the Institute's computer tracking system and represent the 56-day period from September 30, 1995 to November 26, 1995 (see Exercise 1.37 for source); they are on the book's data diskette in the file named EX0137.

Management of the Smithsonian is interested in the relationship between the age of the visitor and the length of the visitation. Do visitors of some age groups tend to stay longer than others? Develop a multiple regression model of the relationship between the average visitation time (response) and the proportions of visitors in the age categories 1–14 years, 15–24 years, 25–44 years, and 45–64 years (predictors). (Note that, if these four proportions are known, the proportion in the 65+ age category is also known. Therefore, only four of the five age categories can be used in the regression model.) Based on this model, do the data provide convincing evidence that the mean visitation time for a day is associated with the age distribution of visitors (as represented by the four predictor variables)?

10.22 The passing performances of National Football League quarterbacks are rated according to a complex formula based on their statistics for four categories: percentage of completed passes relative to attempts, average yards gained per pass attempt, percentage of touchdown passes relative to attempts, and percentage of pass interceptions relative to attempts. Interestingly, an NFL publication, "National Football League Passer Rating System," provides extensive tables for looking up the rating rather than providing the actual formula used.

The following data are the career passing ratings and the values on the four ratings criteria

for the 20 highest rated NFL quarterbacks through the 1992–1993 season among those with 1,500 or more attempts (*Sports Illustrated 1994 Sports Almanac*, p. 155). They are also contained on the book data diskette in a file named EX1022.

Name	Rating	Passing Attempts	Percent Completions
Joe Montana	93.5	4,600	63.67
Steve Young	90.4	1,506	60.29
Dan Marino	87.8	5,284	59.20
Jim Kelly	86.9	3,024	60.32
Mark Rypien	84.3	1,888	57.10
Roger Staubach	83.4	2,958	56.96
Neil Lomax	82.7	3,153	57.63
Sonny Jurgensen	82.6	4,262	57.09
Len Dawson	82.6	3,741	57.10
Dave Krieg	82.1	3,989	58.31
Ken Anderson	81.9	4,475	59.31
Boomer Esiason	81.8	3,378	56.16
Bernie Kosar	81.8	3,012	58.90
Danny White	81.7	2,950	59.69
Ken O'Brien	81.0	3,465	58.85
Warren Moon	81.0	4,026	57.85
Bart Starr	80.5	3,149	57.42
Fran Tarkenton	80.4	6,467	57.00
Dan Fouts	80.2	5,604	58.83
Randall Cunningham	79.9	2,641	55.43

Name	Yardage per Attempt	% Touchdowns to Attempts	% Interceptions to Attempts
Joe Montana	7.63	5.30	2.67
Steve Young	7.88	5.05	2.79
Dan Marino	7.47	5.49	3.12
Jim Kelly	7.61	5.32	3.57
Mark Rypien	7.63	5.14	3.44
Roger Staubach	7.67	5.17	3.68
Neil Lomax	7.22	4.31	2.85
Sonny Jurgensen	7.56	5.98	4.43
Len Dawson	7.67	6.39	4.89
Dave Krieg	7.33	5.26	4.01
Ken Anderson	7.33	4.40	3.58
Boomer Esiason	7.59	5.15	3.82
Bernie Kosar	7.00	3.69	2.59
Danny White	7.44	5.25	4.47
Ken O'Brien	7.03	3.58	2.74
Warren Moon	7.50	4.35	3.60
Bart Starr	7.84	4.83	4.38
Fran Tarkenton	7.26	5.29	4.11
Dan Fouts	7.68	4.53	4.32
Randall Cunningham	6.88	4.77	3.10

(a) Develop a multiple linear regression model for predicting a quarterback's rating given his statistics on the four ratings criteria.

(b) Evaluate the model. How close does your model in part (a) explain the actual ratings? Is it clear that all four criteria contribute to the rating? Justify your answer.

10.23 A marketing firm has been hired to estimate family food expenditures based on family income and family size. The following data represent monthly food expenditures Y (in thousands of dollars) versus monthly income X_1 (in thousands of dollars) and family size X_2 for 15 families that were randomly selected in a geographic region of interest.

Y	X_1	X_2	Y	X_1	X_2
.43	2.1	3	1.29	8.9	3
.31	1.1	4	.35	2.4	2
.32	.9	5	.35	1.2	4
.46	1.6	4	.78	4.7	3
1.25	6.2	4	.43	3.5	2
.44	2.3	3	.47	2.9	3
.52	1.8	6	.38	1.4	4
.29	1.0	5			

Determine whether family income and size appear to contribute to the explanation of variation among sample food expenditures.

10.24 The paper "Effects of Computer System Components on the Price of Notebook Computers" (*Information and Management*, Vol. 27, 1994, pp. 151–160) examines the relationship between the retail price of notebook computers and their attributes. The purpose of the study was to develop a model to identify system attributes that influence prices. Such a model could be used to assist managers in conducting a price/performance analysis for making purchasing decisions. The data represented 91 notebook computer models (all CPU type 486) marketed by 63 different vendors. The notebook computer characteristics considered included CPU clock speed (megahertz), RAM standard ("random-access memory" in megabytes), RAM maximum, and hard drive capacity (megabytes). The data for the study are included on the book data diskette in the file EX1024.

(a) Fit an appropriate multiple regression model to these data. For each predictor variable in your model, interpret its regression coefficient. As part of your interpretation, com-

ment on whether each coefficient has the sign (+ or −) that one would expect.

(b) Which predictor variables seem most predictive of retail price? Which seem least predictive of retail price?

(c) To what extent do these data explain the variation among retail prices of the notebook computer models?

10.25 The paper "Analysis of the Association Between Pollution Performance and Input Cost Factors: The Case of Electric Utility Plants" (*Journal of Accounting and Public Policy*, Vol. 13, 1994, pp. 31–48) examined the possible association between pollution performance by fossil-fuel-burning power plants and several cost factors. One of the key questions was whether reducing pollution emissions requires increased costs, and therefore a negative impact on economic performance in the short run. This study involved pollution and cost factors for 87 fossil-fuel-burning plants. The pollution data that were observed were 1975 emissions of sulfur dioxide. The 1975 cost data included fuel costs per megawatt hour, labor costs per megawatt hour, and other production costs (such as equipment maintenance) per megawatt hour. The cost data were adjusted based on regional producer price indices to reflect regional price differences in 1975. Also included as a predictor variable is plant capacity per megawatt hour. The data are included on the book data diskette in the file EX1025.

(a) Develop a multiple linear regression model of the association between the power plants' 1975 emissions of sulfur dioxide and their corresponding cost and capacity variables.

(b) Do the data contradict a null hypothesis of no association between the emission of sulfur dioxide and the set of four predictor variables?

(c) For each predictor variable, do the data provide convincing evidence that it makes a marginal contribution in explaining variation in emissions of sulfur dioxide?

(d) Interpret the model. What does it suggest about the relationship between a plant's emissions of sulfur dioxide and its fuel, labor, and other costs?

10.26 The paper "Fair Values of Equity and Debt Securities and Share Prices of Property-Liability Insurers" (*The Journal of Risk and Insurance*, Vol. 62, No. 4, 1995, pp. 719–737) investigated the relationship between share prices of property-liability insurers with the fair values of their equity investments and the fair values of their fixed-maturity debt securities. Of chief interest is whether prices are affected when these fair values differ from historical costs. The sample for this exercise consists of 56 publicly held property-liability insurers operating from 1985 through 1991. The sample represents greater than 50% of the premiums earned by the industry over this period. The data were simulated to match the characteristics of the data reported in the paper. They include the following variables representing 1991 performance of the sample insurers: (1) Price = share price of common stock on March 31; (2) Equitydif = difference between fair value of equity investments and the historical cost of equity investments; and (3) Fixeddif = difference between fair value and book value for fixed-maturity debt securities. The data are on the book data diskette in the file EX1026.

(a) Develop a multiple linear regression model for relating an insurer's share price to the given predictor variables.

(b) To what extent does the set of predictor variables explain the variation among insurers' share prices?

(c) To what extent do these data contradict a claim that share price is unrelated to differences between fair value and historical cost for either equity investments or fixed-maturity debt securities?

(d) Evaluate the marginal contribution of each predictor variable. That is, do these data provide convincing evidence that the difference between fair value and book value for fixed-maturity debt securities (Fixeddif) provides incremental information for predicting share price beyond that provided by the other predictor variable? Justify your answer.

Answer the same question for the difference between fair value of equity investments and the historical cost of equity investments (Equitydif).

10.27 The paper "State-Local Revenue Diversification, Balance, and Fiscal Performance" (*Public Finance Quarterly*, Vol. 22, No. 2, 1994, pp. 168–194) investigated the relationship between the diversity balance of a state's revenue sources and its fiscal performance. Diversity is the reliance on a variety of sources for tax revenue. Balanced diversity is the degree to which tax revenues are balanced across all sources. Diversity is measured in this paper by an index for which a value of 1.00 indicates maximum diversity balance and 0.00 indicates total reliance on a single source. One dimension of fiscal performance is tax effort. Based on prior knowledge, it was expected that balanced diversification supports greater tax effort. Another dimension of fiscal performance is per capita expenditure, which is also believed to be associated with tax effort. The data are on the book data diskette in the file EX1027.

(a) Develop a multiple linear regression model of the relationship between tax effort (response) and per capita expenditures and the diversification index (predictors). Interpret the regression coefficient for the diversification index. Is your interpretation consistent with expectation based on prior knowledge?

(b) Do the data provide convincing evidence that tax effort is related to the per capita expenditures and the diversification index variables?

(c) Do the data provide convincing evidence that each predictor variable makes a marginal contribution in explaining the variation in tax effort?

EXERCISES FOR SECTION 10.5

10.28 A regression model is being developed for a county property assessor. The assessor wishes to include as predictor variables the heated space (in square feet), the number of bathrooms, the architectural style (contemporary, colonial, or traditional), and whether or not the house has a fireplace. The response variable is the assessed value. Construct the model that the county assessor should attempt to fit to the representative sample of data.

10.29 The R. L. Williams Company leases minicomputers and also maintains them through ser-

vice contracts. The service manager wants a model of the relationship between a service representative's years of experience and the average time (in hours) it takes to complete a repair. Some minicomputer models typically require more repair time than others. The company uses three models: A, B, and C. Based on a representative sample, the following least squares equation is determined for the average repair time:

$$\hat{Y} = 20 - .2X_1 + 1.1X_2 - .5X_3$$

where X_1 represents the number of years of experience of the service representative and X_2 and X_3 are dummy variables defined as follows:

$$X_2 = \begin{cases} 1 & \text{if average repair time is for model A} \\ 0 & \text{Otherwise} \end{cases}$$

$$X_2 = \begin{cases} 1 & \text{if average repair time is for model B} \\ 0 & \text{Otherwise} \end{cases}$$

(a) Interpret the least squares coefficient values $b_2 = 1.1$ and $b_3 = -.5$.

(b) Express the least squares equation as three equations, each representing the relationship between average repair time and years of experience for a given minicomputer model. Describe the difference among these three equations.

(c) Interpret the least squares coefficient $b_1 = -.2$.

10.30 Consider the least squares equation $\hat{Y} = 60 + 2X_1 - 5X_2 + 22X_3 - 3.5X_4$, where X_4 is a quantitative variable and X_1, X_2, and X_3 are dummy variables representing a qualitative variable with condition levels as follows:

$$X_1 = \begin{cases} 1 & \text{if condition 1} \\ 0 & \text{if not} \end{cases}$$

$$X_2 = \begin{cases} 1 & \text{if condition 2} \\ 0 & \text{if not} \end{cases}$$

$$X_3 = \begin{cases} 1 & \text{if condition 3} \\ 0 & \text{if not} \end{cases}$$

Given that $X_4 = 10$, use this model to predict Y when:

(a) The qualitative variable is at condition 1.
(b) The qualitative variable is at condition 2.
(c) The qualitative variable is at condition 3.
(d) The qualitative variable is at condition 4.
(e) Could the differences between the results you got in parts (a)–(d) have been anticipated solely from knowledge of the least squares coefficient values $b_1 = 2$, $b_2 = -5$, and $b_3 = 22$ without substituting into the least squares equation? Explain.

10.31 An insurance executive wished to estimate the relationship between $Y =$ the number of days of work lost by auto accident victims and $X_1 =$ age, $X_2 =$ gender. A sample of 25 loss reports was selected, resulting in the following estimated regression model:

$$\hat{Y} = 21.4 - .072X_1 - 1.5X_2$$

For this equation, $SST = 4.750$, $SSE = 3.810$, $SE(b_1) = .11$, and $SE(b_2) = .99$.

(a) Do you detect an association between the response variable Y and the predictor variables X_1 and X_2? Support your answer.

(b) Is the marginal contribution of age useful, given the person's gender?

(c) Is the marginal contribution of gender useful, given the person's age?

(d) What do your conclusions in parts (a)–(c) suggest about basing premiums for income replacement on the age and gender of the insured when work time is lost due to an automobile accident?

10.32 A computer systems manager is interested in the relative efficiency of a computer during the busiest time of day (10:00 A.M.–3:00 P.M.) versus "light" times (8:00–10:00 A.M. and 3:00–5:00 P.M.). Efficiency is measured by "job throughput time" (total time to complete a computer job). Data are collected for a sample of 36 jobs, 18 during the busy period and 18 during the light period. Since the size and complexity of a job can be expected to affect its throughput time, the CPU time (actual time spent by the computer processor to complete a job, apart from delays such as waiting for other jobs to be processed) is also included in the model. Thus, the variables are:

$$Y = \text{Throughput time}$$

$$X_1 = \begin{cases} 1 & \text{if busy period} \\ 0 & \text{if light period} \end{cases}$$

$$X_2 = \text{CPU time}$$

The resulting estimated regression model is

$$\hat{Y} = 14.3 + 4.5X_1 + .33X_2$$

with $R^2 = .77$, $SST = 3{,}225$, $SE(b_1) = .091$, and $SE(b_2) = .11$.

(a) Determine SSE and SSR.

(b) Do you detect an association between Y and X_1 and X_2 as a group? Support your answer.

(c) Are the marginal contributions of X_1 and X_2 helpful? State your conclusion about each variable.

(d) Are the signs of b_1 and b_2 consistent with the direction of the expected relationships among throughput time, busy/light time, and CPU time?

(e) What is the least squares equation for the busy period? The light period?

10.33 The location of a service station is critical to its success. The following regression model was developed by an oil company to help evaluate potential sites. It was based on a study of 46 service stations in a city.

$$\hat{Y} = -17.4 + 20X_1 + .0033X_2 + 3.1X_3 + 2.2X_4$$

where

Y = Average gasoline sales per day (thousands of dollars)

X_1 = Price per gallon (dollars, for regular unleaded)

X_2 = Traffic volume (average number of cars passing the site per day)

X_3 = Access (1 if accessible in both directions, 0 if in only one direction)

X_4 = Brand image (1 if a name brand, 0 if an "off" brand)

For this model, SST = 180, SSE = 35, SE(b_1) = 14, SE(b_2) = .0005, SE(b_3) = .60, and SE(b_4) = 1.8.

(a) Determine R_a^2. Based on this value, would you say this is a good prediction equation? Explain.

(b) As a group, are the predictor variables related at all to average daily sales? Support your answer.

(c) With respect to the marginal contribution of each predictor variable, which one appears to be the most influential? The least influential?

(d) Based on your answer to part (c), which, if any, of the predictor variables might you consider deleting and why?

(e) What is the least squares equation for a service station that sells brand-name gasoline and is accessible in both directions?

10.34 In a certain locality, five residential houses that were recently sold were selected at random from each of three distinct neighborhoods (A, B, and C) in the city, and the selling price Y was compared to the property valuation X_1 as determined by the local real estate assessor's office. The sample data are as follows, where selling price and property valuation are in thousands of dollars:

Y	X_1	Neighborhood
62.5	53.1	A
56.8	62.0	A
62.6	67.8	A
61.2	73.4	A
68.6	79.6	A

Y	X_1	Neighborhood
95.2	83.9	B
103.4	88.4	B
103.3	92.3	B
136.8	97.8	B
134.3	100.8	B
142.8	116.5	C
145.6	121.8	C
152.5	126.2	C
147.4	132.6	C
167.8	140.5	C

Fit an appropriate model to these data, evaluate it, and revise as necessary.

10.35 The paper "Consumers' Perception of Risk and the Purchase of Apparel from Catalogs" (*Journal of Direct Marketing*, Vol. 8, No. 2, Spring 1994) examined the role that perceived risk plays in consumers' purchases of apparel from catalogs. A sample of 236 college students was given a questionnaire. Each respondent was asked to provide the number of orders for apparel from a catalog placed in the past 12 months. They were also asked to respond to statements regarding several aspects of perceived risk that had been suggested in the literature, including (1) the ability to inspect merchandise is important to me (Inspect); (2) I have more self-confidence/self-esteem than most people (Confidence); (3) I actively seek information about apparel (Seekinfo); (4) brand names are important to me (Brand); and (5) I am able to visualize myself in a garment (Visual). Each of these perceived risk variables was measured on a 1–4 scale, where 1 = completely disagree, 2 = disagree, 3 = agree, and 4 = completely agree that this is a factor for me. The data have been simulated to match the characteristics described in the paper; they are on the book data diskette in the file named EX1035.

(a) Develop and evaluate a multiple linear regression model of the relationship between orders and the given set of predictor variables.

(b) Based on the evaluation of the regression model in part (a), which of the predictor variables appear to explain the variation in these data involving purchasing frequency?

10.36 Comparisons of women's and men's earnings have consistently demonstrated a substantial gender inequality. The paper "Gender, Earnings, and Proportions of Women" (*Gender and Society*, Vol. 10, No. 2, Apr. 1996, pp. 168–184) investigated the reasons for such differences. The sample consisted of 420 computer professionals working in 14 organizations in a western Canadian city. A questionnaire was completed by each professional (or, for some items, by his or her manager). Information obtained included the professional's income, gender, position, years of work experience, and level of education. Position was coded on a 1–3 scale reflecting increasing levels of responsibility (3 = a manager; 2 = a supervisor; 1 = everyone else). Education was coded on a 1–6 scale reflecting increasing levels of education. Each professional's income, gender, position, years of experience, and education level are on the book data diskette in the file EX1036.

(a) Develop a simple linear regression model of the relationship between income and gender for this population. Interpret the model.

(b) To what extent do these data contradict a null hypothesis that income is not linearly related to gender?

(c) Develop a multiple linear regression model of the relationship between income and all other variables (gender, position, experience, and education level) for this population. Interpret the model.

(d) To what extent do these data contradict a null hypothesis that income is not related to any of the predictor variables in part (c)?

(e) Evaluate the evidence that each predictor variable makes a marginal contribution for explaining the variation in income.

(f) Based on your analysis in parts (a)–(e), what do these data suggest about the role of gender in determining income for this population? Explain.

10.37 Regression analysis can be used to model the relationship of monthly electrical consumption to home size, family size, and possession of various appliances. The paper "Estimating End-use Demand: A Bayesian Approach" (*Journal of Business and Economic Statistics*, Vol. 12, No. 2, Apr. 1994, pp. 221–231) explored the use of several different approaches to developing such a model. The data represent a sample of 174 households in Sydney, Australia, in July 1987. July is the winter month of peak demand in Sydney. The response variable is total weekend electrical consumption per day (Consump). The predictor variables that were considered included dummy variables for the presence/absence of a separate freezer (Freezer), an automatic defrost refrigerator (Refrige), an electric oven (Oven), a dishwasher (Dishwash), a clothes dryer (Dryer), electric heating (Elecheat), a water heater (Waterht), a pool pump (Poolpump), a microwave oven (Microwav), and another major appliance (Otherapp). Other predictor variables included the area of the home (Homesize), the number of household members (People), and annual before-tax income (Income). The data for this exercise have been recreated to simulate the characteristics of the data used in the paper; they appear on the book data diskette in the file EX1037.

(a) Based on your personal knowledge of energy consumption, which of the predictor variables would you expect to have the strongest relationship to weekend electrical consumption?

(b) Fit a multiple linear regression model of the relationship between weekend electrical consumption and this set of predictor variables; interpret the model. Specifically, which of the appliances seem to account for the largest amounts of electrical consumption? Are your findings consistent with your prior expectation?

(c) Evaluate the marginal contributions of the predictor variables for explaining the variation in weekend electrical consumption.

10.38 The paper "Is Revenue-Neutral Tax Reform Revenue Neutral?" (*Public Finance Quarterly*, Vol. 22, No. 1, Jan. 1994, pp. 65–85) explored whether tax reforms that are intended to be revenue-neutral turn out that way. In their study of the effect of the United States' Tax Reform Act of 1986, the authors developed a regression model of the relationship between the quarterly income tax rate—the ratio of tax revenues to Gross National Product (TAX/GNP—and the dummy variable TREFORM, where TREFORM = 0 before 1987 and 1 afterward. (The 1986 tax reform became effective in 1987.) The years studied were 1982 to 1990; thus, there were 36 observations. Real GNP (RGNP) was included as an additional predictor. (RGNP is the quarterly GNP in millions of dollars, adjusted for inflation.) Also included was a time trend variable (YEAR = 1982, 1983, . . . , 1990). The estimated equation is as follows, with *T*-values in parentheses below the corresponding coefficients:

TAX/GNP =
.00129 − .0992 RGNP + .000000607 YEAR + .0000879 TREFORM
     (.58)   (.10)   (3.54)

(a) Interpret the coefficient of TREFORM. What does it suggest about the revenue-neutrality of the 1986 Tax Reform Act?

(b) If the 1986 Tax Reform Act were truly

neutral, what is the probability that the coefficient of TREFORM would be as great as or greater than .0000879 by chance? Based on this probability, do these data provide convincing evidence against the claim that the 1986 Tax Reform Act was actually "revenue-neutral"? (Assume that all necessary assumptions are valid.)

(c) Do these data establish that RGNP and YEAR make marginal contributions in explaining the variation of TAX/GNP?

10.39 The paper "Key Issues Facing European Car Manufacturers and Their Strategic Responses" (*Business Economics,* Oct. 1994) claimed that a ". . . severe drop in demand for European cars in 1993 forced the auto industry to face underlying structural problems that had been growing for several years . . . ." Based on the following data, the paper claimed that reduced utilization of production capacity in 1993 led toward loss positions.

Manufacturer	Year	Utilization (%)	Net Increase to Sales %
PSA	1992	69	2.16
PSA	1993	57	−.97
Renault	1992	79	3.2
Renault	1993	65	.6
GM Europe	1992	93	5.29
GM Europe	1993	73	2.09
Ford Europe	1992	75	−2.99
Ford Europe	1993	63	−2.19
VW Group	1992	91	.002
VW Group	1993	61	−2.52
Fiat Auto	1992	78	.016
Fiat Auto	1993	51	−3.22

(a) Construct a scatter diagram for percent net increase to sales vs. percent utilization of capacity, using a different plotting symbol for each manufacturer. What does this graph suggest about the relationship between a manufacturer's percent net increase to sales and its percent utilization of capacity?

(b) Develop a multiple linear regression model for the association between net increase to sales, using as predictor variables percent utilization of capacity and dummy variables identifying the manufacturer. Interpret the relationship between the mean net increase to sales and percent utilization in the context of this model.

(c) Interpret the coefficient of each dummy vari-

able and evaluate its inclusion in the model.

10.40 The paper "Assessing the Time-Squeeze Hypothesis: Hours Worked in the United States, 1969–89" (*Industrial Relations,* Vol. 33, No. 1, Jan. 1994) assessed the degree to which hours of work have increased in recent decades. A component of the paper was the study of factors determining the number of unpaid hours worked by women in 1980–1981. The factors considered include age, number of children, the number of paid hours worked per week, marital status (married/single), homemaker (yes/no), head of household (yes/no), family income, and race (white, black, other). The data are simulated to match the characteristics of the data reported in the paper, which were taken from a national sample of 228 women. They are on the book data diskette in the file EX1040.

(a) Develop a multiple linear regression model for the relationship between the number of unpaid hours worked per week by U.S. women and the given predictor variables. For each predictor variable, describe its relationship to unpaid hours per week by interpreting its estimated coefficient.

(b) Identify the predictor variables that clearly provide useful marginal information for explaining the variation of unpaid hours per week.

10.41 Over the past three decades, women have represented an increasing proportion of newly employed graduates of Japanese four-year colleges. The paper "Equal Employment Opportunity and the 'Managerial Woman' in Japan" (*Industrial Relations,* Vol. 33, No. 1, Jan. 1994) analyzed the determinants of female representation among these new recruits. The data for the study (*Sources: Statistics Bureau,* 1989a, p. 90; *Statistics Bureau,* 1990, p. 90; and *Japan Labor Bulletin,* Jan. 1991) are Japanese employment data over the period 1955–1990. Variables studied include Newhires, the year-to-year change in the number of newly employed female university graduates. The potential predictor variables were as follows: Grads is the year-to-year change in the number of female university graduates; the more female graduates, the more that are available to be new recruits. Marriage is the 5-year moving average of the annual percent change in marriage rates; it is intended to measure the changing consciousness of Japanese women concerning the legitimacy of pursuing careers. Shortage is the difference between the rate of growth in real gross domestic product and the rate of growth in the number of university-educated men; it was thought that the shortage of men to fill jobs as technical specialists has pressured employers to hire more women. EEOL is a dummy variable indicating the passage of the Japanese Equal Opportunity Employment Act. EEOL = 1 if during the previous year the act had been passed (1985) or was in effect (1985–1990); otherwise, EEOL = 0. The data used in the study are provided on the book data diskette in the file EX1041.

(a) Develop a multiple linear regression model of the relationship between the year-to-year change in the number of newly employed female university graduates (Newhires) and this set of predictor variables.

(b) Evaluate the marginal contribution of each predictor variable. Which appear to account for the increase over the years in the number of newly employed women graduates?

(c) Interpret the regression coefficient for each variable cited in part (b).

EXERCISES FOR SECTION 10.6

10.42 Consider the least squares equation $\hat{Y} = 110 + 4.5X - .25X^2$ to represent the relationship between sales (Y) and price (X). Suppose that SST = 400, SSR(X, X^2) = 300, n = 15, SE(b_1) = .5, and SE(b_2) = .06.

(a) If the range of the X-values used to determine this equation was 5 to 20, show and explain the problem if you attempted to predict sales when X = 40.

(b) Determine the values of R^2 and R_a^2 for this equation.

(c) Should the quadratic term be included? Support your answer.

10.43 Consider determining a least squares equation for the following data:

X:	10	15	22	28	40	45	55	60
Y:	20.1	21.4	23.2	29.9	33.9	38.9	45.3	53.7

(a) Graph the data. Based on the scatter diagram, what model do you believe is appropriate to represent the relationship between Y and X?

(b) Fit the model from your answer in part (a) to the sample data and evaluate the resulting least squares equation.

10.44 Suppose we wish to determine an appropriate model to represent the relationship between monthly sales (Y) in a sales territory and the number of sales representatives (X) that are assigned to the territory. The following representative data are obtained for 12 territories:

Number of reps (X):	2	2	2	3	3	4
Sales (Y):	41	52	48	66	56	77

Number of reps (X):	4	5	6	7	9	9
Sales (Y):	72	85	80	90	92	85

(a) Graph the data. Based on the scatter diagram, what model do you believe is appropriate to represent the relationship between Y and X?

(b) Fit the model from your answer in part (a) to the sample data and evaluate the resulting least squares equation.

10.45 The demand for a product is changing because of a change in its unit price. The following data consist of the demand Y for the product as a potential function of a fairly wide price range X:

X (dollars):	8.8	9.7	9.9	10.3	11.0	12.5
Y (units):	360	305	230	242	180	172

X (dollars):	13.2	14.8	15.8	17.4	18.2
Y (units):	121	83	122	91	105

Answer both parts of Exercise 10.44 for these data.

10.46 The winning times (in seconds) for the gold medal in 100-meter freestyle swimming in the modern Olympic Games for men as reported in the *1998 Sports Almanac* are as follows:

Year	X*	Time	Year	X*	Time
1896	1	82.2	1956	16	55.4
1904	3	62.8	1960	17	55.2
1908	4	65.6	1964	18	53.4
1912	5	63.4	1968	19	52.2
1920	7	60.4	1972	20	51.22
1924	8	59.0	1976	21	49.99
1928	9	58.6	1980	22	50.40
1932	10	58.2	1984	23	49.80
1936	11	57.6	1988	24	48.63
1948	14	57.3	1992	25	49.02
1952	15	57.4	1996	26	48.74

*Each unit of X is equivalent to 4 years.

(a) Graph the winning times (Y) versus year (X). What form of model do you believe is appropriate to represent the relationship between winning times and year?

(b) Fit the model from your answer in part (a) to the given data, and evaluate it.

(c) Do you think it would it be appropriate to use your model from part (b) to predict the winning time for year 2000? Explain.

10.47 In Exercise 9.46, you analyzed data related to the article "A Textbook Case of Hype: Despite the Talk, Our Schools Aren't Failing" (*Washington Post,* Apr. 7, 1996). You developed a simple linear regression model of the relationship between the mean 1990 SAT scores by state and the percentage of students who took the SAT test. A plot of residuals indicated some curvature in that relationship. The data are on the book diskette in file EX0946.

(a) Develop a regression model that accounts for this curvature.

(b) Use hypothesis testing to evaluate the component of the model that deals with the curvature.

(c) Graph the residuals and then comment on the appropriateness of your regression model.

(d) A positive residual indicates that a state achieved a greater mean SAT score than would be predicted based solely on its percentage of students tested. Thus (as in Exercise 9.46), the residuals could be considered to be measures of the effectiveness of the states' educational systems after adjusting for their percentages of students tested. Using residuals in this way, which states now appear to have the most effective educational systems?

(e) Suppose a state had a negative residual, indicating that its actual mean SAT score was lower than predicted by this model, given its percentage of students who took the SAT. Can you suggest any other factors that might explain the negative residual, other than the effectiveness of its educational system? What does your answer suggest about ways to improve the regression model?

EXERCISES FOR SECTION 10.7

10.48 Use the ice cream parlor example data (given in Section 10.3) to fit a straight-line model using price (X_1) as the only predictor variable. Graph the resulting residuals against the corresponding temperature values. In view of what you already know about this problem, are you surprised by the results? Explain your answer.

10.49 Refer to Exercises 9.14 and 9.33 in Chapter 9. These exercises involve the relationship between percent taxes paid (Y) and gross annual income (X). Based on your answer to part (c) of Exercise 9.33, include in the assumed model the term that you believe should be included, fit the new model to the sample data, and evaluate the resulting least squares equation.

10.50 A large construction company wishes to study the relationship between the size of a bid X (in millions of dollars) and the cost to the company for preparing the bid Y (in thousands of dollars). The following 12 recent bids are considered as a representative sample:

X:	2.43	1.61	11.40	6.40	6.0	7.31
Y:	20.5	16.1	67.6	40.4	29.9	33.1

X:	3.37	3.75	10.89	1.50	4.76	8.40
Y:	20.0	28.2	47.0	15.0	25.0	52.5

(a) Construct a scatter diagram and fit what you think is a reasonable model to these data.

(b) Evaluate the resulting least squares equation, and in particular graph the residuals against X.

(c) In view of what the residual graph reveals, would you use this least squares equation for estimation or prediction? Support your answer.

10.51 It is suspected that absenteeism because of the illness of managers could be reduced by their participation in a supervised exercise program or by reduced caffeine consumption. In an experiment involving 20 managers who drink coffee and do not exercise regularly, 10 managers reduce their coffee consumption to no more than one cup per day and participate in a supervised exercise program. The other 10 continue their usual habits. For all 20 managers, the number of absences from work over a 1-year period is recorded. The resulting least squares model is $\hat{Y} = 2.1 - .66X_1 - 15.4X_2$, where Y = the number of absences, X_1 = average coffee consumption per day (ounces), and X_2 = 1 if the manager participated in an exercise program, 0 if not. The model seems to fit well ($R_a^2 = .85$, and for H_0: $\beta_1 = \beta_2 = 0$, P-value = .001 for the F statistic). Yet the sign of b_1 seems wrong. The negative value of b_1 suggests that decreasing coffee consumption increases absences. In addition, $b_2 = -15.4$ suggests a reduction of 15.4 days as a result of the exercise program (a reduction this large seems unrealistic). Explain these results.

10.52 The following sample data consist of the apparent temperature Y (how warm it actually feels), air temperature X_1, and relative humidity X_2:

Y (°F)	X₁ (°F)	X₂ (%)	Y (°F)	X₁ (°F)	X₂ (%)
66	70	20	78	80	30
72	75	20	68	70	40
77	80	20	74	75	40
67	70	30	79	80	40
73	75	30			

(a) Determine the correlation coefficient between X_1 and X_2 using a computer. Based on this result, what is the extent of the linear association between X_1 and X_2?

(b) Fit the model $Y = \beta_0 + \beta_1 X_1 + \beta_2 X_2 + \epsilon$ to the sample data and evaluate the resulting least squares equation. Do you detect collinearity between X_1 and X_2?

(c) Fit a straight line to the sample data first using only X_1 and then using only X_2. Compare the least squares coefficients that you have determined in this part with those that you determined in part (b).

(d) In view of your result in part (a), are you surprised by your findings for parts (b) and (c)? Explain your answer.

10.53 An experiment is being planned to determine the relationship between the grade point averages of college students and (1) the number of hours spent studying per week and (2) the number of hours spent watching TV per week. Each of these variables would be observed over a semester for a sample of 50 students. Can you envision any difficulties that might arise with the resulting least squares equation? What suggestions do you have?

10.54 Suppose two predictor variables in a regression equation are highly correlated. In what way is this likely to damage the regression equation?

10.55 Refer to Exercise 10.23. Use family income (X_1) as the only predictor variable and fit the model $Y = \beta_0 + \beta_1 X_1 + \epsilon$ to the sample data. Plot the residuals of the resulting least squares line against the corresponding values of X_2 (family size). What do you see? Explain what this means.

10.56 Suppose you were asked to fit the model

$Y = \beta_0 + \beta_1 X_1 + \beta_2 X_2 + \beta_3 X_3 + \epsilon$ to the following sample data:

Y	X₁	X₂	X₃	Y	X₁	X₂	X₃
17	.297	.310	.290	17	.099	.092	.074
17	.360	.390	.369	73	.420	.452	.425
35	.075	.058	.047	17	.189	.178	.153
69	.114	.100	.081	35	.369	.391	.364
69	.229	.213	.198	69	.142	.124	.105
173	.315	.304	.267	35	.094	.087	.072
173	.477	.518	.496	35	.171	.161	.145
17	.072	.063	.047	52	.378	.420	.380

(a) Do you detect an association between Y and the three predictor variables as a group? Support your answer.

(b) Do you detect any collinearity among these predictor variables? Support your answer.

(c) Suppose you were to eliminate X_3 from the model. Refit the sample data and determine whether the exclusion of X_3 has improved the situation.

10.57 In the study "... Correlated Variables Are Not Always Redundant" (*The American Statistician*, Vol. 41, No. 2, May 1987, pp. 129–132), the following data were reported on two predictor variables X_1 and X_2 to show the effect of multicollinearity on the response variable Y:

Y	X₁	X₂
12.37	2.23	9.66
12.66	2.57	8.94
12.00	3.87	4.40
11.93	3.10	6.64
11.06	3.39	4.91
13.03	2.83	8.52
13.13	3.02	8.04
11.44	2.14	9.05
12.86	3.04	7.71
10.84	3.26	5.11
11.20	3.39	5.05
11.56	2.35	8.51
10.83	2.76	6.59
12.63	3.90	4.90
12.46	3.16	6.96

(a) Fit two straight lines to the sample data, first using only X_1 as a predictor of Y and then using only X_2. Is there strong evidence that either X_1 or X_2 helps to explain the variation in the sample Y-values? Justify your answer.

(b) Fit a model to the sample data using both X_1 and X_2 and answer the same question as in part (a). Based on your answers to this part and part (a), should either X_1 or X_2 be dropped from the equation? Explain.

10.58 In the "Report of Tar, Nicotine, and Carbon Monoxide of the Smoke of 1,107 Varieties of Domestic Cigarette" (Federal Trade Commission, 1995), one finds tar, nicotine, and carbon monoxide contents (in milligrams) in cigarette smoke of all domestic cigarettes available in 1993. The following data consist of the smoke characteristics of a sample of 28 popular filter brands, distinguished by their lengths: king size (80–85 mm) and 100 mm. They are also on the book' s data disk in the file named EX1058.

Carbon Monoxide	Tar	Nicotine	Length
14	16	1.2	100
13	14	1.0	King
16	15	1.2	100
15	16	1.2	King
17	16	1.1	100
15	16	1.1	King
16	18	1.2	100
18	18	1.3	King
17	15	1.2	100
14	15	1.1	King
15	15	.9	100
15	17	1.0	King
11	11	.8	100
11	11	.8	King
13	13	1.1	100
13	13	1.0	King
14	16	1.1	100
14	16	1.1	King
11	9	.7	100
10	8	.6	King
18	18	1.3	100
17	17	1.2	King
16	17	1.2	100
14	16	1.2	King
18	17	1.2	100
18	18	1.3	King
17	17	1.1	100
14	17	1.4	King

(a) Treating tar, nicotine, and length as potential predictor variables, do they help explain the variation in carbon monoxide levels? Support your answer.

(b) Suppose the order of entry for the predictor variables is nicotine, tar, and length. Com-

ment on any differences you see between this order of entry and the order tar, nicotine, and length.

(c) Based on your answers to parts (a) and (b), which of these predictor variables substantively helps explain the variation in carbon monoxide? Support your answer.

10.59 In Exercise 10.20, you developed a multiple linear regression model of the relationship between the wealth of a locality and four demographic characteristics. The data are contained in the file EX0212 on the book's data diskette (see Exercise 2.12 for source). Evaluate the adequacy of the model for estimation and prediction by carrying out a thorough analysis of the residuals.

10.60 Exercise 10.21 dealt with the visitation process at the Information Age Exhibit of the Smithsonian Institute in Washington, D.C. The data for this exercise are on the book's data diskette in the file named EX0137 (see Exercise 1.37 for source). You developed a multiple linear regression model of the relationship between the average visitation time (response) and the proportions of visitors in the age categories 1–14 years, 15–24 years, 25–44 years, and 45–64 years (predictor variables). Evaluate the adequacy of this model for estimation and prediction by carrying out a thorough analysis of the residuals.

10.61 In Exercise 10.22, you developed a multiple linear regression model of the relationship between the passing ratings of leading NFL quarterbacks and their statistics for four categories. The data are the career passing ratings and the values on these four ratings criteria for the 20 highest rated NFL quarterbacks through the 1992–1993 season among those with 1,500 or more attempts (*Sports Illustrated 1994 Sports Almanac*, p. 155). They are also contained on the book data diskette in a file named EX1022. How sound is your model? Carry out a residual analysis and use it to evaluate the adequacy of the model for estimation and prediction.

10.62 In Exercise 9.37, you investigated the relationship between the infant mortality rate per 1,000 births (Y) and the percentage of population with a bachelor's degree (X_1) for a sample of 20 states. In addition to X_1, suppose we consider the median income in constant 1993 dollars (in thousands) X_2 and the percentage of minority population (X_3) for the same 20 states. The data are as follows (*Statistical Abstract of the United States, 1995*):

Y	X_1	X_2	X_3
5.9	16.4	38.0	2.0
8.8	13.2	31.7	25.6
8.4	16.0	40.5	21.7
9.4	11.1	31.3	12.2
7.2	12.1	31.8	7.8
7.1	15.6	33.7	5.6
8.5	11.7	28.7	12.3
7.4	13.1	31.0	6.2
9.8	15.6	39.9	29.0
9.5	15.4	36.4	22.6
10.6	12.0	28.8	24.4
12.1	9.7	22.2	36.5
11.1	10.5	26.3	32.7
8.1	13.9	28.7	24.8
8.7	12.4	31.0	5.6
5.9	15.4	35.8	6.2
7.8	15.9	35.7	11.5
10.4	11.2	26.1	31.0
10.3	10.5	25.1	17.0
7.2	15.4	31.1	1.4

(a) Show whether the inclusion of X_2 and X_3 helps to explain substantively more of the variation in infant mortality rates for these 20 states.

(b) Suppose you introduced X_2 (median income) as the first predictor variable; is your result the same as in part (a)? Investigate and explain what is going on here.

10.63 In Exercise 10.24, you developed a multiple linear regression model of the relationship between a notebook computer's price and its components and capabilities. The data for the study are included on the book data diskette in the file EX1024 (see Exercise 10.24 for source).

(a) Use an analysis of residuals to evaluate the adequacy of the regression model you developed in Exercise 10.24.

(b) Develop a plot of residuals versus vendor. What does this plot suggest about the pricing policies of the various vendors?

EXERCISES FOR SECTION 10.8

10.64 Discuss the most useful criteria to use for determining how good a least squares equation is.

10.65 Discuss whether the least squares equation resulting from the application of a variable selection technique should be regarded necessarily as the best regression equation to use for estimation and prediction.

10.66 Outline all possible linear least squares models that can be determined if there are four predictor variables in the set.

10.67 Refer to Exercise 10.56. Use the modified forward and backward elimination variable selection procedures to determine the best set of predictor variables to use in a regression equation. Explain your findings.

10.68 The *Baseball Encyclopedia* (9th edition, 1993, Macmillan Publishing Company) presents the following data consisting of number of games won (Y), batting average (X_1), number of stolen bases (X_2), fielding average (X_3), and earned runs allowed (X_4) for each of the then 26 Major League teams for the 1992 season.

Y	X_1	X_2	X_3	X_4
96	.255	110	.984	3.35
87	.252	196	.980	3.25
83	.262	208	.985	3.38
78	.254	77	.982	3.39

Y	X_1	X_2	X_3	X_4
72	.235	129	.981	3.66
70	.253	127	.978	4.11
98	.254	126	.982	3.14
90	.260	125	.984	3.46
82	.255	69	.982	3.56
81	.246	139	.981	3.72
72	.244	112	.982	3.61
63	.248	142	.972	3.41
96	.263	129	.985	3.91
92	.268	256	.986	3.43
89	.259	89	.985	3.79
76	.266	144	.978	4.11
76	.261	78	.982	4.21
75	.256	66	.981	4.60
73	.246	44	.978	3.58
96	.258	143	.979	3.73
90	.277	123	.985	3.70
86	.261	160	.979	3.82
77	.250	81	.975	4.09
72	.243	160	.979	3.84
72	.256	131	.980	3.81
64	.263	100	.982	4.55

Determine which of these potential predictor variables help to explain the variation in the number of games won.

10.69 In Exercises 10.20 and 10.59, you developed a multiple regression model to assist a developer in evaluating Virginia localities as potential locations for expansion. The model dealt with the relationship between a location's wealth and four demographic characteristics. The data (see Exercise 2.12 for source) are contained in the file EX0212 on the book's data diskette. Use backward elimination to determine the variables that should be used in the final model.

SUPPLEMENTARY EXERCISES

10.70 A personnel director has developed a model of Y = manager's job satisfaction (on a scale from 1 to 10) as a function of X_1 = age, X_2 = most recent performance rating (on a 1-to-5 scale), X_3 = salary (in thousands of dollars per month), and X_4 = time in current job (in years). The estimated regression model is $\hat{Y} = 3 + .05X_1 + 1.1X_2 - .6X_3 + .11X_4$.

(a) What satisfaction rating is predicted by this model for a 40-year-old employee who was rated 4 on his most recent performance evaluation, earns $3,950 per month, and has been in his current position for 3 years?

(b) Do the estimated coefficients make sense? Determine for each whether its sign seems appropriate intuitively. If any seem wrong, can you suggest the cause?

10.71 The director of a business school graduate program wished to identify the best predictors of performance in the school's MBA program. Using information from 25 current students in the MBA program, he develops a regression model relating Y = student's GPA (converted to a 4.0 maximum) to X_1 = student's undergraduate GPA (converted to a 4.0 maximum) and X_2 = student's score on the GMAT (a standardized test given to business school applicants). The least squares equation is $\hat{Y} = -.25 + .5X_1 + .0082X_2 - .0000081X_2^2$.

(a) The 25 students had undergraduate GPAs ranging from 2.8 to 3.85, and GMAT scores ranging from 475 to 650. The director now has an applicant with an undergraduate GPA of 3.71 and a GMAT of 750. Would you use the model to predict the MBA GPA of this applicant? Explain your answer.

(b) Try using the model to predict the performance of the applicant in part (a) and of another applicant whose undergraduate GPA is 3.69 and whose GMAT is 650. What do these results tell you about the form of the relationship between Y and X_2 in the model?

For the following exercises, your ultimate goal is to determine whether there is a relationship between the response variable and the given predictor variables and, if yes, to evaluate the regression model completely for the purpose of determining whether the best regression equation is adequate for estimation and prediction.

10.72 A hospital staff analyst investigated the degree to which the length of a Medicare patient's hospital stay is determined by the patient's age.* It was also suspected that men tend to stay longer than women.

Women		Men	
Age	Length of Stay (days)	Age	Length of Stay (days)
63	3	66	9
66	16	70	8
67	6	72	10
68	9	77	17
68	3	77	18
69	4	78	12
69	8	78	9
69	19		
70	9		
70	6		
72	7		
73	10		
74	7		
83	16		
84	21		
85	8		
88	10		

10.73 The XRX Corporation conducts an ongoing research program to improve the copy quality of its copiers. It is important to determine what characteristics of a copy contribute to customers' perceptions of copy quality. In a survey, customers rated the overall copy quality of a sample of copies (Y, on a 0–10 scale). Each copy was also analyzed in the lab, receiving ratings on a 0–10 scale for X_1 = grayness of background, X_2 = number of spots in background, X_3 = image sharpness, and X_4 = image blackness. Given the

---

* Courtesy of Trent Crable.

following sample data, determine an appropriate regression equation:

Y	X_1	X_2	X_3	X_4	Y	X_1	X_2	X_3	X_4
6	10	8	5	4	6	6	4	7	5
2	8	1	2	5	4	8	4	3	5
6	5	9	5	4	4	5	5	3	3
6	4	9	4	5	6	3	7	5	6
8	0	6	9	6	3	7	0	3	5
7	10	5	5	8	5	1	2	6	5
5	5	4	4	6	7	4	6	8	5
5	7	2	6	6	4	3	4	5	4
8	5	7	9	6	4	5	1	7	2
5	1	6	4	4	4	1	2	2	6

10.74 In Exercise 9.78, you were asked to analyze employee absenteeism at each of two plants, Richmond and Louisville. Suppose that in addition to years of service, the gender of the employee in the sample is recorded. For the following sample data, determine an appropriate regression equation that considers gender and plant location.

	Richmond			Louisville	
Absences	Years of Service	Gender	Absences	Years of Service	Gender
18	9	M	24	9	M
14	9	M	0	31	M
24	21	M	18	17	M
5	15	F	28	19	M
7	15	F	30	19	F
0	15	M	51	16	M
8	17	F	48	24	M
13	21	M	3	30	F
2	18	F	14	17	M
0	16	M	19	19	F
5	15	M	50	7	M
11	9	M	9	13	M
10	14	F	13	7	M
1	8	M	9	7	M
7	10	F	4	20	M
2	15	M	50	16	F
21	9	M	49	9	M
18	12	M	15	12	M
2	15	M	11	11	M
12	16	F	15	18	F
9	14	F	9	7	F
5	14	M	13	24	M
9	14	F	5	18	F
13	8	M	6	12	M
16	8	M	33	7	F
11	15	F	64	7	M
9	13	M	12	16	F
23	10	F	8	14	M
5	8	M	0	15	M
13	14	M	3	17	M

10.75 An analyst for a regional telephone company studied the relationship between the annual residential telephone line gain in a given locality and the annual state employment in the construction industry.* The gain is the change in the number of telephones in place that occurs from one year to the next. The analyst also believes that the consumer price index (CPI) might be indicative of annual gain. The annual gains for a recent 10-year period are listed here along with an index for the total annual state employment in the construction industry and the consumer price index. Determine an appropriate regression equation.

CPI	Construction Employment	Area Gain
195.4	130.2	446
217.4	138.4	591
246.8	128.3	569
272.4	116.3	490
289.1	103.8	262
298.4	113.9	688
311.1	132.8	667
322.2	152.0	757
328.4	168.1	899
340.4	173.6	741

10.76 In many corporations, the problem of identifying important factors to predict the job effectiveness of potential employees is a continuous process. The usual procedure is to administer to a potential employee a battery of appropriate tests and to base the hiring decision on the test scores. The key question is to know a priori which tests can predict the job effectiveness of an individual. Suppose the human resources office of a large corporation has developed four tests for a given job classification. These tests were administered to 20 individuals who were hired by the company. After a 2-year period, each of these employees was rated for job effectiveness. The job effectiveness score and the scores on the four tests are listed here. Determine an appropriate regression equation.

Employee	Effectiveness Score	Test 1	Test 2	Test 3	Test 4
1	94	122	121	96	89
2	71	108	115	98	78
3	82	120	115	95	90
4	76	118	117	93	95

---

* Courtesy of Faye Eure.

Employee	Effectiveness Score	Test 1	Test 2	Test 3	Test 4
5	111	113	102	109	109
6	64	112	96	90	88
7	109	109	129	102	108
8	104	112	119	106	105
9	80	115	101	95	88
10	73	111	95	95	84
11	127	119	118	107	110
12	88	112	110	100	87
13	99	120	89	105	97
14	80	117	108	99	100
15	99	109	125	108	95
16	116	116	122	116	102
17	100	104	83	100	102
18	96	110	101	103	103
19	126	117	120	113	108
20	58	120	77	80	74

10.77 The following data represent the average temperatures in January for 24 weather stations in Virginia. Each station is identified by latitude, longitude, and elevation. Determine an appropriate regression equation.

Temperature	Latitude	Longitude	Elevation
37.9	37.35	79.52	975
28.7	38.52	78.43	3,535
38.3	37.08	77.95	440
37.3	37.53	79.68	870
31.5	37.08	81.33	3,300
35.0	37.38	80.08	1,890
36.0	38.03	78.52	870
37.4	36.83	79.37	700
40.4	37.28	75.97	11
35.8	37.77	78.15	300
35.3	38.47	78.00	420
33.2	38.45	78.93	1,400
41.3	36.90	76.20	25
34.7	38.45	77.67	300
38.0	37.33	78.38	450
34.2	36.93	80.30	2,600
35.4	38.30	77.47	100
35.7	37.37	80.00	1,524
39.7	36.68	76.78	80
40.5	37.30	77.30	40
31.6	38.00	79.83	2,238
40.0	37.08	76.35	10
36.1	37.78	79.43	1,060
34.1	39.12	77.72	500

10.78 A graduate student studied the prices of business textbooks for the spring 1992 semester.* He identified the following potential predictor variables: number of pages, type of book cover (hard or soft), and business major (economics, accounting, management, management information systems, and other). The following data were collected:

Price	Pages	Cover	Major
$20.65	486	S	Acc
18.95	522	S	Acc
52.50	826	H	Acc
55.65	810	H	Acc
64.95	1,336	H	Acc
56.25	857	H	Acc
16.95	417	S	Econ
13.95	207	S	Econ
35.15	460	S	Econ
48.75	826	H	Econ
42.95	828	H	Econ
48.75	644	H	Econ
50.95	986	H	Other
18.30	558	S	Other
46.90	1,398	H	Other
25.95	518	S	Mgt
50.00	1,070	H	Mgt
48.50	586	H	Mgt
47.95	732	H	Mgt
47.85	679	H	Mgt
51.65	668	H	Mgt
50.00	440	H	Mgt
48.95	888	H	Mgt
50.65	690	H	Mgt
45.95	1,011	H	Mgt
30.00	507	H	Mgt
45.00	814	H	Mgt
19.95	182	S	MIS
29.95	731	S	MIS
44.95	866	S	MIS
56.25	826	H	MIS
44.95	797	H	MIS
48.75	308	H	MIS
37.95	585	H	MIS
27.20	340	S	Other
48.75	792	H	Other
45.00	829	H	Other
50.00	1,100	H	Other
54.95	1,181	H	Other
15.00	354	S	Other

10.79 A recent study investigated factors that affect the number of complaints about long-term care for

* Courtesy of Wei Zhang.

the aging in Virginia.* One potential factor is how complaint resolution is handled. Currently, it is handled either by a local program with ostensibly different resources depending on the locality, or directly by the state department for the aging. Additional factors that may influence the number of complaints received were the number of beds available at a particular long-term care facility, and where the facility is located (rural, urban, or a mixture of the two). The following data are based on the complaints investigated during 1990:

Area	Number Complaints	of Beds	Location	Program
1	36	412	Rural	Local
2	22	280	Rural	Local
3	211	989	Rural	Local
4	5	650	Rural	State
5	77	1,789	Urban	Local
6	1	1,259	Rural	State
7	15	820	Rural	State
8	176	3,388	Mixed	Local
9	13	582	Rural	State
10	64	800	Urban	Local
11	28	648	Rural	State
12	3	1,364	Rural	State
13	3	494	Rural	State
14	0	475	Rural	State
15	273	3,117	Mixed	Local
16	14	698	Urban	State
17	8	801	Rural	State
18	4	810	Mixed	State
19	17	3,292	Mixed	State
20	5	356	Mixed	State

10.80 In a recent study, it was of interest to estimate the monthly manufacturing expenses for a manufacturing company.† Four quantities were considered as potential predictor variables: (1) the manufacturing value of production, which represents the accumulation of all job costs in a month (X_1); (2) net monthly sales (X_2); (3) payroll costs (X_3); and (4) the percentage of employee-paid hours that were directly applied to customers' jobs (X_4). The following information is based on data from the most recent 18 months:

Month	Actual Manufacturing Expenses	X_1	X_2	X_3	X_4
1	765,715	736,932	1,070,857	431,313	70.9%
2	866,646	868,731	1,166,572	488,672	76.0
3	795,762	768,923	1,084,584	466,110	75.4
4	880,175	802,044	1,152,015	471,759	73.7
5	840,308	768,753	1,102,914	466,955	74.5
6	813,588	738,084	1,209,486	442,674	75.5
7	915,828	830,697	1,093,130	518,724	72.7
8	844,200	772,550	1,178,449	473,927	72.6
9	939,497	865,235	1,246,947	540,264	73.3
10	857,316	778,727	1,026,848	478,457	72.5
11	867,235	835,969	1,283,029	489,242	74.4
12	871,289	814,294	1,421,233	475,405	75.8
13	875,872	862,820	1,006,106	487,189	75.4
14	945,866	1,005,529	1,258,522	544,505	75.5
15	875,960	887,690	1,177,637	489,028	77.0
16	1,014,107	1,031,243	1,252,445	578,567	75.3
17	939,557	978,892	1,227,701	525,516	76.9
18	850,136	816,093	1,221,124	478,830	75.6

10.81 This exercise is an extension of Exercise 7.82, an investigation of the benefit of attending a study session prior to taking a literature test. It was believed that another factor in student test performance, besides whether a student attended the study session, was simply the quality of the student. Students' grade point averages (GPAs) were used to characterize student quality. Finally, it was suspected that a student's class (freshman, sophomore, etc.) might explain some of the observed variation among test grades. The data[‡] follow.

Grade:	75	88	75	95	95	75	75	75	85	65	75	95
Attend?	1	1	0	1	0	0	0	1	0	0	0	0
GPA:	3.02	3.2	2.2	2.9	4.0	2.4	2.0	2.5	1.5	2.5	2.29	3.0
Class:	1	1	1	1	1	2	2	2	2	2	2	2

Grade:	85	88	72	82	82	82	85	92	98	78	85	78
Attend?	1	1	0	0	0	0	0	0	1	1	1	0
GPA:	2.75	2.2	2.1	3.9	2.3	2.0	2.27	2.75	3.23	3.16	2.15	2.5
Class:	2	2	2	2	2	2	2	2	2	2	2	2

Grade:	95	95	85	75	72	78	65	75	72	95	98	88
Attend?	1	1	0	0	0	0	0	0	0	1	1	1
GPA:	3.62	3.56	2.0	2.4	2.72	2.8	2.6	2.4	1.93	3.0	3.5	1.5
Class:	2	2	2	2	2	2	2	2	2	2	2	2

Grade:	75	82	85	78	88	92	65	78	88	82	88	78
Attend?	1	0	0	1	1	1	0	0	1	1	0	0
GPA:	2.5	3.2	2.1	2.8	3.2	2.1	2.2	2.75	3.0	3.0	2.0	3.4
Class:	2	2	2	2	2	2	2	2	2	2	2	2

Grade:	75	75	85	95	92	75	95	75	88	85	82	95
Attend?	0	0	0	1	0	0	1	0	1	1	0	0
GPA:	2.9	2.75	2.01	2.82	2.7	3.4	3.7	2.8	2.8	2.7	1.9	2.35
Class:	2	2	2	2	2	2	2	2	2	2	2	2

Grade:	85	95	65	82	75	98	65	98	75	85	85	78
Attend?	0	0	0	0	0	0	0	1	0	0	0	1
GPA:	3.3	3.4	2.7	2.1	1.96	2.6	2.2	3.65	2.6	2.7	2.9	2.4
Class:	2	3	3	3	3	3	3	3	3	3	3	3

---

* Courtesy of John J. Cotter.

† Courtesy of Neil Callan.

‡ Courtesy of Heather Burke.

Grade:	85	85	75	88	95	92	95	92	88	78	72	75
Attend?	1	0	1	0	1	0	1	1	0	0	0	1
GPA:	2.2	3.2	2.3	2.75	2.25	2.4	3.2	3.2	3.4	3.0	3.02	2.9
Class:	3	3	3	3	3	3	3	3	3	3	4	4

Grade:	92	72	78	92	92	82
Attend?	0	0	0	1	1	1
GPA:	2.7	2.8	2.8	3.7	3.45	3.1
Class:	4	4	4	4	4	4

Note: For Attend: 1 = attended the study session; 0 = did not attend.
For Class: 1 = freshman; 2 = sophomore; 3 = junior; 4 = senior.

10.82 This exercise is an extension of Exercises 2.106 and 8.54, which deal with the work process of associates at the law firm Northup and Bauers. It had been thought that the number of billable hours might be related to an associate's number of years of experience and his or her department. The more experience, it was conjectured, the more billable hours. The following data are the number of billable hours over a 9-month period for each of 43 associates along with the department and the number of years of experience.

Hrs.:	802	1,287	1,225	1,178	1,275	767
Yrs.:	3	10	5	9	7	4
Dept.:	1	1	1	2	1	1

Hrs.:	1,424	1,328	1,223	790	1,399	1,434
Yrs.:	9	7	2	4	4	7
Dept.:	3	2	1	1	4	4

Hrs.:	1,050	796	1,308	1,464	1,389	1,316
Yrs.:	3	5	5	8	5	6
Dept.:	5	6	6	6	7	4

Hrs.:	1,325	1,494	1,096	1,482	1,493	1,452
Yrs.:	6	7	3	15	2	7
Dept.:	8	1	1	3	7	3

Hrs.:	1,060	1,407	1,067	934	901	1,400
Yrs.:	3	12	5	5	4	6
Dept.:	6	6	8	3	1	1

Hrs.:	1,320	1,132	1,256	858	1,346	885
Yrs.:	4	10	4	2	6	4
Dept.:	7	1	3	1	8	1

Hrs.:	1,084	1,065	1,211	1,379	1,340	1,098
Yrs.:	5	4	4	10	8	7
Dept.:	5	5	1	3	6	5

Hrs.:	1,407
Yrs.:	5
Dept.:	1

Dept. Code: 1 = Business/commercial litigation
2 = Labor relations
3 = Real estate
4 = Banking/finance
5 = Administrative
6 = Corporate
7 = Insurance/product liability
8 = Trusts/estates

10.1 Case Study
The Effectiveness of a Medical Device

A firm that manufactures medical devices* has developed a monitor that gives a surgeon new information on the patient's condition during an operation. The company and some physicians strongly believe that the device improves patient outcomes. For example, they theorize that it may lead to less bleeding, fewer blood transfusions, and fewer complications for some patients, thus leading to shorter operations. An analyst at the firm has some data for past surgeries (convenience data), some of which used the monitor and some of which did not. He has been given two goals:

1. To identify positive statements the firm can make about their product.
2. To identify those issues that should be considered next quarter when they start planning a definitive "prospective" study (i.e., a designed experiment).

You have been asked to assist the analyst on a consulting basis. The analyst emphasizes that these data are *retrospective,* i.e., they were not collected as a result of

---

* The identity of the firm and its monitor have been withheld for reason of confidentiality.

a statistically designed experiment (with randomization, blocking, etc.) but were collected from operations performed at two different time periods:

1. Data from period 1 represent the results of surgeries *before* the new monitor was available.

2. Data from period 2 represent the results of surgeries *after* the hospital started using the monitor.

Your assignment is to explore and analyze the data with goals of (1) identifying truthful, positive statements the firm can make about their monitor and (2) understanding the situations where the monitor helps and those where it does not help, if any. You should use as appropriate the methods you have studied thus far from Chapters 1–10.

The data are contained on the data diskette in a file named CASE1001. The following are the variables in the data set with the associated column indicators and brief comments.

Patient Variables

c_1:   Patient gender (0 = male; 1 = female)
c_2:   Patient size (body surface area in square inches)
c_3:   Patient age (years)

Operative Procedure Variables

c_4:   Surgeon ID (labeled 1, 4, and 5)
c_5:   Type of procedure (0 = regular; 1 = emergency)
c_6:   Monitor use (0 = no; 1 = yes)

Intra-Operative Measurements

c_7:   Total time to complete operation (minutes)
c_8:   Blood count B measured pre-op (prior to operation)

Post-Operative Variable

c_9:   Blood count B measured 24 hours post-op (after operation)

Peri-Operative (during operation) Variables

c_{10}:   Blood drained from chest (units)
c_{11}:   Transfusion of count B required (0 = no; 1 = yes)

Comments on the Variables

- c_1 and c_2: Patient gender and body size. Clinicians theorize that small women are more prone to excessive bleeding during this procedure.

- c_3: Patient age. Elderly patients are more likely to have difficulties during surgery.

- c_4: Physician. Physicians may differ in their techniques, familiarity with the monitor, and patient populations.

- c_5: Type of procedure. Emergency cases are more likely to have poor outcomes for this procedure.

- c_6: Monitor. The manufacturer hypothesizes that using this monitor improves patient outcomes.

- c7: Length of operation. Emergency cases and cases where complications develop can take longer.

- c8: Pre-op level of blood component B. This gives a basis of comparison for changes in component B counts due to intra-operative bleeding. Additionally, if this value starts extremely low, it could mean that the patient was in poor shape when the operation began.

- c9: Post-op level of blood component B 24 hours after surgery. Some physicians think that greater decreases in blood component B are undesirable.

- c10: Blood drainage. The more blood that must be drained from the patient's chest during or after the operation, the worse for the patient.

- c11: Transfusions of blood component B. Blood component B is one type of transfusion that is sometimes indicated. In these days of HIV, transfusions are not given unless really necessary.

Comments on the Data:

- Occasionally, data values are missing.
- All data are listed in the order in which surgery was performed.

10.2 Case Study
Analysis of Home Team Advantage in the National Football League

It is widely believed that the home team has an advantage in most sporting events. This case study is an opportunity for you to investigate whether such an advantage exists in the National Football League (NFL) and, if so, its magnitude, the extent to which it is attributable to differences in the type of surface used for the teams' home playing fields, and the extent to which it depends on the relative strengths of the competing teams.

The data represent all 224 NFL games of the 1992 season; they are taken from *The Sports Encyclopedia: Pro Football** and are contained on the data diskette in a file named CASE1002. The file consists of 224 rows of data, one row for each game played. The variables (columns) are:

c1:	Indicator of order of home game (1 through 8)
c2:	Home team name
c3:	Visiting team name
c4:	Outcome (0 = visiting team victory; 1 = home team victory)
c5:	Points for home team
c6:	Points for visiting team
c7:	Margin of home team victory (or loss) = c5 − c6
c8:	Home team playing surface (0 = grass; 1 = artificial turf)
c9:	Visiting team playing surface (0 = grass; 1 = artificial turf)

---

* *The Sports Encyclopedia: Pro Football*, St. Martin's Press, New York, 1993.

c10:   Home team winning percentage at end of the 1992 season
c11:   Visiting team winning percentage at end of the 1992 season

You are to explore and analyze the data using statistical thinking and methods you have studied in Chapters 1–10. You are to develop a sound model of the relationship between home field advantage (if any) and (1) the playing surfaces of the two teams' home fields and (2) the relative strengths of the competing teams. In your report, you should state and justify your conclusions regarding the existence and magnitude of a possible home field advantage, the effects on the home team advantage of the playing surfaces of the two teams' home fields (e.g., is a visiting team that plays its home games on artificial turf at an increased disadvantage when playing a road game on grass?), and the relationship between home team advantage and the strength of the competing teams as measured by their season's end winning percentages.

In developing a model, you will use multiple regression analysis. Be thoughtful about your choice of a response variable. It must be either interval or ratio scaled to conform to the necessary assumptions; therefore, you cannot use c4 (won or lost) as the response variable.

Appendix 10

Computer Instructions for Using MINITAB, EXCEL, and JMP IN

We use the ice cream parlor example (see Tables 10.1, 10.2, 10.8, 10.9, 10.10), and Example 10.4 (see Tables 10.6, 10.7 and Figures 10.4, 10.5) to illustrate Minitab, Excel, and JMP IN instructions that produce the computer outputs (or similar outputs) for these problems.

MINITAB

Fitting Regression Models: Ice Cream Parlor Example

To produce the various Minitab outputs for the ice cream parlor example, first enter the data; put the sales data into c1, the price data into c2, the temperature data into c3, the type-of-day data (0 for weekdays, 1 for weekends) into c4, and the relative humidity data into c5. Name c1, c2, c3, c4, and c5 Sales, Price, Temp, Day, and Humid, respectively. You can produce the regression output in Table 10.1 by choosing STAT–REGRESSION–REGRESSION . . . . In the dialogue box, specify c1 as the RESPONSE variable, and specify c2 and c3 as the PREDICTORS variables; then click the RESULTS button. In the RESULTS dialogue box, click the button for IN ADDITION, THE FULL TABLE OF FITS AND RESIDUALS, and click OK twice.

If you wish to compute and store the predicted values and the residuals, click (in the REGRESSION dialogue box) the STORAGE . . . button. In the STORAGE dialogue box, click the boxes for RESIDUALS and FITS, and click OK. This will place the predicted values and residuals in c6 (with the column name FITS1) and c7 (with the column name RESI1), respectively.

Estimation and Prediction: Ice Cream Parlor Example

Suppose that you wish to use the model to estimate the mean of Y and predict the value of Y corresponding to specific values of X_1 and X_2, such as price = 40 and temperature = 75 as in Section 10.4.4. While in the REGRESSION dialogue box, click the OPTIONS . . . button. In the OPTIONS dialogue box, enter 40 75 in the PREDICTION INTERVALS FOR NEW OBSERVATIONS box; click the FITS, SDS OF FITS, CONFIDENCE LIMITS, and PREDICTION LIMITS buttons, and click OK. This also provides the standard error, confidence interval (for the mean), and prediction interval (for an individual Y-value). Repeat for other values of X_1 and X_2.

Fitting a Quadratic Model: Example 10.4

To produce the output in Table 10.7 and Figure 10.5, enter the manufacturing unit cost data into cl, the production rate data into c2, and the material/labor cost data into c3. Name cl, c2, and c3 Cost, Rate, and Labor, respectively. For Table 10.7, you also need to create a new column containing the squares of the values in c2, and name this column Ratesqrd. Choose CALC–CALCULATOR . . . . In the STORE RESULT IN VARIABLE box, enter c4, and in the EXPRESSION: box, type c2**2 and click OK.

To produce the Minitab output in Table 10.7, choose STAT–REGRESSION–REGRESSION . . . . In the dialogue box, specify cl as the RESPONSE variable, specify c2–c4 as the PREDICTORS variables, and click OK.

Constructing Residual Plots: Example 10.4

To produce the Minitab graph in Figure 10.5, click GRAPHS . . . while you are in the REGRESSION dialogue box. Enter c2 in the RESIDUALS VERSUS THE VARIABLES box, and click OK.

Stepwise Regression: Example 10.5

To produce the stepwise regression output in Table 10.10, choose STAT–REGRESSION–STEPWISE . . . . In the dialogue box, specify cl in the RESPONSE box, c2–c5 in the PREDICTORS box, and click OK. By default, Minitab uses 4.0 as the F-value required to enter or remove a variable.

To use Minitab for the backward elimination procedure, choose STAT–REGRESSION–STEPWISE . . . ; in the dialogue box, specify cl in the RESPONSE box and c2–c5 in the PREDICTORS box as before. Additionally, list c2–c5 in the ENTER box (to place all predictor variables in the model initially) and click the OPTIONS . . . button. Enter 100000 in the F TO ENTER box. (This prevents a variable from reentering the model.) Then click OK.

EXCEL

Fitting Regression Models: Ice Cream Parlor Example

To use Excel to produce regression output as in Table 10.1, enter the data in five columns. Put the sales data into cells a2 through a11; put the price data into cells b2 through b11; put the temperature data into cells c2 through c11; put the type-of-day data into cells d2 through d11; and put the relative humidity data into cells e2 through e11. Enter the variable names Sales, Price, Temp, Day, and Humidity in cells a1, b1, c1,

d1, and e1, respectively. Choose TOOLS—DATA ANALYSIS . . . and click REGRES-
SION. In the dialogue box, specify in the INPUT Y RANGE: box the range of cells
containing the variable name and data for sales (a1:a11); in the INPUT X RANGE:
box, specify the range of cells containing the variable names and data for price and
temperature (b1:c11); and click the LABELS and RESIDUALS boxes. The output
includes not only the regression results in Table 10.1, but also the predicted values, the
residuals, and lower and upper 95% confidence limits for each population coefficient.

Estimation and Prediction: Ice Cream Parlor Example

Suppose you wish to use the regression model to estimate the mean of Y and predict
the value of Y corresponding to specific values of X_1 and X_2, as in Section 10.4.4. Start
with the data in cells a2:e11 as described in the preceding paragraph. Enter the price
values for which you want predictions (40, 50, 60, 40, 50, 60) into cells b12:b17, and
enter the temperature values for which you want predictions (75, 75, 75, 90, 90, 90)
into cells c12:c17. Select cell a12, and click the PASTE FUNCTION button. In the
dialogue box, select the STATISTICAL function category and the function name
TREND. In the TREND dialogue box, enter \$a\$2:\$a\$11 for KNOWN Y'S; enter
\$b\$2:\$c\$11 for KNOWN X'S; enter b12:c12 for NEW X'S; and enter 1 for CONST,
and click OK. Select cell a12 and fill down through cell a17. This places the predicted
Y-values into cells c12:c17. Currently, Excel does not provide standard errors,
confidence intervals, or prediction intervals for a mean Y-value or an individual
Y-value, respectively.

Fitting a Quadratic Model: Example 10.4

To produce outputs similar to those in Table 10.7 and Figure 10.5, enter the
manufacturing unit cost data into cells a2 through a21, the production rate data into
cells b2 through b21, and the material/labor cost data into cells c2 through c21. Enter
the variable names Cost, Rate, and Labor in cells a1, b1, and c1, respectively. You will
also have to create an additional column containing the squares of the Rate values.
First, put the name Ratesqrd in cell d1. Then select cell d2 and type: =B1^2. (This
places the square of cell b1 into cell d1.) With cell d2 selected, fill down through cell
d21. To produce the regression output in Table 10.7, use the previously described
procedure for fitting regression models. Be sure to specify in INPUT X RANGE
portion of the REGRESSION dialogue box the range of cells for Rate, Labor, and
Ratesqrd (b1:d21).

Constructing Residual Plots: Example 10.4

Suppose you wish to produce a plot of residuals similar to Figure 10.5. While in the
REGRESSION dialogue box, simply click the RESIDUAL PLOTS button. This
produces plots of the residuals versus each predictor variable.

Stepwise Regression

Currently, Excel does not provide for stepwise regression.

JMP IN

Fitting Regression Models: Ice Cream Parlor Example

To produce the regression output in Table 10.1, enter the sales data into COLUMN 1, the price data into COLUMN 2, the temperature data into COLUMN 3, the type-of-day data into COLUMN 4, and the relative humidity data into COLUMN 5. Name these columns Sales, Price, Temp, Day, and Humidity, respectively. Set the role of Sales to Y and the roles of Price and Temp to X. Choose ANALYZE–FIT MODEL. In the dialogue box, you will see Sales in the upper right-hand box and Price and Temp in the EFFECTS IN MODEL box. Simply click RUN MODEL. In the MODEL FIT window, click PARAMETER ESTIMATES. Finally, click the check mark popup box, located on the bottom border of the MODEL FIT window, and select SEQ SS (TYPE 1). To determine 95% confidence limits for the regression coefficients, click the PARAMETER ESTIMATES check mark box and select 95% CONFIDENCE LIMITS.

Estimation and Prediction: Ice Cream Parlor Example

Suppose you wish to use the model to estimate the mean of Y and predict the value of Y corresponding to specific values of X_1 and X_2, such as price = 40 and temperature = 75, as in Section 10.4.4. After entering the data as previously described, add three additional rows. Append the price values for which you want predictions (40, 50, 60, 40, 50, 60) to COLUMN 2 and the temperature values for which you want predictions (75, 75, 75, 90, 90, 90) to COLUMN 3. Do not append corresponding salary values to COLUMN 1. Choose ANALYZE–FIT MODEL and complete the MODEL dialogue box as previously described. In the resulting MODEL FIT window, click the $ button at the lower left corner of the window and click SAVE PREDICTED VALUES. Repeat sequentially for SAVE PREDICTION CONFIDENCE, SAVE INDIV CONFIDENCE, SAVE STD ERROR OF PREDICTED, and SAVE STD ERROR OF INDIVIDUAL. This adds the desired values to the data window.

Fitting a Quadratic Model: Example 10.4

To produce outputs similar to those in Table 10.7 and Figure 10.5, enter the manufacturing unit cost data into COLUMN 1, the production rate data into COLUMN 2, and the material/labor cost data into COLUMN 3. Name these columns COST, RATE, and LABOR, respectively. Set the role of COST to Y and the roles of RATE and LABOR to X. You need to create a new column containing the squares of the RATE values. Choose ANALYZE–FIT MODEL; in the MODEL dialogue box, select RATE from the variable list on the upper left. Click the EFFECT MACROS check mark box and select POLYNOMIAL TO DEGREE. Enter 2 in the DEGREE box. Now review the EFFECTS IN MODEL list. You should see RATE, LABOR, and RATE*RATE. (If RATE appears twice, select either RATE and click the REMOVE button.) Now click RUN MODEL. In the MODEL FIT window that results, click PARAMETER ESTIMATES.

Constructing Residual Plots: Example 10.4

Suppose you wish to produce a plot of residuals similar to Figure 10.5. After clicking PARAMETER ESTIMATES in the MODEL FIT window (as just described), click the "$" popup box, located on the bottom border of the MODEL FIT window, and select SAVE RESIDUALS. This places the residuals in a new column of the data window. Set the role of RESIDUAL COST (the new column) to Y; set the role of COST to NONE; and leave the roles of RATE and LABOR as X. Choose ANALYSIS—FIT Y BY X. This produces a residual plot similar to Figure 10.5.

Stepwise Regression: Example 10.5

To produce stepwise regression output like that in Table 10.10, set the role of SALES to Y and the roles of PRICE, TEMP, DAY, and HUMIDITY to X. Choose ANALYZE–FIT MODEL; in the MODEL dialogue box, click the STANDARD LEAST SQUARES button and select STEPWISE. In the MODEL FIT dialogue box, click GO.

JMP IN runs forward selection by default. If you want backward elimination, click the FORWARD check mark box and select BACKWARD; click ENTER ALL; and click GO.

Chapter 11

Goodness-of-Fit Procedures and Contingency Tables

CHAPTER OUTLINE

11.1 BRIDGING TO NEW TOPICS

In this chapter, we introduce two new statistical procedures whose common feature is that they deal with sample data that have been placed in categories. The sample data may be qualitative, such as the type of defect for a manufactured part, the region of the country where a customer resides, and choice of major for a college student. Sample data may also be quantitative. For example, it is common for surveys to request salary information in categories ($20,000–$30,000, $30,000–$50,000, etc.). Consequently, these procedures deal with *proportions;* that is, we wish to reach conclusions about the proportion of items falling into each category. Statistical inferences on categorical data are usually based on a sampling distribution called the **chi-square distribution,** introduced in the next section.

In Section 11.2, we extend the procedure for inferences on a single population proportion (Section 6.4) to inferences involving two or more proportions in a population. For example, we might wish to compare the proportions of customers who were referred by various sources. Based on sample data, can we safely conclude that some sources refer more customers than others? The method used for this purpose is known as a **goodness-of-fit** procedure because it compares the

Table 11.1

Observed and expected numbers of customers

	Manufacturing	Banking	Insurance	Government	Medical	Total
Observed	13	7	8	10	12	50
Expected	10	10	10	10	10	50

distribution of observed outcomes of a random sample with the distribution one would *expect* to observe if the claim of a null hypothesis were correct.

In Section 11.3, we examine the relationship between two variables whose outcomes are placed in categories. For example, suppose an engineer wishes to determine whether there is a relationship between the type of part and the kinds of defect that tend to occur. Perhaps some part types are more prone to a certain defect than are other parts. This method entails an analysis of a *two-way contingency table*. The purpose of analyzing contingency tables is to determine whether the two variables, such as type of part and kind of defect, can be regarded as independent of each other and, therefore, unrelated.

11.2 The Chi-Square Goodness-of-Fit Procedure

Consider the following example in which we compare several proportions. A marketing analyst wishes to determine whether the proportion of industrial customers is evenly distributed over the five major industrial classifications her company deals with. If some industries were found to provide more customers than others, this might influence marketing strategy. For a sample of 50 customers, she determines the industry type of each. The numbers of customers by industry type are as follows:

Manufacturing	Banking	Insurance	Government	Medical	Total
13	7	8	10	12	50

Notice that there were 13 customers from manufacturing compared to only 7 from banking. Does this show conclusively that a higher proportion of customers come from manufacturing, or could a discrepancy this large have occurred simply by chance?

As in most statistical applications, it is advisable to graph the sample data prior to using statistical inference. Since a total of $n = 50$ customers were studied, an even distribution would imply that the proportion of this total for any industry type would be the same as the proportion for each other industry type except for fluctuations due to random sampling. Thus, for a given industry type, we would *expect* to observe 20% of the total number of customers. Using binomial distribution theory (Section 4.2), we determine the expected value of the number of customers for each of the five industry types to be $\mu = n\pi = (50)(.20) = 10$. The observed numbers of customers and the expected numbers of customers (assuming an even distribution) are given in Table 11.1.

We can gain insight by graphing the sample data as in Figure 11.1. Compare the observed and expected numbers of customers for each of the five industry types. Do you believe that the disparities are greater than can be attributed to random sampling variation? Although the numbers for manufacturing and medical are somewhat higher than the expected values and those for banking and insurance are somewhat lower, the disparities do not appear to be appreciable. It seems they could easily have occurred by chance, considering the relatively small sample size of $n = 50$ customers. Thus, it seems plausible that the number of customers for the population studied is evenly distributed over the five industry types. (If the sample size were much larger—say, 500 customers—such equivalent disparities could hardly be attributed to chance and would in all likelihood constitute strong evidence that customers are *not* evenly distributed over the five industry types. This illustrates the need for the inferential methods about to be presented in assessing sample data in addition to graphical analysis.) Notice that, as shown on the right vertical axis of Figure 11.1, we can convert the observed and expected numbers of customers into proportions and plot the proportions, with no changes in the graph.

Figure 11.1

Observed and expected numbers of customers by industry type

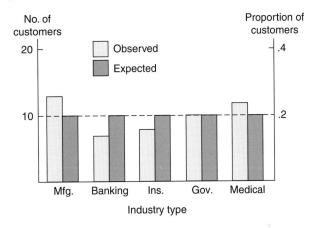

The Goodness-of-Fit Statistic and Its Sampling Distribution

For inference, we need to develop an appropriate statistic. For goodness-of-fit methods, inferences are based on comparisons of observed and expected numbers for each category. Suppose π_1, π_2, π_3, π_4, and π_5 are the population proportions of customers that correspond to the five industry types. An even population distribution means that $\pi_1 = \pi_2 = \pi_3 = \pi_4 = \pi_5 = .2$. Therefore, we may state the null hypothesis as

$$H_0: \quad \pi_1 = \pi_2 = \pi_3 = \pi_4 = \pi_5 = .2$$

against the alternative

$$H_a: \quad \text{At least one } \pi_i \text{ differs from the rest}$$

Now, if the null hypothesis is correct, the expected *number* of customers for each of the five industry types is $(50)(.2) = 10$, since all population proportions are equal to .2 based on the null hypothesis. It is desirable that the statistic have a value of 0 when the observed and expected numbers agree perfectly and a large value when the disparities between them are large. Therefore, a large value of the statistic produces a small *P*-value, indicating that the sample data contradict the null hypothesis.

Now let's develop the best statistic. Let O_i be the observed number of occurrences (customers) for the *i*th category (industry type), and let E_i be the corresponding expected number of occurrences. For k categories (five industry types), the best statistic is given by the expression

$$\sum_{i=1}^{k} \frac{(O_i - E_i)^2}{E_i}$$

(11.1)

Statistical theory shows that, if each expected number of occurrences E_i is at least 5, the sampling distribution of the statistic (11.1) is closely approximated by a chi-square distribution with $k - 1$ degrees of freedom. If any of the expected numbers is less than 5, the use of the chi-square distribution should be avoided. Therefore, assuming each expected number is at least 5, we determine the value of this statistic and use the chi-square distribution with $k - 1$ degrees of freedom to determine the corresponding P-value.

The Chi-Square Distribution

The chi-square distribution is of considerable importance in applied statistics (comparable to that of the T distribution). Like the T distribution, a chi-square distribution is a function of its degrees of freedom. But, unlike the T, the chi-square distribution is skewed to the right and a chi-square random variable can never take on a value less than 0. Theoretically, its range is from 0 to infinity. This range is apparent if we examine Expression (11.1). Since for each category the numerator is a squared quantity and the denominator is the expected number of occurrences (another positive quantity), the value of Expression (11.1) can never be negative; but it can be quite large. The mean of a chi-square distribution is the number of degrees of freedom. The positive skewness of this distribution is illustrated in Figure 11.2. The skewness of a chi-square distribution is considerable when the number of degrees of freedom is small, but it diminishes as the number of degrees of freedom increases.

Figure 11.2

The shape of the chi-square distribution

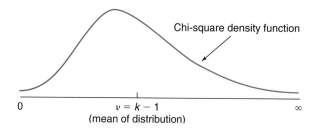

The chi-square distribution is found in most statistical software packages, in addition to being widely tabulated. Table E in the Appendix gives quantile values associated with specific probabilities that represent areas to the left of the given quantile value.

As we did for the Student's T distribution, we can bypass Table E and use Minitab, Excel, or JMP IN to determine chi-square quantile values or chi-square probabilities. Computer instructions are found in the chapter appendix. For example, suppose $\nu = 19$ degrees of freedom and we wish to find the first and 95th percentile values. The desired values are 7.63 and 30.14, respectively; they are illustrated in Figure 11.3.

Symbolically, we may write

$$P(\chi^2_{19} \leq 7.63) = .01$$

Figure 11.3

Illustration of chi-square quantile values for 19 degrees of freedom

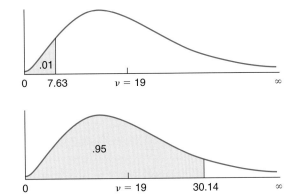

and

$$P(\chi^2_{19} \le 30.14) = .95$$

where the label χ is the lowercase Greek letter chi. It follows from the probability rule for complementary events that

$$P(\chi^2_{19} > 7.63) = .99$$

and

$$P(\chi^2_{19} > 30.14) = .05$$

Alternatively, we may use Table E in the Appendix. The structure of Table E parallels that for the Student's T distribution; that is, we first identify the desired number of degrees of freedom given in the first column of the table, under the heading "ν." Next we choose the desired probability from those that are given as column headings. For the row indicated by the appropriate degrees of freedom and the column for the desired probability, the table gives the corresponding quantile value. For our example with $\nu = 19$ degrees of freedom, the first percentile value is found under the .010 column, and the 95th percentile value is found under the .950 column.

Expression (11.1) requires the following three steps to determine the value of the statistic:

STEPS TO COMPUTE THE VALUE OF THE GOODNESS-OF-FIT STATISTIC (EXPRESSION 11.1)

1. For each of the k categories, square the difference between the observed and expected frequencies $(O_i - E_i)^2$.
2. Divide each squared difference by the expected frequency for that category:

$$\frac{(O_i - E_i)^2}{E_i}$$

3. Sum the k quantities in step 2.

The statistic given by Expression (11.1) is known as **Pearson's chi-square goodness-of-fit statistic.** If there is perfect agreement between the observed and expected frequencies, the statistic has the value 0. The greater the disparities between the observed and expected frequencies, the greater the value of the statistic.

Let's return now to the example at hand. We wish to verify inferentially the preliminary conclusion derived from the graph in Figure 11.1. To do this, we apply the chi-square analysis just described. From Table 11.1, we have

$$n = 50, k = 5; \ O_1 = 13, O_2 = 7, O_3 = 8, O_4 = 10, O_5 = 12; \ E_1 = E_2 = E_3 = E_4 = E_5 = 10$$

The value of the goodness-of-fit statistic is

$$\frac{(13 - 10)^2}{10} + \frac{(7 - 10)^2}{10} + \frac{(8 - 10)^2}{10} + \frac{(10 - 10)^2}{10} + \frac{(12 - 10)^2}{10} = 2.6$$

Since evidence against the null hypothesis is found only in large values of the goodness-of-fit statistic, the value of 2.6 offers no apparent support for contradicting the null hypothesis. Let's confirm this reasoning now by determining the P-value. For $k - 1 = 4$ degrees of freedom, the P-value is the probability of a chi-square value greater than 2.6 (the value determined from the sample); it is determined by computer to be

$$P\text{-value} = P(\chi_4^2 > 2.6) = .6268$$

Since a P-value of .6268 is certainly not small, our tentative conclusion based on the graphical analysis is confirmed: The sample data do not contradict the null hypothesis. Therefore, this sample offers no real support for a marketing strategy that assumes a larger proportion of customers is from manufacturing.

Before we continue, why do you think there are 4 degrees of freedom here? The answer rests on a concept first presented in Section 2.5.3 of Chapter 2. In our example, a total of 50 customers were selected. If we know the number of customers for any four industry types, the number of customers for the remaining industry type is automatically determined to produce the total of 50. Thus, a single degree of freedom is lost, and there are 4 degrees of freedom. In general, therefore, the chi-square distribution for a goodness-of-fit analysis has $k - 1$ degrees of freedom.

The Multinomial Distribution

There is a similarity between the conditions under which the goodness-of-fit procedure is appropriate and those that give rise to the binomial distribution, introduced in Section 4.2. There you learned that a binomial distribution deals with the number of "successes" X that occur out of a fixed number n of trials. Notice that there were $k = 2$ categories of outcomes, "success" and "failure." The necessary condition for the binomial distribution to apply is that the probability π of success on any trial remains constant throughout the set of n independent trials.

The goodness-of-fit procedure is an extension of this idea. Suppose we perform an experiment over n independent trials and classify the outcomes into k distinct categories, where k can be greater than 2. Suppose further that the probability of an outcome falling in the ith category is π_i for $i = 1, 2, \ldots, k$ and that these proportions remain constant throughout the n independent trials. That is, on every trial, π_1 is the probability that the outcome lies in category 1, π_2 is the probability of category 2, etc. This situation is identical to that of the binomial except that there can be more than two possible outcomes on each trial. It gives rise to what is known as a **multinomial distribution.** Thus, the binomial distribution is a special case of the multinomial distribution when $k = 2$.

The probabilities $\pi_1, \pi_2, \ldots, \pi_k$ are the long-run proportions of occurrence for the k categories (applying the relative frequency interpretation of probability), just as π and $1 - \pi$ are the long-run proportions of "successes" and "failures," respectively, in a binomial situation. Suppose $O_1, O_2, \ldots, O_k$ represent the *observed* frequencies of occurrence for the k categories. If the experiment is performed n independent times, the observed frequencies for the categories must sum to n, and the probabilities of the k classes must sum to 1. That is,

$$O_1 + O_2 + \cdots + O_k = n \quad \text{and} \quad \pi_1 + \pi_2 + \cdots + \pi_k = 1 \qquad \textbf{(11.2)}$$

For a binomial experiment, the statements equivalent to Expression (11.2) are

$$X + (n - X) = n \quad \text{and} \quad \pi + (1 - \pi) = 1$$

As discussed previously, if we know the number of observed outcomes for any $k - 1$ categories, we can infer the number of observed outcomes for the remaining category, and thus there are $k - 1$ degrees of freedom. In reality, therefore, the statistic given by Expression (11.1) allows us to test a null hypothesis in which the specified values for $\pi_1, \pi_2, \ldots, \pi_k$ are the parameters of a multinomial distribution.

Using the Computer

EXAMPLE 11.1

The monitoring of market share is a continuous activity for any competitive organization. If an increasing trend in market share can be verified, then an organization has taken positive steps to improve its posture relative to its competitors. On the other hand, if a decreasing trend in market share is apparent, the organization has to act quickly to reestablish its posture relative to its competitors. So keeping a close watch on market share is a very important activity. This example illustrates such a situation with regard to domestic automobile production.

Over the past few years, the market shares for domestic new automobile sales in the United States have been 40%, 35%, and 25% for manufacturers A, B, and C, respectively. A random sample of 200 recent sales of new automobiles revealed the following breakdown:

A	B	C	Total
65	95	40	200

Does this sample information provide convincing evidence that recent market shares have changed from the historical percentages?

Solution

Let π_1, π_2, and π_3 denote the current market shares (proportions) of sales for A, B, and C, respectively. We wish to test the null hypothesis that

$$H_0: \quad \pi_1 = .4, \ \pi_2 = .35, \ \pi_3 = .25$$

against the alternative

$$H_a: \quad \text{Not this arrangement}$$

For $n = 200$, the expected value of the number of sales for manufacturer A (assuming the null hypothesis is true) is $n\pi_1 = (200)(.4) = 80$, whereas those for B and C are $n\pi_2 = (200)(.35) = 70$ and $n\pi_3 = (200)(.25) = 50$, respectively. The observed numbers of sales are $O_1 = 65$, $O_2 = 95$, and $O_3 = 40$, respectively. We compare the observed and expected numbers graphically in Figure 11.4. This figure reveals that the difference between observed and expected values might be appreciable. In particular, it appears as though manufacturer B has gained market share. However, we should not expect the observed proportions to match the expected proportions perfectly because of sampling error. Could these differences have resulted simply by chance, although the underlying process proportions have not actually changed?

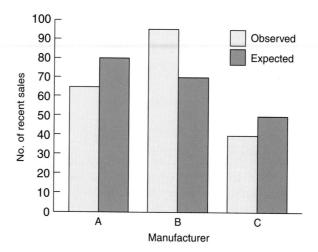

Figure 11.4

A comparison of observed and expected numbers of auto sales

Let's attempt to confirm the initial conclusion by applying Pearson's goodness-of-fit procedure using JMP IN. The output is as follows. Notice that the observed frequencies are given under the column "Count," the historical proportions as indicated by the null hypothesis are found under the column "Hypoth Prob," the value of the goodness-of-fit statistic [Expression (11.1)] is 13.7411 (found under the column "Chi-square" and across the "Pearson" row), and the corresponding P-value is .0010 (found under the column "Prob>Chisq" and across the "Pearson" row). A P-value of .001 provides convincing evidence against the null hypothesis. Therefore, this random sample strongly suggests that the market shares for A, B, and C have indeed changed from their historical values.

Frequencies

Level	Count	Probability	Cum Prob
A	65	0.32500	0.32500
B	95	0.47500	0.80000
C	40	0.20000	1.00000
Total	200		
	3 Levels		

Test Probabilities

Level	Estim Prob	Hypoth Prob
A	0.32500	0.40000
B	0.47500	0.35000
C	0.20000	0.25000

Test	Chi-square	DF	Prob>Chisq
Likelihood Ratio	13.1779	2	0.0014
Pearson	13.7411	2	0.0010

11.3 Analysis of Two-Way Contingency Tables: The Chi-Square Procedure for Independence

It is often of interest to determine whether there is a relationship between two variables whose outcomes are inherently categories, or whose outcomes are placed in categories. We considered such an example in Section 2.7.2 and continued with it in Example 3.3. Table 11.2 (a repeat of Table 2.3) shows a cross-classification of a sample of university students by gender and by school.

Table 11.2

Number of students by gender and by school

	Schools of Business	Schools of Arts & Sciences	Total
Male	130	130	260
Female	70	170	240
Total	200	300	500

As illustrated in Figure 2.16, the proportion of female students in schools of arts and sciences is considerably greater than that in schools of business. Based on this graph as well as on Example 3.3, it appears that gender and the enrollments at these two types of schools are related. The purpose of this section is to present a statistical inference procedure to determine whether two variables such as these are related.

Table 11.2 is an example of what is known as a **two-way contingency table.** Such a table consists of the observed frequencies of occurrence of all combinations of categories of the two variables. Thus, based on the sample data, Table 11.2 contains the observed frequency (enrollment) for each combination of gender and type of school being considered. The analysis of a two-way contingency table addresses the question of whether the two variables are unrelated and thus independent of each other. Consequently, the null hypothesis for analysis of a two-way contingency table is that the two variables are independent. The statistic we develop measures how greatly the observed frequencies differ from the frequencies expected if the variables are independent. If these differences are sufficiently large, the null hypothesis of independence is contradicted. Therefore, the analysis of a contingency table is based on the goodness-of-fit concept.

For our example, we wish to test the null hypothesis

H_0: Type of school enrollments are independent of gender

against the alternative

H_a: Type of school enrollments are not independent of gender

To help you understand the method we are about to present, let's first graph the relative frequencies with regard to enrollments at each of the two types of schools separately for each gender. For example, the relative frequencies for the females are $70/240 = .292$ for schools of business and $170/240 = .708$ for schools of arts and sciences. This graph is given in Figure 11.5.

Figure 11.5

Relative frequencies of enrollments for types of schools by gender

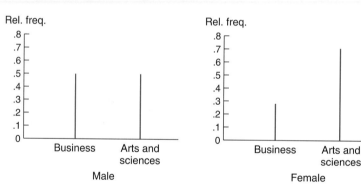

Notice that these proportions do not look the same. If the null hypothesis were true, the proportion of females attending schools of business should be essentially the same as the proportion of females attending schools of arts and sciences because there would be no preference for one school over the other. For this example, it seems fairly clear that this is not the case; thus, the sample data appear to contradict the claim of independence. The contradiction of independence means that preference for schools of business or schools of arts and sciences depends on gender, with a higher proportion of females choosing schools of arts and sciences over schools of business.

Could this difference simply reflect random chance? To address this question, we must develop an inferential method based on an appropriate statistic. But what is an appropriate statistic here? In essence, it is the same as the goodness-of-fit statistic discussed in Section 11.2. Thus, it is based on the disparities between the observed frequencies in Table 11.2 and the corresponding expected frequencies, if enrollments at these two types of schools are independent of gender.

Let's think about what frequencies should be expected here. Notice in Table 11.2 that, for the entire sample of 500 students, the proportions in schools of business and schools of arts and sciences are $200/500 = .4$ and $300/500 = .6$, respectively. If the null hypothesis is true, then the expected enrollment proportions are the same for each gender. To illustrate, for the 260 males in the sample, the expected frequencies are

$$(260)(200/500) = 104 \text{ males in schools of business}$$

$$(260)(300/500) = 156 \text{ males in schools of arts and sciences}$$

For the 240 females in the sample, the expected frequencies are

$$(240)(200/500) = 96 \text{ females in schools of business}$$

$$(240)(300/500) = 144 \text{ females in schools of arts and sciences}$$

Notice the simple pattern that provides the expected frequencies. For each combination, we have simply multiplied the row total (the total number of male or female students) by the column total (the total number of students in each school type), and then divided by the total number of students in the sample. The observed and expected frequencies for the four combinations are given in Table 11.3.

Table 11.3

Observed and expected frequencies for gender by type of school example

		Schools of Business	Schools of Arts & Sciences	Totals
Male	Observed	130	130	260
	Expected	104	156	260
Female	Observed	70	170	240
	Expected	96	144	240
Totals	Observed	200	300	500
	Expected	200	300	500

Let's now extend this procedure and develop a general method for dealing with any two-way contingency table. Assume there are c columns and r rows. Let O_{ij} and E_{ij} be the observed and expected frequencies, respectively, in the ith row and jth column. In Table 11.3, for example, $c = 2$, $r = 2$, $O_{11} = 130$, $E_{11} = 104$, $O_{12} = 130$, $E_{12} = 156$, $O_{21} = 70$, $E_{21} = 96$, and so on.

As we have mentioned, the simple formula for determining any expected frequency for a particular row–column combination is to multiply the row total by the column total and then divide by the overall sample size. In Table 11.3, for example, the expected frequency E_{12} for the first row and second column is found by multiplying the first row total (260) by the second column total (300) and dividing the product by $n = 500$. That is,

$$E_{12} = \frac{(\text{Row 1 total})(\text{Column 2 total})}{\text{Sample size}} = \frac{(260)(300)}{500} = 156$$

In general, therefore, the expected frequency for the ith row and the jth column is determined by

$$E_{ij} = \frac{(\text{Row } i \text{ total})\,(\text{Column } j \text{ total})}{\text{Sample size}}$$ **(11.3)**

Remember, the objective here is the same as for the other goodness-of-fit method of this chapter: to compare the observed and expected frequencies for each combination of categories, and, based on a P-value, to determine whether the differences between them are sufficient to contradict the null hypothesis of independence. The statistic for contingency table analysis is defined to be

$$\Sigma\Sigma\, \frac{(O_{ij} - E_{ij})^2}{E_{ij}}$$ **(11.4)**

where the double summation in Expression (11.4) simply indicates that the quantities $(O_{ij} - E_{ij})^2/E_{ij}$ must be summed over all row–column combinations. After the value of this statistic is determined, we determine the corresponding P-value. If it is sufficiently small, the claim of independence is contradicted.

The statistic given by Expression (11.4) is a random variable whose sampling distribution is adequately approximated by a chi-square distribution with $(r - 1)(c - 1)$ degrees of freedom *under certain conditions*. The necessary condition is that the sample size must be large enough so that each expected frequency is at least 5. For example, notice in Table 11.3 that none of the expected frequencies is less than 5. If one or more of the expected frequencies is less than 5 in a two-way contingency table, the reasonable alternative is to take a larger sample size. If this is not feasible, then two categories may be combined, which in turn combines their expected frequencies.

As we illustrate shortly, the use of a computer is the preferred method of computation. Alternatively, the value of the statistic for our example is determined as follows:

<table>
<tr><td></td><td>1st column</td><td>2nd column</td></tr>
<tr><td>1st row:</td><td>$\dfrac{(130 - 104)^2}{104}$ +</td><td>$\dfrac{(130 - 156)^2}{156}$</td></tr>
<tr><td>2nd row: +</td><td>$\dfrac{(70 - 96)^2}{96}$ +</td><td>$\dfrac{(170 - 144)^2}{144}$</td></tr>
<tr><td></td><td>= 22.569</td><td></td></tr>
</table>

Then for $(2 - 1)(2 - 1) = 1$ degree of freedom, the P-value is $P(\chi_1^2 > 22.569) = .000$. Since the P-value is virtually zero, this sample strongly contradicts the null hypothesis of independence. The inference confirms the conclusion we reached from examining the graphs of Figures 2.16 and 11.5 and Example 3.3.

Using the Computer

We illustrate the use of Minitab and JMP IN for two-way contingency tables with the following examples.

Table 11.4

Two-way contingency table for shareholder opinion versus number of shares held

Shares Held	Opinion			Totals
	Favor	**Oppose**	**Undecided**	
Under 200	38	29	9	76
200–1,000	30	42	7	79
Over 1,000	32	59	4	95
Totals	100	130	20	250

EXAMPLE 11.2

A corporation is evaluating a proposed merger. The board has surveyed a sample of shareholders to determine whether shareholder opinion concerning the proposed merger is related to the number of shares held. The information in Table 11.4 (above) represents a random sample of 250 shareholders. Does this sample information provide convincing evidence that opinion on the proposed merger is not independent of the number of shares held?

Solution

Before we proceed with the computer output, let's first examine Table 11.4. It appears that the proportion of stockholders who oppose the merger increases as the number of shares held increases. For example, 62% of stockholders holding over 1,000 shares oppose the merger, in comparison to only 38% of those holding fewer than 200 shares. If opinion were independent of the number of shares held, the proportion opposed should be about the same for all three shares-held groups. This pattern is illustrated in Figure 11.6. Could the apparent pattern of opinion have resulted by chance? That is, could the observed pattern simply reflect random sampling variation, while opinion and number of shares held are independent phenomena?

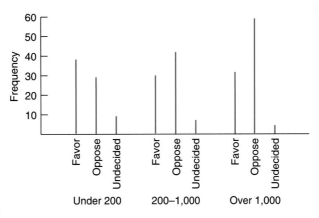

Figure 11.6

Distribution of opinions by number of shares held

Let's state the hypotheses as follows:

H_0:   Opinion is independent of the number of shares held

H_a: Opinion is not independent of the number of shares held

Table 11.5

Minitab and Excel computer outputs for Example 11.2

Minitab

Expected counts are printed below observed counts

	favor	oppose	undecid	Total
1	38	29	9	76
	30.40	39.52	6.08	
2	30	42	7	79
	31.60	41.08	6.32	
3	32	59	4	95
	38.00	49.40	7.60	
Total	100	130	20	250

Chi-Sq = 1.900 + 2.800 + 1.402 +
       0.081 + 0.021 + 0.073 +
       0.947 + 1.866 + 1.705 = 10.796
DF = 4, P-Value = 0.029

Excel

	A	B	C	D	E
1	**Contingency Table**				
2					TOTAL
3		38	29	9	76
4		30	42	7	79
5		32	59	4	95
6	TOTAL	100	130	20	250
7	Test Statistic CHI-Squared = 10.7957				
8	P-Value = 0.029				

The computer outputs for Minitab and Excel are provided in Table 11.5.

Notice that, as in Table 11.3, the Minitab output in Table 11.5 includes the observed and expected frequencies, in that order. The value of the statistic (10.796) is found at the end of the table along with the contribution to this value of each combination of share category and opinion category. The degrees of freedom (df = 4) and the P-value (.029) are given on the last row of the output. The P-value of .029 is small enough to contradict convincingly the claim of independence and confirm our tentative conclusion based on Figure 11.6 that opinion is not independent of the number of shares held. The Excel output in Table 11.5 is briefer. In addition to the observed frequencies, it simply provides the value of the chi-square statistic and the corresponding P-value.

EXAMPLE 11.3

In an experiment, a random sample of 200 students in a statistics course kept track of their total study time for an entire semester. The purpose was to learn about any apparent relationship between study time and grades. Table 11.6 is a contingency

Table 11.6

Two-way contingency table for study time and grade

	Course Grade					
Study Time	**A**	**B**	**C**	**D**	**F**	**Totals**
<20 hr	1	6	15	13	15	50
20–50	3	8	24	15	8	58
50–100	8	10	21	7	2	48
>100 hr	13	14	13	3	1	44
Totals	25	38	73	38	26	200

table that summarizes the results. It includes four categories of study time and five letter grades. Does this sample information provide convincing evidence that grade received is not independent of study time?

Solution

We wish to test the null hypothesis

H_0: Grade is independent of study time

against the alternative

H_a: Grade and study time are not independent

Following the procedure in Example 11.2, we graph the relative frequencies of grades by study time interval, as in Figure 11.7. For this example, it is very clear that the sample data contradict the claim of independence because the distribution of grades look distinctly different in Figure 11.7 for different study time intervals.

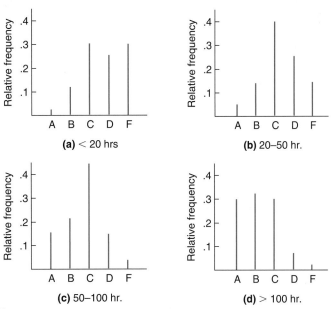

Figure 11.7

Relative frequencies for grades by study time interval

Crosstabs

			Grade				
Count Expected	A	B	C	D	F	
0 - 20	1	6	15	13	15	50
	6.25	9.5	18.25	9.5	6.5	
21 - 50	3	8	24	15	8	58
	7.25	11.02	21.17	11.02	7.54	
51 - 100	8	10	21	7	2	48
	6	9.12	17.52	9.12	6.24	
>100	13	14	13	3	1	44
	5.5	8.36	16.06	8.36	5.72	
	25	38	73	38	26	200

(Study Time — row labels on left)

Tests

Source	DF	-LogLikelihood	RSquare (U)
Model	12	25.72484	0.0931
Error	185	250.50980	
C Total	197	276.23464	
Total Count	200		

Test	ChiSquare	Prob>ChiSq
Likelihood Ratio	51.450	<.0001
Pearson	50.609	<.0001

The JMP IN computer output is given in Table 11.7. This output resembles that of Minitab in Table 11.5. The value of the statistic [Expression (11.4)] is 50.609 (found under the column "ChiSquare" and across the "Pearson" row), and the P-value is less than .0001 (found under the column "Prob>ChiSq" and across the "Pearson" row). The degrees of freedom are given under the column "DF" and across the row "Model"; you should disregard the rest of the output outside the table. Since the P-value is virtually zero, this sample strongly contradicts the null hypothesis of independence, thus confirming the initial conclusion based on Figure 11.7. For the population studied, therefore, the grade received in a statistics course is strongly related to the amount of time spent studying during the term.

11.4 Summary

In this chapter, we introduced two methods for statistical inference involving categorical data. The first is called a goodness-of-fit procedure. The purpose of goodness-of-fit procedures is to determine whether the distribution of sample data, after being classified into a number of distinct categories, conforms to a distribution specified by a null hypothesis. We also introduced graphical approaches that provide insight into this question. We showed that the goodness-of-fit procedure is a generalization of the procedure in Section 6.4 for inferences on a single population proportion. It is based on the multinomial distribution, which is an extension of the binomial distribution. Under certain conditions, the sampling distribution of the goodness-of-fit statistic is adequately approximated by a chi-square distribution.

Second, we introduced a procedure for the analysis of two-way contingency tables. Its purpose is to determine whether two variables whose outcomes are placed in categories can be regarded as independent and thus unrelated. The inferential analysis of two-way contingency tables uses the goodness-of-fit concept by comparing observed frequencies to the corresponding frequencies one would expect to observe if the two variables were indeed independent.

EXERCISES FOR SECTION 11.2

11.1   In the application of Pearson's chi-square procedure, describe how the expected frequencies are determined.

11.2   Suppose there is a relatively large disparity between the observed frequencies and the corresponding expected frequencies.
   (a) Will the value of the chi-square goodness-of-fit statistic be large or small? Explain.
   (b) Will the corresponding P-value be large or small? Explain.

11.3   Describe the condition under which the sampling distribution of the goodness-of-fit statistic would not be approximated adequately by a chi-square distribution.

11.4   Describe the nature of a situation that gives rise to the multinomial distribution.

11.5   Consider a multinomial experiment in which the outcomes are classified into k distinct categories. Explain why there are $k - 1$ degrees of freedom when using the chi-square goodness-of-fit procedure.

11.6   Suppose a die is rolled 300 times with the following results:

Value rolled:	1	2	3	4	5	6
Observed frequency:	45	56	52	46	42	59

   (a) Assuming a balanced die, determine the expected frequencies and compare them graphically to the corresponding observed frequencies. Is it apparent to you that the die is not balanced?
   (b) Does this sample contradict a claim that the die is balanced? Support your answer by applying an appropriate method of statistical inference.

11.7   On Saturdays, a large supermarket has all of its eight regular checkout stands (not counting the express lane) open. On a given Saturday, the manager observes the checkout preferences of 200 customers.
   (a) Do you believe that the chi-square goodness-of-fit procedure is appropriate to determine whether checkout stand preference is evenly distributed? Support your answer.
   (b) Suppose the manager observed the following frequencies. Does this sample contradict the claim of no difference in stand preference? [Proceed here as if your answer to part (a) were "yes."]

Checkout counter:	1	2	3	4	5	6	7	8
Observed frequency:	42	18	38	29	16	22	18	17

11.8   The final grades earned by 100 students in a business statistics class at a university are as indicated in the following table:

Grade:	A	B	C	D	F
Observed frequency:	9	16	48	12	15

   The professor knows that, for this course at this university, the grade distribution over the last 4 years has been stable, yielding the following proportions: 15% A's, 20% B's, 40% C's, 15% D's, and 10% F's.
   (a) Graph the observed and expected frequencies. Is it apparent to you that the grade distribution for this group of students is different for reasons other than random chance?
   (b) Does this sample contradict the claim that the grade distribution for this group is the

same as the historical distribution for this course except for random variation? Support your answer.

11.9 A wine shop manager conducted a survey in which 240 randomly selected customers were asked their taste preferences among six differently priced Chardonnays without their having knowledge of the price. The following information was obtained:

Preferred wine:	A	B	C	D	E	F
Observed frequency:	36	46	42	34	42	40

(a) Assuming no difference in the proportions of customers preferring the six wines, determine the expected frequencies and compare them graphically to the corresponding observed frequencies. Is it apparent to you that differences do, in fact, exist in the proportions?

(b) Does this sample contradict the claim of no differences in the proportions preferring the six wines? Support your answer.

11.10 In the recent past, the market shares for U.S. coffee producers have been as follows:

Brand:	A	B	C	Other
Share:	20%	30%	35%	15%

A current sample of 250 coffee purchases revealed the following proportions preferring each producer's coffee:

Brand:	A	B	C	Other
Number preferring:	75	55	70	50

(a) Assuming the same market shares as in the recent past, determine the expected preferences. Compare them graphically to the corresponding observed preferences. Are differences not attributable to chance variation apparent to you?

(b) Does the current sample contradict a claim that the market shares have not changed? Support your answer.

11.11 The long-term historical distribution of average daily temperature (in degrees Fahrenheit) at a specific location during the month of January is as follows:

Temperature category:	<30	30–39	40–49	≥50
Proportion of days:	10%	45%	37%	8%

For the past 4 Januarys, the following distribution of average daily temperature was observed in this location:

Temperature category:	<30	30–39	40–49	≥50
Number of days:	7	48	56	13

(a) Assuming the historical distribution still holds, determine the expected frequencies and compare them graphically to the corresponding observed frequencies. Are any differences apparent to you that cannot be attributed to random variation?

(b) Based on the last 4 Januarys, is the evidence convincing that there has been a change in the distribution of average temperature for the month of January at this location? Support your answer.

11.12 There are several common methods for controlling a computer cursor. The paper "A Comparison of Three Computer Cursor Control Devices: Pen on Horizontal Tablet, Mouse, and Keyboard" (*Information and Management*, No. 27, 1994, pp. 329–339) reported the result of an experiment comparing the electronic pen to two more familiar methods, a keyboard and a mouse. In the experiment, 63 subjects (university students) performed several cursor-control tasks. After becoming familiar with the use of all three devices, each student was asked which device he or she preferred to use under normal conditions. Their responses are summarized as follows.

Keyboard	Pen	Mouse	Total
21	8	34	63

To what extent do these sample results contradict a claim that the three devices are equally preferred?

11.13 The study "Consumption Imagery in Music Television: A Bicultural Perspective" (*Journal of Advertising*, Vol. XXII, No. 4, 1993, pp. 21–33) reported on the distribution of music videos played in U.S. music television. Based on a sample of program material over 24 hours, the following number of music videos were noted with regard to six music types: classic, dance, metal, new wave, rap, and top 40.

Classic	Dance	Metal	New Wave	Rap	Top 40
40	25	33	35	33	26

(a) Assuming a uniform distribution of music

videos played across music types, determine the expected frequencies and compare them graphically to the corresponding observed data. Is it apparent to you that the distribution is not uniform?

(b) Do these sample data contradict a claim that the distribution is uniform? Support your answer.

11.14 The director of the cooperative education program at Virginia Commonwealth University wished to understand the distribution of academic majors for students in the program. Data* for this exercise consist of the majors for 116 students who were in the program during the Fall 1997 semester. The numbers of students by major are the following:

Major	No. Students
Political Science	7
Accounting	19
Information Systems	42
Computer Science	12
Communication Arts and Design	20
Finance	5
Mass Communications	6
Chemistry	5

(a) Assuming a uniform distribution of students over the eight majors, determine the expected frequencies and compare them graphically to the corresponding observed data. Is it apparent to you that the distribution is not uniform?

(b) Do these sample data contradict a claim that the distribution of academic majors for students in this program is uniform? Support your answer.

---

* Courtesy of Kim Hale.

EXERCISES FOR SECTION 11.3

11.15 The quantities in the following two-way contingency table are expected frequencies. Complete the table of expected frequencies under the assumption of row and column independence.

			Total
40			100
	50		
Total		20	200

11.16 The row and column totals of a two-way contingency table are as follows. Assuming independence, determine the table of expected frequencies.

				Totals
				15
				20
				20
				15
Totals	20	25	10	15	70

11.17 Two hundred randomly selected adults were asked whether TV shows as a whole are primarily entertaining, educational, or a waste of time. (Only one answer could be chosen.) The respondents were categorized by gender. Their responses are given in the following table:

	Opinion		
Gender	Entertaining	Educational	Waste of time
Female	52	28	30
Male	28	12	50

(a) For each gender, graph the indicated opinions. Is it apparent to you that a relationship exists between gender and opinion? If so, describe it.

(b) Is this evidence convincing that there is a relationship between gender and opinion in the population studied? Support your answer with an appropriate statistical inference.

11.18 In a large university, 500 seniors were randomly selected and classified according to their major and their current grade point average. The study resulted in the following information:

	Major			
GPA	Business	Education	Engineering	Science
2.0–2.5	35	10	50	55
2.5–3.0	50	15	60	75
3.0–3.5	50	35	10	15
3.5–4.0	15	15	5	5

(a) For each GPA range, graph the observed numbers of students in the four majors. Is a relationship between GPA and major apparent to you? If so, describe it.

(b) Is this evidence convincing that there is a relationship between GPA and major at this university? Support your answer.

11.19 During a 3-month period, a large automobile retailer observed the sales transacted by the top three salespersons and classified them according to the size of the automobile sold, thereby producing the following cross-classification table:

Salesperson	Size of Automobile			
	Subcompact	Compact	Intermediate	Large
A	15	14	18	13
B	9	16	16	9
C	6	10	16	8

(a) For each salesperson, graph the observed numbers of automobiles sold for the four sizes. Is a relationship between salesperson and automobile size apparent to you? If so, describe it.

(b) Is this evidence convincing that there is a relationship between salesperson and size of automobile? Support your answer.

(c) Describe the population or process to which your inference in part (b) applies.

11.20 A manufacturing plant of automobile parts operates three shifts. Periodically, the plant manager selects random samples of assembled parts and inspects them to affirm that the quality of production is the same for all three shifts. The results of the current sample for a particular part reveal the following breakdown:

Shift	Number of parts	
	Acceptable	Defective
First	95	4
Second	89	12
Third	86	11

(a) For each shift, graph the observed numbers of acceptable and defective parts. Is a relationship apparent to you? If so, describe it.

(b) Do these data provide convincing evidence that the quality of production is not the same for the three shifts? Support your answer with an appropriate statistical inference.

(c) Describe the population or process to which your inference in part (b) applies.

11.21 In Exercises 1.37, 2.57, 6.19, 8.15, and 10.21, you studied several aspects of the visitation process at the Information Age Exhibit of the Smithsonian Institute in Washington, D.C. (see Exercise 1.37 for source). The data for this exercise are the total number of visitors over the observation period by age category for each day of the week; they are on the book's data disk in the file named EX1121.

Management of the Smithsonian is interested in understanding the relationship between the day of the week and the ages of the visitors. Are age and day of the week independent? That is, is the distribution of ages the same for all days of the week (except for random variation)? Or do some age groups tend to visit on weekends and others on weekdays? One might suspect, for example, that persons who have regular jobs might tend to come on weekends, whereas retired visitors and schoolchildren might tend to visit during the week.

(a) For each day of the week, graph the observed number of visitors for the 5 age categories. Based on this graph, is a relationship apparent? If so, describe it.

(b) Do these data contradict a null hypothesis that the age distribution of visitors is independent of the day of the week? Support your answer.

11.22 This exercise refers to Exercises 6.45 and 7.57, in which the Gallup Organization (*The Gallup Poll Monthly*, March 1995) asked a random sample of adults whether they favored President Clinton's proposal to increase the minimum wage. In a sample of 1,010 adults, 732 said they favored the proposal. But it is of interest to understand how this support is distributed over various segments of society. For example, is support for this proposal related to one's level of education? Among 147 in the sample with no college education, 123 supported the proposal. Among 453 in the sample with some college work, 331 supported it. Among 321 college graduates in the sample, 221 supported it. And among 89 in the sample with some postgraduate work, 57 supported it. To what extent do these data contradict a null hypothesis of independence between opinion on this issue and level of education?

11.23 This exercise refers to Exercise 6.46 and 7.58, in which the Gallup Organization (*The Gallup Poll Monthly*, March 1995) asked a sample of 553 responding adults a number of questions about their retirement plans. One interesting result was that 23 of 205 respondents with incomes over $50,000 said they had saved nothing for retirement in the last year. Among the 158 respondents in the $30,000 to $50,000 group, 33 had saved nothing. For the $20,000 to $30,000 group, 37 of the 96 respondents had saved nothing. And 68 of the 94 under $20,000 respondents had saved nothing for retirement. To what extent do these data provide convincing evidence against a claim of independence between income and not having saved?

11.24 Crime has become a major concern in America, especially for teenagers. Eric Donovan, co-director of Teens, Crime, and the Community, which runs violence prevention programs in 40 states, was quoted in the *New York Times* as saying "Crime has become this generation's Vietnam." A 1995 survey by Louis Harris and Associates (*New York Times*, Jan. 17, 1996) asked a random sample of 2,000 teenagers if they considered crime in their neighborhood to be serious. Among the 1,500, 300, and 200 sampled students from public, private, and parochial schools, respectively, 585, 78, and 88 students answered that crime was either serious or somewhat serious in their neighborhoods. All others responded that they did not consider crime in their neighborhood to be serious. Do these results contradict a null hypothesis that teenagers' perceptions about crime are independent of the kind of school they attend? Support your answer.

11.25 The study "Consumption Imagery in Music Television: A Bicultural Perspective" (*Journal of Advertising*, Vol. XXII, No. 4, 1993, pp. 21–33) reported on the distribution of music videos played in U.S. and Swedish music television. Based on similar time samples taken in Sweden and in the United States for a total of 24 hours of program material in each country, the following number of music videos were noted in each country with regard to six music types: classic, dance, metal, new wave, rap, and top 40.

	Classic	Dance	Metal	New Wave	Rap	Top 40
U.S.	40	25	33	35	33	26
Sweden	46	43	19	29	22	49

(a) For each country, graph the observed number of music videos played for the six music types. Is a relationship between country and music type apparent to you? If so, describe it.

(b) Do these data provide convincing evidence against a claim of no relationship between country and music type? Support your answer.

11.26 The paper "Can Information Technology Improve Managerial Problem Finding?" (*Information Management*, No. 27, 1994, pp. 377–390) investigated the use and effectiveness of computerized information and communications support in 90 problem and opportunity finding episodes within the banking industry. The 90 episodes were obtained from bank branch managers in two large banks that used a range of information and communications support tools. Each episode was categorized by the level of information support and the manager's rating of "timeliness." For information support, "none" means no computerized information was used; "low" means the manager used systems that support structured decision making such as MIS; and "high" means the manager used systems that support unstructured decision making, such as decision support systems. For timeliness, the manager judged the timeliness with which a problem was identified (either "far in advance," "just in time," or "late"). The following is a cross-tabulation of the 90 episodes over the three levels of information support and communications support.

	Timeliness			
Information Support	Far in Advance	Just in Time	Late	Total
None	7	8	3	18
Low	28	20	6	54
High	12	6	0	18
Total	47	34	9	90

(a) For each level of information support, graph the timeliness frequencies. Is a relationship apparent between the timeliness of problem finding and the level of information support? If so, describe it.

(b) Test the null hypothesis that information support and timeliness are independent. (*Hint:* If some expected frequencies are less than 5, form new categories by combining some of the existing categories.)

SUPPLEMENTARY EXERCISES

11.27 Based on the records of a boutique, 50% of the dresses bought by the shop for a season will be sold at the full retail price. Twenty-five percent will be sold at 20% off the retail price, 15% will be sold after a 40% price reduction, and the remaining dresses will be sold with a 60% reduction. For the current season, 300 dresses were bought and sold as follows:

Full Price	20% Off	40% Off	60% Off
140	90	30	40

Using both graphical and inferential analyses, determine whether the data indicate that this season's distribution of sales differs from that of past seasons beyond random variation.

11.28 In a large hospital, the observed number of births for each month of a given year is as follows:

Jan.	Feb.	Mar.	Apr.	May	June	July	Aug.	Sept.	Oct.	Nov.	Dec.
105	95	80	75	70	95	110	90	95	110	105	110

Using both graphical and inferential analyses, determine whether the distribution of births over the 12 months of the year is not uniform.

11.29 A manufacturer claims that a process produces 5% defective units. A large buyer randomly selected 100 such units and finds 10 to be defective.

(a) Use the chi-square goodness-of-fit procedure to determine whether there is sufficient reason to contradict the claim.

(b) Use the inferential method discussed in Section 6.4 for testing the null hypothesis that the proportion defective for the process is .05. Compare your answer to your answer in part (a).

(c) Is there any relationship between the values of the statistics obtained in part (a) and part (b)? Explain.

11.30 A traffic safety organization wanted to determine whether the occurrence of fatal automobile accidents is related to the color of the automobiles involved in such accidents. The organization obtained a random sample of 600 automobile accidents in which at least one fatality occurred, and noted the color of the automobile. The following breakdown was determined:

Red	Brown	Yellow	White	Gray	Blue
75	125	70	80	135	115

(a) Use graphical and inferential analyses to determine whether the proportions of accidents involving the six colors differ by more than can be attributed to chance.

(b) Does your analysis in part (a) indicate that autos with some colors are safer to drive than others? (Think carefully; this conclusion is tempting but *might* not be valid.)

11.31 In a medical study spanning 20 years and conducted to determine, among other things, whether smoking habits may influence the development of heart disease, 160 men developed heart disease during this period. These 160 men were classified as heavy smokers, moderate smokers, light smokers, and nonsmokers. The observed number of men in each category is given in the following table:

Heavy Smoker	Moderate Smoker	Light Smoker	Non-smoker
58	54	36	12

(a) Use graphical and inferential analyses to determine whether a claim that the proportions for these categories are the same is contradicted.

(b) Does your analysis in part (a) indicate that the development of heart disease is related to degree of smoking? If not, what information would be needed to address this question?

11.32 In a production process, a random sample of 100 units is taken from each day's production and inspected for defective units. For a given week the following numbers of defective units are observed for the five operating days:

Monday	Tuesday	Wednesday	Thursday	Friday
12	7	6	5	10

Use graphical analysis and statistical inference to determine whether a claim that the process produces equal daily proportions of defectives is contradicted.

11.33 The row and column totals of a two-way contingency table are as follows:

					10
					12
					15
8	14	10	5		37

Under the assumption of independence, determine the table of expected frequencies.

11.34 In Exercise 2.98, a random sample of 135 breakdowns from a stable production process that uses four machines was classified according to machine and the shift in which the breakdown occurred. The data are as follows:

	Machine			
Shift	A	B	C	D
1	10	12	8	14
2	15	8	13	8
3	12	9	14	12

Use a graphical method and statistical inference to determine whether there is a relationship between the shift in which the breakdown occurred and the machine involved. If you detect a relationship, describe it.

11.35 In Exercise 2.103, a random survey of voting citizens was conducted to determine whether there is a relationship between party affiliation and opinion on gun control. The data are given in the following table. Use graphical analysis and statistical inference to assess whether a claim of independence between opinion and party affiliation is contradicted by the data. If the claim is contradicted, describe the apparent relationship.

	Favor	Oppose	Undecided
Democrat	110	64	26
Republican	90	116	14
Independent	55	35	10

11.36 In Exercise 2.105, a random sample of recent college graduates was classified according to two traits: grade point average and SAT score. The data are given in the following table. Use graphical analysis and statistical inference to assess whether a claim of independence between SAT score and grade point average is contradicted. If the claim is contradicted, describe the apparent relationship.

	SAT Score		
GPA	901–1100	1101–1300	1301–1500
> 3.5	50	65	38
3.0–3.5	78	72	42
2.5–3.0	97	80	25
2.0–2.5	105	25	18

11.37 In Exercise 2.97, a random sample of 300 automobile accidents was classified by the size of the automobile and the outcome (whether a fatality had occurred). The data are given in the following table. Use graphical analysis and statistical inference to assess whether a claim of independence between accident outcome and the size of the automobile is contradicted. If the claim is contradicted, describe the apparent relationship.

Outcome	Small	Medium	Large
At least one fatality	42	35	20
No fatality	78	65	60

11.38 A survey was conducted to determine whether consumer preferences for three competing brands—brands A, B, and C—vary by the geographic region of the consumer. The following information was obtained from a random sample of consumers from three distinct regions. Use graphical analysis and statistical inference to assess whether a claim of independence between brand preference and geographic region is contradicted. If it is, describe how consumer preferences depend on the region.

	Region 1	Region 2	Region 3
Brand A	40	52	25
Brand B	52	70	35
Brand C	68	78	60

11.39 Interest in quality of work, life, and productivity has led to the exploration of alternative work schedules. The paper "Flexible Work Schedules, Work Attitudes, and Perceptions of Productivity" (*Public Personnel Management*, Vol. 15, No. 1, Spring 1986) explored the impact of one of the most popular innovations, flextime. With flextime, employees are allowed to depart from a rigidly fixed schedule to better accommodate individual needs. Three agencies in New York State government were chosen for this study. In one agency, a staggered fixed schedule was used in which employees scheduled their arrival anytime between 8:00 and 9:30 A.M.. They could depart 8 hours later. In a second agency, a flextime schedule allowed employees to arrive anytime between 7:00 and 9:00 A.M. and depart anytime between 3:00 and 5:00 P.M. after working a 7½-hour day. Employees could vary their schedules daily. In the third agency, employees worked a fixed schedule—9:00 A.M. to 5:00 P.M. Otherwise, the three agencies were involved in the same aspect of government, were located in the same geographical area, and had similar personnel policies. The samples included 120 employees working the staggered fixed-hours schedule, 135 working a true flextime schedule, and 43 working a fixed schedule. The sampled employees were given a survey that queried them about their attitudes toward their work environment and productivity.

(a) Regarding satisfaction with the workday, the responses are presented in the following table. Do these data provide convincing evidence to contradict a claim that schedule method and attitude toward the work environment are independent? If so, describe the apparent nature of the dependence.

Satisfaction with Work Environment	Flex-time	Staggered Fixed Hours	Standard Fixed Hours
Low satisfaction	15	15	8
Indifference	42	61	20
High satisfaction	78	44	15

(b) Regarding perception of productivity, the following results were observed. Do these data provide convincing evidence to contradict a claim that schedule method and perception of productivity are independent? If so, describe the apparent nature of the dependence.

Productive Work Hours?	Flextime	Staggered Fixed Hours	Standard Fixed Hours
Yes	116	93	29
No	19	27	14

11.40 The paper "Gender and Family Effects on the 'Second Shift' Domestic Activity of College-Educated Young Adults" (*Gender and Society*, Vol. 10, No. 1, Feb. 1996, pp. 78–93) examined gender differences in the extent and type of household activity within a sample of young college-educated adults. The sample consisted of graduates of a northeastern liberal arts college with an upper-middle-class student body. All graduated between 1979 and 1989. The men entering this college are similar to male collegians in general in their attitudes toward gender, but the women are typically more feminist in their values than are undergraduate females nationwide. The respondents were categorized by their family status: single with no children, has a partner or is married with no children, and married with children. They reported whether they had performed a variety of domestic chores, such as washing clothes, preparing dinner, and car maintenance, in the last 48 hours. The data for washing clothes are summarized as follows.

Washed Clothes Last 48 Hours?	Men		
	Single, No Children	Partner/Married, No Children	Married with Children
Yes	114	120	64
No	62	58	66
Total	176	178	130

Washed Clothes Last 48 Hours?	Women		
	Single, No Children	Partner/Married, No Children	Married with Children
Yes	95	126	27
No	39	29	5
Total	134	155	32

(a) Do these data contradict a null hypothesis that, for the population of men studied, washing clothes is independent of family status?

(b) Do these data contradict a null hypothesis that, for the population of women studied, washing clothes is independent of family status?

(c) Summarize what the table and your analyses in parts (a) and (b) tell us about gender differences and family status with respect to washing clothes.

11.41 Refer to Exercise 11.30. That study does not provide enough information to determine whether some automobile colors are safer to drive than others. If color were not a factor, the distribution of accidents with fatalities over the six colors would not necessarily be uniform; it would mirror the distribution of automobile colors in the driving population. The accompanying table is a contingency table showing the proportions of automobiles involved/not involved in fatal accidents in a given year by color for a sample of 20,000 automobiles. Use graphical methods and statistical inference to determine whether a relationship exists between color and fatal accidents.

	Red	Brown	Yellow	White
Accident	16	13	5	18
No accident	3,528	787	682	5,012
Total	3,544	800	687	5,030

	Gray	Blue	Total
Accident	77	18	147
No accident	8,493	1,351	19,853
Total	8,570	1,369	20,000

11.1

Case Study
Analysis of Issues Involving Choice of Manufacturing Process

Manufacturers may choose from job shop, repetitive (batch, line), and continuous processes. The choice has important implications for business and corporate performance. Effectiveness is best when manufacturing processes are congruent with corporate goals and market needs. For example, assembly line (continuous) processes are preferred by most automobile manufacturers, who produce a relatively small number of product types and wish to achieve economies of scale. On the other hand, manufacturers who emphasize flexibility and variety in their products must use a process conducive to frequent new product introductions and rapid changeovers. Elliott Minor* studied the data from a large survey of manufacturers to determine whether their choices of processes were consistent with those generally prescribed by manufacturing strategy literature. The study was initiated out of a suspicion that rapid changes in the competitive environment have outpaced manufacturers' ability to adapt their processes appropriately.

The data were the result of a survey conducted by the National Association of Accountants; they are described by Howell, Brown, Soucy, and Seed.[†] The purpose of the survey was to evaluate management accounting in the face of a changing manufacturing environment. The sample consisted of 61 respondents who identified themselves as using a job shop process only, 92 who used a repetitive process only, and 44 who used a continuous process only. Respondents who said they used more than one process were excluded from the analysis. The relevant questions taken from the survey are provided at the end of this case description.

You are to conduct an exploratory analysis in which the primary interest concerns possible associations between the variables in the study. Specific possible associations of interest include those between process type and (1) volume; (2) number of product types; and (3) make to stock/make to order. In addition, it is of great interest to understand the relationship between the process type and the distribution of manufacturing costs to material, direct labor, and overhead. Conduct appropriate statistical inference procedures to substantiate the existence of the suspected relationships and associations, and provide any conjecture you can about what your findings indicate about the manufacturing environment.

The data for this case are on the data diskette in a file named CASE1101. The data consist of 197 observations (rows), with each row representing a respondent. Each column represents a variable. The variables are c_1 = process type (1: job shop; 2: repetitive; 3: continuous); c_2 = unit volume (1: high; 2: low); c_3 = number of product types (1: many; 2: few); c_4 = make to stock/to order (1: to stock; 2: to order); c_5 = cost allocation percent for material; c_6 = cost allocation percent for direct labor; c_7 = cost allocation percent for overhead.

---

* Minor, E. D., *Manufacturing Process Choice: An Empirical Analysis of Relevant Issues.* Working paper, Virginia Commonwealth University.

† Howell, R. A., J. D. Brown, S. R. Soucy, and A. H. Seed. *Management Accounting in the New Manufacturing Environment.* National Association of Accountants, Montvale, NJ, 1987.

Appendix 11

Computer Instructions for Using MINITAB, EXCEL, and JMP IN

MINITAB

Goodness-of-Fit Procedure

Minitab does not provide a menu choice to perform the one-variable goodness-of-fit procedure. However, it is not difficult to carry out this procedure directly using the CALC function. This approach has the additional benefit of reinforcing your understanding of the logic of these methods.

Consider Example 11.1. To produce a chart like Figure 11.4, enter six category names (such as A-obs, A-exp, B-obs, B-exp, C-obs, and C-exp) into c1, and enter into c2 the observed and expected frequencies for A, followed by the observed and expected frequencies for B, followed by the observed and expected frequencies for C. Choose GRAPH–CHART . . . . In the dialogue box, select SUM under FUNCTION; enter c2 under Y; and enter c1 under X. Then click OK.

To develop output like that for Example 11.1, you will need to enter the data differently. For the three categories, enter the observed frequencies into c3 and the expected frequencies into c4. Choose CALC–CALCULATOR . . . . In the STORE RESULT IN VARIABLE: box, enter c5. In the EXPRESSION: box, type ((c3-c4)**2)/c4; then click OK. This puts the individual terms of Expression (11.1) into c5. To determine the value of the chi-square statistic, you must add the values in c5. To do so, choose CALC–COLUMN STATISTICS . . . . In the dialogue box, click the SUM button (under STATISTIC); enter c5 in the INPUT VARIABLE: box; and click OK. The chi square value will appear in the SESSION window. To obtain the P-value, choose CALC–PROBABILITY DISTRIBUTIONS–CHISQUARE . . . . In the dialogue box, click the CUMULATIVE PROBABILITY button; enter 2 in the DEGREES OF FREEDOM box; click the INPUT CONSTANT button and type 13.74 (the chi-square value); and click OK. The probability (.9990) will appear in the SESSION window. To obtain the P value, subtract this value from 1.

Contingency Tables

Consider Example 11.2. To produce a chart like Figure 11.6 using Minitab, enter all of the contingency table frequencies into cl. (Start with the first row of frequencies, then the second row, then the third row. Do not enter the totals.) Enter corresponding category names in c2. For example, the first category might be named "<200, Favor" or, more briefly, "1,1" (meaning row 1, column 1). Choose GRAPH—CHART . . . . In the dialogue box, select SUM under FUNCTION; specify cl as Y and c2 as X; then click OK.

To produce the output in Table 11.5, enter the observed frequencies for those who are in favor, opposed, and undecided into c3, c4, and c5, respectively. Choose STAT—TABLES—CHISQUARE TEST . . . . In the dialogue box, select c3-c5 in the COLUMNS CONTAINING THE TABLE: box, and click OK.

You can carry out a contingency table analysis starting with raw data as well. Suppose you were starting with the raw sample data for Example 11.2, that is, $n = 250$ observations. Enter the 250 categorical values for shares held into cl, and enter the corresponding 250 categorical values for opinion into c2. All of these categorical values must be coded numerically (i.e., 1, 2, 3). Select SAT—TABLES—CROSS TABULATION. In the dialogue box, select cl c2 for the CLASSIFICATION VARIABLES box; click the buttons for COUNTS (under DISPLAY), CHISQUARE ANALYSIS, and ABOVE AND EXPECTED COUNT (under CHI-SQUARE ANALYSIS).

EXCEL

Excel does not provide a menu choice to perform the one-variable goodness-of-fit procedure. However, it is not difficult to carry out this procedure directly using Excel functions. This approach has the additional benefit of reinforcing your understanding of the logic of this method.

Goodness-of-Fit Procedure

Consider Example 11.1. To produce a chart like Figure 11.4, enter the category names in al:a3, the observed frequencies in bl:b3, and the expected frequencies in cl:c3. Choose INSERT—CHART. For the four steps of the CHART WIZARD: (1) under chart type, select COLUMN; and for the chart subtype, select the upper-left option (CLUSTERED COLUMN); (2) In the DATA RANGE box, enter the cell range containing the data (al:c3); (3) add title and axis labels as desired; (4) specify where you wish to place the chart.

To develop output like that for Example 11.1, enter the three observed frequencies into al:a3 and the three expected frequencies into bl:b3. To determine the P-value for the goodness-of fit procedure, select cell c5 and click the FUNCTION PASTE (f_x) button on the toolbar. In STEP l, select STATISTICAL—CHITEST and click NEXT. In STEP 2, enter al:a3 in the ACTUAL RANGE box; enter bl:b3 in the EXPECTED RANGE box; and click OK. This approach does not provide the value of the chi square statistic. To obtain this value in addition to the P-value, select cell c1 and type: $= (al - bl)^2/bl$. With cell c1 selected, fill down through c3. This places in cl:c3 the three terms of Expression (11.1). Select a4, click the Σ button of the toolbar, and press ENTER. This places into a4 the sum of the observed values in a1:a3. With a4 selected, drag its fill handle through c4. This places into b4 the sum of the expected values in b1:b3 and places into c4 the sum of the values in c1:c3. Thus, c4 contains the value of the chi-square statistic for this example.

Contingency Tables

Consider Example 11.2. To produce a chart like Figure 11.6, enter the first row of observed frequencies in b1:b3; enter the second row of observed frequencies in b5:b7; enter the third row of observed frequencies in b9:b11. (Note that cells b4, b8, and b12 are kept empty to provide desired spacing in the chart.) Enter corresponding category names in a1:a3, a5:a7, and a9:a11. For example, the first category might be named "<200, Favor" or, more briefly, "1,1" (meaning "row 1, column 1"). Choose INSERT–CHART. For the four steps of the CHART WIZARD: (1) under chart type, select COLUMN; and for the chart subtype, select the upper left option (CLUSTERED COLUMN); (2) in the DATA RANGE box, enter the cell range containing the data (a1:b11); (3) add title and axis labels as desired; (4) specify where you wish to place the chart.

To produce the output in Table 11.5, enter the observed frequencies in cells a1:c3 as shown in Table 11.4. Select TOOLS–DATA ANALYSIS PLUS–CHI-SQUARE TEST OF A CONTINGENCY TABLE. In the BLOCK COORDINATES dialogue box, specify the range of cells containing the observed frequencies (a1:c3) and click OK.

You can carry out a contingency table analysis starting with raw data as well. Suppose you were starting with the raw sample data for Example 11.2, that is, $n = 250$ observations. Enter the 250 categorical values for shares held in a1:a250, and enter the corresponding 250 categorical values for opinion in b1:b250. All of these categorical values must be coded numerically (i.e., 1, 2, 3). Select TOOLS–DATA ANALYSIS PLUS–CHI-SQUARE TEST OF A CONTINGENCY TABLE (RAW DATA). In the BLOCK COORDINATES dialogue box, specify the range of cells containing the raw data (a1:b250) and click OK.

JMP IN

Goodness-of-Fit Procedure

Consider Example 11.1. To produce a chart like Figure 11.4, first enter the labels A, B, and C (the categories) in the first three rows of COLUMN 1, and name this column MANUFAC. Set its data type and modeling type to CHARACTER and NOMINAL, respectively, and set its role to X. Enter 65, 95, and 40 (the observed frequencies) in the first three rows of COLUMN 2, and name this column OBSERVED. Enter 80, 70, and 50 (the expected frequencies) in the first three rows of COLUMN 3, and name this column EXPECTED. Set the roles of OBSERVED and EXPECTED to Y. Choose GRAPH–OVERLAY PLOTS. Click the OBSERVED check mark box (below the graph) and select BAR CHART; also click the EXPECTED check mark box and select BAR CHART.

To obtain the JMP IN output given in Example 11.1, set the role of MANUFAC to Y, the role of OBSERVED to FREQ, and the role of EXPECTED to NONE. Choose ANALYZE–DISTRIBUTION OF Y. Click the MANUFAC check mark box (above the graph) and select TEST PROBABILITIES . . . . In the dialogue box, click each of the question marks (?) and enter the expected proportions corresponding to A, B, and C (as specified in the null hypothesis); then click DONE.

Contingency Tables

Consider Example 11.3. To produce a chart like Figure 11.7, enter A, B, C, D, F in the first five rows of COLUMN 1. Name this column GRADE; set its data type to CHARACTER, the modeling type to ORDINAL, and the role to X. Enter the observed frequencies for the <20, 20–50, 50–100, and >100 study hours groups into COLUMN 2, COLUMN 3, COLUMN 4, and COLUMN 5, respectively. Name these columns <20 hrs, 20–50 hrs, 50–100 hrs, and >100 hrs, respectively. Set their roles to Y. Choose GRAPH–BAR/PIE CHARTS. Click the "v" border check mark box and select NEEDLE.

To produce the output given in Table 11.7, you must reenter the data or rearrange the data entered as described above. To reenter the data, enter the 20 observed frequencies (starting in the first row) in COLUMN 1 and enter the corresponding study time and grade categories in COLUMN 2 and COLUMN 3. To rearrange the data, use TABLES–STACK COLUMNS. Name the three new columns COUNT, STUDY TIME, and GRADE, respectively. For COUNT, set the role to FREQ. For STUDY TIME, set the data type to CHARACTER, the modeling type to ORDINAL, and the role to Y. For GRADE, set the data type to CHARACTER, the modeling type to ORDINAL, and the role to X. Choose FIT Y BY X. Click the CROSSTABS check mark box and select EXPECTED.

Chapter 12

Time Series Analysis and Forecasting

CHAPTER OUTLINE

12.1 Bridging to New Topics

You have now completed Chapters 1–11, which may be thought of as the backbone of statistical thinking and methods. This chapter and the chapter that follows, on the other hand, deal with more specialized topics that today can be extremely important. Chapter 12 is intended primarily to provide statistical support for the planning process that takes place in all functional areas of a business.

Planning is a central activity of management. In almost all companies, a great deal of effort goes into manpower planning decisions (e.g., the number of employees required to support various functions), production planning decisions (e.g., the number of units of a given item to produce each month), and a host of others. The appropriate decision usually depends to some degree on variables that are not under the control of management. For example, the number of sales representatives needed for the coming year depends on the future demand for a company's products. The appropriate production level for the next month depends on the number of orders to be received. Before many planning decisions can be made, these uncontrollable variables must be forecasted. Thus, forecasting is an essential element of the planning process.

Forecasting methods may be classified as either judgmental or quantitative. Judgmental forecasts are derived in the mind of a judge or judges. Many quantitative models are statistical in nature. With statistical methods, the forecast is produced by an equation derived from observed data. Most statistical forecasting methods are based on **time series analysis.** Time series data consist of observations taken regularly over time. Some business examples are monthly sales, daily number of invoices processed, weekly requests for service, and quarterly housing starts. Although a time series analysis can involve the simultaneous analysis of several time series, we focus on the more common application involving only one variable at a time. In this chapter, we present several relatively simple time series forecasting methods that are used frequently by forecasters. Interestingly enough, recent forecasting research indicates that the methods presented here are typically at least as accurate as methods that are much more sophisticated mathematically. Furthermore, greater accuracy is achieved by using the average of the forecasts of several simple methods than by using the forecast of a more sophisticated, complex approach. It now appears that in the future the most effective forecasting efforts will derive from the intelligent use of simple methods such as those in this chapter rather than from methods that require great technical expertise.

The crucial assumption underlying time series forecasting is that the future will look like the past. We assume that some underlying pattern exists in historical data. The strategy is to identify the pattern and project it to the future. It follows that time series projection methods are most effective when the environment remains stable. If the environment does not remain stable, the future will not look like the past. Thus, time series projection methods are most effective for short-term forecasting. In business applications, time series methods are commonly used for forecasting horizons ranging to about 2 years.

12.2 Time Series Patterns

We assume that time series data consist of an underlying pattern accompanied by random fluctuations. This may be expressed in the following form:

$$Y_t = \text{Pattern}_t + \epsilon_t \qquad \textbf{(12.1)}$$

| Actual value at t | Mean value at t | Random deviation from mean at t |

where Y_t is the forecast variable at period t, pattern$_t$ is the mean value of the forecast variable at period t and represents the underlying pattern, and ϵ_t is the random fluctuation or deviation from the pattern that occurs for the forecast variable at period t.

12.2.1 Specific Elements of Time Series Patterns

Time series patterns usually consist of a combination of several fairly simple elements; these elements are *trend, cycle,* and *seasonality.*

1. **Trend** is growth or decline in the mean of the forecast variable Y over time. Trend growth may be long-term or transitory. The rate of trend growth usually varies over time.

2. **Cycles** are upward and downward swings of uncertain duration and magnitude. For business time series, cycles are usually related to the economic business cycle. A business cycle is usually greater than 1 year but less than 5 to 7 years, and the magnitude of its peaks and troughs varies.

3. **Seasonality** is a special case of a cycle in which the magnitude and duration of the cycle do not vary but recur in a regular fashion each year. For example, mean sales for a retail store may increase greatly every December for the holidays.

The simplest pattern is a flat pattern in which, in the absence of trend, cycle, and seasonality, the mean of Y remains constant over time. The basic types of pattern, including the flat pattern, are illustrated in Figure 12.1.

Figure 12.1

Elements of time series patterns: (a) flat series, (b) trend pattern, (c) cyclic pattern with no trend, (d) cyclic pattern with trend, (e) seasonal pattern with no trend, and (f) seasonal pattern with trend

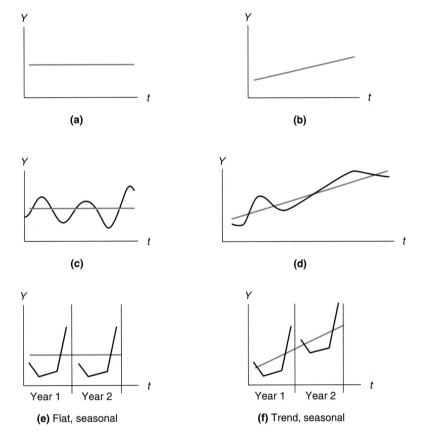

We often use mathematical expressions to characterize these patterns.

1. The equation that represents a flat pattern with no trend is $Y_t = \mu + \epsilon_t$, where μ is the mean of the forecast variable, which is constant over time, and ϵ_t is the random fluctuation at period t.

2. A linear trend pattern may be represented by the equation $Y_t = \beta_0 + \beta_1 t + \epsilon_t$. Notice that this equation is like a simple linear regression model in which the predictor variable t is an indicator of the time period. The rate of trend growth (the slope of the line) is β_1 units per period. The parameter β_0 represents the level of the series at period $t = 0$.

3. Usually, cycles cannot be represented by simple mathematical equations. More complicated methods, such as spectral analysis (not covered here), can fit historical cycles but are not very accurate when projected to the future.

4. Seasonal cycles can be modeled fairly simply. For each period of the year, we develop a *seasonality factor* (SF) that explains by how much Y_t tends to be consistently above or below the mean during that period of the year. For instance, suppose $SF_4 = .90$ represents the seasonality factor for April. This means that April data tend to be 10% lower than average. A model that incorporates seasonality within a flat, no-trend series is $Y_t = (\mu \times SF_t) + \epsilon_t$. Seasonality factors can also be additive, leading to the model $Y_t = \mu + SF_t + \epsilon_t$. The multiplicative form is more common, however, and is the form we deal with in this chapter.

These equations are fairly simple mathematically. The difficulty in forecasting arises from the fact that patterns change. The mean of a no-trend pattern may shift; the rate of trend growth may change; and seasonality factors may shift. Thus, forecasting methods must focus on *current status:* What are the level, rate of trend growth, and seasonal factors *now*? And where within a cycle do we currently stand? The dynamic nature of time series patterns makes their identification difficult, but interesting.

12.2.2 Identifying the Pattern: Classical Decomposition

The purpose of decomposition methods is to break a time series into its component parts: trend, cycle, seasonality, and, of course, randomness. Decomposition methods help us to understand a series and provide a solid basis for forecasting, but they do not themselves provide a forecast.

It is assumed that the time series components interact according to the following multiplicative model:

$$Y_t = T_t \times C_t \times SF_t \times \epsilon_t \tag{12.2}$$

where T_t represents the trend component at period t, and C_t, SF_t, and ϵ_t are factors that respectively represent the effects of cycles, seasonality, and randomness at period t.

Consider a time series that consists of the monthly sales values for several years. Suppose the actual sales value for period 23 is $Y_{23} = 417.9$. This value might eventually be broken down into its component parts as shown in the following box.

In this example, the mean sales at period 23 is 405. However, the effect of the current cycle (.94) is to depress sales by 6%, and the seasonality of the series at period 23 (1.12) boosts sales by 12%. Thus, barring random fluctuation, the expected value of sales for period 23 is $405 \times .94 \times 1.12 = 426.4$. Now, random influences depress sales by 2% in this period, thus providing the actual sales value of $426.4 \times .98 = 417.9$. The components in Expression (12.2) can also be expressed as additive terms, but this is less common and is not considered here.

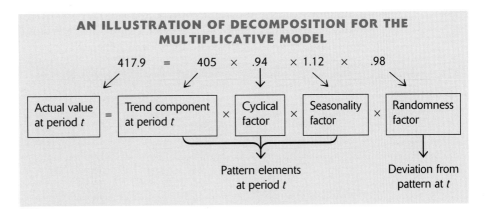

It is important for you to realize that seasonality factors represent deviations that can be explained by the time of year. Overall, they must offset each other; thus, the average of the seasonality factors for a year must equal 1.0.

The goal of decomposition is to identify the components T_t, C_t, SF_t, and ϵ_t for all periods of a series. Several decomposition methods are currently popular. We present **classical decomposition,** which is the oldest and simplest method but still appears to perform about as well as the others. This method is based on the concept of a *moving average.*

Moving Averages

If a series has a flat pattern with a stable mean, the best estimate of the mean is provided by $\bar{Y}$, the mean of the entire time series sample. However, if the mean shifts or if there is trend, then the value of $\bar{Y}$ adjusts too slowly to the current level. This problem is illustrated in Figure 12.2, in which the term *forecast* is abbreviated FC.

Figure 12.2

An illustration of the slow adjustment of the overall mean to a change in level

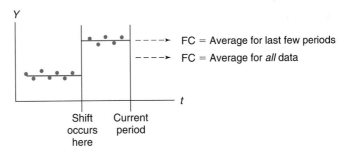

To ensure that the predicted mean reflects the current mean value of the series, we may compute the mean of only the most recent n data values, instead of using all the historical data. Thus, if $n = 3$, then only the most recent three data values are used to estimate the current mean value of the series. This is called a *moving average* because the specific data values used change as new data become available. The process is illustrated graphically in Figure 12.2 for a flat pattern with a shift in level. It is also demonstrated for a data set with trend in Table 12.1, where M_t represents the moving average value at time period t. The moving average of Table 12.1 is called a **centered moving average** because M_t is placed in the middle period of the average computation. Thus, $M_5 = 20.67$ is the average for periods 4, 5, and 6. Centering is necessary to ensure that the moving average does not systematically lag behind the real mean value when trend is present. Figure 12.3 illustrates the smoothing effect of a centered moving average for the data in Table 12.1.

Table 12.1

A centered moving average with $n = 3$

t	Y_t	M_t ($n = 3$)
1	10	—
2	16	12.67
3	12	15.33
4	18	18.00
5	24	20.67
6	20	25.33
7	32	28.33
8	33	—

Figure 12.3

Excel graph illustrating the smoothing effect of a centered moving average

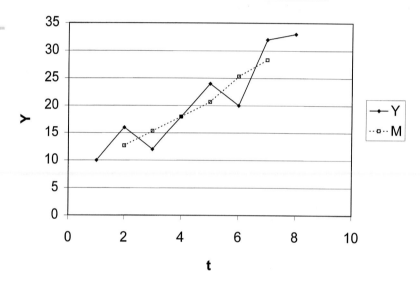

Classical Decomposition Methodology

In classical decomposition, the trend and cycle components of a time series are combined into a single component called the **trend-cycle.** This is done because no effective statistical method has been developed to distinguish between a cycle and a trend whose growth rate can shift over time. The key difference is that a cycle eventually returns to the long-term trend pattern, whereas a shifting trend may never return to a former rate of growth. The trend-cycle in a given period represents the level of the series after seasonal and random influences have been removed. What follows is a step-by-step description of how this is achieved by the method of classical decomposition. In following these steps, you may wish to refer to the example of classical decomposition provided in Table 12.3.

Step 1: Estimate the Trend-Cycle

To estimate the trend-cycle (TC), we compute a moving average in which n is the number of periods in a year. Thus, for monthly data we use $n = 12$, and for quarterly data we use $n = 4$. Now, if a moving average is to represent the trend-cycle, it must be free of both seasonal and random variation in the data. A moving average with $n =$ the number of periods in a year eliminates seasonality and randomness in the following way:

1. *Removal of seasonal effects.* Since n is the number of periods in a year, each moving average calculation uses one data value from each period of the year. Thus, each moving average computation is affected equally by all seasonal influences.

2. *Removal of randomness.* Each data value used in a moving average contributes a random influence. Some are positive and some are negative. The positive and negative random influences tend to cancel each other in the averaging process. Although the resulting moving average is not completely free of random influences (because the positive and negative random influences do not balance perfectly in a sample), much of the randomness is removed.

Consider the quarterly data in Table 12.2, which exhibit a perfect linear trend with no randomness. The moving average computation for $n = 4$ is shown in the third column. Notice that, unfortunately, the moving average cannot be centered because the number of quarters in a year is an even number. (The midpoint would be at "period 2.5," but there is no such period.) Since we have placed the moving average M_t one-half period later than desired, it lags behind the actual trend. We compensate for this lag by computing a *double moving average,* a moving average of the original moving average. The second moving average uses the most recent two values of the first moving average, so it is referred to as a $2 \times n$ *moving average* and is labeled as M'_t. The $2 \times n$ moving average is placed so that it is centered as shown in the fourth column of Table 12.2.

Table 12.2

Example of a moving average and a double moving average when trend is present

t	Y_t	M_t ($n = 4$)	M'_t (2×4)
1	10	—	—
2	20	—	—
3	30	25	30
4	40	35	40
5	50	45	50
6	60	55	60
7	70	65	—
8	80	—	—

Let's take a closer look at the $2 \times n$ moving average. Suppose we have quarterly data, so that $n = 4$. Then the first moving average M_3 (placed at period 3) is an average of the first four data values, and the second moving average M_4 is the average of data values 2 through 5:

$$M_3 = \frac{Y_1 + Y_2 + Y_3 + Y_4}{4} \quad \text{and} \quad M_4 = \frac{Y_2 + Y_3 + Y_4 + Y_5}{4}$$

The first computation for the 2×4 moving average (also placed at period 3) is

$$M_3' = \frac{M_3 + M_4}{2}$$

$$= \frac{1}{2}\left(\frac{Y_1 + Y_2 + Y_3 + Y_4}{4} + \frac{Y_2 + Y_3 + Y_4 + Y_5}{4}\right)$$

Combining terms, we see that M_3' is a weighted average of the first five data values; that is,

$$M_3' = \frac{1}{8}Y_1 + \frac{1}{4}Y_2 + \frac{1}{4}Y_3 + \frac{1}{4}Y_4 + \frac{1}{8}Y_5 \qquad (12.3)$$

An example of classical decomposition with real data is given in Table 12.3; it is produced using Excel (see the chapter appendix for instructions). Let's use it to confirm this result. We have

$$M_3' = \frac{1}{8}(288) + \frac{1}{4}(374) + \frac{1}{4}(528) + \frac{1}{4}(689) + \frac{1}{8}(1,134) = 575.5$$

which is also the average of $M_3 = 469.75$ and $M_4 = 681.25$, shown in the table.

Table 12.3

An example of classical decomposition using Excel

	A	B	C	D	E	F	G	H
1					Prelim	Final		
2		Original		T-C	y	Seasonality	Randomness	
3		Data	n=4 MA	2x4 MA	Factors	Factors*	Component	Deseasonalized
4	t	Y	M	M'	Y/M'	SF	e	Y'
5	1	288				1.188		242
6	2	374				1.207		310
7	3	528	469.75	575.50	0.917	0.754	1.217	700
8	4	689	681.25	819.75	0.841	0.851	0.988	810
9	5	1134	958.25	1004.25	1.129	1.188	0.950	954
10	6	1482	1050.25	1156.00	1.282	1.207	1.062	1228
11	7	896	1261.75	1426.00	0.628	0.754	0.833	1188
12	8	1535	1590.25	1700.00	0.903	0.851	1.062	1805
13	9	2448	1809.75	1873.75	1.306	1.188	1.100	2060
14	10	2360	1937.75	1978.75	1.193	1.207	0.988	1955
15	11	1408	2019.75			0.754		1867
16	12	1863				0.851		2190
17								
18		* The numbers in this column are developed in the following table.						
19								
20					Quarter			
21				First	Second	Third	Fourth	Total
22		Preliminary				0.917	0.841	
23		Seasonality		1.129	1.282	0.628	0.903	
24		Factors		1.306	1.193			
25		Unadjusted final factors		1.218	1.237	0.773	0.872	4.100
26		Final seasonality factors		1.188	1.207	0.754	0.851	4

For example, consider the final second-quarter seasonality factor, 1.207. We first obtained the tentative factor by averaging $[1.237 = \frac{1}{2}(1.282 + 1.193)]$. This number is then adjusted by multiplying by $4.000/4.100$ to obtain the final factor, 1.207.

M_3' is centered at period 3 because it is an average of Y_t values for periods 1 through 5. Notice that greater weight is placed on the three periods in the center, which seems reasonable. Now our trend-cycle estimate is an average of five data values. But are the seasonal effects still balanced? The answer is yes. In Expression (12.3), notice that first-quarter observations appear twice (Y_1 and Y_5), whereas those of the other quarters appear only once. (Since we are dealing with quarterly data, observations Y_1 and Y_5 both represent the first quarter.) But the first quarter data values are given only half the weight assigned to the others. Therefore, the total weight given to each of the four quarters is $\frac{1}{4}$, thus maintaining the seasonality balance.

Step 2: Compute Preliminary Seasonality Factors

Seasonality factors are estimated by dividing each observation by the corresponding trend-cycle estimate M_t'. This computation provides a preliminary estimate of the seasonality factor for each period and is expressed as follows:

$$\text{Preliminary seasonality (estimate)} = \frac{Y_t}{M_t'} = \frac{TC_t \times SF_t \times \epsilon_t}{TC_t} = SF_t \times \epsilon_t$$

(12.4)

For example, consider the classical decomposition shown in Table 12.3. The first preliminary estimate of third-quarter seasonality is $528/575.5 = .917$. Since 528 is below the estimated trend-cycle, we have an early indication that the third-quarter seasonality effect is to depress the data. But this is an unreliable conclusion because the low value could have been caused by randomness. In general, dividing Y_t by M_t' removes the trend-cycle component of Y_t but leaves intact both the seasonality and randomness factors. Therefore, the preliminary seasonal estimates Y_t/M_t' are imprecise because randomness has not been removed.

Step 3: Estimate Final Seasonality Factors

Tentative final seasonality factors are now obtained by averaging the preliminary seasonality factors over all periods that represent the same season. In Table 12.3, for example, a tentative final seasonality factor for the third quarter is obtained by averaging the preliminary seasonality factors for all third-quarter data (periods 3 and 7)—that is, $(.917 + .628)/2 = .773$. Finally, the tentative final factors are adjusted to ensure that they conform to the stipulation that seasonality factors must average to 1.0. This means that they must sum to 4.0 for quarterly data and to 12.0 for monthly data. The tentative seasonal factors obtained in Table 12.3 sum to 4.100. Thus, they are multiplied by the adjustment factor $4.000/4.100 = .9756$ to obtain the final seasonality factors. The final seasonality factors, denoted SF_t, sum to 4.000 as desired. In general, the adjustment factor is

$$\text{Adjustment factor} = \frac{\text{Number of periods in a year}}{\text{Sum of tentative final seasonality factors}}$$

(12.5)

Figure 12.4 is an Excel-generated graph that shows an overlay of the original data and the trend-cycle for the data in Table 12.3. In addition to providing an example of

Figure 12.4

Excel overlay of original data and trend-cycle for data in Table 12.3

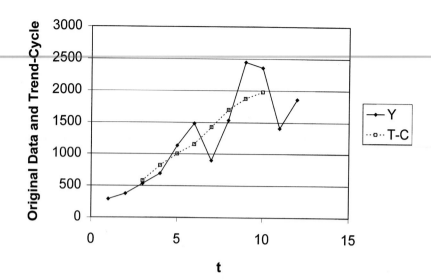

classical decomposition, Table 12.3 shows the development of seasonally adjusted data, described in the next subsection.

Seasonally Adjusted Data

The classical decomposition technique we have presented does not itself provide a forecast. Typically, we obtain forecasts by first removing seasonality from the data (with classical decomposition) and then forecasting the resulting *seasonally adjusted* data with another method such as exponential smoothing (introduced in Section 12.3). Removing seasonality is often called *deseasonalizing* the data. Seasonally adjusted data are determined by dividing the original value by the corresponding final seasonality factors. Let Y'_t be a seasonally adjusted value and let e_t be a randomness component estimate; then

$$Y'_t = \frac{Y_t}{SF_t} = \frac{TC_t \times SF_t \times e_t}{SF_t} = TC_t \times e_t \qquad \textbf{(12.6)}$$

As indicated in Expression (12.6), seasonally adjusted data consist of only the trend-cycle and randomness components. The seasonal component has been removed.

Once a forecast of seasonally adjusted data has been obtained, it is reseasonalized by multiplying by the appropriate seasonality factors. In the example in Table 12.3, suppose the forecast of the seasonally adjusted data for period 13 (the first quarter of the fourth year) were 2,500. Then the forecast of the actual result for this period is $F_{13} = 1.188(2,500) = 2,970$, where 1.188 is the seasonality factor for the first quarter of each year.

12.3 Forecasting with Exponential Smoothing

In this section, we assume that the time series to be forecasted is either nonseasonal or has been deseasonalized. We introduce two versions of a forecasting method called exponential smoothing. **Simple exponential smoothing** is designed for flat, no-trend patterns in which the mean is unstable (that is, it might shift over time). **Linear exponential smoothing** is designed to forecast series with a linear trend in which the rate of growth or decline is unstable—that is, series that grow linearly at a given rate for some time, but for which at any point the rate of growth might change. When either the mean or the slope is unstable, it becomes important to know what their values are currently for the purpose of forecasting.

12.3.1 Simple Exponential Smoothing

Exponential smoothing is based on the same premise as moving averages: If a pattern is unstable, pattern estimates should be based on recent data. The more recent a data value, the more indicative it is of the current pattern. But instead of averaging the most recent n data values and thereby giving them equal influence, we calculate a *weighted average* in which the weight given each data value is proportional to how recent it is. The term *smoothing* refers to the smoothing out of random fluctuations that occur when we compute an average. *Exponential* refers to the type of expression by which the weights are determined.

The Simple Exponential Smoothing Updating Equation

For simple exponential smoothing, the weighted average at period t is given by the equation

$$A_t = wY_t + (1 - w)A_{t-1} \qquad \textbf{(12.7)}$$

where A_t represents the weighted average computed at period t. Expression (12.7) indicates that the current weighted average A_t can be expressed as a weighted average of the current observation Y_t and the previous average A_{t-1}, which was determined in period $t - 1$. The weight given the most recent observation is denoted by w and can be given any value between 0 and 1. The nearer w is to 1, the greater the emphasis placed on the current observation and the less the emphasis placed on the previous weighted average.

Let F_{t+m} represent a forecast made at period t of the value of Y for m periods in the future. For example, if $m = 2$, then F_{t+2} is a forecast of the value of Y for two periods beyond period t. Since we assume a flat pattern when we choose simple exponential smoothing, the forecast (for $m = 1, 2, 3, \ldots$) is

$$F_{t+m} = A_t \qquad \textbf{(12.8)}$$

Exponential smoothing computations based on Expressions (12.7) and (12.8) can be carried out by using either Excel or Minitab (but not JMP IN), as described in Appendix 12. Here is an example. Suppose we wish to forecast demand for each of the next four months using simple exponential smoothing with $w = .5$. We have monthly demand data for the past 10 months. The forecast is developed in Table 12.4 using Excel.

1. *Calculating A_t.* Notice that Expression (12.7) is recursive; that is, each value depends on the preceding value. Therefore, we must find a value of A_1 to get started. It is customary to set A_1 either to the first data value (Y_1) or to the average of the first few data values. In this example, we have chosen $A_1 = Y_1 = 19$.

Then $A_2 = .5(25) + (1 - .5)(19.0) = 22.0$; $A_3 = .5(17) + (1 - .5)(22.0) = 19.5$; and so on.

2. *Calculating F_t.* The one-step-ahead forecast for any period equals the smoothed average from the previous period. Thus, $F_2 = A_1 = 19.0$; $F_3 = A_2 = 22.0$; and so on.

3. *Calculating forecast error.* The error of the one-step-ahead forecast in period t is $e_t = Y_t - F_t$. There is no error for period 1 because there is no forecast. We have $e_2 = 25 - 19.0 = 6.0$; $e_3 = 17 - 22.0 = -5.0$; and so on.

As we did with the regression models of Chapters 9 and 10, we can also characterize the performance of models in this context by the mean square for error (MSE) criterion. Here we determine the MSE based on the one-period-ahead forecasting errors over the historical data using the expression

$$MSE = \frac{\Sigma e_i^2}{k}$$

(12.9)

where k is the number of one-period-ahead forecasts. Thus, for the data in Table 12.4, the mean square for error works out to be MSE = 78.13.

Table 12.4

An example of simple exponential smoothing

	A	B	C	D	E	F	G	H
1	t	Y	A	F	e = Y - F	e-sq		
2	1	19	19					
3	2	25	22.00	19.00	6.00	36.00		
4	3	17	19.50	22.00	-5.00	25.00		
5	4	22	20.75	19.50	2.50	6.25		
6	5	32	26.38	20.75	11.25	126.56		
7	6	41	33.69	26.38	14.63	213.89		
8	7	49	41.34	33.69	15.31	234.47		
9	8	40	40.67	41.34	-1.34	1.81		
10	9	48	44.34	40.67	7.33	53.70		
11	10	42	43.17	44.34	-2.34	5.46		
12	11			43.17		703.14	MSE =	703.14 / 9
13	12			43.17			=	78.13
14	13			43.17				
15	14			43.17				

Figure 12.5 is an Excel graph showing the original data Y_t, and the forecast F_t. Notice that the forecast is always flat for simple exponential smoothing (based on the assumption of a flat pattern).

The Error Correction Formulation of Simple Exponential Smoothing

By rearranging the terms in the simple exponential smoothing expression, we obtain further insight into the method of exponential smoothing. Since $F_{t+1} = A_t$, we can rewrite Expression (12.8) as follows:

$$F_{t+1} = wY_t + (1 - w)F_t$$

Figure 12.5

An Excel graph of the data and forecast in Table 12.4

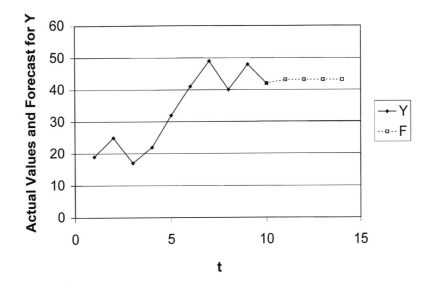

or

$$F_{t+1} = wY_t + F_t - wF_t$$

By factoring the weight w, we can reduce this expression to

$$F_{t+1} = F_t + w(Y_t - F_t) = F_t + we_t \qquad \textbf{(12.10)}$$

where $e_t = Y_t - F_t$ is the forecasting error that occurred in period t (that is, the difference between the actual value in period t and the forecast for period t that was made one period earlier). Expression (12.10) shows that the forecast for the next period is obtained by adjusting the current forecast to correct for the current forecasting error. For this reason, exponential smoothing is called an *adaptive* forecasting method.

Expression (12.10) can be used for updating as well. For example, we can update the forecasts in Table 12.4 using Expression (12.10) with $w = .5$ as follows:

$$F_3 = F_2 + .5(e_2) = 19.0 + .5(6.0) = 22.0$$
$$F_4 = F_3 + .5(e_3) = 22.0 + .5(-5.0) = 19.5$$

Choosing the Value of w

The error-adjustment formulation given by Expression (12.10) provides insight into the choice of w. The larger w is, the more responsive the model is to forecasting errors. Forecasting errors are caused by (1) shifts in the mean and (2) random fluctuation in the data. If the major concern is an unstable mean, then a responsive model is desired. This suggests that a large value of w be chosen. But if the data are very "noisy," with much random fluctuation, then a model that is less responsive to forecasting errors is desirable. That is, we want more smoothing, which is achieved by choosing a smaller value of w. In a given situation, the choice of w involves a tradeoff between our desire to respond to shifts in the mean and our need to smooth random fluctuations. If a great deal of randomness is present, w should be small; if little randomness is present, w should be large. Traditionally, the value of w has usually been selected from the range .05 to .3. However, recent studies indicate that higher values are often warranted.

A common practice is to choose the value of w for which the error mean square for one-step-ahead forecasts is minimized. The calculation of the MSE was illustrated in the demand forecasting example of Table 12.4. In that example, notice the large shift in the mean that seems to have occurred in periods 5 and 6. This suggests that a fairly large w is best for this series. In fact, if $w = .1$ were considered, the mean square for error would be 235.12, whereas for $w = .5$ the mean square for error was 78.13. Clearly, $w = .1$ caused the model to respond too slowly to the shift that occurred in the mean. By trying many values of w, we can discover the value that appears to minimize the MSE.

Simple Exponential Smoothing As a Weighted Average of Historical Data

Part of the beauty of simple exponential smoothing is its simplicity. Given a new data value, a new average can be found by making a simple adjustment to the previous average. However, it is probably not obvious to you that Expressions (12.7) and (12.10) provide a weighted average of all historical data, as claimed earlier. To demonstrate this property, consider simple exponential smoothing with $w = .4$. Expression (12.7) then reduces to

$$A_t = .4Y_t + .6A_{t-1} \qquad\qquad \textbf{(12.11)}$$

This expression applies at any period. By applying it at period $t-1$, we can express A_{t-1} as a weighted average of Y_{t-1} and the previous average A_{t-2}; that is,

$$A_{t-1} = .4Y_{t-1} + .6A_{t-2} \qquad\qquad \textbf{(12.12)}$$

Substituting the right-hand side of Expression (12.12) for A_{t-1} in Expression (12.11), we have

$$A_t = .4Y_t + .6(.4Y_{t-1} + .6A_{t-2}) = .4Y_t + .4(.6)Y_{t-1} + .6^2A_{t-2}$$

Now, repeating the process by substituting this time for A_{t-2}, we have

$$A_t = .4Y_t + .4(.6)Y_{t-1} + .6^2(.4Y_{t-2} + .6A_{t-3})$$
$$= .4Y_t + .4(.6)Y_{t-1} + .4(.6^2)Y_{t-2} + .6^3A_{t-3}$$

Notice what is happening. The weight on the most recent data value Y_t is .4. The weight on Y_{t-1} is $.4(.6) = .24$. The weight on Y_{t-2} is $.4(.6^2) = .144$. If we continued this process, we would see that the weight for Y_{t-3} is $.4(.6^3)$, the weight for Y_{t-4} is $.4(.6^4)$, and so on. Thus, the weight given to a data value for period $t-k$ is $.4(.6^k)$, for $k = 0, 1, 2, \ldots$. It follows that, in general, the weight given to a data value for period $t-k$ is

$$\text{Weight}_{t-k} = w(1-w)^k \qquad\qquad \textbf{(12.13)}$$

Since the weight for each successively older data value is $w(1-w)^k$, the weights decrease as the exponent k (the "age" of a data value) increases. This property is the basis for the name "exponential" smoothing. It can be shown mathematically that the weights sum to 1, as is necessary for a weighted average, as long as w is between 0 and 1.

Table 12.5

Weights applied to recent data for various *w*-values

Period	Age of Observation	Weight for Observations				
		w = .05	*w* = .1	*w* = .3	*w* = .5	
t	0	.05	.1	.3	.5	
t − 1	1	.048	.09	.21	.25	
t − 2	2	.045	.081	.147	.125	
t − 3	3	.043	.073	.103	.063	
t − 4	4	.041	.066	.072	.031	
t − 5	5	.039	.059	.050	.016	
Beyond *t* − 5	>5	.734	.531	.118	.015	⇒ (This is the *sum* of the weights given to data values older than period *t* − 5.)

Table 12.5 shows the weights placed on the six most recent observations, and Figure 12.6 depicts these weights graphically for several values of *w*. Notice that the *total* weight given to older data (say, those more than five periods old) becomes much greater as *w* becomes smaller. This is consistent with our previous comment about the choice for *w*. When we want more smoothing of random fluctuations rather than responsiveness to a shift in the mean, we choose *w* to be small. Thus, the weights of preceding observations decrease slowly and older observations have almost as much weight as recent observations. But when *w* is large and responsiveness to shifts in the mean is desired, the weights of the most recent observations account for most of the total weight.

12.3.2 Forecasting Trends: Holt's Linear Exponential Smoothing

If a time series contains trend, simple exponential smoothing is unsuitable because its forecasts consistently lag behind the true level of the series. (Exercises 12.8 and 12.9 illustrate this phenomenon.) If the trend is positive, simple exponential smoothing forecasts are usually too low; if the trend is negative, its forecasts are usually too high. Holt's method corrects the problem by estimating at each period both the current level of the series and the current rate of trend growth or decline. Its forecasts are achieved by projecting the estimated trend, using the estimated current level as a takeoff point. The level at a given period is the value the series would take on if it were not for randomness.

Holt's method applies simple exponential smoothing separately to both the level and the rate of trend growth. Since the level and the trend are smoothed separately, we need not use the same smoothing constant for both. We use the symbol *w* to represent the constant for smoothing the level and the symbol *v* to represent the constant for smoothing the trend.

We present now the general updating expressions for Holt's method. First, notice that the general concept of simple exponential smoothing can be expressed as

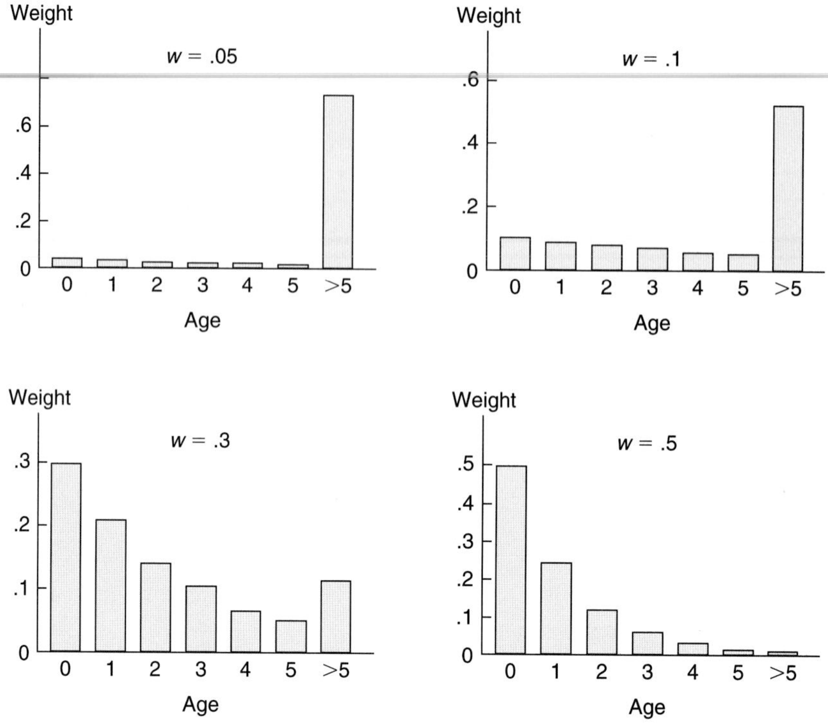

Figure 12.6

A graphical depiction
of weights vs. age
of data for several
values of w

$$\text{Smoothed average} \atop \text{computed at } t = \text{Weight} \times \left\{ {\text{New observation} \atop \text{at } t} \right\} + (1 - \text{Weight}) \times \left\{ {\text{Forecast for } t \atop \text{computed at } t - 1} \right\}$$

That is, at period $t-1$, the estimated level for period t is simply our forecast for period t. The actual result at period t then provides additional information about the level at period t. With this new information, we update the estimated level by forming a weighted average of the current actual result and the previously forecasted level. Now let's see how this concept applies to Holt's method. Let A_{t-1} represent the estimated level of the series at period $t-1$, and let B_{t-1} represent the estimated rate of trend growth at period $t-1$. Then at period $t-1$, the forecasted level for period t is $A_{t-1} + B_{t-1}$ (i.e., the level at period $t-1$ plus one period's growth). The current observation Y_t provides additional information about the level at period t. The new estimated level at period t is a weighted average of the new observation at period t and the level for period t previously forecasted from period $t-1$:

$$A_t = wY_t \quad + \quad (1-w)\underbrace{(A_{t-1} + B_{t-1})} \qquad \textbf{(12.14)}$$

$\underbrace{}$

New observation   Forecasted mean level at t
of mean level   computed at $t-1$

Now consider how simple exponential smoothing is used to update the estimated trend. The estimated rate of trend growth at period $t-1$ is B_{t-1}. At period t, we get new information about trend. This new observation of trend growth is the change in level from period $t-1$ to t—that is, $A_t - A_{t-1}$. Therefore, the updated smoothed estimate of the rate of trend growth is a weighted average of the new observation of trend $(A_t - A_{t-1})$ and the previous estimate of trend B_{t-1}, where v represents the weight assigned to the new observation of trend:

$$B_t = \underbrace{v(A_t - A_{t-1})}_{\substack{\text{New observation of} \\ \text{trend growth}}} + \underbrace{(1-v)(B_{t-1})}_{\substack{\text{Previous estimate of trend} \\ \text{growth computed at } t-1}} \qquad (12.15)$$

The forecasts must project trend growth over the lead time of the forecast. Thus, the forecast one period ahead is the current level A_t plus one period's trend growth B_t. The forecast for two periods ahead is $A_t + 2B_t$; for three periods ahead, $A_t + 3B_t$; and so forth. The forecast m periods ahead is given by

$$F_{t+m} = A_t + mB_t \qquad (12.16)$$

Table 12.6 provides an example of Holt's method. The computations can be carried out by using Excel or Minitab, as described in Appendix 12. This example continues the forecasting problem of Section 12.2 presented in Table 12.3. In that example, we applied classical decomposition and ultimately developed seasonally adjusted data. Now we construct a forecast of the deseasonalized data with Holt's method using $w = .5$ and $v = .4$ (chosen arbitrarily). The deseasonalized data are shown in the column labeled Y. Since the equations are recursive, we require a way of getting started. It is common to fit the equation $Y = \beta_0 + \beta_1 t$ using the forecast variable as the response variable and a time index $(t = 1, 2, \ldots)$ as the predictor variable. We may use only the early data—say, the first year's data—for this purpose, or we may use all the data. The initial value A_1 is $b_0 + b_1$ (the estimated intercept plus one period's growth); the initial value B_1 is simply b_1, the estimated slope. In Table 12.6, all the data were used to obtain the regression equation $\hat{Y} = 71.45 + 185.28\,t$. Thus, the initial values are $A_1 = 71.45 + 185.28 = 256.73$ and $B_1 = 185.28$. Figure 12.7 shows an overlay of the original data and forecast values for the data in Table 12.6.

Table 12.6

An example of forecasting with Holt's Linear Exponential Smoothing, developed with Excel

	A	B	C	D	E	F	G	H	I
	t	Y	A	B	F	e = Y - F	e-sq		
1	1	242	256.73	185.28					
2	2	310	376.00	158.87	442.01	-132.01	17425.85		
3	3	700	617.44	191.90	534.88	165.12	27265.17		
4	4	810	809.67	192.03	809.34	0.66	0.44		
5	5	954	977.85	182.49	1001.70	-47.70	2275.35		
6	6	1228	1194.17	196.02	1160.34	67.66	4577.65		
7	7	1188	1289.10	155.58	1390.19	-202.19	40882.36		
8	8	1805	1624.84	227.65	1444.68	360.32	129829.65		
9	9	2060	1956.24	269.15	1852.49	207.51	43060.98		
10	10	1955	2090.20	215.07	2225.39	-270.39	73113.24		
11	11	1867	2086.13	127.42	2305.27	-438.27	192079.43		
12	12	2190	2201.78	122.71	2213.55	-23.55	554.70		
13	13				2324.48		531,064.80	MSE =	519,056.13 / 11
14	14				2447.19			=	48,278.62
15	15				2569.90				
16	16				2692.60				

Figure 12.7

Excel graph of
deseasonalized data
and forecast in
Table 12.6

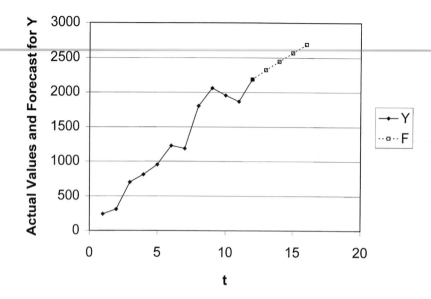

12.4 Forecasting with Regression Models

Regression models can be very useful in forecasting. Sometimes regression analysis is used to develop a model of long-term linear trend, much like Holt's model except that the rate of trend growth is considered to be constant over time. More commonly, causal models are developed that show the relationship between the forecast variable Y_t and several predictor variables. These applications are presented in the next two subsections.

12.4.1 Regression Models for Long-Term Trend

When regression analysis is used to estimate long-term trends, the predictor variable is a time index denoted by X. To represent periods $1, 2, \ldots, t$, we define $X = 1, 2, \ldots, t$. We then develop a least squares regression equation of the form

$$\hat{Y} = b_0 + b_1 X \tag{12.17}$$

For example, consider the following data, which represent per capita final sales (national totals, expressed in terms of 1982 dollars to account for inflation) annually from 1958 through 1989.

Year	X	Sales	Year	X	Sales
1958	1	8,375	1974	17	12,215
1959	2	8,632	1975	18	12,120
1960	3	8,654	1976	19	12,581
1961	4	8,746	1977	20	13,056
1962	5	9,052	1978	21	13,681
1963	6	9,317	1979	22	13,998

Year	X	Sales	Year	X	Sales
1964	7	9,664	1980	23	13,902
1965	8	10,092	1981	24	13,968
1966	9	10,471	1982	25	13,742
1967	10	10,710	1983	26	14,002
1968	12	11,104	1984	27	14,551
1969	12	11,258	1985	28	15,137
1970	13	11,179	1986	29	15,426
1971	14	11,382	1987	30	15,773
1972	15	11,898	1988	31	16,309
1973	16	12,412	1989	32	16,665

The least squares trend line for these data is

$$\hat{Y} = 7,954.75 + 256.67X \qquad \textbf{(12.18)}$$

A forecast of per capita sales can be obtained by extending the trend line. The forecast for 1990 is achieved by substituting $X = 33$ into Expression (12.18) to obtain

$$\hat{Y} = 7,954.75 + 256.67(33) = 16,424.86$$

A Warning About Forecasting with Long-Term Trend Lines

Using regression methods to develop a long-term trend line is usually not a good idea. In many applications, there is no constant, long-term linear trend. For example, company sales may grow at different rates at different times. In many instances, it may be more reasonable to believe that the current rate of growth will continue than to expect a resumption of an overall long-term trend line. If this is the case, then Holt's linear exponential smoothing model is preferred because it emphasizes recent data to estimate the current trend line. The regression line given by Expression (12.18), in contrast, places equal weight on all data, both recent and old. Figure 12.8 illustrates this issue. Notice that a change in the trend occurred about one-third of the way through the time series, with the rate of trend growth declining significantly at this time. A forecast of long-term linear trend based on Expression (12.18) is likely to be too high if the current lower rate continues.

Figure 12.8

A comparison of forecasts based on projections of long-term linear trend versus current linear trend

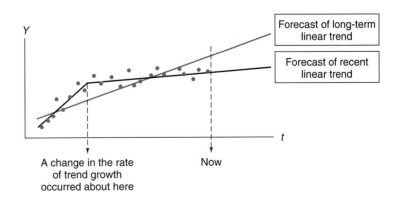

12.4.2 Causal Models

Regression analysis can also be used to develop *causal* forecasting models. A **causal model** is one in which the behavior of the forecast variable Y is explained to some degree by one or more predictor variables. For example, the number of new telephone installations in a geographic region depends to a great extent on the number of housing starts in that region. It makes sense therefore to base a forecast of new telephone installations on a forecast of the number of new housing starts.

Suppose that a regional telephone company has developed the following least squares regression equation based on annual data for the last 18 years:

$$\hat{Y} = 11.44 + 3.2X \qquad\qquad \textbf{(12.19)}$$

where Y is the number of new telephone installations in a year for a given region and X is the number of housing starts in a year for that region. Suppose the forecast of the number of new housing starts (X) for next year is 1,115. Then the forecasted number of new telephone installations is obtained by substituting $X = 1,115$ into Expression (12.19), yielding the value $\hat{Y} = 3,579.44$.

The use of a regression model requires a forecast of the predictor variable(s). This may be accomplished in various ways. One possibility is to use time series methods such as exponential smoothing. Forecasts of a wide range of economic indicators (such as the number of new housing starts) can also be obtained for a fee from econometric forecasting firms. Or the predictor variables can be forecasted judgmentally. The "judges" may be managers within an organization or outside experts.

A distinct advantage of regression models is that they provide a logical basis for forecasting under alternative future scenarios. Thus, a regression model can be used to answer "what-if" questions posed by management. In the telephone installations example, suppose management desires a forecast of telephone installations corresponding to a pessimistic forecast of $X = 800$ housing starts, a "best bet" forecast of $X = 1,115$ housing starts, and an optimistic forecast of $X = 1,500$ housing starts. By substituting these values into Expression (12.19), we obtain the following three forecasts corresponding to possible alternative futures:

$$X = 800 \text{ (pessimistic forecast):} \quad \hat{Y} = 11.44 + 3.2(800) \ \ = 2,571$$
$$X = 1,115 \text{ (best bet forecast):} \quad \hat{Y} = 11.44 + 3.2(1,115) = 3,579$$
$$X = 1,500 \text{ (optimistic forecast):} \quad \hat{Y} = 11.44 + 3.2(1,500) = 4,811$$

Such "what-if" forecasts provide a basis for contingency planning.

Using the Computer

In virtually any application of regression analysis to a forecasting situation, the computer is extremely helpful in determining the least squares equation, evaluating it, and using it to make the desired forecast. The following example illustrates such a situation.

EXAMPLE 12.1

Consider using a regression model to forecast per capita sales (the example used in Section 12.4.1 to illustrate the development of long-term trend models). The predictor variable is per capita disposable personal income, expressed in 1982 dollars to account for inflation. The data for per capita sales and per capita disposable personal income are listed here. Use the computer to determine the appropriateness of a linear model for the relationship between per capita sales and per capita disposable personal income, and forecast the former when the latter is predicted to be $12,000.

Year	Per Capita Sales	Per Capita Disposable Personal Income	Year	Per Capita Sales	Per Capita Disposable Personal Income
1958	8,375	5,641	1974	12,215	8,502
1959	8,632	5,769	1975	12,120	8,613
1960	8,654	5,771	1976	12,581	8,851
1961	8,746	5,831	1977	13,056	9,139
1962	9,052	5,983	1978	13,681	9,435
1963	9,317	6,096	1979	13,998	9,656
1964	9,664	6,439	1980	13,902	9,602
1965	10,092	6,745	1981	13,968	9,760
1966	10,471	7,006	1982	13,742	9,732
1967	10,710	7,213	1983	14,002	9,930
1968	11,104	7,412	1984	14,551	10,419
1969	11,258	7,522	1985	15,137	10,625
1970	11,179	7,744	1986	15,426	10,905
1971	11,382	7,947	1987	15,773	10,970
1972	11,898	8,211	1988	16,309	11,337
1973	12,412	8,692	1989	16,665	11,680

Solution

For this analysis, the abbreviations PCSALES and PCDPI were used to represent per capita sales and per capita disposable personal income, respectively. The Minitab output is given in Table 12.7. Based on the P-values for the T and F statistics (both are .000), there is a strong linear relationship between per capita sales and per capita disposable income. The least squares line is $\hat{Y} = 1,069.7 + 1.32195X$. If the forecast is $X = \$12,000$, the forecasted value of Y is $\hat{Y} = 1,069.7 + 1.32195(12,000) = \$16,933.1$.

Table 12.7

Minitab output for Example 12.1

```
The regression equation is
PCSALES = 1070 + 1.32 PCDPI

Predictor        Coef        Stdev      t-ratio           p
Constant        1069.7       140.9         7.59       0.000
PCDPI          1.32195     0.01638        80.68       0.000

s = 166.9    R-sq = 99.5%    R-sq(adj) = 99.5%

Analysis of Variance

SOURCE          DF            SS            MS           F          p
Regression       1      181373632     181373632     6509.88      0.000
Error           30        835839         27861
Total           31     182209472
```

Notice that the data for both Y and X in Example 12.1 were time series (32 years of annual data). In forecasting applications, time series data are often used in developing a regression model. The use of time series data for regression analysis introduces two issues of particular concern in forecasting applications: (1) the presence of seasonality and (2) nonindependent residuals. The first issue is discussed in the following subsection; the second issue is beyond the scope of this book.

12.4.3 Incorporating Seasonality in Regression Models

Seasonal variation in the predictor variable(s) or the response variable must be taken into account; otherwise, a genuine relationship may be masked because, as we saw in Chapter 9, a regression model will treat it as random error. One way to deal with seasonal effects is to use dummy variables in the same manner as in Section 10.5. For quarterly data, the four seasonal effects can be represented by the following three dummy variables:

$$D_2 = \begin{cases} 1 & \text{if the period is second quarter} \\ 0 & \text{otherwise} \end{cases}$$

$$D_3 = \begin{cases} 1 & \text{if the period is third quarter} \\ 0 & \text{otherwise} \end{cases}$$

$$D_4 = \begin{cases} 1 & \text{if the period is fourth quarter} \\ 0 & \text{otherwise} \end{cases}$$

The first quarter is the "default" quarter, for which D_2, D_3, and D_4 all equal 0.

Suppose a manufacturer of lawn mowers developed the following least squares equation for forecasting quarterly sales:

$$\hat{Y} = 145.3 + 1.75X + 35.1D_2 + 11.6D_3 - 21.5D_4$$

This model indicates that sales are growing at an average rate of 1.75 units per quarter, except for the effects of seasonality. The interpretation of the coefficients of D_2, D_3, and D_4 is the same as for any dummy variable. Consider the second quarter. Since $b_2 = 35.1$, aside from the effects of trend and randomness, sales, on average, tend to be 35.1 units higher in the second quarter than in the first quarter. Similarly, third-quarter sales tend to be 11.6 units higher, and fourth-quarter sales tend to be 21.5 units lower than in the first quarter, apart from the effects of randomness and trend growth. To forecast, we simply substitute into the least squares equation the desired values of X, D_2, D_3, and D_4, as we did in Chapter 10.

The Choice of Regression Models Versus Time Series Models

Given the choice, which kind of statistical model is better, a time series model such as exponential smoothing or a regression model? Many studies indicate that time series models forecast as accurately as regression models for short lead times. As a result, time series models are usually preferred for short-term forecasting because they require fewer resources (time, computer, data). On the other hand, regression models are generally more accurate for long-range forecasting. At what lead time do regression models become more accurate? There is no absolute answer to this question, but we offer some rough guidelines for monthly series such as company (or product) sales. Time series models are generally preferred for forecasting horizons up to about 2 years. Regression models are generally superior for forecasting horizons longer than about 3 years. Between 2 and 3 years, you are on your own!

12.5   Summary

In this chapter, we discussed statistical forecasting methods. These methods are based on time series analysis, where time series data consist of observations taken regularly over time.

Certain basic patterns are usually found in time series data: trend, cycle, and seasonality. Trend is growth or decline over time. Cycles are upward and downward swings of uncertain duration and magnitude. Seasonality is movement that recurs in a regular fashion each year. Decomposition methods provide an understanding of these patterns, but they do not provide a forecast. The forecasts are made based on time series models (such as exponential smoothing) or regression models.

EXERCISES FOR SECTION 12.2

12.1   Describe the purpose of classical decomposition.

12.2   What are the components of a time series, according to the classical decomposition model?

12.3   For the following quarterly series, use classical decomposition:

Quarter	Data	Quarter	Data
1	15	7	15
2	11	8	9
3	15	9	13
4	13	10	9
5	14	11	14
6	10	12	8

(a) Determine the final seasonality factors.
(b) Describe the seasonality pattern verbally.
(c) Deseasonalize the original data.

12.4   Why is it important to compute a double moving average to estimate the trend-cycle? That is, why is a single moving average not adequate?

12.5   Explain why the seasonal and randomness components are eliminated by the computation of a moving average with $n =$ the number of periods in a year.

12.6   Suppose the seasonality factor for January sales, estimated with classical decomposition, is 1.25. The forecast for January seasonally adjusted sales is 750 units. What is the corresponding forecast of actual January sales?

12.7   A moving average allows us to concentrate on recent data. Consider two possible choices of n: $n = 3$ and $n = 10$. What are the characteristics of a time series for which $n = 3$ is the better choice? (*Hint:* What pattern component would be dominant for this series?) On the other hand, what are the characteristics of a time series for which $n = 10$ is the better choice?

EXERCISES FOR SECTION 12.3

12.8   Given here are nonseasonal data for periods 1–5. Use simple exponential smoothing with $w = .2$ to forecast for periods 6 and 7. Then repeat the process, using $w = .7$.

Period	Data
1	10
2	25
3	35

Period	Data
4	40
5	55

12.9   Consider the work you did in Exercise 12.8.
(a) Determine the error mean square for one-step-ahead forecasts, with $w = .2$ and $w = .7$.
(b) Why is the error mean square smaller when $w = .7$? Explain.

(c) Do you see any evidence to suggest that neither of these models is adequate for forecasting this series? If so, explain. (See first sentence of Section 12.3.2.)

(d) For simple exponential smoothing with $w = .2$, determine the weights placed on the data for periods 5, 4, 3, 2, and 1 in computing A_5.

12.10 The following are deseasonalized monthly data:

Period	Data
1	20
2	50
3	10
4	70
5	20
6	40

(a) Construct a forecast for periods 7 and 8, using simple exponential smoothing with $w = .2$. Repeat the process with $w = .7$.

(b) Determine the error mean square for one-step-ahead forecasts, with $w = .2$ and $w = .7$.

(c) Why is the error mean square smaller when $w = .2$? Explain.

(d) Forecast the actual result for periods 7 and 8, assuming their seasonality factors are .75 and 1.10, respectively.

12.11 Suppose you are forecasting with simple exponential smoothing, $w = .15$. The forecast for the current month, made last month, is 150. The actual value for this month turns out to be 40 units lower. Use the error formulation to determine the new forecast for next month.

12.12 Consider the choice of w. Describe the characteristics of a time series for which $w = .2$ would be preferred to $w = .6$. Now describe how a time series for which $w = .6$ is better differs from one for which $w = .2$ is better.

12.13 One way to choose w is to find the value that minimizes the mean square for error. What are the merits of this approach compared to choosing w subjectively? Are there any situations in which using MSE as the choice criterion might be unwise?

12.14 Suppose you are forecasting with simple exponential smoothing, $w = .3$. The forecast for the current month, made one month ago, is 220. The actual value this month turns out to be 227. Update the model and compute a new forecast for next month.

12.15 Consider the data of Exercise 12.8.

(a) Forecast periods 6 and 7, using Holt's method with $w = .2$ and $v = .1$. Use the traditional method of initialization: $A_1 = Y_1$ and $B_1 = 0$.

(b) Compute the error mean square in part (a).

(c) How does this error mean square compare to that of simple exponential smoothing with $w = .2$, from Exercise 12.8?

(d) Now repeat part (a), using as initial factors $A_1 = 10$ and $B_1 = 12.5$.

(e) Compute MSE for part (d). Why is this MSE lower than that reached in part (b)?

(f) If MSE is the criterion for choosing a model, is the method of initialization important?

12.16 Consider the data of Exercise 12.10.

(a) Forecast with Holt's method, $w = .2$, $v = .1$.

(b) Compute the error mean square for part (a).

(c) Compare the error mean square in part (b) to the error mean square for simple exponential smoothing with $w = .2$, found in Exercise 12.10. Based solely on this comparison of mean squares for error, which model is preferable?

12.17 When would it be advisable to utilize a larger value of v in Holt's method? That is, for what pattern characteristics would $v = .3$ be preferred to $v = .1$?

12.18 A key determinant in many business and economic considerations is future energy consumption. The following data represent annual energy consumption in the United States over 1970–1989, measured in millions of tons of oil equivalent (*Source: Energy Ergonomics,* Jan. 1995).

Year	1970	1971	1972	1973	1974
Energy	1,218	1,243	1,315	1,332	1,289

Year	1975	1976	1977	1978	1979
Energy	1,245	1,318	1,366	1,382	1,388

Year	1980	1981	1982	1983	1984
Energy	1,319	1,297	1,231	1,218	1,288

Year	1985	1986	1987	1988	1989
Energy	1,277	1,278	1,324	1,382	1,393

(a) Construct a run chart of annual U.S. energy consumption. Describe any patterns that you see.

(b) Determine a forecast of annual U.S. energy consumption for 1990–1995 using simple exponential smoothing.

(c) Determine a forecast of annual U.S. energy consumption for 1990–1995 using Holt's linear exponential smoothing.

(d) Evaluate your forecasting models in parts (b) and (c). In which forecast do you have more confidence? What concerns do you have about these models, if any?

EXERCISES FOR SECTION 12.4

12.19 The following regression model has been developed: $\hat{Y} = 2.2 + .77X$.
   (a) If X is forecasted to equal 77, 80, and 85 in the next three periods, forecast Y for those periods.
   (b) Typically, with what kinds of methods might X be forecast?

12.20 What special considerations arise when using regression models based on time series data?

12.21 Consider the forecasting of a variable Y with a regression model relating Y to a time index.
   (a) How is this approach similar to forecasting Y with Holt's linear exponential smoothing model?
   (b) How is this approach different from forecasting Y with Holt's linear exponential smoothing model?
   (c) What is the danger of forecasting Y with a regression model that relates Y to a time index?
   (d) Does the danger mentioned in part (c) apply to Holt's linear exponential smoothing model? Explain.

12.22 Consider the following quarterly data:

Period	Y	X	Period	Y	X
1	121	10	7	144	21
2	92	14	8	114	25
3	135	12	9	138	30
4	104	16	10	106	28
5	128	15	11	155	32
6	99	18	12	125	36

   (a) Fit a linear regression model of Y versus X. Based on the P-value, determine whether a discernible relationship seems to exist.
   (b) Refit the regression model, including dummy variables to incorporate quarterly seasonality. Compare the P-value for a test of this overall model to the P-value in part (a). What does your answer suggest about the importance of incorporating seasonality in regression models?
   (c) Interpret the coefficients of the dummy variables for the regression model in part (b).

12.23 Discuss the relative advantages of time series methods versus causal regression methods for forecasting, and the conditions under which each method would be typically preferred.

12.24 Forecasting future earnings of a corporation is an essential component of evaluating its future stock price. The following data are Exxon Corporation's quarterly earnings per share (*Source: Wall Street Journal*) for 1989–1995. Since one might expect earnings to vary with sales, Exxon's sales (in millions) over this period are also included.

Year	Qtr.	EPS	Sales
1989	1	.99	20,115
1989	2	.80	19,928
1989	3	.87	21,473
1989	4	.99	25,140
1990	1	1.01	24,457
1990	2	.87	23,444
1990	3	.85	23,432
1990	4	1.23	34,186
1991	1	1.78	26,383
1991	2	.90	24,251
1991	3	.88	24,238
1991	4	.89	27,975
1992	1	1.07	24,475
1992	2	.76	24,547
1992	3	.90	27,452
1992	4	1.12	26,686
1993	1	.94	24,504
1993	2	.98	24,702
1993	3	1.09	24,455
1993	4	1.20	25,843
1994	1	.87	23,223
1994	2	.70	24,463
1994	3	.92	26,373
1994	4	1.19	27,400
1995	1	1.33	26,709
1995	2	1.30	28,429
1995	3	1.20	27,417
1995	4	1.28	27,065

   (a) Develop a regression model of the relationship between Exxon's earnings per share and its sales. Consider the possible need for dummy variables to explain seasonal variation in the data. Do the data provide convincing evidence that quarterly sales is useful in predicting quarterly earnings per share?
   (b) Use your regression model to forecast Exxon's quarterly earnings per share for 1996 if sales turn out to be $28,000 million for each quarter.

12.25 The winning discus throws (in feet) for the gold medal for men in the modern Olympic Games as reported in the *1998 Sports Almanac* are as follows:

Year	X^*	Distance	Year	X^*	Distance
1896	1	95.63	1952	15	180.50
1900	2	118.25	1956	16	184.92
1904	3	128.88	1960	17	194.17
1908	4	134.17	1964	18	200.08
1912	5	148.25	1968	19	212.50
1920	7	146.58	1972	20	211.25
1924	8	151.33	1976	21	221.42
1928	9	155.25	1980	22	218.67
1932	10	162.33	1984	23	218.50
1936	11	165.58	1988	24	225.75
1948	14	173.17	1992	25	213.67
			1996	26	227.67

*Each unit is equivalent to 4 years.

(a) Fit and evaluate a simple linear regression model to the winning distances (Y) versus year (X).
(b) Fit a quadratic model to the winning distances (Y) versus year (X). Evaluate the marginal contribution of the quadratic term.
(c) Based on the least squares equation in part (b), forecast the winning distance in the Olympic Games of 2004. Do you believe that your forecast is likely to be achieved? Explain.
(d) Use Holt's method $(w = .5, v = .3)$ to forecast the winning distance in the Olympic Games

of 2004. Do you have more confidence in this forecast or that of part (c)? Explain.

12.26 In the study "Working Less and Living Longer: Long-Term Trends in Working Time and Time Budgets" (*Technological Forecasting and Social Change*, Vol. 50, No. 3, Nov. 1995, pp. 195–213), the following data were reported on the hours worked in the United States per person per year for nine different years from 1870 to 1987.

Year	X^*	Hours Worked
1870	1	2,964
1890	2	2,789
1913	3.15	2,605
1929	3.95	2,342
1938	4.40	2,062
1950	5	1,867
1960	5.5	1,795
1973	6.15	1,717
1987	6.85	1,608

*Each unit of X is equivalent to 20 years.

(a) Fit a simple linear regression model of hours worked (Y) versus year (X). Does the straight-line relationship seem sufficient? Explain.
(b) Show how you might be able to improve the model.

SUPPLEMENTARY EXERCISES

12.27 The elements of time series patterns dealt with by the methods of this chapter are trend, cycle, seasonality, and randomness. Considering classical decomposition, simple exponential smoothing, and Holt's linear exponential smoothing, which model or combination of models should be used in forecasting series with the following patterns?
(a) A flat, nonseasonal pattern
(b) A flat, seasonal pattern
(c) A nonseasonal trend pattern
(d) A trend pattern with seasonality

12.28 Consider the choice of smoothing coefficients for deseasonalized time series. In each of the following cases, indicate whether a low smoothing value (.1) or a higher value (.5) is likely to be better.
(a) Choice of w in simple exponential smoothing, for a no-trend series with little random fluctuation and a very unstable mean level
(b) Choice of w in simple exponential smoothing, for a no-trend series with a great deal of random fluctuation and a steady mean level

(c) Choice of v in Holt, for a series with a stable trend and much random fluctuation
(d) Choice of v in Holt, if the series has *no* trend and moderate randomness

12.29 Consider forecasting the following quarterly data:

Period	Data	Period	Data
1	100	7	100
2	115	8	220
3	70	9	150
4	210	10	195
5	120	11	120
6	165	12	270

(a) Plot the data versus the period index $(t = 1, 2, \ldots, 12)$. Describe the elements of the pattern underlying this time series.
(b) Which method or combination of methods is most appropriate for forecasting this series? Choose from simple exponential smoothing.

Holt's linear exponential smoothing, simple exponential smoothing applied to deseasonalized data (from classical decomposition), or Holt's linear exponential smoothing applied to deseasonalized data (from classical decomposition). Justify your answer.

(c) Using your chosen method from (b), develop a forecast of the actual data to occur in periods 13, 14, 15, and 16.

(d) Determine the error mean square for your chosen forecasting method.

12.30 Your company's sales average about 1,200 units per month. This month's sales are only 650 units. Management is very concerned about the possibility that demand has dropped drastically. Can you suggest some possible alternative explanations for this month's low sales figure? (*Hint:* Consider the possible effects of components of time series.)

12.31 You have been asked to establish a model for forecasting the demand of product XT-100. You will use simple exponential smoothing. You have no historical data, since this product has just been introduced. Thus, you must choose the smoothing coefficient judgmentally. Which value would you choose from $w = .05$, $w = .2$, and $w = .4$? Explain your thinking.

12.32 Why does simple exponential smoothing lag when a series has trend? Explain.

12.33 Consider the initialization of a simple exponential smoothing model for a series with 15 data points.

(a) Describe the conventional approach to initializing A_t and at least one alternative approach.

(b) Does the method of initialization have much impact on the forecast for period 16?

(c) Does the method of initialization have much impact on the choice of w if we wish to minimize mean square for error?

12.34 An analyst at a regional telephone company was assigned the task of forecasting the annual telephone line gain (the increase in the number of telephone lines in service in a given year over the previous year). She is considering the use of a time series model and a regression model. The regression model would use as a predictor a forecast of statewide employment in the construction industry. (Regional data were not available.) Her data are provided here.*

* Courtesy of Fay Eure.

Year	Gain	Employment (in thousands)
1978	446	130.2
1979	591	138.4
1980	569	128.3
1981	490	116.3
1982	262	103.8
1983	688	113.9
1984	667	132.8
1985	757	152.0
1986	899	168.1
1987	741	173.6

(a) Forecast the gains for 1988, 1989, and 1990, using Holt's linear exponential smoothing with $w = .4$ and $v = .4$.

(b) Forecast statewide construction employment for 1988, 1989, and 1990, using Holt's linear exponential smoothing with $w = .4$ and $v = .4$.

(c) Determine the least squares regression line for predicting gain, given statewide construction employment. Based on the P-value, determine whether a linear relationship seems to exist between gain and statewide construction employment.

(d) Use your regression model from part (c) to forecast gain for 1988, 1989, and 1990, based on your forecast of statewide construction employment from part (b).

(e) In which forecast are you more confident, the Holt forecast or the regression forecast? Explain. (There is no "right" answer to this question.)

12.35 The State Girl Scout Council has a retail store. The store manager is responsible for all purchasing, inventory, and sales. Budget restrictions are numerous, and every department is evaluated on its ability to meet and plan for very specific budget criteria. The store manager has the opportunity to order large quantities of supplies in June from Girl Scout national headquarters in New York City. Supplies ordered in June can be purchased at a significant discount. However, State Council budget requires that inventory in the store be very low by the end of the fiscal year in December. If fall sales can be accurately forecasted, the shop manager could achieve considerable savings by ordering the merchandise at the June discount level.

A key sales item is membership pins, because sales for many other items are related to sales of pins. Monthly sales of pins were available for

January 1989 through April 1992 and are provided as follows.*

Year	Jan.	Feb.	Mar.	Apr.	May	June
1989	171	219	263	290	278	238
1990	219	252	280	279	313	353
1991	250	274	347	301	260	174
1992	265	320	342	353		

Year	July	Aug.	Sep.	Oct.	Nov.	Dec.
1989	125	147	349	449	381	251
1990	102	172	362	491	428	315
1991	152	171	408	562	480	341
1992						

(a) Plot the data in time sequence (i.e., a run chart). Describe the pattern, if any.

(b) Apply classical decomposition to (1) estimate the seasonal factors and (2) obtain deseasonalized data.

(c) If Holt's method were used to forecast the deseasonalized data, which values of v and w would be most appropriate, smaller values such as $v = .2$, $w = .1$, or larger values such as $v = .5$, $w = .2$? Explain.

(d) Forecast the deseasonalized data for the period from May 1992 through December 1992 with Holt's method, using $v = .5$, $w = .2$. Determine the error mean square.

(e) Forecast the deseasonalized data for the period from May 1992 through December 1992 with Holt's method, using $v = .2$, $w = .1$. Determine the error mean square.

(f) Select the forecast for deseasonalized sales of pins based on the choices for v and w above that provide the smaller error mean square. Use the seasonality factors from part (b) to transform to a forecast of actual sales of pins for May 1992 through December 1992.

---

* Courtesy of Ann Kiernan.

Appendix 12

Computer Instructions for Using MINITAB, EXCEL, and JMP IN

MINITAB

Moving Averages

The moving average in Table 12.1 and Figure 12.3 can be developed with Minitab as follows. Enter the data in c1. Select STAT–TIME SERIES–MOVING AVERAGE . . . . In the dialogue box, specify the original variable to be c1, and specify 3 as the MA LENGTH. Click the CENTER THE MOVING AVERAGES button. Click the RE-SULTS . . . button; in the dialogue box, click PLOT SMOOTHED VS. ACTUAL and SUMMARY TABLE AND RESULTS TABLE, then click OK twice.

Classical Decomposition

Minitab's version of classical decomposition differs somewhat from that of Chapter 12. (Minitab's version uses an additive randomness component rather than a multiplicative one.) Consequently, the Minitab results for the data in Table 12.3 differ slightly from those given in the book. We prefer the approach used in Chapter 12, but both approaches are legitimate and both are used in practice. You can obtain the Minitab classical decomposition results for these data and a graph like Figure 12.4 as follows. Enter the original data in c1. Select STAT–TIME SERIES–DECOMPOSITION . . . . In the dialogue box, specify c1 as the VARIABLE and 4 as the SEASONAL LENGTH. Click the MULTIPLICATIVE button, and click the TREND PLUS SEASONAL button. For FIRST OBS. IS IN SEASONAL PERIOD, enter 1. Click the RESULTS . . . button; in its dialogue box, click the DISPLAY PLOT button and the SUMMARY TABLE AND RESULTS TABLE button, and click OK. To store the components in the DATA window, click the STORAGE . . . button; in its dialogue box, click the buttons for TREND LINE, SEASONALS, SEASONALLY ADJUSTED DATA, and RESIDUALS; and click OK twice.

Simple Exponential Smoothing

The simple exponential smoothing results in Table 12.4 and Figure 12.5 can be obtained using Minitab as follows. Enter the data into c1. Select STAT–TIME SERIES–SINGLE EXP SMOOTHING . . . . In the dialogue box, enter c1 as the VARIABLE; click the USE button and enter .5 as the WEIGHT TO USE IN SMOOTHING; click the GENERATE FORECASTS button and enter 4 as the NUMBER OF FORECASTS. Click the OPTIONS button and in its dialogue box click PLOT PREDICTED VERSUS ACTUAL; click SUMMARY TABLE AND RESULTS TABLE; and enter 1 under USE AVERAGE OF FIRST__OBSERVATIONS to establish the initial value A1, and click OK. To store the components in the DATA window, click the STORAGE . . . button; in its dialogue box, click the buttons SMOOTHED DATA, FITS, RESIDUALS, and FORECASTS; and click OK twice. [Note that Minitab's mean square for error (which it calls MSD) differs from the MSE in Table 12.4 because Minitab includes a forecasting error associated with period 1.]

Holt's Method of Linear Exponential Smoothing

Minitab results for Holt's method differ slightly from those of Table 12.6 because of differences in the way initial values are determined. (Minitab automatically fits a regression equation to *all* the data to determine the initial values of A_1 and B_1.) The Minitab results for these data are obtained as follows. Enter the data into c1. Select STAT–TIME SERIES–DOUBLE EXP SMOOTHING . . . . In the dialogue box, enter c1 as the VARIABLE; click the USE button and enter .5 FOR LEVEL and .4 FOR TREND; click the GENERATE FORECASTS button and enter 4 as the NUMBER OF FORECASTS. Click the RESULTS button and in its dialogue box click PLOT PREDICTED VERSUS ACTUAL, click SUMMARY TABLE AND RESULTS TABLE, and click OK. To store the components in the DATA window, click the STORAGE . . . button; in its dialogue box, click the buttons for LEVEL ESTIMATES, TREND ESTIMATES, FITS, RESIDUALS, and FORECASTS; and click OK twice.

EXCEL

Moving Averages

The methods in this chapter can best be executed with Excel by using formulas, rather than selecting from the Excel data analysis functions found under the TOOLS–DATA ANALYSIS . . . menu. Only some of the methods of Chapter 12 can be executed this way, and even those are rather inflexible and differ somewhat from the methods in the chapter. Using formulas takes advantage of Excel's powerful spreadsheet capability, a capability not offered by statistical software. The use of Excel formulas also reinforces your understanding of the mechanics of the particular method.

The moving average in Table 12.1 can be developed with the AVERAGE formula as follows. Enter the data in cells a1 through a8. In cell b2, place the first moving average value by typing the formula: = AVERAGE(a1:a3). With cell b2 selected, fill down through cell b7. This places the moving average values in cells b2 through b7. To produce the graph in Figure 12.3, choose INSERT–CHART . . . . In step 1 of the CHART WIZARD, select LINE CHART and the first CHART SUB-TYPE option that appears on the second row. In step 2, indicate a1:b8 as the DATA RANGE. In step 3, specify chart title and axis labels as desired; then click FINISH.

Classical Decomposition

To produce the classical decomposition results in Table 12.3, use the following sequence of steps:

1. Enter the original data into cells a1 through a12.
2. Compute the $n = 4$ moving average by typing the formula = AVERAGE(a1:a4) in cell b3 and then filling down from cell b3 through cell b11.
3. Compute the 2×4 moving average by typing the formula = AVERAGE(b3:b4) in cell c3 and then filling down from cell c3 through cell c10.
4. Compute preliminary seasonality factors by typing the formula = a3/c3 in cell d3 and then filling down from cell d3 through cell d10.
5. Arrange the preliminary seasonality factor results elsewhere in the spreadsheet as shown in the bottom portion of Table 12.3. Compute averages as shown, and adjust as indicated to obtain final seasonality factors.
6. Enter the final seasonality factors into cells e1 through e12.
7. Compute random component factors by typing into cell f1 the formula = a1/(c1*e1) in cell f3 and then filling down from cell f1 through cell f12.
8. Finally, compute deseasonalized data by typing the formula = a1/e1 in cell g3 and then filling down from cell g1 through cell g12.

To produce the graph in Figure 12.4, choose INSERT−CHART . . . . In step 1 of the CHART WIZARD, select LINE CHART and the first CHART SUB-TYPE option that appears on the second row. In step 2, indicate a1:a12,c1:c12 as the DATA RANGE. In step 3, specify chart title and axis labels as desired; then click FINISH.

Simple Exponential Smoothing

The simple exponential smoothing results in Table 12.4 and Figure 12.5 are obtained using Excel formulas as follows. Enter the data into cells a1 through a10. In cell b1, enter the initial smoothed value, in this case 19. In cell b2, type the formula = .5*a2 + 5*b1. Fill down from b2 through cell b10; this places the smoothed values in cells b1:b10. Now produce the forecast values. In cell c2, type the formula = B1. With cell c2 selected, fill down from c2 through cell c11. This places the forecast values in cells c2 through c11. To put a forecast value into c12, type into cell c12 the formula = c11. Now produce the one-step-ahead forecasting error values. In cell d2, type the formula = a2-c2, and fill down from d2 through cell d10. This places the error values in cells d2:d10. The squared error values are produced in similar fashion. To produce the graph in Figure 12.5, first delete the forecast values in cells c2 through c10 (leaving forecast values only in cells c11 and c12). Choose INSERT−CHART . . . . In step 1 of the CHART WIZARD, select LINE CHART and the first CHART SUB-TYPE option that appears on the second row. In step 2, indicate a1:a12,c1:c12 as the DATA RANGE. In step 3, specify chart title and axis labels as desired; then click FINISH.

Holt's Method of Linear Exponential Smoothing

To obtain the Holt's method results in Table 12.6 and Figure 12.7, enter the data into cells a1:a12. In cell b1, enter the initial level, in this case 256.73. In cell c1, enter the initial trend value of 185.28. In cell d2, compute the first forecast value by typing the formula $= b1 + c1$. To update the level, type in cell b2 the formula $= .5*a2 + .5*d2$. With cell b2 selected, fill down through cell b12. This places the smoothed values for level in cells b1 through b12. To update trend, type in cell c2 the formula $= .4*(b2 - b1) + .6*c1$. With cell c2 selected, fill down through cell c12. This places the smoothed values for trend in cells c1 through c12. To update the one-step-ahead forecasts, select cell d3 and fill down through cell d13. This places the forecast values in cells d2 through d13. To put forecast values into d14, d15, and d16, type into cell d14 the formula $= d13 + \$c\$12$; then select cell d14 and fill down through d16. To produce the error values, type in cell e2 the formula $= a2\text{-}d2$. With cell e2 selected, fill down through cell e12. The squared error values are produced in similar fashion. To produce the graph in Figure 12.7, first delete the forecast values in cells c2 through c12 (leaving forecast values only in cells c13 through c16). Choose INSERT—CHART . . . . In step 1 of the CHART WIZARD, select LINE CHART and the first CHART SUB-TYPE option that appears on the second row. In step 2, indicate a1:a16,d1:d16 as the DATA RANGE. In step 3, specify chart title and axis labels as desired; then click FINISH.

JMP IN

Currently, JMP IN does not include the time series methods covered in this book.

Chapter 13

Methods for Process Improvement and Statistical Quality Control

13.1 Bridging to New Topics

In the late 1970s, American business showed many signs of trouble. Japanese products were rapidly increasing their markert share because of their superior quality and competitive prices. Japanese success was achieved through the use of business practices different from those of American companies. In the early 1980s, faced with a genuine crisis, American management began to adopt some of the practices of the Japanese, one of which was a commitment to a continual improvement in the quality of goods and services. This commitment required a shift of mind-set away from an emphasis on outcomes and toward a focus on the processes that produce the outcomes. Statistics became a crucial tool for this purpose, providing a way to assess current process performance and evaluate the effect of possible process innovations. For this reason, this chapter may be more central to "modern statistics" than many of the inferential methods presented in Chapters 6–8.

The use of statistical thinking for process improvement was introduced in Section 1.5. In this chapter we extend this discussion, focusing in particular on key tools that support statistical thinking for process improvement. These include flow diagrams and cause-and-effect diagrams, which help us to identify opportunities for process improvement, and control charts, which provide the chief method used for assessing process performance.

In Section 13.2, we elaborate on the process improvement strategies introduced in Section 1.5, and in Sections 13.3–13.5 we explain the development of control charts to investigate the stability of process parameters such as the process mean, the process standard deviation, and the process proportion of outputs having a specified characteristic.

13.2   Process Improvement Strategies

In the past, many organizations have focused almost entirely on process outcomes with the purpose of catching unacceptable product before it gets out the door. But this is not an effective strategy; attempting to "inspect quality in" is an inadequate strategy. Instead it has been found that substantive quality improvement is achievable only by improving the process that produces the outcomes. Quality improvement can be achieved by improvements to any component of a process.

13.2.1   Opportunities for Study and Improvement

Recall that a process was defined in Section 1.2 to be *a set of conditions that repeatedly come together to transform inputs into outcomes.* Inputs are provided by *suppliers.* Outcomes go to the *customers* of the process. The quality of outcomes is determined by how well they serve the needs of the customers of the process. Much can be learned by studying not only a process's outcomes, but also its inputs, factors within the process, and customer feedback about process outcomes. The flow of inputs and outcomes from supplier to process to customer and the associated opportunities for study are depicted by the diagram in Figure 13.1.

Figure 13.1

The extended process with opportunities for statistical study toward process improvement

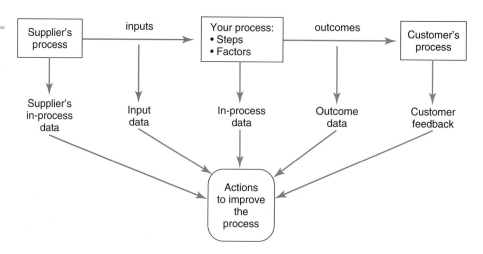

This diagram describes any business process, such as sales, service, administrative functions, or manufacturing. It applies to processes that serve internal as well as external customers and suppliers. For example, suppose your job involves providing a monthly financial report to a manager in your company. Then your customer is this manager, and your suppliers include all who provide information to you. The factors and steps in your process include all the activities you perform in producing the report. Notice also that, from the point of view of your supplier, you are a customer. Their outcomes are your inputs, and the quality of their outcomes is defined by how well they satisfy your needs. Similarly, from the perspective of the manager receiving your report, you are a supplier. Thus, your outcomes are the manager's inputs. As this interrelationship of processes suggests, communication and cooperation of the managers of a process with its suppliers and its customers can lead to substantial opportunities for improvement.

As Figure 13.1 illustrates, there are many possible process improvement opportunities to consider. But choosing good opportunities can be difficult. Two tools have proven to be quite effective for this purpose, the flow diagram and the cause-and-effect diagram. They are introduced later in this section.

Reducing Variation

Recall from Section 1.5 that the quality of a process can be ascertained by observing variables (called quality characteristics) that represent the outcomes of a process. A certain amount of variation in a quality characteristic is natural and unavoidable. The key to determining whether a process is stable is to determine what causes this variation among outcomes. Variation attributable to factors that are part of the process's design or its normal operating conditions is called common cause variation. If only common cause variation is present, a process is regarded as being stable. On the other hand, variation can also result from special or assignable causes. These could be machine malfunctions, an improperly trained worker, poor quality of raw material, a rare blizzard, and so on. The occurrence of special causes of variation constitutes an unstable process, which will usually remain unstable unless corrective action is taken to remove the special causes.

The distinction between stable processes and unstable processes is important because different actions are required to achieve improvement. The greatest opportunity to improve an unstable system is to identify the special causes of variation and remove them—that is, to bring an unstable process into a stable condition. We can think of this as *fixing the process*. Indeed, this is the first step toward long-term process improvement. If a process is unstable (i.e., it is subject to various special causes of variation), it is difficult to evaluate the effect of changes introduced to the process. If we changed the process and then observed a change in the range of outcomes, how would we know whether the changed outcomes were caused by the process change or by some special cause? It helps considerably to bring a process to a stable condition before we attempt to improve it. The most useful tool for ascertaining whether a process is stable or unstable (in regard to a particular quality characteristic) is the *control chart*, which is introduced in the next section.

To improve an unstable process, we must identify the special causes of variation. The persons who work in the process are best able to do this. For instance, they are most likely to know that a late invoice was caused by a computer crash, or that a machine malfunctioned and needs repair. On the other hand, workers in a process are less likely to identify ways to improve a stable process, partly because the occurrence of an outcome near the limits of normal variation cannot be explained by a single causal event. When a process is stable, process improvement can be achieved only by changes in the process itself. Process engineers and managers are better equipped for this task. They are in a better position to understand the process as a whole, and they are more likely to have training in the more involved statistical methods required. By testing a process under various trial conditions, reliable evidence can be obtained that can lead to sustainable process improvement.

Many common business practices violate these principles of process management. A pervasive error in the management of processes is **tampering**—reacting to common cause variation as if it were produced by a special cause. If we adjust a process in reaction to common cause variation, we only increase variation. For example, a thermostat controls the temperature inside a house within a range of, say, 2 degrees. If you set it at 70°, the temperature might vary between 69° and 71°. Now suppose you discover the temperature to be 69° and therefore adjust the thermometer upward by 1 degree. Such a practice of continual adjustment can cause the temperature range to increase to, perhaps, 68°–72°. We consider a few illustrations of tampering in Example 13.1.

EXAMPLE 13.1

Each of the following examples represents a possible lack of statistical thinking. Evaluate each management practice in light of the principles of process management just discussed.

(a) Each morning, a plant manager and his staff review the defective items produced the previous day. Their intent is to identify and remove the causes of the problems.

(b) An economic analyst concludes that " . . . the good times are over" because the August trade deficit rose to $10.8 billion after being $8.2 billion in July.

(c) Because sales have been below expected levels, a sales manager decides to run a special promotion.

Solution

(a) The manager is assuming that each defective item reflects a special cause of variation. It is normal that the production process, when stable, produces some defective product. Trying to identify a special cause for each defective item would be tampering unless it were first established that an unusually large number of defective items was produced. Otherwise, this is a waste of management time and could increase process variation.

(b) The monthly trade deficit is expected to vary. Only if the change from July to August was beyond the established range of month-to-month variation would the analyst's conclusion be justified.

(c) The sales manager should first determine whether the sales process is stable. If it is, then the special sale could constitute tampering and might do more harm than good.

The elimination of special causes often brings about relatively fast improvement. But the greatest improvement over the long term usually is derived by reducing

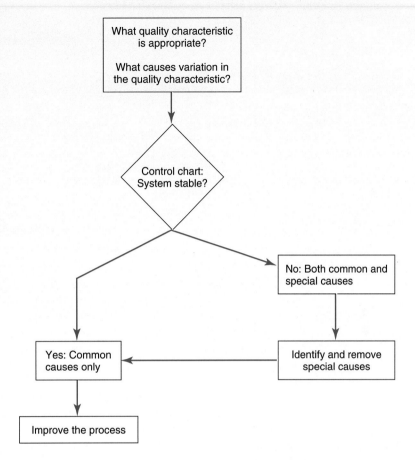

Figure 13.2

An overview of the improvement of processes

common cause variation through changes to the design of the process. Figure 13.2 depicts the improvement of processes as discussed in this section.

For many products, management sets a target value and specification limits which set the range of variation that is considered acceptable. Similar to the discussion in Section 2.3.5, if the actual range of variation exceeds the specification limits, as in Figure 13.3(a), then a reduction of variation will decrease the fraction of unacceptable outcomes. If the range of variation already lies entirely within specification limits, as in Figure 13.3(b), continued improvement efforts will result in more and more outcomes that are near the target value, as in Figure 13.3(c), thereby continuing to improve quality. It is usually the case that, even for outcomes deemed to be acceptable, the nearer the target value, the better the performance. For example, automobile engines made from parts that are selected because they are right at the target value have been found to be vastly superior to engines made from randomly selected parts that are within specification limits. Indeed, the principle of continual reduction of variation around a target value has been a key to many of the remarkable improvements in quality in the 1980s and 1990s.

13.2.2 Flow Diagrams and Cause-and-Effect Diagrams

Flow diagrams and cause-and-effect diagrams are the most effective and commonly used tools for identifying opportunities for quality improvement.

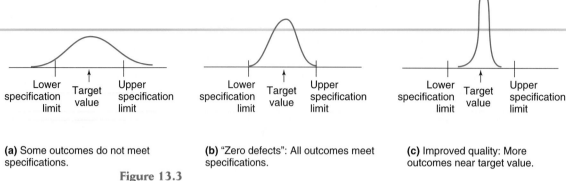

(a) Some outcomes do not meet specifications.

(b) "Zero defects": All outcomes meet specifications.

(c) Improved quality: More outcomes near target value.

Figure 13.3

Range of variation of a quality characteristic compared to specification limits and target value

Flow Diagrams

A flow diagram depicts the interaction of the steps in a process and the decisions that arise along the way. To improve a process, you must understand it. Consequently, many people believe the flow diagram to be perhaps the single most important tool leading to process improvement. Examples of business processes subject to improvement efforts include end-of-day processing of bank transactions, loading of trucks for delivery of products, employee performance appraisal, and manufacture of bottle caps.

The development of a flow diagram should involve people with different perspectives. The right people include those who work in various aspects of the process, the suppliers to the process, the customers of the process, and the managers of the process. Indeed, the great value of a flow diagram is the shared understanding it brings about. Frequently, processes are not clearly understood. Interpretations of how a process works often differ. Some steps may lack adequate operational definitions. Once the time is taken to develop a shared understanding, opportunities for improvement often become obvious. And cooperation is enhanced because people better understand each other's roles and needs.

There are no hard-and-fast rules governing flow diagrams. Any symbols that communicate effectively the workings of the process are appropriate. The following steps are recommended for the construction of any flow diagram:

1. Define the beginning and endpoints of the process being modeled.
2. Identify specific aspects of the process that might influence an outcome of the process.
3. Describe the outcomes of the process. What characteristics are important?
4. Identify the suppliers to the process and the customers of the process.

A flow diagram should indicate its starting and ending points, actions to be taken, and decisions to be made. The symbols shown in Figure 13.4 are commonly used to represent these items.

Suppose you have experienced difficulty getting to school or work on time in the morning. To address this problem, you might begin by developing a flow diagram of your morning routine. Figure 13.5 is an example of such a flow diagram. Notice that the diagram could be made more complex; there is no mention of reading the

Figure 13.4

Symbols commonly
used in flow diagrams

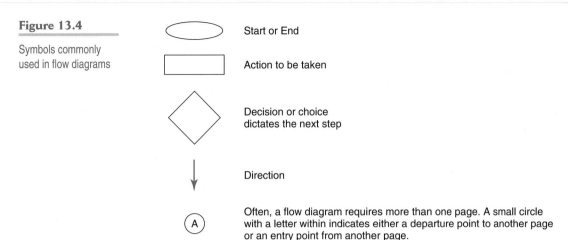

Start or End

Action to be taken

Decision or choice
dictates the next step

Direction

Often, a flow diagram requires more than one page. A small circle
with a letter within indicates either a departure point to another page
or an entry point from another page.

newspaper, watching morning television, etc. Notice also that actions in the process
are processes themselves, for which a flow diagram could be developed, if you
thought it would be helpful to do so. For example, you might develop flow diagrams
for preparing breakfast or cleaning up the kitchen.

Cause-and-Effect Diagram

If we understand the workings of a process, we can target areas for improvement and
problems for resolution. Often enough, the area for improvement is quite clear!
However, before deciding what ought to be done to resolve a problem, you first need
to consider its possible causes. A little work at this point often yields good ideas that
could otherwise be easily missed. Cause-and-effect diagrams are extremely useful in
this regard. They are sometimes called fishbone diagrams because the completed
diagram resembles the skeleton of a fish. They are also called Ishikawa diagrams after
their developer, Kaoru Ishikawa.

A **cause-and-effect diagram** links an "effect"—a problem or desired result—to
its various causes. First, major categories of causes are determined. These are
diagrammed as diagonal lines off a long horizontal line. Then the factors associated
with each major cause category are identified, where each factor may in turn suggest
more detailed causes, with the procedure continuing until all significant lower-level
causes have been included. Thus, developing a cause-and-effect diagram is a kind of
organized brainstorming, in which the initial presence of the major categories makes
it less likely that important causes will be overlooked.

Suppose you decided that improvement in the "drive to school/work" component
of the flow diagram in Figure 13.5 offered the best opportunity for reducing the time
it takes to get to school or work in the morning. Let's use this example to illustrate the
step-by-step development of a cause-and-effect diagram.

1. First write the "effect"—a problem or desired result—on the right-hand side of a
   sheet of paper and enclose it in a box. In this example, the effect is "Time to
   drive to school/work," as shown in Figure 13.6. Then draw a long, horizontal
   line leading to this effect.

2. List major categories of causes. One set of categories that is commonly used
   includes environment, people, machines, measurement, methods, and materials; you can use others if you think they apply better to your process. Draw a

Figure 13.5

An example of a flow diagram

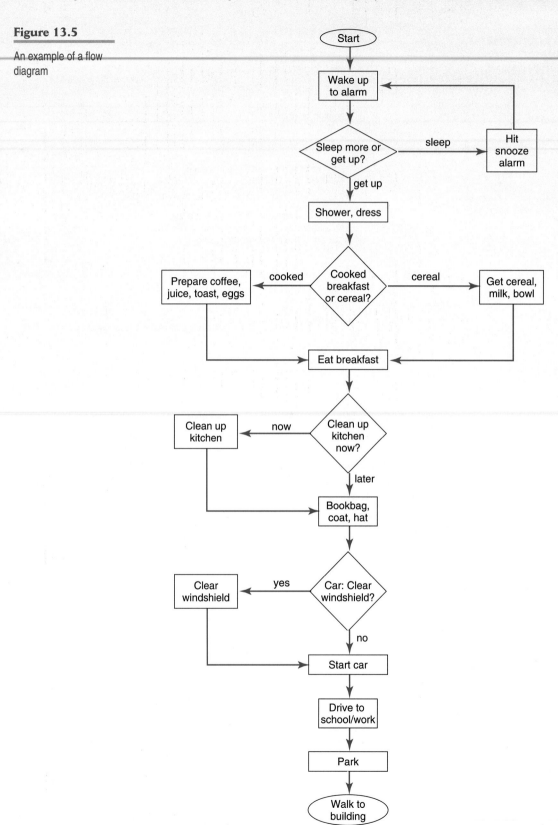

Figure 13.6

Starting point for developing a cause-and-effect diagram

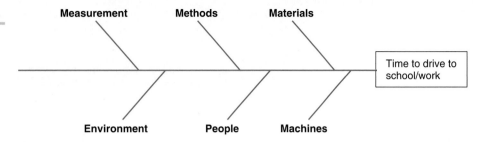

slanted line to connect each major cause category to the main horizontal line, as illustrated in Figure 13.6. The slanted lines constitute the "major bones" of the fishbone diagram.

3. Now generate a list of the possible causes in each main cause category, and connect each of these causes to its associated main cause with a horizontal line. For each cause generated, consider possible subcauses by asking what specific aspects of the cause create variation among outcomes. Continue until all meaningful causes and subcauses have been included. Figure 13.7 illustrates the result of this work for the "Time to drive to school/work" example. Consider the major cause category "methods." Four causes are listed under this main heading: "route driven," "speed," "departure time," and "aggressiveness." For "route driven," the key choice is streets or expressway. Under "expressway," a factor that creates variation in driving time is the lane selected for driving.

Figure 13.7

Cause-and-effect diagram for time to drive to school/work

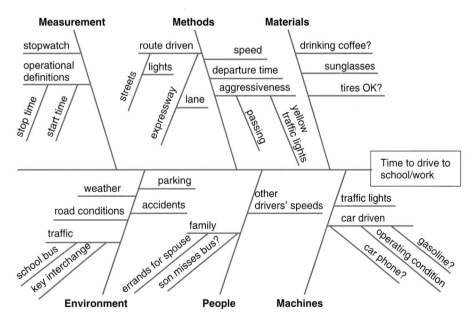

Cause-and-effect diagrams are most effective if developed by a team, using brainstorming to identify causes and place them properly on the diagram. Alternatively, a manager or team leader might post the diagram in a common area, with main causes indicated, and others can add contributing causes over time. The information generated often provides an insightful basis for process improvement actions and experiments. For example, Figure 13.7 might suggest an experiment involving the time it takes you to drive to school/work using alternative routes and departure times.

Statistical Control Charts

A control chart is a powerful tool for assessing the stability or instability of a process. Control charts are effective not only for studying process outcomes but also for measurements at earlier stages of the process, as indicated in Figure 13.1. For any process that is being studied, control charts can be used to monitor the stability of process parameters such as the *average* of the outcomes, the *variation* among outcomes, and the *proportion* of outcomes having some specified characteristic. The usual procedure is to select small samples of outcomes on a regular basis. These periodic samples are called *rational subgroups;* they were mentioned briefly in Section 1.4 and are discussed in more detail at the end of this section. By tracking the appropriate statistic in a control chart, we can determine whether the process is stable with respect to the associated parameter.

A control chart (see Figure 13.8 for an example) contains a center line that represents the parameter value for a stable process, and upper and lower control limits that indicate the usual range of variation of the relevant statistic while the process is stable. The center line and control limits are usually determined from past values of the statistic, observed from rational subgroup samples selected while the process was believed to be stable. It has been standard practice to have the upper and lower control limits correspond to "three standard errors" above and below the mean of the statistic of interest. These are commonly referred to as "three-sigma" limits, and are the ones we shall use throughout this chapter.

The manner with which the values of a statistic fluctuate over time indicates whether a process can be regarded as stable. If a process is stable, a control chart should exhibit no discernible pattern among the values of a statistic. In other words, the values should exhibit a random behavior with the majority of them being relatively close to the center line, some found above it, others found below it, with no long runs of increasing or decreasing values, and all values contained within the upper and lower control limits. The reason why we expect a stable process to behave in this manner should be apparent to you by now. If a process is stable, the behavior is predictable because there exists only variation that is due to common causes, the normal or usual factors within a process. Consequently, the sample values of the statistic of interest should deviate from the center line only because of random sampling variation.

On the other hand, any discernible patterns such as trends (long runs of increasing or decreasing values), consistent oscillation of the values above and below the center line ("sawtooth" pattern), an unusually long sequence of values all above or all below the center line, or a value outside of the control limits, suggest the presence of special cause variation and thus an unstable process.

Traditionally, control charts have been used primarily to monitor process stability, the purpose being to detect and remove special causes of variation. This is known as using a control chart in a "passive manner." Companies involved in continual process improvement efforts also use control charts in an "active manner." That is, they introduce an innovation to a heretofore stable process and use the control chart to see whether it has the desired effect on process outcomes. Since the innovation can be considered a special cause relative to the original process, its effect should be detected by the control chart.

Rational Subgroups

When we study the behavior of a process, we look for variation in its outcomes and attempt to determine its causes. We are interested in the variation among outcomes that were produced at approximately the same time and under the same conditions; we are equally interested in variation among outcomes produced at different times and/or under different conditions. To observe both kinds of variation, we use a sampling procedure called the method of **rational subgroups.** With this method, we select a series of small samples, where (1) the outcomes within a given sample were produced as nearly as possible at the same time and under the same conditions and (2) the samples themselves are selected at different times and/or under different process conditions. For example, we might select a sample every hour from a production process. If the process involved three machines performing the same task, we might select samples every hour from the outputs of each machine. The variation of data *within* a rational subgroup represents the innate common cause variation of the process. The variation *among* different rational subgroups allows us to detect changes in the process. The sampling intervals and/or process conditions are chosen subjectively, based on our knowledge of the process.

13.4 Control Charts for the Average and Variation of Process Outputs: $\overline{X}$ and S Charts

To assess the stability of a process with regard to the average of the outputs, we use an $\overline{X}$ chart. As the name implies, an $\overline{X}$ chart is a graph of the values of the statistic $\overline{X}$ stemming from the rational subgroups, where the upper and lower control limits are determined by taking into account the standard error of $\overline{X}$ when the process is stable.

To assess the stability of a process with regard to variation, we use an S chart. As you would expect, an S chart is a graph of the values of the sample standard deviation S, where, as in the $\overline{X}$ chart, the upper and lower control limits are determined by taking into account the standard error of S when the process is stable. Traditionally, the range R has been used in control charts to characterize the variation of process outputs because of its ease of computation. Indeed, R charts remain common today. Nevertheless, the S chart is better for assessing variation and poses no computational problem today because of the wide availability of computers.

In the construction of $\overline{X}$ and S charts, two distinct cases arise: (1) the process mean and standard deviation are known, and (2) the process mean and standard deviation are unknown. We cover the first case only briefly because, as in similar situations in Chapters 6 and 7, we are not likely to know the values of process parameters.

13.4.1 Process Mean and Standard Deviation Known

In certain situations, the process mean μ and the process standard deviation σ for a quality characteristic are known. Knowledge of these process parameters usually means that a stable process has been methodically observed over time through the use of rational subgroups to the point where the parameters can be regarded as known.

It is important to understand that the process standard deviation σ represents the inherent variation of the quality characteristic stemming from the usual and normal factors within the process that occur naturally over time. In other words, σ measures common cause variation.

$\bar{X}$ Charts

To establish a control chart for the average of process outputs, we of course use the statistic $\bar{X}$. In Chapter 5, we showed that the expected value of $\bar{X}$ is μ, so μ is the center line of the **$\bar{X}$ chart.** Also in Chapter 5, we showed that the standard error of $\bar{X}$ is $\sigma/\sqrt{n}$, where n is the size of each periodic sample. Therefore, since $E(\bar{X}) = \mu$ and $SE(\bar{X}) = \sigma/\sqrt{n}$, the upper and lower control limits corresponding to three standard errors above and below the mean of $\bar{X}$ are

$$\mu \pm 3 \frac{\sigma}{\sqrt{n}} \tag{13.1}$$

In other words, the upper control limit is $\mu + 3\sigma/\sqrt{n}$, the lower control limit is $\mu - 3\sigma/\sqrt{n}$, and the center line is μ.

Recalling the empirical rule or even the considerably more conservative Tchebysheff's finding (see Chapter 2), we can easily understand why the three-sigma limits have traditionally been used in control charts. In a stable process, we expect virtually all values of a statistic to be within three standard errors of the mean of the statistic. This is especially true of the statistic $\bar{X}$, because its sampling distribution approaches symmetry relatively fast (central limit theorem) regardless of the process distribution.

S Charts

To check the stability of a process relative to the variation of outputs, we can use an **S chart.** A process is said to be stable with respect to the variation of its outputs if values of the statistic S are within the usual range of variation as defined by the control limits and no pattern is discernible.

As we have said before, a control chart depends on the average of the corresponding statistic (the center line) and the standard error of the statistic. Although we have used the sample standard deviation S throughout this book, we have not determined its mean and its standard error. The determination of these two quantities is beyond the scope of this book; however, we can state that the average value of S is

$$E(S) = c_4\sigma \tag{13.2}$$

and the standard error of S is

$$SE(S) = c_5\sigma \tag{13.3}$$

where c_4 and c_5 are two constants (traditionally denoted in this manner) that depend only on the sample size n. In Table 13.1, the values of c_4 and c_5 are given for sample sizes typically used in control charts.

From Expression (13.2), notice that the sample standard deviation S is not an unbiased estimator for the process standard deviation σ (because c_4 is less than 1). You may think of this as an unexpected result, when considering that the sample variance

Table 13.1

Values of c_4 and c_5 for typical sample sizes

n:	4	5	6	7	8	9	10	12	15	20
c_4:	.9213	.9400	.9515	.9594	.9650	.9693	.9727	.9776	.9823	.9869
c_5:	.3889	.3412	.3076	.2820	.2622	.2459	.2321	.2105	.1873	.1613

S^2 is an unbiased estimator for σ^2. Nevertheless, the sample standard deviation remains a reliable estimator for σ.

Since the expected value of S is $c_4\sigma$ and the standard error of S is $c_5\sigma$, the center line of an S chart is $c_4\sigma$, and the three-sigma control limits are

$$c_4\sigma \pm 3c_5\sigma \tag{13.4}$$

From Expression (13.4), notice that since σ is known, the control limits depend only on the sample size n.

13.4.2 Process Mean and Standard Deviation Unknown

We now consider the development of $\overline{X}$ and S charts when the values of the process parameters μ and σ are not known. As you would expect, this is the situation that is much more likely to be encountered in an actual application. Obviously, we need to estimate these values. But how should we go about doing this? Because of our need to establish the center line and the upper and lower control limits, our estimates cannot be based on only one sample, nor can they be based on only a few samples. To develop the control limits and the center line for this case, W. A. Shewhart, the originator of statistical control charts, argued that at least 20 samples are needed. Shewhart suggested that only a few observations (about five) of the quality characteristic need be taken at any one time. Perhaps a slightly larger size (say, about ten observations) is advisable to assure reasonable accuracy of the estimates, especially with regard to σ.

The relatively small sample size implies that it is better to take a few observations of the quality characteristic at frequent intervals than to take a large number of observations less frequently. Of course, this is the justification for rational subgroups. The samples must reflect not only variation of the process outputs produced at as nearly the same time as possible, but also variation of the process outputs produced at different times. Finally, it is most important to understand that whatever number of samples we use to establish the center line and the control limits, these samples must come from a stable process. The reason is simple enough: The center line and control limits are to be used to gauge stability for products in the near future. Consequently, the samples used to determine these quantities must come from a stable process.

$\overline{X}$ Charts

To construct an $\overline{X}$ chart when μ and σ are unknown, suppose we take $m \geq 20$ samples, with each sample consisting of n observations of the quality characteristic. For the ith sample, let $\bar{X}_i$ be the sample mean and S_i be the sample standard deviation. For all m samples, we define the statistics

$$\bar{\bar{X}} = \frac{\bar{X}_1 + \bar{X}_2 + \cdots + \bar{X}_m}{m} \tag{13.5}$$

and

$$\bar{S} = \frac{S_1 + S_2 + \cdots + S_m}{m} \tag{13.6}$$

Notice that the statistic $\bar{\bar{X}}$ is the average of the m sample means, and the statistic $\bar{S}$ is the average of the m sample standard deviations.

To establish the center line and control limits, we need to determine the mean and standard error of the statistic $\bar{\bar{X}}$. We can show that $\bar{\bar{X}}$ is an unbiased estimator of μ—that is, $E(\bar{\bar{X}}) = \mu$. Therefore, the value of $\bar{\bar{X}}$ serves as the center line for the $\bar{X}$ chart. From Expression (13.2), we know that for the ith sample standard deviation S_i, $E(S_i) = c_4\sigma$. Indeed, over all m samples, the expected value of the statistic $\bar{S}$ is also $c_4\sigma$. As a statistic for estimating the process standard deviation, let's consider $\bar{S}/c_4$. Since $E(\bar{S}) = c_4\sigma$, we have

$$E\left(\frac{\bar{S}}{c_4}\right) = \frac{1}{c_4} E(\bar{S}) = \frac{1}{c_4}(c_4\sigma) = \sigma$$

As a result, the statistic $\bar{S}/c_4$ is an unbiased estimator of σ.

Since $\bar{S}/c_4$ is a statistic for estimating σ, the standard error of $\bar{\bar{X}}$ is estimated by

$$SE(\bar{\bar{X}}) = \frac{1}{\sqrt{n}}\left(\frac{\bar{S}}{c_4}\right) = \frac{\bar{S}}{c_4\sqrt{n}} \tag{13.7}$$

As usual, the upper and lower control limits correspond to three standard errors above and below $\bar{\bar{X}}$. They are

$$\bar{\bar{X}} \pm 3\frac{\bar{S}}{c_4\sqrt{n}} \tag{13.8}$$

In summary, for an $\bar{X}$ chart when the process parameters μ and σ are unknown, the center line is the value of $\bar{\bar{X}}$, the upper control limit is $\bar{\bar{X}} + 3[\bar{S}/(c_4\sqrt{n})]$, and the lower control limit is $\bar{\bar{X}} - 3[\bar{S}/(c_4\sqrt{n})]$, where c_4 is found in Table 13.1.

Before we illustrate this procedure, we establish the center line and control limits for an S chart.

S Charts

To construct an S chart when σ is unknown, recall Expression (13.4), which gives the three-sigma limits for an S chart when σ is known. Since the statistic for estimating σ based on m samples is $\bar{S}/c_4$, substituting this statistic for σ in Expression (13.4) yields

$$c_4\left(\frac{\bar{S}}{c_4}\right) \pm 3c_5\left(\frac{\bar{S}}{c_4}\right) = \bar{S} \pm 3\frac{c_5\bar{S}}{c_4} \tag{13.9}$$

These are the three-sigma limits for an S chart when σ is unknown. The center line is the value of $\bar{S}$, the upper control limit is $\bar{S} + 3(c_5\bar{S}/c_4)$, and the lower control limit is $\bar{S} - 3(c_5\bar{S}/c_4)$.

Using the Computer

We use the following example to illustrate the use of Excel and Minitab for determining $\bar{X}$ and S charts.

EXAMPLE 13.2

Recall Exercise 5.8 in Chapter 5, in which we had 25 samples, each with five observations, taken from a process that produces a certain kind of yarn. The observations represented the measured tensile strengths of the yarn specimens (in pounds). The observations for the 25 samples are given in the table, along with the mean and standard deviation for each sample. Construct $\bar{X}$ and S charts using these $m = 25$ samples.

Sample Number	Sample Values					$\bar{X}$	S
1	44	46	48	52	49	47.8	3.033150
2	44	47	49	46	44	46.0	2.121320
3	47	49	47	43	44	46.0	2.449490
4	45	47	51	46	48	47.4	2.302173
5	44	41	50	46	50	46.2	3.898718
6	49	46	45	46	49	47.0	1.870829
7	47	48	50	46	47	47.6	1.516575
8	49	46	51	48	46	48.0	2.121320
9	47	42	48	44	46	45.4	2.408319
10	46	48	45	51	50	48.0	2.549510
11	45	47	51	48	46	47.4	2.302173
12	52	51	48	48	45	48.8	2.774887
13	45	45	47	49	44	46.0	2.000000
14	46	47	43	48	45	45.8	1.923538
15	48	49	52	46	51	49.2	2.387467
16	44	46	45	47	52	46.8	3.114482
17	48	50	47	46	49	48.0	1.581139
18	48	52	51	47	46	48.8	2.588436
19	47	51	50	46	49	48.6	2.073644
20	45	46	48	47	49	47.0	1.581139
21	45	48	46	45	49	46.6	1.816590
22	46	49	50	46	48	47.8	1.788854
23	49	48	46	52	45	48.0	2.738613
24	47	49	45	46	50	47.4	2.073644
25	44	51	50	48	46	47.8	2.863564

Solution

The Excel and Minitab $\bar{X}$ and S charts are as given in Figures 13.8 and 13.9, respectively.

XBar-Chart

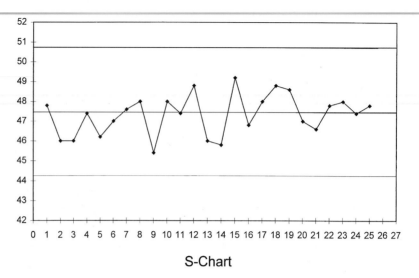

S-Chart

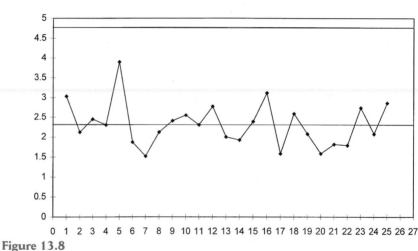

Figure 13.8

Excel $\bar{X}$ and S charts for Example 13.2

Notice that in each chart, the center line and the upper and lower control limits are indicated. (The control limits are labeled 3.0SL and −3.0SL by Minitab, where SL stands for "sigma limit.")

It is important to notice from Figures 13.8 and 13.9 that no pattern is discernible in either graph, and no value of $\bar{X}$ or S is outside the respective control limits. So the process appears to have been stable when these 25 samples were taken. Therefore, to assess the stability of the process with regard to the average of process outputs and the variation of process outputs in the near future, we will use the $\bar{X}$ and S charts in Figures 13.8 and 13.9.

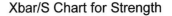

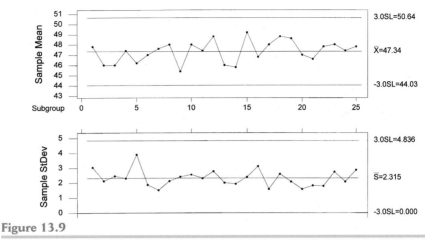

Figure 13.9

Minitab $\overline{X}$ and S charts for Example 13.2

13.4.3 Tests for Detecting Assignable Causes with $\overline{X}$ Charts

We said in Section 13.3 that, if a process is stable, a control chart for a process parameter should exhibit no discernible pattern over time. For $\overline{X}$ charts, Lloyd S. Nelson* studied a series of tests to use for detecting assignable cause variation, and thus instability, in a process. These tests are designed specifically for $\overline{X}$ charts because of the nature of the statistic $\overline{X}$.

Recall from Chapter 5 that the sampling distribution of $\overline{X}$ approaches a normal distribution for a large enough sample size no matter what the process distribution happens to be. For this reason, values of $\overline{X}$ based on rational subgroups tend to conform to the empirical rule if a process is stable. Approximately 68%, 95%, and 99% of the values of $\overline{X}$ should lie within one, two, and three standard deviations of the control chart center line, respectively.

In the context of $\overline{X}$ charts, the area that is between two and three standard deviations of the center line is known as Zone A. The area between one and two standard deviations of the center line is known as Zone B. And the area that makes up the middle 68% (that is, within one standard deviation of the center line) is known as Zone C. These three zones are illustrated in Figure 13.10.

Nelson proposed eight tests to detect assignable cause variation using an $\overline{X}$ chart. These tests are based on what one expects the behavior of an $\overline{X}$ chart to be for a stable process. In particular, the tests look for detectable patterns. If a process is stable, the behavior of an $\overline{X}$ chart is easily predictable when we take into consideration the empirical rule. For example, we expect approximately 68% of the $\overline{X}$-values to be in Zone C, about 27% (.95 – .68) to be in Zone B, about 4% (.99 – .95) to be in Zone A, and virtually all $\overline{X}$-values to be within the control

---

* "The Shewhart Control Chart—Tests for Special Causes," *Journal of Quality Technology,* Vol. 16, No. 4, October 1984.

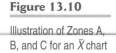

Figure 13.10

Illustration of Zones A,
B, and C for an $\bar{X}$ chart

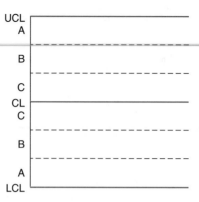

limits. Keeping this breakdown in mind, it should be fairly straightforward to understand why an assignable cause variation is indicated by each one of these tests. For example, if 15 consecutive values of $\bar{X}$ are in Zone C (Test 7), it may be due to deliberate tampering, because this breakdown implies that it is very unlikely to have as many as 15 consecutive values of $\bar{X}$ fall in Zone C.

For each of the eight tests that follow, an assignable cause variation is indicated in the cases given:

Test 1: One value of $\bar{X}$ is beyond Zone A.

Test 2: Nine consecutive values of $\bar{X}$ are in Zone C or beyond (on one side of the center line).

Test 3: Six consecutive values of $\bar{X}$ are all increasing or all decreasing.

Test 4: Fourteen consecutive values of $\bar{X}$ are alternating up and down.

Test 5: Two out of three consecutive values of $\bar{X}$ are in Zone A or beyond (on one side of the center line).

Test 6: Four out of five consecutive values of $\bar{X}$ are in Zone B or beyond (on one side of the center line).

Test 7: Fifteen consecutive values of $\bar{X}$ are in Zone C (above and below the center line).

Test 8: Eight consecutive values of $\bar{X}$ are beyond Zone C (above and below the center line).

These eight tests are illustrated in Figure 13.11. It is important to emphasize that these tests have been designed only for $\bar{X}$ charts. It is generally permitted, however, to use the first four tests in the context of a p chart, the subject of the next section.

It should be noted that the use of these tests tends to increase the chance for a false alarm—that is, an unstable signal for a stable process. This is especially true for Test 3; in fact, this test has been shown not to be particularly effective in detecting unstable processes.

These tests can be carried out with a computer using either Minitab or JMP IN. The application of these tests to the data of Example 13.2 reveals no assignable cause variation.

Figure 13.11

Illustration of the eight tests for detecting assignable cause variation with $\overline{X}$ charts

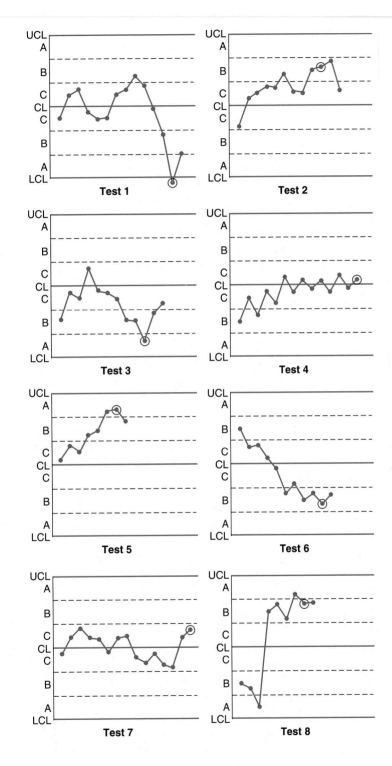

13.5 Control Charts for Process Proportions: p Charts

In the preceding section, we discussed procedures for creating control charts to monitor the average and variation of process outputs. Both $\bar{X}$ and S charts depend on measuring the *magnitude* of a quantity of interest such as fill amount, breaking strength, or sales revenues. Alternatively, we are often interested in the *proportion* of process outputs that have a specified characteristic. For example, we may wish to monitor the proportion of manufactured items that are defective, the proportion of invoices that contain errors, or the proportion of students who receive an A. In such cases, the parameter of interest is the process proportion π, and the best statistic is the sample proportion p. Thus, using the values of p based on periodic samples (rational subgroups), we can construct a **p chart** to assess the stability of a process with regard to the proportion of interest.

As was the case for $\bar{X}$ and S charts, two distinct cases arise in constructing p charts: (1) the process proportion π is known, and (2) π is unknown; the second case is the one that is likely to occur in practice.

13.5.1 Process Proportion Known

In some situations, we can regard the proportion parameter π as known based on substantial observation of a stable process over time. When π is considered known, the determination of a p chart is a straightforward extension of the properties of the statistic p as detailed in Chapter 5. Recall that the expected value of p is π; thus, π is the center line of the p chart. We also showed in Chapter 5 that the standard error of p is $\sqrt{\pi(1-\pi)/n}$, where n is the number of units inspected in each periodic sample for the characteristic of interest. It follows, therefore, that the upper and lower control limits corresponding to three standard errors above and below the mean of p are

$$\pi \pm 3\sqrt{\frac{\pi(1-\pi)}{n}} \tag{13.10}$$

So, to assess the stability of a process with regard to a proportion of interest, we plot the values of p on a control chart whose center line is the established value of π, and where the upper and lower control limits are $\pi + 3\sqrt{\pi(1-\pi)/n}$ and $\pi - 3\sqrt{\pi(1-\pi)/n}$, respectively.

13.5.2 Process Proportion Unknown

We now consider p charts when the process proportion π is not known. As for $\bar{X}$ and S charts, we need to have at least 20 periodic samples taken from a stable process to determine the center line and the control limits. Each sample consists of n units that are inspected for the characteristic of interest.

Suppose we select $m \geq 20$ rational subgroups. Let X_i be the number of units among the n units of the ith sample that possess the characteristic of interest. The sample proportion of the ith sample is

$$p_i = \frac{X_i}{n} \qquad \text{(13.11)}$$

and the average of the sample proportions over all m samples is

$$\bar{p} = \frac{p_1 + p_2 + \cdots + p_m}{m} \qquad \text{(13.12)}$$

$$= \frac{X_1 + X_2 + \cdots + X_m}{mn} \qquad \text{(13.13)}$$

To establish the center line and the control limits, we need to determine the mean and standard error of $\bar{p}$. Since the statistic $\bar{p}$ is also a proportion, it follows that the average value of $\bar{p}$ is π, and the standard error of $\bar{p}$ is estimated by $\sqrt{\bar{p}(1-\bar{p})/n}$. Accordingly, the three-sigma control limits are found by using $\bar{p}$ to estimate π in Expression (13.10). They are

$$\bar{p} \pm 3\sqrt{\frac{\bar{p}(1-\bar{p})}{n}} \qquad \text{(13.14)}$$

So for a p chart when the process population π is unknown, the center line is the value of $\bar{p}$, the upper control limit is $\bar{p} + 3\sqrt{\bar{p}(1-\bar{p})/n}$, and the lower control limit is $\bar{p} - 3\sqrt{\bar{p}(1-\bar{p})/n}$.

As before, you need to keep in mind that the m samples used to determine $\bar{p}$ must have come from a stable process if these control limits and center line are to be used for near-future considerations. Also, it is permissible to use the first four tests presented in Section 13.4.3 for detecting assignable cause variation with a p chart.

Using the Computer

The following example illustrates the determination of a p chart using JMP IN.

EXAMPLE 13.3

The proportion of defective units produced by a manufacturing process is monitored periodically. Specifically, 100 units are selected from the process at a given time and inspected for defective units. The table lists the observed numbers of defective units for 25 samples. Construct a p chart and determine whether it should be used for near-future considerations.

Sample number:	1	2	3	4	5	6	7	8	9	10	11	12	
Number defective:	2	1	4	3	2	2	0	2	3	2	1	2	

Sample number:	13	14	15	16	17	18	19	20	21	22	23	24	25
Number defective:	3	2	1	2	3	3	4	3	5	5	6	5	7

Solution

Since $m = 25$, $n = 100$, and $X_1 = 2$, $X_2 = 1, \ldots, X_{25} = 7$, from Expression (13.13) we determine that

$$\bar{p} = \frac{2 + 1 + \cdots + 7}{(25)(100)} = .0292$$

which serves as the center line of the p chart. From Expression (13.14), the upper and lower control limits are $.0292 \pm (3)\sqrt{(.0292)(.9708)/100} = .0292 \pm .0505$, or $.0797$ and 0 (since a proportion can never be negative).

Using JMP IN, the p chart and the application of Nelson's first four tests are illustrated in Figure 13.12.

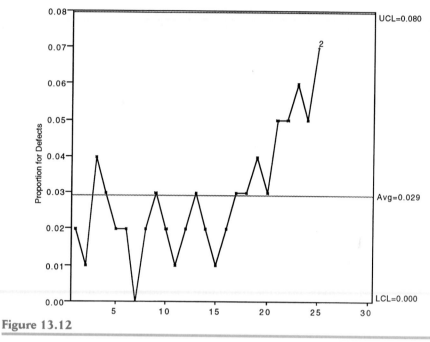

Figure 13.12

JMP IN p chart for Example 13.3

In Figure 13.12, notice that with sample number 17, a generally upward trend in the number of defective units begins to emerge and continues through sample number 25. It is detected by Test 2—the "2" in the figure at sample 25. Therefore, the process appears not to have been stable, at least during the last 7 to 8 samples. Consequently, action is needed to identify and eliminate the apparent assignable cause.

13.6

Summary

In this chapter, we elaborated on opportunities for process improvement by focusing on tools such as flow diagrams and cause-and-effect diagrams. In addition, we developed statistical control charts for assessing process performance with regard to the process parameters μ, σ, and π based on the corresponding statistics $\bar{X}$, S, and p.

A control chart is the most useful statistical method for assessing the stability of a process with respect to important process parameters. A control chart is a graph of the values of a corresponding statistic over time. The determination of a control chart depends on periodic samples from a process. These periodic samples are known as rational subgroups. The manner with which the values of a statistic fluctuate over time indicates whether a process can be regarded as stable. If a process is stable, a control chart should exhibit no discernible pattern, and the values of the statistic should be within the usual range of variation.

EXERCISES FOR SECTION 13.2

13.1 For the following processes, construct a flow diagram based on your knowledge of the process. It should be of a suitable level of detail to guide a visiting foreign student who is unfamiliar with the process.
   (a) Preparing a meal for yourself and a friend— you determine the menu
   (b) Preparing for a statistics test
   (c) Buying gasoline for your car
   (d) Buying a hamburger at a fast-food drive-through restaurant
   (e) Making a telephone call to a friend

13.2 For one of the processes that you diagrammed in Exercise 13.1:
   (a) Identify an appropriate quality characteristic.
   (b) Identify at least three points or stages in the process where opportunities for improvement might exist. Describe how each improvement could ultimately lead to improvement in the quality characteristic.

13.3 Think of a process in which you are often involved that includes at least one other person. Collaborating with the other person(s), develop a flow diagram.

13.4 For each process in Exercise 13.1, develop a cause-and-effect diagram for either getting a better outcome or reducing the time taken to complete the process (whichever seems more appropriate).

13.5 For the process you identified in Exercise 13.3, identify one problem or desired improvement and, in collaboration with the other person(s) involved, construct a cause-and-effect diagram.

13.6 Construct a cause-and-effect diagram to explain variation in your test grades. Based on the diagram, suggest at least one possible action to improve your grades.

13.7 Construct a cause-and-effect diagram to explain variation in the time it takes to pay your bills. Based on the diagram, suggest at least one possible action to reduce variation.

EXERCISES FOR SECTION 13.3

13.8 What is the purpose of a control chart and what are its features?

13.9 When can we regard a process as stable?

13.10 When can we regard a process as unstable?

13.11 Is it sufficient to say that a process is stable as long as values of the statistic of interest remain within the control limits? Explain.

13.12 How can a stable process be improved?

13.13 How can an unstable process be made stable?

13.14 What function do the control limits serve on a control chart?

EXERCISES FOR SECTION 13.4

13.15 What is the purpose of $\bar{X}$ and S charts?

13.16 Explain why a stable process may not be acceptable.

13.17 In the production of certain welded material, it is known from substantial observation that the process average breaking strength is 400 pounds and the process standard deviation is 30 pounds. Each operating day, nine welded specimens are selected from the day's production and their breaking strengths are recorded. The average breaking strengths for 12 days are as follows:

Day:	1	2	3	4	5	6
Sample mean:	393	418	406	419	387	391

Day:	7	8	9	10	11	12
Sample mean:	410	374	425	408	372	386

Construct an $\bar{X}$ chart based on three-sigma limits and determine whether the process was stable relative to the average strength during this time.

13.18 In Exercise 13.17, suppose the sample standard deviations for the 12 days were as follows:

Day:	1	2	3	4	5	6
Sample standard deviation:	9.2	12.6	38.8	25.9	18.2	48.3

Day:	7	8	9	10	11	12
Sample standard deviation:	42.6	22.9	31.7	44.2	8.6	19.4

Construct an S chart based on three-sigma limits and, along with your answer to Exercise 13.17, determine whether the process was stable with regard to average and variation during this time.

13.19 The mean and standard deviation of a process are known to be 100 and 20, respectively. If $\bar{X}$ and S control charts are maintained based on samples of size $n = 8$, determine the center lines and the three-sigma limits for these charts.

13.20 Periodically, samples of $n = 6$ water specimens are taken from a lake to monitor water pollution. For each of 30 samples, the sample mean and sample standard deviation of a certain pollutant are determined. After the 30 samples, we find that

$$\sum_{i=1}^{30} \bar{X}_i = 1,350 \quad \text{and} \quad \sum_{i=1}^{30} S_i = 157.5$$

(a) Determine three-sigma control limits for $\bar{X}$ and S charts.
(b) Estimate the process standard deviation σ and interpret the value.
(c) If an individual measurement must be below 50 to be safe, what can you say about this process?
(d) If it must be below 65, what can you say about the process?

13.21 Forty samples of size $n = 8$ each are taken at regular intervals during a week from a filling process to check the amount of product being poured into containers. After the sample means and sample standard deviations are computed, the following quantities are determined:

$$\sum_{i=1}^{40} \bar{X}_i = 810 \quad \text{and} \quad \sum_{i=1}^{40} S_i = 12.8$$

(a) Determine three-sigma control limits for $\bar{X}$ and S charts.
(b) Estimate the process standard deviation σ and interpret the value.
(c) If the amount in the containers must be between 19.0 and 21.4, what can you say about this process?

13.22 In the assembly of washing machines, assembly time is an important quantity. For each production day, the actual assembly times of four machines are measured. The following table consists of the measured assembly times in minutes for 20 consecutive production days:

Day:	1	2	3	4	5
Assembly times:	18	17	19	20	18
	18	18	21	19	20
	19	16	20	17	21
	21	19	19	18	17

Day:	6	7	8	9	10
Assembly times:	18	23	17	19	21
	19	22	18	21	16
	16	24	17	20	18
	18	23	18	17	19

Day:	11	12	13	14	15
Assembly times:	19	18	20	20	19
	19	17	20	19	17
	20	19	18	19	18
	17	18	17	17	18

Day:	16	17	18	19	20
Assembly times:	18	21	17	16	19
	20	18	18	18	20
	20	16	18	19	18
	19	19	19	19	20

(a) Determine three-sigma control limits for $\bar{X}$ and S charts. Does the process appear to have been stable during this time?
(b) Apply Nelson's eight tests for assignable causes to the $\bar{X}$ chart. What do you find?
(c) Should we use these control limits to gauge stability in the near future? Explain.

13.23 Five bearings are selected twice a day and their inside diameters are measured. The following table contains sample information for 10 production days. Answer the three parts of Exercise 13.22.

Sample number:	1	2	3	4	5
Observed diameters:	1.52	1.47	1.49	1.52	1.49
	1.51	1.49	1.48	1.51	1.52
	1.48	1.49	1.51	1.51	1.52
	1.49	1.51	1.52	1.50	1.51
	1.51	1.48	1.52	1.50	1.48

Sample number:	6	7	8	9	10
Observed diameters:	1.48	1.51	1.52	1.47	1.49
	1.49	1.51	1.48	1.48	1.48
	1.50	1.48	1.48	1.51	1.47
	1.50	1.47	1.49	1.52	1.47
	1.52	1.49	1.47	1.48	1.50

Sample number:	11	12	13	14	15
Observed diameters:	1.47	1.51	1.48	1.47	1.49
	1.48	1.51	1.52	1.48	1.50
	1.51	1.47	1.49	1.47	1.51
	1.50	1.48	1.51	1.51	1.51
	1.50	1.48	1.49	1.51	1.52

Sample number:	16	17	18	19	20
Observed diameters:	1.51	1.50	1.48	1.50	1.49
	1.49	1.51	1.49	1.50	1.47
	1.49	1.49	1.47	1.51	1.52
	1.52	1.49	1.51	1.48	1.51
	1.47	1.48	1.51	1.47	1.50

EXERCISES FOR SECTION 13.5

13.24 Explain the purpose of a p chart.

13.25 State why you think not all eight of Nelson's tests are recommended to be used with p charts.

13.26 In the manufacture of automobile tires, it has been established through substantial observation that the proportion of defective tires produced by the process is .05. A sample of $n = 50$ tires is taken from a day's production, and the sample proportion of defective tires is determined. Sample information for 10 days is as follows:

Day:	1	2	3	4	5
Sample proportion:	.08	.06	.04	.06	.04

Day:	6	7	8	9	10
Sample proportion:	.10	.12	.16	.10	.06

Construct a p chart. Be sure to identify the center line and determine whether the process was stable with regard to the proportion of defective tires during this time.

13.27 A control chart for the proportion of bath towels with unacceptable flaws is to be constructed based on periodic samples of size $n = 60$ towels chosen in a textile plant. To determine the control chart, 40 samples are selected, and the total number of towels with unacceptable flaws found in all 40 samples is 96. Determine the control limits and the center line for a p chart.

13.28 With reference to Exercise 13.27, suppose the next sample of $n = 60$ towels contains seven towels with unacceptable flaws. Based on the control limits found in Exercise 13.27, can we regard the process that produces such a sample to be stable? If not, what should we do next?

13.29 In the manufacture of fine china, 100 dinner plates are selected periodically and the number of plates with unacceptable flaws is recorded. For 20 such samples, the number of plates found with unacceptable flaws in each sample is given in the table that follows:

Sample number:	1	2	3	4	5
Unacceptable plates:	2	0	1	2	1

Sample number:	6	7	8	9	10
Unacceptable plates:	1	3	1	2	1

Sample number:	11	12	13	14	15
Unacceptable plates:	0	3	7	1	0

Sample number:	16	17	18	19	20
Unacceptable plates:	0	2	1	3	1

(a) Based on these data, construct a p chart.

(b) Apply Nelson's first four tests for assignable causes. What do you find? Explain.

(c) Should we use these control limits to gauge stability in the near future? Explain.

13.30 Suppose the numbers of college-age students who smoke for 40 consecutive samples, each sample consisting of $n = 50$ college-age students, are as follows:

Sample number	1	2	3	4	5	6	7
Smokers	7	10	10	9	6	9	11

Sample number	8	9	10	11	12	13	14
Smokers	7	9	7	10	11	8	12

Sample number	15	16	17	18	19	20
Smokers	8	8	11	11	10	15

Sample number	21	22	23	24	25	26
Smokers	7	7	7	9	8	8

Sample number	27	28	29	30	31	32
Smokers	8	8	10	4	9	10

Sample number	33	34	35	36	37	38
Smokers	9	13	14	14	10	8

Sample number	39	40
Smokers	9	15

Answer the three parts of Exercise 13.29.

13.31 The following are average breaking strengths based on periodic samples of six metal specimens:

Sample:	1	2	3	4	5
Sample mean:	498.6	508.3	484.6	505.7	491.7

Sample:	6	7	8	9	10
Sample mean:	495.4	482.6	515.2	510.8	503.7

Based on substantial observation, the average breaking strength and standard deviation are 500 and 20 pounds, respectively.

(a) Construct an $\bar{X}$ chart. Can you regard the process as having been stable relative to the average breaking strength?

(b) Use Nelson's tests to support your answer to part (a).

(c) Determine the control limits and the center line for the sample standard deviation.

13.32 The data in the table that follows consist of 20 samples of four observations each on the diameters of ball bearings produced by a manufacturing process.

Sample Number	Sample Values (centimeters)			
1	4.01	4.03	3.98	4.04
2	3.97	3.99	3.99	4.02
3	4.06	4.05	3.97	4.02
4	3.96	3.98	4.07	4.03
5	3.98	3.99	3.99	4.00
6	4.01	4.02	3.96	3.99
7	3.95	3.98	4.02	4.03
8	4.03	4.00	3.96	4.04
9	4.07	3.96	3.98	4.05
10	3.98	3.97	4.02	4.04
11	3.92	4.03	4.05	3.99
12	3.97	4.05	4.04	4.01
13	4.04	4.04	3.96	3.99
14	4.03	4.00	4.02	4.05
15	3.95	3.96	3.95	4.02
16	4.05	4.09	4.07	4.02
17	3.98	4.06	4.04	4.03
18	4.01	4.02	4.00	3.97
19	4.02	4.01	4.05	3.99
20	3.99	3.99	4.01	4.00

(a) Construct $\bar{X}$ and S control charts. Does the process appear to have been stable during this time?

(b) Apply Nelson's eight tests for assignable causes to the $\bar{X}$ chart. What do you find?

(c) State why you think Nelson's tests should not be used with the S chart.

(d) Should we use these control limits to gauge stability in the near future? Explain.

13.33 The $\bar{X}$ and S control charts are maintained on the amount poured into a container by a filling process. Based on 25 periodic samples, with each sample consisting of five such containers, it is determined that $\bar{X} = 400.2$ grams and $\bar{S} = 15.3$ grams.

(a) For a stable process, what are the control limits for the sample mean and the sample standard deviation?

(b) What is an estimate of the process standard deviation?

13.34 In Exercise 13.33, suppose each sample was based on the weights of six containers. How would this change your answers to parts (a) and (b)?

13.35 In an audit, 100 accounts are selected monthly and the number of accounts that contain errors is recorded. The following is the number of accounts with errors for the last 24 months:

Month:	1	2	3	4	5	6
Accounts with errors:	2	1	4	3	2	2

Month:	7	8	9	10	11	12
Accounts with errors:	5	3	4	2	1	5

Month:	13	14	15	16	17	18
Accounts with errors:	2	3	2	1	0	6

Month:	19	20	21	22	23	24
Accounts with errors:	4	5	2	1	8	3

(a) Based on this information, construct a p chart for the proportion of accounts with errors.

(b) Use Nelson's first four tests to determine whether the process was stable at the time these samples were taken.

(c) Should you use these control limits to gauge stability in the near future with regard to the proportion of accounts that contain errors? Explain.

Appendix 13

Computer Instructions for Using MINITAB, EXCEL, and JMP IN

MINITAB

$\bar{X}$ and S Charts When the Values of μ and σ Are Unknown

Consider Example 13.2. To obtain the $\bar{X}$ and S charts in Figure 13.9, enter the data into column c1 in stacked format. That is, the first five observations in the column are those from subgroup 1 (sample 1); the next five are from subgroup 2; and so on. Select STAT–CONTROL CHARTS–XBAR-S . . . . In the dialogue box, enter c1 in the SINGLE COLUMN box, enter 5 in the SUBGROUP SIZE box, and click OK.

The eight tests for detecting special causes with $\bar{X}$ charts, illustrated in Figure 13.11, can be accomplished as follows. While you are in the STAT–CONTROL CHARTS– XBAR-S . . . dialogue box, click the TESTS . . . button. In the TESTS dialogue box, either click the PERFORM ALL EIGHT TESTS button, or click the CHOOSE SPECIFIC TESTS TO PERFORM button and click the boxes for specific tests, and click OK twice.

$\bar{X}$ and S Charts When the Values of μ and σ Are Known

When the values of μ and σ are considered to be known, we obtain the Minitab $\bar{X}$ and S charts in a similar fashion to when μ and σ are unknown. Enter the data into c1 in stacked format, starting with values of the first subgroup (the first sample) followed by those of the second subgroup, and so on. Select STAT–CONTROL CHARTS–XBAR-S . . . . In the dialogue box, enter c1 in the SINGLE COLUMN box, enter the subgroup size in the SUBGROUP SIZE box; enter the known value of μ in the HISTORICAL MEAN box, enter the known value of σ in the HISTORICAL SIGMA box, and click OK.

p Charts When the Value of π Is Unknown

Consider Example 13.3. To obtain a p chart like that in Figure 13.12, enter the data for the 25 samples into column c1. That is, c1 contains 25 values, the number of defectives for each of the 25 samples. Select STAT–CONTROL CHARTS–P .... In the dialogue box, enter c1 in the VARIABLE BOX, enter 100 in the SUBGROUP SIZE box, and click the TESTS ... button. In the TESTS dialogue box, click the PERFORM ALL FOUR TESTS button, and click OK twice.

p Charts When the Value of π Is Known

When the value of π is considered to be known, we obtain a p chart in a similar fashion to when π is unknown. The only difference is that, in the STAT–CONTROL CHARTS–P ... dialogue box, you enter the known value of π in the HISTORICAL p box.

EXCEL

$\bar{X}$ and S Charts When the Values of μ and σ Are Unknown

Consider Example 13.2. To obtain the $\bar{X}$ and S charts in Figure 13.8, enter the strength data into cells a1:a125. That is, the first five observations in the column are those from subgroup 1 (sample 1); the next five are from subgroup 2; and so on. Select TOOLS–DATA ANALYSIS PLUS. In the dialogue box, select STATISTICAL PROCESS CONTROL, and click OK. In the BLOCK COORDINATES dialogue box, enter a1:a125, the range of cells containing the data, and click OK. In the next dialogue box, click XBAR CHART. In the next dialogue box, enter 5, the sample size, and click OK. In the next dialogue box, click S. This produces the chart and executes the eight tests for detecting special causes with $\bar{X}$ charts, illustrated in Figure 13.11. To produce the S chart, repeat this process, clicking S CHART instead of XBAR CHART in the appropriate dialogue box.

$\bar{X}$ and S Charts When the Values of μ and σ Are Known

Excel does not produce $\bar{X}$ and S charts for cases in which the values of μ and σ are considered to be known.

p Charts When the Value of π Is Unknown

Consider Example 13.3. To obtain a p chart like that in Figure 13.12, enter the 25 values representing the number of defectives for each of the 25 samples into cells a1:a25. Select TOOLS–DATA ANALYSIS PLUS. In the dialogue box, select STATISTICAL PROCESS CONTROL, and click OK. In the BLOCK COORDINATES dialogue box, enter a1:a25, the range of cells containing the data, and click OK. In the next dialogue box, click P CHART. In the next dialogue box, enter 100, the sample size for each sample, and click OK.

p Charts When the Value of π Is Known

Excel does not produce p charts for cases in which the value of π is considered to be known.

JMP IN

$\bar{X}$ and S Charts When the Values of μ and σ Are Known

Consider Example 13.2. To obtain $\bar{X}$ and S charts like those in Figures 13.8 and 13.9, enter the data into COLUMN 1 in stacked format. That is, the first five observations are those from subgroup 1, the next five are from subgroup 2, and so on. Name this column STRENGTH, and set its role to Y. Select GRAPH–CONTROL CHARTS. In the dialogue box, select STRENGTH (in the upper left, variable selection box) and click the PROCESS button. Click the CONSTANT button and enter 5 in the associated box. (This indicates the subgroup sizes.) Click the MEAN and S buttons (in the CHART TYPE box); click the ALL button (in the TESTS area); and click CHART.

$\bar{X}$ and S Charts When the Values of μ and σ Are Known

When the values of μ and σ are considered to be known, we obtain the JMP IN $\bar{X}$ and S control charts in a similar fashion to when μ and σ are unknown. Enter the data into COLUMN 1 in stacked format. Set its role to Y. Select GRAPH–CONTROL CHARTS. Complete the dialogue box as described previously and, in addition, click the SPECIFY STATS . . . button. In the dialogue box, enter the known values of the standard deviation and the mean in the SIGMA box and the MEAN (MEASURE) box, respectively. Enter the expected value of the standard deviation in the MEAN (STD DEV) box; to obtain this value, you must multiply the known value of σ (already entered above) by the appropriate value of c_4 (from Table 13.1). Click DONE, then click CHART.

p Charts When the Value of π Is Unknown

Consider Example 13.3. To obtain the p chart in Figure 13.12, enter the 25 values representing the number of defectives for each of the 25 samples into COLUMN 1. Name this column DEFECTS, and set its role to Y. Select GRAPH–CONTROL CHARTS. In the dialogue box, select DEFECTS (in the upper left, variable selection box) and click the PROCESS button. Click the CONSTANT button and enter 100 in the associated box. (This indicates the sample sizes.) Click the CHART TYPE button and select P. Click the ALL button (in the TESTS area), and click CHART.

p Charts When the Value of π Is Known

When the value of π is considered to be known, we obtain a p chart in a manner similar to that when π is unknown. Enter the sample counts into COLUMN 1, and set its role to Y. Select GRAPH–CONTROL CHARTS. Complete the dialogue box as described previously and, in addition, click the SPECIFY STATS . . . button. In the dialogue box, enter the known value of π as indicated. (Note that JMP IN uses the notation P rather than π.) Click DONE, then click CHART.

Appendix

Statistical Tables

Table A

Values of the binomial cumulative distribution function $P(X \le x) = F(x; n, \pi)$

n	x		.01	.05	.10	.20	.30	.40	.50	.60	.70	.80	.90	.95	.99
		π													
2	0		.9801	.9025	.8100	.6400	.4900	.3600	.2500	.1600	.0900	.0400	.0100	.0025	.0001
	1		.9999	.9975	.9900	.9600	.9100	.8400	.7500	.6400	.5100	.3600	.1900	.0975	.0199
	2		1.0000	1.0000	1.0000	1.0000	1.0000	1.0000	1.0000	1.0000	1.0000	1.0000	1.0000	1.0000	1.0000
3	0		.9703	.8574	.7290	.5120	.3430	.2160	.1250	.0640	.0270	.0080	.0010	.0001	.0000
	1		.9997	.9928	.9720	.8960	.7840	.6480	.5000	.3520	.2160	.1040	.0280	.0072	.0003
	2		1.0000	.9999	.9990	.9920	.9730	.9360	.8750	.7840	.6570	.4880	.2710	.1426	.0297
	3		1.0000	1.0000	1.0000	1.0000	1.0000	1.0000	1.0000	1.0000	1.0000	1.0000	1.0000	1.0000	1.0000
4	0		.9606	.8145	.6561	.4096	.2401	.1296	.0625	.0256	.0081	.0016	.0001	.0000	.0000
	1		.9994	.9860	.9477	.8192	.6517	.4752	.3125	.1792	.0837	.0272	.0037	.0005	.0000
	2		1.0000	.9995	.9963	.9728	.9163	.8208	.6875	.5248	.3483	.1808	.0523	.0140	.0006
	3		1.0000	1.0000	.9999	.9984	.9919	.9744	.9375	.8704	.7599	.5904	.3439	.1855	.0394
	4		1.0000	1.0000	1.0000	1.0000	1.0000	1.0000	1.0000	1.0000	1.0000	1.0000	1.0000	1.0000	1.0000
5	0		.9510	.7738	.5905	.3277	.1681	.0778	.0313	.0102	.0024	.0003	.0000	.0000	.0000
	1		.9990	.9774	.9185	.7373	.5282	.3370	.1875	.0870	.0308	.0067	.0005	.0000	.0000
	2		1.0000	.9988	.9914	.9421	.8369	.6826	.5000	.3174	.1631	.0579	.0086	.0012	.0000
	3		1.0000	1.0000	.9995	.9933	.9692	.9130	.8125	.6630	.4718	.2627	.0815	.0226	.0010
	4		1.0000	1.0000	1.0000	.9997	.9976	.9898	.9688	.9222	.8319	.6723	.4095	.2262	.0490
	5		1.0000	1.0000	1.0000	1.0000	1.0000	1.0000	1.0000	1.0000	1.0000	1.0000	1.0000	1.0000	1.0000
6	0		.9415	.7351	.5314	.2621	.1176	.0467	.0156	.0041	.0007	.0001	.0000	.0000	.0000
	1		.9985	.9672	.8857	.6554	.4202	.2333	.1094	.0410	.0109	.0016	.0001	.0000	.0000
	2		1.0000	.9978	.9841	.9011	.7443	.5443	.3438	.1792	.0705	.0170	.0013	.0001	.0000
	3		1.0000	.9999	.9987	.9830	.9295	.8208	.6563	.4557	.2557	.0989	.0159	.0022	.0000
	4		1.0000	1.0000	.9999	.9984	.9891	.9590	.8906	.7667	.5798	.3446	.1143	.0328	.0015
	5		1.0000	1.0000	1.0000	.9999	.9993	.9959	.9844	.9533	.8824	.7379	.4686	.2649	.0585
	6		1.0000	1.0000	1.0000	1.0000	1.0000	1.0000	1.0000	1.0000	1.0000	1.0000	1.0000	1.0000	1.0000

(continued)

Table A

(continued)

n	x	.01	.05	.10	.20	.30	.40	.50	.60	.70	.80	.90	.95	.99
7	0	.9321	.6983	.4783	.2097	.0824	.0280	.0078	.0016	.0002	.0000	.0000	.0000	.0000
	1	.9980	.9556	.8503	.5767	.3294	.1586	.0625	.0188	.0038	.0004	.0000	.0000	.0000
	2	1.0000	.9962	.9743	.8520	.6471	.4199	.2266	.0963	.0288	.0047	.0002	.0000	.0000
	3	1.0000	.9998	.9973	.9667	.8740	.7102	.5000	.2898	.1260	.0333	.0027	.0002	.0000
	4	1.0000	1.0000	.9998	.9953	.9712	.9037	.7734	.5801	.3529	.1480	.0257	.0038	.0000
	5	1.0000	1.0000	1.0000	.9996	.9962	.9812	.9375	.8414	.6706	.4233	.1497	.0444	.0020
	6	1.0000	1.0000	1.0000	1.0000	.9998	.9984	.9922	.9720	.9176	.7903	.5217	.3017	.0679
	7	1.0000	1.0000	1.0000	1.0000	1.0000	1.0000	1.0000	1.0000	1.0000	1.0000	1.0000	1.0000	1.0000
8	0	.9227	.6634	.4305	.1678	.0576	.0168	.0039	.0007	.0001	.0000	.0000	.0000	.0000
	1	.9973	.9428	.8131	.5033	.2553	.1064	.0352	.0085	.0013	.0001	.0000	.0000	.0000
	2	.9999	.9942	.9619	.7969	.5518	.3154	.1445	.0498	.0113	.0012	.0000	.0000	.0000
	3	1.0000	.9996	.9950	.9437	.8059	.5941	.3633	.1737	.0580	.0104	.0004	.0000	.0000
	4	1.0000	1.0000	.9996	.9896	.9420	.8263	.6367	.4059	.1941	.0563	.0050	.0004	.0000
	5	1.0000	1.0000	1.0000	.9988	.9887	.9502	.8555	.6846	.4482	.2031	.0381	.0058	.0001
	6	1.0000	1.0000	1.0000	.9999	.9987	.9915	.9648	.8936	.7447	.4967	.1869	.0572	.0027
	7	1.0000	1.0000	1.0000	1.0000	.9999	.9993	.9961	.9832	.9424	.8322	.5695	.3366	.0773
	8	1.0000	1.0000	1.0000	1.0000	1.0000	1.0000	1.0000	1.0000	1.0000	1.0000	1.0000	1.0000	1.0000
9	0	.9135	.6302	.3874	.1342	.0404	.0101	.0020	.0003	.0000	.0000	.0000	.0000	.0000
	1	.9966	.9288	.7748	.4362	.1960	.0705	.0195	.0038	.0004	.0000	.0000	.0000	.0000
	2	.9999	.9916	.9470	.7382	.4628	.2318	.0898	.0250	.0043	.0003	.0000	.0000	.0000
	3	1.0000	.9994	.9917	.9144	.7297	.4826	.2539	.0994	.0253	.0031	.0001	.0000	.0000
	4	1.0000	1.0000	.9991	.9804	.9012	.7334	.5000	.2666	.0988	.0196	.0009	.0000	.0000
	5	1.0000	1.0000	.9999	.9969	.9747	.9006	.7461	.5174	.2703	.0856	.0083	.0006	.0000
	6	1.0000	1.0000	1.0000	.9997	.9957	.9750	.9102	.7682	.5372	.2618	.0530	.0084	.0001
	7	1.0000	1.0000	1.0000	1.0000	.9996	.9962	.9805	.9295	.8040	.5638	.2252	.0712	.0034
	8	1.0000	1.0000	1.0000	1.0000	1.0000	.9997	.9980	.9899	.9596	.8658	.6126	.3698	.0865
	9	1.0000	1.0000	1.0000	1.0000	1.0000	1.0000	1.0000	1.0000	1.0000	1.0000	1.0000	1.0000	1.0000

π

Table A

(continued)

n	x	π												
		.01	.05	.10	.20	.30	.40	.50	.60	.70	.80	.90	.95	.99
10	0	.9044	.5987	.3487	.1074	.0282	.0060	.0010	.0001	.0000	.0000	.0000	.0000	.0000
	1	.9957	.9139	.7361	.3758	.1493	.0464	.0107	.0017	.0001	.0000	.0000	.0000	.0000
	2	.9999	.9885	.9298	.6778	.3828	.1673	.0547	.0123	.0016	.0001	.0000	.0000	.0000
	3	1.0000	.9990	.9872	.8791	.6496	.3823	.1719	.0548	.0106	.0009	.0000	.0000	.0000
	4	1.0000	.9999	.9984	.9672	.8497	.6331	.3770	.1662	.0473	.0064	.0001	.0000	.0000
	5	1.0000	1.0000	.9999	.9936	.9527	.8338	.6230	.3669	.1503	.0328	.0016	.0001	.0000
	6	1.0000	1.0000	1.0000	.9991	.9884	.9452	.8281	.6177	.3504	.1209	.0128	.0010	.0000
	7	1.0000	1.0000	1.0000	.9999	.9984	.9877	.9453	.8327	.6172	.3222	.0702	.0115	.0001
	8	1.0000	1.0000	1.0000	1.0000	.9999	.9983	.9893	.9536	.8507	.6242	.2639	.0861	.0043
	9	1.0000	1.0000	1.0000	1.0000	1.0000	.9999	.9990	.9940	.9718	.8926	.6513	.4013	.0956
	10	1.0000	1.0000	1.0000	1.0000	1.0000	1.0000	1.0000	1.0000	1.0000	1.0000	1.0000	1.0000	1.0000
11	0	.8953	.5688	.3138	.0859	.0198	.0036	.0005	.0000	.0000	.0000	.0000	.0000	.0000
	1	.9948	.8981	.6974	.3221	.1130	.0302	.0059	.0007	.0000	.0000	.0000	.0000	.0000
	2	.9998	.9848	.9104	.6174	.3127	.1189	.0327	.0059	.0006	.0000	.0000	.0000	.0000
	3	1.0000	.9984	.9815	.8389	.5696	.2963	.1133	.0293	.0043	.0002	.0000	.0000	.0000
	4	1.0000	.9999	.9972	.9496	.7897	.5328	.2744	.0994	.0216	.0020	.0000	.0000	.0000
	5	1.0000	1.0000	.9997	.9883	.9218	.7535	.5000	.2465	.0782	.0117	.0003	.0001	.0000
	6	1.0000	1.0000	1.0000	.9980	.9784	.9006	.7256	.4672	.2103	.0504	.0028	.0001	.0000
	7	1.0000	1.0000	1.0000	.9998	.9957	.9707	.8867	.7037	.4304	.1611	.0185	.0016	.0000
	8	1.0000	1.0000	1.0000	1.0000	.9994	.9941	.9673	.8811	.6873	.3826	.0896	.0152	.0002
	9	1.0000	1.0000	1.0000	1.0000	1.0000	.9993	.9941	.9698	.8870	.6779	.3026	.1019	.0052
	10	1.0000	1.0000	1.0000	1.0000	1.0000	1.0000	.9995	.9964	.9802	.9141	.6862	.4312	.1047
	11	1.0000	1.0000	1.0000	1.0000	1.0000	1.0000	1.0000	1.0000	1.0000	1.0000	1.0000	1.0000	1.0000

(continued)

Table A

(continued)

n	x		.01	.05	.10	.20	.30	.40	.50	.60	.70	.80	.90	.95	.99
									π						
12	0		.8864	.5404	.2824	.0687	.0138	.0022	.0002	.0000	.0000	.0000	.0000	.0000	.0000
	1		.9938	.8816	.6590	.2749	.0850	.0196	.0032	.0003	.0000	.0000	.0000	.0000	.0000
	2		.9998	.9804	.8891	.5583	.2528	.0834	.0193	.0028	.0002	.0000	.0000	.0000	.0000
	3		1.0000	.9978	.9744	.7946	.4925	.2253	.0730	.0153	.0017	.0001	.0000	.0000	.0000
	4		1.0000	.9998	.9957	.9274	.7237	.4382	.1938	.0573	.0095	.0006	.0000	.0000	.0000
	5		1.0000	1.0000	.9995	.9806	.8822	.6652	.3872	.1582	.0386	.0039	.0001	.0000	.0000
	6		1.0000	1.0000	.9999	.9961	.9614	.8418	.6128	.3348	.1178	.0194	.0005	.0000	.0000
	7		1.0000	1.0000	1.0000	.9994	.9905	.9427	.8062	.5618	.2763	.0726	.0043	.0002	.0000
	8		1.0000	1.0000	1.0000	.9999	.9983	.9847	.9270	.7747	.5075	.2054	.0256	.0022	.0000
	9		1.0000	1.0000	1.0000	1.0000	.9998	.9972	.9807	.9166	.7472	.4417	.1109	.0196	.0002
	10		1.0000	1.0000	1.0000	1.0000	1.0000	.9997	.9968	.9804	.9150	.7251	.3410	.1184	.0062
	11		1.0000	1.0000	1.0000	1.0000	1.0000	1.0000	.9998	.9978	.9862	.9313	.7176	.4596	.1136
	12		1.0000	1.0000	1.0000	1.0000	1.0000	1.0000	1.0000	1.0000	1.0000	1.0000	1.0000	1.0000	1.0000
13	0		.8775	.5133	.2542	.0550	.0097	.0013	.0001	.0000	.0000	.0000	.0000	.0000	.0000
	1		.9928	.8646	.6213	.2336	.0637	.0126	.0017	.0001	.0000	.0000	.0000	.0000	.0000
	2		.9997	.9755	.8661	.5017	.2025	.0579	.0112	.0013	.0001	.0000	.0000	.0000	.0000
	3		1.0000	.9969	.9658	.7473	.4206	.1686	.0461	.0078	.0007	.0000	.0000	.0000	.0000
	4		1.0000	.9997	.9935	.9009	.6543	.3530	.1334	.0321	.0040	.0002	.0000	.0000	.0000
	5		1.0000	1.0000	.9991	.9700	.8346	.5744	.2905	.0977	.0182	.0012	.0000	.0000	.0000
	6		1.0000	1.0000	.9999	.9930	.9376	.7712	.5000	.2288	.0624	.0070	.0001	.0000	.0000
	7		1.0000	1.0000	1.0000	.9988	.9818	.9023	.7095	.4256	.1654	.0300	.0009	.0000	.0000
	8		1.0000	1.0000	1.0000	.9998	.9960	.9679	.8666	.6470	.3457	.0991	.0065	.0003	.0000
	9		1.0000	1.0000	1.0000	1.0000	.9993	.9922	.9539	.8314	.5794	.2527	.0342	.0031	.0000
	10		1.0000	1.0000	1.0000	1.0000	.9999	.9987	.9888	.9421	.7975	.4984	.1339	.0245	.0003
	11		1.0000	1.0000	1.0000	1.0000	1.0000	.9999	.9983	.9874	.9363	.7664	.3787	.1354	.0072
	12		1.0000	1.0000	1.0000	1.0000	1.0000	1.0000	.9999	.9987	.9903	.9450	.7458	.4867	.1225
	13		1.0000	1.0000	1.0000	1.0000	1.0000	1.0000	1.0000	1.0000	1.0000	1.0000	1.0000	1.0000	1.0000

Table A

(continued)

π

n	x	.01	.05	.10	.20	.30	.40	.50	.60	.70	.80	.90	.95	.99
14	0	.8687	.4877	.2288	.0440	.0068	.0008	.0001	.0000	.0000	.0000	.0000	.0000	.0000
	1	.9916	.8470	.5846	.1979	.0475	.0081	.0009	.0001	.0000	.0000	.0000	.0000	.0000
	2	.9997	.9699	.8416	.4481	.1608	.0398	.0065	.0006	.0000	.0000	.0000	.0000	.0000
	3	1.0000	.9958	.9559	.6982	.3552	.1243	.0287	.0039	.0002	.0000	.0000	.0000	.0000
	4	1.0000	.9996	.9908	.8702	.5842	.2793	.0898	.0175	.0017	.0000	.0000	.0000	.0000
	5	1.0000	1.0000	.9985	.9561	.7805	.4859	.2120	.0583	.0083	.0004	.0000	.0000	.0000
	6	1.0000	1.0000	.9998	.9884	.9067	.6925	.3953	.1501	.0315	.0024	.0000	.0000	.0000
	7	1.0000	1.0000	1.0000	.9976	.9685	.8499	.6047	.3075	.0933	.0116	.0002	.0000	.0000
	8	1.0000	1.0000	1.0000	.9996	.9917	.9417	.7880	.5141	.2195	.0439	.0015	.0004	.0000
	9	1.0000	1.0000	1.0000	1.0000	.9983	.9825	.9102	.7207	.4158	.1298	.0092	.0042	.0000
	10	1.0000	1.0000	1.0000	1.0000	.9998	.9961	.9713	.8757	.6448	.3018	.0441	.0301	.0003
	11	1.0000	1.0000	1.0000	1.0000	1.0000	.9994	.9935	.9602	.8392	.5520	.1584	.1530	.0084
	12	1.0000	1.0000	1.0000	1.0000	1.0000	.9999	.9991	.9919	.9525	.8021	.4154	.5123	.1313
	13	1.0000	1.0000	1.0000	1.0000	1.0000	1.0000	.9999	.9992	.9932	.9560	.7712	.5123	.1313
	14	1.0000	1.0000	1.0000	1.0000	1.0000	1.0000	1.0000	1.0000	1.0000	1.0000	1.0000	1.0000	1.0000
15	0	.8601	.4633	.2059	.0352	.0047	.0005	.0000	.0000	.0000	.0000	.0000	.0000	.0000
	1	.9904	.8290	.5490	.1671	.0353	.0052	.0005	.0000	.0000	.0000	.0000	.0000	.0000
	2	.9996	.9638	.8159	.3980	.1268	.0271	.0037	.0003	.0000	.0000	.0000	.0000	.0000
	3	1.0000	.9945	.9444	.6482	.2969	.0905	.0176	.0019	.0001	.0000	.0000	.0000	.0000
	4	1.0000	.9994	.9873	.8358	.5155	.2173	.0592	.0093	.0007	.0000	.0000	.0000	.0000
	5	1.0000	.9999	.9978	.9389	.7216	.4032	.1509	.0338	.0037	.0001	.0000	.0000	.0000
	6	1.0000	1.0000	.9997	.9819	.8689	.6098	.3036	.0950	.0152	.0008	.0000	.0000	.0000
	7	1.0000	1.0000	1.0000	.9958	.9500	.7869	.5000	.2131	.0500	.0042	.0000	.0000	.0000
	8	1.0000	1.0000	1.0000	.9992	.9848	.9050	.6964	.3902	.1311	.0181	.0003	.0000	.0000
	9	1.0000	1.0000	1.0000	.9999	.9963	.9662	.8491	.5968	.2784	.0611	.0022	.0001	.0000
	10	1.0000	1.0000	1.0000	1.0000	.9993	.9907	.9408	.7827	.4845	.1642	.0127	.0006	.0000
	11	1.0000	1.0000	1.0000	1.0000	.9999	.9981	.9824	.9095	.7031	.3518	.0556	.0055	.0000
	12	1.0000	1.0000	1.0000	1.0000	1.0000	.9997	.9963	.9729	.8732	.6020	.1841	.0362	.0004
	13	1.0000	1.0000	1.0000	1.0000	1.0000	1.0000	.9995	.9948	.9647	.8329	.4510	.1710	.0096
	14	1.0000	1.0000	1.0000	1.0000	1.0000	1.0000	1.0000	.9995	.9953	.9648	.7941	.5367	.1399
	15	1.0000	1.0000	1.0000	1.0000	1.0000	1.0000	1.0000	1.0000	1.0000	1.0000	1.0000	1.0000	1.0000

(continued)

Table A

(continued)

π

n	x	.01	.05	.10	.20	.30	.40	.50	.60	.70	.80	.90	.95	.99
16	0	.8515	.4401	.1853	.0281	.0033	.0003	.0000	.0000	.0000	.0000	.0000	.0000	.0000
	1	.9891	.8108	.5147	.1407	.0261	.0033	.0003	.0000	.0000	.0000	.0000	.0000	.0000
	2	.9995	.9571	.7892	.3518	.0994	.0183	.0021	.0001	.0000	.0000	.0000	.0000	.0000
	3	1.0000	.9930	.9316	.5981	.2459	.0651	.0106	.0009	.0000	.0000	.0000	.0000	.0000
	4	1.0000	.9991	.9830	.7982	.4499	.1666	.0384	.0049	.0003	.0000	.0000	.0000	.0000
	5	1.0000	.9999	.9967	.9183	.6598	.3288	.1051	.0191	.0016	.0002	.0000	.0000.	.0000
	6	1.0000	1.0000	.9995	.9733	.8247	.5272	.2272	.0583	.0071	.0015	.0000	.0000	.0000
	7	1.0000	1.0000	.9999	.9930	.9256	.7161	.4018	.1423	.0257	.0070	.0001	.0000	.0000
	8	1.0000	1.0000	1.0000	.9985	.9743	.8577	.5982	.2839	.0744	.0267	.0005	.0000	.0000
	9	1.0000	1.0000	1.0000	.9998	.9929	.9417	.7728	.4728	.1753	.0817	.0033	.0001	.0000
	10	1.0000	1.0000	1.0000	1.0000	.9984	.9809	.8949	.6712	.3402	.2018	.0170	.0009	.0000
	11	1.0000	1.0000	1.0000	1.0000	.9997	.9951	.9616	.8334	.5501	.4019	.0684	.0070	.0000
	12	1.0000	1.0000	1.0000	1.0000	1.0000	.9991	.9894	.9349	.7541	.6482	.2108	.0429	.0005
	13	1.0000	1.0000	1.0000	1.0000	1.0000	.9999	.9979	.9817	.9006	.8593	.4853	.1892	.0109
	14	1.0000	1.0000	1.0000	1.0000	1.0000	1.0000	.9997	.9967	.9739	.9719	.8147	.5599	.1485
	15	1.0000	1.0000	1.0000	1.0000	1.0000	1.0000	1.0000	.9997	.9967	.9719	.8147	.5599	.1485
	16	1.0000	1.0000	1.0000	1.0000	1.0000	1.0000	1.0000	1.0000	1.0000	1.0000	1.0000	1.0000	1.0000

Table A

(continued)

π

n	x	.01	.05	.10	.20	.30	.40	.50	.60	.70	.80	.90	.95	.99
17	0	.8429	.4181	.1668	.0225	.0023	.0002	.0000	.0000	.0000	.0000	.0000	.0000	.0000
	1	.9877	.7922	.4818	.1182	.0193	.0021	.0001	.0000	.0000	.0000	.0000	.0000	.0000
	2	.9994	.9497	.7618	.3096	.0774	.0123	.0012	.0001	.0000	.0000	.0000	.0000	.0000
	3	1.0000	.9912	.9174	.5489	.2019	.0464	.0064	.0005	.0000	.0000	.0000	.0000	.0000
	4	1.0000	.9988	.9779	.7582	.3887	.1260	.0245	.0025	.0001	.0000	.0000	.0000	.0000
	5	1.0000	.9999	.9953	.8943	.5968	.2639	.0717	.0106	.0007	.0000	.0000	.00a0	.0000
	6	1.0000	1.0000	.9992	.9623	.7752	.4478	.1662	.0348	.0032	.0001	.0000	.0000	.0000
	7	1.0000	1.0000	.9999	.9891	.8954	.6405	.3145	.0919	.0127	.0005	.0000	.0000	.0000
	8	1.0000	1.0000	1.0000	.9974	.9597	.8011	.5000	.1989	.0403	.0026	.0000	.0000	.0000
	9	1.0000	1.0000	1.0000	.9995	.9873	.9081	.6855	.3595	.1046	.0109	.0001	.0000	.0000
	10	1.0000	1.0000	1.0000	.9999	.9968	.9652	.8338	.5522	.2248	.0377	.0008	.0000	.0000
	11	1.0000	1.0000	1.0000	1.0000	.9993	.9894	.9283	.7361	.4032	.1057	.0047	.0001'	.0000
	12	1.0000	1.0000	1.0000	1.0000	.9999	.9975	.9755	.8740	.6113	.2418	.0221	.0012	.0000
	13	1.0000	1.0000	1.0000	1.0000	1.0000	.9995	.9936	.9536	.7981	.4511	.0826	.0088	.0000
	14	1.0000	1.0000	1.0000	1.0000	1.0000	.9999	.9988	.9877	.9226	.6904	.2382	.0503	.0006
	15	1.0000	1.0000	1.0000	1.0000	1.0000	1.0000	.9999	.9979	.9807	.8818	.5182	.2078	.0123
	16	1.0000	1.0000	1.0000	1.0000	1.0000	1.0000	1.0000	.9998	.9977	.9775	.8332	.5819	.1571
	17	1.0000	1.0000	1.0000	1.0000	1.0000	1.0000	1.0000	1.0000	1.0000	1.0000	1.0000	1.0000	1.0000

(continued)

Table A

(continued)

n	x	π												
		.01	.05	.10	.20	.30	.40	.50	.60	.70	.80	.90	.95	.99
18	0	.8345	.3972	.1501	.0180	.0016	.0001	.0000	.0000	.0000	.0000	.0000	.0000	.0000
	1	.9862	.7735	.4503	.0991	.0142	.0013	.0001	.0000	.0000	.0000	.0000	.0000	.0000
	2	.9993	.9419	.7338	.2713	.0600	.0082	.0007	.0000	.0000	.0000	.0000	.0000	.0000
	3	1.0000	.9891	.9018	.5010	.1646	.0328	.0038	.0002	.0000	.0000	.0000	.0000	.0000
	4	1.0000	.9985	.9718	.7164	.3327	.0942	.0154	.0013	.0003	.0000	.0000	.0000	.0000
	5	1.0000	.9998	.9936	.8671	.5344	.2088	.0481	.0058	.0014	.0000	.0000	.0000	.0000
	6	1.0000	1.0000	.9988	.9487	.7217	.3743	.1189	.0203	.0061	.0002	.0000	.0000	.0000
	7	1.0000	1.0000	.9998	.9837	.8593	.5634	.2403	.0576	.0210	.0009	.0000	.0000	.0000
	8	1.0000	1.0000	1.0000	.9957	.9404	.7368	.4073	.1347	.0596	.0043	.0000	.0000	.0000
	9	1.0000	1.0000	1.0000	.9991	.9790	.8653	.5927	.2632	.1407	.0163	.0000	.0000	.0000
	10	1.0000	1.0000	1.0000	.9998	.9939	.9424	.7597	.4366	.2783	.0513	.0002	.0000	.0000
	11	1.0000	1.0000	1.0000	1.0000	.9986	.9797	.8811	.6257	.4656	.1329	.0012	.0000	.0000
	12	1.0000	1.0000	1.0000	1.0000	.9997	.9942	.9519	.7912	.6673	.2836	.0064	.0002	.0000
	13	1.0000	1.0000	1.0000	1.0000	1.0000	.9987	.9846	.9058	.8354	.4990	.0282	.0015	.0000
	14	1.0000	1.0000	1.0000	1.0000	1.0000	.9998	.9962	.9672	.9400	.7287	.0982	.0109	.0000
	15	1.0000	1.0000	1.0000	1.0000	1.0000	1.0000	.9993	.9918	.9858	.9009	.2662	.0581	.0007
	16	1.0000	1.0000	1.0000	1.0000	1.0000	1.0000	.9999	.9987	.9984	.9820	.5497	.2265	.0138
	17	1.0000	1.0000	1.0000	1.0000	1.0000	1.0000	1.0000	.9999	1.0000	1.0000	.8499	.6028	.1655
	18	1.0000	1.0000	1.0000	1.0000	1.0000	1.0000	1.0000	1.0000	1.0000	1.0000	1.0000	1.0000	1.0000

Table A

(continued)

π

n	x	.01	.05	.10	.20	.30	.40	.50	.60	.70	.80	.90	.95	.99
19	0	.8262	.3774	.1351	.0144	.0011	.0001	.0000	.0000	.0000	.0000	.0000	.0000	.0000
	1	.9847	.7547	.4203	.0829	.0104	.0008	.0000	.0000	.0000	.0000	.0000	.0000	.0000
	2	.9991	.9335	.7054	.2369	.0462	.0055	.0004	.0000	.0000	.0000	.0000	.0000	.0000
	3	1.0000	.9868	.8850	.4551	.1332	.0230	.0022	.0001	.0000	.0000	.0000	.0000	.0000
	4	1.0000	.9980	.9648	.6733	.2822	.0696	.0096	.0006	.0000	.0000	.0000	.0000	.0000
	5	1.0000	.9998	.9914	.8369	.4739	.1629	.0318	.0031	.0001	.0000	.0000	.0000	.0000
	6	1.0000	1.0000	.9983	.9324	.6655	.3081	.0835	.0116	.0006	.0000	.0000	.0000	.0000
	7	1.0000	1.0000	.9997	.9767	.8180	.4878	.1796	.0352	.0028	.0000	.0000	.0000	.0000
	8	1.0000	1.0000	1.0000	.9933	.9161	.6675	.3238	.0885	.0105	.0003	.0000	.0000	.0000
	9	1.0000	1.0000	1.0000	.9984	.9674	.8139	.5000	.1861	.0326	.0016	.0000	.0000	.0000
	10	1.0000	1.0000	1.0000	.9997	.9895	.9115	.6762	.3325	.0839	.0067	.0000	.0000	.0000
	11	1.0000	1.0000	1.0000	1.0000	.9972	.9648	.8204	.5122	.1820	.0233	.0003	.0000	.0000
	12	1.0000	1.0000	1.0000	1.0000	.9994	.9884	.9165	.6919	.3345	.0676	.0017	.0002	.0000
	13	1.0000	1.0000	1.0000	1.0000	.9999	.9969	.9682	.8371	.5261	.1631	.0086	.0020	.0000
	14	1.0000	1.0000	1.0000	1.0000	1.0000	.9994	.9904	.9304	.7178	.3267	.0352	.0132	.0000
	15	1.0000	1.0000	1.0000	1.0000	1.0000	.9999	.9978	.9770	.8668	.5449	.1150	.0665	.0000
	16	1.0000	1.0000	1.0000	1.0000	1.0000	1.0000	.9996	.9945	.9538	.7631	.2946	.2453	.0009
	17	1.0000	1.0000	1.0000	1.0000	1.0000	1.0000	1.0000	.9992	.9896	.9171	.5797	.6226	.0153
	18	1.0000	1.0000	1.0000	1.0000	1.0000	1.0000	1.0000	.9999	.9989	.9856	.8649	.6226	.1738
	19	1.0000	1.0000	1.0000	1.0000	1.0000	1.0000	1.0000	1.0000	1.0000	1.0000	1.0000	1.0000	1.0000

(continued)

Table A

(continued)

n	x	π												
		.01	.05	.10	.20	.30	.40	.50	.60	.70	.80	.90	.95	.99
20	0	.8179	.3585	.1216	.0115	.0008	.0000	.0000	.0000	.0000	.0000	.0000	.0000	.0000
	1	.9831	.7358	.3917	.0692	.0076	.0005	.0000	.0000	.0000	.0000	.0000	.0000	.0000
	2	.9990	.9245	.6769	.2061	.0355	.0036	.0002	.0000	.0000	.0000	.0000	.0000	.0000
	3	1.0000	.9841	.8670	.4114	.1071	.0160	.0013	.0000	.0000	.0000	.0000	.0000	.0000
	4	1.0000	.9974	.9568	.6296	.2375	.0510	.0059	.0003	.0000	.0000	.0000	.0000	.0000
	5	1.0000	.9997	.9887	.8042	.4164	.1256	.0207	.0016	.0000	.0000	.0000	.0000	.0000
	6	1.0000	1.0000	.9976	.9133	.6080	.2500	.0577	.0065	.0003	.0000	.0000	.0000	.0000
	7	1.0000	1.0000	.9996	.9679	.7723	.4159	.1316	.0210	.0013	.0000	.0000	.0000	.0000
	8	1.0000	1.0000	.9999	.9900	.8867	.5956	.2517	.0565	.0051	.0001	.0000	.0000	.0000
	9	1.0000	1.0000	1.0000	.9974	.9520	.7553	.4119	.1275	.0171	.0006	.0000	.0000	.0000
	10	1.0000	1.0000	1.0000	.9994	.9829	.8725	.5881	.2447	.0480	.0026	.0000	.0000	.0000
	11	1.0000	1.0000	1.0000	.9999	.9949	.9435	.7483	.4044	.1133	.0100	.0001	.0000	.0000
	12	1.0000	1.0000	1.0000	1.0000	.9987	.9790	.8684	.5841	.2277	.0321	.0004	.0000	.0000
	13	1.0000	1.0000	1.0000	1.0000	.9997	.9935	.9423	.7500	.3920	.0867	.0024	.0003	.0000
	14	1.0000	1.0000	1.0000	1.0000	1.0000	.9984	.9793	.8744	.5836	.1958	.0113	.0026	.0000
	15	1.0000	1.0000	1.0000	1.0000	1.0000	.9997	.9941	.9490	.7625	.3704	.0432	.0159	.0000
	16	1.0000	1.0000	1.0000	1.0000	1.0000	1.0000	.9987	.9840	.8929	.5886	.1330	.0755	.0000
	17	1.0000	1.0000	1.0000	1.0000	1.0000	1.0000	.9998	.9964	.9645	.7939	.3231	.2642	.0010
	18	1.0000	1.0000	1.0000	1.0000	1.0000	1.0000	1.0000	.9995	.9924	.9308	.6083	.6415	.0169
	19	1.0000	1.0000	1.0000	1.0000	1.0000	1.0000	1.0000	1.0000	.9992	.9885	.8784	.6415	.1821
	20	1.0000	1.0000	1.0000	1.0000	1.0000	1.0000	1.0000	1.0000	1.0000	1.0000	1.0000	1.0000	1.0000

Table A

(continued)

		π												
n	x	.01	.05	.10	.20	.30	.40	.50	.60	.70	.80	.90	.95	.99
25	0	.7778	.2774	.0718	.0038	.0001	.0000	.0000	.0000	.0000	.0000	.0000	.0000	.0000
	1	.9742	.6424	.2712	.0274	.0016	.0001	.0000	.0000	.0000	.0000	.0000	.0000	.0000
	2	.9980	.8729	.5371	.0982	.0090	.0004	.0000	.0000	.0000	.0000	.0000	.0000	.0000
	3	.9999	.9659	.7636	.2340	.0332	.0024	.0001	.0000	.0000	.0000	.0000	.0000	.0000
	4	1.0000	.9928	.9020	.4207	.0905	.0095	.0005	.0000	.0000	.0000	.0000	.0000	.0000
	5	1.0000	.9988	.9666	.6167	.1935	.0294	.0020	.0001	.0000	.0000	.0000	.0000	.0000
	6	1.0000	.9998	.9905	.7800	.3407	.0736	.0073	.0003	.0000	.0000	.0000	.0000	.0000
	7	1.0000	1.0000	.9977	.8909	.5118	.1536	.0216	.0012	.0000	.0000	.0000	.0000	.0000
	8	1.0000	1.0000	.9995	.9532	.6769	.2735	.0539	.0043	.0001	.0000	.0000	.0000	.0000
	9	1.0000	1.0000	.9999	.9827	.8106	.4246	.1148	.0132	.0005	.0000	.0000	.0000	.0000
	10	1.0000	1.0000	1.0000	.9944	.9022	.5858	.2122	.0344	.0018	.0001	.0000	.0000	.0000
	11	1.0000	1.0000	1.0000	.9985	.9558	.7323	.3450	.0778	.0060	.0004	.0000	.0000	.0000
	12	1.0000	1.0000	1.0000	.9996	.9825	.8462	.5000	.1538	.0175	.0015	.0000	.0000	.0000
	13	1.0000	1.0000	1.0000	.9999	.9940	.9222	.6550	.2677	.0442	.0056	.0001	.0000	.0000
	14	1.0000	1.0000	1.0000	1.0000	.9982	.9656	.7878	.4142	.0978	.0173	.0005	.0000	.0000
	15	1.0000	1.0000	1.0000	1.0000	.9995	.9868	.8852	.5754	.1894	.0468	.0023	.0000	.0000
	16	1.0000	1.0000	1.0000	1.0000	.9999	.9957	.9461	.7265	.3231	.1091	.0095	.0002	.0000
	17	1.0000	1.0000	1.0000	1.0000	1.0000	.9988	.9784	.8464	.4881	.2200	.0334	.0012	.0000
	18	1.0000	1.0000	1.0000	1.0000	1.0000	.9997	.9927	.9264	.6593	.3833	.0980	.0072	.0000
	19	1.0000	1.0000	1.0000	1.0000	1.0000	.9999	.9980	.9706	.8065	.5793	.2364	.0341	.0001
	20	1.0000	1.0000	1.0000	1.0000	1.0000	1.0000	.9995	.9905	.9095	.7660	.4629	.1271	.0020
	21	1.0000	1.0000	1.0000	1.0000	1.0000	1.0000	.9999	.9976	.9668	.9018	.7288	.3576	.0258
	22	1.0000	1.0000	1.0000	1.0000	1.0000	1.0000	1.0000	.9996	.9910	.9726	.9282	.7226	.2222
	23	1.0000	1.0000	1.0000	1.0000	1.0000	1.0000	1.0000	.9999	.9984	.9962	1.0000	1.0000	1.0000
	24	1.0000	1.0000	1.0000	1.0000	1.0000	1.0000	1.0000	1.0000	.9999	.9962	1.0000	1.0000	1.0000
	25	1.0000	1.0000	1.0000	1.0000	1.0000	1.0000	1.0000	1.0000	1.0000	1.0000	1.0000	1.0000	1.0000

Table B

Values of the standard normal cumulative distribution function
$$P(Z \le z) = F(z;\ 0,1)$$

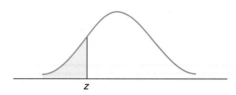

z	.00	.01	.02	.03	.04	.05	.06	.07	.08	.09
−3.5	.0002	.0002	.0002	.0002	.0002	.0002	.0002	.0002	.0002	.0002
−3.4	.0003	.0003	.0003	.0003	.0003	.0003	.0003	.0003	.0003	.0002
−3.3	.0005	.0005	.0005	.0004	.0004	.0004	.0004	.0004	.0004	.0003
−3.2	.0007	.0007	.0006	.0006	.0006	.0006	.0006	.0005	.0005	.0005
−3.1	.0010	.0009	.0009	.0009	.0008	.0008	.0008	.0008	.0007	.0007
−3.0	.0013	.0013	.0013	.0012	.0012	.0011	.0011	.0011	.0010	.0010
−2.9	.0019	.0018	.0018	.0017	.0016	.0016	.0015	.0015	.0014	.0014
−2.8	.0026	.0025	.0024	.0023	.0023	.0022	.0021	.0021	.0020	.0019
−2.7	.0035	.0034	.0033	.0032	.0031	.0030	.0029	.0028	.0027	.0026
−2.6	.0047	.0045	.0044	.0043	.0041	.0040	.0039	.0038	.0037	.0036
−2.5	.0062	.0060	.0059	.0057	.0055	.0054	.0052	.0051	.0049	.0048
−2.4	.0082	.0080	.0078	.0075	.0073	.0071	.0069	.0068	.0066	.0064
−2.3	.0107	.0104	.0102	.0099	.0096	.0094	.0091	.0089	.0087	.0084
−2.2	.0139	.0136	.0132	.0129	.0125	.0122	.0119	.0116	.0113	.0110
−2.1	.0179	.0174	.0170	.0166	.0162	.0158	.0154	.0150	.0146	.0143
−2.0	.0228	.0222	.0217	.0212	.0207	.0202	.0197	.0192	.0188	.0183
−1.9	.0287	.0281	.0274	.0268	.0262	.0256	.0250	.0244	.0239	.0233
−1.8	.0359	.0351	.0344	.0336	.0329	.0322	.0314	.0307	.0301	.0294
−1.7	.0446	.0436	.0427	.0418	.0409	.0401	.0392	.0384	.0375	.0367
−1.6	.0548	.0537	.0526	.0516	.0505	.0495	.0485	.0475	.0465	.0455
−1.5	.0668	.0655	.0643	.0630	.0618	.0606	.0594	.0582	.0571	.0559
−1.4	.0808	.0793	.0778	.0764	.0749	.0735	.0721	.0708	.0694	.0681
−1.3	.0968	.0951	.0934	.0918	.0901	.0885	.0869	.0853	.0838	.0823
−1.2	.1151	.1131	.1112	.1093	.1075	.1056	.1038	.1020	.1003	.0985
−1.1	.1357	.1335	.1314	.1292	.1271	.1251	.1230	.1210	.1190	.1170
−1.0	.1587	.1562	.1539	.1515	.1492	.1469	.1446	.1423	.1401	.1379
−.9	.1841	.1814	.1788	.1762	.1736	.1711	.1685	.1660	.1635	.1611
−.8	.2119	.2090	.2061	.2033	.2005	.1977	.1949	.1922.	.1894	.1867
−.7	.2420	.2389	.2358	.2327	.2297	.2266	.2236	.2206	.2177	.2148
−.6	.2743	.2709	.2676	.2643	.2611	.2578	.2546	.2514	.2483	.2451
−.5	.3085	.3050	.3015	.2981	.2946	.2912	.2877	.2843	.2810	.2776
−.4	.3446	.3409	.3372	.3336	.3300	.3264	.3228	.3192	.3156	.3121
−.3	.3821	.3783	.3745	.3707	.3669	.3632	.3594	.3557	.3520	.3483
−.2	.4207	.4168	.4129	.4090	.4052	.4013	.3974	.3936	.3897	.3859
−.1	.4602	.4562	.4522	.4483	.4443	.4404	.4364	.4325	.4286	.4247
−.0	.5000	.4960	.4920	.4880	.4840	.4801	.4761	.4721	.4681	.4641

Table B (continued)

Values of the standard normal cumulative distribution function
$$P(Z \le z) = F(z;\ 0,1)$$

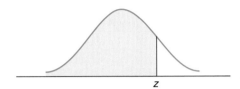

z	.00	.01	.02	.03	.04	.05	.06	.07	.08	.09
.0	.5000	.5040	.5080	.5120	.5160	.5199	.5239	.5279	.5319	.5359
.1	.5398	.5438	.5478	.5517	.5557	.5596	.5636	.5675	.5714	.5753
.2	.5793	.5832	.5871	.5910	.5948	.5987	.6026	.6064	.6103	.6141
.3	.6179	.6217	.6255	.6293	.6331	.6368	.6406	.6443	.6480	.6517
.4	.6554	.6591	.6628	.6664	.6700	.6736	.6772	.6808	.6844	.6879
.5	.6915	.6950	.6985	.7019	.7054	.7088	.7123	.7157	.7190	.7224
.6	.7257	.7291	.7324	.7357	.7389	.7422	.7454	.7486	.7517	.7549
.7	.7580	.7611	.7642	.7673	.7703	.7734	.7764	.7794	.7823	.7852
.8	.7881	.7910	.7939	.7967	.7995	.8023	.8051	.8078	.8106	.8133
.9	.8159	.8186	.8212	.8238	.8264	.8289	.8315	.8340	.8365	.8389
1.0	.8413	.8438	.8461	.8485	.8508	.8531	.8554	.8577	.8599	.8621
1.1	.8643	.8665	.8686	.8708	.8729	.8749	.8770	.8790	.8810	.8830
1.2	.8849	.8869	.8888	.8907	.8925	.8944	.8962	.8980	.8997	.9015
1.3	.9032	.9049	.9066	.9082	.9099	.9115	.9131	.9147	.9162	.9177
1.4	.9192	.9207	.9222	.9236	.9251	.9265	.9279	.9292	.9306	.9319
1.5	.9332	.9345	.9357	.9370	.9382	.9394	.9406	.9418	.9429	.9441
1.6	.9452	.9463	.9474	.9484	.9495	.9505	.9515	.9525	.9535	.9545
1.7	.9554	.9564	.9573	.9582	.9591	.9599	.9608	.9616	.9625	.9633
1.8	.9641	.9649	.9656	.9664	.9671	.9678	.9016	.9693	.9699	.9706
1.9	.9713	.9719	.9726	.9732	.9738	.9744	.9750	.9756	.9761	.9767
2.0	.9772	.9778	.9783	.9788	.9793	.9798	.9803	.9808	.9812	.9817
2.1	.9821	.9826	.9830	.9834	.9838	.9842	.9846	.9850	.9854	.9857
2.2	.9861	.9864	.9868	.9871	.9875	.9878	.9881	.9884	.9887	.9890
2.3	.9893	.9896	.9898	.9901	.9904	.9906	.9909	.9911	.9913	.9916
2.4	.9918	.9920	.9922	.9925	.9927	.9929	.9931	.9932	.9934	.9936
2.5	.9938	.9940	.9941	.9943	.9945	.9946	.9948	.9949	.9951	.9952
2.6	.9953	.9955	.9956	.9957	.9959	.9960	.9961	.9962	.9963	.9964
2.7	.9965	.9966	.9967	.9968	.9969	.9970	.9971	.9972	.9973	.9974
2.8	.9974	.9975	.9976	.9977	.9977	.9978	.9979	.9979	.9980	.9981
2.9	.9981	.9982	.9982	.9983	.9984	.9984	.9985	.9985	.9986	.9986
3.0	.9987	.9987	.9987	.9988	.9988	.9989	.9989	.9989	.9990	.9990
3.1	.9990	.9991	.9991	.9991	.9992	.9992	.9992	.9992	.9993	.9993
3.2	.9993	.9993	.9994	.9994	.9994	.9994	.9994	.9995	.9995	.9995
3.3	.9995	.9995	.9995	.9996	.9996	.9996	.9996	.9996	.9996	.9997
3.4	.9997	.9997	.9997	.9997	.9997	.9997	.9997	.9997	.9997	.9998
3.5	.9998	.9998	.9998	.9998	.9998	.9998	.9998	.9998	.9998	.9998

Table C

Quantile values of the
Student's T distribution

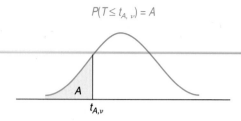

$P(T \le t_{A,\,\nu}) = A$

ν	$t_{.001}$	$t_{.005}$	$t_{.010}$	$t_{.025}$	$t_{.050}$	$t_{.100}$	$t_{.200}$
1	−318.309	−63.657	−31.821	−12.706	−6.314	−3.078	−1.376
2	−22.327	−9.925	−6.965	−4.303	−2.920	−1.886	−1.061
3	−10.215	−5.841	−4.541	−3.182	−2.353	−1.638	−.978
4	−7.173	−4.604	−3.747	−2.776	−2.132	−1.533	−.941
5	−5.893	−4.032	−3.365	−2.571	−2.015	−1.476	−.920
6	−5.208	−3.707	−3.143	−2.447	−1.943	−1.440	−.906
7	−4.785	−3.499	−2.998	−2.365	−1.895	−1.415	−.896
8	−4.501	−3.355	−2.896	−2.306	−1.860	−1.397	−.889
9	−4.297	−3.250	−2.821	−2.262	−1.833	−1.383	−.883
10	−4.144	−3.169	−2.764	−2.228	−1.812	−1.372	−.879
11	−4.025	−3.106	−2.718	−2.201	−1.796	−1.363	−.876
12	−3.930	−3.055	−2.681	−2.179	−1.782	−1.356	−.873
13	−3.852	−3.012	−2.650	−2.160	−1.771	−1.350	−.870
14	−3.787	−2.977	−2.624	−2.145	−1.761	−1.345	−.868
15	−3.733	−2.947	−2.602	−2.131	−1.753	−1.341	−.866
16	−3.686	−2.921	−2.583	−2.120	−1.746	1.337	−.865
17	−3.646	−2.898	−2.567	−2.110	−1.740	−1.333	−.863
18	−3.610	−2.878	−2.552	−2.101	−1.734	−1.330	−.862
19	−3.579	−2.861	−2.539	−2.093	−1.729	−1.328	−.861
20	−3.552	−2.845	−2.528	−2.086	−1.725	1.325	−.860
21	−3.527	−2.831	−2.518	−2.080	−1.721	−1.323	−.859
22	−3.505	−2.819	−2.508	−2.074	−1.717	−1.321	−.858
23	3.485	−2.807	−2.500	−2.069	−1.714	−1.319	−.858
24	−3.467	−2.797	−2.492	−2.064	−1.711	−1.318	−.857
25	−3.450	−2.787	−2.485	−2.060	−1.708	−1.316	−.856
26	−3.435	−2.779	−2.479	−2.056	−1.706	−1.315	−.856
27	−3.421	−2.771	−2.473	−2.052	−1.703	−1.314	−.855
28	−3.408	−2.763	−2.467	−2.048	−1.701	−1.313	−.855
29	−3.396	−2.756	−2.462	−2.045	−1.699	−1.311	−.854
30	−3.385	2.750	−2.457	−2.042	−1.697	−1.310	−.854
35	−3.340	−2.724	−2.438	−2.030	−1.690	−1.306	−.852
40	−3.307	−2.704	−2.423	−2.021	−1.684	−1.303	−.851
45	−3.281	−2.690	−2.412	−2.014	−1.679	−1.301	−.850
50	−3.261	−2.678	−2.403	−2.009	−1.676	−1.299	−.849
60	−3.232	−2.660	−2.390	−2.000	−1.671	−1.296	−.848
70	−3.211	−2.648	−2.381	−1.994	−1.667	−1.294	−.847
80	−3.195	−2.639	−2.374	−1.990	−1.664	−1.292	−.846
90	−3.183	−2.632	−2.369	−1.987	−1.662	−1.291	−.846
100	−3.174	−2.626	−2.364	−1.984	−1.660	−1.290	−.845
200	−3.131	−2.601	−2.345	−1.972	−1.652	−1.286	−.843
500	−3.107	−2.586	−2.334	−1.965	−1.648	−1.283	−.842
1,000	−3.098	−2.581	−2.330	−1.962	−1.646	−1.282	−.842
∞	−3.090	−2.575	−2.326	−1.960	−1.645	−1.282	−.842

Table C (continued)

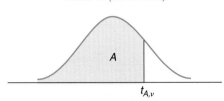

ν	$t_{.800}$	$t_{.900}$	$t_{.950}$	$t_{.975}$	$t_{.990}$	$t_{.995}$	$t_{.999}$
1	1.376	3.078	6.314	12.706	31.820	63.656	318.294
2	1.061	1.886	2.920	4.303	6.965	9.925	22.327
3	.978	1.638	2.353	3.182	4.541	5.841	10.214
4	.941	1.533	2.132	2.776	3.747	4.604	7.173
5	.920	1.476	2.015	2.571	3.365	4.032	5.893
6	.906	1.440	1.943	2.447	3.143	3.707	5.208
7	.896	1.415	1.895	2.365	2.998	3.499	4.785
8	.889	1.397	1.860	2.306	2.896	3.355	4.501
9	.883	1.383	1.833	2.262	2.821	3.250	4.297
10	.879	1.372	1.812	2.228	2.764	3.169	4.144
11	.876	1.363	1.796	2.201	2.718	3.106	4.025
12	.873	1.356	1.782	2.179	2.681	3.055	3.930
13	.870	1.350	1.771	2.160	2.650	3.012	3.852
14	.868	1.345	1.761	2.145	2.624	2.977	3.787
15	.866	1.341	1.753	2.131	2.602	2.947	3.733
16	.865	1.337	1.746	2.120	2.583	2.921	3.686
17	.863	1.333	1.740	2.110	2.567	2.898	3.646
18	.862	1.330	1.734	2.101	2.552	2.878	3.610
19	.861	1.328	1.729	2.093	2.539	2.861	3.579
20	.860	1.325	1.725	2.086	2.528	2.845	3.552
21	.859	1.323	1.721	2.080	2.518	2.831	3.527
22	.858	1.321	1.717	2.074	2.508	2.819	3.505
23	.858	1.319	1.714	2.069	2.500	2.807	3.485
24	.857	1.318	1.711	2.064	2.492	2.797	3.467
25	.856	1.316	1.708	2.060	2.485	2.787	3.450
26	.856	1.315	1.706	2.056	2.479	2.779	3.435
27	.855	1.314	1.703	2.052	2.473	2.771	3.421
28	.855	1.313	1.701	2.048	2.467	2.763	3.408
29	.854	1.311	1.699	2.045	2.462	2.756	3.396
30	.854	1.310	1.697	2.042	2.457	2.750	3.385
35	.852	1.306	1.690	2.030	2.438	2.724	3.340
40	.851	1.303	1.684	2.021	2.423	2.704	3.307
45	.850	1.301	1.679	2.014	2.412	2.690	3.281
50	.849	1.299	1.676	2.009	2.403	2.678	3.261
60	.848	1.296	1.671	2.000	2.390	2.660	3.232
70	.847	1.294	1.667	1.994	2.381	2.648	3.211
80	.846	1.292	1.664	1.990	2.374	2.639	3.195
90	.846	1.291	1.662	1.987	2.368	2.632	3.183
100	.845	1.290	1.660	1.984	2.364	2.626	3.174
200	.843	1.286	1.652	1.972	2.345	2.601	3.131
500	.842	1.283	1.648	1.965	2.334	2.586	3.107
1,000	.842	1.282	1.646	1.962	2.330	2.581	3.098
∞	.842	1.282	1.645	1.960	2.326	2.575	3.090

Table D

Quantile values of the
F distribution

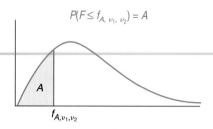

$$P(F \le f_{A, \nu_1, \nu_2}) = A$$

A

f_{A,ν_1,ν_2}

					A = .01					
						ν_1				
ν_2	**1**	**2**	**3**	**4**	**5**	**6**	**7**	**8**	**9**	**10**
1	.00	.01	.03	.05	.06	.07	.08	.09	.09	.10
2	.00	.01	.03	.06	.08	.09	.10	.12	.12	.13
3	.00	.01	.03	.06	.08	.10	.12	.13	.14	.15
4	.00	.01	.03	.06	.09	.11	.13	.14	.16	.17
5	.00	.01	.04	.06	.09	.11	.13	.15	.17	.18
6	.00	.01	.04	.07	.09	.12	.14	.16	.17	.19
7	.00	.01	.04	.07	.10	.12	.14	.16	.18	.19
8	.00	.01	.04	.07	.10	.12	.15	.17	.18	.20
9	.00	.01	.04	.07	.10	.13	.15	.17	.19	.20
10	.00	.01	.04	.07	.10	.13	.15	.17	.19	.21
11	.00	.01	.04	.07	.10	.13	.15	.17	.19	.21
12	.00	.01	.04	.07	.10	.13	.15	.18	.20	.21
13	.00	.01	.04	.07	.10	.13	.16	.18	.20	.22
14	.00	.01	.04	.07	.10	.13	.16	.18	.20	.22
15	.00	.01	.04	.07	.10	.13	.16	.18	.20	.22
16	.00	.01	.04	.07	.10	.13	.16	.18	.20	.22
17	.00	.01	.04	.07	.10	.13	.16	.18	.20	.22
18	.00	.01	.04	.07	.10	.13	.16	.18	.21	.22
19	.00	.01	.04	.07	.10	.13	.16	.19	.21	.23
20	.00	.01	.04	.07	.10	.14	.16	.19	.21	.23
21	.00	.01	.04	.07	.10	.14	.16	.19	.21	.23
22	.00	.01	.04	.07	.11	.14	.16	.19	.21	.23
23	.00	.01	.04	.07	.11	.14	.16	.19	.21	.23
24	.00	.01	.04	.07	.11	.14	.16	.19	.21	.23
25	.00	.01	.04	.07	.11	.14	.17	.19	.21	.23
26	.00	.01	.04	.07	.11	.14	.17	.19	.21	.23
27	.00	.01	.04	.07	.11	.14	.17	.19	.21	.23
28	.00	.01	.04	.07	.11	.14	.17	.19	.21	.23
29	.00	.01	.04	.07	.11	.14	.17	.19	.21	.23
30	.00	.01	.04	.07	.11	.14	.17	.19	.22	.24
35	.00	.01	.04	.07	.11	.14	.17	.19	.22	.24
40	.00	.01	.04	.07	.11	.14	.17	.20	.22	.24
50	.00	.01	.04	.07	.11	.14	.17	.20	.22	.24
60	.00	.01	.04	.07	.11	.14	.17	.20	.22	.24
80	.00	.01	.04	.07	.11	.14	.17	.20	.23	.25
100	.00	.01	.04	.07	.11	.14	.17	.20	.23	.25
200	.00	.01	.04	.07	.11	.14	.18	.20	.23	.25
500	.00	.01	.04	.07	.11	.14	.18	.20	.23	.25
1,000	.00	.01	.04	.07	.11	.15	.18	.21	.23	.26

Table D
(continued)

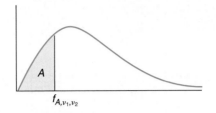

f_{A, ν_1, ν_2}

					$A = .01$					
					ν_1					
ν_2	**11**	**12**	**15**	**20**	**25**	**30**	**40**	**50**	**100**	**1,000**
1	.10	.11	.12	.12	.13	.13	.14	.14	.15	.15
2	.14	.14	.16	.17	.18	.19	.19	.20	.21	.22
3	.16	.17	.18	.20	.21	.22	.23	.24	.25	.26
4	.18	.18	.20	.23	.24	.25	.26	.27	.28	.30
5	.19	.20	.22	.24	.26	.27	.28	.29	.31	.33
6	.20	.21	.23	.26	.28	.29	.30	.31	.33	.35
7	.20	.22	.24	.27	.29	.30	.32	.33	.35	.38
8	.21	.22	.25	.28	.30	.32	.33	.35	.37	.40
9	.22	.23	.26	.29	.31	.33	.35	.36	.39	.41
10	.22	.23	.26	.30	.32	.34	.36	.37	.40	.43
11	.22	.24	.27	.30	.33	.34	.37	.38	.41	.44
12	.23	.24	.27	.31	.33	.35	.38	.39	.42	.45
13	.23	.24	.28	.31	.34	.36	.38	.40	.43	.47
14	.23	.25	.28	.32	.35	.36	.39	.41	.44	.48
15	.24	.25	.28	.32	.35	.37	.40	.41	.45	.49
16	.24	.25	.29	.33	.36	.38	.40	.42	.46	.50
17	.24	.25	.29	.33	.36	.38	.41	.43	.46	.50
18	.24	.26	.29	.33	.36	.38	.41	.43	.47	.51
19	.24	.26	.29	.34	.37	.39	.42	.44	.48	.52
20	.24	.26	.30	.34	.37	.39	.42	.44	.48	.53
21	.25	.26	.30	.34	.37	.40	.43	.45	.49	.53
22	.25	.26	.30	.35	.38	.40	.43	.45	.49	.54
23	.25	.26	.30	.35	.38	.40	.43	.45	.50	.55
24	.25	.26	.30	.35	.38	.41	.44	.46	.50	.55
25	.25	.27	.31	.35	.38	.41	.44	.46	.51	.56
26	.25	.27	.31	.35	.39	.41	.44	.46	.51	.56
27	.25	.27	.31	.36	.39	.41	.45	.47	.52	.57
28	.25	.27	.31	.36	.39	.41	.45	.47	.52	.57
29	.25	.27	.31	.36	.39	.42	.45	.47	.52	.58
30	.25	.27	.31	.36	.39	.42	.45	.48	.53	.58
35	.26	.27	.32	.37	.40	.43	.46	.49	.54	.60
40	.26	.28	.32	.37	.41	.43	.47	.50	.56	.62
50	.26	.28	.32	.38	.42	.45	.49	.51	.58	.65
60	.26	.28	.33	.38	.42	.45	.50	.52	.59	.67
80	.27	.29	.33	.39	.43	.46	.51	.54	.61	.70
100	.27	.29	.34	.39	.44	.47	.52	.55	.63	.72
200	.27	.29	.34	.40	.45	.48	.53	.57	.66	.78
500	.28	.30	.35	.41	.46	.49	.55	.58	.68	.84
1,000	.28	.30	.35	.41	.46	.50	.55	.59	.69	.86

Table D
(continued)

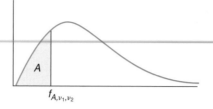

	A = .025									
	ν_1									
ν_2	**1**	**2**	**3**	**4**	**5**	**6**	**7**	**8**	**9**	**10**
1	.00	.03	.06	.08	.10	.11	.12	.13	.14	.14
2	.00	.03	.06	.09	.12	.14	.15	.17	.17	.18
3	.00	.03	.06	.10	.13	.15	.17	.18	.20	.21
4	.00	.03	.07	.10	.14	.16	.18	.20	.21	.22
5	.00	.03	.07	.11	.14	.17	.19	.21	.22	.24
6	.00	.03	.07	.11	.14	.17	.20	.21	.23	.25
7	.00	.03	.07	.11	.15	.18	.20	.22	.24	.25
8	.00	.03	.07	.11	.15	.18	.20	.23	.24	.26
9	.00	.03	.07	.11	.15	.18	.21	.23	.25	.26
10	.00	.03	.07	.11	.15	.18	.21	.23	.25	.27
11	.00	.03	.07	.11	.15	.18	.21	.24	.26	.27
12	.00	.03	.07	.11	.15	.19	.21	.24	.26	.28
13	.00	.03	.07	.11	.15	.19	.22	.24	.26	.28
14	.00	.03	.07	.12	.15	.19	.22	.24	.26	.28
15	.00	.03	.07	.12	.16	.19	.22	.24	.27	.28
16	.00	.03	.07	.12	.16	.19	.22	.25	.27	.29
17	.00	.03	.07	.12	.16	.19	.22	.25	.27	.29
18	.00	.03	.07	.12	.16	.19	.22	.25	.27	.29
19	.00	.03	.07	.12	.16	.19	.22	.25	.27	.29
20	.00	.03	.07	.12	.16	.19	.22	.25	.27	.29
21	.00	.03	.07	.12	.16	.19	.22	.25	.27	.29
22	.00	.03	.07	.12	.16	.19	.23	.25	.27	.30
23	.00	.03	.07	.12	.16	.20	.23	.25	.28	.30
24	.00	.03	.07	.12	.16	.20	.23	.25	.28	.30
25	.00	.03	.07	.12	.16	.20	.23	.25	.28	.30
26	.00	.03	.07	.12	.16	.20	.23	.25	.28	.30
27	.00	.03	.07	.12	.16	.20	.23	.26	.28	.30
28	.00	.03	.07	.12	.16	.20	.23	.26	.28	.30
29	.00	.03	.07	.12	.16	.20	.23	.26	.28	.30
30	.00	.03	.07	.12	.16	.20	.23	.26	.28	.30
35	.00	.03	.07	.12	.16	.20	.23	.26	.28	.30
40	.00	.03	.07	.12	.16	.20	.23	.26	.29	.31
50	.00	.03	.07	.12	.16	.20	.23	.26	.29	.31
60	.00	.03	.07	.12	.16	.20	.24	.26	.29	.31
80	.00	.03	.07	.12	.16	.20	.24	.27	.29	.32
100	.00	.03	.07	.12	.16	.20	.24	.27	.29	.32
200	.00	.03	.07	.12	.17	.20	.24	.27	.30	.32
500	.00	.03	.07	.12	.17	.21	.24	.27	.30	.32
1,000	.00	.03	.07	.12	.17	.21	.24	.27	.30	.32

Table D
(continued)

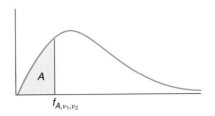

| | A = .025 | | | | | | | | | |
| | | | | | ν_1 | | | | | |
ν_2	11	12	15	20	25	30	40	50	100	1,000
1	.15	.15	.16	.17	.18	.18	.18	.19	.19	.20
2	.19	.20	.21	.22	.23	.24	.25	.25	.26	.27
3	.22	.22	.24	.26	.27	.28	.29	.29	.31	.32
4	.23	.24	.26	.28	.30	.31	.32	.33	.34	.36
5	.25	.26	.28	.30	.32	.33	.34	.35	.37	.39
6	.26	.27	.29	.32	.34	.35	.36	.37	.39	.41
7	.27	.28	.30	.33	.35	.36	.38	.39	.41	.43
8	.27	.28	.31	.34	.36	.38	.40	.41	.43	.45
9	.28	.29	.32	.35	.37	.39	.41	.42	.45	.47
10	.28	.30	.33	.36	.38	.40	.42	.43	.46	.49
11	.29	.30	.33	.37	.39	.41	.43	.44	.47	.50
12	.29	.31	.34	.37	.40	.41	.44	.45	.48	.51
13	.29	.31	.34	.38	.40	.42	.44	.46	.49	.52
14	.30	.31	.35	.38	.41	.43	.45	.47	.50	.53
15	.30	.31	.35	.39	.41	.43	.46	.47	.51	.54
16	.30	.32	.35	.39	.42	.44	.46	.48	.52	.55
17	.30	.32	.36	.40	.42	.44	.47	.49	.52	.56
18	.31	.32	.36	.40	.43	.45	.47	.49	.53	.57
19	.31	.32	.36	.40	.43	.45	.48	.50	.54	.57
20	.31	.33	.36	.41	.43	.46	.48	.50	.54	.58
21	.31	.33	.36	.41	.44	.46	.49	.51	.55	.59
22	.31	.33	.37	.41	.44	.46	.49	.51	.55	.59
23	.31	.33	.37	.41	.44	.47	.49	.51	.56	.60
24	.32	.33	.37	.42	.45	.47	.50	.52	.56	.60
25	.32	.33	.37	.42	.45	.47	.50	.52	.56	.61
26	.32	.33	.37	.42	.45	.47	.50	.52	.57	.61
27	.32	.33	.37	.42	.45	.48	.51	.53	.57	.62
28	.32	.34	.38	.42	.45	.48	.51	.53	.58	.62
29	.32	.34	.38	.42	.46	.48	.51	.53	.58	.63
30	.32	.34	.38	.43	.46	.48	.51	.54	.58	.63
35	.32	.34	.38	.43	.47	.49	.53	.55	.60	.65
40	.33	.34	.39	.44	.47	.50	.53	.56	.61	.67
50	.33	.35	.39	.44	.48	.51	.55	.57	.63	.69
60	.33	.35	.40	.45	.49	.52	.55	.58	.64	.71
80	.34	.35	.40	.46	.50	.53	.57	.59	.66	.74
100	.34	.36	.40	.46	.50	.53	.57	.60	.67	.76
200	.34	.36	.41	.47	.51	.54	.59	.62	.70	.81
500	.35	.36	.41	.48	.52	.55	.60	.64	.73	.86
1,000	.35	.37	.42	.48	.52	.56	.61	.64	.73	.88

Table D
(continued)

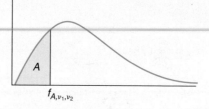

					$A = .05$					
					ν_1					
ν_2	1	2	3	4	5	6	7	8	9	10
1	.01	.05	.10	.13	.15	.17	.18	.19	.20	.20
2	.01	.05	.10	.14	.17	.19	.21	.22	.23	.24
3	.00	.05	.11	.15	.18	.21	.23	.25	.26	.27
4	.00	.05	.11	.16	.19	.22	.24	.26	.28	.29
5	.00	.05	.11	.16	.20	.23	.25	.27	.29	.30
6	.00	.05	.11	.16	.20	.23	.26	.28	.30	.31
7	.00	.05	.11	.16	.21	.24	.26	.29	.30	.32
8	.00	.05	.11	.17	.21	.24	.27	.29	.31	.33
9	.00	.05	.11	.17	.21	.24	.27	.30	.31	.33
10	.00	.05	.11	.17	.21	.25	.27	.30	.32	.34
11	.00	.05	.11	.17	.21	.25	.28	.30	.32	.34
12	.00	.05	.11	.17	.21	.25	.28	.30	.33	.34
13	.00	.05	.11	.17	.21	.25	.28	.31	.33	.35
14	.00	.05	.11	.17	.22	.25	.28	.31	.33	.35
15	.00	.05	.11	.17	.22	.25	.28	.31	.33	.35
16	.00	.05	.12	.17	.22	.25	.29	.31	.33	.35
17	.00	.05	.12	.17	.22	.26	.29	.31	.34	.36
18	.00	.05	.12	.17	.22	.26	.29	.32	.34	.36
19	.00	.05	.12	.17	.22	.26	.29	.32	.34	.36
20	.00	.05	.12	.17	.22	.26	.29	.32	.34	.36
21	.00	.05	.12	.17	.22	.26	.29	.32	.34	.36
22	.00	.05	.12	.17	.22	.26	.29	.32	.34	.36
23	.00	.05	.12	.17	.22	.26	.29	.32	.34	.36
24	.00	.05	.12	.17	.22	.26	.29	.32	.34	.37
25	.00	.05	.12	.17	.22	.26	.29	.32	.35	.37
26	.00	.05	.12	.17	.22	.26	.29	.32	.35	.37
27	.00	.05	.12	.17	.22	.26	.29	.32	.35	.37
28	.00	.05	.12	.17	.22	.26	.30	.32	.35	.37
29	.00	.05	.12	.17	.22	.26	.30	.32	.35	.37
30	.00	.05	.12	.17	.22	.26	.30	.32	.35	.37
35	.00	.05	.12	.17	.22	.26	.30	.33	.35	.37
40	.00	.05	.12	.17	.22	.27	.30	.33	.35	.38
50	.00	.05	.12	.18	.22	.27	.30	.33	.36	.38
60	.00	.05	.12	.18	.23	.27	.30	.33	.36	.38
80	.00	.05	.12	.18	.23	.27	.30	.33	.36	.38
100	.00	.05	.12	.18	.23	.27	.31	.34	.36	.39
200	.00	.05	.12	.18	.23	.27	.31	.34	.37	.39
500	.00	.05	.12	.18	.23	.27	.31	.34	.37	.39
1,000	.00	.05	.12	.18	.23	.27	.31	.34	.37	.39

Table D
(continued)

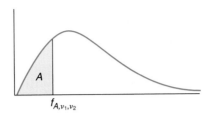

$$f_{A, \nu_1, \nu_2}$$

	A = .05									
	ν_1									
ν_2	**11**	**12**	**15**	**20**	**25**	**30**	**40**	**50**	**100**	**1,000**
1	.21	.21	.22	.23	.24	.24	.24	.25	.25	.26
2	.25	.26	.27	.29	.30	.30	.31	.31	.32	.33
3	.28	.29	.30	.32	.33	.34	.35	.36	.37	.38
4	.30	.31	.33	.35	.36	.37	.38	.39	.41	.42
5	.31	.32	.34	.37	.38	.39	.41	.42	.43	.45
6	.32	.33	.36	.38	.40	.41	.43	.44	.46	.47
7	.33	.34	.37	.40	.42	.43	.44	.45	.48	.50
8	.34	.35	.38	.41	.43	.44	.46	.47	.49	.51
9	.35	.36	.39	.42	.44	.45	.47	.48	.51	.53
10	.35	.36	.39	.43	.45	.46	.48	.49	.52	.54
11	.35	.37	.40	.43	.45	.47	.49	.50	.53	.56
12	.36	.37	.40	.44	.46	.48	.50	.51	.54	.57
13	.36	.38	.41	.44	.47	.48	.51	.52	.55	.58
14	.37	.38	.41	.45	.47	.49	.51	.53	.56	.59
15	.37	.38	.42	.45	.48	.50	.52	.53	.57	.60
16	.37	.38	.42	.46	.48	.50	.53	.54	.57	.60
17	.37	.39	.42	.46	.49	.51	.53	.55	.58	.61
18	.37	.39	.42	.46	.49	.51	.54	.55	.59	.62
19	.38	.39	.43	.47	.49	.51	.54	.56	.59	.63
20	.38	.39	.43	.47	.50	.52	.54	.56	.60	.63
21	.38	.39	.43	.47	.50	.52	.55	.56	.60	.64
22	.38	.40	.43	.48	.50	.52	.55	.57	.61	.64
23	.38	.40	.44	.48	.51	.53	.55	.57	.61	.65
24	.38	.40	.44	.48	.51	.53	.56	.58	.61	.65
25	.38	.40	.44	.48	.51	.53	.56	.58	.62	.66
26	.39	.40	.44	.48	.51	.53	.56	.58	.62	.66
27	.39	.40	.44	.49	.52	.54	.57	.58	.63	.67
28	.39	.40	.44	.49	.52	.54	.57	.59	.63	.67
29	.39	.40	.44	.49	.52	.54	.57	.59	.63	.68
30	.39	.41	.45	.49	.52	.54	.57	.59	.64	.68
35	.39	.41	.45	.50	.53	.55	.58	.60	.65	.70
40	.40	.41	.45	.50	.53	.56	.59	.61	.66	.71
50	.40	.42	.46	.51	.54	.57	.60	.63	.68	.73
60	.40	.42	.46	.51	.55	.57	.61	.63	.69	.75
80	.40	.42	.47	.52	.56	.58	.62	.65	.71	.78
100	.41	.43	.47	.52	.56	.59	.63	.66	.72	.79
200	.41	.43	.48	.53	.57	.60	.64	.67	.75	.84
500	.41	.43	.48	.54	.58	.61	.66	.69	.76	.88
1,000	.41	.43	.48	.54	.58	.61	.66	.69	.77	.90

Table D
(continued)

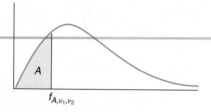

	$A = .10$									
	ν_1									
ν_2	**1**	**2**	**3**	**4**	**5**	**6**	**7**	**8**	**9**	**10**
1	.03	.12	.18	.22	.25	.26	.28	.29	.30	.30
2	.02	.11	.18	.23	.26	.29	.31	.32	.33	.34
3	.02	.11	.19	.24	.28	.30	.33	.34	.36	.37
4	.02	.11	.19	.24	.28	.31	.34	.36	.37	.38
5	.02	.11	.19	.25	.29	.32	.35	.37	.38	.40
6	.02	.11	.19	.25	.29	.33	.35	.37	.39	.41
7	.02	.11	.19	.25	.30	.33	.36	.38	.40	.41
8	.02	.11	.19	.25	.30	.34	.36	.39	.40	.42
9	.02	.11	.19	.25	.30	.34	.37	.39	.41	.43
10	.02	.11	.19	.26	.30	.34	.37	.39	.41	.43
11	.02	.11	.19	.26	.30	.34	.37	.40	.42	.43
12	.02	.11	.19	.26	.31	.34	.37	.40	.42	.44
13	.02	.11	.19	.26	.31	.35	.38	.40	.42	.44
14	.02	.11	.19	.26	.31	.35	.38	.40	.43	.44
15	.02	.11	.19	.26	.31	.35	.38	.41	.43.	.45
16	.02	.11	.19	.26	.31	.35	.38	.41	.43	.45
17	.02	.11	.19	.26	.31	.35	.38	.41	.43	.45
18	.02	.11	.19	.26	.31	.35	.38	.41	.43	.45
19	.02	.11	.19	.26	.31	.35	.38	.41	.43	.45
20	.02	.11	.19	.26	.31	.35	.39	.41	.44	.45
21	.02	.11	.19	.26	.31	.35	.39	.41	.44	.46
22	.02	.11	.19	.26	.31	.35	.39	.41	.44	.46
23	.02	.11	.19	.26	.31	.35	.39	.42	.44	.46
24	.02	.11	.19	.26	.31	.35	.39	.42	.44	.46
25	.02	.11	.19	.26	.31	.36	.39	.42	.44	.46
26	.02	.11	.19	.26	.31	.36	.39	.42	.44	.46
27	.02	.11	.19	.26	.31	.36	.39	.42	.44	.46
28	.02	.11	.19	.26	.31	.36	.39	.42	.44	.46
29	.02	.11	.19	.26	.31	.36	.39	.42	.44	.46
30	.02	.11	.19	.26	.32	.36	.39	.42	.44	.46
35	.02	.11	.19	.26	.32	.36	.39	.42	.45	.47
40	.02	.11	.19	.26	.32	.36	.39	.42	.45	.47
50	.02	.11	.19	.26	.32	.36	.40	.43	.45	.47
60	.02	.11	.19	.26	.32	.36	.40	.43	.45	.47
80	.02	.11	.19	.26	.32	.36	.40	.43	.46	.48
100	.02	.11	.19	.26	.32	.36	.40	.43	.46	.48
200	.02	.11	.19	.27	.32	.37	.40	.43	.46	.48
500	.02	.11	.19	.27	.32	.37	.40	.44	.46	.48
1,000	.02	.11	.19	.27	.32	.37	.40	.44	.46	.49

Table D
(continued)

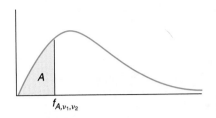

f_{A,v_1,v_2}

	A = .10									
	v_1									
v_2	**11**	**12**	**15**	**20**	**25**	**30**	**40**	**50**	**100**	**1,000**
1	.31	.31	.33	.34	.34	.35	.35	.36	.36	.37
2	.35	.36	.37	.39	.40	.40	.41	.41	.42	.43
3	.38	.38	.40	.42	.43	.44	.45	.46	.47	.48
4	.39	.40	.42	.44	.46	.47	.48	.49	.50	.51
5	.41	.42	.44	.46	.48	.49	.50	.51	.52	.54
6	.42	.43	.45	.48	.49	.50	.52	.53	.55	.56
7	.43	.44	.46	.49	.51	.52	.53	.54	.56	.58
8	.43	.45	.47	.50	.52	.53	.55	.56	.58	.60
9	.44	.45	.48	.51	.53	.54	.56	.57	.59	.61
10	.44	.46	.49	.52	.54	.55	.57	.58	.60	.62
11	.45	.46	.49	.52	.54	.56	.58	.59	.61	.63
12	.45	.47	.50	.53	.55	.56	.58	.60	.62	.64
13	.46	.47	.50	.53	.56	.57	.59	.60	.63	.65
14	.46	.47	.50	.54	.56	.58	.60	.61	.64	.66
15	.46	.48	.51	.54	.56	.58	.60	.61	.64	.67
16	.46	.48	.51	.55	.57	.59	.61	.62	.65	.68
17	.47	.48	.51	.55	.57	.59	.61	.62	.65	.68
18	.47	.48	.52	.55	.58	.59	.62	.63	.66	.69
19	.47	.48	.52	.55	.58	.60	.62	.63	.66	.69
20	.47	.49	.52	.56	.58	.60	.62	.64	.67	.70
21	.47	.49	.52	.56	.58	.60	.63	.64	.67	.71
22	.47	.49	.52	.56	.59	.61	.63	.64	.68	.71
23	.48	.49	.53	.56	.59	.61	.63	.65	.68	.71
24	.48	.49	.53	.57	.59	.61	.64	.65	.68	.72
25	.48	.49	.53	.57	.59	.61	.64	.65	.69	.72
26	.48	.49	.53	.57	.60	.62	.64	.66	.69	.73
27	.48	.49	.53	.57	.60	.62	.64	.66	.69	.73
28	.48	.50	.53	.57	.60	.62	.64	.66	.70	.73
29	.48	.50	.53	.57	.60	.62	.65	.66	.70	.74
30	.48	.50	.53	.58	.60	.62	.65	.67	.70	.74
35	.48	.50	.54	.58	.61	.63	.66	.68	.71	.75
40	.49	.50	.54	.59	.61	.64	.66	.68	.72	.77
50	.49	.51	.55	.59	.62	.64	.67	.69	.74	.79
60	.49	.51	.55	.60	.63	.65	.68	.70	.75	.80
80	.50	.51	.55	.60	.63	.66	.69	.71	.76	.82
100	.50	.52	.56	.61	.64	.66	.70	.72	.77	.84
200	.50	.52	.56	.61	.65	.67	.71	.74	.80	.87
500	.51	.52	.57	.62	.65	.68	.72	.75	.81	.91
1,000	.51	.52	.57	.62	.66	.68	.72	.75	.82	.92

Table D
(continued)

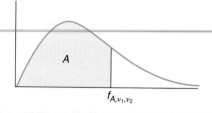

	A = .90									
					ν_1					
ν_2	1	2	3	4	5	6	7	8	9	10
1	39.86	49.50	53.59	55.83	57.24	58.20	58.91	59.44	59.86	60.19
2	8.53	9.00	9.16	9.24	9.29	9.33	9.35	9.37	9.38	9.39
3	5.54	5.46	5.39	5.34	5.31	5.28	5.27	5.25	5.24	5.23
4	4.54	4.32	4.19	4.11	4.05	4.01	3.98	3.95	3.94	3.92
5	4.06	3.78	3.62	3.52	3.45	3.40	3.37	3.34	3.32	3.30
6	3.78	3.46	3.29	3.18	3.11	3.05	3.01	2.98	2.96	2.94
7	3.59	3.26	3.07	2.96	2.88	2.83	2.79	2.75	2.72	2.70
8	3.46	3.11	2.92	2.81	2.73	2.67	2.62	2.59	2.56	2.54
9	3.36	3.01	2.81	2.69	2.61	2.55	2.51	2.47	2.44	2.42
10	3.29	2.92	2.73	2.61	2.52	2.46	2.41	2.38	2.35	2.32
11	3.23	2.86	2.66	2.54	2.45	2.39	2.34	2.30	2.27	2.25
12	3.18	2.81	2.61	2.48	2.39	2.33	2.28	2.24	2.21	2.19
13	3.14	2.76	2.56	2.43	2.35	2.28	2.23	2.20	2.16	2.14
14	3.10	2.73	2.52	2.39	2.31	2.24	2.19	2.15	2.12	2.10
15	3.07	2.70	2.49	2.36	2.27	2.21	2.16	2.12	2.09	2.06
16	3.05	2.67	2.46	2.33	2.24	2.18	2.13	2.09	2.06	2.03
17	3.03	2.64	2.44	2.31	2.22	2.15	2.10	2.06	2.03	2.00
18	3.01	2.62	2.42	2.29	2.20	2.13	2.08	2.04	2.00	1.98
19	2.99	2.61	2.40	2.27	2.18	2.11	2.06	2.02	1.98	1.96
20	2.97	2.59	2.38	2.25	2.16	2.09	2.04	2.00	1.96	1.94
21	2.96	2.57	2.36	2.23	2.14	2.08	2.02	1.98	1.95	1.92
22	2.95	2.56	2.35	2.22	2.13	2.06	2.01	1.97	1.93	1.90
23	2.94	2.55	2.34	2.21	2.11	2.05	1.99	1.95	1.92	1.89
24	2.93	2.54	2.33	2.19	2.10	2.04	1.98	1.94	1.91	1.88
25	2.92	2.53	2.32	2.18	2.09	2.02	1.97	1.93	1.89	1.87
26	2.91	2.52	2.31	2.17	2.08	2.01	1.96	1.92	1.88	1.86
27	2.90	2.51	2.30	2.17	2.07	2.00	1.95	1.91	1.87	1.85
28	2.89	2.50	2.29	2.16	2.06	2.00	1.94	1.90	1.87	1.84
29	2.89	2.50	2.28	2.15	2.06	1.99	1.93	1.89	1.86	1.83
30	2.88	2.49	2.28	2.14	2.05	1.98	1.93	1.88	1.85	1.82
35	2.85	2.46	2.25	2.11	2.02	1.95	1.90	1.85	1.82	1.79
40	2.84	2.44	2.23	2.09	2.00	1.93	1.87	1.83	1.79	1.76
50	2.81	2.41	2.20	2.06	1.97	1.90	1.84	1.80	1.76	1.73
60	2.79	2.39	2.18	2.04	1.95	1.87	1.82	1.77	1.74	1.71
80	2.77	2.37	2.15	2.02	1.92	1.85	1.79	1.75	1.71	1.68
100	2.76	2.36	2.14	2.00	1.91	1.83	1.78	1.73	1.69	1.65
200	2.73	2.33	2.11	1.97	1.88	1.80	1.75	1.70	1.66	1.63
500	2.72	2.31	2.09	1.96	1.86	1.79	1.73	1.68	1.64	1.61
1,000	2.71	2.31	2.09	1.95	1.85	1.78	1.72	1.68	1.64	1.61

Table D
(continued)

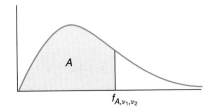

f_{A, ν_1, ν_2}

					A = .90					
					ν_1					
ν_2	**11**	**12**	**15**	**20**	**25**	**30**	**40**	**50**	**100**	**1,000**
1	60.47	60.71	61.22	61.74	62.06	62.26	62.53	62.69	63.00	63.29
2	9.40	9.41	9.42	9.44	9.45	9.46	9.47	9.47	9.48	9.49
3	5.22	5.22	5.20	5.19	5.17	5.17	5.16	5.15	5.14	5.13
4	3.91	3.90	3.87	3.84	3.83	3.82	3.80	3.80	3.78	3.76
5	3.28	3.27	3.24	3.21	3.19	3.17	3.16	3.15	3.13	3.11
6	2.92	2.90	2.87	2.84	2.81	2.80	2.78	2.77	2.75	2.72
7	2.68	2.67	2.63	2.59	2.57	2.56	2.54	2.52	2.50	2.47
8	2.52	2.50	2.46	2.42	2.40	2.38	2.36	2.35	2.32	2.30
9	2.40	2.38	2.34	2.30	2.27	2.25	2.23	2.22	2.19	2.16
10	2.30	2.28	2.24	2.20	2.17	2.16	2.13	2.12	2.09	2.06
11	2.23	2.21	2.17	2.12	2.10	2.08	2.05	2.04	2.00	1.98
12	2.17	2.15	2.10	2.06	2.03	2.01	1.99	1.97	1.94	1.91
13	2.12	2.10	2.05	2.01	1.98	1.96	1.93	1.92	1.88	1.85
14	2.07	2.05	2.01	1.96	1.93	1.91	1.89	1.87	1.83	1.80
15	2.04	2.02	1.97	1.92	1.89	1.87	1.85	1.83	1.79	1.76
16	2.01	1.99	1.94	1.89	1.86	1.84	1.81	1.79	1.76	1.72
17	1.98	1.96	1.91	1.86	1.83	1.81	1.78	1.76	1.73	1.69
18	1.95	1.93	1.89	1.84	1.80	1.78	1.75	1.74	1.70	1.66
19	1.93	1.91	1.86	1.81	1.78	1.76	1.73	1.71	1.67	1.64
20	1.91	1.89	1.84	1.79	1.76	1.74	1.71	1.69	1.65	1.61
21	1.90	1.87	1.83	1.78	1.74	1.72	1.69	1.67	1.63	1.59
22	1.88	1.86	1.81	1.76	1.73	1.70	1.67	1.65	1.61	1.57
23	1.87	1.84	1.80	1.74	1.71	1.69	1.66	1.64	1.59	1.55
24	1.85	1.83	1.78	1.73	1.70	1.67	1.64	1.62	1.58	1.54
25	1.84	1.82	1.77	1.72	1.68	1.66	1.63	1.61	1.56	1.52
26	1.83	1.81	1.76	1.71	1.67	1.65	1.61	1.59	1.55	1.51
27	1.82	1.80	1.75	1.70	1.66	1.64	1.60	1.58	1.54	1.50
28	1.81	1.79	1.74	1.69	1.65	1.63	1.59	1.57	1.53	1.48
29	1.80	1.78	1.73	1.68	1.64	1.62	1.58	1.56	1.52	1.47
30	1.79	1.77	1.72	1.67	1.63	1.61	1.57	1.55	1.51	1.46
35	1.76	1.74	1.69	1.63	1.60	1.57	1.53	1.51	1.47	1.42
40	1.74	1.71	1.66	1.61	1.57	1.54	1.51	1.48	1.43	1.38
50	1.70	1.68	1.63	1.57	1.53	1.50	1.46	1.44	1.39	1.33
60	1.68	1.66	1.60	1.54	1.50	1.48	1.44	1.41	1.36	1.30
80	1.65	1.63	1.57	1.51	1.47	1.44	1.40	1.38	1.32	1.25
100	1.64	1.61	1.56	1.49	1.45	1.42	1.38	1.35	1.29	1.22
200	1.60	1.58	1.52	1.46	1.41	1.38	1.34	1.31	1.24	1.16
500	1.58	1.56	1.50	1.44	1.39	1.36	1.31	1.28	1.21	1.11
1,000	1.58	1.55	1.49	1.43	1.38	1.35	1.30	1.27	1.20	1.08

Table D
(continued)

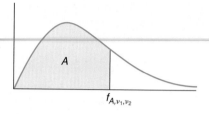

f_{A,ν_1,ν_2}

					A = .95					
						ν_1				
ν_2	**1**	**2**	**3**	**4**	**6**	**6**	**7**	**8**	**9**	**10**
1	161.45	199.50	215.71	224.58	230.16	233.99	236.77	238.88	240.54	241.88
2	18.51	19.00	19.16	19.25	19.30	19.33	19.35	19.37	19.38	19.40
3	10.13	9.55	9.28	9.12	9.01	8.94	8.89	8.85	8.81	8.79
4	7.71	6.94	6.59	6.39	6.26	6.16	6.09	6.04	6.00	5.97
5	6.61	5.79	5.41	5.19	5.05	4.95	4.88	4.82	4.77	4.73
6	5.99	5.14	4.76	4.53	4.39	4.28	4.21	4.15	4.10	4.06
7	5.59	4.74	4.35	4.12	3.97	3.87	3.79	3.73	3.68	3.64
8	5.32	4.46	4.07	3.84	3.69	3.58	3.50	3.44	3.39	3.35
9	5.12	4.26	3.86	3.63	3.48	3.37	3.29	3.23	3.18	3.14
10	4.96	4.10	3.71	3.48	3.33	3.22	3.14	3.07	3.02	2.98
11	4.84	3.98	3.59	3.36	3.20	3.09	3.01	2.95	2.90	2.85
12	4.75	3.89	3.49	3.26	3.11	3.00	2.91	2.85	2.80	2.75
13	4.67	3.81	3.41	3.18	3.03	2.92	2.83	2.77	2.71	2.67
14	4.60	3.74	3.34	3.11	2.96	2.85	2.76	2.70	2.65	2.60
15	4.54	3.68	3.29	3.06	2.90	2.79	2.71	2.64	2.59	2.54
16	4.49	3.63	3.24	3.01	2.85	2.74	2.66	2.59	2.54	2.49
17	4.45	3.59	3.20	2.96	2.81	2.70	2.61	2.55	2.49	2.45
18	4.41	3.55	3.16	2.93	2.77	2.66	2.58	2.51	2.46	2.41
19	4.38	3.52	3.13	2.90	2.74	2.63	2.54	2.48	2.42	2.38
20	4.35	3.49	3.10	2.87	2.71	2.60	2.51	2.45	2.39	2.35
21	4.32	3.47	3.07	2.84	2.68	2.57	2.49	2.42	2.37	2.32
22	4.30	3.44	3.05	2.82	2.66	2.55	2.46	2.40	2.34	2.30
23	4.28	3.42	3.03	2.80	2.64	2.53	2.44	2.37	2.32	2.27
24	4.26	3.40	3.01	2.78	2.62	2.51	2.42	2.36	2.30	2.25
25	4.24	3.39	2.99	2.76	2.60	2.49	2.40	2.34	2.28	2.24
26	4.23	3.37	2.98	2.74	2.59	2.47	2.39	2.32	2.27	2.22
27	4.21	3.35	2.96	2.73	2.57	2.46	2.37	2.31	2.25	2.20
28	4.20	3.34	2.95	2.71	2.56	2.45	2.36	2.29	2.24	2.19
29	4.18	3.33	2.93	2.70	2.55	2.43	2.35	2.28	2.22	2.18
30	4.17	3.32	2.92	2.69	2.53	2.42	2.33	2.27	2.21	2.16
35	4.12	3.27	2.87	2.64	2.49	2.37	2.29	2.22	2.16	2.11
40	4.08	3.23	2.84	2.61	2.45	2.34	2.25	2.18	2.12	2.08
50	4.03	3.18	2.79	2.56	2.40	2.29	2.20	2.13	2.07	2.03
60	4.00	3.15	2.76	2.53	2.37	2.25	2.17	2.10	2.04	1.99
80	3.96	3.11	2.72	2.49	2.33	2.21	2.13	2.06	2.00	1.95
100	3.94	3.09	2.70	2.46	2.31	2.19	2.10	2.03	1.97	1.93
200	3.89	3.04	2.65	2.42	2.26	2.14	2.06	1.98	1.93	1.88
500	3.86	3.01	2.62	2.39	2.23	2.12	2.03	1.96	1.90	1.85
1,000	3.85	3.01	2.61	2.38	2.22	2.11	2.02	1.95	1.89	1.84

Table D
(continued)

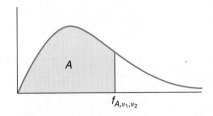

$$f_{A, v_1, v_2}$$

					$A = .95$					
					v_1					
v_2	11	12	15	20	25	30	40	50	100	1,000
1	242.98	243.91	245.96	248.01	249.26	250.08	251.15	251.77	253.01	254.17
2	19.40	19.41	19.43	19.45	19.46	19.46	19.47	19.48	19.49	19.50
3	8.76	8.74	8.70	8.66	8.63	8.62	8.59	8.58	8.55	8.53
4	5.94	5.91	5.86	5.80	5.77	5.74	5.72	5.70	5.66	5.63
5	4.70	4.68	4.62	4.56	4.52	4.50	4.46	4.44	4.41	4.37
6	4.03	4.00	3.94	3.87	3.84	3.81	3.77	3.75	3.71	3.67
7	3.60	3.57	3.51	3.44	3.40	3.38	3.34	3.32	3.27	3.23
8	3.31	3.28	3.22	3.15	3.11	3.08	3.04	3.02	2.97	2.93
9	3.10	3.07	3.01	2.94	2.89	2.86	2.83	2.80	2.76	2.71
10	2.94	2.91	2.85	2.77	2.73	2.70	2.66	2.64	2.59	2.54
11	2.82	2.79	2.72	2.65	2.60	2.57	2.53	2.51	2.46	2.41
12	2.72	2.69	2.62	2.54	2.50	2.47	2.43	2.40	2.35	2.30
13	2.63	2.60	2.53	2.46	2.41	2.38	2.34	2.31	2.26	2.21
14	2.57	2.53	2.46	2.39	2.34	2.31	2.27	2.24	2.19	2.14
15	2.51	2.48	2.40	2.33	2.28	2.25	2.20	2.18	2.12	2.07
16	2.46	2.42	2.35	2.28	2.23	2.19	2.15	2.12	2.07	2.02
17	2.41	2.38	2.31	2.23	2.18	2.15	2.10	2.08	2.02	1.97
18	2.37	2.34	2.27	2.19	2.14	2.11	2.06	2.04	1.98	1.92
19	2.34	2.31	2.23	2.16	2.11	2.07	2.03	2.00	1.94	1.88
20	2.31	2.28	2.20	2.12	2.07	2.04	1.99	1.97	1.91	1.85
21	2.28	2.25	2.18	2.10	2.05	2.01	1.96	1.94	1.88	1.82
22	2.26	2.23	2.15	2.07	2.02	1.98	1.94	1.91	1.85	1.79
23	2.24	2.20	2.13	2.05	2.00	1.96	1.91	1.88	1.82	1.76
24	2.22	2.18	2.11	2.03	1.97	1.94	1.89	1.86	1.80	1.74
25	2.20	2.16	2.09	2.01	1.96	1.92	1.87	1.84	1.78	1.72
26	2.18	2.15	2.07	1.99	1.94	1.90	1.85	1.82	1.76	1.70
27	2.17	2.13	2.06	1.97	1.92	1.88	1.84	1.81	1.74	1.68
28	2.15	2.12	2.04	1.96	1.91	1.87	1.82	1.79	1.73	1.66
29	2.14	2.10	2.03	1.94	1.89	1.85	1.81	1.77	1.71	1.65
30	2.13	2.09	2.01	1.93	1.88	1.84	1.79	1.76	1.70	1.63
35	2.07	2.04	1.96	1.88	1.82	1.79	1.74	1.70	1.63	1.57
40	2.04	2.00	1.92	1.84	1.78	1.74	1.69	1.66	1.59	1.52
50	1.99	1.95	1.87	1.78	1.73	1.69	1.63	1.60	1.52	1.45
60	1.95	1.92	1.84	1.75	1.69	1.65	1.59	1.56	1.48	1.40
80	1.91	1.88	1.79	1.70	1.64	1.60	1.54	1.51	1.43	1.34
100	1.89	1.85	1.77	1.68	1.62	1.57	1.52	1.48	1.39	1.30
200	1.84	1.80	1.72	1.62	1.56	1.52	1.46	1.41	1.32	1.21
500	1.81	1.77	1.69	1.59	1.53	1.48	1.42	1.38	1.28	1.14
1,000	1.80	1.76	1.68	1.58	1.52	1.47	1.41	1.36	1.26	1.11

Table D
(continued)

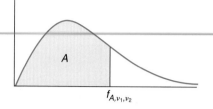

$$f_{A,v_1,v_2}$$

					$A = .975$					
					v_1					
v_2	1	2	3	4	5	6	7	8	9	10
2	38.51	39.00	39.17	39.25	39.30	39.33	39.36	39.37	39.39	39.40
3	17.44	16.04	15.44	15.10	14.88	14.74	14.63	14.54	14.47	14.42
4	12.22	10.65	9.98	9.61	9.36	9.20	9.07	8.98	8.90	8.85
5	10.01	8.43	7.76	7.39	7.15	6.98	6.85	6.76	6.68	6.62
6	8.81	7.26	6.60	6.23	5.99	5.82	5.70	5.60	5.52	5.46
7	8.07	6.54	5.89	5.52	5.29	5.12	5.00	4.90	4.82	4.76
8	7.57	6.06	5.42	5.05	4.82	4.65	4.53	4.43	4.36	4.30
9	7.21	5.71	5.08	4.72	4.48	4.32	4.20	4.10	4.03	3.96
10	6.94	5.46	4.83	4.47	4.24	4.07	3.95	3.85	3.78	3.72
11	6.72	5.26	4.63	4.28	4.04	3.88	3.76	3.66	3.59	3.53
12	6.55	5.10	4.47	4.12	3.89	3.73	3.61	3.51	3.44	3..37
13	6.41	4.97	4.35	4.00	3.77	3.60	3.48	3.39	3.31	3.25
14	6.30	4.86	4.24	3.89	3.66	3.50	3.38	3.29	3.21	3.15
15	6.20	4.77	4.15	3.80	3.58	3.41	3.29	3.20	3.12	3.06
16	6.12	4.69	4.08	3.73	3.50	3.34	3.22	3.12	3.05	2.99
17	6.04	4.62	4.01	3.66	3.44	3.28	3.16	3.06	2.98	2.92
18	5.98	4.56	3.95	3.61	3.38	3.22	3.10	3.01	2.93	2.87
19	5.92	4.51	3.90	3.56	3.33	3.17	3.05	2.96	2.88	2.82
20	5.87	4.46	3.86	3.51	3.29	3.13	3.01	2.91	2.84	2.77
21	5.83	4.42	3.82	3.48	3.25	3.09	2.97	2.87	2.80	2.73
22	5.79	4.38	3.78	3.44	3.22	3.05	2.93	2.84	2.76	2.70
23	5.75	4.35	3.75	3.41	3.18	3.02	2.90	2.81	2.73	2.67
24	5.72	4.32	3.72	3.38	3.15	2.99	2.87	2.78	2.70	2.64
25	5.69	4.29	3.69	3.35	3.13	2.97	2.85	2.75	2.68	2.61
26	5.66	4.27	3.67	3.33	3.10	2.94	2.82	2.73	2.65	2.59
27	5.63	4.24	3.65	3.31	3.08	2.92	2.80	2.71	2.63	2.57
28	5.61	4.22	3.63	3.29	3.06	2.90	2.78	2.69	2.61	2.55
29	5.59	4.20	3.61	3.27	3.04	2.88	2.76	2.67	2.59	2.53
30	5.57	4.18	3.59	3.25	3.03	2.87	2.75	2.65	2.57	2.51
35	5.48	4.11	3.52	3.18	2.96	2.80	2.68	2.58	2.50	2.44
40	5.42	4.05	3.46	3.13	2.90	2.74	2.62	2.53	2.45	2.39
50	5.34	3.97	3.39	3.05	2.83	2.67	2.55	2.46	2.38	2.32
60	5.29	3.93	3.34	3.01	2.79	2.63	2.51	2.41	2.33	2.27
80	5.22	3.86	3.28	2.95	2.73	2.57	2.45	2.35	2.28	2.21
100	5.18	3.83	3.25	2.92	2.70	2.54	2.42	2.32	2.24	2.18
200	5.10	3.76	3.18	2.85	2.63	2.47	2.35	2.26	2.18	2.11
500	5.05	3.72	3.14	2.81	2.59	2.43	2.31	2.22	2.14	2.07
1,000	5.04	3.70	3.13	2.80	2.58	2.42	2.30	2.20	2.13	2.06

Table D
(continued)

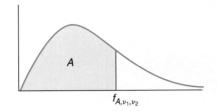

$$f_{A,\nu_1,\nu_2}$$

	A = .975									
	ν_1									
ν_2	**11**	**12**	**15**	**20**	**25**	**30**	**40**	**50**	**100**	**1,000**
2	39.41	39.41	39.43	39.45	39.46	39.46	39.47	39.48	39.49	39.50
3	14.37	14.33	14.26	14.17	14.11	14.08	14.04	14.01	13.96	13.91
4	8.79	8.75	8.66	8.56	8.50	8.46	8.41	8.38	8.32	8.26
5	6.57	6.53	6.43	6.33	6.27	6.23	6.17	6.14	6.08	6.02
6	5.41	5.37	5.27	5.17	5.11	5.06	5.01	4.98	4.92	4.86
7	4.71	4.67	4.57	4.47	4.40	4.36	4.31	4.28	4.21	4.15
8	4.24	4.20	4.10	4.00	3.94	3.89	3.84	3.81	3.74	3.68
9	3.91	3.87	3.77	3.67	3.60	3.56	3.51	3.47	3.40	3.34
10	3.66	3.62	3.52	3.42	3.35	3.31	3.26	3.22	3.15	3.09
11	3.47	3.43	3.33	3.23	3.16	3.12	3.06	3.03	2.96	2.89
12	3.32	3.28	3.18	3.07	3.01	2.96	2.91	2.87	2.80	2.73
13	3.20	3.15	3.05	2.95	2.88	2.84	2.78	2.74	2.67	2.60
14	3.09	3.05	2.95	2.84	2.78	2.73	2.67	2.64	2.56	2.50
15	3.01	2.96	2.86	2.76	2.69	2.64	2.59	2.55	2.47	2.40
16	2.93	2.89	2.79	2.68	2.61	2.57	2.51	2.47	2.40	2.32
17	2.87	2.82	2.72	2.62	2.55	2.50	2.44	2.41	2.33	2.26
18	2.81	2.77	2.67	2.56	2.49	2.44	2.38	2.35	2.27	2.20
19	2.76	2.72	2.62	2.51	2.44	2.39	2.33	2.30	2.22	2.14
20	2.72	2.68	2.57	2.46	2.40	2.35	2.29	2.25	2.17	2.09
21	2.68	2.64	2.53	2.42	2.36	2.31	2.25	2.21	2.13	2.05
22	2.65	2.60	2.50	2.39	2.32	2.27	2.21	2.17	2.09	2.01
23	2.62	2.57	2.47	2.36	2.29	2.24	2.18	2.14	2.06	1.98
24	2.59	2.54	2.44	2.33	2.26	2.21	2.15	2.11	2.02	1.94
25	2.56	2.51	2.41	2.30	2.23	2.18	2.12	2.08	2.00	1.91
26	2.54	2.49	2.39	2.28	2.21	2.16	2.09	2.05	1.97	1.89
27	2.51	2.47	2.36	2.25	2.18	2.13	2.07	2.03	1.94	1.86
28	2.49	2.45	2.34	2.23	2.16	2.11	2.05	2.01	1.92	1.84
29	4.48	2.43	2.32	2.21	2.14	2.09	2.03	1.99	1.90	1.82
30	2.46	2.41	2.31	2.20	2.12	2.07	2.01	1.97	1.88	1.80
35	2.39	2.34	2.23	2.12	2.05	2.00	1.93	1.89	1.80	1.71
40	2.33	2.29	2.18	2.07	1.99	1.94	1.88	1.83	1.74	1.65
50	2.26	2.22	2.11	1.99	1.92	1.87	1.80	1.75	1.66	1.56
60	2.22	2.17	2.06	1.94	1.87	1.82	1.74	1.70	1.60	1.50
80	2.16	2.11	2.00	1.88	1.81	1.75	1.68	1.63	1.53	1.41
100	2.12	2.08	1.97	1.85	1.77	1.71	1.64	1.59	1.48	1.36
200	2.06	2.01	1.90	1.78	1.70	1.64	1.56	1.51	1.39	1.25
500	2.02	1.97	1.86	1.74	1.65	1.60	1.52	1.46	1.34	1.17
1,000	2.01	1.96	1.85	1.72	1.64	1.58	1.50	1.45	1.32	1.13

Table D
(continued)

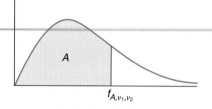

					$A = .99$					
						ν_1				
ν_2	1	2	3	4	5	6	7	8	9	10
2	98.50	99.00	99.17	99.25	99.30	99.33	99.36	99.37	99.39	99.40
3	34.12	30.82	29.46	28.71	28.24	27.91	27.67	27.50	27.34	27.22
4	21.20	18.00	16.69	15.98	15.52	15.21	14.98	14.80	14.66	14.55
5	16.26	13.27	12.06	11.39	10.97	10.67	10.46	10.29	10.16	10.05
6	13.75	10.92	9.78	9.15	8.75	8.47	8.26	8.10	7.98	7.87
7	12.25	9.55	8.45	7.85	7.46	7.19	6.99	6.84	6.72	6.62
8	11.26	8.65	7.59	7.01	6.63	6.37	6.18	6.03	5.91	5.81
9	10.56	8.02	6.99	6.42	6.06	5.80	5.61	5.47	5.35	5.26
10	10.04	7.56	6.55	5.99	5.64	5.39	5.20	5.06	4.94	4.85
11	9.65	7.21	6.22	5.67	5.32	5.07	4.89	4.74	4.63	4.54
12	9.33	6.93	5.95	5.41	5.06	4.82	4.64	4.50	4.39	4.30
13	9.07	6.70	5.74	5.21	4.86	4.62	4.44	4.30	4.19	4.10
14	8.86	6.51	5.56	5.04	4.69	4.46	4.28	4.14	4.03	3.94
15	8.68	6.36	5.42	4.89	4.56	4.32	4.14	4.00	3.89	3.80
16	8.53	6.23	5.29	4.77	4.44	4.20	4.03	3.89	3.78	3.69
17	8.40	6.11	5.18	4.67	4.34	4.10	3.93	3.79	3.68	2.59
18	8.29	6.01	5.09	4.58	4.25	4.01	3.84	3.71	3.60	3.51
19	8.18	5.93	5.01	4.50	4.17	3.94	3.77	3.63	3.52	3.43
20	8.10	5.85	4.94	4.43	4.10	3.87	3.70	3.56	3.46	3.37
21	8.02	5.78	4.87	4.37	4.04	3.81	3.64	3.51	3.40	3.31
22	7.95	5.72	4.82	4.31	3.99	3.76	3.59	3.45	3.35	3.26
23	7.88	5.66	4.76	4.26	3.94	3.71	3.54	3.41	3.30	3.21
24	7.82	5.61	4.72	4.22	3.90	3.67	3.50	3.36	3.26	3.17
25	7.77	5.57	4.68	4.18	3.85	3.63	3.46	3.32	3.22	3.13
26	7.72	5.53	4.64	4.14	3.82	3.59	3.42	3.29	3.18	3.09
27	7.68	5.49	4.60	4.11	3.78	3.56	3.39	3.26	3.15	3.06
28	7.64	5.45	4.57	4.07	3.75	3.53	3.36	3.23	3.12	3.03
29	7.60	5.42	4.54	4.04	3.73	3.50	3.33	3.20	3.09	3.00
30	7.56	5.39	4.51	4.02	3.70	3.47	3.30	3.17	3.07	2.98
35	7.42	5.27	4.40	3.91	3.59	3.37	3.20	3.07	2.96	2.88
40	7.31	5.18	4.31	3.83	3.51	3.29	3.12	2.99	2.89	2.80
50	7.17	5.06	4.20	3.72	3.41	3.19	3.02	2.89	2.78	2.70
60	7.08	4.98	4.13	3.65	3.34	3.12	2.95	2.82	2.72	2.63
80	6.96	4.88	4.04	3.56	3.26	3.04	2.87	2.74	2.64	2.55
100	6.90	4.82	3.98	3.51	3.21	2.99	2.82	2.69	2.59	2.50
200	6.76	4.71	3.88	3.41	3.11	2.89	2.73	2.60	2.50	2.41
500	6.69	4.65	3.82	3.36	3.05	2.84	2.68	2.55	2.44	2.36
1,000	6.66	4.63	3.80	3.34	3.04	2.82	2.66	2.53	2.43	2.34

Table D
(continued)

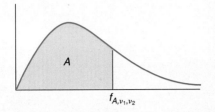

					A = .99					
					v_1					
v_2	**11**	**12**	**15**	**20**	**25**	**30**	**40**	**50**	**100**	**1,000**
2	99.41	99.42	99.43	99.45	99.46	99.46	99.47	99.48	99.49	99.51
3	27.12	27.03	26.85	26.67	26.58	26.50	26.41	26.35	26.24	26.14
4	14.45	14.37	14.19	14.02	13.91	13.84	13.75	13.69	13.58	13.48
5	9.96	9.89	9.72	9.55	9.45	9.38	9.30	9.24	9.13	9.03
6	7.79	7.72	7.56	7.40	7.29	7.23	7.15	7.09	6.99	6.89
7	6.54	6.47	6.31	6.16	6.06	5.99	5.91	5.86	5.75	5.66
8	5.73	5.67	5.52	5.36	5.26	5.20	5.12	5.07	4.96	4.87
9	5.18	5.11	4.96	4.81	4.71	4.65	4.57	4.52	4.41	4.32
10	4.77	4.71	4.56	4.41	4.31	4.25	4.17	4.12	4.01	3.92
11	4.46	4.40	4.25	4.10	4.00	3.94	3.86	3.81	3.71	3.61
12	4.22	4.16	4.01	3.86	3.76	3.70	3.62	3.57	3.47	3.37
13	4.02	3.96	3.82	3.66	3.57	3.51	3.43	3.38	3.27	3.18
14	3.86	3.80	3.66	3.51	3.41	3.35	3.27	3.22	3.11	3.02
15	3.73	3.67	3.52	3.37	3.28	3.21	3.13	3.08	2.98	2.88
16	3.62	3.55	3.41	3.26	3.16	3.10	3.02	2.97	2.86	2.76
17	3.52	3.46	3.31	3.16	3.07	3.00	2.92	2.87	2.76	2.66
18	3.43	3.37	3.23	3.08	2.98	2.92	2.84	2.78	2.68	2.58
19	3.36	3.30	3.15	3.00	2.91	2.84	2.76	2.71	2.60	2.50
20	3.29	3.23	3.09	2.94	2.84	2.78	2.69	2.64	2.54	2.43
21	3.24	3.17	3.03	2.88	2.78	2.72	2.64	2.58	2.48	2.37
22	3.18	3.12	2.98	2.83	2.73	2.67	2.58	2.53	2.42	2.32
23	3.14	3.07	2.93	2.78	2.69	2.62	2.54	2.48	2.37	2.27
24	3.09	3.03	2.89	2.74	2.64	2.58	2.49	2.44	2.33	2.22
25	3.06	2.99	2.85	2.70	2.60	2.54	2.45	2.40	2.29	2.18
26	3.02	2.96	2.81	2.66	2.57	2.50	2.42	2.36	2.25	2.14
27	2.99	2.93	2.78	2.63	2.54	2.47	2.38	2.33	2.22	2.11
28	2.96	2.90	2.75	2.60	2.51	2.44	2.35	2.30	2.19	2.08
29	2.93	2.87	2.73	2.57	2.48	2.41	2.33	2.27	2.16	2.05
30	2.91	2.84	2.70	2.55	2.45	2.39	2.30	2.24	2.13	2.02
35	2.80	2.74	2.60	2.44	2.35	2.28	2.19	2.14	2.02	1.90
40	2.73	2.66	2.52	2.37	2.27	2.20	2.11	2.06	1.94	1.82
50	2.62	2.56	2.42	2.27	2.17	2.10	2.01	1.95	1.82	1.70
60	2.56	2.50	2.35	2.20	2.10	2.03	1.94	1.88	1.75	1.62
80	2.48	2.42	2.27	2.12	2.01	1.94	1.85	1.79	1.65	1.51
100	2.43	2.37	2.22	2.07	1.97	1.89	1.80	1.74	1.60	1.45
200	2.34	2.27	2.13	1.97	1.87	1.79	1.69	1.63	1.48	1.30
500	2.28	2.22	2.07	1.92	1.81	1.74	1.63	1.57	1.41	1.20
1,000	2.27	2.20	2.06	1.90	1.79	1.72	1.61	1.54	1.38	1.16

Table E

Quantile values of the chi-square distribution

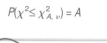

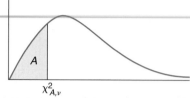

$$P(\chi^2 \leq \chi^2_{A, \nu}) = A$$

ν	$\chi^2_{.005}$	$\chi^2_{.010}$	$\chi^2_{.025}$	$\chi^2_{.050}$	$\chi^2_{.100}$
1	.00	.00	.00	.00	.02
2	.01	.02	.05	.10	.21
3	.07	.11	.22	.35	.58
4	.21	.30	.48	.71	1.06
5	.41	.55	.83	1.15	1.61
6	.67	.87	1.24	1.63	2.20
7	.99	1.24	1.69	2.17	2.83
8	1.34	1.64	2.18	2.73	3.49
9	1.73	2.09	2.70	3.32	4.17
10	2.15	2.55	3.24	3.94	4.86
11	2.60	3.05	3.81	4.57	5.58
12	3.06	3.57	4.40	5.22	6.30
13	3.56	4.10	5.01	5.89	7.04
14	4.07	4.65	5.62	6.57	7.79
15	4.59	5.23	6.26	7.26	8.55
16	5.14	5.81	6.90	7.96	9.31
17	5.69	6.40	7.56	8.67	10.08
18	6.25	7.00	8.23	9.39	10.86
19	6.82	7.63	8.90	10.11	11.65
20	7.42	8.25	9.59	10.85	12.44
21	8.02	8.89	10.28	11.59	13.24
22	8.62	9.53	10.98	12.34	14.04
23	9.25	10.19	11.69	13.09	14.85
24	9.87	10.85	12.40	13.84	15.66
25	10.50	11.51	13.11	14.61	16.47
26	11.13	12.19	13.84	15.38	17.29
27	11.79	12.87	14.57	16.15	18.11
28	12.44	13.55	15.30	16.92	18.94
29	13.09	14.24	16.04	17.70	19.77
30	13.77	14.94	16.78	18.49	20.60
35	17.16	18.49	20.56	22.46	24.79
40	20.67	22.14	24.42	26.51	29.06
45	24.28	25.88	28.36	30.61	33.36
50	27.96	29.68	32.35	34.76	37.69
60	35.50	37.46	40.47	43.19	46.46
70	43.25	45.42	48.75	51.74	55.33
80	51.14	53.52	57.15	60.39	64.28
90	59.17	61.74	65.64	69.13	73.29
100	67.30	70.05	74.22	77.93	82.36

Table E
(continued)

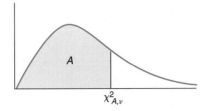

ν	$\chi^2_{.900}$	$\chi^2_{.950}$	$\chi^2_{.975}$	$\chi^2_{.990}$	$\chi^2_{.995}$
1	2.71	3.84	5.02	6.64	7.90
2	4.60	5.99	7.38	9.22	10.59
3	6.25	7.82	9.36	11.32	12.82
4	7.78	9.49	11.15	13.28	14.82
5	9.24	11.07	12.84	15.09	16.76
6	10.65	12.60	14.46	16.81	18.55
7	12.02	14.07	16.02	18.47	20.27
8	13.36	15.51	17.55	20.08	21.94
9	14.69	16.93	19.03	21.65	23.56
10	15.99	18.31	20.50	23.19	25.15
11	17.28	19.68	21.93	24.75	26.71
12	18.55	21.03	23.35	26.25	28.25
13	19.81	22.37	24.75	27.72	29.88
14	21.07	23.69	26.13	29.17	31.38
15	22.31	25.00	27.50	30.61	32.86
16	23.55	26.30	28.86	32.03	34.32
17	24.77	27.59	30.20	33.43	35.77
18	25.99	28.88	31.54	34.83	37.21
19	27.21	30.14	32.87	36.22	38.63
20	28.42	31.42	34.18	37.59	40.05
21	29.62	32.68	35.49	38.96	41.45
22	30.82	33.93	36.79	40.31	42.84
23	32.01	35.18	38.09	41.66	44.23
24	33.20	36.42	39.38	43.00	45.60
25	34.38	37.66	40.66	44.34	46.97
26	35.57	38.89	41.94	45.66	48.33
27	36.74	40.12	43.21	46.99	49.69
28	37.92	41.34	44.47	48.30	51.04
29	39.09	42.56	45.74	49.61	52.38
30	40.26	43.78	46.99	50.91	53.71
35	46.06	49.81	53.22	57.36	60.31
40	51.80	55.75	59.34	63.71	66.80
45	57.50	61.65	65.41	69.98	73.20
50	63.16	67.50	71.42	76.17	79.52
60	74.39	79.08	83.30	88.40	91.98
70	85.52	90.53	95.03	100.44	104.24
80	96.57	101.88	106.63	112.34	116.35
90	107.56	113.14	118.14	124.13	128.32
100	118.49	124.34	129.56	135.82	140.19

Answers to Selected Odd-Numbered Exercises

CHAPTER 1

1.1 A statistical analysis can enhance one's understanding of a business environment, or it can assist directly in making a specific decision.

1.3 Statistical thinking provides us a fundamental understanding of the use of data to acquire new knowledge and make better decisions.

1.5 Variation; discovering patterns and relationships is the key to learning about business phenomena.

1.7 A statistical variable is a precisely defined characteristic to be observed and studied.

1.9 A parameter is a numerical quantity that summarizes some aspect of a population or process. A statistic is a numerical quantity that summarizes a sample.

1.11 In estimation we guess the value of a parameter. In hypothesis testing we assess the plausibility of some *claim* about the value of a parameter.

1.13 Sampling error; a sampled population that does not match the intended population; treating process data as if they represent a population that has not changed over time; poor operational definitions of variables; measurement error. The consequences are erroneous conclusions, leading to poor decisions.

1.15
Sampled population	Stat. variable
Population	Sample
Sampling units	Statistic
Statistic	Parameter

1.17 Sampling error; sampled population does not match intended population; failure to measure accurately and consistently.

1.21 It eliminates bias, provides a statistical basis for determining the confidence associated with inferences, and allows for the control of sampling error.

1.23 Flow diagrams and cause-and-effect diagrams. A flow diagram is a systematic way of showing how the factors in a process transform in-

puts into outcomes. A cause-and-effect diagram focuses on an effect and attempts to identify its potential causes.

1.25 Common causes are the normal or usual factors within a process that naturally vary over time. Assignable causes are unusual occurrences that are not ordinarily part of the process and which usually affect one or only a few outcomes.

1.27 A run chart is a very useful tool in identifying an unstable process when data are time-sequenced.

1.29 No. As a run chart indicates, offensive production has steadily increased and now appears to be averaging at least 85 points. The overall average of 75 points is not indicative of likely future outcomes.

1.31 (a) The process appears to be fairly stable.
   (b) It would be difficult to decide what constitutes a book without a more specific operational definition. For example, there could be confusion over whether a book of maps should be counted as a book.
   (c) Some possible causes of variation are day of the week, sales promotions, and availability of heavily demanded books.
   (d) Day of the week would be a common cause (i.e., normal daily variation). A sales promotion and an out-of-stock condition for heavily demanded books would be special causes.

1.33 Based on a run chart, the transaction process does not appear to be stable. Business activity on Fridays is considerably higher than on the other days. For a given day of the week, however, the transaction process does appear to be stable.

1.35 The run chart exhibits no obvious signs of instability.

CHAPTER 2

2.1   The two types of data are qualitative and quantitative.

2.3   (a) Parts a and f
       (b   Parts c and e
       (c) Parts b and d

2.5   To discern the meaning of the data

2.7   If fewer than five classes are used, we lose sensitivity to portray appropriately the distribution of the data.

2.9   (a) The distribution should be fairly symmetrical.
       (b) Skewed to the left
       (c) Skewed to the right

2.11   All but three of the changes in profit are no more than 22%. The majority are between 17% and 22%.

2.13   (a) Total costs for 30-year mortgages are much greater than for 15-year mortgages. The distributions are slightly skewed.
       (b) While there is some overlap, 15-year rates tend to be lower than 30-year rates. The distributions are slightly skewed.
       (c) For most banks, the difference in interest rates is between .25% and .5%. The distribution is fairly symmetric.

2.15   (b) Overall, the Turkish banks exhibit better performance ratios than the foreign banks. The ratios of the Turkish banks also exhibit considerable variation among themselves.

2.17   The distribution of the number of persons is skewed slightly to the right. The number of nights stayed is typically three and ranges from one to four nights. The distributions of (1) lodging expenditures, (2) meal expenditures, (3) entertainment expenditures, (4) shopping expenditures, and (5) transportation expenditures are single-peaked and slightly skewed to the right.

2.19   (c) Single-peaked and skewed to the left

2.21   (c) Single-peaked and fairly symmetric
       (d) No. It does not appear to be stable, as runs in temperature seem to occur.
       (f) As expected, January temperatures were much colder than April temperatures.

2.23   (c) Single-peaked and skewed to the right. Most transaction times are between 1 and 3 minutes; the distribution ranges from 1 to 10 minutes.
       (d) Inferences based on these results apply to the current process of transaction times at this bank.

2.25   (c) The distribution is single-peaked and symmetric. Demand varies between 25 and 78 books per day and centers around 50 books per day.
       (d) No pattern is apparent. Demand seems to vary randomly.

2.29   (a) Inferences based on this information apply to this manufacturer's current process of producing beads.
       (b) $p = \dfrac{24}{200} = .12$
       (d) The focus should be on defect types C, S, and BD.

2.31   (c) The distribution is single-peaked and skewed to the left.
       (d) Factors include assigned workload, the department within the firm, the partner to whom the associate is assigned, work habits of the associate.

2.33   To determine a value around which data tend to be centered

2.35   The mean; the median

2.37   The median would be preferred because it is not affected by outlier data values.

2.39   (a) 1. Mean = 3.000; median = 3.000
             2. Mean = 12.00; median = 3.00
             3. Mean = 184.2; median = 220.0
       (b) In cases 2 and 3, the values 50 and 1, respectively, are definitely outliers, thus having a pronounced effect on the mean but not on the median.

2.41   (a) Suny 1000: Mean = 4.688; median = 4.150; Saban XL100: Mean = 4.280; median = 4.200
       (b) The Suny downtimes exhibit slightly more variation than those of the Saban.
       (c) Given the wide range of downtimes in each sample, there seems to be no justification for predicting that either model would have shorter downtimes than the other in the future.

2.43   (a) The distribution of cash carried by students is likely to be single-peaked and skewed to the right.

2.45   The statements are true for all the situations described.

2.47   The mode. Example: the data set 6, 6, 10, 12, and 15

2.49 (a) Mean = 1,208.1; median = 1,275.0
(b) The mean is less than the median because the distribution of billable hours is single-peaked and skewed to the left.

2.51 Because the standard deviation is expressed in the units of the original data

2.53 The advantage is simplicity in determining its value. The disadvantage is its reliance upon only two values in the data set.

2.55 (a) The first data set exhibits greater variation because its values are more dispersed than those of the second data set.
(b) 1. St. dev. = 45.6; variance = 2,083.33; range = 100.0; MAD = 37.5   2. St. dev. = 1.826; variance = 3.334; range = 4.0; MAD = 1.5

2.57 (a) Total attendance tends to be greatest on Saturdays and least on Mondays–Thursdays.

(b)
Day	Mean	Median	St. dev.
1	422.0	389.5	157.5
2	359.7	388.0	108.0
3	407.3	411.0	83.0
4	468.6	467.5	157.4
5	658.0	630.0	161.1
6	1,067.3	1,078.0	176.8
7	765.7	713.5	208.4

(c) Attendance varies by day of the week, with the greatest number on Saturdays and the least on Tuesdays.

(d)
Day	Mean	Median	St. dev.
1	31.14	31.05	2.23
2	31.55	31.35	3.69
3	28.83	28.95	3.43
4	29.20	28.95	5.22
5	28.42	28.40	3.60
6	33.70	33.95	1.54
7	33.95	33.70	3.60

2.59 (a) The distribution is single-peaked and very skewed to the right.
(b) The mean will be considerably greater than the median because of the skewed-to-the-right distribution.
(c) Mean = $1,186 thousand; median = $500 thousand

2.61
Variable	Type (ID)	Mean	Median	St. dev.
Comm500	1	240.67	242.50	10.67
	2	231.50	231.00	3.42
	3	65.4	60.5	32.7
FeeTrans	1	3.000	3.500	1.789
	2	3.250	3.000	1.258
	3	4.87	0.00	11.46
Analysts	1	101.2	63.5	88.6
	2	22.50	23.00	9.54
	3	3.12	0.00	8.84
Offices	1	411.3	401.5	101.4
	2	1,017	439	1,481
	3	73.6	41.5	88.9

2.63 (a) Mean = 72.40; median = 73.50; mode = 58, 81, and 85
(b) The modal class is 77.5–82.5.
(c) Range = 37.0; st. dev. = 10.23; MAD = 8.573

2.65 (a) 1.225 standard deviations above the mean
(b) At most 33.32% (assuming symmetry) beyond 1.225 s.d.
(c) Less than 16%

2.67 (b) Machine A: Mean = .498; median = .50.
Machine B: Mean = .507; median = .505.
The means and medians are approximately the same.
(c) Machine A: St. dev. = .02251; range = .08.
Machine B: St. dev. = .0474; range = .14.
Machine B exhibits greater variation in breaking strengths.
(d) The empirical rule is not reliable for such small data sets.

2.69 (a) Successive statistics textbooks have been of steadily increasing length.
(b) Mean = 889.0; median = 938.0; st. dev. = 279.8; MAD = 214

2.71 (a) Patient waiting times are increasing.
(b) Mean = 29.13; st. dev. = 9.18
(c) Prediction is difficult for unstable processes. It appears that the next patient will wait about 40 to 45 minutes.

2.73 Because they indicate the standing of a particular data value relative to the entire data set

2.75 $Z = .5$. The starting salary is .5 standard deviation units (that is, $1,000) above the average starting salary.

2.77 The 10th percentile is 50 sets. Thus 10% of the monthly sales will be no more than 50 sets. The 90th percentile is 150 sets; thus 90% of the monthly sales will be no more than 150 sets.

2.79 Yes; the distribution is skewed to the right.

2.81 Yes; the distribution is fairly symmetric.

2.83 Yes; the distribution is skewed to the right.

2.85 The box plot is consistent with the histogram; the distribution is skewed to the left.

2.87 (b) As the day's high temperature increases, the power generated also increases.
  (c) To some degree, a day's high temperature governs amount of power generated.
  (f) It is not prudent to make April prediction based on August data.

2.89 Median income is slightly related to the proportion of housing units that are renter-occupied. Median income is strongly related to the proportion of housing units with incomes below the poverty line. Median income is fairly strongly related to the proportion of housing units with a telephone.

2.93 (a) None of the performance indicators exhibit much, if any, relationship to the ratio of Medicaid patient-days.
  (b) These data provide no indication that treating Medicaid patients puts hospitals at a disadvantage.

2.97 The proportion of accidents in which there is at least one fatality seems to be greater when small or medium automobiles are involved.

2.99 (a) Mean = 247.68; median = 245.50; st. dev. = 32.81
  (b) Single-peaked and skewed slightly to the right

2.101 (a) Mean = 26.027; median = 25.693; st. dev. = 3.814; min = 20.023; max = 37.036; $Q_1 = 23.175$, median $(Q_2) = 25.693$, $Q_3 = 28.352$

2.103 Yes. A majority of Democrats and Independents appear to favor gun control, whereas a majority of Republicans appear to oppose gun control.

2.105 (a) Yes. Grade point averages change as the SAT changes.

2.107 (a) Most startups involve four or fewer employees; the number of startups declines rapidly as the number of employees increases to about 15.
  (b) Smaller companies had easily the best rate of survival. The rate drops quickly as the initial number of employees increases.

CHAPTER 3

3.1 To obtain information through observation or measurement of a phenomenon whose outcome is not certain. Example: the measurement of time lengths for providing typical banking transactions to customers.

3.3 An event. For the banking transactions example: the set consisting of all time lengths of at most 2 minutes.

3.5 (a) The possible face values when the die is tossed. Possible simple events: 1, 2, 3, 4, 5, and 6.
  (b) The set of possible outcomes when three coins are tossed. Simple events: HHH, HHT, HTH, HTT, THH, THT, TTH, and TTT.

3.7 (a) Let H and L denote higher and lower for the respective companies A, B, and C. The possible simple events are HHH, HHL, HLH, HLL, LHH, LHL, LLH, and LLL.
  (b) The simple events are HHL, HLH, and LHH.
  (c) The simple events are HHH, HHL, HLH, and LHH.
  (d) The simple events are HHL, HLH, HLL, LHH, LHL, LLH, and LLL.

  (e) The simple events are HLL, LHL, and LLH.

3.9 A probability is a numerical measure of the degree of certainty associated with an event.

3.11 The interval from 0 to 1. If an event cannot happen, the probability of the event is 0. If an event is certain to happen, the probability of the event is 1.

3.13 Two events are statistically independent if the probability of one is not affected by knowledge regarding the occurrence or nonoccurrence of the other. If the probability is affected, the events are statistically dependent.

3.15 (a) $\frac{1}{6}$ (b) $\frac{3}{6}$
  (c) The classical interpretation

3.17 (a) The probability is estimated to be $\frac{25}{80}$.
  (b) The relative frequency interpretation

3.19 (a) $\frac{3}{5}$ (b) The subjective assessment interpretation

3.21 (a) "At most two boys"; $\frac{11}{16}$
  (b) "Both genders present"; $\frac{14}{16}$

3.23 (a) $\frac{3}{4}$ (b) Relative frequency
  (c) $\frac{9}{16}$ (d) $\frac{1}{16}$

(e) $\frac{15}{16}$ (f) By $\frac{3}{16}$

3.25   (a) $\frac{1}{4}$ (b) Subjective assessment

(c) $\frac{40}{86}$ (d) Relative frequency

(e) $\frac{30}{40}$ (f) Relative frequency

3.27   (a) A: .925; B: .875; Airline A

(b) Airline B (.864)

(c) Airline B is best overall; Airline A is best only for Atlanta.

3.29   (a) Football: .07788; soccer: .06452; baseball: .05568; basketball: .07143.

(b) No, because probability of being injured regardless of sport is 153/2,237 = .0684.

3.31   For banking transactions: The time length of a transaction; continuous; any value greater than 0.

3.33   (a) The number of home runs a player hits in a game; discrete; 0, 1, 2, 3, 4, and 5.

(b) The time length that the water pump lasts in one's car; continuous; any value greater than 0.

(c) The amount of gasoline pumped into the car; continuous; the interval 0 to 25 gallons

(d) The number of tax returns found to contain errors; discrete; possible values 0, 1, 2, ... , 500

(e) The proportion of defective units; continuous, if n is large; the interval 0 to 1

(f) The number of defective units found; discrete; possible values 0, 1, 2, ... , 100

3.35   Probability values cannot be negative and must sum to 1.

3.37   (a) Yes   (b) No   (c) No   (d) Yes

3.39   (b) .5695   (c) .8131   (d) .3826

3.41   (b) .40   (c) .05

3.43   A probability function of a discrete random variable generates directly the probabilities for each value of the random variable. A probability density function provides the means by which interval probabilities can be determined.

3.45   (a) No   (b) Yes

3.47   (a) $\frac{1}{4}$ (b) $\frac{1}{4}$ (c) $\frac{1}{2}$

3.51   The long-run average value of the random variable

3.53   (a) 1.5

(b) Var(X) = .75; SD(X) = .866

3.55   (a) .5

(b) Var(X) = .45; SD(X) = .6708

3.57 $250

3.59 $\frac{12}{2,652}$

3.61 $(\frac{1}{2})^{10}, \frac{1}{2}$

3.63   (a) P(0) = .0498, P(1) = .1494, P(2) = .2240, P(3) = .2240, P(4) = .1680, P(5) = .1008, P(6) = .0504, P(7) = .0216

(c) F(0) = .0498, F(1) = .1991, F(2) = .4232, F(3) = .6472, F(4) = .8153, F(5) = .9161, F(6) = .9665, F(7) = .9881

3.65   (a) $\frac{3}{4}$ (b) $\frac{1}{4}$ (c) $\frac{3}{16}$ (d) $\frac{7}{16}$

3.67   E(X) = −$0.80; should not play

3.69   E(X) = −$2.63; stay away from the roulette wheel!

3.73   First configuration, the desired probability is .857375; second configuration, .999875; third configuration, .947625; fourth configuration, .995125

3.75   .24

CHAPTER 4

4.1   A random experiment consisting of n identical trials, where the outcome of each trial is either a success or failure such that the probability of success (and thus of failure) remains constant from trial to trial.

4.3   Sampling randomly with replacement

4.5   To generate the probabilities for the values of the random variable

4.7   The value of the parameter π

4.9   Example: the number of houses you sell out of a given set of listings

4.11   Example: the number of air bags that fail to activate upon impact out of a given number selected for testing

4.13

(a)

X	P(X)
0	.2401
1	.4116
2	.2646
3	.0756
4	.0081

(b)

X	P(X)
0	.1681
1	.3601
2	.3087
3	.1323
4	.0283
5	.0024

(c)

X	P(X)	X	P(X)
0	.1176	4	.0595
1	.3025	5	.0102
2	.3241	6	.0007
3	.1852		

4.15 (a) $P(X \le 1) = .6517$; $P(X \ge 2) = .3483$;
$P(X < 3) = .9163$; $P(X \ge 3) = .0837$
(b) $P(X \le 1) = .5282$; $P(X \ge 2) = .4718$;
$P(X < 3) = .8369$; $P(X \ge 3) = .1631$
(c) $P(X \le 1) = .4202$; $P(X \ge 2) = .5798$;
$P(X < 3) = .7443$; $P(X \ge 3) = .2557$

4.17 (a) .6482   (b) .1876   (c) .0611
(d) .9958   (e) .6020   (f) .0035

4.19 (a) .009   (b) .0573
(c) .1894   (d) 7.5 and 2.29

4.21 (a) .345
(b) $E(X) = 12.5$; $SD(X) = 2.5$; P(within 2 s.d.) $= .9568$
(c) Since 7 is *not* within 2 s.d. of the mean, the race is unlikely to be a dead heat (that is, candidate A appears to be behind based on this poll).

4.23 (a) $E(X) = 100$; $SD(X) = 8.94$
(b) $Z = 4.47$; occurrence is highly unlikely

4.25 (a) .7288   (b) $750   (c) No; $Z = 2.78$

4.27 (a) 37.9; 6.00   (b) No; $Z = -3.15$

4.29 Symmetrical, bell-shaped curve with a dense concentration around the central value and tailing off without bound to the left and right

4.31 Because 99.74% of all normal distribution values will lie within 3 standard deviations of the mean

4.33 Because the normal random variable is continuous

4.35 A normal random variable would be the inside diameter of a ball bearing.

4.37 Example: the quantity of a certain staple item

supplied to the restaurants over a specified period of time.

4.39 (a) .3454   (b) .8599
(c) .975   (d) .95

4.41 (a) .4649   (b) .2204
(c) .0228   (d) .8643

4.43 (a) $z = 1.03$ (b) $z = -.44$
(c) $z = -1.58$ (d) $z = 2.03$

4.45 (a) $x = -36.5$ (b) $x = -9.6$
(c) $x = -22.1$ (d) $x = -34.7$

4.47 (a) .0062
(b) Since the probability of at least that amount is so small, the IRS is likely to audit the return.

4.49 87.36

4.51 $z_{.25} = -.67$; $z_{.75} = .67$. The first quartile is $932; the third quartile is $1,468.

4.53 $Z = -4$, a bad day in terms of sales volume.

4.55 (a) .0712   (b) $5,080
(c) Yes; skewed distribution

4.57 (a) 134.9   (b) 256.32

4.59 (a) .1887   (b) .9245   (c) .6415

4.61 .2122

4.63 (a) $E(X) = 1,000$; $SD(X) = 30$
(b) The minimum number needed per day is 2 standard deviations *below* the average. The company has a good chance of success.

4.65 95.44% are usable; 2.28% are scrapped; 2.28% can be reworked

4.67 $\mu = 61.47$ and $\sigma = 45.87$

4.69 $228,000

4.71 (a) $\sigma = 3.8835$ is the desired maximum value.
(b) $\sigma = 1.9417$

CHAPTER 5

5.1 To provide knowledge about some characteristic of a population or process in conjunction with statistical inference

5.3 A sampling distribution depicts the distribution of the sample-to-sample outcomes of a statistic.

5.5 The relative frequency distribution of sample values approximates the distribution of the population from which they arose. The sampling distribution of $\bar{X}$ depicts the sample-to-sample fluctuation of values of $\bar{X}$.

5.7 Because the sampling distribution of $\bar{X}$ depicts the fluctuation of the possible values of $\bar{X}$

5.9 Mostly random variation ranging between 45.5 lb and 49.5 lb

5.11 The proportion of defective units is increasing over time.

5.13 No

5.15 What is the best statistic for the parameter of interest? What is the sampling distribution of the best statistic?

5.17 (a) "9.9" is an estimate
(b) μ, the population mean
(c) Yes; it provides a range within which the value of μ is likely to be contained.

5.19 Over *many* samples, the values of $\bar{X}$ *average* out to the value of μ. For *one* sample, $\bar{X}$ might be above or below μ.

5.21 (a) $\bar{X}$ (b) S (c) p

5.23   No
5.25 $\bar{X}$; it has less variation than the other statistic.
5.27   (a) SE($\bar{X}$) = 151.79; E($\bar{X}$) = 1,400 for all parts
        (b) SE($\bar{X}$) = 75.89   (c) SE($\bar{X}$) = 37.95
5.29 n = 1,600
5.31   By increasing the sample size to n = 400 (four times n = 100)
5.33   .1587
5.35   (a) Z (b) The T distribution
        (c) (Approximately) Z
        (d) (Approximately) the T distribution
5.37   (a) About .001   (b) Yes
5.39   (a) .0025   (b) Yes
5.41   (a) About .20   (b) No
5.43   (a) .006   (b) Yes
5.45   (a) No effect on mean; standard error decreases for increasing sample size.
        (b) For fixed n, standard error of p decreases as π decreases (or increases) from the value $\pi = .5$.

5.47   (a) Approximately normal with mean .5 and standard deviation .0316
        (b) .2643
        (c) No
5.49   (a) Approximately normal with mean .019 and standard deviation .00788
        (b) .0808
5.51   (a) .0019   (b) Yes
5.53   (a) .0003   (b) Claim is not correct.
5.55   (a) .0089   (b) Proportion is exceeded.
5.57   .0256
5.59   (a) .002
        (b) The manufacturer's claim is not plausible. It appears that the average nicotine content exceeds .6 mg per cigarette.
5.61   (a) .0968
        (b) A chance occurrence is plausible.
5.63   (a) .1894
        (b) It is plausible that this higher rate resulted from random sampling variation.

CHAPTER 6

6.1   The important provisions are: a point estimate, the amount of its possible error, and the degree of confidence in the statement that the parameter value lies within a specified range.
6.3   (a) 10   (b) By 2 units, plus or minus
        (c) From 8 to 12
6.5   The claim is plausible.
6.7   When action or change of belief would result if a parameter value were shown to depart from the null hypothesis value in only one specific direction
6.9   (a) H_0: π = .4 vs. H_a: $\pi \neq .4$
        (b) We compare the value of the sample proportion p to the value claimed by the null hypothesis.
6.11   (a) H_0: π = .3 vs. H_a: $\pi < .3$
6.13   (a) 11.87; (110.13, 133.87)
        (b) 5.5; (116.50, 127.50)
        (c) 14.15; (107.85, 136.15)
        (d) 6.55; (115.45, 128.55)
6.15   (a) (14.19, 19.41)   (b) No
        (c) n = 134
6.17   Only part b would be correct.
6.19   (a) 30.97 min.; (29.918, 32.022)
        (b) No, 35 is not included in interval.
        (c) .49865; (.48647, .51082)
        (d) Cannot contradict null, P-value = .82.
6.21   (a) $\bar{X}$ = 20.83 tons   (b) (18.53, 23.13)
        (c) n = 53

6.23   (a) There is some indication that the mean breaking strength has decreased.
        (b) P-value = .13; sample evidence does not convincingly contradict the claim of the null hypothesis.
6.25   (a) P-value = .27
        (b) P-value = .098
        (c) P-value = .0045
        (d) The greater the sample size, the stronger the evidence favoring H_a.
6.27   (a) (136.38, 2,083.62)
        (c) P-value = .77. The evidence does not contradict the claim of the null hypothesis.
6.29   (a) H_0: μ = 15 vs. H_a: $\mu < 15$; P-value = .1135. The data fail to show that the target is not being met.
6.31   (a) The graph offers some indication that the average wage of auto mechanics has decreased.
        (b) P-value = .13
6.33   (a) The mean spending level might have decreased, but this could simply be a chance phenomenon.
        (b) Yes, because 165 is within the 95% confidence limits
        (c) P-value = .05
        (d) P-value = .05
6.35   (a) Increase is not apparent.
        (b) P-value = .23; no contradiction of claim.

6.37   Employees: (5.215, 8.051);
        sales: (109.822, 182.773)
6.39   (a) (−1.382, 7.775)
        (b) No, zero is included in interval.
        (c) (−5.342, 8.323)
        (d) No, zero is included in interval.
6.41   (a) Margin of error increases as n decreases.
        (b) Margin of error is maximum for $p = .5$.
        (c) Approximate; sampling distribution approximated by a normal distribution.
6.43 $\pi = .5$ produces maximum margin of error.
6.45   (.6972, .7523)
6.47   (a) Bars: 37.83%; museums: 28.31%
        (b) For bars: ±.0489; for museums: ±.0454
6.49   (a) (.54, .58); yes, if election were held now
        (b) (.4985, .6215); yes
6.51   (a) $Z = 1.4$, P-value = .081; marginal P-value
6.53 $Z = −.96$, P-value = .17; cannot contradict claim.
6.55   (a) (.6512, .7838)
        (b) No, value of .75 lies within interval.
6.57   Yes, $Z = 2.05$, P-value = .02
6.59   (a) 1. (.5632, .7168); 2. (.4067, .5667); 3. (.4942, .6525).
        (b) Assuming $\pi = .5$, $n = 601$.
6.61   Margin of error decreases as sample size increases for estimates of mean and proportion.
6.63   (a) 90%: (2.699, 2.904); 95%: (2.678, 2.925); 99%: (2.632, 2.971).
        (b) Not essential if population distribution is not severely skewed
6.65   (a) (.577, .781)   (b) 385
667   (a) Claim appears to be incorrect.
        (b) $T = 3.51$, P-value = .0024; claim is contradicted.
6.69   (a) Process appears to be underfilling.
        (b) (9.7859, 9.9791)
        (c) Yes, 10 oz. is not included in interval.
6.71   (a) Yes, $Z = 2.83$, P-value = .002   (b) Yes
6.73   (a) (.8387, .8815).   (b) .0214

CHAPTER 7

7.1   The reduction of random sampling variation by accounting for the variation in the data due to a background variable
7.3   To minimize random variation by controlling as much as possible the causes of variation
7.5   (a) Randomization assures that no condition of the factor under investigation is systematically favored over another.
        (b) Blocking isolates the effect of a background variable, thereby reducing random variation.
        (c) Replication provides the opportunity to assess the extent of random variation in the data.
7.7   (a) Better: send similar packages to the same locations using both the U.S. Postal Service and the private carrier.
        (b) Each location becomes a block. Differences among locations are isolated, thereby reducing random error variation.
7.9   Independent samples
7.11   It is used when the assumption of equal population variances is made.
7.13   (a) Difference not very apparent; spreads are about the same.
        (b) Yes, P-value = .044
7.15   (a) Yes, P-value = .047; spreads are different.
7.17   (a) Difference in average is not apparent; but new process has much more spread.
        (b) No, P-value = .30
7.19   (a) No, but there is more variation in Suny.
        (b) No difference, P-value = .58
7.21   (a) Average appears to be lower with new system; spread is also less.
        (b) Marginally convincing, P-value = .061
        (c) Yes, if there were a day-of-the-week effect
7.23   Differences are not apparent; more variation for western banks. P-value = .64.
7.25   (a) Average appears to be higher for abstainers; spread is also more.
        (b) Contradict claim of no difference, P-value = .014.
7.27   (a) Differences in averages not apparent; about the same spreads.
        (b) Claim of no difference not contradicted, P-value = .15.
7.29   (a) Average appears to be higher for mature group; spreads about the same.
        (b) Claim of no difference is contradicted, P-value = .0012.
7.31   (a) Average listening score appears to be greater for distance learning.
        (b) (1.12, 2.10), based on the pooling procedure. Difference is discernible.
        (c) Average writing score is greater for distance learning.
        (d) (.97, 2.93), based on the pooling procedure. Difference is discernible.

7.33 (a) Average number of orders appears to be greater for women. Variation also is greater for women.
      (b) Claim of no difference is contradicted, P-value = .0046.
      (c) Difference is not apparent; spreads are about the same. Claim of no difference cannot be contradicted, P-value = .45.

7.35 (a) For less than 35% women, no difference is apparent; but difference is apparent for more than 35% women. Spreads are roughly the same.
      (b) Claim of no difference cannot be contradicted, P-value = .58.
      (c) Evidence of a difference is strongly convincing, P-value = .000.

7.37 (a) Average return appears to be slightly greater for pre-holidays; variation also appears to be less for pre-holidays.
      (b) Evidence is convincing, P-value = .0000.

7.39 (a) Variation among requests can be considerable.
      (b) (–7.21, –.99); interval suggests a difference.
      (c) (–6.79, .39); interval suggests no difference.

7.41 (a) New system seems to be faster.
      (b) Claim of no improvement is contradicted, P-value = .027.
      (c) Considerable job-to-job variation.

7.43 (a) Knox tends to be more highly rated.
      (b) (–.2623, –.0577); difference is discernible.
      (c) Claim of no difference is contradicted, P-value = .0064.
      (d) Considerable faculty-to-faculty variation

7.45 (a) Rates in 1989 are uniformly higher.
      (b) Strong contradiction of no change, P-value = .000.

7.47 (a) Longer times-to-exhaustion with caffeine.
      (b) Strong support that mean is greater with caffeine, P-value = .000.
      (c) Doubtful; subjects in study were athletes.

7.49 In hypothesis testing, the claim is that they are the same and, thus, equal to a common value. For confidence intervals, no claim is made about the population proportions.

7.51 We must know (at least approximately) the sampling distribution of this statistic to make inferences possible.

7.53 Pooled proportion: .0401; using p_1 and p_2 separately: .042. Not much difference here.

7.55 (a) (.0077, .1907)
      (b) Because 0 does not lie within interval, the sample data suggest a difference.

7.57 Yes, P-value = .000

7.59 (a) Observed differences could be due to random sampling error; P-value = .223.
      (b) Not necessarily; other factors should be considered.

7.61 (a) (–.1306, .0124); no difference.
      (b) Cannot contradict, P-value = .106.
      (c) Viewer habits can change over time.

7.63 (a) (–.005, .0722); no difference.
      (b) Evidence against claim not convincing, P-value = .093.

7.65 Yes, P-value = .000.

7.67 (a) Yes, P-value = .000.
      (b) Yes, P-value = .000.
      (c) Not consistent with fact.

7.69 (a) Costs are somewhat less for victims with seats belts; spreads differ.
      (b) Evidence not convincing, P-value = .09.

7.71 (a) Research uses more computer time for most months.   (b) Yes, P-value = .013.

7.73 (a) No, P-value = .11.

7.75 Yes, P-value = .022.

7.79 (a) The juniors seem to have outperformed the sophomores at least slightly on each test. The spreads are about the same.
      (b) Test 1: P-value = .021; test 2: P-value = .0040. In both cases, the data contradict a claim that the mean performance is the same for juniors and sophomores.
      (c) Juniors: P-value = .077; not convincing evidence that a difference exists
      (d) Sophomores: P-value = .0009; strong evidence of a difference
      (e) Juniors: (–.58, 10.16); no difference since 0 is included in interval. Sophomores: (3.49, 11.29); a difference exists because 0 is not included in interval.

7.81 (a) Differences are apparent; spreads not the same.
      (b) Claim of no difference contradicted, P-value = .0046.

7.83 (a) Differences are not apparent; spreads about the same.
      (b) Cannot contradict claim, P-value = .39.
      (c) Consider a player's position.

7.85 (a) Differences are very apparent; spreads not the same.
      (b) Higher maximal oxygen uptake for males, P-value = .0001.

CHAPTER 8

8.1 The treatments are either (1) the populations or processes being studied or (2) the levels of a factor to be studied.

8.3 (a) Treatment differences, on average, and random error

(b) The amount of among-sample variation (MSTR) and the amount of within-sample variation (MSE)

8.5 The amount of among-sample variation (MSTR), the amount of within-sample variation (MSE), and their ratio

8.7 (a) For $H_0: \mu_1 - \mu_2 = 0$ vs. $H_a: \mu_1 - \mu_2 \neq 0$, $T = -3.51$ and P-value $= .002$. The data contradict H_0 convincingly.

(b) $H_0: \mu_1 = \mu_2$ vs. H_a: The means differ. The F statistic is $F = 12.35$ with P-value $= .002$ (as in part a). Same conclusion as in part a.

8.9 (a) Yes

(b) The three machines (treatments), plus any factors that caused the fills of any one machine to vary (collectively called random error)

(c) $H_0: \mu_1 = \mu_2 = \mu_3$ vs. H_a: These means are not all equal. The F statistic is $F = 57.05$ with P-value $= .000$. The data contradict H_0 convincingly.

(d) Each treatment population is assumed to be normally distributed with equal variances. The graph helps.

8.11 The F statistic is $F = 17.00$ with P-value $= .000$. The data contradict H_0 convincingly.

8.13 The F statistic is $F = 10.42$ with P-value $= .000$. The data contradict H_0 convincingly.

8.15 Claim of no differences is strongly contradicted, P-value. $= .000$.

8.17 (a) Differences are apparent.

(b) Yes, P-value $= .000$.

8.19 (a) Differences are not apparent.

(b) Claim cannot be contradicted, P-value $= .353$.

8.21 (a) Differences are not apparent.

(b) Claim cannot be contradicted, P-value $= .187$.

8.23 (a) Processes appear to be stable.

(b) Differences are apparent; mean of Location A is greatest.

(c) Claim of no differences contradicted; P-value $= .000$.

8.25 (a) Differences are not very apparent for orders or dollars.

(b) Claim of no differences cannot be contradicted, P-value $= .136$.

(c) Claim is contradicted, P-value $= .005$.

8.27 There may exist a background variable whose effect on the response variable can be isolated through blocking. Blocking permits an apples-to-apples comparison of the treatments.

8.29 The amount of variation attributed to random error would be enlarged, thereby preventing the detection of differences among the treatment means, if they exist.

8.31 (a) Yes

(b) $H_0: \mu_1 = \mu_2 = \mu_3$ vs. H_a: The treatment means are not all equal. The F statistic is $F = 11.40$ with P-value $= .009$. The data contradict H_0 convincingly.

8.33 $H_0: \mu_1 = \mu_2 = \mu_3 = \mu_4 = \mu_5$ vs. H_a: The treatment means are not all equal. The F statistic is $F = 10.00$ with P-value $= .0008$. The data contradict H_0 convincingly.

8.35 (a) Yes

(b) Brands, supermarkets, random variation in purchases for a given supermarket and brand

(c) $H_0: \mu_1 = \mu_2 = \mu_3$ vs. H_a: The treatment means are not all equal. $F = 4.65$ with P-value $= .037$. The data contradict H_0 convincingly.

8.37 (a) Shift A appears to be different.

(b) Yes, P-value $= .003$.   (c) No

8.39 (a) Yes

(b) Differences are suggested, P-value $= .000$.

8.43 (a) Yes, Route 2 takes longer, on average.

(b) Yes, slightly less variation for Route 2.

(c) Traffic lights, road conditions, traffic intensity

(d) Claim contradicted, P-value $= .021$.

8.45 (a) Yes, tensile strength increases as carbon content increases.

(b) There is a carbon content effect, P-value $= .000$

8.47 The within-area salaries vary substantially. A better plan would use blocking on factors such as size of the companies or the type of industry.

8.49 (a) Yes; device C yields greater mileage.

(b) Because mileage varies greatly by automobiles.

(c) Differences exist, P-value $= .000$.

8.51 (a) The subjects who breathed the mixture Air + CO consistently walked a shorter distance.

(b) If not blocked, variation among subjects could mask variation caused by gas mixtures.

(c) H_0: $\mu_1 = \mu_2 = \mu_3 = \mu_4$ vs. H_a: The treatment means are not all equal. $F = 16.48$ with P-value $= .000$. The data show convincingly that mean distances walked vary for the different gas mixtures.

8.53 (a) Yes; on average, sales for professional referrals are larger.

(b) H_0: $\mu_1 = \mu_2 = \mu_3$ vs. H_a: The treatment means are not all equal. $F = 9.21$ with

P-value $.000$. The data contradict strongly the claim of no differences in mean sales for the three sources of referral.

8.55 (a) Brazil is higher in three of the four indicators.

(b) Differences are suggested; $F = 5.72$, P-value $= .041$.

CHAPTER 9

9.1 The response variable is the variable to be predicted; the predictor variable is the variable upon which predictions are based.

9.3 This requires a careful experiment in which the value of the predictor variable is changed while all other factors are held constant.

9.5 Scatter diagrams

9.7 (a) Since $X = 0$ (no experience) is outside the range of values for these data, the interpretation of the number 28.9 (the intercept) is not meaningful in this relationship.

(b) 1.26 (or \$1,260) is the average differential in salary for each additional year of experience.

(c) No

9.9 (1) To gain insight into relationships; (2) for prediction and estimation

9.11 (a) Yes; an approximately linear relationship

(b) Positive

9.13 (a) Yes; an approximately linear relationship. In years when prices were higher, consumption tended to be lower.

(b) Negative; see the explanation in part a.

9.17 (a) $S_e^2 = 70.71$. This is a measure of the closeness of fit of the data to the least squares line and the best estimate of the population error variance σ_e^2.

(b) SST $= 552.8$; the total variation among the Y values. SSR $= 340.66$; the amount of variation in the Y values that is explained by the relationship between Y and X—that is, the variation among the $\hat{Y}$ values. SSE $= 212.14$; the amount of the variation in the Y values that remains unexplained by the relationship between Y and X—that is, the variation among the residuals.

(c) $r^2 = .62$. Thus 62% of the variation in the sample Y values is explained by the relationship between Y and X.

9.19 (b) $\hat{Y} = -3.5 + 3.5X$

(c) Least squares line represents the sample Y values the best.

(e) The sum of the residuals is not a useful measure of fit, because the result is 0 for all three lines.

(f) $\Sigma e_A^2 = 1.5$; $\Sigma e_B^2 = 6$; $\Sigma e_C^2 = 26$. The sum of squared residuals is smallest for the least squares line (line A).

9.21 It allows for the observation of Y-values within a range of interest for X.

9.23 If the data are not representative, the least squares equation does not represent the environment of interest and can give very misleading results.

9.25 (a) It is highly unlikely that β_1 equals 0.

(b) The presence of a linear relationship between Y and X

9.27 (a) It is plausible that β_1 is 0.

(b) A lack of evidence of a linear relationship between Y and X

9.29 (a) $\hat{Y} = 51.5 - 1.92X$. For the slope, on average, Y decreases by 1.92 units for each unit increase in X. Null hypothesis of no linear association cannot be contradicted; $F = 4.82$, P-value $= .116$.

(b) $\hat{Y} = -3.5 + 3.5X$. For the slope, on average Y increases by 3.5 units for each unit increase in X. Null hypothesis of no linear association cannot be contradicted; P-value $= .154$.

9.31 (a) Predicted Salary $= -1.63 + 8.12$GPA. On average, Salary increases by 8.12 units (\$ thousands) for each unit increase in GPA. The interpretation of the intercept estimate is not meaningful here.

(b) (5.08, 11.16). The slope is not being estimated very accurately here.

(c) H_0: $\beta_1 = 0$ vs. H_a: $\beta_1 \neq 0$. $F = 33.18$, P-value $= .000$. The data provide convincing evidence of a linear relationship.

(d) The residuals seem to be scattered in random fashion above and below 0.

9.33 (a) (.083, .148). This is a fairly wide range; the upper limit has almost twice the magnitude of the lower limit.

(b) $H_0: \beta_1 = 0$ vs. $H_a: \beta_1 \neq 0$. $F = 61.29$; P-value = .000. The data provide convincing evidence of a linear relationship.

(c) The plot indicates that a nonlinear equation would represent better the relationship between Tax and Income.

(d) It is likely, based on the results in part c, that better estimation and prediction can be achieved through a quadratic equation.

9.35 (a) Profit = −.64 + .0963Sales. For the slope, on average profit increases by .0963 unit for each unit increase in sales.   (b) 171.935

(c) Null hypothesis of no linear association is contradicted; $F = 11.71$, P-value = 009.

(d) (.0314, .1612)   (e) No

9.37 (a) Some linear association is apparent.

(b) Rate = 15.9 − .535Degree. On average, the rate decreases by .535 unit for each percentage increase in percent holding bachelor's degrees.   (c) Yes, P-value = .001

9.39 (a) Response is sales, predictor is test score.

(b) A degree of linear association is apparent.

(c) Sales = −11.7 + .404Score. For the slope, on average sales increase by .404 unit for each unit increase in test score. Claim is contradicted; $F = 9.57$, P-value = .021

(d) No, (.084, .724)

9.41 (a) No linear relationship is apparent. Null hypothesis of no linear relation cannot be contradicted; P-value = .201. No reasonable accuracy in estimating slope, interval is (−7.17, 30.87).

(b) 11.849 hundred images

9.43 (a) Any relationship is not discernible.

(b) Score = 8.11 + .0104Return. On average, score increases by .0104 unit for each percentage increase in return.

(c) No, P-value = .407. Result is not surprising.

9.45 (a) A degree of linear association is apparent.

(b) Rate = −30.4 + .765Count. On average, rate increases by .765 unit for each unit increase in count.

(c) Yes, P-value = .000

9.47 (a) A degree of linear association is apparent.

(b) Sales = −9.56 + .136Utilization

(c) Yes, P-value = .022   (d) 42.5%

9.49 (a) $\hat{Y} = 6.648$

(b) (5.73, 7.57). The confidence interval seems relatively narrow.

(c) $\hat{Y} = 6.648$; no

(d) (4.3, 8.99). The upper limit of the prediction interval is about twice the lower limit.

(e) The interval for prediction of an individual Y value is wider.

9.51 (a) Predicted Weight = 128.05

(b) (121.06, 135.04). The confidence interval seems relatively narrow.

(c) $\hat{Y} = 128.05$; no

(d) (108.69, 147.41). The prediction interval seems relatively narrow.

(e) The interval for prediction of an individual Y value is wider.

9.53 (a & c) $\hat{Y} = 20.29$; $\hat{Y} = 22.73$; $\hat{Y} = 25.17$

(b) $X = 2.7$: (19.02, 21.57); $X = 3.00$: (21.98, 23.48); $X = 3.30$: (24.08, 26.25). The greatest accuracy occurs when $X = 3.00$ because this value is nearest the sample mean $\bar{X} = 3.04$.

(d) $X = 2.7$: (17.16, 23.42); $X = 3.00$: (19.77, 25.69); $X = 3.30$: (22.10, 28.23). The greatest accuracy occurs when $X = 3.00$ because this value is nearest the sample mean $\bar{X} = 3.04$.

(e) Interval for individual Y is wider.

9.55 (a & c) $\hat{Y} = 13.2789$; $\hat{Y} = 16.875$; $\hat{Y} = 23.352$

(b) $X = 11$: (11.99, 14.59); $X = 42$: (16.03, 17.72); $X = 98$: (21.35, 25.36). The greatest accuracy occurs when $X = 42$ because this value is nearest the sample mean $\bar{X} = 41.6$.

(d) $X = 11$: (9.87, 16.71); $X = 42$: (13.6, 20.15); $X = 98$: (19.61, 27.10). The greatest accuracy occurs when $X = 42$ because this value is nearest the sample mean $\bar{X} = 41.6$.

(e) Intervals for individual Y values are wider.

9.57 (a) $\hat{Y} = 70.97$

(b) $X = 1$: (15.60, 126.33)

(c) Not very useful. The manager could only count on the actual press speed being between 15.60 and 126.33.

9.59 (a) half should be chosen at the lower end of the range and half at the upper end. This maximizes $SS(X)$, which in turn minimizes the width of all confidence and prediction intervals.

(b) No. To check for curvature, it would be important to select some families with incomes near the center of the range.

9.61 (a) 210.35   (b) (146.5, 274.2)

(c) Yes, the value 2,850 is outside the range of X values in the data.

9.63 (a) 10.077 and 7.401
(b) (9.166, 10.989) and (6.513, 8.29)

9.65 (a) Perfect linear relation with negative slope
(b) Total absence of linear relation
(c) Perfect linear relation with positive slope

9.67 −.91

9.69 (b) $r = 0$; no, because relation is entirely nonlinear.

9.71 X_2 because the magnitude of its correlation coefficient is greater than that for X_1.

9.73 17.64%; 82.36% remains unexplained.

9.75 (1) The scatter diagram indicates a positive relationship between GPA and SAT score, possibly not linear. There is substantial random variation.
(2) SAT = 515 + 149 GPA. On average, SAT increases by 149 points for each 1-point increase in GPA. The interpretation of the intercept estimate is not meaningful here.
(3) For H_0: $\beta_1 = 0$ vs. H_a: $\beta_1 \neq 0$, $T = 4.50$, $F = 20.23$, and P-value = .000. The sample data indicate strongly the presence of a linear relationship.
(4) (81.28, 217.14). We can be 95% confident that the population slope lies between 81.28 and 217.14.
(5) $r^2 = 42\%$. The variation among GPAs explains 42% of the variation among SAT scores.
(6) The residuals appear to be scattered in random fashion above and below 0.
(7) The least squares line is not adequate for estimation and prediction.

9.77 (1) The scatter diagram indicates a negative linear relationship between scrap and yards printed. There is substantial random variation.
(2) Scrap = 53.4 − .000867 Yards. On average, Scrap decreases by .000867 unit for a

1-yard increase in Yards. The interpretation of the intercept estimate is not meaningful here.
(3) For H_0: $\beta_1 = 0$ vs. H_a: $\beta_1 \neq 0$, $T = -3.48$, $F = 12.10$, and P-value = .002. The sample data indicate clearly the presence of a linear relationship.
(4) (−.00139, −.000348). We can be 95% confident that the population slope lies between −.00139 and −.000348.
(5) $r^2 = 36.5\%$. The variation in yards per shift explains 36.5% of the variation in scrap.
(6) These residuals appear to be consistent with regression assumptions.
(7) The least squares line is not adequate for estimation and prediction.

9.79 (1) The scatter diagram indicates a strong positive relationship between the 52-week high price and the 52-week low price. There is relatively little random variation.
(2) High = 3.56 + 1.48Low. On average, High increases by $1.48 for a $1.00 increase in Low. The interpretation of the intercept estimate is not meaningful here.
(3) For H_0: $\beta_1 = 0$ vs. H_a: $\beta_1 \neq 0$, $T = 12.17$, $F = 148.04$, P-value = .000. The data indicate strongly the existence of a linear relationship between the high and low prices.
(4) (1.22, 1.75). We can be 95% confident that β_1 lies between 1.22 and 1.75.
(5) $r^2 = 91.9\%$. The variation in low prices explains 91.9% of the variation in high prices.
(6) The plot of residuals does not appear to be consistent with regression assumptions. Two observations are possible outlier values, causing most residuals to be negative. If they could be explained by other factors, the model might be improved greatly.
(7) Upon the resolution of part (6), the least squares line may be adequate for estimation and prediction.

CHAPTER 10

10.1 (a) The average maintenance cost increases by 1.2 thousand dollars for each additional automobile rented, if the average number of miles driven remains constant. The average maintenance cost increases by $.15 for each 1-mile increase in the average number of miles driven, if the number of automobiles rented remains constant.

(b) $X_1 = 200$
$X_2 = 20$: $\hat{Y} = 244.5$; $X_2 = 30$: $\hat{Y} = 246$; $X_2 = 40$: $\hat{Y} = 247.5$
$X_1 = 400$
$X_2 = 20$: $\hat{Y} = 484.5$; $X_2 = 30$: $\hat{Y} = 486$; $X_2 = 40$: $\hat{Y} = 487.5$
$X_1 = 600$
$X_2 = 20$: $\hat{Y} = 724.5$; $X_2 = 30$: $\hat{Y} = 726$; $X_2 = 40$: $\hat{Y} = 727.5$

10.3 (a) Linear
(b) Linear
(c) Not linear because the parameter β_1 appears as an exponent
(d) Not linear because the parameter β_2 appears as an exponent

10.5 (a) SSE = 265.6; $S_e^2 = 88.52$
(b) $R^2 = 83\%$; $R_a^2 = 77.3\%$
(c) X_2 does not contribute to the prediction of Y if X_1 is known.

10.7 (a) $R^2 = 91.59\%$. The variation among the sample values of the four predictor variables explains 91.59% of the variation among the sample Y values.
(b) Further analysis is necessary to determine adequacy. There might exist models that are better for predicting Y.
(c) $R_a^2 = 89.61\%$
(d) R_a^2 takes into consideration the number of terms in the regression model; it is more useful for comparing models with different numbers of terms.

10.9 SSE = 144.3, SST = 855.1, SSR = 710.8; $R^2 = 83.12\%$, $R_a^2 = 82.6\%$. We cannot say for certain without further analysis.

10.11 1. (a) SSE = 504; $S_e^2 = 100.8$
(b) $R^2 = 41.1\%$; $R_a^2 = 29.3\%$
(c) This residual plot shows that much of the variation unexplained by X_1 can be explained by the variation among X_2 values.
2. (a) SSE = 403.24; $S_e^2 = 80.65$
(b) $R^2 = 52.9\%$; $R_a^2 = 43.4\%$
(c) This residual plot shows that much of the variation unexplained by X_2 can be explained by the variation among X_1 values.
(d) A model including both X_1 and X_2 is superior to a model including either X_1 alone or X_2 alone. X_2 explains variation in Y that cannot be explained by X_1, and vice versa.

10.13 $R_a^2 = 65\%$

10.15 (a) H_0: $\beta_1 = \beta_2 = \beta_3 = 0$ vs. H_a: At least one of the parameters is not equal to 0. $F = 23.33$, P-value = .0001. The sample evidence strongly contradicts the null hypothesis of no relationship between Y and any of the predictor variables.
(b) $R_a^2 = 83.75\%$
(c) For H_0: $\beta_1 = 0$ vs. H_a: $\beta_1 \neq 0$, $F = 20.0$. P-value = .0012. The sample data provide evidence that X_1 is helpful.

(d) For H_0: $\beta_2 = 0$ vs. H_a: $\beta_2 \neq 0$ (in the presence of X_1): $F = 47.0$, P-value = .0000. The sample data provide strong evidence that X_2 is helpful in predicting Y in the presence of X_1.
(e) For H_0: $\beta_3 = 0$ vs. H_a: $\beta_3 \neq 0$ (in the presence of X_1 and X_2): $F = 3.0$, P-value = .1139. The sample data do not provide evidence that X_3 is helpful.

10.17 Evaluation of the overall model: The null hypothesis H_0: $\beta_1 = \beta_2 = 0$ is contradicted by the sample evidence based on the analysis of variance (P-value = .000). Thus, either GPA or age or both contribute to the explanation of the variation in the sample starting salary. Evaluation of the contributions of individual predictor variables: The null hypothesis H_0: $\beta_1 = 0$ (in the presence of X_2) is contradicted based on the T statistic (P-value = .000). So, GPA helps to explain variation not explained by age. Similarly, the hypothesis H_0: $\beta_2 = 0$ (in the presence of X_1) is also contradicted (P-value = .030). Thus, age helps to explain variation not explained by GPA.

10.19 (a) The coefficient b_1 is positive and b_2 is negative; both make sense.
(b) H_0: $\beta_1 = \beta_2 = 0$ vs. H_a: At least one of these parameters is not 0. $F = 90.0$. P-value = .0000. The sample evidence contradicts strongly the null hypothesis; either X_1 or X_2 or both are associated with Y.
(c) 95% CI for β_1: (5.149, 7.851). 95% CI for β_2: (−4.072, −2.328). Neither confidence interval contains 0, thus both X_1 and X_2 appear to make incremental contributions to the prediction of Y.

10.21 Yes, for the four predictor variables, $F = 3.5$ and P-value = .013.

10.23 $\hat{Y} = -.1605 + .1487X_1 + .0769X_2$. Both make discernible marginal contributions, $T_1 = 14.92$, P-value = .000; $T_2 = 3.83$, P-value = .002.

10.25 (b) Yes, $F = 27.12$, P-value = .000.
(c) All predictor variables make discernible marginal contributions (P-values of .001 or .000).

10.29 (a) $b_2 = 1.1$: When the repair involves model A, the estimated average repair time is 1.1 hours more than for model C if years of experience are held constant.
$b_3 = -.5$: When the repair involves model B, the estimated average repair time is .5 hour less than for model C if years of experience are held constant.

(b) For model A: $\hat{Y} = 21.1 - .2X_1$; for model B: $\hat{Y} = 19.5 - .2X_1$; for model C: $\hat{Y} = 20 - .2X_1$.
These equations have the same slope estimate and different estimates of the intercept.

(c) The average repair time decreased by .2 hour for an additional year of experience for a given model being repaired.

10.31 (a) $H_0: \beta_1 = \beta_2 = 0$ vs. H_a: At least one of these parameters $\neq 0$. $F = 2.71$, P-value = .0887. The evidence is not convincing that there is an association.

(b) $T_1 = -.65$. P-value = .5224. There is little evidence of a marginal contribution of age.

(c) $T_2 = -1.52$. P-value = .1428. There is little evidence of a marginal contribution of gender.

(d) Bad idea; the model could not be defended.

10.33 (a) $R_a^2 = 78.66\%$. We cannot say; other equations might predict better; R_a^2 is primarily useful for comparisons.

(b) $H_0: \beta_1 = \beta_2 = \beta_3 = \beta_4 = 0$ vs. H_a: At least one of these parameters is not 0. $F = 42.46$. P-value = .0000. Strong evidence that there is an association between Y and $X_1, X_2, X_3,$ and X_4 as a group.

(c) $T_1 = 1.43$; P-value = .1602; there is little evidence that X_1 makes a marginal contribution.

10.35 (b) The predictor variables Inspect and Brand make discernible marginal contributions; $T_1 = -3.05$, P-value = .003; $T_B = -5.83$, P-value = .000. The others do not.

10.37 (a) Appliances used most frequently on weekends; also oven, dishwasher, dryer, etc.

(b & c) Yes; the clearly discernible marginal contributions are: oven (P-value = .001), dryer (P-value = .034), water heater (P-value = .024), and people (P-value = .000).

10.39 (a) For some—but not all—manufacturers, there is a stong relation between percent net increase to sales and percent utilization of capacity.

(b) Discernible marginal contribution for percent utilization (P-value = .01), somewhat discernible contributions for the manufacturers PSA (P-value = .069), Renault (P-value = .053), and GMEur (P-value = .042).

10.41 (b) The predictor variables Grads (P-value = .000) and EEOL (P-value = .014) make discernible marginal contributions. The others do not.

10.43 (a) A quadratic model seems appropriate.

(b) X does not provide marginal contribution ($T = .58$, P-value = .586). Using only the quadratic term (X^2) in the model, a better fit is obtained ($T = 19.26$, P-value = .000).

10.45 (a) A quadratic model is appropriate.

(b) Both X and X^2 provide marginal contributions, P-values = .000 in both cases.

10.47 (a) Mean SAT = $1,067 - 6.09$ Tested + $.0495$ Tested − sq.

(b) Discernible marginal contribution provided by Tested − sq. ($T = 5.67$, P-value = .000).

(d) The five states with the largest positive residuals are: Iowa, Oregon, Minnesota, Montana, and North Dakota.

10.49 When the quadratic term X^2 is included, the model improves considerably. R_a^2 improves to 94.5%, MSE decrease to .657, and the P-value for the X^2 term is .000.

10.51 The two predictor variables X_1 and X_2 are collinear. This causes b_1 to be negative and b_2 to be larger than a value that makes sense.

10.53 Hours studied and hours of TV are likely to be collinear. This problem can be avoided by a carefully designed experiment.

10.55 The residuals, when plotted against X_2, reveal an upward linear trend.

10.57 (a) $\hat{Y} = 12 + .004X_1$; no evidence that X_1 helps (P-value = .993). $\hat{Y} = 10.6 + .195X_2$; only slight evidence that X_2 helps (P-value = .106).

(b) $\hat{Y} = -4.52 + 3.1X_1 + 1.03X_2$. Strong evidence that both provide marginal contributions, P-values = .000. Thus, X_1 and X_2 should be retained.

10.59 The model does not appear to be adequate for estimation and prediction. There is a distinct outlier (Roanoke). The model could be refitted with Roanoke deleted; but then it would not apply to this locality.

10.61 The residual plots do not reveal any problems. Thus, based on the earlier analysis, the model is adequate for estimation and prediction.

10.63 (a) The residual plots do not reveal any problems. But the model is not adequate for estimation and prediction because about 60% of the variation in the sample prices remains unexplained.

(b) The residuals reveal much unexplained variation in prices.

10.65 No. Automatic variable selection techniques do not recognize violations of the required regression assumptions, the presence of outlier values, or nonlinearities in relationships. They also do not deal effectively with collinearity.

10.67 Predictor variables X_1 and X_2 are retained in the model; X_3 is removed.

10.69 Only % poverty remains in the model ($T = -4.77$).

10.71 (a) No; $X_2 = 750$ is well outside the range of the sample X_2 values. Predictions for X_2 values outside the sample range 475 to 650 are especially suspect because of the quadratic term.

(b) For $X_1 = 3.71$ and $X_2 = 750$: $\hat{Y} = 3.2$; for $X_1 = 3.69$ and $X_2 = 650$: $\hat{Y} = 3.5$.

The predicted GPA for the applicant with GMAT = 750 is less than that for the applicant with GMAT = 650; a counterintuitive result is caused by the quadratic term.

10.73 The final regression equation is $\hat{Y} = -.541 + .305X_2 + .454X_3 + .415X_4$. Each predictor variable in this model has a very low P-value and therefore clearly explains variation in copy quality not explained by the other variables. R_a^2 equals 95%. A plot of residuals vs. the predictor variables indicated no problems. Model is adequate for estimation and prediction.

10.75 The final regression equation is Gain $= -235 + 6.24$Employm. A plot of residuals vs. construction employment reveals no problems. Because too much of the variation is left unexplained, model is not adequate.

10.77 Longitude does not appear to make a marginal contribution ($T = -1.18$, P-value $= .252$). The model containing Latitude ($T = -8.88$, P-value $= .000$) and Elevation ($T = -13.09$, P-value $= .000$) is much better.

10.79 $X_1 =$ Number of beds,

$$X_2 = \begin{cases} 1 & \text{if rural} \\ 0 & \text{otherwise,} \end{cases}$$

$$X_3 = \begin{cases} 1 & \text{if urban} \\ 0 & \text{otherwise,} \end{cases}$$

$$X_4 = \begin{cases} 1 & \text{if local} \\ 0 & \text{otherwise} \end{cases}$$

For a model including X_1, X_2, X_3, and X_4, the P-values for X_1 (number of beds) and X_4 (program) are low, indicating they both make marginal contributions. To study the contribution of location, we compare to a model excluding X_2 and X_3. We discover that the adjusted R^2 statistic decreases from 63.06% to 60.8%. A marginal F analysis shows that $F = .0365$ with P-value .9642. There is no indication that location makes a marginal contribution, so X_2 and X_3 are eliminated. Upon refitting the model, the final regression equation is $\hat{Y} = -22.7 + .0336X_1 + 93.7X_4$. An analysis of residuals reveals no serious problems, though the variation among residuals appears to increase as the number of beds increases.

10.81 The final regression equation is Grade $= 68.9 + 5.90$ Attend $+ 4.40$ GPA. The estimated effect of attending the session is an additional 5.90 points on the test, on average, after adjusting for the effect of GPA. A residual analysis indicated no problems with the model. However, because nearly 80% of the variation in grades is left unexplained, model is not adequate.

CHAPTER 11

11.1 For each category, the expected frequency is obtained by multiplying the proportion claimed for that category (in the null hypothesis) by the sample size n.

11.3 The expected frequency must be at least 5 for every category.

11.5 If the frequencies in $k - 1$ of the categories were known, the number in the remaining category must cause the sum of the frequencies to equal n, the total sample size. Thus, there are $k - 1$ degrees of freedom.

11.7 (b) The expected frequency for each checkout stand is $(200)(1/8) = 25$. The goodness-of-fit statistic equals 29.04, with a P-value of .0001 for 7 degrees of freedom. These data strongly contradict a null hypothesis that there are no differences among preferences for the eight checkout stands.

11.9 (b) The expected frequency for each wine is $(240)(1/6) = 40$. The goodness-of-fit statistic equals 2.4, with a P-value of .7914 for 5 degrees of freedom. These data fail to contradict a null hypothesis that there are differences among customers' taste preferences for the wines.

11.11 (b) The expected frequencies are found by multiplying the hypothesized proportions by 124. The goodness-of-fit statistic equals 6.63 with a *P*-value of .0847 for 3 degrees of freedom. The data fail to contradict a null hypothesis that the distribution of days over the temperature range in recent years is the same as the historical pattern.

11.13 (a) Graph shows no discernible differences among the six music types; apparently distribution is uniform.
   (b) Null hypothesis cannot be contradicted, *P*-value = .416.

11.15 (The required frequencies are in boldface.)

				Total
40	**50**	**10**	100	
40	50	**10**	**100**	
Total **80**	**100**	20	200	

11.17 (a) Yes; adult men appear to regard TV as a waste of time, while adult women regard it as entertaining.
   (b) Strong contradiction of independence of opinion, *P*-value = .000.

11.19 (a) Although some differences exist among the salespersons, relationship is not apparent.
   (b) Null hypothesis of independence (no relationship) cannot be contradicted, *P*-value = .794.

11.21 (a) Strong relationship is apparent.
   (b) Null hypothesis of independence (no relationship) is strongly contradicted, *P*-value = .000.

11.23 Claim of independence strongly contradicted, *P*-value = .000.

11.25 (a) A relationship is apparent.
   (b) Null hypothesis of independence (no relationship) is contradicted, *P*-value = .003.

11.27 (b) A null hypothesis of no change in distribution is contradicted by these data, *P*-value = .007.

11.29 (a) These data contradict the null hypothesis that the proportion of defectives for the process is .05 as claimed, *P*-value = .022.
   (b) For H_0: $\pi = .05$ vs. H_a: $\pi \neq .05$, the *Z* statistic equals 2.2942, with a *P*-value = .022, the same *P*-value as in part (a).
   (c) Yes; the value of the chi-square statistic equals the square of the value of the *Z* statistic.

11.31 The null hypothesis is H_0: $\pi_1 = .25$; $\pi_2 = .25$; $\pi_3 = .25$; $\pi_4 = .25$. These data strongly contradict the null hypothesis, *P*-value = .000.
   (b) Not necessarily. We need to know the number of men who belong to each of the four groups of this study.

11.33 (The required frequencies are in boldface.)

2.162	**3.784**	**2.703**	**1.351**	10
2.595	**4.541**	**3.243**	**1.622**	12
3.243	**5.676**	**4.054**	**2.027**	15
8	14	10	5	37

11.35 The null hypothesis is that party affiliation and attitude toward restricting handguns are independent. These data convincingly contradict the null hypothesis, *P*-value = .000.

11.37 The null hypothesis is that automobile size and the proportion of accidents involving a fatality are independent. The sample data fail to contradict the claim of the null hypothesis, *P*-value = .262.

11.39 (a) Yes, null hypothesis of independence is strongly contradicted, *P*-value = .004.
   (b) Yes, null hypothesis of independence is contradicted, *P*-value = .022.

11.41 Null hypothesis of independence is strongly contradicted, *P*-value = .000.

CHAPTER 12

12.1 To reveal the elements of pattern governing the behavior of a time series. Classical decomposition provides a basis from which a forecast can be developed.

12.3 (a) The final seasonality factors are Q_1: 1.112938; Q_2: .806704; Q_3: 1.195601; Q_4: .884758.
   (b) Values tend to be somewhat below trend-cycle in the second and fourth quarters, and above trend-cycle in the first and third quarters.

(c) The deseasonalized data for periods 1–12 are (in rows):
   13.48 13.64 12.55 14.69 12.58 12.40
   12.55 10.17 11.68 11.16 11.71 9.04

12.5 When a moving average's length equals the number of periods in a year, each period or season is always represented by exactly one data value. The averaging process causes random effects to offset each other, thereby reducing significantly (but not eliminating entirely) the effect of randomness.

12.7 For series dominated by randomness, with little trend-cycle variation, $n = 10$ would be preferred because averaging a larger number of data values causes more randomness to be eliminated.

12.11 $F_{t+1} = 144$

12.13 The choice of w is based on the relative amount of randomness in a series compared to its instability in level. If this relationship does not change in the future, then minimizing the error mean square will result in an appropriate choice of w. However, since relationships often change, many believe it wise to simply select "benchmark" values of w rather than minimizing MSE for historical data.

12.15 (a) $F_6 = 31.88$; $F_7 = 33.67$
   (b) MSE = 533.23
   (c) For simple exponential smoothing (Ex. 12.8), MSE = 578.51. The MSE of Holt's method is less than that of simple exponential smoothing.
   (d) $F_6 = 70.31$; $F_7 = 82.62$
   (e) MSE = 21.09. MSE is lower in part d because the initial trend factor was approximately correct. This avoided large early errors that were experienced in part a.
   (f) Yes

12.17 For very unstable trend, i.e., when large changes in trend were thought likely, then $v = .3$ would be preferred to $v = .1$.

12.19 (a) 61.49; 63.8; 67.55
   (b) Judgment, some form of exponential smoothing, economic model, etc.

12.21 (a) Both assume linear association between Y and time.
   (b) This approach assumes rate of trend growth is constant over period of observation. Holt's method assumes rate of trend growth might vary over time.
   (c) The forecast reflects the historical rate of trend growth, rather than the current rate.
   (d) Not much. Holt's method projects the best estimate of the current rate of trend growth.

12.25 (a) Distance = $112 + 4.72X$
   (b) A slightly better equation is obtained by including the X^2 term:
   Distance = $104 + 6.63X - .0708X^2$. MSE is reduced from 61 to 49.
   (c) For 2004, predicted distance is 233.62 based on part b.
   (d) With Holt's method, a distance of 229.06 is predicted for 2004.

12.27 (a) Simple exponential smoothing
   (b) Classical decomposition to produce deseasonalized data, which can then be forecasted with simple exponential smoothing
   (c) Holt's method
   (d) Classical decomposition to produce deseasonalized data, which can then be forecasted with Holt's method

12.29 (a) Strong seasonality; up in second quarter, down in third, way up in fourth. Steady trend—about 30 units per year.
   (b) First apply classical decomposition to develop deseasonalized data; then forecast with Holt's method.
   (c) The seasonality factors are Q_1: .855661, Q_2: 1.095996, Q_3: .598008, and Q_4: 1.450334. The deseasonalized values are: 116.87, 104.93, 117.06, 144.79, 140.24, 150.55, 167.22, 151.69, 175.3, 177.92, 200.67, 186.16. Applying Holt's method with $w = .5$, $v = .2$ (chosen arbitrarily) and starting values $A = 116.87$, $B = .00$: the forecasts of the deseasonalized data for the next four periods are 200.07, 206.93, 213.79, and 220.65. To obtain a forecast of the actual data, we multiply by the seasonal factors: $F_{13} = 171.19$, $F_{14} = 226.79$, $F_{15} = 127.85$, and $F_{16} = 320.02$
   (d) MSE = 331.07. Notice that MSE should reflect error from the *combination* of Holt's method and classical decomposition.

12.31 Since there are no data, it is desirable to shed the effects of the initial conditions quickly. Therefore $w = .4$ would be the preferred value until the sales level settles down.

12.33 (a) The conventional approach is $A_1 = X_1$. An alternative is to set A_1 equal to the average of the first few data values.
   (b) This depends on the value of w. If w is large, the effects of initialization wear off quickly. If w is small, the effect of initialization takes quite a while to wear off.
   (c) Yes

12.35 (a) There is a steady upward trend and a distinct seasonal pattern. Sales consistently tended to increase the first 3 months of a year; they were very low in July and August; they increased to a peak in October, then declined through January.

13.9   By noting how the values of a statistic fluctuate over time. If these values exhibit no discernible pattern with the majority of them being relatively close to the center line, some above it, others below it, with no long runs of increasing or decreasing values, and all values contained within the upper and lower control limits, then the process is stable.

13.11   No, because discernible patterns would indicate an unstable process even though all values remain within the control limits.

13.13   An unstable process can be made stable by identifying and removing the assignable causes of variation.

13.15   The purpose of $\bar{X}$- and S-charts is to assess the stability of a process with regard to the average and the variation of the outcomes.

13.17   The process was stable with respect to average strength.

13.19   For the $\bar{X}$-chart, the center line is $\mu = 100$. The upper and lower control limits are 121.21 and 78.79, respectively. For the S-chart, the center line is 19.3, and the upper and lower control limits are 35.032 and 3.568, respectively.

13.21 $\bar{\bar{X}} = 20.25$; $\bar{S} = .32$.
   (a) The upper and lower control limits for the $\bar{X}$-chart are 20.60 and 19.90, respectively. The upper and lower control limits for the S-chart are .58 and .06, respectively.
   (b) An estimate is .3316.

13.23   (a) For the $\bar{X}$-chart, the upper and lower limits are 1.519 and 1.472, respectively. For the S-chart, the upper and lower limits are .03453 and .000, respectively.
   (b) Tests do not indicate any assignable-cause variation.
   (c) Yes

13.25   The eight tests are based on the variation of the statistic $\bar{X}$ under stable conditions and not on that of the statistic p.

13.27   The center line is .04. The upper and lower control limits are .116 and 0, respectively.

13.29   (b) Test 1: one point beyond upper control limit. Test failed at point 13.
   (c) No, because of instability

13.31   (a) Yes
   (b) Tests do not indicate any assignable cause.
   (c) S-chart: center line = $E(S) = 19.03$; upper control limit = 37.486; lower control limit = .574.

13.33   Since $n = 5$, $c_4 = .9400$, and $c_5 = .3412$.
   (a) The upper and lower control limits for the $\bar{X}$-chart are 422.04 and 378.36, respectively. The upper and lower control limits for the S-chart are 31.96 and 0, respectively.
   (b) 16.28

13.35   (b) Tests do not indicate any assignable cause. The process appears to have been stable with respect to the proportion of accounts that contain errors.
   (c) Yes

Index

Photo Credits

This page constitutes an extension of the copyright page. We have made every effort to trace the ownership of all copyrighted material and to secure permission from copyright holders. In the event of any question arising as to the use of any material, we will be pleased to make the necessary corrections in future printings. Thanks are due to the following for permission to use the material indicated.

TO THE OWNER OF THIS BOOK:

We hope that you have found *An Introduction to Modern Business Statistics*, Second Edition, useful. So that this book can be improved in a future edition, would you take the time to complete this sheet and return it? Thank you.

School and address: _____

Department: _____

Instructor's name: _____

1. What I like most about this book is: _____

_____

_____

2. What I like least about this book is: _____

_____

_____

3. My general reaction to this book is: _____

_____

4. The name of the course in which I used this book is: _____

_____

5. Were all of the chapters of the book assigned for you to read? _____

   If not, which ones weren't? _____

6. In the space below, or on a separate sheet of paper, please write specific suggestions for improving this book and anything else you'd care to share about your experience in using the book.

_____

_____

_____

_____

_____

_____

Optional:

Your name: _____ Date: _____

May Brooks/Cole quote you, either in promotion for *An Introduction to Modern Business Statistics,* Second Edition, or in future publishing ventures?

Yes: _____ No: _____

Sincerely,

George C. Canavos
Don M. Miller

FOLD HERE

FOLD HERE

IMPORTANT

If the CD-ROM packaging has been opened, the purchaser cannot return the book for a full refund!
The CD-ROM is subject to this agreement!

LICENSING AND WARRANTY AGREEMENT

For Technical Support:
Voice: 1-800-423-0563
Fax: 1-606-647-5045
E-mail: support@kdc.com